BUTLER'S
LIVES OF THE SAINTS

BUTLER'S
LIVES OF THE SAINTS
COMPLETE EDITION

EDITED, REVISED AND SUPPLEMENTED BY

HERBERT J. THURSTON, S.J.
AND DONALD ATTWATER

Foreword by Cardinal Basil Hume, O.S.B.
Archbishop of Westminster

VOLUME III
JULY · AUGUST · SEPTEMBER

General Index in Volume IV

CHRISTIAN CLASSICS
Westminster, Maryland
1988

NIHIL OBSTAT : PATRICIVS MORRIS, S.T.D., L.S.S.
CENSOR DEPVTATVS
IMPRIMATVR : E. MORROGH BERNARD
VICARIVS GENERALIS
WESTMONASTERII : DIE XXIII FEBRVARII MCMLIII

Christian Classics, Inc.

P.O. BOX 30
WESTMINSTER, MD. 21157

Lives of the Saints originally published 1756-9.
Revised edition by Herbert J. Thurston, S. J.,
published 1926-38. Copyright by Burns & Oates.
Second Edition, by Herbert J. Thurston, S. J. and
Donald Attwater, published 1956.
Copyright © Burns & Oates 1956.
Reprinted 1981
Foreword copyright © Burns & Oates 1981

LIBRARY OF CONGRESS CATALOG CARD NUMBER: 56-5383

ISBN: Cloth 0 87061 0457, Paperback 0 87061 1372

PRINTED IN THE UNITED STATES OF AMERICA

CONTENTS OF VOLUME III

JULY

AUGUST

SEPTEMBER

BIBLIOGRAPHICAL ABBREVIATIONS

Acta Sanctorum—This without qualification refers to the *Acta Sanctorum* of the Bollandists.

BHG.—The *Bibliotheca hagiographica graeca* of the Bollandists.

BHL.—The *Bibliotheca hagiographica latina* of the Bollandists.

BHO.—The *Bibliotheca hagiographica orientalis* of the Bollandists.

Burton and Pollen, LEM.—*Lives of the English Martyrs*, second series, ed. E. H. Burton and J. H. Pollen.

Camm, LEM.—*Lives of the English Martyrs*, first series, ed. Bede Camm.

CMH.—H. Delehaye's Commentary on the Hieronymian Martyrology, in the *Acta Sanctorum*, November, volume ii, part 2.

DAC.—*Dictionnaire d'Archéologie chrétienne et de Liturgie*, ed. F. Cabrol and H. Leclercq.

DCB.—*A Dictionary of Christian Biography*, ed. William Smith and Henry Wace.

DHG.—*Dictionnaire d'Histoire et de Géographie ecclésiastiques*, ed. A. Baudrillart *et al.*

DNB.—The *Dictionary of National Biography*, ed. Leslie Stephen *et al.*

DTC.—*Dictionnaire de Théologie catholique*, ed. A. Vacant *et al.*

KSS.—*Kalendars of Scottish Saints*, ed. A. P. Forbes.

LBS.—*Lives of the British Saints*, by S. Baring-Gould and John Fisher.

LIS.—*Lives of the Irish Saints*, by John O'Hanlon.

Mabillon—*Acta Sanctorum Ordinis Sancti Benedicti*, ed. J. Mabillon.

MGH.—*Monumenta Germaniae Historica*, ed. G. H. Pertz *et al.*

MMP.—*Memoirs of Missionary Priests*, by Richard Challoner, referred to in the edition of 1924, ed. J. H. Pollen.

PG.—*Patrologia graeca*, ed. J. P. Migne.

PL.—*Patrologia latina*, ed. J. P. Migne.

REPSJ.—*Records of the English Province of the Society of Jesus*, ed. Henry Foley.

Ruinart—*Acta primorum martyrum sincera et selecta*, ed. T. Ruinart.

Stanton's *Menology*—*A Menology of England and Wales*, by Richard Stanton.

VSH.—*Vitae Sanctorum Hiberniae*, ed. Charles Plummer.

Father Delehaye's *Les origines du culte des martyrs* is referred to in the " deuxième édition revue " of 1933.

There is an English translation by Mrs. V. M. Crawford of Father Delehaye's *Les légendes hagiographiques* (" The Legends of the Saints "), made from the first edition. The third French edition (1927) is revised and is therefore sometimes referred to.

The English title of the work herein referred to as " Léon, *L'Auréole séraphique* (Eng. trans.) " is *Lives of the Saints and Blessed of the Three Orders of St Francis* (1885-87), by Father Léon (Vieu) de Clary. A corrected and enlarged edition of this work in Italian, by Father G. C. Guzzo, began publication in 1951 : *Aureola serafica*. By 1954 four volumes had appeared, covering January-August.

It has not been deemed necessary to give every reference to such standard works as the *Dictionary of Christian Biography*, the *Dictionnaires* published by Letouzey,

and A. Fliche and V. Martin's *Histoire de l'Église*, though these are often referred
to in the bibliographical notes.   The first two volumes of Fliche and Martin, by
J. Lebreton and J. Zeiller, have been translated into English by Dr E. C. Messenger
(*The History of the Primitive Church*, 4 vols.), and the first two English volumes of
the continuation, *The Church in the Christian Roman Empire*, are also published.

The reader may here be reminded once for all that for all modern saints and
beati the surest source of information on the more strictly spiritual side is the *summarium de virtutibus* with the criticisms of the *Promotor fidei* which are printed in
the process of beatification.   Copies of these are occasionally to be met with in
national or private libraries, though they are not published or offered for sale to the
general public.

For all saints named in the Roman Martyrology the standard shorter reference
is in the *Acta Sanctorum, Decembris Propylaeum : Martyrologium Romanum ad
formam editionis typicae scholiis historicis instructum* (1940).   This great work provides a running commentary on the entries in the Roman Martyrology, correcting
where necessary conclusions expressed in the sixty-odd volumes of the *Acta
Sanctorum*, and anticipating much that will be said at greater length in those
volumes that have yet to appear ; and there are summary bibliographies throughout.
It is indispensable for all serious study and reference.

BUTLER'S
LIVES OF THE SAINTS

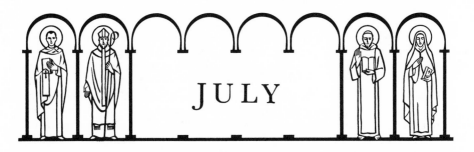

JULY

1: THE PRECIOUS BLOOD OF OUR LORD JESUS CHRIST

THOUGH the Precious Blood of our Lord has been used as a synonym for the Redemption from the times of the Apostles, spread of a special devotion in its honour was due in the main to St Caspar del Bufalo (January 2). But the celebration of a feast of the Precious Blood was observed in some few churches long before his time. For example, an office " of the Blood of Christ " was conceded to the archdiocese of Valencia in Spain in 1582, and a similar office was approved for the diocese of Sarzana in Tuscany in 1747 ; the feast was granted to St Caspar's congregation early in the nineteenth century. Pope Pius IX extended it to the whole Western church in 1849, amid the trials of the revolution which had driven him from Rome. The feast was at first fixed for the first Sunday of July ; this was altered by Pope Pius X to the first day of the month. By the Passionists and some others a second feast is kept on the Friday after *Laetare* Sunday. The cathedral-church of the archdiocese of Westminster is dedicated to the Most Precious Blood.

In this feast, as Dom Guéranger has pointed out, the Church rejoices in the celebration of her birthday, for the stream of blood and water which issued from the Lord's pierced side is mystically the beginning of the Church. It was a stream of new life poured out over the world. St John Chrysostom says in a homily read at Matins : " It was therefore out of the side of Christ that the Church was built, just as it was out of the side of Adam that Eve was raised up to be his bride . . . for even as God made the woman out of the side of the man so Christ gave to us the water and blood from His own side whence was the Church raised up." St Augustine, whose homily is read at the third nocturn, speaks to the same effect.

See F. G. Holweck, *Calendarium festorum Dei et Dei Matris* (1925), p. 235 ; Moroni, *Dizionario di Erudizione*, vol. lxi, pp. 40–48 ; Nilles, *Kalendarium manuale* (1896–97), vol. ii, pp. 493–495 ; Buchberger, *Lexikon für Theologie und Kirche*, vol. ii, cc. 401–404.

ST SHENUTE, ABBOT   (*c*. A.D. 466)

EGYPT was the original home of communal monastic life, and St Shenute (Shenoudi) was, after St Antony and St Pachomius, the most considerable force in its early development, as well as the only prominent original writer in Coptic. He was born about the middle of the fourth century at Shenalolet and became a monk at Dair-al-Abiad, founded near Atripe in the Thebaid by his uncle, whom he succeeded as abbot in 385. The monks were numerous, chiefly recruited from rough and ignorant peasants, and the superior had to be a strict disciplinarian. It is not surprising to learn that Shenute was a martinet ; and his difficulties were increased by his being naturally quick-tempered and of a rigorous, indeed, violent, disposition. His policy was to strengthen regularity, to maintain order by increasing the severity of the austere rule imposed by St Pachomius, and he instituted something in the nature of monastic vows as we now understand them. By the fact of entering on the monastic life the monk or nun took on certain obligations ; Shenute legislated for these to be expressed in a formula, in which the religious covenanted to observe continence, not to steal or bear false witness or lie, and to do no secret evil, upon pain of the wrath of God and the loss of salvation. Shenute also permitted religious of proved worth, who so wished, to pass from the communal to the solitary life in the neighbourhood of the monastery. So far from discouraging aspirants, St Shenute's severity was an attraction : his successor and biographer, Bêsa, says that he had at one time 2200 monks and 1800 nuns. He enforced his will with great strictness, and discouraged any study among his subjects (very few of them were capable of it) ; he was not learned himself, but wrote many letters of direction and some powerful sermons ; on the other hand he set himself against undisciplined exercises of penitence and all false mysticism, at a time and place when monastic life was prone to degenerate into competitive austerity.

It is said, though it is far from certain, that St Shenute was present at the Council of Ephesus in 431. He came to be archimandrite, a sort of abbot general, over all the monasteries that had sprung up in imitation of the one at Atripe. As all the monks of a monastery, living in their groups of huts, were subject to their abbot, so the abbots were subject to the archimandrite. The exact date of his death is unknown, but it is believed that he lived to the age of 118. In spite of numberless sackings and raidings St Shenute's monastery was still in existence a hundred years ago, and its ruins are still called Dair Anba-Shenute. In 1833 the excellent and Honourable Robert Curzon, junior, found three Coptic monks living there ; but " who the great Abou Shenood had the honour to be, I could meet with no one to tell me. He was, I believe, a Mahomedan saint, and this Coptic monastery had been in some sort placed under the shadow of his protection in the hopes of saving it from the persecutions of the faithful." Mr Curzon was no more fortunate in getting ancient manuscripts (which was what he was after) than in getting information about Anba Shenute : the Mamelukes had destroyed the last of them in 1812.

Shenute's sanctity is perhaps somewhat compromised by the suspicion that in his last days he became a monophysite, and on the other hand the conspicuous part attributed to him at the Council of Ephesus is not free from difficulties. See P. Peeters in the *Analecta Bollandiana*, vol. xxiv (1905), p. 146. M. Amélineau has published a French translation of the eulogistic biographies by Bêsa and others ; these abound in extravagant miracles. The learned essay of J. Leipoldt published in *Texte und Untersuchungen* is based on a very exhaustive study of the materials, but a truer picture may be found in the book of P. Ladeuze, *Étude sur le cénobitisme pakhomien* (1898), and in his article in the *Revue d'histoire ecclésiastique*, vol. vii (1906), pp. 76–83. Reference should also be made to the articles " Cénobitisme " and " Deir-el-Abiad " in DAC., and to De L. O'Leary, *The Saints of Egypt* (1937), pp. 251–255.

ST THEODORIC, or THIERRY, Abbot   (A.D. 533)

THEODORIC was born in the district of Rheims, his father being a man of evil character. He married under the compulsion of his relations, but persuaded his wife to renounce her rights ; and, becoming himself a priest under St Remigius he eventually formed a religious community at "Mont d'Or" (*Mons Or*), near Rheims. Theodoric became famous by the many remarkable conversions he wrought through the zeal wherewith he exhorted sinners to repentance; among these was his own father, who persevered under the direction of his son and died in his monastery. He is said miraculously to have cured King Theodoric I of ophthalmia. According to the most common opinion he died on July 1, 533.

Flodoard in the tenth century gives some account of Theodoric, and there are two brief Latin biographies which are printed both by Mabillon and by the Bollandists in the *Acta Sanctorum*. These are sources in which very little confidence can be placed.

ST CARILEFUS, OR CALAIS, ABBOT   (*c*. A.D. 540 ?)

CARILEFUS was born in Auvergne and was brought up in the monastery of Menat near Riom, where he became a friend of St Avitus. They became monks together and migrated to the abbey of Micy, near Orleans, where they were ordained to the priesthood. But Calais longed for greater solitude, so with two companions he went to Maine, where he revived the vigorous discipline of the ancient eastern hermits. But as he was constantly visited by numbers who sought to live under his direction, he at length consented to receive them; his monastery was called Anisole, from the river Anille on which it was situated. The small town which grew up around it is now known by the name of its founder, Saint-Calais, who is honoured as the pioneer of monasticism in that neighbourhood.

The oldest life of St Carilefus has been edited by B. Krusch in MGH., *Scriptores merov.*, vol. iii. The others are of little value. See also the important article of Father Albert Poncelet on the Saints of Micy in the *Analecta Bollandiana*, vol. xxiv (1905), especially p. 84. The little town of Saint-Calais in the department of Sarthe is, of course, quite distinct from Calais opposite Dover.

ST GALL, BISHOP OF CLERMONT   (A.D. 551)

THIS Gall was born about the year 486 at Clermont in Auvergne, his father being of one of the first families of that province. He took special care in the upbringing of his son, and when he arrived at a proper age, proposed to have him married to the daughter of a senator. Gall, who had resolved to consecrate himself to God, fled from his father's house to the monastery of Cournon, and asked to be admitted among the monks. The abbot refused until he should have obtained the consent of his father, which, rather surprisingly, he was able to do and so was received into the abbey. Here he attracted the notice of the bishop, Quintian, who ordained him deacon, attached him to his cathedral-church, and sent him as his representative at the royal court, where for his good singing he was made a cantor in King Theodoric's chapel. Quintian dying about 526, St Gall was appointed to succeed him. Under new responsibilities his humility, charity, and zeal increased: conspicuous above all was his patience under injuries, to which several stories bear witness. On one occasion a man hit him over the head, but the bishop showed no anger or resentment, and by his meekness disarmed the bad temper of his assailant. At another time one Evodius, who from a senator became a priest, having so far forgotten himself as to treat his bishop in the most insulting manner, Gall, without making any reply, got up quietly from his seat and went to visit the churches of the city. Evodius was so touched that he ran after him and fell on his knees in the middle of the street to ask the saint's pardon. During the last few years of his life St Gall was much concerned in the upbringing of his nephew, who became famous as St Gregory of Tours.

This St Gall is, of course, to be distinguished from the more famous St Gall, the Irishman, who has given his name to one of the Swiss cantons and who lived about a century later. The former is hardly known to us except from the account furnished in the *De vitis patrum* by his nephew St Gregory of Tours. All that is relevant is quoted in the *Acta Sanctorum*, July, vol. i.

ST EPARCHIUS, or CYBARD   (A.D. 581)

CYBARD quitted the world in spite of his parents, and retired to a monastery, perhaps at Saint-Cybard in the Dordogne. He there served God some time under Abbot Martin, and soon became known and sought after because of his virtues and miracles. In dread of the seduction of vainglory, he left his monastery to hide himself in absolute solitude near Angoulême. But his virtues were too striking for concealment, and the bishop obliged him to accept the priesthood. Moreover, although a recluse, he did not refuse to admit disciples ; but he would not allow them manual labour, as he wished that they should be constantly occupied in prayer in a literal sense. When any of them complained for want of necessaries, he would remind them of St Jerome's saying that " faith never feared hunger " : and, indeed, he found abundance for himself and his disciples in the beneficence of the faithful, by whom his miracles were greatly appreciated.

That a considerable cult of this saint existed in the sixth century we know from St Gregory of Tours. Gregory calls him Eparchius, which in the popular speech became Separcus and eventually Cybard. We know little of him in reality beyond what Gregory tells us. The. Latin biography which has been printed by the Bollandists and by Bruno Krusch is pronounced by the latter editor to be a forgery of the ninth century : but *cf.* L. Duchesne in the *Bulletin critique*, 2nd series, vol. iii (1897), pp. 471–473. See also J. de la Martinière, *S. Cybard* (1908), who criticizes the view of H. Esmein that some of our materials date from the sixth century.

ST SIMEON SALUS   (SIXTH CENTURY)

SIMEON, with his friend, a certain St John, retired to the desert near the Dead Sea, where he remained twenty-nine years in the constant practice of a most penitential life. He could never forget that we must love humiliations if we would be truly humble ; that at least we should receive those which God sends us with resignation, and remember that they are less than we deserve ; that it is even sometimes commendable to seek them, and that human prudence should not always be our guide in this regard. His application of these principles was such that, when he went to live at Emesa, on the Orontes in Syria, he received the nickname of *Salos*, which in Greek signifies " mad " ; for by affecting the manners of those who want sense, he passed for a fool, and his love of humility was not without reward, for God bestowed on him extraordinary graces, and even honoured him with the gift of miracles. The year of his death is unknown, but it was some time after the earthquake of 588. Some of his eccentricities were indeed surprising ; Alban Butler comments that although we are not obliged to imitate St Simeon's behaviour in all respects, and it would be rash even to attempt it without a special call, yet his example ought to make us ashamed when we consider with what an ill-will we suffer the least thing that hurts our pride. But indeed it seems likely that at times the saint's mind was unhinged.

4

A reasonably full account of St Simeon is furnished by the church historian Evagrius who was a contemporary, and there is also a long Greek life by Leontius, Bishop of Neapolis in Cyprus, who lived a century later.   The text is printed in the *Acta Sanctorum*, July, vol. i.   There is a useful bibliography of St Simeon and " fools for Christ's sake " in general in Baudot and Chaussin, *Vies des saints . . .*, t. vii (1949), pp. 18–19.

ST SERF, OR SERVANUS, BISHOP   (SIXTH CENTURY ?)

THE history of this saint is a confused mass of legends, from which even the century in which he flourished cannot be clearly learned.   The old Aberdeen Breviary says that he was a Scot (*i.e.* an Irishman), consecrated by Palladius.   According to Joscelyn's Life of St Kentigern, that bishop was educated and formed by Serf in the monastery he had founded at Culross, his mother having been cast up on the shore near by.   He was venerated as the patron and apostle of the Orkneys, but the evidence that he ever preached in those islands is very slight : Culross in Fifeshire and his monastery there was the centre of his activity and of his *cultus* in medieval Scotland.   Some of the legends connected with St Serf are astonishingly wild : one says that his mother was a daughter of the king of the Picts (or of Arabia) and that his father was the king of Canaan ; that he gave up his right to that throne, studied at Alexandria, was made patriarch of Jerusalem, and eventually pope—which dignity he resigned in order to preach to the Scots.   A lesson in the Aberdeen Breviary tells how, a poor man having killed his only pig to feed the saint and his monks, Serf restored flesh and life to its bones to recompense him for his hospitality ;   other tales of his wonders are simply absurd and are apparently adaptations of local folk-tales.   St Serf apparently died and was buried at Culross ; a former pilgrimage has preserved at Dysart knowledge of the cave wherein he worsted the Devil.

Besides the lessons of the Aberdeen Breviary, a medieval fiction which purports to be a biography of the saint has been printed in Skene's *Chronicles of the Picts*, pp. 412–420, and elsewhere.   See also KSS., pp. 445–447.

BD THOMAS MAXFIELD, MARTYR   (A.D. 1616)

THOMAS MAXFIELD (or Macclesfield) was born at The Mere, Enville, in the county of Stafford, about the year 1590.   His father William was a confessor of the faith, and at the time of Thomas's birth was actually under sentence of death for harbouring priests.   Thomas himself was eventually ordained and sent on the mission in 1615.

Within three months he was arrested in London, and lodged in the Gatehouse at Westminster.   After the usual interrogations he was left there for eight months, when, with the help of another prisoner, a Jesuit, he attempted to escape by means of a rope let down from a high window.   But he landed right in the arms of a passer-by, who raised the alarm.   The turnkeys seized him and " thrust him under a table, girding about his neck a massive collar of iron ; to this again they fasten a ponderous chain of an hundredweight . . . and in this painful posture they keep him for some hours till the morning ".   Then he was removed to a filthy and verminous underground dungeon, and fastened in wooden stocks, in such fashion that he could neither stand nor lie down properly ; and so he was left from before daybreak on Friday until Monday night.   Some of his fellow prisoners managed to get a blanket for him, and his Jesuit confessor spoke words of encouragement through a hole in the roof—and found the sufferer in very good heart.

At his trial Mr Maxfield refused to take the oath of allegiance to King James in the form it was tendered, while protesting that he was loyal to him as his true and lawful sovereign ; and the next day he was condemned for his priesthood to be hanged, drawn and quartered.   The Spanish ambassador, the Duke of Gondomar, made a personal intervention at court to obtain Mr Maxfield's pardon or at least a reprieve ; but without avail.

Unusual crowds of people watched Bd Thomas dragged to Tyburn the next ·day, July 1, many following him to the scaffold, including a number of Spaniards. To the great vexation of the authorities it was found that someone had decked the gibbet with garlands of flowers, and covered the ground about it with leaves and sweet-smelling herbs.   Bd Thomas addressed the crowd from the cart, declaring that he had had no other object " but only to be serviceable to the souls of my dear countrymen " by preaching the faith that St Augustine had preached to their ancestors.   In spite of the sheriff's peremptory order to the hangman to cut him down quickly, the bystanders insisted that he should be allowed to hang till he was dead, and so be spared the horrors of disembowelling.

Special precautions were taken to prevent any relics of Bd Thomas Maxfield being preserved.   Nevertheless the Spanish ambassador was able to recover the body, part of which is still at Gondomar and the other part at Downside.

In the year of his death a life of Bd Thomas, by Dr Kellison, was published at Douay, and in the following year an eye-witness account of his execution : see Catholic Record Society publications, vol. iii.   See also MMP., pp. 344–353 ; DNB., vol. xxxvii ; and the *Downside Review*, vol. xxxiv.

2 : THE VISITATION OF THE BLESSED VIRGIN MARY

THE angel Gabriel, in the mystery of the Annunciation, told the mother of God that her cousin Elizabeth had conceived, and was then in the sixth month of her pregnancy.   Our Lady concealed the wonderful dignity to which she was raised by the incarnation of the Son of God in her womb, but in her joy and gratitude she would go to congratulate the mother of the Baptist. " Mary therefore arose ", says St Luke, " and with haste went into the hill country into a city of Juda ; and entering into the house of Zachary saluted Elizabeth." She made this visit to a saint because the company of the servants of God is to be sought, from whose example and very silence the heart will always treasure up something, and the understanding receive some new light.   In this journey, too, the holy Virgin gives us a lesson in humility.   She had been saluted mother of God, and exalted above all creatures ; yet far from being elated with the thoughts of her incomprehensible dignity, she appears but the more humble, and the mother of God pays a visit to the mother of her Son's servant ; the Redeemer of the world goes to His forerunner.

When charity called upon Mary, she thought of no dangers or difficulties in so painful and long a journey from Nazareth in Galilee to the southern part of the mountainous country of Judea.   Being arrived at the house of Zachary, she entered it, and saluted Elizabeth.   At the voice of the mother of God, but by the power and grace of her divine Son, Elizabeth was filled with the Holy Ghost, and the infant in her womb was sanctified, and he leapt and exulted within his mother.   If

Abraham and all the ancient prophets exulted only to foresee in spirit that day when it was at the distance of so many ages, what wonder the little Baptist felt so great a joy to see it then present.   And he himself was there and then cleansed from original sin and filled with sanctifying grace, was made a prophet, and worshipped the Messiah before he was yet born.

And Elizabeth was likewise filled with the Holy Ghost ; and by His infused light she understood the great mystery of the incarnation which God had wrought in Mary, and called her blessed above all other women ; and the fruit of her womb she called blessed infinitely more, He being the source of all graces, by whom Mary herself was blessed.   And of herself Elizabeth cried out, " Whence is this to me that the mother of my Lord should come to me ? "   She had conceived barren and by a miracle ; but Mary a virgin, and by the Holy Ghost ; she conceived one greater than the prophets, but Mary the eternal Son of God, himself true God. The Baptist, her son, used the like exclamation to express his confusion and humility when Christ came to be baptized by his hands.   In the like words and sentiments ought we to receive the visits of God in His graces, especially in the holy sacraments.   Elizabeth styles Mary Mother of her Lord, that is, Mother of God ; and she foretells that all things would befall her and her Son which had been spoken by the prophets.   Mary, hearing her own praise, answered in that wonderful song we call the *Magnificat*, the most perfect thanksgiving and praise for the incarnation of the Son of God, and the most precious monument of Mary's humility.   She praises God with all the powers of her soul, and gives glory to Him alone.

This feast was first observed by the Friars Minor in the thirteenth century and was extended to the whole Western church in 1389.   In the East it is unknown, except among the Catholic Melkites, the Maronites, and the Malabarese in India.   For the liturgical celebration, see F. G. Holweck, *Calendarium festorum Dei et Dei Matris* (1925), pp. 213–214.

SS. PROCESSUS AND MARTINIAN, Martyrs   (Date Unknown)

THESE martyrs were publicly venerated in Rome from at least the fourth century, but of their history and passion nothing is known.   No credence can be given to the legend in their sixth-century *acta*, adopted by the Roman Martyrology and Breviary.   According to this, while SS. Peter and Paul were confined in the Mamertine prison, their warders, Processus and Martinian, and forty others, were converted by the miracles and teaching of the apostles, to whom they offered their liberty.   A flow of water miraculously sprang from the rock to enable St Peter to baptize them.   The officer in charge, Paulinus, tried to persuade Processus and Martinian from their new faith, and afterwards subjected them to cruel tortures when they would not offer incense on the altar of Jupiter ; their sufferings only wrung from them the words, " Blessed be the name of the Lord ".   So they were slain with the sword.   Whoever these two martyrs may actually have been, they were buried, it is said, by a woman called Lucina on her own property, near the second milestone on the Via Aurelia, and in the fourth century a basilica was built over their tomb, wherein St Gregory the Great preached his thirty-second homily on their feast-day, in the course of which he said that at that place the sick were healed, the possessed were freed, and the forsworn were tormented.   In the beginning of the ninth century Pope St Paschal I translated their relics to St

Peter's, where they still rest under the altar dedicated in their honour in the south transept.

The alleged *acta* of these martyrs are printed in the *Acta Sanctorum*, July, vol. i.   This legend has been exhaustively discussed by Pio Franchi de' Cavalieri in *Studi e Testi*, vol. xix, pp. 97–98, and xxii, 35–39.   He shows that in the fourth century there was no idea of their having been the gaolers of the two apostles.   He also suggests that the baptism episode probably took its rise from the frescoes in the catacombs which depicted St Peter, in the character of Moses, striking the rock and quenching the thirst of two soldiers who represented the multitude.   See also Delehaye's CMH., pp. 347–348.

ST MONEGUNDIS, WIDOW   (A.D. 570)

THIS saint was a native of Chartres, married, and with two daughters, who were the objects of her happiness and greatest interest in this world.   She was deprived of them by death, and in the excess of her sorrow she resolved to abandon the world and give herself entirely to God's service, lest in her grief she should become so centred in herself as to be unmindful of Him.   With her husband's consent, she built herself a cell at Chartres in which she shut herself up, having no other furniture than a mat on the floor on which she took her short repose, and allowing herself no other food than coarse oat bread with water.   She afterwards removed to Tours, where she continued the same manner of life in a cell near St Martin's shrine.   Many fervent women joining her, this cell grew into a nunnery, St Pierre-le-Puellier, and many miracles of healing were reported at her tomb.

St Gregory of Tours has given an account of St Monegundis in his *De vitis patrum*. See also the *Acta Sanctorum*, July, vol. i, and Y. Delaporte, *Les principaux saints du diocèse de Chartres*.

ST OTTO, BISHOP OF BAMBERG   (A.D. 1139)

OTTO belonged to the family of Mistelbach in Swabia, and while still young was ordained priest and entered the service of the Emperor Henry IV, by whom he was chosen in due course to be chancellor.   In the struggle between the Holy See and the emperor, Henry set up an antipope ; Otto laboured to bring him to repentance and submission, and refused to approve his schism or other crimes, while supporting his politics in so far as they were lawful.   When the emperor nominated him bishop of Bamberg in 1102 he refused to be consecrated until some years later when he was able to go to Rome and receive episcopal orders from Pope Paschal II himself.   Under the succeeding emperor Otto worked to heal the breach with the Holy See and the harms which it produced, for Henry V altered his own policy of conciliation and followed that of his father.   Yet Otto always enjoyed the trust of both parties, so strongly does virtue command respect and such is the power of meekness in disarming tyrants, and amid all his political activities he discharged his episcopal duties with the greatest care, established many monasteries and other religious foundations, and led an exemplary private life.

Boleslaus III of Poland, having conquered part of Pomerania, he entreated St Otto to undertake a mission among the idolaters of that country.   The bishop in 1124 took with him a number of priests and catechists and passed into eastern Pomerania.   Over 20,000 persons are said to have been baptized, and he returned to Bamberg for Easter the following year, having appointed clergy to attend to the converts and finish the work he had so happily begun   The towns of Stettin and

Julin having relapsed into idolatry, Otto again went into Pomerania in 1128, brought those cities back to the faith, and through hardships and dangers carried the light of the gospel into other remote places.   He returned again to the care of his own flock, amidst which he died on June 30, 1139.   He was canonized fifty years later.

The material available for the life of St Otto is considerable, as the list in BHL (nn. 6392–6407) would alone suffice to show.   Apart from the important *Relatio de piis operibus Ottonis*, edited by Holder-Egger in MGH., *Scriptores*, vol. xv (†156–1166) we have a *Vita* by Ebo, a *Dialogus* by Herbord, and another *Vita* by a monk of Prüfening.   The book of C. H. Robinson, *The Life of Otto, Apostle of Pomerania* (1920), must be read with caution in the light of the *Analecta Bollandiana*, vol. xlii (1924), pp. 452–453. See also A. Hofmeister, *Das Leben des Bischofs Otto von Bamberg von einem Prüfeninger Mönch* (1928).

BD PETER OF LUXEMBURG, Bishop of Metz and Cardinal (a.d. 1387)

PETER was son to Guy of Luxemburg, Count of Ligny, and his wife Mahaut de Châtillon, and was born in 1369.   He was left an orphan when only four years old ; his piety and intelligence attracted notice, and at ten he was sent to Paris to pursue his studies, where he was made a canon of Notre Dame, in accordance with an abuse all too common in those days.   In 1380–81 he spent some months at Calais as hostage for the payment of the ransom of his elder brother, who was a prisoner in English hands.

Peter strove to advance in humility and Christian perfection : this was the point which he had in view in all his actions and undertakings, and he was far from seeking ecclesiastical dignity.   But a consideration of his powerful relatives, which the troubles of the times made it prudent to take into account, moved Clement VII at Avignon, who in the " great schism " was acknowledged by France for true pope, to nominate him in 1384 bishop of Metz and, two months later, cardinal.   To take possession of his see against the supporters of Urban VI, Peter had to rely on the armed help of his brother Valeran, to his deep distress.   But even his sanctity could not make up for lack of orders (he was a deacon), and a Dominican was given him for his assistant and consecrated bishop.   With him Peter performed the visitation of his diocese, in which he everywhere corrected abuses and gave proofs of his zeal and prudence.   But political disturbances soon drove him from Metz, and in the autumn of 1386 Clement VII called him to Avignon.

Here Peter continued all his former austerities, till Clement commanded him to mitigate them for the sake of his health.   His answer was, " Holy Father, I shall always be an unprofitable servant, but I can at least obey."   He compensated for what he lost in the practices of penance by redoubling his alms-deeds.   By his charities his purse was always empty ; his table was frugal, his household small, his furniture simple, and his clothes poor.   It seemed that he could not increase his alms, yet he found means to do it by distributing his little furniture and selling the episcopal ring which he wore.   Everything about him breathed a spirit of poverty and showed his affection for the poor.   An ancient picture of the saint was kept in the collegiate church of our Lady at Autun, in which he is painted in an ecstasy and on which are written these words, which he was accustomed frequently to repeat : " Contempt of the world, contempt of yourself : rejoice in your own contempt, but despise no other person."

Early in 1387 increasing ill-health made Bd Peter seek better air, at Villeneuve on the other side of the Rhône, where he lodged at a Carthusian monastery. Here he died on July 2, after writing a last letter to his beloved sister, Joan. His tomb soon became a place of pilgrimage, miracles were reported there, and he was eventually beatified, by the true Pope Clement VII, in 1527. Bd Peter was only eighteen at his death.

The principal source of information is the process of beatification, the greater part of which is printed in the *Acta Sanctorum* (July, vol. i). This is of exceptional interest because very few such documents containing the depositions of the witnesses are preserved to us from the middle ages. Strange to say most of these are concerned with youthful saints belonging to royal or very noble families, *e.g.* this Peter of Luxemburg, St Louis of Anjou who was consecrated archbishop of Toulouse and died at the age of twenty-three, and St Margaret of Hungary who was not twenty-nine. A brief account of Bd Peter, based upon the process, was published by H. François in 1927, *Vie du B. Pierre de Luxembourg.*

3 : ST IRENAEUS, Bishop of Lyons (*c.* A.D. 203) See p. *656ff, Vol. II (June 28)*

ST LEO II, Pope   (A.D. 683)

THIS Leo was a Sicilian by birth and was elected to succeed Pope St Agatho early in 681. His short pontificate is chiefly remembered for his confirmation of the acts of the sixth oecumenical council, which had condemned the heresy of Monothelism and anathematized the memory of Pope Honorius I for having "hedged" and not denounced this heresy outright when he ought to have done. Leo translated the relics of many martyrs from the catacombs to a chapel he built to receive them, and another church that he built was identified by Mgr Duchesne with St George *in Velabro*, the titular church of Cardinal Newman. The *Liber Pontificalis* speaks of this pope's zeal as a teacher and preacher and of his concern for the needy ; he was eloquent, and skilled in music, and the same authority thinks it worth while to mention that he was as proficient in Greek as in Latin—which is only to be expected in a seventh-century Sicilian. The feast of St Leo II was observed on June 28 until 1921. In a Motu Proprio of John XXIII dated July 25, 1960, this feast was dropped from the Roman Calendar.

Almost all that we know of Pope St Leo II is derived from the *Liber Pontificalis* (ed. Duchesne, vol. i, pp. 359–362). There is an excellent article on this pope in DTC., vol. ix, cc. 301–304. See also Mann, *Lives of the Popes*, vol. ii, pp. 49–52.

ST ANATOLIUS, Bishop of Laodicea   (*c.* A.D. 283)

THIS Anatolius, an Alexandrian, is remembered by his services to his fellow citizens at a time when he was conducting an Aristotelian school in that place. A rebellion broke out in the city and the Roman troops closely invested that part of it called the Bruchium, where Anatolius was living : the people were threatened both by starvation and disease. He communicated with his friend Eusebius, a deacon, who was outside the beleaguered area, and he induced the Roman general to permit all who would to leave the Bruchium without molestation. The rebel leaders would not at first allow anyone to take advantage of this, but Anatolius prevailed on them to the extent of letting non-combatants leave, and many others got away at the same time. Anatolius subsequently went to Palestine and became assistant to the bishop of Caesarea. Eusebius meanwhile had become bishop of Laodicea in Syria, and on his death Anatolius was chosen in his place.

Anatolius was eminent as a philosopher, as a physical scientist, and as a mathematician. Among his works which have survived are parts of ten treatises on arithmetic, and the Roman Martyrology says of his writings that they " are admired not only by religious men but also by philosophers ".

Eusebius, the church historian, is our chief authority, but St Jerome also speaks of Anatolius in terms of warm appreciation. Eusebius quotes a considerable fragment of his book about Easter, but the Latin treatise, *Liber Anatoli de ratione paschali*, purporting to be a translation, is pronounced a forgery, compiled probably in Ireland in the sixth century.

SS. IRENAEUS AND MUSTIOLA, MARTYRS   (THIRD CENTURY ?)

THIS Irenaeus was said to be a deacon who buried the body of St Felix, priest of the church of Sutri, who had been put to death for the faith. This coming to the ears of the officer Turcius, who was charged with executing the laws against Christians in that district, he ordered the arrest of Irenaeus ; the deacon was manacled and made to run with bare feet before the chariot of Turcius the whole way from Sutri to Chiusi, where he was put in prison. He and the other Christians with him were ministered to by a noble lady, Mustiola, and she was brought before Turcius to give an account of herself and her doings. Being a woman of great beauty, Turcius put aside his duty and pestered her with unwelcome attentions, but she refused to have anything to do with him. Thereupon Turcius worked off his annoyance on the Christians under his charge, and in particular on Irenaeus. He had him racked in Mustiola's presence, and when the martyr gave way to nothing but courage and patience, had his flesh torn with spikes and branded with hot irons until he died under the torture. Mustiola fiercely denounced Turcius for his barbarity and called down the wrath of Heaven on him, whereat his desire was turned to loathing and he had her beaten to death with clubs. Their legend says this took place under Aurelian. Mustiola was buried in a catacomb at Chiusi and she is venerated at that place and at Pesaro as a virgin martyr, but the Roman Martyrology refers to her as a matron.

The brief *acta* are printed by the Bollandists, July, vol. i. So far at least as concerns Mustiola, we seem to have here an interesting example of legendary accretions which have attached themselves to an historic *cultus*. An inscription (fourth century) found in the catacombs of Chiusi pays honour to a married lady " ex genere Mustiolae sanctae ". See Liverani, *Spicilegium Liberianum*, p. 778 ; Leclercq in DAC., vol. iii, cc. 1389–1392 ; Delehaye, *Les Origines du Culte des Martyrs*, p. 319, and his Commentary on the *Hieronymianum*, p. 617.

SS. JULIUS AND AARON, MARTYRS   (A.D. 304 ?)

THESE were Britons who are said to have glorified God by martyrdom at Caerleon in Monmouthshire in the persecution of Diocletian. St Gildas speaks of their triumph as having been most illustrious, and the Venerable Bede adds, " Very many others of both sexes by unheard-of tortures attained to the crown of heavenly glory " in Britain at that time, but only the names of these and of Alban have come down to us. However, some doubt attaches to this alleged martyrdom : Bede here seemingly is only quoting Gildas, and there is reason for thinking that Diocletian's edicts of persecution were not carried out in Britain. The feast of SS. Julius and Aaron is observed in the archdiocese of Cardiff on this date.

St Julian's farm near Caerleon, once the home of Edward, Lord Herbert of Chirbury, is said to be really St Julius's, and there are other local evidences of medieval *cultus*.

See Haddan and Stubbs, *Concilia*, vol. i, p. 6 ; LBS., vol. i, pp. 101–103 ; A. W. Wade-Evan's edition of Nennius (1938), p. 131 ; and W. Coxe, *Historical Tour through Monmouthshire*, pp. 103–104 (1904 ed.).

ST HELIODORUS, Bishop of Altino   (*c.* A.D. 400)

HELIODORUS, who had been a soldier, met St Jerome at Aquileia about the year 372 and became his disciple.   He went with Jerome and others to the East, but refused to accompany him into retirement in the desert, going back home in answer to the call of duties there instead.   Heliodorus was in consequence sharply rebuked by St Jerome in a celebrated letter that was greatly treasured by the early ascetics as a manifesto of their principles.

Soon after his return to Aquileia Heliodorus was named bishop of his native Altino, and the choice proved an excellent one ; when his nephew Nepotian was ordained priest, St Jerome—who never lost his affection for the friend he felt had deserted him—wrote telling him to take his uncle Heliodorus as a model of a Christian pastor.   St Heliodorus joined with St Chromatius of Aquileia in giving Jerome great encouragement and practical assistance with money and goods in his work of translating the Bible into Latin, help which he acknowledged gratefully in the preface to the books of Solomon.

See the *Acta Sanctorum*, July, vol. i, though the short Latin biography there printed is of little value.   The letters of St Jerome remain our chief authority, and *cf.* DCB., vol. ii, pp. 887–888.

ST ANATOLIUS, Patriarch of Constantinople   (A.D. 458)

WHEN St Flavian died as the result of the ill-treatment he had received at the Robber Council of Ephesus, Anatolius was appointed to succeed him in the see of Constantinople and was consecrated by Dioscorus of Alexandria, who was a monophysite.   He was a native of Alexandria and had distinguished himself at the Council of Ephesus in his opposition to Nestorianism.   Almost at once Anatolius held a synod at Constantinople, at which he formally accepted Pope St Leo's dogmatic letter (" The Tome ") sent to St Flavian, and he sent copies of the letter, together with a condemnation of Nestorius and Eutyches, to be signed by all his metropolitans.   This done, he informed the pope of his action, protested his orthodoxy, and asked to be recognized as Flavian's legitimate successor.   To this Leo agreed, but expressly " rather in mercy than in justice ", because of his association with and acceptance of consecration from a heretic, Dioscorus.   In the following year, at the great Council of Chalcedon, which defined the Catholic faith as against Monophysism and Nestorianism and recognized in unequivocal terms the authority of the Holy See, Anatolius took a prominent part ; he occupied the first place after the papal legates and earnestly seconded their efforts on behalf of the true faith of the Church.   It is disappointing to find that at the fifteenth session, from which the pope's legates were absent, Anatolius with the Eastern bishops decreed that the see of Constantinople was second only to that of Old Rome, in defiance of the historical rights of the reputedly apostolic sees of Alexandria and Antioch.   St Leo refused to accept this twenty-eighth canon and wrote to Anatolius that " a Catholic, especially if he be a priest of the Lord, should not be corrupted by ambition any more than involved in error ".

It is unfortunate that nothing is known of the private life of Anatolius, for his public career is rather equivocal for one who is acclaimed as a saint. Indeed, Baronius condemned him outright for the way he received his see, for ambition, for conniving at heresy, and on other grounds ; the Bollandists, on the other hand, acquit him of these charges, and Catholics of the Byzantine rite have always kept his feast on July 3, the day of his death in 458.

The very laudatory Greek life printed from a Paris manuscript by the Bollandists seems to be of no great authority, but there is abundant material in other more general sources. See Hergenröther's *Photius*, vol. i, pp. 66 *seq.*, DHG., vol. ii, cc. 1497–1500, and works dealing with the period.

ST RUMOLD, OR ROMBAUT, MARTYR   (*c.* A.D. 775)

IT is the view of the Bollandists that, if this Rumold came from the west at all, it was from England : but he is commonly credited to Ireland, where his feast is kept on this date. There is nothing known of him before the twelfth century, and most of it has no historical value. According to Abbot Theodoric he had faithfully served God for many years as a monk in his own country, when zeal for the salvation of souls induced him to preach the faith to the idolaters. He made a journey first to Rome, to receive his mission from the chief pastor, who consecrated him bishop, and with the apostolic blessing went into Brabant, a great part of which country about Malines he converted. He had a great desire to give his blood for Christ, an offering which was accepted, for having rebuked two men for the wickedness of their lives, they slew him and cast his body into the river. It was miraculously recovered and a great church built around his shrine, whereat many miracles were recorded. This church was dedicated in his honour and is now the cathedral of the city.

The life of St Rumold, by Theodoric of Saint-Trond, is printed in the *Acta Sanctorum* under July 1. His commemoration in the Roman Martyrology occurs on June 24 where he is described as " bishop of Dublin and martyr " as well as " son of a king of the Scots " (*i.e.* Irish). The most thorough discussion of this mythical story is to be found in the work of Canon J. Laenen, *Histoire de l'Église métropolitaine de S. Rombaut* (1919–20), and *cf. Analecta Bollandiana*, vol. liv (1936), pp. 12, 17.

ST BERNARDINO REALINO   (A.D. 1616)

BERNARDINO was born at Carpi, near Modena, in 1530 and had a somewhat lively youth, softening the rigour of successful studies by excursions into humanist literature. After having been engaged in the profession of the law, he entered the Society of Jesus when he was thirty-four years old. He was admitted at Naples by Father Alphonso Salmeron, one of the first companions of St Ignatius. Father Realino worked for ten years at Naples, preaching, catechizing, devoted to the sick, the poor and the inmates of prisons ; he was then transferred to the college at Lecce in Apulia, of which he became rector and where he died at the age of eighty-six. His self-sacrificing zeal and apostolical fervour had long before earned the veneration of the people, who recognized him as a saint, and a spontaneous *cultus* sprang up which helped to provide evidence for some of the remarkable occurrences which were testified to on oath in the process of beatification.

Six years before his death St Bernardino had a bad fall resulting in two wounds which would not heal ; during his last illness the blood discharged from these was collected and kept in phials on account of the great veneration in which he was held. This blood behaved in various extraordinary ways : in some vessels it kept liquid for over a century, in others it even foamed and appeared to increase in volume ; in one, according to witnesses at the process, it " boiled " and frothed on the anniversary of Bernardino's death and when it was brought near a reliquary containing his tongue. In 1634 his tomb was opened by the ecclesiastical authorities and a good deal of fleshy tissue was found unimpaired ; this was separated from the bones and put in two glass receptacles which were reburied in the same coffin as the skeleton. Seventy-eight years later (ninety-five after his death), in 1711, the contents of the coffin were inspected by the bishop of Lecce, before witnesses, to enable him to verify the relics. One of the glass vessels was found to be broken, but in the other the tissues were in an apparently unaltered state but floating in an inch and a half of dark red liquid ; this was carefully examined by physicians and pronounced to be human blood, giving off a sweet smell ; moreover, they stated that its preservation and smell under such conditions was miraculous—but there they exceeded their competence. Just over two years later a commission of three bishops, appointed by the Congregation of Sacred Rites to investigate the matter, took the evidence of the witnesses of 1711 and examined the blood : it was then liquid, crimson, and foaming into tiny bubbles. Don Gaetano Solazzo who had charge of a phial of the blood (probably that of 1616) in the cathedral of Lecce in 1804 left a statement to the effect that it was liquid, had twice foamed and bubbled, and was regarded by all as miraculous ; some nuns saw it do the same thing, and a Jesuit father stated in a sworn deposition that he had personally witnessed the like twice during the year 1852.

It has seemed worth while to give these details, which may not have anything whatever to do with the holiness of St Bernardino Realino, because they are a well-authenticated example of such prodigies, which raise an interest and excitement out of all proportion to their importance or significance. In 1895, however, St Bernardino's biographer could find no relic of the blood preserved in a liquid state. At the same time it may be pointed out that, just as the mortal flesh of many saints, known to have been preserved supple, incorrupt and almost life-like for long years after their decease, eventually hardens, blackens and crumbles away, so it seems only reasonable to expect that any similar immunity from putrefaction in the case of the blood, if such immunity be really granted in some instances, should only be temporary in its character.

See the biographies in Italian by E. Venturi (1895) and G. Germier (1943) ; *Lettere spirituali inedite* . . . (1854), ed. G. Boero ; and for the " blood miracles ", Father Thurston in *The Month*, January-March, 1927. An English biography by Fr F. Sweeney appeared in 1951. The canonization took place in 1947.

4 : ST BERTHA, Widow   (*c.* A.D. 725)

THIS Bertha at twenty years of age married a nobleman by whom she had five daughters. After her husband's death, she retired to the nunnery which she had built at Blangy in Artois, with her two elder daughters, Gertrude and Deotila. After establishing regular observance in her community, she left Deotila abbess in her stead, and shut herself in a cell, to be employed only in prayer.   No confidence can, however, be put in the historical accuracy of these particulars, for which the evidence is very late and unreliable.   Another story, of her pursuit by a certain Roger who wished to marry her by force, is equally worthless.

The so-called life is printed in the *Acta Sanctorum*, July, vol. ii ; see also Van der Essen, *Étude critique*, pp. 420–421.

ST ANDREW OF CRETE, ARCHBISHOP OF GORTYNA   (A.D. 740 ?)

THIS Andrew was born at Damascus about the middle of the seventh century.   In contrast with the ready tongue of his later years, he is said to have been quite dumb until he received holy communion when he was seven years old.   At the age of fifteen he went to Jerusalem (after which city he is sometimes named) and became a monk of St Sabas and of the Holy Sepulchre, where he received the orders of lector and subdeacon.   He in 685 was sent to Constantinople by Theodore, Patriarch of Jerusalem, to reiterate the adhesion of his church to the sixth oecu-menical council, which had recently condemned the monothelite heresy.   Andrew remained in the city and was ordained a deacon of the Great Church, and put in charge of an orphanage and of a hospice for old men.   His character and all-round abilities caused him soon to be advanced to the bishopric of Gortyna, the metro-politan see of Crete.   Here he became himself involved in the final recrudescence of Monothelism in 711, when Philippicus Bardanes seized the imperial throne, burned the acts of the sixth oecumenical council, restored the names of those it had anathematized to the diptychs in the liturgy, and summoned a synod to approve his actions.   Andrew was present at this synod in 712, but came to his senses in the following year and doubtless associated himself with the long letter of apology and explanation (pleading *force majeure*) which his patriarch sent to Pope Constan-tine, when the orthodox Anastasius II had driven out Bardanes.

For the rest of his life St Andrew distinguished himself as a preacher and hymnographer.   More than twenty of his discourses are extant, which have been edited and published ; but it is as a writer of hymns that he has left a permanent mark on the Byzantine liturgy.   He is said to have introduced that form of hymnody called a *kanon ;* certain it is that he wrote a large number of these and associated compositions, some of which are still sung.   Unfortunately the *kanon* is a form that lends itself to empty verbosity ; St Andrew himself wrote one of 250 strophes, sung in Lent, " with much hard work and weariness of the lungs ", wrote Combefis. St Andrew's homilies are of importance in the history of the development of Mariology.   This saint must not be confused with another Andrew of Crete, " the Calybite " (October 17).

The panegyric of Nicetas Quaestor (BHG., 16) tells us something of the life of St Andrew, and *cf.* S. Vailhé in *Échos d'Orient*, vol. v (1902), pp. 378–387.   Upon Andrew as homilist and hymn-writer see Bardenhewer, *Patrology* (Eng. trans.), p. 567 ; DTC., vol. i, cc. 1183–1184 ; DAC., vol. i, cc. 2034–2041 ; Nilles, *Kalendarium manuale*, vol. ii, pp. 147–156 ; and J. M. Neale, *Hymns of the Eastern Church*.   For a very free rendering of one of St Andrew's hymns, see no. 91 in *Hymns Ancient and Modern*.

ST ODO, ARCHBISHOP OF CANTERBURY   (A.D. 959)

ODO was born in East Anglia of Danish parents.   While bishop of Ramsbury he was present at the great battle of Brunanburh, when King Athelstan defeated the

Danes, Northumbrians and Scots, and shortly afterwards was translated to the see of Canterbury. As archbishop he was very active in both civil and ecclesiastical affairs ; he made his native East Anglia into a separate diocese, and encouraged the monastic reforms of St Dunstan at Glastonbury. Odo himself had received the religious habit at Fleury-sur-Loire.

He was popularly known as " Odo the Good ", and several miracles are recorded of him, one of which, at Canterbury, was a demonstration of the Real Presence against some doubting clergy. He died in 959, having lived in the reigns of six kings, and his name appears in several ancient calendars of the church of Canterbury.

The most reliable information about St Odo comes from the life of his nephew, St Oswald of York, by a contemporary monk of Ramsey ; it is printed in *Historians of the Church of York*, vol. i, in the Rolls Series. A life of Odo himself by Eadmer (*Acta Sanctorum*, July, vol. ii) is valuable, but much later in date. See also DNB., vol. xli. Odo's prefatory epistle to Frithegod's metrical Life of St Wilfrid is a curiosity of Anglo-Saxon learning ; *cf. Analecta Bollandiana*, vol. lxx (1952), p. 400.

ST ULRIC, Bishop of Augsburg (A.D. 973)

St Ulric was born at Augsburg in 890, and was educated in the abbey of St Gall. St Wiborada, a recluse who lived near that monastery, is said to have foretold that he would one day be a bishop, and would meet with severe trials, though the young man was so delicate that others who knew him judged he could never live long. Regularity and temperance preserved a life and strengthened a constitution which the excessive tenderness of parents and care of physicians would probably have worn out : a thing which Cardinal Lugo shows by several instances to have often happened in austere religious orders. When he had made progress in his studies his father removed him to Augsburg, where he placed him under the care of his uncle St Adalbero, bishop of that city ; and in due course Ulric himself was raised to the see.

The Magyars had lately pillaged the country, murdered his old friend Wiborada, plundered Augsburg, and burnt the cathedral. The new bishop, not to lose time, built for the present a small church, in which he assembled the people, who in their distress stood in extreme need of instruction, comfort, and relief, all which they found abundantly in Ulric, who devoted himself, so far as his other obligations would allow, entirely to his spiritual functions. He rose every morning at three o'clock to assist at Matins and Lauds, and only left the church after None ; then he went to the hospital, where he comforted the sick and every day washed the feet of twelve poor people, giving to each of them a liberal alms. The rest of the day he employed in instructing, preaching, visiting and discharging all the duties of a vigilant pastor. He made every year the visit of his whole diocese.

During his last years the saint earnestly desired to resign his bishopric and retire to the monastery of St Gall, and with this object appointed his nephew Adalbero in his place ; this was judged to be an uncanonical act, for which he had to answer before a synod at Ingelheim. In his last illness Ulric caused himself to be laid on ashes strewed on the floor in the form of a cross, and thus he died amidst the prayers of his clergy on July 4, 973. Miracles were recorded at his tomb, and he was canonized by Pope John XV in 993, the first solemn canonization by a pope of which there is record.

Abundant materials are available for the life of St Ulric.   The most important is the biography by the provost Gerhard, a contemporary, printed in the *Acta Sanctorum*, July, vol. ii, and in MGH., *Scriptores*, vol. iv.   There is also a life by Berno, abbot of Reichenau (in Migne, PL., cxlii, 1183–1204), as well as other early sources.   St Ulric seems to have left no writings ; a letter against clerical celibacy attributed to him is admittedly a forgery belonging to the period of the *Libelli de Lite* (see *The Month*, March, 1908, pp. 311–313) : this letter was exploited by the Reformers.   A German translation of it was printed and circulated in 1521, and an English version appeared in London about 1550.   There are several modern lives in German, *e.g.* those of Raffler, Stützle, and U. Schmid (1904), and a full and able article in the *Kirchenlexikon*, vol. xii.

BD WILLIAM OF HIRSCHAU, Abbot   (A.D. 1091)

In the year 1065 Bd Frederick, a monk of Einsiedeln, was sent with twelve companions to re-people the abbey of Hirschau in Würtemberg, which for sixty years had been in the hands of the counts of Calw and was falling into decay.   Pope St Leo IX, who belonged to the family of Calw, had ordered Count Adalbert to restore the abbey to the Benedictines, which he did very slowly and with a bad grace, and obtained such an influence over part of the new community that after four years they deposed Frederick.   In his place was elected William, a monk of the abbey of St Emmeram at Ratisbon, who protested against the deposition of Bd Frederick and refused to regard himself as other than his vicar until after his death.   After dealing with Count Adalbert, Abbot William turned his attention to the reform of his monks and the building up of a stable and observant community.   Bernard, abbot of Saint Victor at Marseilles who had been sent into Germany as papal legate, advised him to adopt the usages and observance of Cluny, which William accordingly did.   His own personal reputation attracted numbers of suitable subjects and he was able to re-establish the school for which Hirschau had formerly been famous ; and, knowing that idleness is a chief enemy of monks and that good books cannot be too often multiplied, he staffed a large *scriptorium*.   He himself drew up the " Constitutions of Hirschau ", which for long remained the norm of observance in that monastery and in many others, and set an example of such careful observance of them that he completely reformed his own community and attracted so many aspirants that other monasteries had to be founded for them.

One of the outstanding characteristics of William's life and one by no means shared by all the great abbots of the middle ages, was his concern for the spiritual and material well-being of the serfs both of the monastery and of neighbouring manors ; and by aggregating its servants to the monastic community he had a significant part in the development of the institution of *fratres conversi* (lay-brothers). Bd William strongly appreciated the value of learning, and had seen how often bad morals go with lack of instruction and of intelligence ; hence on the one hand his interest in the schooling of the common people and on the other his urgency for a learned episcopate : when asked to recommend men suitable for a bishopric he always, other things being equal, named a scholar.   His own accomplishments, after that science of the saints, knowledge of God and holy living, in which he excelled, were of a variousness more common in his time than in ours : astronomy, music, mathematics, poetry ; he invented an ingenious clock, revised and rewrote several of the office hymns, and among other works wrote a treatise *De musica et tonis*.   But his great public work was the establishment of his " school of the Lord's service ", whose charter he wrote down in the constitutions which continued to be in force at Hirschau until the beginning of the fifteenth century.

There is a biography by a contemporary, said to be Haymo, Prior of Hirschau. As printed in the *Acta Sanctorum* (July, vol. ii) it seems to be overlaid with legendary matter. The more historical portions have been re-edited in MGH., *Scriptores*, vol. xii. See also B. Albers in *Festschrift zum Jubiläum des deutschen Campo Santo*, pp. 115–129, and the articles in the *Catholic Encyclopedia*, vol. xv, p. 629, and vol. vii, p. 363. There are modern lives by Kerker (1863) and Helmsdörfer (1874) and a valuable study of Bd William's musical theories by Hans Müller (1883).

BB. JOHN CORNELIUS AND HIS COMPANIONS, THE DORCHESTER MARTYRS (A.D. 1594)

ON July 4, 1594 was hanged, drawn and quartered at Dorchester in Dorset Bd JOHN CORNELIUS (*alias* Mohun), priest, and with him were simply hanged BB. THOMAS BOSGRAVE, JOHN CAREY and PATRICK SALMON, laymen. Mr Cornelius was born of Irish parents at Bodmin in 1557 and was sent to Oxford by Sir John Arundell of Lanherne : but not liking the " new learning " of that university he went overseas to the English College at Rheims and afterwards to Rome, where he was ordained. He worked on the English mission from Lanherne for nearly ten years, and both then and during his earlier days abroad he was known as a man of unusual zeal and recollection.

On April 25, 1594, he was arrested at Chideock Castle, the seat of Lady Arundell, by the sheriff of Dorset. While he was being hurried away, bareheaded and unprepared, Mr Thomas Bosgrave, a gentleman of Cornwall, nephew of Sir John Arundell, offered him his hat, saying, " The honour I owe to your function may not suffer me to see you go bare-headed ". This innocent act of kindness and respect was sufficient to implicate him, and he also was arrested. At the same time were carried off two of the castle serving-men, John Carey and Patrick Salmon, both Dubliners. Cornelius was taken to London and examined before the Privy Council, which ordered him to be racked that he might betray the names of those who had harboured or assisted him ; but he remained mute, and was returned to Dorchester for trial. On July 2 he was found guilty of high treason, in that he was a priest who had come into the realm and remained there, and the other three for felony in aiding and abetting him. After sentence had been pronounced they were offered a reprieve if they would apostatize.

Two days later they were executed. The laymen, each of whom made a final profession of faith, suffered first ; Bd John Cornelius kissed the feet of his companions, but was not allowed to speak to the people ; he was, however, able to declare that he had been admitted into the Society of Jesus and would have gone to Flanders for his novitiate but for his arrest.

There also suffered at Dorchester Bd HUGH GREEN, a secular priest who on August 19, 1642, was hanged, drawn and quartered with peculiarly revolting circumstances, for his priesthood. The feast of the Dorchester martyrs is kept in the diocese of Plymouth.

See MMP., pp. 198–202. But fuller details concerning these martyrs may be found in an article contributed by Fr Leo Hicks to *Studies*, December, 1929, pp. 537–555 ; and *cf.* A. L. Rowse, *Tudor Cornwall* (1941), pp. 358, 363–367.

BB. WILLIAM ANDLEBY AND HIS COMPANIONS, MARTYRS (A.D. 1597)

ON July 4, 1597, there suffered at York Bd WILLIAM ANDLEBY, a secular priest, and BB. HENRY ABBOT, THOMAS WARCOP and EDWARD FULTHROP, laymen. Mr Andleby (or Anlaby) was born at Etton, near Beverley, and brought up a Protestant, being educated at St John's College, Cambridge. When some twenty-five years old, while on his way to join the Dutch in their wars with the Spaniards, he visited Douay and had an interview with Dr Allen. Within twenty-four hours the prayers and discourses of the rector of the seminary had such an effect on the young man, who hitherto had been strongly averse from the Church and even from religion at all in his behaviour, that he not only made his submission but remained in Douay and was in due course ordained in 1577.

He worked on the mission in Yorkshire and Lincolnshire for twenty years, and was concerned with the Ven. Thomas Atkinson in ministering under conditions of the greatest difficulty and danger to the Catholic prisoners in Hull Castle. He was at last arrested and condemned to be hanged, drawn and quartered for being a priest. The same death was inflicted on Edward Fulthrop, a Yorkshire gentleman, for having been reconciled to the Church, and Thomas Warcop was hanged for sheltering Mr Andleby. Henry Abbot, of Holden in the East Riding, was hanged, drawn and quartered for persuading another to join the Catholic Church. Into this he had been tricked by a Protestant minister who, being imprisoned in York Castle for some offence or other, had pretended that he wished to abjure his heresy to ingratiate himself with some recusant fellow prisoners. These at his release referred him to Mr Abbot as a likely person to know of a priest who would reconcile him. At the minister's request, therefore, Abbot tried to find one at a certain house, and, though he did not succeed, this was sufficient to ensure his death and that of the recusants in the jail (the Ven. George Errington, William Knight and William Gibson) when the treacherous minister had commended himself to his superiors by informing on those whom he had deceived.

See Challoner, *Memoirs of Missionary Priests*, pp. 231–232.

5: ST ANTONY ZACCARIA, FOUNDER OF THE CLERKS REGULAR OF ST PAUL (A.D. 1539)

THE early part of the sixteenth century, before the Council of Trent, was one of the saddest periods of the Church's history ; nevertheless it produced some figures of outstanding sanctity and beauty, and among these that of Antony Mary Zaccaria is one of the noblest. He was born at Cremona in 1502 and his father died while he was yet young ; but his mother made admirable compensation for that early loss and in particular encouraged that side of her son's character which was moved to compassion by the sufferings of the poor. He was sent to the University of Padua to study medicine ; when he was twenty-two he graduated, and returned to his home to practise. Here he soon learned that his vocation was to heal souls as well as bodies, and he began seriously to study theology, meantime continuing to exercise his profession, to give spiritual help to the dying, to teach Christian doctrine to the young, and to be at the service of all. In 1528 he was ordained priest, and his spiritual and corporal ministry was so successful that he was encouraged to extend its possibilities by removing to the bigger city of Milan.

Here Antony joined the Confraternity of Eternal Wisdom and met people like-minded with himself, among them Louisa Torelli, Countess of Guastalla, who under his direction founded the congregation of women called the Angelicals, for the protection and rescue of girls who were in danger or had fallen into evil ways ; these sisters were an auxiliary of the saint in all his works of mercy. In 1530 he decided, with two other priests, the Ven. Bartholomew Ferrari and the Ven. James Morigia, to start a body of clerks regular (*i.e.* priests who are bound by rule and vows but are neither monks nor friars), whose object should be to " regenerate and revive the love of divine worship, and a properly Christian way of life by frequent preaching and faithful ministering of the sacraments ". This was done with five members, who preached in any place, church or street, and particularly on our Lord's passion and death for men, of which St Antony reminded people every Friday evening by the tolling of a bell. While Luther was attacking both the truths of the faith and the iniquities of churchmen, while the people were oppressed physically by the wars which ravaged Italy and spiritually by the neglect of the clergy, this faithful band laboured heroically to reform the Church from within by reviving the Christian spirit and care for souls among the clergy and by ministering to the dual needs of the laity. They worked among the plague-stricken Milanese and infused such vigour into the spiritual life of their city that in 1533 the new congregation was approved by Pope Clement VII under the name of the Clerks Regular of St Paul. The founder was its first provost general, but three years later he resigned the office to Father Morigia and went to inaugurate its work at Vicenza, where he is said to have introduced from Milan the custom of exposing the Blessed Sacrament for three continuous days.

In the last year of his life St Antony acquired for the headquarters of his congregation the church of St Barnabas at Milan, whence the common name of Barnabites for his followers. While on a mission at Guastalla he was taken ill and, his body worn out by mortifications and unceasing work, he quickly became worse ; he was carried to his mother's house at Cremona and there died at the age of thirty-seven. He was canonized by Pope Leo XIII in 1897. After considerable troubles in their early days the Barnabites prospered, but have never been a large order ; they still labour in modest obscurity among the outcasts of great towns ; they educate, for wherever is a Barnabite community there is a centre of learning ; and following their founder they preach the gospel with special reference to the epistles of St Paul.

See P. A. Dubois, *Antoine Marie Zaccharia* (1890) ; F. T. Moltedo, *Vita di S. Antonio Maria Zaccaria* (1897) ; and O. M. Premoli, *Le lettere e lo spirito religioso di S. Antonio Zaccaria* (1909), and *Storia dei Barnabiti nel cinquecento* (1913).

ST ATHANASIUS THE ATHONITE, Abbot   (*c.* A.D. 1000)

FOR a thousand years Athos, the Holy Mountain, the most easterly of the three large headlands which the peninsula of Chalcidice thrusts out into the Aegean Sea, has been the chief centre of Byzantine monasticism ; for nearly all that time this " monastic republic " has been out of communion with the Holy See, but at the time of its inception and organization, and during the preceding centuries when it was occupied by little colonies of hermits, Athos was Catholic and a stronghold of orthodoxy in a different sense from that in which it is so today. The father of Mount Athos as a congeries of regular monasteries was one Athanasius, who was born at Trebizond about the year 920, the son of an Antiochene, and baptized Abraham. He studied at Constantinople, where he became a professor ; and while he was teaching he met St Michael Maleinos and his nephew, Nicephorus Phocas, who as emperor was to be Abraham's patron. He received the monastic habit in St Michael's monastery at Kymina in Bithynia, taking the name of Athanasius, and lived there till about the year 958. Kymina was a *laura*, the name then reserved for monasteries wherein the monks lived in separate cells grouped more or less closely round their church. When the abbot St Michael Maleinos died Athanasius saw that he would be pretty surely elected in his place ; he there-fore fled, and eventually found his way to Mount Athos, to avoid this responsibility —only to find that God was reserving for him a greater.

He disguised himself as an ignorant fellow, assuming the name of Dorotheos, and hid in a cell near Karyes, but he was soon traced and found by his friend Nicephorus Phocas. He was about to undertake an expedition against the Saracens, and persuaded Athanasius to come to Crete to help him organize it (it is so often found that the contemplative soul is a capable man of affairs—which, after all, is only to be expected) and to support it with his blessing and prayers. Athanasius was very unwilling to make this sally out into the world and its concerns, but he went ; the expedition was victorious, and Athanasius asked permission to return to Athos. But before he was allowed to he was forced to accept a large sum of money, with which he was to build a monastery. This, the first monastery proper on Athos, was begun in the spring of 961 and the church two years later ; it was dedicated in honour of the All-holy Mother of God, but is now called " of St Athanasius ", or, more often, simply Laura, " The Monastery ".

When Nicephorus Phocas became emperor, Athanasius feared that he might be called to court or to other honours and disturbing offices, so he ran away from Athos to Cyprus. Phocas again found him and told him to go back and govern his monastery in peace, giving him more money, with which was built a harbour for Athos. In adopting the *laura* system for his monks, Athanasius had deliberately reversed the policy of St Basil and St Theodore Studites and returned in a measure to the ancient monastic tradition of Egypt ; his monks were to be as " out of the world " as is possible for human beings (even now the Athonite monks are still extraordinarily " out of touch with things ", as a general rule). But in spite of this he was involved in great difficulties with the solitaries who had been on Athos long before he came and who felt, understandably, that generations of predecessors had given them a prescriptive right to have the place to themselves ; they resented his coming there and building monasteries and churches and harbours, imposing rules and keeping order generally. Twice attempts were made to murder St Athanasius. Criminal violence spoils the best of causes, and the Emperor John Tzimisces interfered ; he confirmed the donations and rights granted by Nicephorus Phocas, forbade opposition to Athanasius, and recognized his authority over the whole of the mountain and its inhabitants. He thus became superior general over fifty-eight communities of hermits and monks, and the monasteries of Iviron, Vatopedi and Esphigmenou were founded, which still exist as living communities. St Athan-asius died about the year 1000, being killed with five of his monks by the falling of a keystone of the vault of the church on which they were working. He is named daily in the preparation of the Byzantine Liturgy, and is sometimes called " the Lauriote " or " of Trebizond ".

There exists a very full Greek life of St Athanasius the Athonite which was edited in Russia by J. Pomialovsky in 1895. The author was a monk, also named Athanasius, who lived in close relation with the saint's immediate successor in office. Another long biography in Greek, based upon the earlier text, was published by L. Petit in the *Analecta Bollandiana*, vol. xxv (1906), pp. 1–89, with the addition of valuable notes ; a French translation appeared in *Irénikon*, t. viii and ix (1931–32). Mount Athos and its monasteries has always had a great interest for scholars of the Anglican Church ; Messrs Athelstan Riley, Kirsopp Lake, F. Hasluck and R. M. Dawkins may be mentioned among writers of more recent date ; but there is a very extensive literature upon the subject in French and German. See especially P. de Meester, *Voyage de deux Bénédictins* (1908), F. Perilla, *Le Mont Athos* (1927), and T. Belpaire in *Irénikon*, t. vi (1929).

6 : ST ROMULUS, BISHOP OF FIESOLE, MARTYR   (*c.* A.D. 90 ?)

ACCORDING to a late tradition, the apostle and first bishop of Fiesole was Romulus, a Roman convert of St Peter, who was martyred under Domitian. Nothing is known of him historically, and his name was added to the Roman Martyrology only in the sixteenth century.

St Romulus is the hero of a rather tiresome romance, of uncertain *provenance*, but seemingly a work of fiction of not earlier than the eleventh century. In this we are told that a certain citizen of Rome had a daughter named Lucerna who gave her affections and herself to one of her father's slaves, Cyrus. By him a son was born to her, whom she abandoned in a wood, where the baby was adopted and suckled by a wolf. The unnatural sight was seen by some verderers of the Emperor Nero, who reported it to him and were ordered to capture the child. For three days the hunt pursued the couple without catching them, whereupon the emperor consulted St Peter. Peter provided himself and some fellow Christians with fishing nets and went into the wood, where they were confronted by the child and his foster-mother. Peter adjured the boy, " If you are born of a wolf, go hence ; but if of a human woman, come to me ". The quarry did not stir, the Christians shot their nets, and the two were caught and safely shut up. To eat they gave them a sheep, which the wolf straightway killed and both fed on its raw flesh. Thereupon St Peter ordered the wolf to be liberated and driven off, and the child was baptized ; at the suggestion of Peter's companion Justin it was, with a nice appropriateness, given the name of Romulus. He was civilized and educated first by a noble Roman lady and then by the same Justin, and at eight years of age this prodigy was preaching, exorcizing and working miracles. Romulus was later consecrated bishop, he evangelized at Fiesole, Sutri, Nepi, Florence, Pistoia, etc., and after sundry adventures and doing of marvels he was ordered to be put to death by the governor Repertian. On the way to execution Romulus begged a drink of water from a girl at a wayside spring ; she, for fear of the soldiers, refused, and the martyr rebuked her and ordained that for the future the spring should still run fresh water for Christians, but to every heathen man drinking of it should be turned to blood. With St Romulus were executed Carissimus, Dulcissimus and Crescentius.

It is a curious fact that despite the wild extravagance of the above legend, there is evidence of the historical existence and early *cultus* of a St Romulus at Fiesole. The story has been critically studied by A. Cocchi, *San Romolo, vescovo di Fiesole ; Storia e Leggende* (1905). The one element of historical interest is a fragmentary epitaph said to be of the end of the fourth century. But *cf.* M. C. Cipolla in *Rivista storico-critica delle scienze teologiche*, vol. i, pp. 422–428.

ST DOMINICA, VIRGIN AND MARTYR   (*c.* A.D. 303 ?)

THIS is the best known of several saints of the name, but her existence, so far as the Western legend is concerned, is more than doubtful. Baronius inserted her name in the Roman Martyrology with this notice : " In Campania, of the holy Dominica, virgin and martyr, who was a breaker of idols under the Emperor Diocletian and was therefore condemned to the beasts ; but being not at all hurt by them she was at last beheaded and passed to the Lord. Her body is preserved with great honour at Tropea in Calabria." The lessons of her office tell us further that she was born in the Campagna, suffered on the banks of the Euphrates, and that her body was carried by angels to Tropea. But in that city it is said that she was born, lived and died there—whereas actually she seems to have been unheard of there before the sixteenth century. It is possible that she must be identified with St Cyriaca (*Κυριακή* = Dominica), a virgin martyr whom the Byzantines venerate on July 7 ; her acts are worthless, but they state that she suffered by beheading at Nicomedia in Bithynia. What started her *cultus* at Tropea, or whether there is a confusion of two Dominicas, is not known.

See the *Acta Sanctorum*, July, vol. ii. What little can be said in defence of the legend will be found in a booklet of Mgr Taccone-Gallucci, *Memoria storica di Santa Domenica* (1893).

ST SISOES   (*c.* A.D. 429)

AFTER the death of St Antony, St Sisoes was one of the most shining lights of the Egyptian deserts. He was an Egyptian by birth, and having quitted the world in his youth he retired to the desert of Skete. The desire of finding a more unfrequented retreat induced him to cross the Nile and hide himself in the mountain where St Antony had died, and the memory of that great man's virtues wonderfully supported his fervour and encouraged him to persevere. He imagined he saw him and heard the instructions he was wont to deliver to his disciples ; and he strained every nerve to imitate his most heroic exercises : the austerity of his penance, the rigour of his silence, the ardour of his prayer, so that the reputation of Sisoes spread among the neighbouring solitaries, and some came a great distance to be guided in the ways of perfection, and he was forced to submit his love of silence and retreat to the greater duty of charity.

His zeal against vice was without bitterness ; and when his disciples fell into faults he did not affect astonishment or the language of reproach, but helped them to rise again with patience and tenderness. Sisoes in all his advice and instruction held out humility constantly as a most necessary virtue. A recluse saying to him one day, " Father, I always place myself in the presence of God ", he replied. " It would be much better for you to put yourself below every creature, in order to be securely humble." Thus, while he never lost sight of the divine presence, it was ever accompanied with the consciousness of his own worthlessness. To another who complained that he had not yet arrived at the perfection of St Antony, he said, " Ah ! if I had but one only of that man's feelings, I should be one flame of divine love ". On a visit of three solitaries wanting instruction, one of them said, " Father, what shall I do to avoid hell-fire ? " Sisoes made no reply. " How shall I ", asked another, " escape the gnashing of teeth and the worm that dieth not ? " " What will become of me ? " asked the third, " for every time I think of outer darkness I am ready to die with fear." Then the saint answered : " I confess that these are subjects which I never think about, and as I know that God is merciful, I trust He will have compassion on me. You are happy ", he added, " and I envy your virtue. You speak of the torments of Hell, and your fears must be strong guards against sin. It is I should exclaim, What shall become of me ? for I am so insensible as never even to reflect on the place of torment. This perhaps is the reason I am guilty of so much sin." He said another time : " I am now thirty years praying daily that my Lord Jesus may preserve me from saying an idle word, and yet I am always relapsing."

Being at length worn out with sickness and old age, Sisoes yielded to his disciple Abraham's advice, and went to reside a while at Clysma, a town near the Red Sea. Here he received a visit from Ammon, abbot of Raithu, who, seeing him miserable at being absent from his retreat, tried to comfort him by pointing out that his present state of health wanted the remedies which could not be had in the desert. " What do you say ? " replied the saint. " Was not the ease of mind I enjoyed there everything for my comfort ? " and he was not at ease till he returned to his retreat.

The solitaries assisting at his death-bed heard him cry out, " Behold ! Abbot Antony, the choir of prophets, and the angels are come to take my soul ! " At the same time his countenance shone, and being some time interiorly recollected with God, he cried out anew, " Behold ! our Lord comes for me ! " And so he died, about the year 429, after a retreat of at least sixty-two years in St Antony's Mount. His feast is observed in the Byzantine calendar.

This saint must not be confused with another SISOES, surnamed the Theban, who lived in the same age at Calamon, in the territory of Arsinoe. It is related of him that a certain recluse, having received some offence, went to tell him that he must be avenged. The holy old man recommended him to leave his revenge to God, to pardon his brother, and forget the injury. But seeing that his advice had no weight, " At least ", said he, " let us both join in speaking to God ". Then, standing up, he prayed thus aloud : " O Lord, we no longer want your care of our interests or your protection, since this monk maintains that we can and ought to be our own avengers."

What we know of St Sisoes comes to us mainly through the *Apophthegmata Patrum*, a collection of utterances of the fathers of the desert, to which of late years much attention has been devoted. See particularly W. Bousset, *Apophthegmata ; Studien zur Geschichte des ältesten Mönchtums* (1923), with the review of this in the *Analecta Bollandiana*, vol. xlii (1924), pp. 430–435 ; Wilmart in *Revue Bénédictine*, vol. xxxiv (1922), pp. 185–198. The Greek text is in Migne, PG., vol. lxv, cc. 71–440. The Latin, differently arranged, is in Migne, PL., vol. lxxiii, cc. 855–1022.

ST GOAR   (*c.* A.D. 575)

GOAR was born in Aquitaine and for years worked as a parish priest in his own country. But he heard the call of solitude and eventually settled down on the banks of the Rhine near the small town of Oberwesel. Here he lived for years in quietness till it happened to him as it has happened to so many other solitaries—he was " discovered " and people came to consult him. The peasants of the neighbourhood were particularly fond of him : they listened to his preaching, wondered at his way of life, marvelled at his holiness and patience, and then went away and attributed all sorts of miracles to him. Probably no notice would have been taken had he not been a priest, but some busybody reported his irregular ministry to the bishop of Trier, and evil-disposed persons added the information that the holy hermit was a humbug, who over-ate himself, got drunk, and deceived the people. The bishop, Rusticus, thereupon sent for Goar, who obediently came and was accused not only of hypocrisy but of sorcery and other crimes. How he cleared himself is not known : according to the legend God Himself interfered and caused a three-day-old child not only to vindicate the hermit but also to convict the bishop of most irregular living. There was at once an outcry, and Sigebert I, King of Austrasia, hearing what had happened, sent for St Goar to come to him at Metz. The hermit's modesty and innocence greatly impressed the king, and having deposed the unworthy Rusticus, he wished to put him in his place. But the idea of being a bishop so upset Goar that he was taken ill ; he asked for time to think it over, and went back to his cell, where death overtook him before the king succeeded in getting his acceptance. His home became a place of pilgrimage, and is now marked by a small town which bears his name and has a church dedicated in his honour.

The curious legend of St Goar, in the form in which we have it, is probably older than 768, but it cannot be regarded as a historical document. There can have been no Rusticus, bishop of Trier, in the time of Childebert and Sigebert I. The primitive text, in very barbarous Latin, has been critically edited by B. Krusch in MGH., *Scriptores Merov.*, vol. iv, pp. 402–423 ; a more readable recension is in the *Acta Sanctorum*, July, vol. ii. See also J. Depoin, *La légende de S. Goar* in the *Revue des Études historiques*, vol. lxxv (1909), pp. 369–385.

ST SEXBURGA, ABBESS OF ELY, WIDOW (*c.* A.D. 699)

ST SEXBURGA was daughter of Anna, King of the East Angles, and therefore the sister of SS. Etheldreda, Ethelburga and Withburga, and half-sister of St Sethrida. She was given in marriage to Erconbert, King of Kent, a prince of excellent dispositions which she contributed for twenty-four years to improve by her counsels and example. Her virtue commanded the reverence, and her humility and devotion raised the admiration, of her subjects ; and her goodness and charity gained her the love of all. She became the mother of two princes and of two saints, Ercongota and Ermenilda. Because she had a longing to consecrate herself wholly to God in religious retirement, and that others might attend divine service without impediment, she began in her husband's lifetime to found a monastery at Minster in the isle of Sheppey, which she finished after his death in 664. Here she assembled seventy-four nuns, and herself joined them. After some years she appointed her daughter Ermenilda to rule the house, and, being desirous to live in greater obscurity and to be more at liberty to employ all her thoughts on Heaven, she left Kent and went to the abbey of Ely, where she was chosen to succeed her sister St Etheldreda in the government of that house. Sixteen years after she caused the body of that saint to be taken up, when it was found incorrupt, and was enshrined in a white marble coffin found at Cambridge. Sexburga herself passed to bliss in a good old age, on July 6, at the end of the seventh century. Her monastery of Minster-in-Sheppey was destroyed by the Danes, but rebuilt in 1130, and consecrated in honour of our Lady and St Sexburga, continuing to be occupied by Benedictine nuns until the dissolution.   She was also honoured in Sweden.

See Bede's *Ecclesiastical History*, bk iii, cap. 8 and iv, 19.   A Latin life of Sexburga described by Hardy, *Catalogue of British History* (vol. i, pp. 361–362), seems to be of no historical value apart from its quotation from Bede.   There is some mention of Sexburga in certain Anglo-Saxon fragments printed by Cockayne in vol. iii of his *Leechdoms*.   See also the *Acta Sanctorum*, July, vol. ii, and Stanton's *Menology*, p. 313.

ST MODWENNA, Virgin   (Seventh Century ?)

The St Modwenna, or Monenna, formerly venerated at Burton-on-Trent and elsewhere, may have lived in the middle of the seventh century and been a recluse on an islet called Andresey in the Trent.   But not only are other and conflicting things alleged of her, but her legend has been conflated with that of the Irish St Darerca, or Moninne, said to have been the first abbess of Killeavy, near Newry, and to have died in 517 ; and she has perhaps been confused with others as well. Capgrave and others speak of St Modwenna as having charge of St Edith of Poles-worth, which were it true would throw no useful light on either saint.   The most valuable information we possess about St Moninne seems to be the entry in the *Félire* of Oengus : " Moninne of the mountain of Cuilenn was a fair pillar ; she gained a triumph, a hostage of purity, a kinswoman of great Mary ", with the gloss.

It would seem hopeless to unravel the tangle.   Baring-Gould and Fisher (LBS., vol. iii, pp. 490–497, and *cf*. i, pp. 286–287) only seem to make confusion worse confounded.   Two Latin lives are printed in the *Acta Sanctorum* under July 6—the one is anonymous, from the Codex Salmanticensis, the other attributed to Conchubranus.   The latter has been again edited by M. Esposito in the *Proceedings of the Royal Irish Academy*, vol. xxxviii (1910), pp. 202–251.   There is a later *vita* in manuscript by Geoffrey of Burton.   For those who can read Anglo-Norman texts " le romanz de la vie seinte Modwenne noneyne ", ed. A. T. Baker and A. Bell (*St Modwenna* ; 1947), will be of interest.   See also KSS., pp. 404–407 ; and for Moninne, J. Ryan, *Irish Monasticism* (1931), p. 136.

ST GODELEVA, Martyr   (A.D. 1070 ?)

According to the narrative written by a contemporary priest, Drogo, the story of Godeleva is an example of that wanton persecution and cruelty shown towards an innocent victim which is as shocking to reasonable, not to say Christian, human beings as it is unexplainable ; no adequate motive is given or even suggested for the behaviour of the offender at first, though afterwards his desire to get rid of his wife is clear enough.

Godeleva was born at Londefort-lez-Boulogne about 1049, of noble parentage. She grew up beautiful both in person and character, and was particularly beloved by the poor, to whose welfare she constantly devoted herself.   At the age of eighteen she married a Flemish lord, Bertulf of Ghistelles, who conducted his bride home, where she was received with insults by his mother ; apparently she had had other plans for her son, and was furious that he had disregarded them in favour of this girl from the Boulonnais.   Bertulf, the days of the wedding festivities yet unfinished, deserted Godeleva, leaving her in charge of his mother, who was not content with petty persecutions, but treated her who should have been mistress of the house with fanatic brutality.   She at length contrived to escape and returned to her parents, who took the case to the count of Flanders and the bishop of

Tournai.   It was ruled that Bertulf should receive back his wife, and henceforward treat her properly, which he promised to do.

But once she was back at Ghistelles, Bertulf was first indifferent and then again openly violent to her, and to get rid of her he resolved on more direct action. First of all he shammed penitence and a desire for reconciliation, with the object both of averting suspicion from himself and to enable him the more easily to entrap the girl.   Then at the appointed time Godeleva was induced by a trick to go out of the castle by a back-door at night ; she was seized by two of Bertulf's servants and smothered by having her head held down in a pond, with a thong drawn tight round her neck.   When she was dead, the ruffians replaced her body in bed, meaning it to be supposed she had died a natural death.   It was obvious that she had not, but Bertulf had absented himself in Bruges at the time of the crime and Godeleva's parents were unable to bring it home to him.   He at once married again, but his wickedness haunted him, and he ended his days in a monastery at Bergues-St-Winoc.

The scene of the murder of Godeleva soon had a reputation for miracles, and the sudden recovery of sight by Bertulf's blind daughter by his second wife was attributed to her intercession.   In 1084 her body was dug up and enshrined in the church, which is still a place of pilgrimage, the people drinking the water of her well and appropriately invoking her intercession against sore throats.   It is difficult to see why (except in popular estimation) Godeleva is venerated as a martyr : she did not endure death for any article of the faith or for the preservation of any Christian virtue or for any other act of virtue relating to God—unless indeed her supernatural patience finally provoked her husband to his wicked violence.

The Bollandists in the *Acta Sanctorum* (July, vol. ii) have treated St Godeleva at great length, printing not only the life by Drogo, but also another, more diffuse, narrative of her history.   A copy of the formal verification of the saint's relics made when they were " elevated " in 1084, shortly after her death, has been preserved, and its authenticity has been established by the tattered fragments of a later deed which recites it.   This was found when the shrine was examined in 1907.   See the *Analecta Bollandiana*, vol. xliv (1926), pp. 102–137, for an earlier text of the Drogo *vita*, ed. by Father Coens, and vol. lxii (1944), pp. 292–295 ; and also the charming little book of M. English, *Les quatre couronnes de Ste Godelieve de Gistel* (1953).

BD THOMAS ALFIELD, Martyr   (A.D. 1585)

THOMAS ALFIELD (his name is variously spelt) was born in Gloucester and educated at Eton and King's College, Cambridge.   He was brought up a Protestant, and on becoming a Catholic went to Douay in 1576 to study for the priesthood.   He was ordained at Rheims in 1581 and sent on the English mission, where he was associated with Bd Edmund Campion.   By the spring of 1582 he was already in the Tower of London, and here he endured torture without failing ; but later for a short time he succumbed to temptation, and outwardly conformed to the Established Church.   After his release he withdrew to Rheims, where he made amends, and then came back to England.

In the early part of 1584 Alfield was concerned in a curious episode.   He was employed by John Davys, the navigator who explored for the North-West Passage, to communicate an offer of his (Davys's) services to the court of Spain—a proposal that may be assumed not to have been seriously meant.   Later in the year, with the help of Thomas Webley, also of Gloucester, and a dyer by trade, Alfield was busy circulating copies of Dr Allen's *True and modest Defence*, written in answer to *Execution of Justice*, in which Burghley had sought to prove that Catholics were being proceeded against in England not for their religion but for treason.   This soon landed him in the Tower again, and both he and Webley were tortured, with the object of making them disclose to whom they had distributed the book.   They were both tried and condemned for this offence, and were hanged at Tyburn on July 6, 1585, after being offered their freedom if they would acknowledge the queen's ecclesiastical leadership.   A reprieve had in fact been issued for Bd Thomas—it is not known why—but it arrived too late.   A third man who had been concerned with them, one Crabbe, purchased his life by apostasy ; Alfield's brother, Robert, also became a renegade.

Bd Thomas Alfield was beatified in 1929 ; the Venerable Thomas Webley's cause is still under consideration.

See MMP., pp. 105–106 ; Burton and Pollen, LEM. ; and Catholic Record Society's *Publications*, vol. v.

ST MARY GORETTI, Virgin and Martyr   (A.D. 1902)

MARY GORETTI was born in 1890 at Corinaldo, a village some thirty miles from Ancona, the daughter of a farm-labourer, Luigi Goretti, and his wife Assunta Carlini.   They had five other children, and in 1896 the family moved to Colle Gianturco, near Galiano, and later to Ferriere di Conca, not far from Nettuno in the Roman Campagna.   Almost at once after settling down here, Luigi Goretti was stricken with malaria and died.   His widow had to take up his work as best she could, but it was a hard struggle and every small coin and bit of food had to be looked at twice.   Of all the children none was more cheerful and encouraging to her mother than Mary, commonly called Marietta.

On a hot afternoon in July 1902 Mary was sitting at the top of the stairs in the cottage, mending a shirt.   She was not yet quite twelve years old, and it must be remembered that in Italy girls mature earlier than in more northern countries. Presently a cart stopped outside, and a neighbour, a young man of eighteen named Alexander, ran up the stairs.   He beckoned Mary into an adjoining bedroom ; but this sort of thing had happened before and she refused to go.   Alexander seized hold of her, pulled her in, and shut the door.

Mary struggled and tried to call for help, but she was being half-strangled and could only protest hoarsely, gasping that she would be killed rather than submit.   Whereupon Alexander half pulled her dress from her body and began striking at her blindly with a long dagger.   She sank to the floor, crying out that she was being killed : Alexander plunged the dagger into her back, and ran away.

An ambulance fetched Mary to hospital, where it was seen at once that she could not possibly live.   Her last hours were most touching—her concern for where her mother was going to sleep, her forgiveness of her murderer (and she now disclosed that she had long been going in fear of him, but did not like to say anything lest she cause trouble with his family), her childlike welcoming of the holy viaticum. Some twenty-four hours after the assault, Mary Goretti died.   Her mother, the parish priest of Nettuno, a Spanish noblewoman and two nuns, had watched by her bed all night.

Alexander was sentenced to thirty years' penal servitude.   For long he was surly, brutal and unrepentant.   Then one night he had a dream or vision in which

Mary Goretti appeared gathering flowers and offering them to him.   From then on he was a changed man, and so exemplary a prisoner that at the end of twenty-seven years he was released.   His first act when free was to visit Mary's mother to beg her forgiveness.

Meanwhile the memory of his victim had become more and more revered. The sweetness and strength of her life before her untimely end was recalled, people prayed for her intercession in Heaven, answers, even miracles, were attributed to that intercession, and in response to a widespread wish the cause of her beatification was introduced.   On April 27, 1947, Mary Goretti was declared blessed by Pope Pius XII.   When he afterwards appeared on the balcony of St Peter's he was accompanied by Mary's mother, Assunta Goretti, then eighty-two years old, together with two of Mary's sisters and a brother.   Pilgrims came from all over Italy and the pope addressed them, presenting Bd Mary as a new St Agnes and calling down woe on the corrupters of chastity in press and theatre and cinema and fashion-studio : " in our day ", he said, " women have been thrown even into military service—with grave consequences ."   Three years later the same pope canonized Mary Goretti, in the piazza of St Peter's, before the biggest crowd ever assembled for a canonization.   Her murderer was still alive.

A number of " popular " canonizations of early times notwithstanding, a violent and unjust death alone is not sufficient to constitute martyrdom.   (The common idea that St Joan of Arc, for example, was a martyr is mistaken.)   But St Mary Goretti was killed in defence of a Christian virtue, and so was every bit as much a martyr as if she had died for the Christian faith.   And it was Cardinal Salotti's opinion that, " Even had she not been a martyr she would still have been a saint, so holy was her everyday life ".

The case of Mary Goretti seems to be unique in hagiology, and at the time of the beati-fication her short and moving story was noticed in the newspaper press of the world, from the London *Times* downwards.   Among the published accounts of her in English are those of Mother C. E. Maguire, Father J. Carr and Marie C. Buehrle.   In *L'art sacré*, May-June 1951, p. 14, are printed some pictures illustrating the iconographical evolution of the saint. There is a good essay by Eric B. Strauss in *Saints and Ourselves* (1953).

7 : ST. CYRIL AND ST. METHODIUS, ARCHBISHOP OF SIRMIUM   (A.D. 869 AND 884)

THESE brothers, natives of Thessalonika, are venerated as the apostles of the Southern Slavs and the fathers of Slavonic literary culture.   Cyril, the younger of them, was baptized Constantine and assumed the name by which he is usually known only shortly before his death, when he received the habit of a monk.   At an early age he was sent to Constantinople, where he studied at the imperial university under Leo the Grammarian and Photius.   Here he learned all the profane sciences but no theology ; however, he was ordained deacon (priest probably not till later) and in due course took over the chair of Photius, gaining for himself a great reputation, evidenced by the epithet " the Philosopher ". For a time he retired to a religious house, but in 861 he was sent by the emperor, Michael III, on a religio-political mission to the ruler of the judaized Khazars between the Dnieper and the Volga.   This he carried out with success, though the number of converts he made to Christianity among the Khazars has doubtless been much exaggerated.　The elder brother, Methodius, who, after being governor of one of the Slav colonies in the Opsikion province, had become a monk, took part in the mission to the Khazars, and on his return to Greece was elected abbot of an important monastery.

In 862 there arrived in Constantinople an ambassador charged by Rostislav, prince of Moravia, to ask that the emperor would send him missionaries capable of teaching his people in their own language.　Behind this request was the desire of Rostislav to draw nearer to Byzantium as an insurance against the powerful German neighbours on his west, and this was a good opportunity for the Eastern emperor to counterbalance the influence of the Western emperor in those parts, where German missionaries were already active.　It favoured too the ecclesiastical politics of Photius, now patriarch of Constantinople, who decided that Cyril and Methodius were most suitable for the work : for they were learned men, who knew Slavonic, and the first requirement was the provision of characters in which the Slav tongue might be written.　The characters now called " cyrillic ", from which are derived the present Russian, Serbian and Bulgarian letters, were invented from the Greek capitals, perhaps by the followers of St Cyril ; the " glagolitic " alphabet, formerly wrongly attributed to St Jerome, in which the Slav-Roman liturgical books of certain Yugoslav Catholics are printed, may be that prepared for this occasion by Cyril himself, or, according to the legend, directly revealed by God.*

In 863 the two brothers set out with a number of assistants and came to the court of Rostislav ; they were well received and at once got to work.　But the position was very difficult.　The new missionaries made free use of the vernacular in their preaching and ministrations, and this made immediate appeal to the local people.　To the German clergy this was objectionable, and their opposition was strengthened when the Emperor Louis the German forced Rostislav to take an oath of fealty to him.　The Byzantine missionaries, armed with their pericopes from the Scriptures and liturgical hymns in Slavonic, pursued their way with much success, but were soon handicapped by their lack of a bishop to ordain more priests.　The German prelate, the bishop of Passau, would not do it, and Cyril therefore determined to seek help elsewhere, presumably from Constantinople whence he came.

On their way the brothers arrived in Venice.　It was at a bad moment.　Photius at Constantinople had incurred excommunication ; the East was under suspicion ; the *protégés* of the Eastern emperor and their liturgical use of a new tongue were vehemently criticized.　One source says that the pope, St Nicholas I, sent for the strangers.　In any case to Rome they came, bringing with them the alleged relics of Pope St Clement, which St Cyril had recovered when in the Crimea on his way back from the Khazars.　Pope Nicholas in the meantime had died, but his successor, Adrian II, warmly welcomed the bearers of so great a gift.　He examined their cause, and he gave judgement : Cyril and Methodius were to receive episcopal consecration, their neophytes were to be ordained, the use of the liturgy in Slavonic was approved.

Although in the office of the Western church both brothers are referred to as bishops, it is far from certain that Cyril was in fact consecrated.　For while still

---

* Like so much to do with these brothers, the history of these alphabets is a matter of debate.　The southern Slavonic of SS. Cyril and Methodius is to this day the liturgical language of the Russians, Ukrainians, Serbs and Bulgars, whether Orthodox or Catholic.

in Rome he died, on February 14, 869. The " Italian legend " of the saints says that on Cyril's death Methodius went to Pope Adrian and told him, " When we left our father's house for the country in which, with God's help, we have laboured, the last wish of our mother was that, should either of us die, the other would bring back the body for decent burial in our monastery. I ask the help of your Holiness for me to do this." The pope was willing ; but it was represented to him that " It is not fitting that we should allow the body of so distinguished a man to be taken away, one who has enriched our church and city with relics, who by God's power has attracted distant nations towards us, who has been called to his reward from this place. So famous a man should be buried in a famous place in so famous a city." And so it was done. St Cyril was buried with great pomp in the church of San Clemente on the Coelian, wherein the relics of St Clement had been enshrined.

St Methodius now took up his brother's leadership. Having been consecrated, he returned, bearing a letter from the Holy See recommending him as a man of " exact understanding and orthodoxy ". Kosel, prince of Pannonia, having asked that the ancient archdiocese of Sirmium (now Mitrovitsa) be revived, Methodius was made metropolitan and the boundaries of his charge extended to the borders of Bulgaria. But the papal approval and decided actions did not intimidate the Western clergy there, and the situation in Moravia had now changed. Rostislav's nephew, Svatopluk, had allied himself with Carloman of Bavaria and driven his uncle out. In 870 Methodius found himself haled before a synod of German bishops and interned in a leaking cell. Only after two years could the pope, now John VIII, get him released ; and then John judged it prudent to withdraw the permission to use Slavonic (" a barbarous language ", he called it), except for the purpose of preaching.* At the same time he reminded the Germans that Pannonia and the disposition of sees throughout Illyricum belonged of old to the Holy See.

During the following years St Methodius continued his work of evangelization in Moravia, but he made an enemy of Svatopluk, whom he rebuked for the wickedness of his life. Accordingly in 878 the archbishop was delated to the Holy See both for continuing to conduct divine worship in Slavonic and for heresy, in that he omitted the words " and the Son " from the creed (at that time these words had not been introduced everywhere in the West, and not in Rome). John VIII summoned him to Rome. Methodius was able to convince the pope both of his orthodoxy and of the desirability of the Slavonic liturgy, and John again conceded it, with certain reservations, for God, " who made the three principal languages, Hebrew, Greek and Latin, made others also for his honour and glory ". Unfortunately, in accordance with the wishes of Svatopluk, the pope also nominated to the see of Nitra, which was suffragan to Sirmium, a German priest called Wiching, an implacable opponent of Methodius. This unscrupulous prelate continued to persecute his metropolitan, even to the extent of forging pontifical documents. After his death, Wiching obtained the archiepiscopal see, banished the chief disciples of his predecessor, and undid much of his work in Moravia.

During the last four years of his life, according to the " Pannonian legend ", St Methodius completed the Slavonic translation of the Bible (except the books of

* For Methodius, as a Byzantine, the alternative to Slavonic was of course not Latin but Greek.

Machabees) and also of the *Nomokanon*, a compilation of Byzantine ecclesiastical and civil law. This suggests that circumstances were preventing him from devoting all his time to missionary and episcopal concerns ; in other words, he was fighting a losing battle with the German influence. He died, probably at Stare Mesto (Velehrad), worn out by his apostolic labours and the opposition of those who thought them misdirected, on April 6, 884. His funeral service was. carried out in Greek, Slavonic and Latin : " The people, carrying tapers, came together in huge numbers ; men and women, big and little, rich and poor, free men and slaves, widows and orphans, natives and foreigners, sick and well—all were there. For Methodius had been all things to all men that he might lead them all to Heaven."

The feast of SS. Cyril and Methodius, always observed in the land of their mission, was extended to the whole Western church in 1880 by Pope Leo XIII. As orientals who worked in close co-operation with Rome they are regarded as particularly suitable patrons of church unity and of works to further the reunion of the dissident Slav churches ; they are venerated alike by Catholic Czechs and Slovaks and Croats and Orthodox Serbs and Bulgars. According to Slavonic usage they are named in the preparation of the Byzantine Mass.

The political and ecclesiastical rivalries behind these events have a long and complex history, and in spite of all the recent work on the conflicting evidence it is difficult to disentangle the details. The task is complicated by the judgements of some writers on the subject having tended to be moved by nationalist considerations. The sources represent a double tradition. For the so-called Pannonian legend there are lives of Constantine (Cyril) and of Methodius (Miklosich, *Die Legende von hl. Cyrillus* and *Vita S. Methodii russico-slovenice et latine*, Vienna, 1870), and a Greek life of St Clement of Okhrida (Migne, PG., vol. cxxvi, cc. 1194–1240). For the so-called Italian legend, there is the life of St Cyril *cum translatione sancti Clementis*, in *Acta Sanctorum*, March, vol. ii. The " Moravian legend " is of a much later date than the ninth and tenth centuries represented above. For discussion of these sources reference may be made to F. Dvornik, *Les Slaves, Byzance et Rome au IXe siècle* (1926) and *Les légendes de Constantin et de Méthode vues de Byzance* (1933), with bibliographies. See also J. B. Bury, *History of the Eastern Roman Empire* (1912) ; A. Lapôtre, *Le pape Jean VIII* (1895) ; L. K. Goetz, *Geschichte der Slavenapostel K. und M.* (1897) ; F. Grivec, *Die hl. Slawenapostel K. und M.* (1928) ; *Analecta Bollandiana*, vol. xlvii (1929), pp. 178–181 ; and Fliche and Martin, *Histoire de l'Église*, t. vi, pp. 451–463.

ST PANTAENUS   (*c.* A.D. 200)

THIS learned father and apostolic man flourished in the second century, and had been a Stoic philosopher. He is commonly spoken of as becoming head of the catechetical school at Alexandria, where by his learning and excellent manner of teaching he raised its reputation above all the schools of the philosophers, and the lectures which he read, gathered from the flowers of the prophets and apostles, conveyed light and knowledge into the minds of all his hearers, as Clement says of him. That he taught with success at Alexandria is almost all that is known of the life of Pantaenus ; there he had, it is said, the formation of the more famous Clement of Alexandria. The historian Eusebius records on hearsay that St Pantaenus had been a missionary to India (perhaps the Yemen and Ethiopia) and had there met Christians who had received from St Bartholomew the Apostle the Gospel of St Matthew in Hebrew (this statement, repeated by St Jerome, has been much used by supporters of the theory of an apostolic foundation for the Church in India proper). Eusebius knows of him as a man of great learning, ardent and zealous in the preaching of the word ; and his nickname of " the Sicilian bee " not only bears witness to his industry and to the sweetness of his teaching, but suggests the place of his origin.   None of his writings have survived.

See the *Acta Sanctorum* (July, vol. ii) and DCB., vol. iv, pp. 181–184.   The relations of Pantaenus and Clement of Alexandria have been much discussed by Zahn, Harnack and Bardenhewer.   But see especially G. Bardy on the origins of the Alexandrian school in *Recherches de science religieuse*, t. xxvii (1937), pp. 65-90.   Pantaenus has been suggested as the writer of the *Epistle to Diognetus* : *cf.* H. I. Marrou, *A Diognète* (1951), p. 266.

ST PALLADIUS, Bishop   (A.D. 432)

St Prosper of Aquitaine in his chronicle tells us that when Agricola had corrupted the British Christians by Pelagian doctrine it was at the instance of the deacon Palladius that St Germanus of Auxerre was sent into Britain to combat the heresy. This was in 429.   In 431 Prosper says that " Palladius was consecrated by Pope Celestine and sent to the Irish believing in Christ, as their first bishop ", and he landed at Arklow in Leinster.   He met with opposition at once, but he managed to make some converts, as we learn from an ancient Life of St Patrick, and built three churches, which have been identified as Cilleen Cormac, near Dunlavin, Tigroney beside the Avoca, and Donard in the west of County Wicklow.   Before the end of the year Palladius " seeing that he could not do much good there and wishing to return to Rome, departed to the Lord in the country of the Picts. Others, however, say that he was crowned with martyrdom in Ireland."   That is to say, he crossed over into Scotland and there died.   He was not a martyr (except in the non-technical sense of one who must have suffered very great hardships and trouble of spirit in trying to spread the gospel of Christ among an opposed people), and the story of his twenty-three years' mission in Scotland cannot be maintained : the early Irish writers state plainly that he died soon after leaving their country, at Fordun, near Aberdeen, where his relics were venerated in the middle ages.   The feast of St Palladius is still kept by the diocese of Aberdeen. He was probably a Gallo-Roman or Romano-Briton.

See the *Acta Sanctorum*, July, vol. ii, but more recent scholarship has revised the speculations of that date ; see Fr P. Grosjean in *Analecta Bollandiana*, vol. lxiii (1945), pp. 73–86, 112–117.   *Cf.* note to St Patrick on March 17.

ST FELIX, Bishop of Nantes   (A.D. 582)

Among the illustrious bishops of Nantes was St Felix, a nobleman of Aquitaine, who was eminent in virtue, eloquence and learning.   He was married when he was called to the see of Nantes, towards the close of the year 549, when he was thirty-six years of age, but his wife retired to a convent and he received holy orders.   His zeal for discipline and good order appeared in the regulations he made for his diocese, and his charity to the poor had no bounds but those of their necessities. His predecessor had formed a project of building a cathedral within the walls of Nantes, which Felix executed in the most magnificent manner.   More than once he had to deal with his troublesome Breton neighbours.   St Gregory of Tours, though sometimes disagreeing with his suffragan, bore testimony to his sanctity, and Fortunatus, in particular, praised Felix, especially for public works, in panegyrics that did not err on the side of coolness.   The holy prelate died on January 6, in 582, the day on which his feast is kept, July 7, being the anniversary of the translation of his relics.

We know little of Felix beside what has been recorded in Gregory of Tours and in the poems of Venantius Fortunatus. Both writers are cited at length in the *Acta Sanctorum*, July, vol. ii. Delanoue, *St Félix de Nantes* (1907), cannot be recommended as serious history.

SS. ETHELBURGA, ERCONGOTA AND SETHRIDA, VIRGINS
(*c.* A.D. 664 AND 660)

THIS Ethelburga was one of the children of the family of Anna, King of the East Angles. Having received the grace of a religious vocation she went to Gaul with her half-sister St Sethrida, and was received by St Burgundofara, or Fare, in the abbey afterwards known as Faremoutier, in the forest of Brie. Sethrida succeeded the foundress as abbess of the monastery, and after her death Ethelburga succeeded Sethrida. She began to build a new abbey church, but did not live to see it completed and was buried in the unfinished building ; as the building was not carried on, her body was taken up after seven years, when it was found to be incorrupt, and translated to the church of St Stephen.

St Ethelburga is mentioned in the Roman, French (under the name of Aubierge) and some English martyrologies. With her was her niece St Ercongota. She was the daughter of Erconbert, King of Kent, and St Sexburga. Bede states that the reason she, her two aunts, and others went to Faremoutier, Chelles, and other abbeys in Gaul, either to lead the religious life or to be educated, was because there were so few monasteries in the territory of the Angles. The same chronicler says that Ercongota was famed for marvels, and that she was divinely forewarned of her death by a vision of angels : so that she made a farewell visit to each of her sisters, recommending herself to their prayers, and then died in great peace. Her body also was enshrined in the church of St Stephen.

Bede, *Historia Ecclesiastica*, bk. iii, ch. 8, is our principal authority ; see also Plummer's notes. The names of the princesses here mentioned appear in Bede as Aedilberg, Earcongota and Saethryd ; the last two seem to have had no *cultus* in England. *Cf.* Stanton's *Menology*, pp. 13–14, 319–321, 324 ; and especially H. M. Delsart, *Ste Fare* (1911), pp. 112–113 and 181–185.

ST HEDDA, BISHOP OF WINCHESTER   (A.D. 705)

HEDDA was a monk, probably, of the monastery of St Hilda at Whitby, and was made bishop of the divided diocese of the West Saxons in 676. He resided first at Dorchester, near Oxford, but afterwards removed his see to Winchester. He was consecrated by St Theodore of Canterbury, who had great regard for him. Hedda, while on a visit to the hermit St Guthlac, at Croyland, consecrated his chapel and ordained him priest. He was one of the first benefactors of the abbey of Malmesbury, endowing it with land. King Ine in his famous laws, enacted in a council of bishops and ealdormen in 693, declared that in drawing them up he had been assisted by the counsels of St Hedda and St Erconwald. St Hedda governed his church with great prudence about thirty years, exercising his episcopal office, says Bede, rather by his innate love of virtue than by what he had acquired from study. After his death in 705 many miraculous cures were reported at his tomb, and the men of Wessex took thence dust and earth which they mixed with water and sprinkled on, or gave to drink to, sick men and animals. St Hedda is commemorated liturgically on this date in the archdiocese of Birmingham.

What little we know of St Hedda comes mainly from Bede and from William of Malmesbury.

BD BENEDICT XI, POPE   (A.D. 1304)

NICHOLAS BOCCASINI was born at Treviso in the year 1240. He was educated there and at Venice, where at seventeen years of age he took the habit of St Dominic. In 1268 he was appointed professor and preacher at Venice and Bologna, where he fruitfully communicated to others those spiritual riches which he had treasured up in silence and retirement, while always advancing in the way of perfection himself. He composed a volume of sermons, and wrote commentaries on the Holy Scriptures, which are still extant. He was chosen prior provincial of his order for Lombardy and, in 1296, elected ninth master general of the whole Order of Preachers. Two years later Brother Nicholas was created cardinal and soon after bishop of Ostia, and he went as legate *a latere* to Hungary to endeavour to compose the differences which divided that nation ; he had some temporary success, for his learning, prudence and selflessness everywhere gained respect : but his services were urgently required in Rome.

Trouble had long been brewing between the Holy See and King Philip of France, who had been heavily taxing ecclesiastical persons and property to help carry on his war with England ; the king entered into an alliance with the Colonna cardinals against Pope Boniface VIII who, the French king having circulated a forged document in the place of his statement of the pope's prerogatives, in 1302 issued the famous bull " Unam sanctam ", in which, *inter alia*, the relationship between the spiritual and temporal powers were set out. In the following year Philip appealed to a general council to judge the pope on a number of astounding charges, as infamous as they were false, preferred by the royal councillor William of Nogaret and a knight, William du Plessis.* A storm was raised against Boniface, who withdrew to Anagni, deserted by all who should have supported him, excepting only the cardinal-bishop of Sabina and the cardinal-bishop of Ostia, Nicholas Boccasini. With their advice and assistance Boniface acted with vigour and promptness, and prepared a bull of excommunication against Philip. But the very day before its promulgation Nogaret and the Ghibelline leader, Sciarra Colonna, broke into the papal residence with a rabble of hired troopers and seized the person of the pontiff, on September 7. Three days later he was released by the citizens of Anagni, returned to Rome, and on October 11 he died.

To such a troubled heritage did Cardinal Nicholas Boccasini succeed, for within a fortnight he was elected to the apostolic chair, and took the name of Benedict. He set himself straightway to deal with the situation, with the confidence engendered by trust and submission to God and unimpeachable personal uprightness : but his pontificate was too short for him to do more than take the first steps towards restoring peace ; Bd Benedict's policy was one of conciliation without compromising the memory of his predecessor. He favoured the mendicant friars, and all the three cardinals created by him were Dominicans ; two, moreover, were Englishmen : William Maklesfield of Canterbury, who died at Louvain before he

* These gentlemen were experts in such work, and later played a similar part in the arraignment of the Knights Templars on terrifying charges.

heard of his elevation, and Walter Winterburn of Salisbury.   In his private life Benedict continued the mortifications and penances of a friar, and abated none of his humility and moderation ; when his mother came to see him at the papal court and dressed herself up for the occasion, he refused to see her until she had changed into the simple clothes which she ordinarily wore.   But he only ruled for eight months and a few days, in which short space, as the Roman Martyrology says, he " wonderfully promoted the peace of the Church, the restoration of discipline, and the increase of religion " ; he died suddenly at Perugia on July 7, 1304.   His *cultus* was confirmed in 1736.

Various short lives of Blessed Benedict are mentioned in BHL., nn. 1090–1094, including a notice by Bernard Guy incorporated in the *Liber Pontificalis*, vol. ii, pp. 471–472.   See also Mortier, *Maîtres Généraux O.P.*, vol. ii ; H. Finke, *Aus den Tagen Bonifaz VIII* (1902) ; the *Regesta* of Benedict, edited by C. Grandjean ; and A. Ferrero, *B. Benedetto XI* (1934).

BB. ROGER DICKENSON and his Companions, Martyrs (A.D. 1591)

In this year there suffered at Winchester, on July 7, BB. Roger Dickenson and Ralph Milner, and on a date unknown Bd Laurence Humphrey.   Milner was a small farmer, or even a farm-labourer, and brought up a Protestant.   Upon contrasting the lives led by his Protestant and Catholic neighbours, to the great disadvantage of the first, he put himself under instruction and was received into the Church ; but on the very day of his first communion he was committed to prison for the change of religion.   Here he was kept for a number of years, but his confinement was not strict and he was often released on *parole*, when he would obtain alms and spiritual ministrations for his fellow prisoners, and also use his knowledge of the country to facilitate the movements and work of missionary priests.   In this way he made the acquaintance of Father Stanney, s.j., who afterwards wrote a memoir of him in Latin, and with the same priest's assistance a secular priest, Mr Roger Dickenson, came to live in Winchester.   He was a Lincoln man, who had made his studies at Rheims, and for several years he worked in the Winchester district, helped by Milner.

The first time Mr Dickenson was arrested his guards got so drunk that he was able to escape, but the second time, Milner being with him, they were both committed for trial : Dickenson for being a priest, Milner for " relieving " him. At the trial the judge, being somewhat pitiful for Blessed Ralph, who was old and had a wife and eight children looking to him, recommended him to make one visit as a matter of form to the Protestant parish church, and so secure his release.   But, says Challoner, Milner answered, " Would your lordship then advise me, for the perishable trifles of this world, or for a wife and children, to lose my God ?   No, my lord, I cannot approve or embrace a counsel so disagreeable to the maxims of the gospel."   As Father Stanney states that Milner was entirely illiterate, we must assume that this is a paraphrase of his reply.   These two suffered together, one of the most moving couples in the whole gallery of English martyrs.

At the same assizes seven maiden gentlewomen were sentenced to death for allowing Bd Roger to celebrate Mass in their houses, but were immediately re-prieved ; whereupon they asked that they might die with their pastor, seeing that they undoubtedly shared his supposed guilt and should share also in his punish-ment : but they were returned to prison.

Laurence Humphrey was a young man of Protestant upbringing and good life who, having undertaken to dispute with Father Stanney (referred to above), was instead himself converted.   Father Stanney in a brief memoir speaks very highly of the virtues of his neophyte and his energy in instructing the ignorant and relieving the needs of those in prison for their faith.   But Humphrey being taken seriously ill, he was heard to say in delirium that " the queen was a whore and a heretic " ; his words were reported to the authorities, and before he was well recovered he was committed to Winchester gaol.   At his trial he confessed his religion, but denied memory of ever having spoken disrespectfully of the queen ; he was nevertheless condemned, and hanged, drawn, and quartered in his twenty-first year.

See MMP., pp. 168–169, 592–596, and Burton and Pollen, LEM.

8 : ST ELIZABETH OF PORTUGAL, Widow   (A.D. 1336)

THIS Elizabeth was daughter of Peter III, King of Aragon.   She was born in 1271, and received at the font the name of Elizabeth, from her great-aunt, St Elizabeth of Hungary, but she is known in her own country by the Spanish form of that name, Isabella.   Her birth was an omen of that title of " the Peacemaker " which she was to earn in after-life, for by it was established a good understanding between her grandfather James, who was then on the throne, and her father, whose quarrelling had divided the whole kingdom.   The young princess was of a sweet disposition, and from her early years had relish for anything that was conducive to devotion and goodness.   She desired to emulate every virtue which she saw practised by others, for she had been already taught that mortification of the will is to be joined with prayer to obtain the grace which restrains our tendency to sin.   This is often insufficiently considered by those parents who excite the wilfulness and self-indulgence of their children by teaching them a love of worthless things and giving in to every whim and want.   Certainly, fasting is not good for them ; but submission of the will, obedience, and consideration for others are never more indispensable than at this time ; nor is any abstinence more fruitful than that by which children are taught not to drink or eat between meals, to bear little denials without impatience, and never to make a fuss about things.   The victory of Elizabeth over herself was owing to this early training.

At twelve years of age she was married to Denis, King of Portugal.   That prince admired her birth, beauty, riches and personality more than her virtue ; yet he allowed her an entire liberty in her devotion, and esteemed her piety without feeling called on to imitate it.   Elizabeth therefore planned for herself a regular distribution of her time, which she never interrupted unless extraordinary occasions of duty or charity obliged her.   She rose early every morning, and recited Matins, Lauds and Prime before Mass ; in the afternoon she had other regular devotions after Vespers.   Certain hours were allotted to her domestic affairs, public business, or what she owed to others.   She was abstemious in her food, modest in her dress, humble and affable in conversation, and wholly bent upon the service of God.   Frequent attempts were made to induce her to modify her life, but without success.   Charity to the poor was a distinguishing part of her character.   She gave orders to have pilgrims and poor strangers provided with lodging and necessaries, and made it her business to seek out and relieve persons who were reduced to necessity.   She provided marriage dowries for girls, and founded in different parts of the kingdom charitable establishments, particularly a hospital at Coïmbra, a house for penitent women at Torres Novas, and a refuge for foundlings.   Nor with it all did Elizabeth neglect any of her immediate duties, especially those of respect, love and obedience to her husband, whose neglect and infidelity she bore with much patience.

For Denis, though a good ruler, was a bad subject : just, brave, generous and compassionate in public life, devoted to his realm, but in his private relations selfish and sinful.   The queen used all her endeavours to reclaim him, grieving deeply for the offence to God and the scandal given to the people ; she never ceased to pray for his conversion.   She strove to gain him by courtesy and constant sweetness, and cheerfully cherished his natural children and took care of their education.

St Elizabeth had two children, Alfonso, who afterwards succeeded his father, and a daughter, Constance.   This son when he grew up showed a very rebellious spirit, partly due to the favour in which his father held his illegitimate sons.   Twice he rose in arms and twice his mother brought about a reconciliation, riding out between the opposing forces.   But evil tongues suggested to the king that she secretly favoured her son and for a time she was banished from the court.   Her love for concord and qualities as a peacemaker were indeed very notable ; she stopped or averted war between Ferdinand IV of Castile, and his cousin, and between that prince and her own brother, James II of Aragon.

Her husband Denis became seriously ill in 1324, and Elizabeth gave all her attention to him, scarcely ever leaving his room unless to go to the church.   During his long and tedious illness the king gave marks of sincere sorrow for the disorders of his life, and he died at Santarem on January 6, 1325.   After his burial the queen made a pilgrimage to Compostela, after which she wished to retire to a convent of Poor Clares which she had founded at Coïmbra.   However, she was dissuaded, and instead she was professed in the third order of St Francis, and lived in a house which she built near to her convent, leading a life of great simplicity.

The cause of peace that had been so dear to her all her life was the occasion of Elizabeth's death, which came about on July 4, 1336 at Estremoz, whither she had gone on an errand of reconciliation in spite of her age and the great heat.   She was buried in the church of her monastery of Poor Clares at Coïmbra, and honoured by miracles ; and eventually in 1626 her *cultus* was crowned by canonization.

The Bollandists in the *Acta Sanctorum*, July, vol. ii, have printed a life of the queen which seems to be of almost contemporary date, and a good deal of information may also be found in the chronicles of the period.   See also P. de Moucheron, *Ste Elisabeth d'Aragon* (1896) ; and a short sketch by Fr V. McNabb (1937).   The story (told by Butler in company with many others) of the innocent page saved miraculously from death in a lime-kiln is a mere fiction which can be traced back to the folk-lore of ancient India.   See Cosquin in the *Revue des Questions historiques*, vol. lxxiii (1903), pp. 3–12, with vol. lxxiv, pp. 207–217 ; and Formichi in *Archivio delle tradizioni popolari*, vol. xxii (1903), pp. 9–30.   It is only in 1562 that we find it christianized and told in connection with St Elizabeth.

SS. AQUILA AND PRISCA, OR PRISCILLA   (FIRST CENTURY)

WHAT little is known of these two is to be found in the Holy Scriptures.   They were disciples of St Paul and, like their master, constrained to undertake many journeys and changes of residence ; when we first hear of them (Acts xviii 1–3) they had recently left Italy in consequence of the decree of the Emperor Claudius whereby Jews were prohibited to foregather in Rome.   Aquila was a Jew of Pontus, and when he and his wife Prisca left Rome he took a house at Corinth.   St Paul coming thither from Athens called on them, and when he found that Aquila was, like himself, a tent-maker (every Jewish rabbi had a trade) he decided to live with them during his stay in Corinth ; it is possible that they received the faith from him at this time, or they may have been Christians already. Aquila and Prisca went on with Paul to Ephesus and stopped on there when he continued his voyage ; in his absence they instructed Apollo, a Jew of Alexandria, " mighty in the Scriptures ", who knew of our Lord only through some of the disciples of St John Baptist. They continued in Ephesus during St Paul's third missionary journey, he using their house as his headquarters, and in it they had a church (1 Cor. xvi 19). Later they returned to Rome, and there also had a church in their house, for writing to the Romans, St Paul says : " Salute Prisca and Aquila, and the church which is in their house ", and adds a testimony of gratitude for all they had done : " My helpers in Christ Jesus, who have for my life laid down their own necks : to whom not I only give thanks but also all the churches of the Gentiles." But soon the devoted couple were at Ephesus again, and in his second letter to Timothy Paul sends greetings to them there. The Roman Martyrology states that SS. Aquila and Prisca died in Asia Minor, but there is a tradition that they were martyred in Rome, a late legend associating them with the *Titulus Priscae*, now the church of St Prisca on the Aventine.

Certain alleged " acts " of SS. Aquila and Priscilla dating from the seventh century have been edited by J. Ebersolt (1902). See also R. Schumacher in *Theologie und Glaube*, vol. xii (1920), pp. 86–89.

ST PROCOPIUS, MARTYR (A.D. 303)

AN account of the passion of St Procopius, the protomartyr of the persecution of Diocletian in Palestine and one of several martyrs distinguished in the East as " the Great ", was written by a contemporary, Eusebius, Bishop of Caesarea, who narrates it in the following words :

The first of the martyrs of Palestine was Procopius, a man filled with divine grace, who had ordered his life so well that from childhood he had devoted himself to chastity and the practice of all the virtues. He had reduced his body until he had given it so to speak the appearance of a corpse, but his soul drew from the word of God so great a vigour that the body itself was refreshed by it. He lived on bread and water and only ate every two or three days ; sometimes he prolonged his fast during a whole week. Meditation on the divine word so filled his being that he remained absorbed in it day and night without fatigue. Filled with goodness and gentleness, regarding himself as the least of men, he edified everyone by his discourses. The word of God was his sole study, and of profane science he had but little knowledge. Born at Aelia [Jerusalem], he had taken up his residence at Scythopolis [Bethsan], where he filled three ecclesiastical offices. He was reader and interpreter in the Syriac language, and cast out evil spirits by the imposition of hands.

Sent with companions from Scythopolis to Caesarea [Maritima] he had scarcely passed the city gates when he was conducted into the presence of the governor, and even before he had had a taste of chains or prison walls he was urged by the judge Flavian to sacrifice to the gods. But he, in a loud voice, proclaimed that there are not several gods, but One alone, the creator and author of all things. This answer made a vivid impression on the judge. Finding nothing to say in reply, he tried to persuade Procopius at least to sacrifice to the emperors. But the martyr of God despised his entreaties. " Listen ", he said, " to this verse of Homer : It is not good to have several masters ; let there be one chief, one king."

Οὐκ ἀγαθὸν πολυκοιρανίη· εἷς κοίρανος ἔστω,
εἷς βασιλεύς. *(Iliad*, ii, 204.)

At these words, as though he had uttered imprecations against the emperors, the judge ordered him to be led to execution. They cut off his head, and he passed happily to eternal life by the shortest road, on the 7th of the month of Desius, the day that the Latins call the nones of July, in the first year of our persecution. This was the first martyrdom that took place at Caesarea.

It is hardly believable that this simple and impressive narrative should have been the seed of the incredible legends which afterwards grew up around the name of Procopius : astonishing and absurd fables and trimmings that eventually transformed the austere cleric into a mighty warrior, and even split him into three people, the ascete, the soldier, and a martyr in Persia. In his earlier legend he was made to argue with the judge and to refer to Hermes Trismegistus, Homer, Plato, Aristotle, Socrates, Galen and Scamandrus in support of the oneness of God, to suffer torture in most ingenious fashions, and to paralyse his executioner ; later he becomes a duke of Alexandria and the hero of more legendary marvels (afterwards borrowed for the "acts" of St Ephysius of Cagliari and the unknown martyr John of Constantinople), undergoing a miraculous conversion (combined of the visions of St Paul and of the *Labarum*), slaying six thousand marauding barbarians with the aid of a wonder-working cross, converting in prison a band of soldiers and twelve noble matrons, and the like. The evolution, if such arbitrary leaps can be called evolution, of the story of St Procopius is a " leading case " in hagiology ; but in the dignified account of Eusebius we may be certain that we have what really happened.

Father Delehaye devotes a whole chapter (ch. v) of his book *The Legends of the Saints* to this transformation of St Procopius into a military saint. The most noteworthy Greek text has been edited by him in *Les légendes grecques des saints militaires*, pp. 214–233.

SS. KILIAN AND HIS COMPANIONS, MARTYRS   (*c*. A.D. 689)

KILIAN was an Irish monk who, having been consecrated bishop already or later, set out with eleven companions to Rome in 686 and obtained of Pope Conon a commission to preach the gospel in Franconia (Baden and Bavaria). With Colman, a priest, and Totnan, a deacon, he converted and baptized numbers at Würzburg, and among others Gosbert, the duke of that place. The circumstances of their martyrdom are given by a medieval life as follows. The duke had married his brother's widow Geilana and, being told by St Kilian that such a marriage was condemned by the law of the gospel, he promised to leave her. Geilana was furious, and took the opportunity of Gosbert's absence on a military expedition to have the three missionaries beheaded. That Kilian, Colman and Totnan were evangelists in Franconia and East Thuringia is certain, as is their martyrdom : but doubt has been thrown on the authenticity of the details of the above story. Some writers have attributed the crime to Gosbert and, if the story be true, it must be regretfully admitted, in view of the times and circumstances, that it is very likely that the disappointed man and woman may have conspired together to remove their troublesome teachers. St Kilian is venerated in the dioceses of Würzburg and Vienna and elsewhere, including the country of his birth.

Two medieval accounts of St Kilian are printed in the *Acta Sanctorum*, July, vol. ii. See also Gougaud, *Gaelic Pioneers of Christianity*, pp. 140–141, and *Les saints irlandais hors d'Irlande*, pp. 125-129. For more recent references, *cf. Analecta Bollandiana*, vol. lxxi (1953), pp. 450-463.

ST WITHBURGA, Virgin   (*c.* A.D. 743)

SHE was the youngest of the holy daughters of Anna, King of the East Angles. Like her sisters, she devoted herself to the divine service, and led an austere life in solitude for several years at Holkham, near the sea-coast in Norfolk, where a church dedicated in her honour was afterwards built.   After the death of her father she changed her dwelling to Dereham, now a market-town in Norfolk but then an obscure retired place.   Withburga assembled there some devout maidens, and laid the foundation of a church and nunnery, but did not live to finish the buildings. Her death happened on March 17, 743.   Her body was interred in the churchyard at East Dereham, and fifty years after found incorrupt and translated into the church.   In 974, Brithnoth, Abbot of Ely, removed it to Ely, and deposited it near the bodies of her two sisters.   In 1106 the remains of four saints were translated into the new church and laid near the high altar.   The bodies of SS. Sexburga and Ermenilda were reduced to dust, except the bones.   That of St Etheldreda was entire, and that of St Withburga was not only sound but also fresh, and the limbs flexible.   This is related by Thomas, monk of Ely, in his history of Ely, which he wrote the year following ; he also tells us that in the place where St Withburga was first buried, in the churchyard of Dereham, a spring of clear water gushed forth : it is to this day called St Withburga's well.

Thomas of Ely's narrative is printed in Wharton's *Anglia Sacra*, and there is also a reference to Withburga in Malmesbury's *Gesta Pontificum*.   See Stanton's *Menology*, pp. 325 and 328.

ST ADRIAN III, Pope   (A.D. 885)

THIS pope succeeded Marinus I in 884 during a troubled period in the history of the papacy.   He adopted Carloman, King of France, as his spiritual son, took steps to stop the bishop of Nîmes annoying the monks of St Giles's abbey, and, it is alleged, punished with a ferocity that matched their crimes the ex-official George of the Aventine and the wealthy widow of another official, whose husband had been murdered in the forecourt of St Peter's—there were some remarkably bad characters in Rome at that time.   In 885 Adrian was invited by the emperor, Charles the Fat, to be present at a diet at Worms ; what specific reasons he had for desiring the pope's presence is not known.   Whatever they were they came to nothing, for Adrian fell ill on the journey and died near Modena on July 8, or else in September. He was buried in the abbey church of St Silvester at Nonantula.   There is nothing in the little that is known of his pontificate of fourteen (or sixteen) months to gauge the grounds on which Adrian was venerated as a saint, but he has received a continual liturgical *cultus* in the diocese of Modena, which was confirmed in 1891. During his brief reign there was famine in Rome, the hardships of which for the people he tried by every means to avert, and Flodoard, historian of the church of Rheims, praises him as a kind father to his fellow bishops.

See the *Liber Pontificalis*, vol. ii, p. 225 ; and Mann, *Lives of the Popes*, vol. iii, pp. 361–367.

ST GRIMBALD   (A.D. 903)

THIS holy man was born at Saint-Omer in Flanders and became a monk at Saint-Bertin, where he met King Alfred of England when that prince was going to Rome. The king afterwards, by the advice of Eldred, Archbishop of Canterbury, invited Grimbald over into England, where he arrived in the year 885.

Upon the death of Eldred, Alfred pressed Grimbald to accept the see of Canterbury, but was not able to get his consent, and was obliged to allow him to retire to the church of Winchester.   King Alfred's son and successor, Edward, in compliance with his father's will, built the New Minster there, close to the old, in which he placed secular canons and appointed St Grimbald superior over them (later they were replaced by Benedictine monks, and King Henry I removed this monastery of Newminster outside the walls of the city to the place called Hyde, which still continued sometimes to be called St Grimbald's monastery).   Grimbald in his last sickness, though extremely feeble, gathered strength when the sacred viaticum was brought, rose out of bed, and received it prostrate on the ground. Among the few things recorded of St Grimbald is that he was a very good singer.

There are slight references to Grimbald in Malmesbury's *Gesta Regum* and *Gesta Pontificum* as well as in Simeon of Durham ; see Stanton's *Menology*, pp. 325 and 658, and D. Knowles, *The Monastic Order in England* (1949), pp. 33, 551.

SS. SUNNIVA AND HER COMPANIONS   (TENTH CENTURY ?)

THIS popular Norse legend is a sort of local version of the story of St Ursula. Sunniva, daughter of an Irish king, in order to avoid marriage or to escape dishonourable intentions or flying before an invader, put to sea with a number of followers in a boat without rudder, sail or oars.   They were cast up on the island of Selje, off the coast of Norway, where they lived in caves and fed upon fish ; presumably they got tired of this diet, for the inhabitants of the neighbouring mainland began to miss beasts from among their cattle left to graze on the island. Suspecting that the strangers were responsible they sent an armed party across to see about it ; but when they arrived they found that the caves occupied by the refugees had been blocked up and the occupants entombed by a landslide—miraculously closed against their pursuers at the prayer of Sunniva.   Some time afterwards passers-by in boats noticed a strange light streaming from the spot where the strangers had died.   This story reached King Olaf Tryggvason (then engaged on an attempt to christianize the land), and he went to investigate, accompanied by a bishop.   The caves were opened and bones found ; but the body of Sunniva was intact and incorrupt.   Olaf built a church there to shelter the body. This was in 995.   In 1170 her relics were translated to the cathedral of Bergen, and the feast of the Selje-men was celebrated every year on this day during the middle ages.   What truth lies behind the story it is impossible to tell.   The bones discovered have been speculated to be those of slain sea-rovers ; but why did King Olaf trouble to disinter them and build a church there ?

The Latin legend, not older than the eleventh century seems to have been written by an Anglo-Saxon missionary bishóp, Sigurd or Sigward.   The text has been printed by G. Storm, *Monumenta Historiae Norvegiae*, pp. 147–152.   See also the *Analecta Bollandiana*, vol. xvii (1898), p. 347, and S. Undset, *Saga of Saints* (1934), pp. 68-86.   For further references, see *Analecta Bollandiana*, vol. lii (1934), pp. 120-121.

ST RAYMUND OF TOULOUSE   (A.D. 1118)

RAYMUND GAYRARD was born at Toulouse about the middle of the eleventh century and was put by his parents in the service of the church of St Sernin.   Here he became a chorister, and married a woman with whom he lived happily until her death.   He then devoted himself and his goods to the relief of the poor, the suffering and the unfortunate, in the true Christian spirit of withholding his charity from none who required it ;   he caused comment by extending it even to the Jews, not only because the Jews are well known to look after their own people with care and efficiency, but also because the common people of those days by no means followed the example of the Apostolic See in its generally benevolent and protective attitude towards that people.   He also founded and endowed an almshouse for thirteen poor clerics, in memory of our Lord and His twelve apostles, and built two stone bridges.

Raymund was at length accepted as a canon of the collegiate church of St Sernin, where he was a model of canonical discipline and the observance of common life under a rule ;   but he is remembered best for his enthusiasm and industrious labours in carrying on the building of St Sernin's church (the number and nature of whose relics of saints made it one of the most famous shrines of the middle ages). St Raymund died on July 3, 1118 (the Canons Regular of the Lateran keep his feast today, the 8th), and was buried in the almshouse which he had founded.   His tomb was the scene of many miraculous cures, and his ancient *cultus* was approved in 1652.

Most of what we know concerning this saint is derived from the Latin lessons of an office compiled a century or more after his death.   See the *Acta Sanctorum*, July, vol. i ; and M. Aubert, *L'église Saint-Sernin de Toulouse* (1933).

BD EUGENIUS III, POPE   (A.D. 1153)

EUGENIUS III, called by St Antoninus " one of the greatest and one of the most afflicted of the popes ", was born at Montemagno between Pisa and Lucca, probably of the noble family of Paganelli, and was baptized Peter.   While holding office in the episcopal *curia* of Pisa he was moved, in 1135, to become a Cistercian monk at Clairvaux ;   he took in religion the name of Bernard, his great namesake being his superior at Clairvaux.   When Pope Innocent II asked for some Cistercians for Rome, St. Bernard sent the other Bernard in charge of a band who occupied the monastery of St Anastasius (Tre Fontane), where the new abbot earned the love and admiration of all ;   one of his difficulties was the unhealthy situation of the monastery, and St Bernard in one of his letters to the community expresses his sympathy, but warns them against excessive use of medicines, which excess was both contrary to their vocation and bad for their health.

On the death of Pope Lucius II in 1145 the cardinals elected Bernard, Abbot of St Anastasius, to the supreme pontificate ;   the election was a surprise to the abbot and to everybody else, and the reasons which moved the cardinals are not known :   it may be suggested that they knew a saint when they saw one.   Not the least surprised was St Bernard of Clairvaux, who wrote to the electors : " May God forgive you for what you have done. . . . You have involved in cares and thrown among the multitudes of men a man who had fled from both. . . . Was there no wise and experienced man among you more fitted for such things ?   It seems indeed absurd that a humble and ill-kempt man should be taken to preside over kings, to govern bishops, to dispose realms and empires. Is it ridiculous or miraculous ? " And he wrote plainly to the new pope : " If Christ has sent you, you will feel that you are come not to be served but to serve . . . [the Lord] will allow me to see before I die the Church of God as in the days of old, when the Apostles let down their nets for a draught, not of silver and gold, but of souls." Bernard the Pope took the name of Eugenius, but before he could be consecrated the Roman senate threatened to challenge his election unless he recognized their usurped sovereign rights over the city. He was powerless to oppose them, and fled to the abbey of Farfa, where he was consecrated, and then to Viterbo. There came to him Arnold of Brescia, the opponent of St Bernard and critic of the higher clergy, who had been condemned with Peter Abelard. He recanted his errors and promised obedience, and Bd Eugenius absolved him, sending him on a penitential pilgrimage to Rome—unfortunately.

Unfortunately because the atmosphere of Rome speedily destroyed Arnold's good resolutions, and he became a leader in the faction opposed to Eugenius. The pope had to leave Rome a second time, and in January 1147 gladly accepted an invitation from King Louis VII to go to France to forward a crusade. In the summer the Second Crusade began under Louis, and was a dismal failure. Eugenius was intimidated by its lack of success and disturbed by the loss of life involved, and refused to back St Bernard and the Abbot Suger, regent of France, when they wanted it promoted with renewed vigour. He continued in France until the news of the lost crusade raised popular feeling against him, and during the time held synods at Paris, Trier and Rheims ; these dealt chiefly with promoting Christian life ; and he concerned himself about the reorganization of the schools of philosophy and theology. At the suggestion of St Bernard he encouraged the mystical writer St Hildegard, to whom he wrote : " We congratulate ourselves in this grace of God [her revelations] and we congratulate you ; but we would have you remember that God resists the proud and gives grace to the humble. Take good care of this grace that is within you, so that what you are spiritually urged to proclaim may be set out with caution." In May 1148 he returned to Italy and, as negotiations were unavailing, excommunicated Arnold of Brescia (who at his worst was the prototype of later ethical democratic demagogues and doctrinaires), and prepared to use force against the Romans. They suddenly got frightened and came to terms, and at the end of 1149 the pope re-entered his city.

It was at this time that St Bernard wrote for Bd Eugenius that ascetical treatise entitled *De consideratione*, one of the writer's most famous works. Its argument was that the pope must not allow the " accursed activities " in which he was necessarily involved (*e.g.* dealing with the litigation of " ambitious, avaricious, simoniacal, sacrilegious, lecherous, incestuous men, and all sorts of human monsters ") get in the way of his principal business, the consideration of spiritual things. The pope is " watchman over all ", " chief of ministers ", head of " the Universal Church throughout the world " ; on the other hand, he is also only a human man and must be humble, yet no respecter of persons, industrious, yet not relaxing amid the achievements of industry. He must not lord it over men, or use the sword when spiritual weapons failed—that was the emperor's office ; justice and punishment of injustice must rule in the papal courts and virtue in the papal household. But chiefly and above all God must be directly sought, and that by prayer rather than by arguments. A pope who followed such counsel as this could hardly fail to attain sanctity, and perhaps it was under its direct influence that in the summer of 1150 Eugenius again left Rome, and lived for two and a half years in Campania, while he negotiated for help with the Emperor Conrad III and his successor Frederick Barbarossa.

Some of the minor troubles of Eugenius's pontificate were concerned with the Church in England. King Stephen forbade the English bishops to attend the Synod of Rheims in 1148, and Theobald of Canterbury was banished for disobeying; the king narrowly escaped excommunication. At the same synod was deposed William, Archbishop of York, for irregularities in connection with his election and consecration and the indiscreet zeal of his supporters; William took his misfortunes in such good part that he was canonized after his death, and his feast is still kept in several English dioceses (June 8). Eugenius approved the rule drawn up for the order founded by St Gilbert of Sempringham in Norfolk, and in 1152 sent as legate to Scandinavia Cardinal Nicholas Breakspear, who was to return with the title of " the Apostle of the North " and be his second successor in the papacy as Adrian IV, the only English pope. Eugenius had a high opinion of the ability of the English, but thought they spoiled it by levity. When he sent a legate to the synod of Kells, with *pallia* for the metropolitans of Armagh, Dublin, Cashel and Tuam, the pope confirmed an arrangement that endures to this day.

Bd Eugenius survived his final return to Rome by only seven months, dying on July 8, 1153, at Tivoli; his *cultus* was approved in 1872. Roger of Hoveden, a contemporary English chronicler, writes of him that " he was worthy of the highest dignity of the popedom. His mind was always kindly disposed, his discretion always to be relied on, his looks always not only cheerful but even joyous "—which, considering what he went through, was no small matter. Under the dignity of the pontiff there was always the heart of the monk; he never put off his monastic habit or Cistercian austerities. Peter of Cluny wrote of him to St Bernard : " Never have I known a more true friend, a more trustworthy brother, a more kind father. His ear is ever ready to hear, and his tongue is quick and capable in speech. And he carries himself not as one's superior, but rather as an equal or even as an inferior. There is in him no arrogance, no domineering, no regality : justice, humility and reason claim the whole man."

The contemporary Cardinal Boso wrote a short life, preserved in the *Liber Pontificalis* (ed. Duchesne, ii, 236), and there is further information in the *Historia Pontificalis* by John of Salisbury (in MGH., *Scriptores*, vol. xx, pp. 516–545). Also there is much material in the chronicles, particularly those concerned with Arnold of Brescia. See further Mann, *The Lives of the Popes*, vol. ix, pp. 127-220 ; G. Sainati, *Vita del B. Eugenio III* (1874) ; and H. Gleber, *Papst Eugen III* (1936), for his politics.

9 : ST JOHN FISHER, BISHOP OF ROCHESTER AND CARDINAL, MARTYR (A.D. 1535)

BEVERLEY, in Yorkshire, from which one St John, in the eighth century, derived his surname, was the native place nearly eight hundred years later of another and perhaps a greater, *viz.* St John Fisher, bishop, cardinal and martyr. Born in 1469, the son of a small mercer who died when his children were very young, John Fisher was sent to Cambridge University at the age of fourteen. There he distinguished himself greatly in his studies, was elected a fellow of Michaelhouse (since merged into Trinity), and was ordained priest by special permission when he was only twenty-two. He became successively senior proctor, doctor of divinity, master of Michaelhouse, and vice-chancellor of the university. In 1502 he resigned his mastership to become the chaplain of the king's mother, Lady Margaret Beaufort, Countess of Richmond and Derby. She appears first to have made his acquaintance seven years earlier, when as senior proctor he had visited the court at Greenwich on business; and, like everyone else who knew him, she was deeply impressed by his scholarship and by his sanctity. She was herself a capable and learned woman of great wealth, who, during the lifetime of three husbands, had been involved in many political intrigues: now finally a widow, she vowed to dedicate her remaining years to God under the direction of Dr Fisher.

Under his guidance she made a noble use of her fortune. By founding Christ's College and St John's College, Cambridge, to supersede earlier and decadent institutions; by establishing there, as well as at Oxford, a Lady Margaret divinity chair, and by other princely gifts, she has come to be regarded—and justly so—as the greatest benefactress Cambridge has ever known. The university's debt to St John Fisher is not so universally recognized. When he went to Cambridge its scholarship had sunk to a low ebb: no Greek or Hebrew was taught, and the library had been reduced to 300 volumes. Not only did all the administrative work in connection with Lady Margaret's benefactions fall upon his shoulders during her life and after her death, but he did much, entirely on his own initiative, to foster learning in the university. He endowed scholarships, he re-introduced Greek and Hebrew into the curriculum, and he brought Erasmus over to teach and to lecture.

In 1504 he was elected chancellor of the University of Cambridge—a post which he continued to hold until his death. Later in that same year King Henry VII nominated him to the bishopric of Rochester, although he was only thirty-five years of age. He accepted with reluctance an office which added the cares of a diocese to his work for Cambridge. Nevertheless, he carried out his pastoral duties with a zeal and thoroughness exceptional in those days. He held visitations, administered confirmation, disciplined his clergy, visited the sick poor in their hovels, distributed alms with his own hands, and exercised generous hospitality. Moreover, he found time to write books and to continue his studies. He was forty-eight when he began to learn Greek, and fifty-one when he started upon Hebrew. The sermons he preached in 1509 for the funerals of Henry VII and of Lady Margaret Beaufort have been preserved to us. Both of them are recognized as English classics of the period; that on the king is particularly remarkable as a noble and sincere tribute to the memory of a sovereign, with little trace of the exaggerated and adulatory language almost universally employed in such circumstances. St John Fisher's private life was most austere: he limited his sleep to four hours, used the discipline freely and, though his fare was of the scantiest, he kept a skull before him at meal-times to remind himself of death. Books were his one earthly pleasure: and, with a view to bequeathing his books to Cambridge, he formed a library which was among the finest in Europe.

Personal ambition he had none and, when offered preferment in the shape of wealthier sees, he refused them, saying that " he would not leave his poor old wife for the richest widow in England ". Because of his learning and eloquence, he was specially selected to preach against Lutheranism when it was found to be making headway—particularly in London and in the universities. He also wrote four weighty volumes against Luther which can claim the distinction of being the first books to be published in refutation of the new doctrines. These and other literary works helped to spread his fame abroad as well as at home. But when a Carthusian monk afterwards congratulated him on the service he had thus rendered to the Church, he expressed his regret that the time he had devoted to writing had not been spent in prayer : prayer, he thought, would have done more good and was of greater merit. Such was the man whom the Emperor Charles V's ambassador described as " the paragon of Christian bishops for learning and holiness ", concerning whom young King Henry VIII was wont to boast that no other prince or kingdom had so distinguished a prelate. With unclouded vision John Fisher apprehended the evils of the time and the dangers that threatened the Church of God. He was himself a reformer, but of abuses and evils, not a deformer of religious truth. At a synod called by Cardinal Wolsey in 1518 he boldly protested against the worldliness, the laxity and the vanity of the higher clergy, the greater part of whom had won their preferments through secular service to the state or by private interest. Because, unlike them, he was not trying to serve two masters, he had no hesitation, some nine years later, in upholding the validity of King Henry's marriage to Catherine of Aragon when other men in high office were temporizing or yielding.

He was chosen to be one of the queen's counsellors in the nullity suit begun before Cardinal Campeggio at Blackfriars in 1529, and he proved to be her ablest champion. In an eloquent speech before the court he demonstrated that the marriage was valid and that it could be dissolved by no power, human or divine, winding up with the reminder that the Baptist of old had died in defence of the marriage tie. To his arguments, embodied in literary form and presented to the king, Henry sent a furious reply, which with Fisher's marginal comments may still be seen at the Record Office. Shortly afterwards the case was recalled to Rome and Fisher's immediate connection with it ceased. He had upheld the sanctity of marriage : he now became the champion of the rights of the Church and the supremacy of the Pope. As a member of the House of Lords he denounced the measures against the clergy which were being forced through the Commons : " With them ", he exclaimed, " is nothing but ' Down with the Church ! ' " He uttered another great protest in Convocation when that assembly was called upon to agree that Henry VIII was head of the Church in England. To him it was due that the words " So far as the law of Christ allows " were added to the form of assent that was eventually signed, but he regarded even that as too much in the nature of a compromise.

The warnings of friends and the threats of his enemies were not necessary to bring home to Bishop Fisher the danger he now ran by his opposition to the ruling powers. Twice already he had suffered short terms of imprisonment, at least one attempt was made to poison him, and on another occasion a shot fired from across the river penetrated his library window. Then came an unsuccessful effort on the part of Thomas Cromwell to connect him with the affair of Elizabeth Barton, the " Holy Maid of Kent ". Eventually the passage into law of the bill of succession provided his enemies with the means of securing his downfall. He was summoned to Lambeth to subscribe to it, although he was so ill that he fainted on the road between Rochester and London. To the actual succession he would have been willing to agree, but he absolutely refused to take the oath in the form presented because it was so worded as to make it practically an oath of supremacy. " Not that I condemn any other men's conscience ", he had written to Cromwell. " Their conscience may save them, and mine must save me." For the other bishops took the oath.   John of Rochester was immediately arrested and conveyed to the Tower.

An act of attainder of misprision of treason was then passed against the prisoner : he was declared to be degraded from his office and his see was pronounced vacant. He was sixty-six years of age, but so reduced by physical ill-health, by his austerities, and by all he had gone through that he looked more like a man of eighty-six. His wasted body, we are told, could scarcely bear the weight of his clothes.   Three years earlier Cardinal Pole had reckoned him a dying man, and he afterwards expressed his wonder that Fisher should have survived the ordeal of a ten-months' imprisonment in the Bell Tower.   In November 1534, a second act of attainder was passed upon him, but he still lingered on in prison.   By sending him the cardinal's hat, six months later, Pope Paul III infuriated Henry VIII and hastened the end.   " Let the pope send him a hat ", the king exclaimed, " I will so provide that whensoever it cometh he shall wear it on his shoulders, for head he shall have none to set it on."   After that the result of his so-called trial was a foregone conclusion, for the king's will was law.   Though some of the judges wept when the sentence was declared, John Fisher was condemned to death on June 17, 1535.

Five days later, at five in the morning, he was roused with the intelligence that he was to be executed that day.   He asked to be allowed to rest a little longer and he slept soundly for two hours.   He then dressed, putting on a fur tippet " to keep me warm for the while until the very time of execution " ; then he took his little New Testament, and, with great difficulty owing to his excessive weakness, went down the steps to the entrance from whence he was conveyed in a chair to the Tower gate.   There, as he leant against a wall before proceeding to the place of execution, he opened his book with a prayer for some word of comfort.   The first words he saw were, it is said, those spoken by our Lord before His passion : " This is life everlasting that they may know thee, the only true God, and Jesus Christ whom thou hast sent.   I have glorified thee upon the earth : I have finished the work that thou gavest me to do."   Thus fortified, he walked up Tower Hill, mounted the scaffold unassisted, and in the customary terms pardoned his executioner.   As he stood up to address the crowd his tall emaciated figure made him appear like a living skeleton.   With a clear voice he said that he was dying for the faith of Christ's holy Catholic Church, and he asked the people to pray that he might be steadfast to the end.   After he had recited the *Te Deum* and the psalm *In te Domine speravi*, he was blindfolded, and with one blow from the axe his head was severed from his body.   Henry's vindictive spirit pursued the martyr even beyond his death.   His body, after lying exposed all day, was thrust without shroud or rites into a hole in All Hallows Barking churchyard, and his head was impaled for fourteen days on London Bridge with the heads of the Carthusian martyrs, seeming " as though it had been alive, looking upon the people coming into London ".   A fortnight later it was thrown into the river, to make room for More's.

In May 1935, almost exactly four hundred years after his death, John Fisher was solemnly numbered among the saints, together with his friend and fellow martyr, Sir Thomas More ; and on July 9 the feast of these two martyrs is kept together throughout England and Wales, and in the Scottish diocese of Dunkeld.

It might be said that to a very large extent the *Letters and Papers, Foreign and Domestic, of the Reign of Henry VIII*, published by the Record Office, supply the best materials for the life of St John Fisher, but there is also an important biography written by one who was in part a contemporary. In 1891–93 an accurate edition of it, based upon a collation of the available manuscripts and of the Latin translation, was produced by the Bollandist, Fr van Ortroy, and printed in the *Analecta Bollandiana*, vol. x and vol. xii. Another text was printed in 1915 by the Early English Text Society. Both these preserved the original spelling, but in 1935 an edition for popular perusal with modernized spelling was brought out, together with an excellent introduction and occasional notes, by Fr Philip Hughes. The author of this biography was not, as was for a long time supposed, Richard Hall, though it was he who made the Latin version, but, most probably, Dr John Young, vice-chancellor of Cambridge in Mary's reign. It seems to have been written some time after 1567. But nearly all the materials available for Fisher's life have been utilized in the great work of Fr T. Bridgett; his *Life of John Fisher* (3rd ed., 1902) is extremely thorough, discerning and spiritual, altogether a model biography. See also the admirable lecture of E. A. Benians, entitled *John Fisher* (1935); N. M. Wilby's popular sketch (1929); R. L. Smith, *John Fisher and Thomas More* (1935). The E.E.T.S. has published *Bishop Fisher's English Works* (pt. i, ed. J. E. B. Mayor, 1876; pt. ii, ed. R. Bayne, 1915).

ST THOMAS MORE, MARTYR (A.D. 1535)

AT either end of the medieval monarchy in England stands the figure of a great martyr: one gave his life to make the Church in this country safe from royal aggression for three hundred and fifty years, the other in a vain effort to save it from the like aggression; each was named Thomas, each was chancellor of the realm, each was a royal favourite who loved God more than his king; the coincidence is remarkable, though on closer examination the resemblance seems suddenly to end: yet the contrast is after all largely one of difference in time— between the late twelfth century and the full tide of the Renaissance—and in status; Thomas Becket was a churchman, Thomas More a layman.

More's father was Sir John More, barrister-at-law and judge, and he was born of his first wife Agnes, daughter of Thomas Grainger, in Milk Street, Cheapside, on February 6, 1478. He was sent as a child to St Antony's School in Threadneedle Street, and at thirteen was received into the household of Morton, Archbishop of Canterbury, who had sufficient opinion of his promise to send him to Oxford, where he was entered at Canterbury College (afterwards absorbed into Christ Church). Sir John was strict with his son, allowed him money only against bills for necessaries, and with nothing for himself; if young Thomas grumbled about this (and no doubt he did), he afterwards saw the sense of it: it had kept him out of mischief and he was not tempted away from the studies which he loved. But his father called him home when he had been only two years at the university. In February 1496, being now eighteen, he was admitted a student of Lincoln's Inn; he was called to the bar in 1501, and in 1504 he entered Parliament. He was already bosom friends with Erasmus, Dean Colet was his confessor, he made Latin epigrams from the Greek Anthology with William Lilly, lectured on St Augustine's *de Civitate Dei* at St Lawrence Jewry. He was a brilliant and successful young man and popular.

On the other hand, he was for a time very seriously perturbed about his vocation in life. For four years he lived at the London Charterhouse, and was indubitably drawn to the Carthusian life; alternatively, the possibility of becoming a Friar Minor engaged his attention. But he could find no assurance of his calling either to the monastic life or the secular priesthood; to be an unworthy priest was the last thing he wanted; and so in the early part of 1505 he married. Nevertheless, though a man of the world in the good sense of that expression, he had none of that contempt for asceticism which characterized so many at the Renaissance: from somewhere about his eighteenth year he wore a hair-shirt (to the amusement of his daughter-in-law, Anne Cresacre), and used the discipline on Fridays and vigils ; he assisted at Mass every day and daily recited the Little Office. " I never saw anyone ", says Erasmus, " so indifferent about food. . . . Otherwise, he has no aversion from what gives harmless pleasure to the body."

Thomas More's first wife, " *uxorcula Mori* ", as he called her, was Jane, the eldest daughter of John Colt of Nether-hall in Essex. We learn from his son-in-law, William Roper, that More's mind " most served him to the second daughter, for that he thought her the fairest and best favoured, yet when he considered that it would be both great grief and some shame also to the eldest to see her younger sister preferred before her in marriage, he then, of a certain pity, framed his fancy toward her, and soon after married her ". That, surely, was an act of *pietas* rather than pity and is worth recording both for what it tells about More and also as an instructive example of the shifting standards of what may be required of an English gentleman. They were happy together, and they had four children, Margaret, Elizabeth, Cecilia and John. More's household was a seat of learning and accomplishment which, from its lack of dilettantism, would today be dubbed " high-brow " ; he was all for educating women, not from any doctrinaire feminism, but as a reasonable thing, recommended by the prudent and holy ancients, such as St Jerome and St Augustine, " not to speak of the rest ". All the family and servants met together for night-prayers, and at meals a pericope from the Scriptures, with a short commentary, was read aloud by one of the children : this done, discussion and jesting followed ; but cards and dicing he forbade in his house. He endowed a chapel in his parish church of Chelsea, and even when chancellor would sing in the choir, dressed in a surplice. " More was used, whenever in his house or in the village he lived in there was a woman in labour, to begin praying, and so continue until news was brought him that the delivery had come happily to pass. . . . He used himself to go through the back lanes and inquire into the state of poor families. . . . He often invited to his table his poorer neighbours, receiving them . . . familiarly and joyously ; he rarely invited the rich, and scarcely ever the nobility " (Stapleton, *Tres Thomae*). But if the rich and great were rarely seen at his house, such men as Grocyn, Linacre, Colet, Lilly, Fisher, the religious and learned, not only of London but from the continent as well, were ever-welcome visitors, and no one was more frequent or more welcome than Desiderius Erasmus. Attempts have been made to misrepresent this friendship : some Protestants by maximizing the alleged unorthodoxy of Erasmus, some Catholics by minimizing the warmth of the friendship. There is no testimony better than More's own : " For had I found with Erasmus my darling the shrewd intent and purpose that I find in Tyndale, Erasmus my darling should be no more my darling. But I find in Erasmus my darling that he detesteth and abhorreth the errors and heresies that Tyndale plainly teacheth and abideth by, and therefore Erasmus my darling shall be my darling still."

During his first period of married life More lived in Bucklersbury, in the parish of St Peter Walbrook. In 1509 Henry VII died. More had led the opposition in Parliament to this king's monetary exactions, and his success had caused his father to be imprisoned in the Tower and fined £100. The accession of Henry VIII was to mean an accession of worldly fortune to the young lawyer, and in the next year it was presaged by his being elected a reader of Lincoln's Inn and appointed under-sheriff of the City of London ; but almost at the same time the " little Utopia of his own " was abruptly shaken : his beloved wife, Jane Colt, died.   Within a few weeks he had married another, Alice Middleton.   Quite a lot of nonsense has been written about this second and so quick marriage, but the position is clear.   More was a man of sense as well as of sensibility, and he had four young children on his hands : so he married a widow, seven years older than himself, an experienced housewife, talkative, kindly and full of unimaginative common sense.   Some writers have tried to see a double martyrdom for More : but it is no reproach to Mistress Alice that she could not live up to her second husband ; she was no Xanthippe, and probably his only real complaint (if he can be imagined complaining) would be that she did not appreciate his jokes—an undeniable trial of patience. More now moved from Bucklersbury to Crosby Place, in what was then Bishops-gate Street Within ; he did not go to his new house in Chelsea until some twelve years later.

In 1516 he finished writing *Utopia*.   This is not the place to discuss the sig-nificance of that book ; it is enough to say with Sir Sidney Lee that, " More's practical opinion on religion and politics must be sought elsewhere than in the *Utopia* ".   The king and Wolsey were now determined to have More's services at court ; if the idea was not repugnant to him, he was at least unwilling : he knew too much about kings and courts, and that the good life was not there.   But he did not refuse, and he received a rapid succession of preferments till he became, in October 1529, lord chancellor, in succession to the disgraced Wolsey.   Contem-porary records enable us to see Sir Thomas from two different sides at this period. Erasmus wrote : " In serious matters no man's advice is more prized, while if the king wishes to recreate himself, no man's conversation is gayer.   Often there are deep and intricate matters that demand a grave and prudent judge.   More unravels them in such a way that he satisfies both sides.   No one, however, has ever pre-vailed on him to receive a gift for his decision.   Happy the commonwealth where kings appoint such officials !   His elevation has brought with it no pride. . . . You would say that he had been appointed the public guardian of all those in need." From a yet more intimate knowledge, the Carthusian John Bouge wrote in 1535 : " Item, as for Sir Thomas More, he was my parishioner at London. . . . This Mr More was my ghostly child ; in his confession [he used] to be so pure, so clean, with great study, deliberation and devotion, I never heard many such.   A gentleman of great learning both in law, art, and divinity. . . ."   Yet Sir Thomas was as good a courtier as a Christian man and a saint can be, and that does not mean to say he was not a very good one.   Nor yet was the friendship with Henry VIII one-sided : More retained his master's familiar affection, and never failed in it—but he had no illusions about him : " Son Roper, I may tell thee, I have no cause to be proud thereof, for if my head would win him a castle in France, it should not fail to go."

At the time when he was appointed lord chancellor, Sir Thomas More was engaged in writing against Protestantism, and particularly in opposition to Tyndale. Though some complained at the time that his controversial writing was insufficiently solemn, and others have complained since that it was insufficiently refined, his tone was much more moderate than was usual in the sixteenth centruy ; " integrity and uprightness " characterized his polemics, and he always preferred ridicule to denunciation when sober and pitiless argument would not serve.   But if More had the best of the argument, Tyndale was the better writer : More could not match his clear, terse English and perfect phrasing ; he took six pages to say what Tyndale could say in one.   Statements to the contrary notwithstanding, there is no doubt that More's attitude towards heretics was one of scrupulous fairness and notable moderation. It was to heresy and not the persons of heretics that he was opposed and " of all that ever came in my hand for heresy, as help me God, saving (as I said) the sure keeping of them . . . had never any of them any stripe or stroke given them, so much as a fillip on the forehead." It is interesting, too, to read his view of the then acute question of free circulation of vernacular Bibles. He advocated the dissemination of certain books thereof, but the reading of others should be at the discretion of each individual's ordinary, who would probably " suffer some to read the Acts of the Apostles, whom he would not suffer to meddle with the Apocalypse " : just as " a father doth by his discretion appoint which of his children may for his sadness [*i.e.* seriousness] keep a knife to cut his meat, and which shall for his wantonness have his knife taken from him for cutting of his fingers. And thus am I bold, without prejudice of other men's judgement, to show you my mind in this matter, how the Scripture might without great peril, and not without great profit, be brought into our tongue and taken to lay men and women both, not yet meaning thereby but that the whole Bible might for my mind be suffered to be spread abroad in English. . . . Among [the clergy] I have perceived some of the greatest and of the best of their own minds well inclinable thereto."

When King Henry VIII imposed on the clergy the acknowledgement of himself as " Protector and Supreme Head of the Church of England ", to which Convocation managed to add, " so far as the law of Christ allows ", More, according to Chapuys, the ambassador of the emperor, wished to resign his office, but was persuaded to retain it and also to give his attention to Henry's " great matter ". This was the petition for a declaration of nullity *ab initio* of his marriage with Catherine of Aragon, commonly called in English history the king's " divorce ". The matter was involved, both as to the facts and the law, and was one in which men of good-will might well disagree ; More upheld the validity of the marriage, but was allowed at his own wish to stand aside from the controversy. When in March 1531 he had to announce the then state of the case to the Houses of Parliament, he was asked for and refused to give his own opinion. But the position was fast becoming impossible. In 1532 the king proposed to forbid the clergy to prosecute heretics or to hold any meeting without his permission, and in May a parliamentary bill was introduced to withhold from the Holy See the firstfruits of bishoprics (*annates*) ; Sir Thomas opposed all these measures openly, and the king was greatly angered. On May 16 he accepted his chancellor's resignation, after he had held office for less than three years.

The loss of his official salary reduced More to little better than poverty ; he had drastically to reduce his household and state, and gathering his family around him he explained the position to them in a good-humoured statement, ending up, " then may we yet with bags and wallets go a-begging together, and hoping that for pity some good folk will give us their charity, at every man's door to sing ' *Salve regina* ', and so still keep company and be merry together ". For eighteen months he lived very quietly, engaging himself in writing, and he refused to attend the coronation of Anne Boleyn. His enemies missed no opportunity to harass him, as when they implicated him in the case of Elizabeth Barton, the " Holy Maid of Kent ", and caused his name to be included in her bill of attainder, for misprision of treason ; but the Lords wished to hear him in his own defence, which did not suit the king and he withdrew the charge. But the time was soon at hand. On March 30, 1534, the Act of Succession provided for the taking of an oath by the king's subjects recognizing succession to the throne in the offspring of Henry and Anne Boleyn ; to which were later added particulars that his union with Catherine of Aragon had been no true marriage, that his union with Anne Boleyn was a true marriage, and repudiating the authority of " any foreign authority, prince or potentate ". To oppose the act was high treason, and only a week before Pope Clement VII had pronounced the marriage of Henry and Catherine to be valid. Many Catholics took the oath with the reservation " so far as it be not contrary to the law of God ". On April 13 Sir Thomas More and John Fisher, Bishop of Rochester, were tendered the oath before the commission at Lambeth ; they refused it. Thomas was committed to the custody of the Abbot of Westminster. Cranmer advised the king to compromise, but he would not ; so the oath was again tendered and again refused, and More was imprisoned in the Tower—in itself an illegal proceeding on the part of the commissioners, for the proffered oath did not agree with the statute.

During the fifteen months that Thomas was in the Tower two things stand out, his quiet serenity under so unjust a captivity and his tender love for his eldest daughter, Margaret. The two are seen together in his letters to and recorded conversations with her there, as in the beautiful passage quoted by Roper, ending, " I find no cause, I thank God, Meg, to reckon myself in worse case here than at home, for methinks God maketh me a wanton and setteth me on His lap and dandleth me ". The efforts of his family to induce him to come to terms with the king were fruitless ; his custody was made more rigorous and visitors forbidden, so he began to write the *Dialogue of Comfort against Tribulation*, the best of his spiritual works, in which a French writer, the Abbé Bremond, sees a forerunner of St Francis de Sales, and an Englishman, the late W. H. Hutton, of Jeremy Taylor. In November he was attainted of misprision of treason and, but for a small pension from the Order of St John of Jerusalem, rendered penniless by forfeiture of the lands formerly granted by the Crown ; Lady More had to sell her clothes to buy necessaries for him, and twice in vain petitioned the king for his release, pleading his sickness and poverty. On February 1, 1535, the Acts of Supremacy came into operation, which gave the title of " only supreme head of the Church of England " to the king and made it treason to deny it. In April Cromwell came to ask More his opinion of this bill, but he would not give one. On May 4 his daughter visited him for the last time, and together they watched the first three Carthusian monks and their companions go to martyrdom : " Lo ! dost thou not see, Meg, that these blessed fathers be now as cheerfully going to their deaths as bridegrooms to their marriage ? . . . Whereas thy silly father, Meg, that like a most wicked caitiff hath passed forth the whole course of his miserable life most sinfully, God, thinking him not so worthy so soon to come to that eternal felicity, leaveth him here yet still in the world further to be plagued and turmoiled with misery." When a few days later Cromwell and others again examined him on the statute and taunted him for his silence, he replied : " I have not been a man of such holy living as I might be bold to offer myself to death, lest God for my presumption might suffer me to fall."

On June 19 the second three Carthusians suffered, and on the 22nd, the feast of St Alban, protomartyr of Britain, St John Fisher was beheaded on Tower Hill. Nine days later St Thomas More was indicted and tried in Westminster Hall ; he was very weak from illness and long captivity, and was permitted to sit during the proceedings. The charge was that he had in divers ways opposed the Act of Supremacy in conversation with the members of the council who had visited him in prison and in an alleged conversation with Rich, the solicitor general. St Thomas maintained that he had always kept silence on the subject and that Rich was swearing falsely; and he reminded the jury that, " Ye must understand that, in things touching conscience, every true and good subject is more bound to have respect to his said conscience and to his soul than to any other thing in all the world beside . . .". He was found guilty and condemned to death. Then at last he spoke, categorically denying that " a temporal lord could or ought to be head of the spirituality ", and ending that, as St Paul had persecuted St Stephen " and yet be they now both twain holy saints in Heaven, and shall continue there friends for ever, so I verily trust, and shall therefore right heartily pray, that though your lordships have now here on earth been judges of my condemnation, we may yet hereafter in Heaven merrily all meet together to everlasting salvation ". On his way back to the Tower he said farewell to his son and daughter, most movingly described by Roper, and the martyr referred to it four days later in a last letter which he sent to her with his hair-shirt (most of which relic is now in the care of the Austin canonesses at Newton Abbot, founded at Louvain by the daughter of More's adopted child, Margaret Clement) : " I love when daughterly love and dear charity hath no desire to look to worldly courtesy."

Early on Tuesday, July 6, Sir Thomas Pope came to warn him that he was to die that day at nine o'clock (the king had commuted the sentence from hanging and quartering to beheading) ; whereupon St Thomas thanked him, said he would pray for the king, and comforted his weeping friend. He then put on his best clothes, walked quietly to Tower Hill, speaking to sundry persons on the way, and mounted the scaffold, with a jest for the lieutenant. He invoked the prayers of the people, protested that he died for the Holy Catholic Church and was " the king's good servant—but God's first ", and said the psalm *Miserere ;* he kissed and encouraged the headsman, covered his own eyes and adjusted his beard, and so was beheaded at one stroke. He was fifty-seven years old.

His body was buried somewhere in the church of St Peter ad Vincula within the Tower ; his head, after being exposed on London Bridge, was begged by Margaret Roper and laid in the Roper vault in the church of St Dunstan, outside the West Gate of Canterbury, beneath the floor at the east end of the south aisle.

More was equivalently beatified with other English martyrs in 1886, and canonized in 1935. But, as has been pointed out more than once, had he never met his death as he did he would have been a good candidate for canonization as a confessor. Some saints have attained their honours by redeeming an indifferent or even sinful life by martyrdom ; not so Thomas More. He was from first to last a holy man, living in the spirit of his own prayer : " Give me, good Lord, a longing to be with thee : not for the avoiding of the calamities of this wicked world, nor so much for the avoiding of the pains of Purgatory, nor of the pains of Hell neither, nor so much for the attaining of the joys of Heaven in respect of mine own commodity, as even for a very love of thee." And this when his ways were cast, not in the cloister, but in the ordinary places of the world—home 'and family, among scholars and lawyers, in tribunals, council-chambers, and royal courts.

The earliest formal biography of St Thomas More, that by Nicholas Harpsfield, has been edited by E. V. Hitchcock and R. W. Chambers (1932), and that by his son-in-law, Wm. Roper, by E. V. Hitchcock (1935), both published by the E.E.T.S. The first printed life was Thomas Stapleton's in *Tres Thomae* (1588 ; Eng. trans., 1928). The very valuable life by " Ro : Ba : " (*c.* 1599) was edited by Miss Hitchcock, Mgr Hallett and Prof. A. W.

Reed in 1950 (E.E.T.S.). A fourth life, by his great-grandson, Cresacre More, appeared before 1631. An edition of his *English Works*, ed. W. E. Campbell and others, is in progress ; *The Dialogue . . . concerning Tyndale* (with valuable supplementary matter) and the *Early Works* are issued. A. Taft edited the *Apologye* for the E.E.T.S. (1930) ; it contains in text and notes much useful detail bearing on More's dealings with heretics. Father Bridgett's *Life of Sir Thomas More* (1891), with his supplementary booklets, still remain the fullest source of information for the reader who is not a specialist ; but the best general life of all is R. W. Chambers's *Thomas More* (1935) ; *cf.* review in *Analecta Bollandiana*, vol. liv (1936), p. 245. There are shorter recent biographies by J. Clayton, C. Hollis, D. Sargent, T. Maynard and others ; and an excellent work by E. E. Reynolds (1953). More's *Correspondence* has been edited by E. F. Rogers (Princeton, 1947). But the bibliography of More is very long.

ST EVERILD, Virgin   (*c.* A.D. 700)

ALL we know of this maiden is derived from the breviary lessons for her feast in the church of York. She was the daughter of a noble family converted some time after the baptism of Cynegils, King of Wessex, and in order to devote herself perfectly to the service and love of God she fled from the house of her parents to seek some monastery of nuns. She was joined by two other maidens named Bega and Wulfreda. They arrived at York, where St Wilfrid gave her a spot called the Bishop's Farm. Here she trained up many nuns to the perfection of divine love, the summit of Christian virtue, by animating them with the true spirit of the gospel ; and continually encouraged them in the faithful discharge of all the duties and exercises of their holy state, until she was called to God.

See the *Acta Sanctorum*, July, vol. ii ; and Stanton, *Menology*, p. 328, who points out that three medieval northern English calendars insert the name of St Everildis on this day. On the strength of the name, Everingham in the East Riding has been claimed as the site of the nunnery, but E. Ekwall gives no support to such a derivation (*Oxford Dictionary of English Place-Names*.) The name Everild still exists as Averil.

BD JANE OF REGGIO, Virgin   (A.D. 1491)

JANE SCOPELLI was born in 1428 at Reggio in Emilia, and while still young wished to become a nun. This her parents would not allow, so she put on the religious habit and led an ascetical life at home. When the death of both father and mother left her free, she set about founding a convent of Carmelites in Reggio ; but she refused to make use for this purpose of the wealth she had inherited insisting that all must be done by means of alms and charitable bequests. She laboured unceasingly, and at the end of four years the monastery of our Lady of the People was established, with Bd Jane as prioress. In spite of the ties of administration and the choir-office she spent five hours a day in private prayer, while adding austerities to those prescribed by the rule. She fasted all the year round, and from Holy Cross day till Easter ate nothing but bread and water ; her mortifications were indeed astonishing.

Several stories are told of the wonders she worked by prayer. She thus cured of bodily disease the noble lady Julia Sessi, whom the doctors had given up as hopeless, and of spiritual sickness a young man called Augustine. This youth was attached to Albigensian and other heretical opinions, and his distressed mother brought him to Bd Jane, who used all arguments and the most moving appeals to turn him from them ; her efforts were vain, but when they had gone she made the matter a subject of fervent prayer, and Augustine opened his heart to the proffered grace.   There is also attributed to her the miracle related of St Dominic, among other saints : coming to table one day the nuns were met by bare boards, for there was no food in the house.   But at the prayer of the holy prioress the larder which a few minutes before had been empty was found to contain bread more than sufficient for them all.   Bd Jane died in 1491 at the age of sixty-three, after having with her last breath urged her sisters to join rigid observance of their rule to their love of God and of one another.   Her *cultus* was confirmed in 1771.

A biography of moderate length written in Italian by Fr Benedict Mutti has been translated into Latin by the Bollandists and will be found in the *Acta Sanctorum*, July, vol. ii.

SS. NICHOLAS PIECK AND HIS COMPANIONS, THE MARTYRS OF GORKUM   (A.D. 1572)

NINETEEN priests and religious, taken by Calvinists in Gorkum, near Dordrecht, were hanged on account of their religion.   Of these, eleven were Franciscan friars of the Observance of the convent of Gorkum, amongst whom were ST NICHOLAS PIECK, the guardian, and ST JEROME WEERDEN, vicar.   With them were taken SS. LEONARD VECHEL, NICHOLAS JANSSEN and GODFREY VAN DUYNEN, secular priests, and JOHN VAN OOSTERWYK, a canon regular of St Augustine of great age.   Vechel was the parish priest at Gorkum.   To these fifteen were afterwards added ST JOHN VAN HOORNAER, a Dominican, who came to the assistance of his Franciscan brethren when he heard that they were taken ; two Premonstratensians, SS. ADRIAN VAN HILVARENBEEK and JAMES LACOPS, the last of whom had been very slack in his religious observance and contumacious under reproof ; and ST ANDREW WOUTERS, a secular priest, who went straight from an irregular life to imprisonment and martyrdom.

In June 1572 the anti-Spanish Calvinist forces called the *Watergeuzen*, " Sea-Beggars ", or *Gueux*, " Ragamuffins ", seized Gorkum, and from June 26 to July 5 the Franciscans and four other priests were at the mercy of the soldiers, who treated them with incredible cruelty, partly out of contempt for their religion and partly in order to discover the whereabouts of the hidden church vessels.   Then word came from the admiral, Lumaye, Baron de la Marck, to bring them to Briel, where they disembarked in the early morning of the 7th and, half-naked as they were, marched to the market-place with the caricatured circumstance of a religious procession, and there contemptuously ordered to sing the Litany of the Saints, which they did gladly enough.   That evening and the next morning they were interrogated before the admiral and, confronted by Calvinist ministers, invited to purchase their freedom by abandoning the Catholic doctrine of the Blessed Sacrament ; this they refused to do.   Letters now arrived to the Baron de la Marck from the magistrates of Gorkum, complaining of the detention of the prisoners, and from the Prince of Orange, ordering that they be released ; at the same time two brothers of Nicholas Pieck made personal appeal for him.   The admiral said that all should at once be set free if they would abjure the primacy of the pope : again they refused, and all the efforts of his brothers could not induce Father Pieck to abandon either his faith or his religious brethren.   Soon after midnight an apostate priest of Liège was sent to lead the prisoners to a sacked and deserted monastery at Ruggen, in the outskirts of Briel.

Here they were gathered in a turf-shed where were two convenient beams.   At this last moment, when already Father Pieck had been flung off the ladder, speaking words of encouragement, the courage of some failed them ; it is a significant warning against judging the character of our neighbour or pretending to read his heart that, while a priest of blameless life recanted in a moment of weakness, the two who had been an occasion of scandal gave their lives without a tremor.   All the nineteen were hanged, St James Lacops from a ladder, the rest from the beams ; one, St Antony van Willehad, was ninety years old.   The execution was the sheerest butchery : all hung long before they were dead, St Nicasius van Heeze till after dawn, and the bodies were mutilated before they were cold, some before life was extinct.

Like the martyrs of England and Wales, these men gave their lives for the Catholic faith in general, and for the truth of its eucharistic teaching and the primacy of the Roman pontiff in particular.   Their bodies were ignominiously cast into two ditches and there lay till 1616, when, during a truce between Spain and the United Provinces, they were dug up and the remains translated to the Franciscan church in Brussels.   The martyrs of Gorkum were canonized in 1867.

The story of the martyrdom was told in detail by William Estius, the Scripture commentator, himself a native of Gorkum and a nephew of Father Pieck.   His account with other illustrative matter is printed in the *Acta Sanctorum*, July, vol. ii.   See also the modern narratives of Kronenburg, Spilbeek, and in particular Hubert Meuffels.   This last volume, written in French, which belongs to the series " Les Saints ", contains a quite formidable bibliography.

ST VERONICA GIULIANI, Virgin   (A.D. 1727)

Ursula Giuliani was born at Mercatello in Urbino in 1660, her parents being gentlefolk of that city.   She is said to have begun to show signs of unusual piety at a very early age ; at six and seven she was concerned to give away her own food and clothing to the needy, and at eleven devotion to our Lord's passion had begun to colour her own life.   She had the not uncommon fault of resenting when others did not join in her religious practices, which was cured by a vision in which she saw her own heart made, as it were, of steel.   When her father received a public office at Piacenza she took a good deal of pleasure in the increased dignity and more affluent circumstances which this meant for the family ; no bad thing in itself, but she made it a matter of self-reproach in after years.

In consequence of a vision of our Lady, Ursula made a vow to become a nun, but met with strong opposition from her father, Francis Giuliani : he not only wanted her to marry, but insisted on presenting eligible suitors.   This worried her into an illness ; Francis gave way, and in 1677 she was clothed a Capuchiness in the convent of Città di Castello, in Umbria, taking the name of Veronica.   Her noviciate was a difficult one ; in addition to interior trials she was subjected to severe discipline by her superiors, for her holy ambition was such that it required careful testing ; moreover, the bishop who clothed her had predicted that she would be a saint.   After her profession her absorption in the Passion deepened, she had a vision of our Lord bearing the cross, and she began to have acute pain over her heart.   In 1693 she experienced another vision in which the chalice of Christ's sufferings was offered to her ; after a great struggle she accepted it, and henceforth reproduced in her own body and soul something of the sufferings of the divine Master.   In the following year the imprint of the crown of thorns appeared on her head, and on Good Friday, 1697, the impress of the five sacred wounds. These physical manifestations were subjected to medical treatment, but without any effect on them. These things being reported to the Bishop of Città di Castello, he referred to the Holy Office for direction, and was told to do nothing and to say no more about it. But when the phenomena became more pronounced he decided to examine them for himself, which he did at the convent *grille* in the presence of four nuns, and was convinced of their objective reality. To get rid of any possibility of fraud he had every moment of Sister Veronica's time controlled; she was forbidden to receive holy communion, to mix with the other nuns, or to have any sort of communication with the outside world; and she was to be day and night under the eye of a lay-sister. The bishop, moreover, ordered that the wounds were to be dressed and bandaged, and her hands put into gloves with the fastenings sealed with his signet. Veronica suffered these prudent precautions with exemplary patience. They made no difference at all to the phenomena, and the bishop having communicated this and the nun's obedient and humble demeanour to the Holy Office, it was ordered that she should be allowed to return to the normal life of her community.

St Veronica was of the type of St Teresa of Avila and all the greatest contemplatives, adding to her devotion and supernatural gifts common sense and ability in affairs. She was novice-mistress of her convent for thirty-four years, which itself shows how well she fulfilled the office, and eleven years before her death was elected abbess. She would not allow the novices under her to read any books of advanced mysticism. She bade them be content with such practical works as the *Christian and Religious Perfection* of Rodriguez, and thought that during that time of preparation they had enough to do in laying the foundations of humility, obedience and charity. It may also be supposed that this saint, herself a mystic, knew the damage that may be done to unformed minds and aspiring souls by being excited and puffed up by the doctrine of the great masters, which is as yet too high for them. We expect to find that such a woman improved the convent's water-supply by having it piped in, and that she enlarged the conventual buildings—and so she did.

At the end of her life this " spouse of the Lord " who for nearly fifty years had suffered with patience, resignation, and joy, was afflicted with apoplexy, and she died of this disorder on July 9, 1727. She left an account of her life and spiritual experiences, written by order of her confessor, and this was much used in the process of beatification; she was canonized in 1839. Long before her death she had told her confessor that the instruments of our Lord's passion were imprinted on her heart, giving him more than once, for they, as she averred, shifted their position, a rough plan of a heart on which they were sketched. A *post-mortem* examination in the presence of the bishop, the mayor, surgeons, and other witnesses, revealed in the right ventricle a number of minute objects corresponding to those she had drawn.

So far as concerns the evidence of mystical phenomena, the case of St Veronica is perhaps the most remarkable known to Catholic hagiology. The writer of this note, Father Thurston, had the opportunity in the Bollandist library of consulting the very rare *summarium* of the evidence presented for her beatification. The sworn testimony of the saint's confessor and fellow religious goes to show that her stigmatic wounds opened and bled at command, and that they closed again and healed perfectly in a short space of time while the bishop waited. And there were many other phenomena of levitations, perfumes, etc., not mentioned above. The least unsatisfactory life is probably that of Father F. M. Salvatore (1839), founded on the process ; it was translated into English in 1874. Father Pizzicaria has edited St Veronica's spiritual diary in ten volumes, and there is a good selection therefrom by Fr Désiré des Planches, *Le journal de Ste Véronique Giuliani* (1931), with medical comment by J. F. Gentili ; other extracts in *Franciscan Annals* for 1944 and 1945. See also an article by Fr L. Veuthey in *Vita Cristiana*, vol. xv (1943), pp. 481–489, 566–589.

THE MARTYRS OF ORANGE (A.D. 1794)

AT the time of the French Revolution there were in the little town of Bollène in the Comtat-Venaissin two convents, one of Ursulines and the other of Perpetual Adorers of the Blessed Sacrament, the congregation founded at Marseilles by the Venerable Antony Le Quien in 1639. When in April 1794 the local authorities tendered the republican oath to these nuns they refused to take it, for both Christians and others attributed to it an anti-religious significance. Twenty-nine of them were accordingly arrested and lodged in jail at Orange where, amid numerous other women prisoners, they organized so far as possible a communal religious life, beginning with the Little Office at 7 a.m.

The first victim was BD MARY ROSE DELOYE, a Benedictine, who on July 6 was sentenced to death for having tried " to destroy the republic by fanaticism and superstition ". The first Sacramentine was BD IPHIGENIA DE GAILLARD DE LAVALDÈNE the next day, and the first Ursulines BD MELANIA DE GUILHERMIER and BD ANGELA DE ROCHER on the 9th. Others followed almost daily till nearly the end of the month. In all, thirty-two nuns suffered on the guillotine at this time, sixteen of them being Ursulines, thirteen Sacramentines, two Bernardines and one Benedictine.

We have the testimony of one who was released from the prison that each day the dwindling band of survivors said together the prayers for the dying for the day's victims and then sang the *Te Deum*. BD PELAGIA BÈS after her sentence shared out a box of sweets, " For my wedding " ; BD THEOCTISTA PÉLISSIER wrote a song in prison, welcoming the guillotine ; while BD MARTHA CLUSE, a pretty lay-sister, refused to save her life at the last moment at the price of marrying one of the executioners. " These jades die laughing ", commented the guards.

These thirty-two martyrs were beatified in 1925. After the fall of Robespierre the notorious Orange tribunal was condemned in its turn : two of its judges and the public prosecutor were reconciled with the Church before execution. In 1802 the Sacramentine house at Bollène was reopened, and sisters from there had for a time a convent at Taunton, opened in 1863.

See Redon, *Les trente-deux religieuses guillotinées à Orange* . . . .: H. Leclercq, *Les martyrs*, t. xii (1913). Summary in Baudot and Chaussin, *Vies des Saints* . . ., t. vii (1949), pp. 209–215.

THE MARTYRS OF CHINA, II, UNDER THE BOXERS (A.D. 1900)

THE modern era in Chinese missions dates from the middle of the nineteenth century, when by the Treaty of Nanking and other international agreements " Forbidden China " at last opened her doors to the outside world and guaranteed tolerance for Christianity. A period of great missionary enterprise and expansion followed—but not missionary only, for by the end of the century four-fifths of the country's external trade was in English hands. The prospect of European merchants making of China another India caused alarm, and there was a reaction against the " foreign devils " after the encouragement given them by the chief minister, Li Hungchang.

With the support of the dowager empress, Tzu-hsi, a secret society was formed to drive the Europeans out. It was called *Yi Ho Chuan*, meaning " Righteous Harmony Boxers ", and so its members are referred to in English as Boxers. In 1900 they took up arms ; foreign diplomatic bodies were besieged in their legations, and large numbers of merchants, missionaries and others were massacred. Among the victims were five bishops, twenty-nine priests and nine nuns (all Europeans) and between twenty and thirty thousand other Catholics. The cases of nearly three thousand of them are under examination at Rome, and the first twenty-nine were beatified in 1946.

At the time of the Boxer outbreak the vicar apostolic of Northern Shansi was BD GREGORY GRASSI, Titular Bishop of Orthosias. He was sixty-seven years old, a native of the Piedmont, and a Friar Minor. He had been a missionary in China for forty years, and at the midsummer of 1900 was in Taiyuanfu, where the seminary of his vicariate was situated. In the previous May a notorious enemy of Christianity, Yu Hsien, had been made governor of Taiyuanfu, and week by week the situation there became more threatening. Among the Friars Minor was a herculean lay-brother, BD ANDREW BAUER, an Alsatian who had served in the 7th Cuirassiers, and he, together with a Christian mandarin, Li Fu, wanted to organize armed resistance. But their superiors would have none of it. " If it be God's will that we should be martyred, then we must accept it ", declared BD FRANCIS FOGOLLA. He was the coadjutor bishop of Mgr Grassi, and like him an Italian Franciscan, but from Tuscany, where he was born in 1839.

On June 27 the Boxers raided the Protestant missions of the neighbourhood. That night Mgr Grassi shut up the seminary, telling the students to disperse to their homes, and all but five succeeded in getting away. Those five were BB. JOHN CHANG, PATRICK TONG, PHILIP CHANG, JOHN CHANG junior, and JOHN WANG, of whom the eldest was twenty-three and the youngest sixteen. They were stopped at the town gate, arrested, and taken before the sub-prefect, who called on them to repudiate Christianity. They refused, and after some days in prison were taken to the courtyard of Yu Hsien's house.

Meanwhile Mgr Grassi was very perturbed for the nuns, Franciscan Mission-aries of Mary,* for whom he was responsible. He told them to dress in Chinese clothes, to give them a better chance to escape. But they showed no particular desire to be spared : " Don't stop us from dying with you, Monsignor ", they said. " If we are not brave enough, God will give us strength." Their superioress was BD MARY HERMINA GRIVOT, who was a Burgundian from Beaune, born in 1866, and she had been in China only fifteen months. The witnesses agree that it was her strength and courage above all that nerved the rest, under God, to face their terrible ordeal. Two of her nuns were Italian, BB. MARY GIULIANI and CLARE NANETTI, one French, MARY ST JUST MOREAU, one Breton, NATALIA KERGUIN, one Belgian, AMANDINE JEURIS, and one Dutch, ADOLPHINE DIERKX. They were all between twenty-five and thirty-five years old. Mgr Grassi got some carts, and told the nuns to take their orphan charges off in them to Christian households ; but they were turned back, and after a day or two the children were forcibly carried away by soldiers. An order came from Yu Hsien forbidding Christians to meet

---

* This congregation was founded in 1877 by Mother Mary Helen de Chappotin de Neuville. They first came to China nine years later.

together for prayer; the bishop refused to confirm such an order. Mother Hermina was anxious to do something to protect her orphans, but her nuns implored her to take some rest. " Rest ! " she retorted. " Time enough to rest in Heaven!" The flames of burning houses were coming nearer, and the little group around Bishop Grassi was completely cut off from the outer world.

On July 5 the two bishops and the nuns were made to go to a building adjoining Yu Hsien's house. With them were two Franciscan priests, Fathers Elias and Theodoric, and the Brother Andrew mentioned above. BD ELIAS FACCHINI was an old man, born near Bologna, who had been training young clergy in Shansi for over thirty years. BD THEODORIC BALAT was a Frenchman from near Albi, a man of gentle and reserved character, whose reliability and knowledge of the Chinese language had caused his being entrusted for ten years with a remote and difficult mission-post in the mountains.

In the afternoon of July 9 an attack was made on a number of devoted Protestants in a neighbouring building,* and all knew the end was at hand. The Boxers broke in and drove the Catholics out just as Bishop Grassi had given the last absolution. There was no pretence of a trial. Yu Hsien himself cut down the two bishops. The nuns knelt, singing the *Te Deum* and drawing back their veils for the death-blow ; but they were cruelly hoisted up by their hands behind their backs before their throats were cut. Mother Clare was the first to die, she who had long before foreseen her death for Christ. The three Friars Minor and the five Chinese seminarians perished by the sword ; and with them the nine mission servants and others, who could have saved themselves and would not, humble and obscure men whose names are written in the Church's roll of holiness as BB. THOMAS SEN, SIMON CHEN, PETER U NGANPAN, FRANCIS CHANG YUN, MATTHIAS FUN TE, JAMES YEN KUTUN, PETER CHANG PANNIEN, JAMES CHAO SIUENSIN, and PETER YANOL MAN. Of these twenty-six, the seminarians and the nuns were the protomartyrs of the Chinese seminaries and the Franciscan Missionaries of Mary respectively. And the building where they were all gathered together at the end was known in Chinese, with nice appropriateness, as the " Inn of Heavenly Peace ".

Four days earlier, at Hengchowfu in the province of Honan, another Franciscan, Father CESIDIO GIACOMANTONIO, going to a place of greater safety, had turned back to remove the Blessed Sacrament from the tabernacle in his chapel. He was caught by the Boxers, severely beaten, wrapped in sacking soaked with oil and slowly burned to death. Bd Cesidio had been in China only seven months and he is the first martyr and the first *beatus* of the international Franciscan College of St Antony at Rome.

The news of this priest's death had brought the vicar apostolic of Southern Honan, Bishop ANTONY FANTOSATI, hurrying to Hengchowfu, accompanied by another friar, Father JOSEPH GAMBARO. In their boat on the river they were recognized. Boxer boats surrounded them and pushed their boat aground, where they were met with showers of heavy stones. Bd Joseph was killed first, but Bd Antony lingered for two hours before a spear put an end to his life.

Before these twenty-nine persons could be beatified as martyrs it had to be

---

* These were the thirty-three victims (including two of her own step-daughters) referred to by the wife of an American Protestant missionary, Ernest Atwater, in a letter from Fenchufu on August 3. She adds, " The following [same ?] day the Roman Catholic priests and nuns, Taiyuan, were also beheaded ". Mrs Atwater and her husband and two more children were themselves martyred about August 15.

proved that they had been killed out of hatred of the Christian faith, and not simply because they—or some of them— were foreigners, or for other political reasons. The principal piece of evidence adduced was a proclamation of the governor, Yu Hsien, in which he said : " The European religion is wicked and cruel, it despises the spirit and oppresses peoples.   All [Chinese] Christians who do not sincerely repudiate it will be executed. . . . Christians, hear and tremble !   Give up this perverse religion !   Let all Christians fear and obey : the Boxers will not hurt persons—it is this religion they hate."

And so the beatification of the first group of martyrs in China in 1900 duly took place in the archbasilica of St Peter at Rome, on November 24, 1946.   Among the Franciscan Missionaries of Mary from China who were present were two Chinese nuns who had been witnesses of some of the martyrdoms.   One of them, seventy years of age, had been without the use of her thumbs for forty-six years, for the Boxers had hung her up by them for an hour, and then forced the blood of one of their victims down her throat.   Another nun was the granddaughter of one of the martyrs.

Five years later took place the beatification of ALBERIC CRESCITELLI, an Italian missionary, born near Naples in 1863, who came to China in 1888.   His huge field was along the Han river, where for over ten years he travelled from village to village, preaching and establishing schools.   He eventually reached southern Shansi, after a three-months' journey by boat, on horseback and on foot.   When the Boxer rising happened Father Crescitelli was seized by a howling mob ; for twenty-four hours he was tortured, and finally hacked to death on July 22, 1900.

There were a number of eye-witnesses of the passion of these martyrs whose testimony is extant.   In 1902 there was published in Rome a *Vie de la Mère Marie-Hermine de Jésus et de ses compagnes ;* it is a small-royal 8vo volume of 580 pages, and it narrates the lives of the seven nuns in considerable detail.   An abbreviation of this (146 pages), by M. T. de Blarer, appeared in Paris in 1946.   Both these books contain some particulars of the other Franciscan martyrs.   See also *Les vingt-neuf martyrs de Chine* . . . (1946).   A list of European missionaries killed in China between 1815 and 1923 can be found in *Missions de Scheut* (1924).   For other martyrs in China, see under February 17.

10 : THE SEVEN BROTHERS AND ST FELICITY, MARTYRS
(SECOND CENTURY ?)

THE feast of St Felicity, widow and martyr, is observed on November 23, but it is convenient to speak of her here with those seven commonly referred to as her sons.   According to their legend, Felicity was a noble Christian woman who, after the death of her husband, served God in a state of widowhood and employed herself in prayer and works of charity.   By the example of this lady and her family many idolaters were moved to embrace the faith of Christ.   This angered the pagan priests, who complained to the Emperor Antoninus Pius that the boldness with which Felicity practised the Christian religion drew many from the worship of the immortal gods, who on that account would be angry with the city and state.   The emperor was prevailed upon to send an order to Publius, the prefect of Rome, and he caused the mother and her sons to be apprehended and brought before him.   He took Felicity aside and used the strongest inducements to bring her to sacrifice to the gods, that he might not be obliged to proceed with severity against her and her sons ; but she answered, " Do not think to frighten me by threats, or to win me by fair speeches. The spirit of God within me will not suffer me to be overcome, and will make me victorious over all your assaults." " Unhappy woman ", replied Publius, " if you wish to die, die ; but do not destroy your children."   " My children ", said she, " will live eternally if they are faithful, but must expect eternal death if they sacrifice to idols."

The next day the prefect sent for Felicity and her sons again, and said, " Take pity on your children, Felicity, they are in the bloom of youth."   The mother answered, " Your pity is impiety, and your words cruel."   Then, turning towards her children, she said, " My sons, look up to Heaven, where Jesus Christ with His saints expects you.   Be faithful in His love, and fight courageously for your souls." Publius commanded her to be beaten, saying, " You are insolent to give them such advice in my presence, in contempt of the orders of our prince."   He then called the boys to him one after another, and mixed promises with threats to induce them to worship the gods ; but they all refused and, after being whipped, were remanded to prison.   The prefect laid the whole process before the emperor, who gave an order that they should be sent to different judges and be condemned to different deaths.   Januarius was scourged to death, Felix and Philip were beaten with clubs, Silvanus was thrown headlong into the Tiber, and Alexander, Vitalis and Martial were beheaded ; the same sentence was executed upon the mother last of all.

Of the death of St Felicity, St Augustine says : " Wonderful is the sight set before the eyes of our faith.   We have heard with our ears and seen with our minds a mother choosing for her children to finish their course before herself, contrary to human instincts.   But she did not send away her sons, she sent them on ; she looked on them as beginning life, not as finishing it.   They gave up a life in which they had to die, and began to live the life that is endless.   It was not enough that she had to look on ; we are yet more astonished that she encouraged them.   She was more fruitful in her courage even than in her womb : seeing them contend, she contended, and in the victory of each one she was victorious."   St Gregory the Great delivered a homily on the festival of St Felicity in the church built over her tomb on the Via Salaria.   In it he says that this saint, " having seven children, was as much afraid of leaving them behind her on earth, as other mothers are of surviving theirs.   She was more than a martyr, for seeing her seven children martyred before her eyes, she was in some sort a martyr in each of them.   She was the eighth in the order of time, but was from the first to the last in anguish, beginning her martyrdom in the eldest and finishing it in her own death.   She received a crown not only for herself, but likewise for all her children.   Seeing them in torments she remained constant, feeling their agony by nature as their mother, but rejoicing for them in her heart by hope."   The same father takes notice how weak faith is in us : in her it was victorious over flesh and blood, but in us it is not able to check our passions or wean our hearts from a wicked world.

The force of the eloquence of St Augustine, St Gregory and Alban Butler himself, and of the lessons which they draw from this story, is not weakened by the fact that it cannot be regarded as historical.   It is known that a woman named Felicity suffered martyrdom, she was buried in the cemetery of Maximus on the Salarian Way, and her feast was on November 23, as it still is.   But there is no evidence, apart from the very doubtful *acta*, that the Seven Brothers were her sons, or indeed that they were brothers at all.   From at least the middle of the fourth century, seven martyrs were commemorated on July 10 ; two of them, Felix and Philip, were buried in the cemetery of St Priscilla ; Martial, Vitalis and Alexander in the cemetery " Jordanorum " ; Januarius in that of Praetextatus, where in 1863 de Rossi discovered a frescoed chapel with a *graffito* invoking the saint ; and Silanus (Silvanus) in the catacomb of Maximus. The contiguity of this last tomb to that of St Felicity may have given rise to the whole identification of the seven martyrs as seven brothers and her sons.

The question of St Felicity and her seven sons was very keenly debated at the close of the last century. Though the " acts ", as stated above, are certainly late and of questionable authority, and though there is reason to suspect the influence of the biblical account of the mother of the Machabees, still the early *cultus* is attested by the Philocalian calendar, the epitaph of St Damasus and the *Hieronymianum*. The text of the " acts " is in Ruinart's *Acta sincera*, and has been re-edited in modern times by Doulcet and by Künstle. For the more destructive criticism see J. Führer, *Ein Beitrag zur Lösung der Felicitas-Frage* (1890) with his subsequent brochure in reply to Künstle. On the other side *cf.* Duchesne in the *Bulletin critique*, 1890, p. 425 ; and the very full discussion of the subject by Leclercq in DAC., vol. v, cc. 1259–1298. Fr Delehaye returned to the question in his CMH. (pp. 362–364) and his *Étude sur le légendier romain* (1936), pp. 116–123 ; he concludes that the undoubted seven martyrs of July 10 were arbitrarily made brothers by a hagiographer as a Christian parallel to the seven Machabees (August 1).

SS. RUFINA AND SECUNDA, VIRGINS AND MARTYRS   (A.D. 257 ?)

ACCORDING to their unhistorical " acts ", these were sisters, daughters of Asterius, a man of senatorial rank in Rome. They were engaged to be married, the one to Armentarius, the other to Verinus, who were also Christians. But when the persecution of the Emperor Valerian fell upon the Church, these two men apostatized. The two girls refused to follow their example and fled secretly from Rome. Their flight being soon discovered, they were overtaken not far from the city and haled before the prefect, Junius Donatus. He imprisoned them with the object of making them apostatize, and when he found that they were unmoved either by arguments or threats, he ordered Rufina to be scourged ; whereupon Secunda cried out, " Why do you judge my sister to honour and me to dishonour ? Be pleased to beat us both together, for together we declare that Christ is God." After they both had been tortured in divers ways, they were put to death by beheading. A pagan lady named Plautilla gave their bodies burial at a spot eleven miles from Rome on the Aurelian Way, and herself became a Christian from their example. The place where they lay was at that time called *Silva Nigra*, the Black Forest, but from these martyrs that name was changed to *Silva Candida*, the White Forest. A church was built over their tomb and a town grew up around it, which also was called Silva Candida, or Santa Rufina ; it was made an episcopal see and became appurtenant to the cardinalate in after years. The relics of the martyrs were translated in 1154 to the Lateran basilica, near the baptistery of Constantine. The church dedicated in honour of SS. Rufina and Secunda in the City purports to be built over the site of their dwelling-house. Except their existence, their martyrdom and their early *cultus* nothing is certainly known of these maidens.

The text of the *passio* is printed in the *Acta Sanctorum*, July, vol. iii. See also F. Lanzoni, *Le origini delle diocesi antiche d'Italia* (1923), pp. 320–321, and Delehaye's CMH., p. 364.

ST AMALBURGA, OR AMELBERGA, WIDOW   (c. A.D. 690)

AMALBURGA (Amelia), born in Brabant, was married to Count Witger, by whom she had three holy children, SS. Gudula, Reineldis, and Emebert of Cambrai. When eventually Witger became a Benedictine monk at Lobbes, Amalburga became a nun of the same rule at the convent of Maubeuge, where she was professed by St Aubert, Bishop of Cambrai.   She passed the rest of her life very ascetically, and after her death was buried beside her husband at Lobbes.   There is much confusion between this saint, St Amalburga of Susteren, and the one who follows ; the invocation of Amalburga for the cure of bruises is probably due to the second of these confusions.

No trust can be placed in the life printed in the *Acta Sanctorum*, July, vol. iii, and elsewhere ; but there is no reason to doubt that Amalburga did end her days as a nun at Maubeuge.

ST AMALBURGA, Virgin   (*c*. A.D. 770)

On this day is commemorated another Amalburga, who has been sometimes confused with the above.   She was a native of the Ardenne, and according to a worthless story her charm and beauty attracted the notice of King Pepin, who asked her hand in marriage for his son Charles.   She refused, and was thereupon pursued for a long time with an assiduity and unscrupulousness which did no credit to the medieval hagiographer's idea of either the dignity or the decency of the future Charlemagne.   On one occasion, it is related, he broke her arm while trying to carry her off from a church where she had taken refuge.   St Amalburga was in fact a nun of Munsterbilzen in Belgium, having been clothed while young by St Willibrord.   Her relics were translated to the abbey church of St Peter at Ghent in 1073.

The Latin life, printed in the *Acta Sanctorum*, July, vol. iii, is a pure romance, but there was an earlier outline by Radbod in the tenth century which is of some value.   See the *Analecta Bollandiana*, vol. xxxi (1912), pp. 401–409.   Bächtold-Staubli, *Handwörterbuch des deutschen Aberglaubens*, vol. i, p. 358, discusses the folk-lore elements of the story.

SS. ANTONY and THEODOSIUS PECHERSKY, Abbots of the Caves of Kiev   (A.D. 1073 and 1074)

The period of the evangelization of Russia was one during which Byzantine monasticism was particularly flourishing, when the monastery of Studius at Constantinople and its offshoots were still at the height of their influence (though decay was at hand) and the great foundations on Mount Athos were just beginning. But in Russia the earliest monasteries, foreign foundations made at the instance of the grand-princes and Greek bishops, did not have much significance.   The great monasticism of Russia began only with the foundation of a monastery which at first owed nothing to the great ones of the earth but was established by Russian monks for their own people, that of the Caves of Kiev (Kiev-Pecherskaya Lavra) : " the first *Russian* monastery in point of time, and first also in importance by reason of the amount of spiritual good that it poured into the treasury of Russian religion ", says Mgr Alexander Sipiaguin.   Its founders, " the first great candles lighted in the name of Russia before the universal image of Christ ", were St Antony and St Theodosius Pechersky.

Antony was born in 983 at Lubech, near Chernigov, and early in life made an experiment at living as a solitary after the pattern of the Egyptian anchorites ; but he soon realized that one must be trained for that life as for any other, and he went on pilgrimage to Mount Athos, where he became a hermit attached to the monastery

of Esphigmenou.   After some years there he was unwilling to leave, but his abbot
bade him return to his own land.   " The Lord has strengthened you in the way of
holiness ", he said, " and you must now lead others.   Go back home, with the
blessing of the Holy Mountain on you.   You will be a father of many monks."

Antony did as he was told, but finding insufficient peace and solitude in the
prince-founded monasteries, after the strictness of Athos, he took up his abode in
a cave in a wooded cliff beside the river Dnieper at Kiev.   Here he lived on bread
and vegetables and water, passing his time in contemplation and tilling his little
patch of land.   People came to consult him and ask his blessing, and sometimes
made him gifts, which he straightway passed on to the poor.   Some of these
visitors stayed on with him, the first being the monk Nikon, who was a priest ; and
after a time there were other aspirants, who dug caves for themselves and larger
ones to serve as chapel and dining-room.   Unlike the other abbots of that time,
St Antony accepted anybody who showed the right dispositions, rich or poor, free
men or serfs, with the result that the community outgrew its accommodation.
Prince Syaslav offered to give them the land on the hill above their caves, and here
the monks built of wood a monastery and a church, dedicated in honour of the
Falling-asleep of the All-holy Mother of God.   " Many monasteries ", says the
Chronicle of Nestor, " were built with the wealth of princes and nobles ; this was
the first built with tears and fasting and prayer.   Antony had no gold or silver :
he used these means instead."

St Antony had early given up the direction of the community to one Barlaam
and, disturbed by strife among the nobles of Kiev, he retired after a while to
Chernigov and established another monastery there.   But he eventually came
back to the Pecherskaya Lavra and died in his cave there in 1073 ; he was ninety
years old.

Forty years before there had come to Pechersk a certain Theodosius, and he it
was rather than the severe and solitude-loving Antony who first struck the Russian
imagination and gave an impress to indigenous monasticism.   He was the son of
well-to-do parents, and as a young man had put on serf's clothes and joined the
labourers in his father's fields.   His mother was horrified, and said so.   " My dear
mother, listen to me," he replied to her protests.   " Our Lord Jesus Christ humbled
Himself and underwent degradation, and we have got to follow His example in this
too."   Later, in face of blows and attempts to shut him up, Theodosius apprenticed himself to a baker and learned how to make the bread for the Holy Mysteries,
and then about 1032 he joined the monks at the Caves of Kiev.

St Theodosius soon succeeded Barlaam as abbot, and he was the real organizer
of the monastery, who gave the direction to the first generations of Russian monks.
He completed and enlarged the buildings and put the community under the
discipline and rule given by St Theodore to the " Studion ".   Emphasis was put,
not on personal sanctification solely by means of prayer and mortification, but on
the necessity of the corporal works of mercy and on the need of identifying oneself
with all the suffering children of Christ.   He followed both the liturgical prescriptions and the social activities of the Studites : a hospital for the sick and disabled
and a hostel for travellers were established at the monastery, and every Saturday a
cartload of food was sent to the city jails.   Nor was Theodosius, as were so many
early monks, afraid of contact with the ordinary world of men ; his monks played
a part in the evangelization of Kiev and he took part in the general life of the
country, with the result that his influence was not confined to his community but

was felt all over Varangian Russia : he was able to defend the rights of the poor and oppressed and to protest to his face when Svyatoslav drove his own brother from the throne of Kiev. Moreover, to Theodosius may be traced the beginnings of the institution of *startsy*, " spiritual directors ", so characteristic of Russian religious life ; he encouraged the lay people of Kiev, without distinction of sex or age or rank, to come to him with their problems and difficulties, and we are told of a man and wife, John and Mary, of whom he was particularly fond, " because they loved God and loved one another ".

To an invitation to dine with the usurper Svyatoslav, St Theodosius replied, " I will not go to Jezebel's table and eat food contaminated by blood and murder ". Svyatoslav, he said, had acted against justice and the law, and in a long letter to him compared him to Cain. Svyatoslav considered banishing Theodosius, but decided he did not dare to and instead made a personal appeal to him to withdraw his opposition. The reply of St Theodosius, as one having no worldly authority but bound to uphold the gospel of Christ, was humble and direct : " What can our anger do against your power, my good lord ? Nevertheless it is our duty to admonish, and to declare whatever is good for the saving of souls ; and it is your duty to give heed."

A few short homilies and extracts from the sermons of Theodosius have come down to us, and they are of a piece with the rest that is known about him. He had found the cave monastery of St Antony " narrow and depressing ", and he sought spiritual as well as physical enlargement . " Christ's love is overflowing upon us unworthy ones ", he said, and love must be met with love and it must flow beyond the cloister. " Mindful of the commandment of the good Lord, my unworthy self declares to you that it is good for us to feed the hungry and the tramps with the fruits of our labour. . . . If God's grace does not uphold and nourish us through the poor, what should we do with all our works ? " In his view monks are not a people apart, spiritual and corporal works of charity cannot be separated : and so equally, " If I could I would not let a day pass without throwing myself in tears at your feet and imploring you not to neglect a single hour of prayer ". But certainly one of the most effective and one of the best known of his " exhortations " was a single sentence, a question he asked as he listened to the minstrels in the hall of the ruler of Kiev : " Sir, will it sound the same in the life to come ? " St Theodosius of Pechersk has been seen as a forerunner of St Francis of Assisi, a western saint with a great appeal for Russians ; and the abbot's gentleness, humility and patience were rooted in love of Jesus Christ as the light of a world that is at the same time beautiful and wicked : " What good have we done to Him that He should choose us and rescue us from this transitory life ? Have we not, all of us, erred and become useless for His service ? . . . He sought us out, found us, carried us on his shoulders, and set us at the right hand of the Father. Is He not merciful and the lover of mankind ? It was not we who sought Him, but He us. . . ."

It has been pointed out that whereas St Antony Pechersky followed the Egyptian hermits, unsociable, rather frightening, their life sometimes degenerating into a sort of competition in fantastic penances, St Theodosius Pechersky looked for his pattern rather to the monks of Palestine and such saints as Sabas and Euthymius the Great and his namesake Theodosius the Cenobiarch, who never forgot that physical austerity is only a means towards purity of heart and spirit. Virtue, goodness, and therefore closeness to God, is the aim of religion : " The young ", said Theodosius, " must love their fellows and learn humbly and obediently from their elders ; the old must love and help and teach the young, nor must any man make public his own mortifications." He emphasized, too, the importance of community life and the holding of all things in common, so much so that one of his monks declared that a " Lord, have mercy on us " prayed from the heart collectively by the community is of greater spiritual value than the whole psalter said alone in one's cell ; nevertheless, there must be times of solitude and retirement (as during Lent). Theodosius thus sought to harmonize the contemplative and the active life, just as he sought to harmonize the needs of men as they are (and not as they ought to be) with the call to bring about the kingdom of God on earth. In all these things he was following the Palestinian tradition and the spirit of St Basil, father of Eastern monks.

Even when he had all the responsibility of ruling a large community and caring for the welfare of numerous spiritual children, St Theodosius still did his share of the ordinary daily work, whether in the fields or in the house. In particular he made it his business for two years to look after the needs of an old monk, Isaac, who was so infirm that he could neither sit up nor turn in his bed nor do anything for himself: Abbot Theodosius fed him, washed him, changed his clothes, did the least honourable offices for him—and then went out to sit at table with the grand-prince in the city. It is not surprising to read that his community was like one family, " where the young respected the old and the old were considerate to the young ", where when one was at fault three or four were always at hand to share his penance.

St Theodosius celebrated the Easter of 1074 with his brethren as usual, and a week later he was dead. At his own wish he was buried in one of the caves that formed the original monastery, but in 1091 his body was translated to the principal church and in 1108 he was canonized by the bishops of the Kiev province—the second Russian canonization and the first of the *prepodobny*, " very-like ones ", that is, Christlike monks. His feast is kept by the Catholic Ukrainians and Russians on May 3, and that of St Antony on July 10. The names of both these saints occur in the preparation of the eucharistic liturgy according to Slavonic usage.

Some bibliographical notes for the Kievan saints are given on September 25, under St Sergius. There are notices of St Antony and many of his disciples in the Kiev *paterik*, but for St Theodosius there still exists a detailed *vita :* it is translated in G. P. Fedotov's *Treasury of Russian Spirituality* (1950). The Monastery of the Caves was devastated by the Tartars in 1240, in 1299, and again in 1316, and each time it recovered to take its place at the head of Russian monasteries and as one of the chief places of pilgrimage in the country. But never again did it touch the level of Christian life that it attained under the guidance of St Theodosius : it became too wealthy in this world's goods. Until the eighteenth century the monks of the Caves wore a habit resembling that of the Benedictines and had many other special customs, some developed under Western influence. Their great printing-press, established in 1651, and the hospice for pilgrims founded by St Theodosius (which in the nineteenth century could accommodate 20,000 people) remained until our own day. Somewhere about its nine-hundredth birthday revolutionary fury brought the monastery to an end ; but in 1945 permission was given to the authorities of the Russian Orthodox Church to restore it, the buildings having been destroyed during the second world-war.

BB. EMMANUEL RUIZ, FRANCIS MASABKI AND THEIR COMPANIONS, THE MARTYRS OF DAMASCUS   (A.D. 1860)

AFTER the Crimean War the Congress of Paris required of Turkey certain reforms within the Ottoman empire, particularly with regard to the treatment of Christian minorities, and in 1856 the sultan signed a decree whereby all subjects of the empire, without distinction of race or religion, were put on a level in the matter of taxation and public offices. This was an outrage to Mohammedan sentiment : for twelve hundred years the Christian communities had been *rayahs*, " herds ", people of the " lesser breeds without the law ", and now the *khalifa* required them to be treated as equal with the children of the Prophet ; resentment smouldered and was aggravated, it is said, by news of the Indian Mutiny. The native Moslems of Syria, notably the Druses, a sect of the Lebanon, were covertly encouraged by the Turks, especially by Khursud Pasha, governor of Bairut, and in 1860 the fire flared up at Bait Mari ; the occasion was a quarrel between a Druse and a young Christian, one of the large Catholic body of Maronites which was to suffer more than any other in what followed. A massacre began. The Druses were armed and prepared, but Christians allowed themselves to be disarmed by the Turkish authorities on the plea of restoring order. From May 30 to June 26 every Maronite village of the main and southern Lebanon was pillaged and burned, and six thousand Christians were murdered, mutilated, or outraged ; at Zahleh five Jesuits were strangled and at Dair al-Kamar the abbot of the Maronite monastery was flayed alive and his twenty monks pole-axed. Khursud Pasha marched into the district with six hundred soldiers, fired a single gun, and then left his troops to join in the massacre. On July 9 it broke out in Damascus. The governor, Ahmed Pasha, did nothing, but was shamed by the noble Algerian emir Abd-al-Kadar, the champion of Islam, who now in open defiance of his co-religionists gave shelter in his palace to fifteen hundred Christians, including a number of Europeans. In three days thousands died from violence and terror, adult males alone numbering three thousand. Of all these victims, eleven, eight Friars Minor and three Maronite laymen, were shown by the circumstances of their death, the testimony of approved miracles having been dispensed with, to be specially worthy to be raised to the altars of the Church, and they were accordingly beatified in 1926. When the mob invaded the quarter of the city in which the Franciscan friary was situated, the father guardian gathered into it all the school-children and a number of other Christians ; he encouraged them to fortitude, and they said the litany of the saints before the Blessed Sacrament exposed ; then they all received absolution and communion. The monastery was a stout building, well protected by heavy doors, and it is probable that the inmates would have been safe but for the treachery of a man, one who had received kindnesses from the friars, who directed the mob to a forgotten back entrance.

The guardian, BD EMMANUEL RUIZ, was a Spaniard born of humble parents in the province of Santander in 1804. When the mob broke into the house on the night of July 9, 1860, he ran to the church and consumed the Blessed Sacrament, then knelt at the altar and awaited his end. He was seized, amid shouts of " Affirm ! Affirm ! " *viz.* that there is no god but God, and Mohammed is the prophet of God. " I am a Christian and I will die a Christian ! " he replied, and laid his head on the altar, where it was split open with axes.

All the other friars were also Spaniards, except BD ENGELBERT KOLLAND, who was an Austrian. After four years in the diocesan seminary he had had to leave because of his restlessness and excessive liveliness ; he had then pulled himself together, been accepted by the Friars Minor, and spent the years of his ministry in the Custody. On this night he took refuge on the roof of the house, where somebody wrapped a woman's large veil over his habit ; but his sandals gave him away, he was dragged down to the courtyard, refused to apostatize, and was slain. BD CARMEL VOLTA was half-killed by a blow on the head ; he lay for an hour, when two Mohammedans, friends of his, found him and offered the shelter of their house, provided he became a renegade.   He refused, and they killed him.   BD NICANOR ASCANIO had arrived in Syria only in the previous year, and, but for the orders of Father Emmanuel on account of the dangers of the road, would have been in Jerusalem at the time of the massacre.   BD PETER SOLER started life in a factory at Cuevas, where he was a missionary among his fellows.   Two young boys who heard him in broken Arabic refusing to give up his faith and saw him murdered in consequence, in after years gave evidence in the process of beatification.   BD NICHOLAS ALBERCA, who was only thirty years old, was found in a corridor of the burning monastery and was shot.   The other two Franciscan martyrs were lay-brothers.   BD FRANCIS PINAZO had been a shepherd, but, when disappointed in his projected marriage, became a lay-brother in the third order regular at Cuelva ; thence he was admitted to the first order.   BD JOHN JAMES FERNANDEZ received the habit at Hebron, and lived in Spain until he was sent to the East in 1857.   On the night of the massacre they hid on the upper floor of the belfry of the church. Here they were found and both were thrown out of the window to the ground. Brother Francis was killed at once, but Brother John lingered in agony all night, till early in the morning a Turkish soldier found him and despatched him with his sword.

Most of the lay-people in the house escaped or were spared, but three Maronite laymen were slain and were beatified with the friars.   These were three brothers, BB. FRANCIS, ABDUL-MUTI and RAPHAEL MASABKI.   The eldest, Francis, was about seventy years old, head of his family and a wealthy and influential man. Muti, a widower, having retired from commerce, lived with his elder brother and helped the Franciscans by teaching school.   Raphael, the youngest, was unmarried and from being the assistant of Francis in his business, had become a sort of unofficial sub-sacristan at the friary.   The circumstances of the beatification of these three are remarkable, because the process was complete in less than six months.   The cause of the Franciscans was introduced in 1885, but the names of the Masabkis were not added to it until the spring of 1926, at the suggestion of Mgr Giannini, delegate apostolic in Syria.   Happily a complete *dossier* of their case had been kept by the Maronite bishop of Damascus, and it was enabled to be completed at the same time as that of the friars on October 10, 1926.

Fuller details are supplied in H. Lammens, *La Syrie* (1921), vol. ii, pp. 180ff.; P. Paoli, *Il beato Emmanuele Ruiz . . .* (1926) ; P. Seeböck, *P. Engelbert Kolland* (1904) ; and C. Salotti, *L'eroismo di tre martiri maroniti* (1926).   A general account of the outbreak may be found in the *Annals of the Propagation of the Faith* for 1860, pp. 308-326.

11 : ST PIUS I, POPE AND MARTYR   (A.D. 155 ?)

THIS Pius succeeded St Hyginus in the see of Peter, and the *Liber Pontificalis* states that he was the son of one Rufinus and a native of Aquileia ; some authorities add further that he was a brother of that Hermas who wrote the famous work called *The Shepherd* : if the account of himself given by the author of this book be not a pious fiction, and if his relationship to the pope be true, then St Pius will have been likewise born a slave.   During his pontificate the Roman church was troubled by the allied heresies of the Valentinians and Marcionites ; Pius accordingly had energetically to oppose these heresies, and in these controversies the true faith had a great champion in the Jewish convert St Justin Martyr, who was in Rome at that time.   St Pius ordained twelve bishops and eighteen priests and is said to have turned the Baths of Novatus into a place for worship.   That he is venerated liturgically as a martyr seems to be due to Cardinal Baronius : there is no early reference to his martyrdom.

Nearly all that is known concerning St Pius will be found in the text and notes of Mgr Duchesne's edition of the *Liber Pontificalis*, vol. i, pp. 132 *seq.*, and in his *Histoire ancienne de l'Eglise*, vol. i, pp. 236 *seq.*   For the historical situation *cf.* G. Bardy, " L'Eglise romaine sous le pontificat de S. Anicet " in *Recherches de science religieuse*, vol. xvii (1927), pp. 481–511.

ST DROSTAN, ABBOT OF DEER   (*c.* A.D. 610)

ALL that is known of this saint is found in the old Aberdeen Breviary and in the " Book of Deer ", and there are discrepancies between the two sources.   He was of blood royal in Ireland, of the family of Cosgrach, and followed the religious life under St Columba.   When a foundation was made at Deer in Aberdeenshire, Drostan was the first abbot.   It is also said that he went to Glenesk in Angus and lived there as a hermit ; his holiness and kindness to the needy were noised about the countryside and miracles were attributed to him.   After his death his body was transferred to a shrine at Aberdour, and his feast is still kept in the dioceses of Aberdeen and Argyll on this day.

See the *Acta Sanctorum*, July, vol. iii ; Forbes, KSS., pp. 326–327 ; DCB., vol. i, p. 907. The " Book of Deer ", believed to date from the close of the ninth century, was printed by the Spalding Club in 1869.

ST JOHN, BISHOP OF BERGAMO   (*c.* A.D. 690)

THIS John, having been elected to the see of Bergamo because of his holiness and learning, set himself to get rid of the heresies, particularly the remnants of Arianism, which were polluting the faith of his diocese.   He was present at the synod held by Pope St Agatho in 679 at Rome at which St Wilfrid of York appealed against the division of his diocese.   It has been alleged, though erroneously, that St John met his death through the malice of heretics, and he was venerated as a martyr, *e.g.* in the Roman Martyrology, which refers to him as " slain by the Arians for defending the Catholic faith ".   He died peacefully *c.* 690.   It is related that·on one occasion St John of Bergamo was at Pavia, dining with the duke of Benevento, when he openly rebuked the duke's son for an act of injustice of which he was guilty.   The young man, Cunibert by name, took the reproof badly and concocted a scheme to revenge himself.   Professing much friendliness for the bishop, he sent him a present of a saddle-horse, but in fact one so vicious that no one dare get on its back.   When St John set out from Pavia he decided to ride the new horse, and when he was in the saddle the servants of Cunibert standing round expected every minute to see him thrown off and savaged on the flagstones of the courtyard ; but nothing of the sort occurred, the beast was quite quiet and obeyed every touch of the bridle.

See the *Acta Sanctorum*, July, vol. iii ; and Ughelli, *Italia Sacra*, vol. iv, p. 590.   Ughelli describes him as the thirteenth bishop of Bergamo.   His historical existence is made certain by à reference to him in Paulus Diaconus, *Historia Langobardorum*, bk vi, ch. 3.

ST HIDULF, Bishop   (*c.* A.D. 707)

St Hidulf was born at Regensburg in Bavaria and was consecrated bishop at Trier, probably as a *chorepiscopus* or auxiliary in that diocese.   In the midst of his duties he was strongly drawn to monastic retirement, being affected by the example and conversation of many men who then adorned the Church and maintained in it the true spirit of Christ by the sanctity which their minds and example spread, and who were raised to this virtue by a monastic life.   He was, in fact, himself called to the religious life, and he retired to the Vosges mountains and settled in a hermitage, where he soon after, about the year 676, built the monastery of Moyenmoutier. This name was given it from its situation between the abbeys of Senones, Etival, Bonmoutier and Saint-Dié : these formed a cross and Moyenmoutier was established at the intersection.   The subjects of these monasteries were very numerous and many had a reputation for great sanctity.   Several of these monks lived in solitude, and manual work was held in honour, St Hidulf himself spending time at it daily, old and otherwise busy though he was.   He died about 707, and nine hundred years later his monastery at Moyenmoutier became the second house of the Benedictine reform of Saint-Vanne at Verdun, the congregation receiving the name of SS. Vanne and Hidulf.

The principal sources for the life of St Hidulf will be found in the *Acta Sanctorum*, July, vol. iii, but these legendary materials should be studied in the light of the comments of C. Pfister, *Annales de l'Est*, vol. iii (1889), and of L. Jérôme in his *L'abbaye de Moyenmoutier* (1902).

ST OLGA, Widow   (A.D. 969)

St Olga is venerated with her grandson St Vladimir as the first-born of the new Christian people of Russia : the monk Jacob in the eleventh century grandiloquently refers to them as " the new Helen and the new Constantine, equals of the Apostles ".   Olga was before her conversion no less cruel and barbarous than Vladimir ; her husband, Prince Igor of Kiev, was assassinated, and she punished his murderers by scalding them to death with hot steam and treacherously slew hundreds of their followers.

Olga is popularly regarded as the first in Russia ever to be baptized.   This is now seen to be far from the truth ; but it is still generally held that her baptism took place at Constantinople, about 957.   Nevertheless she does in some measure represent the Germanic element in Russia's evangelization, for she about 959 sent a request for missionaries for " the land of Kiev'" to the emperor Otto I, which resulted in the abortive mission of St Adalbert of Magdeburg.   Her efforts for the conversion of her own son, Svyatoslav, came to nothing : " My men would laugh at me if I took up with a strange religion ", he declared feelingly.

St Olga died at an advanced age in 969.   Her feast is observed by the Russians, Ukrainians and others.

Among the scattered sources are Constantine Porphyrogenitus, *De cerimoniis aulae byzantinae*, ii, 15, in PG., vol. cxii, and the chronicle of Cedrenus, p. 329 of vol. ii in the Bonn edition.   See the bibliography of St Vladimir, July 15.

BD ADRIAN FORTESCUE, Martyr   (A.D. 1539)

Sir Adrian Fortescue was born in 1476, of an old Devonshire family, and was a cousin, on his mother's side, of Anne Boleyn ; he himself married, first, Anne

Stonor of Stonor, by whom he had two daughters, and twelve years after her death, Anne Rede of Boarstall, who bore him three sons.

His early and middle life was that of a gentleman of his time. He was a justice of the peace for the county of Oxford and a knight of the Bath, he attended at the royal court, fought in France in 1513 and again in 1523 ; was in Queen Catherine's train when she went to Calais during the " Field of the Cloth of Gold ", and attended upon Anne Boleyn at her coronation. He was always a religious man and, subsequent to becoming a knight of devotion of the Sovereign and Sacred Order of St John of Jerusalem (the " Knights of Malta "), he was enrolled as a tertiary of the Dominicans at Oxford.

With respect to the king's religious proceedings Sir Adrian seems to have behaved with circumspection and prudence, but on August 29, 1534, he was, for a reason that does not appear, arrested and confined in the Marshalsea prison ; but he was released sometime probably in the spring of 1535, the year that saw the martyrdom of More and Fisher and the Carthusians. What these foreboded Sir Adrian must perfectly well have understood, but he was not again arrested till February 1539, when he was sent to the Tower.

Parliament met in April, and Fortescue, without trial, was attainted for that he " not only most traitorously refused his duty of allegiance, which he ought to bear to your Highness, but also hath committed divers and sundry detestable and abominable treasons, and put sedition in your realm ". The nature of these treasons is not stated, but that they had reference to his religious duty to the Holy See is sufficiently indicated by the names of those attainted with him : Cardinal Pole, Thomas Goldwell and Friar William Peto, among others.

Bd Adrian was beheaded with the Ven. Thomas Dingley at Tower Hill on July 8 or 9 following. Ever since his death there was a *cultus* of him among the Knights of Malta, and this was the basis of his beatification in 1895. His feast is kept in the archdiocese of Birmingham.

On the morrow is observed the anniversary of another martyred knight of St John, BD DAVID GONSON. He was condemned by attainder for denying the royal supremacy over the Church, and was executed at Southwark in 1541.

Fr John Morris in *The Month*, June and July 1887 (and in a separate reprint) collected most of the information available. See also Camm, LEM., vol. i, pp. 413–461. Bodley's Library at Oxford possesses a manuscript of *Piers Plowman* transcribed by Bd Adrian's hand.

BD OLIVER PLUNKET, ARCHBISHOP OF ARMAGH, MARTYR   (A.D. 1681)

THE last Catholic to die for his faith at Tyburn and the first of the Irish martyrs to be beatified was born in 1629 at Loughcrew, in county Meath ; through his father he was connected with the earl of Fingall and the barons of Dunsany and Locriff, and his mother was a Dillon and near kin to the earl of Roscommon. He was given his name after that young Oliver Plunket who had been done to death when the Spanish prisoners were massacred at Smerwick in Kerry in 1580. His youth was spent in the turmoil and confusion of parties consequent on the rebellion against King Charles I in England, the Plunkets naturally being among those Catholic nobles and gentry who were for the king's prerogative and freedom for the Irish ; but Oliver himself was already destined for the priesthood and studied under his kinsman Patrick Plunket, Benedictine abbot of St Mary's, in Dublin.

In 1645, when he was sixteen, he went to Rome with four other young men who had been chosen to be educated at his own expense for the priesthood by Father Pierfrancesco Scarampi, the Oratorian who had been sent in 1643 by Pope Urban VIII to assist at the supreme council of the Irish Confederate party. He did brilliantly under the Jesuits at the then lately established Irish College, followed the course of civil and canon law at the *Sapienza,* and was ordained in 1654. The state of affairs in Ireland made it impossible for him at once to go on the mission there, so by the good offices of Father Scarampi he was appointed to the chair of theology in the College *de Propaganda Fide.* At first he lodged with the Oratorians, and Father Marangoni said of him that he was " among the most illustrious persons whose virtues have adorned this house " ; he was appointed a consultor of the Sacred Congregation of the Index and procurator for the Irish bishops to the Holy See. He thus lived a busy and devoted life in Rome for twelve years.

In March 1669 died in exile in France Edmund O'Reilly, Archbishop of Armagh and Primate of All Ireland. Pope Clement IX chose to succeed him Dr Oliver Plunket, " a man of tried virtue, long experience, and ripe learning ", and in November of that year he was consecrated at Ghent. He then went on to London, where he was weather-bound and was secretly lodged in his own apartments by Father Philip Howard, o.p. (afterwards cardinal), almoner of Charles II's queen, Catherine of Braganza. She was very amiable to the new archbishop and he did what he could to obtain some amelioration of the rigour, not to say vindictiveness, with which the penal laws were applied in Ireland. He reached Dublin in March 1670, where he was received by his noble relatives, including his former tutor, Dom Patrick Plunket, now bishop of Meath. He was one of the two bishops in Ireland, the aged and worn-out bishop of Kilmore being the other ; there were only three others, and they were in exile : Bd Oliver's predecessor, O'Reilly, had been able to pass only two of his twelve years of episcopate in the country. The disorder, enforced neglect, and clerical timidity that the papal nuncio Rinuccini had reported twenty years before was now twenty years worse. The new archbishop within three months held a provincial synod of his clergy and two ordinations, and confirmed ten thousand persons of all ages—and still there were fifty thousand unconfirmed in his province. The first two years of his rule were peaceful, owing to the fairness and moderation of the viceroy, Lord Berkeley of Stratton ; he was tolerant to Catholics and personally friendly towards Bd Oliver. Unhappily this peace was marred, as in similar circumstances it has been in other times and places, by a domestic dispute among Catholics, in this case between the Archbishop of Armagh and his cousin the Archbishop of Dublin, Peter Talbot, as to the extent and implications of Armagh's primacy. It was no mere vulgar squabble about personal precedence, but a matter of considerable canonical importance to the Church in Ireland. Bd Oliver interpreted his primacy as being not merely titular but carrying with it primatial jurisdiction over the other metropolitans ; Dr Talbot saw in it only a precedence of rank. " They are both one and the other touchy and of a hot disposition ", wrote Dr John Brennan, later archbishop of Cashel, at the time, so it is the more to the credit of both parties that their differences were so much controlled by charity and humility. Bd Oliver, indeed, interfered in 1671 to prevent the viceroy, who for his own reasons wanted to banish Dr Talbot.

These two years were not otherwise uneventful, but a period of tremendously hard and difficult work, of clearing the ground for an improvement of the spiritual state of the people which the new primate was not to see. The Synod of Clones legislated rigorously against abuses among both clergy and laity ; Plunket himself went out into the wilds of Ulster to reason with the *tories*, men who had taken to brigandage as a desperate last resort for making a living, but were reinforced by bad characters of all sorts : many of these he reformed and others he enabled to go abroad ; he established the Jesuits in Drogheda, where they ran a school for boys and a college for ecclesiastical students ; he even aspired to extend his ministry to the Gaelic-speaking Catholics of the highlands and isles of Scotland, but the difficulties were too great ; he laboured to maintain discipline among his clergy, to put into force the decrees of the Council of Trent, and to forestall Jansenist infiltration through those who had been trained in France and Flanders, to enforce better observance among the friars, and to adjust the strained relationships both between seculars and regulars and between the orders themselves, whose differences were deliberately aggravated by the civil authorities for political ends. All this, the day-to-day care of his flock, and much more, had to be done with one eye all the time on the likelihood of incurring the penalties of *praemunire* for acknow-ledging the Pope's jurisdiction and resorting to the Holy See ; moreover, it had to be done under conditions of " astounding poverty ", which Bd Oliver shared with all his brother bishops and clergy. In this connection one of his complaints is particularly significant for all who live in non-Catholic countries : " The poverty of the bishops prevents their associating with the Protestants from which great good might be derived." He himself was on friendly terms with the Protestant bishops and gentry of Ulster, who had great regard for him and for his sake were disposed not to oppress Catholics ; the Synod of Clones expressed its gratitude to the Holy See for sending them " a pastor so assiduous in good works, so exemplary in life and conduct, that he has won for himself and his clergy the love and reverence even of the enemies of our faith ".

In 1673 the well-meant but tortuous politics of King Charles II provoked a fresh outbreak of persecution. Archbishop Talbot was banished and the Arch-bishop of Tuam fled to Spain ; at first Bd Oliver was not interfered with, but he went into hiding with Dr Brennan, Bishop of Waterford, who was in 1676 advanced to the see of Cashel. These two were in continual danger of arrest and lived under circumstances of grinding physical hardship and penury, carrying on their pastoral work to the best of their ability. It was made even more difficult for Bd Oliver by the enmity of a section of schismatic or quasi-schismatic Catholics who, beginning with Friar Peter Walsh, o.s.f., of " Remonstrance " notoriety, had been a grave trouble to the archbishop, and had support from some of the abettors of the *tories*. A number of serious charges were framed by Friar Fitzsymons and other malcontents against the primate, and these Dr Brennan was deputed by the Holy See to examine ; his report entirely exonerated Bd Oliver.

In 1678 the miserable conspiracy called after its promoter Oates's Plot matured, and in August was launched. The panic which it caused in England had its repercussions in Ireland, where an order of expulsion was made against all Catholic bishops and regular priests, and people were officially encouraged by proclamation to " make any further discovery of the horrid popish plot ". Lord Shaftesbury's agent, Hetherington, MacMoyer, an expelled Franciscan, and Murphy, an excom-municated secular priest, all jail-birds, put their heads together, " informed " against Bd Oliver in London, and the lord lieutenant was ordered to arrest him. On December 6, 1679, he was shut up in Dublin Castle : here he was able to help his old opponent, Dr Talbot, on his death-bed, for the archbishop of Dublin had been allowed to return to Ireland, but was arrested for complicity in the " popish plot ", although he was actually a dying man.   Oliver Plunket was put on trial at Dundalk for conspiring against the state by plotting to bring 20,000 French soldiers into the country and levying a tax on his clergy to support 70,000 armed men for rebellion.   For two days no witnesses turned up for the prosecution, and on the third day only MacMoyer, who was drunk, and asked for a remand until the other witnesses could be procured.   It was obvious to Shaftesbury that the archbishop would never be convicted on so absurd an indictment in Ireland ; he was therefore removed to Newgate prison in London.   He was allowed no inter- course with any but his warders, from whom a fellow-prisoner, Dom Maurus Corker, o.s.b., learned that during his nine months' imprisonment Bd Oliver spent his time in almost continual prayer, fasted several days a week, and was always quietly cheerful and courteous.

The first time his trial came on the grand jury found no true bill ; he was not released, but it was adjourned till June 1681 to enable the accused's witnesses to arrive in London, but even then they could not come in time ; from the rapscallion Irish in London who were prepared to swear away their primate's life, the prose- cution selected nine, of whom the chief were MacMoyer and his confederate Duffy, of whom Bd Oliver said that they were " two friars, whom I have endeavoured to correct for seven years, renegades from our religion, and dastard apostates ". There is a doubt if the court had jurisdiction over the Irishman, and the trial was conducted with only a semblance of justice, so that Lord Campbell, writing of the judge, Sir Francis Pemberton, calls it " a disgrace to himself and country " : the jury found the accused guilty of high treason ; and judgement was reserved.   It was pronounced a week later, and the Primate of All Ireland was condemned to be hanged, disembowelled and quartered ; in delivering sentence Pemberton gave expression to the hatred of that faith for which the martyr died : " . . . the bottom of your treason was your setting up of your false religion . . . the most dishonour- able and derogatory to God and His glory of all religions or pretended religions whatsoever . . . a greater crime cannot be committed against God than for a man to endeavour the propagation of that religion. . . ."

During his last two weeks of life the archbishop was allowed the ministrations of Dom Maurus Corker, and both he and Oliver's own letters to his friends and ecclesiastical superiors testify to the glorious frame of mind in which he was ; one letter contains a very gratifying tribute to the generosity and constancy of the English Catholics.   The execution took place on Friday, July 1 (o.s.), 1681 ; there was a huge crowd at Tyburn to whom the martyr protested his innocence of treason and his loyalty to the king, praying for him and for his own enemies.   He was dead before he was cut down from the scaffold.   The mutilated body was buried in the churchyard of St Giles-in-the-Fields, whence it was taken to the English Bene- dictine abbey of Lamspring in Westphalia in 1684 ; two hundred years later the relics were translated to Downside Abbey, where they are now enshrined ; the martyr's head is preserved in St Peter's church at Drogheda.   Bd Oliver Plunket was beatified in 1920 ; his feast is observed throughout Ireland, Australia and New Zealand, and in the English diocese of Clifton wherein his shrine is situated.

The life history and martyrdom of Bd Oliver Plunket were for the first time adequately recounted from the available sources by Dr Patrick Moran, afterwards cardinal. His book, entitled *Memoirs of the Most Rev. Oliver Plunket*, was printed in 1861, and a second revised edition appeared in 1895. There had, however, already been an Italian life written by Marangoni (1712), as well as long notices by Dodd and Bishop Challoner. Of the more important documents many are printed in Cardinal Moran's *Spicilegium Ossoriense*. See Mrs H. Concannon's biography (1935) and an important volume of historical studies under his name (1937). There are short popular lives by a sister of Notre Dame (1920) and by Fr H. Gaffney (*Oliver*, 1946). The *Downside Review* for January 1921 gives an account of the martyr's relics and their translation, with a more complete text of some of his letters. See also Alice Curtayne, *The Trial of Oliver Plunkett* (1953); and an important article by Fr John Brady in the *Irish Ecclesiastical Record* for 1954.

THE MARTYRS OF INDO-CHINA, I   (A.D. 1745-1840)

AMONG the martyrs of Indo-China beatified in 1906 were four, all Dominicans, who suffered before the nineteenth century. BD FRANCIS GIL and BD MATTHEW LEZINIANA were beheaded in 1745, on January 22. During his eight years of captivity Father Francis conducted an apostolate from his prison that resulted in numerous conversions; Father Matthew, on the other hand, had been a fugitive for thirteen years, during which he never ceased to minister in secret to the native Christians. BD HYACINTH CASTENEDA and BD VINCENT LIEM suffered twenty-eight years later, on November 7, 1773. Hyacinth had been sent from Spain to the Philippines (the voyage took him two years), and gone thence to China. Here he was arrested and taken from prison to prison, being dragged before the judges and ordered to apostatize fourteen times before he was finally deported from the country. Then he was sent to Tongking (Viet-Nam). After three years he was arrested when he went aboard a ship on the river at Ke-Uang to administer the sacraments. He was joined in his prison (his cell was too small to stand up in) by Vincent Liem, a priest and the first Indo-Chinese Dominican to suffer martyrdom. His parents were Christians of good position, and he was a missionary among his fellow-countrymen for fourteen years before he was taken, cruelly ill-treated, and put to death. BB. Francis, Matthew and Hyacinth were Spaniards.

Thus fertilized with the blood of martyrs, Christianity during the first two decades of the nineteenth century made great progress in Indo-China, but this was at once followed from 1820 to 1841, by a period of violent persecution by which the Annamite sovereign, Minh-Mang, tried to stamp out the faith. He was at first held in check by the governor of Cochin-China, who was well disposed towards the Christians, but after his death in 1832 Minh-Mang gave full rein to his violence. All new missionaries had long been excluded; Christians were now ordered publicly to renounce their religion by trampling upon the crucifix, churches were to be destroyed, and teachers suppressed. In 1836 all ports except one were closed to Europeans, death was decreed for all priests, and a systematic hunting-out of missionaries began; lay people as well gave their lives in large numbers. In 1900 Pope Leo XIII beatified seventy-seven of these martyrs, among the principal of whom were BB. IGNATIUS DELGADO Y CEBRIAN, vicar apostolic of Eastern Tongking, and DOMINIC HENAREZ, his coadjutor, both Dominicans of Spanish nationality who had worked in that mission for nearly fifty years. The persecution having broken out anew in 1838 the two bishops went into hiding, but Bd Ignatius was at once caught and carried in a small cage to Nam-Dinh; a crucifix had been thrown on to the road outside the city for the bearers to carry him over, but at his earnest entreaty it was removed; however, it was put back immediately he had passed and none of his devoted followers were allowed to go in after him except they trod upon it as they passed. Bd Ignatius was sentenced to be beheaded, but he was seventy-six years old and infirm, and he died on July 12 before the sentence was carried out, from hunger and thirst and exposure to the sun and dust in a cage too small for him to stand up in. His titular episcopal see was Melipotamus, and he was succeeded in it two years later by Nicholas Wiseman, afterwards cardinal and first archbishop of Westminster, who on being given a choice of titular sees chose this out of the regard and honour he had for the martyr.

Bd Dominic and his Annamite Catechist, BD FRANCIS CHIEN, were also confined in a cage, and beheaded on June 25. Another catechist, BD THOMAS TOAN, twice gave way under torture, but each time repented and earned his crown by dying in prison of lack of food, June 27, 1840. Among the other Indo-Chinese beatified were three secular priests, BB. PETER TUAN, BERNARD DUE and JOSEPH NIEN; a physician, BD JOSEPH CANH; a tailor, BD THOMAS DE; and two peasants, BB. AUGUSTINE MOI and STEPHEN VINH; these while in prison converted and baptized a number of their fellow countrymen. Many of these martyrs were subjected to most ingenious and horrible tortures, and under this pressure three of them, who were all soldiers by trade, and had been suffering for over a year, gave in and trampled on the crucifix. It is alleged that they did this under the influence of a drug, administered with the idea of making an impression on the people, who had been greatly moved by the constancy of the martyrs, by a public apostasy of this sort—how history sometimes seems to repeat itself! Afterwards, anyway, all three disavowed their action and were put to death, two being sawn in twain and the third strangled; they are venerated as BB. AUGUSTINE HUY, NICHOLAS THE and DOMINIC DAT. All the above and twelve others were Dominican friars or tertiaries or otherwise closely associated with the Order of Preachers.

One of the best known of the martyrs of Annam was BD JOSEPH MARCHAND, a priest of the Paris Society of Foreign Missions. Because he was captured at Saigon when the town was in the hands of some rebels (who had in vain tried to get his countenance and support), he was treated with extra and unbelievable barbarity, and died while his flesh was being torn off his body with red-hot tongs. A representative martyr of these seventy-seven, a member of the same society, was BD PETER DUMOULIN-BORIE. To carry on under the stress of persecution it was necessary often and secretly to change his residence, and he wrote at the time : " I travel by night by bridle-ways and indirect foot-paths, rain and wind notwithstanding, often thick with mud or up to my middle in water. Where are you going like that ? you ask. To find the lost sheep and rescue them from the maw of that wolf, the Devil. . . . But my height makes me easily recognizable ; I am too long and they will shorten me." At last he went into hiding but was betrayed, and in July 1838 thrown into prison with two Annamite priests, BB. PETER KOA and VINCENT DIEM. In addition to cross-questioning them about their religion their captors blasphemed and talked obscenely in their presence. " You can rip up my body if you want to ", said Bd Peter, " but at least stop talking like that." While in prison he learned of his nomination to the titular see of Acanthus as vicar apostolic. People were freely allowed to come and see him, and Christian and

heathen alike were struck by his gaiety and patience. When he refused to disclose
to a mandarin the names of those who had sheltered him, an officer remarked, "You
hold your tongue now, but what about when you are flogged ? " " I shall see
what I will do then. I won't flatter myself in advance ", replied the bishop elect.
A few days after he was again examined, and in reply to their questions said, " I am
thirty and a half years old. I came to Tongking in a ship belonging to a well-
known mandarin. I have lived in the province of Quang-Binh five or six years
and visited nearly every place in it. The names of the places don't matter."
Thereupon he was beaten with bamboos so savagely that his flesh was laid open
in strips. The mandarin asked if he felt the pain, and was told, " I am made of
skin and bone like any other man, so why shouldn't I feel the pain ? " He wrote
from prison to one of his fellow-missionaries : " As to a hope of seeing one another
again in this world, we must not think of it. The tiger eats his victim, he doesn't
let him go ; and I tell you frankly I should be sorry to miss so good an opportunity. . . . I ask you to say the usual three Masses for me. . . . As I am so soon
to appear before God's judgement-seat the merits of our divine Saviour reassure
me and the prayers of the good associates of the Propagation of the Faith give me
confidence. . . . I have no books with me and not even a rosary, only a piece of
string in which I have tied knots." During four months he was often flogged and
tortured for refusing to name his *confrères* or to trample on the crucifix, and the
other two priests shared his constancy and his sufferings. On November 24, 1838,
they were led out to die. On the way a mandarin asked if they were not afraid.
" Why should we be ? We're neither rebels nor brigands, so we need fear
only God." Fathers Koa and Diem were strangled. Peter Dumoulin-Borie
was to be decapitated, but the headsman was half-drunk and butchered him with
seven blows.

Another young member of the Paris Society of Foreign Missions had given
his life in the previous year. He had been ordained at Macao at the age of twenty-
five in 1834. This was BD JOHN CHARLES CORNAY. The principal scene of his
labours was Ban-no in Annam, where unfortunately a brigand chief sought to take
refuge, but was imprisoned and expelled by the inhabitants, largely composed of
Christians. Out of revenge this man denounced the commune to the mandarins,
stating that in defiance of the laws they were keeping a Catholic priest in hiding
amongst them. The mandarins were not fanatical and took no action. Then
the man's wife made a pretence that she wanted to become a Christian, and by
that means obtained evidence of the Abbé Cornay's presence in the village and
information as to his manner of living. During the night she buried a number of
weapons in the plot of ground he cultivated, and then laid an information that an
armed insurrection was being plotted by the priest. The story was believed,
soldiers were sent, the arms were found, the missionary arrested, and put in a *cang*.
He seems to have been treated with a curious mixture of severity and kindness.
He was at first left without food and exposed to the terrible rays of the sun ; it was
June, and Annam is well within the tropics. On the other hand, as time went on,
some little indulgence was shown him. The gaiety of this youth of twenty-eight
seems quite to have won the hearts of those who had more immediately to do with
him. He had a beautiful voice, and the various commanders and mandarins before
whom he was brought nearly always made him sing to them, though he must often
have been near to fainting from hunger, illness and want of sleep. The cage, or
rather the series of cages, in which he was kept for three months, loaded moreover

with chains for part of the time, did not allow of his lying down at full length. On two occasions he was most cruelly beaten, in an attempt to extort from him a confession of the conspiracy for which he had been denounced. Not the least part of his sufferings was the brutal treatment of two or three faithful Christians who were flogged and tortured in his presence.

In the end the sentence to be passed upon him was referred to higher authority, and the reply having come by mounted courier, it was carried out the same day, September 20, 1837. And now history again seems to repeat itself. It is recorded of the Spanish martyr St Fructuosus, who died in the third century, that on the day that he suffered he was still careful to observe the fasts of the Church. They offered him food before the lawful hour, but he announced that he would break his fast in Heaven. Similarly, September 20 being an ember day, the Abbé Cornay, in spite of the sufferings of his confinement and of ill-health, would not dispense himself from the common law. A huge crowd assembled, for no European had ever suffered there before. A large body of soldiers took part in the procession and kept order. The sentence was displayed upon a placard and ran in these terms :

> The culprit called Tan, whose true name is Cao-Lang-Ne (*i.e.* Cornay),* of the kingdom of Flu-Lang-Sa (*i.e.* France) and of the town of Loudun, has been found guilty as the teacher of a false religion masquerading in this country, and as the head of an insurrection. The supreme tribunal decrees that he is to be hewn to pieces and that his head, after being exposed for three days, is to be thrown into the river. May this exemplary sentence be a warning to all. The 21st of the eighth moon of the eighteenth year of the reign of Minh-Mang.

The penalty enjoined was an extreme form of punishment, reserved for cases of high treason. The limbs of the condemned man were usually cut off joint by joint, and it was only after he had been thus mutilated that his head was stricken off and the trunk quartered. In this case the presiding magistrate, seemingly at some risk to himself of royal disfavour, showed mercy, and the martyr was decapitated by a single blow of the sword before the rest of the sentence was carried out. During the long procession which preceded the execution the holy missionary sang hymns and canticles alond with all the strength which remained to him, and his courage made a deep impression on pagans and Christians alike.

Today, July 11, is the feast of Bd Ignatius Delgado and his companions. Other martyrs in Indo-China are mentioned under November 6.

The earliest first-hand information regarding these martyrdoms will be found in the *Annales de la Propagation de la Foi*, vols. xi and xii (1839–1840). More detailed accounts are supplied in the various books of A. Launay, *Les 52 serviteurs de Dieu* (1893), *Les 35 vénérables serviteurs de Dieu* (1907), *Les bienheureux de la Société des Missions Étrangères* (1900), and in his *Histoire de la Société des Missions Étrangères* (1894). See also the *Analecta O.P.*, vol. iv (1900), pp. 577–645 ; H. Walter, *Leben, Wirken und Leiden der 77 sel. Martyrer von Annam und China* (1903) ; and J. R. Shortland, *The Persecutions of Annam.* For the earlier period see D. Collantes, *Hist. de la Prov. del S. Rosario de Filipinas, China e Tunkin, O.P.* (1785). For Marchand there is a life by Fr J. Chauvin (1936), and for Cornay one by Fr R. Plus (1947), both in French.

* The Chinese always confuse the letters *r* and *l*. Thus both the *r* of Cornay and the *r* of France are rendered by a sound which is here written *lang*.

12: ST JOHN GUALBERT, Abbot, Founder of the Vallombrosan Benedictines (A.D. 1073)

S T JOHN GUALBERT was born at Florence towards the end of the tenth century, the son of a nobleman.   Hugh, his elder and only brother, was murdered by a man reputed to be his friend, and John conceived it to be his duty to avenge his brother.   Under the influence of his resentment, heightened by the sorrow and persuasion of his father, he listened to the voice neither of reason nor of religion.   The motive of revenge is criminal if it be present even in demanding the just punishment of an offender ; much more if it push men to vindicate their own cause themselves by returning injury for injury and by wreaking wrongs on those that inflict them.   But John was persuaded that his honour in the world required that he should not suffer so flagrant an outrage to pass unpunished.   One day he came upon the murderer in so narrow a passage that it was impossible for either to avoid the other.   John drew his sword and advanced upon the defenceless man, who fell upon his knees, his arms crossed on his breast.   The remembrance of Christ, who prayed for His murderers on the cross seized the heart of the young man ; he put up his sword, embraced his enemy, and they parted in peace.

John went on his road till he came to the monastery of San Miniato, where, going into the church, he offered up his prayers before a crucifix.   And as he continued his prayer the crucifix miraculously bowed its head, as it were to give a token how acceptable were the sacrifice of his revenge and his sincere repentance. Divine grace so took possession of his heart that he went to the abbot and asked to be admitted to the religious habit.   The abbot was apprehensive of his father's displeasure ; but after a few days John cut off his hair himself, and put on a habit which he borrowed.   John devoted himself to his new state in the dispositions of a true penitent, so that he became entirely a new man.

When the abbot of San Miniato died John, apparently on account of a scandal concerning the abbatial succession, left the house with one companion in quest of a closer solitude.   He paid a visit to the hermitage of Camaldoli, and while there decided to make a new foundation of his own.   This he did in a pleasant place near Fiesole, called Vallis Umbrosa, where with his companions he built a small monastery of timber and mud walls and formed a little community serving God according to the primitive austere rule and spirit of St Benedict.   The abbess of Sant' Ellero gave them ground on which to build.   The saint added to the original Rule of St Benedict certain constitutions, one of which was the provision of *conversi*, lay-brothers, and the abolition of manual work for choir-monks.   Vallombrosa was perhaps the first monastery in which the institution of *conversi* appeared.   The life of this congregation was one of great austerity, and for some time it flourished and established other houses ; but though it still exists it now numbers but few monks.

St John Gualbert feared no less the danger of too great lenience and forbearance than of harshness, and was a true imitator of both the mildness and zeal of Moses, whom the Holy Ghost calls " a man exceeding meek above all men that dwelt upon earth ".   His humbleness would not allow him to receive even minor orders ; he was zealous for poverty, and would not allow any of his monasteries to be built on a costly or imposing scale, thinking such edifices not agreeable to a spirit of poverty.   His kindness to the poor was not less active than his love for poverty.

He would have no poor person sent from his door without an alms, and often emptied the stores of his monasteries in relieving them; in a famine he supplied, sometimes by miracle, the multitudes of people that flocked to Rozzuolo. The saint was endowed with the spirit of prophecy, and by his prayers restored many sick persons to health. Pope St Leo IX went to Passignano on purpose to converse with him and Stephen X had the greatest esteem for him. Pope Alexander II testified that the whole country where he lived owed to his zeal the extinction of simony, for John's enthusiasm for the purely contemplative life did not prevent him and his monks from taking an active part in putting down that disorder, which was rife at the time.

St John Gualbert died on July 12, 1073, the only certain date in his history, being eighty or more years old. Pope Celestine III enrolled him among the saints in 1193.

The materials for St John's life are in a sense abundant : see the long list in BHL., nn. 4397–4406. Still we do not get from them much significant detail. The earliest is that by Bd Andrew of Strumi (*d.* 1097) : unfortunately the only manuscript is mutilated. Another biography, by Bd Atto, must have been written within half a century of the saint's death. Perhaps another narrative belonging to the twelfth century, which was edited by Davidsohn in his *Forschungen zur älteren Geschichte von Florenz* (1896), is not the least valuable of our available sources. Curiously enough this last omits all reference to the pardon accorded to the murderer, from which incident St John's conversion is said to date. The two lives first named are printed in the *Acta Sanctorum*, July, vol. iii, and that by Andrew of Strumi has been re-edited in the folio continuation of MGH., *Scriptores*, vol. xxx, part 2 (1929). There is a popular sketch in Italian by D. F. Tarani (1903), and see Lugano, *L'Italia Benedettina* (1929), pp. 307–356.

ST VERONICA   (First Century)

Few Christian legends are better known and more valued than that of St Veronica, who compassionately wiped the face of Jesus when He fell beneath the load of His cross on the way to Calvary. Nor is that to be wondered at, for it is a most touching story that appeals at once to the heart of every Christian and, in the version which makes her the wife of a Roman officer, is a moving example of contempt of public opinion and human respect. But the legend, though ancient, has only a vague tradition to support it, and the identifications of the woman to whom the name Veronica has been given are several and various. In its origins the story seems to have been more concerned with the miraculous image of our Lord's face imprinted on the cloth with which it was wiped than with the love and charity that prompted the action. Thus in a widespread western version Veronica came to Rome and cured the Emperor Tiberius with the precious relic, which at her death she left to Pope St Clement. In France, on the other hand, she is called the wife of Zacchaeus (Luke xix 2–10), who when her husband becomes a hermit (under the name of Amadour at Rocamadour), helps to evangelize the south of France. Other versions make her the same person as Martha, the sister of Lazarus, the daughter of the woman of Canaan (Matt. xv 22–28), a princess of Edessa, or the wife of an unknown Gallo-Roman officer. The earliest version of the Veronica story is found in a later Latin addition to the fourth or fifth-century apocryphal work *The Acts of Pilate* or *Gospel of Nicodemus ;* it is called there *Cura Sanitatis Tiberii*, and in it Veronica is identified with the woman who had an issue of blood (Matt. ix 20–22), and this identification occurs elsewhere.

The name Veronica has been the subject of a good deal of speculation. It has been suggested and widely received that among several alleged authentic likenesses of our Lord (generally " not-made-with-hands ") the one on the handkerchief of the kind woman was distinguished as *vera icon*, the " true image " ; this became *veronica* and was transferred to the woman as a personal name.   Certainly such images were and are called holy veronica, corrupted in Middle English to " vernicle ".   But it is significant that in the East the *haemorrhoïssa* was called by the name Berenike (victory-bringer) before ever there was any indication of an association with a miraculous image.   Origen, in the first quarter of the third century, in his polemic *Contra Celsum*, speaks of the Valentinians regarding the *haemorrhoïssa* as a type of Wisdom under the name of Prounike, whom Celsus had confounded into a Christian virgin.

St Veronica is not mentioned in any of the earliest historical martyrologies, nor is she named in the Roman Martyrology today, and St Charles Borromeo removed her feast and office from the church of Milan.   A house of Veronica was pointed out at Jerusalem in the early fifteenth century, when the devotion of the stations of the cross was beginning to take its present form ; but the Veronica incident, in common with several others, only gradually became a permanent station in the series.   It was omitted in Vienne so late as 1799.

That a compassionate woman wiped the face of our suffering Lord may well have happened, and Christians do well to ponder her action and revere her traditional memory.   The existence of a cloth claimed to be the original veil of Veronica in St Peter's at Rome is a greatly venerated witness to the tradition, but from the nature of the case there can be no guarantee of its authenticity.

The Bollandists discuss this legend in two different places, first in February, vol. i, and then again in July, vol. iii, dealing with the supposed identity of Veronica with the woman whom our Lord healed of an issue of blood.   A considerable literature has grown up in connection with the Veronica legend.   After K. Pearson, *Die Fronika* (1887), we have the excellent investigation of von Dobschütz in his *Christusbilder,* continued in his article " Das Schweisstuch der Veronica " in *Monatschrift f. k. Kunst* (1909) ; and see P. Perdrizet, " De la Véronique et de Ste Véronique ", in *Seminarium Kondakovianum* (1932), pp. 1–16.   See also H. Leclercq in DAC., vol. vii, cc. 224–225 and 2458–2459.   The suggestion that Veronica = *vera icon* has sometimes been attributed to Mabillon, but it is found already in the *Speculum Ecclesiae* of Giraldus Cambrensis : see Thurston, *Holy Year of Jubilee* (1900), pp. 58, 152–153 and 193–195, where the passage is quoted in full.   In the time of Dante and Petrarch an immense devotion centred in this supposed relic kept in St Peter's ; there is some evidence that the cloth, the lineaments depicted upon which are now completely effaced, has been preserved there ever since the time of Pope John VII, A.D. 705–707.   For the sixth station in Jerusalem, see *Revue biblique*, t. i (1892), pp. 584 *seq.*, and H. Vincent in *Le Lien*, February 1951, pp. 18–26.

ST JASON   (First Century)

WHILE on his second missionary journey St Paul stayed at Salonika, in the house of one Jason.   In consequence of Paul's successful preaching, the Jews, " moved with envy and taking unto them some wicked men of the vulgar sort, and making a tumult, set the city in an uproar ; and besetting Jason's house sought to bring them out unto the people.   And not finding them, they drew Jason and certain brethren to the rulers of the city, crying, ' They that set the city in an uproar are come hither also, whom Jason hath received.   And these all do contrary to the decrees of Caesar, saying that there is another king, Jesus.'   And they stirred up the people and the rulers of the city, hearing these things.   And having taken satisfaction of Jason and of the rest, they let them go " (Acts xvii 5–9).   This is probably the Jason referred to with Lucius and Sosipater as the kinsmen of St Paul in his letter to the Romans (xvi 21), and in the Greek legend he is represented as bishop of Tarsus in Cilicia, going with St Sosipater, bishop of Iconium, to Corfu, evangelizing that island, and dying there. After preaching successfully for some time the two missionaries were thrown into prison, where they converted seven thieves who afterwards achieved martyrdom (their apocryphal story is mentioned in the Roman Martyrology on April 29). The Syrians, however, venerate Jason as the apostle of the district round Apamea and as a martyr who was thrown to the beasts. The Roman Martyrology wrongly identifies him with the Mnason of Acts xxi 16, " an old disciple " with whom St Paul was to lodge in Jerusalem, and makes Cyprus the place of his death as well as of his birth.

The confusion of Mnason and Jason seems to have originated in a mention in Ado's martyrology of " Mnaso, antiquus Christi discipulus ". The Bollandists, *Acta Sanctorum*, July, vol. iii, point out that in one manuscript known to them the name was written Naso. This might easily have been misread. Baronius in his notes to the Roman Martyrology conveniently assumes that there were two Jasons, one of whom lived in Thessalonica, the other in Cyprus.

SS. HERMAGORAS AND FORTUNATUS, MARTYRS   (FIRST CENTURY ?)

THERE is an eighth-century tradition that St Mark the Evangelist, before he went to found the church of Alexandria, was sent from Rome by St Peter to be the apostle of Aquileia, where he preached, strengthened his testimony by miracles, and made many converts. When he left he chose for their pastor an " elegant person " called Hermagoras, who was consecrated bishop by St Peter and is venerated in Istria and the neighbourhood as first bishop of Aquileia. Together with his deacon, St Fortunatus, he first preached the gospel in Belluno, Como, Ceneda and other places. The late and quite untrustworthy acts of St Hermagoras narrate that Nero sent his envoy Sebastius to Aquileia to carry out the edicts against Christians, who tortured Hermagoras and threw him into prison. At midnight his dungeon was illuminated by a celestial light which so impressed the gaoler that he was converted ; but the man very imprudently ran about the city, crying out, " Great is the God of Hermagoras ! Behold His wonders ! " Many people flocked to the prison, saw the radiance, and were also converted, so that Sebastius sent an executioner who beheaded the bishop and his deacon under cover of darkness. Although a St Fortunatus was undoubtedly honoured as a martyr at Aquileia, there seems to be nothing to connect him with any Hermagoras.

See the *Acta Sanctorum*, July, vol. iii ; Delehaye's CMH., pp. 371–372 and his *Origines du Culte des Martyrs*, pp. 331–332.

SS. NABOR AND FELIX, MARTYRS   (A.D. 303 ?)

ST AMBROSE greatly praised these martyrs and multitudes of people flocked to Milan to venerate them. Late legends say that they were Moorish soldiers in the army of Maximian Herculeus, stationed at Milan, and that they were beheaded for their faith at Lodi ; but these legends are imitated from those of other soldier martyrs, such as St Victor of Marseilles, and are historically worthless. The names of SS. Nabor and Felix occur in the canon of the Milanese Mass, and their *cultus* was widespread in northern Italy.

The short Latin text which professes to preserve the " acts " of SS. Nabor and Felix has been printed in the *Acta Sanctorum*, July, vol. iii. The martyrs are duly commemorated in the " Hieronymianum ", and it is impossible to doubt the antiquity of their cult at Milan. See Delehaye's Commentary on that martyrology, and his *Les Origines du Culte des Martyrs*, pp. 335–337.

ST JOHN THE IBERIAN, ABBOT   (*c.* A.D. 1002)

THE little-known Church of Georgia (Iberia) was distinguished in its early ages by the vigour of its monastic life, not only in Georgia but also in Syria, Palestine, Sinai, Bithynia, Greece and its islands ; and finally, when St Athanasius the Athonite was organizing the religious life on Mount Athos, a foundation was made there. The beginning of this monastery of Iviron was due to St John the Iberian and his son St Euthymius, and we are fortunate in having an account of them written by a monk, George, who was almost their contemporary there.

John belonged to a noble Iberian family and was distinguished alike by his personal attraction, military valour, intellectual ability and uprightness of life. But in early middle-age he parted from his wife and family, gave up his fortune and official post, and retired to a monastery on Mount Olympus in Bithynia. From here he had to visit the court at Constantinople, for his son Euthymius had been given, with other young Georgian nobles, as hostages to the emperor. He was able to retrieve him and take him back to Olympus, whence after a time the attentions of his followers consequent on his growing reputation for sanctity drove them to seek greater seclusion in the *laura* of St Athanasius on the Holy Mountain of Athos. Here he was employed for two·years as cook, until he was joined by his brother-in-law, John Thornikios, who had given up a brilliant military career to serve God as a monk, when the three compatriots were given permission to build separate cells and a chapel for themselves. About the year 980 it was decided to establish an independent monastery for Iberians, who were now coming to the mountain in numbers. This was done, much of the expense being met by the ex-general's share of the booty of his last campaign. But after his death St John resolved to take flight, with his son and a few specially dear disciples, to Spain ; he had never been keen on starting the new monastery, and now his friend was no longer there to share them, the bustle and worry were more than he could bear. They got as far as Abydos, where the prefect learned of their plan, reported it to Constantinople, and John was ordered to go there. Come into the presence of the emperors, Basil II and Constantine VIII, they said to him, " Holy father, we have testified to our regard for your goodness by great marks of esteem and affection. Why then do you run away from us and try to emigrate to a strange land ? " To whom he replied, " Religious and most mighty emperors, I am a poor layman and I find myself badly off in this world, overcome by all sorts of wickedness. That is why I wish to go to some far country where I can concern myself with my soul's salvation. There I can live in poverty and get rid of the crowd of cares and visitors which came to me with the coming of my brother-in-law." However, with great trouble he was persuaded to return to Athos and the government of Iviron.

During the last years of his life St John was kept to his bed by gout and general debility ; he bore his sufferings with great patience, praising God for sending him so painful an affliction. When his strength entirely failed, he handed the government of the monastery over to his son, but till the end nothing was done without his authorization. On his death-bed, *c.* 1002, he exhorted his brethren : " Let no one distract you from our holy work and from the love of God, that is, from humble obedience and a close unity and harmony of souls ; so will you be saved in this mortal life and gain for the future eternal life by the love which our Lord Christ bears towards human kind. May the kind and all-pitiful God have mercy on you and lead you in the way of His divine teaching and holy will, by the intercession of the all-holy Mother of God and of all the saints. Amen. Never fail to receive guests well and share with the poor, according as you are able, those things which God in His goodness has given to you. Observe the memory of our spiritual father Athanasius every year. . . . Pray for me, my children and brethren, and do not forget me. . . ." He asked and received the blessing of his son Euthymius, and peacefully gave his soul to God. His biographer says of him : " Truly our blessed father John was a man dear to God and worthy of all veneration. Like Abraham he went forth from his own country, to lead a life of exile and poverty. He gave himself into the hands of the spiritual fathers, and God made him the equal of those whom he took for his pattern." And of the monastery which he unwillingly co-operated in founding : " Behold this famous *laura*, magnificently built and dignified by all kinds of decoration—these blessed men raised it with great labour and endless industry to be a place of refuge for many souls. They built heavenly churches, which they filled with holy books and venerable images. They endowed it with lands, with farms, with dependencies and cells, and provided for the most fitting celebration of the sacred rites. From the most pious emperors they obtained for it protection and charters. They gathered therein monks of angelic life, who by their translation of the sacred texts become an ornament of our country and the flower of our language." It was in this work that St Euthymius particularly distinguished himself, translating over fifty religious works from Greek into Iberian.

St John extended his benefactions to Leo the Roman, who founded on Mount Athos a monastery of Benedictines, the first and only Latin institution ever established at the headquarters of Byzantine monasticism ; this abbey was swept away centuries ago, but St John's own monastery of Iviron still flourishes, though it has been transferred from the Georgians to the Greeks.

The history of St John the Iberian, or " the Hagiorite ", was first published in the language of the original by G. M. Sabinin in 1882 at Petersburg, but a more critical text appeared at Tiflis in 1901. More recently Fr Paul Peeters made a copiously annotated Latin translation, printed in vol. xxxvi of the *Analecta Bollandiana* (1922), pp. 8–68, and a French translation appeared in *Irénikon*, vol. vi (1929) and vii (1930). Fr Peeters is of opinion (*Analecta Bollandiana*, vol. xlix, 1931, p. 284) that St John died at latest in 1002, and that the life above summarized, which also contains an account of John's son and successor, St Euthymius, must have been written by George the Hagiorite about forty years later. See also Hasluck, *Athos and its Monasteries* (1924), pp. 162–164 ; M. Tamarati, *L'Église Géorgienne* (1910), pp. 318–332 ; and D. Attwater, *Book of Eastern Saints* (1938), for a popular account of St John and his son.

BD ANDREW OF RINN (A.D. 1462)

ANDREW was born in 1459, the son of Simon and Maria Oexner, peasants of Rinn, near Innsbruck. At two years old his father died and the boy was confided to the care of his uncle, Mayer, an innkeeper of the village. On July 12, 1462, the child disappeared, and his mother eventually found him hanging dead from a tree, his body terribly slashed with knife-cuts. Mayer explained that he had sold him to some Jewish pedlars as the boy was a nuisance to him, and showed the payment he had received—but the gold pieces were turned to yellow willow leaves ; the man was out of his mind, he had to be confined, and died raving.

It must be noticed that at the time no active notice was taken of Mayer's statement that Andrew had been taken away by Jews ; but when in 1475 certain Jews of Trent were tortured into a confession that they had murdered a Christian boy, Simon, of that city, the peasants of Rinn accused them of like dealings with Andrew. The place where his body was found was named the Judenstein, miracles were reported, the veneration of the child as a martyr spread all over the northern Tirol, and in 1670 a chapel was built to shelter his relics. In 1750 Pope Benedict XIV allowed the *cultus* and granted a local office in honour of Andrew ; but five years later the same pope refused the request of the bishop of Brixen for the canonization of the boy. It may reasonably be held that he was not a victim of the Jews at all, but was killed by his mad uncle in an outburst of homicidal mania.

See the *Acta Sanctorum*, July, vol. iii ; where also may be found the reproduction of a curious set of engravings, published at Innsbruck in 1658, depicting the principal incidents of the story of the martyrdom. For a reference to some similar cases of alleged ritual murder see March 24 herein, under Simon of Trent, and August 27, Little St Hugh.

BD JOHN JONES, Martyr   (A.D. 1598)

John Jones, known on the mission as John Buckley and having the names in religion of Godfrey Maurice, came of a Catholic family of Clynog Fawr in Caernarvonshire. He became a Friar Minor of the Observance in Rome, and in 1592 he was sent at his own request to the English mission and lodged for a time in London. He worked in various parts of the country until 1596, when he was arrested on an order of the priest-hunter Topcliffe, and subjected to cruel tortures. He was kept in prison for two years, during which time he contrived to reconcile Bd John Rigby, a layman who for a time conformed to Protestantism and suffered death in 1600 for his repentance. On July 3, 1598, Bd John was tried for having been ordained overseas and returned to the realm. He protested that he had never been guilty of any treason, and asked that his case should be referred to the conscience of the judges, rather than to an ignorant jury. Mr Justice Clinch pointed out to him that his offence was treason by statute, whereto the prisoner replied, " If this be a crime I must own myself guilty ; for I am a priest and came over into England to gain as many souls as I could to Christ ". The place fixed for his execution was St Thomas Waterings in the Old Kent Road, the place where in days not then long past pilgrims to the shrine of St Thomas Becket had made their first halt and watered their horses at a ford (Chaucer mentions it in the prologue to the *Canterbury Tales*). When the martyr had been dragged to this place on a hurdle, the hangman was found to have forgotten the rope, and it took an hour to fetch it ; Bd John passed the time in prayer and in talking to the people, asserting that he had prayed daily for the queen's welfare. His head was displayed in Southwark and his members in the Lambeth and Newington roads ; two young men were committed to prison for trying to rescue these relics, but where they failed others succeeded.

See Challoner, MMP., pp. 234–239 ; Catholic Record Society *Publications*, vol. v, pp. 362–375 ; *The Rambler*, January 1859, pp. 49–55 ; Mason, *Certamen Seraphicum* (1885 ed.), p. 17.

13 :* ST SILAS   (First Century)

IN the Roman Martyrology under July 13 is the entry : " In Macedonia, the death of the blessed Silas, who, being one of the first brethren and sent by the Apostles to the churches of the Gentiles with Paul and Barnabas, was full of the grace of God and readily fulfilled the office of preaching ; and, glorifying Christ in His sufferings, was afterwards at rest."

Silas is first mentioned in chapter xv of the Acts of the Apostles, when he was chosen with Judas as " chief men among the brethren " to go with Paul and Barnabas to Antioch bearing the letter from the Council of Jerusalem to the Gentile converts in Syria.   Judas and Silas, " being prophets also themselves ", took part in the exhortation and confirming of the brethren, and Silas remained with Paul and Barnabas at Antioch until the disagreement arose between those two, when he was chosen by Paul to go with him in his visitation of the other churches of Syria and Cilicia, and ultimately into Macedonia.   At Philippi he shared St Paul's beating and imprisonment, and with him was miraculously delivered.   He stopped behind with Timothy at Berea, but they received a message from the apostle at Athens that they should join him again, and they overtook him at Corinth.   Here St Paul wrote his two letters to the Thessalonians, in each of which he refers to Silas in the full form of his name, Silvanus.   Nothing more is known of him, but traditionally he lived the rest of his life in Europe and died, as the martyrology says, in Macedonia.   It is possible that St Peter's secretary, Silvanus (1 Peter v 12), is the same disciple.

We know nothing of St Silas beyond what is told us in the New Testament.   See the *Acta Sanctorum*, July, vol. iii, and *cf.* Vigouroux, *Dictionnaire de la Bible*, and Hastings, *Dictionary of the Bible*.

SS. MAURA and BRIGID   (Fifth Century ?)

THERE is an old *cultus* of these maidens in Picardy, but scholars have found it impossible to give a satisfactory account of them from the sources available. According to these legends they were British princesses from Northumbria, who made a pilgrimage to Rome ; on their way home through Gaul they were set upon by heathen outlaws or Frankish raiders and put to death at Balagny-sur-Thérain. Here they were buried and there arose a *cultus* of them as martyrs.   In the middle of the seventh century St Bathildis, the queen of King Clovis II, who came from England and (especially as she was a slave-girl) may have been a Briton, attempted to translate their relics to her monastery at Chelles ; she was prevented by divine intervention, and forced to leave them at Nogent-les-Vierges (Oise), where they were solemnly enshrined in 1185.   St Louis IX had a great devotion to these saints and was a benefactor of their shrine and church, to which he made pilgrimage, and a cessation of the plague at Beauvais attributed to their intercession further endeared them to the people.

St Gregory of Tours relates of his predecessor, St Euphronius, that, having heard of a mysterious light seen over a bramble-covered hill and of a vision of two maidens asking for a chapel to be built on the hill because two holy virgins were

---

* St Analectus, pope, appears in many calendars on this day.   He is now recognized to be the same person as St Cletus, April 26.   The separate name of Anacletus has now been expunged from the general calendar and the Roman Martyrology.

buried there, he himself visited the spot, and it was revealed to him that the maidens were called Maura and Britta ; they had been solitaries at Ariacum (now Sainte-Maure), and had died in the fifth century, not long after St Martin. The relics were found, the chapel built, and a *cultus* begun in Touraine which still exists : their feast is kept at Tours on January 28. Because of the likeness in names and era attempts have been made to show them identical with the saints of Nogent.

See the *Acta Sanctorum*, January, vol. ii ; Stanton, *Menology*, pp. 659–660 ; Renet, *S. Lucien et les autres SS. du Beauvaisis* (1895), vol. iii, pp. 573–579 ; *Mémoires de la Soc. des Antiquaires de Picardie*, vol. x, pp. 117–119.

ST EUGENIUS, BISHOP OF CARTHAGE (A.D. 505)

THE Roman provinces in Africa were for a long time one of the richest and most noble portions of the empire, but when its rulers, to preserve Italy, abandoned its extremities, Genseric, King of the Vandals, in 428, passed into this country and in a short time became master of those fertile provinces. The Vandals, who were mostly Christians but infected with the Arian heresy, laid the country waste, plundered churches and monasteries, burned alive two bishops and tortured others to extort from them the treasures of their churches, razed the public buildings at Carthage, and banished St Quodvultdeus, bishop of that city, with many others. But for the brief episcopate of St Deogratias, the episcopal see of Carthage had remained vacant for fifty years, when in 481 Huneric, who had succeeded Genseric, permitted the Catholics on certain conditions to choose one who should fill it. The people pitched upon Eugenius, a citizen of the place, eminent for his learning, zeal, piety and prudence ; and he became so dear to his flock that every one of them would have thought it a happiness to lay down his life for him. His charities to the distressed were very great, especially considering his poverty. But he always found resources for their necessities in the hearts of his people, and he refused himself everything that he might give all to the poor. When others reminded him that he ought to reserve something for his own necessities, his answer was, " If the good shepherd must lay down his life for his sheep, can it be excusable for me to trouble about the passing needs of my body ? "

The influence of St Eugenius was so strong that the king became alarmed, and he ordered the bishop not to occupy his episcopal chair or to preach in public or to allow any Vandals into his churches. Eugenius replied that the law of God commanded him not to shut the door of a church against any who wished to enter it. Huneric then posted guards at the doors of the Catholic churches, who when they saw any man or woman going in recognizable as a Vandal by his clothes and long hair, used forked sticks which, twisted into the hair and violently drawn back, tore off hair and skin together. Some thus lost their eyes, others died, and women who had been scalped in this way were led through the streets as a warning to others. A fierce persecution was thus initiated.

Bishop Eugenius was spared in the first storm, and he was soon informed by Huneric that the orthodox Catholics were to meet in a conference with the Arian bishops at Carthage. Eugenius answered that the terms were not equal, seeing their enemies· were to be judges ; and that as it was the common cause of all churches, other churches ought to be invited and consulted, " especially the Church of Rome, which is the head of all churches. I will write to my fellow bishops, who will be able with me to show you our common faith." It is said that about this time one Felix, who had been long blind, addressed himself to St Eugenius, desiring him to pray over him that he might recover his sight, saying he had been told in a vision so to do. The bishop showed great reluctance, but at length, after blessing the font for the administration of baptism on the eve of the Epiphany, he turned and said to the blind man, " I have told you that I am a sinner, and the least of all men ; but I pray God that He show you mercy according to your faith, and restore to you your sight ". Then he made the sign of the cross on his eyes, and the blind man saw. Huneric sent for Felix, and examined the circumstances of the miracle, which he found too evident to be called in question ; but the Arian bishops told him that Eugenius had performed it by magic.

The conference, when it assembled in 484 to discuss the divisions between Catholics and Arians, was a farce ; and Huneric took the opportunity of so many bishops assembled in Carthage to plunder them, and then deport them to forced labour. St Eugenius, after having long encouraged others to the conflict, was himself suddenly carried into exile, without being allowed to take leave of his friends. He found means, however, to write a letter to his flock, which St Gregory of Tours has preserved. In it he says : " I with tears beg, exhort and implore you, by the dreadful day of judgement and the aweful light of the coming of Christ, that you hold fast the Catholic faith. Keep the grace of baptism and the anointing of chrism. Let no man born again of water return to the water." This he mentions, because the Arians in Africa, like the Donatists, rebaptized those that came over to their sect. St Eugenius protests to his flock that, if they remain constant, no distance nor death could separate him from them in spirit ; but that he was innocent of the blood of those that should perish, and that this his letter would be read before the tribunal of Christ at the last day for the condemnation of apostates. " If I return to Carthage "says he, " I shall see you in this life ; if not, I shall meet you in the other. Pray for us, and fast ; fasting and almsdeeds have never failed to move God to mercy. Above all things, remember that we are not to fear those who can only kill the body."

St Eugenius was carried into the desert country in the province of Tripoli and committed to the care of Antony, an Arian bishop who treated him with barbarity. At this time apostates signalized themselves above others by the cruelties which they exercised upon the orthodox. Elpidophorus, one of this number, was appointed judge at Carthage ; and St Muritta, the deacon who had assisted when he was baptized in the Catholic Church, being brought before him, took with him the white garment with which he had clothed the apostate coming out of the font. Holding it up before the whole assembly, he said, " This robe will accuse you when the Judge shall appear in majesty at the last day. It will bear testimony against you to your condemnation." This Muritta, with the archdeacon St Salutaris, is mentioned together with St Eugenius in the Roman Martyrology on this day.

King Huneric died in 484, and his nephew Gontamund who succeeded him recalled St Eugenius to Carthage in 488 ; some years later the orthodox churches were reopened and the other clergy allowed to return. But the next king, Thrasimund, was again a persecutor. He eventually condemned Eugenius to death ; but he was reprieved and banished to Languedoc, which was then subject to Alaric, King of the Visigoths, who was also an Arian. He died in exile in 505 in a monastery near Albi.

The principal authority is Victor of Vita, *Historia persecutionis Vandalicae* (the best edition is that of Petschenig in the *Corpus ss. eccles. Lat.*, vol. vii) ; but the more relevant matter is reprinted in the *Acta Sanctorum*, July, vol. iii, together with a few passages from Gregory of Tours, etc. See also S. Mesnage, *L'Afrique chrétienne* (1912) ; Ludwig Schmidt, *Geschichte der Vandalen* (1901) ; Hefele-Leclercq, *Conciles*, vol. ii, pp. 930–933 ; and Duchesne, *Histoire ancienne de l'Église*, vol. iii.

ST MILDRED, Abbess of Minster-in-Thanet, Virgin   (*c.* A.D. 700)

OUR forefathers had an extraordinary veneration for St Mildred, though the scanty records we have of her life give no clue to the reason for this popular devotion. William of Malmesbury says that her remains, which were translated (or rather carried off by stratagem) in 1033 to St Augustine's at Canterbury, were venerated above all the relics in that holy place.   Furthermore, the rock which received St Augustine's first footprints was known until comparatively recent times, not as his, but as St Mildred's rock.   She was the second daughter of Merewald, an Anglian ruler, and of St Ermenburga or Domneva, a Kentish princess, and she had two sisters, Milburga and Mildgytha, as well as a brother, who were also reckoned as saints.

Egbert, King of Kent, had caused two nephews to be secretly murdered in the Isle of Thanet.   He was filled with compunction, and sending for their sister Ermenburga from western Mercia, he paid her the wergild, the penalty for murder which the law ordained should be paid to the relatives of the victim.   In satisfaction for the crime he settled land on her, upon which she founded a monastery in which prayers should be continually offered for the souls of the two princes. The monastery was called Minster, in the Isle of Thanet, and Ermenburga at first took charge of it herself.   As her daughter Mildred gave evidence of a vocation for the religious life, she sent her to the convent of Chelles in France to be educated. Here she was persecuted by the unwelcome attentions of a young nobleman, who sought to induce her to marry him.   She stood firm and eventually returned to England and rejoined her mother.   St Theodore, Archbishop of Canterbury, received her into the community.   Soon St Ermenburga gave over her charge to her daughter, who appears to have been the first abbess of Minster, under which title she attended a council in Kent.   Her aunt Ermengytha served God in the same house with such fervour that she was ranked among the saints and her tomb became a place of pilgrimage.

Of St Mildred's life we are told that she fasted often and was intensely humble. " She was merciful to widows and orphans, and a comforter to all the poor and afflicted, and in all respects of easy temper and tranquil."   She died of a lingering and painful illness probably towards the close of the seventh century, but the date is quite uncertain.   During the reign of Canute her relics were taken, more or less forcibly, to St Augustine's abbey at Canterbury, whence some portion of them later found their way to Deventer in Holland.   Thence a small relic was sent in 1882 to the Catholic church at Minster, where her feast is observed as its titular saint.   In 1937 Minster Court, on the site of the successor of St Mildred's monastery, was occupied by Benedictine nuns from the ancient St Walburga's abbey at Eichstätt, thus reviving monastic life there after a thousand years.

It is curious that Bede seems nowhere to mention St Mildred, but lives of her were written at a much later date by Goscelin, Thorn and Capgrave.   See the *Acta Sanctorum*, February, vol. iii, and especially Stanton's *Menology*, pp. 332–333.   St Augustine's Abbey, Ramsgate, publishes a useful pamphlet on St Mildred and her sisters.

BD JAMES OF VORAGINE, ARCHBISHOP OF GENOA   (A.D. 1298)

THIS James took his name from the village of Viraggio, now Varazze, near Genoa, where he was born about the year 1230.   He entered the Order of Preachers at the age of fourteen, and after some years of the most devoted study and spiritual exercises began to preach in the churches of Lombardy and was soon famous for his power.   He taught theology and Sacred Scripture in various houses of his order, became prior at Genoa, and in 1267 was elected prior provincial of the Lombard province.   To be given this office when only thirty-seven years old gave rise to some adverse comment which he silenced by the prudence and ability with which he discharged it : so much so that he held it for an unbroken period of nineteen years, and when he laid it down was appointed definitor.   On the death of Charles Bernard, Archbishop of Genoa, in 1286, the chapter wished Bd James to succeed to the see, but he refused.   Two years later he was entrusted by Pope Nicholas IV with the duty of raising the interdict and removing the censures imposed on the same city for having helped the revolting Sicilians against the king of Naples.   In 1292 the see again became vacant, again the chapter elected Bd James, and again he refused ; but this time he was obliged to withdraw his refusal and he was consecrated at Rome.   His episcopate of six years was troubled by continuous hostilities between Guelfs and Ghibellines, represented respectively by the *rampini* and the *mascarati*, and the new archbishop laboured without ceasing to bring about political and social peace ; in this he did not succeed, for an apparent reconciliation in 1295 proved to be only a truce, and in the following year the feud broke out as badly as ever.   Bd James did not forget his religious vow of poverty, and liberally bestowed the revenues of his great see on the needy and those suffering from civil strife, in the endowment of hospitals and monasteries, and for the repair of churches ;   he was a model to the bishops of northern Italy, some of whom adopted his measures to maintain the discipline of their clergy.

But it is as a writer that James of Voragine is chiefly famous.   One work attributed to him, the translation of the Bible into Italian, cannot by any means be proved ; if he did it, every copy has perished.   It is as the author of *Legenda Sanctorum*, now everywhere known as *Legenda Aurea*, " The Golden Legend ", that his name is known and venerated ; it is the most famous, and for the mind of the people the most influential, collection of legends or " lives " of the saints that has ever been put together.   From the point of view of history it is entirely un-critical and worthless—except as a sidelight on the unsophistication and simple mentality of the folk for whom it was written.   But as a book of devotion, of edification, it is a superb work of art : the author perfectly accomplished what he set out to do, to write a book which people would read and whose message of love for God and hatred for sin they could not misunderstand ; but for the Reformation, Caxton's beautiful translation might have had the same effect on English thought and writing as the Jacobean Bible and the *Imitation of Christ* have had, or as other versions had in other countries.   It is illustrative of the narrowness of historical Humanism when contrasted with the true scientific spirit that, whereas Luis Vives, Melchior Cano and others roundly condemned the *Legenda Aurea*, the Bollandists have shown a nice appreciation of it.   Father Delehaye says :

For a long time the Golden Legend, which is so accurately representative of the hagiographic labours of the middle ages, was treated with supreme disdain, and scholars showed no mercy towards the worthy James of Voragine. " The man who wrote the Legend ", declared Luis Vives, " had a mouth of iron and a heart of lead."

It would in fact be hard to speak of it too severely if it were conceded that popular works are to be judged according to the standards of historical criticism. But people are beginning to realize that this is an injudicious method, and those who have penetrated into the spirit of the Golden Legend are very far from referring to it in scornful terms.

I confess that, when reading it, it is somewhat difficult at times to refrain from a smile. But it is a sympathetic and tolerant smile, and in no way disturbs the religious emotion excited by the picture of the virtues and heroic actions of the saints.

In this picture God's friends are represented for us as what is greatest on earth ; they are human creatures lifted up above matter and above the miseries of our little world. Kings and princes honour and consult them, mingling with the people in order to kiss their relics and implore their protection. They live, even here on earth, in God's intimacy, and God bestows upon them, with His consolations, something also of His power ; but they only make use of it for the good of mankind, and it is to them that men have recourse in order to be delivered from sufferings both of body and soul. The saints practice all the virtues in a superhuman degree ; gentleness, mercy, the forgiveness of injuries, mortification, renunciation, and they render these virtues lovable, and they urge Christians to practise them. Their life is, in truth, the concrete realization of the spirit of the Gospel, and from the very fact that it brings home to us this sublime ideal, legend, like all poetry, can claim a higher degree of truth than history itself " (*The Legends of the Saints*, cap. vii, pp. 229-231).

The book was exceedingly popular and widely distributed in the middle ages, and in 1470 the first printed edition of the original Latin was published at Basle ; within ten years printed versions had appeared in Low German, Italian, French and Czech. Caxton made the first edition printed in English at Westminster in 1483. No other book was reprinted more often between 1470 and 1530 ; by 1500 there were over seventy editions in Latin, fourteen in Low German, eight in Italian, five in French and three each in English and Czech—it was indeed the first printed best-seller. The *cultus* of Bd James began at once after his death in 1298 and was confirmed in 1816.

For a devotional account of the incidents of the life of Bd James, the illustrated biography by M. de Waresquiel, *Le B. Jacques de Voragine* (1902), may be recommended. Most other books and essays deal predominantly with the literary side of his career. Among these may be mentioned the two articles of E. C. Richardson in the *Princeton Theological Review*, 1903 and 1904 ; P. Butler, *Legenda aurea, Légende dorée, Golden Legend* (1899) ; and the article in DTC. For a fuller bibliography see Taurisano, *Catalogus hagiographicus O.P.* On E. C. Richardson's *Materials for a Life of Jacopo da Varagine* (1935), see *Analecta Bollandiana*, vol. liv (1936), pp. 440-442. Several modernized versions of Caxton's *Golden Legend* have been published in recent times, and a new translation appeared in New York (2 vols.) in 1941.

ST FRANCIS SOLANO   (A.D. 1610)

THIS saint was born at Montilla in Andalusia in 1549, did his studies in the school of the Jesuits, and in 1569 joined the Franciscan Observants at his birthplace. He was duly professed and in 1576 ordained priest. Full of zeal and charity and an ardent desire for the salvation of souls, he divided his time between silent retirement and the ministry of preaching. His sermons, though without the ornaments of studied eloquence, had a great effect in reforming his hearers. The saint was appointed master of novices, and when his charges were at fault he gave a penance not to them but to himself, for if they transgressed, he said, the blame must be his.

Francis exercised his ministry in southern Spain for many years and heroically during the plague of 1583 at Granada, when he himself was struck down but made a quick recovery. After the epidemic was passed he asked to be sent as a missionary into Africa ; this was refused, but when in 1589 King Philip II wanted more friars of the Observance in the West Indies, Francis was selected to go with Father Balthazar Navarro to Peru. The missionaries sailed to Panama, crossed the isthmus, and again took ship on the other side. But in approaching Peru they ran into a bad storm and were driven aground on a sandbank. The ship looked as if she were going to pieces, and the master ordered that she be abandoned, leaving aboard her a number of Negro slaves for whom there was no room in the single lifeboat. Francis had these men under instruction and he now refused to leave them, so he remained behind on the ship, which was breaking up. He gathered them around him, encouraged them to trust in the mercy of God and the merits of Jesus Christ, and then baptized them. This he had scarcely done when the vessel parted amidships, and some of the Negroes were drowned. The remainder were on the part of the hull that was firmly aground, and there they remained for three days, Francis keeping up their courage and rigging signals of distress. When the weather broke the ship's boat returned and took them off to join the others in a place of safety, whence they eventually were conveyed to Lima.

Now began twenty years of untiring ministry among the Indians and Spanish colonists. First of all Francis was sent to Tucuman, in the north of what is now the Argentine Republic ; he set himself to learn the Indian languages and dialects, and from thence went on a missionary journey through the Chaco to Paraguay, where in after years were to be the famous " reductions " of the Society of Jesus. In these days it is difficult to realize what such a journey meant in those ; this friar not only did it, but made numerous converts as well. After a time he was made *custos* of the houses of his order in Tucuman and Paraguay, and so was able to supervise the missions he had planted, but when his term in that office was ended he was appointed guardian of the Lima friary. Here there was plenty of work of another kind for him to do among the Peruvian Spaniards of that port, of Trujillo, and other towns. In 1604 his preaching in the public square against the corruptions of Lima and his comparison of the fate of a sinful soul to that of a doomed city had so powerful an effect on the people that their consciences caused them to fear an impending calamity like to that of Ninive, and a panic threatened. The viceroy was alarmed and consulted St Turibius, archbishop of the city, who with the Franciscan commissary general required of St Francis that he should calm the people, who had already had examples of his gift of prophecy, by declaring his true meaning, which was not to foretell a material destruction of buildings but a spiritual loss of souls.

It is said that St Francis had the gift of tongues, and for his miracles he was called the " Wonder-worker of the New World " ; in his funeral sermon Father Sebastiani, s.j., said that God had chosen him to be " the hope and edification of all Peru, the example and glory of Lima, the splendour of the Seraphic order ".

A habit of his, very reminiscent of his religious father and namesake, was to take a lute and sing to our Lady before her altar. He died on July 14, 1610, while his brethren were singing the conventual Mass, at the moment of consecration, saying with his last breath, " Glory be to God ". His whole life, says Alvarez de Paz, was a holy uninterrupted course of zealous action, yet at the same time a continued prayer. St Francis Solano was canonized in 1726.

There is a very full account of this great missionary in the *Acta Sanctorum*, July, vol. v, which includes a reprint of the life by Tiburtio Navarro, together with a number of documents submitted in the process of beatification. A still more copious life by Fray Diego de Cordova appeared twenty years after the saint's death. There are modern biographies in most languages : a translation of the short sketch by F. Courtot was included in the Oratorian series in 1847, an English life appeared in New York in 1888, and a German one by O. Maas in 1938. Some of these, notably that of A. M. Hiral in French (1906), are devotional rather than critical. There is a sketch by J. Wilbois in the series " Profils franciscains " (1942). The saint's feast is observed on differing dates ; he is named in the Roman Martyrology on the day of his death, July 14.

BD THOMAS TUNSTAL, Martyr   (A.D. 1616)

THOMAS TUNSTAL was born at Whinfell, near Kendal. He entered the English College at Douay in 1606, was ordained priest, and sent on the mission in 1610. He was arrested almost at once and spent the rest of his life in various prisons. He contrived to escape from Wisbech Castle by sliding down a rope, and took refuge with a friend near King's Lynn ; but he was immediately discovered, under the following circumstances. In sliding down the rope he had very badly skinned his hands, and for lack of attention the raw places had gone septic. His host recommended him to consult a certain kindly woman, who did many medical services for the poor, and this he did. Lady L'Estrange, for that was her name, cleaned and dressed his hands, not without some curiosity as to who the poorly dressed but well-bred stranger might be ; unfortunately she did not keep her curiosity to herself but mentioned the man to her husband, Sir Hammond L'Es-trange. He was a justice of the peace and knew that there was hue and cry for a priest escaped from Wisbech, and when he heard that the injured man was staying in the house of a recusant he at once ordered his arrest, in spite of the entreaties of his wife to forget what she had said.

Bd Thomas was committed to Norwich gaol, and brought up at the next assizes in that city, when he was condemned on the evidence of a single false witness, one Symons. This fellow swore that the prisoner had reconciled two Protestants and tried to do the same with himself. The alleged converts were called and deposed that they were still Protestants, but that Mr Tunstal had urged them in general terms to holiness of life. Mr Justice Altham offered the oath of supremacy, which Bd Thomas refused, asking, however, that he might have opportunity to expose his faith and reasons before a minister. The request was disregarded and sentence pronounced. At the scaffold the next morning he was met by Sir Hammond L'Estrange, whom he heartily forgave, saying, " I beseech God that my guiltless blood may not lie heavy upon you and yours ". When he was asked if he were a Jesuit he replied that he was not, but a secular priest who had made a vow to join the Order of St Benedict, and he therefore asked the sheriff that his head might be set up on St Benet's gate. He answered a nagging question from a minister about whether he expected salvation from his good works, called for a glass of water, and enquired the hour ; when told eleven o'clock, he said, " Then it is near dinner-time. Sweet Jesus, admit me though most unworthy to be a guest this day at thy table in Heaven." He quietly blessed the fire and the rope, and with the prayer, " Jesu, have mercy on me ! " upon his lips, he was turned off ; he was left to hang till he was dead and his head was displayed on St Benet's gate of Norwich as he had wished.

The account of Bd Thomas given in Challoner, MMP., is not quite satisfactory owing to some confusion into which he was betrayed by Raissius, but the difficulties have been cleared up and all the available evidence collected in the account published by Dom Bede Camm under the title of *Nine Martyr Monks* (1931), pp. 238–257. But there is still some uncertainty about the day of the month on which he suffered.

14 : ST BONAVENTURE, Cardinal-Bishop of Albano, Doctor of the Church   (A.D. 1274)

O F the youth of this greatest successor of St Francis of Assisi nothing is known beyond the facts that he was born at Bagnorea, near Viterbo, in the year 1221, the son of John Fidanza and Mary Ritella. He was clothed in the order of Friars Minor and studied at the University of Paris under an Englishman, Alexander of Hales, " the Unanswerable Doctor " ; Bonaventure, who was to become known as the Seraphic Doctor, himself taught theology and Holy Scripture there from 1248 to 1257. His penetrating genius was balanced by the most careful judgement by which, while he dived to the bottom of every subtle inquiry, he cut off whatever was superfluous, dwelling only on that knowledge which is useful and solid, or at least necessary to unravel the false principles and sophistry of erroneous opinions. Thus he became a proficient in scholastic philosophy and theology. Whilst he referred all his studies to the divine honour and his own sanctification, he was careful not to lose the end in the means or to let his application degenerate into dissipation of mind and idle curiosity. Not content to make his studies a continuation of prayer, he devoted to formal prayer a great part of his time, knowing this to be the key of all spiritual life. For only the Spirit of God, as St Paul teaches, can lead us into the secrets and designs of God, and engrave His teachings on our hearts. Such was the innocence and purity in which Brother Bonaventure lived, that Alexander of Hales used to say of him that he " seemed not to have sinned in Adam ". A remarkable cheerfulness always appeared in his countenance, which resulted from the inward peace of his soul, for as he himself says, " A spiritual joy is the greatest sign of the divine grace dwelling in a soul ".

He had no eyes to see anything in himself but faults and imperfections, and this humility sometimes withheld him from holy communion, notwithstanding the desire of his soul to be united to the object of his love and to approach the fountain of grace. But God by a miracle overcame his fears. " Several days had passed ", say the acts of his canonization, " nor durst he yet presume to present himself at the heavenly banquet. But whilst he was assisting at Mass, and meditating on the passion of Jesus Christ, our Saviour, to crown his humility and love, put into his mouth by the ministry of an angel part of the consecrated Host, taken from the hand of the priest." From this time his communions were without scruple and sources of great joy and grace. Bonaventure prepared himself to receive the priesthood by long fasts and fervent prayer, that he might obtain an abundant measure of grace for that sacred dignity which he looked forward to with fear and trembling, so high and incomprehensible did it appear to him. A prayer which he composed for his own use after Mass, beginning with the words, *Transfige dulcissime Domine Iesu*, " Pierce, dearest Lord Jesus, the inmost depths . . ." is recommended by the Church to us all at that most solemn time.

Bonaventure was called by the obligations of his priestly character to labour for the salvation of his neighbour, and to this he devoted himself with enthusiasm. He announced the word of God to the people with an energy which kindled a flame in the hearts of those that heard him ; everything was burning with love that came from his mouth. While at the University of Paris he produced one of the best-known of his written works, the *Commentary on the Sentences* of Peter Lombard, which covers the whole field of scholastic theology. Of it Pope Sixtus IV said that " he uttered such things on sacred science that the Holy Ghost would seem to have spoken by his mouth ". The years of his public lecturing at Paris were greatly disturbed by the attack made on the mendicant friars by the other professors at the university. Jealousy of their pastoral and academical success and the standing reproof to worldliness and ease of the friars' lives were in part behind this attempt to get them excluded from the schools. The leader of the secular party was William of Saint-Amour, who made a bitter onslaught on the mendicants in a book called *The Perils of the Last Times*, and other writings. Bonaventure, who had to suspend lecturing for a time, replied in a treatise on evangelical poverty, named *Concerning the Poverty of Christ*. The pope, Alexander IV, appointed a commission of cardinals to go into the matter at Anagni, and on their findings ordered Saint-Amour's book to be burnt, vindicated and reinstated the friars, and ordered the offenders to withdraw their attack. A year later, in 1257, St Bonaventure and St Thomas Aquinas received the degree of doctor of theology together.

For Blessed Isabella, St Louis IX's sister, and her nunnery of Poor Clares at Longchamps, St Bonaventure wrote *Concerning Perfection of Life*. Other mystical works of his are the *Soliloquy* and *Concerning the Threefold Way*. The love which every word breathes in the writings of this doctor pierces the heart, and Gerson, the learned and devout chancellor of the University of Paris, writes of his works, " Among all the Catholic doctors Eustachius (for so we may translate his name of Bonaventure) seems to me the best for enlightening the understanding and at the same time warming the heart. In particular his *Breviloquium* and *Itinerarium mentis in Deum* are written with so much force, art and conciseness that nothing can be beyond them." In another book he says : " Bonaventure's works seem to me most suitable for the instruction of the faithful. They are solid, safe and devout ; and he keeps as far as he can from niceties, not meddling with logical or physical questions which are foreign to the matter in hand. Nor is there any doctrine more sublime, more divine, or more conducive to religion." Trithemius, a learned Benedictine, writes, " Whoever would be both learned and devout, let him read the works of Bonaventure ". This is particularly to be understood of his spiritual treatises. The joys of Heaven were the frequent meditation of his soul, and he endeavoured by his writings to excite in others the same fervent desire for our heavenly country. He writes that " God Himself, all the glorious spirits, and the whole family of the eternal King wait for us and desire that we should be with them ; and shall not we long above all things to be admitted into their happy company ? He who had not in this valley of tears continually raised his soul above visible things to become already, in ardent desire, an inhabitant of those blessed regions, would be considerably abashed upon appearing amongst them." Bonaventure puts the perfection of Christian virtue, not so much in the more heroic life of a religious state, as in performing our ordinary actions well. " The perfection of a religious man ", he says, " is to do common things in a perfect manner. A constant fidelity in small things is a great and heroic virtue." It is a continual crucifixion of self-love, a complete sacrifice of all our actions, moments and affections, and the reign of God's grace throughout our whole lives ; St Bonaventure's deep appreciation of this is illustrated by an anecdote related of him and Bd Giles of Assisi (April 23).

In 1257 Bonaventure was chosen minister general of the Friars Minor. He was not yet thirty-six years old, and the order was torn by dissensions, some of the friars being for an inflexible severity, others demanding certain mitigations of the rule ; between the two extremes were a number of other interpretations. Some of the extreme rigorists, the so-called Spirituals, had even fallen into error and disobedience, and thus given a handle to the friars' opponents in the Paris dispute. The new minister general wrote a letter to his provincials in which he made it clear that he required a disciplined observance of the rule, involving a reformation of the relaxed, but giving no countenance to the excesses of the Spirituals. At Narbonne in 1260, the first of the five general chapters which he held, he produced a set of constitutions on the rule, which were adopted and had a permanent effect on Franciscan life, but they failed to pacify the excessive rigorists. At the request of the friars assembled in this chapter, he undertook to write the life of St Francis, which he compiled with a spirit which shows him to have been filled with the virtues of the founder whose life he wrote. St Thomas Aquinas, coming one day whilst he was employed in this work, saw him through the door of his cell in contemplation, and going away, said, " Let us leave a saint to work for a saint ". The resulting biography, the " Greater Legend ", is a work of great value for the life of St Francis ; but St Bonaventure can hardly be acquitted of a tendency sometimes to strain his material so as to tell against those who favoured a moderation of the strict Franciscan life. He governed his order for seventeen years and has been justly called its second founder.

In 1265 Pope Clement IV nominated St Bonaventure to be archbishop of York in succession to Geoffrey of Ludham ; he induced the pope to accept his refusal, but in 1273 Bd Gregory X created him cardinal-bishop of Albano, adding a command to accept that charge without alleging any pretext against it, and immediately to come to Rome. He sent legates to meet him on the road with the hat and other insignia of the office, and it is said that they found the saint in a convent of his order in the Mugello near Florence, washing the dishes. He desired them to hang the cardinal's hat on the bough of a tree, because he could not decently take it in his greasy hands, and left them to walk in the garden till he had finished his work. Then taking up the hat he went to the legates, and paid them the respect due.

Gregory X ordered him to prepare the matters to be dealt with in the general council which he had called to meet at Lyons for the reunion of the Greeks, the Emperor Michael Palaeologus having made proposals to Pope Clement IV for union. All the best theologians were sent for : St Thomas Aquinas died on the way thither. But St Bonaventure was the outstanding figure in this great assembly.

He arrived with the pope some months before it began, and between the second and third sessions he held his last general chapter of his order, in which he abdicated the office of minister general.   When the Greek delegates arrived he conferred with them, and the reunion with Rome was duly effected.   In thanksgiving the pope sang Mass on the feast of SS. Peter and Paul, and the epistle, gospel and creed were sung first in Latin then in Greek; St Bonaventure preached.   But amidst all this triumph, on the night of July 14–15, the Seraphic Doctor died; his mortal eyes were spared the pain of seeing Constantinople speedily repudiate the union it had sought and he had laboured to make good.   Peter of Tarentaise, a Dominican friar, afterwards Pope Innocent V, preached his panegyric, in which he said : " No one ever beheld Bonaventure who did not conceive a great regard and affection for him ; and even strangers were desirous to follow his counsel and advice, simply from hearing him speak : for he was gentle, courteous, humble, pleasing to all, compassionate, prudent, chaste and adorned with all virtues."

There is a story told that when St Bonaventure, as minister general, visited the friary of Foligno there was a certain friar who wished to talk with him, but his humility and shyness would not allow him to force himself on his superior's notice. When, however, Bonaventure had gone, and the friar realized that he had missed his chance, he plucked up courage, pursued the general down the road, and catching him up, begged for a few words alone.   The saint at once withdrew with him to the roadside, and their conversation was a long one.   When at length the friar had returned home, comforted and rejoicing, Bonaventure noticed signs of impatience among those waiting for him.   He smiled and gently rebuked them.   " My brethren ", he said, " I could not do otherwise.   I am at the same time both prelate and servant, and that poor brother is both my brother and my master.   These are the words of the rule : ' The ministers shall receive the brethren with charity and kindness, and so hold themselves towards them that the brethren shall be able to treat with them as masters with their servants, for the ministers must be the servants of all the friars.'   And so I, as minister and servant, must be at the disposal of this poor brother who is my master, and help him according to my ability and his needs ".   In this spirit did he discharge the office which he had taken up with the words, " I well know my own incapacity, but I also know that it is hard to kick against the goad.   And so, in spite of my want of understanding, my inexperience in affairs, and my great unwillingness, I will not persist in opposition to the wish of a numerous family and the order of the supreme pontiff, for fear lest at the same time I should resist the will of God.   Therefore I take upon my weak shoulders a heavy, nay, an almost intolerable, burden.   I hope for help from Heaven and count on all the help your good-will can give me."   In those two passages is Bonaventure the saint, simply humble and simply charitable.   Had he never been a member of the Seraphic order he would still deserve the title of Seraphic Doctor because of the angelic virtues with which he adorned his learning.   He was declared a doctor of the Church in 1588, having been canonized in 1482.

There is no formal contemporary or quasi-contemporary life of St Bonaventure, but there are abundant references to him in the chronicles of the Franciscan Order and in other early sources.   The most important notices of this kind, extracted *e.g.* from Salimbene, Bernard of Besse, Angelo Clareno, " the Chronicle of the XXIV Generals ", etc., have been carefully re-edited in vol. x of the monumental Quaracchi edition of the works of the Seraphic Doctor.   The text of the canonization process instituted at Lyons in 1479–1480 (the canonization itself only took place in 1482 under Sixtus IV) has been printed in *Miscellanea*

Francescana di storia, di lettere, di arti, vols. xvii and xviii (1916 and 1917), but it deals mainly with miracles. Of the numerous modern biographies, the most reliable seems to be that of L. Lemmens as published in an Italian version at Milan in 1921. In this edition the original German text (1909) has been extensively revised in deference to criticisms, notably those made in the *Archivum Franciscanum Historicum* (vol. iii, pp. 344–348). The life written in Italian by D. M. Sparacio (1921) emphasizes the point of view of the Conventual Franciscans and is not free from a certain animus. Similarly that of Leonard de Carvalho e Castro (1923, in French), though admirably presented, rather minimizes the active part taken by St Bonaventure at Paris in opposition to Dominican teaching. On the other hand this theological combativeness of the great Franciscan is somewhat exaggerated by the Capuchin Father Jules d'Albi in his book, *S. Bonaventure et les luttes doctrinales de 1267–1277* (1923). An important study of the chronology of St Bonaventure, 1257 to 1274, by P. Glorieux, in the *Archivum Franciscanum Historicum* (vol. xix, pp. 145–168), seems to leave little room for the contention of A. G. Little in the same volume (pp. 289–291) that the Seraphic Doctor visited Oxford towards the close of the year 1259. Finally mention should be made of two other biographies in French, that of E. Clop (1922) and E. Gilson (1927), as also of the excellent appreciation of St Bonaventure in P. Gratien, *Histoire de la fondation et de l'évolution de l'Ordre des Frères Mineurs . . .* (1928), pp. 249–333. A good bibliography is provided in the work last named, as also in DTC. See also É. Longpré in DHG., t. ix, cc. 741–788, and in *Dictionnaire de spiritualité,* t. i, cc. 1768–1843. Bonaventure's *Breviloquium,* a concise summary of his teaching, was translated into English in 1946.

ST DEUSDEDIT, ARCHBISHOP OF CANTERBURY   (A.D. 664)

WHEN St Honorius, the last of the companions of St Augustine to govern the church of Canterbury, died in 653, he was succeeded as sixth archbishop by Frithona, who took the name of Deusdedit. He came from the territory of the South Saxons and was the first Englishman to become primate ; he was consecrated by St Ithamar, the first English bishop of Rochester. Of his life or the events of his episcopate nothing is known. He consecrated Ithamar's successor at Rochester, but the two or three other official acts attributed to him are very uncertain. He died during the plague, probably on October 28, 664, and was buried in the abbey-church of SS. Peter and Paul, outside the walls of Canterbury.

See Plummer's edition of Bede's *Historia Ecclesiastica,* text and notes ; a life by Goscelin (see Hardy, *Catalogue,* vol. i, pp. 261–262) adds nothing to Bede " but declamation or inference ".

ST MARCHELM   (*c.* A.D. 762)

MARCHELM (Marceaumes, Marculf, Marcellinus) was one of several young Englishmen who in the early part of the eighth century followed St Willibrord into Holland to evangelize the Frisians. The statement in the forged life of St Suitbert (professedly written by Marchelm) that he was one of the eleven original companions of that great missionary is not credible. He was put at the disposition of St Gregory of Utrecht, and accompanied him and St Boniface to Rome. For fifteen years he laboured in Friesland and Guelderland, making converts by the force of his preaching and his example. After the martyrdom of St Boniface the district of Utrecht was put under the administration of St Gregory, and he chose Marchelm to join St Lebuin, newly come from England, in working among the barbarians of Overyssel. Before long he had built the first church at Deventer, and he was so successful that the more stubborn of the pagans burned down the church and scattered the Christians. St Marchelm continued his mission undismayed, but God shortly after called him to his reward. He died at Oldenzaal and his relics were afterwards translated to Deventer; his feast is kept in Holland, and in England and elsewhere by the Canons Regular of the Lateran.

There is considerable uncertainty about this saint; but see the *Acta Sanctorum*, July, vol. iii, and Mabillon, *Annales O.S.B.*, vol. ii.

ST ULRIC OF ZELL, Abbot   (A.D. 1093)

ULRIC was born at Ratisbon about the year 1020, and went to court, where he was a page to the Empress Agnes.   But he had no ambition for a secular career, and after a time was received by his uncle Notker, Bishop of Freising.   When he was ordained to the diaconate he was appointed archdeacon and provost of the cathedral. In this office he distinguished himself by the care with which he provided for the proper celebration of divine worship within the cathedral and for the cure of souls without.   No one appealed to his charity in vain, and in a time of distress he distributed his fortune lavishly to the sufferers.   After going on pilgrimage to Rome and to Jerusalem, finding his office had been given to another, he decided to become a monk.   He therefore went to Cluny and there received the habit from St Hugh himself in 1052.

Soon after he had been professed and ordained he was appointed chaplain to the nuns at Marcigny, having already been confessor at Cluny.   These early responsibilities were the cause of jealousy among some unworthy brethren, to which trial were added violent headaches and no less violent temptations.   Ulric bore these with patience and without reproach, but when he lost the use of an eye he resigned his office and returned to Cluny.   But his talents were required elsewhere, and he was sent to found a priory on the Rüggersberg and worked with great success for the conversion of sinners in the canton of Bern until he came into collision with the bishop of Lausanne, Burchard, who was supporting teh Emperor Henry IV against the Holy See.   Thereupon he was recalled to Cluny and ordered to start a new foundation at Grüningen, near Breisach.   He found the place unsuitable for a monastery and carried out the work instead at Zell, in the Black Forest.   Here he was more fortunate in his bishop, Gebhard of Basle, who appreciated Ulric and seconded him in all his good works.   This included the establishment of a monastery of nuns at Bollschweil, near Zell; it was at their prayers that he was enabled miraculously to cure a young girl of cancer.

To advance the monastic life, and the monastic life in all its rigour, was the work of St Ulric.   When one of his monks found him in tears and asked the reason, he was told, " I weep for my sins.   I weep to find myself still not called to the happiness of the heavenly kingdom.   But I weep most of all because I see there are several monks here who have only the name and dress of religious."   He wrote down in three books the constitutions and customs of the abbey of Cluny, and it was on this recension that his friend Bd William based the observance of his abbey at Hirschau.   St Ulric died on July 10, 1093, after having been totally blind for the last two years of his life.

There is a good deal of information available concerning St Ulric of Zell, though the earliest text of his life has only come down to us in a fragmentary condition.   It is edited in MGH., *Scriptores*, vol. xii.   On the other hand a second life, which seems to be older than the year 1120, was also written, and this latter has been printed by Mabillon, as also by the Bollandists under July 10, this being the day upon which his feast was kept among the Cluniac monks.   See also F. Hauviller, *Ulrich von Cluny* (1896); Ratzinger, *Forschungen zur bayerischen Geschichte* (1898), pp. 577 *seq.* ; and P. Schmitz, *Histoire de l'Ordre de St Benoît* (1942), t. i.

BD HROZNATA, Martyr   (A.D. 1217)

HROZNATA was one of those men the course of whose blameless life was changed by a succession of misfortunes.   He was a nobleman at the court of Ottokar I of Bohemia, happily married, with an heir for whom he had great affection, and enjoying the prospect of an honourable and prosperous career.   But when he was still only about thirty years of age his young son sickened and died, and was followed to the grave shortly after by his mother.   Hroznata was overcome ; left the court ; and made a vow to become a crusader and go to the Holy Land.   But he changed his mind, going to Rome to get released from his vow, which Pope Celestine III commuted for the foundation of a monastery.   He therefore found a suitable site and built the abbey of Tepl, in western Bavaria, which he peopled with canons regular of Prémontré from Strahov, and founded two other religious houses, one to shelter his sister, who had been left a widow.   These undertakings having been successfully carried through, Hroznata himself became a canon of Tepl.   But the presence of the founder in the house, and under an abbot who was shallow and unimaginative, soon led to trouble and a position of such discomfort that Hroznata left for a time, and only returned when the abbot had apologized and promised to amend his ways.   The death of Hroznata is alleged to have been due to his defence of ecclesiastical immunities, and he is venerated as a martyr : for he was kidnapped, thrown into a dungeon at Alt-Kinsburg, near Eger, and there left to die.

Premonstratensian canons still live in the abbey of Tepl, where the body of their founder is preserved.   His *cultus* was confirmed in 1897.

An account of his life, including a short Latin contemporary biography, is printed in the *Acta Sanctorum*, July, vol. iii.   The official *confirmatio cultus* will be found in the *Analecta Ecclesiastica*, vol. v (1897), pp. 452–453.   See also *Zum 700 jahrigen Todestage des sl. Hroznata* (1917).

BD BONIFACE OF SAVOY, Archbishop of Canterbury   (A.D. 1270)

BONIFACE OF SAVOY, the forty-sixth archbishop of Canterbury, was a member of the ducal family of Savoy and the grandson of Bd Humbert of Savoy.   Remarkable for his physical beauty, which gained for him the nickname of " the Absalom of Savoy ", he was said to be one of the most accomplished noblemen of his time— although the English chronicler Wykes describes him as " not very learned ".   At an early age he entered the Grande Chartreuse near Grenoble, desiring to give himself up to prayer and study ; but before he had completed his noviciate he was compelled, much against his will, to become prior of Mantua.   When still only a subdeacon he was appointed administrator of the diocese of Belley in Burgundy, and seven years later of Valence.

In 1241 St Edmund, Archbishop of Canterbury, died, and Boniface, who was the uncle of Queen Eleanor, the consort of King Henry III, was elected through her influence.   Owing to the unexpected deaths of two popes the election could not be confirmed until 1243, and it was not until the following year that the new archbishop went to England for the first time.   He found his see heavily in debt owing to the sequestration of its revenues during the primacy of St Edmund, and his first action was to effect economies in every possible direction.   Sinecures and unnecessary offices were abolished, and the clergy and tenants were ordered to contribute towards the paying off of the debt. Those, however, who attempt to curtail expenses and to attack vested interests are always unpopular, and Boniface was no exception to the rule. In 1244 he had set out for the Council of Lyons, at which he was consecrated bishop.

Upon his return to England he was enthroned at Canterbury, and soon afterwards started upon a visitation of his diocese, correcting abuses and levying charges. As soon, however, as he attempted to visit the dioceses of his suffragans, he encountered determined opposition. The dean and chapter of St Paul's in London raised the contention that the bishop of London, and no one else, was their visitor. At the priory of St Bartholomew the Great which Boniface visited the following day, he was met by the sub-prior and the canons, who expressed their willingness to receive him as a prelate, but not as a visitor. They declared that they were under the jurisdiction of their own bishop, without whose permission they were not disposed to submit to anyone else. The indignant archbishop is said to have struck the sub-prior a blow which felled him to the ground, and this was the signal for a general scuffle. The archbishop's clothes were torn, and it was noted against him that he wore chain-mail under his clerical garb. Rescued by his bodyguard, he escaped by barge to Lambeth, where he excommunicated the bishop of London and the clergy of St Bartholomew's. As soon as he announced his intention of holding a visitation at Saint Albans, the suffragans met together and decided to make resistance, whilst the clergy of the diocese taxed themselves in order to institute proceedings against him at Rome. Apprised of their intention and resolved to be beforehand, Boniface set out for the curia to make a counter-appeal, in which he was only partly successful. Pope Innocent IV indeed allowed him to continue his visitations, but subject to great restrictions, and he was compelled to withdraw the excommunications which he had launched.

King Henry held Boniface in esteem : on one occasion he appointed him regent during his own absence, and on another he induced him to accompany him to France in order to assist him in delicate negotiations. In his own country he was more appreciated than by the English clergy, and when grave dissensions arose in Savoy during the minority of the successor of Amadeus IV, Boniface came to the rescue and restored harmony. He died at the castle of Sainte-Hélène des Millières when on a visit to his native land, and was buried with his ancestors at the Cistercian monastery of Hautecombe.

The character of Boniface has been variously estimated by English chroniclers, but none deny the purity of his life and his extraordinary goodness to the poor. It has been said of him by a modern writer that in the twenty-five years of his administration of the province of Canterbury he certainly did three good things—he paid off a debt of 22,000 marks, he built and endowed the hospital at Maidstone, and he constructed the great hall of the archiepiscopal palace. His *cultus*, which had long been general in Savoy, was approved by Gregory XVI at the instance of King Charles Albert in 1838, on the ground that honour had been paid him from time immemorial ; he is liturgically commemorated in Savoy, Sardinia and by the Carthusians.

For our information we are largely dependent upon the English contemporary chroniclers, most of them violently prejudiced against " imported prelates " and Henry III's foreign favourites ; but see also the letters of Grosseteste and Adam de Marisco. Amongst modern authorities Mgr Mann's *Lives of the Popes*, vols. xiv and xv, Cardinal Gasquet's *Henry III*, and Joseph Strickland's *Ricerche storiche sopra il B. Bonifacio di Savoia* should be consulted ; see also Fr Thurston in *The Tablet*, 1913, pp. 601–604 ; and M. Powicke, *The Thirteenth Century* (1953), *passim*.

BD HUMBERT OF ROMANS   (A.D. 1277)

HUMBERT was born at Romans, near Valence, about the year 1200, and went to Paris to study, where he took the degree of doctor of law, and in 1224 was clothed as a Dominican with the encouragement of his professor, Hugh of Saint-Cher. He was sent as lector to the house of his order at Lyons, of which he became prior, and in 1240 was elected provincial of the Roman province, after a pilgrimage to the Holy Land.   On the elevation of Hugh of Saint-Cher to the cardinalate he was elected provincial of France and held that office until he was in 1254 appointed fifth master general of the Order of Preachers.   He held ten general chapters and devoted himself to the encouragement of studies, to the final revision of the Dominican liturgy, and to the development of missions in the East.   This was a matter particularly near to his heart ; friars went to Barcelona to learn Arabic and missions were undertaken to the Cumans and Tartars.   The same interest is evinced in his writings, of which two were directed to encouraging a crusade against the Saracens and to discussing the question of the East in view of the second council of Lyons.   As a man of great charity, devotion, and rectitude himself, he had hard things to say about the need of reform among the clergy.   His spirit is shown in a joint pastoral which he wrote with Bd John of Parma, the Franciscan minister general, to the two orders in 1255 : " Just think, dearest brethren, with what sincerity and true friendship we ought to love one another, we whom our holy Mother the Church has brought forth together and who are together sent by Eternal Charity to work for the salvation of men.   How are the faithful to know us as the messengers of Christ if not by His mark of charity ?   And how can we hope to kindle this charity in their souls if it is weak and uncared for in our own ? "

At the general chapter held in London in 1263 he resigned from his generalate and retired to the priory of Valence, devoting himself to study and preaching. He came out of retirement at the order of Pope Clement IV to help in the settlement of domestic difficulties among the Cistercians, but went back to Valence and died there on July 14, 1277, revered by all as a man of great holiness, " sure in counsel ".

The early Dominican chronicles, such, for instance, as are printed in the *Monumenta O.P. Historica*, make frequent reference to Bd Humbert, but there is no text devoted to his individual life and work.   See, however, Mortier, *Maîtres Généraux O. P.*, vol. i, pp. 415–664; a short life by M. de Waresquiel (1901) ; and F. Heintke, *Humbert von Romans* (1933). Fr Berthier reprinted several of his ascetical tractates (1889), and Fr Bede Jarrett explains his moral and social teaching in *Social Theories of the Middle Ages* (1926).   Humbert's *Treatise on Preaching* is available in English (1951) ; his sermons were very popular during the middle ages and were more than once reprinted before the Reformation.   For a fuller bibliography see Taurisano's *Catalogus*.   Though called " Blessed " by some writers there has been no confirmation of *cultus*.

BD CASPAR DE BONO   (A.D. 1604)

CASPAR DE BONO was born at Valencia in Spain in the year 1530, of poor and un-distinguished parents.   When he grew up he went into the silk trade, but he was unsuccessful, so he gave it up and took to soldiering.   He already had a suspicion of where his true vocation lay, and he spent as much time in prayer and meditation as his duties would allow, and contrived by the grace of God and his own firm will to lead a virtuous life, which was certainly no easier to do in an army in the sixteenth century than in the twentieth. During the course of a battle he was badly wounded, and he made a vow that if he recovered he would join the Minims, the order of very austere and humble friars whose founder, St Francis of Paula, had been canonized a few years before Caspar's birth. This he accordingly did in 1560, and his superiors were so impressed by his virtues and ability that he was professed and ordained in the following year. Throughout his religious life he suffered acute bodily pain which he not only bore with patience and equanimity, but added to it by voluntary mortifications. He was twice elected corrector provincial of the Spanish province of his order, an office he filled with much efficiency, correcting, in accordance with its name, with prudence and charity and encouraging his brethren to an unmitigated observance of their penitential rule. He died in the friary at Valencia on July 14, 1604, and was beatified in 1786.

There is a modern life by Roberti (1904); and an older one by P. A. Miloni, who was postulator of the cause, written for the beatification.

15 : ST HENRY THE EMPEROR (A.D. 1024)

S T HENRY II was son of Henry, Duke of Bavaria, and Gisela of Burgundy, and was born in 972. He was educated by St Wolfgang, Bishop of Ratisbon, and in 995 succeeded his father in the duchy of Bavaria; in 1002, upon the death of his cousin Otto III, he was chosen emperor. He had always before his eyes the dangers to which those who move in places of power are exposed. He studied the extent and importance of the obligations which attended his dignity, and by prayer maintained in his heart the necessary spirit of humility and fear, and was able without being spoiled to bear the tide of prosperity and honour. He knew the end for which alone he was exalted by God to the highest temporal dignity, and worked his hardest to promote the peace and happiness of his realm. Nevertheless, Henry at times made use of the Church for political ends, in accordance with the imperial policy of his predecessor Otto the Great. He refused his support to ecclesiastical aggrandizement in temporal concerns, while maintaining the Church's proper authority; but some of his politics look equivocal when examined from the point of view of the welfare of Christendom.

He had to engage in numerous wars for the defence and consolidation of the empire, as for example in Italy, before he could receive that crown; Arduin of Ivrea had had himself crowned king at Milan, so the emperor crossed the Alps and drove him out. In 1014 he went in triumph to Rome, where he was crowned emperor by Pope Benedict VIII. Henry munificently repaired and restored the episcopal sees of Hildesheim, Magdeburg, Strasburg and Meersburg, and made benefactions to the churches of Aachen, Basle and others. It is sometimes mistakenly asserted that he brought about the conversion of St Stephen, King of Hungary, who in fact was born of Christian parents; but he promoted his endeavours for the conversion of his people. In 1006 Henry founded the see of Bamberg and built a great cathedral there, in order to solidify German power among the Wends. In this he was opposed by the bishops of Würzburg and Eichstätt, whose dioceses were thus dismembered, but Pope John XIX approved, and Benedict VIII consecrated the cathedral in 1020. Henry also built and endowed a monastery at Bamberg, and made foundations in several other places, that the divine honour and the relief of the poor might be provided for to the end of time. In 1021 the emperor again came to Italy, on an expedition against the Greeks in Apulia ; on his way back he was taken ill at Monte Cassino, where he was said to have been miraculously cured at the intercession of St Benedict, but he contracted a lameness which never left him.

Henry was attentive to the smallest affairs amidst the multiplicity of business which attends the government of the state, and whilst he was most active and vigilant in every duty which he owed to the public, he did not forget that the government of himself was his first obligation. He identified himself in time with those ideas of ecclesiastical reform which radiated from the great monastery of Cluny, and in support of them he even opposed himself to his kinsman, friend, and former chaplain, Aribo, whom he had appointed archbishop of Mainz and who in synod had condemned appeals to Rome without episcopal permission. It is a well-known story of Henry that, wishing to become a monk, he promised obedience to the abbot of Saint-Vanne at Verdun, whereupon the abbot put him under obedience to continue the administration of the empire. This and similar accounts of his ascetic practices do not entirely accord with what is known of his character and life ; Henry was one of the great rulers of the Holy Roman Empire, and triumphed precisely as a Christian statesman and soldier, whose ways were, in the nature of things, not those of the cloister. Edifying legends were invented about him by the Bambergers, and such a work as Adalbert's life of the emperor does not give us the real Henry. What we know of him is mostly a matter of general history ; unlike St Louis of France, St Henry II did not have a Joinville. He clearly promoted ecclesiastical reform, taking great care about episcopal appointments and supporting such great monks as St Odilo of Cluny and Richard of Saint-Vanne.

St Henry was canonized by Bd Eugenius III in 1146, and St Pius X declared him the patron of Benedictine oblates.

As the most important ruler in Europe at the beginning of the eleventh century, Henry was bound to fill a great place in the chronicles of the time, *e.g.* those of Raoul Glaber and Thietmar. But there are also two Latin biographies, attributed respectively to Adalbold, Bishop of Utrecht, and Adalbert, a deacon of Bamberg. These will be found in the *Acta Sanctorum*, July, vol. iii, and in MGH., *Scriptores*, vol. iv. The best life of St Henry from a religious point of view is that of H. Gunter, *Kaiser Heinrich der Heilige* (1904). For the part he took in secular history, Hauck, *Kirchengeschichte Deutschlands*, vol. iii, and the *Cambridge Medieval History*, vol. iii, may be consulted ; see also F. Dvornik, *The Making of Central and Eastern Europe* (1949), pp. 185–222. On St Henry's alleged " celibate marriage ", see the notice of St Cunegund, his wife, herein under March 3, and the bibliographical note thereto.

ST JAMES, BISHOP OF NISIBIS   (A.D. 338)

THIS is one of the cases in which all Alban Butler's diligence and learning could not save him from error, for it was not till long after his time that the life of St James of Nisibis received the critical study that it demanded ; accordingly he accorded several pages to an account of a saint about whom very little is in fact known.

That James was an important figure, venerated throughout the East from early times, is quite certain ; he is recognized liturgically in practically every Eastern church, and he is mentioned in the Hieronymian martyrology. He became the first bishop of Nisibis in Mesopotamia about the year 308, and St Ephraem, his disciple, refers to the importance of his services to that church, for which he built a great basilica and perhaps inaugurated its famous theological school. He was present at the Council of Nicaea in 325, and St Athanasius, the historian Theodoret and others record that he was an outstanding opponent of Arianism. (The Roman Martyrology refers to the fable that St James's prayers contributed to bring Arius to a shocking end at Constantinople.) When the Persian king, Sapor II, made his first attack on Nisibis in 338, the bishop was still alive, but there is good evidence that he died in the same year.

Butler remarks that St James's learning and writings have procured him a rank next to St Ephraem among the doctors of the Syrian church, and that the Armenians too honour him as a doctor; but it is now known that the writings formerly attributed to him are not his. He is named in the canon of the Syrian and Maronite Mass, and in the festal litany of the Chaldean.

It is only of recent years that the Bollandist, Father Paul Peeters, after a critical examination of all the sources, Greek, Latin and, more especially, Syriac and Armenian, has shown that the traditional story recounted in the original Butler's *Lives* is for the most part no better than a work of fiction, compiled out of elements borrowed from other hagiographical legends, particularly the Syriac Life of St Ephraem. To give details would be impossible here, but the whole case is made clear in the *Analecta Bollandiana*, vol. xxxviii (1920), pp. 285–373. See also DTC., t. viii, cc. 292–295.

ST BARHADBESABA, Martyr   (A.D. 355)

IN the year 340 the Church in Persia began to undergo one of the most intense persecutions that any body of Christians has suffered. In the fifteenth year of the persecution, by the command of Sapor Tamsapor, governor of Adiabene, Barhadbesaba, deacon of the city of Arbela, was apprehended and put on the rack. Whilst he was tormented, the officers continually cried out to him, " Worship fire and water, and eat the blood of beasts, and you shall be set at liberty ". But the deacon said to the judge, " Neither you nor your king nor any manner of suffering shall ever be able to separate me from the love of Jesus : Him alone have I served from my childhood to this old age." The tyrant condemned him to be beheaded, and commanded Aggai, an apostate Christian, to be his executioner. Barhadbesaba stood bound, waiting with joy for the moment which was to associate him with the angels ; but Aggai trembled so as not to be able to give the blow. He struck, however, seven times at the martyr's neck, and not being able to sever his head from his body, ran his sword into him. The judge set guards to watch the body, but two clerks carried it off in the night, and buried it.

See Assemani, *Acta martyrum orientalium*, pp. 129–130 ; and P. Peeters in *Analecta Bollandiana*, vol. xxvii (1908), p. 188, and xliii (1925), pp. 276, 279, 281. This martyr seems to be mentioned in the ancient Syriac martyrology under the form Barsabas, though he is by error included among the priests.

ST DONALD   (Eighth Century)

ALL that is recorded of this saint, whose name is so common in Scotland, is that he lived at Ogilvy in Forfarshire in the eighth century, that his wife bore him nine daughters, and that on her death they formed a sort of community who led the religious life under his direction. But if no more is known of him, he has nevertheless left his mark otherwise, for the often found natural features, wells, hills, and so on, which are known as the "Nine Maidens", are so called in memory of his daughters. They are said to have afterwards entered a monastery founded by St Darlugdach and St Brigid at Abernethy, and were commemorated on July 18. The popularity of the name in Scotland must be attributed, not to veneration for the saint, but to the ubiquity of the sons of Somerled of the Isles, Clan Donald.

See Forbes, KSS., pp. 324–325 ; and *cf.* what is said *ibid.* of St Mazota, pp. 395–396.

ST SWITHUN, Bishop of Winchester   (A.D. 862)

SWITHUN was born in Wessex at the end of the eighth century or beginning of the ninth, and passed his youth in the study of grammar, philosophy and the Holy Scriptures at the Old Monastery in Winchester, of which, however, he was probably never a member. Being ordained priest, his learning, piety and prudence moved Egbert, King of the West Saxons, to make him his chaplain, under which title the saint subscribed a charter granted to the abbey of Croyland in 833. That prince also committed to his care the education of his son Ethelwulf, and made use of his counsels in the government of his kingdom.

On the death of Egbert, Ethelwulf succeeded, and he governed his kingdom by the prudent advice of Aelfstan, Bishop of Sherborne, in temporal affairs, and of St Swithun in ecclesiastical matters, especially those which concerned his own soul. Bearing always the greatest reverence to Swithun, he procured him, upon the death of Helmstan, to be chosen bishop of Winchester, to which see he was consecrated by Ceolnoth, Archbishop of Canterbury, in 852. William of Malmesbury says that this good bishop was a treasury of all virtues, and those in which he took most delight were humility and charity to the poor ; in the discharge of his episcopal functions he omitted nothing belonging to a true pastor. He built several churches and repaired others ; and when he had to dedicate any church, he used to go barefoot to the place. He died on July 2, 862, and at his own request was buried in the churchyard, where his grave might be trodden by passers-by and the rain fall upon it.

But his feast is observed in the dioceses of Portsmouth and Southwark on July 15, on which date, over a hundred years after, his relics were taken up and translated into the church, which legend says was done in accordance with a vision of the saint granted to a poor labourer. Malmesbury affirms that a great number of miraculous cures of all kinds were wrought on this occasion. In the reign of William the Conqueror, Walkelin, Bishop of Winchester, laid the foundation of a new cathedral church, and on July 15, 1093, the shrine of St Swithun was translated from the old to the new church. Swithun is still in the memory of the English people by reason of the superstition that if it rains on his feast-day it will rain for forty days after, and the opposite. Many ingenious attempts have been made to explain this belief, but no one of them is convincing. Other saints elsewhere have the same story attaching to their day, for example, SS. Gervase and Protase, and St Medard in France and St Cewydd in Wales.

The scanty sources available for the life of St Swithun have been printed by the Bollandists in the *Acta Sanctorum*, July, vol. i, and in the *Analecta Bollandiana*, vol. iv, pp. 367–410, vol. vii, pp.373–380, and vol. lviii, pp. 187–196. There are also some fragments in Anglo-Saxon, for which see Earle, *Gloucester Fragments*, vol. i (1861), and G. H. Gerould in the periodical *Anglia*, vol. xx, pp. 347–357. Most of this material, particularly the account by Santfrid and the long Latin poem by Wolstan (ed. Alistair Campbell, 1951), deals only with the translation and miracles of the saint. For the little we know concerning his life we are indebted mainly to William of Malmesbury and Simeon of Durham. That a genuine *cultus* of Swithun existed in England is shown by the fact that, in contrast to many others commonly styled " saints ", his feast and translation day are entered in many of our native calendars. Churches were dedicated in his honour even in Scandinavia.

ST ATHANASIUS, BISHOP OF NAPLES   (A.D. 872)

THIS Athanasius became bishop of Naples about the year 850, when he was not yet twenty years old. He was a native of the city, of which his father had been *dux*, and took much trouble both for its material and moral improvement; he repaired or built anew the buildings overset and despoiled by the Saracens, founded a hospice for pilgrims and the aged, and set on foot a scheme for the ransom of Christians captured by the Mohammedans. In 863 he took part in the council at the Lateran, summoned by Pope St Nicholas I, whereat St Ignatius was declared to be lawful patriarch of Constantinople. But St Athanasius, having thus assisted the Father of Christendom to vindicate justice on behalf of a bishop oppressed by the civil power, became himself victim of a similar oppression. The dukedom of Naples had come into the hands of Sergius II, an ambitious and troublesome tyrant, whose private life was as unscrupulous as his public politics. On every count he was no friend of the good Athanasius, and his enmity was aggravated by the fact that the bishop was his uncle and so had personal as well as official right to call him to order : and he was not afraid to do so, but sharply rebuked his nephew for simoniacal dealings and other disorders. Thereupon, instigated by his wife, Sergius clapped Athanasius into jail at Sorrento. The indignation of the Neapolitans frightened him into setting him at liberty again, but he continued to pursue the bishop with threats and hampered his work in every possible way, so that in 871 Athanasius left Naples and installed himself on the Island of the Saviour nearby.

Here Sergius promised him peace and freedom from persecution if he would resign his see. When Athanasius refused he sent troops to bring him back by force, which they were prevented from doing by the intervention of the Western emperor, Louis II, who had the bishop taken in safety to Benevento by the duke of Amalfi. Sergius retorted by plundering the episcopal treasury at Naples and venting his anger on the bishop's supporters with such violence that the pope, Adrian II, excommunicated him. The Emperor Louis again took up the bishop's cause and was about to restore him to his see by the force of the imperial authority and strength, when death overtook St Athanasius at Veroli, near Monte Cassino, on July 15, 872.

Most of the relevant material may be found in the *Acta Sanctorum*, July, vol. iv, and also in MGH., *Scriptores rerum Langobardicarum*. It does not seem to be true that the expanded Life (BHL. 736) is a fabrication by Peter the Deacon of Monte Cassino, as has been maintained by E. Caspar in his monograph on Peter the Deacon's forgeries ; see on this the *Analecta Bollandiana*, vol. xxix (1910), p. 169.

ST EDITH OF POLESWORTH   (TENTH CENTURY ?)

FROM the conflicting references to St Edith of Polesworth it has sometimes been supposed that there were several English women thus styled, one of whom is mentioned in the lives of St Modwenna (July 6). Goscelin in his Life of St Edith of Wilton speaks of her holy aunt, Edith of Polesworth, sister of King Edgar ; while another suggestion is that she is that sister of King Athelstan, said to have been called Edith, who in 925 married Sihtric, the Viking king at York. He died in the following year ; and his widow, who seems to have had the repute of holiness, was eventually buried at Tamworth, only a few miles from Polesworth. On the whole she may be regarded as probably the one and only St Edith called " of Polesworth ".

These perplexities are set out in some detail by Stanton in his *Menology*, pp. 337–338. But *cf. Analecta Bollandiana*, vol. lvi (1938), p. 53, n. 4, and vol. lxv (1947), p. 315.

ST VLADIMIR OF KIEV (A.D. 1015)

THE earliest saints of Russia, princes and monks, were connected with Kiev in the south-west, " the God-protected mother of Russian cities ", now the capital of what we call The Ukraine and in those days centre of a principality whose Finnish-Slav people were ruled by princes of Scandinavian origin, Varangians, who as pirates and traders had penetrated into Russia by its waterways. During the last quarter of the tenth century the grand-prince of Kiev was Vladimir, a man not only reared in idolatry but one who freely indulged in the barbarous excesses that were available to one in his position : he was brutal and bloodthirsty, and a contemporary Arabian chronicler, ibn-Foslan, comments on his five wives and numerous female slaves, which supports the statement of the Chronicle of Nestor that Vladimir's " desire for women was too much for him ". The circumstances of this prince's conversion to Christianity have been and still are much debated, but converted he was, probably in the year 989, when he was about thirty-two ; and he then received in marriage Anne, daughter of the emperor Basil II at Constantinople—the two events were closely connected. And the conversion of the Russian people is dated from then.

The fact that pious writers have attributed perfect purity of motive to Vladimir, when undoubtedly he was moved in great measure by the prospect of political and economic advantages from an alliance with the Byzantines and the Christian Church, must not be allowed to obscure that, once having accepted Christianity, he is said to have been wholehearted in his adherence to it. He put away his former wives and mistresses and amended his life ; he had idols publicly thrown down and destroyed ; and he supported the Greek missionaries with energy and enthusiasm—indeed, with an excess of energy, for at times he did not stop short of " conversion " by force : to refuse baptism was to incur penalties. But quite apart from that sort of thing, the speed with which the Russians became Christian has been much exaggerated, and during the reign of Vladimir the new religion probably did not penetrate far beyond the Kievan nobility and wealthy merchants. Nor was its subsequent spreading so fast as has been represented : paganism gave ground but slowly. Nevertheless he was revered in after years not only because he was a sinner who repented but because he brought about the reconciliation of the Russian people with God, he was the Apostle of Russia, chosen from on high for that end.

" The Devil was overcome by fools and madmen ", says the Chronicle of Nestor, and emphasizes that St Vladimir received God's grace and forgiveness, while " many righteous and godly men strayed from the path of uprightness and perished ". And it would seem that his repentance and understanding of his new obligations were of that simple, straightforward kind which will forever remain at the heart of the most developed and complex Christianity : " When he had in a moment of passion fallen into sin he at once sought to make up for it by penitence and almsgiving ", says a chronicler. It is said that he even had scruples whether, now that he was a Christian, he was entitled to punish robbers or even murderers by putting them to death. Such ideas astonished the sophisticated Greek ecclesiastics, who appealed to examples in the Old Testament and Roman history to show that punishment of the wicked was the duty of a Christian prince. But Vladimir seems to have been only half convinced.

The circumstances of Vladimir's conversion brought his people within the Byzantine patriarchate, but he was not particularist. He exchanged ambassadors with the apostolic court of Rome; he helped the German bishop St Boniface (Bruno) of Querfurt in his mission to the Pechenegs; and he even borrowed certain canonical features from the West, notably the institution of tithes, which were unknown to the Byzantines. Not till the Mongol invasions was Christian Russia cut off from the West.

St Vladimir died in 1015, after, as is said, giving away all his personal belongings to his friends and to the poor. His feast is solemnly celebrated by the Russians, Ukrainians and others.

The original Russian sources are indicated in some detail in the bibliography of vol. iv of the *Cambridge Medieval History*, pp. 819–821. The Chronicle of Nestor has been translated by S. H. Cross, *The Russian Primary Chronicle* (1930). See N. de Baumgarten, *Orientalia Christiana*, vol. xxiv, no. i, 1931 (*Olaf Tryggwison* . . .) and vol. xxvii, no. i, 1932 (*St Vladimir* . . .); G. Fedotov, " Le baptême de St. Vladimir . . ." in *Irénikon*, t. xv (1938), pp. 417 *seq.* ; M. Jugie, " Les origines romaines de l'Église russe " in *Échos d'Orient*, no. 187 (1937). Summaries in Fliche and Martin, *Histoire de l'Église*, vol. vii, pp. 444-451, and DTC., s.v. Russie. For Christians before Vladimir, see also M. de Taube, *Rome et la Russie* . . ., vol. i (1947). And see F. Dvornik, *The Making of Central and Eastern Europe* (1949), pp. 170 *seq.*

ST DAVID OF MUNKTORP, Bishop   (*c.* A.D. 1080)

This David is said to have been an English monk who had a passionate desire to give his life for Christ by martyrdom. When he heard of the death at the hands of the heathen of St Sigfrid's three nephews, he offered himself to the English mission in Sweden which was trying to rebuild the spoiled work of St Anskar. He came to St Sigfrid, who was bishop at Växiö, and was sent to Västmanland; here he laboured for the conversion of the people, and to help in the work established a monastery, whence the place was afterwards known as Munktorp. He gave himself whole-heartedly to his mission, with great success; he received the gift of miracles and the even more valuable gift of tears—but the grace of martyrdom for which he longed was denied him. He lived instead to a considerable age and died peacefully, his sanctity being again confirmed by miracles at his tomb. David is commonly said to have been the first bishop of Västeras, and is one of the saints of whom it was told that he hung a garment on a sunbeam— in this case, his gloves. Davö, where he lived for a time, gets its name from St David.

There is a short life printed in the *Scriptores rerum Suecicarum*, vol. ii, pt. 1, pp. 408–411. See also C. J. A. Oppermann, *English Missionaries in Sweden* (1937), pp. 112–117; and *cf.* the note to St Sigfrid, under February 15 herein.

BD BERNARD OF BADEN   (A.D. 1458)

Among the descendants of Herman von Zähringen, who gave up the margravate of Baden to become a Cluniac monk, was the Margrave James I, who was known in his day as " the Solomon of Germany "; he married Catherine, the daughter of Charles II of Lorraine and Margaret of Bavaria, and to them was born a son Bernard, about the year 1429. He turned out a brilliant young man, with a taste both for letters and for soldiering, but he refused to betroth himself to the daughter of the King of France; and when his father died in 1453 he turned his responsibilities and rights as margrave over to his brother Charles and went from court to court of Europe trying to stir up their sovereigns to a crusade against the Turks, who on May 29, 1453 had captured Constantinople. Bernard set out for Rome to get the support of Pope Callistus III, but just after leaving Turin he was attacked by the plague and died in the Franciscan monastery at Moncalieri, being less than thirty years old. On account of his great reputation for sanctity, supported by miracles reported at his tomb, he was beatified in 1479 by Pope Sixtus IV, in the presence of his mother and brothers.

There is some account in the *Acta Sanctorum*, July, vol. iv; and a fuller biography by O. Ringholz (1892), who prints the contemporary attestations of a number of miracles submitted in the process of beatification; an abridgement of this appeared in 1907. Two, more popular, small lives by J. Franck and H. Mohr were published in 1929, the fifth centenary of Bernard's birth.

BB. IGNATIUS AZEVEDO AND HIS COMPANIONS, MARTYRS   (A.D. 1570)

IGNATIUS AZEVEDO came from a family of wealth and rank on both his father's and mother's side; he was born at Oporto in 1528, and joined the Society of Jesus when he was twenty. He proved to be a model novice, except that his physical mortifications made him so thin that the Portuguese provincial Father Simon Rodriguez had to remonstrate with him. When he was still only twenty-five he was made rector of the college of St Antony at Lisbon. Here he did not confine himself to the strict limits of his official duties, but was active in every good work; it is recorded that on one occasion he personally tended three men in such advanced stages of some loathsome disease that the ordinary hospitallers would not touch them: and by caring for their bodies he converted their souls. With a brief interval as vice-provincial of Portugal, Father Azevedo persevered in this office for ten years, and was then removed to a similar post at the college in Braga founded by the famous Dominican archbishop Bartholomew Fernandez (" a Martyribus ").

All this time he had been beset by a desire—kindled by a Japanese student at Lisbon—to preach the gospel to the heathen; and at length, in 1566, he was appointed to go to Brazil as visitor, to inspect and advise on the Jesuit missions there. He was away on this commission for two years; the first missionaries had landed in Brazil only seventeen years previously, but the Jesuits had already established residences among several of the cannibal tribes of that huge country. On his return to Rome he recommended to St Francis Borgia that more missionaries be sent out there, and the general ordered him to select suitable subjects for the work from the Spanish and Portuguese provinces and to go with them to Brazil as their superior. The band which Father Azevedo enlisted set out on June 5, 1570. The superior and thirty-nine (at first forty-two) others of the party were on a merchant vessel, the *Santiago*, and the others on one of a squadron of men-o'-war going out under the command of Dom Luis Vasconcelos, governor of Brazil.

They reached Madeira, and here Vasconcelos decided to stop for a time in order to get the advantage of more favourable winds; the master of the *Santiago*,

however, intended to continue the voyage to the Canaries.   This put Father
Azevedo into a quandary.   There was no room for the rest of the Jesuits on the
other warships ; but if he went on he would not have them under his care and there
was very grave danger from pirates.   However, he decided to proceed with his
ship, but seems to have had a premonition of what would happen, for before leaving
Madeira he delivered a stirring address on the glory of martyrdom, and warned
his own party of their danger.

When within a few miles of her destination the *Santiago* was overtaken by a
French privateer, commanded by James Soury, an implacable Huguenot, who
directly he heard of the convoy of Jesuits going to Brazil had set out in chase from
La Rochelle.   The *Santiago* put up a good fight, and the missionaries helped in
every possible way, short of actually bearing arms and shedding blood ; after she
was boarded there was a fierce hand-to-hand struggle, but on the death of her
captain she was constrained to strike her flag.   Thereupon Soury demonstrated
his hatred of the Catholic religion by sparing the remainder of the crew and
passengers but ordering the death of the missionaries.   Bd Ignatius and his thirty-
nine companions were then and there brutally massacred in cold blood, meeting
their death with heroism and joy ; their leader was thrown into the sea clasping
a picture of our Lady given to him by Pope St Pius V.   Of these martyrs nine
were Spaniards and the rest Portuguese.   Several contemporary revelations of
this massacre were reported, of which the chief were to Bd Ignatius's brother,
Don Jerome, in the East Indies, and to St Teresa at Avila, whose kinsman, BD
FRANCIS GODOY, was among the martyrs.   Their beatification took place in 1854.

A popular account may be found in the small volumes by Father Cordara in Italian
and by Father de Beauvais in French in 1854.   See also Astrain, *Historia de la Compañia
de Jesús en la Asistencia de España*, vol. ii, p. 244 ; and J. Brodrick, *The Progress of the Jesuits*
(1946), pp. 220–230.   For bibliography, De Guilhermy, *Ménologe de Portugal*, vol. ii,
pp. 39–43.

ST POMPILIO PIRROTTI   (A.D. 1756)

POMPILIO MARY PIRROTTI was born in 1710 of a good family at Montecalvo in
Campania.   He had a good education, and struck by the need of schools, especially
among the poor, he decided to give his life to teaching.   He therefore joined the
clerks regular of the Religious Schools (" Piarists " or *Scolopini*), founded by St
Joseph Calasanctius for that work, and was professed in 1728, taking the name of
Mary-of-St-Nicholas.   He was ordained, and taught for some years in Apulia, and
then on account of his sanctity and enthusiasm was appointed missioner apostolic
in Emilia and Venetia.   At Naples his zeal got him into trouble, and a campaign
of slander and persecution was worked up against him by those who feared his
influence or were jealous of his success.   He was expelled from Naples, but such
was the indignation of the people that the king had to revoke the decree of banishment.   St Pompilio continued his work with a splendid patience, until his superiors
recalled him to the house of his order at Campo, near Lecce, where he died at the
age of forty-six.   Ferdinand II, King of the Two Sicilies, took a keen interest
in the cause of his beatification, which was achieved in 1890, and he was canonized
in 1934.

See Seeböck, *Die Herrlichkeit der Katholischen Kirche in ihren Heiligen und Seligen des
19 Jahrhunderts* (1900), p. 431 ; Heimbucher, *Die Orden und Kongregationen*, vol. iii ; and
the *Acta Apostolicae Sedis*, vol. xxvii (1935), pp. 223–234.

BD ANNE MARY JAVOUHEY, Virgin, Foundress of the Congregation of St Joseph of Cluny　　(A.D. 1851)

Of the many remarkable women beatified or canonized during the second quarter of the twentieth century one of the most outstanding was Anne Mary Javouhey. She was born in 1779 at Jallanges in Burgundy, where her father was a well-to-do farmer, and she early showed the forcefulness of her character : though the fifth of a large family she dominated the rest of the children. Another characteristic that soon showed itself was courage, and during the revolution she often helped clergy and others at no little risk. It was at a Mass celebrated secretly in the house in 1798 that Nanette (as she was commonly called) made a vow of celibacy, together with a promise to devote her life to the education of children and help of the poor.

When religious communities were again allowed in France Nanette joined the Sisters of Charity at Besançon. But she had no vocation there. She went to the Cistercian nuns at Val-Sainte in Switzerland, with a like result. But here she was directed by a well-known monk, Dom Augustine Lestrange (he introduced the Cistercians into the United States), who told her that her vocation was to found a new congregation. Nanette had told him of her vision at Besançon of a room full of coloured boys and girls, and the voice which said to her, " These are the children God gives you. I am Teresa, and I will look after your congregation." So she returned to France, and Javouhey *père*, who alternated between opposition and a generous help of his daughter, set her up with rooms at Chamblanc where she and her three sisters could start a school. When Pope Pius VII passed through Chalon in 1805 he received the four young women and gave them every encouragement. Two years later Anne, her sisters and five others were clothed in a blue and black habit by the Bishop of Autun. Other schools and establishments were soon in demand, and in 1812 Mr Javouhey bought a former Franciscan friary at Cluny to be the novitiate and mother-house of the enterprise.

A school was opened in Paris, where Mother Javouhey's educational methods excited comment, favourable and other, and brought her to the notice of the government.* The governor of the island of Bourbon (now Réunion, east of Madagascar) asked her to send some sisters there, and in September 1817 their first missionary school for coloured children was begun. This led to similar requests from elsewhere, and Mother Javouhey herself spent two years in Senegal, extending her work to Gambia and Sierra Leone to take over hospitals for the British authorities. She supervised the inauguration of a large plantation for Africans up the Senegal river, and carried through a scheme for educating Senegalese in France for the priesthood. This last undertaking had eventually to be abandoned, and it was said with reference to it that " Mother Javouhey was before her time ". The truth is just the opposite. Establishment of a " native clergy " is no new policy of twentieth-century popes, but a return to the earlier and normal practice of the Church in mission lands.

With the passing of time Nanette's youthful forcefulness became inflexible determination, and a girl's pluck became adult fortitude in an heroic degree. To these were added a clear and receptive mind and intellectual ability. Those qualities have their dangers, even for a fervent religious ; but they were balanced

* She owed something to the work of Joseph Lancaster (d. 1838), one of the founders of the British and Foreign School Society.

by a simplicity and humility in her dealings with men and women no less than towards God. This can be clearly seen from her simple charity combined with firmness when things went wrong : the period of " schism " among the sisters in Bourbon, the long and bitter disagreement with Bishop d'Héricourt of Autun, and, partly as a consequence of this, the extraordinary behaviour of the prefect apostolic in Guiana, who for two years deprived Anne of the sacraments. " The Cross is found wherever there are servants of God, and I rejoice to be reckoned among them," she said; but to the priest who refused her the sacraments as she left Guiana on her last voyage to Europe she spoke out : " Very well. But if anything goes wrong, you will answer to God for it."

If she received a heavy cross in French Guiana, there also was the field of Mother Javouhey's most striking achievements. Her congregation already had establishments in Guadaloupe, Martinique, Saint-Pierre, Pondicherry—hospitals, schools, workshops—and at Cayenne and New Angoulême in Guiana, when in 1828 the government asked her to undertake a task in which men had already failed badly—the colonization of the Mana district there. With thirty-six sisters, a number of French artisans and prospective colonists, and fifty Negro labourers she set to work according to a plan she had drawn up for the approval of the authorities. Those four years were doubtless temporally the four hardest years she ever knew, planting not simply civilization but a Christian civilization in the forests of South America ; and, as her success became apparent, doing it in the teeth of the jealousy of those in Guiana who had failed, and of lack of support from the government after the abdication of King Charles X in 1830. She was tireless as well as intrepid, and would buy up a score of runaway slaves to save them from the lash, or establish a village for lepers, as it were " in passing ".

Mother Javouhey had not been back in France two years when an even more surprising service was asked of her. Much to the indignation of some of the Europeans there, several hundred Negro slaves in Guiana were to be emancipated ; they were a rough lot, and their sudden freedom might lead to grave difficulties. Would Mother Javouhey, during the time before their liberation, train them in the ways of true religion and civilized society ? After much thought and more prayer she replied that, with God's help, she would do her best. Nothing in her life aroused more general interest than this, and there was adverse criticism too. Lamartine, Chateaubriand, Lamennais all came to her defence. And King Louis-Philippe made the remark, " Madame Javouhey is a great man ! "

Back she went to Mana, and the Negroes were brought along in instalments as she was ready for them—not under armed guard, as was proposed, but in charge of a nun. There were 200 men, 200 women and 111 children, afterwards increased to a round 600. Their day was mapped out almost like that of a religious community ; the greatest domestic difficulty was their disinclination to work, but Mother Javouhey took on herself to be foreman, as well as guide, philosopher, friend and magistrate. She was clearly going to justify in practice the abstract arguments in favour of emancipation, and the hostility of the French planters increased. They even bribed a Negro to upset a boat and drown the nun in the river. Mother Javouhey was warned of this, but she would not defer the journey or change the crew. Nothing happened. And on May 21, 1838 the first 185 Negro slaves were solemnly and publicly freed. For each family a cottage, a piece of land and a sum of money were waiting—Mother Javouhey had looked after that.   And also, at their own earnest request, a pair of white-man's boots : but never having worn such things before they were quite unable to walk in them.

Mother Javouhey was now sixty-four.   In 1843 she left Guiana, and spent the last eight years of her life supervising her now large congregation, and arranging new foundations in Tahiti, Madagascar and elsewhere and the admission of Indian postulants in India.   There was, too, ecclesiastical opposition to be met.   She hoped to go to Rome to lay her work at the feet of the Father of Christendom ; but she learned that " I have a different journey in front of me, and I must make it alone ".   Anne Mary Javouhey died on July 15, 1851.   She was beatified ninety-nine years later, when the congregation she had founded had spread to thirty-two countries and colonies of the world.

Among the biographies in French are those of P. Kieffer (2 vols., 1915) ; V. Caillard (1909) ; G. Goyau (1934) ; and G. Bernoville (1942).   Father Plus studies her " physionomie morale " in *Une passionnée de la Volonté de Dieu* (1950).   In English, see J. A. Mullins, *In Journeys Often;* and C. C. Martindale, *Mère Anne-Marie Javouhey* (1953).

16 : THE COMMEMORATION OF OUR LADY OF MOUNT CARMEL

THE patronal feast of the Carmelite Order was originally the Assumption of the Blessed Virgin Mary on August 15 ; but between 1376 and 1386 the custom arose of observing a special feast of our Lady, to celebrate the approbation of their rule by Pope Honorius III in 1226.   This custom appears to have originated in England ; and the observance was fixed for July 16, which is also the date that, according to Carmelite tradition, our Lady appeared to St Simon Stock and gave him the scapular.   At the beginning of the seventeenth century it became definitely the " scapular feast " and soon began to be observed outside the order, and in 1726 it was extended to the whole Western church by Pope Benedict XIII.   In the proper of the Mass for the day no mention is made of the scapular or of St Simon's vision, but they are referred to in the lessons of the second nocturn at Matins ; and our Lady's scapular is mentioned in the proper preface used by the Carmelites on this feast.

See B. Zimmerman, *Monumenta historica Carmelitana* (1907), pp. 334 *seq.* ; and A. G. Forcadell, " De cultu B.M.V. in liturgia Carmelitana ", in *Analecta Ordinis Carmelitarum,* vol. x (1940), pp. 437–445.   For the scapular question refer to the bibliographical note to St Simon Stock on May 16.   Pope Benedict XIV's projected reform envisaged the removal of this feast from the general calendar.

ST ATHENOGENES, BISHOP AND MARTYR   (c. A.D. 305)

THE Roman Martyrology has on January 18, " In [Pontus], the birthday of the holy Athenogenes, an old theologian, who, when about to consummate his martyrdom by fire, sang a hymn of joy, which he left in writing to his disciples " ; and again on July 16, " At Sebaste in Armenia, the birthday of the holy martyrs Athenogenes the Bishop and his ten disciples, under the Emperor Diocletian ". These are a double of the same martyr, of whom St Basil speaks in his treatise on the Holy Spirit, praising the hymn referred to.   St Gregory the Enlightener is said to have established a feast in honour of St Athenogenes and St John Baptist in Armenia in order to displace a pagan festival.

The occurrence of the martyr's name in the ancient Syriac martyrology and in the "Hieronymianum" is a proof of the genuineness of the cult. See Delehaye, *Les Origines du Culte des Martyrs*, pp. 177–178 ; DAC., vol. i, cc. 3104–3105 ; and DHG., vol. i, cc. 44–46. The hymn of Athenogenes was one in which he professed his faith in the divinity of the Holy Spirit ; it was not the Byzantine Vespers hymn, *Phôs hilaron*.

ST EUSTATHIUS, Bishop of Antioch (*c.* A.D. 340)

St Eustathius was a native of Side in Pamphylia, and confessed the faith of Christ before the persecutors, as St Athanasius assures us. He was learned, eloquent and virtuous. Being made bishop of Beroea in Syria, he began to be highly considered in the Church ; and in due course he was translated to the see of Antioch, in dignity the next to Alexandria, and then the third in the world. He at the same time was called on to assist at the general Council of Nicaea, where he was received with much honour and distinguished himself by his opposition to Arianism. Amidst his external work for the service of others he did not forget that charity must begin at home, and he laboured in the first place to sanctify his own soul ; but after watering his own garden he did not confine the stream there, but let it flow abroad to enrich the neighbouring soil, and to dispense plenty and fruitfulness all around. He sent into other dioceses that were subject to his oversight men capable of instructing and encouraging the faithful, and was greatly alarmed to find that Eusebius, Bishop of Caesarea in Palestine, favoured the new heresy (this same Eusebius is known and honoured as "the father of church history"). The distrust of Eustathius for the doctrine of this and other bishops, and his accusation that they altered the Nicene creed, provoked a storm against him among the Arians, who about the year 330 obtained his deposition.

The holy pastor assembled the people before his departure from Antioch, and exhorted them to remain steadfast in the true doctrine : which exhortations were of so great weight in preserving many in the orthodox faith that a body of "Eustathians" was formed, who refused to recognize bishops appointed over them by the Arians. But this loyal behaviour afterwards developed into a factious and troublesome sectarianism in the face of orthodox prelates. St Eustathius was exiled with several priests and deacons to Trajanopolis in Thrace, but the place and date of his death are alike somewhat uncertain. Most of his copious writings have perished ; his principal extant work is a disquisition against Origen, in which the powers of the pythoness of Endor (1 Kings xxviii 7–23) are criticized. Sozomen commends these works both for their style and their matter—but nothing shows his virtue so well as the patience with which he suffered first lying accusations in matters of weight, and then unjust deposition and banishment. St Eustathius bore his exile with resignation and submission, greater under its disgrace and hardships than whilst his virtues shone with lustre on the episcopal chair. He is named in the canon of the Syrian and Maronite Mass.

Since Canon Venables wrote an account of this bishop in DCB., vol. ii, much has been written upon the controversies in which St Eustathius played so prominent a part ; but it must suffice here to indicate the bibliographical references supplied in DTC., vol. v, cc. 1554–1565 ; and the *Lexikon für Theologie und Kirche*, vol. iii, c. 864. See also especially F. Cavallera, *Le Schisme d'Antioche* (1905) ; L. Duchesne, *History of the Early Church*, vol. ii (1912) ; and R. V. Sellers, *Eustathius of Antioch* (1928).

ST HELIER, Martyr   (Sixth Century)

In the isle of Jersey and on the coasts of Normandy the name of this servant of God has been in veneration from the time of his death, but little is certainly known of him.   He is said to have belonged to Tongres in Belgium, and to have been brought up to Christianity by a priest, Cunibert, who was afterwards murdered by the boy's heathen father.   He then fled for refuge to St Marcou at Nanteuil in the Cotentin.   Another tradition says he was converted by this abbot.   Seized with an ardent desire of serving God in solitude, Helier retired to the isle of Jersey and, choosing for his abode a cave on the summit of a rock of difficult access, there led an eremetical life of fasting and prayer.   In this lonely retreat he was murdered by robbers or infidel barbarians to whom he had tried to preach the gospel.   The chief town in the island bears his name and he is commemorated on July 16 in the diocese of Portsmouth, which includes the Channel Islands ; his feast is also kept by Rennes and by Coutances, the island having been formerly subject to the jurisdiction of that see.

There is a Life of St Helier printed in the *Acta Sanctorum*, July, vol. iv, though its historical value is not very great.   See also E. A. Pigeon, *Vies des SS. du diocèse de Coutances*, t. ii, pp. 136–145, and Stanton, *Menology*, pp. 342 and 661.

ST REINELDIS, Virgin and Martyr   (*c.* A.D. 680)

Reineldis was the daughter of St Amalberga, mentioned on the tenth of this month, and her acts are contained in an unreliable life not older then the eleventh century.   When her parents embraced the religious life and her sister St Gudula retired to Morzelle, she followed her father to the abbey of Lobbes, hoping to be allowed to join him there.   When she found this to be impossible she spent three days and nights in prayer in the church, and then, according to her biographer, went on a pilgrimage to the Holy Land, whence she returned after seven years.   She then lived at Saintes, near Hal, her birthplace, spending her time in works of piety and benevolence, helped by a subdeacon named Grimoald and her servant Gundulf.   All three were put to death by raiding barbarians, probably at Kontich in the province of Antwerp, and were venerated as martyrs.

The life is in the *Acta Sanctorum*, July, vol. iv ; see also, for the translation of her relics, the *Analecta Bollandiana*, vol. xxii (1903), pp. 439–445, and for the place of her death, the same, vol. lxix (1951), pp. 348–387.   *Cf.* Van der Essen, *Saints Mérovingiens*, pp. 299–301 ; and E. de Moreau, *Histoire de l'Église en Belgique*, vol. i (1945), pp. 197–198.

ST FULRAD, Abbot   (A.D. 784)

The abbey of Saint-Denis near Paris was one of the most famous monasteries of Europe in the middle ages ; St Fulrad was the most famous of its abbots and the only one to be venerated as a saint.   He was born in Alsace, where he founded three monasteries, Lièvre and Saint-Hippolyte and Salone, which were afterwards affiliated to Saint-Denis, and in 750 he was elected abbot of that house.   In this office his sanctity and talents had full scope to make themselves felt, and they were recognized by his sovereigns with the added honours and responsibilities that they put upon him ; he was a royal councillor and the archchaplain (that is, head of the court clergy) under Pepin, Carloman and Charlemagne, and in these capacities he received the trust of popes and princes and did great service to church and state.

In 750 he was appointed with St Burchard of Würzburg to go to Rome to lay before Pope St Zachary the question of the succession to the throne of the Franks, and brought back a reply favourable to Pepin, who accordingly became king of the Franks and promised to support the pope against the Lombards.

In 756 St Fulrad was Pepin's representative for the handing over to the Holy See of the exarchate of Ravenna and the duchy of the Pentapolis, which the king had taken by force of arms from the Lombard Aistulf (who had wrongfully seized them from their Byzantine governors); St Fulrad solemnly laid the deed of gift, with the keys of the cities, on the altar of St Peter. Thus he was closely connected with the early development of the papal states and with the shifting of the dependence of the Apostolic See for temporal support from the Byzantine emperor to the Frankish sovereigns. Among the saint's benefactions to his own monastery, of which his holy life and paternal government were the chiefest, was the enshrining of the reputed relics of St Vitus, the fourth-century martyr, which he brought from Italy; in the next century they were given to the abbey of Corvey. St Fulrad died, full of years and diversified labours for the Lord, in 784.

Although there is no formal life of St Fulrad, Mabillon in his *Acta Sanctorum O.S.B.*, vol. iii, pt. 2, has printed various documents concerning him with a sketch of his activities. See also the Bollandist *Acta Sanctorum*, February, vol. iii. There are modern accounts of the saint in French by Rapp (1883) and by Dubruel (1902).

BD ERMENGARD, VIRGIN (A.D. 866)

ERMENGARD was born about 832, the daughter of King Louis the German, grandson of Charlemagne, and his queen Emma. Her name, with those of her three sisters and of her mother, is found in the book of the confraternity of the monastery of Saint-Gall. Louis, having established two of his other daughters as abbesses of convents (according to the custom of those times), appointed Ermengard to govern first the monastery of Buchau and then the royal abbey of Chiemsee in Bavaria. She was a model of virtue and penance, and of charitable care for the maidens over whom she ruled. She died on July 16, 866, and was buried in her monastery church.

The nuns of the abbey and people of the neighbourhood at once began to venerate Ermengard as a saint, a veneration which has continued without interruption to this day. In 1928 Pope Pius XI confirmed the *cultus*, which had been established by the findings of the court of the Archbishop of Munich and Freising at the instance of the present Chiemsee community.

This Ermengard must not be confounded with Bd Irmgard or Ermengard honoured in the diocese of Cologne on September 4, who died about 1100.

The decree for the confirmation of the *cultus* is printed in the *Acta Apostolicae Sedis*, vol. xxi (1929), pp. 24–26 ; it contains a brief sketch of the life of Bd Ermengard. See also Dümmler, *Gesch. d. Ostfränk. Reiches*, vol. ii, pp. 425 *seq.*, and the *Abhandlungen* of the Munich Academy, 1873, pp. 6 *seq.*

BD MILO OF SÉLINCOURT, BISHOP OF THÉROUANNE (A.D. 1158)

DURING the second quarter of the twelfth century north-western Europe saw a revival of religion centring round the monasteries established by St Norbert at

Prémontré and other places, spreading thence over France, Germany and the Netherlands, and to England and elsewhere. Milo of Sélincourt, who for some years lived as a hermit with several others at Saint-Josse-au-Bois in the Pas-de-Calais, felt himself called to the common life ; he therefore offered his little group to the Premonstratensians, they were accepted, and in 1123 he was advanced to the government of the monastery, being instituted by St Norbert himself. He held office for eight years, discharging it in perfect accordance with the constitutions of his order, dividing his time between the worship of God in choir and active work for souls. In 1131 he was appointed bishop of Thérouanne, and his first episcopal act was to give the canonical benediction to Simon, the new abbot of the famous monastery of Saint-Bertin at Saint-Omer. As befitted a canon regular Bd Milo insisted on the strictest discipline in his diocese, and he was quick to check any infringement of a bishop's prerogative : one Arnoul built a castle at Thérouanne which Milo saw as a threat to the independent position of the bishop and a menace to his people's peace—so he made him pull it down. Milo also showed himself very critical of the Cluniac monks, for which he was rebuked by Bd Peter the Venerable. Nevertheless he is said to have been personally a humble man.

In the controversy about the teaching of Gilbert de la Porrée, Milo ranged himself on the side of St Bernard (they were also personal friends) and vigorously supported his attack ; he appeared against Gilbert before Pope Eugenius III at the Council of Rheims in 1148. The English pope, Adrian IV, appointed Milo to be his delegate in 1157 to judge a dispute between the bishop of Amiens and the abbot of Corbie. Cardinal Baronius highly praised the goodness and learning of Milo, but it is not decided which of the works attributed to him are authentic. Peter Cantor, a contemporary, in his *Verbum Abbreviatum* quotes a sermon said to be his in which the following passage occurs : " It is not decent that Christian women should trail at their heels long skirts which pick up filth off the roadway. Surely you realize, dear ladies, that if a gown of this kind were necessary to you, Nature would have met the case by attaching to you something more suitable with which to sweep the ground."

See Corblet, *Hagiographie d'Amiens*, vol. iii, pp. 254–277 ; Le Paige, *Bibliotheca Prae-monstratensis*, pp. 459 *seq.* ; Goovaerts, *Dictionnaire bio-bibliographique*, vol. i, pp. 590 *seq.* The title " Blessed " seems to have been accorded to Milo chiefly on account of the miracles reported at his tomb.

ST MARY-MAGDALEN POSTEL, Virgin, Foundress of the Sisters of the Christian Schools of Mercy   (A.D. 1846)

JOHN POSTEL and Teresa Levallois his wife were members of the *bourgeoisie* in the small port of Barfleur, to whom on November 28, 1756, was born a daughter, who was baptized with the names Julia Frances Catherine. This child was of a pious disposition, and several illustrative anecdotes are told, of the sort that may be found in the childhood of some who grew up to be anything but saints ; however, it may be noted that she was allowed to make her first communion when she was eight, four years earlier than was customary in those days. She was sent to a local school and afterwards to that of the Benedictine convent at Valognes, and while there she determined to devote her life to the direct service of God and her neigh-bour and took a private vow of perpetual virginity. On leaving school when she was eighteen she returned to Barfleur, where she opened a school for girls, and her pupils in after life were a consistent witness to the grounding they had received from their first teacher.

Julia carried on quietly for five years, and then the revolution burst. In 1790 the National Assembly imposed an oath on the clergy to maintain the civil constitution, which oath Pope Pius VI forbade as detrimental to the freedom of the Church. Nevertheless, many clergy (the " constitutionals ") took it and the Church in France was torn by a schism. In Barfleur the constitutional clergy had the upper hand, and Julia Postel was a leader among those who refused to attend their services or accept their ministrations. She made a secret chapel under the stairs in her house, and here Mass was offered by the abbé Lamache, rector of Notre Dame de Barfleur, who had been proscribed as " refractory ". M. Lamache trusted her to the extent of reserving the Blessed Sacrament in the chapel, and Julia made the secret arrangements necessary to enable him to minister to his flock. After a time it was deemed imprudent to reserve the Blessed Sacrament there any longer and, in accordance with the law of the Church in time of persecution or other extreme need, Julia was allowed to carry it on her person and to administer it as viaticum to the dying when no priest was at hand : a veritable " maiden-priest ", as St Pius X did not hesitate to call her in the decree of beatification. Admiration for her was not confined to the " refractories ". Once when her house had been searched the comment of the disappointed soldiers was, " Let her alone. She does nobody any harm, and is very kind to the children ." Year after year of such danger, responsibility, and nervous strain could be supported only by an intense inner life. And if Julia was always with God, God showed time and again that He was always with her.

For four years after the concordat of 1801 Julia was one of those devoted workers who laboured at whatever task came next to repair the ravages of revolution in the religious life of the people ; she taught, she catechized, she prepared children and adults to receive the sacraments, she organized works of mercy, and always she prayed. Then, in her fifty-first year, armed with her reputation and a testimonial from a priest, but with no material resources beyond her own hands and head, she went to Cherbourg where she heard the municipality was in need of school-teachers. She told a local chaplain, the abbé Cabart, that " I want to teach the young and to inspire them with the love of God and liking for work. I want to help the poor and relieve some of their misery. These are the things I want to do, and for long I've seen that I must have a religious congregation to do it." M. Cabart was not the man to discourage enthusiasm or fail to recognize ability. He told Julia she was just the woman he had been looking for and he would find her a house. One was soon rented ; it was dedicated in honour of our Lady, Mother of Mercy (the patron of that former chapel under the stairs) ; pupils were got together ; and three other teachers joined her, Joan Catherine Bellot, Louisa Viel and Angelina Ledanois. In 1807 these four took the vows of religion before M. Cabart, representing the bishop, and Julia took the name of Mary-Magdalen. Three years later it was reported to the charity commissioners that two hundred little girls were being instructed by them in sacred and profane knowledge, handicrafts being taught to others, ragamuffins rescued from the streets, and ten thousand francs a year given in alms.

In 1811, when the community numbered nine sisters, the Sisters of Providence returned to Cherbourg, and, rather than appear to emulate and rival them, Mother Mary-Magdalen withdrew her family to Octeville-L'Avenel, where they lived for six months in great hardship in a barn adjoining the school-house. Then they migrated to Tamerville, and looked after orphans and the poor there until their lease fell in. Again they migrated, this time to Valognes, where it looked as if the foundress's undertaking would come to nothing. There were already three convents of nuns teaching in the town, and Mother Mary-Magdalen and her six sisters had to subsist on the work of their hands, they and their twelve orphans. Sister Rosalia died, and when an untrue rumour that she had starved to death got around, the abbé Cabart thought it was the last straw, wished to sever his connection with them, and told the community it was time to give up. The superioress thought otherwise. " Tell monsieur l'abbé ", she said, " that I am so certain that our Lord desires the realization of my aims that I shall not cease to pursue them with the greatest ardour. He who has given my daughters to me and who watches over the birds of the air can easily provide me with the means to support them. So long as God gives me strength to work I shall never leave one of them." That act of faith turned the tide—but not yet. For two years they lived at Hamel-au-Bon, in extreme poverty, doing any work that came along, needlework, repairs, in the fields, and then Prince Le Brun offered them their former house at Tamerville and the charge of a school.

Almost at once a famine broke out, which gave Mother Mary-Magdalen's sisters their chance to earn a permanent place in the hearts of the people, and then in 1818 in consequence of a new by-law she had, at sixty-two years old, to sit down and pass an examination to qualify as a head teacher. Though the community was reduced by deaths to four, a school was started at Tourlaville : and with this expansion of activity the community began to grow in numbers ; by 1830 a larger convent was imperatively needed. Mother Mary-Magdalen obtained the dilapidated abbey of Saint-Sauveur-le-Vicomte, which had been founded in the eleventh century and abandoned at the Revolution. Here in the first twelve months the community received ten postulants, before whose coming its total number was only fifteen ; among them was Bd Placida Viel. In 1837 the rule by which Mother Mary-Magdalen had governed her sisters for twenty-eight years was laid aside (not on her own initiative, but without a word of protest from her) and that approved by the Holy See for the Brothers of the Christian Schools was formally adopted ; a canonical novitiate was begun, and at the end of the year their vows were received by Mgr Delamare, Bishop of Coutances, who was the devoted friend and adviser of the community.

The last eight years of the foundress's life, though they had their trials, setbacks, and crosses, was a period of expansion and achievement : the congregation grew, the number of its pupils increased, and the great abbey church of St-Sauveur-le-Vicomte, which had been in ruins, began to rise again. She died when this last work was not yet finished on July 16, 1846, at the age of ninety years. Miracles were not wanting to confirm her reputation for sanctity ; and in 1925 she was canonized. For forty-one years the life of St Mary-Magdalen Postel was the vicissitudes and progress of the institute that she founded ; had she never been raised to the altars of the Church her name would still be rendered illustrious by the Sisters of the Christian Schools.

See the life by Mgr Grente (Eng. trans., 1928) and his *Une sainte normande* (1946). There are other lives in French, *e.g.* by Mgr Legoux (1908, in two volumes) and by P. de Crisenoy (1938).

17 : ST ALEXIS, THE MAN OF GOD   (FIFTH CENTURY)

EARLY in the fifth century there is said to have lived at Edessa in Syria a man who, whether from choice or necessity, lived the life of a beggar, and was of such virtue that he was revered as a saint. After his death an unknown writer wrote an account of him. He called him by no name but simply " the Man of God ", and stated that he lived during the episcopate of Rabbula, who died in 436. According to this writer, he lived by begging alms at the church doors, which he shared with other poor people, existing himself on what little was left over from their needs, and when he died was buried in the common grave of the city ; but before his death he had confided to an attendant in the hospital that he was the only son of noble Roman parents, and when the bishop heard of this he ordered the body to be exhumed ; but only the ragged garments of the Man of God could be found. His fame spread westward, and before the ninth century was known in Greece with sundry embroideries, including the name of the saint, Alexis, and was related in a *kanon* by St Joseph the Hymnographer (d. 883) ; the *cultus* in the West, though known before, *e.g.* in Spain, was popularized in Rome towards the end of the tenth century by an exiled metropolitan of Damascus, Sergius ; to him was given the church of St Boniface on the Aventine, and he established a monastery of Greek monks there, adding the name of St Alexis to the church as contitular. As an alleged citizen of Rome the saint soon had a vast popularity, and this popularity has persisted : in the twelfth century his story is said to have had a deep influence on the heretic Peter Waldo ; in the fifteenth, he was chosen as the patron of the nursing congregation commonly called the Alexian Brothers, and so late as 1817 as a lesser patron of the Congregation of the Sacred Hearts of Jesus and Mary (Picpus Fathers) ; while in the East he is still greatly venerated as the " Man of God ". The legend of this forerunner of St Joseph Benedict Labre as it came to be received in the West, with its resemblance to that of St John Calybites, may be told in the summarized words of Alban Butler :

St Alexis was the only son of a rich senator of Rome, Euphemian, and his wife Aglaë, born and educated in that capital in the fifth century. From the charitable example of his parents he learned that the riches which are given away to the poor remain with us for ever, and that alms-deeds are a treasure transferred to Heaven, with the interest of an immense reward. Whilst yet a child he was intent on the relief of all whom he saw in distress, and thought himself obliged to those who received his charity and regarded them as his benefactors. Fearing lest the distraction of earthly honours might at length divide or draw his heart too much from more noble objects, he decided to renounce the advantages of his birth and retire from the world. Having, in compliance with the will of his parents, married a wealthy girl, he on the very day of the wedding parted from her with her consent. In disguise he travelled into Syria, embraced extreme poverty, and resided in a hut adjoining a church dedicated to the Mother of God at Edessa. Here he lived for seventeen years until an image of our Lady spoke and revealed his holiness to the people, calling him " the Man of God ". Thereupon he fled back to his home ; his father did not recognize him, but received him as a beggar and gave him employment, allotting a corner under the staircase as his quarters. For another seventeen years he thus lived unknown in his father's house, bearing the ill-treatment of the other servants in patience and silence. After his death a writing was found upon him, giving his name and family and an account of his life.

The extraordinary paths in which the Holy Ghost is pleased sometimes to conduct certain privileged souls are rather to be admired than imitated. If it cost them so much to seek humiliations, we ought diligently to make a good use of those which Providence sends us. It is only by humbling ourselves on all occasions that we can walk in the path of true humility and root out of our hearts all secret pride. The poison of this vice infects all states and conditions : it often lurks undiscovered in the heart even after a man has got the mastery over all his other passions. Pride always remains even for the most perfect to fight against ; and unless we watch continually against it, nothing will remain sound or untainted in our lives : it will creep into our best actions, infect the whole circle of our works, and become a mainspring of everything ; and the deeper its wounds, the more is the soul stupefied and the less capable of knowing her disease and weakness. St John Climacus writes that when a young novice was rebuked for his pride, he said, " Excuse me, father, I am not proud ". To whom the experienced director replied, " And how could you give me a surer proof of your pride than by not seeing it yourself ? "

This warning against pride comes very fitly *à propos* of the story just related, but the same story is also an apt illustration of a quite different matter, namely, of how a legend is embellished in the course of time and travelling. To draw attention to only a few points: the flight on the wedding-day, so common an incident in hagiography; when a man wishes to avoid marriage he does not wait till after the wedding, but the popular form is so much more spectacular and impressive to simple minds ; the speaking image provides an edifying reason for his coming back to Rome and being buried there ; and the finding of his relics—somebody's relics were certainly found at the church of St Boniface in Rome in 1217 ; but the only things which are reasonably certain about St Alexis are that he lived (if indeed he ever lived), died, and was buried in Edessa : his name is found in no ancient Roman liturgical book or martyrology and was apparently not heard of there before about 972.

The fifth-century Syriac text recounting how " the Man of God " who had edified Edessa revealed before his death that he had come from Rome, has been edited by A. Amiaud, *La légende syriaque de S. Alexis* (1889). The most widely diffused recension of the Greek legend (though this particular type of text seems to have taken shape in Rome) has been printed in the *Analecta Bollandiana*, vol. xix (1900), pp. 241–256. For the Latin versions see the *Acta Sanctorum*, July, vol. iv. But the literature of the subject is vast and brings us into contact with the early developments of almost every European language. The articles of Poncelet in *Science Catholique*, t. iv (1890), and of Mgr Duchesne in *Mélanges d'Archéologie*, t. x (1890), are especially worthy of mention. For the treatment of the subject in art *cf.* Künstle, *Ikonographie der Heiligen*, ii, pp. 48–49, and for its folk-lore aspects Bächtold-Stäubli, *Handwörterbuch des deutschen Aberglaubens*, vol. i, cc. 261–262. See also *Analecta Bollandiana*, vol. lxii (1944), pp. 281–283 ; vol. lxiii (1945), pp. 48–55 ; and vol. lxv (1947), pp. 157–195. In this last Fr B. de Gaiffier refers to twenty-one other hagiological examples of a newly-married husband who goes away " intactam sponsam relinquens ", or of a couple forced to marry who agree to live together in virginity ; these range from the *Acta Thomae* to St Bernard of Montjoux. Fr de Gaiffier then discusses the evolution of the story of St Alexis's departure.

SS. SPERATUS AND HIS COMPANIONS, THE SCILLITAN MARTYRS (A.D. 180)

THESE martyrs suffered in the last year of the persecution of Marcus Aurelius, but actually under Commodus. Their *acta*, indubitably authentic, are the earliest in existence for the Church in Africa and have suffered little from later editorial " improvement ". They were of Scillium, a place in what is now Tunisia, and twelve in number, seven men and five women, namely Speratus, Nartzalus, Cittinus, Veturius, Felix, Aquilinus, Laetantius, Januaria, Generosa, Vestia, Donata, and Secunda.

They were brought prisoners to Carthage and presented before the proconsul Saturninus, who offered them the emperor's pardon if they would worship the gods of the Romans. Speratus answered in the name of all : " We have never committed any crime, we have injured no one ; we have given thanks for the evil treatment we have received, because we hold our own sovereign in honour." " We also are religious people ", said the proconsul, " and moreover our religion is simple. We swear by the divine spirit of our lord the emperor and pray for his safety. Do you the like : it is your duty." " If you will listen a moment patiently, I will explain the mystery of true simplicity ", replied Speratus. But Saturninus again urged them to swear by the emperor's *genius*. Speratus replied : " I know not the empire of this world, but I serve that God whom no mortal man has ever seen or can see. I never have stolen ; I pay the public duties for whatever I buy, because I know my Master, who is the King of kings, and sovereign over all the nations in the world." Saturninus called on them all to give up their belief, and Speratus exclaimed, " It is a bad belief that allows murder and false witness ". The proconsul turned to the others and urged them to dissociate themselves from Speratus. But Cittinus answered : " We have nobody to fear save the Lord our God in Heaven " ; and Donata said : " We give to Caesar the honour that is due to Caesar ; but we fear God alone " ; and Vestia said : " I am a Christian " ; and Secunda said : " I wish to be none other than what I am " ; and so all the others. The proconsul then said to Speratus : " Are you still resolved to remain a Christian ? " Speratus replied : " Yes, I am a Christian." The proconsul said : " Will you deliberate upon the matter ? " Speratus replied : " When the right is thus clear, there is nothing to deliberate upon." Then Saturninus asked : " What have you got in that box ? " referring to a case that had been brought into the court, and Speratus answered : " The sacred books, and the letters of a righteous man, one Paul."

Then Saturninus offered them a remand of thirty days for further consideration, but they all persisted with Speratus in his dogged reply : " I am a Christian." The proconsul then, seeing their constancy and resolution, pronounced sentence against them in these terms : " Speratus, Nartzalus, Cittinus, Veturius, Donata, Vestina, Secunda, and the rest, having acknowledged themselves Christians, and having refused an opportunity of returning to the Roman customs, it is our sentence that they perish by the sword." This sentence being read, Speratus said : "Thanks be to God " ; and Nartzalus said : " This day we are martyrs in Heaven. Thanks be to God." And when a herald read out the names of all who were to die, all exclaimed, " Thanks be to God ". Having said this, they were led to the place of execution, where their heads were struck off. The faithful who transcribed their acts out of the public registers add : " And so all were crowned with martyrdom together, and reign with the Father and the Son and the Holy Ghost for ever and ever. Amen."

For the *passio* of the Scillitan martyrs, if we compare the texts registered in BHL., nn. 7527–7534, and in BHG., 1645, the most ancient and reliable seems to be that edited by Dean Armitage Robinson in *Texts and Studies*, vol. i, pt. 2 (1891). See also Delehaye,

Les Passions des Martyrs et les Genres littéraires, pp. 60–63 ; and for their relics Pio Franchi de' Cavalieri in the *Römische Quartalschrift*, vol. xvii (1903), pp. 209–221, and *Analecta Bollandiana*, vol. xxiii (1904), pp. 344 *seq.* Popular but scholarly accounts of these martyrs are furnished also by P. Monceaux in *La vraie légende dorée* (1928) and in L. Bertrand, *Martyrs africains* (1930). An English translation of the *passio* will be found in E. C. E. Owen, *Acts of the Early Martyrs* (1927).

ST MARCELLINA, Virgin   (*c.* A.D. 398)

MARCELLINA was sister to St Ambrose of Milan and born before him, probably at Trier, their father being prefect of the Gauls. She went to Rome with her family, and at an early age sought with her whole heart the only thing for which she was created and sent into the world. Being charged with the care of her two brothers, she inspired them by words and example with love of virtue. She kindled in their breasts a desire, not of the appearance of virtue, but to become truly virtuous ; and in her whole conduct all her view was only the glory of God. The better to pursue this end she resolved to renounce the world ; and on the Epiphany in the year 353, she received the veil of the consecrated virgin from the hands of Pope Liberius, in St Peter's basilica. The pope in a discourse on that occasion exhorted her to love only our Lord Jesus Christ, to live in continual recollection and mortification and always to behave herself in church with the utmost respect and awe : in reporting this address St Ambrose did not hesitate to heighten the eloquence of Liberius where he thought it insufficient. It was to his sister that St Ambrose addressed and dedicated his work on the excellence of virginity, and after he became bishop she several times visited him at Milan to confer with him on the spiritual life, helping him in his dealings with dedicated maidens.

Marcellina in her practice went beyond the most perfect lessons. She fasted every day till evening, and the greater part both of the day and night she devoted to prayer and spiritual reading. St Ambrose advised her in the decline of her life to moderate her austerities, but to redouble her prayer, especially in often reciting the psalms, the Lord's Prayer, and the creed, which he calls the seal of a Christian and the guard of our hearts. She continued at Rome after the death of her mother, living not in a community but in a private house with another woman, the faithful companion of all her exercises. Marcellina outlived St Ambrose, but the exact year of her death is not known ; in his funeral sermon for his elder brother, Satyrus, he had referred to her as " . . . a holy sister, worshipful for her innocence, equally so for her uprightness, and no less so for her kindness to others ".

See the *Acta Sanctorum*, July, vol. iv, where in addition to certain passages extracted from the works of St Ambrose, a Latin panegyric is reprinted which has been preserved to us by Mombritius.

ST ENNODIUS, Bishop of Pavia   (A.D. 521)

MAGNUS FELIX ENNODIUS was descended of an illustrious family, settled in Gaul ; he seems to call Arles the place of his birth, but he passed his first years in Italy, and had his education at Milan under the care of an aunt, after whose death he married. After a short time he heard a call to receive holy orders, and his wife, a wealthy young woman who had saved him from destitution, became a nun. Ennodius was already an accomplished rhetor and, being ordained deacon by St Epiphanius of Pavia, he took up sacred studies and taught in the schools. He wrote an apology for Pope St Symmachus and the synod which had pronounced against the schism formed in favour of Laurence ; " God ", he says, " certainly ordained that men should settle the affairs of men ; but the passing of judgement on the pontiff of the supreme see He reserved to Himself." He was selected to make a panegyric upon King Theodoric, whom he commends only for his victories and temporal success. He wrote the life of St Epiphanius of Pavia, who died in 496, and of St Antony of Lérins, besides letters and other works, both in prose and verse. Ennodius was one of the last representatives of the ancient school of rhetoric, and, though they have historical value, his writings tend to be verbose, turgid, and at moments unintelligible, and he clung to the old mythological literary conventions of pagan Rome. He tells us that, under a violent fever in which he was given up by the physicians, he had recourse to the heavenly Physician through the intercession of his patron St Victor (of Milan), and that he found himself restored to perfect health. To perpetuate his gratitude, he wrote a work called *Eucharisticon*, or " Thanksgiving ", in which he gives a short account of his life, especially of his conversion from the world.

St Ennodius was advanced to the episcopal see of Pavia about the year 514, and governed his church with a zeal and authority worthy of a disciple of St Epiphanius. He was made choice of by Pope St Hormisdas to go twice to Constantinople where the Emperor Anastasius II was favouring the monophysite heretics. Neither mission had any success, and after the second one St Ennodius was obliged to put to sea in an old rotten vessel, and all were forbidden to suffer him to land in any port of the Eastern empire, whereby he was exposed to much danger. Nevertheless he arrived safe in Italy and returned to Pavia. The glory of suffering for the faith which his zeal and constancy had procured him was now a spur in the more earnest pursuit of virtue. He exerted himself in the conversion of souls, in relieving the poor, in building and adorning churches, and in composing poems on sacred subjects : on our Lady, St Ambrose, St Euphemia, on the mysteries of Pentecost and on the Ascension, on a baptistery adorned with the pictures of martyrs whose relics were deposited in it, and so on. Others of his poems are simply mythological, *e.g.* on Pasiphaë and the bull. It has been said of the writings of St Ennodius that " He seems to shrink from making himself intelligible lest he should be thought commonplace ". He wrote two new hymns of praise to be sung at the lighting of the paschal candle, in which the divine protection is implored against winds, storms, and all dangers through the malice of our invisible enemies. St Ennodius died in 521, being only forty-eight years old.

Although Ennodius is not commonly honoured with the title of " Saint ", he is commemorated on this day in the Roman Martyrology. Most of what we know of his life is derived from his *Eucharisticon*, a title not given to this tractate by himself, but suggested apparently by his editor, Sirmond. His works have been twice re-edited in modern times, first by Hartel in the Vienna *Corpus scriptorum Latinorum*, and then by Vogel in MGH. See the *Acta Sanctorum*, July, vol. iv, as well as D'T'C., and the *Patrologie* of Bardenhewer, and G. Bardy in *Le Christianisme et l'Occident barbare* (1945), pp. 229–264. A French translation of Ennodius's letters was published by S. Léglise in 1906, with the Latin text.

ST KENELM   (*c.* A.D. 812)

THERE is no historical evidence for the story of this young " martyr ", but it was the simple sort of tale that attracted our ancestors and, decked out with astonishing details, made him widely venerated in England in the middle ages. According to it, Kenelm succeeded to the throne of his father, Kenulf of Mercia, at the age of seven years, and thereby incurred the jealousy of his sister Quendreda. So, in order that she might succeed to the throne, she bribed Ascebert, his preceptor, to remove him, and this man, taking the young king into the forest of Clent under the pretence of hunting, there killed him. The crime was discovered, and the body was taken up and enshrined at Winchcombe, in Gloucestershire ; St Kenelm's chapel, near Halesowen in Worcestershire, marks the site of the murder.

Among the marvels with which later writers have adorned this narrative is Kenelm's prevision of his fate and the flowering of his staff at the spot where Ascebert should slay him ; and the discovery of his body by the roundabout means of a letter dropped by a dove on the high altar of St Peter's basilica in Rome. The *Golden Legend* supplies the text of this letter :

> In Clent in Cowbage, Kenelm, king born
> Lieth under a thorn,
> His head off shorn,

and tells us there was strife between the shires of Worcester and Gloucester about who should have the body, and how God settled the question.

Kenelm (Cynhelm), with his father King Kenulf (Coenwulf) and his sister Quendreda (Quoenthryth), are historical characters. But Kenelm did not die at seven, for in 798 Pope St Leo III confirmed to him the ownership of Glastonbury, and he signed certain charters up to 811. He was, like Kenulf, buried at Winchcombe Abbey, but he seems certainly to have predeceased his father : he may perhaps have been killed in battle ; as we have seen elsewhere, it was not unusual in earlier times for one killed fighting for a just cause, or one who suffered death unjustly, to be venerated as a martyr. St Kenelm is still commemorated on this day in the dioceses of Birmingham and Clifton.

Numerous calendars from about 975 onwards include the name of St Kenelm, martyr, on July 17 : William of Malmesbury states that St Dunstan sanctioned his being honoured as a martyr. The alleged circumstances of his murder are told in the eleventh century, but the original text of the legend (T. D. Hardy, *Descriptive Catalogue*, vol. i, 2, p. 508) has not been published ; there is an abbreviated version by John of Tynemouth in *Nova Legenda Angliae*. See E. S. Hartland in the *Transactions* of the Bristol and Gloucestershire Archaeological Society, vol. xxxix (1916) ; J. Humphrey, *Studies in Worcester History* (1938) ; W. Levison, *England and the Continent* . . . (1946), pp. 32, 249–251 ; and G. T. Haig, *History of Winchcombe Abbey* (1948). There is a Life of Kenelm in the Gotha MS. : cf. *Analecta Bollandiana*, vol. lxviii (1950), p. 94.

ST LEO IV, POPE   (A.D. 855)

LEO was a Roman by birth, but probably of Lombardic descent, and was educated at the Benedictine monastery of St Martin, near St Peter's. The attention of Gregory IV having been called to his good qualities he was made a subdeacon of the Lateran basilica and afterwards cardinal-priest of the title of the Quatuor Coronati. Immediately after the death of Sergius II in 847 Leo was elected to succeed him, and the new pope was consecrated without reference to the emperor, the Romans being in terror of the Saracen invasions and in a hurry to have a good and strong man, albeit an unwilling one, occupying the chair of Peter. Leo's first care was necessarily to deal with these attacks, and he at once set about repairing and strengthening the walls of the city, for in the previous year the Saracens had come up the Tiber and plundered the city. The list of Leo's benefactions to churches takes up twenty-eight pages of the *Liber Pontificalis*, and he also brought the relics of many saints into the city, including those of the Four Crowned Ones, which he enshrined in his rebuilt titular basilica.   But his ecclesiastical material achievements, great as they were, were eclipsed by the civil ones, for while considering how best to fortify Rome he decided to surround St Peter's and the Vatican hill with a wall, thus making the new quarter which has ever since been known as the Leonine City.

But St Leo never forgot that mighty walls are no defence against the wrath of God upon a sinful people, and that a slack or rebellious clergy corrupts its flock. So in 853 he summoned at Rome a synod of bishops who passed forty-two canons, most of which were concerned with clerical discipline and studies.   They had also to take measures against Cardinal Anastasius, who was intriguing with the Emperor Lothair I for the succession to the papacy.   Leo had to deal with the rebellious and violent John, Archbishop of Ravenna, and his brother, the duke of Emilia, who had murdered a papal legate.   Leo went to Ravenna, where the duke was tried and, with two accomplices, condemned to death ; but the fact that it was paschal time, when by law no executions could take place, enabled them to avoid the penalty of their crimes.   Leo was also in difficulties with Nomenoë, duke of Brittany, who presumed to erect a metropolitan see at Dol in his own territory ; with St Ignatius, Patriarch of Constantinople, over his deposition of the bishop of Syracuse ; and with one Daniel, a soldier, who maliciously accused him to the emperor of intriguing with the Greeks against the Franks.   Finally he had trouble with Hincmar, Archbishop of Rheims, whom he had accused of preventing appeals from deposed clerics being referred to the Holy See : in the midst of this the energetic and much-tried pontiff died on July 17, 855.

St Leo IV was a man of liberality and justice combined with patience and humility ; if his known achievements appear to be chiefly in a political and quasi-temporal sphere allowance must be made for the times in which he lived and for the fact that spiritual greatness is so often hidden or forgotten by man.   He was a good preacher, so much so that the instruction on sacerdotal duties, the Homily on Pastoral Care in the *Pontificale*, has been attributed to him, though probably wrongly.   In his enthusiasm for the chant of the Roman church he was a precursor of St Pius X, and there is extant a letter which he sent to an abbot who erred on the subject : " A quite incredible story has reached our ears. . . . It is alleged that you have such an aversion from the sweet chant of St Gregory . . . that you are at variance in this matter not only with this see, which is near to you, but with almost every other church in the West, in fact, with all those who use the Latin tongue to pay their tribute of praise to the King of Heaven. . . ."   He proceeds to threaten excommunication if the recipient continues to differ from " the supreme head of religion " and his proper rite in his manner of worship.   St Leo was credited with a number of miracles, including the stopping of a great fire in the English quarter of Rome, the Borgo, by the power of the cross.   In spite of critical objections it seems to be true that Alfred, afterwards the Great, was brought to Rome at this time at the age of four, and was invested by St Leo with the honorary dignity of a Roman consul (not a royal consecration).   Leo is often wrongly credited with the institution of the rite of the " Asperges " before Mass on Sundays.

The main authority is the *Liber Pontificalis*, with Duchesne's notes, but there is also some information to be gleaned from such chroniclers as Hincmar of Rheims and from the pope's own letters.   See especially Mann, *Lives of the Popes*, vol. ii, pp. 258–307, and the *Acta Sanctorum*, July, vol. iv.

SS. CLEMENT OF OKHRIDA AND HIS COMPANIONS, THE SEVEN APOSTLES OF BULGARIA (NINTH-TENTH CENTURY)

IN origin the Bulgars were probably a Turanian people from central Asia, related to the Avars and Huns. They established an independent kingdom (khanate) in their present country and its borders during the seventh century of our era, subduing the peoples whom they found already settled there but intermarrying with them and adopting the Slavonic language. They are now reckoned among the Slav peoples.

In or about the year 865 their ruler, the khan Boris I, moved principally by political motives, accepted Christianity from Constantinople and imposed it on his nobles and people. This revived the old disagreement between Rome and Constantinople about patriarchal jurisdiction in Illyricum and the Balkans; it was aggravated by Boris, whose policies were directed towards having a national church independent of either. When in 869 Pope Adrian II had appointed St Methodius archbishop over Moravia and Pannonia he had deliberately extended his jurisdiction to the very borders of Bulgaria, not, as Pope John VIII later carefully explained to Boris, because the religion of Rome and Constantinople was not one and the same, but because, he said, the Byzantines were inclined to separation and schism. Methodius in fact had to keep an eye on the Bulgars, most of whom were still heathen; and for this reason he and his brother St Cyril (July 7) are reckoned the first two of their seven apostles. But it does not seem that either of them actually ever preached among the Bulgars.

After the death of St Methodius violent and cruel persecution by Svatopluk and his archbishop, Wiching, drove his principal followers into exile from Moravia. Among them was ST GORAZD, whom Methodius had designated as his successor; it is uncertain what became of him, but he is reputed to have been a great missionary, and relics supposed to be his are venerated at Berat, in modern Albania. Others were welcomed to Bulgaria by Boris, who saw in them a valuable help for his own plans; they evangelized many of the people, and are held in memory as ST CLEMENT, ST NAHUM, ST SABAS and ST ANGELARIUS.

Of these Clement, who probably was in origin a Slav from southern Macedonia, was clearly the most important, and much apostolic and educational work is attributed to him. Under the khan Simeon he became bishop at a place (Velitsa) which very likely was close to Okhrida where he established a monastery: later he was regarded as the founder of that primatial see, which was to be very important in subsequent history, and as the first man of Slav race to receive the episcopate. Certain extant sermons in Slavonic seem to be properly attributed to St Clement, though some of them may be simply translations from Greek: they are clearly intended for people newly converted to Christianity. Clement died at Okhrida in the year 916 (July 27 is his feast-day). Some say that his colleague St Nahum succeeded him as bishop; he was a convert of Cyril and Methodius in Moravia, helping them with their translations and accompanying them to Rome, and he is venerated in Russia as well as Bulgaria as a wonder-worker.

By these men the work of St Cyril and St Methodius, which had been so hampered and at last overturned further north, was planted and carried on in territory far removed from its original scene of action. The Bulgarian Orthodox Church honours these missionaries in a body on this date and individually on the dates of their death, as do the few Bulgarian Catholics of Byzantine rite.

There is a considerable literature about St Clement, called Slovensky, in Russian and Bulgarian. His life in Migne, PG., vol. cxxvi, 1193–1240, is a late eleventh-century Greek rewriting of a work written in Slavonic soon after his death by one of his disciples. See M. Jugie in *Échos d'Orient*, vol. xxiii (1924), pp. 5 *seq.* ; F. Dvornik, *Les Slaves, Byzance et Rome* . . . (1926), pp. 312–318 ; S. Runciman, *History of the First Bulgarian Empire* (1930) ; and an article by M. Kusseff in the *Slavonic Review*, 1949, pp. 193–215. *Cf.* also DTC., vol. iii, cc. 134–138 ; and DHG., vol. x, *s.v.* " Bulgarie ".

ST NERSES LAMPRONATSI, Archbishop of Tarsus (A.D. 1198)

THERE are several saints named Nerses in the Armenian calendar. This one was born in 1153, son of the prince of Lampron in Cilicia and nephew of St Nerses Klaietsi. He was educated at the monastery of Skeyra and soon showed himself a man of many great parts : he was a poet and scholar, knowing Latin, Greek, Syriac and Coptic, and became a theologian and scriptural exegete. At first he did not intend an ecclesiastical life, but on the death of his father received holy orders and lived for a time as a hermit. In 1176 he was consecrated archbishop of Tarsus, having already identified himself with the party in his church which sought to remedy their ecclesiastical isolation. For a time they turned their attention towards the Orthodox, and in 1179 the Greek and Armenian bishops met in council at Hromkla. At this council Nerses made a great speech, still extant, on behalf of the orthodox faith, but owing to the death of the emperor, Manuel Comnenus, in the following year the meeting was fruitless.

Nerses and the bishops of Lesser Armenia now looked towards Rome once more, in which they were backed for political reasons by the prince of Cilicia, Leo II, and in the negotiations which led to reunion the saint was very active. As a public sealing of the return of so large a part of Armenia from schism Leo II was, on the feast of the Epiphany, 1198, crowned king of Little Armenia by the papal legate, Cardinal Conrad von Wittelsbach (the crown being sent by Pope Celestine III), and anointed by the Armenian katholikos of Sis, Gregory IV Abirad. Crowned also was the work of Nerses, and he died in peace six months later. Among the works which caused him to share his uncle's place of literary eminence was his translation into Armenian of the Rule of St Benedict and of the *Dialogues* of St Gregory.

See Nilles, *Kalendarium manuale* . . ., vol. ii, p. 598, but more fully in F. Tournebize, *Histoire politique et religieuse de l'Arménie* (1900), especially pp. 259–262 and 272–277. Some confusion prevails concerning the councils of Hromkla and Tarsus. In Hefele-Leclercq, *Conciles*, vol. v, the council of 1179 is called wrongly the council of Tarsus ; this latter seems to have been held in 1196. *Cf.* also the article " Arménie " in DHG., and Max of Saxony, *Nerses von Lampron* (1929).

BD CESLAUS (A.D. 1242)

CESLAUS was of the house of the counts of Odrowatz, in Silesia, and is reputed to have been brother to St Hyacinth. Having devoted himself to God in the ecclesiastical state, he became eminent for piety and learning, and was instituted to a canonry at Cracow and to be provost of St Mary's at Sandomir. His prebends he employed on the poor, leading himself a most abstemious and penitential life. In Rome he came under the spell of St Dominic, and together with St Hyacinth received the habit of the Order of Preachers. After his novitiate at Santa Sabina he was, at his own urgent request, sent into Poland, where he preached penance with much fruit. He also preached in Silesia, Pomerania and Bohemia, and became provincial of his order in Poland, directing both St Hedwig and Bd Zdislava Berka in the paths of perfection.

In 1240, while he was governing the priory of Breslau, the Tartars fell like a torrent on all those parts. The inhabitants prepared for the sack of their city. But Bd Ceslaus never ceased with tears to implore the divine protection, and God was pleased to hear his prayers. The Christians made a sally, and the troops of the barbarians took flight and abandoned their enterprise. Thus they who had overturned so many thrones, and trampled to the ground so many powerful armies, saw themselves tumbled down from their victories and pride by the prayer of one humble servant of God. Ceslaus died in 1242, and his popular *cultus* was confirmed in 1713.

See the *Acta Sanctorum*, July, vol. iv ; B. Altaner, *Die Dominikanermissionen des 13 Jahrhunderts* (1924), pp. 212–218 ; Procter, *Lives of Dominican Saints*, pp. 197–201.

THE CARMELITE MARTYRS OF COMPIÈGNE   (A.D. 1794)

THE Carmelite nuns of the Teresian reform first came to France in 1604, and in 1641 Mme de Louvancourt founded the fifty-third convent of the order in that country, at Compiègne, and from the first it was noted for the excellence of its religious observance.

In 1789 the Revolution broke out, and early in the following year religious communities were suppressed, except those engaged in teaching and nursing. The Carmelites of Compiègne were " visited " in August : their goods were impounded, they had to put on secular dress, and they were driven from their monastery. They divided into four groups, led respectively by the prioress, the sub-prioress, the novice-mistress, and another professed nun. They lodged in four different houses, all near to the church of St Antony, and in this situation they continued so far as was possible and consistent with the circumstances to observe their rule and to keep up a community life ; the groups were in constant touch one with another, but the greatest care had to be taken to avoid arousing the suspicion of the authorities that they were doing their best to follow an unlawful way of life. But in June 1794 the nuns were arrested on the grounds that they continued their former life and had plotted against the Republic ; at the same time Mulot de La Ménardière was arrested for abetting them. They were imprisoned in the former Visitation convent at Compiègne, in the same house but separate from the English Benedictine nuns from Cambrai, who had been confined there since the previous October. When these last were allowed to return to England in 1795 they were wearing the secular clothes which the Carmelites had left at Compiègne ; to this is due the preservation of a number of relics of the martyrs (at Stanbrook, Darlington, Lanherne, Chichester, Oulton, New Subiaco in New South Wales, and elsewhere), and the testimony of the archives of Stanbrook Abbey was of much value in the process of beatification.

In 1790 the nuns had taken the oath to maintain the nation, liberty, and equality, about the lawfulness of which for Catholics there was considerable difference of opinion. The prioress now sent for the mayor, and they all made a formal retractation of this oath before a notary public, it having been condemned by, among others, the Bishop of Soissons. Three weeks later, under circumstances of brutality and insult, they were removed to the Conciergerie at Paris ; they wore their religious habits, their secular clothes referred to above being left " in the wash ". During the short time they were in this prison they continued to observe their rule so far as possible, reciting the Divine Office together at the proper hours, and greatly impressing and strengthening their fellow-prisoners. They were arraigned before three judges, Fouquier-Tinville prosecuting ; no legal assistance was allowed for the defence. The charges and the evidence produced were either frivolous or unproven, but Fouquier-Tinville accused them of being fanatics. Sister Mary Henrietta took him up and asked what he meant by the word. " I mean by it ", he replied, " your attachment to childish beliefs and your silly religious practices." The nun turned to her sisters. " You see ! " she said, " we are condemned for cling-ing to our holy religion. We have the happiness to die for God." They, together with M. de La Ménardière, who also was executed, were condemned for having made themselves " enemies of the people by conspiring against its sovereign rule ". Their journey in tumbrils to the guillotine in the Place du Trône Renversé (now the Place de la Nation) took more than an hour, and the nuns sang *Miserere, Salve Regina, Te Deum*, and recited the prayers for the dying. Their demeanour awed both the mob and the officials, as they mounted the scaffold one by one singing " Laudate Dominum omnes gentes ". There were sixteen victims : ten professed choir-nuns, one novice, three lay-sisters, and two extern-sisters or *tourières*. They met their deaths in the reverse order of seniority, the novice first, the prioress last ; and the bodies were straightway thrown into a pit with those of 1282 other victims of the Terror. This was all done on July 17, 1794.

The prioress, BD TERESA (Madeleine Ledoine), was forty-two years old, and had been a novice under Madame Louise de France at Saint-Denis. In the depositions for the process of beatification it was stated that she merited to be beatified quite apart from martyrdom. She was lively, charming, well-educated, a woman of parts. The sub-prioress, BD SAINT-LOUIS (Mary Anne Brideau), was by contrast silent and given to a meticulous observance of the letter of law and order. BD CHARLOTTE (Anne Mary Thouret) had as a girl no idea of entering on the monastic life. But at the age of twenty some unknown incident occurred which had the result of sending her into Carmel, where she was professed only after a long and difficult novitiate. BD EUPHRASIA (Mary Claude Brard) was a restless and lively person, whose temperament manifested itself on the one hand in excessive austerities and on the other in practical jokes at the expense of royal visitors. She was a great letter-writer (some correspondence from her cousin, La Ménardière, contributed to the nuns' denouncement), and a number of her correspondents' replies are extant. BD HENRIETTA (Gabrielle de Croissy) was a great-niece of Colbert. BD JULIA LOUISA was the widow of Chrétien de Neufville. Her husband had died after some years of great happiness and she had been prostrated with grief ; after going into the convent it was long before she showed any real disposition to persevere there. A sentence of hers may be well applied to others who in other times are called on to suffer, even though not physically, much less to death, for the faith : " We are the victims of the age, and we ought to sacri-fice ourselves to obtain its return to God." It was BD MARY HENRIETTA (Annette Pelras) who had pulled up the public prosecutor and elicited the fact that they were condemned on account of religion. The two *tourières* were sisters, BB. CATHERINE and TERESA SOIRON ; Teresa was very good-looking and had refused a place with the Princess de Lamballe to serve the Carmelites of her native town.   Only one of these victims was under thirty, and the eldest was seventy-eight.

These martyrs were beatified in 1906, the first authoritative declaration of the Church that there were true martyrs among the victims of the French Revolution. During the process the tribunal of information twice sat at Stanbrook Abbey, near Worcester, where the English Benedictine dames of Cambrai settled in 1838.

See the convenient little book of V. Pierre in the series "Les Saints" (1905), that of C. de Grandmaison (1906), and the articles of H. Chérot in *Études* for 1904 and 1905.   One member of the community, Mother Josephine (Frances Philippe), formerly prioress, deserted her fellows in the spring of 1794.   She was readmitted to Carmel at Sens in 1823, and wrote a most valuable account of the events, which was published in 1836 after her death.   There is a short sketch in English by E. M. Willson ; and see Fr Bruno, o.d.c., *Le Sang du Carmel* (1954).

18 : ST CAMILLUS DE LELLIS, Founder of the Ministers of the Sick   (A.D. 1614)

CAMILLUS DE LELLIS was born in 1550 at Bocchianico in the Abruzzi, when his mother was nearly sixty.   He grew to be a very big man—6 feet 6 inches tall and the rest in proportion—and when he was seventeen he went off with his father to fight with the Venetians against the Turks ; but soon he had contracted that painful and repulsive disease in his leg that was to afflict him for the rest of his life.   In 1571 he was admitted to the San Giacomo hospital for incurables at Rome, as a patient and servant ; after nine months he was dismissed, for his quarrelsomeness among other things, and he returned to active service in the Turkish war.   Though Camillus habitually referred to himself as a great sinner, his worst disorder was an addiction to gambling that continually reduced him to want and shame.   All playing at lawful games for exorbitant sums, and all games of hazard for considerable sums, are forbidden by the law of nature, by the laws of civilized nations, and by the canons of the Church.   No contract is justifiable in which neither reason nor proportion is observed.   Nor can it be consistent with justice for a man to stake any sum on blind chance, or to expose, without a reasonable equivalent or necessity, so much of his own or opponent's money, that the loss would notably distress himself or any other person.   A spirit of gaming often springs from avarice ; it is so hardened as to rejoice in the losses of others and is the source and occasion of many other vices.   Such considerations, if they were ever put plainly before Camillus, left him cold : in the autumn of 1574 he gambled away his savings, his arms, everything down to the proverbial shirt, which was stripped off his back in the streets of Naples.

The indigence to which he had reduced himself, and the memory of a vow he had made in a fit of remorse to join the Franciscans, caused him to accept work as a labourer on the new Capuchin buildings at Manfredonia, and there a moving exhortation which the guardian of the friars one day made him completed his conversion.   Ruminating on it as he rode upon his business, he at length fell on his knees, and with tears deplored his past unthinking life, and cried to Heaven for mercy.   This happened on Candlemas day in the year 1575, the twenty-fifth of his age ; and from that time he never interrupted his penitential course.   He entered the novitiate of the Capuchins, but could not be admitted to profession on account of the disease in his leg.   He therefore returned to the hospital of San Giacomo and devoted himself to the service of the sick.   The administrators, having been witnesses to his charity and ability, after some time appointed him superintendent of the hospital.

In those days the spiritual and physical conditions in hospitals were such as it is now difficult to credit, conditions largely due to the necessity of employing any staff that could be got, even criminals.   Camillus, grieving to see the unscrupulousness and slackness of hired servants in attending the sick, formed a project of associating for that office some of the attendants who desired to devote themselves to it out of a motive of charity.   He found several persons so disposed, but met with great obstacles in the execution of his design, particularly from that jealousy and suspicion that are so often provoked by disinterested reformers.   To make himself more useful in spiritually assisting the sick, he resolved, with the approval of his confessor, St Philip Neri, to receive holy orders, and was ordained by the vicegerent of Rome, Thomas Goldwell, Bishop of St Asaph, the exiled last bishop of the old English hierarchy.   A certain gentleman of Rome named Fermo Calvi gave him an annuity as his title of ordination.   Camillus decided to sever connection with San Giacomo and start on his own, though to do so was contrary to the advice of St Philip ; so with two companions he laid the foundations of his congregation : he prescribed certain short rules, and they went every day to the great hospital of the Holy Ghost, where they served the sick with so much affection and diligence that it was visible to all who saw them that they considered Christ Himself as lying sick or wounded in his members.

They made the beds of the patients, paid them every office of charity, and by their exhortations disposed them for the last sacraments and a happy death.   The founder had powerful adversaries and great difficulties to struggle with, but by confidence in God he conquered them all.   In 1585 he hired a larger house, and the success of his undertaking encouraged him to extend his activities : so he ordained that the members of his congregation should bind themselves to serve persons infected with the plague, prisoners, and those who lie dying in private houses ; later, in 1595 and 1601, some of his religious were sent with the troops fighting in Hungary and Croatia, thus forming the first recorded " military field ambulance ".   Nothing can deprive Henry Dunant of his honour for the part he played in the foundation of the International Red Cross ; but the memory should not be lost of those who before him concerned themselves with the wounded in battle, who include St Camillus de Lellis as well as Florence Nightingale.

In 1588 Camillus was invited to Naples, and with twelve companions founded there a new house.   Certain galleys having the plague on board were forbidden to enter the harbour, so the Ministers of the Sick (for that was the name they took) went on board, and attended them : on which occasion two of their number died of the pestilence, and were the first martyrs of charity in this institute.   St Camillus showed a like charity in Rome when a pestilential fever swept off great numbers, and again when that city was visited by a violent famine.   In 1591 Gregory XIV erected this congregation into a religious order, for perpetually serving the sick. They are now reckoned as clerks regular, are about equally divided between priests and lay-brothers, and follow their original work of nursing all sick persons without distinction, privately or in hospitals, or elsewhere.   The founder was, as has already been said, himself afflicted with many corporal sufferings : the disease in his leg for forty-six years ; a rupture for thirty-eight years ; two sores in the sole of one of his feet, which gave him great pain ; and, for a long time before he died, a distaste for food and inability to retain it.   Under this complication of infirmities he would not suffer anyone to wait on him, but sent all his brethren to serve others. When he was not able to stand he would creep out of his bed, even in the night, and crawl from one patient to another to see if they wanted anything.   Among many evils and dangers which the zeal of St Camillus prevented, his attention to the care of the dying soon made him discover that in hospitals many were buried alive.   Hence he ordered his religious to continue the prayers for souls yet in their agony for at least a quarter of an hour after they seemed to have drawn their last breath, and not to suffer their faces to be covered so soon as was usual, lest those who were not dead should be smothered.   St Camillus saw the foundation of fifteen houses of his brothers and eight hospitals, and Almighty God acknowledged his zeal and selflessness by the spirit of prophecy and the gift of miracles, and by many heavenly communications and favours.

The saint laid down the canonical leadership of his order in 1607.   But he assisted at the general chapter in Rome in 1613, and after it, with the new superior general, visited the houses, giving them his last exhortations.   At Genoa he was extremely ill : he recovered so as to be able to finish the visitation of his hospitals, but soon relapsed, and his life was now despaired of.   He received viaticum from the hands of Cardinal Ginnasi, and when he received the last anointing he made a moving exhortation to his brethren ; he expired on July 14, 1614, being sixty-four years old.   St Camillus de Lellis was canonized in 1746, and was, with St John-of-God, declared patron of the sick by Pope Leo XIII, and of nurses and nursing associations by Pope Pius XI.

The earliest account we possess of the saint's activities is the life which Father S. Cicatelli published in 1615, a year after his death ; Cicatelli had been his companion for twenty-six years.   This life was translated into English in the Oratorian series edited by Father Faber. There have been many others since, notably those by Bäumker in German, and by Blanc and Latarche in French ; but by far the fullest, based on a study of letters and original documents, is that by Mario Vanti, *S. Camillo de Lellis* (1929)´ ; see also his *San Giacomo degl' Incurabili di Roma* . . . (1938).   There is an excellent biography in English by Fr C. C. Martindale (1946) ; and *cf.* A. C. Oldmeadow, *Camillus : the Red Cross Saint* (1923).

SS. SYMPHOROSA AND HER SEVEN SONS, MARTYRS   (DATE UNKNOWN)

ACCORDING to her legend St Symphorosa was the widow of a martyr, St Getulius, living with her seven sons at Tivoli (Tibur), near Rome, during the reign of the Emperor Hadrian.   They attracted imperial notice when the emperor learned by oracle that the durability of his new palace at Tivoli depended on their sacrificing to the gods.   This Symphorosa refused to do, and after surviving torments she was drowned in the river Anio.   The next day the emperor had no better success with her sons, Crescens, Julian, Nemesius, Primativus, Justin, Stacteus and Eugenius ; and they too were put to death, each in a different way.   A Symphorosa was in fact buried at the ninth milestone on the Via Tiburtina, as were seven men called brothers, with names as above.

The resemblance between this case and that of St Felicity and her alleged seven sons (July 10) is obvious, and presents a problem that there would be no point in detailing here.   It is sufficient to quote Father Delehaye (*Origines du culte des martyrs*, pp. 278–279) :

Popular tradition, no doubt helped by the hagiographers, seems to have taken the same course on the Via Tiburtina which, in another place, has led to the endowment of St Felicity with a family of seven martyrs.   Seven saints, who probably had no other connexion than the proximity of their graves or of the anniversaries of their deaths, have been made into brothers and given to St Symphorosa as sons.   One may well ask if Symphorosa is anything but a doublet of St Felicity.

There is an old *cultus* of these martyrs at Tivoli (where the remains of a basilica were explored in 1877), and their *passio* was included by Ruinart in his *Acta sincera* and has found defenders in Paul Allard and some others ; but it is now generally held to belong in Delehaye's historical-romance category.   See his CMH., pp. 338, 382 ; *Étude sur le légendier romain*, pp. 121–123 ; and *Origines . . .*, *loc. cit.*   The *passio* is in Ruinart and in the *Acta Sanctorum*, July, vol. iv.   See also H. Stevenson on the basilica of St Symphorosa in his *Studi in Italia* (1878), vols. i and ii.

ST PAMBO   (*c.* A.D. 390)

ONE of the founders of the Nitrian group of monasteries in the deserts of Egypt was this St Pambo ; he became in his youth a disciple of St Antony, and was a fellow worker of such great fathers of the desert as the two Macarii and St Isidore of Pelusium and instructor of the " tall brothers ", Dioscorus, Ammon, Eusebius and Euthymius, who were persecuted for supporting Origenism.   He sharply rebuked their oppressor, Theophilus of Alexandria, when reproached for not speaking to that archbishop : " If he will not learn a lesson from my silence, neither will he from my words."   St Pambo had the usual characteristics of the monks of the Thebaïd : assiduous manual labour, usually in the making of mats from palm-leaf strips, long fasts, and other severe physical mortifications, and prayer uninterrupted over long periods of time ; his personal appearance was so majestic as to divert attention from the rags with which he was clothed : he would wear only such cast-offs as no one else would trouble to pick up.   His particular exercise was control of the tongue, both by silence and by careful consideration before speech, and, as with others, this sometimes led him into a pointed brusqueness which to more polished folk sounds somewhat discourteous.   Self-training in this respect was the result of his very first reading lesson.   His teacher began with the 38th psalm : " I said, I will take heed to my ways that I sin not with my tongue."   " That will do for to-day," said Pambo, and went off to think about it ; when he had considered the implications of that single text for about six months he came back to continue his lessons.

The world is prone to attribute wisdom to those who speak little, from that fact alone, regardless that silence may as much be due to emptiness as to understanding or strength ; but the numerous people who came to consult Pambo were not deceived : his mouth spoke wisdom, and some of his sayings are what is chiefly known of his life.   Rufinus visited him in 374, and later St Melania the Elder, the Roman widow who founded a convent in Jerusalem.   On her first visit she brought a gift of three hundred pounds of silver as a present for St Pambo ; he accepted it and said it should be for the benefit of poor monasteries—but no word of thanks.   Melania gently reminded ˙him : " There is three hundred pounds of silver, my father."—" He to whom you have offered this gift has no need for you to tell Him its value," was the reply.   Another time, when asked to count some money given to him to distribute in alms, he said : " God does not ask how much, but *how*."

Unlike some monks and ascetics St Pambo had no narrow outlook on other ways of life.   To two monks who disputed as to which were better of two men, one of whom had spent a fortune to become a monk and the other had done the same on corporal works of mercy, he said, " Before God both are perfect.   There are other roads to perfection besides being a monk."   And when two men came to him, detailing their austerities and alms-deeds and asking if thus they would save their souls, he replied, " I do the like, but am not thereby a good monk.   Seek never to offend your neighbour, and you will be saved."

Death came to St Pambo while he was plaiting a basket for his disciple Palladius. " Since I came into the desert I have eaten nothing that I have not earned by work, and I do not remember that I have ever said anything for which I had need to be sorry afterwards.   Nevertheless I must now go to God, before I have even begun to serve Him."   St Melania was there when he died ; she provided for his funeral, and took away the unfinished basket as a precious relic.

The references to Pambo in Rosweyde's *Vitae Patrum* have been printed in the *Acta Sanctorum*, July, vol. i.   Most of these derive ultimately from Palladius's *Lausiac History*, and from the *Historia Monachorum*, the Greek text of which has been edited by Preuschen. There is a convenient English translation of the *Lausiac History* by Lowther Clarke, and see Abbot Butler's edition.

ST PHILASTRIUS, BISHOP OF BRESCIA   (BEFORE A.D. 397)

WE know nothing certain of this saint's country, but he quitted it and the house and inheritance of his ancestors, like Abraham, the more perfectly to disengage himself from the ties of the world.   He travelled through many provinces to oppose infidels and heretics, especially the Arians, whose errors were at that time dispersed over the whole Church.   His zeal and faith gave him courage to rejoice with the Apostle in suffering for the truth, and to bear in his body the marks of a severe scourging which he underwent for asserting the true godhead of Jesus Christ.   At Milan he vigorously opposed the endeavours of Auxentius, the Arian, who laboured to destroy the flock of Christ there ; and he preached and held disputations with heretics in Rome itself, and afterwards went to Brescia.   Being chosen bishop of this see, he exerted himself with such vigour as even to outdo himself.   Alban Butler is understating when he says that Philastrius was not equal in learning to the Ambroses and Augustines of that age ; but what was wanting in that respect was abundantly made up by the example of his life, his spirit of humility and piety, and his unwearied application to every pastoral duty : he is an instance of what eminent service moderate abilities may be capable of when they are joined with a high degree of virtue.

To caution his flock against the danger of errors in faith St Philastrius wrote his *Catalogue of Heresies*, in which he does not take that word in its strict sense and according to the theological definition, but includes among his hundred and twenty-eight " heresies " a number of opinions which are matters of dispute : not only that, but he branded as heretics those who, for example, call the days of the week by heathen names (he would have approved the practice of the Society of Friends in this respect).   The work has little value in itself, but is of interest to scholars for the light it may throw on the work of other writers, *e.g.* Hippolytus. St Gaudentius in a panegyric of St Philastrius praises his modesty, quietness and sweetness towards all men ; he extended his liberality, not only to all that were reduced to beggary, but also to tradesmen and others, whom he generously enabled to carry on or to enlarge their business. St Augustine met St Philastrius at Milan with St Ambrose about the year 384. He died before St Ambrose, his metropolitan, who after his death placed his disciple St Gaudentius in the see of Brescia.

See the *Acta Sanctorum*, July, vol. iv. The authenticity of the panegyric by St Gaudentius, which is the source of most of our scanty information about Philastrius, has been questioned, but it is vindicated by Knappe and Poncelet : see the *Analecta Bollandiana*, vol. xxviii (1909), p. 224 ; and *cf.* Bardenhewer, *Patrologie*, § 89. See also P. de Labriolle and G. Bardy, *Histoire de la littérature latine chrétienne* (1947), pp. 432–434.

ST ARNULF, OR ARNOUL, BISHOP OF METZ   (*c.* A.D. 643)

THIS Arnulf, born of noble parents and educated in learning and piety, was called to the court of King Theodebert II of Austrasia, in which he was equally admired for prudence in council and valour in the field : he joined the virtues of a Christian with the duties of a statesman. Having married a noble lady called Doda, he had by her two sons, Clodulf and Ansegisel ; by the latter's marriage with a daughter of Bd Pepin (called " of Landen ") the Carlovingian kings of France descended from St Arnoul.

Fearing the danger of entangling his soul in the many affairs which passed through his hands, he wanted to retire to the monastery of Lérins, but was stopped by the clergy and people of Metz demanding him for their bishop. He was therefore consecrated about the year 610, and while fulfilling his new duties with exactness, he continued to take a prominent part in public affairs : as, for example, on the death of Theodebert and his brother Thierry, when with other nobles he called Clotaire of Neustria to the throne of Austrasia. Ten years later Clotaire divided his dominions, and giving charge of Austrasia to his son Dagobert, appointed St Arnoul his chief counsellor. The holy bishop did not for long continue to guide this prince ; he asked and received permission to quit the court, which he had long wished to do (Dagobert at first threatened to cut Arnoul's son's head off if he went away). He then resigned his bishopric, and retired with a friend, St Romaricus, to a hermitage in the Vosges mountains, later the monastery of Remiremont. Here he died.

Nearly all the material which is relevant will be found in the *Acta Sanctorum*, July, vol. iv. The contemporary Latin life has been re-edited by B. Krusch in MGH., *Scriptores Merov.*, vol. ii, pp. 426–446. On the genealogies see Saltet in *Mélanges Léonce Couture*, pp. 77–95 ; and *cf.* the articles of J. Depoin in the *Revue Mabillon*, vols. xi and xii.

ST FREDERICK, BISHOP OF UTRECHT, MARTYR   (A.D. 838)

FREDERICK was trained in piety and sacred learning among the clergy of the church of Utrecht. Being ordained priest, he was charged by Bishop Ricfried with the care of instructing converts, and about 825 he was chosen to succeed him as bishop of Utrecht. The new bishop at once began to establish order everywhere, and sent St Odulf and other zealous and virtuous labourers into the northern parts to dispel the paganism which still subsisted there.

According to tradition St Frederick became involved in the difficulties between the sons of the emperor, Louis the Debonair, and their father and step-mother. During these disturbances the party of the young princes charged the Empress Judith with numerous immoralities. Whatever may have been the truth of these stories, St Frederick is said to have admonished her of them, with charity but with the effect of drawing upon himself the fury and resentment of the empress. He also got himself disliked elsewhere. The inhabitants of Walcheren were barbarous and most averse from the gospel. On which account St Frederick, when he sent priests into the northern parts of his diocese, took this most dangerous and difficult part chiefly to himself; and nothing gave him more trouble than marriages contracted within the forbidden degrees and the separation of the parties (that the union of Louis and Judith was itself incestuous was an afterthought of hagiographers).

The story goes on that, on July 18, 838, after St Frederick had celebrated Mass and was about to make his thanksgiving, he was stabbed by two assassins. He died in a few minutes, reciting that verse of Psalm 114, " I will praise the Lord in the land of the living ". The eleventh-century author of his life says these assassins were employed by the Empress Judith, who could not pardon the liberty he had taken to reprove her sins, and was incited thereto by her husband. William of Malmesbury and others repeat the same; but later writers, such as Baronius and Mabillon, think that they were rather sent by some of the inhabitants of Walcheren. And this seems the more likely opinion : for no contemporary makes the charge against Judith and it is not at all in consonance with the attitude of Louis towards episcopal authority and Christian conduct.

St Frederick composed a prayer to the Blessed Trinity which for many ages was used in the Netherlands. The reputation of his sanctity appears from a poem of Rabanus Maurus, his contemporary, in praise of his virtue.

The Life of St Frederick, with other materials, is printed in the *Acta Sanctorum*, July. vol. iv, and it has also been re-edited in MGH., vol. xv. *Cf.* Duchesne, *Fastes Épiscopaux*, vol. iii, p. 196. There is a notice of Frederick in DNB., vol. xiii, *s.v.* Cridiodunus ; his nationality is uncertain, but he may have been of Wessex descent.

ST BRUNO, BISHOP OF SEGNI   (A.D. 1123)

BRUNO was of the family of the lords of Asti in Piedmont, and born near that city. He made his studies in the university of Bologna, and was made a canon of Siena. He was called to Rome and there, in the council of 1079, he defended the doctrine of the Church concerning the Blessed Sacrament against Berengarius of Tours ; Pope Gregory VII nominated him bishop of Segni in the following year, Bruno's humbleness prompting him to refuse a cardinalate. Bruno served his flock with unwearied zeal ; he was a personal friend of St Gregory and entered with fearless enthusiasm into all his projects for the reform of the Church, suffering imprisonment for three months at the hands of Count Ainulf, a partisan of the Emperor Henry IV. He went with Bd Urban II into France in 1095, and assisted at the Council of Clermont-Ferrand, and returning into Italy he continued to labour for the sanctification of his flock till, not being able any longer to resist his inclination for solitude and retirement, and still persecuted by Ainulf, he withdrew to Monte Cassino and received the monastic habit. The people of Segni demanded him back ; but the abbot of Monte Cassino prevailed upon the pope to allow his retreat, but not the resignation of his see. In 1107 he was elected abbot of the monastery.

Bruno by his writings laboured to support ecclesiastical discipline and to extirpate simony. This abuse, together with that of lay investiture to ecclesiastical offices, he looked upon as a main source of the disorders which saddened zealous pastors in the church, by filling the sanctuary with hirelings and by corrupting with avarice and ambition those in whom, above all others, a perfect freedom from earthly things ought to lay a foundation of the gospel temper and spirit.   He indeed took it upon himself to rebuke Pope Paschal II, who had been persuaded by the emperor elect, Henry V, to make concessions in the matter of ecclesiastical privileges and investiture in Germany.   The pope retorted by ordering Bruno to resign his abbacy and return to his bishopric, and was at once obeyed.   He continued faithfully in the discharge of his duties and in writing, especially commentaries on the Holy Scriptures, until his death in 1123.   He was the greatest scriptural commentator of his age, but in theology he maintained the extreme and erroneous view that the sacraments administered by bishops or priests who had been guilty of simony were invalid.   Bruno was canonized in 1183.

There are two lives of Bruno printed in the *Acta Sanctorum*, July, vol. iv, the shorter and earlier being the work of that historically unscrupulous writer Peter the Deacon ; but the main facts given above may be trusted.   See B. Gigalski, *Bruno Bischof von Segni* (1898). Bruno is noticed in both DTC. and DHG.

19 : ST VINCENT DE PAUL, FOUNDER OF THE CONGREGATION OF THE MISSION AND THE SISTERS OF CHARITY   (A.D. 1660)

EVEN in the most degenerate ages, when the truths of the Gospel seem almost obliterated among the generality of those who profess it, God fails not to raise to himself faithful ministers to revive charity in the hearts of many.   One of these instruments of the divine mercy was St Vincent de Paul. He was a native of Pouy, a village near Dax, in Gascony.   His parents occupied a very small farm, upon the produce of which they brought up a family of four sons and two daughters, Vincent being their third child.   His father was determined by the strong inclinations of the boy and the quickness of his intelligence to give him a school education.   He therefore placed him under the care of the Cordeliers (Franciscan Recollects) at Dax.   Vincent finished his studies at the university of Toulouse, and in 1600 was ordained priest at the extraordinary age of twenty.

In the little we know of Vincent at this time there is nothing to suggest his future fame and sanctity.   Indeed, the outstanding event, his trip to Marseilles and the captivity in and romantic escape from Tunisia that is said to have followed it, raises such delicate questions and has been so controverted that—without wishing to indulge any improper suppressions—it seems better to ignore it and to get on more solid ground.

On his own showing, Vincent's ambition at that time was to be comfortably off.   He was already one of the chaplains of Queen Margaret of Valois and, according to the bad custom of the age, he was receiving the income of a small abbey.   He went to lodge with a friend in Paris.   And there it was that we first hear of a change in him.   His friend was robbed of four hundred crowns.   He charged Vincent with the theft, thinking it could be nobody else ; and in this persuasion he spoke against him with the greatest virulence among all his friends, and wherever he went.   Vincent calmly denied the fact, saying, " God knows the truth ".   He bore this slander for six months, when the true thief confessed.   St Vincent related this in a spiritual conference with his priests, but as of a third person ; to show that patience, humble silence, and resignation are generally the best defence of our innocence, and always the happiest means of sanctifying our souls under slanders and persecution.

At Paris Vincent became acquainted with the holy priest Peter de Bérulle, afterwards cardinal. Bérulle conceived a great esteem for Vincent, and prevailed with him to become tutor to the children of Philip de Gondi, Count of Joigny. Mme de Gondi was attracted by Vincent, and chose him for her spiritual director and confessor.

In the year 1617, whilst they were at a country seat at Folleville, Monsieur Vincent was sent for to hear the confession of a peasant who lay dangerously ill. He discovered that all the former confessions of the penitent had been sacrilegious, and the man declared before many persons and the Countess of Joigny herself, that he would have been eternally lost if he had not spoken to Monsieur Vincent. The good lady was struck with horror to hear of such past sacrileges. Far from the criminal illusion of pride by which some masters and mistresses seem persuaded that they owe no care, attention or provision for their dependants, she realized that masters lie under strict ties of justice and charity towards all committed to their care ; and that they are bound to see them provided with the necessary spiritual helps for their salvation. To Vincent himself also appears to have come at that moment an enlightening as to the terrible spiritual state of the peasantry of France, and Mme de Gondi had no difficulty in persuading him to preach in the church of Folleville, and fully to instruct the people in the duty of repentance and confession of sins. He did so ; and such crowds flocked to him to make general confessions that he was obliged to call the Jesuits of Amiens to his assistance.

With the help of Father de Bérulle, St Vincent left the house of the countess in 1617 to become pastor of Châtillon-les-Dombes. He there converted the notorious Count de Rougemont and many others from their scandalous lives. But he soon returned to Paris, and began work among the galley-slaves who were confined in the Conciergerie. He was officially appointed chaplain to the galleys (of which Philip de Gondi was general), and in 1622 gave a mission for the convicts in them at Bordeaux ; but the story that Monsieur Vincent once took the place of one of them at the oar has no evidence to support it.

Mme de Gondi now offered him an endowment to found a perpetual mission among the common people in the place and manner he should think fit, but nothing at first came of it, for Vincent was too humble to regard himself as fit to undertake the work. The countess could not be easy herself whilst she was deprived of his direction and advice ; she therefore obtained from him a promise that he would never abandon the direction of her conscience so long as she lived, and that he would assist her at her death. But being extremely desirous that others, especially those who were particularly entitled to her care and attention, should want nothing that could contribute to their sanctification and salvation, she induced her husband to concur with her in establishing a company of able and zealous missionaries who should be employed in assisting their vassals and tenants, and the people of the countryside in general. This project they proposed to their brother, who was archbishop of Paris, and he gave the Collège des Bons Enfants for the reception of the new community. Its members were to renounce ecclesiastical preferment, to devote themselves to the smaller towns and villages, and to live from a common fund. St Vincent took possession of this house in April 1625.

Vincent attended the countess till her death, which happened only two months later; he then joined his new congregation. In 1633 the prior of the canons regular of St Victor gave to this institute the priory of Saint-Lazare, which was made the chief house of the congregation, and from it the Fathers of the Mission are often called Lazarists, but sometimes Vincentians, after their founder. They are a congregation of secular priests, who make four simple vows of poverty, chastity, obedience and stability. They are employed in missions, especially among country people, and undertake the direction of diocesan and other seminaries; they now have colleges and missions in all parts of the world. St Vincent lived to see twenty-five houses founded in France, Piedmont, Poland and other places, including Madagascar.

This foundation, though so extensive and beneficial, could not satisfy the zeal of this apostolic man. He by every other means studied to procure the relief of others under all necessities, whether spiritual or corporal. For this purpose he established confraternities of charity (the first had been at Châtillon) to attend poor sick persons in each parish, and from them, with the help of St Louise de Marillac, sprang the institute of Sisters of Charity, whose "convent is the sickroom, their chapel the parish church, their cloister the streets of the city". He invoked the assistance of the wealthy women of Paris and banded them together as the Ladies of Charity to collect funds for and assist in his good works. He procured and directed the foundation of several hospitals for the sick, foundlings, and the aged, and at Marseilles the hospital for the galley-slaves, which, however, was never finished. All these establishments he settled under excellent regulations, and found for them large sums of money. He instituted a particular plan of spiritual exercises for those about to receive holy orders; and others for those who desire to make general confessions, or to deliberate upon the choice of a state of life; and also appointed regular ecclesiastical conferences on the duties of the clerical state, to remedy somewhat the terrible slackness, abuses and ignorance that he saw about him. It appears almost incredible that so many and so great things could have been effected by one man, and a man who had no advantages from birth, fortune, or any of those more obvious qualities which the world admires and esteems.

During the wars in Lorraine, being informed of the miseries to which those provinces were reduced, St Vincent collected alms in Paris, which were sent thither to the amount of thousands of pounds. He sent his missionaries to the poor and suffering in Poland, Ireland, Scotland, the very Hebrides, and during his own life over 1200 Christian slaves were ransomed in North Africa, and many others succoured. He was sent for by King Louis XIII as he lay dying, and was in high favour with the queen regent, Anne of Austria, who consulted him in ecclesiastical affairs and in the collation of benefices; during the affair of the Fronde he in vain tried to persuade her to give up her minister Mazarin in the interests of her people. It was largely due to Monsieur Vincent that English Benedictine nuns from Ghent were allowed to open a house at Boulogne in 1652.

Amidst so many and so great matters his soul seemed always united to God. Under set-backs, disappointments and slanders he preserved serenity and evenness of mind, having no other desire but that God should be glorified in all things. Astonishing as it may seem, Monsieur Vincent was "by nature of a bilious temperament and very subject to anger". This would seem humble exaggeration but that others besides himself bear witness to it. But for divine grace, he tells us, he would have been "in temper hard and repellent, rough and crabbed"; instead, his will co-operated with grace and he was tender, affectionate, acutely sensible to the calls of charity and religion. Humility he would have then to be the basis of his congregation, and it was the lesson which he never ceased to repeat. When two persons of unusual learning and abilities once presented themselves, desiring to be admitted into his congregation, he refused them both, saying, " Your abilities raise you above our low state. Your talents may be of good service in some other place. Our highest ambition is to instruct the ignorant, to bring sinners to repentance, and to plant the gospel spirit of charity, humility, meekness and simplicity in the hearts of Christians." He laid it down that, if possible, a man ought never to speak of himself or his own concerns, such discourse usually proceeding from, and nourishing in the heart, pride and self-love.

St Vincent was greatly concerned at the rise and spread of the Jansenist heresy. " I have made the doctrine of grace the subject of my prayer for three months ", he said, " and every day God has confirmed my faith that our Lord died for us all and that He desires to save the whole world." He actively opposed himself to the false teachers and no priest professing their errors could remain in his congregation.

Towards the end of his life he suffered much from serious ill-health. In the autumn of 1660 he died calmly in his chair, on September 27, being fourscore years old. Monsieur Vincent, the peasant priest, was canonized by Pope Clement XII in 1737, and by Pope Leo XIII he was proclaimed patron of all charitable societies, outstanding among which is the society that bears his name and is infused by his spirit, founded by Frederic Ozanam in Paris in 1833.

The abundant materials for the life of St Vincent have been edited with great care by Fr Pierre Coste, *Saint Vincent de Paul, correspondance, entretiens, documents*, occupying fourteen volumes (1920–25), completed by his *Le grand saint du grand siècle* (3 vols., Eng. trans., 1935). Biographies are numerous, beginning with that of Mgr Abelly published four years after Vincent's death. The lives by Bougaud, de Broglie, and Lavedan have appeared in English ; the last-named, *The Heroic Life of St Vincent de Paul* (1928), though written with great charm of style, is not perhaps historically so accurate as *La vraie vie de S. Vincent de Paul* by A. Redier (1927), or *S. Vincent de Paul* by P. Renaudin (1929). The religious spirit of the saint is very well illustrated in the selection of letters translated by Fr J. Leonard under the title *St Vincent de Paul and Mental Prayer* (1925). See also *St Vincent of Paul and the Vincentians in England*, by P. Boyle ; E. K. Sanders, *Vincent de Paul* (1913) ; T. Maynard, *Apostle of Charity* (1940) ; two studies by A. Ménabréa (1947– 48) ; E. Canitrot, *Le plus familier des saints* (1947) ; and J. Calvet's *St Vincent de Paul* (1948), Eng. trans. by L. C. Sheppard (1952).

SS. JUSTA AND RUFINA, VIRGINS AND MARTYRS   (A.D. 287 ?)

THESE martyrs were two Christian women at Seville in Spain who maintained themselves by selling earthenware. Not to concur in idolatrous superstitions, they refused to sell vessels for the use of heathen ceremonies, and when the worshippers broke up their stock-in-trade Justa and Rufina retorted by overthrowing the image of a false goddess. Whereupon the people impeached them for their faith before the governor. The prefect, after they had boldly confessed Christ, commanded them to be stretched on the rack and their sides to be torn with hooks. An idol was placed near the rack with incense, that if they would offer sacrifice they should be released ; but their fidelity was not to be shaken. Justa died on the rack ; the judge ordered Rufina to be strangled, and their bodies to be burnt. They are greatly venerated in Spain, and no doubt their names represent historical martyrs in that place. But their acts are unreliable and one of the martyrs appears to have undergone a change of sex in the course of the ages, for Justa was originally called Justus.

See the *Acta Sanctorum*, July, vol. iv ; Florez, *España Sagrada*, vol. ix, pp. 338–343 ; Gams, *Kirchengeschichte v. Spanien*, vol. i, pp. 284–288.

ST MACRINA THE YOUNGER, Virgin (A.D. 379)

MACRINA was the eldest of ten children of St Basil the Elder and St Emmelia, and was born at Caesarea in Cappadocia about the year 330. She was brought up with particular care by her mother, who both taught her to read and exercised vigilance over how she used that accomplishment : the Wisdom of Solomon and the Psalms of David were her constant companions. Nor were household duties and the spinning and weaving of wool neglected. At twelve years old she was betrothed, but after the sudden death of the young man she refused all other suitors, and was a great assistant to her mother in educating her younger brothers and sisters. St Basil the Great, St Peter of Sebastea, St Gregory of Nyssa and the rest learned from her contempt of the world, dread of its dangers, and application to prayer and the word of God ; Basil, in particular, we are told, came back from the schools a very conceited young man, and his sister taught him humility ; while to Peter, the youngest, she was " father, teacher, guide, mother, giver of good advice ", for his father died just as he was born. Basil the younger then established his mother and Macrina on an estate by the river Iris in Pontus, and there they were joined by other women in an ascetic communal life.

After the death of St Emmelia, Macrina disposed of all that was left of their estate in favour of the poor, and lived on what she earned by the labour of her hands. Her brother Basil died in the beginning of the year 379, and she herself fell ill nine months after. St Gregory of Nyssa, making her a visit after eight years' absence, found her sick, lying on two boards for her bed. He was exceedingly comforted by her cheerfulness and encouragement, and impressed by the fervour of love with which she prepared herself for death. She died very happily at the hour of the lighting of lamps. Such was her poverty that nothing was found to cover her body when it was carried to the grave but her old hood and coarse veil ; St Gregory therefore provided a special linen robe. Araxius, bishop of the place, and St Gregory, with two priests, themselves carried the bier in the funeral procession, choirs singing psalms all the way to the place of burial ; but the press of the crowd and lamentations of the people, especially of some of the women, much disturbed the solemnity of the chant.

An account of the life of St Macrina, with details of her conversation, death and burial, have been left us by St Gregory himself in the form of a dialogue on the soul and resurrection, and of a panegyric on his sister addressed to the monk Olympius. In the last of these he speaks of two miracles, the one when his sister was cured of a growth at the sign of the cross made by her mother ; the other, when Macrina herself healed the diseased eye of the small daughter of a military officer. He adds : " I do not think it expedient to add to my story all the similar things that we heard from those who lived with her and knew her intimately. . . . Though they seem incredible, they are all believed to be true by those who have carefully investigated them. But they are judged by the carnally-minded to be outside the possible. . . . And so, lest the unbeliever should suffer hurt by being led to disbelieve the gifts of God, I have abstained from a consecutive narrative of these sublime marvels. . . ." The which observation discloses another aspect of the meaning of the saying that it takes a saint to write the life of a saint.

We know little or nothing of St Macrina except what may be gathered from the memoir written by her brother, St Gregory of Nyssa. The Greek text will be found in his works, a Latin translation is given in the *Acta Sanctorum*, July, vol. iv, and there is an English translation by W. K. Lowther Clarke (1916). The feast of St Macrina is kept in the Byzantine rite.

ST ARSENIUS THE GREAT   (*c.* A.D. 450)

WHEN the Emperor Theodosius the Great wanted a man to whom he might entrust the education of his children Pope St Damasus recommended Arsenius, a man of senatorial rank learned in both sacred and profane knowledge. He accordingly went to Constantinople and was appointed to the post by Theodosius who, coming once to see Arcadius and Honorius at their studies, found them sitting whilst Arsenius talked to them standing : at once he caused Arsenius to sit and ordered them to listen to him standing. But neither then nor in after-life were the two *augusti* any credit either to such a father or such a tutor ; added to this Arsenius had always a great inclination to a retired life. When therefore after over ten years at the court he seemed clearly to hear the voice of God saying, " Flee the company of men and you shall be saved ", he left Constantinople and came by sea to Alexandria. After the death of Theodosius the monks with whom he lived taunted him as " Father of the Emperors " ; but the careers of his two pupils and his failure to make decent men of them was the last thing he wanted to be reminded of, and he fled into the wilderness.*

When he first presented himself to the superiors of the monks of Skete they recommended him to the care of St John the Dwarf who, when the rest in the evening sat down to take their meal, took his place among them and left Arsenius standing in the middle without taking notice of him. Such a reception was a severe trial to an ex-courtier ; but was followed by another much rougher, for St John took a loaf of bread and threw it on the ground before him, bidding him with an air of indifference to eat if he would. Arsenius cheerfully sat on the ground and took his meal. St John was so satisfied with his behaviour that he required no further trial for his admission, and said to his brethren, " This man will make a monk ". Arsenius at first used thoughtlessly to do certain things which he had done in the world, which seemed to his new companions to savour of levity or lack of physical recollection, as, for instance, to sit cross-legged. The seniors were unwilling through the respect they bore him to tell him of this in public, so one agreed with another that he should put himself in that posture, and then be rebuked for his immodesty ; nor did the other offer any excuse. Arsenius saw that the reproof was meant for him, and corrected himself of that trick. He employed himself in making mats of palm-tree leaves ; and he never changed the water in which he moistened the leaves, but only poured in fresh water upon it as it wasted. When some asked him why he did not cast away the filthy water, he answered, " I ought to be punished by this smell for the self-indulgence with which I formerly used perfumes ". He lived in the most utter poverty, so that in an illness, having

---

* Of Arcadius Gibbon wrote, " The bold satirist, who has indulged his discontent by the partial and passionate censure of the Christian emperors, violates the dignity rather than the truth of history by comparing the son of Theodosius to one of those harmless and simple animals who scarcely feel that they are the property of their shepherd."

need for a small sum to procure him some little necessaries, he was obliged to beg for it. The sickness continued so long that the priest of this desert of Skete carried him to his apartment and laid him on a bed made of the skins of beasts, with a pillow under his head : but this was considered pampering by some of the hermits. One of the emperor's officers, at another time, brought him the will of a senator, his relation, who was lately dead, and had left him his heir. The saint took the will and would have torn it to pieces, but the officer begged him not to, saying such an accident would get him into trouble. Arsenius, however, refused the estate, saying, " I died before him and cannot be made his heir ". Though no one knew his fasts, they must have been great, for the measure of corn sent him for the year was very small, yet he managed not only to make it suffice for himself, but also to give some to others.

Arsenius often passed the whole night in watching and prayer, and on Saturdays it was his custom to go to prayers at sunset and continue with his hands lifted up to Heaven till the sun beat on his face the next morning. He had two disciples who lived near him. Their names were Alexander and Zoilus : he afterwards admitted a third called Daniel. All three were famous for their sanctity and frequent mention is made of them in the histories of the fathers of the deserts of Egypt. St Arsenius would seldom see strangers who came to visit him, but Theophilus, Archbishop of Alexandria, came one day in company with others to visit him, and begged he would speak on some subject for the good of their souls. The saint asked them whether they were disposed to comply with his directions ; and being answered in the affirmative, he replied, " I entreat you then that, whenever you are informed of Arsenius's abode, you would leave him to himself and spare yourselves the trouble of coming after him ". He never visited his brethren, contenting himself with meeting them at spiritual conferences. The abbot Mark asked him one day why he so much shunned their company. The saint answered, " God knows how dearly I love you all ; but I find I cannot be both with God and with men at the same time ; nor can I think of leaving God to converse with men ". This disposition, however, did not hinder him from giving spiritual instruction to his brethren, and several of his sayings are recorded. He said often, " I have always something to repent of after having talked, but have never been sorry for having been silent " ; and he had frequently in his mouth those words which St Euthymius and St Bernard used also to repeat to themselves to renew their fervour, " Arsenius, why have you forsaken the world, and wherefore are you come hither ? " Being asked one day why he, being so well educated, sought the instruction and advice of a certain monk who was an utter stranger to all literature, he replied, " I am not unacquainted with the learning of the Greeks and Romans ; but I have not yet learned the alphabet of the science of the saints, whereof this seemingly ignorant person is master ". Evagrius of Pontus who, after he had distinguished himself at Constantinople by his learning, had retired into the desert of Nitria in 385, expressed surprise that many learned men made no progress in virtue, whilst many Egyptians, who did not even know the letters of the alphabet, arrived at a high degree of contemplation. Arsenius answered, " We make no progress because we dwell in that exterior learning which puffs up the mind ; but these illiterate Egyptians have a true sense of their own weakness, blindness, and in-sufficiency ; and by that very thing they are qualified to labour successfully in the pursuit of virtue ". Nothing is so much spoken of by ancient writers about Arsenius as his gift of tears, weeping both over his own shortcomings and those of the world, particularly the feebleness of Arcadius and the foolishness of Honorius.

St Arsenius was tall and comely but stooped a little in his old age ; he had a graceful carriage and a certain shining beauty and air of both majesty and meekness ; his hair was all white, and his beard reached down to his girdle, but the tears which he shed continually had worn away his eye-lashes. He was forty years old when he quitted the court, and he lived in the same austere manner from that time to the age of about ninety-five ; he spent forty years in the desert of Skete, till a raid of barbarians compelled him to forsake this abode about the year 434. He retired to the rock of Troë, over against Memphis, and ten years after to the island of Canopus, near Alexandria ; but not being able to bear the neighbourhood of that city, he returned to Troë, where he died. His brethren, seeing him weep in his last hours, said to him, " Father, why do you weep ? Are you, like others, afraid to die ? " The saint answered, " I am very afraid—nor has this dread ever forsaken me from the time I first came into these deserts ". Notwithstanding his fear, St Arsenius died in great peace, full of faith and of that humble confidence which perfect charity inspires, about the year 449 or 450. He is named in the canon of the Armenian Mass.

The Bollandists have published, with a translation, the Greek life written by Theodore Studites. A better text, unknown to them, was edited in 1920 by T. Nissen in the *Byzant. Neugriech. Jahrbuch*, pp. 241–262. See also the commentary in the *Acta Sanctorum*, July, vol. iv, and DCB., vol. i, pp. 172–174.

ST SYMMACHUS, POPE (A.D. 514)

ACCORDING to the *Liber Pontificalis*, this pope was the son of one Fortunatus, and a native of Sardinia. He was baptized at Rome, became archdeacon of the Roman church under Pope Anastasius II, and succeeded him in the Holy See in 498. But there was a minority of the clergy with Byzantine sympathies, and they, on the same day that Symmachus was elected at the Lateran, met at Santa Maria Maggiore and elected one Laurence, the archpriest of St Praxedes ; they were helped with money by Festus, a senator who had been gained by Anastasius, emperor at Constantinople and later a protector of the monophysites, to endeavour to procure papal confirmation of the *Henotikon* of Zeno, an imperial document condemned by the Holy See. Both claimants appealed to Theodoric, the Gothic king at Ravenna (he was an Arian), who decided in favour of Symmachus as the lawful pope because he had been elected first and by the greater number ; he also gave him a testimonial that he " loved the clergy and the poor, and was good, prudent, kindly and gracious". But this far from ended the troubles, which disturbed all the first half of the pontificate.

The name of St Symmachus does not figure in the earlier martyrologies, and little is known of him personally. When the Arian Thrasimund banished many African bishops to Sardinia, Symmachus sent them clothes and money for themselves and their flocks ; there is still extant a letter which he sent to comfort them, accompanied by some relics of martyrs. He established three hospices for the poor, sent relief to those suffering from barbarian raids in northern Italy, and redeemed many captives. He decorated and restored several churches in Rome, and built a new basilica of St Andrew, one of St Pancras outside the walls, and one of St Agnes on the Aurelian Way. According to custom inscriptions were made on the various works ; in one the thankful pope refers to the end of the troubles with Laurence : " The biting of the wolves has ceased." Pope St Symmachus died on July 19, 514, and was buried in St Peter's.

This saint's life is a matter of general church history, and may be found in fuller detail in such works as Hefele-Leclercq, *Conciles*, vol. ii, pp. 957–973, and 1349–1372 ; Grisar, *History of Rome and the Popes*, etc., and *cf.* Duchesne's *L'Église au VIe siècle* (1925), pp. 113–130. See also the *Liber Pontificalis* (Duchesne), vol. i, pp. cxxxiii *seq.*, 44–46 and 260–263. The pope's letters are in Thiel, *Epp. Rom. Pont.*

ST AMBROSE AUTPERT   (A.D. 778 ?)

THIS St Ambrose was a distinguished official at the court of King Pepin the Short. Being sent as the king's envoy into Italy, he had occasion to visit the Benedictine monastery of St Vincent, on the Volturno in the duchy of Benevento, and was so impressed by the spirit and observance of the monks that he received the habit there, and proceeded to profession and ordination. He was a successful preacher and some of his sermons are extant ; he led a holy and uneventful life, devoted to his writings, which were very greatly esteemed in the middle ages : so much so that his treatise on the conflict between the virtues and the vices was attributed to *the* St Ambrose, to St Augustine, to St Leo IX and to St Isidore of Seville in turn. He also wrote lives of the saints and a commentary on the Apocalypse. Of these works Dom Morin writes : " His learning and manner of writing make Ambrose a remarkable phenomenon, and rather a puzzle ; one asks oneself where and how he was able to acquire such a formation, in his time and among such surroundings." His talents did not lack admiration and appreciation : Charlemagne consulted him (Ambrose had been at one time his tutor) and Pope Stephen IV befriended him ; nor was he without love and honour in his own monastery, for about the year 776, the abbacy becoming vacant, the Frankish element among the monks elected him. But unhappily a Lombard *clique* opposed to Ambrose as their choice a certain Potho ; the trouble reached Rome, and Pope Adrian I summoned the rivals to appear before him. On the journey St Ambrose Autpert died. He was buried in St Peter's, but his relics were translated about the year 1044 to the abbey he had ruled for so short a time.

There is a short Latin life which has been printed by Muratori, Mabillon, etc., and which will be found also in the *Acta Sanctorum*, July, vol. iv. See especially G. Morin, *Revue Bénédictine*, vol. xxvii (1910), pp. 204–212, and Morin, *Études, Textes, Découvertes* (1913), pp. 23, 488, 494, 498, 506. See also J. Winandy, *Ambroise Autpert, moine et théologien* (1953).

BD STILLA, VIRGIN   (*c.* A.D. 1140)

BD STILLA was born at Abenberg, near Nuremberg, towards the end of the eleventh century, of the family of the counts of Abenberg, which gave many priests, bishops and holy men to the Church.

Stilla had built at her own expense, on a hill adjoining her home, a church which was consecrated and dedicated in honour of St Peter in 1136 ; she visited this church every day, and therein, in the presence of St Otto, Bishop of Bamberg, she took a vow of virginity. She lived the life of a nun within her father's household, engaging herself in the relief of all unfortunates, and she hoped in time to build a monastery wherein she might end her days. But death overtook her first.

Her brothers wanted to bury her at Heilsbronn, but the two horses drawing the funeral car could not pull it in that direction, turning always towards the church of St Peter, where therefore they buried her. The tomb became a place of pilgrimage, and in 1897 the bishop of Eichstätt was able to establish that the veneration of Stilla had gone on since before 1534. This *cultus* was confirmed in 1927.

A short account of Bd Stilla, with reports of a number of miracles, will be found in the *Acta Sanctorum*, July, vol. iv. The decree confirming the *cultus* and containing a summary of her life is printed in the *Acta Apostolicae Sedis*, vol. xix (1927), pp. 140–142.

20 : ST JEROME EMILIANI, Founder of the Somaschi   ʻ(A.D. 1537)

JEROME was born at Venice in 1481, the son of Angelo Emiliani (*vulgo* Miani) and Eleanor Mauroceni, and served in the armies of the republic during the troubled times of the beginning of the sixteenth century. When the League of Cambrai was formed to resist the Venetians, he was appointed to the command of the fortress of Castelnuovo, in the mountains near Treviso ; at the fall of the town he was taken prisoner and chained in a dungeon. Hitherto he had led a careless and irreligious life, but now he sanctified his sufferings by prayer and turning to God, and, in circumstances which appeared to be miraculous, he was enabled to make his escape. He made his way at once to a church in Treviso and, probably later, hung up his fetters as votive offerings before the altar of our Lady, to whom he had vowed himself ; and was given the post of mayor in the town. But he shortly after returned to Venice to take charge of the education of his nephews and to pursue his own sacerdotal studies, and in 1518 he was ordained.

Famine and plague having reduced many to the greatest distress, St Jerome devoted himself to relieving all, but particularly abandoned orphans. These he gathered in a house which he hired ; clothed and fed them at his own expense, and instructed them himself in Christian doctrine and virtue. After himself recovering from the plague, he resolved in 1531 to devote himself and his property solely to others, and founded orphanages at Brescia, Bergamo, and Como, a shelter for penitent prostitutes, and a hospital at Verona. About 1532 Jerome with two other priests established a congregation of men, and at Somascha, between Bergamo and Milan, he founded a house which he destined for the exercises of those whom he received into his congregation. From this house it took its name, the Clerks Regular of Somascha, and its principal work was the care of orphans. The instruction of youth and young clerics became also an object of his foundation, and continues still to be. It is claimed for St Jerome Emiliani that he was the first to introduce the practice of teaching Christian doctrine to children by means of a set catechism drawn up in the form of questions and answers. He was so unwearying in looking after the peasants around Somascha that they credited him with the gift of healing : he would work with them in the fields and talk of God and His goodness while he worked. While attending the sick in 1537 he caught an infectious disease of which he died on February 8. He was canonized in 1767, and in 1928 was named patron-saint of orphans and abandoned children by Pope Pius XI.

After his death his congregation suffered considerable vicissitudes, but it had the approval of St Charles Borromeo and in 1540 was recognized by Pope Paul III ; today, however, the Somaschi number but few members, who conduct schools and orphanages in Italy.

See the *Acta Sanctorum*, February, vol. ii, where the life of the saint by A. Tortora is printed entire. There are other lives by Scipio Albani (1600), Andreas Stella (1605), and W. Hubert (in German, 1895). But the most recent contributions to the subject are the volume published to commemorate the fourth centenary of the foundation of the Somaschi, *L'Ordine dei Chierici Regolari Somaschi,* 1528–1928 (1928), and the full official biography by G. Landini, *S. Girolamo Miani* (1947).

ST WILGEFORTIS, or LIBERATA   (No Date)

THIS mythical personage was also known as Uncumber (in England), Ontkommer, Kümmernis (in Germany), Regenfledis (in Flanders), Livrade (in France), and by other names. Her story is a curiosity of hagiology and is hardly worth including in a collection of lives of the saints but for the fact that it has the unenviable distinction of being one of the most obviously false and preposterous of the pseudo-pious romances by which simple Christians have been deceived or regaled.

Wilgefortis was one of seven (or nine) children born at one birth by the wife of a heathen king of Portugal, all of whom became Christian and suffered martyrdom. Her father wanted to marry Wilgefortis to the king of Sicily, but she had taken a vow of virginity. She therefore prayed in her distress for help from on high, which came in the form of a beard and moustache growing upon her face, whereupon the king of Sicily withdrew his suit. Her father, enraged at what had happened, had her crucified.

In his *Caractéristiques des saints dans l'art populaire* (1867), Father Charles Cahier, S.J., wrote :

> For my part, I am inclined to think that the crown, beard, gown and cross which are regarded as the attributes of this marvellous maiden [in pictorial representations], are only a pious devotion to the famous crucifix of Lucca, somewhat gone astray. It is known that devotion to this image of Jesus Christ crucified was widely spread in the twelfth century, so that the favourite oath of William Rufus, King of England, was " By the holy face of Lucca ". This famous crucifix was completely dressed and crowned, as were many others of the same period. In course of time, the long gown caused it to be thought that the figure was that of a woman, who on account of the beard was called *Vierge-forte*. We may add that the crucifix of Lucca was shod with silver to prevent the wearing away of the wood by the kissing of the feet by pilgrims. This also has been turned to the glorification of St Wilgefortis. For it is said that a poor minstrel playing an air before the saint's statue was rewarded by her giving him one of her precious shoes.

This is the generally accepted explanation of the legend, but of course there were numerous robed crucifixes besides that of Lucca. The name Liberata represents a separate character, who originally had a different legend. The derivation of the name Wilgefortis has been suggested to be not *Vierge-forte* but a corruption of *Hilge vartz*, " holy face ". The " Uncumber " names signify one who frees from anxiety, because of the belief that clients of this " saint " will be delivered from troubles and die a happy death. In England she was invoked particularly by women who were afflicted by troublesome husbands. " For a peck of oats she would not fail to uncumber them of their husbands ", says St Thomas More.

St Wilgefortis belongs more to the domain of folklore than to hagiology, and a considerable bibliography might be compiled out of the books and periodicals of the former class.

An account of her, however, is given in the *Acta Sanctorum*, July, vol. v, and a long section is devoted to the subject in Detzel and Künstle, *Ikonographie der Heiligen*.   See Delehaye, *Légendes hagiographiques* (1927), pp. 103–104, and the references there indicated.   The standard work on the subject now is G. Schnürer and J. M. Ritz, *Sankt Kümmernis und Volto Santo* (1934).   See also J. Gessler, *La vierge barbue* (1938).

ST MARGARET, or MARINA, VIRGIN AND MARTYR   (NO DATE)

ON July 20 the Roman Martyrology celebrates " the passion at Antioch of the holy Margaret, virgin and martyr ", formerly one of the most famous and widely venerated saints of the Church.   Her *cultus*, under the name of " the very great martyr Marina ", began in the East ; as Margaret she appears in the martyrology of Rabanus Maurus in the ninth century, and in the Bosworth Psalter, and soon her fame spread in England, France and Germany, and continued throughout the middle ages ; she is one of the Fourteen Holy Helpers, and hers was one of the " voices " that spoke to St Joan of Arc.   Her alleged relics were stolen from Antioch in 908 and brought to San Pietro della Valle on the lake of Bolsena, and in 1145 were translated to Montefiascone ; part of them were further translated, to Venice, in 1213, an event noted in the Roman Martyrology on July 17, which is the saint's feast-day among the Greeks.   Many other relics of her are shown throughout Europe.   Her acts are a pure forgery, written by a man who called himself Theotimus and represented himself to be her attendant who had been the spectator of all he related.   They belong to the same family of legends as those of St Pelagia of Antioch (*alias* Margaret, *alias* Marina ; October 8) and her congeners.

The story they tell is briefly this.   Margaret was the daughter of a pagan priest of Antioch in Pisidia, who was put out to nurse with a Christian woman.   Margaret herself became a Christian, and on being driven away in consequence from her father's house she went to live with her old nurse and made a living as a shepherdess. While thus employed she was seen by the prefect Olybrius, who marvelled at her beauty and grace and would have had her as his wife were she free, as his mistress were she a slave.   But she would not have him either way, and in revenge he ordered her to be brought before his tribunal and charged as a Christian ; and after she had been tortured she was cast into prison.   There she underwent a terrible ordeal with the Devil, who appeared to her in the form of a dragon and eventually swallowed her : but the cross which she had in her hand (or the sign of the cross) was an irritation to the dragon's stomach, which opened and emitted her in safety (even the *Golden Legend* says that " this swallowing and breaking of the belly of the dragon is said to be apocryphal ").*   Then she had conflict with another demon, whom she overcame, and they talked together, and he told her how he had been with others like him enclosed in a brazen vessel by Solomon, and how the vessel had been found in Babylon and broken open by people who thought it to contain treasure, so that the demons were released to plague the world—the affinities of which tale are not hard to see.   The next day an attempt was made to slay her in various ways both by fire and by water ; but the only result was to convert thousands of the spectators, who were all put to the sword.   At length she was killed by beheading, the executioner immediately after falling dead also : not, it appears, as a retribution but as a reward whereby he would join her in Heaven,

---

* When it is considered that patron saints are often selected by direct or indirect association, *e.g.* St Vitus, of comedians, St Barbara, of gunners, our Lady of Loreto, of airmen, it is not merely ribald to suggest that this absurd incident may account for St Margaret being a patroness of women in childbirth.

for he had been unwilling to fulfil his office.   And this is stated to have taken place during the persecution of Diocletian.   The faithful Theotimus took up Margaret's body and it was buried by a noble widow of the city.

As may be learnt from BHL., nn. 5303–5313, there are a number of variant Latin texts of this extravagant but highly popular biography ; and there are also many adaptations of the life in French, Provençal, Anglo-Saxon, German, Irish, etc.   For the Latin see the *Acta Sanctorum*, July, vol. v ; also G. H. Gerould in the *Publications of the Modern Language Association of America*, vol. xxxix (1924), pp. 225–256 ; and A. Mabellini, *Leggenda di Santa Margherita* (1925).   *Cf.* also what has been said above in connection with St Marina on February 12 and St Pelagia on October 8, and Delehaye, *Légendes hagiographiques* (1927), pp. 187–192.   St Margaret's name appears in the Bosworth Psalter and other tenth-century English calendars, and at the provincial council of Oxford in 1222 her feast, like that of St Catherine and some other saints, was made a holiday of obligation.   Alban Butler remarks that Marco Girolamo Vida, an almost forgotten poet of the sixteenth century whom he calls " the glory of the Christian muses ", has honoured St Margaret, one of the tutelary saints of his native Cremona, with two hymns.

ST JOSEPH BARSABAS   (First Century)

He was put in competition with St Matthias to succeed the traitor Judas in the apostleship, and from the words used by St Peter before the drawing of the lots it is clear that Joseph had been a close follower of our Lord : " Wherefore of these men who have companied with us, all the time that the Lord Jesus came in and went out among us, beginning from the baptism of John until the day wherein He was taken from us, one of these must be made a witness with us of His resurrection " (Acts i 21–22).   It is probable that he was one of the seventy-two disciples, as Eusebius definitely states he was.   After the dispersion of the disciples he preached the gospel in many places, and, among other miracles, drank poison without receiving hurt (as Papias, and from him Eusebius, testify), in accordance with our Lord's promise (Mark xvi 18).

See the Acts of the Apostles i 15–16, and the *Acta Sanctorum*, July, vol. v.   *Cf.* also J. Renié in *Revue biblique*, vol. lv (1948), pp. 43–53.

ST AURELIUS, Bishop of Carthage   (A.D. 429)

About the year 392, just after St Augustine was ordained priest and appointed to the church of Hippo, a deacon of Carthage, Aurelius, was chosen to be bishop of that see.   At this time the great church of north Africa was at the height of its power and influence, and the bishop of Carthage, being in effect its primate or patriarch, was one of the most important of all Christian prelates.

The new bishop was faced by two great heretical movements, that of the Donatists, which was reaching its last stages, and that of the Pelagians, which was beginning to emerge ; during the thirty-seven years of his episcopate St Aurelius convened numerous provincial and plenary synods of the African bishops to deal with these and other matters.   These meetings and the journeys they involved took up so much of the bishops' time that St Aurelius extended their duty of preaching to the better qualified among the presbyters, which was not yet usual in the Church.

Aurelius was on terms of intimate friendship with St Augustine, and when he complained of the degeneracy of numerous monks, who were simply lazy under pretence of the contemplative life, Augustine wrote a treatise, " Concerning the

Work of Monks ", to help remedy the situation. St Fulgentius of Ruspe, an African bishop of the next generation, wrote in glowing terms of St Aurelius, as did the learned Spaniard, Paul Orosius.

An account of St Aurelius is given in the *Acta Sanctorum* for October, vol. xi, pp. 852–860. He had been omitted in his proper place from failure to observe that his *cultus* was recognized in the Carthaginian calendar of the sixth century in this form : " July 20, depositio sancti Aurili episcopi ". There is no formal biography, but many allusions in St Augustine's letters and in conciliar documents, etc. See Hefele-Leclercq, *Conciles*, vol. ii, pt 1, and Bardenhewer, *Geschichte der altkirchlichen Literatur*, vol. iv, pp. 524–525.

ST FLAVIAN, PATRIARCH OF ANTIOCH, AND ST ELIAS, PATRIARCH OF JERUSALEM (A.D. 518)

ELIAS was an Arab, educated in an Egyptian monastery and in 457 driven out of that country as an orthodox Catholic by the monophysite patriarch of Alexandria, Timothy the Cat. He went to Palestine where, after being given shelter in the *laura* of St Euthymius, he founded a community at Jericho, was ordained priest, and in 494 elected patriarch of Jerusalem. During these years he must have met Flavian, a Syrian hieromonk, who had been used by his patriarch as delegate to the imperial court at Constantinople, and had succeeded him in the see of Antioch in 498.

In the year 482 the Emperor Zeno had issued a document called the *Henotikon*, of which the object was to settle the controversy between Catholics and monophysites. It was condemned at Rome as favouring Monophysism, and was a source of further schism and dissension in the East for years. Both Flavian and Elias accepted the *Henotikon* and in other ways acted equivocally ; but they were both orthodox at heart, and eventually were driven from their sees for their refusal to co-operate with the imperial support of Monophysism.

St Flavian died in exile at Petra in Arabia, and St Elias at Aïla, further south on the shore of the Red Sea, his friend the great St Sabas being with him at the time. In spite of their having subscribed the *Henotikon*, these two hierarchs are named together today in the Roman Martyrology (inserted by Baronius) and their feast is kept by Catholics of the Syrian rite on February 18.

The principal authorities for these facts are the historians Evagrius and Theophanes. See also the *Acta Sanctorum*, July, vol. ii. It must be admitted that the recorded conduct of both patriarchs has laid them open to much criticism. See, for example, the articles devoted to them in DCB., vol. ii, pp. 84 *seq.* and 533 *seq.*

ST VULMAR, ABBOT (*c*. A.D. 700)

ST VULMAR or Wulmar, whom the Roman Martyrology calls a man of wonderful holiness, was born in the territory of Boulogne in Picardy. He was married, but having been separated by force from his wife, he entered himself in the abbey of Hautmont in Hainault, where he was employed to keep the cattle and to hew wood for the community. He was distinguished for his eminent spirit of prayer, and was promoted to the priesthood. He after obtained leave to live alone in a hermitage near Mount Cassel for some years, and then founded near Calais the abbey of Samer, corruptly so called for Saint-Vulmar ; this monastery existed until the French Revolution. St Vulmar also founded a nunnery at Wierre-aux-Bois, a mile from his own monastery. Caedwalla, King of the West Saxons, passing that way in 688 on his journey to Rome to receive baptism, conferred on the abbey an alms towards carrying on the foundation. St Vulmar was glorified by miracles, and his relics were conveyed to Boulogne, and from thence to the abbey of St Peter at Ghent.

The biography which has been printed· in the *Acta Sanctorum* (July, vol. v) and by Mabillon is of no great value : it was written at earliest in the middle of the ninth century. *Cf.* Van der Essen, *Etude critique sur les Vitae des saints mérovingiens* (1907), pp. 412–414.

ST ANSEGISUS, ABBOT   (A.D. 833)

ANSEGISUS was born about 770, probably in the Lyonnais, and at the age of eighteen became a monk in the abbey of Fontenelle, of which a relation of his was abbot. His goodness and learning soon attracted notice, and upon the recommendation of his superior he was appointed by Charlemagne to administer the abbeys of St Sixtus at Rheims and St Menge, near Châlons.   He then was made abbot of St Germer-de-Fly in the diocese of Beauvais, of which both the buildings and the community were in a state of collapse.   He was still only thirty-seven years old, yet he was among the emperor's advisers and was entrusted by him with adminis-trative offices, a trust which was carried on by his successor, Louis the Debonair, who as well named him to the abbacy of Luxeuil.   This famous monastery had not recovered from the effects of its ravaging by the Vandals, and for five years Ansegisus laboured to bring it to its former state of discipline and prosperity. The last benefice of the saint was the house of his profession, Fontenelle, of which he was made abbot in 823, and where he built up both a highly spiritual community and a worthy material edifice.

Under Ansegisus the monks of Fontenelle became famous for their library and their *scriptorium*, and not least for the work of the abbot in making a collection of capitularies, which for long remained an official law-book in the empire.   These capitularies were laws or ordinances promulgated by the Frankish kings, and the collection of Ansegisus was divided into books containing civil and ecclesiastical enactments by Charlemagne and Louis.

At a period the later " lives " of so many of whose saints had to be padded out with doubtful miracles or common-form panegyric, the record of St Ansegisus stands out by its sobriety and solidity.   Nobody who was not himself a great administrator and user of the virtues which he inculcated could have brought three monasteries from decay and slackness to a state of observance and good discipline. He was seized by a paralysis in the month of July 833, and died surrounded by his brethren of Fontenelle on the 20th.

The main authority is the *Gesta sanctorum patrum Fontanellensis coenobii*, from which the biographical matter has been extracted by Mabillon and the Bollandists, July, vol. v. See also the *Dictionnaire de Droit Canonique*, t. i, cc. 564–567, and DHG., t. iii, cc. 447–448.

"BD" GREGORY LOPEZ   (A.D. 1596)

AT the time when the empire of Spain was reaching its widest extent and highest point of power Gregory, who afterwards assumed the name of Lopez, was born at Madrid.   Of his parentage and family nothing is known.   As a youth he served as a page at the court of King Philip II, but the turning-point of his life came in 1562 when he undertook a pilgrimage to the shrine of our Lady of Guadalupe in Estremadura.   While here he doubtless heard of the other shrine of our Lady of

Guadalupe in Mexico, and he determined to go to that country, having an inward conviction that there God would show him what he was to do. At Vera Cruz he sold his possessions and gave the money to the poor, and then wandered off in search of a place where he might live as a hermit. This he found in a lonely valley, where for a time he lived peacefully in prayer and penance, walking twenty-four miles to the nearest mission station to assist at Mass and receive the sacraments on great feasts. Soon, however, Gregory learned that some of the Spaniards were very shocked that he chose to live in a place where he could get to Mass at only irregular intervals ; so, not wishing to appear to set a bad example, he went to a plantation, where he remained till after the earthquake of 1566. Then he returned to his hermitage, which after five years he was persuaded by Friar Dominic de Salazar, a famous missionary, to leave in order to enter the Dominican convent in Mexico City ; a few days of community life was sufficient to show he was not fitted for it, and he returned to solitude, at Guestaca and other places.

Tongues meanwhile were wagging ; the simple Gregory was made into a " mystery man ", and all sorts of things were said. So the archbishop of Mexico appointed a commission to look into the matter ; when he received its report, he unhesitatingly pronounced in public that Gregory Lopez was a man of extraordinary piety and virtue. This made Gregory far too popular both for his convenience and his humility, and he fled to the sanctuary of our Lady " de los Remedios ". For a time Gregory was in the hospital, where he wrote a book on pharmacy for the use of the nursing brothers, for in the desert he had learned much about the properties of herbs. Then, in 1589, with the help of his friend, a priest, Francis Losa, he established himself in a hermitage not far from the church of Michoacan. Here he was joined by Don Losa, and the two lived together there until Gregory's death. Their life was simple and orderly, with nothing startling about it. Gregory's practice of poverty was marked by careful use of what was available rather than by an excessive " going without ", and, unlike some solitaries, he was scrupulously clean in his body and neat in his clothes. Much time was spent in scriptural study : Gregory had a remarkable knowledge both of the text and the sense of the Bible ; and he was often consulted by clergy and lay people of all classes. Naturally he passed long hours in prayer, and that of a high order ; but when conversation once turned to those who enjoy tranquillity in a state of passive union with God, he said : " They are good souls and on a good path. But perfection and merit do not lie in acts of enjoyment, but in the soul's effort to use all her forces in loving God in the most perfect way and with the most perfect acts of which she is capable. This, you see, is rather doing than enjoying, whereas the other is enjoying rather than doing. The soul which loves God perfectly is she who is capable of giving no more than she does ; in that consists the whole Law and the Prophets, and God requires nothing else from her."

Gregory Lopez died on July 20, 1596, at the age of fifty-four. Relics of the dead man were eagerly sought, many well-authenticated miracles were recorded at his tomb, and his *cultus* soon spread all over Mexico ; Don Losa wrote his life, and the book was translated into English in 1675. But this popular *cultus* has never been officially confirmed, and the cause of the beatification seems to have been in abeyance since 1752. Lopez was admired by such diverse people as Bossuet, John Wesley, the Quietists and the German Pietists.

The life by Don Losa was many times reprinted in Spanish ; it was a favourite book of Father Augustine Baker. The unskilful English version of 1675 was replaced in 1876 by a new life written by Canon F. Doyle.   *Cf.* also Father M. Cuevas, *Historia de la Iglesia en Méjico*, vol. ii.   Gregory Lopez wrote a commentary on the Apocalypse of St John which was printed in Madrid in 1678.

21 : ST LAWRENCE OF BRINDISI   *(Transferred from July 23. See p. 172)*

ST PRAXEDES, Virgin   (Date Unknown)

PRAXEDES according to her legend was a Roman maiden, the sister of St Pudentiana, who, when the Emperor Marcus Antoninus was hunting down Christians, sought them out to relieve them with money, care, comfort and every charitable aid.   Some she hid in her house, others she encouraged to keep firm in the faith, and of yet others she buried the bodies ; and she allowed those who were in prison or toiling in slavery to lack nothing.   At last, being unable any longer to bear the cruelties inflicted on Christians, she prayed to God that, if it were expedient for her to die, she might be released from beholding such sufferings. And so on July 21 she was called to the reward of her goodness in Heaven.   Her body was laid by the priest Pastor in the tomb of her father, Pudens, and her sister Pudentiana, which was in the cemetery of Priscilla on the Salarian Way.

This saint was certainly buried in the catacomb of Priscilla, near to St Pudentiana.   But that she was the sister of that saint, or that either of them was the daughter (as later legends aver) of a Roman senator, Pudens, converted by St Peter, there is no reason to believe.   She was at first venerated as a martyr in connection with the *ecclesia Pudentiana*, but afterwards a separate church was built in her honour, on the alleged site of her house, to which, when it was rebuilt by Pope St Paschal I (the present Santa Prassede), her relics were translated.

In the *Acta Sanctorum* the legend of the two sisters is printed in the fourth volume of May.   A commission appointed by Pope Benedict XIV to revise the Breviary declared the " acts " to be spurious and unworthy of credence.   On the cult and " title " of St Praxedes see particularly De Waal in the *Römische Quartalschrift*, vol. xix (1905), pp. 169–180 (archaeological section).   *Cf.* Marucchi, *Basiliques et églises de Rome* (1909), pp. 323 *seq.* and 364 *seq.*, and CMH., pp. 263, 388.

ST VICTOR OF MARSEILLES, Martyr   (A.D. 290 ?)

WHEN the Emperor Maximian, towards the end of the third century, arrived at Marseilles, the most numerous and flourishing church in Gaul, his coming filled the Christians with alarm.   In this general consternation, Victor, a Christian officer in the Roman army, went about in the night-time from house to house, visiting the faithful, and inspiring them with contempt of a temporal death.   His activity was discovered and he was brought before the prefects Asterius and Eutychius who, the prisoner being a person of distinction, sent him to Maximian himself.   The anger of an emperor did not daunt the champion of Christ, and the tyrant, seeing his threats had no effect upon him, commanded him to be bound and dragged through the streets of the city.   Victor was brought back bruised and bloody to the tribunal of the prefects, who again pressed him to worship their gods.   But the martyr, filled with the Holy Ghost, expressed his respect for the emperor and his contempt for their gods, adding, " I despise your deities, and confess Jesus Christ ; torture me how you like ".   Asterius commanded him to be hoisted on to the rack, and most cruelly stretched.   The martyr asked patience and constancy of God, and our Lord appeared to him, holding a cross, and gave him His peace and told him that He suffered in His servants and crowned them after their victory. These words dispelled Victor's pain and fortified his will, and the tormentors being weary, the prefect ordered him to be taken down and thrown into a dungeon. At midnight God visited him by His angels : the prison was filled with a light brighter than the sun, and the martyr heard them singing the praises of God. Three soldiers who guarded the prison, seeing this light, feared greatly, and casting themselves at the martyr's feet they asked his pardon and desired baptism. The martyr sent for priests the same night, and going with them to the sea-side he led them out of the water, that is, was their godfather, and returned with them again to his prison.

When Maximian heard of the conversion of the guards he was furious, and sent officers to bring them all four before him in the market-place. The mob yelled at Victor, trying to make him bring back his converts to the worship of their gods ; but he said, " I cannot undo what is well done ". The three soldiers persevered in the confession of Christ, and were at once beheaded. After having been beaten with clubs and scourged with leather thongs, Victor was carried back to prison, where he continued three more days. Then Maximian called him again before his tribunal, and having caused a statue of Jupiter, with an altar and incense, to be placed by him, he commanded the martyr to offer incense thereon. Victor went up to the altar and (as other martyrs are alleged to have done on like occasions) kicked it over. The emperor ordered his foot to be forthwith chopped off, and he was condemned to be put under the grindstone of a mill, and crushed to death. The executioners turned the wheel, but when part of his body was mutilated the mill broke down. Victor still breathed, so his head was cut off. His and the other three bodies were thrown into the sea, but being cast ashore were buried by the Christians in a cave. The author of the acts adds : " They are honoured to this day with many miracles, and many benefits are conferred by God and our Lord Jesus Christ on those who ask them through their merits."

These acts, on which our knowledge of St Victor depends, belong to the category of " hagiographical romances ", in which truth and fiction are mixed so that it is difficult or impossible to arrive at the real facts ; but St Victor was one of the most celebrated martyrs of Gaul.

The *passio* of St Victor has been printed both in the *Acta sincera* of Ruinart and in the *Acta Sanctorum*, July, vol. v. In spite of the mythical excrescences with which the story has been decorated, we have evidence both in St Gregory of Tours and in Venantius Fortunatus that the tomb of St Victor at Marseilles was one of the best-known places of pilgrimage on French soil, and it is at least probable that the martyr was commemorated in the original text of the *Hieronymianum*. See Delehaye, CMH., p. 389, and E. Duprat in *Mémoires de l'Institut historique de Provence*, t. xx et xxi (1943–1944).

ST ARBOGAST, BISHOP OF STRASBURG   (SIXTH CENTURY)

THIS Frankish bishop has been claimed, as to his origin, by both Scotland and Ireland, but it appears that he belonged to Aquitaine, whence he went into Alsace and lived as a hermit in a wood. He came to the notice of a King Dagobert when his son while hunting was seemingly killed by a wild boar, his recovery being attributed to the prayers of the holy man (but other accounts put this event during his episcopate). The king made Arbogast bishop of Strasburg, and he devoted himself wholeheartedly to governing his flock in apostolic humility, and asked that after his death he might be buried on the side of a hill where only felons were laid.

This was done, and a church built over the place.   Great uncertainty exists about this saint, the facts of whose life have been lost in a confusion of stories.

A life of the saint, attributed to one of his successors, Uto III, is printed in the *Acta Sanctorum*, July, vol. v.   Though late and legendary it seems to be based on some historical tradition.   See R. Forrer, *Strasbourg-Argentorate*, t. ii (1927), pp. 748 *seq.* ; A. Postina, *S. Arbogast* (1928) ; and M. Barth, *Der h. Arbogast* (1940).

BD ODDINO OF FOSSANO   (A.D. 1400)

THE life of a secular priest in a parish gives infinite scope for sanctity, but rarely any opportunity for spectacular achievements.   Things were no different in the middle ages, when numerous priests of heroic virtue lived and died in the obscurity of their own parishes and their names died with them ; except that now and again a local *cultus* has kept them in memory, though generally with no reliable particulars of what sort of men they were or what they did, beyond a common-form catalogue of miracles and virtues.   Of these Bd Oddino Barrotti stands out as rather remark-able because of the variety of activities that he engaged in, despite the fact that he was a humble *parroco*, never called upon to rule a great diocese or to counsel kings in the intricacies of politics, ecclesiastical and secular.   He was in about 1360 appointed to the cure of the parish of St John Baptist in his native town of Fossano in Piedmont.   He was so devoted to the needs of his flock that before long the bishop of Turin had to order him to take some flesh-meat at his meals, notwith-standing any vow he might have made to the contrary, and to retain from the tithes paid over to him whatever was necessary for his own proper support—for the good man was handing over everything to the poor and making himself unfit for his work.   In 1374 he was appointed provost of the collegiate-chapter of Fossano (it has since become cathedral) and rector of the parish served by the canons, but after four years he resigned the double benefice in order to put himself at the disposal of a religious confraternity, of which he had been asked to become director. Then he became a Franciscan tertiary, turned his house into a shelter for the destitute, and in 1381 made a pilgrimage to the Holy Land.   On his return home he was made governor of the Guild of the Cross, an association for the care of the sick and to give hospitality to pilgrims ; by his efforts a free hospital was built, with a hospice attached from which neither poor nor pilgrims were to be turned away : this shelter existed on into the nineteenth century.

Bd Oddino showed such capacity as organizer and builder that his successor in the provostship of the chapter asked him to take on the contract of building their new church.   This he did, and in the course of the work made use of more than natural means to forward it.   The wonders recorded are already familiar in the lives of other saints : an ox-drawn wagon, loaded with a huge beam, got stuck in a bog and nothing would move it ; the saint seized hold of the draught-pole, exclaimed, " In the name of God and of St Juvenal, come out ! " and out it came (St Juvenal was the patron of Fossano).   Another time he was praying in the church when a mason fell from the tower where he was working, and lay apparently dead. Bd Oddino took him by the hand, saying, " Get up and go back to work ", and the man at once recovered, none the worse for the accident.   In 1396 the canons asked Oddino again to become their provost, and he for the second time accepted that office and the care of the parish wherein he was so well known and loved.   But four years afterwards it was visited by a plague which made awful ravages among the people ; Bd Oddino was day and night at the beds of the sick and dying, he was himself infected, and on July 7, 1400, he died—a fitting end in this world for one who had given the whole of his life to the pastoral care of others.   His memory has never gone out of mind in Fossano ; the local *cultus* was confirmed in 1808.

A short account of Bd Oddino, with a translation of an Italian panegyric, and a copy of a rude engraving of the good priest, will be found in the *Acta Sanctorum*, July, vol. v.

BD ANGELINA OF MARSCIANO, Widow   (A.D. 1435)

ANGELINA was born at Montegiove, near Orvieto, in 1377, her father being James Angioballi, Lord of Marsciano, and her mother Anne, of the family of the counts of Corbara, whence Angelina is sometimes called by that name.   When her beloved mother died in 1389 her thoughts turned to the life of the cloister, but when she was fifteen she married, her husband being the count of Civitella, John of Terni.   He, however, lived less than two years longer, leaving his widow *châtelaine* of the castle and estate of Civitella del Tronto.

Angelina now assumed the dress of a tertiary of St Francis and converted her household into what was in effect a body of secular tertiaries living in community. Those of her female attendants, relatives and friends who were able and willing to do so gathered round her, intent on personal sanctification and ministering to the spiritual and material needs of others.   Angelina and her companions travelled about recalling sinners to penance, relieving distress, and putting before young women the call of a life of virginity for Christ's sake.   She was not the first nor the last saint to inculcate celibacy with such vigour that the civil authorities were alarmed ; what happened to St Ambrose happened to her, and she was denounced for sorcery (in her influence over girls) and heresy (in that, they alleged, she taught the Manichean doctrine of the iniquity of marriage).   Ladislaus, King of Naples, summoned her before him at Castelnuovo, having secretly made up his mind that if the woman was guilty she should be burnt, great lady or no.   But Angelina had a premonition of his intention, and when she had demonstrated the orthodoxy of her faith and the lawfulness of her behaviour, she added, " If I have taught or practised error I am prepared to suffer the appropriate punishment ".   Then, it is said, she shook out the folds of her habit, displaying some burning embers that she had concealed there, exclaiming, " Behold the fire ! "   Ladislaus dismissed the charge against her, but complaints of her activities continued to be made, and shortly after he exiled Angelina and her companions from the kingdom.

She was yet only eighteen and now went straight to Assisi.   And there, in Santa Maria degli Angeli, God made plain to her what He would have her do, namely, to found an enclosed monastery of the third order regular of St Francis at Foligno.   The following day she set out, and laid her project before the bishop of that city, who approved it.   When the building was ready, early in 1397, it was dedicated in honour of St Anne (and doubtless in memory of the saint's mother), and Angelina was elected abbess over the community of twelve sisters.   This is generally esteemed to be the first convent of regular tertiaries with vows and enclosure, and its success was immediate.   In 1399 Bd Angelina founded another, St Agnes's, at Foligno, then others at Spoleto, Assisi, Viterbo, and eleven others were begun during her lifetime ; she insisted that for the sake of good observance the communities must be small.

Angelina died at the age of fifty-eight, and her *cultus* was approved in 1825.

Besides frequent references in such great collections as Wadding's *Annales*, there is a popular Italian life by L. Jacobilli (1627) which has been more than once translated and reprinted, another by Nicholas de Prato (1882), and another by Felix da Porretta (1937). See also Mazzara, *Leggendario Francescano* (1679), vol. ii, pp. 107–114, and Léon, *Auréole Séraphique* (Eng. trans.), vol. ii, pp. 491–503.

22 : ST MARY MAGDALEN (First Century)

THE story of St Mary Magdalen, as generally received in the West following St Gregory the Great, is one of the most moving and encouraging in the Holy Scriptures. Mention is made in the gospels of a woman who was a sinner (Luke vii 37–50, etc.), of Mary Magdalen, a follower of our Lord (John xx 10-18, etc.), and of Mary of Bethany, the sister of Lazarus (Luke x 38–42, etc.), and the liturgy of the Roman church by identifying these three as one single individual has set its approval on the ancient tradition and popular belief of Western Catholics.*

Mary Magdalen, whom our English ancestors called " Mawdleyn ", probably received her name from Magdala, a place on the western shore of the sea of Galilee, near to Tiberias, and our Lord first met her when on His Galilean ministry. St Luke records that she was a sinner, and evidently a notorious sinner (though he says nothing to suggest that she was a public harlot, as is commonly supposed), and goes on to describe how, Christ having accepted an invitation to dine with a Pharisee, she came into the house while they were at table, fell weeping before Jesus, and, having wiped His feet with her own hair, anointed them with ointment from an alabaster box. The Pharisee murmured at what seemed to him the unbecoming acquiescence of a prophet in the presence of a great sinner, and Jesus, knowing his thoughts, rebuked him ; first by asking which of two released debtors, a great and a small, had the more cause to be grateful to their creditor, and then directly :

" Dost thou see this woman ? I entered into thy house—thou gavest me no water for my feet. But she with tears hath washed my feet, and with her hairs hath wiped them. Thou gavest me no kiss. But she, since she came in, hath not ceased to kiss my feet. My head with oil thou didst not anoint—but she with ointment hath anointed my feet. Wherefore I say to thee : Many sins are forgiven her, because she hath loved much. But to whom less is forgiven, he loveth less." And to the penitent woman he said, " Thy sins are forgiven thee. Thy faith hath made thee safe. Go in peace."

In his very next chapter St Luke, in speaking of the missionary travels of our Lord in Galilee, tells us that He and His apostles were accompanied and ministered to by certain women, among them (by name) Mary Magdalen, " out of whom seven devils had gone forth ". Later, He entered into a certain town and was received by Martha and her sister Mary, who supposedly had come to live with their brother

* The identification of Mary Magdalen, the sister of Lazarus and the Sinner as one person is still by no means unchallenged in the West. Though most Latin writers since the time of Pope St Gregory have supported the identity, St Ambrose, St Jerome, St Augustine, St Albert the Great and St Thomas leave the question undecided ; most of the Greek fathers distinguish three, or at least two, different persons. This is the common view in the East, not only among the dissidents but also among those in communion with the Holy See. Thus the Catholic Byzantines keep the feast of Mary Magdalen the Myrrh-bearer on July 22, and of the other two on other dates.

Lazarus at Bethany in order to be nearer the Master who, at their instance, had restored him to life.　Martha, busy about the house, appealed to Him to urge Mary to help her, rather than to sit continually at His feet listening to His words, and received that answer which has puzzled and consoled all succeeding ages : " Martha, Martha, thou art careful and art troubled about many things.　But one thing is necessary.　Mary hath chosen the best part, which shall not be taken away from her."　Mary the sinner had become Mary the contemplative.

On the day before the triumphal entry into Jerusalem which was the prelude to His passion, Jesus supped with the family of Lazarus at Bethany (Jesus loved them, St John tells us), and on this occasion Mary again anointed His head and feet and wiped them with her hair, so that " the house was filled with the fragrance of the ointment ".　And again there was a critic present, this time Judas Iscariot the apostle, scandalized not because he was self-righteous but because he was dishonest and avaricious ; and even the other disciples were distressed at what seemed a waste.　And again Jesus vindicated Magdalen :

" Let her alone !　Why do you molest her ?　She hath wrought a good work upon me.　For the poor you have always with you, and whensoever you will you may do them good ; but me you have not always.　She hath done what she could : she is come beforehand to anoint my body for the burial.　Amen, I say to you— wheresoever this gospel shall be preached in the whole world, that also which she hath done shall be told for a memorial of her."　" And behold ! " says St John Chrysostom, " what He said has come to pass.　Wherever you go you will hear her praises sung. . . . The dwellers in Persia, in India . . . in the British isles celebrate this deed."

And yet Mary Magdalen is remembered at least as well for other things.　In the darkest hour of our Lord's life she stood at some distance, watching Him on the cross ; and with " the other Mary " she saw the great stone rolled before the door of the tomb wherein lay the body of the Lord.　But the crowning mercy of the life of Mary Magdalen was yet to come, for it was she who, bearing sweet spices and weeping by the sepulchre early on the first day of the week, was the first to see, to be greeted by, and to recognize, the risen Christ ; she, the contemplative, was the first witness to that resurrection without which our faith and our preaching are alike vain ; it was to the abused flesh of the penitent that the radiant and glorified body of the Son of God was first made manifest.

Jesus saith to her, " Mary ! "　She, turning, saith to Him, " Master ! "　Jesus saith to her : " Do not touch me, for I am not yet ascended to my Father.　But go to my brethren and say to them : I ascend to my Father and to your Father, to my God and to your God."

According to Eastern tradition, Mary Magdalen after Pentecost accompanied our Lady and St John to Ephesus where she died and was buried ; the English pilgrim St Willibald was shown her shrine there in the middle of the eighth century. But according to the tradition of France, in the Roman Martyrology and by the granting of various local feasts, she, with Lazarus, Martha, and others, evangelized Provence.　The last thirty years of her life, it is claimed, she spent in a cavern of a rock, La Sainte Baume, high up among the Maritime Alps, to be transported miraculously, just before she died, to the chapel of St Maximin ; she received the last sacraments from and was buried by that saint.

The earliest known reference to the coming of the Palestinians to France is of the eleventh century, in connection with the relics of St Mary Magdalen claimed by the abbey of Vézelay in Burgundy ; the elaborations of the story seem to have spread in Provence only during the thirteenth.   From 1279 the relics of the Magdalen are said to be in the keeping of the monks of Vézelay and of the Dominican friars of Saint-Maximin, to the shrine in which church and the cave at La Sainte Baume pilgrimage is still popular.   But research, especially by Mgr Duchesne, has demonstrated more and more clearly that neither the relics nor the story of the voyage of the friends of our Lord to Marseilles can be relied on as authentic ; in spite of the defence of those piously concerned on behalf of the local belief, it cannot be doubted that the whole story is a fabrication.

Among the other curious and baseless tales current about the saint in the middle ages is that she was affianced to St John the Evangelist when Christ called him. " She had thereof indignation that her husband was taken from her, and went and gave herself to all delight ; but because it was not fitting that the calling of St John should be the occasion of her damnation, therefore our Lord mercifully converted her to penance, and because He had taken from her sovereign delight of the flesh, He replenished her with sovereign spiritual delight before all other, that is, the love of God " (*The Golden Legend*).

Much has been written on the subject of St Mary Magdalen's coming to Provence, but it is impossible to allow any sort of probability to the view which venerates the Sainte Baume as the home of her last years.   The destructive criticism which began with J. de Launoy in the seventeenth century has been supported and developed by Catholic scholars of the highest name.   The modern Bollandists have many times recurred to the subject (see for example the *Analecta Bollandiana*, vol. xii, 296 ; xvi, 515 ; xvii, 361, etc.), where in reviewing different phases of the controversy they have expressed themselves in the most unequivocal terms.   Particular attention may be directed to the essay of Mgr Duchesne, now reprinted in his *Fastes Épiscopaux*, vol. i, pp. 321–359 ; to the paper of G. de Manteyer in *Mélanges d'archéologie et d'histoire*, vol. xvii (1897), pp. 467–489 ; to G. Morin in the *Revue Bénédictine*, vol. xxvi (1909), pp. 24–33 ; to an article of E. Vacandard in the *Revue des questions historiques* for 1924, pp. 257–305 ; and another by Fr H. Thurston in *Studies*, vol. xxiii (1934), pp. 110–123 (it may be noticed that on the last page of this article, " Saint-Marcellin " has by an oversight been misprinted for Saint-Maximin) ; and H. Hansel, *Die Maria Magdalena-Legende* (1937).   There is an excellent summary in Baudot and Chaussin, *Vies des Saints . . .*, t. vii (1949), pp. 526–543.   The case of the believers in these traditions is presented very fully in books by J. Véran (1868), and by J. Sagette in 1880.   A fuller bibliography may be found in Leclercq, DAC., vol. viii, cc. 2038–2086, *s.v.* " Lazare ", an article which supplies an admirably documented discussion of the whole subject.   There is a well-known Life of St Mary Magdalen by Lacordaire (Eng. trans.), but however excellent it may be from a literary and devotional point of view it is historically quite uncritical.   A discussion of the problem of the Maries in Provence by C. M. Girdlestone appeared in *Blackfriars*, vol. xxxii (1951), pp. 407–414, 478–488.

ST JOSEPH OF PALESTINE   (*c.* A.D. 356)

THE Jews after the destruction of Jerusalem chose one among their chief teachers to whom they gave the title of patriarch or " prince of the captivity ".   The most celebrated person who ever bore this honour was the Rabbi Hillel (who must not be confounded with the more famous Hillel of whom the Talmud speaks) ; he was very learned and a leading founder and ornament of their biblical school at Tiberias. This Hillel a few days before his death sent for a Christian bishop in the character of a physician, who ordered a bath to be prepared in his room, as if it had been for his health, and baptized him in it.   Hillel received the divine Mysteries, and died.   Joseph, one of his assistants, was witness to this secret transaction, and having always been a confidant of Hillel had the care of his son given to him (this youth was " named Judas, I think, but it is some time since I was told and so I'm not sure ", says St Epiphanius, Joseph's biographer), together with the rabbi's books.   These included a number of Christian works, which Joseph read, and was much impressed by them.   But he was by no means converted yet, though feeling from time to time a strong attraction towards Christianity.   He was encouraged by the firm stand of a Christian girl against the amorous overtures of his ward Judas, who failed to seduce her even with the help of magic.   One night he seemed in a dream to see Christ, and to hear from His mouth the words, " I am Jesus whom thy fathers crucified ; believe in me ".   He received another sign when he privately exorcised an indwelling demon in the name of our Lord, and the energumen was delivered.   But still, though practically convinced, he did nothing and allowed himself to be appointed ruler of the synagogue at Tarsus.   In this position he was exceedingly unhappy and excited the suspicions of the Jews, who, already dissatisfied with his conduct, found him one day reading the Gospels.   They beat him and threw him into the river Cydnus.   At the touch of persecution his heart was opened to grace. and he was baptized.

Constantine the Great gave Joseph the rank of *comes* (he is sometimes referred to as " Count Joseph "), with authority to build churches over Galilee, wherever he should judge proper, but particularly in the Jewish towns.   It is said that, the Jews having employed many artifices to hinder the work and stopped his lime-kilns from burning, he, making the sign of the cross upon a vessel of water, poured it on the kilns, and the fire instantly burst forth and burned.   But Joseph eventually had to leave Tiberias, and went to live at Scythopolis (Bethsan), where in 355 he lodged St Eusebius of Vercelli, banished by the Arians.   He harboured other servants of God, among the rest St Epiphanius, who had from his own mouth the particulars here related.   Joseph was then seventy years of age, and died soon after, about the year 356.   It is matter for remark that, though he is mentioned in the Roman Martyrology, his name having been added by Baronius, St Joseph appears to have been venerated liturgically nowhere in the world, not even in the country of which he was so conspicuous a figure.

See the *Acta Sanctorum*, July, vol. v, where a Latin translation is provided of the text of St Epiphanius.

ST WANDREGISILUS, OR WANDRILLE, ABBOT   (A.D. 668)

WANDRILLE (Wandregisilus) was born at the end of the sixth century, or the beginning of the seventh, in the neighbourhood of Verdun, a relative of Bd Pepin of Landen, the ancestor of the Carolingian dynasty ; he was brought up in a sober and Christian home, where he was taught the rudiments of secular learning.   For the Frankish nobility all advancement and successful careers began at the royal court, and when he was old enough to the Austrasian court Wandrille went.   In accordance with the wishes of his parents he married.   He did not want to, for his heart was set on the monastic life, but he found that his bride shared his wishes ; they therefore lived together as brother and sister (though it is also said that they were first the parents of St Landrada), until such time as Wandrille could arrange his secular affairs, when each went into a monastery.   This happened about the year 628, and not without objection from King Dagobert, who did not want to lose so reliable and efficient a servant.   Wandrille first of all put himself under the direction of St Baudry at Montfaucon, near Verdun, and a few months here showed him that he needed a life of complete solitude for a time. So he retired to the wooded banks of the river Doubs, at Saint-Ursanne in the Jura, and there built himself a log hut, in which he lived for five or six years. His way of life and the nature of the austerities he practised (eating only twice a week, sleeping only an hour or two, saying his office with bare limbs on the frozen ground) are very reminiscent of the monks of Ireland, and it has been said that probably the memory of St Columban haunted his mind ; the district in which he was now living had been sanctified by the life and death of St Ursicinus, one of Columban's disciples, and Wandrille even projected a visit to Ireland. He left this place and the disciples who had gradually gathered round him there, and went for a time to St Columban's abbey at Bobbio, and from thence to the abbey of Romain-Moûtier, on the Isère. Here he remained for ten years, perfecting himself in the rules and exercises of the cenobitical life and receiving holy orders from the hands of St Ouen, Archbishop of Rouen, in whose diocese he worked for a time.

Then, the instrument of God's purpose being at last formed, Wandrille learned that the time had come for him to undertake his own particular great work. This was the foundation of the abbey of Fontenelle, near Caudebec-en-Caux. In a short time he was the head of a large community ; the abbey church, dedicated in honour of St Peter, was consecrated by St Ouen in 657. Fontenelle was a characteristic monastery of the early middle ages : in the first place, a home of ascetics ; then, a missionary centre ; then, a school of the fine and useful arts and of letters. St Wandrille was particularly careful for the well-being of the people of the surrounding country ; not content with ministering to the large number of dependents of the monastery he extended his labours to the whole country of Caux, where there were still many heathen. Wandrille's kindliness sweetened and transformed bitter hearts ; his humility encouraged the proud wanderer to return ; his teaching and preaching gained many souls for God.

In July 668 St Wandrille took to his bed with a slight illness, and during it was caught up in an ecstasy. When he came to himself he knew that he was about to die, and gathered his community round him. " Rest assured ", he told them, " that if you are faithful to my teaching, if you remember what I have told you, strengthening yourselves in unity and love and humbleness in such a way that there is no division among you, the house will prosper. The Lord will always be amongst you ; He will be your comfort and your help in every need."

There are two lives of this saint, printed in the *Acta Sanctorum* (July, vol. v) and elsewhere ; but only the first, composed in very barbarous Latin by a monk of Fontenelle about the year 700, is of any historical value. This has been critically edited by B. Krusch in the fifth volume of MGH., *Scriptores Merov.*, pp. 1–24. The other life, which dates only from the middle of the ninth century, is quite worthless. From a misapprehension of the character of this second text a good deal that has been written popularly about St Wandregisilus is unreliable ; this remark applies notably to the life published by Dom Besse in the series " Les Saints ". See also *Gesta sanct. patrum Fontanellensis coenobii*, ed. Lohier-Laporte (1936), pp. 1–14.

BD BENNO, BISHOP OF OSNABRÜCK (A.D. 1088)

THIS Benno was born at Löhningen in Swabia and was educated from an early age under Bd Herman the Cripple at Reichenau. He soon attracted attention by his knowledge of the art of building and was made " official architect " to the Emperor Henry III. His most spectacular performance in this capacity was the saving of the cathedral of Speyer, which had been begun only in 1030, from being under-scoured by the wash of the Rhine. In 1047 he was put in charge of the cathedral school at Hildesheim. He was taken away to accompany his bishop when he followed the emperor in his campaign against the Hungarians, and on his return was made provost of the cathedral and archpriest of Goslar. In 1068 he was appointed to the see of Osnabrück, and eight years later the struggle began between the Emperor Henry IV and Pope St Gregory VII in which the German bishops were inevitably involved. Benno was among those who at first sided with the emperor, and at the Synod of Worms signed the attempted " deposition " of the pope. St Gregory at once retorted by excommunicating all who had taken part in this infamous proceeding, and Benno with other bishops went into Italy to make their peace. Gregory received them at the castle of Canossa, and, upon hearing their explanations and expressions of penitence, absolved them. After Henry had been again excommunicated in 1080 Benno hid himself to avoid having again to take sides against the pope, to whom he was sent more than once as imperial envoy.

These, and other political activities of Bishop Benno are less edifying than the justice, goodness and honesty which were attested by the affection which his flock had for him ; he is said once to have dispersed a plague of grasshoppers by his prayers, and for that reason his intercession against them was sought in after ages. He had the unhappiness of seeing his cathedral, a timber building, burnt to the ground, but his own building days were over, and it was the work of his successor to replace it. The last years of his life were spent in peace at Iburg, where he had founded a monastery, and here he died. An account of his life was written by Norbert, the third abbot of Iburg, who was elected while the bishop was living there, and it was principally at Iburg and Osnabrück that Bd Benno was venerated.

There is no account given of Benno in the *Acta Sanctorum*, though he is mentioned among the *praetermissi* under July 22 ; the Bollandists remarked that they had no life of him or evidence of *cultus*. Later, however, a biography by Norbert was found in a seventeenth-century manuscript, alleged to be a copy of an ancient text destroyed by fire. This was reproduced in MGH., vol. xii. Of recent years a codex of the genuine text of Norbert has been discovered, which shows that the former version was a copy which had been extensively interpolated and falsified, apparently by Maur Rost, abbot of Iburg in 1666. The correct text, first discovered and edited by H. Bresslau, has now been reprinted in the folio continuation of the MGH., 1926, vol. xxx, pt. 2. Benno's work as an architect seems to have been noteworthy.

BB. PHILIP EVANS AND JOHN LLOYD, MARTYRS (A.D. 1679)

PHILIP EVANS was born at Monmouth in 1645, was educated at Saint-Omer, and joined the Society of Jesus at the age of twenty. In 1675 he was ordained at Liège and sent to South Wales. He was soon well known for his zeal, but no active notice was taken by the authorities until the scare of Oates's " plot ", when in the November of 1678 John Arnold, of Llanvihangel Court near Abergavenny, a justice of the peace and hunter of priests, offered a reward of £200 for his arrest. Father Evans refused to leave his flock, and early in December was caught at the house of Christopher Turberville at Sker in Glamorgan. He refused the oath and was confined alone in an underground dungeon in Cardiff Castle. Two or three weeks afterwards he was joined by Mr John Lloyd, a secular priest, who had been taken at Penlline in Glamorgan. He was a Breconshire man, who had taken the missionary oath at Valladolid in 1649 and been sent to minister in his own country.

After five months the two prisoners were brought up for trial at the shire-hall in Cardiff, charged not with complicity in the " plot " but as priests who had come unlawfully into the realm. It had been difficult to collect witnesses against them, and they were condemned and sentenced by Mr Justice Owen, Wynne principally on the evidence of two poor women who were suborned to say that they had seen Father Evans celebrating Mass. On their return to prison they were better treated and allowed a good deal of liberty, so that when the under-sheriff came on July 21 to announce that their execution was fixed for the morrow, Father Evans was playing a game of tennis and would not return to his cell till he had finished it. Part of his few remaining hours of life he spent playing on the harp and talking to the numerous people who came to say farewell to himself and Mr Lloyd when the news got around. The execution took place on Gallows Field (at the north-eastern end of what is now Richmond Road, Cardiff). Bd Philip died first, after having addressed the people in Welsh and English, and saying, " Adieu, Mr Lloyd, though for a little time, for we shall shortly meet again ", to Bd John, who made only a very brief speech because, as he said, " I never was a good speaker in my life ".

See Challoner, MMP., pp. 544–547. Challoner cites the *Florus Anglo-Bavaricus*, and there was also a broadsheet printed the same year (1679), of which there is a copy at the British Museum, describing the martyr's death. See also T. P. Ellis, *Catholic Martyrs of Wales* (1933), pp. 119–125 ; and Catholic Record Society *Publications*, vol. xlvii (1953), pp. 296–299.

23 : ST APOLLINARIS, Bishop of Ravenna, Martyr (Date Unknown)

ST APOLLINARIS was the first bishop of Ravenna, and its only known martyr. His acts say that he was born at Antioch, a disciple of St Peter, and made by him bishop of Ravenna, but this is an invention of the seventh century, when the pretensions of that see were in need of support. He was famous among the earlier martyrs, and the high veneration which the Church paid early to his memory is a sufficient testimony to his sanctity and apostolic spirit ; but no reliance can be put in his legend. According to it he miraculously healed the wife of an official and converted her and her husband, cured one Boniface who was dumb, and made many converts, for which he was flogged and chased from the city ; he preached the gospel in Bologna and converted the household of the patrician Rufinus, and was banished from thence and wrecked on the Dalmatian coast, where his preaching caused him to be ill-treated. Three times he returned to his see, and each time was captured, tortured, and driven out again ; the fourth time the Emperor Vespasian issued a decree of banishment against Christians, and for a time Apollinaris lay in hiding with the connivance of a Christian centurion ; but he was recognized and set upon by the mob at Classis, a suburb of the city, knocked about, and left for dead. St Peter Chrysologus, the most illustrious among his successors, has left a sermon in his honour, in which he styles him martyr; but adds that God preserved him a long time to His Church, and did not suffer the persecutors to take away his life. So he may have been a martyr only by the torments he endured for Christ. The name of St Apollinaris occurs in the canon of the Milanese Mass.

St Peter Chrysologus in his sermons (no. 128) refers to St Apollinaris as first bishop of Ravenna and as a martyr. Beyond this we know very little. The life, printed in the *Acta Sanctorum*, July, vol. 5, is not of older date than the seventh century, and there is no reason to suppose it to be based on any genuine tradition. The subject has been fully discussed by Mgr Lanzoni in his essay *Le fonti della leggenda di Sant' Apollinare di Ravenna* (1915), and again in his book *Le diocesi d'Italia* . . . (1923), pp. 455 *seq.*, and see E. Will, *S. Apollinaire de Ravenne* (1936). *Cf.* also Delehaye, " L'Hagiographie ancienne de Ravenne " in *Analecta Bollandiana*, vol. xlvii (1929), pp. 5–30 ; Zattoni, *La data della Passio S. Apollinaris* (1904), with other later papers ; M. G. Loreta, *Le chiese di S. Apollinare* (1924) ; and CMH., pp. 390–392.

THE THREE WISE MEN (First Century)

That the Wise Men or Magi were three in number, though this is not directly stated in the gospel, appears to be a tradition of great antiquity, founded, no doubt, upon the fact that three kinds of gifts are specified. They are represented as three in some of the oldest catacomb paintings (though there are a few exceptions, in which we find two, four, and even six—apparently from a motive of artistic symmetry), and several of the fathers—*e.g.* Origen (*Hom. in Genesim*, xiv 3), St Maximus of Turin, and St Leo—seem to take the number three for granted. The fact that the adoration of the Magi is often balanced against the Old Testament scene of the three youths in the fiery furnace may also have helped to stereotype the convention.

In the catacomb frescoes and sarcophagus sculptures of early date the Magi are always depicted as wearing Phrygian caps. The idea of their royal character developed later, being probably suggested by the wording of Psalm lxxi 10 : " The kings of Tharsis and the islands shall offer presents ; the kings of the Arabians and of Saba shall bring gifts." It seems to occur first in a sermon attributed to St Caesarius of Arles (Migne, PL., vol. xxxix, c. 2018), who died in 543 ; anyhow, from the eighth century onwards we find them in Christian art commonly represented with crowns.

Still later the Magi acquire definite names. A Paris manuscript of the eighth century calls then " Bithisarea, Melchior and Gathaspa " ; in a miniature of the Codex Egberti (*c.* 990) we find written against two of them " Pudizar " and " Melchias ". Despite these *prima-facie* divergences, there can be no doubt that these represent some common form from which have come the Balthasar, Melchior and Caspar now popularly received. In the later middle ages one often notices that in pictures of the Magi one is represented as a youth, another as an old man, and the third as middle-aged. Lastly, the practice of painting one of them as a Negro only developed in the fifteenth century.

The bones of these three holy " kings " are now believed by some to rest in Cologne cathedral, in a shrine which is one of the finest examples of the craft of the medieval metal-worker. There is no reason to doubt that these relics are identical with those which were brought to Cologne in 1164 from the basilica of St Eustorgius at Milan, having been given to the archbishop of Cologne by Frederick Barbarossa. But the earlier history is much less satisfactorily attested, although the identification of the relics at Milan with those of the three kings may probably be traced back to the ninth century. The bones are said to have come to Milan from Constantinople, possibly in the time of the Emperor Zeno (474–491), but we know nothing of how they were identified with the kings nor of how they got to Constantinople. No one can dispute that the three kings were enthusiastically venerated, especially in Germany during the middle ages, the devotion being probably fostered by the many pilgrimages made to their shrine at Cologne and by the mystery plays in which the coming of the Magi to Bethlehem was a favourite theme. They were naturally often venerated as the special patrons of travellers.

See Hugo Kehrer, *Die heiligen Drei Könige* in *Literatur und Kunst* . . . (2 vols., 1909) ; Kraus, *Geschichte der christl. Kunst*, vol. i, p. 151, and many other passages ; H. Detzel, *Christliche Ikonographie* (1896), vol. ii, pp. 473–475 ; and G. Messina, *I Magi a Betlemme* (1933). The traditional English form of the name Caspar is Jasper.

ST LIBORIUS, BISHOP OF LE MANS   (FOURTH CENTURY)

NOTHING at all is known about St Liborius except that he was bishop of Le Mans, apparently for nearly fifty years, during the fourth century. St Martin of Tours was present at his funeral, and in 836 his relics were translated to Paderborn. St Liborius is invoked against gravel and allied complaints, and this, curiously enough, accounts for his commemoration in the liturgy of the Western church on July 23 : the observance was instituted by Pope Clement XI (d. 1721), who suffered from that painful disease.

See the *Acta Sanctorum*, July, vol. v, but the lives there printed are of little service ; *cf.* A. Ledru, *Les premiers temps de l'église du Mans* (1913). A long account of the translation of the relics to Paderborn is edited in the *Analecta Bollandiana*, vol. xxii (1903), pp. 146–172, and a collection of historical and archaeological essays was published in 1936, *Sankt Liborius, sein Dom und sein Bistum*. And *cf. Analecta Bollandiana*, vol. lxxi (1953), p. 480.

ST JOHN CASSIAN, ABBOT   (*c*. A.D. 433)

THIS patriarch of monachism, commonly known simply as Cassian, was born about 360, probably in the Dobruja (Rumania), and may have fought against the Goths at the battle of Adrianople. Somewhere about the year 380 he set out with a friend, Germanus, to visit the holy places of Palestine. In Bethlehem they became monks, but in those days the heart of the contemplative life was in Egypt, and before long they went into that country, and visited in turn the famous holy men who from their solitudes " had a great mission to the world, not only a mission of prayer for the needs of the world, but a great mission to edify and instruct the ages after them " (Ullathorne). For a time they lived as hermits under Archebius, and then Cassian penetrated into the desert of Skete, there to hunt out the anchorites concealed among its burning rocks and live with the monks in their *cenobia*. For some reason unknown, about the year 400 he crossed over to Constantinople. He became a disciple of St John Chrysostom, by whom he was ordained deacon, and when that great saint wsa uncanonically condemned and deposed Cassian was among those sent to Rome to defend the archbishop's cause to Pope St Innocent I. It is possible that he was ordained priest while in Rome, but nothing more is known of his life until several years later, when he was in Marseilles.

Here Cassian founded two monasteries, one, whose church was built over the tomb of St Victor the martyr, for monks, the other for nuns ; and there radiated from him and his foundations the spirit and ideal of Egyptian asceticism which had great effect on the Church of southern Gaul. For the instruction and guidance of religious he drew up his *Institutes of the Monastic Life* and *Conferences* * *on the Egyptian Monks*, and these were destined to have an influence far beyond anything within the intention of the author ; for, with the *Vitae patrum* and the Rule of St Basil, they were recommended by St Benedict as the most suitable reading for his monks after the Bible, and had the greatest influence on his rule, both in the planning of its life and the adumbration of its spirituality.   Through St Benedict, Cassian has left his mark on all Christendom.   In the first four books of the *Institutes* he describes a way of living as a pattern for the monastic state ; the rest of the work is devoted to the virtues which the monk must strive for and the deadly sins that lie in wait for him in common with all Christians.   He prefaces the book with the declaration that, " I shall make no attempt to relate anecdotes of miracles and prodigies.   For although I have heard of many unbelievable marvels from my elders and have seen some with my own eyes, I have wholly omitted them because they contribute nothing but astonishment to the instruction of the reader in the perfect life."   That sobriety is characteristic of Cassian.

It is surprising that Cassian is not named in the Roman Martyrology ; but doubtless he was not included by Baronius because he came to be regarded as the originator and leading exponent of that teaching which is now known as Semi-Pelagianism.   His views were expressed in the course of a controversy about St Augustine's *On Rebuke and Grace*, and may more fairly be called " anti-Augustinian ".   All St John Cassian's later life was passed at Marseilles, where he died about 433 ; there his feast is kept today and by the Byzantines on February 29.

There is no ancient life of Cassian, but a good deal of information may be found collected in the *Acta Sanctorum*, July, vol. v ; see also the introduction to Petschenig's edition of his works in the Vienna *Corpus script. eccl. Lat.* English trans. of works by E. C. S. Gibson (1894).   Most writers who are concerned with early monasticism make frequent reference to him, *e.g.* Herwegen, Albers and C. Butler.   Cassian has received a good deal of attention lately, *e.g.* L. Cristiani's *Cassien* (2 vols., 1946) ; but an even better book on the strictly biographical side is O. Chadwick's *John Cassian* (1950), with full bibliography.   *Cf.* also DHG., vol. xi.

SS. ROMULA AND HER COMPANIONS, VIRGINS   (SIXTH CENTURY)

ON July 23 the Roman Martyrology mentions " the holy maidens Romula, Redempta and Herundo, of whom St Gregory the Pope has written ".   St Redempta was brought up by St Herundo in the ways of virtue and the solitary life, and when she had grown old went from the hills near Palestrina to live with St Romula and another woman in a small house near the church of St Mary Major, about the year 575.   St Gregory, who knew them personally, says that they showed a perfect humility and obedience, and hardly opened their mouths to speak except in prayer.   During the last years of her life Romula suffered from a general paralysis, which kept her motionless in bed ; she turned this infirmity to her advantage, guarding her tongue that she should never complain of it, especially as it enabled her to concentrate on prayer and worship of God free from the distraction of any other duties.   Doubtless her disease was the cause of Romula dying the first, for she was considerably younger than Redempta.   One night the two active ones

---

* *Collationes*, a word which has crept into our common speech.   For " collation ", in the sense of a meal, derives from the monastic custom of reading *collationes* (not necessarily Cassian's) while food is taken.

were aroused by Romula crying out, and running to her room they found it full with a wonderful light, and heard a noise as it were of people about to enter the room. They were rather frightened, but reassured by Romula, who said : " Do not fear ; I shall not die yet." Three nights later, she called them again, and this time asked for viaticum, which was brought to her. She had scarcely received it, when again a noise was heard : it seemed as if a heavenly choir were outside the door, singing in alternate strophes the most perfect music. And so Romula died, and the singing gradually became fainter, as though the singers were moving away and away, bearing her soul to Paradise.

See the *Dialogues* of St Gregory, bk iv, ch. 15, and his Homilies, 40, ch. 11.

ST ANNE, OR SUSANNA, VIRGIN (*c.* A.D. 918)

ANNE, also called Susanna, was born at Constantinople about the year 840. Her father died while she was young, leaving a large fortune to her mother, who brought her up with care. Anne added personal beauty to her material riches, but refused several offers of marriage. One suitor, Agarenus, was backed by the emperor himself, Basil the Macedonian, and when Anne again refused she was subjected to persecution and ill-treatment. Hitherto she had led a monastic life in the world, but now she fled to Leucadia, the promontory in Epirus, and there passed the rest of her life in complete solitude. She was then about twenty-eight years of age and died fifty years later. Long afterwards her tomb was the scene of such marvellous cures, especially of those possessed by evil spirits, that it was opened ; her body was found quite undecayed and giving off a sweet smell, and thenceforth St Anne was held in great veneration by the Greeks.

It is interesting to note that Leucadia is also known as Saint Maura, the name of a town thereon, after a virgin martyr of whom nothing at all is known except that veneration for her memory was so great that the apostate Emperor Julian, in order to overcome it, gave it out that the *cultus* was really a disguised worship of Aphrodite. The Roman Martyrology mentions her on November 30, and puts her at Constantinople ; it does not name this St Anne.

See the *Acta Sanctorum*, July, vol. v. It is noted by Martynov, *Annus Ecclesiasticus Graeco-Slavicus* (in *Acta Sanctorum*, October, vol. xi), that in certain texts of the synaxaries the virgin is named Susanna, not Anna.

BD JOAN OF ORVIETO, VIRGIN (A.D. 1306)

JOAN was a peasant girl of Carnaiola, and was, and is at Orvieto, commonly called Vanna. She was left an orphan at the age of five, and her companions tried to frighten her by telling her that now she would have no one to look after her and she would starve. This did not disturb her and she retorted on them that " I've got a better father than you have ! " When asked what she meant she led them to the church and pointed triumphantly to an image of a guardian angel : " He will look after me ! " Her trust was justified, for she was adopted by a family in Orvieto, who brought her up and arranged a marriage for her. But Joan had different ideas. She ran away to the house of a friend and joined the third order of St Dominic. Henceforward her life was one of unwearied devotion to God and attention to the poor ; it was known that she bore particular good will towards those who were unkind to her, doing penance for their sins, and it became a byword in Orvieto that anyone who wanted Sister Joan's prayers should do her a bad turn. Numerous ecstasies and other unusual occurrences were reported of her. For some years she was under the spiritual direction of Bd James of Mevania, who was stationed at the Dominican priory in Orvieto ; and there is a remarkable story told of Joan confessing to him at Orvieto, when he was in fact lying dead at Bevagna. Joan predicted among other things some of the miracles that would happen after her own death, but made every effort to conceal the supernatural favours that were accorded her ; her detachment from the world, her humility and her sweetness she could not hide. She always maintained great devotion to the holy angels, and died in their care on July 23, 1306. Her *cultus* was approved in 1754.

Bd Joan is known to us primarily by a Latin life that was written by James Scalza ; this was edited in 1853, and other editions in Italian were issued by L. Fumi and by L. Passarini. See also Procter, *Dominican Saints*, and M. C. Ganay, *Les bienheureuses Dominicaines* (1913).

ST LAURENCE OF BRINDISI   (A.D. 1619)   *(Transferred to July 21)*

CESARE DE ROSSI was born at Brindisi in the kingdom of Naples in 1559, of a Venetian family of good standing. He was educated first by the Conventual Franciscans in his birthplace and then by his uncle in the college of St Mark at Venice. He made rapid progress, both in studies and in the spiritual life, and when he was sixteen received the Capuchin Franciscan habit at Verona, taking the name of Laurence. He made his philosophical and theological studies at the University of Padua, displaying a marvellous gift for languages : he learned Greek, Hebrew, German, Bohemian, French and Spanish, and had an extraordinary knowledge of the text of the Bible. While still a deacon he preached a Lenten course of sermons, and after his ordination preached with great fruit in Padua, Verona, Vicenza and other towns of northern Italy. In 1596 he went to fill the office of definitor general of his order in Rome, and was charged by Pope Clement VIII to work for the conversion of the Jews. In this he had considerable success, his knowledge of Hebrew being a valuable adjunct to his learning and holy life. He was sent with Bd Benedict of Urbino into Germany to establish the Capuchins there as a bulwark against Lutheranism ; they began this work by nursing those sick of the plague, and before they left they had founded friaries at Prague, Vienna and Gorizia, which developed into the provinces of Bohemia, Austria and Styria. At the chapter of 1602 he was elected minister general of the Capuchins, and administered his charge with both vigour and charity, setting out at once on a visitation of the provinces. But when his term of office was up, in 1605, he refused to accept re-election ; nor was there other work lacking for him to do.

While still vicar general Laurence had been sent by the emperor, Rudolf II, to enlist the help of the German princes against the Turks who were threatening the whole of Hungary. He was successful in his mission, an army was got together, and Laurence was appointed chaplain general of the forces. He even fulfilled in some respects the duties of chief-of-staff as well : before the battle of Szekes-Fehervar in 1601 the friar was consulted by the generals ; he advised assault, gave a rousing address to the troops, and himself rode before the army—armed with a crucifix. The crushing defeat of the Turks was attributed on all hands to St Laurence. There is a story that on his way back from this campaign he stayed with his brethren at Gorizia, where our Lord appeared to them in choir and gave all holy communion with His own hand. Having spent some time preaching and reconciling heretics in Germany he was commissioned by the emperor to induce Philip III of Spain to join the Catholic League, and took the opportunity to found a house of Capuchins in Madrid. Then he was sent to Munich as nuncio of the Holy See at the court of Maximilian of Bavaria, head of the League; from here he administered two provinces of his order and continued his work of pacification and conversion. After settling two more royal quarrels he retired in 1618 to the friary at Caserta, hoping there to be free from exterior distractions, though he had had the will and the grace never to allow his activities in secular affairs to get in the way of the principal business of self-sanctification. He frequently fell into ecstasy while saying Mass, and his personal devotion was the starting-point of all his achievements.

But princes and governors, however irreligious themselves, often value the service of truly religious men. The chief men of Naples came to Laurence and complained of the tyranny of the Spanish viceroy, the Duke of Osuna; they feared a rising of the people; would he go to the court of King Philip and put their case before him? The saint was still not very old, but he was worn out and he was ill; moreover, he predicted that if he went he would never return. He set out. When at last he arrived in Madrid the king was not there: he had gone to Lisbon. So Laurence followed him across Spain and Portugal in the heat of summer. He used all his eloquence and power of persuasion on behalf of the Neapolitans, and gained his point; the Duke of Osuna should be recalled.

Then Laurence returned to his lodging, and there, on his birthday, July 22, in the year 1619, he died. He was buried in the cemetery of the Poor Clares at Villafranca, and was beatified in 1783; when in the course of the process his writings were examined, it was recorded of them that " Indeed, he is fit to be included among the holy doctors of the Church ". These writings consist for the most part of sermons, but include also a commentary on the book of Genesis and some works against Luther; until recently but little of them had been printed. St Laurence of Brindisi was canonized in 1881.

An English *Life of St Laurence of Brindisi* was published in 1911 by Father Anthony Brennan; it is founded, as the author tells us in his preface, mainly upon the biography of Father Bonaventure of Coccaleo, who had before him the documents of the beatification process. Nine volumes of St Laurence's *Opera omnia* have now been published (1928–45) by the Capuchins of the Venetian province. This great work provides authentic materials for a fuller study of the saint's career, and a critical biography will in due course be added. For his Mariology, see Fr Jerome, *La doctrine mariale de St Laurent de Brindes* (1933), and Fr Serafino, *S. Lorenzo da Brindisi : discorsi mariani* (1950). A collection of testimonies concerning the saint's life and work, ed. Fr Jerome of Fellette, was published at Venice in 1937.

24 : ST CHRISTINA, Virgin and Martyr   (Date Unknown)

THE legend of the Western martyr of this name is summarized in the Roman Martyrology. She was a young girl belonging to the Roman family of the Anicii who became a Christian and broke up the gold and silver images of the gods in her father's house, selling the fragments to relieve the poor. He beat her and threw her, with a stone round her neck, into the lake of Bolsena, which their home adjoined. Being miraculously preserved from drowning she was brought before the magistrate, who ordered her to be put to death by being shot through with arrows, after her tongue had been cut out and she had overcome serpents by the strength of Christ and remained unharmed in a burning furnace for five days. This is supposed to have happened under Diocletian. St Christina was formerly a popular saint in the West, but her story has been hopelessly mixed up with that of the equally popular Eastern martyr, St Christina of Tyre, whose feast is kept on the same date. An attempt has been made to identify them as one by an imaginary translation of the Tyrian relics to Bolsena (those of the Western Christina are claimed principally by Palermo), while Alban Butler records the legend that her martyrdom was " at Tyro, a city which formerly stood in an island in the lake of Bolsena in Tuscany, but has long since been swallowed up by the waters ".

The Christina of the Eastern story, which is a collection of absurd and pointless marvels, was imprisoned for refusing to sacrifice to the gods ; when her mother came to argue with her she spurned her, and refused, as a child of God, to be called her daughter. Her flesh was torn with hooks from her body and she picked up a piece and threw it in the judge's face ; a fire was kindled under her, but it got out of hand and slew hundreds of men without harming her ; and when she was thrown into the sea, our Lord Himself came down into the water and baptized her, " in the name of God my Father and of myself His Son, and of the Holy Ghost ". And then the archangel Michael brought her safely to land. That same night the judge died and his successor put her into a tub full of boiling pitch and oil, with four men to rock it ; and this Christina regarded as no more uncomfortable than a cradle ; so her head was shaved and she was led naked through the city to the temple of Apollo, whereat the image of the god fell headlong and was broken. And the second judge died. And his successor caused venomous serpents to be cast upon her, which did her no injury, but instead attacked and killed the snake-charmer who stood by ; him Christina raised again to life. Then the judge ordered her breasts to be cut off, and milk flowed therefrom ; and her tongue to be cut out, but she spoke none the less clearly, and, picking up her tongue, threw it at the judge, so that he lost the sight of one eye. But at last being shot through the heart with an arrow she achieved her crown.

The substantial identity of the two stories is clear. Nothing is known of Christina of Bolsena ; her feast was doubtless assigned to this date through confusion with Christina of Tyre, and she entered into the further inheritance of childish fables outlined above. Whether there ever was a virgin named Christina and connected with Tyre who was martyred is very doubtful. But there is good evidence for the tradition that a maiden martyred at Bolsena in Italy was afterwards held in great honour and was believed to have been called Christina. Excavations at Bolsena have proved the existence of a sort of catacomb there with a shrine.

The archaeological evidence is summarized in the article " Bolsena " in DAC., t. ii. The extravagant legend in its various forms will be found most conveniently in Pennazi, *Vita e martirio . . . della gloriosa S. Cristina* (1725). *Cf.* also Delehaye, *Origines du culte des martyrs*, pp. 181, 320 ; CMH., p. 394 ; and *Lexikon für Theologie und Kirche*, vol. ii, cc. 923–924.

ST LEWINA, VIRGIN AND MARTYR   (DATE UNKNOWN)

LEWINA is supposed to have suffered martyrdom under the Saxons in Britain before their conversion to Christ. Nothing is heard of her till 1058 when, on or about July 24, her relics, with those of St Ideberga, virgin, and part of those of

St Oswald, were translated from Seaford in Sussex to the church of St Winnoc at Bergues in Flanders.   They were honoured by many miracles, especially at the time of this translation, as Drogo, an eye-witness to several, testifies.   Lewina was among the saints represented on the walls of the chapel of the English College at Rome in the sixteenth century.

There is an account of St Lewina in the *Acta Sanctorum*, July, vol. v, but it is mainly concerned with the translation of her relics.

ST DECLAN, Bishop   (Sixth Century ?)

Declan was born in the territory of the Desi (now Decies, in county Waterford) and was baptized by one of the many Irish saints named Colman.   His traditional life contains a number of chronological contradictions, and it is not decided whether he preached before or after the coming of St Patrick.   Many miracles are ascribed to him, and two visits to Rome, on the second of which he met St David while passing through Wales, but these voyages are probably legendary.   He was consecrated bishop and had his episcopal church at Ardmore, where he was held in great veneration.   St Declan's feast is observed throughout Ireland.

A Latin Life of St Declan will be found in the *Acta Sanctorum*, July, vol. v, but a better text is provided in Plummer, VSH., vol. ii, pp. 32–59.   An ancient Irish version has been edited by the Rev. P. Power for the Irish Texts Society (1914).

SS. BORIS and GLEB, Martyrs   (A.D. 1015)

After the death of the first Christian prince in Russia, St Vladimir of Kiev, the inheritance should, according to the custom of succession at that time and place, have passed to all his sons and been divided among them.   But the elder, Svyatopolk, had other ideas on the subject and determined to remove the two young princes Boris and Gleb, Vladimir's sons by Anne of Constantinople, daughter of the Emperor Basil II the Bulgar-slayer.   Boris was on his way back from an expedition against some troublesome nomadic tribes when he learned what was in the wind, and his military following prepared to defend him.   But he would not allow it.   " It is not right ", he said, according to a chronicler, " that I should raise my hand against an elder brother who now stands for me in the place of my father " : like Jesus Christ he would be an innocent victim rather than spill the blood of his brothers in the flesh and in God.   " It is better for me to die alone than to be the occasion of death to many."

So Boris dismissed his followers, and sat down to wait with one attendant on the bank of the river Alta.   During the night he meditated on those martyrs who had been put to death by near relatives, on the emptiness of all earthly things " except good deeds and true love and right religion ", and he was sad to think that he must leave the " marvellous light " of day and his " good and beautiful body ".   One of his biographers professes to give the very words of his prayer, which are valuable as showing how the Russians of following generations looked on SS. Boris and Gleb : " Lord Jesus Christ, who came on earth in this bodily form for our salvation and who suffered your passsion and let your hands be nailed to the cross for our sins, give me strength to bear my passion.   It does not come from enemies but from my own brother : but, Lord, do not count it to him for wickedness."

Early in the morning a gang of ruffians sent by Svyatopolk found Boris and set upon him ; they ran him through with spears, while he called down peace on them. As they approached Kiev with the body, Boris was found still to be breathing, so two Varangians finished him with their swords.

St Gleb, younger than Boris, met his end soon after. Svyatopolk, shamming friendliness, had invited him to come to Kiev. On his way down the Dneiper, near Smolensk, his boat was boarded by strange men, armed and threatening. Gleb was terrified and besought them to spare him : with tears streaming down his face, calling on his father and his brother, he threw himself on his knees and promised to be their slave if only they would not kill him. But he would not resist ; and when he saw that appeals were useless he resigned himself quietly to death. " I am in your hands and the hands of my brother, your prince. I am being slain ; I know not what for ; but thou, Lord, knowest. And I know, O my Lord, that thou didst say to thine apostles that for thy name's sake hands would be laid on them and they would be betrayed by kinsmen and friends, and that brother would bring death to brother." The final blow is said to have been given by his own cook, who crept up behind him and cut his throat, " like a butcher killing a sheep ".

Five years later, in 1020, another son of St Vladimir, Yaroslav, buried the incorrupt bodies of Boris and Gleb in the church of St Basil at Vyshgorod ; their tomb became a place of pilgrimage and miracles were reported there. The Greek metropolitan of Kiev was asked to declare their formal canonization, but he was more than dubious, for they did not come under any of the categories of saints with which he was familiar : they had not been great ascetics, they had not been bishops or teachers, they had not been martyrs, for they did not die for the faith. But the Russians saw them as *strastoterptsy*, " passion-bearers ", innocent men who, unwilling to die, had yet repudiated violence and quietly accepted suffering and death in the unresisting spirit of Christ. It was a conception characteristically Russian, as it is characteristically Christian,* and popular feeling was so strong that the Greek ecclesiastical authorities in Russia submitted to what they seem not to have understood, and Boris and Gleb were enrolled among the saints. This verdict was confirmed by Pope Benedict XIII in 1724.

These brothers are sometimes referred to as SS. Romanus and David, names they were given at baptism. Liturgically they are called martyrs.

There are three sources if not for the life at any rate for the death of these brothers. (1) The chronicle compiled at or near Kiev and attributed to the monk Nestor, now generally referred to as the " Primary Chronicle " ; (2) " An Account of the Passion and Glory of the Holy Martyrs Boris and Gleb ", attributed to a monk called Jacob who lived at the end of the eleventh century ; (3) " A Reading of the Life and Assassination of the Blessed Sufferers Boris and Gleb ", by a Nestor who was probably not the same as the one named above. See Behr-Sigel in *Irénikon*, vol. xii (1935), no. 6. *Cf.* also bibliographical notes under St Sergius on September 25, especially Fedotov's *Russian Religious Mind*. There is a reproducttion of an interesting picture of these brothers in the " King Penguin " booklet of Russian eikons.

ST CHRISTINA THE ASTONISHING, Virgin   (A.D. 1224)

CHRISTINA was born at Brusthem in the diocese of Liège, in 1150, and at the age of fifteen was left an orphan, with two elder sisters. They belonged to the peasant class. When she was about twenty-two Christina had a seizure, which was probably

* Non-violent resistance to evil has persisted throughout Christian history : there were, for instance, conscientious objectors to military service among the early saints, *e.g.* St Victricius, St Martin of Tours and the martyr St Maximilian.

a cataleptic fit, was assumed to be dead, and in due course was carried in an open coffin to the church, where a Mass of requiem was begun. Suddenly, after the *Agnus Dei*, Christina sat up, soared to the beams of the roof, " like a bird ", as her biographer says, and there perched herself. Everyone fled from the church except her elder sister, who, though thoroughly frightened, gave a good example of recollection to the others by stopping till the end of Mass, *immobilis perseverans*. The priest then made Christina come down (it was said that she had taken refuge up there because she could not bear the smell of sinful human bodies), and she averred that she had been actually dead ; that she had gone down to Hell and there recognized many friends, and to Purgatory, where she had seen more friends, and then to Heaven ; that she had been offered the choice of stopping there or of returning to earth and liberating by her prayers and sufferings those whom she had seen in Purgatory ; that she had elected to return, and that within the space of the threefold *Agnus Dei* her soul had been restored to her body.

This was only the beginning of a series of hardly less incredible occurrences. Christina fled into remote places, climbed trees and towers and rocks, and crawled into ovens, to escape from the smell of humans. She would handle fire with impunity and, in the coldest weather, dash into the river, or into a mill-race and be carried unharmed under the wheel. She prayed balancing herself on the top of a hurdle or curled up on the ground in such a way that she looked like a ball. Not unnaturally, everyone thought she was mad or " full of devils ", and attempts were made to confine her, but she always broke loose. Eventually she was caught by a man who had to give her a violent blow on the leg to do it, and it was thought her leg was broken. She was therefore taken to the house of a surgeon in Liège, who put splints on the limb and chained her to a pillar for safety. She escaped in the night. On one occasion when a priest, not knowing her and frightened by her appearance, had refused to give her communion, she rushed wildly through the streets, jumped into the Meuse, and swam away. She lived by begging, dressed in rags, and in many ways behaved in a very terrifying manner. There is even a faint hint of relief in her biographer when he says that, when she had climbed into the font at Wellen and sat down in the baptismal water, " after that her way of living was more conformed to that of men, she was quieter, and better able to bear the smell of human beings ".

The last years of her life Christina passed in the convent of St Catherine at Saint-Trond, and there she died at the age of seventy-four. Even while she lived there were some who regarded her with great respect. Louis, Count of Looz, treated her as a friend, welcoming her to his castle, accepting her rebukes, and on his deathbed insisting on manifesting his conscience to her. Bd Mary of Oignies had regard for her, the prioress of St Catherine's praised her obedience, and St Lutgardis sought her advice.

The things narrated above are not from the *acta* of a saint written up from all sorts of sources long after her death ; we have the first-hand evidence of Cardinal James de Vitry, and Christina's biographer was also a contemporary, a Dominican friar, Thomas de Cantimpré, who, if he did not know her personally, got his information from those who did. Allowances must be made for exaggeration, misunderstanding and the desire to be edifying according to the mind of the writer and his time ; but even when this has been done, there is little in the recorded history of Christina of Brusthem to make us think she was other than a pathological case.

By far the most valuable testimony we possess to Christina's extraordinary phenomena is that of Cardinal James de Vitry in the preface to his life of Mary of Oignies. This is extracted in the *Acta Sanctorum*, July, vol. v, and printed together with the biography by Thomas de Cantimpré. See also the *Analecta Bollandiana*, vol. xix (1900), pp. 58 and 365; Fr Thurston in *The Month*, August 1922, pp. 122–131; and E. Michael, *Geschichte des deutschen Volkes seit dem* 13 *Jahrh.*, vol. iii, pp. 160 seq.

BD CUNEGUND, or KINGA, Virgin   (A.D. 1292)

CUNEGUND, whose Magyar name was Kinga, was born in the year 1224, daughter of Bela IV, King of Hungary, and niece of St Elizabeth; her mother, who had suffered greatly at former births, was on this occasion delivered with ease, and other marvels of a more unlikely nature are recorded of her birth and infancy, as that her first cry took the form of a salutation to the Queen of Heaven. Cunegund was brought up at the court, learning " Latin and the fear of the Lord ", and in her sixteenth year was married to Boleslaus V, King of Poland. She had agreed to the marriage, but on her wedding night asked the king to observe continence towards her, as she had given herself to God; to this he agreed for one year, and at the end of that time took with her a vow of perpetual chastity before the bishop of Cracow, whence he is known in history as Boleslaus the Chaste.

The queen led a most austere life, wearing a hair-shirt under her royal garments and giving much time to the care of the needy and sick. When her husband died in 1279 she refused the wish of the nobles that she should carry on the government of the kingdom and became a Poor Clare in the convent she had founded at Sandeck, and there passed the rest of her life, dying on July 24, 1292. She built churches and hospitals, paid the expenses of chapters of the Friars Minor, and ransomed Christians from the Turks. When in 1287 Poland was overrun by the Tartars, the nuns of Sandeck had to take refuge in the castle of Pyenin which was besieged by the invaders; but at the prayers of Cunegund they drew off. Her last years were marked by many miracles and supernatural manifestations. Her popular *cultus* was approved in 1690.

Of this saint there are two medieval biographies. The first, attributed erroneously to a Franciscan named Stanislaus, has been printed in the *Monumenta Polon. histor.*, vol. iv, pp. 682–744; the second, by Jan Dlugosz, may be found in the *Acta Sanctorum*, July, vol. v, and in the collected edition of the works of Dlugosz (1863–1887). *Cf.* F. Banfi, *Sponsus Marianus filius regis Hungariae* (1930).

BD NICHOLAS, Bishop of Linköping   (A.D. 1391)

IN spite of the labours of St Anskar in the ninth century, and the activities of English and German missionaries during the eleventh, Christianity had not an extensive and permanent hold in Sweden until the twelfth, and even then its progress was laborious. Until Uppsala was made a metropolitan see by Pope Alexander III, Linköping was the principal ecclesiastical centre, and even afterwards its position was to a considerable extent maintained by a succession of capable and energetic bishops, of whom Bd Nicholas Hermansson was one of the most noteworthy. He was born in 1331 and was educated at the University of Paris and at Orleans. After his ordination to the priesthood he was taken into the royal household and appointed tutor to the young princes.

When he was promoted to the bishopric of Linköping, Nicholas soon was noted both for his reforming zeal and his personal example of austerity. He enforced the celibacy of the clergy, which was still a cause of discontent in the Swedish church, and stoutly upheld the very extensive prerogatives of clerics in the country ; but unlike some of the later Swedish bishops he used the episcopal power and wealth solely for the good of religion and the poor. Bd Nicholas was a poet and wrote several liturgical offices in rime ; such compositions were very popular in the middle ages, and amid a large number, of which most are anonymous and of no credit to their writers, the contributions of several known Swedish prelates stand out as better than most ; Nicholas was the best of these, and after the death of St Bridget he wrote an office in her honour which included his best verse, the hymn *Rosa rorans bonitatem.* The abbey of Vadstena, the headquarters of the Bridgettine Order which she had founded, was in his diocese, and he received her body when it was brought thither from Rome by her daughter St Catherine in 1374, the first year of his episcopate. He died on May 2, 1391, and is generally referred to as Bd Nicholas, though it has been claimed that he was canonized.

A complete Latin life of this holy bishop, compiled about twenty-five years after his death by one of the canons of Linköping, has been edited by H. Schück in *Tva svenska biografier från medeltiden* (1895). We have also in the same volume a fragment of another biography and a letter from Bishop Canute of Linköping addressed to the pope and cardinals at Constance urging the beatification of Nicholas. Naturally the bishop is frequently mentioned in the various lives of St Bridget of Sweden.

BD FELICIA OF MILAN, Virgin (A.D. 1444)

FELICIA MEDA was born at Milan in 1378, the eldest of three children of good family. The sudden death of both her parents when she was a child disposed her mind to serious things, and soon after she was twelve she bound herself to a life of chastity and direct service of God, which she followed in the world for ten years. Then she became a Poor Clare in the convent of St Ursula at Milan ; shortly afterwards her sister followed her example and her brother became a Friar Minor. For twenty-five years Bd Felicia led the hidden and austere life of her order, remarkable in the community for her faultless observance of the rule and her perseverance in prayer and penance in spite of the diabolical influences that were active against her. The gentle nun overcame these fierce trials, and her experience and tempered character caused her to be elected abbess. Under her loving and skilful direction the devotion and virtue of the nuns of St Ursula's became famous, and when, some fourteen years later, in 1439, the wife of Galeazzo Malatesta, Duke of Pesaro, wished to found a Poor Clare convent in that city she asked for an affiliation from Milan. The Franciscan minister general sent Felicia herself to make the new foundation. The sadness with which the Milanese nuns parted from their abbess was equalled by the rejoicing with which she was received at Pesaro, whither her reputation had preceded her. The wife of Galeazzo, accompanied by the townspeople, came out to meet her and her seven nuns, but could not persuade them to get into the ducal carriages and drive in in state, so they made their entry into the city all together on foot. Bd Felicia presided over the new convent for only four years, in which time she filled it with devoted religious, and died on September 30, 1444. The people of Pesaro, who had

attributed their deliverance from war and plague to her prayers, flocked to venerate her tomb and were rewarded by many miracles. This *cultus* was approved
in 1812.

In the *Acta Sanctorum*, September, vol. viii, a tolerably full account, based mainly on
Mark of Lisbon, is given of this *beata*. An article, however, in the *Archivum Franciscanum
Historicum*, vol. xx (1927), pp. 241–259, supplies a more thorough discussion of the sources,
and points out with reference to the sending of Bd Felicia to Pesaro that the minister general's,
Guglielmo da Casale, letter imposing this obedience is still preserved. A life of the *beata*
by Fra Agostino Gallucci was printed in 1637.

BD JOHN OF TOSSIGNANO, BISHOP OF FERRARA   (A.D. 1446)

JOHN TAVELLI is generally called "of Tossignano" after his birthplace, near
Imola. He studied at the University of Bologna and then joined the Jesuats
(*Gesuati*), a lay nursing congregation, of whose founder, Bd John Colombini, he
wrote a biography. He also made translations into Italian of parts of the Bible, of
the *Moralia* of St Gregory, and of the sermons of St Bernard, and himself wrote
several devotional works, including a treatise on perfection in the spiritual life.
In 1431 he was chosen bishop of Ferrara, and seven years later welcomed to his
cathedral city and assisted at the council, convoked by Pope Eugenius IV at the
suggestion of the emperor, John VIII Palaiologos, to effect a union of the Western
and Eastern churches against the encroachments of Islam ; until the council was
removed to Florence he was the host of the pope, the emperor and the patriarch
of Constantinople. But his duties to the Church at large did not prevent him
from having a tender care for those committed to his special charge in his own
diocese, and he was loved for his charity and benevolence. In 1444 he devoted
the whole of a big legacy to building a hospital. Bd John died two years later,
and his popular *cultus* was approved in 1748.

There is a Latin life written by one of the *Gesuati* which is printed, with introductory
matter, in the *Acta Sanctorum*, July, vol. v. Cf. also the *Analecta Bollandiana*, vol. iv,
pp. 31–41 ; and Ughelli, *Italia sacra*, vol. ii, cc. 591–592.

BD AUGUSTINE OF BIELLA   (A.D. 1493)

AUGUSTINE FANGI was born in 1430 at Biella in Piedmont and became a Dominican
at his birth-place. His life was outwardly uneventful, being passed in a careful
observance of his duties as a religious. For a long time he suffered from a painful
illness, which was made more painful by the remedies of the physicians, and his
patience was the admiration both of them and his brethren. He was in turn the
prior of several friaries, which he governed capably and restored to a stricter
observance when it had become lax. The success of his preaching and a reputation
for miracles earned him a publicity that was most distasteful to him ; having borne
it humbly and patiently for some time he was allowed to withdraw to the house
of his order at Venice, and there in retirement spent the last ten years of his
life. With the words, " Praise be to God ! Praise be to the Most High ! " on
his lips he died on July 22, 1493. The *cultus* of Bd Augustine was approved
in 1872.

Besides a life by D. Riccardi, *Il beato Agostino di Biella* (1874), there is also a sketch by
M. Cicognani (1873). See further, Procter, *Dominican Saints*, pp. 208–210, and cf. Mortier,
Maîtres Généraux O.P., vol. iv, p. 648.

THE DURHAM MARTYRS OF 1594

In the year 1594 four men in the county of Durham gave their lives for the Church, and they were beatified with other English martyrs in 1929. The first, on February 4, was a layman, BD JOHN SPEED (*alias* Spence), who was hanged in the city of Durham for " being aiding and assisting to priests, whom he used to serve in guiding and conducting from one Catholic house to another. He died with constancy, despising the proffers that were made to him to bring him to conform " (Challoner).

BD JOHN BOSTE was born at Dufton in Westmorland about the year 1544 and educated at Queen's College, Oxford, of which he became fellow. He was received into the Church in 1576 and four years later went to Rheims, where he was ordained priest in the following year and returned to England. He laboured with such energy and success in the North that he became one of the most sought-after of priests, whether by his friends or his enemies. He was betrayed by one Francis Ecclesfield. To forward his purpose by inspiring confidence in Mr Boste, this Ecclesfield had sacrilegiously received the sacraments from his hands ; he then informed Sir William Bowes, and the priest was taken in his hiding-place at Waterhouses, the residence of Mr William Claxton, near Durham.

He was taken up to London, where he was so terribly racked in the Tower to induce him to betray his friends that he was permanently crippled. He was sent back to Durham for trial at the July assizes. With him was arraigned BD GEORGE SWALLOWELL, a converted Protestant minister ; he was wavering in his resolution, but the sight of Mr Boste's " resolute, bold, joyful and pleasant " bearing encouraged him to stand firm and make in open court a declaration of his faith, whereupon the priest equally publicly absolved him. The man suffered a few days later at Darlington. Mr Boste was condemned for his priesthood, and on July 24, 1594, was put to death at Dryburn, outside Durham. An eye-witness (the Ven. Christopher Robinson, afterwards martyred) states that he recited the *Angelus* as he mounted the ladder, and that he was cut down so soon (" after the space of a *Paternoster* ") that he revived while being carried for dismemberment, which was begun while he was yet living. Another witness states that he prayed, " Jesus, Jesus, Jesus forgive thee ! " for his executioner even as his heart was being torn from his body.

Two days after the passion of John Boste there was hanged, drawn, and quartered for his priesthood at Gateshead BD JOHN INGRAM, who had been condemned at Durham at the same time as Boste and Swallowell. He was born at Stoke Edith, in Herefordshire, and educated at New College, Oxford. After his conversion he went to the English College at Rheims and afterwards to Rome, where he was ordained in 1589 and three years later was sent on the Scottish mission. At the end of 1593 he was arrested on Tyneside and sent to London, where he was tortured under the eye of Topcliffe but, in his own words, " I take God to witness that I have neither named house, man, woman, or child, in time of or before my torments ".

See Challoner's MMP., pp. 197, 202–208, and 597–600. *Cf.* also the many references to these martyrs which occur in the Catholic Record Society *Publications*, vol. v. Bd John Ingram was an expert in Latin verse and many of his " Epigrams " are there printed (pp. 270–285), together with two letters to his fellow prisoners.

25 : ST JAMES THE GREATER, Apostle   (A.D. 44)

S T JAMES, the brother of St John Evangelist, son of Zebedee, was called the Greater to distinguish him from the other apostle of the same name, surnamed the Less because he was the younger. St James the Greater was by birth a Galilean, and by trade a fisherman with his father and brother, living probably at Bethsaida, where St Peter also dwelt at that time. Jesus walking by the lake of Genesareth saw Peter and Andrew fishing, and He called them to come after Him, promising to make them fishers of men. Going a little farther on the shore, He saw two other brothers, James and John, in a ship, with Zebedee their father, mending their nets, and He also called them ; who forthwith left their nets and their father and followed Him. Probably by conversing with Peter, their townsman, and by other means, they had before this call a conviction that Jesus was the Christ ; and no sooner did they hear His invitation, and felt the divine will directing them, but the same moment they quitted all things to answer this summons.

St James was present with his brother St John and St Peter at the cure of Peter's mother-in-law, and the raising of the daughter of Jairus from the dead, and in the same year Jesus formed the company of His apostles, into which He adopted James and John. He gave these two the surname of Boanerges, or " Sons of Thunder ", seemingly on account of an impetuous spirit and fiery temper. For example, when a town of the Samaritans refused to entertain Christ, they suggested that He should call down fire from Heaven to consume it ; but our Redeemer gave them to understand that meekness and patience were the arms by which they were to conquer. " You know not of what spirit you are. The Son of Man came not to destroy souls but to save." But the instruction and example of the Son of God did not fully enlighten the understanding of the apostles nor purify their hearts, until the Holy Ghost had shed His light upon them : their virtue was still imperfect, as appeared when the mother of James and John, imagining that He was going to set up a temporal monarchy, according to the notion of the Jews concerning the Messias, asked Him that her two sons might sit, the one on His right hand, and the other on His left, in His kingdom. The two sons of Zebedee spoke by the mouth of their mother as well as by their own, but Christ directed His answer to them, telling them they knew not what they asked ; for in His kingdom prefer-ments are attainable, not by the forward and ambitious, but by the most humble, the most laborious, and the most patient. He therefore asked them if they were able to drink of His cup of suffering. The two apostles, understanding the condition under which Christ offered them His kingdom and ardent for His sake, without hesitation answered, " We can ". Our Lord told them they should indeed have their portion of suffering ; but He could make no other disposal of the honours of His kingdom than according to the proportion of every one's charity and patience in suffering : " The Son of Man also is not come to be ministered unto, but to minister and to give His life a redemption for many."

Nevertheless, those apostles who from time to time acted impetuously, and had to be rebuked, were the very ones whom our Lord turned to on special occasions. Peter, this James and John alone were admitted to be spectators of His glorious transfiguration, and they alone were taken to the innermost recesses of Gethsemani on the night of agony and bloody sweat at the beginning of His passion.

Where St James preached and spread the gospel after the Lord's ascension we have no account from the writers of the first ages of Christianity. According to the tradition of Spain, he made an evangelizing visit to that country, but the earliest known reference to this is only in the later part of the seventh century, and then in an oriental, not a Spanish source. St Julian of Toledo himself resolutely rejected this alleged visit of the apostle to his country. At no time has the tradition been unanimously received, and there are grave arguments against it, *e.g.* in St Paul's letter to the Romans xv 20 and 24. St James was the first among the apostles who had the honour to follow his divine Master by martyrdom, which he suffered at Jerusalem under King Herod Agrippa I, who inaugurated a persecution of Christians in order to please the Jews. Clement of Alexandria, and from him Eusebius, relate that his accuser, observing the courage and constancy of mind wherewith the apostle underwent his trial, was so impressed that he repented of what he had done, declared himself a Christian, and was condemned to be beheaded. As they were both led together to execution, he begged pardon of the apostle for having apprehended him. St James, after pausing a little, turned to him and embraced him, saying, " Peace be with you ". He then kissed him, and they were both beheaded together. The Holy Scriptures simply say that Agrippa " killed James, the brother of John, with the sword " (Acts xii 2). He was buried at Jerusalem, but, again according to the tradition of Spain, dating from about 830, the body was translated first to Iria Flavia, now El Padron, in Galicia, and then to Compostela, where during the middle ages the shrine of Santiago became one of the greatest of all Christian shrines. The relics still rest in the cathedral and were referred to as authentic in a bull of Pope Leo XIII in 1884. Their genuineness is seriously disputed, but it does not depend in any way on the truth or falseness of the story of St James's missionary visit to Spain.

Nothing reliable is known of the life of St James except what has been quoted above. Certain apocryphal " acts " in Greek, which cannot be earlier than the eighth century, have been edited by J. Ebersolt, *Les Actes de St Jacques* (1902). They are relatively sober, but quite fictitious. An immense controversy has raged over the connection of St James with Spain. Two entirely distinct questions are involved : first, whether the apostle preached in Spain during his life-time ; secondly, whether his remains were conveyed thither after his death and are now enshrined at Santiago de Compostela. Outside of Spain almost all eminent scholars and critical students of history answer both questions in the negative. See for example Mgr Duchesne's article " S. Jacques en Galice " in the *Annales du Midi*, t. xii (1900), pp. 145–180 ; as well as H. Leclercq's article " Espagne " in DAC., vol. v, cc. 412–416, and *cf.* the *Analecta Bollandiana*, vol. xlviii (1930). They urge that not only is such a visit in itself improbable, seeing that St James was martyred at Jerusalem in A.D. 44, but that it was unheard of in Spain before the end of the seventh century. Again it is quite possible that the relics now recovered, after they had been lost, are identical with those which were venerated at Compostela in the middle ages, but the authenticity of medieval relics is always difficult to establish and in this case it is more than dubious. On the other hand Spanish scholars champion the traditional view most strenuously. See, for example, the huge work of A. Lopez Ferreiro, *Historia de la S. Iglesia de Santiago de Compostela*, in ten volumes (1898–1908) ; also the articles of Father Fidel Fita in the early years of *Razón y Fe* ; and Z. Garcia Villada, *Historia eclesiastica de España* (1929), vol. i. A book of miscellaneous and curious interest bearing on the subject is that of J. S. Stone, *The Cult of Santiago* (1927) ; but the standard work on the Compostela pilgrimage is the three detailed volumes published in 1949 by the Madrid Institute of Medieval Studies. *Cf. Analecta Bollandiana*, vol. lxx (1952), pp. 214–218.

ST CHRISTOPHER, Martyr   (Date Unknown)

" Christopher before his baptism was named Reprobus, but afterwards he was named Christopher, which is as much as to say as bearing Christ, for that he bare Christ in four manners : he bare Him on his shoulders by conveying and leading, in his body by making it lean, in mind by devotion, and in his mouth by confession and preaching.

" Christopher was of the lineage of the Canaanites, and he was of a right great stature and had a terrible and fearful face and appearance. And he was twelve cubits of length, and as it is read in some histories that, when he served and dwelled with the king of Canaan, it came in his mind that he would seek the greatest prince that was in the world, and him would he serve and obey. And so far he went that he came to a right great king, of whom the renown generally was that he was the greatest of the world. And when the king saw him, he received him into his service, and made him to dwell in his court. Upon a time a minstrel sang before him a song in which he named oft the Devil, and the king, who was a Christian man, when he heard him name the Devil, made anon the sign of the cross on his visage. And when Christopher saw that, he had a great marvel what sign it was and where-fore the king made it, and he demanded of him. And because the king would not say, he said : ' If thou tell me not, I shall no longer dwell with thee ' ; and then the king told him, saying : ' Alway when I hear the Devil named I fear that he should have power over me, and I garnish me with this sign that he grieve me not nor annoy me.' Then Christopher said to him : ' Doubtest thou the Devil that he hurt thee ? Then is the Devil more mighty and greater than thou art. I am then deceived of my hope and purpose, for I had supposed I had found the most mighty and the most greatest lord in the world, but I commend thee to God, for I will go seek him for to be my lord, and I his servant.'

" And then he departed from this king and hasted him for to seek the Devil. And as he went by a great desert he saw a great company of knights, of which a knight cruel and horrible came to him and demanded whither he went, and Christopher answered him and said : ' I go seek the Devil, for to be my master.' And he said : ' I am he that thou seekest.' And then Christopher was glad, and bound him to be his servant perpetual and took him for his master and lord. And as they went together by a common way, they found there a cross erect and standing. And anon as the Devil saw the cross he was afeared and fled, and left the right way, and brought Christopher about by a sharp desert. And after, when they were past the cross, he brought him to the highway that they had left. And when Christopher saw that, he marvelled, and demanded whereof he doubted and had left the high and fair way and had gone so far about by so rough a desert. And the Devil would not tell him in no wise. Then Christopher said to him : ' If thou wilt not tell me, I shall anon depart from thee and shall serve thee no more.' Wherefore the Devil was constrained to tell him, and said : ' There was a man called Christ which was hanged on the cross, and when I see His sign I am sore afraid and flee from it wheresoever I see it.' To whom Christopher said : ' Then He is greater and more mightier than thou, when thou art afraid of His sign, and I see well that I have laboured in vain when I have not founden the greatest lord of the world. And I will serve thee no longer ; go thy way then, for I will go seek Christ.'

" And when he had long sought and demanded where he should find Christ at last he came into a great desert, to an hermit that dwelt there, and this hermit preached to him of Jesu Christ and informed him in the faith diligently and said to him : ' This King whom thou desirest to serve requireth the service that thou must oft fast.' And Christopher said to him : ' Require of me some other thing and I shall do it, for that which thou requirest I may not do.' And the hermit said : ' Thou must then wake and make many prayers.' And Christopher said to him : ' I wot not what that is ; I may do no such thing.' And then the hermit said to him : ' Knowest thou such-and-such a river, where many be perished and lost ? ' To whom Christopher said : ' I know it well.' Then said the hermit : ' Because thou art noble and high of stature and strong in thy members thou shalt be resident by that river, and thou shalt bear over all them that shall pass there, which shall be a thing right pleasing to our Lord Jesu Christ whom thou desirest to serve, and I hope He shall show Himself to thee.' Then said Christopher : ' Certainly this service may I well do, and I promise to Him for to do it.' Then went Christopher to this river and made there a dwelling-place for himself, and bare a great pole in his hand instead of a staff by which he sustained himself in the water, and bare over all manner of people without ceasing. And there he abode, thus doing, many days.

" And in a time, as he slept in his lodge, he heard the voice of a child which called him and said : ' Christopher, come out and bear me over.' Then he awoke and went out, but found no man. And when he was again in his house he heard the same voice, and he ran out and found nobody. The third time he was called and came thither and found a child beside the edge of the river, which prayed him goodly to bear him over the water. And then Christopher lift up the child on his shoulders, and took up his staff, and entered into the river for to pass. And the water of the river arose and swelled more and more ; and the child was heavy as lead, and alway as he went farther the water increased and grew more, and the child more and more waxed heavy, insomuch that Christopher had great anguish and was afeared to be drowned. And then he was escaped with great pain, and passed the water and set the child aground, he said to the child : ' Child, thou hast put me in great peril ; thou weighest almost as I had all the world upon me : I might bear no greater burden.' And the child answered : ' Christopher, marvel thee nothing ; for thou hast not only borne all the world upon thee, but thou hast borne Him that created and made all the world, upon thy shoulders. I am Jesu Christ, the King whom thou servest in this work. And because that thou know what I say to be the truth, set thy staff in the earth by thy house and thou shalt see to-morrow that it shall bear flowers and fruit,' and anon He vanished from his eyes. And then Christopher set his staff in the earth, and when he arose on the morn he found his staff like a palm tree, bearing flowers, leaves and dates.

" And then Christopher went into the city of Lycia, and understood not their language. Then he prayed our Lord that he might understand them and so he did. And as he was in this prayer, the judges supposed that he had been a fool, and left him there. And then when Christopher understood the language, he covered his visage and went to the place where they martyred Christian men, and comforted them in our Lord. And then the judges smote him in the face, and Christopher said to them : ' If I were not a Christian, I should avenge mine injury.' And then Christopher pitched his rod in the earth and prayed to our Lord that for to convert the people it might bear flowers and fruit ; and anon it did so. And then he converted eight thousand men. And then the king sent two knights for to fetch him, and they found him praying, and durst not tell him so. And anon after the king sent as many more, and anon they set them down for to pray with him. And when Christopher arose, he said to them : ' What seek ye ? ' And when they saw him in the visage, they said to him : ' The king hath sent us, that we should lead thee bound unto him.' And Christopher said to them : " If I would, ye should not lead me to him, bound or unbound.' And they said to him : ' If thou wilt go thy way, go quit, where thou wilt. And we shall say to the king that we have not found thee.' ' It shall not be so,' said he, ' but I shall go with you.' And then he converted them in the Faith, and commanded them that they should bind his hands behind his back and lead him so bound to the king. And when the king saw him he was afeared and fell down off the seat ; and his servants lifted him up again. And then the king enquired his name and his country ; and Christopher said to him : ' Before I was baptized I was named Reprobus, and after I am Christopher ; before Baptism, a Canaanite, now a Christian man.' To whom the king said : ' Thou hast a foolish name, that is, to wit, of Christ crucified, who could not help Himself and may not profit to thee. How therefore, thou cursed Canaanite, why wilt thou not do sacrifice to our gods ? ' To whom Christopher said : ' Thou art rightfully called Dagnus, for thou art the death of the world and fellow of the Devil, and thy gods be made with the hands of men.' And the king said to him : ' Thou wert nourished among wild beasts and therefore thou mayst not say but wild language and words unknown to men. And if thou wilt now do sacrifice to the gods, I shall give to thee great gifts and great honours, and if not, I shall destroy thee and consume thee by great pains and torments.' But for all this he would in no wise do sacrifice, wherefore he was sent into prison, and the king did behead the other knights, that he had sent for him, whom he had converted.

" And after this he sent into the prison to St Christopher two fair women, of whom the one was named Nicaea and the other Aquilina, and promised to them many great gifts if they could draw Christopher to sin with them. And when Christopher saw that, he set him down in prayer, and when he was constrained by them that embraced him to move, he arose and said : ' What seek ye ? For what cause be ye come hither ? ' And they, which were afraid of his appearance and clearness of his visage, said : ' Holy saint of God, have pity on us so that we may believe in that God that thou preachest.' And when the king heard that, he commanded that they should be let out and brought before him. To whom he said : ' Ye be deceived. But I swear to you by my gods that, if ye do no sacrifice to my gods, ye shall anon perish by evil death.' And they said to him : ' If thou wilt that we shall do sacrifice, command that the places may be made clean and that all the people may assemble at the temple.' And when this was done they entered into the temple, and took their girdles and put them about the necks of the gods, and drew them to the earth and brake them all in pieces ; and said to them that were there : ' Go and call physicians and leeches, for to heal your gods.' And then, by the commandment of the king, Aquilina was hanged, and a right great and heavy stone was hanged at her feet so that her members were most piteously broken. And when she was dead and passed to our Lord, her sister Nicaea was cast into a great fire, but she issued out without harm, all whole, and then they made to smite off her head, and so suffered death.

" After this Christopher was brought before the king, and the king commanded that he should be beaten with rods of iron, and that there should be set upon his head a cross of iron red hot and burning, and then after he had made a seat of iron and had Christopher bound thereon, and after fire set under it, and cast therein pitch. But the seat melted like wax, and Christopher issued out without any harm or hurt. And when the king saw that, he commanded that he should be bound to a strong stake and that he should be through-shotten with arrows by forty knights archers. But none of the knights might attain him, for the arrows hung in the air about, nigh him, without touching. Then the king weened that he had been through-shotten by the arrows of the knights, and addressed him for to go to him. And one of the arrows returned suddenly from the air and smote him in the eye and blinded him. To whom Christopher said : ' Tyrant, I shall die to-morrow. Make a little clay, mixed with my blood, and anoint therewith thine eye, and thou shalt receive health.' Then by the commandment of the king he was led for to be beheaded, and then there made he his orison, and his head was smitten off, and so suffered martyrdom. And the king then took a little of his blood and laid it on his eye, and said : ' In the name of God and of St Christopher ! ' and was anon healed. Then the king believed in God, and gave commandment that if any person blamed God or St Christopher, he should anon be slain with the sword."

That, with a few verbal alterations, is the story of St Christopher from the *Golden Legend* as put into English by William Caxton, a story known all over Christendom, both East and West. From it arose the popular belief that he who looked on an image of the saint should not that day suffer harm : a belief that was responsible for the putting of large statues or frescoes representing him opposite the doors of churches (some of which remain in our own country), so that all who entered might see it ; he was the patron-saint of travellers and was invoked against perils from water, tempests and plagues ; and in recent times has found a revived popularity as the patron of motorists.

The legend of St Christopher did not take its final forms until the middle ages : his name, " Christ-bearer ", from having a spiritual meaning was given a material one as well, and the story was embroidered by the liveliness of medieval fancy. Except that there was a martyr Christopher, nothing is certainly known about him : the Roman Martyrology says that he suffered in Lycia under Decius, shot with arrows and beheaded after he had been preserved from the flames.

The many interesting points which arise in connection with St Christopher are discussed very thoroughly by Dr R. Hindringer in the *Lexikon für Theologie und Kirche*, vol. ii, cc. 934–936, and by H. F. Rosenfeld, *Der hl. Christophorus* (1937). There undoubtedly was a St Christopher whose cult was pretty widely spread in East and West. A church in Bithynia was dedicated to him A.D. 452. The primitive legend tells us nothing about Christopher's search for a master or about his task of transporting wayfarers across a river, but his gigantic stature and terrible appearance are dwelt upon, and also the staff which grew and blossomed when struck into the earth. The incident of Aquilina and her companion is likewise prominent, and we have the same preposterous series of fruitless attempts to put the martyr to death. The Latin and Greek texts of the earlier legend in various recensions have been printed in the *Acta Sanctorum*, July, vol. vi ; in the *Analecta Bollandiana*, vol. i, pp. 121–148, and x, 393–405 ; and in H. Usener's *Acta S. Marinae et S. Christophori*. There is also a Syriac text among the manuscripts of the British Museum (Addit. 12, 174). For St Christopher in art see Künstle, *Ikonographie*, vol. ii, pp. 154–160, and Drake, *Saints and their Emblems ;* and from the point of view of folk-lore Bächtold-Stäubli, *Handwörterbuch des deutschen Aberglaubens*, vol. ii, pp. 65–75 ; but the majority of the folk-lorists, H. Günther for instance, are only intent upon finding alleged pagan origins for medieval devotional practices.

SS. THEA, VALENTINA AND PAUL, MARTYRS　　(A.D. 308)

FIRMILIAN, the successor of Urban in the government of Palestine under Maximinus II, carried on the persecution of Christians with great cruelty. When fourscore and seventeen confessors, men, women and children, were brought before him at Caesarea, he commanded the sinews of the joint of their left feet to be burnt with a hot iron and their right eyes to be put out, and the eye-holes burnt. In this condition he sent them to work at the quarries in the Lebanon. Many others were brought before this inhuman judge from different towns of Palestine, and were tormented in various ways.

Among the Christians taken at Gaza, whilst they were assembled to hear the Holy Scriptures read, was a maiden named Thea, a native of the place, whom the judge threatened with prostitution in the public brothel. She reproached him for such infamous injustice, and Firmilian, enraged at her liberty of speech, caused her to be scourged and otherwise tormented. Valentina, a Christian girl of Caesarea who was present, cried out to the judge from the midst of the crowd, " How long will you thus torture my sister ? " She was seized at once and dragged to the pagan altar, which she kicked over, together with the fire and incense which stood ready upon it. Firmilian, provoked beyond bounds, commanded her to be more cruelly tortured than the other, and then ordered the two girls to be tied together and burnt, which was done.

At the same time and place, Gaza, on July 25, 308, one Paul was beheaded for the faith. At the place of execution he prayed aloud for his fellow countrymen, for the spread of Christianity, for those there present, for the emperor, and for the judge and the headsman.

This account comes from Eusebius, *De Mart. Palaestin.*, ch. viii. He names Valentina, but does not mention the name of the other maiden, who in later documents is sometimes called Ennatha. But Thea seems undoubtedly correct. See the extract from the Life of St Porphyrius quoted by Delehaye, *Origines du Culte des Martyrs*, p. 187, and also the *Synaxarium eccl. Const.*, c. 822 *et al.*

ST MAGNERICUS, BISHOP OF TRIER　　(A.D. 596)

THIS saint was born at the beginning of the sixth century and brought up in the household of St Nicetius, Bishop of Trier, who gave him the priesthood and made him his confidant. When Nicetius was expelled from his see by King Clotaire I because he had excommunicated him for his profligacy, Magnericus accompanied him into exile ; they were recalled by Sigebert the following year, and six years later Magnericus succeeded to the bishopric of Trier. A great enthusiasm of St Magnericus was devotion to St Martin of Tours, and he built several churches and founded the monastery dedicated in his honour. In the course of his pilgrimages to the shrine at Tours he formed a close friendship with St Gregory, bishop of that city, who testified in his writings to the sanctity of Magnericus. When Theodore, Bishop of Marseilles, was in 585 exiled by Guntramnus of Burgundy, he took refuge at Trier, and St Magnericus took St Gregory with him to plead the cause of the oppressed bishop before King Childebert II, who had a great regard for the bishop of Trier. So too had another saint who knew him well, Venantius Fortunatus, who was impressed by his shining piety and sound learning and praises him as an ornament of the Church ; he attracted numerous fervent disciples, among others St Gaugeric (Géry), whom he made one of his deacons and who became bishop of Cambrai.   St Magnericus died at a great age in 596.

The relatively copious life of the saint, written by Eberwin, abbot of Saint-Martin at Trier, is printed with introductory matter in the *Acta Sanctorum*, July, vol. vi.   The more historical portions have been re-edited in MGH., and by H. V. Sauerland, *Trierer Geschichts-quellen* (1889).   See also Fortunatus, in MGH., *Epistolae*, vol. iii, p. 128.

26 : ST ANNE, Matron   (First Century b.c.)

O F the mother of our Lady nothing is certainly known ; even for her name and that of her husband Joachim we have to depend on the testimony of the apocryphal *Protevangelium of James* which, though its earliest form is very ancient, is not a trustworthy document.   The story there told is that his childlessness was made a public reproach to Joachim, who retired to the desert for forty days to fast and pray to God.   At the same time Anne (*Hannah*, which signifies " grace ") " mourned in two mournings, and lamented in two lamentations ", and as she sat praying beneath a laurel bush an angel appeared and said to her, " Anne, the Lord hath heard thy prayer, and thou shalt conceive and bring forth, and thy seed shall be spoken of in all the world ".   And Anne replied, " As the Lord my God liveth, if I beget either male or female I will bring it as a gift to the Lord my God ; and it shall minister to Him in holy things all the days of its life ".   Likewise an angel appeared to her husband, and in due time was born of them Mary, who was to be the mother of God.   It will be noticed that this story bears a startling resemblance to that of the conception and birth of Samuel, whose mother was called Anne (1 Kings i) ; the early Eastern fathers saw in this only a parallel, but it is one which suggests confusion or imitation in a way that the obvious parallel between the parents of Samuel and those of St John the Baptist does not.

The early *cultus* of St Anne in Constantinople is attested by the fact that in the middle of the sixth century the Emperor Justinian I dedicated a shrine to her. The devotion was probably introduced into Rome by Pope Constantine (708–715). There are two eighth-century representations of St Anne in the frescoes of S. Maria Antiqua ; she is mentioned conspicuously in a list of relics belonging to S. Angelo in Pescheria, and we know that Pope St Leo III (795–816) presented a vestment to St Mary Major which was embroidered with the Annunciation and St Joachim and St Anne.   The historical evidence for the presence of the relics of St Anne at Apt in Provence and at Düren in the Rheinland is altogether untrust-worthy.   But though there is very little to suggest any widespread *cultus* of the saint before the middle of the fourteenth century, this devotion a hundred years afterwards became enormously popular, and was later on acrimoniously derided by Luther.   The so-called *selbdritt* pictures (*i.e.* Jesus, Mary and Anne—" herself making a third ") were particularly an object of attack.   The first papal pronounce-ment on the subject, enjoining the observance of an annual feast, was addressed by Urban VI in 1382, at the request, as the pope said, of certain English petitioners, to the bishops of England alone.   It is quite possible that it was occasioned by the marriage of King Richard II to Anne of Bohemia in that year. The feast was extended to the whole Western church in 1584.

The *Protevangelium of James*, which appears under various names and in sundry divergent forms, may be conveniently consulted in the English translation of B. H. Cowper, *Apocryphal Gospels* (1874), but the text here in question is called by him " The Gospel of Pseudo-Matthew " ; this translation is reprinted in J. Orr's handy *N.T. Apocryphal Writings* (1903). The Greek text may be consulted in vol. i of *Évangiles apocryphes* (1911), ed. H. Hemmer and P. Lejay ; see also E. Amann, *Le Protévangile de Jacques et ses remaniements* (1910). The most complete work dealing with St Anne and devotion to her from every point of view is that of Fr B. Kleinschmidt, *Die hl. Anna* (1930) ; but see also H. M. Bannister in the *English Historical Review*, 1903, pp. 107–112 ; H. Leclercq in DAC., t. i, cc. 2162–2174 ; and P. V. Charland, *Ste Anne et son culte* (3 vols.). M. V. Ronan, *St Anne : her Cult and her Shrines* (1927) is rather uncritical. The spelling " Ann " was formerly commoner in England than it is today.

ST SIMEON THE ARMENIAN   (A.D. 1016)

ST SIMEON was said to have been an Armenian who in the year 982 started on pilgrimage and went to Jerusalem, and passed from thence to Rome. Here he was accused of being a heretic, and by order of Pope Benedict VII he was examined, and declared to be orthodox. For a time he wandered about Italy, then visited the shrines of St James at Compostela and St Martin of Tours, and so returned to Lombardy. Already he had earned a reputation for miracles, and charity : he greatly impressed the people of Mantua by playing unharmed with a lion which was being exhibited as a curiosity. He settled at the Cluniac Benedictine monastery of Padilirone, where he passed the rest of his life. The miracles attributed to him caused notice to be taken at Rome, and Simeon's *cultus* was allowed by Pope Benedict VIII.

The author of the Life of Simeon, which is printed by Mabillon and also in the *Acta Sanctorum*, July, vol. vi, may have been a contemporary, but he seems to have been extremely credulous. It is very questionable, then, whether we may trust his statement that in the course of his wanderings the saint visited " Britannia ".

BD WILLIAM WARD, MARTYR   (A.D. 1641)

BD WILLIAM's family name was really Webster, and he was born at Thornby in Westmorland, went to Douay in 1604, and was sent upon the English mission after his ordination in 1608. At this time he was well over forty years of age, but we have no particulars of his early life. Being driven by the weather to land in Scotland, he was at once arrested and spent three years in prison. Immediately after his release he went into England to try again to begin his labours for the Church and was soon after again imprisoned. Of his thirty-three years on the mission, twenty were passed in one prison or another. A number of details of the personal character, trial, and passion of Mr Ward are given by a secular priest who called himself " his ghostly child ", and are printed by Challoner.

" He . . . was ever known to be of an excellent spirit, exceeding zealous in God's service. . . . He did not use to preach set sermons, though his whole life was a continual preaching ; but in confessions, wherein he spent most of his time, he would exhort much to virtue and the love of God, and dissuade from vice and the vanity of the world ; and seldom spared a threat of damnation if the party were vain, as many of his penitents have told me themselves. . . . And however some men held him to be passionate, because his speech was earnest and his face somewhat fiery upon any fervent speaking, yet to those that knew he was truly *vir dolorum* being in perpetual pain of two infirmities. . . . The sole and true reason why he did wear no better clothes, nor covet better diet than he used himself to, was only by reason he did in his own conscience not think himself worthy of better. . . . In all the time I knew this holy man, I could never hear him relate any passage or speak of any subject, but it either began or ended with a memory of Almighty God's service, if his whole speech were not upon that theme. . . ."

On April 7, 1641, Parliament issued a proclamation banishing all priests under pain of death, but Mr Ward refused to leave London, and was arrested on July 15 following ; and within ten days tried and condemned at the Old Bailey for his priesthood. He was dragged to Tyburn on a sledge by four horses, and after maintaining before the people that he died for the true religion and for no other cause, he gave forty shillings to the sheriff to be distributed among poor Catholics, half a crown to the hangman, and a florin to the sledge-driver, and so met his end, crying, " Jesu, Jesu, Jesu receive my soul ".

A very full account of this martyr is given by Challoner in MMP., pp. 382–392. See also the *Douay Diaries*, vol. i.

ST BARTHOLOMEA CAPITANIO, Virgin, Co-Foundress of the Sisters of Charity of Lovere (A.D. 1833)

Bartholomea was no more than twenty-six when she died. But in those few years she had founded a religious congregation, had sown the seeds of virtue in the hearts of countless young people, and had left behind her a mass of spiritual notes and instructions which, having been subsequently published under the title of *Scritti spirituali*, fill two very stout volumes, not to speak of some three hundred letters which have been brought together to form a separate book. Born at Lovere in the Brescian Alps, not far from Castiglione, the ancestral home of the Gonzagas, Bartholomea at an early age conceived an intense devotion for St Aloysius. She acquired nothing of piety from her father, a rough corn-factor, who was given to heavy drinking. It was one of her greatest spiritual triumphs that her gentleness and self-sacrificing devotion to him, at a time when she herself was ill, changed his heart completely, so that he died in a state of fervent contrition. Her mother, on the other hand, was a most exemplary Christian woman, and the child learnt from her and from the nuns whose school she attended to put God before everything else and to aim at a high standard of perfection. She could not obtain her parents' leave to become a nun, so after making, with her director's sanction, a vow of perpetual chastity, she devoted herself to the work of education, obtaining an elementary teacher's diploma from the secular authorities. In this way she definitely set about consecrating her life to the apostolate of the young, and organized for the purpose a guild or sodality of St Aloysius, which, spreading to other districts, produced marvellous effects. That there was something strangely inspiring about her simplicity, her straightforwardness, her tact, and her force of character is proved by the spell she exercised over a number of devoted women, her relations with whom stand revealed in her correspondence.

Seeing the need of creating some kind of religious institute to perpetuate the good she had most at heart, St Bartholomea joined forces with another earnest worker of the same district, Catherine Gerosa (now, in virtue of the name she took in religion, known as St Vincentia Gerosa), a woman twenty years her senior. Catherine's main interest was in nursing and relieving the sick poor, for whom she had already founded a hospital, taking the heaviest burdens upon herself. But now both activities, of teaching and nursing, were combined, and to facilitate matters it was decided at the suggestion of ecclesiastical authority that the two friends should adopt the rule of the Sisters of Charity of St Vincent de Paul. Certain difficulties, mainly it seems of a political character, stood in the way of any foundation being made at Lovere which would be dependent upon another house outside the Austrian frontier, for Lovere was then under Austrian rule, so a new institute was begun which took the name of " Suore della Carità ", and which, being encouraged by the bishop from the first, eventually obtained papal approval. The congregation is now widely diffused, having its mother house at Milan, wearing a habit strikingly in contrast to the white *cornette* familiar in England and France, and with modifications of the Vincentian constitutions which bring them into much closer accord with the rule originally outlined by St Bartholomea and written down some time before her death. She never spared herself; her endless correspondence and outside activities left her no moment of leisure, and though for four months before the end she obeyed her doctor, who prohibited the writing of letters, she was already far gone in consumption, and the relief came too late. She died on July 26, 1833, and was canonized in 1950.

There is a very full life by Father L. I. Mazza (2 vols., 1905), and one in French by C. Carminati (1934). *Cf.* also Kempf, *Holiness of the Church in the Nineteenth Century*, pp. 204–207.

27 : ST PANTALEON, OR PANTELEIMON, MARTYR   (c. A.D. 305 ?)

THAT there was a martyr of this name (*Παντελεήμων*: the all-compassionate) there can be little doubt, but the legends which have come down to us are without any value. According to them he was the son of a pagan father, Eustorgius of Nicomedia, brought up in the faith by his Christian mother, Eubula. He became learned in medicine and was physician to the Emperor Galerius Maximian at Nicomedia. For a time he failed under a temptation which is sometimes more dangerous than the severest trials or fierce torments, bad example, which, if not shunned, insensibly weakens and at length destroys the strongest virtue. Pantaleon, being perpetually obsessed by it in a wicked and idolatrous court, and deceived by often hearing the false wisdom of the world applauded, fell into apostasy. But a zealous Christian, called Hermolaos, by his prudent admonitions awakened his conscience to a sense of his guilt, and brought him again into the Church. When Diocletian's persecution broke out at Nicomedia in 303, he distributed all his possessions among the poor Christians, and was shortly after denounced to the authorities by some jealous fellow-physicians ; he was arrested together with Hermolaos and two others. The emperor wished to save him and urged him to apostatize, but Pantaleon refused, and miraculously cured a paralytic as a sign of the truth of the faith. After suffering many torments they were all condemned to lose their heads, but St Pantaleon suffered the day after the rest. He was subjected to six different attempts to kill him, by burning, liquid lead, drowning, wild beasts, the wheel, and the sword ; all of these, with the help of the Lord under the appearance of Hermolaos, he frustrated, till at length he permitted himself to be beheaded : there poured from his severed veins milk instead of blood, and the olive tree to which he was bound sprang into fruit.

St Pantaleon is one of the Fourteen Holy Helpers and is honoured in the East. as the " Great Martyr and Wonder-worker " and one of the Holy Moneyless Ones (ἀνάργυροι), who treated the sick without payment. In the past he has been almost as famous in the West. Alleged relics of his blood are preserved at Constantinople, Madrid and Ravello, and these are said to liquefy on his feast-day exactly as does that of St Januarius at Naples.

In spite of the extravagant legends of the saint which exist both in Latin and in Greek in many redactions (see BHL., 6429–6448, and BHG., 1413–1418) his early *cultus* is well attested and seems to be predominantly connected with Nicomedia and Bithynia. See Delehaye, *Les Origines du Culte des Martyrs*, p. 189, etc. That the wildly fabulous story of St Pantaleon was in early circulation is proved by the fact that a translation of it into Syriac exists at the British Museum in a manuscript which is dated sixth century (Addit., 12,142). At the same time the Syrians wanted to have a Pantaleon of their own ; so they borrowed many features of his legend and bestowed them upon a fictitious creation called Asia (the word means " physician "), making him a resident of Antioch, in which city also he is represented as ending his days. See the *Analecta Bollandiana*, vol. xxxviii (1920), p. 408. For a present-day account of the liquefaction of the blood of St Pantaleon at Ravello see Ian Grant, *The Testimony of Blood* (1929), pp. 17–44 ; J. H. Newman, when a newly-ordained priest, wrote about the phenomenon to Henry Wilberforce from Naples in August 1846.

THE SEVEN SLEEPERS OF EPHESUS (No Date)

" The Seven Sleepers were born in the city of Ephesus. And when Decius the Emperor came into Ephesus for the persecution of Christian men he commanded to build up the temples in the middle of the city, so that all should come with him to do sacrifice to the idols, and did so seek all the Christian people and bind them for to make them to do sacrifice, or else to put them to death ; in such wise that every man was afeared of the pains that he promised, that the friend forsook his friend, and the son repudiated his father, and the father the son. And then in this city were found seven Christian men, that is to wit, Maximian, Malchus, Marcian, Denis, John, Serapion and Constantine [in the East they are Maximilian, Jamblichus, Martin, John, Dionysius, Constantine and Antoninus, and there are other lists]. And when they saw this, they had much sorrow and, because they were the first in the palace that despised the sacrifices, they hid them in their houses and were in fastings and in prayers. And then they were accused before Decius, and came thither and were found very Christian men. Then was given them space for to repent them, unto the coming again of Decius. And in the meanwhile they expended their patrimony in alms to the poor people, and assembled themselves together and took counsel, and went to the mount of Celion and there ordained to be more secretly and hid themselves a long time. And one of them administered and served them always ; and when he went into the city he clothed him in the habit of a beggar.

" When Decius was come again he commanded that they should be fetched, and then Malchus, which was their servant and ministered to them meat and drink, returned in great dread to his fellows and told and showed to them the great fury and madness of them, and then they were sore afraid. . . . Suddenly, as God would, they slept, and when it came on the morn they were sought and could not be found. . . . Then Decius thought what he should do with them and, as our Lord would, he enclosed the mouth of the cave wherein they were with stones, to the end that they should die therein for hunger and lack of meat. Then the ministers and two Christian men, Theodore and Rufinus, wrote their martyrdom and laid it subtly among the stones. And when Decius was dead, and all that generation, three hundred and sixty-two years after and the thirtieth year of Theodosius the Emperor, when the heresy of them that denied the resurrection of dead bodies began to grow . . . God, merciful and piteous, seeing, would comfort them that were sorrowful and weeping and give to them esperance and hope of the resurrection of dead men, and opened the precious treasure of His pity and raised the foresaid martyrs in the manner following.

" He put into the will of a burgess of Ephesus that he would make in that mountain, which was desert and rough, a stable for his pasturers and herdmen. And it happed that of adventure the masons that made the said stable opened the cave. And then these holy saints that were within awoke, and got up and saluted one another and supposed verily that they had slept but one night only and remembered of the heaviness that they had the day before. . . . [Maximian] commanded Malchus to go and buy bread in the city, and bade him bring more than he did yesterday and also to enquire and demand what the emperor had commanded to do. And then Malchus took five shillings and issued out of the cave, and when he saw the masons and the stones before the cave he began to bless him and was much amarvelled. But he thought little on the stones, for he thought on other things. Then came he all doubtful to the gates of the city, and was all amarvelled. For he saw the signs of the cross above the gate, and then, without tarrying, he went to that other gate of the city and found there also the sign of the cross thereon, and then he had great marvel, for upon every gate he saw set up the sign of the cross, and therewith the city was garnished. And then he blessed him and returned to the first gate and weened he had dreamed ; and after he advised and comforted himself and covered his visage and entered into the city. And when he came to the sellers of bread and heard the men speak of God, yet then was he more abashed and said, ' What is this that no man durst yesterday name Jesu Christ, and now every man confesseth him to be Christian ? I trow this is not the city of Ephesus, for it is all otherwise builded. It is some other city ; I wot not what.' And when he demanded and heard verily that it was Ephesus he supposed that he had erred and thought verily to go back again to his fellows, and then went to them that sold bread. And when he showed his money, the sellers marvelled and said that one to that other, that this young man has found some old treasure. And when Malchus saw them talk together he doubted not that they would lead him to the emperor, and was sore afeared and prayed them to let him go and keep both money and bread, but they held him and said to him, ' Of whence art thou ? For thou hast found treasure of old emperors ; show it to us, and we shall be fellows with thee and keep it secret.'

" And Malchus was so afeared that he wist not what to say to them for dread. And when they saw that he spake not they put a cord about his neck and drew him through the city unto the middle thereof. . . . And when St Martin, the bishop, and Antipater, the consul, which were new come into this city, heard of this thing, they sent for him that they should bring him wisely to them and his money with him. And when he was brought to the church he weened well he should have been led to the Emperor Decius. And then the bishop and the consul marvelled of the money and they demanded him where he had found this treasure unknown. And he answered that he had nothing founden but it was come to him of his kindred and patrimony. . . . And then said the judge, ' How may we believe that this money is come to thee of thy friends when it appeareth in the scripture that it is more than three hundred and seventy-two years sith it was made and forged and is of the first days of Decius the emperor and it resembleth nothing of our money ? . . .' And Malchus said : ' Sir, hereof I am greatly abashed and no man believeth me, for I wot well that we fled for fear of Decius the emperor, and I saw him that yesterday he entered into this city, if this be the city of Ephesus.' Then the bishop thought in himself and said to the judge that this is a vision that our Lord will have showed by this young man. Then said the young man : ' Follow ye me, and I will show you my fellows which be in the mount of Celion, and believe ye them. This I know well, that we fled from the face of the Emperor Decius.' And then they went with him and a great multitude of the people of the city with them. And Malchus entered first into the cave to his fellows and the bishop next after him. And there found they among the stones the letters sealed with two seals of silver. And then the bishop called them that were come thither and read them before them all, so that they that heard it were all abashed and marvelled. And they saw the saints sitting in the cave and their visages like unto roses flowering, and they, kneeling down, glorified God. And anon the bishop and the judge sent to Theodosius, the emperor, praying him that he would come anon for to see the marvels of our Lord that He had late showed. . . .

" And as soon as the blessed saints of our Lord saw the emperor come, their visages shone like to the sun. And the emperor entered then and glorified our Lord and embraced them, weeping upon each of them, and said, ' I see you now like as I should see our Lord raising Lazarus '. And then Maximian said to him, ' Believe us, for forsooth our Lord hath raised us before the day of the great resurrection. And to the end that thou believe firmly the resurrection of the dead people, verily we be raised as ye here see, and live. And in like wise as the child is in the womb of his mother without feeling harm or hurt, in the same wise we have been living and sleeping in lying here without feeling of anything.' And when they had said all this they inclined their heads to the earth and rendered their spirits at the command of our Lord Jesus Christ, and so died. Then the emperor arose and fell on them, weeping strongly, and embraced them and kissed them debonairly. And then he commanded to make precious sepulchres of gold and silver and to bury their bodies therein. And in the same night they appeared to the emperor and said to him that he should suffer them to lie on the earth, like as they had lain before till that time that our Lord had raised them, unto the time that they should rise again. Then commanded the emperor that the place should be adorned nobly and richly with precious stones, and all the bishops that would confess the resurrection should be assoiled. It is in doubt of that which is said that they slept three hundred and sixty-two years, for they were raised the year of our Lord four hundred and seventy-eight, and Decius reigned but one year and three months, and that was in the year of our Lord two hundred and seventy, and so they slept but two hundred and eight years."

So William Caxton translated Bd James of Voragine's version of the famous tale of the Seven Sleepers of Ephesus, which does more justice to it than any bald summary. After Baronius first began to question its truth in the sixteenth century, it was generally put forward as the explanation of the genesis and rise of the legend that there was a finding, not of living martyrs, but of their relics at Ephesus under Theodosius II. This was quite a good surmise, but there is no record or rumour of any such finding, and everything points to the story being a purely imaginative romance, a Christian version of a well-known theme, looking back to pagan and Jewish legends and forward to Rip van Winkle ; a theme, moreover, found in one " folk " form or another throughout Europe and Asia. In the sixth century it was written down by James of Sarug in the East and St Gregory of Tours in the West, and a *cultus* of the mythical saints began to arise and develop. It soon spread throughout the East, where the Sleepers are generally regarded as children, and their feast is kept to this day in the Byzantine and other rites ; the Greek *Euchologion* has a prayer invoking their aid against sleeplessness. In the West they also achieved a wide popularity : they are still named in the Roman Martyrology and their feast is observed in two or three places, as it was in England in earlier times.

There has been much discussion as to the provenance of the story and as to the language in which it first took the shape of a contribution to hagiography. The theme of the sleeper who after long years awakes to find the face of the world around him entirely changed seems to have its roots in the folk-lore of ages. See, with regard to the tale of Epimenides in particular, H. Demoulin, *Épiménide de Crète* (1901). The christianized version must have been in circulation at a relatively early date. It was the subject of one of the metrical homilies of James of Sarug who died in 521, and a portion of the prose legend in Syriac is found in a manuscript at the British Museum which is assigned to the sixth century. St Gregory of Tours in the same century recounted the episode of the Seven Sleepers at full length in Latin, *Syro quodam interpretante*, which may only mean that the man who translated it for him was an oriental. Still B. Krusch in his critical edition of Gregory's version, printed in the *Analecta Bollandiana*, vol. xii, pp. 372–388, inclined to the opinion that the interpreter was a Syrian, though the narrative itself had first been compiled in Greek. That the Greek is the oldest is also the view of the Bollandist Fathers Peeters and Delehaye. Ignazio Guidi, when he first published the oriental texts, also gave precedence to the Greek, but from his article in the *Encyclopedia of Religion and Ethics*, vol. xi, pp. 426–428, he seems to have modified his earlier conclusions. A. Allgeier in *Oriens Christianus* (vols. iv to vii) argues for the priority of the Syriac ; Dom M. Huber somewhat paradoxically holds that the Latin was the original. Gratitude is, however, due to Dom Huber for the vast collection of materials he has brought together in his book *Die Wanderlegende von den Siebenschläfern* (1910). See also J. Koch, *Die Siebenschläferlegende* . . . (1883). For the legend of the Sleepers in Islam, see *Analecta Bollandiana*, vol. lxviii (1950), pp. 245–260. There is a translation of Gregory of Tours on the subject in *Selections* from his minor works (University of Pennsylvania Press, 1949). See E. Honigmann, *Patristic Studies* (1953), pp. 125–168 (*Studi e testi*, 173) : very important.

SS. AURELIUS, NATALIA, AND THEIR COMPANIONS, MARTYRS (*c.* A.D. 852)

DURING the eighth century the Christians of Spain, as elsewhere in the early stages of Mohammedan domination, were treated tolerantly, provided they did not make converts from Islam or openly abuse the law of Mohammed. But after the setting up of the independent emirate at Cordova, the Emirs Abdur Rahman II and Mohammed I carried on a more positive persecution. Among its victims was St Eulogius of Toledo, who before he was beheaded in 859 had been assiduous in fortifying the harassed Christians and in waiting upon the confessors in prison ; he moreover wrote accounts of their lives, sufferings and deaths, and among others of these martyrs who are today commemorated at Cordova. The first of them, Aurelius, was the son of a Moor and of a Spanish woman, people of distinction ;

they both died while he was yet a boy, confiding him to the care of his mother's sister who brought him up a Christian. When he grew up he conformed outwardly, so far as he conscientiously could, to Islam, but continued to practise his religion in secret and converted his half-Moorish wife, Sabigotho, who at her baptism took the name of Natalia. One day this Aurelius saw a certain Christian merchant, one John, who had been cruelly beaten for having publicly asserted the falseness of the Mohammedan religion and its prophet, and who was being led through the streets on a donkey as a spectacle and an example. The sight of this confessor moved Aurelius to compunction, and he began to be ashamed of his own careful hiding of the fact that he was a Christian ; at the same time he was much troubled as to what he should do, as he had two small children. He talked it over with his wife, and together they consulted St Eulogius, who advised them that, before they made open avowal of their religion, they should make material provision for their children and arrange for them, in case their parents were killed, to be brought up in the faith ; they were, in fact, commended to the care of Eulogius himself. Their example fired a kinsman of Aurelius, Felix, who had been brought up a Christian but apostatized to Islam, although his wife, Liliosa, had remained faithful. He returned to the Church (thus automatically making himself liable to death as a renegade), and all four took to visiting and ministering to the Christian captives, getting to know, among others, the merchant John and two girls, SS. Flora and Mary, who were in prison at Seville.

At this time there had come into Spain a monk called George ; he belonged to the monastery of St Sabas near Jerusalem, and had been sent, first to Egypt and then to Europe, to beg alms for his house. When he came to Cordova he met Aurelius, was received into his house, and they became great friends ; it is recorded of George that he had not washed for twenty-five years, a form of mortification better thought of in those days than in these. Flora and Mary duly received the crown of martyrdom, and soon after appeared in a vision to Aurelius and Natalia, telling them that they would before long have a like happy fate. Taking this as an indication of the will of God, Natalia and her friend Liliosa gave themselves away as Christian women by visiting the churches of Cordova (there were even then seven of them) with their faces open and unveiled. They were all arrested, with other Christians, while assisting at Mass in the house of Aurelius, and the monk George putting himself forward as one of the rest was taken along too. They were charged with apostasy from Islam, but as no such charge could be laid against George who was a foreigner, he would have been released ; but he openly before the court reviled the name of Mohammed, so he was condemned with the rest. They were all beheaded before the emir's palace.

The *Memorialis sanctorum* of St Eulogius is practically our only source of information. The relevant matter is quoted in the *Acta Sanctorum*, July, vol. vi, but under the heading " Georgii monachi, Aurelii, etc." *Cf.* however, Florez, *España Sagrada*, vol. x ; and Simonet, *Historia de los Mozarabes de España*, pp. 428 *seq*. On St Eulogius, see March 11.

BD BERTHOLD OF GARSTEN, ABBOT   (A.D. 1142)

BERTHOLD was born about the year 1090 on the shores of Lake Constance. His wife dying when he was some thirty years old, he became a monk at Sankt Blasien and was promoted to be prior of Goettweig in the Black Forest. Ottokar, Margrave of Styria, had some years previously founded a house of secular canons at Steyer-Garsten, but the institution had not come up to his expectations and fulfilled his intentions, so he determined to dismiss the canons and people the house with Benedictines.   This he did about 1111, and put at their head Bd Berthold, who at once established a rigorous discipline, and the reputation of the abbot and his monks soon made the monastery a place of pilgrimage.   To shelter and entertain them Berthold built a hospice and added thereto a hospital for the benefit of the sick poor of the whole neighbourhood as well as of travellers.   These charities, and the succour of the numerous indigent folk who asked for help, were a great strain on the resources of the monastery, but on several occasions it appeared that God had intervened to supply their needs miraculously.   Berthold led the ordinary life of a monk, dividing his time between prayer and study and the work of the house ; but this life is designed to be a means of sanctity, and by it Berthold became a saint : in secret he led a life of great penitence, he never ate meat or fish, and spent hours of his short night in private prayer.   People came from far and wide to hear him preach and to ask his blessing ; and it is particularly interesting to note, in view of the period at which he lived, that Berthold's zeal manifested itself especially in hearing confessions, both of his own religious and of lay people.

The full life of Bd Berthold which we possess was written about twenty years after his death, and has been printed with much illustrative matter in the *Acta Sanctorum*, July, vol. vi.

ST THEOBALD OF MARLY, Abbot   (A.D. 1247)

This monk, by his virtue the great ornament of the illustrious family of Montmorency in France, was born in the castle of Marly.   His father, Bouchard de Montmorency, gave him an education suitable to his birth, trained him for arms, and sent him for a time to the court of King Philip Augustus II.   But Theobald manifested a strong inclination to a state of retirement ; he spent a great part of his time in prayer, and resorted often to the church of the nunnery called Port Royal, which had been founded in 1204 by the wife of Matthew de Montmorency, and on which his father Bouchard had bestowed so many estates that he was regarded as a second founder.   Theobald took the Cistercian habit at Vaux-de-Cernay in 1220, and was chosen abbot in 1235.   He lived in the midst of his brethren as the servant of every one, and surpassed all others in his love of poverty, silence and prayer.   He was known to and much venerated by St Louis.   Theobald died on December 8, 1247, but the Cistercians observe his feast on July 27.

We do not know very much about Theobald of Marly, but some biographical material has been printed by André Duchesne in his *Historiae Francorum Scriptores*, vol. v, pp. 406–407.   See also Lenain, *Histoire de Cîteaux*, vol. ix, and especially G. Müller's article " Der hl. Theobald, Abt von Vaux de Cernay ", in *Cistercienser-Chronik*, vol. xv (1903), pp. 321–336.

BD LUCY OF AMELIA, Virgin   (A.D. 1350)

Lucy Bufalari was born at Castel Ponziano in Umbria, and was a sister of Bd John of Rieti.   Like her brother, she joined the order of the Hermits of St Augustine (Augustinian Friars), and she became prioress of the convent of Amelia.   She practised the most severe mortifications and displayed heroic virtues in the service of God in the cloister.   After her death she was invoked by the people, and her cult was confirmed in 1832.

See Lupidi, *Memorie storiche riguardanti la B. Lucia Bufalari* (1938) ; and Seeböck, *Herrlichkeit der Katholischen Kirche* (1900).

BB. RUDOLF AQUAVIVA and his Companions, Martyrs (A.D. 1583)

THESE five martyrs of the Society of Jesus were RUDOLF AQUAVIVA, ALFONSO PACHECO, PETER BERNO, ANTONY FRANCISCO, priests, and FRANCIS ARANHA, temporal coadjutor. Father Aquaviva was son of the Duke of Atri, related to the family of St Aloysius Gonzaga, and nephew of Claud Aquaviva, the fifth general of the Jesuits. He was admitted at the age of eighteen, in 1568, and after being ordained priest at Lisbon was sent to Goa, in India. In 1579 a request was received from the Great Mogul Akbar that missionaries should be sent to his court at Fatehpur Sikri, near Agra. Father Aquaviva, a man " of very sweet and simple disposition . . . perpetually conscious of God ", was one of the two chosen for this mission, and he spent till 1583 in strenuous efforts to convert Akbar and his subjects ; he had no success, and in that year was recalled to be put in charge of the Salsette mission, north of Bombay. Father Pacheco, a Castilian, and Father Berno, a Swiss, accompanied two punitive expeditions of the Portuguese against the village of Cuncolim ; on these occasions they were both conspicuous for their energy in the destruction of Hindu sacred buildings, and no doubt the people made a note of it. Father Francisco was Italian ; Brother Aranha was the mission architect at Goa and at his death had been twenty-three years in India.

These five Jesuits, then, were all in the district of Salsette, and they determined together to make a " frontal attack " on Cuncolim, which was the heart of Hindu opposition in that mission. On July 15, 1583, they met at Orlim and, together with other Christians, set out for Cuncolim, intending to choose there a piece of ground for a church and to plant a cross thereon. On their arrival the notables of the village hurriedly took counsel, and then approached the missionaries with an armed force. A Portuguese layman, Rodriguez, would have fired on them, but he was stopped by Father Pacheco with the words, " We are not here to fight ". The villagers then fell on the party. Bd Rudolf and Bd Alfonso were killed praying for their murderers, and the other two priests were likewise slain outright. The coadjutor, Bd Francis, was left for dead, but found living the next day ; he was given the chance to venerate an idol, and on refusing was tied to a tree and shot through with arrows. There were put to death at the same time Gonçalo Rodriguez and fourteen Indian Christians, two of whom were lads. There is now no means of judging the reasons on account of which these fifteen were omitted from the cause of the martyrs by Mgr Menezes, Archbishop of Goa, in 1600 but, from what is known of the methods of that prelate, they would probably be found unconvincing today.

Even the cause of the five Jesuits was subjected to long delay. The promoter of the faith raised the doubt that the destroying of Hindu pagodas and other aggressive acts had brought about what was in effect a state of war which, rather than hatred of the faith, involved the massacre. It was not till 1741 that Pope Benedict XIV declared the martyrdom proved, and even then the formal beatification did not take place till 1893.

The best popular account of the Martyrs of Salsette is that written in German by Father H. Grüber, *Der selige Rudolf Aquaviva und seine Gefährten* (1894) ; but see also P. Suau, *Les BB. martyrs de Salsette* (1893), and in English F. Goldie, *The First Christian Mission to the Great Mogul* (1897), and J. S. Narayan, *Aquaviva and the Great Mogul* (Patna, 1946). From the point of view of secular history valuable sidelights may be obtained from Sir Edward Maclagan's article in the *Journal* of the Asiatic Society of Bengal (vol. lxv) on " Jesuit Missions to the Emperor Akbar ", and from C. H. Payne's *Akbar and the Jesuits* (1926).

BD MARY MAGDALEN MARTINENGO, Virgin   (A.D. 1737)

Mary Magdalen Martinengo da Barco was born into a noble family at Brescia in northern Italy in 1687.   At five months old she lost her mother, and her childhood showed a considerable precocity of religious devotion, self-inflicted mortifications and spiritual, or psychological, disturbances.   Her determination " to imitate *everything* in the lives of the saints ", though heroic, could hardly be called a wise programme at any age.   When she was eighteen Mary Martinengo joined the Capuchinesses of Santa Maria della Neve in her native town.   She was professed in 1706, and her responsibilities varied between novice-mistress (three times) and portress ; in 1732 and again in 1736 she was superior of the convent, and was admirable in all these offices.   Her humility and selfless love of God were adorned with the divine recognition of unusual mystical experiences and the gift of miracles ; she had a particular personal devotion towards our Lord's sufferings from the crown of thorns, and after her death a fillet of sharp points was found bound about her own brow.

This was the simplest and most " ordinary " of Bd Mary's practices, which to detail would not necessarily tend to edification ; not without reason has a Benedictine written that to many they might seem like " the feats of a fakir ".   But they were so many witnesses to her love for the crucified Redeemer who had suffered so much for her, " for everybody to love whom with one single heart is too little, much too little ".   And all this was joined with capability as novice-mistress and abbess, with a love of silence, with a quiet sweetness of speech.   Bd Mary Magdalen died in 1737, in her fiftieth year, and was beatified in 1900.

Several biographies, mostly based upon the documents of the cause, were published about the time of Bd Mary's beatification, notably that by Fr Ladislaus of Vannes in French (1901).   Others, in Italian, were by Fr Ludovic of Leghorn (1899), Fr Antonino of Bergamo (1900), and Fr Sisto of Pisa (1900).

28 : SS. NAZARIUS and CELSUS, Martyrs   (Date Unknown)

ST NAZARIUS'S father was a heathen, and an officer in the Roman army. His mother was a zealous Christian, and he was instructed by St Peter, or his disciples.   Nazarius out of zeal for the salvation of others left Rome, his native city, and preached the faith in many places with a fervour and disinterestedness becoming a disciple of the apostles.   Arriving at Milan he was there beheaded, together with Celsus, a youth whom he took with him to assist him on his travels.   These martyrs suffered soon after Nero had raised the first persecution.   Their bodies were buried separately in a garden outside the city, where they were discovered and taken up by St Ambrose soon after the year 395.   In the tomb of St Nazarius the saint's blood was found as fresh and red as if it had been spilt that day.   St Ambrose conveyed the bodies of the two martyrs into the church of the Apostles, which he had just built, and a woman was delivered from an evil spirit in their presence.

This brief account is taken by Alban Butler from a sermon of the saint's feast by St Ennodius, another wrongly attributed to St Ambrose, and the biography of the last named by the deacon Paulinus.   It may represent a tradition current in Milan at the end of the fourth century, which led to St Ambrose's search for the bodies, but the only historically certain points are his discovery and translation of them.   In later versions the legend is much embroidered, and abounds in inconsistencies and fables.   SS. Nazarius and Celsus are united in one feast with the holy popes Victor and Innocent (see below), and are named in the canon of the Milanese Mass.

This legend has been very thoroughly studied by Father Fedele Savio, first in the volume issued under the title *Ambrosiana,* to do honour to the St Ambrose centenary of 1897, and secondly in his work *Gli antichi vescovi d'Italia,* pt. 1 (1913).   He shows that the four Latin and two Greek texts which we possess probably derive from an original fabricated in Africa in the fourth century.   See also the *Acta Sanctorum,* July, vol. vi, and Delehaye, *Les Origines du Culte des Martyrs,* pp. 79–80, etc.

ST VICTOR I, POPE AND MARTYR   (*c.* A.D. 199)

ST VICTOR was a native of Africa, and succeeded St Eleutherius in the pontificate about the year 189.   Those virtues which had prepared him for that dignity made him a true successor of the Apostles, and he vigorously grappled with the difficulties of the times.   Among these was a group of Asiatic Christians at Rome who insisted on celebrating Easter on a date that accorded with their own traditions, even if a week-day.   Certain Asiatic bishops interfered to support them, and were threatened by the pope with excommunication.   St Irenaeus of Lyons and others protested against this severity, pointing out that differences of disciplinary custom had not hitherto been allowed to compromise Christian brotherhood.   The protest appears to have been successful ; but St Victor naturally insisted on maintaining uniformity of observance in his own province without being meddled with by bishops from outside it.   Other troubles were caused by the arrival in Rome from Byzantium of a man called Theodotus, a leather-merchant, who taught that Jesus Christ was only a supernaturally endowed man.

Pope St Victor died before the persecution of Septimius Severus began, and there is no good reason to suppose he was martyred ; but his energy and zeal exposed him to persecutions for which alone he might deserve the honours of a martyr which are accorded him liturgically.   This pope is named in the canon of the Ambrosian Mass, he is said by St Jerome to have been the first in Rome to celebrate the Mysteries in Latin, and he was formerly held in special veneration in Scotland, being fabled to have sent missionaries thither.

The little we know of St Victor comes to us mainly from Eusebius and the *Liber Pontificalis.*   It is the latter authority which describes him as a martyr.   See also the *Acta Sanctorum,* July, vol. vi, and Duchesne, *History of the Early Church,* vol. i, cap. 16.

ST INNOCENT I, POPE   (A.D. 417)

INNOCENT I was a native of Albano, near Rome, and succeeded Pope St Anastasius I in the year 401.   For sixteen years he played an active part in ecclesiastical affairs, and his actions show him to have been a very capable man, energetic and vigorous, but otherwise little is known of him personally.   He informed the bishop of Rouen, St Victricius, that " greater causes " were to be referred to Rome, writing to the Spanish bishops in the same sense ; he also directed several bishops that their clergy should be celibate, after the Roman example.   He did his best to uphold St John Chrysostom, who had been unjustly removed from his see of Constantinople by the Synod of The Oak in 403, the pope refusing to recognize his intruded successors and vainly trying to get the Emperor Arcadius to have him reinstated.   After the bishops of Africa had condemned Pelagianiam at the councils of Carthage and Milevis in 416 they wrote asking the pope to confirm their decisions. In his reply Innocent said that " in all matters of faith bishops throughout the world should refer to St Peter ", and commended the Africans for so doing.   The papal confirmation was announced by St Augustine to his flock at Hippo : " Two councils have written to the Apostolic See about this matter, and the reply has come back : the question is settled "—whence the adage *Roma locuta, causa finita est.*

During this pontificate, on the night between the years 406 and 407, the Great Raid of barbarians crossed the Rhine ; four years later Rome was taken and sacked by the Goths.   Innocent was in Ravenna at the time, whither he had gone with a deputation to persuade the Emperor Honorius to try and make peace by buying off the invaders.   He died on March 12, 417.

As in the preceding entry, the life of St Innocent I belongs less to hagiography than to the general history of the Church.   We have a fair amount of evidence from his own letters and contemporary documents.   See the *Acta Sanctorum*, July, vol. vi ; L. Duchesne, *History of the Early Church*, vol. iii ; DCB., vol. iii, pp. 243–249 ; DTC., vol. vii, cc. 1940–1950 ; and Fliche and Martin, *Histoire de l'Église*, t. iv, pp. 243–247.   For Innocent's liturgical enactments, *cf.* R. Connolly in the *Journal of Theological Studies*, vol. xx (1919), pp. 215–226.

ST SAMSON, BISHOP OF DOL   (*c.* A.D. 565)

ST SAMSON was one of the most important of the British missionary bishops of the sixth century, and he is to this day venerated liturgically in South Wales and Brittany.   He was born about the year 485, his father, Amon, being of the Welsh province of Dyfed, and his mother, Anna, from Gwent, he being a " child of promise " after his parents' long childlessness.   Out of gratitude the child was, at the age of five years, dedicated to God in the monastery founded and governed by St Illtud at Llantwit in Glamorgan, a very nursery of saints.   The young Samson was most virtuous in his life, quick in his studies, and austere in his monastic observance, so he was early made deacon and priest by St Dyfrig (Dubricius). This excited the jealousy of two brothers, monks and nephews of St Illtud, one of whom aspired to succeed his uncle as abbot of the house.   They therefore tried to remove Samson by poison ; but he remained unharmed, whereupon one of the brothers repented, as did the other after he had had a seizure when receiving communion from his victim's hand and been cured at his prayer.   Samson obtained the abbot's permission to go to an island where was a small community governed by one Piro.   This island is usually identified with Caldey (Ynys Byr), off the coast of Pembrokeshire.   Here he " ceased not by day or night from prayer and communion with God, leading with untiring patience a wonderful, isolated, and above all, heavenly life, spending the whole day in working with his hands and in prayer ".   His father being, as he supposed, near death, sent for Samson to administer the last rites.   At first he was unwilling to go out into the world, but Piro rebuked him and appointed a deacon to bear him company, and when he had ministered the sacraments to his father, the man recovered. Whereupon Amon and his wife wished to retire from the world, and when provision had been made for her, Samson with his father and his uncle Umbrafel and the deacon returned to the island. Here they found St Dubricius spending Lent in retreat there, according to his custom, and when he heard of certain marvels that had happened on their journey, he had Samson appointed cellarer to the community. Shortly afterwards Piro died * and Samson was made abbot in his stead. In this office, while himself being regarded as a hermit, he brought the monks gently into better discipline, and also made a journey to Ireland ; a monastery which was there confided to him he put in charge of Umbrafel. But on his return he refused to continue as abbot and retired, with Amon and two others, to somewhere near the river Severn and there they lived as hermits.

But his peace was not for long undisturbed. He was made abbot of the monastery " which, it is said, had been founded by St Germanus ", and was consecrated bishop by St Dubricius. He soon after, on Easter eve, had a vision in which he was told to go beyond the seas. Accordingly he went into Cornwall, with his companions, and landed " with a favourable wind, after a happy passage " at or near Padstow. He proceeded towards the monastery called Docco (now Saint Kew), and when the monks heard of his approach they sent one of their number, the most prudent and a man with the gift of prophecy, Winiau, to meet him. This was not, however, the sign of an eager welcome, for when St Samson proposed to stay at the monastery for a little, Winiau tactfully intimated that it was not convenient, " for our discipline is not what it was. Go on your way in peace. . . ."

Samson took his words as an indication from God, and went on across Cornwall, travelling by means of a car or chariot which he had brought from Ireland. Going through the district of Trigg he converted a number of idol-worshippers by restoring miraculously a boy who had been thrown from a horse ; he founded a church at Southill and another at Golant, coming by way of the Fowey river to its mouth, whence he took ship to Brittany, leaving his father in charge of a monastery at Southill. It is possible that before leaving Cornwall, where he must have spent a considerable time, he visited the Scilly Islands, for one of them is named after him.

Of Samson's work in Brittany his biographers speak most of his miracles ; he made missionary journeys in all directions, including the Channel Islands, where a town on Guernsey bears his name, and founded two monasteries, one for himself at Dol and another at Pental in Normandy. He helped to restore to Brittany its rightful prince, Judual, against his rival Conmor in the year 555. Upon visiting Paris Samson attracted the favourable notice of King Childebert, who is said to have nominated him bishop of Dol, and he is probably the " Samson, peccator, Episcopus " who signed the acts of the Council of Paris in 557 ; but Dol was not a regular episcopal see until the ninth century. St Samson died peacefully among his monks about the year 565.

There has been much discussion concerning the date and the value of the life of St Samson printed by Mabillon and in the *Acta Sanctorum*, July, vol. vi. The text has been

---

* Not for mere wantonness but as an illustration of the change of manners and standards, it is worth recording that Piro is reported to have died as the result of falling into a well " owing to stupid intoxication ". The biographer says with satisfaction of Samson that " no one ever saw him drunk ".

re-edited in modern times by Robert Fawtier, *La vie de S. Samson* (1912), who arrives at the conclusion that it was written by a monk of Dol at the end of the eighth or beginning of the ninth century, and that its data as a whole are historically worthless. Other specialists in Celtic hagiography by no means share this view. F. Duine (*Origines Bretonnes : la Vie de S. Samson*, 1914) adheres to the opinion of M. de la Borderie that the life was compiled about 610–615 at the latest. It seems that Mgr Duchesne, who at first pronounced for the ninth century date, afterwards changed his mind and came over to the side of La Borderie. Canon T. Taylor, who published a translation with an admirable introduction, *The Life of St Samson of Dol* (1925), also adheres to the view that the text is a genuine memorial of the early seventh century. *Cf.* LBS., vol. iv, pp. 130 *seq. ;* Burkitt in *Journal of Theological Studies*, vol. xxvii (1925), pp. 42–57 ; A. W. Wade-Evans, *Welsh Christian Origins* (1934), pp. 205–233 ; and G. H. Doble, *St Samson in Cornwall* (1935). Samson's name occurs in many medieval English calendars.

ST BOTVID (A.D. 1100)

BOTVID was a Swedish layman, born in the province of Södermannland and brought up a pagan, who was converted to the faith in England. He preached in his own countryside and in Vestmannland and Norrland and met his death by an example of the basest treachery and ingratitude. He bought a Finnish slave whom he instructed, baptized, and then set free, telling him to spread the gospel in his own land. With a man called Asbjorn, Botvid then set out in a boat to take the Finn across the Baltic, but during the night, when they had gone ashore to sleep, the slave murdered both of them and decamped with the boat. According to the legend the search party sent out to find the missing Swedes was guided by a bird which perched on the prow of the boat, singing until the bodies were found. Botvid was buried at Botkyrka and an account of him written by a monk of Bodensee ; he is venerated as a martyr and as one of the apostles of Sweden.

See the *Acta Sanctorum*, July, vol. vi ; but there are fuller texts of the life which have been edited in the *Scriptores rerum Suecicarum*, vol. ii, pt 1, pp. 377–387 ; *cf.* also I. Collijn's paper on the " Kalendarium Munkalivense " in the H. Degering *Festgabe* (1926).

BD ANTONY DELLA CHIESA (A.D. 1459)

ANTONY was born in 1395 at San Germano, near Vercelli, of the noble family of della Chiesa di Roddi, which was afterwards to give to the Church Pope Benedict XV (Giacomo della Chiesa). His religious vocation was opposed by his parents, and he was already twenty-two when he took the habit of the Friars Preachers at Vercelli. He was a very successful preacher and director of souls, and for some years accompanied the Franciscan St Bernardino of Siena on his missions. While prior at Como he completely reformed the life and morals of that town, and was sent successively to govern the friaries at Savona, Florence and Bologna, where he insisted on a rigorous observance of their rule. Each time he relinquished office with joy and had soon to take it again, saying sadly that he who could not even manage an oar was entrusted with the tiller. From 1440 to 1449 the Church was troubled by an antipope, Amadeus of Savoy, calling himself Felix V, who had a large following in Savoy and Switzerland. Bd Antony stoutly opposed himself to this man and succeeded in winning over a number of his adherents to lawful authority. He also preached with great energy against usury, using as a terrible warning the story of a usurer who at his death had lost not only his soul but even his body, which had been carried off by a troop of diabolic horsemen, so that his relatives had had to bury an empty coffin. Stories of this sort, some entertaining, some touching, some to our ideas merely silly, were part of the stock-in-trade of every medieval preacher. While going by sea from Savona to Genoa with a fellow friar, the ship in which they were was captured by corsairs ; they had no reason to look for anything but death or slavery, but the pirates were so impressed by the demeanour of the two religious that they set them free without ransom. Bd Antony received the gift of miracles and of discernment of spirits, and predicted the day of his own death, which was at Como on January 22, 1459. His *cultus* was approved in 1819, his feast being kept on July 28, the date of the translation of his relics to his birthplace in 1810.

An account of Bd Antony is furnished in Procter, *Lives of the Dominican Saints*, pp. 210–213. See further V. Pellazza, *Elogio storico del B. Antonio* (1863) ; Taurisano, *Catalogus Hagiographicus O.P.*, p. 40 ; and L. Ferretti, *Vita del B. Antonio* (1919).

29 : ST MARTHA, Virgin (First Century)

MARTHA was sister to Mary (who is usually identified with Magdalen) and Lazarus, and lived with them at Bethany, a small town two miles distant from Jerusalem, a little beyond Mount Olivet. Our blessed Redeemer had made His residence usually in Galilee, till in the third year of His public ministry He preached frequently in Judaea, during which interval he frequented the house of these three disciples, who perhaps had removed from Galilee to be nearer Him. St John particularly tells us that " Jesus loved Martha and her sister Mary and Lazarus ". Martha seems to have been the eldest, and to have had the chief care and direction of the household, for, when Jesus visited them, St Luke tells us that Martha showed great solicitude to entertain and serve Him, to be herself busy in preparing everything for their guest. Mary sat all the while at our Saviour's feet, feeding her soul with heavenly doctrine.

With so great love did Martha wait on our Redeemer that, as we cannot doubt, she thought that if the whole world were occupied in attending to so great a guest, all would be too little. She wished that all men would employ their hands, feet and hearts, all their faculties and senses, with their whole strength, in serving their Creator who was made for us our brother. Therefore she asked Him to bid her sister Mary help her. Our Lord was indeed well pleased with the affection and devotion wherewith Martha waited on Him ; yet He commended more the quiet repose with which Mary attended only to that which is of the greatest importance, the attendance of the soul on God. " Martha, Martha," said He, " thou art careful and troubled about many things ; but one thing is necessary. Mary hath chosen the best part. . . ." In active works the soul is often distracted or entirely drawn off, whereas in heavenly contemplation the heart is wholly taken up in God, and united to Him by worship and love. This is the novitiate of Heaven, where it is the uninterrupted occupation of the blessed. In this sense Christ so highly commends the choice of Mary, affirming that her happy employment would never be taken from her. He added, " One thing is necessary ", that is, " Eternal salvation is our only concern ".

See Luke x 38–42, and John xi and xii 1–2. In the Provençal legend referred to under St Mary Magdalen on the 22nd of this month, St Martha accompanied her sister to France and evangelized Tarascon, where her alleged relics were found in 1187 and enclosed in a shrine where they are still venerated. Most of what is said in the note appended to the account of St Mary Magdalen above applies to the legends connecting St Martha with Provence and particularly with Tarascon.

SS. SIMPLICIUS, FAUSTINUS AND BEATRICE, MARTYRS (A.D. 304 ?)

OF these martyrs in Rome no reliable particulars are known. The legend relates that Simplicius and Faustinus were brothers who refused to sacrifice to the gods ; they were therefore beaten, tortured, beheaded and their bodies thrown into the Tiber ; another version says that they were drowned therein. The bodies were recovered by their sister Beatrice (Viatrix) and buried in the cemetery of Generosa on the road to Porto. For seven months after she lived with a woman called Lucina, but was then denounced as a Christian by her neighbour Lucretius, who coveted her estate. When brought before the judge she was ordered to sacrifice, but she replied boldly that she would do no act of worship towards demons, for she was a Christian. On the night of May 11 she received her crown, being strangled in prison, and was buried with her brothers. Retribution overtook Lucretius in miraculous fashion. On the strength of his ill-gotten property, he gave a feast to his friends, and while they were all enjoying themselves a suckling babe suddenly jumped up in its mother's lap and denounced the host : " You, Lucretius, are a thief and a murderer and the Devil's own ! " And after being in agony for three hours Lucretius died, and all those present were converted. The relics of these three martyrs were translated by Pope St Leo II in the seventh century to the church of Santa Bibiana, and later to St Mary Major's ; joined to them in their liturgical commemoration is St Felix, martyr (see below).

This is another case in which the uncertainty or the extravagance of later accounts create no presumption against the genuineness of the cult or the fact of the martyrdom. In the *Hieronymianum* we find the bare entry that on " July 29 on the road to Porto at Sextum Philippi " was celebrated the memory of Simplicius, Faustinus and Viatrix (not Beatrix). But in 1868 the cemetery of Generosa was discovered beside the road to Porto with a little basilica dating from the time of Pope Damasus, which preserved frescoes and fragments of inscriptions. These give the names Simplicius, Faustinianus, Viatrix, and add another martyr, Rufinianus. See J. B. de Rossi, *Roma Sotterranea*, vol. iii, pp. 647–697 ; or more compendiously in Leclercq, DAC., vol. vi, cc. 866–900. The brief " acts " of these saints are in the *Acta Sanctorum*, July, vol. vii.

ST FELIX " II " (A.D. 365)

THE history of this individual is confused, uncertain and surprising. When in the year 355 the Emperor Constantius dragged Pope Liberius to Milan and thence banished him to Thrace for upholding the definitions of the Council of Nicaea and refusing to condemn St Athanasius (" Who are you to stand up for Athanasius against the world ? "), he caused to be intruded in the pope's place the senior deacon of Rome, one Felix, who was quietly consecrated by three Arian bishops. Felix accepted the office, but he was acknowledged by only some of the clergy of the City and by very few of the laity, and by nobody at all outside except at the imperial court ; when Constantius visited Rome he was petitioned to reinstate Liberius. In 357 the true pope was allowed to return and was enthusiastically received by the people ; Felix fled, after vainly trying to maintain his position, and was forbidden by the senate ever to return. He died near Porto on November 22, 365.

This is not very promising material for the life of one honoured as a pope, saint and martyr, as he is represented in certain spurious documents of the early sixth century, the *Gesta Felicis* and *Gesta Liberii*. The measure of the error and confusion may be seen in the Roman Martyrology, which has on this day : " At Rome, on the Aurelian Way, the burial-day of the holy Felix the Second, pope and martyr, who was cast out of his see for his defence of the Catholic faith by the Arian Emperor Constantius, and died gloriously, being secretly slain by the sword at Cera in Tuscany. His body was taken thence by the clergy and buried on the same road, but having been afterwards taken to the church of SS. Cosmas and Damian, it was found there under the altar by Pope Gregory XIII, together with the relics of the holy martyrs Mark, Marcellian and Tranquillinus, and all together buried in the same place again on July 31." Here Felix has clearly been confounded with Pope Liberius (or their respective roles deliberately exchanged). The *Liber Pontificalis* speaks of the archdeacon Felix building a church on the Aurelian Way, a road on which there was the tomb of a martyred St Felix, and this doubtless has been a further source of mistake and derangement.

Since 1947 the *Annuario Pontificio* in its list of popes has noted " Felix II " among the antipopes.

The surprising entry in the Roman Martyrology quoted above is a sad memorial to the still backward state of critical scholarship at the time when Cardinal Baronius was editing this official service book. The insertion of Felix as Pope and Martyr was not any oversight, for Baronius in his annotated edition of the martyrology refers his readers for an elucidation of the matter to the volume of his great work, the *Annales*, which was on the point of appearing. Mgr Duchesne has discussed the whole subject at length in the introduction to his edition of the *Liber Pontificalis*, §§ 59–66. It is plain that the text of the *Liber Pontificalis* is the source of all the trouble. In the middle ages this book passed for authoritative : its strange inversion of the roles of Felix and Liberius consequently imposed themselves upon the first compilers of the martyrology. It may be that the account of Felix in the *Liber Pontificalis* is simply an interpolation, or that it is due to a confused memory of the *Gesta Liberii*. Upon this last document, see Abbot Chapman in the *Revue Bénédictine*, vol. xxvii (1910), pp. 191–199. See also Saltet, " La Formation de la légende des papes Libère et Félix ", in *Bulletin de littér. ecclés.*, 1905, pp. 222 *seq.*, and J. P. Kirsch, " Die Grabstätte der Felices duo pontifices et martyres an der Via Aurelia ", in *Röm. Quartalschrift*, vol. xxviii (1925), pp. 1–20.

ST LUPUS, BISHOP OF TROYES   (A.D. 478)

ST LUPUS, called in French Loup, was born at Toul about the year 383. He married a sister of St Hilary of Arles, but after six years spent in wedlock, desirous of serving God with greater perfection, they parted by mutual consent. Lupus sold his estate for the benefit of the poor and went to the famous abbey of Lérins, then governed by St Honoratus ; but very shortly afterwards, about the year 426, he was chosen as bishop of Troyes. In this position he continued the same humility, mortification, and as much as possible poverty as in the monastery. He never wore any other than the most simple garments, slept upon bare boards, passed many hours in private prayer and many days in voluntary fasts. Thus he lived for over fifty years, labouring at the same time in all his pastoral functions with unremitting zeal.

When in 429 St Germanus of Auxerre passed over into Britain to combat the Pelagian heresy, St Lupus was appointed to accompany him. The two bishops accepted the commission the more willingly as it seemed laborious and painful, and by their prayers, preaching and miracles put down the false teaching, at any rate for a time. Lupus after his return set himself with fresh vigour to reform his own flock, and displayed so great prudence and piety that St Sidonius Apollinaris calls him " The father of fathers and bishop of bishops, chief of the prelates of Gaul, the rule of morals, the pillar of truth, the friend of God, and the intercessor to Him for men ". He spared no pains to save one lost sheep, and he often had a success which seemed miraculous. Among other instances it is recorded that a man of his diocese, named Gallus, had deserted his wife and gone to live at Clermont. St Lupus wrote to St Sidonius, Bishop of Clermont, a strong letter, but so prudently tempered with sweetness that Gallus by reading it was at once persuaded, and set out to return to his home. Upon which Sidonius remarked, " What is more wonderful than a single reprimand which both moves a sinner to repentance and makes him love his reprover ! "

At that time Attila with a numberless army of Huns overran Gaul, so that he came to be called " the scourge of God ", sent to punish the sins of the people. Rheims, Cambrai, Besançon, Auxerre and Langres had already felt his fury, and Troyes was the next place threatened. The bishop, after fervent prayer to God on behalf of his people, went out to meet the invader, and prevailed on him to spare the whole province. But Lupus was forced to accompany Attila as a hostage, and after the barbarians had been beaten on the plains of Châlons he was accused of having favoured the escape of Attila, and he was obliged to leave Troyes for two years—an early victim of " anti-collaborationist " hysteria. He spent that time as a hermit among the mountains, in great austerity and contemplation ; when his charity and patience had overcome the malice of men, he went back to his church, which he governed with renewed enthusiasm until his death in 478.

On account of his association with St Germanus, St Lupus was formerly venerated in England. Some doubt has been cast on the story of his resistance to Attila and its consequences ; but the moral to be drawn from it is unimpaired : it was by prayer that the saints became holy and performed great wonders. By it Moses could ward off the destruction of many thousands. By it Elias called down fire and rain from the heavens ; Manasses in chains found mercy ; Ezechias saw his health restored ; the Ninivites were preserved from destruction ; Judith and Esther saved God's people ; Daniel was delivered from the lions, St Peter from his chains.

The document which purports to be the earliest Life of St Lupus has long been regarded with suspicion, and Bruno Krusch in a definitive edition of the text (MGH., *Scriptores Merov.*, vol. vii, 1920, pp. 284–302) claims to have demonstrated that it is no older than the eighth century. If so, it can have little authority in bearing witness to incidents alleged to have occurred three hundred years earlier. It was written, Krusch avers, in the Carolingian era to defend the temporal possessions of the see of Troyes. For Lupus's relations with his contemporaries see the *Acta Sanctorum*, July, vol. vii.

ST OLAF OF NORWAY, Martyr　　(A.D. 1030)

OLAF was the son of Harold Grenske, a lord in Norway, and after eight years of piracy and fighting succeeded to his father in 1015 at the age of twenty, at a time when most of Norway was in the hands of the Danes and Swedes. These parts he conquered and then set about the subjection of the realm to Christ, for he himself had already been baptized at Rouen by Archbishop Robert ; the work had been begun, but had not made much real progress, by Haakon the Good and by

Olaf Tryggvason, whose methods of " evangelization " seem to have been preposterous and wicked. In 1013 Olaf Haraldsson had sailed to England and assisted King Ethelred against the Danes, and he now turned to that country for help in his more peaceable task. He brought over from England a number of priests and monks, one of whom, Grimkel, was chosen bishop of Nidaros, his capital. Olaf relied much on the advice of this prelate, and by his counsel published many good enactments and abolished ancient laws and customs contrary to the gospel. Unfortunately, like St Vladimir of Russia and other princes who sought to convert their people, he was not content with exhortation, his zeal was often more than his prudence, and he used force without compunction. To his enemies he was merciless, added to which some of his legislation and political objects were not everywhere approved. Therefore many rose in arms, and, with the assistance of Canute, King of England and Denmark, defeated and expelled him. St Olaf fled, but returned with a few Swedish troops to recover his kingdom ; he was slain by his rebellious and infidel subjects in a battle fought at Stiklestad, on July 29, 1030.

The king's body was buried in a steep sandbank by the river Nid, where he had fallen ; here a spring gushed out whose waters became credited with healing power and the bishop, Grimkel, in the following year ordered that he was to be there venerated as a martyr and a chapel built over the place. Miracles were reported at the shrine, and on the return of his son Magnus to power the veneration of St Olaf became widespread ; in 1075 the chapel was replaced by a bishop's church, dedicated to Christ and St Olaf, which in time became the metropolitan cathedral of Nidaros (Trondhjem), which was, both as a building and a shrine, to Scandinavia what Canterbury was to England : and just as pilgrims to the one dismounted on Harbledown Hill to greet the first sight of England's greatest shrine, so pilgrims to the other did the like on what is still known as Feginsbrekka, the Hill of Joy. During the middle ages the *cultus* of " the perpetual King of Norway " spread to Sweden, Denmark, the British Isles and beyond, and he is still regarded by Norwegians as the patron and national hero of his country. The name Tooley of a London street is a corruption of St Olaf's, and marks the former Scandinavian and Danish colony in Southwark ; and the churches of St Olave in Hart Street and of St Olave Upwell in Old Jewry were named after him.

See the *Acta Sanctorum*, July, vol. vii, where a text of the life by Archbishop Eystein is printed. This and other documents are also given in Metcalfe, *Passio et miracula b. Olavi* (1881). There is an English account by F. Vicary, *Olav the King* . . . (1887) ; a short life in French by C. Riesterer (1930) ; a translation into French by G. Sautreau of Snorre Sturluson's Saga of St Olaf (1930) ; and S. Undset's *Saga of Saints* (1934), pp. 87–148. See also F. M. Stenton, *Anglo-Saxon England* (1943), pp. 396–399, etc. ; and for Olaf's *cultus* in the British Isles articles by Professor Bruce Dickins in *Saga Book of the Viking Society*, vol. xii (1939), pp. 53–80, and in *The Norseman*, vol. ii (1944), no. 5.

BD URBAN II, POPE   (A.D. 1099)

It has been said that the Benedictine reform of Cluny was " by far the most potent international influence of the eleventh century ". Not all this influence was directly effected by the various Cluniac houses and the activities of their inmates ; much of it came through the popes, particularly in the first place St Gregory VII, who was brought up in the Cluniac monastery of St Mary on the Aventine and was a personal friend of St Odilo and St Hugh, and after him by the pontificate of Bd

Urban II.   Odo (Eudes) of Lagery was born at Châtillon-sur-Marne in 1042, and made his studies in the school of Rheims under St Bruno, the founder of the Carthusians ; perhaps by him he was inspired with a love for the religious life, for after being canon and archdeacon of Rheims he retired to Cluny and there received the habit.   He afterwards wrote to his abbot, St Hugh : " You and yours do I love in particular, for through you I learnt the elements of the monastic life and in your monastery I was re-born by the life-giving grace of the Holy Spirit." He became prior of the house and was called from that office in 1078 to be cardinal-bishop of Ostia and one of the chief advisers of St Gregory VII.   Hildebrand's successor, Bd Victor III, on his death-bed named the Cardinal-bishop of Ostia to succeed himself ; such a nomination has no canonical effect, but it had great weight with the conclave, which on March 12, 1088 elected Odo pope by acclamation. He took the name of Urban, and announced to the world his intention of following closely in the footsteps of Gregory VII ; among others, he wrote to Bd Lanfranc, Archbishop of Canterbury, calling him " the most noble and truest of the distin-guished sons of your mother, the Holy Roman Church ", and asking for his support.

He needed all he could get.   When St Peter Damian wrote, urbanely con-gratulating him in a Latin epigram on being made a poor bishop at Rome, his statement that " [Peter] is ever cleaning his fishing-gear and ploughing through deep waters " was more than just rhetoric.   Rome itself was in the hands of the antipope Guibert (" Clement III ") and it was not till November that Urban was able to enter the city, and more military force had to be used before he could take possession of St Peter's.   But soon afterwards the Emperor Henry IV invaded Italy : Urban abandoned Rome, and the antipope Clement was again welcomed by the citizens.   Urban retired to southern Italy, where he worked for the im-provement of local ecclesiastical discipline and for the peace of the Church at large ; but the continued use of the sword by the principal of his adherents did not hasten an agreement, and Henry was egged on in his course by the bishops of Germany. At the end of 1093 Urban re-entered Rome, living in the fortified palace of the Frangipani family, for Guibert's followers still held the castle of Sant' Angelo and the pope was unwilling to take up arms against the Roman citizens.   He was reduced to the direst poverty and indebtedness, from which he was in a measure rescued by the generosity and devotion of a French abbot, Geoffrey of Vendôme.

In the spring of 1095 a synod was convened at Piacenza.   After the fathers had dealt with two royal marriage cases, Urban promulgated the Gregorian decrees concerning clerical celibacy, lay investitures and simony, and first broached the subject of a crusade in consequence of an appeal from the Eastern emperor, Alexius I Comnenus, for help to drive out the Seljuk Turks.   This matter was taken up seriously later in the year at the Council of Clermont-Ferrand in France, and it was received with immense enthusiasm.   The idea of the Emperor Alexius was " to call in the barbarians of the West to destroy the barbarians of the East ". Among the considerations on the Western side was the appeal to churchmen of the prospect of finding a more distant outlet for the energies and ambitions of the feudal lords ; while the people at large welcomed the aim of making the road across Asia Minor safe for pilgrims and traders and rescuing Jerusalem and the churches of Asia from the power of the Saracens.

It was decided to raise an army ; a plenary indulgence was granted to all who joined it solely from religious motives, and their goods were to be inviolable ; the " Truce of God " was extended ; and clergy and young married men were discouraged from going. Bd Urban in an eloquent appeal to the religious spirit and military valour of the Franks carried the people away : the multitude replied with shouts of " God wills it ! " and large numbers there and then " took the cross ". The pope himself for the next nine months preached the crusade up and down France, and in the words of William of Malmesbury : " The Welshman left his hunting, the Scot his comradeship with lice, the Dane his drinking fellows, the Norwegian his raw fish. Lands were left by their husbandmen, houses by those who dwelt in them ; even whole cities were on the move." During the spring of 1097 the four official armies of the First Crusade assembled at Constantinople, and a fortnight before the death of Bd Urban, in July 1099, Jerusalem was taken. Thus began the Crusades, a series of expeditions which, had they all been undertaken and carried out in the spirit of the holy pope who initiated the first, might have been of permanent value to the Church and the cause of Christianity ; as it was, the good they did was on the whole ephemeral, while some of their evil results subsist to this day. Before ever the first official army set out, bands of undisciplined enthusiasts had prejudiced its reputation by pillaging and murdering through the valley of the Danube, terrorizing Constantinople, and been left for the Turks to annihilate ; while the capture of the Holy City was celebrated by a frightful massacre of Jews and Moslems.

Before returning to Italy the pope reduced some of the French bishops to order and received a promise of amendment from the adulterous King Philip (which he did not keep), and in May 1097 the rebellious Emperor Henry IV finally returned to Germany ; somewhat over a year later the antipope's party in Sant' Angelo surrendered the fortress, and at last the pope occupied the apostolic city in peace. The antipope Guibert was at Ravenna. At the same time, to solve the problems of church and state in the south, Urban constituted Count Roger of Sicily and his heir his legate in Sicily ; the exact terms of the commission are uncertain, but later the office was interpreted as residing in each and every successor to Roger as ruler of the Two Sicilies, and their privileges and " rights " were only finally extinguished by the Treaty of the Lateran in 1929. The last considerable act of Bd Urban's troubled but fruitful pontificate was the holding of a council at Bari, of which the ostensible object was the healing of the ecclesiastical divisions between Rome and Constantinople. But the Emperor Alexius had his hands full at the time, and, though there seem to have been Byzantine bishops present, the council resolved itself into a successful attempt to resolve the difficulties of the Italo-Greek bishops of southern Italy ; the question of the procession of the Holy Ghost from the Son was thrashed out to their satisfaction, chiefly owing to the eloquence and learning of St Anselm of Canterbury, who, being in Italy to inform the pope of the iniquities of King William Rufus, was called on by Bd Urban to explain and defend the Catholic teaching.

No account of Urban can end without a further reference to his association with St Bruno, his former master, although so little is known about it. When Urban ascended the papal chair Bruno had been already four years in the wilds of the Grande Chartreuse, and two years after he was called away to be " at the service of the Apostolic See ". It may be safely assumed that until the end of his life the pope depended much on the counsels of Bruno, for he would never let him go again out of Italy. For some time he lived with Urban himself, and was then allowed to found and reside at a hermitage on the lands of Count Roger in Calabria ; he makes no public appearances that are recorded in Urban's reign, but is always there at the pope's need—an outstanding example of religious obedience and of the function of the contemplative in the Church's life. Doubtless Bruno was at Urban's side when he had to deal with the delicate business of the relations of St Robert with his abbey of Molesme and the new foundation at Cîteaux, whose monks " make profession of keeping the Rule of St Benedict in all particulars, [so] let them not by another change return to a system which they now hold in contempt " ; and his influence, as well as his own upbringing, probably contributed to Urban's notable partiality for monks and the privileges he granted to monasteries everywhere.

Urban held a last council at Rome after Easter in 1099, at which Guibert was once more condemned and at which the pope pleaded for the crusade with such effect that the antipope's own brother took the cross. Three months later he died, and his *cultus* seems to have been from the day of his death, but he was formally beatified only in 1881. His story is one of great events in which, from the circumstances of the case, secular politics played a distressingly large part ; but what is known of Urban's private life bears out the uncompromising but not hard Christianity of his public life : in particular was he solicitous for the poor and devoted to our Lady—and his reliance on St Bruno and Bruno's faithful service have their own significance.

Bd Urban's life involves the whole history of his times and no criticism of the sources would be possible here. There is a relatively full account of his pontificate in the *Liber Pontificalis* (Duchesne, vol. ii, 293–295) by Petrus Gulielmus ; and Urban figures, of course, prominently in all the chronicles of the period. English readers will find a painstaking narrative in Mann, *The Lives of the Popes in the Middle Ages*, vol. vii, pp. 245–346. The biography by Lucien Paulot, *Un Pape français, Urbain II* (1903), should be read in the light of Poncelet's comments in *Analecta Bollandiana*, vol. xxiii (1904), pp. 372–375. The estimate of Urban in such modern authorities as Hauck, *Kirchengeschichte Deutschlands*, vol. iii, pp. 858–881, and the *Cambridge Medieval History*, vol. iv, pp. 87–95, shows a not unappreciative sense of the services he rendered to the Church and to the political problems of his time. *Cf.* also Fliche and Martin, *Histoire de l'Eglise*, t. viii, pp. 199–337, and S. Runciman, *History of the Crusades*, vol. i (1951).

ST WILLIAM PINCHON, Bishop of Saint-Brieuc   (A.D. 1234)

Of this bishop, St William Pinchon, we are told that his virtues and miracles were remarkable, but of the actual events of his life very little is known. He received holy orders at the hands of Josselin, Bishop of Saint-Brieuc, served that church under his two successors, Peter and Silvester, and succeeded himself to the see about the year 1220. The poor were his treasurers, and not content to exhaust on them whatever he possessed, he borrowed stores of corn and other necessary provisions for their relief ; his application to all the duties of his charge was no hindrance to his nourishing within himself the spirit of recollection and holy prayer. Being pertinacious in defending the rights of the Church and its bishops against the encroachments of Peter Mauclerc, Duke of Brittany, he was expelled from his diocese for two years and took refuge at Poitiers. He returned in 1230 and died four years later at Saint-Brieuc. His body was deposited in his cathedral and taken up incorrupt in 1248, the year after he was canonized.

See the *Acta Sanctorum*, July, vol. vii, where a short life is printed, attributed to Godefrid Calvus. *Cf.* also Lobineau, *Vies des saints de Bretagne*, vol. ii, pp. 426–455, and J. Arnault, *S. Guillaume, évêque de Saint-Brieuc* (1934).

30 : SS. ABDON AND SENNEN, MARTYRS   (A.D. 303 ?)

THEY were Persians who courageously confessed the faith of Christ in the persecution of Decius, ministering to their fellows and burying the bodies of the martyrs. They were brought to Rome as prisoners, refused to sacrifice, and spat upon the images of the gods, wherefore they were exposed to the beasts ; as neither lions nor bears would touch them they were hewn into pieces by gladiators. But the more their bodies were mangled and covered with wounds the more were their souls adorned and beautified with divine grace, and rendered glorious in the sight of Heaven. The Christians at Rome did not treat them as strangers, but as brethren united to them in the hope of the same blessed country ; and their bodies were buried by night at the house of a subdeacon called Quirinus. In the reign of Constantine their relics were removed to the burying-place of Pontian (called also, from some sign, the " Bear and Cap ", *Ad Ursum Pileatum*), situated near the Tiber on the road to Porto ; this translation took place in consequence of a vision wherein the martyrs revealed their place of burial. These particulars are derived from their late and unreliable " acts ", but the veneration of SS. Abdon and Sennen in Rome can be traced back to the fourth century.

The acts state that they gave burial in Persia to SS. Olympias (Olympiades) and Maximus, and these two victims of persecution are mentioned in the Roman Martyrology on April 15.

The *passio* of Abdon and Sennen is printed in the *Acta Sanctorum*, July, vol. vii. Opinion inclines to the view that these martyrs suffered in the Diocletian persecution, for the mention of Decius in their acts is of no authority and is in contradiction with other statements in the same account. The date of their feast and their burial in the cemetery of Pontian are already mentioned in A.D. 354 in the " Depositio Martyrum " written in that year. Moreover, in the cemetery of Pontian may still be seen on the wall of a subterranean baptistery in that catacomb a fresco (sixth or seventh century) representing SS. Abdon and Sennen with one or two other martyrs, the names being painted with the figures. See Mgr Wilpert, *Die Malereien der Katakomben Roms*, pl. 258, and also DAC., vol. i, cc. 42–45, and vol. ii, cc. 402–408. *Cf.* also *Bolletino della Commissione Archaeologica Communale di Roma*, An. li (1923), fasc. i–iv ; P. Franchi de' Cavalieri, *Note agiografiche*, vol. viii (1935) ; *Analecta Bollandiana*, vol. lvi (1938), pp. 296–300 ; and CMH., p. 404.

ST JULITTA, WIDOW AND MARTYR   (*c.* A.D. 303)

THE Emperor Diocletian by the edicts which he issued against the Christians in 303 declared them infamous, debarred from protection of the laws and from the privileges of citizens. St Julitta was a widow of Caesarea in Cappadocia, and possessed of farms, cattle, goods and slaves. A powerful man of the town got possession of a considerable part of her estate : and when he could not make good his title before the magistrate, charged her with being a Christian. The judge caused incense to be brought into the court, and commanded her to offer sacrifice to Zeus ; but she courageously made answer, " May my estates be ruined or given to strangers ; may I lose my life, and may my body be cut in pieces, rather than that by the least impious word I should offend God that made me. If you take from me a little portion of this earth, I shall gain Heaven for it." The judge without more ado confirmed to the usurper the estates to which he unjustly laid claim, and condemned Julitta to the flames. She was led to the fire, walked boldly into it, and was killed, it would seem, by the smoke stifling her, for her body was drawn out dead before the flames reached it.   Julitta was buried by her fellow Christians, and St Basil, in a homily written about the year 375, says of her body, " It enriches with blessings both the place and those who come to it ", and he assures us that " the earth which received the body of this blessed woman sent forth a spring of most pleasant water, whereas all the neighbouring waters are brackish.   This water preserves health and relieves the sick."

We know practically nothing of St Julitta beyond what is contained in the homily of St Basil (Migne, PG., vol. xxxi, cc. 237–261).   The *Acta Sanctorum*, July, vol. vii, give a Latin translation with introductory matter.

BD MANNES   (*c*. A.D. 1230)

OF the three sons of Felix de Guzman and Bd Joan of Aza, Mannes was the middle one, Antony being the elder, and St Dominic, founder of the Friars Preachers, the younger.   Mannes was born at Calaruega, in the province of Burgos, in the middle of the twelfth century and had already devoted himself to God when Dominic was born in 1170.   Of most of his life nothing is known, but he was among his younger brother's first followers, one of the sixteen who adopted the Rule of St Augustine in 1216 and made their profession at Prouille in the following year. These men were " all in fact and in name excellent preachers ", and Mannes had already shared his brother's labours in Languedoc.   After they had made their vows Dominic decided on the bold stroke of sending them straight out into the world, and Mannes with six others went to Paris and made the first French foundation, under Brother Matthew of France, near the university.   He is next heard of as chaplain to the nuns at Prouille, whom St Dominic had established in 1207, and later on was put in charge of their new convent at Madrid ; the founder refers to him in a letter to the sisters : " Our very dear brother, Brother Mannes, who has spared no pains to bring you to this high state, will take what steps seem to him necessary to secure its continuance.   He has authority from us to make visitation of the convent, to correct what he finds amiss, and if he so judge fitting, to change the prioress, so long as the greater number of the sisters consent thereto."

Dominic evidently had a very high opinion of the qualities of his brother, who had always had an attraction to the contemplative life, making him a particularly suitable director for the Madrid nuns, an office he filled for a dozen years.   He clearly shared the peaceful gentle disposition and personality which so strongly attracted men to St Dominic, and had a similar serene and reasonable knowledge of the difficulties of souls.   Bd Mannes outlived his great brother, but the year of his death is not certain ; it is generally given as 1230, but there is a story that he visited Calaruega after St Dominic's canonization in 1234 and urged the people to build a chapel in his honour, saying, " Be satisfied with a small one for the present : my brother will know how to enlarge it when he chooses to ", a prophecy fulfilled by King Alfonso X thirty years after.   Bd Mannes was buried at the Cistercian church of St Peter at Gamiel d'Izan, and his *cultus* was approved in 1834.

See Mortier, *Maîtres Généraux O.P.*, vol. i, pp. 2, 29, 90 ; Procter, *Dominican Saints*, pp. 213–215 ; *Année Dominicaine*, vol. vii, p. 819.

BD ARCHANGELO OF CALATAFIMI   (A.D. 1460)

ARCHANGELO was born, a member of the family of Placentini, in Sicily, about the year 1390.   From his childhood he was of a religious and retiring disposition and it caused no surprise when in his early manhood he withdrew himself to a cave, there to live in solitude. As so often happens, many people invaded his retreat to seek his advice and conversation, and when it was said that miracles had taken place there, they came in greater numbers. This distressed Archangelo ; his charity was evoked by the needs of his visitors, but his humility represented him to himself as ill-equipped to help them. So he removed to Alcamo ; here he was asked to revive and organize a decayed hospice for the poor, which he undertook, but when it was firmly re-established he once more returned to the solitary life.

It happened that Pope Martin V saw fit to order all the hermits in Sicily, of which there were many, to return to the world or to accept the religious life in an approved order. Obedient to this decree, Bd Archangelo went to Palermo and there received the habit of the Friars Minor of the Observance from Bd Matthew of Girgenti. After profession he was sent to the hospital at Alcamo to establish it as a house of the order, which was done. Archangelo accepted the Rule of St Francis in all its primitive austerity, and he was withdrawn from Alcamo to be minister provincial of the Sicilian Observants. In that office he was able to come to the help of Bd Matthew when, after resigning the see of Girgenti, he was shown the door by the father guardian who had succeeded Archangelo at Alcamo. Worn out with penance and work for souls, Archangelo died on April 10, 1460, and Pope Gregory XVI confirmed his *cultus* in 1836.

The fullest source of information is the volume of Fr A. Gioia, *Il beato Arcangelo Placenza da Calatafimi* (1926). The author has been able to use the materials submitted for the *confirmatio cultus*, and also a rare biography of the *beatus* by P. Longo printed in 1804. See also Léon, *Auréole Séraphique* (Eng. trans.), vol. ii, pp. 59–64.

BD JOHN SORETH (A.D. 1471)

JOHN SORETH was born in Normandy about the year 1405, and at sixteen years old became a Carmelite ; after being ordained he went to study at the University of Paris, where he took his doctor's degree in 1438. Two years later he was appointed prior provincial of his order in France, and in this office he had to deal with a dispute that broke out between the mendicant friars and the University of Paris, and was called in to settle a schism in the Carmelite province of Lower Germany ; both of these difficult tasks he brought to a successful conclusion after he was unanimously elected prior general of the whole order in 1451. He was confirmed in the generalate in 1456, 1462 and 1468, and he carried out its arduous duties with unabating energy. At this time the Carmelites, in common with the other mendicant friars, were in most urgent need of a reform, in part because of the ravages of the Black Death and of the " great schism of the West ". The lack of reality in their religious life was testified to by the slackening of the strictness of the law of personal poverty and by the exemption of those engaged in teaching from the obligations of choir office, common table, etc., dispensations from the rule which were regarded as " privileges " by those who had voluntarily undertaken its observance for the service of God and the good of their own souls.

Bd John was a forerunner of St Teresa, and, though he was not the first to attempt improvement, he tried to do it without compromising the unity of the order. Religious, like other reformers, meet opposition even from men of good will. In every province he visited he established one or more houses where the constitutions and rule were to be strictly observed, and every facility was given to those friars who wished to join these houses ; to guide them he published a revised and up-to-date edition of the constitutions in 1462. At the same time he was responsible for the institution of convents of Carmelite nuns, which began about 1452 when several communities of *béguines* in the Netherlands asked to be affiliated to the order ; he gave them the unrelaxed rule of the friars, with the addition of some special constitutions relative to their sex and state. The first of such convents was at Gueldre in Holland, and he established others at Liège, Dinant, Huy, Namur, Vilvorde and elsewhere. By the end of the century the movement had spread to Italy and to Spain, where later it was to attain to its greatest glory.

Bd John's efforts at reform among the friars met with only a limited success ; but his sanctity and abilities were recognized by Pope Callistus III, who wished to make him a bishop and a cardinal. John however had not taught humility to others at the expense of his own, and the Holy See accepted his refusal of these honours, leaving him free to persevere with his own task ; in the service of his order he went up and down Europe, to Germany, to England, to Italy, to Sicily. He made his journeys accompanied by only one friar and a muleteer, and exposure to the weather had so tanned and lined his face that the common people are said to have known him as " the nigger ", or even as " the devil ". Liège seems to have been his chief headquarters and he returned there nearly every year, taking an active interest in the affairs of the city, which was anything but quiet and peaceful ; when it was pillaged in 1468 by Charles the Bold of Burgundy, Bd John had to go to one church and at the peril of his life rescue the Blessed Sacrament from the sacrilegious troopers. A contemporary Benedictine eulogist says of him : " He was a man deeply versed both in sacred science and in profane philosophy. But over and above such gifts, it was his religion and goodness that made him the glory and the most illustrious reformer of the Carmelite order. By word and example he attained that high indifference to the vanities of the world that is only reached by chosen souls. He was a model of regular observance and of Christian virtues."

Though doubtless there were local fraternities before his time, it seems that the institution of a Carmelite third order must be credited to Bd John Soreth. At Liège in 1455 he drew up a short rule for tertiaries which, with much added, is still the basis of the rule of Calced Carmelite tertiaries. He died at Angers on July 25, 1471, and it is often stated that he was poisoned by a friar who did not favour stricter observance, but the allegation is untrue ; worn out with work and travelling, he succumbed to cholera brought on by eating unripe mulberries. There was always some *cultus* of John Soreth and, when the process of the beatification of Bd Frances d'Amboise in 1863 brought his name to the fore, it was confirmed by the Holy See in 1865.

Much information concerning Bd John Soreth was brought together by B. Zimmerman in his *Monumenta historica Carmelitana* (1907) ; see especially pp. 410–411. There is also an account of Soreth in Fr Daniel, *Speculum Carmelitarum*, reprinted in *Analecta Ordinis Carmelitarum*, vol. xi, pp. 24 *seq.*, with valuable notes. *Cf.* also Fr Francis, *Les plus vieux textes du Carmel*, where the original version of the tertiary rule is printed on pp. 236–243.

BD SIMON OF LIPNICZA (A.D. 1482)

HE was born at Lipnicza, in Poland, not far from Cracow, in the university of which city he made his studies. In 1453 St John Capistran began to preach a mission in Cracow, and one of the first-fruits of his heart-searching appeals was young Simon, who had just graduated. He offered himself to the Friars Minor, who seemed to him the most humble, mortified, and devoted to the cause of Christ and their neighbour; he was accepted, clothed by St John, and after ordination worked in his own city, his preaching and prayers bringing many sinners to repentance within a few years. Like the holy father Francis before him he visited the Holy Land in the hope that there his life might be asked of him, but God did not destine him to martyrdom, and he took up his apostolate at home with renewed energy.

Bd Simon lived in an age of great Franciscan preaching, and among so many who were famed he was not the least eminent. In the face of a certain amount of local opposition he followed St Bernardino in fostering devotion to the holy name of Jesus, at the end of every sermon asking the people to pronounce it three times aloud. That which he preached in public he practised in private, and his virtues were recognized by his superiors and brethren, who made him in turn novice-master, guardian and provincial. When the plague broke out in Cracow his devotion to our Lord and solicitude for the suffering drove him into the most pestiferous places, where he waited on the sick and dying by day and night. He himself became a victim, and he died in the midst of his labours on July 18 in 1482. Miracles were multiplied at his tomb and he was beatified in 1685.

There is a full account in the *Acta Sanctorum*, July, vol. iv, including a life by L. Strobcowicz which was printed in 1636, but the greater part of the notice devoted to him is a record of posthumous miracles from a contemporary manuscript source. See also Mazzara, *Leggendario Francescano* (1679), vol. ii, 122–125 ; and Léon, *Auréole Séraphique* (Eng. trans.), vol. ii, pp. 503–506.

BD PETER OF MOGLIANO (A.D. 1490)

THIS Peter was born at Mogliano in the March of Ancona in the year 1442, and studied law for three years at the University of Perugia. In 1467 he was touched by the preaching of Friar Dominic of Leonissa, an Observant Franciscan from Ancona, and after careful reflection offered himself and was accepted by that order. He was sent as a preaching companion to St James della Marca, who was, after St John Capistran, the most distinguished of the disciples of St Bernardino of Siena. Bd Peter was an effective preacher and director, and was chosen as con-fidant and counsellor by the Duke of Camerino, whose daughter, Bd Baptista Varani, owed much to her father's friend. Peter was vicar provincial of the Franciscan province of the Marches for three terms, and once for the province of Rome, and in 1472 he was sent as commissary to Crete ; in all these charges he showed himself a man of high prudence, understanding in the light of divine charity both men and affairs.

Six years after his death in 1490, Bd Baptista wrote an account of his last days to the Duchess of Urbino ; on the feast of the Visitation he had a premonition of his death, and some days later was struck down by a painful illness. True to the tradition of St Francis, Peter bore his sufferings in such a way that his attendant said to him, " Father, you will die laughing ". " You must know, dear lady," goes on Bd Baptista, " that for three years before his death he was known in this town and throughout the province simply as ' the holy father ' ; people loved him so much that he was followed by a crowd wherever he went. When he had to go to the chapter at Urbino he passed through Camerino and stopped at our monastery; when he left there was such a mob waiting for him that, had it not been for the help of several kind young men, he would have been killed by their well-meant attentions. . . . His happy and holy soul went to God on the night of Saturday-Sunday, July 25 [1490], the feast of St James the apostle, just at the time of the *Te Deum* at Matins. As he breathed his last he several times murmured the name of Jesus, and so went from this world with that sweet name on his lips by whose virtue he had wrought so many wonders during his life." The *cultus* of Bd Peter of Mogliano was confirmed in 1760.

Bd Peter is perhaps best known through his connection with the more famous Baptista Varani. See Mazzara, *Leggendario Francescano* (1679), vol. ii, pp. 153–155 ; Léon, *Auréole Séraphique* (Eng. trans.), vol. iii, pp. 1–8 ; and *Le opere spirituali della B. Battista Varani* (1894), pp. 61–101.

BB. EDWARD POWELL AND RICHARD FETHERSTON, MARTYRS
(A.D. 1540)

EDWARD POWELL, born in Wales about 1478, was a fellow of Oriel College, Oxford, where he took his doctorate in theology in 1506 and was styled *perdoctus vir* by the authorities. He accepted the living of Bleadon in Somerset, prebendal stalls at Lincoln and Salisbury, and other preferments.

In 1523 he wrote a book against Luther, which was praised by his university both to the bishop of Salisbury and to the king : " It seems proper to select the work of Dr Powell as a chief and brilliant gem." And his reputation was such that he was one of the four canonists appointed as counsel to Queen Catherine in the matter of the king's nullity suit (" divorce ") ; he spoke in favour of the marriage before Convocation in 1529, and wrote a book on the same subject, which was one of the causes against him. His eloquent preaching made him enemies among Henry's party, who extracted compromising information from his servant, and by the April of 1534 he was in gaol at Dorchester, where his bed was taken from him and he was confined in the stocks. In the following month he was removed to the Tower, and at the end of the year was sentenced to forfeiture and imprisonment for refusing to take the oath of succession. He was kept in strict confinement for six years, when the king sanctioned his attainder for alleged high treason in denying his supremacy over the Church in England and " adhering unto the Bishop of Rome ".

Of the origins and early life of Bd Richard Fetherston nothing is known, but he became a secular priest, a doctor in theology of Cambridge, and was in 1523 appointed archdeacon of Brecon. Shortly after, because of his piety and learning, he was made tutor in Latin to the Princess Mary, a post which he still held ten years later. In the Convocation of 1529 he spoke and voted in favour of the validity of Queen Catherine's marriage, and was named in the bill of attainder for misprision of November, 1534, which condemned Cardinal Fisher, Dr Powell, and others, and was cast into the Tower. He was eventually attainted for high treason, as above, and was hanged, drawn and quartered at Smithfield, together with Bd Edward Powell and Bd Thomas Abel, on July 30, 1540. Three Protestants were burnt at the stake at the same time and place. BB. Edward and Richard were equivalently beatified in 1886, and their feast is kept throughout Wales on the day of their martyrdom.

The substance of all that is known concerning these martyrs will be found in section xiii of *Lives of the English Martyrs*, vol. i, edited by Bede Camm ; the author of this chapter is Father J. H. Pollen. See especially pp. 484–501.

BD THOMAS ABEL, Martyr   (A.D. 1540)

THIS secular priest was master of arts and doctor of divinity in the University of
Oxford and became a chaplain and tutor of music and languages to Queen Catherine.
When King Henry desired to get hold of the original brief of dispensation by Pope
Julius II for his marriage to Catherine, he sent Dr Abel into Spain to obtain it from
the Emperor Charles V, carrying a letter from the queen asking for it; but she
secretly instructed the messenger to tell the emperor that the delivery of the brief
would injure her cause, and he accordingly refused to give it up.   For his services
in this matter the queen presented Dr Abel to the living of Bradwell in Essex; but
his action must have been suspected, for in 1532 we find him appealing to the pope
for protection against the king's vindictiveness; Clement VII had a brief prepared
appointing him a preacher apostolic, but it was never published.   But apparently
Abel thought he might as well " be hanged for a sheep as a lamb ", for about the
same time he wrote a book called *Invicta Veritas*, in which he opposed the opinion
of the universities about Henry's marriage.   For this he was imprisoned in the
Tower.   He was released on Christmas eve, but a year later was again confined,
and in February, 1534, lodged in the Beauchamp tower, where his rebus, Thomas
A and a representation of a bell, may still be seen carved on the wall.   Henry had
been trying to lay him by the heels for the past six months, and the ostensible reason
for the second arrest was implication in the affair of the " Holy Maid of Kent ";
there is no evidence that he ever had anything to do with her, yet he was accused
of and attainted for misprision of treason in that he had given " such firm and
constant credit " to her alleged revelations that he had on the strength of them
written against the divorce and encouraged Catherine in her opposition thereto.

In the spring of 1537 he was still in prison and wrote a respectful letter to Cromwell, pointing out that he had been in close confinement for over three years
without trial, and asking for a change of quarters and permission to celebrate Mass,
he being ill and in great poverty.   Apparently nothing was done (though he may
have been moved to another prison), but after another three years his gaoler took
it on himself to let Dr Abel and Dr Powell go out on *parole* to beg; for this the
gaoler was committed to the Marshalsea, and the bishop of Chichester (Richard
Sampson) and a Dr Wilson were sent to the Tower for having given them alms.
On July 24, 1540, he was attainted of high treason for " adhering unto the Bishop
of Rome ", and denying the king's supremacy, and, as has been said above, suffered
on the 30th, with BB. Edward Powell and Richard Fetherston, who were attainted
by the same act.   There is extant a long letter from the French ambassador,
Marillac, to King Francis in which he expresses the popular disgust and indignation
at the scene on Smithfield.

The same reference may be given as for the preceding notice, but Bd Thomas Abel is
more particularly spoken of on pp. 461–483.

BD EVERARD HANSE, Martyr   (A.D. 1581)

EVERARD HANSE was born in Northamptonshire of Protestant parents, studied in
the University of Cambridge, and " then was made a minister and promoted to a
good fat living ".   He was a popular preacher, very proud of his own success, and
on the surface quite unmoved by the conversion and appeals of his brother William,
who was sent on the English mission from Rheims in 1579.   But in the same year

Everard was taken by a dangerous illness : he was face to face with death and could look into his own heart unprejudiced by the presence of an admiring congregation ; the example and words of his brother now bore fruit and strengthened him to co-operate with God's grace.   He sent for him, made his submission, and was received into the Church.   Directly his health was mended he resigned his benefice and went over to the English College, then at Rheims, where he studied for nine months, showing himself especially apt in moral theology.   On March 25, 1581, he was ordained priest, and on the following April 24 he left for England with three other priests, assuming the name of Evans Duckett.

He was destined to exercise his ministry for only about three months.   Having occasion to go to the Marshalsea prison to visit the Catholic prisoners there, a turnkey noticed that his shoes were of French make and denounced him as a suspicious person, whereupon a magistrate committed him to Newgate.   He was treated with great cruelty here, but the gaol delivery took place only a few days after and he was brought before the recorder of London, Fleetwood, the lord mayor, Sir John Branch, and others.   There was no charge laid against him, for his priesthood, which he admitted, was not at that time an offence.   So the recorder, by skilful questioning, proceeded to make him commit a capital felony on the spot. After Bd Everard had declared that his mission was to save souls and that he had been ordained at Rheims, Fleetwood said : " Then you are a subject to the pope ? "

" So I am, sir."

" Then the pope hath some superiority over you ? "

" That is true."

" What ! in England ? "

" Yea, in England ; for he hath as much authority and right in spiritual government in this realm as ever he had, and as much as he hath in any other country, or in Rome itself."

This reply was contrary to the Act of Supremacy.   He was then asked if the pope could err : the reply was the same in 1581 as it would be in this current year : " In life and manners he might offend, as also err in his private doctrine or writing ; but in judicial definitions for deciding matters of controversy he cannot err."   Then was read an extract from the bull of Pope Pius V excommunicating Queen Elizabeth, referring to her as a heretic and fautor of heresy ; did he err when he said that ? This concerned a question of fact, on which he might be wrong, so Bd Everard simply said to this, " I hope he did not ".   " Have you ", asked Fleetwood, " given the answers we have heard to persuade other men who hear you to be of the same mind ? "   " I know not what you mean by persuading ; but I would have all men to believe the Catholic faith as I do."   This was what they wanted, and there and then an indictment was drawn charging Everard Hanse, otherwise Everard Duckett, with having, intending to withdraw the queen's subjects from their obedience and religion over to the Romish religion, uttered malicious and slanderous words, saying that he was subject to the pope in ecclesiastical matters, that the pope had the same authority in England as ever, that he cannot err, that it is true he can depose princes, that he hoped the pope did not err in calling the queen a heretic and deposing her, that these things were said with the purpose of persuading others, etc.   This indictment was read over to the prisoner, who was told to plead to it.   He replied, " I am not altogether guilty in those things as they are set down, but I acknowledge the substance and the sense thereof ".   This was taken as a plea of guilty (which in law it was not), and sentence of death was pronounced on the count of " persuasion " by virtue of 23 Eliz. c. 1. He wrote a farewell letter to his brother ; it is quiet and confident : " The comforts at the present instant are unspeakable ; the dignity too high for a sinner ; but God is merciful." He remembers his parents ; asks that his debts be paid (he owed 10s. 2d.) and borrowed books returned ; then, " The day and hour of my birth is at hand, and my Master saith, ' Tolle crucem tuam et sequere me '. Vale in Domino. Yours, Everard Hanse."

Pridie obitus is printed after this letter in Allen's *Briefe Historie of the glorious Martyrdom of xij Reverend Priests.* He was drawn to Tyburn, where " he desired humbly all Catholics to pray for him and with him ". He was cut down and disembowelled while fully conscious, and is said to have been heard to murmur, " O happy day ! " while the butcher was at work ; while several witnesses stated that his heart leaped from the fire and could not be consumed. Not a particle of the blood-stained earth was left by the faithful, but none is known to be preserved today. Bd Everard Hanse was beatified with the others in 1886, and his feast is kept in the diocese of Northampton on July 30, the day before that on which he suffered.

See Challoner's MMP., pp. 13–19 and 587, and B. Camm, LEM., vol. ii, pp. 249–265.

31 : ST IGNATIUS OF LOYOLA, FOUNDER OF THE SOCIETY OF JESUS (A.D. 1556)

S T IGNATIUS was born, probably in 1491, in the castle of Loyola at Azpeitia, in Guipuzcoa, a part of Biscay that reaches to the Pyrenees. His father, Don Beltran, was lord of Oñaz and Loyola, head of one of the most ancient and noble families of that country, and his mother, Marina Saenz de Licona y Balda, was not less illustrious. They had three daughters and eight sons, and Ignatius (Iñigo he was christened) was the youngest child ; he was trained to arms and saw some service against the French in northern Castile ; but his short military career came to an abrupt end on May 20, 1521 when, in the defence of Pamplona, a cannon ball broke his right shin and tore open the left calf. At his fall the Spanish garrison surrendered.

The French used their victory with moderation, and sent him carried in a litter to the castle of Loyola. His broken leg had been badly set, and the surgeons therefore thought it necessary to break it again, which he suffered without any apparent concern. But a violent fever followed the second setting, which was attended with dangerous symptoms ; on the eve of the feast of SS. Peter and Paul it was believed he could not hold out till the next morning, but he suddenly took a turn for the better, though he was convalescent for many months. After the second setting of his leg, the end of a bone stuck out under his knee, a visible deformity. Though the surgeons told him the operation would be very painful, this protuberance he had sawn off, and would neither be bound nor held, and scarce ever changed countenance whilst the operation was performed. Because his right leg remained shorter than the left, he would be for many days together with weights attached to stretch it out. It is not surprising that he limped for the rest of his life.

While he was confined to his bed, finding the time tedious, Ignatius called for some book of romances, for he had always been much delighted with stories of knight-errantry. None such being then found in the castle of Loyola, a book of the life of our Saviour and another of legends of the saints were brought him. He read them first only to pass away the time, but afterward began to relish them and to spend whole days in reading them. He said to himself : " These men were of the same frame as I ; why then should I not do what they have done ? " and in the fervour of his good resolutions he thought of visiting the Holy Land and becoming a Carthusian lay-brother. But these ideas were intermittent ; and his passion for glory and inclination for a lady of high degree again filled his mind till, returning to the lives of the saints, he perceived in his own heart the emptiness of all worldly glory, and that only God could content the soul. This fluctuation of mind continued some time : but he observed this difference, that the thoughts which were from God filled his soul with consolation, peace, and tranquillity ; whereas the others brought indeed some sensible delight, but left a certain bitterness and heaviness in the heart. Taking at last a firm resolution to imitate the saints at least in some respects, he began to treat his body with all the rigour it was able to bear, and spent his retired hours in weeping for his sins.

One night, Ignatius saw the Mother of God surrounded with light, holding the infant Jesus in her arms ; this vision replenished his soul with delight and, being cured of his wounds, he went on pilgrimage to the shrine of our Lady at Montserrat, resolved thenceforward to lead a life of penance. Three leagues from Montserrat is the small town of Manresa, and here he stayed, sometimes with the Dominican friars, sometimes in a paupers' hospice ; and there was a cave in a neighbouring hill whither he might retire for prayer and penance. So he lived for nearly a year. After enjoying much peace of mind and heavenly consolation he was soon visited with the most terrible trial of fears and scruples. He found no comfort in prayer, no relief in fasting, no remedy in disciplines, no consolation from the sacraments, and his soul was overwhelmed with sadness. He apprehended some sin in every step he took, and seemed often on the very brink of despair. During this time he began to note down material for what was to become the book of his *Spiritual Exercises*. At length his tranquillity of mind was restored, and his soul overflowed with spiritual joy. From this experience he acquired a particular talent for curing scrupulous consciences, and a singular light to discern them. He afterward assured Father Laynez that he learned more of divine mysteries by prayer in one hour at Manresa than all the doctors of the schools could ever have taught him. So imperfect was his knowledge of his duties when he first renounced the world, that hearing a Moor speak somewhat injuriously of the holy Mother of God, he deliberated whether, as a Christian knight, he ought not to kill him, but divine Providence preserved him from so criminal an action.

In February 1523, Ignatius started on his journey to the Holy Land ; begging his way, he took ship from Barcelona, spent Easter at Rome, sailed from Venice to Cyprus, and thence to Jaffa. He went by donkey from thence to Jerusalem, with the firm intention of staying there. But after visiting and spiritually rejoicing in the scenes of the passion of Jesus, the Franciscan guardian of the Holy Places commanded him to leave Palestine, lest his reckless attempts to convert Mohammedans should cause him to be kidnapped and held to ransom. Ignatius gave up his project and obeyed, with no knowledge of what he was going to do.

He returned to Spain in 1524 ; and he now set himself to study, " as a means of helping him to work for souls ", and began at Barcelona with Latin grammar, being assisted by the charities of a pious lady of that city, called Isabel Roser. He was then thirty-three years old : and it is not hard to imagine what difficulties he went through in learning the rudiments of grammar at that age.   At first his mind was so fixed only on God that he forgot everything he read, and conjugating *amo*, for example, could only repeat to himself, " I love God ; I am loved by God ", and the like ; but he began to make some progress, still joining contemplation and austerities with his studies.   He bore the jeers and taunts of the little boys, his schoolfellows, with patience and even amusement.

After studying two years at Barcelona he went to the University of Alcala, where he attended lectures in logic, physics and divinity : by which multiplicity he only confounded his ideas, and learned little, though he studied night and day. He lodged at a hospice, lived by begging, and wore a coarse grey habit.   He catechized children, held assemblies of devotion in the hospice, and by his mild reprehensions converted many loose livers.   Those were the days of strange cults in Spain, and Ignatius, being a man without learning or authority, was accused to the bishop's vicar general, who confined him to prison two-and-forty days, but declared him innocent of any fault at the end of it ; but forbidding him and his companions to wear any singular dress, or to give any instructions in religious matters for three years.   So he migrated with his three fellows to Salamanca, where he was exposed again to suspicions of introducing dangerous doctrines, and the inquisitors imprisoned him ; but after three weeks declared him innocent.   Ignatius looked upon prisons, sufferings and ignominy as trials by which God was pleased to purge and sanctify his soul.   Recovering his liberty again, he resolved to leave Spain, and in the middle of winter travelled on foot to Paris, where he arrived in the beginning of February 1528.

He spent two years improving himself in Latin ; in vacation time he went into Flanders, and once into England, to procure help from the Spanish merchants settled there, from whom and from some friends at Barcelona he received support. He studied philosophy three years and a half in the college of St Barbara, where he induced many of his fellow-students to spend the Sundays and holy days in prayer, and to apply themselves more fervently to good works.   Pegna, his master, thought he hindered their studies and prepossessed Gouvea, principal of the college, against him, so that he was ordered to undergo a public flogging, that this disgrace might deter others from following him.   Ignatius offered himself joyfully to suffer all things ; yet fearing lest the scandal of this disgrace should make those whom he had reclaimed fall back, he went to the principal and modestly laid open to him the reasons of his conduct.   Gouvea made no answer, but taking him by the hand led him into the hall, where the whole college stood assembled.   He then turned to Ignatius and begged his pardon for having too lightly believed false reports. In 1534 the middle-aged student—he was forty-three—graduated as master of arts of Paris.

At that time six students in divinity associated themselves with Ignatius in his spiritual exercises.   They were Peter Favre, a Savoyard ; Francis Xavier, a Basque like Ignatius ; Laynez and Salmeron, both fine scholars ; Simon Rodriguez, a Portuguese ; and Nicholas Bobadilla.   These fervent students, moved by the exhortations of Ignatius, made all together a vow to observe poverty and chastity and to go to preach the gospel in Palestine, or if they could not go thither to offer themselves to the pope to be employed in the service of God in what manner he should judge best.   They pronounced this vow in a chapel on Montmartre, after they had all received holy communion from Peter Favre, who had been lately ordained priest. This was done on the feast of the Assumption of our Lady in 1534. Ignatius continued by frequent conferences and joint exercises to animate his companions, and a simple rule of life was adopted. But his theological studies were soon interrupted, for he was ordered by the physicians to try his native air for the improvement of his health. He left Paris in the spring of 1535, and was joyfully received in Guipuzcoa, where, however, he refused to go to the castle of Loyola, taking up his quarters in the poor-house of Azpeitia.

Two years later they all met in Venice, but hostilities between Venice and the Turks had then reached an acute phase and it was impossible to find a ship to sail to Palestine. Ignatius's companions (now numbering ten) therefore went to Rome, where Pope Paul III received them well, and granted them an indult that those who were not priests might receive holy orders from what bishop they pleased. They were accordingly ordained and then retired into a cottage near Vicenza to prepare themselves for the holy ministry of the altar. The rest celebrated their first Masses in September and October, but Ignatius deferred his own from month to month till he had employed over a year in preparing himself to offer the adorable Sacrifice. There being no likelihood of their being able soon to go to the Holy Land, it was at length resolved that Ignatius, Favre and Laynez should go to Rome and offer the services of all to the pope, and they agreed that if anyone asked what their association was they might answer, " the Company of Jesus ",* because they were united to fight against falsehood and vice under the standard of Christ. On his road to Rome, praying in a little chapel at La Storta, Ignatius saw our Lord, shining with an unspeakable light, but loaded with a heavy cross, and he heard the words, *Ego vobis Romae propitius ero*, " I will be favourable to you at Rome ". Paul III appointed Favre to teach in the Sapienza and Laynez to explain the Holy Scriptures ; Ignatius laboured by means of his spiritual exercises and instructions to reform the manners of the people and the others were likewise employed in the city—that none of them yet spoke Italian properly did not deter them.

With a view to perpetuate their work, it was now proposed to form themselves into a religious order. It was resolved, first, besides the vows of poverty and chastity already made by them, to add a third of obedience, the more perfectly to conform themselves to the Son of God who was obedient even unto death ; and to appoint a superior general whom all should be bound to obey, who should be for life and his authority absolute, subject entirely to the Holy See. They likewise determined to prescribe a fourth vow, of going wherever the pope should send them for the salvation of souls. It was agreed that the celebration of the Divine Office in choir (as distinct from the obligatory private recitation) should be no part of their duties, " lest they be withdrawn from those works of charity to which we have wholly dedicated ourselves ". And in the forefront of those works of charity was put " that children or any others whosoever are to be taught the commandments of God ". The cardinals appointed by the pope to examine the affair of this new order at first opposed it, thinking religious orders already too much multiplied, but after a year changed their opinions, and Paul III approved it by a bull, dated September 27, 1540. Ignatius was chosen the first general superior, but only acquiesced in obedience to his confessor. He entered upon his office on Easter-

---

* This expression is still in use in France, Spain and Italy ; it was altered to " Society " when the bull of foundation was drawn up. " Jesuit " was at first a rather hostile nickname, never used by Ignatius himself.

day, 1541, and the members all made their religious vows in the basilica of St Paul-outside-the-Walls a few days later.

For the rest of his life Ignatius lived in Rome, tied there by the immense work of directing the activities of the order which he ruled till his death. Among the establishments which he made there, he founded a house for the reception of converted Jews during the time of their instruction, and another for penitents from among women of disorderly life. When one told him that the conversion of such sinners is seldom sincere, he answered, " To prevent only one sin would be a great happiness though it cost me ever so great pains ". Already in 1540 Rodriguez and Francis Xavier had been sent to Portugal, and under the protection of King John III Xavier went into the East Indies where he began to gain a new world to the faith of Christ. Fathers Gonçalves and John Nuñez Barreto were sent into Morocco to instruct and assist the Christian slaves ; four others to the Congo ; others to Ethiopia ; and others into the Portuguese settlements in South America. Pope Paul III commissioned Fathers Laynez and Salmeron to assist as his theologians at the Council of Trent. Before their departure St Ignatius instructed them to visit the sick and poor, and in all disputations to be careful to preserve modesty and humility, and to shun all confidence, contentiousness, or empty display of learning. But among the first disciples of St Ignatius who distinguished themselves in Europe, there was none with greater reputation for learning and piety than St Peter Canisius, now venerated as a doctor of the Church. St Francis Borgia in 1550 gave a considerable sum towards building the Roman College for the Jesuits ; St Ignatius made this the model of all his other colleges and took care that it should be supplied with able masters and all possible helps for the advancement of learning. He also directed the foundation of the German College in Rome, originally intended for scholars from all countries seriously affected by Protestantism. Other universities, seminaries and colleges were established in other places ; but the work of education for which the Jesuits are so famous was a development that only came by degrees, though well established before the founder's death.

Two Jesuits sent to the British Isles landed in Ireland so early as 1542, but the first efforts of the Society were not successful. Ignatius ordered prayers for the conversion of England (still said by his sons " for all Northern nations "), and of the English and Welsh martyrs of penal times who have been beatified, twenty-six were Jesuits. The activity of the Society in England was characteristic of the tremendous part played by St Ignatius and his religious in the work of the so-called Counter-Reformation : by reformation and consolidation within the Church, and by opposing Protestantism without. " It was exactly what was wanted at the time to counteract the revolt of the sixteenth century. The revolt was disobedience and disorder in the most aggressive form. The Society was obedience and order in the most solid compactness. It may be said, with historical truth, that the Jesuits charged, threw back and defeated the Lutheran revolt. They also won back souls by their preaching and spiritual guidance. They preached ' Jesus Christ and Him crucified '. This has been their central message, and by it they have deserved and won the confidence and obedience of souls " (Cardinal Manning). In this connection may be noted Ignatius's instructions about relations with Protestants, given to fathers going to found a college at Ingolstadt : " Great care must be taken to show forth orthodox truth in such a way that if any heretics happen to be present they may have an example of charity and Christian moderation. No

hard words should be used nor any sort of contempt for their errors be shown."
And he wrote in the same spirit to Father Broët and Father Salmeron before they
set out for Ireland.

One of the most famous and fruitful works of St Ignatius was the book of his
Spiritual Exercises, begun at Manresa and first published in Rome in 1548 with
papal approval.   The spirit which reigns in this book was that of all the saints.
Frequent religious retirement had been practised in imitation of Christ from the
beginning, and the use and method of spiritual meditation were always known ;
but the excellent order of these meditations, prescribed by Ignatius, was new : and,
though the principal rules and maxims are found in the lessons and lives of the
ancient Fathers, they are here judiciously chosen, methodically digested, and
clearly explained.   The particular scope and object of " The Exercises " is to
induce a state of interior calm and disinterestedness in order that the retreatant
may be able to make a choice, " either as to some particular crisis or as to his
general course of life, unbiased by any excessive like or dislike ; and guided solely
by the consideration of what will most conduce to the one end for which he was
created—the glory of God and the perfection of his own soul."   In the words of
Pope Pius XI, the Ignatian methods of prayer " lead a man by the safe paths of
self-abnegation and the removal of bad habits up to the supreme heights of prayer
and divine love ".

The prudence and charity of St Ignatius in his conduct towards his religious
won him all their hearts. He always showed the affection of the most tender parent
towards his brethren, especially towards the sick, for whom he procured every
spiritual and temporal succour and comfort, which it was his great delight to give
them himself.   Though he was superior, he submitted to inferiors with meekness,
when he could do it without prejudice to his necessary authority.   In things of
which he was not certain, he readily acquiesced in the judgement of others, and was
a great enemy to positiveness and to the use of superlatives in discourse.   He
received rebukes from anyone with cheerfulness ; but would not from a false
delicacy abstain from rebuking others who clearly stood in need of it.   He particularly reprimanded those whom learning had made conceited, tiresome, or
lukewarm in religion, but at the same time he encouraged every branch of learning
and would have the fathers in his Society applied to that work, whether in teaching,
preaching or the missions, for which God seemed chiefly to qualify and destine
them by their genius, talents and particular graces.   Charity, the most ardent and
pure love of God, was the crown of all his virtues.   He had often in his mouth
these words, which he took for his motto, " To the greater glory of God "—to
which end he referred himself, his Society, and all his actions.   He often said,
" Lord, what do I desire, or what can I desire, besides thee ? "   True love is never
idle ; and always to labour for God, or to suffer for His sake, was all his happiness.
The " military spirit " and inspiration of St Ignatius and the Society of Jesus has
perhaps been exaggerated.   On the other hand, in admiring the grandeur of his
strength and his achievements it is not uncommon to overlook the attractiveness
of Ignatius's character and his great gift of friendship.

In the fifteen years that he directed his order St Ignatius saw it grow from ten
members to one thousand, in nine countries and provinces of Europe, in India and
in Brazil.   And in those fifteen years he had been ill fifteen times, so that the sixteenth time caused no unusual alarm.   But it was the last.   He died suddenly, so
unexpectedly that he did not receive the last sacraments, early in the morning of

July 31, 1556. He was canonized in 1622, and by Pope Pius XI he was declared the heavenly patron of spiritual exercises and retreats.

From the love of God sprang the enthusiasm of St Ignatius for the salvation of men, for which he undertook so many and so great things, to which he devoted his watchings, prayers, tears and labours. To gain others to Christ he made himself all things to all men, going in at *their* door, and coming out at *his own*. He received sincere penitents with the greatest sweetness, often taking upon himself part of their penance, and endeavouring to bring them to make the perfect sacrifice of themselves to God, telling them that it is not to be expressed what precious treasures God reserves for those who give themselves to Him with their whole heart. He proposed to them for their model this prayer, which he used often to recite : " Receive, Lord, all my liberty, my memory, my understanding and my whole will. You have given me all that I have, all that I am, and I surrender all to your divine will, that you dispose of me. Give me only your love and your grace. With this I am rich enough, and I have no more to ask."

By the publication of the *Monumenta Historica Societatis Jesu* an immense mass of documents has been rendered accessible which includes practically everything which can throw light upon the biography of the founder of the order. More particularly important are the twelve volumes which contain his correspondence, both private and official, and also all the written memorials of a personal nature which have been discovered. Chief amongst these is the account of his early life which, with great reluctance but at the earnest solicitation of his spiritual sons, he was persuaded in his last days to communicate in a sort of dictation. A Latin version of this " autobiography " was printed in the *Acta Sanctorum*, July, vol. vii, but it has now been edited in the *Monumenta* in the original Spanish and Italian, and it has also been translated into English, French, German, and other languages. By the publication of so much new material in the *Monumenta*, the older lives by Orlandini, Maffei, Bartoli, Genelli, etc., are in some sense superseded, though that written by Father Pedro Ribadeneira retains its value as the personal appreciation of one who was in an especially close relation with the saint. Father Astrain's *Historia de la Compañía de Jesús en la Asistencia de España*, vol. i (1902), is from the nature of the case almost a history of the founder's career and activities, but Father Astrain also published a valuable little summary, translated into English by Fr R. Hull. The accounts by Fr J. H. Pollen (1922) and Christopher Hollis (1931) are in their different ways excellent, and an admirable life in French by Fr de Grandmaison appeared in 1930. Among more recent publications may be mentioned *Iñigo de Loyola* (Eng. trans.), in which Fr Leturia studies the saint's conversion ; Fr H. Pinard de la Boullaye, *St Ignace de Loyola, directeur d'âmes* (1947) ; an English translation of Fr P. Dudon's standard life (1949) ; and a new edition of the biography by the poet Francis Thompson (1950). For those who do not want a formal biography, Fr J. Brodrick's *Origin of the Jesuits* (1940) is a splendid work. The same writer says of the lives of the saint by H. D. Sedgwick (1923) and P. van Dyke (1926), " The two books are easily the fairest Protestant accounts of Ignatius ever written, and, as history, are far superior to many Catholic accounts ". A new English version of the *Spiritual Exercises* was published by Fr J. L. Puhl in U.S.A. in 1950, and another by W. H. Longridge in England.

ST NEOT (DATE UNKNOWN)

ACCORDING to the medieval legends St Neot was a monk of Glastonbury in the ninth century, who while there received holy orders. Desiring greater solitude he went into the western country and settled at the place now called Saint Neot, in Cornwall, where he was visited by King Alfred, who greatly valued his counsel. According to some he was a relative of the king, and it is to a work called the *Chronicle of the Sanctuary of St Neot* that we owe the story of Alfred and the burnt cakes. He went on pilgrimage to Rome, and by his intercession Alfred triumphed over the Danes. After his death he appeared in a vision to the custodian of his shrine in Cornwall and commanded him to remove his relics and take them to a certain place ; this the man did and the relics found a resting-place in a monastery at the place we call Saint Neots in Huntingdonshire.

This in brief outline is the story of St Neot as told, with variations and additions of miraculous and other incidents, in an Old English homily and two Latin lives of the saint.   The austerities attributed to him are those associated with most Celtic saints, *e.g.* the reciting of psalms while immersed in icy water, and it has been pointed out that his life is a collection of some of the most distinguishing features of Celtic hagiology.   None of the lives are in any degree trustworthy, and nothing certainly true is known of Neot : it has, indeed, been suggested, with some reason, that there were two holy men of that name, a British saint (Niet) in Cornwall and an English one in Huntingdon.

It seems impossible to disentangle the confusions and contradictions which beset the so-called biographies of St Neot.   The best attempt to cope with the difficulties of the problem is that made by G. H. Doble in his little book, *St Neot* (1929), in which he had the assistance of another expert, C. Henderson.   The texts are to be found in the *Acta Sanctorum*, July, vol. vii, and G. C. Gorham, *History of Eynesbury and Saint Neots* (1820). *Cf.* also LBS., vol. iv, pp. 4 *seq.*

ST HELEN OF SKÖVDE, Widow   (*c.* A.D. 1160)

St Helen was a lady of noble birth of Västergötland in Sweden, who after the death of her husband gave her time and goods to the service of the poor and of religion.   She made a pilgrimage to Rome, and upon her return was put to death by the relatives of her son-in-law on a false charge that she had connived at his death, he having been murdered by his servants on account of his cruel tyranny. Her body was brought from Götene and interred in the church she had built at Skövde, and on the strength of the miracles of healing there reported Pope Alexander III authorized her *cultus* in 1164.   She was honoured on July 31, as a martyr, in her country, and also at Tüsvilde on the island of Zealand in Denmark, which claimed to have her relics ; but, though there is a worthless legend of their miraculous transportation, there is no record of their having been translated thither. At both places her veneration persisted after the Reformation, being in either case associated with a healing well.

A Latin life, partly reproduced in the *Acta Sanctorum*, July, vol. vii, has been critically edited in the *Scriptores rerum Suecicarum*, vol. iii, pt. 2, pp. 135–138.   See, in Swedish, T. Schmid, *Den hl. Sigfrid* (1931).   Of J. Dunney's *Saint of the Snows* (1937), Fr P. Grosjean, Bollandist, writes, " surely the last word in American romantic hagiography ".

BD JOHN COLOMBINI   (A.D. 1367)

More than two-thirds of this saint's years on earth had passed before he began to live other than a worldly life ; he inclined to avarice, was ambitious, and gave way to a bad temper without scruple.   He was born about 1304 in Siena, and as a successful merchant married Biagia Cerretani, by whom he had two children. One day, after being taken up the whole morning with business he came home, much fatigued, and not finding dinner ready, flew into a rage.   His wife (perhaps from a human point of view a little tactlessly) put a book of saints' lives into his hands ; but he threw it on the ground.   The next moment, being ashamed of his temper, he took it up again, and sitting down to read, fell on the life of St Mary of

Egypt. He read it with so much interest that he forgot his dinner, and his wife in her turn was kept waiting, but she had the sense not to draw attention to the fact. The reading did its work and made a way for the grace of God, and he found his heart pierced with remorse for his past sins and unthinking conduct. Being sensible that the first sacrifice which God requires of a sinner is that of a contrite and humble heart, he spent much time in prayer and penitential exercises. He sold his rich clothes and furniture, giving the money to the poor ; he slept on a bench, and his house seemed converted into a hospital, so great was the number of the poor and sick that he caused to be brought thither and attended. In defiance of the iron laws of economics and the general custom of traders, he even bought goods for more than was asked and sold them for less than market price. Naturally, every one was astonished at so great a change. One day seeing a leper lying at the door of the church, the saint carried him to his own home, attending him till he had overcome the abhorrence which naturally besets man at the sight of so loathsome a disease, and continued his care of this patient till he was able to be removed. But it was said by some that the leper disappeared miraculously, leaving only a heavenly fragrance.

But John's good wife was by no means pleased at the excess of his conversion, and would often remonstrate with him to be more prudent. And when he answered, " You prayed to God that I might become charitable and good, and now you are annoyed because I make a little amends for my avarice and other sins ", she would reply, " I prayed for rain, but this is a flood ". After some years, their son having died and their daughter become a nun, Biagia agreed to let him go his ways without hindrance. He thereupon divided his fortune between a convent, a hospital and a confraternity of women, the gifts being first charged with the proper maintenance of his wife, and having thus reduced himself to poverty he gave himself up to serve the poor in the hospitals, and to the exercises of devotion and penance.

Bd John was joined in this renunciation by Francis Vincenti, who had been his partner in good works, and several others became his faithful imitators and companions. There seems to have been a strong element of " fools for Christ's sake " in their earlier practices. They exhorted to repentance and fervour in the divine service ; and the charity and disinterestedness with which they ministered corporal relief and comfort gave great force to their instructions. But when members of respectable families threw in their lot with them, the Sienese authorities became alarmed and John was banished. He therefore left the city with some followers and visited Arezzo, Città di Castello, Viterbo and other places : in the last-named they were given the nickname *Gesuati*, " Jesuats ", because of their devotion to the Holy Name and frequent ejaculation of " Praise be to Jesus Christ ". They converted many to a Christian life (including an episcopal notary, who joined the band), brought about the restitution of goods and reputations, and composed long-standing quarrels.

Bd John had been recommended to obtain ecclesiastical sanction for his activities, but on being assured by the bishop of Città di Castello that they were doing nothing irregular, the matter was let drop : " they were poor, simple, and right-minded men, with no material cares, and so they might well leave all in God's hands ". In 1367, however, Pope Urban V came to Viterbo on his way back from Avignon, and John and his followers, crowned with garlands and carrying olive branches, but dressed in rags, went to meet him, soliciting an audience. This was granted and the pope was greatly impressed, but considered it advisable to order Cardinal William Sudre and others to examine John and the life of the brothers, as they were now accused by some of holding the errors of the *Fraticelli*. Of this they were acquitted, and Pope Urban approved the Jesuats as a new congregation under the formal title of Apostolic Clerics of St Jerome, because of their particular veneration for that saint. In spite of this name they were to be an institute of lay-brothers, whose life was to be one of great physical austerity and devoted to the care of the sick and burial of the dead, and they were to be dispersed among the towns and villages. Only a few days later, when the brothers were gathered together by the Lake of Bolsena, their founder was taken ill; he was taken to Acquapendente, where he received the last sacraments, and then they tried to remove him to Siena, but he died on the way. In the presence of his wife and his spiritual children he was buried at the convent of SS. Abundio and Abundanzio (" Santa Bonda "), wherein his daughter had died and which by his influence had been brought back to the observance of common life. His friend and companion, Francis Vincenti, died a fortnight later.

John Colombini's name was inserted in the Roman Martyrology by Pope Gregory XIII. His congregation flourished for a time, and then began to languish; in 1606 an attempt was made to revive it by allowing members to be in priest's orders, but sixty-two years later it was entirely suppressed by Pope Clement IX, it being no longer useful to the Church because of the fewness of its members. Some of Bd John's letters are still extant, and in his life of the saint, written in 1449, Feo Belcari, a Florentine citizen, has reported some of his exhortations. They are full of evangelical fervour and show strongly the influence of the earlier Franciscans.

A short life by Bd John Tossignano (see above, July 24), has been printed by Mansi among the *Miscellanea* of Baluzius (vol. iv, pp. 566–571). In the *Acta Sanctorum*, July, vol. vii, is a seventeenth-century biography compiled by Fr J. B. Rossi, together with much other illustrative matter. The Florentine poet Feo Belcari in 1449 also wrote a life of Bd John in Italian prose of great literary merit—see R. Chiarini, who in 1904 brought out a new edition—which is not without some historical value. It is possible even that Belcari had previously translated Tossignano's *Compendio*, though L. Albertazzi thinks otherwise. P. Misciatelli has published 114 letters written by John Colombini, many of them previously unknown; they appeared as vol. viii in the series of *Libri della Fede* issued at Florence under the direction of G. Papini. There are some modern popular lives, notably that by the Countess de Rambuteau in French (1893). Father Delehaye in his *Légendes Hagiographiques* has called attention to the curious coincidence that July 31 is the heavenly birthday both of St Ignatius Loyola and Bd John Colombini, the one the founder of the *Jesuitae*, the other of the *Jesuati*. Both were converted from a worldly career by reading the lives of the saints, both established a religious order, and while the earlier order was suppressed by Clement IX that of St Ignatius was suppressed by Clement XIV, though it was subsequently restored by Pius VII.

BD JUSTIN DE JACOBIS, Titular Bishop of Nilopolis   (A.D. 1860)

ETHIOPIA (the proper name of the country commonly called Abyssinia) has a population of which about half is Christian and the rest Mohammedan, Jewish and heathen. The Ethiopians were first evangelized in the fourth century, from Syria and Egypt, and ever since then their church has had a certain dependence on the Coptic patriarch of Alexandria. When, therefore, most of the Egyptians and Syrians followed the monophysite schism after 451 the Ethiopians also were involved. For centuries, and even still in a measure, they were the most isolated and neglected of all Christian bodies.

During the sixteenth century, however, Portuguese military-trading expeditions were active in the Red Sea, and eventually, early in the seventeenth century, the Ethiopian *negus* (king), Susneyos, entered into communion with the Catholic Church. But this promising movement was completely spoiled by the irreligious methods used by Susneyos to impose the reunion on his people ; these methods were, unhappily, not repudiated by the Portuguese clergy of the Society of Jesus in the country, who indeed made matters worse by their clumsiness and unnecessary intransigence. The upshot was that a violent counter-persecution began in 1632, and for two hundred years no Catholic priest was allowed to enter Ethiopia. Some did, from time to time, and paid for their courage with their lives ; among them were the two Capuchins, BB. Agathangelo and Cassian (August 7).

In the nineteenth century things got a bit easier, and in 1839 the Irish-French travellers, Arnauld and Antony d'Abbadie d'Arrast, used their influence to get a Catholic mission established at Adua. It was entrusted to the Congregation of the Mission, founded by St Vincent de Paul and hence often called Vincentians in English, but more commonly known as Lazarists from their college of St Lazarus in Paris. The first prefect and vicar apostolic of this mission was Justin de Jacobis, who was born in the year 1800 at San Fele in the Basilicata, the seventh of the fourteen children of his parents, and while still a child was taken to live in Naples. His mother was a religious woman, and no doubt it was partly due to her example and care that young Justin offered himself to the Congregation of the Mission at the age of eighteen. A fellow student at the seminary, who himself was to become archbishop of Smyrna, has left a testimony to the virtue of Justin's life at this time and the high regard in which he was held by all who came in contact with him : he was " beloved of God and man ". After his ordination he was in constant demand as a mission preacher and confessor, and he concerned himself particularly with the poor people of the countryside. He was chosen to help in the establishment of a new house of his congregation at Monopoli, and a few years later was made superior at Lecce, after he had been subjected to very unkind treatment by a new superior at the first-named house. There is good evidence that already at this period Father de Jacobis was distinguished by happenings outside the ordinary course of nature. During the short time he was stationed in Naples there was an outbreak of cholera, when he devoted himself with tireless energy and courage to the care of the sufferers. " Everybody loved him ", says a contemporary, and when he was appointed to take charge of the new Ethiopian mission a Neapolitan newspaper wrote, " Mr de Jacobis is one of those evangelical workers who knows how to bring the works of nature under the dominion of religion and to attract to Jesus Christ the wise man and the scholar no less than the ignorant and simple ".

Father de Jacobis arrived in Ethiopia in September 1839. There were two other priests with him, and these he stationed at the Amharic capital, Gondar, settling himself at Adua, capital of the Tigrai. The ruler of this province, Ubia, was quite well disposed towards him, but among the clergy and people at large the events of the sixteenth century were not forgotten and the name Catholic was bitterly detested. For two years Father de Jacobis set himself to learn about the country, its people and its languages, and to break down prejudice by kindness and quiet humility. Early in 1840 he ventured on his first conference with some dissident clergy, whom he addressed with beautiful simplicity, emphasizing that he came among them as a friend and a servant, because he loved them and wanted to help them. Then and thereafter he did not fail to make a deep impression : but the obstacles in his way were huge—not least, human respect and a widespread corruption of life—and those who asked to be reconciled with the Catholic Church were very few indeed.

At this time the notables of Ethiopia were arranging to send a deputation to Egypt to ask the Coptic patriarch of Alexandria to appoint, according to custom, one of his monks as primate (*abuna*) of the Ethiopian Church : the sole episcopal see had been vacant for twelve years. And it occurred to them to ask Father de Jacobis to accompany this deputation, so that the presence of a respected European might make a suitable impression in Egypt. This proposal produced some qualms of conscience in Father de Jacobis—could a Catholic priest associate himself quasi-officially with such a mission ? But he agreed to do as he was asked on condition that Ubia furnished him with a letter to the patriarch urging reunion with the Catholic Church and that the deputation should go on to Rome as an official mission from Ethiopia to the Holy See. This was agreed to, and early in 1841 the party set out, the other principal members being a lay minister of state, a priest and a monk of the Ethiopian Church, and a secretary. The monk was Abba Gabra Mika'el. It would have been a hardy speculator who could have surmised that this dissident monk was to die a martyr for unity and be raised to the altars of the Church thirteen years before another of the deputation, Father Justin himself.

At first his companions were inclined to ignore Father Justin as a " Frank " and a heretic ; but his courtesy and consideration won them over, and the testimony of the chief secretary shows that they had not been in Cairo long before they were comparing him favourably with the Coptic patriarch. This prelate flatly and rudely refused to have anything to do with the Holy See, and threatened the deputies with excommunication if they did not dissociate themselves from Father de Jacobis ; he then presided over an election at which flagrant intrigue conferred the Ethiopian see on a young and ignorant monk who was below the canonical age. At his consecration he took the name of Salama—we shall meet him again. Meanwhile it looked as if the visit to Rome would fall through. But some of them, including Gabra Mika'el, defied the patriarch and accompanied Father de Jacobis thither. They were warmly received by Pope Gregory XVI, assisted at Mass in St Peter's on the Assumption, and came away exceedingly impressed. Only one of them had yet repudiated schism, on the way back at Jerusalem, but Father de Jacobis was sowing good seed. And so the deputation returned home. As Bd Justin said, " That visit to Rome altered the ideas of my poor Ethiopians : it was the best possible course of theology for them ".

For a time at this period the outlook for the mission in Ethiopia was not un-favourable, in spite of grave difficulties presented by misunderstanding, ignorance and slander. A nucleus of indigenous Catholics was formed, and it included such influential and respected men as the monks Gabra Mika'el and Takla Haimanot. Even from the Galla country, where a European priest had never been seen, Antony d'Abbadie sent an encouraging report to Montalembert in Paris. And so already Father de Jacobis experienced the need for a college to educate and train a future generation of clergy ; in a letter to the superior general of the Congregation of the Mission he described how for a year he had been looking for a site towards

Massawa (which is on an island in the Red Sea) that would be suitable both for a religious centre and as a place of refuge for the faithful in the event of persecution. Eventually he obtained a suitable property on land belonging to the monastery of Gunda-Gunda : several of the monks of this house had become Catholics and its abbot was well disposed towards Abba Jacob, as Father de Jacobis was called. Here, at Guala, near Adigrat, the college was begun in 1845. Bd Justin had as his staff his colleague Father Biancheri, three Ethiopian priests and two monks, and an Italian laybrother ; and an Ethiopian layman in charge of the boys' school. The seminary had soon made sufficient progress for Bd Justin to represent to Rome the need for a bishop, and before the end of 1846 a vicariate apostolic " of the Galla " had been set up. It was entrusted to the Capuchin friars minor, and the first bishop was Mgr (afterwards Cardinal) William Massaia.

The popularity of " the Frank Jacob " and his activities at Guala had not escaped the notice of the head of the national church, Abuna Salama,* and he published an excommunication of all who should " give him food and drink when travelling, or accept money from him ". This had no particular effect ; but the arrival of a Catholic bishop excited Salama to more effective action. Making use of the political situation and the parties to which his own unpopularity had given rise, he brought about a state of open persecution. The college and groups of faithful were dispersed, Catholicity was proscribed, Mgr Massaia had to withdraw to Aden, and Bd Justin was a hunted man : Salama's patron, Subagadis, wrote to his chiefs, " Kill Abba Jacob and all his people. To kill only one who follows his religion is to earn seven heavenly crowns hereafter. . . ." In such conditions Father de Jacobis, whose prefecture had been made a vicariate, received episcopal consecration, secretly at Massawa, at the hands of Mgr Massaia in 1848. Though remaining a priest of the Latin rite he was given faculties to celebrate Mass and administer the sacraments, especially holy orders, according to the Ethiopic rite whenever that should be desirable. The first priest he ordained was Bd Gabra Mika'el, who was sixty years old at the time.

Not all those who had been reconciled with the Catholic Church were constant under persecution, others were constant to death : and in spite of all, Bd Justin's work developed, a little here and a little there. By 1853 there were a score of Ethiopian priests and 5,000 other faithful, and for a time Bd Gabra Mika'el was able to reopen the college, at Alitiena. Among those who befriended Mgr de Jacobis at this time was a young Scot named John Bell, who was in the service of the viceroy of Beghemeder, Ras Ali. It is said to have been Bell's intention to become a Catholic, but in the disturbed state of the country he was killed in a skirmish, in 1860, before putting his determination into effect. These disturbances were brought about when the commander of Ras Ali's troops, Kedaref Kassa, began the conquests which were to bring him to the throne of Ethiopia as Negus Neghesti (King of Kings) Theodore II. Kassa bought the support of Abuna Salama by promising to banish all Catholic clergy, and again persecution flared up.

Bd Justin was arrested in Gondar and jailed for several months with common criminals. He was then dispatched under escort to the frontier post of Senaar, where it was intended that he should either " disappear " or fall a victim to Mohammedan fanaticism. Instead, his guards set him at liberty ; and after

---

* It is common form in some hagiography to represent the persecutors of the saints to have been as wicked in all respects as their victims were virtuous. Of course they weren't always. But this Salama was a very bad lot.

undergoing great suffering and in continual danger he arrived safely at Halai, towards the coast in southern Eritrea, from whence he wrote to his superiors referring to his " almost miraculous deliverance ". On the very day, August 28, 1855, Bd Justin wrote this letter, Bd Gabra Mika'el died in chains (see September 1).

Mgr de Jacobis tried to get back to his harried little flock in the Tigrai province, but in vain ; for the few remaining years of his life he had to confine his ministry to the Red Sea coast. Towards the end of 1859 the French government sent an envoy extraordinary, Count de Russel, on a political mission to Negusie, ruler of the Tigrai. This action provoked considerable excitement in Ethiopia ; Russel's position was very awkward, and Mgr de Jacobis gave the mission shelter in his house at Halai. The action was prompted by charity and not by political considerations ; but Bd Justin was seized when about to celebrate the Holy Mysteries, and kept shut up for over three weeks in a stable or beast house. Russel ransomed him in March 1860 ; but the imprisonment, forced marches and change of climate from the mountains at Halai to low-lying Emkullo had been too much for a body already worn out by twenty years of grinding toil in Ethiopia.

On July 19 he was seized by a fever. He knew it meant the end, but insisted on setting out on the difficult journey of return to Halai on July 29, accompanied by Father Delmonte, several monks, and a dozen young students. On the 31st they reached the valley of Alghedien, but Bd Justin could no longer keep in the saddle. Lying on the ground, surrounded by his weeping disciples, he was anointed ; then, sitting up, with his head leaning against a rock, he spoke to them for the last time : " Pray hard, little ones, for I'm going to die. I won't forget you . . . I am dying." He drew his cloak over his face, and so died.

St Vincent de Paul once said to the priests of his congregation, " Suppose a missionary were to be found worn out with toil and weakness, having nothing of his own, sitting under a hedge. And that he were asked, ' Poor priest, what has brought you to this state ? ' And that he were able to reply, ' Love '. What a happiness that would be ! " Justin de Jacobis was certainly that priest, even to the detail of sitting on the ground ; and Father Delmonte's letter to his superiors from Emkullo, dated August 3, began, " I have to announce the death of a saint ". Yet his devoted and self-sacrificing life can be paralleled over and over again in the lives of missionaries whom no one has ever suggested canonizing : the difference between him and them is not in their external lives and experiences, but in the man himself, what he *was*. Reading a long memorandum written by Mgr Massaia, it is Bd Justin's humility that keeps on cropping up and that seems to have been *the* characteristic of his heroic virtue : not simply a gentlemanly modesty or a creaking adherence to copybook maxims, but an ingrained virtue that enabled him to be as it were " one of themselves " among the people to whom he was sent—and they were not a people with any surface attractiveness about them. Over and over again priests and monks and notables, who had been told that he was an emissary of the arrogant " Franks " and the even more arrogant Pope of Rome, found that he talked and behaved as if he looked on himself as their servant—which of course is exactly what he did. Mgr Massaia wrote, " He was chosen by God to be a teacher, not only in words but even more by example ; and to be a model of the perfection that is possible to mortal man, amid a people terribly corrupted by falsehood, pride, lasciviousness and every kind of wickedness. And God raised this great figure of human perfection on a base of humility, to be a lesson to Ethiopia, and to the apostles who should carry on the work he began, for ever after."

Bd Justin was buried in the church at Hebo, which had to be enlarged to accommodate the tomb ; it has ever since been regarded as the shrine of a saint by the people, both Catholic and dissident, of the neighbourhood, who have never forgotten Abuna Jacob. And on May 14, 1939, the Church put her seal on their tradition by declaring Justin de Jacobis blessed.

In 1866 there was published in Paris an anonymous [A. Devin] life of Justin de Jacobis, *L'Abyssinie et son apôtre ;* it is somewhat disconnected and has awkward gaps, but it is a most valuable work since it consists almost entirely of verbatim passages from the letters of Antony d'Abbadie d'Arrast, Mgr Massaia and other contemporaries and from the letters and journals of Bd Justin himself. See also Massaia's *Trenta anni in Abissinia ;* Coulbeaux, *Vers la Lumière,* a biography of Bd Gabra Mika'el (1926) ; Arata, *Vita del B. Giustino de Jacobis* (1939) ; and the biographies in French by M. Demimuid (1906) and J. Baeteman (1939). For the background, Archbishop Mathew's *Ethiopia* (1947) is excellent ; see also Attwater, *Christian Churches of the East,* vol. i, cap. v (1947). The John T. Bell mentioned above married an Ethiopian princess ; their daughter married a Swiss missionary, and *their* daughter, Princess Asfa Yilma, wrote an account of the *negus* Haile Salassie in English, published in 1936. See also C. Korolevsky in *Roma e l'Oriente,* July 1919, pp. 23–36, January 1920, pp. 35–52 ; and for Salama, J. B. Coulbeaux in *Revue anglo-romaine,* vol. i (1896), pp. 625–636, 673–696.

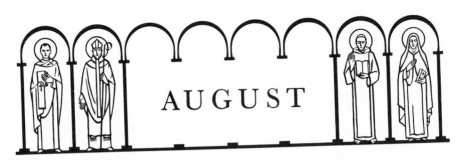

AUGUST

1 : ST PETER *AD VINCULA*

IT has been related in the life of St James the Greater that Herod Agrippa, having put to death that apostle in order to please his people, by an action still more agreeable to them caused St Peter to be cast into prison. It was his intention to put him to death after the Passover. The whole church at Jerusalem sent up its prayers to God without ceasing for the deliverance of the chief pastor of His flock. The king took all precautions possible to prevent the escape of his prisoner, as he and the other apostles had once before been delivered out of prison by an angel. St Peter, in complete tranquillity of mind and entire resignation of himself, lay fast asleep on the very night before the day on which he was to be brought before the people, when it pleased God to deliver him out of the hands of his enemies. He was fastened by two chains, and slept between two soldiers. In the middle of the night a bright light shone in the prison and an angel appeared and, striking him on the side, awaked him out of his sleep, and bade him instantly arise, gird his coat about him, put on his sandals, and follow him. The chains dropped off from his hands, and Peter rose up and went after the angel, thinking that he was in a vision. He passed after him through the first and second ward, and through the iron gate which led into the city, which opened to them of its own accord. The angel conducted him through one street ; then suddenly disappeared. Till then the apostle doubted whether the whole thing was not a dream, but now he knew in very deed that the Lord had sent His angel and delivered him from Herod and from the expectation of the Jews. He went directly to the house of Mary the mother of John Mark, where several disciples were together, praying for his deliverance. As he stood knocking, a young woman came to the door, and, perceiving it was his voice, ran in and told the others that Peter was outside ; and when she persisted, they thought it must be his angel sent by God, until, being let in, he told them the whole manner of his escape. And having enjoined them to tell what had happened to St James and the rest of the brethren, he withdrew to a place of more security. The next day, when he was not to be found, Agrippa commanded the keepers to be put to death, supposing them to be, either by connivance or carelessness, accessory to St Peter's escape.

It would be gathered from the proper of the Mass and Office of today's feast that it commemorates the event of St Peter's life that has just been narrated. It is, however, in origin the commemoration of the dedication in Rome of a church on the Esquiline Hill in honour of SS. Peter and Paul. The notice of it in the "Martyrology of Jerome" runs : "At Rome the dedication of the first church which was built and consecrated by blessed Peter." This is, of course, a misconception. The *titulus Apostolorum*, the earliest name by which the parish was known, possibly came into existence at the end of the fourth century, and it had reference to the two apostles Peter and Paul, as inscriptions prove. The church having been rebuilt, it was consecrated between 432 and 440 by Pope St Sixtus III, and was then known as the *titulus Eudoxiae*, in honour of the Byzantine princess who was the principal benefactress. It is not till nearly a century later that we first find it referred to as St Peter *ad Vincula*, " St Peter's where the Fetters are ", with reference to the chains wherewith the apostle had been bound when a prisoner in Rome. Later these came to be regarded as the chains which had fallen from his hands in Jerusalem, and the legend grew up that the Empress Eudoxia had sent one of these chains from Jerusalem to Rome, where it had miraculously united with its fellow already there. This story still figures in the second nocturn of Matins on August 1, in lessons which Pope Benedict XIV intended to have removed from the office.

August 1 was formerly called in England Lammas-day, *i.e.* Loaf-Mass, from Old English *hláfmæsse*, it being a sort of early harvest-thanksgiving, at which a Mass of thanksgiving for the first-fruits of the earth, or of the corn, was celebrated and loaves made from the new flour blessed. The blessing of new grapes was common both among the Greeks and Latins, in some places on the 1st, in others on the 6th day of August, and is mentioned in ancient liturgical books.

In a Motu Proprio of John XXIII dated July 25, 1960, this feast was dropped from the Roman Calendar.

See H. Grisar, *History of Rome and the Popes*, vol. i, p. 190 ; also H. Grisar in the *Civiltà Cattolica*, vol. iii of 1898, pp. 204–221 ; DAC., vol. iii, cc. 3–19 ; J. P. Kirsch, *Die römischen Titelkirchen*, pp. 45–52 ; and CMH., pp. 409 seq.

THE HOLY MACHABEES, Martyrs   (168 B.C. ?)

MACHABEE was the surname of Judas, the third son of that Mathathias who was the first leader of the Jews in their revolt against King Antiochus IV Epiphanes ; the name was afterwards extended to the whole family and descendants of Mathathias, and was applied to those who followed them in their rising against the king of Syria, among them the martyrs who are celebrated on the first day of August. These Machabean martyrs are the only saints of the Old Law who are commemorated liturgically throughout the Universal Church, and the only ones to figure in the general calendar of the Western church ; feasts of Old Testament saints are common in the East, but, apart from the Machabees, are unknown in the West, except for a few proper to religious orders or places, *e.g.* SS. Elias and Eliseus among the Carmelites, and others in the Latin diocese of Jerusalem.

The cause of the rebellion of the Jews was the efforts of Antiochus to impose Greek paganism upon them ; but the occasion of the first actual outbreak was a persecution of the Jews undertaken by Antiochus in rage and mortification when his second campaign against Egypt was stopped by the Roman senate in 168 B.C. He sent a general, Apollonius, with twenty-two thousand men to Jerusalem, whose orders were to hellenize the city by killing the Jews who would not apostatize and importing foreigners in their place. Among the martyrs who preferred torments and death to violation of the divine law one of the most eminent was St Eleazar. He was one of the chief among the Scribes or doctors of the law, an aged man of a comely aspect. The persecutors thought that they could gain the rest if they succeeded in perverting this holy man, and they therefore tried by bribery, threats, and violence to make him commit an act of apostasy, but he remained firm. Certain bystanders, moved with pity for the old man, desired that flesh might be brought which it was lawful for him to eat, that the people might believe that he had eaten swine's flesh, and the king be satisfied by such a pretended obedience. He rejected the subterfuge, saying that by such dissimulation the young would be tempted to transgress the law, thinking that Eleazar, at the age of fourscore and ten years, had gone over to the rites of the heathen, and that if he should be guilty of such a crime he could not escape the hand of the Almighty, either alive or dead. He was forthwith carried to execution, and as he was dying under the stripes he exclaimed, " O Lord, whose holy light pierces the most secret recesses of our hearts, thou seest the pains I endure ; but my soul feels joy in suffering these things for the sake of thy law, because I fear thee ".

The confession of St Eleazar was followed by the martyrdom of seven brothers, who suffered tortures one after another with invincible courage, whilst their heroic mother stood by, encouraging and strengthening them. The youngest brother was put to death with yet more cruelty than the others, and last of all their mother, having given the lives of all her children, yielded up her own rather than desert the law of the Most High. Neither the names of these martyrs nor the place of their suffering are known.

See the second Book of Machabees, vi 18–31 and vii ; CMH., pp. 408–409 ; DAC. vol. xi, cc. 12–13. Presumably because they typified and in some sense were taken to represent the vast army of Christian martyrs who amid similar torments were to follow their example, the Machabees seem to have been honoured in every part of the Church at a very early date. We find them mentioned and connected with Antioch in the Syriac " breviarium " of the first years of the fifth century. They are also in the *Fasti* of Polemius Sylvius, in the Carthaginian calendar and in the *Hieronymianum*. It is curious that in the church of St Peter *ad Vincula*, just mentioned, there should be preserved a great stone sarcophagus divided into seven compartments and bearing an inscription which says that the bones and ashes of the seven brothers with their parents had been buried therein. It should be noted also that St Leo the Great preaching on August 1, probably in that church, mentions the double celebration of the dedication of the building and the passion of the seven brothers. One difficulty which defies solution is that raised by St Jerome. He had seen the relics of the Machabees at Modin, and he asks how they could be exposed for veneration at Antioch. Cf. Delehaye, *Les origines du culte des martyrs*, pp. 201–202.

SS. FAITH, HOPE AND CHARITY, AND THEIR MOTHER WISDOM, MARTYRS   (NO DATE ?)

THE Roman widow St Wisdom and her three daughters are said to have suffered for the faith under the Emperor Hadrian. According to a spurious legend St Faith, aged twelve, was scourged, thrown into boiling pitch, taken out alive, and beheaded ; St Hope, aged ten, and St Charity, aged nine, being unhurt in a furnace, were also beheaded ; and their mother suffered while praying over the bodies of her children. That the whole story is a myth is very likely, the legend spreading to the East from Rome, where there is reference to two groups : a family martyred under Hadrian and buried on the Aurelian Way, where their tomb under the church of St Pancras was afterwards resorted to : their names were Greek, Sophia, Pistis, Elpis and Agape ; and another group of martyrs of an unknown date, Sapientia, Fides, Spes and Caritas, buried in the cemetery of St Callistus on the Appian Way. The Roman Martryology names Faith, Hope and Charity on August 1, and their mother (of whose martyrdom it says nothing) on September 30. The great church of St Sophia at Constantinople has nothing to do with this saint or with any other of her name ; it is dedicated in honour of the Holy Wisdom (ἡ ἁγία σοφία), that is, to Christ as the Word of God.

Father Delehaye, commenting upon these supposed martyrs, remarks : " Every one will agree that it would need very strong evidence to lend verisimilitude to even a single group of this kind, but no such evidence is here forthcoming " (*Les origines du culte des martyrs*, pp. 286–287) ; J. P. Kirsch also, in the *Lexikon für Theologie und Kirche*, vol. iii, cc. 1035–1036, seems to concur in this verdict. The cult cannot be called ancient. No earlier evidence has been adduced than the *Index oleorum*, which dates only from the end of the sixth century.

ST ALED, EILUNED OR ALMEDHA, VIRGIN AND MARTYR (SIXTH CENTURY)

" NOT far from Brecon is the church called St Almedha's, after the holy maiden who, refusing an earthly husband, was wedded to the Eternal King, and there triumphed in a happy martyrdom. A solemn feast is held in her honour every year at the beginning of August, and it is attended by many people from distant parts ; those who suffer from various diseases receive wished-for health through the merits of the blessed maiden. Certain things which happen at this anniversary seem remarkable to me. In the church or in the churchyard, during the dance which is led round the churchyard with a song, you may see men and girls suddenly fall to the ground as in a trance ; then, as if frenzied, they jump up and represent to the people with their hands and feet whatever work they have unlawfully done on great feasts. You may see one man put his hand to the plow, and another as it were goad on the oxen, lightening their labour with the usual uncouth song ; one imitates the trade of a cobbler, another that of a tanner. You may see a girl with a distaff, drawing out the thread and winding it again on the spindle ; another as she walks arranges the threads for the web ; another throws the shuttle and seems to weave. Then, on coming into the church and being led to the altar with their offerings, you will be astonished to see them suddenly come to their senses again. Thus, by the divine mercy which rejoices not at the death of sinners but at their conversion, many, convicted by their own actions, are corrected and amended on these feast days."

This interesting passage comes from the *Itinerary through Wales* of Giraldus Cambrensis, who was archdeacon of Brecon from 1175 for over twenty years and lived at Llanddew only a couple of miles away ; he was therefore well placed for verifying the details of the phenomena which he describes. The passage is well known, and has often raised questions about the identity and story of St Almedha, or Aled as she was more usually called locally—the name is found in a score of forms. Gerald himself states that she was one of the children of Brychan, that prolific father of saints, but the name figures in only some lists of these children ; and it is odd that, while she appears in at least one Latin calendar, she is unknown to the Welsh ones.

The legend of St Aled as it was current in the seventeenth century has a suspicious resemblance to the story of St Winifred (November 3). While still young she dedicated herself completely to God, and when a young prince, supported by her family, urged her to marry him, she fled away in disguise to Llanddew. Here she was so badly treated that she withdrew to Llanfillo, and then again to Llechfaen, where she had to sleep in the street as nobody would give her a bed. So she took refuge in the wood on Slwch Tump, by Brecon itself, where the lord of the place helped her to build a cell, and she settled down there, prophesying that " a chastisement would rest on the village of Llanddew for the injuries done to her ; that the village of Llanfillo should be plagued with thieves (as they are to this day above all others) ; and the village of Llechfaen with envy, as indeed they are almost continually in contention and law with one another " (Hugh Thomas, *c.* 1698).

It is not recorded that Aled also foretold her own misfortunes, but soon after her princely suitor sought her out in her retreat. Directly she saw him she ran away down the hill ; he followed, caught her up, and in baffled rage smote off her head with his sword. Where Aled's head fell, a spring of water miraculously welled up from the rock ; and thereafter the maiden was venerated as a saint and martyr.

> The legend of St Aled is set out in a late seventeenth-century manuscript of Hugh Thomas, the Breconshire herald (Harleian MS. 4181) : see *Archaeologia Cambrensis* for 1883, pp. 46–47, 168, and for 1903, pp. 214–223. Gerald the Welshman's *Itinerary through Wales*, bk i, cap. 2 ; Jones's *History of Brecknock*, vol. i, pp. 43–44 (edition of 1909) ; Cressy's *Church History of Brittany* (*i.e.* Britain), published at Rouen in 1668. William of Worcester says that " St Elevetha " was buried at Usk, but other writers agree that it was in her cell, which became the first St Aled's chapel on Slwch hill. This in turn became a small church of some importance in the middle ages ; by 1698 it was roofless and disused, and today its site can with difficulty be identified.

ST ETHELWOLD, BISHOP OF WINCHESTER (A.D. 984)

THIS saint was a native of Winchester. Being moved in his youth to devote himself to the divine service, he submitted himself to St Alphege the Bald, bishop of his native city, who gave him the priesthood, at the same time as St Dunstan, who was about his equal in age. When Dunstan became abbot of Glastonbury in 944 and introduced strict Benedictine observance there, Ethelwold took the habit and was made one of the deans of the house. He was a practitioner of the useful arts, especially bell-founding, and at the same time his zeal for knowledge made him study also the sacred sciences. About 954 Ethelwold was appointed abbot of Abingdon in Berkshire, which with the help of monks from Glastonbury he rendered a model of regular discipline and a nursery of good monks. He procured from Corbie a master of church music, and sent Osgar to Fleury, a monastery which at that time surpassed all others in the reputation of strict observance, to learn its discipline for the benefit of Abingdon. The Danes had made such havoc of religious houses that practically no monks were then left in all England, and the education of youth and every other support of learning and virtue was almost banished by the ravages of the barbarians. These deplorable circumstances awakened the zeal especially of St Dunstan, St Ethelwold and St Oswald of York, and these three set themselves with great industry to restore monasticism and studies.

St Ethelwold was consecrated bishop of Winchester by St Dunstan in 963. The disorders and ignorance which reigned among many of the clergy of England had produced some very scandalous states of affairs, and Ethelwold found these evils obstinate and past recovery among the canons of the cathedral of Winchester. He therefore expelled them, with the approval of King Edgar, placing monks from Abingdon in their room, with whom he kept choir as their bishop and abbot. Three of the former canons took the monastic habit and continued to serve God in that church. The year following, St Ethelwold expelled the seculars out of the

Newminster monastery at Winchester, and placed there Benedictine monks under an abbot, and was the means of peopling Chertsey with monks also. He repaired the nunnery dedicated in honour of our Lady in his cathedral city, and bought of the king the lands and ruins of the great nunnery of St Etheldreda in the isle of Ely, which had been burnt by the Danes a hundred years before, and he established on the same spot an abbey of monks. He likewise purchased the ruins of Thorney in Cambridgeshire, which he restored in like manner about the year 972. He directed and assisted Aldulf to buy the ruins of Peterborough Abbey, and rebuilt and peopled it as well ; this monastery, after having flourished two hundred years, was destroyed by the Danes in 870. Aldulf, chancellor to King Edgar, having buried his only son, gave his whole estate to this house, took the monastic habit in it, and was chosen the first abbot.

Ethelwold's reforming activities, in particular the displacing of slack canons by strict monks, met with a deal of opposition, but to malcontents he was " terrible as a lion ", while the good-willed and persevering found in him a benevolent shepherd, " more gentle than a dove ". He who was fittingly called " the father of monks " and who laboured so strenuously for the divine honour and the sanctification of others, was always solicitous first to adorn his own soul with all virtues, and to make himself a sacrifice agreeable to God ; for it is only the humility and charity of the heart that give a value to exterior actions : without these, to give our goods to the poor and our bodies to the flames would not avail us. The fervour of devotion and compunction must be always nourished and increased, or it grows lukewarm ; in this great bishop interior devotion and exterior actions of virtue supported and gave strength to each other. He rested from his labours on August 1, 984, and was buried in the cathedral of Winchester. Authentic proofs of miracles wrought through his intercession having been made, his body was taken up and solemnly deposited under the altar by St Alphege, his immediate successor, afterwards archbishop of Canterbury and martyr. Several written works are credited to St Ethelwold, of which one was a translation into English of the Rule of St Benedict.

There is a fair amount of historical material for the life of St Ethelwold. The biography by Aelfric has been printed by Stevenson in the *Chronicon de Abingdon* (Rolls Series) ; another, attributed to Wolstan, has been more often printed, but Dean Armitage Robinson was inclined to question the authorship and early date. There are also references in the *Historia Eliensis*, William of Malmesbury, etc. Ethelwold is now generally recognized as the author of the *Regularis Concordia* which was formerly assigned to St Dunstan. See H. W. Keim, " Ethelwold und die Mönchsreform in England " in *Anglia*, vol. xxxix (1917), pp. 405–443 ; Armitage Robinson, *The Times of St Dunstan* (1923) ; D. Knowles, *The Monastic Order in England* (1949), pp. 38–59 and *passim* ; and T. Symons, *Regularis Concordia* (1954).

BB. THOMAS WELBOURN AND WILLIAM BROWN, MARTYRS
(A.D. 1605)

THE little that is known of these martyrs is narrated by Challoner thus : " Thomas Welbourn was a schoolmaster, a native of Kitenbushel [Hutton Bushel], in Yorkshire, and John Fulthering was a layman of the same county, who being zealous Catholics, and industrious in exhorting some of their neighbours to embrace the Catholic faith, were upon that account arraigned and condemned to suffer as in cases of high treason ; as was also William Brown, a native of Northamptonshire, convicted of the same offence. They were all executed according to sentence [by hanging, drawing and quartering] ; Mr Welbourn and Mr Fulthering at York, the 1st of August, 1605 ; Mr Brown at Ripon, the 5th of September, the same year."

The Venerable John Fulthering's cause is among those postponed in 1929.

Challoner's *Memoirs of Missionary Priests* (at p. 280 in the edition of 1924).

2 : ST ALPHONSUS DE' LIGUORI, BISHOP OF SANT' AGATA DEI GOTI, DOCTOR OF THE CHURCH, FOUNDER OF THE CONGREGATION OF THE MOST HOLY REDEEMER   (A.D. 1787)

ST ALPHONSUS was born near Naples in 1696 ; his parents were Don Joseph de' Liguori, captain of the royal galleys, and Donna Anna Cavalieri, both people of virtuous and distinguished life. The boy was baptized Alphonsus Mary Antony John Francis Cosmas Damian Michael Caspar, but preferred to call himself simply Alfonso Maria ; the use of the Latin form of his name has become usual in English. Don Joseph was determined that his first-born should have every advantage that formal education could give him, and he was early put under tutors. At thirteen he began the study of jurisprudence, and when sixteen he was allowed, by dispensation of four years, to present himself before the university of Naples for examination for the doctor's degree in both laws (civil and canon) ; it was granted him with acclamation. His reputation as a barrister is testified by the tradition (not certainly true) that in eight years of practice he never lost a case. In 1717 Don Joseph arranged a marriage for his son, but it came to nothing and Alphonsus continued to work diligently and quietly ; for a year or two some slackness in religious care was observable, coupled with and perhaps due to an affection for " society life " and fashionable amusements, but he had the will to avoid serious sin. He was very fond of the music of the theatre, but music was not the only thing on the Neapolitan stage of the eighteenth century ; however, Alphonsus was very short-sighted and when the curtain went up his spectacles came off, and so he was able to enjoy the good without receiving harm from the dangerous. A retreat with the Lazarists during the Lent of 1722 and reception of the sacrament of Confirmation in the following autumn steadied him and revived his fervour, and at the next Lent he made a private resolution not to marry and to continue in his profession only until it should appear that God wished him to abandon it. What he took to be a clear indication of the divine will was shown him only a few months later.

A certain Neapolitan nobleman was suing the grand-duke of Tuscany for possession of an estate valued at over £100,000. Alphonsus was briefed in the case, for which side we do not now know, but probably for his countryman, and made a great speech on his client's behalf which much impressed the court. When he sat down opposing counsel coolly remarked, " You have wasted your breath. You have disregarded the evidence on which the whole case depends." " What do you mean ? Where ? How ? " asked Alphonsus. He was handed a document which he had read through several times, but with a passage marked that had entirely escaped his notice. The point at issue was whether the estate was held under Lombard law or under the Angevin capitularies : this clause made the point

242

clear, and decided against the client of Alphonsus. For a moment he was silent. Then he said, " I have made a mistake. The case is yours ", and left the court. Braving the fiery indignation of his father, Alphonsus refused either to go on with his profession or to entertain a second project for his marriage. While visiting the sick in the hospital for incurables he twice heard as it were an interior voice, saying, " Leave the world, and give yourself to me " ; he went to the church of our Lady of Ransom, laid his sword on her altar, and then offered himself to the priests of the Oratory. Don Joseph tried every way to dissuade his son, but was at last constrained to agree to his being a priest, provided that, instead of joining the Oratory, he should stay at home. On the advice of his director, Father Pagano, himself an Oratorian, Alphonsus accepted this condition.

He began his theological studies at home, and in 1726 was advanced to the priesthood. For the two following years he was engaged in missionary work throughout the kingdom of Naples, and at once made his mark. The early eighteenth century was a time of pompous oratory and florid verbosity in the pulpit—a fruit of the Renaissance out of control—and of rigorism in the confessional —a fruit of Jansenism ; Don Alphonsus repudiated both these characteristics. He preached simply and without affectation : " It is a pleasure to listen to your sermons ; you forget yourself and preach Jesus Christ ", somebody said to him, and he afterwards instructed his missioners : " Your style must be simple, but the sermon must be well constructed. If skill be lacking, it is unconnected and taste-less ; if it be bombastic, the simple cannot understand it. I have never preached a sermon which the poorest old woman in the congregation could not understand." He treated his penitents as souls to be saved rather than as criminals to be punished or frightened into better ways ; he is said never to have refused absolution to a penitent. This was not pleasing to everybody, and some looked with suspicion on Don Alphonsus. He organized the *lazzaroni* of Naples into groups which met for instruction in Christian doctrine and virtue ; one of the members was reproved by Don Alphonsus for his imprudent fasting, and another priest added, " It is God's will that we should eat in order to live. If you are given cutlets, eat them and be thankful. They will do you good." The remark was taken up and twisted into a matter of offence : the clubs were secret societies of Epicureans, of Quietists, of some other heresy, there was a new sect, " of Cutlets ". The solemn wiseacres of church and state took the matter up, arrests were made, and Don Alphonsus had to make explanations. The archbishop counselled him to be more careful, the " Cutlet clubs " continued undisturbed, and developed into the great Asso-ciation of the Chapels which numbers thousands of working-men who meet daily for prayer and instruction in the confraternity chapels.

In 1729, being then thirty-three years old, Alphonsus left his father's house to become chaplain to a college for the training of missionaries to China. Here he met Thomas Falcoia and became friendly with him ; he was a priest twice his own age, whose life had been devoted to trying to establish a new religious institute in accordance with a vision he claimed to have had in Rome. All he had succeeded in doing was to establish a convent of nuns at Scala, near Amalfi, to whom he had given a version of the rule of the Visitandines. One of the nuns, however, Sister Mary Celeste, alleged that she had received a revelation of the rule which the nuns were to follow, and when Father Falcoia discovered that its provisions tallied with those intimated to him twenty years before he was naturally impressed. In 1730 he got St Alphonsus interested in the matter. About the same time an unexpected turn was given to events by Falcoia's appointment to the see of Castellamare ; this left him free to associate himself with the convent of Scala again, and one of his first episcopal acts was to invite Alphonsus to give a retreat to the nuns, a step that had far-reaching consequences for everybody concerned.

St Alphonsus went to Scala, and in addition to giving the retreat he investigated, with a lawyer's precision, the matter of Sister Mary Celeste's revelation, and came to the conclusion that it was from God and not an hallucination. He therefore recommended, and the nuns agreed, that the convent should be re-organized in accordance with the vision, and the bishop of Scala gave his consent ; on the feast of the Transfiguration 1731 the nuns put on their new habit, of red and blue, and entered upon their strictly enclosed and penitential life. Thus began the Redemptoristines, who still flourish in several lands. The new rule had been expanded and made more explicit by St Alphonsus himself, and Mgr Falcoia proposed that he should now undertake the establishment of a new congregation of missionaries to work especially among the peasants of the country districts. St Alphonsus agreed, but had to face a storm of opposition. At last, after a long and painful leave-taking with his father, he left Naples in November 1732 and went to Scala. There the Congregation of the Most Holy Redeemer was born on the 9th of that month, and its first home was in a small house belonging to the convent of nuns. There were seven postulants under Alphonsus, with Mgr Falcoia as informal superior general, and dissensions began at once, centring chiefly in this very matter of who was in supreme authority ; a party opposed the bishop, and consequently Alphonsus, and a schism was formed in both houses. Sister Mary Celeste went off to found a convent at Foggia, and at the end of five months St Alphonsus was alone but for one lay-brother. But other subjects came, a larger house became necessary, and in the autumn of 1733 successful missions were given in the diocese of Amalfi. In the following January a second foundation was made at Villa degli Schiavi, and here Alphonsus went to reside, and conducted missions. The saint is so well known as a moral theologian, for his writings, and for his efforts in founding the Redemptorists, that his eminence as a missioner has been overshadowed ; but from 1726 till 1752 he was preaching up and down the kingdom of Naples, especially in villages and rural settlements, and with the greatest success. His confessional was crowded, hardened sinners returned to the healing sacraments in great numbers, enemies were reconciled, family feuds healed, and he established the practice, characteristic of the method of his followers, of returning some months after a mission was closed in order to confirm and consolidate the work.

But the troubles of the young Redemptorists were not over : indeed they had hardly begun. In the same year as the foundation at Villa degli Schiavi, Spain re-asserted its authority over Naples, the absolutist Charles III was in power, and he had as his prime minister the Marquis Bernard Tanucci, who was to be the life-long opponent of the new congregation. In 1737 a priest of bad character spread evil reports about the establishment at Villa, the community was attacked by armed men, and it was deemed wise to close the house ; in the following year troubles caused Scala too to be abandoned. On the other hand Cardinal Spinelli, Archbishop of Naples, put St Alphonsus at the head of a general mission throughout his diocese, and for two years the saint organized and conducted this, until the death of Mgr Falcoia recalled him to the work of the congregation. A general chapter was held, at which St Alphonsus was elected rector major (*i.e.* superior general), vows were taken, and rules and constitutions were drawn up. They were now constituted as a religious institute and proceeded in the following years to make several new foundations, all under great difficulties of local and official opposition ; " regalism " was in the ascendant and the implacable anti-clericalism of Tanucci was a sword at all times threatening the existence of the congregation.

The first edition of the *Moral Theology* of St Alphonsus, in the form of annotations to the work of Busembaum, a Jesuit theologian, was published at Naples in 1748, and the second edition, which is properly the first of his own complete work, in 1753–55. It was approved by Pope Benedict XIV and had an immediate success, for with consummate wisdom it steered a middle course between the rigorism of Jansenism and an improper laxity ; seven more editions were called for in the author's lifetime. There is no need here to follow the controversy concerning " probabilism ", with which the name of St Alphonsus is associated. Probabilism is the system in moral theology which holds that, if of two opinions one insists that in certain circumstances a law binds, while the other holds that in these circumstances it does not, one is allowed to follow an opinion favouring liberty provided it be truly and solidly probable, even though the opinion favouring the law be more probable. St Alphonsus eventually favoured what he called Aequiprobabilism, which insists that the law must be obeyed unless the opinion favouring liberty is at least nearly equally probable with that favouring the law, though there would appear to be little practical difference between the two systems. The Church permits the application of either, but the reader may be reminded that Probabilism is primarily a principle for the moral theologian and is not put forward as an ideal of Christian life ; often the more perfect and therefore more desirable course of action is to follow the more probable opinion according to which the law is binding. Attempts have been made to impugn the morality of the teaching of St Alphonsus about lying : his was the ordinary teaching of the Church, namely, that all lies are intrinsically wrong and illicit. Among the consequences of the teachings of the Jansenists was that holy communion can be received worthily only very rarely and that devotion to our Lady is a useless superstition ; St Alphonsus vigorously attacked both these errors, the last-named particularly by the publication in 1750 of *The Glories of Mary.*

From the time of the death of Mgr Falcoia in 1743 St Alphonsus led a life of extraordinary industry : guiding and fostering his new congregation through troubles both external and internal, trying to get it authorized by the king, ministering to individual souls, conducting missions all over Naples and Sicily, even finding time to write hymns, compose music, and paint pictures. After 1752 his health was failing, his missionary vigour decreased, and he devoted much more time to writing. The general opinion of him was voiced by a prebendary of Naples, " If I were pope I would canonize him without process ". " He fulfilled in a most perfect way ", said Father Mazzini, " the divine precept of loving God above all things, with his whole heart and with all his strength, as all might have seen and as I saw better than anyone during the long years I spent with him. The love of God shone forth in all his acts and words, in his devout manner of speaking of Him, his recollection, his deep devotion before the Blessed Sacrament, and his continual exercise of the divine presence." He was strict, but tender and compassionate, and, often suffering acutely from scrupulosity himself, was particularly kind to others afflicted in the same way. Father Cajone testified during the process of beatification of St Alphonsus that " His special and characteristic virtue seemed to me to be purity of intention. In all things and at all times he acted for God without any admixture of self.   He said to us one day, ' By the grace of God I have never confessed having acted from passion.   It may be that I have not noticed what was passing in me, but I have not remarked it so as to confess it.' "   This is the more remarkable when it is considered that Alphonsus was a Neapolitan, and by nature passionate and precipitate, easily moved by anger, pride, or a sudden resolve.

When he was sixty-six years old St Alphonsus was made by Pope Clement XIII bishop of Sant' Agata dei Goti, between Benevento and Capua.   When the messenger of the nuncio apostolic presented himself at Nocera, greeted him as " Most Illustrious Lord ", and handed over the letter announcing the appointment, Alphonsus read it through and handed it back, saying, " Please do not come back again with any more of your ' Most Illustrious ' ; it would be the death of me ". But the pope would take no refusal, and he was consecrated in the church of the Minerva at Rome.   Sant' Agata was only a small diocese, but that was about all that could be said in its favour ; it numbered 30,000 souls with 17 religious houses and 400 secular priests, of whom some did no pastoral work at all, living on the proceeds of an easy benefice, and others were not only slack but positively evil-living.   The laity were to match, and rapidly getting worse ; the results of nearly thirty years of neglect were apparent on all sides.   After having established his own modest household, the new bishop sent out a band of priests to conduct a general mission throughout the diocese : they were recruited from all orders and institutes in Naples except, for reasons of tact and prudence, his own congregation of Redemptorists.   Alphonsus recommended two things only to these missioners, simplicity in the pulpit, charity in the confessional, and after hearing one of the priests neglect his advice he said to him, " Your sermon kept me awake all night. . . . If you wanted to preach only yourself, rather than Jesus Christ, why come all the way from Naples to Ariola to do it ? "   At the same time he set about a reform of the seminary, and of the careless way that benefices were granted.   Some priests were in the habit of saying Mass in fifteen minutes or less ; these were suspended *ipso facto* until they amended their ways, and the bishop wrote a moving treatise on the subject :   " ' The priest at the altar ', says St Cyprian, ' represents the person of Jesus Christ.'   But whom do so many priests today represent ? They represent only mountebanks earning their livelihood by their antics.   Most lamentable of all is it to see religious, and some even of reformed orders, say Mass with such haste and such mutilation of the rite as would scandalize even the heathen. . . . ' Truly the sight of Mass celebrated in this way is enough to make one lose the faith.' "

After he had been at Sant' Agata a short time famine broke out, with its usual accompaniment of plague.   Alphonsus had foreseen this calamity several times in the previous two years, but nothing had been done to avert it.   Thousands were starving, and he sold everything to buy food for the sufferers, down to his carriage and mules and his uncle's episcopal ring ; the Holy See authorized him to make use of the endowment of the see for the same purpose, and he contracted debts right and left in his efforts at relief.   When the mob clamoured for the life of the mayor of Sant' Agata, who was wrongfully accused of withholding food, Alphonsus braved their fury, offered his own life for that of the mayor, and finally distracted them by distributing the rations of the next two days.   The bishop was most vigorous in his concern for public morality ; he always began with kindness, but when amendment was not promised or relapse occurred he took strong measures, invoking the help of the civil authorities. This made him many enemies, and several times his life was in danger from people of rank and others against whom he instituted proceedings. The custom of the courts of banishing hardened offenders, whether public vagabonds or private sinners, must have pressed somewhat hardly on the districts to which they went, and the bishops of neighbouring dioceses probably found scant consolation in the observation of the Bishop of Sant' Agata that, " Each must look after his own flock. When these people find themselves turned out everywhere, in disgrace and without food or shelter, they will come to their senses and give up their sinful lives."

In June 1767 St Alphonsus was attacked by terrible rheumatic pains which developed into an illness from which he was not expected to recover : not only did he receive the last sacraments but preparations were begun for his funeral. After twelve months his life was saved, but he was left with a permanent and incurable bending of the neck, familiar from the portraits of him ; until the surgeons had succeeded in straightening it a little the pressure of the chin caused a raw wound in his chest and he was unable to celebrate Mass, which afterwards he could do with the aid of a chair at the communion. In addition to attacks on his moral theology, he had to face an accusation against the Redemptorists of carrying on the Society of Jesus under another name (the Jesuits had been suppressed in the Spanish dominions in 1767), and an action against them, begun but adjourned some time before, was revived in 1770. The case dragged on for another thirteen years before it was decided in favour of Alphonsus on all counts. Pope Clement XIV died on September 22, 1774,* and St Alphonsus in the following year petitioned his successor, Pius VI, for permission to resign his see. Similar petitions had been refused by Clement XIII and XIV, but the effects of his rheumatic fever were now taken into consideration ; permission was granted, and the aged bishop retired to his Redemptorist's cell at Nocera, hoping to end his days in peace.

But it was not to be. The Redemptorists having in 1777 been subjected to another attack, Alphonsus determined to make another effort to get the royal sanction for his rule (it was as religious rather than as priests that the congregation was objected to) ; † in addition to four houses in Naples and one in Sicily, it had now four others in the Papal States. What followed was nothing less than tragic. Alphonsus agreed with the royal almoner, Mgr Testa, to waive any request to be allowed to hold property in common, but otherwise to submit the rule unchanged, and the almoner would put it before the king. Then Testa betrayed him. He altered the rule in several vital respects, even to the extent of abolishing the vows of religion ; he won over to his plot one of the consultors of the congregation, Father Majone, and this altered rule (*regolamento*) was presented to Alphonsus, written in a small hand and with many erasures. He was old, crippled, deaf, his sight was bad : he read over the familiar opening lines of the document—and signed it. Even his vicar general, Father Andrew Villani, seems to have connived at the cruel

---

* After celebrating Mass on the 21st, Alphonsus became unconscious and so remained for twenty-four hours. On coming round he announced that " I have been assisting the pope, who has just died ". This incident is sometimes put forward as an example of bilocation, but seems simply to have been a clairvoyant trance. It was referred to, but no great importance was attached to it in the process of beatification.

† There were said to be 65,000 priests in the kingdom at this time. On the basis of the Church in England and Wales today that would give the Two Sicilies a population of 30 millions, or two-thirds of the population of all Italy in 1948.

deception, probably through fear of the others.   The king approved the *regolamento*, it became legally binding, and its provisions were made known to the Redemptorists —and to their founder.   The storm broke on him : " You have founded the congregation and you have destroyed it ", he was told.   For a moment he was indignant with Father Villani : " I never thought I could be so deceived by you, Don Andrew ", and then he overwhelmed himself with reproaches for his infirmity and his remissness.   " It was my duty to read it myself, but you know I find it difficult to read even a few lines."   To refuse to accept the *regolamento* now would mean suppression of the Redemptorists by the king ; to accept it would mean suppression by the pope, for the Holy See had already approved the original rule.   Alphonsus cast about in every direction to save a *débâcle*, but in vain ; he would consult the pope, but the Redemptorists in the Papal States had forestalled him, for they had at once denounced the new rule and put themselves under the protection of the Holy See.   Pius VI forbade them to accept the *regolamento*, and withdrew them from the jurisdiction of St Alphonsus ; he provisionally recognized those of the Papal States as the only true Redemptorists, and named Father Francis de Paula their superior general.   In 1781 the fathers of Naples accepted the *regolamento*, with a slight modification which the king had **agreed** ; but this was not acceptable at Rome and the provisional decree was made final.   Thus was St Alphonsus excluded from the order which he had founded.

He bore the humiliation, inflicted by the authority he so loved and respected, with the utmost patience, and without murmuring accepted the apparent end of all his hopes as the will of God.   But there was still one more bitter trial for him : during the years 1784–85 he went through a terrible " dark night of the soul ". He was assailed by temptations against every article of faith and against every virtue, prostrated by scruples and vain fears, and visited by diabolical illusions. For eighteen months this torment lasted, with intervals of light and relief, and was followed by a period when ecstasies were frequent, and prophecy and miracles took the place of interior trials.   The end came peacefully on the night of July 31– August 1, 1787, when he was within two months of his ninety-first birthday. Pius VI, the pope who had condemned him under a misapprehension, in 1796 decreed the introduction of the cause of Alphonsus Liguori, in 1816 he was beatified, in 1839 canonized, and in 1871 declared a doctor of the Church.   St Alphonsus predicted that the separated houses in the Papal States would prosper and spread the Redemptorist congregation, but that reunion would not come about till after his death.   These predictions were verified ; St Clement Hofbauer in 1785 first established the congregation beyond the Alps, and in 1793 the Neapolitan government recognized the original rule and the Redemptorists were again united. Today they are established as missioners throughout Europe and America, and in several other parts of the world.

The first considerable biography of St Alphonsus was that of his devoted friend and religious son Father Tannoia which appeared at Naples in three volumes (1798–1802).   It was long ago translated into English in the Oratorian series of lives of the saints.   For a very valuable criticism of Tannoia see Father Castle's book, vol. ii, pp. 904–905, a note strangely incorporated in the index of the work in the first edition.   The lives by Cardinal Villecourt (1864) and Cardinal Capecelatro (1892) do not offer much that is new, but the German life by Fr K. Dilgskron (1887) was to a considerable extent based on unpublished material and corrected many previous misconceptions.   The most exhaustive biography, however, is that compiled in French by Father Berthe (1900) ; but it was greatly improved, and in many points corrected, by Fr Harold Castle in his English translation, published in two bulky volumes in 1905. An abridged French edition of Berthe's book appeared in 1939, and an up-to-date biography by D. F. Miller and L. X. Aubin in Canada in 1940. Many minor publications exist, studying particular aspects of the life and work of St. Alphonsus. On the question of Probabilism and Aequiprobabilism reference ought to be made to the books *Vindiciae Alphonsianae* (1873) and *Vindiciae Ballerinianae* (1873) ; and on the spiritual teaching of Alphonsus see P. Pourrat, *La spiritualité chrétienne*, t. iv (1947), pp. 449–491. See also the exhaustive work in Spanish by R. Telleria, *San Alfonso M. de Ligorio* (2 vols., 1950–51).

ST STEPHEN I, POPE   (A.D. 257)

St Stephen was by birth a Roman, and was a priest at the time of his succession to Pope St Lucius I. Little is known of him personally, and that little is mostly gathered from the writings of those who disagreed with him. The outstanding event of his short pontificate was a controversy on the subject of baptism administered by heretics. St Cyprian and the African bishops declared that such baptism was null and void, and that one so baptized must be baptized anew upon becoming a Catholic ; and this view was supported by many bishops in Asia. St Stephen upheld the teaching that, other things being equal, baptism given by heretics is valid, and he was violently abused by Firmilian of Caesarea in Cappadocia in consequence ; the great St Cyprian himself may be said to have displayed undue warmth during this controversy, and the pope too appears to have been impatient of argument. " No innovation must be introduced ", he declared, " but let that be observed which tradition has handed down ", and he refused to receive the delegates of the African synod that supported St Cyprian. Stephen threatened the dissentients with excommunication, but, writes St Augustine, " having the pity of holy charity, he judged it better to abide in union. The peace of Christ triumphed in their hearts ", but the disagreement was not yet resolved.

The persecution of Valerian began in the year of Pope St Stephen's death, and a once popular *passio* has caused him to be venerated as a martyr. But the truth of his martyrdom is difficult to sustain, for the earliest relevant sources say nothing about it and the original Roman tradition seems to be that he died in peace.

Mgr Duchesne in his edition of the *Liber Pontificalis* (vol. i, p. 154), and in his *Histoire ancienne de l'Église* (vol. i, pp. 419–432) has called attention to the main points of interest. Our other authorities are Eusebius, *Eccl. Hist.*, bk vii, and the letters of St Cyprian, Firmilian and St Dionysius of Alexandria. A larger fragment of a letter of Dionysius to this pope was recovered from an Armenian source by F. C. Conybeare and printed in the *English Historical Review*, vol. xxv (1910), pp. 111–113. See also DTC., vol. v, cc. 970–973 ; CMH., pp. 412–413 ; and *Acta Sanctorum*, August, vol. i.

ST THEODOTA, MARTYR   (A.D. 304 ?)

St Theodota, named in the Roman Martyrology on this day, was a noble lady of Nicaea. According to the *acta*, which are of no value, she was sought in marriage by the prefect Leucatius, and when she refused to have anything to do with him he denounced her and her three children to Nicetius, proconsul in Bithynia, as Christians. It was at the time of the persecution of Diocletian, and when they were brought before Nicetius he asked Theodota if it were she who had taught her children the new-fangled impiety which they believed. She retorted that they had been taught nothing new, but rather the age-old law. " What ! " asked her questioner, " Did your ancestors know these doctrines ? " At this the eldest boy, Evodius, spoke up and said, " If our ancestors have been in error it is not because

God has hidden the truth from them. Rather they were blind, and wandered into untruth through their blindness. But we are going to follow our mother." " Your mother is going to sacrifice to the gods, whether she likes it or not ", replied Nicetius, and then, blaming Theodota for the offensive candour of her son's words, urged her to sacrifice that they might follow her example and be saved. But when he could in no way move either her or them, he ordered them all to be burned together. Which was done.

Although the so-called " acts ", both in the Greek and Latin recensions, are worthless, there is good reason to believe that the martyrdom of St Theodota at Nicaea with her three sons is an authentic fact. " The sons of Theodota " are mentioned in the Syriac " breviarium " at the beginning of the fifth century, and it is probable that September 2, the date there assigned them, is the true anniversary, though in the " Hieronymianum ", from which our Roman Martyrology derives, August 2 has been erroneously indicated.

See H. Delehaye, CMH., pp. 412–414, and again in *Analecta Bollandiana*, vol. lv (1937), pp. 201 *seq.*

"ST" THOMAS OF DOVER　　(A.D. 1295)

AMONG English holy men of the middle ages who have quite dropped out of memory is Thomas of Hales, a monk of the Benedictine priory of St Martin at Dover, a cell·of Christ Church, Canterbury. On August 2, 1295, a French raid descended on Dover from the sea, and the monks of the priory fled with the exception of this venerable old man, who in accordance with the Rule went to take his mid-day siesta. When the raiders invaded the monastery they found him on his bed and told him to disclose where the church plate and other valuables had been hidden ; he refused, and was at once put to death. Miracles were recorded at his tomb and Simon Simeon, an Irish friar who made a pilgrimage to the Holy Land about 1322, mentions the honour given to him as a martyr " at the Black Monks, under Dover Castle ". King Richard II asked Pope Urban VI to canonize Thomas, and a process was begun in 1382 but never carried out. There was considerable popular *cultus* of Thomas locally, and he was represented among the paintings of martyrs in the English College of Rome ; but to call him Saint is an almost entirely modern practice.

There is a life and *passio* (BHL. 8248 b), and a summary of it and of some miracles (BHL. 8249) ; texts in C. Horstman, *Nova Legenda Anglie* (1901), vol. ii, pp. 555–558 and 403 ; translations in C. R. Haines, *Dover Priory* (1930), on which book see the following article, p. 168, n. 4 and p. 191, n. 2. In *Analecta Bollandiana*, vol. lxxii (1954), pp. 167–191, Fr P. Grosjean provides a fully documented discussion of all that is known of Thomas de la Hale.

3 : THE FINDING OF ST STEPHEN　　(A.D. 415)

THIS second festival in honour of the protomartyr St Stephen was instituted by the Church to commemorate the discovery by the priest Lucian of his relics, together with those of Gamaliel, Nicodemus and Abibo, at Kafr Gamala in Palestine in December 415. According to the narrative attributed to Lucian, this discovery was made in consequence of dreams or visions vouchsafed to himself and to the monk Migetius. Alban Butler narrates the occurrence in some detail, which is not reproduced here ; for it adds nothing to our knowledge of St Stephen, and moreover scholars increasingly incline to the view that there was no supernatural revelation made to Lucian or Migetius : Father Delehaye and others suggest that the discovery was accidental, but that a few years afterwards the incident was " dramatized " by Lucian in accord with the hagiographical precedents of that age.

The wide distribution of relics of the martyr that followed the finding at Kafr Gamala had a great influence, directly and indirectly, on the spread of the cult of St Stephen. God was pleased to glorify His name by miracles wrought through their means and the intercession of His first martyr. Many of them were described by Evodius, Bishop of Uzalum in Africa, and by St Augustine, who said of them to his flock, " Let us so desire to obtain temporal blessings by his intercession, that we may by imitating him deserve those which are eternal ". Our corporal necessities were not the motive which drew our divine Physician down from Heaven ; but in His mortal life He restored many sick to health and delivered demoniacs, to relieve distress, to give men sensible proof of His divine power, and as a sign that He came to relieve spiritual disease.

In a Motu Proprio of John XXIII dated July 25, 1960, this feast was dropped from the Roman Calendar.

The most trustworthy text of Lucian's narrative is the Latin translation by Avitus, which is printed, for example, in the works of St Augustine (see Migne, PL., vol. xli, cc. 805–816), but there are also versions in Greek, Syriac, Armenian and Old Slavonic. The story of the discovery of the relics as narrated by Lucian, and its bearing upon certain traditional sites in Jerusalem, led in the years 1900–1908 to a good deal of lively controversy. For this see especially the *Revue de l'Orient chrétien*, t. xxx, and the article of Fr Peeters in the *Analecta Bollandiana*, vol. xxvii (1908), pp. 359–368. See also F. M. Abel, *La légende apocryphe de S. Etienne* (1931), and H. Delehaye, *Origines du culte des martyrs* (1933), pp. 80–82. Upon the miracles at Uzalum, etc., see the same writer in the *Analecta Bollandiana*, vol. xliii (1925), pp. 74–85, and upon the fact that the "inventio b. Stephani" is commemorated on August 3, see the *Analecta Bollandiana*, vol. xlix (1931), pp. 22–30. A very full article on the "inventio", with copious references, has been contributed by H. Leclercq to DAC., vol. v, cc. 624–671. Pope Benedict XIV's commission proposed to suppress this feast.

ST GERMANUS, Bishop of Auxerre   (A.D. 448)

It is very fitting that the feast of St Germanus (Germain) of Auxerre should be observed in Wales and in several southern English dioceses for, while there is no saint who can be venerated as the apostle of Britain, to him belongs the honour of strengthening and consolidating the British church after the country was abandoned by the Roman empire, of purging it from error, and of converting yet more of the people ; and by his influence on St Patrick no doubt Germanus left his mark on Ireland also. But there was nothing in his youth and early manhood to suggest the future that was before him.

He was born at Auxerre of Christian parents, and attended the Gallic schools ; then he went to Rome, read law and studied eloquence there, and practised at the bar, as we should say, with success. He married—his wife was named Eustochia —and was sent back to Gaul as *dux* of the Armorican border provinces. Germanus was a capable governor, and on the death of St Amator in 418 he was chosen, much against his will, to succeed him as bishop of Auxerre. This sudden change of state imbued him with a deep sense of the obligations of his new dignity (*cf*. St Amator on May 1). He renounced all worldliness, and embraced a life of poverty and austerity. He extended his hospitality to all sorts of persons, washed the feet of the poor and served them with his own hands, while he himself fasted. He built a monastery near Auxerre, on the other side of the river Yonne, in honour of SS. Cosmas and Damian, and endowed the cathedral and other churches of Auxerre, which he found very poor.

At this time the British church was troubled by the heresy of Pelagius. This man was himself a Briton, and he, teaching in Rome, rejected the doctrine of original sin and denied that grace is necessary for salvation. One of his disciples, Agricola, had propagated this false teaching in Britain, and the bishops of Gaul were asked to deal with the trouble. Pope St Celestine and the Gallic bishops nominated St Germanus to go thither in the year 429, and appointed St Lupus, Bishop of Troyes, to accompany him on this mission.

The bishops arrived in Britain after a rough passage, and the fame of their sanctity, doctrine and miracles soon spread abroad. They confirmed the orthodox and converted heretics, preaching wherever the people would listen. A public disputation was held at some unnamed place, where the heretics were allowed to speak first. When they had talked a long time, the bishops answered them with great eloquence, and so supported their arguments with quotations from the Bible and the fathers that their adversaries were reduced to silence. The saints went from this conference to return thanks to God at the tomb of St Alban, and to ask for a smooth passage home. St Germanus caused his sepulchre to be opened, and put therein his box of relics (with which he had just cured a little blind girl), taking out a little of the dust of St Alban. This he carried away with him, and at his return built at Auxerre a church in his honour.

St Germanus found his people burdened with excessive taxes and went to Arles to appeal to Auxiliaris, prefect of Gaul, on their behalf. On the road the people everywhere met him in crowds to receive his blessing. In consequence of the bishop's healing of his sick wife, Auxiliaris granted Germanus the discharge from the taxes which he had asked for his people. About 440 he was called again into Britain to assist that church against Pelagianism, which was again gaining ground. He sought out those who had been seduced by the heretics, and converted many of them ; so that by his teaching and miracles Pelagianism was finally eradicated and its teachers banished. But Germanus knew that ignorance could not be banished, nor the reformation which he had established maintain its ground, without schools for the instruction of the clergy, and is said himself to have founded such institutions, by which means, " These churches continued afterward pure in the faith, and free from heresy ", as Bede observes. And, but for the slight and passing success of Wiclif, free from heresy the Church in these islands remained for a space of eleven hundred years, until the errors of Protestantism took root and were watered by royal corruption in the sixteenth century.

In the proper Mass of St Germanus formerly used in the diocese of Paris, the offertory verse was taken from the Apocalypse xix 1, 3 : " I heard as it were the voice of much people in Heaven, saying, Alleluia. And again they said, Alleluia." This had reference to an incident recorded by Germanus's biographer Constantius. During his first visit to Britain, a plundering expedition of Picts and Saxons descended on the country, and the Britons, having assembled an army, invited the bishop into their camp, hoping to be protected by his prayers and presence. The saint agreed, and employed his time in bringing idolaters to the faith, and the Christians to penance. Many of the former demanded baptism, and they were prepared to receive it at Easter, for it was then Lent. They made a church in the camp, of green boughs twisted together, in which the catechumens received the sacrament of regeneration, and the whole army celebrated the festival with great devotion. After Easter, St Germanus had recourse to a stratagem by which, without bloodshed, he rescued his friends from the danger with which they were threatened. He led the little army into a vale between two high mountains and, when warned of the enemy's approach, ordered his troops to send forth the same shout for which he would give them a sign. When the Saxons came near, he cried out thrice, *Alleluia !* which was repeated by the whole British force, and the sound was carried on by the echo from the hills with an awe-inspiring noise. The barbarians, judging from the shout that they were falling upon the swords of a mighty army, flung down their arms and ran away. According to tradition this " battle " took place near Mold, in Flintshire, where is a meadow called Maes Garmon, though the association is very dubious indeed : other suggested localizations are near the south-east coast (Dr Hugh Williams) and the Chiltern escarpment (R. H. Hodgkin).

To quell a revolt in Armorica, the Roman general Aetius sent a force of barbarians under their chief Goar, and Germanus, fearing for the people in the hands of such savages, went out to meet Goar, stopping his horse by the bridle, at the head of his army. He at first refused to hear the bishop, but Germanus was firm, and Goar agreed not to ravish the province until the matter had been referred to Aetius, who in turn said that Germanus must get the imperial pardon for the people. He therefore undertook a journey to Ravenna. His fame went before him and it was like a triumphal progress, so that he entered the city by night to avoid a public reception. He was received with joy by the bishop, St Peter Chrysologus, by the young Emperor Valentinian III, and by his mother, Galla Placidia ; but unhappily for the cause which had brought Germanus there, news came of a further revolt among the Armoricans. The last great act of charity of his life was done, for while still at Ravenna, God took him, on July 31, 448. The transport of his body to Auxerre was one of the most magnificent funerals of which there is record, and his shrine in the great abbey church of his name at Auxerre was a famous place of pilgrimage. Saint Germans in Cornwall takes its name from this saint, who in a ninth- or tenth-century sacramentary is referred to as " a preacher of the truth and the light and pillar of Cornwall ". A medieval legend associates the foundation of the great abbey of Selby with a vision of St Germanus to the monk Benedict, with many marvels added.

The critical edition published by W. Levison in 1920 of Constantius's *Vita S. Germani* renders the older texts, such as that in the *Acta Sanctorum*, July, vol. vii, to some extent out of date. Like so many of the other biographies edited in MGH., *Scriptores Merov.* (vol. vii, pp. 225–283), the older text is now shown to have been considerably interpolated. Still the substance remains, and it cannot be disputed that Constantius wrote within thirty years of the death of the saint. See also Levison's " Bischof Germanus von Auxerre " in *Neues Archiv*, vol. xxix (1904) ; and, for a good popular work, L. Prunel's book in the series " Les Saints " (1929). The meeting of the Association Bourguignonne des Sociétés Savantes held at Auxerre in 1948 produced a volume of studies, *St Germain d'Auxerre et son temps*, of great value. Baring-Gould and Fisher's hypothesis (LBS., vol. iii, pp. 60–79) of a separate St Germanus, " of Man ", giving his name to Saint Germains on that island and other British churches, cannot be accepted without many reserves : see *Analecta Bollandiana*, vol. xxiii (1904), p. 356, and J. Loth in the *Annales de Bretagne*, vol. xx (1905), p. 351. The *vita* by Constantius is translated in F. R. Hoare, *The Western Fathers* (1954). The feast of St Germanus is kept on August 3 in Wales and on other dates in Westminster, Plymouth and Portsmouth ; his day in the Roman Martyrology is July 31.

ST WALTHEOF OR WALTHEN, ABBOT OF MELROSE   (*c.* A.D. 1160)

WALTHEOF was second son of Simon, Earl of Huntingdon, and Matilda or Maud, daughter to Judith, the niece of William the Conqueror. His elder brother was called Simon, and in their childhood it was the pastime of this Simon to build castles and play at soldiers, but Waltheof's to build churches and monasteries of stones and wood. When grown up, the elder inherited his father's martial disposition together with his title; but Waltheof had a strong inclination for the religious life and was mild and peace-loving. Their mother Maud, after the death of her first husband, was given in marriage by King Henry I to St David I, King of Scotland, and Waltheof followed his mother to that court, where he formed an intimate friendship with St Aelred, who was master of the royal household at that time. When he went out hunting with the king Waltheof used to hide himself in some thicket and there employ the day in meditation or reading. The king, having one day surprised him at this, told the queen that her son was not a man of this world, for he could find no satisfaction in its diversions. Only once did it look as if his vocation might be lost; he had attracted the attention of one of the ladies of the court and accepted from her a ring, which he wore on his finger. Such gages commonly have more serious developments, but when a courtier, noticing the ring, said, " Ha ! At last Waltheof begins to take some notice of women ", he pulled himself together, snatched off the ring, and threw it into the fire.

Soon after he decided to avoid the life of a court cleric and become a religious. He left Scotland, and made his profession among the regular canons of St Augustine in their monastery at Nostell, near Pontefract in Yorkshire. He was soon after chosen prior of Kirkham, in the same county, and, realizing the obligations he now lay under for the sanctification of others as well as for his own, he redoubled his austerity and regularity of observance. In celebrating Mass one Christmas day, after the consecration of the bread he was favoured with a wonderful vision. The divine Word, who on that day had made Himself visible to mankind by His birth, seemed pleased to manifest Himself not only to the eyes of faith but also to the bodily eyes of His servant. Waltheof saw in his hands, not the form of bread, but the radiant form of the child Jesus. When he had laid the Host on the altar he saw only the sacramental form.

Waltheof, impressed by the life and vigour of the Cistercian monks, became anxious to join them; naturally he was encouraged by the advice of his friend St Aelred, then abbot of Rievaulx, and accordingly he took the habit at Wardon in Bedfordshire. Waltheof found Cistercian life excessively severe, and judged it to be therefore less suitable for the salvation of souls than Augustinian discretion. Nevertheless, only four years after profession, he was chosen abbot of Melrose, recently founded on the banks of the Tweed by King David. Whenever he fell into the smallest failing by inadvertence Waltheof immediately had recourse to confession, a practice of perfection which the confessors found rather trying, as one of them admitted to Jordan, the saint's biographer. Yet cheerfulness and spiritual joy always shone in his face, and his words were animated with a fire which penetrated the hearts of those that heard him. His alms supported the poor of all the country round his abbey, and he is said to have twice multiplied bread miraculously. He once went to King Stephen in England, about affairs of his community, carrying a bundle on his back. His brother Simon, who was present, was very annoyed and said to the king, " See how this brother of mine, and cousin of yours, disgraces his family." "Not so," said the king. "If we understand what the grace of God is, he does honour to us and all his kindred."

In 1154 Waltheof was chosen archbishop of Saint Andrews ; but he prevailed on St Aelred to oppose the election and not to oblige him to accept it. Once when giving a conference to his community he had occasion to refer to a vision of the glory of Heaven which had been vouchsafed to him, but he spoke in the third person as of another ; but at last by inadvertence he spoke in the first person : he no sooner realized it than, cutting his discourse short, he withdrew in tears, much afflicted for the word which had escaped him. St Waltheof died at a great age on August 3, about 1160.

Under the Latin form " Walthenus ", a long life, attributed to Joscelin, or Jordan, a monk of Furness (*c.* 1210), is printed in the *Acta Sanctorum*, August, vol. i. Though prolix, the narrative may be considered fairly reliable. See also T. D. Hardy, *Descriptive Catalogue of MSS.* (Rolls Series), vol. ii, p. 285.

BD AUGUSTINE, Bishop of Lucera   (A.D. 1323)

Augustine Gazotich was born at Trogir in Dalmatia about the year 1260 and before he was twenty received the habit of the Friars Preachers. After profession he was sent to Paris, to study at the university, and on his way thither nearly came to an untimely end : while passing through the district of Pavia with a fellow Dominican, Brother James, they were set on by footpads ; James was killed and Brother Augustine recovered only after some weeks' nursing in a near-by country-house. He preached fruitfully in his own country and established several new houses of his order, to which he gave as their motto the words of his patron, St Augustine of Hippo : " Since I began to serve God, as I have hardly ever seen better men than those who live a holy life in monasteries, so I have never seen worse than those in monasteries who live not as they should." After missions in Italy and Bosnia, missions wherein he confirmed his reputation for great charity and prudence, Bd Augustine was sent to Hungary, where the people had been reduced to a bad state of misery and irreligion by continual civil wars. Here he met Cardinal Nicholas Boccasini, the papal legate, who was to become Bd Benedict XI, and attracted his favourable notice, and when Cardinal Boccasini became pope in 1303 he sent for Bd Augustine and consecrated him bishop of Zagreb in Croatia.

His clergy, and in consequence the whole diocese, was badly in need of reform, and he held disciplinary synods whose canons he enforced and supported in frequent visitations, and he encouraged learning and the study of the Bible by establishing a Dominican priory in his cathedral city. He was present at the general council at Vienne in 1311–12 ; and on his return he suffered persecution at the hands of Miladin, governor of Dalmatia, against whose tyranny and exactions he had protested. Bd Augustine had in a marked degree the gift of healing (he had cured of rheumatism the hands that gave him episcopal anointing) and there is a pleasant story told of how he rebuked those who flocked to him for this reason : he planted a lime tree, and suggested that its leaves would be more efficacious than his hands. God and the people took him at his word, and even the invading Turks respected the wonder-working tree.

After ruling the diocese of Zagreb for fourteen years Bd Augustine was translated to the see of Lucera in the province of Benevento. Here his great task was to eradicate the religious and moral corruption which the Saracens had left behind them ; the remainder of the Moslems had been more or less converted in a body in 1300. King Robert of Naples gave him the fullest support and endowed a monastery of Dominicans who zealously assisted their bishop, and within five years the face of the country was changed. Bd Augustine was venerated by all, from the royal family downwards, and when he died on August 3, 1323, a *cultus* began which was formally confirmed in 1702.

The principal source seems to be a Latin life written as late as the seventeenth century by Thomas Marnavich, Bishop of Bosnia ; in this the family name figures as Gozottus. It is printed in the *Acta Sanctorum*, August, vol. i. See also Taurisano, *Catalogus Hagiographicus O.P.*, pp. 27–28, in which *inter alia* a reference is given to Mortier, *Maîtres Généraux O.P.*, vol. iv, pp. 461–467 : the pages in question, however, have nothing to do with this Bd Augustine, but with another Augustine of Zagreb, who lived a century later.

ST PETER JULIAN EYMARD, Founder of the Priests of the Blessed Sacrament   (A.D. 1868)

St Peter Julian was born in 1811 at La Mure d'Isère, a small town in the diocese of Grenoble. His father was a cutler, and Peter Julian worked at his father's trade, and in an oil-press, until he was eighteen ; in his spare hours he studied Latin and had some instruction from a priest at Grenoble for whom he worked for a time, and in 1831 he went to the seminary of Grenoble. He was ordained there in 1834 and for the five following years ministered in the parishes of Chatte and Monteynard. What they thought of him there was expressed in the words of his bishop, Mgr de Bruillard, when the Abbé Eymard asked for permission to join the Marists : " I show my esteem for that congregation by allowing such a priest as yourself to enter it." After his novitiate he was made spiritual director of the junior seminary at Belley, and in 1845 provincial of his congregation at Lyons. Always the Blessed Sacrament had been the centre round which his life revolved, " without It I should have been lost ", and on a certain Corpus Christi Sunday, while carrying the Host in procession, he had an overwhelming experience : " My soul was flooded with faith and love for Jesus in the Blessed Sacrament. Those two hours seemed but a moment. I laid at the feet of our Lord the Church in France and throughout the world, everybody, myself. My eyes were filled with tears : it was as though my heart were under the wine-press. I longed at that moment for all hearts to have been within my own and to have been fired with the zeal of St Paul."

In 1851 Father Eymard made a pilgrimage to Notre-Dame de Fourvières : " One idea haunted me, and it was this : that Jesus in the Blessed Sacrament had no religious institute to glorify His mystery of love, whose only object was entire consecration to Its service. There ought to be one. . . . I promised Mary to devote myself to this end. It was still all very vague, and I had no idea of leaving the society. . . . What hours I spent there ! " His superiors advised him to defer his plans till they were more mature, and he spent four years at La Seyne. During this time he received encouragement from Pope Pius IX and from the Ven. John Colin, founder of the Marists, and he determined to sacrifice his vocation with the Society of Mary and to devote himself to a new society. In 1856, with the approval of the Marist superior general, he submitted his scheme for an institute of priest-adorers of the Blessed Sacrament to Mgr de Sibour, Archbishop of Paris, and at the end of twelve anxious days it was approved. Mgr de Sibour put a house at his disposal, wherein Father Eymard took up his residence with one companion, and on January 6, 1857, the Blessed Sacrament was exposed in its chapel for the first time, and Father Eymard preached to a large assembly.

The first members of the Congregation of Priests of the Most Blessed Sacrament were Father de Cuers and Father Champion, and they began with exposition three times a week. Vocations were slow : many were called but few chosen ; and the difficulties were great. They had to leave their first house, and in 1858 they obtained a small chapel in the Faubourg Saint-Jacques, where during nine years the grace of God was poured out so abundantly that Father Eymard called it the " chapel of miracles ". In the following year Pope Pius IX gave the congregation a laudatory brief and a second house was opened, at Marseilles, and in 1862 a third, at Angers. By this time there were enough members to establish a regular novitiate, and the congregation rapidly expanded. The priests recite the Divine Office in choir and perform all other duties of the clergy, subordinate to their chief business of maintaining perpetual adoration of the Blessed Sacrament exposed, in which they are assisted by lay-brothers. In 1858 Father Eymard established the Servants of the Blessed Sacrament, sisters who are also engaged in perpetual adoration and spreading the love of our Lord ; and he founded the Priests' Eucharistic League, whose members pledge themselves to spend so far as possible about an hour a day in prayer before the Tabernacle. But Father Eymard did not confine his labours to the clergy and religious : in his Work for Poor Adults he put before his congregation the necessity for preparing for first communion all adults who are no longer of an age to attend the parish catechism classes, or who are unable to go to these classes, and he also organized the Archconfraternity of the Blessed Sacrament, whose value is so highly regarded by the Church that by canon law a branch should be erected in every parish ; he also wrote a number of books on the Eucharist which have been translated into several languages.

Of the difficulties which beset St Peter Julian in making his new foundation one of the most trying was the adverse criticism he was subjected to at its very inception, because he had left the Society of Mary, and detractors of the work were not wanting when it was started. He excused them : " They do not understand it, and each one who thinks to oppose it does it a service. For I know well it must be persecuted. Was not our Lord persecuted throughout His life ? " There were other grave difficulties and disappointments, but in spite of all the congregation was approved by the Holy See, as has been said, in his lifetime, and was finally confirmed *in perpetuum* in 1895. He had an engaging spirit of *pietas :* whenever he visited his home at La Mure he regularly made three " stations " : at the font at which he was baptized, at the altar where he received his first communion, and at the tomb of his parents ; and again, in 1867, " For how long have I wanted to see again the dear country of Chatte and Saint-Romans ", scenes of his earliest ministry. Father Eymard had been looked on as a saint even in those days, and throughout his life the impression of his holiness was recognized more and more, in his daily life and virtues, in his works, and in his supernatural gifts : several times he knew the thoughts of persons absent, he read souls, and more than once had prophetic prevision. St John-Baptist Vianney, who knew Eymard personally, said of him, " He is a *saint*. The world hinders his work, but not knowingly, and it will do great things for the glory of God. Adoration *by priests !* How fine ! . . . Tell the good Father Eymard I will pray for the work every day."

During the last four years of his life St Peter Julian suffered from rheumatic gout and insomnia, and his sufferings were added to by saddening difficulties. For

once he allowed his discouragement to be seen. " He opened his heart to us ",
wrote Father Mayet in 1868. " ' This time ', he said, ' I am crushed under the
cross, beaten down, annihilated.' His heart felt the need of seeking relief from a
friend, because, as he explained, ' I am obliged to bear my cross alone, so as not to
frighten or discourage my *confrères* '." The presentiment of approaching death
was strong. " I shall return sooner than you think ", was his reply when his sister
urged him to visit La Mure more often. This was in February, and he began to
go round visiting his penitents and others who looked to him, speaking to them as
one who spoke for the last time. In July he broke down and his doctor ordered
him to leave Paris at once. On the 21st he left Grenoble by coach for La Mure ;
it was very hot and he arrived in a state of collapse and partial paralysis. On
August 1 he died. Miracles took place at his tomb before the end of that year,
and in 1925 Peter Julian Eymard was beatified, and canonized in 1962 during
the Second Vatican Council.

There is a short sketch by Lady Herbert, *The Priest of the Eucharist* (1898) ; an excellent
life by J. M. Lambert in the series " Les Saints " (1925) ; a full biography in French by
F. Trochu (1949), and one in Italian by P. Fossati (1925). See also A. Bettinger, *Pierre-
Julien Eymard et sa méthode d'Adoration* (1927).

4 : ST DOMINIC, Founder of the Order of Preachers (A.D. 1221)

ST DOMINIC was born soon after 1170 at Calaruega, then Calaroga, in
Castile. Practically nothing is known with certainty of his father Felix,
though he is said to have been of the Guzmán family ; his wife was Bd Joan
of Aza, and the few particulars recorded of Dominic's birth and childhood are
mentioned in these pages under the 8th day of this month, which is her feast-day.
When he was fourteen years old he left the care of his uncle, who was the archpriest
of Gumiel d'Izan, and was entered at the school of Palencia. While still a student
he was made a canon of the cathedral of Osma, and after his ordination he took up
his duties there. The chapter lived a community life under the Rule of St Augustine, and their regularity of observance was such as to provide an admirable school
for the young priest. His life there was, so far as is known, undistinguished by
outward event, a gathering of strength and exercising of virtues for the labours that
were to come ; he seldom left the canons' house and spent much time in church,
" weeping for the sins of others, and reading and putting into practice the *Conferences* of Cassian ". When Diego d'Azevedo became bishop of Osma about 1201
he succeeded him as prior of the chapter. He was then thirty-one years old, and
had been leading this contemplative life for six or seven years ; it at last came to
an end, and Dominic began his work in the world in unexpected fashion in 1204.

In that year Alfonso IX, King of Castile, chose the bishop of Osma to go as
ambassador to Denmark to negotiate a marriage for his son. The bishop took
Dominic with him. On their way they passed through Languedoc, which was
then filled with the heresy of the Albigenses. He in whose house they lodged at
Toulouse professed it, and St Dominic, pierced to the heart with compassion for
the man, spent the whole night in discussion with him, and with such effect that
with the light of morning came the light of faith, and the man abjured his errors.
It is generally supposed that from this moment Dominic knew what work God
required of him. Their embassy fulfilled, Bishop Diego and Dominic went to
Rome to ask of Pope Innocent III leave to go to preach the gospel to the Cumans

in Russia.   The pope at once appreciated their zeal and virtue, but apparently
exhorted them rather to choose the neighbouring harvest and to oppose a heresy
which threatened the Church at home.   On their return they made a visit to
Cîteaux, whose monks were the officially appointed organizers and preachers against
the Albigenses, and at Montpellier they met the Abbot of Cîteaux, together with
two monks, Peter of Castelnau and Raoul of Fontefroide, who had been in charge
of the missions in Languedoc ; and Diego and Dominic confirmed their observa-
tions of why all these efforts against the heresy were fruitless.

The Albigensian system was based on the dualism of two opposing principles,
good and evil, and all matter was regarded as in itself evil ; therefore the reality of
the Incarnation was denied and all the sacraments rejected : human perfection,
so far as it was attainable, required complete abstinence from procreation and the
minimum of eating and drinking ; suicide was, indeed, a praiseworthy act.   The
rank and file of the Albigensians did not attempt any such austerity of life, but the
inner circle of the " Perfect " maintained an heroic standard of purity and asceticism, against which the rather easy-going observance of the Cistercian monks looked
mediocre.   In the circumstances a reasonable use of material things was the wrong
weapon for Christian orthodoxy to use : the good common people followed those
who were obviously leading an heroic life for Christ's sake—and these were not the
Cistercian preachers.   When they saw this, St Dominic and the Bishop of Osma
invited these preachers to follow more closely the example of their opponents : to
give up travelling with horses and retinues and staying at the best inns, with servants
to wait on them.   Then, when they had shown themselves worthy of being listened
to, to use persuasion and peaceful discussion, rather than threats and overbearing-
ness.   The task was the more difficult and dangerous in that Albigensianism was a
different religion rather than an heresy from Christianity, and in its more fanatical
forms threatened human society.   Dominic maintained that its spreading torrent
could be stemmed, and God was pleased to make his preaching the instrument of
His grace to open the ears and to soften the hearts of many.   And the example he
urged others to give he was the first to give himself.

A series of conferences was held with the heretics ; they influenced some of the
rank and file, but had little effect on the leaders.   Soon Bishop Diego returned to
Osma, leaving his companion in France.   But before he went St Dominic had
already taken that step which was the first in the definite foundation of his order, by
which the tide of Albigensianism began to be stayed.   He was greatly concerned
by the activities of women in the propagation of Albigensianism, and also by the
fact that many girls were, on the one hand, exposed to evil influences in their homes
and, on the other, were sent to Albigensian convents to be educated.   On the feast
of St Mary Magdalen in 1206 he had a sign from Heaven, and in consequence of it
within six months he had founded at Prouille, near Fanjeaux, a monastery to shelter
nine nuns, all of whom were converts from the heresy.   Near by was a house for
his helpers, and thus St Dominic began to provide for a supply of trained and
virtuous preachers, for a shelter for converted women, for the education of girls,
and for a permanent house of prayer.

The murder of the pope's legate, Peter of Castelnau, who was assassinated by a
servant of the count of Toulouse, and other outrages, let loose a " crusade ", with
all the attendant horrors and savagery of civil war.   The Albigensians were led
by Raymund VI, Count of Toulouse, the Catholics by Simon IV de Montfort,
de iure Earl of Leicester.   Dominic himself had no illusions as to the efficacy or

propriety of inducing Christian orthodoxy by military activity nor, as is sometimes alleged, had he anything to do with the establishment of inquisitions in concert with the civil power, which was done in the Midi from the end of the twelfth century.* He never appears to have in any way concurred in the execution of any of those unhappy persons that then suffered. The original historians mention no other arms to have been used by him against heretics than those of instruction, patience, penance, fasting, tears and prayer; and he rebuked his ex-troubadour supporter, Fulk, Bishop of Toulouse, when he went on a visitation accompanied by soldiers, servants and sumter-mules, with the words, " The enemies of the faith cannot be overcome like that. Arm yourself with prayer, rather than a sword; wear humility rather than fine clothes." Three times efforts were made to raise him to the episcopate; each time he refused firmly. He was called to another work.

St Dominic had now spent nearly ten years preaching in Languedoc, and as leader, though with no canonical status, of a small band of special preachers. All this time he had worn the habit of a regular canon of St Augustine, and followed that rule. But he earnestly desired to revive an apostolic spirit in the ministers of the altar, the want of which in many was a subject of great scandal to the people, and a great source of the overflowing of vice and heresy. With this view he projected a body of religious men not like the monks who were contemplatives and not necessarily priests, but who to contemplation should join a close application to sacred studies and all the functions of a pastoral life, especially that of preaching. The principal aim of the saint was to multiply in the Church zealous preachers, whose spirit and example might be a means more easily to spread the light of faith and the fire of divine charity, and to assist the pastors in healing the wounds which the Church had received from false doctrine and ill-living. In order that he might have means at his disposal Fulk of Toulouse in 1214 gave him an endowment and extended his episcopal approval to the embryonic order in the following year. A few months later Dominic accompanied Fulk to the Fourth Lateran Council.

Pope Innocent III received the saint with great kindness and gave his approbation of the nunnery of Prouille. Moreover, he drew up a decree, which he inserted as the tenth canon of the council, to enforce the obligation of preaching, and the necessity of choosing for pastors men who are powerful in words and works, who will instruct and edify their flocks both by example and preaching, and ordering that fit men be selected specially for this office of preaching. But to get approval for Dominic's project was no easy matter, especially as that very council had legislated against the multiplication of new religious orders. It is said that Innocent had decided to refuse but that, the night following, he dreamed he saw the Lateran church in danger of falling, and that St Dominic stepped in and supported it with his shoulders. Be that as it may, the pope at last gave a guarded approval by word of mouth, bidding the founder return to his brethren and select which of the already approved rules they would follow. They met at Prouille in August 1216, and after consultation with his sixteen colleagues, of whom eight were Frenchmen, seven

* The Dominican order later received charge of the Inquisition with unwillingness. In 1243 they asked to be relieved of the commission, but Pope Innocent IV refused the petition. The provincial chapter of Cahors in the next year forbade the acceptance of any monies accruing from its work. The fifth master general, Bd Humbert of Romans, instructed the friars to avoid its duties whenever possible. Only two of the inquisitors general of Spain were Dominicans : the notorious and somewhat maligned Torquemada was one of them.

Spaniards, and one Englishman (Brother Laurence), he made choice of the Rule of St Augustine, the oldest and least detailed of the existing rules, written for priests by a priest, who was himself an eminent preacher. St Dominic added certain particular constitutions, some borrowed from the Order of Prémontré. Pope Innocent III died on July 18, 1216, and Honorius III was chosen in his place. This change retarded St Dominic's second journey to Rome ; and in the meantime he finished his first friary, at Toulouse, to which the bishop gave the church of St Romain, wherein the first community of Dominicans assembled and began common life under vows.

St Dominic arrived at Rome again in October 1216, and Honorius III confirmed his order and its constitutions the same year : " Considering that the religious of your order will be champions of the faith and a true light of the world, we confirm your order." St Dominic remained in Rome till after Easter, preaching with great effect. It was during this time that he formed his friendships with Cardinal Ugolino, afterwards Pope Gregory IX, and St Francis of Assisi. The story goes that Dominic saw in a vision the sinful world threatened by the divine anger but saved by the intercession of our Lady, who pointed out to her Son two figures, in one of whom St Dominic recognized himself, but the other was a stranger. Next day while at prayer in a church he saw a ragged beggar come in, and recognized him at once as the man of his dream ; going up to him therefore, he embraced him and said, " You are my companion and must walk with me. For if we hold together no earthly power can withstand us." This meeting of the two founders of the friars is commemorated twice a year, when on their respective feast-days the brethren of the two orders sing Mass in each other's churches, and afterwards sit at the same table " to eat that bread which for seven centuries has never been wanting ". The character of St Dominic is sometimes assumed to suffer by comparison with St Francis. The comparison is a meaningless one, for actually the two men complete and are complementary to one another, the one corrects and fills out the other : they meet on the common ground of the Christian faith, tenderness and love.

On August 13, 1217, the Friars Preachers met under their leader at Prouille. He instructed them on their method of preaching and teaching and exhorted them to unremitting study, but in particular reminded them that their first business was their own sanctification, that they were to be the successors of the Apostles in establishing the kingdom of Christ. He added instructions on humility, distrust of themselves and an entire confidence in God alone, by which they were to stand invincible under afflictions and persecutions, and courageously to carry on the war against the world and the powers of Hell. Then, on the feast of the Assumption, to the surprise of all, for heresy was again gaining ground in all the neighbourhood, St Dominic broke up his band of friars and dispersed them in all directions. "Leave it to me ", he said, " I know what I'm about. We must sow the seed, not hoard it." Four were sent to Spain, seven to Paris, two returned to Toulouse, two remained at Prouille, and the founder himself in the following December went back to Rome. He wished that he might now resign his part in the nascent order and go into the East to evangelize the Cuman Tartars ; but this was not to be.

On his arrival in Rome the pope gave him the church of St Sixtus (San Sisto Vecchio), and while making a foundation there the saint lectured on theology, and preached in St Peter's with such eloquence as to draw the attention of the whole city. At this time a large number of nuns lived in Rome without keeping enclosure, and almost without regularity, some dispersed in small monasteries, others in the houses of their parents or friends. Pope Innocent III had made several attempts to assemble all such nuns into one enclosed house, but had not been able, with all his authority, to compass it. Honorius III committed the management of this reformation to St Dominic, who successfully carried it out. He gave the nuns his own monastery of St Sixtus, which was built and then ready to receive them, and which Innocent III had formerly offered them ;* and he received for his friars a house of the Savelli, on the Aventine, with the church of St Sabina. It is related that when, on Ash Wednesday in 1218, the abbess and some of her nuns went to their new monastery of St Sixtus, and were in the chapter house with St Dominic and three cardinals, a messenger ran in to say that the young Napoleon, Cardinal Stephen's nephew, was thrown from his horse and killed. The saint ordered the body of Napoleon to be brought into the house, and bid Brother Tancred make an altar ready that he might offer Mass. When he had prepared himself, the cardinals with their attendants, the abbess with her nuns, the friars, and a great concourse of people went to the church. The Sacrifice being ended, Dominic, standing by the body, disposed the bruised limbs in their proper places, prayed, rose from his knees, and made the sign of the cross over the corpse ; then, lifting up his hands to Heaven, he cried out, " Napoleon, I say to you in the name of our Lord Jesus Christ, arise ". That instant, in the sight of all, the young man arose sound and whole.

A foundation having been successfully made by Friar Matthew of France at the University of Paris, St Dominic sent some brethren to the University of Bologna, where, under the guidance of Bd Reginald of Orleans, one of the most famous of Dominican establishments was set on foot. In 1218–19 the founder journeyed in Spain, France and Italy, establishing friaries in each country, and arrived at Bologna about the end of summer 1219, which city he made his ordinary residence to the end of his life. In 1220 Pope Honorius III confirmed Dominic's title and office as master general, and at Pentecost was held the first general chapter of the order, at Bologna, at which were drawn up the final constitutions which made the organization of the Friars Preachers " the most perfect of all the monastic organizations produced by the middle ages " (Hauck) ; a religious order in the modern sense of the term, wherein the order and not the house is the unit, and all members are subject to one superior general, its regulations bearing the unmistakable mark of the founder, notably in their adaptability and the rejection of property-holding.

Wherever the saint travelled, he preached ; and he never ceased to pray for the conversion of infidels and sinners. It was his earnest desire, if it had been God's will, to shed his blood for Christ, and to travel among the barbarous nations of the earth to announce to them the good news of eternal life. Therefore did he make the ministry of the word the chief end of his institute : he would have all his religious to be applied to it, every one according to his capacity, and those who had particular talents for it never to discontinue the office of preaching, except in intervals allotted to retirement that they might preach to themselves in silence. The vocation of his friars is " to hand on to others the fruits of contemplation ", and for this high work he prepares the religious by long habits of virtue, especially of prayer, humility, self-denial and obedience. It was a saying which St Dominic frequently repeated, " That a man who governs his passions is master of the world.

* Innocent wanted the English Gilbertines to do this work, but they had been unable to undertake it.

We must either rule them, or be ruled by them. It is better to be the hammer than the anvil." He taught his missionaries the art of preaching to the heart by animating them with charity. Being once asked after preaching in what book he had studied his sermon, " In no other ", said he, " than in that of love ". Learning, study of the Bible, and teaching were from the beginning of first importance in the order : some of its chief achievements have been in intellectual work and the founder has been called " the first minister of public instruction in modern Europe ". But an eminent spirit of prayer and recollection has at all times been the characteristic of the Dominicans, as it was of St Dominic, whose constant and most characteristic prayer was that he might have a true love of his neighbour and the ability to help others. He was inflexible in maintaining the discipline he had established. Coming to Bologna in 1220, he was so much offended to find the convent of his friars in that city being built in a stately manner, not consistent with his idea of the poverty which he professed by his rule, that he would not allow the work to be continued. This was the discipline and strength that was behind the rapid spread of his order ; by the second general chapter in 1221 it had some sixty friaries divided into eight provinces ; friars had already got to Poland, Scandinavia and Palestine, and Brother Gilbert with twelve others had established monasteries in Canterbury, London and Oxford. The Order of Preachers is still world-wide.

After the second general chapter Dominic visited Cardinal Ugolino at Venice. On his return he was ill, and he was taken to a country place for the better air. But he knew he was dying. To his brethren he spoke of the beauty of chastity, and, having no temporal goods, made his last testament in these words : " These, my much-loved ones, are the bequests which I leave to you as my sons : have charity among you ; hold to humility ; keep willing poverty." He spoke more at length on this subject of poverty, and then at his request was carried back to Bologna that he might be buried " under the feet of his brethren ". Gathered round him, they said the prayers for the dying ; at the *Subvenite* St Dominic repeated those great words, and died. It was the evening of August 6, 1221 ; he was about fifty-two years old ; and he died in that poverty of which he had so lately spoken : " in Brother Moneta's bed because he had none of his own ; in Brother Moneta's habit, because he had not another to replace the one he had long been wearing." It may be said of him after death what Bd Jordan of Saxony wrote of him in life : " Nothing disturbed the even temper of his soul except his quick sympathy with every sort of suffering. And as a man's face shows whether his heart is happy or not, it was easy to see from his friendly and joyous countenance that he was at peace inwardly. With his unfailing gentleness and readiness to help, no one could ever despise his radiant nature, which won all who met him and made him attract people from the first." When he signed the decree of canonization of his friend in 1234 Pope Gregory IX (Cardinal Ugolino) said that he no more doubted the sanctity of Dominic than he did that of St Peter or St Paul.

Beginning with the life written by Bd Jordan of Saxony, the successor of St Dominic in the generalship of the order, there is a good deal of biographical material of relatively early date. Without particularizing, it may be sufficient to say that the more important elements will be found in the *Acta Sanctorum*, August, vol. i ; in the *Scriptores O.P.* by Quétif and Echard ; and in the *Monumenta O.P. historica*, vols. xv and xvi. Perhaps, however, the most generally useful contribution to the study of the history of the saint is the work in three volumes which Frs Balme and Lelaidier published under the name of *Cartulaire de St Dominique* (1893–1901), consisting largely of extracts and documents with pictorial illustrations. Unfortunately, however, the collection stops short at his death, and the evidence given in the process of canonization by the friars who had lived with him is not included. These testimonies which reveal so much of his interior spirit are printed in the *Acta Sanctorum* and elsewhere. The definitive work is now P. Mandonnet and H. M. Vicaire, *S. Dominique, l'idée, l'homme et l'œuvre* (2 vols., 1937–38). An abridged version of the biography in vol. i was published in English in New York in 1944. See further A. Mortier, *Histoire des maîtres généraux O.P.*, vol. i. The best original lives in English are by Mother Frances Raphael Drane (1891) and Fr Bede Jarrett (1924), and in German by M. Rings (1920), B. Altaner (1922) and H. C. Scheeben (1927). There are lives in French by Lacordaire (1840), J. Guiraud (1899 ; Eng. trans.), H. Petitot (1925) and M. S. Gillet (1942).

SS. IA AND HER COMPANIONS, MARTYRS (*c.* A.D. 360)

In the worst times of Roman persecution of Christians there was never a more cruel and bloody period than that of from about 314 until 379, during which King Sapor II persecuted in Persia ; in proportion to the numbers involved and its duration, this persecution had more victims than any other. Among them was St Ia and those that suffered with her. She was, according to her quite unreliable *passio*, a Greek maiden who made many converts among the Persian women, so that she was denounced and ordered to be put to the torture. Her limbs were first stretched apart and she was remorselessly beaten, at which she only prayed aloud, " Lord Jesus Christ, Son of the living God, strengthen thy handmaiden and save me from the wolves that rend me ". She was put back into prison until she had recovered and then offered her life if she would apostatize. She again refused, and was beaten as before, till she could neither speak nor move. After another six months her tormentors stuck slips of bamboo all over her body and wound her round with ropes, so as to press them into her flesh ; then each was sharply pulled out again. She nearly died from loss of blood, but after another ten days was brought out of prison, hung up by her hands, and lashed until her bones were bare and life was extinct. Then her head was struck off and her body thrown away. The Roman Martyrology records the tradition that those who suffered death with her numbered nine thousand. This St Ia must not be confounded with the maiden Ia who gives her name to Saint Ives in Cornwall.

The best text of the *passio* is that edited by Delehaye in the *Patrologia orientalis*, vol. ii, pp. 453–473, fasc. 4 ; it is also printed in the *Acta Sanctorum*, August, vol. i. The martyr's Syriac name simply meant " violet " (*ἴον*), as Peeters has shown in *Analecta Bollandiana*, vol. xxv (1906), p. 340 ; it has nothing to do with Εὐδοκία.

ST MOLUA, OR LUGHAIDH, ABBOT (A.D. 608)

MOLUA (Lugaid and other forms) was the son of Carthach, of the Hy Fidhgente of Limerick county, and his mother came from Ossory. When a lad he was employed as a herdboy till, as his late *vita* tells us, having distinguished himself by miracles, he was sent to be a monk under St Comgall at Bangor. He was ordained priest and in time sent by his abbot to establish monasteries elsewhere. The most important of them was at Clonfertmulloe, now called Kyle, in the Slievebloom mountains between Leix and Offaly, which had a very large community. He is said to have gone to Rome (" Unless I see Rome I shall soon die "), and taken the opportunity to submit to Pope St Gregory the Great the rule he had drawn up for his monasteries ; it was, like all Celtic monastic rules, extremely arduous and the pope said of it that, " The holy man who drew up this rule has laid a hedge round his family which reaches to Heaven ". On his death-bed St Molua addressed his monks and said, " Dearest brethren, cultivate your land industriously, that you may have a sufficiency of food, drink and clothing ; for where there is sufficient, there is stability ; where is stability, there is true religion ; and the end of true religion is life everlasting " : " *Rerum novarum* " and " *Quadragesimo anno* " in a nut-shell.   Molua, we are told, never killed any living thing, and when he died the birds wept.

There is some confusion between this Molua and other saints of the same name. Killaloe (Cill da Lua) may get its name from this Molua or from another who was called " the Leper ", or they may both be the same person.

There are three Latin recensions of the Life of St Molua ; one has been printed in the *Acta Sanctorum*, August, vol. i ; another in De Smedt's edition of the Codex Salmanticensis, and the third by C. Plummer in VSH., vol. ii, pp. 206–225.   A. P. Forbes in KSS. (pp. 409–411) repudiates any identity between St Moloc (June 25) and St Molua.

5 : THE DEDICATION OF THE BASILICA OF ST MARY MAJOR
" OUR LADY OF THE SNOW "

THIS feast celebrates the dedication of the third of the patriarchal basilicas within the walls of Rome, to which at first the name of " Liberian Basilica " was given, because it was founded in the time of Pope Liberius, in the middle of the fourth century ; it was restored and consecrated under the title of the Virgin Mary by Sixtus III, about the year 435, and is now generally known as St Mary Major (Santa Maria Maggiore ; Great St Mary's), because it is in both age and dignity the first church of the City among those dedicated to God in honour of our Lady.   In the liturgical books it is called St Mary *ad Nives*, or " of the Snow ", from a popular tradition that the Mother of God chose this place for a church under her invocation by a miraculous fall of snow upon this spot in summer and by a vision in which she appeared to a patrician named John, who munificently founded and endowed this church in the pontificate of Liberius at the site thus indicated on the Esquiline Hill.   No mention is found of this miracle until some hundreds of years later, and it is now everywhere recognized as a myth.   A com- mission for the reform of the Breviary recommended to Pope Benedict XIV in 1742 that its old name of " Dedication of St Mary " should be restored to the feast ; this has not been done yet, except in the Benedictine calendar (1915).   This basilica has sometimes also been known by the name of St Mary *ad Praesepe*, from the alleged relic of the crib or manger of Bethlehem, in which Christ was laid at His birth.

See H. Grisar, *Analecta Romana* (1900), p. 70, and the same writer's *Geschichte Roms und der Päpste* (1901), p. 153, n. 1 ; as well as Duchesne, *Liber Pontificalis*, vol. i, pp. 232, 235, and CMH., p. 418.   Stress is rightly laid upon the fact that no mention is made of any miraculous fall of snow in Sixtus III's inscription for the dedication of the basilica.   Though the original has now perished, its text is well known, and has been reprinted, for example, from De Rossi's *Inscriptiones Christianae*, vol. ii, pp. 71, 98, 139, in Duchesne's footnote ; see under St Sixtus III herein, on August 19.

SS. ADDAI AND MARI, BISHOPS   (*c.* A.D. 180 ?)

THERE were inhabitants of Mesopotamia present when St Peter and his com- panions preached at Pentecost, and for all that we know the first East Syrian

Christians were made at that time, but the actual date of the introduction of Christianity into those parts, among the Edessene Jews, is unknown. There is evidence of a Christian colony at Edessa in the second century, but it was probably not till the coming of the Sassanid dynasty that the faith began to spread from there over Mesopotamia, Adiabene and Persia. Local ecclesiastical tradition, however, attributes their evangelization to the apostle St Thomas, and more particularly to St Addai, St Aggai and St Mari. The story of how they came to Edessa, combined from the narratives of Eusebius and of a Syriac document called *The Doctrine of Addai* (written *c.* 400), is as follows.

At the time when our Lord was still incarnate upon earth there reigned in Osroene a king called Abgar the Black, who lived at Edessa. He suffered from some incurable disease and, having heard of the miracles of healing of our Lord, he sent to Him a letter by the hand of his secretary, Hannan. In it he addresses Christ as " the good Physician " and asks Him to come to Edessa and heal him, professing to believe, in consequence of the reported wonders, that, " either thou art God, who hast come down from Heaven, or else the Son of God, who brings all these things to pass ". Hannan found our Lord in the house of Gamaliel, " Chief of the Jews ", and He replied to Abgar that, " Happy art thou who hast believed in me without having seen me, for it is written that they who see me shall not believe and they who see me not shall believe. As for my coming to you, I am about to return to my Father, all for which I was sent into the world being finished. But when I shall have ascended to Him I will send thee one of my disciples, who shall heal thee of thy sickness and bring thee and thine to eternal life." According to Eusebius our Lord wrote out this message Himself and it was accordingly greatly reverenced throughout Christendom during the middle ages ; it is said to have been used as an amulet in England before the eleventh century. The Syriac document states that Hannan also brought back to Abgar a portrait of our Lord which he had painted (later, " not-made-by-human-hands "), and which as the Holy Mandylion is famous in Christian iconography.

After the Ascension, the apostle Thomas accordingly sent one of the seventy-two disciples, Addai (Thaddeus), to the court of King Abgar. He lodged at the house of a Jew, Tobias, and when he was brought before the king he healed him of his disease, and spoke to him of the faith of Christ. Addai converted Abgar and multitudes of his people, among others the royal jeweller, Aggai, whom he made bishop and his successor, and Palut, whom he ordained priest on his death-bed. In due course St Aggai was martyred and Palut had to go to Antioch to be consecrated by Serapion, who in his turn had been made bishop by Pope St Zephyrinus at Rome. Quite apart from any other consideration, this last statement throws the whole of the legend into confusion, for it is known that there was a Serapion, Bishop of Antioch, who was at least contemporary with St Zephyrinus, and was, moreover, contemporary with another Abgar, who was a Christian king of Edessa between about 179 and 213, and probably the first ; so Serapion could not have consecrated a convert of one of the Seventy-two.

The most, then, that can be said of St Addai is that he was perhaps a missionary in Edessa, before the end of the second century. St Mari is an even less satisfactory person, for there are serious doubts of his existence at all. According to his late " acts " he was a disciple of St Addai, who sent him to Nisibis ; he preached there and took up the work of Jonas the prophet at Ninive, then he went down the Tigris, until he began " to smell the smell of the apostle Thomas ", and died near

Seleucia-Ctesiphon, after consecrating as its bishop Papa bar Aggai, another certainly historical personage, the first katholikos of the East Syrian churches—but at the beginning of the fourth century. Wherever he went St Mari made numerous converts, destroyed temples, built churches and founded monasteries, on a scale familiar in spurious legends but rarely, if ever, found in sober history. Nevertheless, SS. Addai and Mari, nebulous as they now are, have from early ages been venerated as the evangelists of the lands around the Tigris and Euphrates, and still are by their successors, the Catholic Chaldeans and the Nestorians of Iraq and Kurdistan; they are referred to as "the Holy Apostles", and the principal *anaphora* of the eucharistic liturgy of those Christians bears this name.

The two primary sources are Eusebius, *Ecclesiastical History*, bk i, ch. 13 ; and the *Doctrine of Addai*, Syriac text with Eng. trans., edited by G. Phillips (1876). The authenticity of the letters exchanged between Abgar and our Saviour was formerly very warmly defended, *e.g.* by the Abbé Paulin Martin in the *Revue des Sciences Ecclésiastiques* for 1888–1889 (several articles), as against Tixeront, R. Duval, R. Lipsius, and others. On the Armenian version and its bearings on the controversy, consult P. J. Dashian, " Zur Abgar Sage ", three articles in the *Vienna Oriental Journal* for 1890. Modern opinion tends strongly to regard the whole incident as apocryphal, see *e.g.* Bardenhewer, *Geschichte der altkirchlichen Literatur*, vol. i, pp. 569 *seq.* and p. 443 ; and *Dictionnaire de la Bible*, Supplement, cc. 540–542. *Cf.* however, Casartelli in *The Dublin Review* for April 1889, and H. Thurston in *The Month*, September 1892, pp. 39–61. See also DCB., *s.v.*, Abgar and Thaddeus, and DHG., *s.v.*, Abgar ; and F. C. Burkitt, *Early Eastern Christianity* (1904), cap. 1.

ST AFRA, MARTYR   (A.D. 304)

THE persecution of Diocletian was carried on with great cruelty by his colleague Maximian in those provinces which fell to his share in the division of the empire. At Augsburg, in Rhaetia, according to her " acts ", the officers apprehended a woman called Afra, known to have formerly been a common prostitute. A later embroidery says she was converted by St Narcissus, bishop of Gerona in Spain, of whom nothing is certainly known. When she was brought to trial the judge, by name Gaius, who knew who she was, said, " Sacrifice to the gods ; it is better to live than to die in torments ". Afra replied, " I was a great sinner before I knew God ; but I will not add new crimes, or do what you command me ". " I am informed ", said Gaius, " that you are a prostitute. Sacrifice therefore, as you are a stranger to the God of the Christians and cannot be accepted by Him." Afra replied, " My Lord Jesus Christ has said that He came down from Heaven to save sinners. The gospel says that a sinful woman washed His feet with her tears and obtained pardon, and that He never rejected the outcasts but welcomed them to eat with him." When he found that she could not be moved, declaring, " Let the body which has sinned suffer ; but I will not ruin my soul by false worship ", the judge passed sentence, and the executioners carried her to an island in the river Lech. There they stripped her and tied her to a stake ; and whilst they were heaping vine branches about her and setting fire to them, Afra was heard to say, " I thank thee, Lord Jesus Christ, for thy goodness in receiving me, a burnt-offering for thy name's sake : thou didst offer thyself upon the cross as a sacrifice for the sins of the whole world ; I offer myself a victim to thee, who livest and reignest with the Father and the Holy Ghost world without end. Amen." Having spoken these words she gave up her spirit, being suffocated by the smoke.

Three servants of the martyr, Digna, Eunomia and Euprepia, who had lived disorderly lives with their mistress, but were converted and baptized at the same time, watched her triumph. With Hilaria, the martyr's mother, they came in the night and carried away the body, which they buried in a sepulchre. Whilst Hilaria and her attendants were still within the tomb, Gaius was informed of what they had done. He therefore dispatched soldiers with an order to persuade the whole company to offer sacrifice, and if they refused to burn them alive without any other formality. The soldiers used both mild words and threats ; but finding all to no purpose they filled the vault with thorns and branches, shut the door, and having set fire to the wood, left them to be roasted to death.

The existence of a martyr called Afra, who suffered at Augsburg and was venerated there from early times, seems established ; but the value of the *acta* from which the above relation is taken is a matter of dispute. According to some scholars they are worthless ; others claim that the part which narrates her trial and martyrdom is an expanded version of an earlier historical narrative, while the separate story of her being a harlot, her conversion, and the execution of her mother and servants is an invention of the Carlovingian era. St Afra is referred to by Venantius Fortunatus, and she is still venerated at Augsburg and elsewhere in Germany.

The two Latin texts of most importance have both been edited by B. Krusch in MGH., *Scriptores Merov.*, vol. iii, pp. 55–64 and vol. vii, pp. 192–204. Much discussion has centred round the question whether the original text of the *acta* is really a Merovingian document as Duchesne contended, or, as Krusch believed, was only elaborated out of the notice in the " Hieronymianum "—" In provincia Retia civitate Augusta Afrae veneriae." A. Bigelmair, A. Poncelet and O. Riedner support Krusch, but in CMH., p. 423, an opposite view is taken ; there are fuller bibliographical references in the same notice.

ST NONNA, Matron   (A.D. 374)

Nonna was born towards the end of the third century and, although she was brought up a Christian, married Gregory, the magistrate of Nazianzus in Cappadocia, who was a member of a Judaic-pagan sect called the Hypsistarians. However, this was a case of a " mixed marriage " turning out for the very best, and the resulting family was one of the most famous and brilliant saintly families of Christian history. By her shining example St Nonna converted her husband, and he became a priest, and then a bishop : in those days the now universal law that a bishop must be single or a widower was not yet everywhere in force ; he is moreover venerated as a saint and is known as St Gregory Nazianzen the Elder. They had three children, all of them saints, and the eldest, St Gregory Nazianzen the Divine, became one of the greatest of the doctors of the Church ; in his writing he often refers to the devoted and virtuous life of his mother Nonna. The next child was a girl, St Gorgonia, who married and had three children. The third was St Caesarius, a physician by profession. St Nonna outlived two of her children : Gorgonia died in her arms, and she heard the funeral sermons preached for her and Caesarius by Gregory the Younger which have continued to be the admiration of succeeding ages. She survived her husband only a few months and died at a considerable age in 374 : a valiant woman, whose children rose up and called her blessed, whose husband praised her.

A sufficient account of St Nonna is given in the *Acta Sanctorum*, August, vol. ii, and in DCB., vol. iv, p. 50.

6 : THE TRANSFIGURATION OF OUR LORD JESUS CHRIST

OUR divine Redeemer, in order to show that the sufferings of His servants are usually intermingled with spiritual comforts and to give us a sensible demonstration of the truth of His promises of an eternal glory reserved for us in the world to come, was pleased to manifest His majesty in the mystery of the Transfiguration. Being in Galilee about a year before His passion, He chose to be witnesses of His glory the same three beloved disciples who were afterward to be witnesses of His agony in the garden, namely St Peter, and the two sons of Zebedee, SS. James and John. He took three, that their evidence might be unexceptionable ; but He would not publicly show His glory, to teach His followers to love the closest secrecy in all spiritual graces and favours. Practices contrary to this are suggested by self-love, not by the spirit of God ; they are a disguised pride and a dangerous illusion. Every true servant of God loves to be hidden ; his motto, even when he most warmly invites all creatures to magnify the Lord with him, is : " My secret to myself, my secret to myself " (Isaias xxiv 16). He fears lest he should be at all considered or thought of in what belongs purely to God alone. Jesus therefore showed this miracle in retirement, and He led these three apostles to a lonely mountain, as He was accustomed to go often to some solitude to pray.

The tradition of the Christians in Palestine, of which St Cyril of Jerusalem, St John Damascene, and other fathers speak, assures us that this was Mount Tabor, which rises, something like a sugar-loaf, in the middle of Galilee. This was the place in which the God-man appeared in His glory. He was transfigured whilst at prayer, because it is usually then that the soul receives the dew of divine con-solations, and tastes how infinitely sweet God is to those who sincerely seek Him. Many Christians indeed are strangers to this effect of prayer because they do not apply themselves to it with perseverance and fervour, or neglect to disengage their affections from creatures by humility, self-denial and mortification of the senses. Without purity of heart no man shall see God ; but a Christian worthily disposed and fitted by the Holy Ghost to receive the spirit of prayer purifies his love more and more, transforms his affections, and renders them ever more spiritual and heavenly. Of this, the transfiguration of our Lord was, among other transcending prerogatives, a most noble and supereminent prototype.

In the East the tendency to commemorate incidents of the gospel history by special feasts is more pronounced than in the Western church, and it is probable that we must look there for the earliest traces of such a celebration as the present. What is certain is that the Transfiguration was widely and solemnly honoured in the Byzantine church on August 6 before the year 1000. See the *Synaxarium Constant.*, edited by Delehaye, p. 897, and Nilles, *Kalendarium Manuale*, vol. i, pp. 235–238. The feast seems to have been adopted sporadically and on different days by certain local churches in the West, but it did not become of general observance until Pope Callistus III, to commemorate the victory gained over the Turks in 1456 by G. Hunyady and St John of Capistrano, required the Trans-figuration to be everywhere honoured on this day. See F. G. Holweck, *Calendarium festorum Dei et Dei Matris* (1925), pp. 258–259.

SS. SIXTUS II, FELICISSIMUS AND AGAPITUS, WITH THEIR COMPANIONS, MARTYRS (A.D. 258)

SIXTUS succeeded Pope St Stephen I in the year 257. In continuation of the dispute begun under Stephen, St Dionysius of Alexandria consulted him by three letters on certain difficulties, and recommended him to bear a little while with the Africans and some among the Asiatics with regard to their error concerning the validity of baptism given by heretics. Accordingly this pope was indulgent towards them, contenting himself with strongly recommending the truth ; his successors pursued the same conduct till the error that heretical baptisms are invalid was condemned in the plenary council mentioned by St Augustine. St Sixtus is referred to by Pontius, the biographer of St Cyprian, as a " good and peaceable priest ".

The Emperor Valerian published his first decree against the Christians in 257, which was followed by the martyrdom of many. The persecution grew more fierce in the following year, the effect of which St Cyprian notified within a month or two to his fellow bishops in Africa : " Valerian has sent an order to the senate, importing that bishops, priests and deacons should forthwith die. . . . You are to understand that Sixtus suffered in a cemetery upon the sixth day of August, and with him four deacons. The officers of Rome are very keen upon this persecution ; and the persons who are brought before them are sure to suffer, and to forfeit their estates to the exchequer. Pray notify these particulars to my colleagues, that so our brethren may everywhere be prepared for their great conflict : that we may all think rather of immortality than death, and derive more joy than fear from this confession, in which we know that the soldiers of Christ are properly not killed but crowned."

St Sixtus suffered in a cemetery, for Christians in times of persecution resorted to those subterraneous caverns to celebrate the divine Mysteries. Here they met, though Valerian had forbidden them to hold assemblies, and here they were hunted out. Sixtus was seized while seated in his chair, addressing the assembly, and was either beheaded immediately or hurried off to a court for sentence and then brought back for execution. He was buried in the cemetery of St Callistus on the Appian Way, across the road from the cemetery of Praetextatus in which he was taken, and a hundred years later Pope St Damasus wrote an inscription for his tomb. St Sixtus was the most highly venerated among the popes martyred after St Peter, and he is named in the canon of the Mass.

Four deacons, SS. Januarius, Vincent, Magnus and Stephen, who were seized with St Sixtus, suffered with him ; two others, SS. Felicissimus and Agapitus, were martyred probably on the same day. The last two were buried in the cemetery of Praetextatus. The seventh deacon of the City, St Laurence, followed them four days later, as St Sixtus is said to have foretold.

The body of evidence which attests the fact that St Sixtus suffered on August 6 and was buried in the catacomb of Callistus is remarkably early and conclusive. In CMH. (pp. 420–421) this evidence has been most effectively summarized. A misunderstood phrase in one of Damasus's inscriptions apparently led Prudentius into the erroneous belief that Sixtus was crucified ; but he was put to death by the sword. Further, the *Liber Pontificalis* is wrong in stating that the " four deacons " as well as Felicissimus and Agapitus were buried in Praetextatus ; see Duchesne's notes (vol. i, pp. 155–156), and P. Franchi de' Cavalieri in *Studi e Testi*, vol. vi, pp. 147–178. On the other hand, the supposed *Passio S. Sixti*, in all its recensions, is a historically worthless document. See also *Analecta Bollandiana*, vol. li (1933), pp. 43–49.

SS. JUSTUS AND PASTOR, MARTYRS   (A.D. 304)

THEY were two brothers who, while still schoolboys, overcame with heroic courage the rage and power of Dacian, governor of Spain under Diocletian and Maximian.

In his progress through his province in search of the servants of God, he arrived at Complutum, now called Alcalà de Henares, and began to put to the torture the Christians that were brought before him.   Justus and Pastor, children who were then learning their elements in the public school of that city (the one being thirteen, the other only nine years old), hearing of the torments which were inflicted on the followers of Christ, were fired to have a share in their triumphs.   They threw down their books, ran to the place where the governor was interrogating the confessors, and by their behaviour showed the faith which they professed.   They were soon taken notice of and presented to the judge.   He, instead of being touched, was furious to see children brave his power and authority and, not doubting that a little correction would dispel their courage, commanded them to be severely whipped.   This was executed in the most barbarous manner ; but He who makes the tongues of infants eloquent in His praise, gave them strength to defy their tormentors.   The spectators were filled with astonishment to see the constancy with which in their turn they encouraged each other to be brave for Christ.   Dacian, to cover his shame, gave an order that they should be at once beheaded.   Their relics are enshrined at Alcalà, of which city and Madrid they are the patrons.

Whatever may be thought of the value of the reputed " acts ", printed by the Bollandists under August 6, there can be no question as to the genuineness and antiquity of the *cultus* of these saints.   St Paulinus of Nola had his little son buried close beside them at Alcalà ; Prudentius numbers them among the most glorious martyrs of Spain.   Their names also are recorded in the " Hieronymianum ", on August 25.   See the *Acta Sanctorum*, August, vol. ii.

ST HORMISDAS, POPE   (A.D. 523)

HORMISDAS, a Campanian by birth, was a widower and a deacon of the Roman church, whose son St Silverius was also to become pope.   He earned the high regard of St Ennodius, Bishop of Pavia, who prophesied that this deacon would one day be pope.   Two days after the death of St Symmachus in 514 the prediction was fulfilled.   Practically the whole of the pontificate of St Hormisdas was devoted to dealing with the delicate and complex situation brought about in the East by the Acacian schism, caused by the attempt of Acacius of Constantinople to placate the monophysites ; and to this pope belongs the honour of having brought it to an end by means of the confession of faith that bears his name, the Formula of Hormisdas.   This document, which has been cited in the deliberations of the Church so lately as at the Vatican Council, is one of the most important pieces of evidence of the recognition of papal authority in the first six centuries.

Nothing is recorded of the less public life of St Hormisdas, but it is clear that he was able and sagacious, and a man of peace : he severely rebuked some African monks for their quarrelsomeness.   His last days were made happy by the cessation of the Vandal persecution in Africa.

Save for the succinct account given in the *Liber Pontificalis*, there is nothing in the nature of a biography of Pope Hormisdas.   A fairly full discussion of his public activities will be found in the *Acta Sanctorum*, August, vol. ii.   See also Mgr Duchesne's notes to the *Liber Pontificalis*, vol. i, pp. 272–274 ; and H. Grisar, *Geschichte Roms und der Päpste*, vol. i, pp. 478–481, and *passim*.

7 : ST CAJETAN, Co-Founder of the Theatine Clerks Regular   (A.D. 1547)

ST CAJETAN (Gaetano) was son of Caspar, Count of Thiene, and Mary di Porto, of the nobility of Vicenza, where he was born in 1480. Two years later his father was killed, fighting for the Venetians against King Ferdinand of Naples, and his widow was appointed guardian of Cajetan and his two brothers. The admirable example and teaching she gave her sons bore quick and abundant fruit, and Cajetan in particular was soon known for his unusual goodness. He went for four years to the University of Padua where the long exercises of devotion which he practised were no hindrance to his studies, but sanctified them and purified his understanding, enabling him the better to judge of truth. He distinguished himself in theology, and took the degree of doctor in civil and canon law in 1504. He then returned to his native town, of which he was made a senator, and in pursuance of his resolve to serve God as a priest he received the tonsure. In 1506 he went to Rome, not in quest of preferment or to live at court, but because of a strong inward conviction that he was needed for some great work there. Soon after his arrival Pope Julius II conferred on him the office of protonotary, with a benefice attached. On the death of Julius II in 1513 Cajetan refused his successor's request to continue in his office, and devoted three years to preparing himself for the priesthood : he was ordained in 1516, being thirty-three years old, and returned to Vicenza in 1518.

Cajetan had re-founded a confraternity in Rome, called " of the Divine Love ", which was an association of zealous and devout clerics who devoted themselves to labour with all their power to promote God's honour and the welfare of souls. At Vicenza he now entered himself in the Oratory of St Jerome, which was instituted upon the plan of that of the Divine Love but consisted only of men in the lowest stations of life. This circumstance gave great offence to his friends, who thought it a reflection on the honour of his family. He persisted, however, and exerted his zeal with wonderful fruit. He sought out the sick and the poor over the whole town and served them, and cared for those who suffered from the most loathsome diseases in the hospital of the incurables, the revenues of which he greatly increased. But his primary concern was for the spiritual life of the members of his oratory : " In this oratory ", he said, " we try to serve God by worship ; in our hospital we may say that we actually find Him." He founded a similar oratory at Verona and then, in obedience to the advice of his confessor, John-Baptist of Crema, a Dominican friar of great prudence and piety, Cajetan went in 1520 to Venice and, taking up his lodgings in the new hospital of that city, pursued his former manner of life there. He was so great a benefactor to that house as to be regarded as its principal founder. He remained in Venice three years, and introduced exposition of the Blessed Sacrament in that city, as well as continuing the promotion of frequent communion : " I shall never be content till I see Christians flocking like little children to feed on the Bread of Life, and with eagerness and delight, not with fear and false shame ", he wrote.

The state of Christendom at this time was not less than shocking. The general corruption weakened the Church before the assaults of Protestantism and provided an apparent excuse for that revolt, and the decay of religion with its accompaniment of moral wickedness was not checked by the clergy, many of whom, high and low, secular and regular, were themselves sunk in iniquity and indifference. The Church was " sick in head and members ". The spectacle shocked and distressed Cajetan, and in 1523 he went back to Rome to confer with his friends of the Oratory of Divine Love. They agreed that little could be done otherwise than by reviving in the clergy the spirit and zeal of those holy pastors who first planted the faith, and to put them in mind what this spirit ought to be, and what it obliges them to, a plan was formed for instituting an order of regular clergy upon the model of the lives of the Apostles. The first associates of St Cajetan in this design were John Peter Caraffa, afterwards pope under the name of Paul IV but at that time bishop of Theate (Chieti) ; Paul Consiglieri, of the family of Ghislieri ; and Boniface da Colle, a gentleman of Milan. The institute was approved by Clement VII, and Caraffa was chosen the first provost general. From his episcopal name of Theatensis these clerks regular came to be distinguished from others as Theatines. On September 14, 1524 the four original members laid aside their prelatical robes and made their profession in St Peter's in the presence of a papal delegate. The principal ends which they proposed to themselves were to preach sound doctrine to the people, assist the sick, restore the frequent use of the sacraments, and re-establish in the clergy disinterestedness, regularity of life, sacred studies (especially of the Bible), preaching and pastoral care, and the fitting conduct of divine worhsip. Life was to be in common, under the usual vows, and poverty was strongly emphasized.

The success of the new congregation was not immediate, and in 1527, when it still numbered only a dozen members, a calamity happened which might well have put an end to it. The army of the Emperor Charles V sacked Rome : the Theatines' house was nearly demolished, and the inmates had to escape to Venice. Caraffa's term as superior expired in 1530, and St Cajetan was chosen in his place. He accepted the office with reluctance, but did not let its cares abate the energy with which he worked to inspire the clergy with his own fervour and devotion, and his charity was made most conspicuous during a plague which was brought to Venice from the Levant, followed by a dreadful famine.

At the end of the three years of office, Caraffa was made superior a second time, and Cajetan was sent to Verona, where both the clergy and laity were tumultuously opposing the reformation of discipline which their bishop was endeavouring to introduce among them. Shortly after, he was called to Naples to establish the clerks regular there. The Count of Oppido gave him a large house, and tried to prevail upon him to accept an estate in lands ; but this he refused. In vain the count pointed out that the Neapolitans were neither so rich nor so generous as the Venetians. " That may be true ", replied Cajetan, " but God is the same in both cities." A general improvement at Naples was the fruit of his example, preaching and labours, and he was foremost in the successful opposition to the activities of three apostates, a layman, an Augustinian and a Franciscan, who, respectively Socinian, Calvinist and Lutheran, were corrupting the religion of the people. During the last years of his life he established with Bd John Marinoni the benevolent pawnshops (*montes pietatis*) sanctioned some time before by the Fifth Lateran Council. Worn out with trying to appease civil strife in Naples, and disappointed by the suspension of the Council of Trent from which he hoped so much for the Church's good, St Cajetan had to take to his bed in the summer of 1547. When his physicians advised him not to lie on the hard boards but to use a mattress, his answer was, " My Saviour died on a cross, allow me at least to die on wood ". He lingered for a week, the end coming on Sunday, August 7. Many miracles wrought by his intercession were approved at Rome after a rigorous scrutiny, and he was canonized in 1671.

St Cajetan was one of the most outstanding figures among the pre-Tridentine Catholic reformers, and his institution of clerks regular, priests bound by vow and living in community but engaged in active pastoral work, played a very great part in the Catholic reformation. Today, with the one tremendous exception of the Jesuits, all their congregations have been reduced to small bodies, but continuing their original life and work. Thomas Goldwell, Bishop of Saint Asaph and last survivor of the old hierarchy of England and Wales, was a Theatine, who entered their house of St Paul at Naples in the year of St Cajetan's death.

No biography of this saint has been left us by anyone who actually knew him. The life which is printed in the *Acta Sanctorum*, August, vol. ii, compiled by A. Caracciolo, was not written until some sixty years after the holy priest's death. Probably St Cajetan's close association with Caraffa, and the extreme unpopularity of the latter's pontificate—he became pope, as Paul IV, eight years after the former went to Heaven—rendered the early history of the Theatines a delicate subject to handle. It is only in recent times that L. von Pastor, G. M. Monti, O. Premoli, and other conscientious investigators have thrown light upon many matters formerly buried in obscurity. Though only a slight sketch, the booklet of O. Premoli, *S. Gaetano Thiene* (1910), perhaps offers the most reliable picture of the saint ; but for the earlier portion of his career, Pio Paschini, *S. Gaetano . . . e le origini dei . . . Teatini* (1926), has provided a study of great value, largely based upon unpublished letters. The life by R. de Maulde la Clavière, which having been translated into English is the most easily accessible, cannot be recommended without reserves : see the reviews of both the original and the revised edition in the *Analecta Bollandiana*, vol. xxii, p. 119, and vol. xxiv, p. 419. Two later biographies in Italian are by P. Chiminelli (1948), very full, and by L. Ruiz de Cardenas (1947), shorter and more popular.

ST CLAUDIA, MATRON   (FIRST CENTURY)

IN his second letter to St Timothy (2 Tim. iv 21), St Paul says, " Eubulus and Pudens and Linus and *Claudia* and all the brethren salute thee ". She was evidently a lady of importance : the *Apostolic Constitutions* (fourth century) state that Claudia was the mother of Linus, and St Irenaeus says that the Linus mentioned by St Paul was he who succeeded St Peter in the supreme pontificate. The poet Martial mentions in his *Epigrams* a British lady, Claudia Rufina, who was the wife of his friend Aulus Pudens, and by some this man has been identified with the Pudens of St Paul. That St Claudia was a Briton is maintained independently by a tradition that she was a daughter of the British King Caractacus, who was defeated by the Roman general Aulus Plautius and sent with his family in chains to Rome in the year 51. They were released by the Emperor Claudius, but one of the daughters remained in Rome, was baptized, and took the name of Claudia, and is the lady whom St Paul mentions. Others think she was the daughter, not of Caractacus, but of Cogidubnus, a British ally of Claudius who adopted the emperor's name. None of these theories have more than the weight of not-impossible suppositions ; it is not even certain that St Claudia was the wife of St Pudens.

Bishop Lightfoot (*Apostolic Fathers*, vol. i, pt 1, pp. 76–79) discusses these identifications in connection with St Clement and Pudens. He finds nothing which can lend them any probability.

ST DONATUS, Bishop of Arezzo   (A.D. 362)

DONATUS was the second bishop of Arezzo in Tuscany. Though the Roman Martyrology refers to him as a martyr at Arezzo under Julian the Apostate, and he is commemorated as such in today's Mass, he seems certainly not to have died for the faith. In the same place Donatus is associated with the martyred monk St Hilarinus, but he seems to have suffered at Ostia ; there too mention is made of the attribution to him by St Gregory the Great of a miracle of restoring a chalice broken up by the heathen. There has also been confusion between St Donatus of Arezzo and another St Donatus, bishop of Euroea in Epirus.

The early *cultus* of this Donatus as a confessor is indubitable, but his so-called *passio* (*Acta Sanctorum*, August, vol. ii) is simply derived from the fictitious story of St Gallicanus, who has a long entry in the Roman Martyrology on June 25.

ST DOMETIUS THE PERSIAN, Martyr   (*c.* A.D. 362 ?)

THE Melkites and other Christians of the East today celebrate the memory of St Dometius who, according to the legend, was a Persian convert who became a monk at Nisibis in Mesopotamia, was ordained deacon, and went to live in a cave, from whence he converted many heathen of the neighbourhood. People flocked to his retreat to ask his blessing and in hope that he would cure their ills ; and the Emperor Julian the Apostate, whom Dometius had reproached for his impiety, accused the holy man of courting popularity. " If these poor harmless folk come to see me, I cannot send them away ", he replied. Julian was so incensed by the answer that he had him stoned to death.

There has been great confusion between this Dometius and another, mentioned in the Roman Martyrology on July 5 as a martyr in Syria, " who by his power affords many benefits to the inhabitants of these parts ". St Dometius has a great reputation in the East as an ascete and wonder-worker ; there is evidence that he was honoured in Cyprus and in southern Italy, and we find him referred to in the Syriac martyrology of Rabban Sliba as a " healer of sciatica ".

The Greek acts have been printed in *Analecta Bollandiana*, vol. xix (1900), pp. 285–320 ; in the Syriac recension, edited by P. Bedjan, the narrative has been transformed in a number of details. In *Analecta Bollandiana*, vol. lvii (1939), pp. 72–104, Fr P. Peeters discusses at length the confusion between the two Dometii.

ST VICTRICIUS, Bishop of Rouen   (*c.* A.D. 407)

AMONG the great bishops of the Western church during the fourth century three stand out conspicuously in Gaul, namely, Hilary of Poitiers, Martin of Tours and Victricius of Rouen. Of these the last-named is the least well known to fame because we have less information about his career, whereas the other two are pretty well documented. It is likely that his birthplace was somewhere not far from the Scheldt, that he was born about the year 330, and that his father or near ancestor was a soldier in one of the Roman legions called *Victrix*. Nothing is known of his early years, but at the age of seventeen he became a soldier and not long afterwards a Christian. At this time the lawfulness of the military profession for a Christian had not yet been decided in the Church, and there were not wanting learned and good men who denied that a Christian could bear arms without blame ; and St Victricius, laying down his weapons one day on parade, asked for his discharge (*cf.* the action of St Martin of Tours in similar circumstances). His period of service was not yet expired, so his tribune treated the request as a breach of discipline and ordered him to be flogged. Unable to move him, the tribune referred the matter to the *comes*, who sentenced Victricius to death for desertion. St Paulinus of Nola says in one of his letters that miraculous intervention prevented the sentence from being carried out ; and Victricius and some Christian comrades were released and discharged.

Then follows a blank in the history of Victricius, and when next heard of he is bishop of Rouen, to which see he must have been elected about the year 386. Within his diocese there were still many heathen, to whose conversion the bishop applied himself with zeal, and he introduced monasticism into Rouen in the loose unorganized form that it had in Gaul at that time : his " flock of ascetes, thin with fasting " and his " choir of maidens ", whose " life is even more splendid than it is, in the world's eyes, hard ". He obtained from St Ambrose at Milan many relics of the saints, which were received by the people in solemn procession and duly enshrined. In connection with these translations he preached or wrote his work *On the Praise of the Saints*, which partakes of the nature both of a panegyric and of a thesis on the *cultus* of the saints ; as a piece of literature it is particularly valuable for the study of the rhythmical *cursus*. Victricius established a number of rural parishes, which in those days were still rare, but progress against paganism was slow among the country people, and it continued for another couple of hundred years. He preached in Artois, western Flanders, Hainault and Brabant ; but his work was largely undone and the religious centres he established destroyed by the barbarian invasions in the fifth century. His reputation for wisdom and holiness had meanwhile crossed the Channel, and about 396 he came over at the request of the British bishops to settle some differences. Their nature is not known. Whatever it was, Victricius, in his own words, " did all he could, even if he did not do all that wanted doing. . . . I inspired the wise with love of peace, I taught it to the teachable, I explained it to the ignorant, I imposed it on the obstinate, insisting on it in season and out of season. . . ."

Towards the end of his life St Victricius came under suspicion of heresy, and he went to Rome to clear himself. This he had no difficulty in doing ; and he received from Pope St Innocent I in 404 a famous decretal on disciplinary matters, including the reference of *causae maiores* from the local bishops to the Holy See. The exact date of the death of this great bishop is not known.

Considering the important position claimed for St Victricius it is curious that we possess no early life of him. We have to be content for the most part with such information as may be gleaned from the letters of St Paulinus of Nola. There is an excellent study of all that is known of Victricius, by E. Vacandard, in the series " Les Saints " (1903). *Cf.* also C. Jullian, *Histoire de la Gaule*, and E. de Moreau, *Histoire de l'Église en Belgique*, t. i (1945). For the saint's influence on St Patrick, see Fr P. Grosjean in *Analecta Bollandiana*, vol. lxiv (1946), pp. 94–99.

ST ALBERT OF TRAPANI (A.D. 1307 ?)

St Albert, also called " of Sicily ", was born at Trapani in that island. It is said that his parents were Benedict Adalberti and Joan of Palizze and that, having been long without issue, they vowed that if they had a male child he should be dedicated to our Lady of Mount Carmel in her order. At any rate, the young Albert became a Carmelite, and after he had been ordained was sent to the priory of Messina, where he preached with much success, especially among the Jews. He added many voluntary austerities to those of his rule, among them the custom of repeating the whole psalter on his knees before a crucifix every night before he went to bed. Unfortunately this and other particulars given by his biographer were written long after he was dead and are far from reliable. He tells us that when the king of Naples was besieging Messina and had blockaded it so effectually that the city was in imminent danger of starvation, Frederick III of Sicily contemplated burning it down to keep it out of the enemy's hands ; certain of the citizens came to St Albert in great distress about this, and the sudden arrival of food ships that had successfully run the blockade was attributed to his prayers.

His biographer records that St Albert made a pilgrimage to Palestine to the cradle of his order, where he became as famous for his miracles as he was at home ; but in fact this journey was never undertaken, and the miracles must be regarded as probably equally apocryphal. During the last years of his life he lived as a hermit near Messina. When, three hundred years later, St Mary Magdalen de' Pazzi was tempted to leave the Carmel at Florence and return to the world, she asked the prayers of St Albert in Heaven ; the temptation left her, and she was confirmed in her good resolution by a vision of the saint. He was never formally canonized, but his *cultus* was approved in 1476.

The Latin life, upon which all the others of more recent date are directly or indirectly founded, has been printed in the *Analecta Bollandiana*, vol. xvii (1898), pp. 317 *seq.* It was only written at the beginning of the fifteenth century. See also B. Zimmerman, *Monumenta historica Carmelitana*, pp. 259, 422, etc.

BB. AGATHANGELO AND CASSIAN, Martyrs (A.D. 1638)

THE foundation and first direction of the Capuchin missions in the Levant in the seventeenth century was the work of Father Joseph of Paris (Joseph Leclerc du Tremblay), known on account of his influence with Richelieu and Louis XIII as " the Grey Cardinal ". Early in 1629 five Capuchins landed at Alexandretta, among them Father Agathangelo of Vendôme.

He had been born in that town in 1598, and at the age of twenty-one entered the Capuchin friary of Le Mans. He was ordained priest in 1625 and was a preacher in his own country until he was asked to go to Syria. At Aleppo he ministered to the French and Italian traders and others while he was learning Arabic, and soon mastered that language sufficiently well to talk and preach ; he cultivated the society of Moslems and dissident Christians, winning the goodwill of such notables as the *imam* of the principal mosque and the superior of the Dervishes, and even explained Christianity to the Turks, in spite of the forbiddance by the Congregation *de Propaganda Fide* of any public preaching among Mohammedans. The fruit of this work was to induce an atmosphere of tolerance and interest : Father Agathangelo was too good a missionary to look for any more tangible results before due time.

In 1630 a Capuchin mission was established at Cairo which did not prosper, and at the end of 1633 Father Agathangelo was sent there to take charge. He was joined by three new missionaries from Marseilles, one of them being Father Cassian of Nantes, a Frenchman by birth but Portuguese by parentage. He soon became the right-hand man of Father Agathangelo and entered whole-heartedly into his efforts to bring about a reunion with the Holy See of the Coptic or native Egyptian church. Agathangelo got into personal touch with the Coptic bishops ; and their patriarch, Matthew, opened all the dissident churches to him ; using powers granted by Rome, he celebrated Mass, preached, and catechized therein and reconciled a number of individual Copts. The friars determined to try and gain the influence of the monks also, from among whom the Coptic bishops were chosen, and in 1636 Father Agathangelo took with him Father Benedict of Dijon and made the long journey to the monastery of Dair Antonios in the Lower Thebaid.

They were well received by the monks and made a stay of four months, Father Agathangelo conducting doctrinal discussions and giving spiritual conferences ; of the two books which he used for the last purpose one was the treatise *On the Holy Will of God*, written by the English Father Benedict of Canfield (William Fitch), the first Capuchin missionary in England in penal times. Two of the community were reconciled to the Church, and Father Agathangelo left them at the monastery in the hope that they would draw their brethren after them. This was his deliberate policy in Egypt, especially as there were no Catholic churches of the Coptic rite for reconciled dissidents to attend : priests were allowed to celebrate the Liturgy in, and lay-people to frequent, the dissident churches whose schism they had repudiated ; thus they were not left without ministration and they might in time leaven the whole. Then *Propaganda* declared the practice illicit. Father Agathangelo asked the opinion of the father custodian of the Holy Land. " I think ", replied the Recollect, " that if those eminent prelates had known the conditions in this country they would never have come to such a decision ; and that is the opinion of all my friars as well." All the missionaries of Palestine and Egypt agreed, and Father Agathangelo wrote a long letter to the cardinal prefect giving theological, canonical and practical reasons for a withdrawal of the decree. The matter was referred to the Holy Office ; there is no record of its reply, but it was probably favourable, for the successors of Father Agathangelo at Cairo followed his policy without hindrance.

Unhappily, and not for the only time in history, the great obstacle to Coptic reunion in a body was the Latin Catholics themselves. Some years before encouraging negotiations had taken place between the Coptic patriarch and the consuls of France and Venice, and the French friars did not hesitate to make the renown and power of his Most Christian Majesty a *point d'appui* of their undertaking. Or rather, they wished to. But the parties to the previous conversations were all dead, and the then consul of France was a man of such shocking life that his house deserved the name given to it by Father Agathangelo, " a synagogue of Satan ". Moreover, the general life of Europeans in Cairo was such that he had to write to his superiors that the public scandals made the Church " so great an object of abomination among the Copts, Greeks and other Christians that it will be very difficult to overcome their aversion for the Latins ". Even the appointment of a new and better consul in 1637 did not mend matters. When the synod of the Coptic patriarch met in the same year to discuss the possibility of reunion, one of his councillors denounced the proposal because of the scandalous lives of Catholics in Cairo : " The Roman Church is in this country a brothel ", he exclaimed. Father Agathangelo was present, but could not deny the truth of what was said ; after gently urging that the sins of individuals, however terrible, could not alter the fact of the truth and holiness of the Church, he left the assembly and wrote a letter to the cardinal prefect of *Propaganda*. After pointing out that for three years he had asked in vain for authority publicly to excommunicate the worst offenders, he said he had done his best and could do no more : " I have appealed, I have reproved, I have threatened. . . . Now my enthusiasm, whether reasonable or indiscreet, can no longer tolerate that those who have authority should not use it. They are dumb dogs, who are afraid to bite. Your Eminence will do whatever your good zeal for God's glory may suggest to you. . . . For the love of our crucified Lord and His holy Mother may your Lordships find a cure for these enormous scandals. As for myself, I shall not be held responsible for them before the judgement-seat of Christ who will judge us all. . . ." A few days later he left Egypt for Abyssinia with Father Cassian.

A Capuchin mission for Abyssinia—or Ethiopia, as it is better called—had been planned in 1637, and Agathangelo and Cassian had been awaiting orders to go and establish it. For some years Father Cassian had been destined for Ethiopia, and with this in view had set himself while in Cairo to learn Amharic, the principal language in use in that country ; he therefore now took the leading place, as Father Agathangelo knew little of the language. They were, of course, fully informed about the dangerous state for Catholics in Ethiopia which had been brought about by recent political and ecclesiastical events there, and they had made certain provisions in view of it ; what they did not know was that a certain German Lutheran physician, Peter Heyling, notorious for his hostility to Catholics, had been at work to upset their plans. Accordingly, when they got to Dibarua, an unidentified place beyond Suakim, in the early summer of 1638, they were arrested and taken, manacled and on foot, to Gondar.

The day after their arrival they were brought, chained and in muddy and torn Franciscan habits, before King Basilides and his court. In reply to his questions Bd Cassian replied, " We are Catholics and religious, natives of France. We have come to invite you to reunion with the Roman Church. We are well known to Abuna Mark, who has had a letter from the Patriarch of Alexandria, and we should like to speak with him." Mark was the newly elected primate of the dissident Church of Ethiopia, who had been friendly with Father Agathangelo in Cairo ; but Heyling had been talking to him, and Mark now refused to see the friars, saying, " I indeed knew this Agathangelo in Egypt and he is an evil and dangerous man. He tried to draw the people there to his religion, and has come to do the same here. I do not wish to see him. I recommend you to hang them both." A Moham- medan remonstrated with the archbishop, but he repeated his words, with abuse. Basilides was inclined to banish the friars, but Peter Heyling with Mark and the king's mother worked on the mob to demand their death, and so they were sen- tenced after they had been given the opportunity to save themselves by abjuring the Catholic faith in favour of that of the monophysites.

When the two martyrs were brought beneath the trees from which they were to be hanged there was some delay. " Why are you so slow ? What are we waiting for ? " asked Bd Cassian. " We have had to send for ropes ", answered the execu- tioner. " But have we not ropes round our clothes ? " And so they were hanged with the cords of their Franciscan habits. But before they were dead the traitor Mark appeared before the crowd, crying out, " Stone these enemies of the faith of Alexandria, or I will excommunicate you ! " Volleys of stones were immediately flung at the swinging bodies, and thus Bd Agathangelo and Bd Cassian died, the one being forty years old, the other thirty. For four nights miraculous light was reported to be seen above the bodies, and Basilides in terror ordered them to be buried ; but some Catholics took them away by stealth and their resting-place is to this day unknown. In 1905, Agathangelo of Vendôme, one of the most remarkable missionaries of the seventeenth century, and his faithful companion, Cassian of Nantes, were declared blessed by Pope Pius X.

A sufficient account of these martyrs is provided in Ladislas de Vannes, *Deux martyrs capucins* (1905); and Antonio da Pontedera, *Vita e martirio dei BB. Agatangelo e Cassiano* (1904).

8 : ST JOHN VIANNEY   (A.D. 1859)

THE beauty of holiness will not be gainsaid, and from time to time some more than usually resplendent example forces the admiration of the whole world. Such were " The Little Flower " and " The holy Curé of Ars ". And of these two the popularity of M. Vianney is the more remarkable, because the halo of sentimentality, with which undisciplined devotees or unscrupulous exploiters can so easily surround Sœur Thérèse, is far less easily fitted to *his* head. His face alone is a difficulty, for little can be done by way of getting superficial " appeal " out of a man whose exterior appearance is that of a sanctified Voltaire. And the life of a country *curé* in France is no less, even if no more, unfamiliar to the average Englishman or American than the inside of a Carmelite convent. The world into which John Mary Vianney was born, at Dardilly, near Lyons, on May 8, 1786, was not an undisturbed one. When he was three the Revolution began and two years later Dardilly found itself saddled with a " constitutional priest ", so the little John and his parents had to assist in secret at the Mass of any fugitive loyal priest who came to the neighbourhood. While the Terror was going on, no less at Lyons than at Paris and elsewhere, he was learning to be a herd-boy, shepherding the cattle and sheep of Matthew Vianney's farm in the meadows on either side of the little river Planches. He was a quiet, well-behaved and religious child, who urged his companions to be good and would always rather " play at church " than at games, though he had skill at quoits, which they played for *sous*. He made his first communion, in secret, when he was thirteen, and very shortly after Mass could be offered again in public at Dardilly. Five years later he broached to his father his project of becoming a priest. But the good man was unwilling ; he could not afford to educate his son, having already had to provide for other members of the family, and could not spare him from the work of the farm, and it was not till he was twenty that John Mary could get permission to leave home for the neighbouring village of Ecully, where the Abbé Balley had established a " presbytery-school ".

His studies were a source of great trouble to him ; he had little natural aptitude and his only schooling had been a brief period at the village school opened at Dardilly when he was nine. Latin above all he found such difficulty in mastering that for a time he and his teacher were discouraged. In the summer of 1806 he made a pilgrimage on foot, over sixty miles and begging his food and shelter on the way, to the shrine of St John Francis Regis at La Louvesc, to implore God's assistance in this unforeseen obstacle. On his return he found his studies no easier, but the deadly disease of discouragement was gone, and in the following year he was further strengthened by the sacrament of confirmation. On this occasion he took the name of Baptist. And this grace came at the right moment, for another and very serious trial was at hand. Through his name not having been entered on the roll of exempt ecclesiastical students, John Mary Vianney was conscripted for the army. In vain M. Balley tried to get the matter put right, in vain Matthew Vianney tried to get a substitute for his son ; he had to report at the depot in Lyons on October 26, 1809. Two days later he was taken ill and sent to hospital, and his draft for the army in Spain left without him. On January 5, being barely convalescent, he was ordered to report at Roanne for another draft on the morrow, and, having gone into a church to pray, arrived only after it had gone. However, he was given his movement-order and set out to catch up the draft at Renaison, having still no military acoutrements but his knapsack (it carried the saint's halo rather than the marshal's baton). John made but poor progress and while he was resting at the approach to the mountains of Le Forez a stranger suddenly appeared, picked up the knapsack, and peremptorily ordered him to follow ; he was too tired to do aught but obey, and presently found himself in a hut near the remote mountain village of Les Noës. He now learned that the stranger was a deserter from the army, and that many more such were hiding in the woods and hills around. John did not know what to do ; he saw at once that his situation was compromising, and after a few days reported himself to the mayor of the commune. M. Fayot was an humane official and a sensible man ; he pointed out to John that he was already technically a deserter, and that of two evils the lesser was to remain in refuge where he was ; and found him a lodging in the house of his own cousin. His hiding-place was in a stable under a hay-loft. For fourteen months John Mary (known as Jerome Vincent) was at Les Noës, persevering with his Latin, teaching the children of his hosts and working on their farm, and earning their love and respect ; several times he was nearly taken by gendarmes, once feeling the point of a sword between his ribs as it was thrust about in the hay of the loft. In March 1810 the emperor, on the occasion of his marriage with the Archduchess Marie-Louise, had proclaimed an amnesty for all defaulters, and early in the following year, on his brother volunteering to join up before his time as a substitute, John Mary was able to return home, a free man.

In 1811 he received the tonsure and at the end of the following year was sent for a year's philosophy to the *petit séminaire* at Verrières. His career there was anything but distinguished, but he plodded on humbly and doggedly, and in the autumn of 1813 went to the *grand séminaire* at Lyons. Here all the instruction and studies were in Latin and, although the authorities recognized his quality and made special provision and allowances for him, John Mary made no headway at all. At the end of the first term he left the seminary to be coached privately by M. Balley at Ecully, and after three months presented himself for examination. In his *viva* he lost his head and broke down ; the examiners could not accept him for ordination but recommended him to try another diocese. M. Balley went off at once to see the Abbé Bochard, one of the examiners, and he agreed to come with the rector of the seminary and interview Vianney privately. After this interview, which was satisfactory, they went to put the case of " the most unlearned but the most devout seminarian in Lyons " before the vicar general, who was governing the diocese in the archbishop's absence. M. Courbon asked one question : " Is M. Vianney good ? " " He is a model of goodness ", was the reply. " Very well. Then let him be ordained. The grace of God will do the rest." On July 2, 1814, John Mary Vianney received the minor orders and subdiaconate, and returned to Ecully to continue his studies with M. Balley. In June 1815 he received the diaconate (five days after the battle of Waterloo), and on August 12 the priesthood. He offered his first Mass the following day, and was appointed curate to M. Balley, to whose clear-sightedness and perseverance is due, under God, the fact that St John Mary Vianney ever attained to the priesthood.

" The Church wants not only learned priests but, even more, holy ones ", the vicar general of Lyons had said at his ordination, and Mgr Simon, Bishop of Grenoble, had seen in the Abbé Vianney a " good priest ". The things that a priest must know he did know : but not necessarily from text-books. Moral theology, for example. When M. Bochard cross-examined him on difficult " cases ", his replies were explicit and accurate : for the Abbé Vianney was a saint and he had common sense ; and moral casuistry is sanctified common sense. A few months after his appointment to Ecully he received his faculties to hear confessions ; his first penitent was his own rector, and very soon the " run " on his confessional was noticeable. Later on the hearing of confessions was to take up three-quarters of his time. Quietly, rector and curate began to have a holy competition in austerity, rather after the manner of monks in the Thebaïd ; the *curé* denounced his *vicaire* to the vicar general for " exceeding all bounds ", while M. Vianney retorted by accusing the rector of excessive mortifications. M. Courbon laughed, and said the people of Ecully were lucky to have two such priests to do penance for them. In 1817, to the infinite sorrow of his pupil, M. Balley died, and early in the following year the Abbé Vianney was made parish-priest of Ars-en-Dombes, a remote and neglected place of 230 souls, " in every sense of the word ' a hole ' ".

There has been a good deal of exaggeration of the debased spiritual state of Ars at the time when M. Vianney took it in hand (just as there has been of the " ignorance " of the good man himself). It seems to have been in just about the same state as many English villages in the third quarter of the twentieth century : little definite immorality and malicious wickedness, but little true religion and love of God ; the greatest scandal at Ars was probably the " deadly scandal of ordinary life ". For the rest, there were several exemplary Christian families ", including that of the mayor, and the " lady of the manor ", Mlle M. A. C. Garnier des Garets (" Mlle d'Ars "), was sincerely, if rather fussily, pious. The new *curé* (he was really at that time only a chaplain to a sort of chapel-of-ease) not only continued but redoubled his austerities, especially the use of a cruel " discipline ", and for the first six years of his incumbency lived on practically nothing but potatoes, seeking to make himself a sacrifice for the shortcomings of his " feeble flock ". The evil spirits of impurity and drunkenness and dishonesty and indifference are " not cast out but by prayer and fasting ", and if the people of Ars would not pray and fast for themselves, well, then their pastor must do so for them.

When he had personally visited every household under his care and provided a regular catechism-class for the children, he set to work in earnest to make a real conversion of Ars, by personal intercourse, in the confessional, and by laboriously and carefully prepared sermons which he delivered naturally, but not quietly.* The people were too sunk in religious indifference and material preoccupations to be amenable to quietness and moderation ; moreover, in those days Jansenism was still something more than a memory and had left its backwash in the methods and teaching of orthodox but rigorist directors and theologians. Consequently it is not

* " Did M. le Curé preach long sermons ? " asked Mgr Convert of gaffer Drémieux. " Yes, long ones, and always on Hell. . . . There are some who say there is no Hell. Ah, well ! He believed in it."

surprising to find that the Curé of Ars was very strict indeed. There were too many taverns in the village, where money was wasted, drunkenness encouraged, evil talk not reprehended : first the two near the church were shut, for lack of enough business ; then two more ; seven new ones were opened in succession, but each one had to close.   He waged relentless war against blasphemy, profanity and obscenity, and was not afraid to utter from the pulpit the words and expressions that offended God, so there should be no mistake as to what he was talking about.   For eight years and more he struggled for a proper observance of Sunday : not merely to get everybody to Mass and Vespers, but to abolish work which at times was done on Sunday without a shadow of necessity.   Above all he set his face against dancing, maintaining that it was of necessity an occasion of sin to those who took part, and even to those who only looked on ; to those who took part in it, whether publicly or privately, he was merciless : they must give it up entirely and keep to their resolution, or absolution was refused them.   M. le Curé waged this battle, and the associated engagement of modesty in clothes, for twenty-five years ; but he won in the end.†

In 1821 the district of Ars was made a succursal parish, and in 1823 it became part of the revived diocese of Belley.   This was an occasion for slanderous attacks on M. Vianney (whose reforming zeal naturally made enemies for him) and his new bishop, Mgr Devie, sent the dean to enquire what it was all about ; but the bishop soon learned to have confidence in the Curé of Ars and later offered him an important parish elsewhere which he refused only after a good deal of hesitation. In the meanwhile the reputation of his holiness and achievements was also becoming known, and he was asked to give several parochial missions, when his confessional was always besieged.   In 1824 there was opened at Ars by the enterprise of the curé a free school for girls, run by Catherine Lassagne and Benedicta Lardet, two young women of the village whom he had sent away to a convent to be trained. From this school sprang, some three years later, the famous institution of *La Providence*, a shelter for orphans and other homeless or deserted children, neither babies on the one hand nor adolescent girls on the other being turned away.   Not a halfpenny was accepted from the inmates, even from girls who could pay, and neither Mlle Lassagne, Mlle Lardet, nor any other helper received any salary ; it was a charity, run on alms, and its final end the saving of souls.   At times there were sixty people thus being provided for, and the *curé* was hard put to it to support such a family.   On one occasion the loft was found full of wheat under circumstances that clearly indicate a miracle, and on another occasion the cook testified to making ten 20 lb. loaves from a few pounds of flour, at the prayer of M. Vianney. Such works as these slowly and surely brought about a change of heart among his parishioners, and visitors noticed and commented on their orderly appearance and good behaviour ; and it was the personal influence and example of the man himself that moved them in the first place : " Our *curé* is a saint and we must obey him." " We are no better than other people, but we live close to a saint."   Some of them doubtless never got beyond that, to " It is the will of God, we must obey Him ", but still they persevered in obeying the *curé* precisely because he was a good man.

And he, while his people were slowly and painfully coming back to a Christian life, was being the object of manifestations which would appear to be nothing less than a persecution by the Devil himself, as M. Vianney believed them to be.   There

† Over the arch of the chapel of St John the Baptist in the parish-church he had painted the words : " Sa tête fut le prix d'une danse ! "

is in history no other record of seemingly diabolical "infestation" so long, so varied, and so cogent; the phenomena ranged from noises and voices to personal violence and the unexplained burning of the saint's bed, and continued intermittently from 1824 for over thirty years, both by day and night, sometimes under conditions in which they were observed by others beside the sufferer. It is not an exaggeration to say he took it as all part of the day's work. "You must get very frightened", the Abbé Toccanier said to him. "One gets used to everything, my friend", was the reply. "The *grappin* and I are almost mates." Not only was the Curé of Ars subjected to supernatural persecution but he also suffered from attacks which, were it not for the infected state of human nature, would be labelled unnatural. Some of the less worthy and less discerning among his brother priests, remembering only his lack of education and formal training, listening perhaps to idle gossip, certainly unable to recognize sanctity when they saw it, criticized his "ill-judged zeal", his "ambition", his "presumption"; he was even a "quack" and an "impostor". "Poor little Curé of Ars!" he commented, "What don't they make him do and say! They are preaching on him now and no longer on the gospel." But they did not stop at verbal criticism and sacristy tittle-tattle: they delated him to the bishop of Belley. The *curé* refused to take any action, nor after enquiry did Mgr Devie; but having heard a priest apply the adjective "mad" to M. Vianney, he referred to it before his clergy assembled at their annual retreat and added, "Gentlemen, I wish that all my clergy had a small grain of the same madness".

Another of the astonishing circumstances of the Abbé Vianney's incumbency of Ars was its becoming a place of pilgrimage even during his lifetime: and that not to the shrine of "his dear little St Philomena", which he had set up, but to himself. No doubt curiosity had its share in starting it, for miracles of loaves and visits of the Devil cannot be kept quiet, but it gathered strength and volume and continued because people wanted the spiritual direction of the village priest in his confessional. This steady stream of penitents, "the pilgrimage", was what chiefly upset his myopic clerical critics: some of them even forbade their people to go to him. People from afar began to consult him so early as 1827; from 1830 to 1845 the daily visitors averaged over three hundred; at Lyons a special booking-office was opened for Ars, and 8-day return tickets issued—one could hardly hope to get a word with the *curé* in less. For him this meant not less than eleven or twelve hours every day in the confessional in winter, and anything up to sixteen in summer; nor was he content with that: for the last fifteen years of his life he gave an instruction every day in the church at eleven o'clock. Simple discourses, unprepared—he had no chance to prepare them—which went to the hearts of the most learned and the most hardened. Rich and poor, learned and simple, good and bad, lay and cleric, bishops, priests, religious, all came to Ars, to kneel in the confessional and sit before the "catechism-stall". M. Vianney did not give long instructions and directions to his penitents; a few words, a sentence even, but it had the authority of holiness and not infrequently was accompanied by supernatural knowledge of the penitent's life: how many times, for example, he was able to correct the number of years since a penitent had last been to confession, or remind him of a sin which he had forgotten. "'Love your clergy very much', was all he said to me", said the Archbishop of Auch; "Love the good God very much", to the superior general of a teaching institute; "What a pity! What a pity!" he would murmur at each accusation, and weep at the tale of sin. This people came hundreds of miles and waited sometimes twelve hours on end, or had to attend in the church day after day, before they could be heard ; and by these simple means numberless conversions were made.

At first the rigour with which the *curé* treated his own flock was extended to outsiders ; but with advancing years came greater experience of the needs and capabilities of souls and deeper insight into moral theology, and pity, kindness and tenderness modified his severity.   He discouraged people from encumbering themselves with a multiplicity of little " devotions ".   The rosary, the *Angelus,* ejaculatory prayer, above all, the Church's liturgy, these he recommended. " Private prayer ", he would say, " is like straw scattered here and there : if you set it on fire it makes a lot of little flames.   But gather these straws into a bundle and light them, and you get a mighty fire, rising like a column into the sky : public prayer is like that."   " There were no affected attitudes, no ' ohs ! ' and ' ahs ! ', no sighs and transports about M. Vianney ; when most interiorly moved he simply smiled—or wept."

Reference has been made to his power of reading souls, and his knowledge of the hidden past and of future events was no less remarkable than his more formal miracles.   None of these things can be brought within the charge of " uselessness ", a criticism so easily and so thoughtlessly made at the marvels attributed to some of the saints ; but the Abbé Vianney's prophecies did not relate to public affairs but to the lives of individuals and were directed to their personal help and consolation. On one occasion he made the interesting admission that hidden things seemed to come to him by way of memory.   He told the Abbé Toccanier that, " I once said to a certain woman, ' So it is you who have left your husband in hospital and who refuse to join him.' ' How do you know that ? ' she asked, ' I've not mentioned it to a soul.'   I was more surprised than she was ; I imagined that she had already told me the whole story."   The Baroness de Lacomblé, a widow, was troubled by the determination of her eighteen-year-old son to marry a girl of fifteen.   She determined to consult the Curé of Ars, whom she had never met.   When she went into the church it was crowded to the doors and she despaired of ever getting a word with him ; suddenly he came out of his confessional, went straight up to her and whispered, " Let them marry.   They will be very happy ! "   A servant-girl was warned by him that a great peril awaited her in Lyons ; a few days later the memory of this warning enabled her to escape from the hands of a murderer of girls, at whose trial she subsequently gave evidence.   To Mgr Ullathorne, Bishop of Birmingham, he in 1854 said with great conviction, " I believe that the Church in England will recover her former greatness ".   He stopped a strange girl in his church one day.   " Is it you who have written to me, my child ? "   " Yes, M. l'abbé."   " Very well.   You must not worry.   You will enter the convent all right.   You will hear from the reverend mother in a few days."   And it was so : nor had he communicated with the abbess concerned.   Mlle Henry, a shopkeeper at Chalon-sur-Saône, came to ask M. Vianney to pray for the cure of her sick aunt. He told her to go back home at once, for " while you are here you are being imposed on ! "   She returned accordingly and found her assistant making free with the stock ; and the aunt recovered.

The numerous miracles of bodily healing reported of the Curé of Ars were mostly attributed by him to the intercession of St Philomena, and his first demand of those that sought them was fervour of faith : something of the faith by which he himself was enabled miraculously to provide money and goods when one or other of his charities was in straits.   But the schoolmaster of Ars, echoing the well-known words about St Bernard, saw where was the greatest miracle of all : " The most difficult, extraordinary and amazing work that the Curé did was his own life." And every day after the noon *Angelus,* when he left the church to go to the presbytery to eat the food brought in from *La Providence,* there was a manifestation of recognition, love and respect for his goodness.   It sometimes took him over twenty minutes to cross that dozen yards.   The sick in soul and body knelt to ask his blessing and his prayers : they seized his hands, they tore pieces from his cassock. It was one of his hardest mortifications : " What misguided devotion ! " he exclaimed at it.   It is not surprising that as time went on M. Vianney longed more and more for solitude and quiet.   But there is more to it than that : every one of his forty-one years at Ars was spent there against his own will ; all the time he had to fight his personal predilection for the life of a Carthusian or Cistercian.   He left the village three times, " ran away " in fact, and in 1843, after a grave illness, it needed the diplomacy of the bishop and of M. des Garets to get him to return.

In 1852 Mgr Chalandon, Bishop of Belley, made M. Vianney an honorary canon of the chapter ;   he was invested almost by force and never again put on his *mozzetta,* which indeed he sold for fifty francs which he required for some charitable purpose.   Three years later well-meaning but insensitive officials obtained for him further recognition in the form of a civil decoration : he was made a knight of the Imperial Order of the Legion of Honour.   But with this he positively refused to be invested, and no persuasion could induce him to have the imperial cross pinned to his cassock, even for a moment.   " What if, when death comes, I were to appear with these toys and God were to say to me : ' Begone !   You have had your reward ? ' "   " I can't think why the emperor has sent it to me," he added, " unless it is because I was once a deserter ! "   In 1853 M. Vianney made his last attempt at flight from Ars.   It is a moving story, of the old and worn-out priest cajoled back to his presbytery on behalf of the numerous poor sinners who were unable to do without him.   " He imagined he was doing the will of God by going away ", said Catherine Lassagne in innocent surprise.   And it may well have been the will of God that his servant should now have some few years of repose and peace, to practise that contemplation which had already borne fruit in some of the highest experiences of ecstasy and vision.   It is not impossible that Bishop Chalandon should have been mistaken in not allowing him to resign his cure.   But such a possibility was not one which M. Vianney would entertain ; he devoted himself to his ministry more assiduously than ever.   In the year 1858-1859 over 100,000 pilgrims visited Ars ; the *curé* was now a very old man of seventy-three, and the strain was too much.   On July 18 he knew the end was at hand, and on the 29th he lay down on his bed for the last time : " It is my poor end.   You must send for M. le curé of Jassans ", he said.   Even now he sent for several souls to kneel by his bed and finish their confessions.   As the news spread people flocked into Ars from all sides : twenty priests accompanied the Abbé Beau when he brought the last sacraments from the church.   " It is sad to receive holy communion for the last time ", murmured the dying priest.   On August 3 the Bishop of Belley arrived in haste, and at two o'clock in the morning of the 4th, amid a storm of thunder and lightning, the earthly life of the Curé of Ars came to a gentle end.

St John Mary Baptist Vianney was canonized by Pius XI in 1925.   The same pope made him principal patron-saint of the parochial clergy throughout the world in 1929.

Mgr F. Trochu's Life of the Curé d'Ars (1928) has been founded upon a careful study of the evidence submitted in the process of beatification and canonization, and is likely for a long time to hold the field. It clears up a number of points left obscure by such earlier biographers as the Abbé Monnin (1899) and Joseph Vianney (1911), and both in its bibliographical introduction and in the footnotes it provides full details concerning the sources which have been utilized. There is an English translation by Dom E. Graf. A volume in Italian of over 800 pages, *Ars e il suo curato*, by A. M. Zecca (1929), is not so much a biography as an agreeable record of the impressions of a pilgrim visiting Ars. Among slighter sketches that of H. Ghéon, translated by F. J. Sheed, *The Secret of the Curé d'Ars*, deserves special commendation. See also Trochu, *L'âme du Curé d'Ars* (1929), and *Autour du Curé d'Ars* (1950) ; and the saint's sermons, edited in 4 volumes by M. A. Delaroche (1925).

SS. CYRIACUS, LARGUS AND SMARAGDUS, MARTYRS (DATE UNKNOWN)

THE legend of St Cyriacus and his companions is a romance devoid of historical value. It relates that Cyriacus was a deacon who, with Sissinius, Largus and Smaragdus, succoured the Christians who were being forced to work on the construction of the baths of Diocletian. Having been arrested, Cyriacus cured the emperor's daughter, Artemia, of demoniac possession, and was rewarded with the present of a house ; herein he established a place of worship, the *titulus Cyriaci*. He was then sent to Persia at the request of its king, whose daughter suffered in the same way as Artemia, and her also he cured. After his return to Rome he was apprehended by order of Maximian, together with Largus and Smaragdus, and on March 16, in company with a score of others, he was tortured and beheaded at a spot on the Salarian Way. On August 8 Pope St Marcellus I translated the bodies to a burial-place, which received the name of Cyriacus, on the road to Ostia.

That Cyriacus was an authentic martyr, honoured on this day in Rome from an early date, is proved from the *Depositio Martyrum* of 354. Therein he is said to rest close beside the seventh milestone on the road to Ostia in company with Largus, " Ixmaracdus ", and three others, who are named. Delehaye shows that this Cyriacus has been confused with another Cyriacus, the founder of the *titulus Cyriaci*, and that a fictitious story was later evolved which is best known to us as an episode in the spurious Acts of Pope St Marcellus.

See on the whole question Delehaye in CMH., p. 425 (with which *cf. ibidem* pp. 190 and 431–433) ; and Duchesne in *Mélanges d'archéologie et d'histoire*, vol. xxxvi, pp. 49–56.

THE FOURTEEN HOLY HELPERS

THIS name represents a group of saints, devotion to whom as a body was German in origin and largely German in diffusion. The idea behind the devotion is sufficiently indicated by its name, and the theoretical qualification for inclusion in the group was a real or alleged divine promise to the saint during life that he or she would have particular intercessory power to help men in need. The usual fourteen names are ACHATIUS (June 22) ; BARBARA (December 4 ; invoked against lightning, fire, explosion, sudden and unprepared death) ; BLAISE (February 3 ; invoked against throat troubles) ; CATHERINE (November 25 ; invoked by philosophers, students, wheelers and others) ; CHRISTOPHER (July 25 ; invoked by travellers in difficulties) ; CYRIACUS (August 8) ; DENIS (October 9 ; invoked against headache and rabies) ; ERASMUS (June 2 ; against colic, cramp, etc.) ; EUSTACE (September

20 ; invoked by hunters) ; GEORGE (April 23 ; protector of soldiers) ; GILES (September 1 ; invoked against epilepsy, insanity and sterility) ; MARGARET (July 20 ; invoked against possession and by pregnant women) ; PANTALEON (July 27 ; invoked against phthisis) ; and VITUS (June 15 ; invoked against epilepsy and his " dance ").

It will be noticed that all these saints except one (Giles) were martyrs. Among the other saints included in the group locally were Dorothy (February 6), Leonard of Noblac (November 6), Magnus of Füssen and Magnus of Altino (October 6), Oswald (August 5), and Nicholas of Myra (" Santa Klaus " ; December 6). All the above will be found referred to herein under their dates. In France the Helpers are fifteen, the extra one being our Lady.

This devotion is an example of the medieval popular tendency to honour the saints more for what they would do for their devotees than for what they had been in their earthly lives. The *cultus* became widely diffused during the fifteenth century ; it spread from the Germanies to Bohemia, Moravia, Hungary, Italy and France ; it does not seem to have reached England. Churches, hospitals and shrines were named after the Holy Helpers, and their feast was permitted in various places, on August 8 and other dates. It is still observed at a few places in Germany, and there is a church under their invocation at Baltimore in Maryland.

The book of H. Weber, *Die Verehrung der hl. vierzehn Nothhelfer* (1886), supplies abundant information. The Bollandists touch upon the subject in dealing with St George, *Acta Sanctorum*, April, vol. iii, pp. 149–150. See also A. Franz, *Die Messe im deutschen Mittelalter*, and Zöckler in the *Realencyklopädie für protestantische Theologie*, vol. xiv, pp. 217–218.

ST HORMISDAS, MARTYR   (*c.* A.D. 420)

THE shocking persecution of Christians carried on by Sapor II, King of Persia, was renewed by Yazdagird I, the occasion being the burning down of a Mazdaean temple by a priest. This unhappy man, who brought so much distress on the faithful, was constrained to admit that persuasion and not violence is the only Christian method, but this did not mollify the anger of the king. It is not easy, says Theodoret, to describe or express the cruelties which were then invented against the disciples of Christ. On the death of Yazdagird the persecution was carried on by his son Bahram ; and Hormisdas (Hormizd) was one of the chief victims. He was of the nobility among the Persians, son to the governor of a province. Bahram sent for him, and commanded him to renounce Jesus Christ. Hormisdas answered him, " Nay ! This would offend God, and be against charity and justice ; whoever dares to violate the supreme law of the sovereign Lord of all would easily betray his king, who is only a mortal man. If that be a crime deserving death, what must it be to renounce the God and ruler of the universe ? " The king at this answer caused him to be deprived of his rank, honours and goods, and even stripped of clothes to his loin-cloth, and ordered him to look after the camels of the army. Some time after Bahram saw Hormisdas all sunburnt and covered with dust, and calling to mind his former position and the high office of his father, he was filled with pity ; so he sent for him, ordered a gown to be given him, and said, " Now lay aside your obstinacy, and renounce the carpenter's Son ". The saint pulled off the gown and threw it away, saying, " Why should you have thought that I should so easily be tempted to abandon the law of God ? Take back your present." The king, incensed at his boldness, sent him back to his camels. It is not known when and how St Hormisdas suffered martyrdom.

See the *Acta Sanctorum*, August, vol. ii, where the passage of Theodoret, bk v, ch. 39, is quoted at length. See also Assemani, *Bibliotheca orientalis*, vol. iii, pt 2, p. 384. There seems to be a reference to this St Hormisdas in the Martyrology of Rabban Sliba on September 1 ; for which *cf.* the *Analecta Bollandiana*, vol. xxvii (1908), p. 193.

ST ALTMAN, BISHOP OF PASSAU   (A.D. 1091)

ST ALTMAN was born at Paderborn during the first quarter of the eleventh century, and studied at Paris. After being ordained he was appointed canon and master of the cathedral-school at Paderborn, then provost of the chapter of Aachen and chaplain to the Emperor Henry III, and confessor and counsellor of the Dowager Empress Agnes. In 1064 he took part in a pilgrimage to the Holy Land, which numbered seven thousand persons (according to a monk who was there) and was led by several archbishops and bishops, and the adventure was a most unhappy one. Having safely traversed Europe and Asia Minor with no more than the misfortunes inevitable to so long a journey on horseback, they were attacked by Saracens in Palestine and sustained a siege in an abandoned village ; lack of food forced them to surrender, and they might all have been massacred but for the intervention of a friendly emir. Though they eventually reached Jerusalem they were not able to visit many of the other holy places because of the enmity of the Saracens, and by the time the pilgrimage reached home again it had lost nearly half of its members, dead from hardship, sickness and murder. It was happenings of this sort which contributed, thirty years later, to the institution of the crusades.

Immediately on his return Altman was nominated to the see of Passau, and he set himself energetically to govern a large and deteriorated diocese. For the increase of learning, the care of the poor, and proper carrying out of divine worship he looked particularly to regular clergy ; at Göttweig he founded an abbey of Augustinian canons, put the same at Sankt Pölten in the place of secular canons, and introduced the Cluniac reform at Kremsmünster. In these works he had the help of the Empresses Agnes and Bertha, and the Emperor Henry IV was a bene-factor of the see ; but St Altman soon found himself in conflict with that monarch. When in 1074 Pope St Gregory VII renewed the pontifical decrees against simony and married clergy, Altman read out the letter in his cathedral. It was very ill received, he had to escape from the ensuing uproar, and found himself opposed in the matter of celibacy by a strong party led by his own provost. The bishop's chief supporters were the Augustinian canons, but the rebels invoked the help of the emperor ; Altman did his best to enforce the decree, excommunicated the provost, and, when in the following year the pope forbade lay investiture, definitely ranged himself against Henry. He was driven from his see, and went to Rome. He had some scruples as to whether he held his own see simoniacally, as he had received it by favour of the Empress Agnes ; but St Gregory VII confirmed him in it and appointed him delegate apostolic for Germany.

St Altman returned to his see in 1081, but was turned out again almost at once ; he spent the remaining years of his life in exile but maintained a footing in the eastern part of his diocese, from whence he exercised a great influence. He had lost all his revenues and was in great poverty, but for all that his charity to the poor did not abate, and in a time of famine he sold his furniture to relieve the suffering.

Nor did the disturbance of his rule and his long banishment entirely spoil his work ; a canon of Göttweig who wrote an account of him not long after his death says that when he was appointed bishop many of his churches were of wood, and so were his priests ; he had stone churches built and, though it was more difficult to reform the clergy than their buildings, he had inspired many priests with an enthusiasm for celibacy and a contempt for riches.   St Altman was an important figure in the early history of canons regular ; in addition to the foundations mentioned above he instituted them at Sankt Florian, at St Nicholas's in his cathedral city, and other places.   He died in 1091, and his *cultus* was approved by Pope Leo XIII.

There are two lives printed in the *Acta Sanctorum*.   The older of these (re-edited in MGH., *Scriptores*, vol. xii, pp. 226–243) was written some fifty years after Altman's death by a canon of Göttweig.   The second for the greater part adds no new facts, but fills some *lacunae* in the narrative towards the end.   An excellent German translation of the earlier document, with abundant notes, has been published by A. Fuchs, *Der heilige Altmann* (1929).   See also Hans Hirsch " Die Vita Altmanni " in *Jahrbuch für Landeskunde von Nieder-Österreich*, vols. xv and xvi, pp. 348–366 ; and A. Stonner, *Heilige der deutschen Frühzeit*, vol. ii (1935).

BD JOAN OF AZA, MATRON   (*c.* A.D. 1190)

THE mother of St Dominic is said to have been born in the castle of Aza, near Aranda in Old Castile ; nothing is known of her childhood, but doubtless her marriage took place when she was very young, according to the custom of the time and country.   Her husband was Felix, perhaps de Guzman, who was warden of the small town of Calaruega in the province of Burgos, of which Dante writes in speaking of St Dominic : " Happy Calaroga ! there where the gentle breeze whispers and wanders among the young flowers that bloom over the garden of Europe, near that shore where the waves break and behind which the great sun sinks at evening."   Here they lived and here were born to them four children, Antony, who became a canon of St James and sold all that he had that he might serve the poor and sick in a hospital ; Bd Mannes, who followed his younger brother, Dominic ; and an unknown daughter, whose two sons became preaching friars.   The greatest of these children was a child of promise, for when Antony and Mannes were already grown up and clerics, Joan wished for another son and prayed to that end in the abbey-church of Silos ; and a vision of St Dominic of Silos is said to have appeared to her in sleep, telling her that a son would be born to her and that he would be a shining light to the Church : and she in thankfulness determined that he should be baptized Dominic.

While the child was yet unborn Bd Joan dreamed " that she bore a dog in her womb and that it broke away from her with a burning torch in its mouth wherewith it set the world aflame " ; this dog became a symbol of the Dominican Order and in later ages gave rise to the pun *Domini canes*, " the watch-dogs of the Lord ". His godmother at his baptism (or, as some say, Bd Joan again) likewise had a dream in which the babe appeared with a shining star upon his forehead, enlightening the world : wherefore is a star often shown upon images of the saint.   Dominic remained under the care of his mother till he was seven years old, and then was sent to school with his uncle, the parish priest of Gumiel d'Izan.   Other stories are told, but by later writers, about the saint's infancy.

It has not been given to many mothers of saints to be themselves beatified, and Joan achieved this distinction by her own virtues and not by those of her children :

it is not unusual for hagiographers to praise the parents of their heroes, but to the mother of St Dominic such praise is due in her own right ; to beauty of soul she added beauty of body, and both were handed on to the greatest of her sons.   Her *cultus* dates from the moment of her death ; a hermitage at Uclés, where she would go to visit the commandery of the Knights of St James, was called after her, and likewise a chapel in the cemetery at Calaruega.   At the request of King Ferdinand VII this *cultus* was confirmed in 1828.

It is to be feared that the little we are told concerning Bd Joan does not rest upon a very sound basis of evidence.   See, however, Ganay, *Les Bienheureuses Dominicaines*, pp. 13 *seq.* ; R. Castaño, *Monografía de Santa Joanna* (1900) ; Procter, *Dominican Saints*, pp. 215–219 ; and the standard lives of St Dominic.

BD JOHN FELTON, Martyr   (A.D. 1570)

ON February 25, 1569–70, Pope St Pius V published a bull, " *Regnans in excelsis* ", directed against Queen Elizabeth, who was at the time ostensibly a Catholic.   By it she was declared excommunicate, deprived of the kingdom which she ruled and all her subjects discharged from their allegiance, because she claimed headship of the Church in England, sheltered heretics, oppressed Catholics, and coerced her subjects into heresy and repudiation of the Holy See, contrary to her coronation oath.   On the following May 25 the citizens of London woke up to find a copy of this bull of excommunication of their sovereign fastened to the door of the bishop of London's house, adjoining St Paul's cathedral ; it had been put there late on the previous night by Mr John Felton, a gentleman of a Norfolk family who lived in Southwark.

It was not long before it was discovered who had done the deed.   Searchers in the chambers of a well-known Catholic lawyer in Lincoln's Inn found a copy of the bull, arrested the lawyer, and racked him, whereupon he confessed that he had had it from Felton.   He was at once seized at Bermondsey, but, although he at once admitted what he had done, he was not brought to trial for three months ; he was kept in prison, Newgate and the Tower, and was three times racked, in the hope that he would confess to some political intrigue with the Spaniards.   But there had been none on his part : he had published the bull as a legitimate pontifical censure for the queen's religious offences.   When brought to trial at the Guildhall on August 4 he pleaded guilty and openly declared the supremacy of the Holy See. Four days later he was dragged to St Paul's churchyard ; the scaffold was set up opposite the door on which the bull had been posted, and at the sight of the barbarous paraphernalia of execution the martyr was seized with a violent spasm of fear.   By an effort of will more violent he overcame it : he pointed at the bishop's door, saying, " The supreme pontiff's letters against the pretended queen were by me exhibited there.   Now I am ready to die for the Catholic faith " ; to that queen, as a token of good-will, he sent a valuable ring off his finger ; then he knelt and said the *Miserere*, commended his soul to God, and was cast off.   The executioner would in pity have let him hang, but the sheriff ordered that he be cut down alive, and as his heart was torn out, Mrs Salisbury, his daughter, heard him utter the name of Jesus twice.

The wife of Bd John Felton had been a personal friend of the queen, who after her husband's death licensed her to have a priest as chaplain in her house : there are few enough acts of this sort to Elizabeth's credit to make this one worth recording, and the circumstance doubtless had its effect in determining the career of the son, Bd Thomas Felton, then a babe of two, who eighteen years later followed his father to martyrdom.　John was equivalently beatified in the decree of 1886. There is no need here to discuss the question of the bull " *Regnans in excelsis* " ; Bd John suffered for publishing a canonical act of the Holy See against a supporter of heresy and a persecutor, who proceeded against him for supporting papal ecclesiastical jurisdiction.　Whether that act was opportune or justifiable under the circumstances is beside the point.　Popes, even when they are saints, as Pius V was, are not immune from errors of judgement, and it is now the general opinion of Catholics that " *Regnans in excelsis* " was a belated attempt to exercise a deposing power already in fact a dead letter.　For the rest, we have the words of another Pope Pius, to the Academy of the Catholic Religion in 1871 : " Though certain popes have sometimes exercised this deposing power in extreme cases, they did so in accordance with the public law of the time and by the agreement of Christian nations, whose reverence for the pope as the supreme judge for Christ extended to his passing even civil judgement on princes and nations.　But the present state of affairs is entirely different. . . . No one now thinks any more of the right of deposing princes which the Holy See formerly exercised ; and the Supreme Pontiff even less than anyone."

A full account is given in B. Camm, LEM., vol. ii (1905), pp. 1–13 ; *cf.* also the introduction, pp. xviii–xx ; and see further J. H. Pollen in *The Month*, February 1902.

9 : ST ROMANUS, Martyr　　(A.D. 258)

ACCORDING to the *Liber Pontificalis* Romanus was a doorkeeper of the Roman church who suffered martyrdom at the same time as St Laurence, whose unreliable *acta* make of him a soldier in Rome at the time of the martyrdom of Laurence. Seeing the joy and constancy with which that holy martyr suffered persecution, he was moved to embrace the faith, and was instructed and baptized by him in prison. Confessing aloud what he had done, he was arraigned, condemned and beheaded the day before the execution of St Laurence.　Thus he arrived at his crown before his guide and master.　The body of St Romanus was buried on the road to Tivoli in the cemetery of Cyriaca, and his grave is mentioned as being there in the itineraries of the seventh century.

Mgr Duchesne's note in his edition of the *Liber Pontificalis*, vol. i, p. 156, supplies all the information which is available ; and see CMH., p. 428.

ST EMYGDIUS, Martyr　　(A.D. 304)

CHIEFLY because he is regarded as patron against earthquakes, St Emygdius (Emidius) is greatly honoured in Italy : for the same reason his *cultus* has, in later years, been extended to San Francisco and Los Angeles in the United States.　The saint's true history has long since been forgotten, but his legend is preserved in his so-called " acts ".　He is there described as a German who, after being converted to Christianity, left his native city of Trier and came to Rome during the pontificate of Pope Marcellus I.　Full of zeal for the faith, Emygdius entered a heathen temple and dashed a statue of Aesculapius to the ground.   The pagans of Rome were so incensed by this action that Pope Marcellus, in order to protect Emygdius from their vengeance, ordained him, consecrated him a bishop, and sent him to evangelize the territory of Ascoli Piceno.   There he laboured with success, making many converts. He was beheaded during the persecution of Diocletian, together with three companions, SS. Eupolus, Germanus and Valentinus.   Seeing that St Marcellus did not occupy the chair of St Peter until 308, he could scarcely have been the pope who ordained St Emygdius, but popular tradition is notoriously indifferent to chronology.   On the other hand, it is possible that a careless scribe may have substituted the name of Marcellus for that of Marcellinus, who was his predecessor. The festival of St Emygdius is kept throughout Italy on August 9 and other dates, in accordance with local use and tradition.

The Bollandists have printed the supposed *passio* of St Emygdius in the *Acta Sanctorum*, August, vol. ii, but they regard the story as altogether untrustworthy.   Several booklets have been written by devout inhabitants of Ascoli and others about their patron, but most of these are entirely uncritical.   The most considerable seem to be the volumes by P. A. Appiani (1702), A. G. Andreucci (1729), G. Masdeu (1794) and G. Levis (1809).

SS. NATHY AND FELIM, Bishops   (SIXTH CENTURY ?)

THOUGH not associated with one another so far as is known, these two saints are celebrated throughout Ireland by a common feast on this day.   St Felim (Fedhlimidh) was the son of Dediva, a lady who was married four times, and had several saints among her children, including Dermot, Abbot of Inis Clothrann, brothergerman to Felim.   We have no particulars or even legends of St Felim, but he is traditionally venerated as the first bishop of Kilmore ; he was probably a regionary bishop in the Breffney country.   Another FELIM, named on the 18th or 28th of this month, was king of Munster in the ninth century ; according to the exploits of his life he must have been included in the Martyrology of **Gorman** either in error or as a penitent.

St Nathy Cruimthir, that is " the Priest ", was a native of the Luighne district in Sligo and is mentioned in the life of St Attracta, who was probably his contemporary.   He is said to have been put at Achonry by St Finnian of Clonard, though the name by which he was known makes it unlikely that he was a bishop.

No biography either in Latin or Irish seems to be available in either case.   Nathy is commemorated under this day in the *Félire* of Oengus.   See O'Hanlon, LIS., vol. viii.

ST OSWALD OF NORTHUMBRIA, Martyr   (A.D. 642)

AFTER the death of King St Edwin in the year 633 in battle against Penda and Cadwallon, Oswald, nephew of Edwin, prepared to regain possession of both parts of Northumbria ; he had received Christianity with his whole heart and, far from forsaking Christ as his unhappy brothers had done to court the favour of his subjects, he wished to bring them to the spiritual kingdom of divine grace.   While Cadwallon ravaged the Northumbrian provinces, Oswald assembled what troops he was able, and marched confidently, though with a small force, against his enemy. In 634 battle was joined some three miles south of Hexham, near Rowley Burn. The evening before the engagement, the king caused a great wooden cross to be made, and he held it up whilst the hole dug in the earth to plant it in was filled up round the foot.   When it was fixed, St Oswald cried out to his army (in which only a handful of individuals were Christians), " Let us now kneel down, and together pray to the almighty and only true God that He will mercifully defend us from our enemy ; for He knows that we fight in defence of our lives and country ". All the soldiers did as he commanded, and that same night Oswald had a vision wherein St Columba of Iona appeared to stretch his cloak over his sleeping troops and to promise them victory on the morrow. And so it fell out. God blessed Oswald's faith and the superior forces of Cadwallon were routed and himself killed in the battle. It was a happy omen, says St Bede, that the place where this cross was set up was called in English *Hefenfelth*, that is, " Heaven field " (though doubtless in fact it was given that name later), because there was erected the first heavenly trophy of faith : before that time no church or altar was known to have been raised in the kingdom of the Bernicians. This cross of St Oswald was afterwards very famous. In St Bede's time little chips of it were steeped in water, and drunk by sick persons, or sprinkled upon them, and many recovered their health. After the death of King Oswald, the monks of Hexham used to come to the place on the day before the anniversary of his death, there to sing the night-office and to celebrate Mass the next morning. A church was built on the spot some time before Bede wrote.

St Oswald immediately set himself to restore good order throughout his dominions, and to plant in them the faith of Christ. Naturally enough he looked not to Canterbury but to Scotland, where he had received the faith himself, for help in this task, and asked for a bishop and assistants by whose preaching the people whom he governed might be grounded in the Christian religion and receive baptism. St Aidan, a native of Ireland and a monk of Iona, was chosen for the arduous undertaking, and he by his mildness repaired the mischief done by another monk, sent before him, whose harshness had alienated many from the gospel which he professed to preach. The king bestowed on Aidan the isle of Lindisfarne for his episcopal see, and, before the bishop could sufficiently speak the English language, he would himself be his interpreter and explain his sermons and instructions to the people. " From that time many of the Scots [Irish] came daily into Britain and preached the word with great devotion to those provinces of the English over which King Oswald reigned. . . . Churches were built in a number of places ; the people gladly gathered to hear the gospel ; money and land were given by the king to build monasteries ; and the English, high and low, were instructed by their Scottish teachers in the rules and observance of regular discipline, for most of them that came to preach were monks " (Bede).

Oswald, whilst he was governing his temporal kingdom, was intent to labour and pray also for an eternal crown ; and by reason of his praying and giving thanks at all times, it is said that whenever he was sitting he would have his hands on his knees turned upwards, toward Heaven. The kingdom of Northumberland then extended as far as the Firth of Forth, and so great was his power that the other kings of England recognized in him some sort of nominal overlordship (*bretwalda*), so that St Adamnan, in his life of St Columba, styles him " Emperor of all Britain ". Bede gives the following example of the charity of this great king amidst his prosperity. One Easter day, whilst he was sitting down to dinner, an officer came in and told him there was a multitude of poor people at his gate, asking alms. The king sent them a large silver dish full of meat, and ordered the dish to be broken into small pieces and distributed among them. Upon this, St Aidan, who happened to be at table, taking him by the right hand, said, " May this hand never perish ".

After St Oswald's death his right arm was cut off and remained incorrupt at least till the time of Simeon of Durham (d. *c.* 1135), when it was kept at the minster of Peterborough.   St Oswald married Cyneburga, daughter of Cynegils, the first Christian king of Wessex ; he stood sponsor for him at his baptism.   They had one child, a son, Ethelwald, who became king of Deira and was little credit to his father.

When St Oswald had reigned some years war broke out with the pagan Penda of Mercia.   Penda again allied himself with the Welsh and the struggle lasted until a decisive battle was fought at Maserfield (probably Oswestry in Shropshire).   St Oswald met him with an inferior force, and was killed in the battle.   When he saw himself surrounded with his enemies, he offered his last prayer for the souls of his soldiers, and it became a proverb : " O God, be merciful to their souls, as said Oswald when he fell."   He was slain in the thirty-eighth year of his age, on August 5, 642.   His relics were eventually distributed to various places and St Bede chronicles some of the many miracles of which they were the occasion ; nor is it to be wondered at that the sick should be healed by him when dead, for while he lived he never ceased to provide for the poor and infirm.   St Oswald was formerly remembered as one of the great national heroes of England, and his veneration extended to Scotland, Ireland, Portugal, northern Italy, Bohemia, southern Germany and Switzerland, where he is patron of Zug.   His memory is now somewhat dim ; but his feast is observed in several English dioceses and in Argyll (with a proper Mass) on August 9 ; and at Meissen and Trier.   He is named in the Roman Martyrology on the 5th.

We know little of St Oswald beyond what has been recorded in Bede's *Ecclesiastical History*, bk iii, but C. Plummer gives (vol. ii, p. 161) a list of subsequent lives of the holy king.   That by Drogo (eleventh century) is printed in the *Acta Sanctorum*, August,vol. ii; that by Reginald of Durham may be found in Arnold's edition of Simeon of Durham (Rolls Series).   Plummer points out in detail (pp. 159–160) how widespread was the *cultus* of St Oswald in central Europe.   Plummer's notes upon Bede's text are also valuable, as well as those in the edition of Mayor and Lumby (1881).   For the Swiss *cultus*, see E. P. Baker's article in *Archaeologia*, vol. xciii (1949), pp. 103–123, and for northern Italy, the same writer in *Archaeologia*, vol. xciv (1951), pp. 167–194.

BD JOHN OF SALERNO   (A.D. 1242)

JOHN GUARNA was born at Salerno about the year 1190.   While studying at Bologna he met St Dominic; they were mutually attracted one to the other, and John received the habit of the new order.   In 1219 thirteen friars were sent to preach in Etruria and of these, though he was easily the youngest, John of Salerno was made superior.   A house was given them at Ripoli, near Florence, from whence they went out to the whole neighbourhood, but particularly to Florence itself, where John every day preached in the streets and sought the sheep that were lost.   This arrangement was soon found to be too inconvenient and wasteful of time, and the community moved to San Pancrazio, adjoining the walls of the city.   Here Bd John had a trying experience with a young woman of undisciplined desires who had given herself up to a passion for him.   She pretended she was ill, went to bed, and sent for Brother John to hear her confession ; the friar went at once, only to discover his " penitent " taking brazen advantage of their being alone.   He rebuked the girl severely and tried to bring her to reason but she took no notice, so he could only go away and leave her.   But he did not forget her, and his prayers eventually brought the girl to repentance towards God and humble apology to himself. This incident is said to have been made public in the following way. A possessed woman was being exorcized by a priest when the evil spirit, speaking by her mouth, exclaimed, " Only he who was unburned in the fire can drive me out ! " He was adjured to explain who and what he meant, and he named the prior of the Dominicans and told the story ; Bd John was sent for and the woman was freed. He had the gift of reading minds and consciences, and would sometimes abash or enlighten a penitent or one of his subjects by his knowledge of them.

In 1221 he found his community turned out of the church in which they had been wont to sing the Divine Office ; he soon established them at Santa Maria Novella, whose famous present church was begun fifty years later. Florence was troubled at this time by the Patarines, a sect which had penetrated into Italy from Bosnia ; Pope Gregory IX commissioned Bd John to deal with these heretics, whose tenets and life were similar to those of the Albigensians who had first exercised St Dominic. They were indignant at his campaign but he refused to be intimidated by their threats or ruffled by their insults, and succeeded in bringing numbers back to the Church and to a Christian life. While he lay dying Bd John reminded his brethren that no action requires so much care, devotion and purity as the reception of holy communion. His *cultus* was approved in 1783.

A life by John Caroli has been printed in the *Acta Sanctorum*, September, vol. iii, but with *lacunae*, which in the *Analecta Bollandiana*, vol. vii (1888), pp. 85–94, have been made good from a recovered copy of the text. Mortier speaks of Bd John in his *Histoire des maîtres généraux O.P.*, vol. i, pp. 106 *seq.* See also Procter, *Lives of Dominican Saints*, pp. 226–228. A fuller bibliography is supplied in Taurisano, p. 11.

BD JOHN OF RIETI (*c.* A.D. 1350)

JOHN BUFALARI was born about the beginning of the fourteenth century at Castel Porziano in Umbria, brother to Bd Lucy of Amelia. Little is known of his life, except that it was uneventful, but none the less significant in that he grew daily in grace and virtue. He early determined to leave the world and joined the Hermits of St Augustine (Austin friars) at Rieti. He was ever at the service of his neighbour, especially the sick and strangers, and delighted to wait on guests who came to the monastery ; he spent long hours in contemplation and especially valued the opportunities provided by serving Mass in the friary church for loving converse with God. He had the gift of tears, not only for his own faults but for those of others ; when walking in the garden he would say, " How can one not weep ? For we see all around us trees and grass and flowers and plants germinating, growing, producing their fruit, and dying back again into the earth in accordance with the laws of their Creator : while men, to whom God has given a reasoning intelligence and the promise of a transcendent reward, continually oppose His will." A simple reflection whose force, if rightly understood, is not lessened by the consideration that the vegetable creation could not do otherwise if it would. The exact date of the death of Bd John is not known, but his holy life and the miracles taking place at his tomb were the cause of a *cultus* which persisted and was formally confirmed in 1832.

See Torelli, *Secoli Agostiniani*, vol. ii, and P. Seeböck, *Die Herrlichkeit der Katholischen Kirche* (1900), pp. 299–300.

10 : ST LAURENCE, Martyr (A.D. 258)

THERE are few martyrs in the Church whose names are so famous as that of St Laurence, in whose praises the most illustrious among the Latin fathers have written, and whose triumph, to use the words of St Maximus, the whole Church joins in a body to honour with universal joy and devotion. He was one among the seven deacons who served the Roman church ; this was a charge of great trust, to which was annexed the care of the goods of the church, and the distribution of its alms among the poor. The Emperor Valerian in 257 published his edicts against Christians and Pope St Sixtus, the second of that name, was apprehended the year following and put to death ; on the fourth day after the faithful Laurence followed him to martyrdom. That is all that is known for certain of the life and death of St Laurence, but Christian piety has adopted and consecrated as its own the details supplied by St Ambrose, the poet Prudentius, and others ; though it must be regretfully admitted that good reasons have been adduced for doubting the historical reliability of such moving incidents as St Laurence's presentation of the goods of the Church, and the manner of his death.

According to these traditions, as Pope St Sixtus was led to execution, his deacon Laurence followed him weeping, and said to him, " Father, where are you going without your deacon ? " The pope answered, " I do not leave you, my son. You shall follow me in three days." Laurence was full of joy, hearing that he should be so soon called to God ; he set out immediately to seek all the poor, widows and orphans, and gave among them the money which he had in his hands ; he even sold the sacred vessels to increase the sum, employing it all in the like manner. When then the prefect of Rome was informed of these charities, imagining that the Christians had hid considerable treasures, he wanted to secure them : for he was no less a worshipper of gold and silver than of Jupiter and Mars. With this view he sent for St Laurence, and said to him, " You Christians often complain that we treat you with cruelty, but no tortures are here thought of ; I only inquire mildly after what concerns you. I am informed that your priests offer in gold, that the sacred blood is received in silver cups, and that in your nocturnal sacrifices you have wax tapers fixed in golden candlesticks. Bring out these treasures ; the emperor has need of them for the maintenance of his forces. I am told that according to your doctrine you must render to Caesar the things that belong to him. I do not think that your God causes money to be coined ; He brought none into the world with Him ; He only brought words. Give us therefore the money, and be rich in words." St Laurence replied, without showing any concern, " The Church is indeed rich ; nor hath the emperor any treasure equal to what it possesses. I will show you a valuable part ; but allow me a little time to set everything in order, and to make an inventory." The prefect did not understand of what treasure Laurence spoke, but, imagining the hidden wealth already in his hands, was satisfied with this answer and granted him three days.

During this interval Laurence went all over the city, seeking out the poor who were supported by the Church. On the third day he gathered together a great number of them, and placed them in rows, the decrepit, the blind, the lame, the maimed, the lepers, orphans, widows and maidens ; then he went to the prefect and invited him to come and see the treasure of the Church. The prefect, astonished to see such an assembly of misery and misfortune, turned to the deacon with threatening looks, asked him what all this meant, and where the treasures were which he had promised to show him. St Laurence answered, " What are you displeased at ? These *are* the treasure of the Church." The prefect's anger was not allayed but redoubled, and in a fury of rage he shouted, " You mock me ! The axes and the fasces, the ensigns of the Roman power, are not to be insulted ! I know that you desire to die : that is your madness and vanity : but you shall not die immediately, as you imagine. You shall die by inches ! " Then he had a great gridiron made ready, and glowing coals put under it, that the martyr might be slowly burnt. Laurence was stripped and bound upon this iron bed over the slow fire, which roasted his flesh by little and little. His face appeared to the Christians to be surrounded with a beautiful light, and his suffering body to give off a sweet smell ; but the unbelievers neither saw this light nor perceived this smell. The martyr felt not the torments of the persecutor, says St Augustine, so passionate was his desire of possessing Christ : and St Ambrose observes that whilst his body burned in the material flames, the fire of divine love was far more active within his breast and made him regardless of the pain. Having suffered a long time, he turned to the judge and said with a cheerful smile, " Let my body be turned ; one side is broiled enough ". When the executioner had turned him, he said, " It is cooked enough, you may eat ". Then, having prayed for the conversion of the city of Rome that the faith of Christ might spread thence throughout the world, St Laurence gave up the ghost.

Prudentius ascribes to his prayer the entire conversion of Rome, and says God began to grant his request at the very time he made it ; for several senators who were present at his death were so moved by his heroic fortitude and piety that they became Christians upon the spot. These noblemen took up the martyr's body on their shoulders and gave it honourable burial on the Via Tiburtina. His death, says Prudentius, was the death of idolatry in Rome, which from that time began to decline ; and now (*c.* 403) the senate itself venerates the tombs of the apostles and martyrs. He describes with what devotion and fervour the Romans frequented the church of St Laurence and commended themselves to his patronage ; and the happy issue of their prayers proves how great his power is with God. St Augustine assures us that God wrought in Rome many miracles through the intercession of St Laurence, and St Gregory of Tours, Fortunatus, and others, relate several in other places. St Laurence has been one of the most venerated martyrs of the Roman church since the fourth century, and he is named in the canon of the Mass. He was certainly buried in the cemetery of Cyriaca *in agro Verano* on the Via Tiburtina, where Constantine built the first chapel on the site of what is now the church of St Laurence-outside-the-Walls, the fifth patriarchal basilica of the city.

Much confusion and inconsistency prevail in what purport to be the " acts " of St Laurence, though in fact this document is only an item in a series of similar narratives. See BHL., n. 6884, as compared with nn. 7801 and 4753. The poem of Prudentius, however, which Ruinart prints among his *Acta sincera*, affords a relatively clear statement, followed in the main above. Is this merely a poetical fiction, or does it represent some genuine tradition handed down either orally or in documents which have perished ? St Ambrose (see *e.g.* his *De Officiis*, i, 41) undoubtedly shared the belief that the martyr was roasted to death, and so did other early fathers. P. Franchi de' Cavalieri (*Römische Quartalschrift*, vol. xiv (1900), pp. 159–176 ; and *Note agiografiche*, vol. v (1915), pp. 65–82) and Delehaye (*Analecta Bollandiana*, vol. xix, 1900, pp. 452–453 ; see also vol. li, 1933, pp. 49–58, and CMH., pp. 431–432) reject altogether the gridiron tradition ; but it still finds defenders. See, for example, H. Leclercq in DAC., article " Gril " (vol. vi, cc. 1827–1831) and article " Laurent " (vol. viii, cc. 1917–1947). The great devotion inspired by the memory of St Laurence in Rome is strikingly illustrated in the Life of St Melania the Younger (see Rampolla's edition, pp. 5–6), as also by the fact of the numerous dedications of churches and oratories. See J. P. Kirsch, *Die römischen Titelkirchen in Altertum*, pp. 80–84, and Huelsen, *Le Chiese di Roma nel medio evo*, pp. 280–297. *Cf.* also Duchesne " Le Sanctuaire de S. Laurent ", in *Mélanges d'archéologie*, vol. xxxix (1921), pp. 3–24. *Lawrence* seems to be the better English spelling of this name.

ST PHILOMENA OR PHILUMENA (DATE UNKNOWN)

ON May 24, 1802, in the catacomb of St Priscilla on the Via Salaria Nova an inscribed *loculus* was found, and on the following day it was carefully examined and opened. The *loculus* was closed with three tiles, on which was the following inscription in red paint :

LUMENA PAXTE CUM FI

together with certain symbols, namely, two anchors, three arrows, a palm and a flower (or torch). One theory about this inscription was that it had originally run :

[*Fi*]*lumena pax tecum fi*[*at*],
" Philumena, peace be with thee. So be it " ;

that the *loculus* had had to be closed in a hurry, and that the mason's tools had obliterated the first two and last two letters. But it is now generally accepted that the tiles were put in a wrong order, again either through hurry or by one who could not read, and that the inscription should read :

Pax tecum Filumena,
" Peace be with thee, Philumena,"

which is obtained by putting the first of the three tiles at the end. Within the *loculus* was found the skeleton of a female of from thirteen to fifteen years old, the principal bones entire except the skull, which was much broken. Embedded in cement was a small glass phial or vase, with vestiges of what was taken to be blood. This was one of the so-called " blood-ampullae " which, before the researches of V. De Buck, Kraus and Rossi, when found in conjunction with the palm symbol were accepted as proof of the grave of a martyr. Accordingly, in accordance with the knowledge of the time and the current regulations of the Congregation of Sacred Rites, the remains were taken to be those of a virgin-martyr named Philomena, they were reverently gathered up, and deposited in the *custodia generalis* of sacred relics.

No more attention was paid to them until the summer of 1805, when Pope Pius VII gave them into the care of the Reverend Don Francis di Lucia, and they were translated to Mugnano del Cardinale in the diocese of Nola and enshrined under one of the altars of the parish-church. Miracles and favours, spiritual and temporal, consequent on invocation of St Philomena and in the presence of her relics, were immediately reported, and with the subsequent increase of devotion marvels multiplied. Her fame spread throughout Italy and was increased by the credence popularly, but not officially, given to certain private revelations claimed by Sister Mary-Louisa-of-Jesus, a canoness of Naples* ; on the strength of these Don Francis di Lucia wrote a " life " of the unknown St Philomena, including a completely

* The value of these alleged revelations may be somewhat gauged by the fact that the nun said the saint told her that her name was derived from Latin and signified " daughter of light " (*Filia luminis*). It is, in fact, a quite well-known name from the Greek φιλουμένη, " beloved ".

fictitious account of her martyrdom. The church of Mugnano became a great pilgrimage shrine, she became known in France, and from thence devotion to her spread throughout the world. The holy alliance, so to say, between St Philomena and St John Vianney is well known ; she was his " dear little saint ", his " agent in Heaven ", she would do anything he asked : " And why not ? For Almighty God Himself obeys me every day upon the altar." Nor was he the only one among the heroes of religion in nineteenth-century France to be distinguished for devotion to St Philomena : St Madeleine Sophie Barat, Bd Peter Julian Eymard, St Peter Louis Chanel, the Venerable Countess de Bonnault d'Houet were among them. But it is likely enough that if the Curé of Ars had not sounded her praises for the space of thirty years she would not have enjoyed the immense popularity that became hers.

On the other hand, the most influential single event in the diffusion of the *cultus*, and the one which did much to move the Roman authorities to action, was the miraculous cure of the Venerable Pauline Mary Jaricot, foundress of the Association for the Propagation of the Faith. During 1834 her life was despaired of, but she determined to make the journey from Lyons to Mugnano, lying at full length in a chaise, to ask the intercession of St Philomena at her shrine. While passing through Rome she stayed at a convent, where she was twice visited by Pope Gregory XVI, who betrayed his idea of her condition by asking her to pray for him as soon as she got to Heaven. Mlle Jaricot, almost at the point of death, arrived at Mugnano on August 8, 1835 ; two days later, when receiving holy communion in St Philomena's church on the saint's feast, she was completely cured of her disease. On her way home she stopped again at Rome, " to show herself to the priest ", and Gregory promised at once to examine the cause of this wonder-working Philomena. On January 30, 1837, he signed a decree authorizing her public *cultus*, with permission for the clergy of the diocese of Nola to celebrate on August 11 in her honour the Mass *Loquebar* and Office from the common of a virgin-martyr, with a proper fourth lesson at Matins ; this feast soon was extended to other dioceses, including Rome itself. In 1855 Pope Pius IX approved a proper Mass and Office for the feast ; but her name has not been inserted in the Roman Martyrology. The lessons of her office remark that " it is to be regretted that her life, her acts, and the kind of martyrdom that she suffered have remained hidden ", but definitely state that she was a virgin and a martyr ; these same lessons do not anywhere say in so many words that the bones found in the sepulchre " wherein the body of St Philomena had been laid " were those of that person ; nevertheless, it cannot be denied that the implication of the lessons is that they were.

The Congregation of Sacred Rites accepted the evidence of the symbols on the inscription and of the phial within the *loculus* as proofs positive of martyrdom ; it must now be recognized in the light of more accurate knowledge that this cannot safely be done. The miracles and spiritual helps granted by God to the faithful who have called on St Philomena cannot, however, be reasonably called in question as proofs of sanctity—but the sanctity of whom ? Professor Marucchi has cast very grave doubt indeed on the identity of the bones in the sepulchre with those of the Philomena commemorated on its outside ; he makes out an exceedingly strong case for the tiles not having been disarranged accidentally, but that they were originally used to close the grave of one Philomena between the middle and end of the second century, and later used again, deliberately in the wrong order, to close another, of a maiden unknown. The real body of the Philomena of the inscription, likely enough a martyr, but not certainly, was probably translated with many others to one of the churches of the city by Pope St Paul I or Pope St Paschal I (eighth to ninth centuries) ; the relics of the second burial in Philomena's grave are, of course, at Mugnano, very imposingly enshrined.

Some devotees of St Philomena, especially those who have received kindness at her hands, view with suspicion and even resentment the results of the efforts of learned men (men not less religious than themselves) to establish the truth about their patron. They fear that the effect of those researches is to " do away with St Philomena ", to nullify the testimony of all who are under practical, spiritual or temporal obligation to her, from the sainted Curé of Ars to her most hidden devotee. This is not so, nor is it possible : but we must not, in the name of piety, deceive ourselves with knowledge we have not got. The miracles and benefactions wrought by God when we ask for the intercession of a certain saint, whom we call on by the name of Philomena, are indubitably known to us : nothing can shake them, or our gratitude to her. But we do not know certainly whether she was in fact named Philomena in her earthly life, whether she was a martyr, whether her relics now rest at Mugnano or in some place unknown. And these questions are of only relative importance : the spiritual influence of her whom we call St Philomena is what really matters ; we may accommodate to this subject (and to others like it) the words of our Lord : " Is not the life more than the meat and the body more than the raiment ? "

In April, 1961, Philomena was removed from the Calendar of Saints by the Sacred Congregation of Rites.

This is one of the cases in which we seem to have on the one side a number of critical scholars agreeing in a practically unanimous verdict, and on the other a devout credulity which is mainly impressed by reputed miracles and revelations. Professor Marucchi's conclusions have not undergone any change since he published in *Miscellanea di Storia Ecclesiastica*, vol. ii (1904), pp. 365–386, his " Osservazioni archeologiche sulla Iscrizione di S. Filomena ", and supplemented this with further arguments in the *Nuovo Bullettino di arch. crist.*, vol. xii (1906), pp. 253–300. On the other hand Fr G. Bonavenia has replied to Marucchi in two essays—*Controversia sul celeberrimo Epitaffio di S. Filomena* (1906), and *La questione puramente archeologica . . .* (1907). Further, the Abbé Trochu, author of the excellent Life of the Curé d'Ars, has also published a monograph, *La " petite Sainte " du Curé d'Ars* (1924), defending the historicity of the martyr. A great deal has been written upon the question of St Philomena, and a very full bibliography may be found in DAC., vol. v, cc. 1604–1606.

11 : SS. TIBURTIUS AND SUSANNA, MARTYRS   (THIRD CENTURY ?)

ST TIBURTIUS is famous from an epitaph by Pope St Damasus, which, however, unfortunately contains no biographical information. He is said to have been a subdeacon of Rome, who was betrayed to the persecutors by an apostate, and brought before the prefect Fabian. He walked unharmed over burning embers by the power of his faith ; but this miracle was set down to magic, and he was beheaded on the Via Labicana, three miles from Rome. These particulars are found in the *acta* of St Sebastian, and therefore no reliance can be placed on them ; but St Tiburtius was certainly buried on the Via Labicana, at the place called The Two Laurels, where a small church was afterwards built.

Together with St Tiburtius the Western church celebrates today the virgin martyr Susanna. We are told that she was the daughter of a learned priest,

Gabinius, and niece of Pope St Caius. She was as beautiful as she was charming, and so highly educated that her scholarship matched her father's. The Emperor Diocletian, who was seeking a wife for his son-in-law Maximian, heard so favourable a report of her that he sent one of her uncles, Claudius, who held a post at court, to intimate to Gabinius that he desired Susanna's hand for Maximian. As soon, however, as Susanna heard of the honour proposed for her she declared that she was the bride of Christ and could take no earthly husband. When her uncle Claudius came to see her about the matter and would have kissed her, she drew back. He explained that it was only a natural token of affection, to which she replied, " It is not your kiss that I object to, but your mouth defiled by idolatrous sacrifices ". " How can I cleanse my mouth ? " asked Claudius. " Repent, and be baptized ", was the reply.

His niece's refusal of a royal marriage made such an impression on Claudius that he sought instruction and was baptized, together with his wife Praepedigna and his two sons. He then liberated his slaves and gave away his property to the poor. As he did not return to court, Diocletian sent his brother Maximus, who also was in the royal household, to find out about Susanna and to inquire after Claudius, who was reported to be ill. He found his brother greatly emaciated by the penances he had undergone. Claudius told him of Susanna's decision. They then went together to visit her and afterwards talked matters over with Gabinius and Pope St Caius. All four brothers agreed that the girl must not be hindered in her vocation, although they realized the great danger to which they were all exposed. Maximus also received baptism and gave away his goods to the poor. When Diocletian was informed of the determination of Susanna and of the conversion of his two officers, he was greatly incensed, and he gave permission to one of his favourites, called Julian, who had a grudge against them, to apprehend them and to deal as he would with the whole family. Possibly fearing lest Diocletian should relent, Julian ordered that Maximus and Claudius, with the latter's wife and sons, should at once be taken to Cumae, where they were burnt alive and their bodies cast into the water. St Susanna was beheaded in her father's house and her father likewise was martyred. The two uncles, St Claudius and St Maximus, are mentioned in the Roman Martyrology on February 18, and St Gabinius on the following day.

This story seems to be fictitious from beginning to end, but the germs of historic truth incorporated in it are of curious interest. The primitive Hieronymian Martyrology would seem to have contained a notice in this form : " In Rome, at the ' Two Houses ' beside the baths of Diocletian, the birthday of St Susanna." These brief data are quite reliable, but they have probably provided the nucleus from which the story of Gabinius and Pope St Caius in their two houses was evolved.

For Tiburtius, see the texts quoted by Delehaye in CMH., pp. 434–435 ; and *cf.* the article of J. P. Kirsch, " Die Martyrer der Katakombe ' ad duas Lauros ' ", in *Ehrengabe deutscher Wissenschaft dargeboten von Katholischen Gelehrten* (1920), pp. 577–601 ; and *Damasi epigrammata* (ed. Ihm), n. 30. The evolution of the story of St Susanna and her uncles was traced by Mgr Duchesne with extraordinary patience and skill. The topographical foundation is in a sense correct, but the names have been taken over from some blundering text of the first recension of the " Hieronymianum ". The extraordinary name Praepedigna simply consists of the last part of a martyr's name, Euprepe, fused with the first part of the name of the place where she suffered—Dinogetia, miswritten Dignae Cotiae. Duchesne shows reason for thinking that the *Passio Susannae* was fabricated somewhere about the year 500. See his article in *Mélanges d'archéologie et d'histoire*, vol. xxxvi (1916), pp. 27–42 ; and *cf.* P. Franchi de' Cavalieri, *Note agiografiche*, vol. vii (1928), pp. 184–202 ; Lanzoni, *I titoli presbiterali di Roma* (1925), pp. 34–50 ; and CMH., p. 435.

ST ALEXANDER THE CHARCOAL-BURNER, Bishop of Comana, Martyr (A.D. 275 ?)

The Christian community of Comana in Pontus having grown to be sufficiently large to require a bishop, St Gregory the Wonder-worker, Bishop of Neocaesarea, went thither to preside at the election. He rejected all the candidates put forward by the clergy and people, especially one who was favoured because of his high birth and wealth, reminding them that the Apostles were poor and common men. Whereat a wag exclaimed, " Very well then. Why not appoint Alexander the charcoal-burner ? " St Gregory, knowing that the Holy Ghost was as likely to make Himself heard by means of this sarcastic suggestion as any other way, was moved to send for the said Alexander, who presented himself all dirty and blackened from his trade. Gregory looked at him and saw through the grime and the rags ; he took him aside and questioned him, and soon discovered that Alexander was a man of good birth and education, who had given away his goods and taken up this trade the more literally to follow Christ ; the Roman Martyrology says that he was " a most learned philosopher ", though there is no reason to think that anything more is meant by this than that he was a man of wisdom. St Gregory accordingly put Alexander forward, he having signified his willingness, as his own choice for the vacant see, it was ratified by the people, and the new bishop was consecrated. St Gregory of Nyssa, who relates this happening, speaks highly of St Alexander as a bishop and teacher. He eventually gave his life for the faith, being martyred by fire. St Alexander was naturally revered as a patron of charcoal-burners.

See the *Acta Sanctorum*, August, vol. ii.

ST EQUITIUS, Abbot (c. A.D. 560)

St Equitius flourished in the Abruzzi at the time when St Benedict was establishing his rule at Monte Cassino, and in his youth suffered greatly from temptations of the flesh. He sought solitude in the province of Valeria, where by prayer and discipline he brought his body into subjection and attained the virtues of the spirit. When he had learned to govern himself he undertook the direction of others and founded first a monastery at Terni (Amiternum) and then other houses, both of men and women. St Gregory the Great describes Equitius from accounts he had received from Albinus, Bishop of Rieti, and others who knew him personally : " Zeal for the salvation of souls so burned in his heart that, in spite of his responsibility for so many monasteries, he travelled about diligently, visiting churches, towns, villages, and particularly men's houses, to stir up the hearts of those that heard him to a love of heavenly joys. His clothes were so poor and shabby that those who did not know who he was would not deign to salute him, even if he greeted them first. He rode on the most forlorn beast he could find, with a halter for bridle and a sheep's skin for saddle. He carried his books of divinity in leather bags, hung on either side of his horse, and to what place soever he came he opened there the spring of Sacred Scripture and refreshed the souls of his hearers with the heavenly water of his words. His grace in preaching was so great that the fame thereof reached Rome itself."

Like many of the early abbots St Equitius was not in holy orders, and a patrician called Felix challenged him for presuming to preach when he was neither ordained nor licensed thereto by the bishop of Rome. " I myself have seriously considered the matter on which you speak," replied Equitius, " but on a certain night a young man stood by me in a vision and touched my tongue with such an instrument as is used in letting blood, and said to me : ' Behold ! I have put my word into your mouth. Go your way and preach.' And since that day I can talk only of God, whether I would or no." This did not satisfy some of the Roman clergy, who complained to the pope that " this countrified fellow has taken on himself authority to preach and, ignorant as he is, usurps the office of our apostolic ruler ", and asked that he be sent for to be dealt with. A cleric called Julian was therefore sent to his monastery to fetch Equitius, and he found the abbot in hobnailed boots, mowing grass, who, when he received the pope's message, prepared to set out at once. Julian was tired with his journey and wanted to stay there the night, and St Equitius agreed, but, " I am very sorry ", he said, " for if we go not to-day, to-morrow we shall not ". And so it fell out, for the next morning a messenger arrived from the pope to tell Julian that he had had a vision from God about Equitius and the holy man was not to be disturbed. St Equitius died on March 7 about the year 560, and on this day his body was translated to the church of St Laurence at Aquila.

The Bollandists have dealt with St Equitius on March 7 (*Acta Sanctorum*, March, vol. i) ; there is a similar collection of fragmentary data in Mabillon, vol. i, pp. 655–658.

ST BLAAN, OR BLANE, BISHOP   (*c.* A.D. 590 ?)

THERE is considerable uncertainty about the chronology of this Scots bishop, who was born in Bute. He is said to have spent seven years in Ireland under the instruction of St Comgall and St Canice, and presumably became a monk there. He then returned to the isle of Bute (" in a boat without oars "), and put himself under the discipline of his uncle St Cathan, who gave him holy orders, and he devoted his life to apostolic work in Scotland. He eventually became a bishop and is said to have gone on pilgrimage to Rome, returning on foot through England. A number of miracles are attributed to him, as that he rekindled the church lights, which had gone out during the night office, by striking fire from his finger-nails. He died and was buried at Kingarth in Bute, and on the site of his monastery the cathedral of Dunblane was built ; his bell is still preserved there. Devotion to St Blaan early became popular, and his feast is still observed today in the dioceses of Saint Andrews, Dunkeld (which includes the former see of Dunblane), and Argyll.

There is an account in the *Acta Sanctorum*, August, vol. ii, which is taken mainly from the lessons of the Aberdeen Breviary ; but see rather KSS., pp. 280–281. St Blane is mentioned in the *Félire* of Oengus, and this as well as the Aberdeen Martyrology enters his name under August 10.

ST ATTRACTA, OR ARAGHT, VIRGIN   (SIXTH CENTURY ?)

As with so many Irish saints, there is much uncertainty about the chronology of St Attracta ; her alleged association with St Patrick would put her in the fifth century, but others mentioned as her contemporaries lived in the sixth. According to her legend she was the daughter of a noble house, and when her father refused to allow her to dedicate herself to God, she fled to Coolavin, where she is said to have received the nun's veil from St Patrick. She then established herself on Lough Gara, and founded a hospice for travellers in a place where seven roads meet, now called after her Killaraght. This hospice continued its good work until 1539. Later, she went into Roscommon, where she wished to have a cell close to St Conall (said to have been her half-brother) at Drum, near Boyle. This was forbidden by him and St Dachonna, and St Attracta expressed her indignation with a freedom which strikes us as Irish rather than holy : she hoped that the time would come when their respective churches would be reduced to insignificance, and their offerings to nothing, by the rising of another church near by, "and many other things that were disagreeable ", some of which are "not set down in her *acta* ". It is fanciful to see a fulfilment of this in the foundation centuries later of the Cistercian abbey of Boyle, but the churches of Drumconnell and Eas Dachonna (Assylin) were soon after overshadowed by the rise of the episcopal churches of Achonry and Elphin.

When a raiding-party of the men of Luighne (Lugna) were fleeing from the king of Connacht, St Attracta enabled them to escape by dividing the waters of Lough Gara ; two natural weirs on the lake are still connected with her name. Another miracle attributed to her is the harnessing of forest deer with her own hair, to drag timber for the construction of a fort by the king of Connacht, when he had unjustly summoned her to take part in the work : doubtless he remembered the affair of the men of Lugna. This saint's feast is now celebrated throughout Ireland on August 11 ; she is patron of the diocese of Achonry.

There is a Latin life, unfortunately mutilated, printed by Colgan, as well as in the *Acta Sanctorum* under February 9, and in the form "Tarahata ". Although St Attracta is mentioned as in personal relation with St Patrick both in Tirechan's Collections and in the Tripartite Life, there seems to be no reference to her in the *Félire* of Oengus.

ST LELIA, VIRGIN   (SIXTH CENTURY ?)

THE diocese of Limerick today keeps the feast of St Lelia, who as well has a commemoration in all other Irish dioceses. Canon O'Hanlon in his *Lives of the Irish Saints* says of this maiden that "Her era and her locality have not been distinctly revealed to us ; but there is good reason for supposing that she lived at a remote period, and most probably she led a life of strict observance, if she did not preside over some religious institution in the province of Munster ". Lelia is now generally identified with the Dalcassian saint Liadhain, great-grand-daughter of the prince Cairthenn whom St Patrick baptized at Singland. There are no particulars or traditions about her (in the seventeenth century she was said to be the sister of St Munchin), but she gives her name to Killeely (Cill Liadaini) just within the borough boundary of Limerick.

See LIS., vol. viii, p. 170, and notes by Mgr Canon M. Moloney in the *North Munster Antiquarian Journal*, 1936, p. 39, and *St Munchin's Folk*, 1948, p. 18.

ST GAUGERICUS, or GÉRY, BISHOP OF CAMBRAI   (c. A.D. 625)

ST GAUGERICUS, in French, Géry, was a native of Yvoi, a small town in the Ardennes. During an episcopal visitation, St Magnericus, the successor of St

Nicetas in the bishopric of Trier, coming to Yvoi, was much delighted with the sanctity and talents of St Géry, and ordained him deacon (but not till he knew the whole psalter by heart, says his biographer) ; from that moment the saint redoubled his fervour in good works, and applied himself with zeal to the functions of his sacred ministry, especially to the instruction of the faithful.

The reputation of his virtue and learning raised him to the episcopal chair of Cambrai, and the saint devoted his episcopate to the rooting out of the paganism which was by no means dead in his diocese. At Cambrai he founded a monastery, called by him after St Médard, and to him is popularly attributed the foundation of the city of Brussels, for he is said to have built a chapel on an island in the Senne (now Place Saint-Géry) around which a village grew up. Among other miracles recounted of him, it is related that at Yvoi a leper was healed by being baptized by him : which aptly represented the interior cleansing of the soul from sin. St Géry was called to rest after occupying his see for thirty-nine years, about the year 625, and was buried in the church which he had built in honour of St Médard, on a hill outside Cambrai.

The oldest life of St Géry was printed in the *Analecta Bollandiana*, vol. vii (1888), pp. 388–398. Since then it has been re-edited by Bruno Krusch in MGH., *Scriptores Merov.*, vol. iii, pp. 652–658. It seems to have been written about fifty or sixty years after the death of the saint, and is in very barbarous Latin. *Cf.* the *Neues Archiv*, vol. xvi (1891), pp. 227 *seq.* ; and E. de Moreau, *Histoire de l'Église en Belgique*, t. i (1945), pp. 60–63.

SS. GERARD OF GALLINARO AND HIS COMPANIONS (DATE UNKNOWN)

GERARD and his companions are commonly enumerated as SS. Gerard, Arduin, Bernard and Fulk. Although the date, history and even the existence of these alleged saints are problematical, still they are honoured locally down to the present time with a liturgical *cultus* in certain Italian townships, and tradition there is agreed in describing them as coming from England. It is supposed that they were pilgrims—according to some in the seventh century, according to others in the twelfth—who journeyed to the Holy Land and also visited the shrine of St Michael at Monte Gargano. On the other hand, the most seemingly trust-worthy of the records now preserved, a document of the early thirteenth century, speaks of St Gerard as coming not from England but from Auvergne, in the time of the First Crusade, with two companions named Peter and Stephen. All seem to have died in the district of the Abruzzi. St Gerard in particular is venerated with a great concourse of people at Gallinaro on August 11 of each year.

See the *Acta Sanctorum*, August, vol. ii, and October, vol. xi ; *The Month*, vol. lxxxv (1895), pp. 72–81, and pp. 408–417 ; and Stanton, *Menology*, pp. 184–185, and pp. 365–367, where we learn that the famous Jesuit John Gerard visited Gallinaro in 1608, and that at his request his family presented the shrine with a silver reliquary in the form of an arm.

BD PETER FAVRE (A.D. 1546)

PETER FAVRE (Faber) was the senior of the first companions of St Ignatius Loyola and held the highest place in his master's estimation with St Francis Xavier ; and he was the first among the Jesuits to come to grips with the Protestant Reformation. He was a Savoyard by birth, born in 1506 of a family of farmers, and while still a shepherd-boy of ten years old longed for a chance to study. To his great joy he was sent to school, first with a priest at Thônes and then to a local college. In 1525 Peter went to Paris and was entered at the college of Sainte-Barbe. Here he shared the lodging of a Navarrese student, one Francis Xavier, and met a backward undergratuate from Salamanca, Ignatius Loyola. The three became firm friends. In 1530 Favre received his licentiate in arts on the same day as Xavier, but for a time he could not make up his mind what profession he should pursue : medicine, law, teaching, by turns attracted him, and he as yet heard no clear call to " leave the world ". At last he decided to throw in his lot with Ignatius ; he was ordained priest in 1534, and on August 15 in the same year celebrated the Mass at Montmartre when the seven first Jesuits took their vows. He was in charge of the little company that met St Ignatius at Venice early in 1537, only to find that their way to the Holy Land, where they planned to be missionaries, was barred by the Turkish war. At the end of the year he went with Ignatius and Laynez to Rome, where they were appointed mission preachers by the Holy See, and for a time he was professor at the university.

At the time the Emperor Charles V was trying to compose the religious troubles of Germany by convoking a series of conferences, called " diets ", of the Catholic and Protestant leaders, and Peter Favre was appointed by Pope Paul III to go to that of Worms, in 1540 ; from this abortive meeting he went on to assist at the equally useless diet of Ratisbon in the following year. But Bd Peter saw clearly what both the emperor and high ecclesiastics could not or would not see, that what Germany needed was not so much discussions with heretics but a reformation in the life and discipline of Catholics, both clergy and lay-people. He was appalled by the state of the country in general and by the lethargy and ill-living of Catholics in particular, and he devoted himself to preaching and direction in Speyer and Ratisbon and Mainz ; at the last-named place Peter Canisius, then a layman, made the " spiritual exercises " under his direction and was received into the Society of Jesus. The Catholicity of the Rhineland today is to a considerable degree due to the work and influence of Peter Favre from Savoy. After having been notably successful in Cologne, whose archbishop, Herman von Wied, was himself a Protestant, and helping to found the first Jesuit residence there, he was called from Germany first to Portugal and then to Spain. While travelling through France he was imprisoned for seven days, and during that time made a vow to accept no stipends for celebrating Mass or preaching whenever he could refuse them without injustice to others. In Spain, as elsewhere, he gave retreats to lay-people as well as to the clergy, using the Spiritual Exercises of St Ignatius with the happiest results ; he made a Latin version of the Exercises for the use of the Carthusians of Cologne. Among those in Spain whose life was permanently influenced by Bd Peter was Francis Borgia, then duke of Gandia.

Pope Paul III wished to have Father Peter as his theologian at the Council of Trent. He was not anxious to go, but " I determined to fall in with the wish of the Archbishop of Mainz, who wanted me to go with him to the Council of Trent, which was to begin on the first day of November. Before I took that determination I had various feelings in my mind and some sadness, from which our Lord delivered me by virtue of holy and unquestioning obedience, which knows better than to consider either one's own insufficiency or the difficulty of the things which are commanded." In 1546 the pope's summons to the same assembly confirmed his resolution of obedience, and he set out at once, though he was sick and the summer heat was overpowering. The effort was too much. Though only forty years old, Bd Peter was exhausted by his laborious journeys and the strain of his work, and soon after his arrival in Rome he died in the arms of St Ignatius.

Bd Peter Faber left behind in his *Memoriale* a detailed account of his spiritual life during a long period, describing the action of God in his soul, especially at Mass and Divine Office, almost from day to day. The following is a characteristic entry : " One day I went to the palace to hear the sermon in the prince's chapel and the porter, not knowing me, would not let me in. So I had to stop outside, and it came into my mind how many times I had given entrance into my soul to vain thoughts and evil imaginings, while refusing it to Jesus who was knocking at the door. I reflected, too, how He is everywhere badly received by the world, and I prayed for myself and for the porter that the Lord would not make us wait long in Purgatory before admitting us to Heaven. Many other good thoughts came to me at that time, and so I felt very kindly towards that porter who had been for me the occasion of so much devotion." The mind that turned to such gentle reflection was naturally opposed to coercion when dealing with Protestants, and he had little faith in diets and formal conferences. When it was required of him he could and would meet such opponents as Bucer and Melancthon face to face, and confute them in argument, and such victories were not without good effect. But he attached far more importance to winning men to a change of heart, to amend their lives, and so lead them back to Christ and His Church. " It is necessary ", he wrote, " that anyone who desires to be serviceable to heretics of the present age should hold them in great affection and love them very truly, putting out of his heart all thoughts and feelings that tend to their discredit. The next thing he must do is to win their good will and love by friendly intercourse and converse about matters on which there is no difference between us, taking care to avoid all controversial subjects that lead to bickering and mutual recrimination. The things that unite us ought to be the first ground of our approach, not the things that keep us apart."

There was a grace and sweetness about Bd Peter that Father Simon Rodriguez met in no other man ; " I am at a loss for words to express the way in which, by his lovable and pleasing manner, he earned everyone's good-will and affection and won all who met him to the love of God. When he spoke of divine things it was as though he had the keys of men's hearts on his tongue, so powerfully did he move and attract them ; and the love he inspired was equalled by the reverence they had for the sweet gravity and firm virtue which informed all he said." The *cultus* of Bd Peter Favre was confirmed in 1872.

Ever since the publication by the Spanish Jesuits of the *Monumenta historica Societatis Jesu*, an immense amount of material has become accessible regarding the activities of St Ignatius's first companions. A special volume of nearly 1,000 pages, under the title *Fabri monumenta*, contains a critically revised text of Bd Peter's letters, of his *Memoriale*, and of the documents of the process of beatification, including a *processus informativus* begun informally in 1596 but ratified in 1607 by the ordinary of Geneva, who was then St Francis de Sales. Modern lives are numerous, including that by Father Boero, translated into English for the Quarterly Series, a French biography by A. Maurel, one in German by R. Cornely, and one in Spanish by F. Maruri. Three new lives in French appeared in 1931–1935, by F. Pochat-Baron, L. Buffet and G. Guitton.

12 : ST CLARE, VIRGIN, FOUNDRESS OF THE POOR CLARES OR MINORESSES (A.D. 1253)

"THE Lady Clare, shining in name, more shining in life, most shining in conversation, was a native of Assisi, of noble birth and by grace nobler, a maiden most pure in heart, young in years but hoary in determination, most steadfast in purpose, but withal wise and meek and a marvellous lover of Christ". She was born about the year 1193. Her mother was Ortolana di Fiumi and her father Faverone Offreduccio, and she had a younger sister, Agnes, and another, Beatrice, but of her childhood, adolescence and home-life there are no certain facts. When she was eighteen St Francis came to preach the Lenten sermons at the church of San Giorgio in Assisi ; his words fired her, she sought him out secretly, and asked him to help her that she too might live " after the manner of the holy gospel ". Francis spoke to her of contempt for the world and love of God, and strengthened her nascent desire to leave all things for Christ. On Palm Sunday in the year 1212 Clare attended at the cathedral of Assisi for the blessing of palms ; when all the rest went up to the altar-rails to receive their branch of olive a sudden shyness kept her in her place, which the bishop seeing, he went from the altar down to her and gave her the branch. In the evening she ran away from home and went a mile out of the town to the Portiuncula, where St Francis lived with his little community. He and his brethren met her at the door of the chapel of our Lady of the Angels with lighted tapers in their hands, and before the altar she put off her fine clothes, and St Francis cut off her hair, and gave her his penitential habit, which was a tunic of sackcloth tied about her with a cord. The holy father not having yet any nunnery of his own, placed her for the present in the Benedictine convent of St Paul near Bastia, where she was affectionately received. It would seem that the relatives of St Clare (her father was probably dead) had proposed a particular marriage that did not recommend itself to her, but that she did not entirely renounce the idea of matrimony in general until the burning words of Francis persuaded her to commit her maidenhood finally to God. Then followed what G. K. Chesterton called this " regular romantic elopement ", in which the bridegroom was Christ and St Francis the " knight-errant who gave it a happy ending ".

No sooner was her action made public but her friends and relations came in a body to draw her out of her retreat. It is said that Clare resisted and held to the altar so fast as to pull its cloths half off when they endeavoured to drag her away ; and, uncovering her head to show her hair cut, she said that Christ had called her to His service and that she would have no other husband, and that the more they should continue to persecute her, the more God would strengthen her to resist and overcome them. And God triumphed in her. St Francis soon after removed her to another nunnery, that of Sant' Angelo di Panzo. There her sister Agnes joined her, which drew on them both a fresh persecution. Agnes's constancy proved at last victorious, and St Francis gave her also the habit, though she was only fifteen years of age. (It may be noted that in the bull of canonization Pope Alexander IV makes no mention of any violence being used in the attempt to dissuade Clare and her sister from their new life.) Eventually St Francis placed them in a poor house contiguous to the church of San Damiano, on the outskirts of Assisi, and appointed Clare the superior. She was later joined by her mother and others, among whom three were of the illustrious family of the Ubaldini in Florence, who held for truer greatness the sackcloth and poverty of St Clare than the estates and riches which they possessed, seeing they left them all to become humble disciples of so admirable a mistress. St Clare saw founded within a few years monasteries of her nuns at several places in Italy, France and Germany. Bd Agnes, daughter to the King of Bohemia, founded a nunnery of the order in Prague, in which she took the habit, and was called by Clare " my half self ".

St Clare and her community practised austerities which till then had scarcely been known among women. They wore neither stockings, shoes, sandals nor any other covering on their feet ; they slept on the ground, observed perpetual abstinence from meat, and never spoke but when they were obliged by necessity and charity. The foundress recommended this holy silence as the means to avoid innumerable sins of the tongue, and to preserve the mind always recollected in God and free from the dissipation of the world which, without this guard, penetrates even the walls of cloisters. Not content with the fasts and other mortifications of the rule, she always wore next her skin a rough shirt of hair ; she fasted on vigils and all Lent on bread and water ; and on some days she ate nothing at all. All Clare's austerities were on the same scale, and after a time it became necessary for Francis and the bishop of Assisi to oblige her to lie upon a mattress and never pass one day without taking at least some bread for nourishment. Discretion came with experience, and years later she wrote to Bd Agnes of Bohemia : " Since our bodies are not of brass and our strength is not the strength of stone but rather are we weak and subject to corporal infirmities, I implore you vehemently in the Lord to refrain from that exceeding rigour of abstinence which I know you practise, so that living and hoping in the Lord you may offer Him a reasonable service and a sacrifice seasoned with the salt of prudence."

St Francis wished that his order should never possess any rents or other property even in common, subsisting on daily contributions, and St Clare possessed this spirit in perfection. Pope Gregory IX desired to mitigate this part of her rule, and offered to settle a yearly revenue on the Poor Ladies of San Damiano ; but she in the most pressing manner persuaded him by many reasons, in which her love of evangelical poverty made her eloquent, to leave her order in its first rigorous establishment. When the pope offered to dispense from the vow of strict poverty St Clare replied, " I need to be absolved from my sins, but I do not wish to be absolved from the obligation of following Jesus Christ ". Gregory accordingly granted in 1228 the *Privilegium paupertatis*, that they might not be constrained by anyone to accept possessions : " He who feeds the birds of the air and gives raiment and nourishment to the lilies of the field will not leave you in want of clothing or of food until He come Himself to minister to you for eternity." The convents of Perugia and Florence also received this privilege, but others thought it more prudent to accept a mitigation.* After the death of Gregory IX (who as Cardinal Ugolino had drawn up the first written rule for the Poor Ladies of San Damiano), Innocent IV in 1247 published another recension of the rule which in some respects brought it nearer to Franciscan than to Benedictine observance, but which permitted the holding of property in common ; he wrote that he did not wish to force this rule on any community unwilling to accept it. St Clare was unwilling, and she, as the living depository of the spirit and tradition of St Francis

---

* Thus began the two observances which have ever since been perpetuated among the Poor Clares. The mitigated houses are called " Urbanist " from the modification of the rule given to them in 1263 by Pope Urban IV.

himself, set to work to draw up a rule which should truly express them, and which unequivocally provides that the sisters shall possess no property, either as individuals or as a community.   It was not until two days before she died that this rule was approved for the convent of San Damiano by Pope Innocent IV.

From the time when she was appointed abbess, much against her will, by St Francis in 1215, St Clare governed the convent for forty years.   But it was her wish always to be the servant of servants, beneath all, washing and kissing the feet of the lay-sisters when they returned from begging, serving at table, attending the sick.   She had as it were wings to fly wherever St Francis directed her, and was always ready to do anything or to put her shoulders under any burden that was enjoined : " Dispose of me as you please ; I am yours by having given my will to God.   It is no longer my own."   Whilst her sisters took their rest she watched long in prayer, and tucked the nuns up when their bed-clothes had come loose ; she was the first that rose, rang the bell in the choir, and lighted the candles.   She came from prayer with her face so shining (like that of Moses coming down from conversing with God) that it dazzled the eyes of those that beheld her ; and she spoke with such a spirit of fervour as to enkindle those who did but hear her voice. She had a wonderful devotion towards the Blessed Sacrament, and even when sick in bed (she ailed grievously for the last twenty-seven years of her life) she made fine linen corporals and cloths for the service of the altar, which she distributed among the churches of Assisi.

The powerful force and efficacy of St Clare's prayer is well illustrated by a story told by Thomas of Celano, which may well be true.   In 1244 the Emperor Frederick II ravaged the valley of Spoleto, because it was the patrimony of the Holy See.   He had in his army many Saracens, and these infidels came once in a body to plunder Assisi, and as San Damiano stood without the walls they first assaulted it.   St Clare, though very sick, caused herself to be carried to the wall and the Blessed Sacrament to be placed there in a pyx in the very sight of the enemies ; prostrating herself before it, she prayed saying, " Does it please thee, O God, to deliver into the hands of these beasts the defenceless children whom I have nour- ished with thy love ?   I beseech thee, good Lord, protect these whom I am now not able to protect."   And she heard a voice like the voice of a little child saying, " I will have them always in my care ".   Then Clare prayed for the city of Assisi, and again the voice came, reassuring her, and she turned to the trembling nuns and said, " Have no fear, little daughters ; trust in Jesus ".   Terror at the same time seized the assailants and they fled with such precipitation that several were hurt without being wounded by any enemy.   Shortly after a general of the same emperor laid siege to Assisi for many days.   St Clare said to her nuns that they, who received corporal necessaries from that city, owed it all assis- tance in their power in its necessity.   She therefore bid them cover their heads with ashes, and in this suppliant fashion to beg of Christ the deliverance of the town.   They continued this with many tears a whole day and night, till " God in His mercy so made issue with temptation that the besiegers melted away and their proud captain with them, for all he had sworn an oath to take the city ".

Another popular story, namely, of St Clare and one of her nuns leaving the cloister of San Damiano and going to the Portiuncula to sup with St Francis, and of the marvellous light which radiated from the room, is less deserving of credence. The event, in itself exceedingly unlikely, is mentioned by no contemporary or by any writer for at least one hundred and fifty years ; and Thomas of Celano, who often heard St Francis warning his followers to avoid any injudicious association with the Poor Ladies, states categorically that St Clare never left the walls of San Damiano. Unhappily even during her life, and for long after her death at intervals, there was disagreement between the Poor Clares and the Friars Minor as to the relations of the two orders : the observant Clares maintaining that the friars were under obligation to serve them in things both spiritual and temporal. In this connection Thomas of Celano has a story which, if it be the source of much trouble to historians, at least is illuminating on the subject of the stalwart and inflexible character of Clare. When Pope Gregory IX in 1230 forbade the friars to visit the convents of nuns without his special licence, she feared that this would mean a loss of the spiritual help to be obtained from the friars and a severing of the ties St Francis had wished should subsist between them. She thereupon dismissed every one of them attached to the convent, saying, " Now that he has deprived us of our spiritual almoners, let him also take them that serve our material needs " : if she couldn't have the one, she wouldn't have the other.

St Clare bore years of sickness with sublime patience, and at last in 1253 the long-drawn-out agony began. Twice during its course she was visited by Pope Innocent IV, who gave her absolution, saying, " Would to God *I* had so little need of it ". For the last seventeen days she was able to eat nothing, " and during that weary time of labour the faith and devotion of the people increased more and more. Every day prelates and cardinals came to call on her, for all men were firmly convinced that this dying woman was truly a great saint." Her sister St Agnes was there, and three of the companions of St Francis, Leo, Angelo and Juniper, who read aloud to her the passion of our Lord according to St John as they had done at his death-bed twenty-seven years before. And when Brother Reginald exhorted her to patience, she replied, " Dear brother, ever since by means of His servant Francis I have known the grace of our Lord Jesus Christ, I have never in my whole life found any pain or sickness that could afflict me ". Seeing her spiritual children weep, she comforted them and tenderly exhorted them to be constant lovers and faithful observers of holy poverty, and gave them her blessing, calling herself the " little plant " of her holy father Francis. And to herself she was heard to say, " Go forth in peace, for you have followed the good road. Go forth without fear, for He that created you has sanctified you, has always protected you, and loves you as a mother. Blessed be thou, O God, for having created me." " Thus was the passing of blessed Clare. It was on the morrow of blessed Laurence that she received her laurel crown, for on that day the temple of her body was dissolved, her most holy soul went forth and, exulting in its freedom, soared on the wings of gladness to the place which God had prepared for it." It was the forty-second year after her religious profession, and the sixtieth of her age. She was buried on the day following, on which the Church keeps her festival. Pope Alexander IV canonized her at Anagni in 1255.

A vast literature has grown up around St Clare, but the sources themselves, apart from the saint's connection with general Franciscan history, are not overwhelmingly abundant. First comes the life commonly attributed to Thomas of Celano, which must have been written before 1261, that is, at latest, within eight years of her death. The short metrical life adds nothing of any value, but there are occasional references in the so-called *Speculum perfectionis* (see the second edition published by the British Society of Franciscan Studies, 1928), in the *Actus B. Francisci* (which supplies so much of the material of the *Fioretti*), and in other early documents. Besides these we have five letters written by St Clare, the Rule which bears her name, and her " Testament ", with a certain number of papal bulls.   An early life of the saint in English was translated from a compilation by Francis Hendricq, and printed at Douai in 1635 under the title of *The History of the Angelicall Virgin, glorious S. Clare*, and dedicated to the Queen's Most Excellent Majesty (*i.e.* Henrietta Maria).   But there have been many admirable books in English since then.   It must suffice to mention *The Life of S. Clare ascribed to Thomas of Celano*, translated by Abp Paschal Robinson, which also contains a translation of the Rule (1910) ; E. Gilliat Smith, *St Clare of Assisi* (1914) ; C. Balfour, *The Life and Legend of the Lady St Clare* (1910) ; L. de Chérancé, *Ste Claire d'Assise* (1911, Eng. trans.).   Later works are R. M. Pierazzi, *Ste Claire* (1937) ; M. Fassbinder, *Die hl. Klara von Assisi* (1934) ; N. de Robeck, *St Clare of Assisi* (1951).   From a more erudite point of view the *Archivum Franciscanum Historicum*, vols. vi, vii, xii and xiii, contains valuable art'cles, particularly that on the canonization of the saint in vol. xiii (1920), pp. 403–507.   See also Fr Cuthbert, *The Romanticism of St Francis* (1915), pp. 83–130.

ST EUPLUS, Martyr   (A.D. 304)

On April 29, 304, during the persecution of Diocletian, at Catania in Sicily, a man called Euplus, or Euplius, was heard shouting outside the governor's court, " I am a Christian, and I am willing to die for it ".   The governor, Calvisian, heard him and ordered that he who had made that noise should be brought in.   Euplus appeared accordingly, carrying a book of the gospels, whereat a bystander remarked, " You have got wicked writings, contrary to the emperors' orders ".   " Where do they come from ? " asked Calvisian, " From your house ? "

Euplus : " I haven't got a house, as the Lord knows."

Calvisian : " Do these writings belong to you ? "

Euplus : " As you see."

Calvisian : " I see that you are carrying them.   What are they ?   Read me something."

Euplus : " I know them well : they are the holy gospels according to the holy Matthew, Mark, Luke and John."

Calvisian : " What is that all about ? "

Euplus : " It is the law of the Lord my God, that I have received from Him."

Calvisian : " Somebody has taught you all this."

Euplus : " I have just said that I learned it from our Lord Jesus Christ, the Son of God." ·

Calvisian : " That is enough.   Take him to prison."

Three months and more later, on August 12, Euplus was again brought before the governor, and Calvisian asked him, " What do you say now ? "

Euplus : " What I have said before, I say again to-day."

Calvisian : " Do you still keep those forbidden writings ? "

Euplus : " I do."

Calvisian : " Where are they ? "

Euplus : " Within me."

Calvisian : " If you have still got them, bring them here."

Euplus repeated, " They are within me ", and showed by a gesture that he knew them by heart, whereupon Calvisian ordered him to be tortured till he should consent to sacrifice to the gods.   He was tormented in vain, and the governor again exhorted him : " The enemies of our great deities, those who defy our emperors and persist in their criminality, must die in their sufferings.   Euplus has said insane things before this court, and I adjure the sacrilegious man to withdraw them if he does not want to die." But he appealed in vain, and Euplus was sentenced to be beheaded ; which sentence was carried out.

The Acts of Euplus or Euplius make a favourable impression. They exist both in Latin and Greek. The former will be found in the *Acta Sanctorum*, August, vol. ii, and in Ruinart ; the latter in Cotelerius, *Ecclesiae Graecae Monumenta*, vol. i, pp. 192–200. But a much improved edition of both, with other new texts, will be found in *Studi e Testi*, vol. xlix (1928), where P. Franchi de' Cavalieri in the seventh series of his *Note agiografiche* has discussed the whole question. St Euplus is duly entered in the " Hieronymianum ", and the notice is discussed in CMH., p. 436. The Acts of Euplus are also to be found in Krüger-Knopf, *Ausgewählte Martyrerakten* (1929), a revised and enlarged edition of Knopf's previous collection.

ST MURTAGH, OR MUREDACH, BISHOP   (SIXTH CENTURY ?)

HE was of the royal family of King Laoghaire, and is reputed to have been the first bishop in Killala, by the appointment of St Patrick. It seems probable, however, that he lived at a later date, for in the life of St Cormac it is stated that the harbour of Killala was blessed in turn by Patrick, Brigid, Colmcille, Kenny and Muredach, which, as Canon O'Hanlon says, doesn't sound as if Patrick and Muredach were contemporaries ; moreover, he is stated to have met St Colmcille at Ballysodare, near Sligo, after Colmcille's conference with the Irish king at Drumkeith in 575. St Muredach's feast is kept throughout Ireland. On the same day was venerated another ST MUREDACH, who was a monk at the monastery of Iniskeen in Lough Erne, in the seventh century.

There seems to be no life of this saint either in Latin or Irish ; but there is a curiously obscure reference to him on this day in the *Félire* of Oengus. See also O'Hanlon, LIS., vol. viii, pp. 177 *seq.*

SS. PORCARIUS AND HIS COMPANIONS, MARTYRS   (*c.* A.D. 732)

AT the beginning of the fifth century the great abbey of Lérins was founded on an island off the coast of Provence now known after the founder as Saint-Honorat, opposite Cannes. By the eighth century the community numbered over five hundred monks, novices, *alumni* and familiars, and about the year 732 the head of this great body, Abbot Porcarius, was warned by an angel that they were threatened by a descent of infidel barbarians from the sea. The medieval account calls these marauders Saracens, that is, probably Moors from Spain or North Africa. Porcarius at once sent off to a place of safety all for whom there was room on ship-board, namely, the *alumni* or boys being educated in the monastery, and thirty-six of the younger religious, and gathered together the remainder of his community and prepared them for death, exhorting them to suffer bravely for the faith of Christ. The pirates landed, broke into the abbey, and slaughtered every one of its inmates with the exception of four, whom they carried off as slaves. St Porcarius and his monks are mentioned in the Roman Martyrology and their feast is kept in the diocese of Fréjus, but the story is not wanting in difficulties.

The texts printed in the *Acta Sanctorum*, August, vol. ii, give all the information which seems obtainable ; they are, however, of very late date. See further B. Munke, " Die vita S. Honorati ", in *Beihefte zur Zeitschrift für romanische Philologie*, no. 32 (1911), pp. 23 *seq.*

13 : ST HIPPOLYTUS, Martyr   (*c.* A.D. 235)

THE Roman Martyrology today mentions that Hippolytus the martyr who is mentioned in the *acta* of St Laurence. According to that very unreliable document Hippolytus was an officer in charge of Laurence when he was in prison, and was by him converted and baptized. He assisted at the burial of the martyr, and for so doing was summoned before the emperor, who rebuked him for disgracing the imperial uniform and commission by " conduct unbecoming an officer and a gentleman ", and ordered him to be scourged. At the same time St Concordia, the nurse of Hippolytus, and nineteen others were beaten to death with leaded whips. St Hippolytus himself was sentenced to be torn apart by horses— a suspicious circumstance in the narrative when we remember the fate of Hippolytus, the son of Theseus who, flying from the anger of his father, met a monster the sight of which affrighted his horses, so that he fell from his chariot and, being entangled in the harness, was dragged along and torn to pieces.* They took a pair of the most furious and unruly horses they could meet with, and tied a long rope between them to which they fastened the martyr's feet. The horses dragged him away furiously over ditches, briers and rocks ; the ground, trees and stones were sprinkled with his blood, which the faithful that followed at a distance weeping dipped up with kerchiefs, and they gathered together all the mangled parts of his flesh and limbs which lay scattered about.

This story would appear to be a romance, and the martyr Hippolytus whose feast is kept by the Church on this day is probably a Roman priest who lived during the early part of the third century. He was a man of great learning and the most important theological writer (he wrote in Greek) in the early days of the Roman church. He may have been a disciple of St Irenaeus, and St Jerome called him a " most holy and eloquent man ". Hippolytus censured Pope St Zephyrinus for being, in his opinion, not quick enough to detect and denounce heresy, and on the election of his successor, St Callistus I, he severed communion with the Roman church and permitted himself to be set up in opposition to the pope. With Pope St Pontian he was banished to Sardinia during the persecution of Maximinus in 235, and was reconciled to the Church. He died a martyr by his sufferings on that unhealthy island, and his body was afterwards translated to the cemetery on the Via Tiburtina.

Prudentius who, led astray by the inscription of Pope St Damasus over his grave, confuses this Hippolytus with another of that name, puts his martyrdom, by wild horses, at the mouth of the Tiber. In a hymn he testifies that as often as he had prayed at the tomb of St Hippolytus for the remedy of his infirmities, whether of body or mind, he had always found relief ; but he was indebted to Christ for this because He gave to his martyr Hippolytus the power to obtain for him the divine succour. He says that not only the inhabitants of Rome but many from remote countries resorted to this place to worship God ; and that especially

---

* The name Hippolytus means " loosed horse ". In the county of Hertford, two miles south-east from Hitchin, is the village of Ippollitts, which takes its name from the parish-church of Hippolytus. Formerly it had a shrine of the saint to which sick horses were brought, " out of the North Street, through the North Gate, and the north door of the church, which was boarded on purpose to bring up the horses to the altar ". Having regard to the story of the martyrdom and the significance of the name it is natural that the saint should be looked on as a patron of horses and their riders.

on the martyr's festival, on the Ides (13th) of August, people came thither to implore the divine mercy. " In the morning they rush to greet him ; all the youth worship ; they come, they go, till the setting of the sun. They press kisses on the shining metal of the inscription ; they pour out spices ; they bedew his tomb with tears. And when . . . his feast-day returns, what throngs are forced thither by their earnest zeal . . . the wide fields can scarce contain the joy of the people." It is further evidence of the great veneration which St Hippolytus enjoyed that he is named in the canon of the Ambrosian Mass of Milan.

In the year 1551 was dug up in the cemetery of St Hippolytus on the road to Tivoli a third-century statue of marble, representing the saint sitting in a chair, on the sides of which are inscribed his tables for computing Easter and a catalogue of his works. This statue is now in the Lateran museum.

It is only in recent times that the true importance of St Hippolytus in the early history of the Roman church has come to be recognized. Butler wrote a hundred years before the discovery of the *Philosophumena*, and even the excellent account of Hippolytus in Mgr Duchesne's *Histoire ancienne de l'Église* (vol. i, pp. 292–323) has to be supplemented by R. H. Connolly's important discovery that the so-called " Egyptian Church Order " dates from Hippolytus and forms the foundation document of the far-famed *Apostolic Constitutions* (see the Cambridge *Texts and Studies*, vol. viii, no. 4, 1916). For the personality and writings of the historical presbyter Hippolytus the reader may be referred to Lightfoot, *Apostolic Fathers*, vol. ii, pp. 316–477, and to Amann's excellent article in DTC., vol. vi, cc. 2487–2511. A. d'Alès, *La théologie de S. Hippolyte* (1906) is also a book of great value. See also G. Dix, *The Treatise of the Apostolic Tradition* (1937) ; G. Bovini, *Sant' Ippolito* (Studi di antichita cristiana, 1943) ; and B. Botte in the series " Sources chrétiennes " (the Apostolic Tradition and the Commentary on Daniel, 1947). Hippolytus's authorship of the *Philosophumena* is still contested by some. Prudentius's hymn is no. xi in the *Peristephanon*, Migne, PL., vol. lx, cc. 530 ss. Whether Hippolytus the writer was identical with the Hippolytus venerated at Porto cannot be certainly determined. The fantastic story of the martyrdom by wild horses seems to be a pure invention ; but as Prudentius testifies, there was already a fresco of the incident painted over the tomb. Hippolytus was buried in a cemetery on the Via Tiburtina, opposite to that of St Laurence, and a story had to be fabricated for him in order to complete the Laurentian cycle. See especially Delehaye in CMH., pp. 439–440 ; and H. Leclercq in DAC., vol. vi, cc. 2409–2483.

ST CASSIAN OF IMOLA, Martyr   (Date Unknown)

IN a single feast with St Hippolytus the Church joins St Cassian, though there was no connection between the two martyrs. He was a Christian schoolmaster, and taught children to read and write at Imola, a city twenty-seven miles from Ravenna in Italy. A violent persecution being raised against the Church, he was taken up and interrogated by the governor of the province. As he refused to sacrifice to the gods, the barbarous judge, learning of what profession he was, commanded that his own scholars should stab him to death with their iron pens.* He was exposed naked in the midst of two hundred boys, " by whom ", says the Roman Martyrology, " he had made himself disliked by teaching them ". Some threw their tablets, pens and knives at his face and head ; others cut his flesh, or stabbed him with their knives ; and others pierced him with their pens, some only tearing the skin and some penetrating more deeply, or making it their barbarous sport to cut letters out of his skin. Covered with blood and wounded in every part of his

* At that time it was the custom in schools to write upon wax laid on a board of boxwood, in which the letters were formed with an iron *stylus* or pen, sharp at one end but blunt and smooth at the other, to erase what was to be effaced or corrected.

body, he cheerfully bade the little fiends not to be afraid and to strike him with greater force : not meaning to encourage them in their sin, but to express the willingness he had to die for Christ. He was buried by the Christians at Imola. Prudentius tells us that in his journey to Rome he visited this martyr's tomb, and before it implored the divine mercy for the pardon of his sins. He describes a picture of the saint's martyrdom over the altar, representing his cruel death in the manner he has recorded it in verse.

The *passio* of the martyr, printed in Mombritius, *Sanctuarium*, vol. ii, seems merely to be a prose resetting of Prudentius's poem in *Peristephanon*, ix. The stylus-prodding by schoolboys is probably a reminiscence of an incident in Apuleius (see P. Franchi de' Cavalieri, *Hagiographica*, p. 131) and bears a more than suspicious resemblance to the torture of St Mark of Arethusa (March 29). But of the historical existence of the martyr of Imola there can be no reasonable doubt. See Lanzoni, *Le leggende di S. Cassiano d'Imola* (1913) ; *Didaskaleion*, vol. iii (1925), pp. 1–44 ; and Delehaye in CMH., pp. 440–441.

ST SIMPLICIAN, BISHOP OF MILAN (A.D. 400)

WHEN a priest of the Roman church of some age and corresponding experience, this Simplician was distinguished by the friendship of St Augustine, in whose life he played an important part. To him Augustine gave an account of the round of his wanderings and errors, and mentioned his reading certain books of the Platonists, which had been translated into Latin by Victorinus, who had been professor of rhetoric in Rome and died a Christian. Simplician commended his choice of these books, and related to him how he himself had been instrumental in the conversion of Victorinus, that very learned old man, who taught most of the senators of Rome and had the honour of a statue set up in the Forum. A fear of offending his friends made him defer his baptism for some time ; but being encouraged by Simplician he was instructed and baptized by him. When Julian the Apostate forbade Christians to teach the sciences, Victorinus quitted his school. Augustine was strongly touched by so generous an example, and the influence of St Simplician and the example of Victorinus led him perceptibly nearer to his own conversion.

In several places in his writings St Ambrose praises the learning, prudent judgement and glowing faith of Simplician, and when he was dying, overhearing someone suggest the priest as his successor, he cried out emphatically, " Simplician is old, but he is a good man ". Simplician in fact succeeded to the see of Milan, but survived to govern it for only three years. Being troubled by certain difficulties found in St Paul's epistle to the Hebrews he referred them to St Augustine ; his work *Quaestiones diversae ad Simplicianum* was written in reply. One of the practices of St Simplician (and of St Augustine) was the wearing of a black leather belt on account of a vision said to have been experienced by St Monica in which our Lady told her to wear such an one in her honour. This belt was adopted as part of the habit of the Augustinian friars. St Simplician is named on August 16 in the Roman Martyrology, but the friars just mentioned keep his feast on the 13th ; neither date is that of his death, which took place in May.

There is no early life of Simplician, but some later accounts with references to SS. Ambrose and Augustine and a quotation from Ennodius will be found in the *Acta Sanctorum*, August, vol. iii ; see also DCB., vol. iv, pp. 688–689.

ST RADEGUND, Matron   (A.D. 587)

" THE figure of St Radegund ", writes Godefroid Kurth in his life of St Clotilde, " is undeniably the most authentic and the best known of her century. All the light which history throws on that period converges on her personality, since her life has been related by two biographers who lived on intimate terms with her, without counting Gregory of Tours, who was in the ranks of her respectful admirers." She was born in 518, probably at Erfurt, the daughter of Berthaire, a pagan king of part of Thuringia, who was assassinated by his brother, Hermenefrid. In 531 Theodoric, King of Austrasia, and his half-brother, Clotaire I, King of Neustria, fell upon Hermenefrid, vanquished him, and carried home a great booty. Among the prisoners, Radegund, then about twelve years old, fell to the lot of King Clotaire, who is said to have had her instructed in the Christian religion and baptized, but it is more probable that she was already a Christian when she was seized from her father. Until her eighteenth year she lived at Athies, near Péronne, distinguished for her personal beauty, her goodness and her devotion to religion ; and then she was called to Vitry to become the wife of the king.

Clotaire I was the youngest son of Clovis, the first Christian king of the Franks, but he was a man of shocking character, " sensual and a brute ", the Abbé Aigrain justly calls him. His matrimonial alliances have never been properly disentangled ; he was married at least five times and it is even possible that his union with Radegund was polygamous. She bore her lot with fortitude and, though now become a queen, she continued no less an enemy to dissipation and vanity than she was before, and divided her time chiefly between the church and care of the poor, the sick and captives. She also founded a hospital for lepers, whom she waited on herself, and was one day seen kissing their diseased bodies. A friend remonstrated, saying that after that no one would dare kiss her. " If you don't want to kiss me, I really do not mind at all ", retorted Radegund. Clotaire allowed her full liberty in her devotions ; but after his affection began to be alienated from her he reproached her, saying he had married a nun rather than a queen, who converted his court into a monastery. His complaints were unjust ; for she made it the first point of her devotion never to be wanting in any duty of her state and to show the king all possible complaisance. She accepted his infidelities and taunts on her childlessness with patience and courtesy, but after six years of marriage Clotaire committed a crime which Radegund could not overlook : he murdered her brother, who had been captured with herself at the battle of the Unstrut and of whom she was very fond.

Radegund asked her husband's leave to retire from the court, which was granted, or he may have sent her away. She went to Noyon and asked the bishop, St Médard, to give her the religious veil. He hesitated, for she was in a somewhat equivocal position and the king was notoriously violent and unscrupulous. But when she appeared before him in church, dressed in a nun's habit, and charged him, " If you will not consecrate me, you fear man more than God, and He will ask you an account of my soul ", Médard gave in and consecrated her a deaconess. St Radegund first withdrew to Saix, an estate of Clotaire's in Poitou, living a penitential life there for six months ; she employed almost her whole revenue in alms, and served the poor with her own hands. She went after to Poitiers, and there built a monastery of nuns, of which she arranged for a friend, named Agnes, to be made the first abbess, and paid her an implicit obedience. King Clotaire about this time went as far as Tours upon a religious pretence but intending to go to Poitiers and carry her again to court. Radegund was alarmed, and wrote to St Germanus of Paris, beseeching his help. The bishop went to the king and implored him to leave his innocent wife alone. Germanus's interference was so effectual that Clotaire sent him to Poitiers to beg Radegund's forgiveness for him and her prayers that he might find God's pardon also. His better frame of mind was only passing ; among other subsequent enormities he burned alive in a cottage his own son and grandchildren. He is said to have died penitent, but it is not surprising to read that during his last illness he showed great alarm and disturbance of mind at the remembrance of his crimes ; but he left St Radegund in peace and was even a benefactor of her monastery.

This abbey, at first called St Mary's but afterwards Holy Cross, was one of the first double monasteries, for men and women, and on this account was also one of the first to insist on a strict and permanent enclosure. The rule chosen was that of St Caesarius of Arles, in accordance with which the nuns had to spend two hours every day in study, and Radegund herself knew some Latin ; under her influence Holy Cross became a meeting-place for scholars and, traditional accompaniment of learning, a centre for the maintenance of peace. Whenever rumours of war were heard, St Radegund sent letters to the combatants, urging them in the name of Christ to desist ; but she used violence unsparingly to her own body. St Caesaria the Younger, abbess of St John's at Arles, sent to Poitiers with a copy of the rule a letter of advice for the nuns. In it she says that every nun shall learn the psalter by heart, and be able to read.

Radegund enriched the church she had built with the relics of a number of saints, but was very desirous to procure a particle of the true cross of our Redeemer, and sent clerks to Constantinople, to the Emperor Justin, for that purpose. The emperor sent her a piece of that sacred wood, adorned with gold and precious stones, a book of the gospels beautified in the same manner, and the relics of several saints. They were carried to Poitiers, and deposited in the church of the monastery with a great procession, wax tapers, incense, and singing of psalms ; this was carried out by St Euphronius, Archbishop of Tours, the bishop of Poitiers having for some reason refused to have anything to do with it. It was for that occasion that St Venantius Fortunatus composed the hymn " *Vexilla regis prodeunt* ", which was solemnly sung for the first time on this November 19, 569. Venantius was at that time a priest at Poitiers, and a close friend of St Radegund, whose life he wrote ; he corresponded freely with her and the Abbess Agnes, writing letters to them in Latin verse about their austerities and their health, acknowledging gifts of food and sending in return flowers.

Much of Radegund's last years was spent in complete seclusion, and she died peacefully on August 13, 587. " When we heard of her death ", writes St Gregory of Tours, " we went to the monastery which she had founded at Poitiers. We found her lying in her coffin, her face shining with a brightness surpassing the beauty of lilies and roses. Around her stood nuns to the number of about two hundred, who, inspired by the words of the saint, led a perfect life within their cloister. In the world many of them had belonged to senatorial families, and some of them were even of royal blood." The nun Baudonivia, who had been brought up by St Radegund and was present at her funeral, relates that during it a blind man recovered his sight, and other miracles were attributed to her both before and after death. On one occasion she cured a sick nun, miraculously or not, by giving her a hot bath—for two hours. Following St Caesarius, she always insisted on the excellent practice of bathing, and when at Saix used to bath sick people twice a week. This Baudonivia wrote a biography of their holy foundress, not, as she says, " to repeat those things which the apostolic bishop Fortunatus wrote in his life of the blessed one, but to record those which he in his prolixity passed over ". " Human eloquence ", he had written, " has in its astonishment but little power to show in what piety, self-denial, charity, sweetness, humility, uprightness, faith and fervour Radegund lived ", but his own eloquence had done its best. St Radegund is named in the Roman Martyrology and her feast is observed in many places ; she is one of the three contitulars of the Cambridge college commonly known as Jesus College.

As stated above, we owe our knowledge of St Radegund to the lives by Venantius Fortunatus and the nun Baudonivia, together with certain passing references in Gregory of Tours. The two former sources have been edited, after Mabillon and the Bollandists, by B. Krusch in MGH., *Scriptores Merov.*, vol. ii, pp. 364–395. There are modern lives by Leroux (1877) and Briand (1899) ; that by R. Aigrain in the series " Les Saints " is mentioned with high commendation in the *Analecta Bollandiana*, vol. xxxix (1921), pp. 192–194. For English readers attention may be called to F. Brittain, *St Radegund* (1925), and to a re-edition (1926) of an English poem (probably by Henry Bradshaw), *The Lyfe of Seynt Radegunde*, published originally by R. Pynson about 1510.

ST MAXIMUS THE CONFESSOR, Abbot (A. D. 662)

MAXIMUS is called " the Confessor " because of his labours and sufferings for the true faith ; he was one of the foremost divines of the seventh century, a pillar of orthodoxy against the monothelite heresy, and a zealous supporter of the teaching authority of the Holy See. He was born about the year 580 and belonged to Constantinople ; when he grew up he was placed at the imperial court and became the principal secretary of the Emperor Heraclius. But after a time he resigned this post (it is likely that he was made uncomfortable by the emperor's support of what he recognized as heretical opinions) and became a monk at Chrysopolis (now known as Skutari) ; there he was elected abbot and wrote some of his mystical treatises. On the death in 638 of St Sophronius, Patriarch of Jerusalem, who had been a hermit and whom Maximus calls his master, father and teacher, Maximus took his place as the champion of orthodoxy against the Monothelism (the attribution of only one, a divine, will to our Lord) of the Emperor Heraclius and his successor Constans II. He defended the memory of Pope Honorius from the charge of having held that heresy, and in a letter about Pyrrhus, who had been exiled from the see of Constantinople, he says, " If the Roman see recognizes Pyrrhus to be a heretic as well as a reprobate, it is quite clear that everyone who anathematizes those who have condemned Pyrrhus, anathematizes the see of Rome, that is, the Catholic Church. . . . Let him hasten before all else to satisfy the Roman see, for if it is satisfied all will agree in calling him pious and orthodox . . . [that] Apostolic See which has received universal and supreme dominion, authority and power of binding and loosing over all the holy churches of God throughout the world, from the incarnate Son of God Himself and also by all holy councils. . . ."

In 645 Gregory, the governor of the African province and a friend of Maximus, arranged a public disputation between the saint and Pyrrhus, as the result of which Pyrrhus went to Rome to abjure his monothelite heresy. Three years later the

Emperor Constans II issued a decree in favour of Monothelism, called the *Typos*, and St Maximus was in Rome at the time of the council summoned by Pope St Martin I at which this document was condemned. In 653 the pope was dragged from Rome by the imperial exarch, banished to the Chersonese, and there bullied and starved to death, the last martyred pope. St Maximus remained in Rome until, having argued against the *Typos* before an imperial legate, he too was seized, being now an old man of seventy-five, and carried off to Constantinople. He was put on trial on a charge of conspiring against the empire ; he said that he supported Rome in the matter of the *Typos*, and when it was objected that he thereby condemned the church of Constantinople he replied, " I condemn no one ; but I would rather lose my life than depart from the least point of the faith ". He was sentenced to banishment at Bizya, in Thrace, where he suffered greatly from cold, hunger and neglect. After some months a commission was sent to interview him, headed by Theodosius, Bishop of Caesarea in Bithynia. Maximus so eloquently demonstrated to them the two natures in Christ and the depravity of keeping silence on the true faith that Theodosius was convinced, gave the confessor money and some clothes (which were taken away by the bishop of Bizya), and promised that he would submit to the Holy See. St Maximus was then removed to a monastery at Rhegium, and there arrived Theodosius of Caesarea and another deputation, offering him honours from the emperor if he would accept the *Typos*. Maximus reminded Theodosius of his promise, which he had ratified " on the holy gospels, on the cross, and on the image of the Mother of God ", to which the bishop could only reply, " What could I do ? The emperor took another view ". Maximus remained firm ; he was struck and spat upon, his few possessions were taken away from him, and the next day he was taken to Perberis, where his two friends and supporters, Anastasius the Abbot and Anastasius the Apocrisiarius, were already in captivity.

Here they remained in great hardship and distress for six years, and then were brought back to Constantinople to appear before a tribunal. All three were condemned, and with them the memory of St Martin I and St Sophronius, and they were sentenced to be scourged, to be deprived of their tongues and their right hands, thus mutilated to be pilloried in each of the twelve quarters of the city, and to be imprisoned for life. Tongueless, they could no longer preach the orthodox faith, handless, they could no longer write it ; but they could still confess it by suffering with patience and dying with fortitude. St Maximus survived only a few weeks, after a terrible journey to Skhemaris, near Batum on the Black Sea ; one Anastasius died even sooner, but the other lived on until 666.

This great confessor of the faith and mystical religious writer suffered thus in his eighty-second year ; he left many writings, including allegorical commentaries on the Scriptures and the works of Denis the Areopagite, a dialogue on the spiritual life between two monks, and a *Mystagogia*, an explanation of liturgical symbolism. St Maximus was not, as is sometimes said, the father of Byzantine mysticism, which originated with the desert monks of earlier ages ; he was, rather, its foremost exponent.

The history of St Maximus is mainly derived from a Greek biography originally edited by Combefis, and now accessible in Migne, PG., vol. xc, cc. 68–109, followed by letters or tractates of his, and other documents concerning him. But of late years better texts have become available which correct prevailing misconceptions in many details, and there has been an increasing interest in the writings of St Maximus. See L. Duchesne, *L'Église au vi^e siècle* (1925), pp. 431 *seq.* ; R. Devreesse in *Analecta Bollandiana*, vol. xlvi (1928), pp. 5–49, and vol. liii (1935), pp. 49 *seq.* ; V. Grumel in DTC., vol. x, cc. 448–459 ; H. Urs von Balthasar, *Liturgie cosmique* (1947) ; the saint's *Centuries sur la charité* (tr. J. Pégon, 1945) ; and a French translation of his Mystagogy in *Irénikon*, t. xiii (1936), no. 4 to t. xv (1938), no. 5. There is a long notice in the Bollandist commentary on the *Mart. Rom.*, pp. 336–337. Dom P. Sherwood's *Date-List of the Works of Maximus the Confessor* (1952) gives more than the title promises.

ST WIGBERT, ABBOT   (*c.* A.D. 738)

THIS Wigbert was an Englishman who, despising the world in his youth, embraced a monastic state.   In due course St Boniface invited him to join in the labours of the conversion of the Germans, and made him abbot of Fritzlar, a monastery three miles from Cassel, where one of his disciples was St Sturmi.   Later he was transferred to Ohrdruf, in Thuringia, and he successfully formed and organized both these foundations, himself setting an impeccable example of monastic observance ; when called out by duty he spoke to no one on the road, and made haste back to his monastery.   His biographer speaks much of St Wigbert's virtues, miracles and accomplishments, but tells us little of the events of his life.   Towards its end St Boniface gave him permission to return to Fritzlar, where he could live more quietly to prepare himself for death.   His last sickness could not make him mitigate the severity of his penances and fasts, and he died about the year 738.   His body was translated to the monastery of Hersfeld by St Lull in 780.   This saint must not be confused with the St Wigbert (Wictbert), a disciple of St Egbert, who tried to evangelize the Frisians at the end of the seventh century.

The life written about 100 years after Wigbert's death by Servatus Lupus, in which the miraculous element is very prominent, after being printed by Mabillon and the Bollandists, was re-edited in MGH., *Scriptores*, vol. xv, pp. 37–43.   See also H. Timerding, *Die christliche Frühzeit Deutschlands*, Zweite Gruppe (1929).

ST NERSES KLAIËTSI, KATHOLIKOS OF THE ARMENIANS   (A.D. 1173)

NERSES, called " Shnorhali ", the Gracious, because of the beauty of his character and his writings, was born at Hromkla in Cilicia, his mother being of the family of Gregory the Enlightener. He was educated by his uncle, the Katholikos Gregory II, who favoured the reunion of his church with Rome, and by a great Armenian doctor, Stephen Manuk.   Nerses was ordained by his elder brother, the Katholikos Gregory III.   This Gregory, whom both Catholic and dissident Armenians venerate as a saint, seems to have been in communion with the prelates of the Western crusaders ; and when in 1166 Nerses succeeded his brother as katholikos (the fourth of his name), he maintained this union, which, however, was not formally confirmed until the coronation of King Leo II at Tarsus in 1198.   Nerses, moreover, worked for the reconciliation of the Orthodox Greeks ; and writing to the Emperor Manuel Comnenos he refers to the pope as " the first of all the archbishops and successor of the apostle Peter ".   He is the most famous writer of the twelfth-century Armenian renaissance, both in prose and verse ; he wrote a book of short prayers for every hour of the day, poems on religious and historical subjects, and liturgical hymns, in one of which the Roman church is apostrophized as " immovably built on the rock of Kephas, invincible by the gates of Hell, and seal of the guardian of the gates of Heaven ".   St Nerses died on August 13, 1173, but his feast is kept on the 3rd, and he is named in the great intercession of the Armenian Mass both by Catholics and dissidents.

A full account of St Nerses and of his attitude to monophysite teaching will be found in Tournebize, *Histoire politique et religieuse de l'Arménie* (1901), especially pp. 239–253 ; references to Armenian authorities are there supplied.   See also Balzy, *Historia doctrinae christianae inter Armenos*, pp. 33 *seq.*, and Nilles, *Kalendarium* . . ., vol. ii, p. 598.   The daily prayers of St Nerses were published by the Armenian monks at Venice in 1862, translated into 32 languages, including English, Irish and " Greenlandish ".   Pope Pius XII quoted from Nerses against Monophysism in the encyclical letter " Sempiternus Christus rex " (1951).

BD NOVELLONE   (A.D. 1280)

THIS is one of those who, from among the numerous lay-people who in all ages and places live a life of heroic sanctity in the world, have been chosen by Almighty God to be withdrawn from their obscurity and raised to the altars of the Church. Novellone was a native of Faenza and by trade a shoemaker.   He did not grow up in the fear of the Lord, and his godless life was in no way altered when he received the sacrament of matrimony.   But at the age of twenty-four he had a serious illness ; fear of death opened his heart to grace ; he resolved to amend his life, and as an aid thereto became a tertiary of St Francis.   He imposed mortifications on himself and gave all he could to the poor, went on pilgrimage to Rome and then, bare-footed, to Compostela, scourging himself as he went.   But now he had much to suffer from his wife, who complained of his long absences from home and of his charity to the poor ; but she was changed one day when, a beggar coming to the door, the larder that a few minutes before had been empty was found to be well stocked with food. After the death of his wife Novellone reduced himself to want by his benefactions and sought to lead the life of a hermit.   In order to do this, he is said by some writers to have entered the Camaldolese order, but he seems simply to have taken up his residence beside the cell of a Camaldolese hermit, one Laurence, at Faenza. After edifying his fellow citizens for fifty-six years Novellone died and was buried in the cathedral of Faenza.   His *cultus* was approved in 1817.

Mgr F. Lanzoni published, first in 1903 a brochure showing that what purported to be a summary of a contemporary biography was really no more than a panegyric delivered 150 years after his death, and then in 1913 a valuable article in the *Archivum franciscanum historicum* (vol. vi, pp. 623–653) which discusses the whole history.   It appears that the details of Bd Novellone's story are untrustworthy.   Our sole reliable authority is the brief notice in Cantinelli's Chronicle of Faenza.   *Cf.* however, A. Marchetti, *Cronotassi dei parroci di Faenza* (1927).

BD GERTRUDE OF ALTENBERG, VIRGIN   (A.D. 1297)

TWO weeks after the death in September 1227 of her husband Louis at Otranto, on his way to the crusade in the Holy Land, St Elizabeth of Hungary gave birth to their third daughter, who was christened Gertrude.   Before his departure Bd Louis had agreed with his wife that their coming child should be dedicated to the service of God as a thank-offering for their years of happiness together : if a girl, with the Premonstratensian canonesses at Altenberg, near Wetzlar.   Friar Conrad of Marburg, ander whose direction the landgravine had put herself and who ruled her rigorously, insisted that this should be done when the child was still short of two years old, and to Altenberg the baby Gertrude was taken.   When she grew up she elected to ratify the wish of her parents, by then both dead ; she was received into the community, and by the age of twenty-two was abbess.   Following in the footsteps of her mother, she expended the inheritance she received from her uncle on building a new church for her monastery and an almshouse for the poor ; the conduct of the last she made her own personal business and, at a time when abbesses, especially royal abbesses, tended to be very great ladies indeed, she was in her works and mortifications indistinguishable from the other nuns.

During the seventh crusade Bd Gertrude, in memory of her father's chivalry, " took the cross ", on behalf of herself and her community :   not indeed with the obligation of going to the Holy Land, but binding themselves to support it unwearyingly by their prayers and penances.   She also obtained permission for the celebration of the feast of Corpus Christi in her monastery ; this was in 1270 and she was in consequence one of the first to introduce it into Germany.   When Dietrich the Dominican was writing his *vita* of St Elizabeth of Hungary in 1289 he noted that her daughter the Abbess Gertrude was still living, and she lived on for another eight years, dying in the fiftieth year of her abbacy.

See the *Acta Sanctorum*, August, vol. iii, and *cf.* the *Stimmen aus Maria Laach* (1893), vol. ii, pp. 415 *seq.*   Most lives of St Elizabeth of Hungary contain some notice of Bd Gertrude.

BD JOHN OF ALVERNIA   (A.D. 1322)

THIS John is sometimes called " of Fermo " in the Marches, where he was born in 1259, but usually " of Alvernia " because he lived for many years and died on the mountain of La Verna.   In 1272 desire for a life of greater perfection caused him to join the Friars Minor, and after his profession he was sent to La Verna, where St Francis had received the *stigmata*.   Here he lived in a cell formed in a cave in the mountain-side, sleeping only a few hours, and then on the bare ground with a stone for pillow.   In this solitude of penance and contemplation he spent some years, and frequent ecstasies and visions of our Lord and of the saints are recorded of him ; one All Souls' day while offering Mass he saw numberless souls released from Purgatory, and for a space of three months he was conscious of the habitual presence of his guardian angel, who conversed with him.   After a time his austerities became excessive and St Francis himself in vision ordered him to moderate them lest he unfit himself for the active service of his neighbour to which he was soon to be called.

This took the form of preaching and pastoral work, first in the towns and villages around La Verna and then throughout central and northern Italy.   He had the gifts of infused knowledge and of reading souls, and his exhortations brought back many who were sinners to Christ and excited the admiration of good and learned men.   He never wrote out his sermons, and when it was pointed out to him that this had its disadvantages he replied, " When I go into the pulpit I just remind myself that it is not I, a poor sinner, who is to preach, but God Himself who will teach divine truth through my mouth.   Do you suppose, dear brethren, that God can ever fail in His words ? "   Bd John was a close friend of the poet Bd Giacopone da Todi and gave him the last sacraments as he lay dying on Christmas day 1306 ; and John himself is alleged to be the author of the proper preface sung by the Friars Minor in the Mass of St Francis.   He was at the friary of Cortona when he felt death approaching ; he therefore hurried to La Verna, and there died on

August 10, 1322.   To the brothers who were present he said, as his last message,
" If you would have a good conscience, wish to know Jesus Christ only, for He
is the way.   If you would have wisdom, wish to know Jesus Christ only, for He
is the truth.   If you wish to have glory, wish to know Jesus Christ only, for He is
the life."

The *cultus* of Bd John of Alvernia was approved in 1880.   The Friars Minor
keep his feast with Bd Novellone (above), and join with it that of BD VINCENT OF
AQUILA, a lay-brother who died at San Giuliano in 1504 : " a man of great humility,
of prayer, temperance and patience, adorned with the spirit of prophecy."   His
cultus was confirmed in 1785.

There is more than one sketch of the life of Bd John printed in the *Acta Sanctorum*,
August, vol. ii, and there is another early account which has been edited in the *Analecta
Franciscana*, vol. iii (1879), pp. 439–447.   See also Léon, *Auréole Séraphique* (Eng. trans.),
vol. ii, pp. 553 *seq.*, and more especially L. Oliger, *Il b. Giovanni della Verna* (1913).   For
Bd Vincent, see the *Acta Sanctorum*, August, vol. ii ; and G. Rivera, *Il b. Vincenzo dall'
Aquila* (1904).

BD WILLIAM FREEMAN, MARTYR   (A.D. 1595)

WILLIAM FREEMAN (*alias* Mason) was born in the East Riding of Yorkshire about
1558, and was educated at Magdalen College, Oxford.   He had been brought up a
Catholic, but took to outward conformity with the new church until 1586.   In that
year he was present at the martyrdom of Bd Edward Stransham at Tyburn, and
he was so deeply impressed that he at once went over to Rheims and was ordained
in the following year.   He was sent to England in 1589 and worked for six years on
the borders of Worcestershire and Warwickshire, where he was in touch with
several of the friends of Shakespeare.   He was then engaged by a Mrs Heath of
Stratford-on-Avon to be tutor to her son, but in January 1595 a special commission
was sent to search her house, and Mr Freeman was arrested.   He managed to
conceal the fact that he was a priest, but he was betrayed by a fellow prisoner, and
at the end of seven months' imprisonment was convicted and sentenced as a seminary priest.   He was accordingly hanged, drawn and quartered at Warwick on
August 13, 1595.   Certain criminals were put to death before him and in his
presence, in the hope that the terrifying sight would make him apostatize ; but he
protested that if he had many lives he would most willingly lay them down for the
sake of Him who had been pleased to die upon a cross for his redemption, and
devoutly recited Psalm xli, " As the hart panteth after the fountains of water ".

See MMP., pp. 227–228, and *Publications* of the Catholic Record Society, vol. v, pp.
345–360.

ST BENILDUS   (A.D. 1862)

IN the fertile plain called the Limagne in the French civil department of Puy-de-
Dôme stands the small town, or large village, called Thuret.   It has a big and
handsome romanesque church of the twelfth century, and in it was christened, on
June 13, 1805, the day of his birth, a boy called Peter Romançon, the second son
of his parents, who were people much respected in the district.   In the same
church, twelve years later, he made his first communion and was confirmed by the
bishop of Clermont.   But long before this, when he was six, the child had begun
to attend the local school and to show a notable spiritual and intellectual intelligence.

One day when he was in Clermont with his father, Peter's attention was caught by a black-habited religious who passed them with flowing cloak. The boy asked who he was and what he did, and was told that he was one of the congregation called the Brothers of the Christian Schools, who had been founded at Rheims in 1684 by St John Baptist de la Salle for the free education of boys, especially the sons of poor parents. The idea struck young Peter and stuck in his head, and he told his parents that he wanted to be one of these brothers ; he was shy about it at first, but later got quite insistent. His parents neither encouraged nor discouraged him, but when the brothers opened a school at Riom they sent him there to finish his schooling.

The atmosphere at Riom suited Peter down to the ground, and when he was fourteen he asked to be admitted as an aspirant to the congregation. In spite of his excellent reputation he was refused, on the ground that he was too small. So he waited patiently and prayerfully for two years, until he had grown bigger, and then tried again : this time successfully. Mr Romançon, to try his son, threatened to cut him off with a shilling if he left home. " I shan't complain if you want to do so ", replied Peter gently, " I should only be exchanging earthly goods for heavenly goods." And so, in the autumn of 1820, he asked and received his parents' blessing and departed for the novitiate at Clermont-Ferrand. During the following twelve months his vocation was clearly confirmed, and his director did not hesitate to declare that " This young brother will be one of the glories of our congregation one day ". Upon being clothed with the religious habit, Peter Romançon had been given the name of Benildus.*

At the end of his novitiate Brother Benildus was sent back to the school at Riom to begin his course of instruction in the art of teaching, and during the following years he was in turn with other Christian Brother communities, sometimes varying his teaching with other tasks, such as that of cook. He had been professed only two years when he was put in charge of the community and school at Billom in the Puy-de-Dôme. One of his pupils here said of him afterwards : " Brother Benildus was as good as an angel and looked like a saint. He was a fine teacher ; a bit strict, but always fair. He would encourage the backward ones, and made us work hard. His pupils were good, and knew their religion properly."

Brother Benildus was so successful in this charge that in 1841, when he was thirty-six years old, he was sent to direct a community and open a school at Saugues, in Haute-Loire ; and it was here he spent the rest of his life. The brothers were welcomed with enthusiasm in the town, and they were soon asked to run evening classes for grown-ups in addition to their main work. The government inspectors became so pleased with the school that they awarded Brother Benildus a silver medal ; but more gratifying to him would have been the golden opinions of his pupils, some of which are still on record. One of them finds it worth mentioning that " the holy head master " used to have the windows opened when he came into class.

It was as a religious teacher that Brother Benildus excelled. " I live for the apostolate ", he wrote. " If through my fault these children don't grow in goodness, what is the use of my life ? If I die teaching the catechism, then I die at my proper work." He had prepared himself for this work by his own personal life and by acquiring a thorough background of theological and other knowledge. More

* The writer has been unable to trace any saint of this unusual name. But there was a woman martyr under the Moors at Cordova, mentioned in the Roman Martyrology on June 15, called Benildis.

than one witness testifies that in his divinity classes the pupils listened with absorbed attention and found the time go too quickly; and they were never dismissed without a few words of exhortation straight from the teacher's loving heart. " Dear Brother Benildus used to speak of the eternal truths with such warmth that I have never forgotten his words. They touched the hearts of us all, and made us sorry for our misdoings." And it was not only his former pupils that appreciated him : their parents and the Presentation sisters who ran the girls' school and the clergy of the town all spoke to the same effect. Said one of the curates of the parish church, " Brother Benildus did not worship God like an angel only when he was in church and saying his prayers, but always and everywhere—even among his cabbages in the garden ".

Enthusiasm for the congregation of which he was a member was very characteristic of Benildus. " Even were I reduced to eating potato-skins ", he said at one moment of difficulty, " I would not give up the congregation—I am too conscious of God's goodness in calling me to His service in it." He never missed an opportunity of encouraging a suitable volunteer for it, but not by putting forward human considerations. " What was he looking for ? An easy life ? The school at Saugues did not promise anything of the kind. The approval of public opinion ? The brothers' life was retired and hidden. But if he wanted personal sanctification, and work for our Lord that was humble but useful, hard but worth doing, then . . ." A priest, who visited the mother house of the Brothers of the Christian Schools in Paris five years after the death of Brother Benildus, found there thirty-two novices from the Saugues neighbourhood, nearly all of them former pupils of Benildus.

In 1855 Brother Benildus wrote to one of his colleagues that, " I have got a complaint that at present hardly allows me to leave my bed. I am very tired, worn out, and almost unable to speak ; I expect the end daily ". But it was not till six years later that he was finally struck down by a painful and serious rheumatic disease. His superiors sent him several times to take the water at Bagnols-les-Bains (where the parish priest said his visits were as good as a mission to his flock), but in January 1862 it was apparent that the end was not far off. On the eve of Trinity Sunday he insisted on getting up to prepare the chapel for the annual renewal of vows on the following day, and he took a last farewell of his pupils. " Boys ", he said, " I know that you are praying for me, and I thank you ; but your prayers are not going to make me get well. God is calling me ; and if He is merciful to me, be sure that I will pray for you in Heaven." About July 30 he struggled into the chapel again. " This is the last time," he said to his companion. " Soon you will be carrying me in." A fortnight later, on August 13, 1862, Brother Benildus died, surrounded by his brethren.

The funeral was on the feast of the Assumption. The parish church of Saugues is large, but on that day it was filled to overflowing. From the moment of burial the humble brother's grave was a place of pilgrimage ; and when in 1884 a new memorial stone was set over it the inscription was " décédé en odeur de sainteté ". There were some who demurred at this, but the former parish priest, Canon Raveyre, was not one of them ; " It won't be surprising if one day the Church raises him to her altars ", he said. And he was right, for in 1896 the process was begun at Le Puy which in 1968 culminated in Rome in the canonization of Bd Benildus Romançon.

See *Le Vénérable Frère Benilde* (1928) ; and G. Rigault, *Un instituteur sur les autels* (1947).

14 : ST EUSEBIUS OF ROME   (FOURTH CENTURY)

S T EUSEBIUS lived in Rome during the latter part of the fourth century, but the story of his life as related in his *acta* is entirely spurious.   This relates that he was a priest who opposed the Arian emperor Constantius, supported " St Felix II " (July 29), and celebrated the Holy Mysteries in his own house after he had been forbidden the churches.   He was therefore imprisoned in a tiny room of the same house, where he died after seven months.   He was buried, we are told, in the cemetery of Callistus on the Appian Way, with the inscription over his tomb : " To Eusebius, the Man of God " : this circumstance may be true, but no trace of the tomb has been found.

This is one of the cases in which we have clear evidence of the historical existence of a person who was afterwards the object of a certain *cultus*, though the story subsequently told is quite untrustworthy.   Eusebius beyond doubt founded what we may call a parish church in Rome which was known as the " titulus Eusebii ". As founder an annual commemorative Mass was offered for him, which in course of time was regarded as a Mass celebrated in his honour, and in 595 we find that the parish was already referred to as the " titulus sancti Eusebii ".

See H. Delehaye, *Sanctus* (1927), p. 149 ; J. Wilpert in *Römische Quartalschrift*, vol. xxii, pp. 80–82 ; J. P. Kirsch, *Die römischen Titelkirchen*, pp. 58–61 ; with the whole discussion in CMH., pp. 443–444.   Alban Butler printed also on this day almost in its entirety the *passio* of a martyred Eusebius, said to be in Palestine.   But the document is worthless and there is no indication of *cultus*, so this strangely obscure martyr is here omitted.

ST MARCELLUS, BISHOP OF APAMAEA, MARTYR   (*c.* A.D. 389)

AMONG the undertakings of the Emperor Theodosius the Great was the attempt completely to christianize the Roman empire, and in 380 he and the co-emperor, Gratian, issued a decree that all their subjects were to profess the faith of the bishops of Rome and Alexandria.   Eight years later he sent an officer into Egypt, Syria, and Asia Minor, whose duty it was to enforce an edict that all pagan temples were to be destroyed ; this violent policy was carried out very roughly and not unnaturally aroused the anger and resentment of the pagans.   When the imperial prefect arrived at Apamaea in Syria he set his soldiers to work to pull down the temple of Zeus there, but it was a large building and well built and the soldiers, being inexpert at systematic demolition, made little progress.   The bishop of the place was one Marcellus ; he told the prefect to take off his men to their next job and in his absence means would be sought efficiently to destroy the temple.   The very next day a navvy came to the bishop and said that, if he would pay him double wages, he could do the work himself.   St Marcellus agreed, and the man proceeded to demolish the temple by the simple device of undermining some of the supporting columns, holding up the foundations with timber, and then burning it away, in much the same way as a tall chimney-stalk is brought down today.

Marcellus proceeded to have other temples dealt with in this manner, until he went to one in a certain unidentified place ; this building was stoutly defended by those who worshipped in it, and the bishop had " to take up a position some way from the scene of conflict, out of the reach of the arrows, for he suffered from gout and so was not able either to fight or to run away ".   But while he was watching from this point of vantage, some of the pagans stole a march on him, seized him, and put him to death by throwing him into the flames. The sons of St Marcellus (he had been married) afterwards wanted to take vengeance on his murderers, but the council of the province forbade them, saying they should rather rejoice that God had accounted their father worthy to die in His cause. This St Marcellus must not be confused with another St Marcellus, born at Apamaea and abbot in Constantinople, whose feast is observed on December 29.

The account in the *Acta Sanctorum*, August, vol. iii, seems to have gathered up all that is known concerning this Marcellus. Theodoret, *Eccles. Hist.*, bk v, ch. 21, is the main authority. It would seem that, because of his aggressive behaviour, Marcellus is hardly entitled to the honours of a martyr.

ST FACHANAN, Bishop   (Sixth Century)

This saint's feast is observed liturgically throughout all Ireland and he is patron of the diocese of Ross, where he was probably the first bishop. He was born at Tulachteann, was one of the pupils of St Ita, and founded the monastery of Molana on an island in the Blackwater, near Youghal. But his great achievement was the establishment of the monastic school of Ross, at what is now Rosscarbery, in county Cork, one of the most famous schools of Ireland, which flourished for three hundred years and survived in some form until the coming of the Normans. Fachanan (Fachtna) suffered for a time from blindness, from which he recovered at the intercession of Ita's sister, who was about to give birth to St Mochoemog. St Fachanan was revered as a " wise and upright man ", with a great gift for preaching ; St Cuimin of Connor said of him that he was " generous and steadfast, fond of preaching to the people and saying nothing that was base or displeasing to God ". The St Fachanan honoured on this day as the patron of Kilfenora diocese may be a different person from him of Ross.

St Fachanan is another Irish saint of whom no early biography survives. He is mentioned, however, on this day in the *Félire* of Oengus and is described as " son of Mongach, the son of the wright, a fair captive ". There is also a passing reference to him and to his school in the Latin life of St Mochoemog. See O'Hanlon, LIS., vol. viii, pp. 191 *seq.*

ST ATHANASIA, Matron   (*c.* A.D. 860)

She was born on the island of Aegina, in the gulf of that name, and married an officer in the army ; but only sixteen days after their union he was killed while fighting against the Arabs, who had made a descent on the Grecian coast. Athanasia was now anxious to become a nun, especially as she had had a dream or vision in which the passingness of all earthly things had been strongly impressed on her. But she was persuaded by her parents to marry again. Her second husband was a devoted and religious man, and shared in and encouraged his wife's good works. She gave alms liberally and helped the sick, strangers, prisoners and all who stood in need ; after the Liturgy on Sundays and holy-days she would gather her neighbours round her and read and explain to them a passage from the Bible. After a time her husband decided he wanted to become a monk, which with Athanasia's consent he did, and she turned her house into a convent, of which she was made abbess.

These nuns followed a life of excessive austerity, till they came under the direction of a holy abbot called Matthias ; he found that they had by mortifications reduced themselves to such weakness that they could hardly walk.   He therefore insisted to St Athanasia that she should modify the austerities of her subjects, and also arranged for the community to move from their noisy house in a town to one more quiet and suited for monastic life at Timia.   Here so many came to them that their buildings had to be enlarged, and the fame of St Athanasia caused her to be called away to the court of Constantinople as adviser to the Empress Theodora.   She had to live there for seven years, being accommodated in a cell similar to that which she occupied in her own monastery.   She had not been allowed to return to Timia long when she was taken ill ; for twelve days she tried to carry on as usual, but at last she had to send her nuns to sing their office in church without her, and when they returned their abbess was dying and survived only long enough to give them her blessing.

The evidence for this history is unsatisfactory, for though the author of the life which the Bollandists have translated from the Greek (*Acta Sanctorum*, August, vol. iii) claims to be virtually a contemporary, such pretensions are not of themselves convincing.   No great *cultus* seems to have existed, but an account of Athanasia is given in some texts of the synaxaries on April 4.   I. Martynov, *Annus Ecclesiasticus Graeco-Slavicus*, pp. 107–108, speaks of her on April 12.   One point of interest in the Greek life is the stress laid upon the commemoration on the fortieth day after burial, which amongst the Greeks corresponded to the " month's mind " in western lands.

BD EBERHARD, ABBOT   (A.D. 958)

BD EBERHARD was of the ducal family of Swabia and became provost of the cathedral of Strasburg.   In the year 934 he gave up this dignity and went to the hermitage of Einsiedeln in Switzerland, to join his friend Benno, who had been bishop of Metz.   Benno already had a few followers there and the coming of Eberhard, who enjoyed a wide reputation for spiritual wisdom and holiness, considerably increased their numbers.   He therefore devoted his fortune to building a monastery to shelter them and a church wherein they might worship, and after the death of Benno he was recognized as first abbot of the monastery of our Lady of the Hermits.   In 942 there was a great famine in Alsace, Burgundy and Upper Germany, and Bd Eberhard and his monks gave a large supply of corn for the relief of the suffering people.   The consecration of the abbey-church of Einsiedeln, which incorporated the hermits' chapel, by our Lord himself, assisted by the four Evangelists, St Peter and St Gregory the Great, is fabled to have taken place in 948, ten years before the death of Bd Eberhard ; actually it seems to have been consecrated in that year by St Conrad of Constance and St Ulric of Augsburg.   Einsiedeln is still a great place of pilgrimage.

See O. Ringholz, *Geschichte des fürstl. Benediktinerstiftes Einsiedeln* (1904), vol. i, pp. 33–43 ; R. Henggeler, *Reliquien der Stiftskirche Einsiedeln* (1927), pp. 7 *seq.*

BB. ANTONY PRIMALDI AND HIS COMPANIONS, MARTYRS   (A.D. 1480)

IN the year 1480 the Turks under Mohammed II captured and pillaged the city of Otranto in southern Italy, putting to the sword many of its inhabitants and defenders.   Some of these victims are regarded as martyrs, principal among them being Bd Antony Primaldi (or Grimaldi) and the eight hundred who suffered with him.   He was an old man, an artisan, and well known in the city as a good workman and a good Christian. When the Turks rounded up those males who had escaped the first massacre, sacking their houses and carrying off their wives, Antony and the others were led out into a valley near the town, and offered the restoration of their liberty, their wives and their goods if they would apostatize and become Moslems. Antony, as spokesman for the rest, replied that they confessed there was only one God, and that the Lord Jesus Christ was His divine Son, and that on no account would they abandon that faith. The Turkish general threatened them with fearful torments and some began to waver, seeing which Antony loudly appealed to them : " We have fought for our city and for our lives. Now we must fight for our souls and for Jesus Christ ; He died for us ; we must die for him." The waverers rallied to him, and it was ordered that all be beheaded. Bd Antony was the first to die, and it is said that his headless body remained upright on its feet, as it were to encourage the others, until all the rest were slain. The place where this massacre took place is to this day called the Valley of the Martyrs, and there their bodies lay unburied during the twelve months that the Turks occupied the country. The *cultus* of these martyrs was confirmed in 1771.

There is a long account of these martyrs in the *Acta Sanctorum*, August, vol. iii, under the heading " Martyres Hydruntini ", at the end of which the evidence of certain witnesses is printed in full. Unfortunately these depositions were not taken until 1539, fifty-nine years after the event. See also DHG., vol. iii, cc. 805–806, which gives further references.

15 : THE BLESSED VIRGIN MARY, On the Feast of her Assumption into Heaven (First Century)

MARY was a Jewish maiden of the house of David and the tribe of Judah, whose parents are commonly referred to as St Joachim and St Anne. At her conception, that is, when God infused a soul into her embryonic body, she was preserved by Him from all taint of original sin (the Immaculate Conception, December 8) ; her birth, which the Church celebrates on September 8, may have taken place at Sepphoris or Nazareth, but a general tradition favours Jerusalem, at a spot adjoining the Pool of Bethesda, close to a gate still called by Mohammedans (but not, curiously enough, by Christians), *Bab Sitti Maryam*, the Gate of the Lady Mary. She is believed to have been a child of promise to her long childless parents, and on November 21 the Church keeps a feast of her presentation in the Temple, though upon what occasion is not certain. According to apocryphal writings she remained within the Temple precincts in order to be brought up with other Jewish children, and at the age of fourteen was betrothed to a carpenter, Joseph, her husband being indicated to the high priest by a miracle. While still only betrothed she was visited by the Archangel Gabriel (the Annunciation, March 25) and the Second Person of the Blessed Trinity became incarnate by the power of the Holy Ghost in her womb. This was at Nazareth, and she journeyed into Judaea to see her cousin St Elizabeth, who also was with child, St John the Baptist (the Visitation, July 2). The marriage with St Joseph was duly ratified, and in due course, going up with him to Jerusalem for the enrolment ordered by Caesar Augustus, Mary gave birth in a rock-hewn stable at Bethlehem to Jesus Christ, the God-man (Christmas day, December 25). Forty days later, in accordance with the Jewish law, she presented herself and her Child in the Temple for her ritual purification (February 2), an observance abrogated by the law of

Christ which sees nought but honour in sanctified child-bearing. Warned by an angel, St Joseph fled with his wife and the holy Child into Egypt, to avoid the jealous rage of King Herod ; it is not known how long they lived there, but when Herod was dead they returned to their old home at Nazareth.

For the thirty years before the public ministry of Jesus began Mary lived the outward life of any other Jewish woman of the common people. There are some who, concentrating their hearts and minds on our Lady in her glorified state as queen of Heaven, or as participating in the chief mysteries of the life of her Son, lose all memory of her day by day life as a woman in this world. The sonorous and beautiful titles given to her in the litany of Loreto ; representations of her in art, from the graceful delicate ladies of Botticelli to the prosperous *bourgeoises* of Raphael ; the efforts of writers and preachers who feel that ordinary language is inadequate to describe her perfections ; these and many other influences help to glorify the Mother of God—but somewhat tend to make us forget the wife of Joseph the carpenter. The Lily of Israel, the Daughter of the princes of Judah, the Mother of all Living, was also a peasant-woman, a Jewish peasant-woman, the wife of a working-man. Her hands were scored with labour, her bare feet dusty, not with the perfumed powder of romance but with the hard stinging grit of Nazareth, of the tracks which led to the well, to the olive-gardens, to the synagogue, to the cliff whence they would have cast Him. And then, after those thirty years, those feet were still tired and dusty, but now with following her divine Son from afar in His public life, from the rejoicings of the wedding-feast at Cana to His dereliction and her desolation on Mount Calvary, when the sword spoken of by Simeon at the purification pierced her heart. The dying Jesus confided her to the care of St John, " and from that hour the disciple took her to his own ". On the day of Pentecost the Holy Ghost descended on our Lady when He came upon the Apostles and other disciples gathered together in the upper room at Jerusalem : that is the last reference to her in the Sacred Scriptures. The rest of her earthly life was probably passed at Jerusalem, with short sojourns at Ephesus and other places in company with St John and during the times of Jewish persecution.

Mary is the mother of Jesus, Jesus is God, therefore she is the Mother of God ; the denial of this was condemned by the third general council at Ephesus in 431. Both before and after her miraculous child-bearing she was a virgin and so remained all her days, according to the unanimous and perpetual tradition and teaching of the Church. That she remained for her whole life absolutely sinless is affirmed by the Council of Trent. As the " second Eve " Mary is the spiritual mother of all living, and veneration is due to her with an honour above that accorded to all other saints ; but to give divine worship to her would be idolatry, for Mary is a creature, like the rest of human-kind, and all her dignity comes from God.

It has been for ages the explicit belief of the Church that the body of the Blessed Virgin was preserved from corruption and taken into Heaven and re-united to her soul, by an unique anticipation of the general resurrection. This preservation from corruption and assumption to glory was a privilege which seems due to that body which was never defiled by sin, which was ever the most holy and pure temple of God, preserved from all contagion of Adam and the common curse of mankind : that body from which the eternal Word received His own flesh, by whose hands He was nourished and clothed on earth, and whom He vouchsafed to obey and honour as His mother. Whether or not our Lady died is not certain ; but it is generally held that she did in fact die before her glorious assumption, some conjecture at Ephesus but others think rather at Jerusalem.   But did this feast commemorate only the assumption of her soul, and not of her body as well, its object would still be the same.   For, as we honour the departure of other saints out of this world, so we have great reason to rejoice and praise God on this day when the Mother of Christ entered into the possession of those joys which He had prepared for her.

At the time that Alban Butler wrote, belief in our Lady's bodily assumption to Heaven was still, in the words of Pope Benedict XIV, a probable opinion the denial of which would be impious and blasphemous ; and so it remained for another two hundred years.   Then, in 1950, after taking counsel with the whole Church through her bishops, Pope Pius XII solemnly declared this doctrine to be divinely revealed and an article of faith.   In the bull " *Munificentissimus Deus* " he declared that :

> The remarkable unanimity of the Catholic episcopacy and faithful in the matter of the definibility of our Lady's bodily assumption into Heaven as a dogma of faith showed us that the ordinary teaching authority of the Church and the belief of the faithful which it sustains and directs were in accord, and thereby proved with infallible certainty that that privilege is a truth revealed by God and is contained in the divine deposit which Christ entrusted to His bride the Church, to be guarded faithfully and declared with infallible certainty.

And on November 1, the feast of All Saints, the pope promulgated the bull publicly in the square before St Peter's basilica at Rome, defining the doctrine in the following terms :

> Having repeatedly raised prayers of urgent supplication to God and having called upon the light of the Spirit of Truth—to the glory of Almighty God, who has bestowed His signal favours on Mary ; in honour of His Son, deathless King of all the ages and conqueror of sin and death ; to the increase of the glory of the same exalted Mother : and to the joy and exultation of the whole Church : By the authority of our Lord Jesus Christ, by that of the blessed apostles Peter and Paul, and by our own authority, We pronounce, declare and define to be divinely revealed the dogma that the immaculate Mother of God, the Ever-virgin Mary, was on the completion of her earthly life assumed body and soul into the glory of Heaven.

The assumption of the Virgin Mary is " St Mary's day " *par excellence*, the greatest of all the festivals which the Church celebrates in her honour, and it is the titular feast of all churches dedicated under her name without any special invocation.   It is the consummation of all the other great mysteries by which her life was made wonderful ; it is the birthday of her greatness and glory, and the crowning of all the virtues of her whole life, which we admire singly in her other festivals.   It is for all these gifts conferred on her that we praise and thank Him who is the author of them, but especially for that glory with which He has crowned her.   Nevertheless, whilst we contemplate the glory to which Mary is raised on this day, we ought to consider how she arrived at this honour and happiness, that we may walk in her steps.   That she should be the mother of her Creator was the most wonderful miracle and the highest dignity ; yet it was not properly this that God crowned in her.   It was her virtue that He considered : her charity, her humility, her purity, her patience, her meekness, her paying to God the most perfect homage of worship, love, praise and thanksgiving.

To discuss in brief space the introduction and development of our Lady's Assumption feast would not be easy. Three points seem clear. First that the building of churches in veneration of Mary, the *Theotokos*, Mother of God, inevitably brought in its train the celebration of some sort of dedication feast. That such churches dedicated to our Lady existed both in Ephesus and at Rome in the first half of the fifth century is certain, and some scholars think it probable that " a commemoration of the ever-virgin Mary, Mother of God " was known at Antioch as early as A.D. 370. Secondly, in such a commemoration or annual feast of the Blessed Virgin no stress was at first laid upon the manner of her departure from this world. In her case, as in the case of the martyrs and other saints, it was simply the heavenly " birthday " (*natalis*) which was originally honoured, and the festival was spoken of indifferently either as the " birthday ", or the " falling-asleep " (*dormitio*), the " passing away " (*transitus*), the " deposition ", or the " assumption". Thirdly, according to an apocryphal but ancient belief, the Blessed Virgin actually died on the anniversary of her Son's birth, *i.e.* on Christmas day. As this day was consecrated to the veneration of the Son, any distinctive commemoration of the Mother had to be postponed. In some parts of the world this separate feast was assigned to the winter season. Thus we know from St Gregory of Tours (*c.* 580) that a great feast in Mary's honour was then kept in Gaul in the middle of January. But it is equally certain that in Syria there was a summer feast on the fifth day of the month Ab, roughly August. This, with some fluctuations, was also adopted in the West, and in England St Aldhelm (*c.* 690) speaks plainly of our Lady's " birthday " being kept in the middle of August.

The only authentic written source for the life of the Blessed Virgin Mary is the New Testament. The facts recorded therein have been " written up " endlessly, and expanded by loving speculation and inference ; the resulting narratives are sometimes happy, more often less happy: no attempt can be made here to pick and choose among them. In the same way theological and devotional books about her defy enumeration. For her bodily Assumption, see the historico-doctrinal study by M. Jugie, *La mort et l'assomption de la Ste Vierge* (1944) ; for a more popular historical and explanatory work, see J. Duhr, *The Glorious Assumption* (1950). That Ephesus was the place of our Lady's death and burial was supported by Tillemont and Pope Benedict XIV ; but Eastern tradition is solid for Jerusalem. For an account of petitions and other movements for the definition of the Assumption, see the *Tablet*, August 26, 1950, and for the bull of definition the same review on November 4, 1950 (Latin text of bull in the *Clergy Review*, vol. xxxiv (1950), pp. 407–420). For the Assumption feast, see H. Thurston in *The Month*, August 1917, pp. 121–134 ; A. Baumstark in *Römische Quartalschrift*, 1897, p. 55 ; Mrs Smith Lewis in *Studia Sinaitica*, vol. xi, p. 59 ; F. Cabrol in DAC., vol. i, cc. 2995–3001 ; and CMH., pp. 444–445. Until modern times it was exceptional for churches to be dedicated in honour of the Assumption ; in the middle ages the patronage was normally simply " St Mary's ". Which of her feasts was chosen for the church's name-day depended on various factors—the Assumption had an advantage because it was not in Lent but in full summer (*cf. Analecta Bollandiana*, vol. lxv (1947), pp. 316–317). Recent books on our Lady and her *cultus* that can be particularly recommended are those of Bp M. Besson, *La Ste Vierge* (1942), Fr L. Bouyer, *Le culte de la Mère de Dieu* . . . (1950), and J. Guitton, *The Blessed Virgin* (1952). In *The Second Eve* (1952) selections from the writings of Cardinal Newman give a sober but eloquent account of the Church's teaching about Mary.

ST TARSICIUS, Martyr   (Third Century)

" At Rome, on the Appian Way, the passion of St Tarsicius the acolyte, whom the heathen met bearing the sacrament of the Body of Christ and asked him what it was that he carried. He judged it a shameful thing to cast pearls before swine, and so was attacked by them for a long time with sticks and stones, until he gave up. the ghost. When they turned over his body the sacrilegious assailants could find no trace of Christ's sacrament either in his hands or among his clothing. The Christians took up the body of the martyr and buried it with honour in the cemetery of Callistus." Thus the Roman Martyrology sums up the later form of the story of St Tarsicius, " the boy martyr of the holy Eucharist ", which is derived from the fourth-century poem of Pope St Damasus, wherein it is stated that one Tarsicius, like another St Stephen stoned by the Jews, suffered a violent death at the hands of a mob rather than give up " the divine Body* to raging dogs ".

This bare fact is certainly true, but we do not know that Tarsicius was a boy or an acolyte. It may be, especially having regard to the reference of St Damasus to the deacon St Stephen, that he was a deacon, for it was the deacon's special office to administer holy communion in certain circumstances and to carry the Blessed Sacrament from one place to another when necessary, *e.g.* that part of the conse-crated Host, called *Fermentum*, which the pope sent from his Mass to the presbyters of the principal Roman churches, symbolizing the unity of the holy Sacrifice and the union subsisting between the bishop and his flock. But then, as now, in times of dire persecution, anybody, cleric or lay, young or old, male or female, may be entrusted with the sacred Host in case of necessity, and the tradition about St Tarsicius since the sixth century is that he was a young acolyte commissioned to take communion to certain Christian prisoners, victims of the persecution of Valerian. He was buried in the cemetery of St Callistus ; his grave has never been positively identified, but his relics are claimed by San Silvestro in Capite. The great increase of devotion to the Blessed Sacrament in recent times has brought about a corresponding extension of the *cultus* of St Tarsicius.

See J. Wilpert, *Die Papstgräber und die Cäciliengruft* (1909), pp. 92–98. *Cf.* also Marucchi in *Nuovo bullettino di arch. christ.*, vol. xvi (1910), pp. 205–225 ; and DAC., vol. iv, c. 174.

ST ARNULF, or ARNOUL, Bishop of Soissons   (A.D. 1087)

This Arnoul was born about 1040 in Flanders and in his youth distinguished himself in the armies of Robert and Henry I of France. He was called to a more noble warfare, resolving to employ for God the labour which till then he had con-secrated to the service of the world. He became a monk in the great monastery of Saint-Médard at Soissons ; and after he had for some time made trial of his

---

* *Tarcisium sanctum Christi sacramenta gerentem,*
  Cum male sana manus peteret vulgare profanis ;
  Ipse animam potius voluit dimittere caesus
  Prodere quam canibus rabidis caelestia membra.

Cardinal Wiseman, who uses the story in *Fabiola*, says of " [Christi] caelestia membra " that the words, " applied to the Blessed Eucharist, supply one of those casual, but most striking, arguments that result from identity of habitual thought in antiquity, more than from the use of studied or conventional phrases ". An example, in fact, of " unity of indirect reference ".

strength in the cenobitic life, he shut himself up in a narrow cell and in the closest solitude, almost without any intercourse with men, and devoted himself to assiduous prayer and the most austere penance.   He led this manner of life until he was called to be abbot of the monastery.   It was in 1081 that a council at the request of the clergy and people of Soissons resolved to place him in that episcopal see.   To the deputies who came to inform him Arnoul said, " Leave a sinner to offer to God some fruits of penance ; and do not compel such a fool as myself to take up a charge which requires so much wisdom."   He was, however, obliged to shoulder the burden.   He set himself with great zeal to fulfil every part of his ministry ; but having been driven from his see by a usurper, he obtained leave to resign his dignity. He afterward founded a monastery at Aldenburg in Flanders, where he died in 1087.   At a council at Beauvais in 1120 the then bishop of Soissons showed a life of St Arnoul to the assembly and demanded that his body should be enshrined in the church.   " If the body of my predecessor were in my diocese ", he said, " it would have been brought in out of the churchyard long ago."   The translation was accordingly made into the abbey-church of Aldenburg in the following year.

The life by Hariulf has been printed by the Bollandists and Mabillon, but has been more critically edited in MGH., *Scriptores*, vol. xv, pt. 2, pp. 872–904.   See also E. de Moreau, *Histoire de l'Église en Belgique*, t. ii (1945), pp. 433–437.

16 : ST JOACHIM   (FIRST CENTURY B.C.)

IN the opinion of St Peter Damian it is unnecessary and blameworthy curiosity to inquire into those things that the evangelists did not tell us, and he specifies the parentage of the Blessed Virgin Mary as an example.   In this matter, those who judge differently can receive little satisfaction for their " curiosity ".   An apocryphal work, the *Protevangelium of James*, which, in spite of its name, has none of the authenticity of Holy Scripture, is with other similar apocryphal works the only source of information we have about the parents of Mary ; even their traditional names, Joachim and Anne, must ultimately be traced to them.   Of St Joachim, as of St Anne, we know absolutely nothing with certainty ; but we are at liberty to retain as pious beliefs anything in an uncanonical book that does not conflict with the teaching of the Church or with other certain truths, and it is a widely held tradition that our Lady was a child of promise as related in the so-called Gospel of James.   This has been referred to herein under St Anne, on July 26.

The feast of both parents of the all-holy Mother of God has been observed in the East, on September 9, from early times, but in the West not till much later. That of St Joachim is not heard of before the fifteenth century, and its present date was fixed only in 1913.   The Benedictines, as well as some Eastern Catholics, celebrate Joachim and Anne together, on July 26.

See the bibliographical note under St Anne on July 26.

ST ARSACIUS   (A.D. 358)

ARSACIUS was a soldier by profession, and was also employed as superintendent of the imperial menagerie.   He became a Christian and suffered for the faith under the Emperor Licinius, but was not put to death.   He then lived as a solitary in a small tower at Nicomedia where, among other marvels, he had prevision of a terrible calamity that was about to overtake the city. He went at once to the clergy and told them to offer public prayer for the averting of disaster and to urge the people to penitence, but no notice was taken and he returned to his tower to pray alone for the city. There was a terrible earthquake, in which the tower of Arsacius was one of the few buildings to escape destruction ; when people ran to it to seek safety he was found on his knees—but dead. Though St Arsacius is named in the Roman Martyrology on this day, the earthquake at Nicomedia took place on August 24, in the year 358. His story is told by the historian Sozomen, who says he got his information from people who had got it from others who knew Arsacius personally, and that many miracles were done at his intercession.

An account of St Arsacius, or Ursacius, is furnished in the *Acta Sanctorum*, August, vol. iii, based upon Sozomen, *Hist. Eccles.*, bk iv, ch. 16. It is curious that no *cultus* of Arsacius seems to be traceable in the Eastern churches. On the other hand through the *Historia Tripartita* of Cassiodorus he found his way into the Western martyrologies ; moreover copious, but very unreliable, accounts are furnished of the translation of his relics.

ST ARMEL, ABBOT (*c.* A.D. 570)

ARMEL, whose name takes various forms (Ermel, Erme, Arzel, Arkel, Arthmael, even Ermyn), is the eponymous saint of Ploërmel and of other places in Brittany. He is supposed to have been a Welshman, who spent his youth under the abbot Carentmael, and he was remarkable for piety and aptness in studies. It is related of him, as of other saints, that one day he entered a church just as the deacon was singing the words, " And whosoever doth not carry his cross and come after me cannot be my disciple " ; and he heard this as a call from God direct to himself to give up all for His sake. He therefore followed the example of so many other Britons of his age and went into Armorica, together with his master and other companions. They landed in Finistère, but while living an evangelical life together at Plouarzel they were disturbed by the activities of the usurper Conmor, who had killed Jonas, the chieftain of those parts. They therefore went to Paris to seek the protection of King Childebert. After the son of Jonas had, with the help of St Samson, defeated and slain Conmor in 555, St Armel was granted some land near Rennes whereon to establish his community anew (Saint-Armel-des-Bochaux). He founded another monastery at Ploërmel in Morbihan and there died in peace. His feast was noted in the Sarum calendar of 1498.

See LBS., vol. i, pp. 170 *seq.*, and F. Duine, *Saints de Brocéliande : S. Armel* (1905).

BD LAURENCE LORICATUS (A.D. 1243)

THIS Laurence was born at Fanello, near Siponto in Apulia, and while still a young man had the misfortune accidentally to kill another. In expiation he made a pilgrimage of penance to Compostela, and on his return in 1209 went to Subiaco, where he joined a community but was soon given permission to be a solitary. He lived in a mountain cave near by the *Sacro Speco* of St Benedict for thirty-three years, and practised terrific mortifications of the body : the name *Loricatus*, " the cuirassier ", was given to him because of the coat of mail studded with sharp points which he wore next his skin. His *cultus* was approved in 1778.

An account of him is given in the *Acta Sanctorum*, August, vol. iii, which possesses interest from the fact that it embodies documents compiled in 1244 during an investigation undertaken at the instance of Pope Innocent IV.

ST ROCK   (*c*. A.D. 1378)

WE find this servant of God venerated in France and Italy during the early fifteenth century, not very long after his death, but we have no authentic history of his life. No doubt he was born at Montpellier and nursed the sick during a plague in Italy, but that is almost all that can be affirmed about him.   His " lives " are chiefly made up of popular legends, which may have a basis in fact but cannot now be checked. According to the one written by a Venetian, Francis Diedo, in 1478, Rock was son of the governor of Montpellier, and upon being left an orphan at the age of twenty he went on a pilgrimage to Rome.   Finding Italy plague-stricken he visited numerous centres of population, Acquapendente, Cesena, Rome, Rimini, Novara, where he not only devoted himself to care of the sick but cured large numbers simply by making the sign of the cross on them.   At Piacenza he was infected himself, and not wishing to be a burden on any hospital he dragged himself out into the woods to die.   Here he was miraculously fed by a dog, whose master soon found Rock and looked after him ;   when he was convalescent he returned to Piacenza and miraculously cured many more folk, as well as their sick cattle.   At length he got back to Montpellier, where his surviving uncle failed to recognize him ; he was there imprisoned, and so he remained five years, till he died.   When they came to examine his body it was recognized who he really was, the son of their former governor, by a cross-shaped birth-mark on his breast.   He was therefore given a public funeral, and he performed as many miracles when dead as he had done when alive.   Another biography, shorter, simpler and perhaps older, says that St Rock was arrested as a spy and died in captivity at Angera in Lombardy.

The popularity and rapid extension of the *cultus* of St Rock, a veneration by no means extinct today, was remarkable, and he soon became the saint *par excellence* to be invoked against pestilence.   St Rock is named in the Roman Martyrology, and his feast is kept in many places ;   there is no evidence that he was a Franciscan tertiary, but the Franciscans venerate him as such.

See the *Acta Sanctorum*, August, vol. iii, and " Le problème de S. Roch ", by A. Fliche, in *Analecta Bollandiana*, vol. lxviii (1950), pp. 343–361.   The saint is very popular, as anyone may learn who consults the long list of books and articles noted in the *Bio-bibliographie* of Chevalier.   A good modern work of general interest is that of G. Ceroni, *San Rocco nella vita . . .* (1927) ;   see also M. Bessodes, *San Rocco, storia e leggende* (1931) ;   and A. Maurino, *San Rocco, confronti storici* (1936) (*cf. Analecta Bollandiana*, vol. lv (1937). p. 193).   It is curious that St Rock seems even to have left traces of *cultus* in England. The present St Roche's Hill in Sussex was St Rokeshill in 1579 ;   and it is said that the Glasgow parliamentary division of Saint Rollox had its name from him.   A short popular account of the saint may be found in Léon, *Auréole Séraphique* (Eng. trans.), vol. iii, pp. 11–21.

17 : ST HYACINTH   (A.D. 1257)

ST HYACINTH (in Polish, Jacek, a form of John) was a Silesian, born in 1185, in the district called Oppeln, between Breslau and Cracow.   He is venerated as an apostle of Poland, and was undoubtedly a great missionary ; but the particulars of the achievements commonly attributed to him unfortunately depend on biographies that are of very little historical value.

He became a Dominican, perhaps in Rome, in 1217 or 1218, and came with other Dominicans to Cracow, where they were given the church of the Holy Trinity by the bishop, Ivo Odrowaz. Hyacinth is recorded as being at this priory again in 1228, and ten years later was preaching a crusade against the heathen Prussians. The field of his labours was doubtless extensive ; but his biographers take him north-east into Lithuania, east to Kiev, south-east to the Black Sea, south to the Danube and north-west to Scandinavia, leaving Silesia, Pomerania and Bohemia to his fellow Dominican, Bd Ceslaus, who was said to be also his brother in the flesh. The miracles with which Hyacinth was credited are no less sensational, some of them being apparently suggested by what had been related of other holy ones in Poland and in his order. During his time the Friars Preachers did penetrate down the Vistula to Danzig and towards Russia and the Balkans, and a number of priories were founded ; but much damage was done to their missions after the Mongols crossed the Volga in 1238, in the repairing of which no doubt St Hyacinth was active.

He died on the feast of the Assumption 1257, after exhorting his brethren to esteem poverty as men that had renounced all earthly things, " For this is the testament, the sealed deed, by which we claim eternal life ". He was canonized in 1594.

What commonly passes current as the life of St Hyacinth partakes more of the nature of a saga than of a sober historical record. This is pointed out both by Knöpfler in the *Kirchenlexikon* and by the modern Bollandists (*e.g.*, in *Analecta Bollandiana*, vol. xlv, 1927, pp. 202–203). The earliest and practically the only source of information down to quite recent times was the account of St Hyacinth's life and miracles, written by Fr Stanislaus of Cracow a hundred years after the saint's death. It is printed in the *Monumenta Poloniae Historica*, vol. iv, pp. 841–894. Later biographers only embroidered this account with further extravagances, and consequently even such lives as that by the Comtesse de Flavigny, *S. Hyacinthe et ses compagnous* (1899), must be read with great caution. The most valuable contribution which has so far been made to the perplexed history of St Hyacinth is that of B. Altaner, *Die Dominikanermissionen des 13 Jahrhunderts* (1924), pp. 196–214. For the traditional account see Mortier, *Histoire des maîtres généraux O.P.*, vol. i, pp. 215–218 and 377–388 ; Procter, *Lives of Dominican Saints*, pp. 229–232 ; and for a fuller bibliography Taurisano, p. 16.

ST MAMAS, MARTYR   (*c.* A.D. 275)

ST BASIL and St Gregory Nazianzen inform us that St Mamas was a shepherd at Caesarea in Cappadocia who, seeking from his childhood the kingdom of God with his whole heart, distinguished himself by his fervour in the divine service. Being apprehended by the persecutors, he suffered cruel torments with joy and attained the crown of martyrdom. According to Eastern tradition he suffered under Aurelian by stoning, while yet a boy ; but the Roman Martyrology says that he underwent " a prolonged persecution from youth to old age ". We can be sure of little but his existence, occupation and the place of his martyrdom.

Among the fables associated with the name of this authentic martyr is an approximation to Orpheus. Mamas went out from among the " wolves " of the city and lived peacefully among the animals of the countryside, feeding on milk and honey. When the persecutors exposed him to wild beasts the animals treated him like sheep their shepherd, " lying down at his feet, and showing their affection by fawning on him with their tails ". Later he was befriended by a " huge lion ", who licked his limbs, weary with bearing chains. Soldiers sent to fetch Mamas were picked up by this lion and deposited at his feet : when told by him to go away to his lair, the lion " wept and sobbed "—and obeyed.

The vogue enjoyed by St Mamas as an object of popular devotion was undoubtedly very great. One has to read the panegyric of St Basil and the allusions of St Gregory Nazianzen to appreciate the depth of feeling involved. See Delehaye, *Origines du culte des martyrs*, p. 174, and *Passions des Martyrs et les genres littéraires*, pp. 198–200 ; and *Analecta Bollandiana*, vol. lviii (1940), pp. 126–141, where an extravagant romance in the guise of a *passio* is printed. *Cf.* too, in the same periodical, vol. lxx (1952), pp. 249-261, the legend of St Zosimus of Anazarbus.

ST EUSEBIUS, POPE   (A.D. 310)

EUSEBIUS was a Greek by birth, the son of a physician, and was elected in succession to Pope St Marcellus, whom he survived by only a few months.   During the episcopate of his predecessor serious trouble had been caused in the Roman church by the question of the treatment which was to be accorded to those who had lapsed from the faith during the persecution of Diocletian.   A party led by a certain Heraclius opposed itself to the pope ; probably Heraclius represented a number of *lapsi* who wanted immediate restoration to communion without further penance. It is recorded in an inscription put by Pope St Damasus over the tomb of St Eusebius in the cemetery of Callistus that this dispute was prolonged into his pontificate and caused disorder and bitter strife in the Church at Rome : probably the repentant *lapsi* tried to force their way into the assemblies of the faithful.   So great was the uproar that the Emperor Maxentius banished both Pope Eusebius and Heraclius from the city.   The pope went to Sicily where he died almost at once, and this exile following on his determined upholding of the canons caused him for a time to be venerated as a martyr, a title which St Damasus accords him.

See the *Acta Sanctorum*, September, vol. vii ; the *Liber Pontificalis* (ed. Duchesne), vol. i, p. 167 ; and J. Carini, *I lapsi e la deportazione in Sicilia del Papa S. Eusebio* (1886).

SS. LIBERATUS AND HIS COMPANIONS, MARTYRS   (A.D. 484)

HUNERIC, the Arian Vandal king in Africa, in the seventh year of his reign published fresh edicts against the Catholics and ordered their monasteries to be everywhere demolished.   Seven monks who lived near Capsa, in the province of Byzacene, were summoned to Carthage.   Their names were Liberatus the abbot, Boniface deacon, Servus and Rusticus subdeacons, Rogatus, Septimus and Maximus, monks. They were first tempted with promises to conform to Arianism, but they answered with one accord, " We confess one Lord, one faith and one baptism.   As to our bodies, do with them what you please, and keep those riches which you promise us, which will surely perish."   They were put in irons and thrown into a dungeon. The faithful having bribed the guards, visited them day and night.   The king being informed of this, he commanded them to be more closely confined, and after a time condemned them to be burnt.   Particular endeavours were used by the persecutors to gain Maximus, who was very young, indeed, a boy, who was being educated by the monks.   But God, who makes the tongues of children to praise His name, gave him strength to withstand all their efforts, and he boldly told them that they would never be able to separate him from his abbot and brethren.   An old vessel was filled with sticks, the seven martyrs were put on board, and it was set adrift ; fire was put to it several times, but it would not kindle, and all their attempts to get the ship burning failed. Huneric therefore ordered that they should be brought back to land, and there the martyrs' brains were brutally dashed out with oars.

All our information comes from a *passio* formerly, but as it would seem wrongly, ascribed to Victor of Vita. The *passio* with comments is printed in the *Acta Sanctorum*, August, vol. iii.

ST CLARE OF MONTEFALCO, Virgin   (A.D. 1308)

THERE has been much discussion between the Franciscans and the Augustinians as to whether this holy nun belonged to one order or the other ; the solution of the difficulty which appears to satisfy both parties is that the community of pious young women, living penitentially in hermitages under the direction of her sister Joan, to which Clare belonged for fifteen years, consisted of secular tertiaries of St Francis : but that when they wished to adopt a regular conventual life the bishop of Spoleto gave them the Augustinian rule. Their convent, of the Holy Cross, was erected in 1290 and, her sister dying, St Clare much against her will was elected abbess. Her life was already notable for its austerities and they were now increased: for a breach of silence she stood barefoot in snow while she said the Lord's Prayer a hundred times. Her words and example kept alive in her community a great desire of perfection, and the union of her heart with God gave them a model of recollection. A number of miracles were attributed to her, frequent ecstasies, and supernatural gifts, which she utilized for the good of those outside her convent as well as those within. St Clare had a very great devotion to the passion of our Lord. She once said to a sister, " If you seek the cross of Christ, take my heart ; there you will find the suffering Lord ". These words were taken literally, and when her heart was examined after death in 1308 an image of the cross was said to have been found imprinted on it.

Apart from her faithful observance and the austerity of her penance, St Clare is alleged to have been honoured by three divine favours of exceptional interest. First, the marvellous incorruption of her remains. See on this John Addington Symonds in the *Cornhill Magazine*, October 1881, p. 446, who describes what he himself had seen at Montefalco : " Only her hands and the exquisitely beautiful pale outline of her face (forehead, nose, mouth and chin, modelled in purest outline, as though the injury of death had never touched her) were visible. Her closed eyes seemed to sleep." Secondly, the cross and other instruments of the Passion formed solidly within her heart in some fibrous tissue, just referred to. The evidence for this strange phenomenon is certainly not contemptible. Thirdly, the alleged liquefaction and ebullition of her blood. St Clare of Montefalco was canonized in 1881.

The Bollandists, having been refused access to the original sources preserved at Montefalco, had to be content with reprinting (*Acta Sanctorum*, August, vol. iii) the life of St Clare by Masconio (1601), which is of no great value. But in presenting the case for the canonization of the saint, the more reliable documents came in the last century to be better known and are now generally accessible in print. The most important is the life, said to have been compiled in 1309 by Berengarius, vicar general of Spoleto. It may be read in Faloci Pulignani, *Vita di santa Chiara da Montefalco* (1885). As to modern literature, see L. Tardi, *Vita della b. Chiara da Montefalco* (Eng. trans., 1884) ; T. de Töth, *Vita* (1908) ; A. N. Merlin, *Ste Claire de la Croix* (1930) ; Faloci Pulignani, *Miscellanea Francescana*, vol. xiv (1913), pp. 129–152. There is a biography in English by E. A. Foran, *St Clare of the Cross* (1935). For the blood phenomenon, consult Ian Grant, *The Testimony of Blood* (1929), pp. 79–122 ; and see *Douleur et stigmatisation* in the series " Études carmélitaines " (1936), pp. 36–41.

BD JOAN DELANOUE, Virgin, Foundress of the Sisters of St Anne of The Providence of Saumur   (A.D. 1736)

CHRISTIAN history is full of penitents, of people who by co-operating with the grace given by God are enabled to turn their backs on a life of sin and shame, and not seldom to climb to the very heights of godliness.   The earlier lives of many penitents have a sort of paradoxical impressiveness in the very enormity of their wickedness, the depth of their depravity ; but Bd Joan Delanoue was one who freed herself, not from the thrall of some " picturesque " iniquity, but from the morass of petty worldliness and selfishness, from the graspingness and avarice of *petit-bourgeois* materialism.   Her father was a draper at Saumur in Anjou, who also dealt in crockery, bloaters and those goods purveyed in what in England are curiously called " Catholic repositories "—these last particularly for the benefit of pilgrims to the near-by shrine of our Lady " des Ardilliers ".   The Delanoues did a brisk trade ; but they were not well off for they had twelve children to support, of whom Joan, the youngest, was born in 1666.

Twenty-five years later her long-widowed mother died, and Joan's share of the estate was the house and shop, with a stock that was small and a capital even smaller.   She at once took into partnership her seventeen-year-old niece, also called Joan Delanoue, who resembled her aunt in more than name.   For one thing, both of them were interested in making money, and the neighbours soon began to see a difference.   Old Mother Delanoue had been a generous soul, kind to beggars ; now they were told, " I have nothing to give you ".   Now too the shop was open on Sundays and feast-days ; a scandalous thing that, for not only was it a contempt of the Third Commandment but it was taking an unfair advantage of the other shopkeepers.   Space was found to accommodate pilgrims, for payment, at the back of the house, in the holes of the cliff whence its building-stone had been quarried. In a word, Joan Delanoue became immersed in money-grubbing, and without seeing that it was involving her in all sorts of little sins and dishonest subterfuges.   As a young girl she had been devout and almost over-scrupulous in her behaviour ; but the religious atmosphere about her was arid and formalized : the love of God too often took the form only of set devotional observances, the doing of His will was a matter simply of rules and regulations.   And now she was grown-up and in a responsible position the uselessness of the letter without the spirit was only too apparent : every one of her neighbours knew that Joan Delanoue sent her niece to buy food only just as they were about to sit down to a meal—so that she could with a clear conscience tell beggars that there was no food in the house.

It was on the eve of the Epiphany in 1693 that a strange old woman first appeared in Saumur, who for several years was to play a curious and rather undefined part in the life of Joan Delanoue.   Frances Souchet was a widow, from Rennes, who spent her time going from shrine to shrine ; opinions differed as to whether she was mentally disordered, a genuine visionary, or " just a bit simple ", for she would relate what she claimed to be heavenly communications in terms that were always oracular and often unintelligible, prefacing them with the statement, " *He* (*scil.*, God) told me . . .".   In a moment of kindness Joan gave this old woman lodgings in the house almost for nothing ; but the only thing at all noticeable that Mrs Souchet said on this occasion was, " God sent me this first time to learn the way ".   However, for the duration of her visit Joan seems to have been specially unhappy and upset, and during the following Lent wandered from church to church, listening disconsolately to the various preachers in hope of help and consolation. Eventually she opened her heart to the Abbé Geneteau, chaplain to the municipal hospital and a man of spiritual perception. The first fruit of his advice was that she ceased to open her shop on Sundays ; within a few weeks reality and fervour had begun to return to her religion, and she undertook voluntarily to fast three days a week : but the spirit of avarice was still stubborn within her.

At Whitsun Mrs Souchet was back again, and after Mass she began to talk to Joan. " *He* says this. . . ." " *He* says that. . . ." What He said or what He meant seemed more and more incomprehensible, but Joan listened attentively ; and it began to dawn on her, not only that God was using this shabby old woman to tell her something, but also what that something was : and it was in effect, " I was hungry, and you did not give me food, thirsty, and you did not give me drink ; I was a stranger, and you brought me not home, naked, and you clothed me not, sick, and you did not care for me. . . ." And then Joan Delanoue saw in a flash that her vocation was not " business " after all but the service of the poor, that she was not to take but give—and to give without distinction. She went to her wardrobe and took out her best dress. " This ", she said, " is for Mrs So-and-so. I know she doesn't need it. But our Lord says I've got to give it to her."

This remarkable conversion was as it were confirmed a fortnight later, when Joan was found by her niece standing motionless and senseless in the shop, hearing, seeing and feeling nothing of what went on around her. That ecstasy, of whatever nature it may have been, lasted three whole days and nights ; and during it Joan saw in figurative form that she was to give herself to the service of the most abandoned, that others would join her in a most difficult and trying work, that the Abbé Geneteau would be her adviser, and the Mother of God her heavenly guide. All of which was in due course fulfilled.

But whereabouts were these poor creatures who were so urgently needing her attention ? Frances Souchet supplied the answer. " *He* told me that you are to go to Saint-Florent and look after six poor children in a stable there." So she went, and there sure enough in a dirty stable found six miserable little wretches and their parents, all ill, all cold, all famished. She filled a cart with food, blankets and clothing, and worked for this family two or three days a week for the next two months. That was the beginning. Other cases of need were soon brought to her notice ; and in 1698 Joan Delanoue shut up her shop—her business was giving, not taking.

Within three years she was looking after a dozen orphans in her small house with its cavernous annexe. People called it Providence House, and wondered where the money came from. Mrs Souchet knew the answer : " The king of France won't give you his purse ; but the King of kings will always keep His open for you." Critics shook their heads, and their incredulity seemed justified when, early one morning in the autumn of 1702, the cliff at the back gave way, burying and destroying the house, and killing one of the children. " So much for Miss Delanoue and her Providence ! " Even the more sympathetic spoke more in the tones of Job's comforters than of Jesus. At first she found shelter for her flock in the stables of the house occupied by the Oratorian fathers ; but the stream of beggars and rapscallions that followed her was too much for their peace and quiet-ness, and after three months the procurator gave Joan notice to quit. For the next three years and more they were crowded into a house of three rooms and a kitchen, with another cave annexe.

During this time Joan and her niece were joined by two other young women, Joan Bruneau and Anne Mary Tenneguin, and eventually she opened her heart to them : our Lord, she said, had revealed to her that she would found a congregation of religious women, who would wear a certain dress and devote themselves to the poor and sick.   She had a simple eloquence, more effective, said the Abbé Cever, than the periods of the most moving preacher, and the three agreed to follow her. The Abbé Geneteau had already been consulted, and on July 26, 1704 they were clothed with the religious habit.   It was the feast of St Anne, and thence they took the name, Sisters of St Anne.

For want of room Sister Joan had continually to refuse orphans and old people who needed a home and care, and for years she had dreamed of her little Providence House becoming Great Providence House, that the mockers should be proved to have spoken more wisely than they knew, " like Balaam's she-ass ", as Mgr Trochu observes.   In 1706 then she took her courage in both hands and asked the Oratorians to lease her their big Fountain House.   They agreed to do so ; and in consideration of the fact that the new tenants were likely to be less quiet and clean than their predecessors, the procurator raised the rent by 150 per cent.   In that same year Saumur was visited by St Louis Grignion de Montfort, who was to be canonized in the same year, 1947, that Joan Delanoue was beatified.   Sister Joan decided to consult him about her life and vocation.   At first he repulsed her, declaring that pride was making her overdo her mortifications : but his final verdict, given before all the sisters, was, " Go on in the way you have begun.   God's spirit is with you ; it is He who is leading you in this penitential way.   Follow His voice, and fear no more."

The next ten years was a period of trials and consolations, of ups and downs. The bishop of Angers, Mgr Poncet de la Rivière, gave his canonical approbation to the rule of the growing community, and the first vows were made, Sister Joan taking the name of Joan-of-the-Cross.   On the other hand, there were difficulties with their Oratorian landlords, who wanted to take over the direction of the sisters and their works.   Jansenism was at work among these priests, and they looked with strong disapproval on such things as Sister Joan's daily communion, which had been allowed her by the Abbé Geneteau long since.   It is an unresolved problem where the money came from to support the institution at this time.   In the famine year of 1709 there were more than a hundred persons in the Providence ; two years later scurvy threatened to wipe out sisters and charges.   Then, when things were looking at their worst, a benefactor appeared, Henry de Vallière, governor of Annecy in Savoy, who did much to put the community on a firm footing.   He bought new and larger premises, Three Angels House, to which three other benefactors added adjoining buildings and paid for repairs and enlargements.   By the time it was finished a guide was needed to find one's way about in it—there was now room to shelter the aged as well as orphans, the sick as well as the aged.   By 1717 Providence House had become Great Providence House.

Before taking possession of The Three Angels, Sister Joan made a ten-day retreat, which was marked by striking spiritual experiences.   About this time the Abbé Geneteau retired, and was succeeded by the Abbé de Tigné, who directed her and her work no less wisely, sympathetically and generously.   He too had somewhat to restrain her mortifications, which Pope Pius XI two hundred years later qualified as " unbelievable " ; practically from the time of her conversion she did not sleep in a bed but sitting in a chair, or curled up on a chest with a stone for pillow.   Even in her lifetime miracles of healing were attributed to her, while she herself suffered atrociously from tooth and ear ache, as well as from pain in hands and feet that seems to have had a less physical origin.

From 1721 the Sisters of St Anne began to make foundations elsewhere, in half a dozen and more places in France, but Bd Joan never felt she had done enough. At last, in September, 1735, her health gave way in a violent fever, which was followed by four months of great spiritual suffering.   Then tranquillity of soul returned, but not strength of body ; and she died very peacefully on August 17, 1736.   She was seventy years old.   " That little shopkeeper did more for the poor of Saumur than all the town councillors put together.   The king told them to build an almshouse for a hundred old people and pay for it out of the rates.   It wasn't done.   Joan Delanoue built one for three hundred with money that she begged. What a woman !   And what a saint ! "   So spoke the citizens of Saumur.   And that holiness was proclaimed throughout the Church when Joan Delanoue was beatified in 1947.

The principal source for the personal life of Bd Joan Delanoue is the memories of Sister Mary Laigle, who was a member of the Saumur Providence from the early years of the eighteenth century.   Her first biographer was the Abbé Cever, in his *Discours*, but the standard life is that of Mgr F. Trochu (1938).   Of this a summary version was issued at the time of the beatification in 1947.   The Sisters of St Anne of the Providence of Saumur must be distinguished from the congregation of the same name but of Turin.

18 : ST AGAPITUS, Martyr   (Date Unknown)

AGAPITUS is said to have been a Christian boy, only fifteen years old, who was brought before the governor Antiochus at Praeneste (Palestrina), and upon refusing to abjure his faith was scourged, imprisoned and beheaded, under the Emperor Aurelian.   In his *acta* embroideries have been added in the usual way : after being beaten he was confined in a foul cell without food or drink for four days ; burning coals were poured over his head and he was hung up by his feet over a smoking fire ; boiling water was poured upon him, and the bones of his jaw broken.   The disappointed Antiochus had a seizure and died before his victim. Agapitus was beheaded only because the beasts in the arena refused to touch him : a sight that so impressed the tribune Anastasius that he was converted on the spot. Actually nothing at all is known of this St Agapitus except that he was a martyr who was buried at Palestrina, for his *acta* are spurious.

The early *cultus* of St Agapitus is well attested, not only by the mention of him under this day in the sacramentaries, but by traces of the ruins of his basilica a mile out of Palestrina and of an epitaph bearing his name.   We may note also the dedication to him of several other churches in the eighth and ninth centuries.   See CMH., pp. 448–449 ; add also A. Kellner, " Der hl. Agapitus von Praeneste ", in *Studien und Mitteilungen* (1930), pp. 404–432 ; and a number of notices by O. Marucchi duly indicated in the Bollandist volume just quoted.

SS. FLORUS and LAURUS, Martyrs   (Date Unknown)

ACCORDING to a Greek tale Florus and Laurus were brothers, stone-masons, who were employed upon the building of a pagan temple in Illyria.   After it was finished those responsible for putting up the temple were converted to Christianity, and their two masons with them, whereupon they broke down the images of the heathen gods and delivered the building over to Christian worship ; they were seized by the governor and all four buried alive in a dry cistern or drowned in a deep well. The story is chiefly interesting because an ingenious attempt has been made to show that we have here a survival of the worship of the Dioscuri, that SS. Florus and Laurus are Castor and Pollux disguised as Christians and that from the earliest times there was a monthly festival in honour of the twins. The theory is based on the coincidence on the 18th and 19th of most months from April to December of the commemorations of martyred brothers with consonant names (*e.g.* Mark and Marcellinus, Gervase and Protase) and of martyrs whose names resemble or are associated with Castor and Pollux (*e.g.* Dioscorus, Polyeuctes, Castor). Florus and Laurus are particularly important to the argument because on their day occurs the feast of St Helen, and Helen was the name of the sister of Castor and Pollux. There is nothing in this speculation, as Father Delehaye has no difficulty in showing. He points out that some of the dates of these martyrs as given by the theorists do not agree with the dates in the martyrologies ; that the 18th of the month in the Julian calendar does not correspond with the 18th in Greek, Syrian or Asiatic calendars ; and that St Helen occurs on August 18 in the Roman Martyrology quite fortuitously. For the day of her celebration traditional in the East is May 21 and was formerly February 8 in many churches of the West ; the concurrence of the three saints on August 18 in the Roman Martyrology is no older than the sixteenth century, before which SS. Florus and Laurus did not appear in it at all.

These are obscure saints whose very existence is doubtful. See, regarding Castor and Pollux, Delehaye, *The Legends of the Saints* (Eng. trans.), pp. 182–184, and sundry other references in the *Analecta Bollandiana*, e.g. vol. xxiii, pp. 427–432. *Cf.* also H. Thurston in *The Month*, August 1906, pp. 202–207, where it is pointed out that there is no real assonance between Florus and Laurus, as Rendel Harris pretends, except for an Englishman who adheres to his native pronunciation of Latin ; and secondly that a much stronger case than any Dr Harris presents could be made out to prove that SS. Cedd and Chad were Dioscuri ; yet nobody dreams of disputing the account which Bede gives of these two bishops of his own time.

ST HELEN, WIDOW   (*c.* A.D. 330)

ST HELEN was born, so far as can be ascertained, at Drepanum in Bithynia, perhaps the daughter of an inn-keeper. Somewhere about 270 the Roman general Constantius Chlorus met her there and, in spite of her humble birth, married her ; but when he was made *caesar*, he was persuaded to divorce her and marry Theodora, the stepdaughter of the Emperor Maximian. Some years earlier Helen had given birth at Naissus (Nish in Serbia) to Constantine the Great, who had a deep regard and affection for his mother, and afterwards conferred on her the title of " Nobilissima Femina ", changing the name of her birth-place to Helenopolis. " We are assured ", says Alban Butler, " by the unanimous tradition of our English historians that this holy empress was a native of our island." This is so ; but the oft-repeated statement of medieval chroniclers that Constantius married Helen, " daughter of Coel of Caercolvin " (Colchester), is without historical foundation. Supported by misunderstood passages in certain panegyrics of Constantine, the legend arose probably from confusion with another Constantine and Helen, namely the British Helen who married Magnus Clemens Maximus, who was emperor in Britain, Gaul and Spain from 383 to 388 (the Maxen Wledig of Welsh romance) ; they had several sons, one of whom was called Constantine (Custennin). This lady received the epithet *Luyddog* (" of the hosts "), later transferred to the other Helen, and already in the tenth century there is a statement that Constantine was the " son of Constrantius [*sic*] and Helen Luicdauc, who went out of Britain to seek the Cross so far as Jerusalem, and brought it thence to Constantinople ". It has been suggested that the churches dedicated in honour of St Helen in Wales, Cornwall and Devon refer to Helen Luyddog, as the name of the ancient Welsh road, Sarn Elen, perhaps does. There is in another part of the dominions of Maximus another and equally erroneous tradition of St Helen : namely, that she was born at Trier.

Constantius Chlorus lived for fourteen years after the repudiation of St Helen, and when he died in 306 their son Constantine was proclaimed *caesar* by his troops at York, and eighteen months later emperor. He entered Rome after the battle of the Milvian Bridge on October 28, 312, and by the Edict of Milan early in the following year Christianity was tolerated throughout the empire. It appears from Eusebius that St Helen was converted only at this time, when she was about sixty-three years old (Constantine himself was a catechumen until his death-bed) : " She became such a devout servant of God under [her son's] influence that one might believe her to have been a disciple of the Saviour of mankind from her very childhood." Though she was so advanced in years before she knew Christ, her fervour and zeal were such as to make her retrieve the time lost in ignorance ; and God prolonged her life many years to edify by her example the Church which her son laboured to exalt by his authority. Rufinus calls her faith and zeal incomparable, and she kindled the same fire in the hearts of the Romans ; she assisted in the churches amidst the people in modest and plain attire, and to attend at the divine offices was her greatest delight. She made use of the treasures of the empire in liberal alms, and was the mother of the indigent and distressed. She built numerous churches, and when after his victory over Licinius in 324 Constantine became master of the East, the noble lady went to Palestine to venerate the places made sacred by the bodily presence of our Lord.

After Golgotha and the holy sepulchre had been laid bare by the removal of the terrace and temple of Venus with which the Emperor Hadrian had over-built them, Constantine wrote to St Macarius, Bishop of Jerusalem, ordering a church to be built, " worthy of the most marvellous place in the world ". St Helen, then fourscore years of age, took the charge on herself to see this work executed, desiring at the same time to discover the sacred cross on which our Redeemer died. Eusebius mentions no other motive for her journey but to give thanks to God for His mercies to her family, and to pray for His continued protection ; but other writers attribute it to visions and to admonitions in her sleep, and St Paulinus of Nola says that one of its definite objects was to find the holy places. Constantine in his letter to Macarius commissions him to make search for the cross on Mount Calvary. The finding of three crosses in a rock-cistern just to the east of Calvary, and the difficulty in deciding which was the cross of Christ, has been related herein under May 3, on which date the Western church celebrates this discovery, and under St Macarius (March 10). On May 3, too, reference is made to the absence of early information about the finding of the cross and of evidence that directly connects its discovery with the name of St Helen. The first known ascription of it to her is in a sermon of St Ambrose, preached in 395, who remarks that St Helen, when she had discovered the holy cross, " worshipped not the wood, but the King, Him who hung on the wood. She burned with an earnest desire of touching the guarantee of immortality." Several other writers about the same time mention her as playing a principal part in the recovery of the cross, but it is noteworthy that St Jerome, who lived near by at Bethlehem, was not among them.

Whether or not she actually took an active part in the finding of the cross, it is beyond dispute that Helen's last days were spent in Palestine and, says Eusebius, " In the sight of all she continually resorted to church, appearing humbly dressed among the praying women ; and she adorned the sacred buildings with rich ornaments and decorations, not passing by the chapels of the meanest towns." He reports that she built two basilicas, the *Eleona* on the Mount of Olives and one at Bethlehem.   She was kind and charitable to all, but especially to religious persons ; to these she showed such respect as to serve them at table and hold them water to wash their hands ; " though empress of the world and mistress of the empire she looked upon herself as servant of the handmaids of Christ ".   Whilst she travelled over the East she heaped all kinds of favours both on cities and persons, particularly on soldiers, the poor, and those who were condemned to the mines, freeing many from oppression, chains and banishment.   The latest coins which, by order of her son, bore her name, Flavia Julia Helena, were minted in 330, which presumably was the year of her death.   This took place apparently somewhere in the East, and her body was taken to Rome.   St Helen is named in the Roman Martyrology on August 18, on which day her feast is kept in the dioceses of Liverpool, Salford and Brentwood ; it is observed universally in the East, but on May 21, with that rather equivocal person, her son Constantine : the Byzantines refer to them as " the holy, illustrious and great emperors, crowned by God and equal with the Apostles ".

The principal source is the life of Constantine by Eusebius, the relevant passages of which are quoted in the *Acta Sanctorum*, August, vol. iii.   See also M. Guidi, *Un Bios di Costantino* (1908) ; and DAC., vol. vi, cc. 2126–2145.   Among more popular accounts of St Helen may be mentioned R. Couzard, *Ste Hélène d'après l'histoire et la tradition* (1911), and A. M. Rouillon, *Sainte Hélène* (1908) in the series " Les Saints ".   In both these books too much stress seems to be laid upon the very questionable translation of the relics of the saint to the monastery of Hautvillers in France.   St Helen, as Delehaye shows (CMH., p. 450), after Duchesne, was buried, not in Constantinople, but in Rome on the Via Lavicana. In the series " L'Art et les Saints " an interesting little brochure has been written concerning St Helen by J. Maurice (1929).   Evelyn Waugh's novel *Helena* (1950) must be read in the light of the author's preface.   *Cf.* also Fr Thurston in *The Month*, May 1892, pp. 88–100.

ST ALIPIUS, BISHOP OF TAGASTE   (c. A.D. 430)

ST ALIPIUS was born about the year 360 at Tagaste in Africa, of which town St Augustine, only a few years older than himself, was also a native.   He studied grammar at Tagaste and rhetoric at Carthage, both under St Augustine, till a disagreement happened between his master and his father.   Alipius still retained a great affection and respect for Augustine, and was reciprocally much beloved by him.   At Carthage Alipius was engrossed by the circus, to which the inhabitants of that city were extravagantly addicted.   Augustine was afflicted that so hopeful a young man should be lost in what was an exceedingly dangerous interest, but he had no opportunity to warn him, as Alipius by that time was not allowed by his father to be any longer one of his scholars.   Alipius happened, however, one day to go into his school, and hear some part of the lecture, as he did sometimes by stealth.   Augustine, in expounding the subject which he had in hand, borrowed a similitude from the shows of the circus, with a smart rebuke for those who were involved in their excesses.   This he did without any thought of Alipius.   But he imagined it had been spoken purely for him and, being a well-disposed youth, was angry with himself for his weakness, and determined to overcome it.

Alipius, pursuing a career in the world according to the wishes of his parents, went to Rome to study the law. He had already moved some distance on the road towards conversion to Christianity, but soon had a serious set-back. Some of his friends meeting him one day led him to some barbarous sports. He resisted all the way, and said to them, " If you haul my body thither, can you force me to turn my mind or my eyes upon these shows ? I shall be absent therefrom, though present in body." Yet they did not desist, but carried him with them. When they had taken their seats Alipius shut his eyes, that his soul might not take any delight in such scenes ; and would to God, says St Augustine, he had shut his ears too. For hearing a great shout, he was overcome by curiosity and opened his eyes, meaning only to see what the matter was, and then shut them again. But, showing us how much our safety depends upon our shunning the occasions of evil and shutting out all dangerous objects from our soul, by this curiosity he fell. One of the combatants was wounded ; and Alipius no sooner saw the blood of the wounded gladiator than, instead of turning away his eyes, he fixed them on the savage sight, sucked in all the fury, and was made drunk with the insensate cruelty of those criminal combats. He was not now the man he came, but one of the multitude with which he mingled. He looked on gloatingly, he shouted, he carried away with him a madness which compelled him to return again and to draw others with him. He relapsed into his former passion for the diversions of the circus, some of them innocent, some barbarous, and some gross. From these misfortunes he learned to fear his own weakness, and trust in God alone, after he had been rescued by the strong and merciful hand of his Creator. But this was long afterwards.

In the meantime Alipius followed his studies, lived chaste, behaved with integrity and honour, and in due course received a judicial office, which he discharged with equity and disinterestedness. When Augustine came to Rome he stuck close to him, went with him to Milan in 384, and shared his conversion. Their names were inscribed together among the *competentes* at the beginning of the Lent of 387. Alipius followed with exactness and fervour the exercises of catechumens before baptism, and received that sacrament with St Augustine from St Ambrose on Easter eve. Some time after they went back to Africa. They lived together at Tagaste, in a small community of devout persons, in the fervent practice of penance and prayer. Worldly habits just discarded stood in need of such a retreat, and habits of virtue were to be formed and strengthened. Such a solitude was also a necessary preparation for the apostolic life, which these holy men afterwards undertook. They lived thus three years at Tagaste when, St Augustine being made priest of Hippo, they all removed thither and continued the same manner of life. Alipius, now a priest, made a pilgrimage of devotion to Palestine, where he met with St Jerome. Upon his return to Africa he was consecrated bishop of Tagaste, about the year 393. He was St Augustine's chief assistant in all his public work, and preached and laboured with indefatigable zeal in the cause of God and His Church. St Augustine in a letter which he wrote to St Alipius in 429 calls him old, and he seems not to have long survived that year. His name occurs in the Roman Martyrology on August 15, but the Augustinian canons regular and others keep his feast on the 18th.

A sufficient account of St Alipius, pieced together mainly from the writings of St Augustine, will be found in the *Acta Sanctorum*, August, vol. iii.

BD ANGELO AUGUSTINE OF FLORENCE　　(A.D. 1438)

ANGELO AUGUSTINE MAZZINGHI was born at Florence in 1377 of a family rivalling in distinction those of the Corsini and Pazzi.　Having entered the Carmelite Order, he was successively appointed prior of the Carmels of Le Selve, Frascati and Florence, and then provincial of Tuscany.　In these offices he showed himself a model of virtue ; his religious devotion warmed the zeal of every monastery with which he came in contact.　He had great success as a preacher, which certain old pictures indicate by representing him with garlands of flowers coming from his mouth and entwining among his hearers.　At the end of his term as provincial he went back to Le Selve and devoted the rest of his life to the reform of his order which had been begun by James Alberti in 1413.　Among its principles on which Bd Angelo insisted was the abolition of the use of all private property and that no friar might accept or retain a post which involved his living outside his monastery. He died at Florence on August 16, 1438, after predicting the day of his death. The ancient *cultus* of Bd Angelo, supported by many miracles, was confirmed in 1761.

A sketch of the life of Bd Angelo was printed at Saragossa at the time of his beatification : R. A. Faci, *Noticia breve de la vida de S.· Angelo Augustini* (1761).　See also Villiers, *Bibliotheca Carmelitana*, vol. i, pp. 104–105, and DHG., vol. iii, c. 40.

BD BEATRICE DA SILVA, VIRGIN, FOUNDRESS OF THE CONCEPTIONIST NUNS　　(A.D. 1490)

THIS Beatrice, known in Portugal as Brites, was born in 1424 and was a sister of Bd Amadeus, initiator of the Franciscan " reform of Marignano ", of whom there is a popular *cultus* at Milan.　She was brought up in the household of the Princess Isabel and at the age of about twenty accompanied her to Spain when she married John II of Castile.　The beauty and attractiveness of Beatrice excited the jealousy of the queen, or, as some say, she listened too readily to the ill-natured gossip of jealous ladies of the court, and Beatrice was imprisoned for three days without food. When she was released she had had enough of court life and she was given leave to retire to the Cistercian convent at Toledo.　Beatrice for long had a project for a new order of women, and in 1484 the Congregation of the Immaculate Conception of the Blessed Virgin Mary was founded.　Queen Isabella the Catholic gave the castle of Galliana to be the house of the first community, who followed an adaptation of the Cistercian rule, and wore a white habit with a blue mantle, after the form in which our Lady had appeared to the foundress.　Bd Beatrice died in 1490.　Soon after, the new order came under the influence of the Franciscan Cardinal Ximenez de Cisneros, Archbishop of Toledo, and it was finally approved with a modification of the rule of the Poor Clares ; it still exists in Spain and elsewhere.　The *cultus* of Bd Beatrice da Silva was confirmed in 1926.

　　Together with Bd Beatrice the Friars Minor today keep the feast of BD PAULA OF MONTALDO, a Poor Clare mystic at Mantua, who died in 1514.　Her *cultus* was approved in 1906.

The decree confirming the cult is printed in the *Acta Apostolicae Sedis*, vol. xviii (1926), pp. 496–499, and contains a short sketch of her history.　See also Jeronymo de Belem, *Chronica Serafica da santa Provincia dos Algarves*, vol. ii, pp. 736–748, where also is a full account of the Bd Amadeus mentioned above.　Upon the Conceptionist Order, of which the famous mystic Maria Coronel d'Agreda was a member, see Heimbucher, *Die Orden und Kongregationen der Kath. Kirche*, vol. ii, pp. 488 *seq.*

BD HAYMO OF SAVIGLIANO (A.D. 1495)

HAYMO TAPARELLI belonged to the family of the counts of Lagnasco and was born at Savigliano in Piedmont in 1395. He was an attractive and quick-witted youth who, after being married for a time, joined the Dominicans and studied at the University of Turin, where he afterwards taught. He preached with much effect throughout Piedmont, for the reconciliation of heretics, the reformation of ill-livers, and the edification of good Christians. He eventually attracted the attention of Bd Amadeus, Duke of Savoy, and was appointed to preach at his court, and he continued to counsel and encourage that holy but unfortunate prince in the troubles which followed his abdication. Bd Haymo's favourite text was, " To serve God is to reign " ; he wrote those words on the wall of his cell, and in a more simple form above the door of the friars' church at Savigliano : " Salvation consists in serving God ; everything else is delusion." His own long life was simply a commentary on that text : all his time he was serving God either directly or by service of his neighbour for God's sake ; and when the world was too much with him he would retreat for a time of uninterrupted contemplation to a mountain near Saluzzo.

And the world and its doings were often very much with him, for northern Italy was overrun by Vaudois and it was the Dominicans' business to deal with them. In 1466 the commissary of the Inquisition, Bd Bartholomew, a fellow-townsman of Bd Haymo, was done to death by heretics at Cervere ; he was the third of the four inquisitors produced by Savigliano, and the third to be martyred. Haymo was appointed to take his place and shortly after was made inquisitor general for Upper Lombardy and Liguria ; the post was as dangerous as it was difficult and laborious, but Haymo, already over seventy, took it up without a word and carried out its duties till the end of his life, nearly thirty years. On August 13, 1495, when reciting the office of the day he came to the words, " The saints shall rejoice in glory ", and it seemed to him that a choir of angels made the response, " They shall be joyful in their beds ", and at once he had a premonition that his death was at hand. And so it was. Two days later, when he had said his office and received the last sacraments, he clasped a crucifix to his breast and quietly died. He was a hundred years old. The people immediately flocked to venerate his body, and the *cultus* that then began was confirmed in 1856.

The case presented for the confirmation of the *cultus* of Bd Haymo seems to have been largely based upon a manuscript chronicle compiled by Father Peronino Sereno at the beginning of the sixteenth century. A full account is given in the *Analecta juris pontificii*, vol. ii (1856), cc. 2337–2346. See also Arnaud, *Vita del b. Aimone* (1802), and Procter, *Lives of Dominican Saints*, pp. 45–47.

19 : ST JOHN EUDES, FOUNDER OF THE CONGREGATIONS OF JESUS AND MARY AND OF OUR LADY OF CHARITY OF THE REFUGE (A.D. 1680)

IN the second half of the sixteenth century there lived at Ri, in Normandy, a certain Isaac Eudes. He was what we should call a yeoman farmer, and he married Martha Corbin ; when after two years they had no children the couple made a pilgrimage to a neighbouring shrine of our Lady, and nine months later a boy was born to them ; subsequently they had five more children. The first-born was baptized John, and he led an exemplary childhood ; it is recorded of him that, when he was nine, a play-mate hit him in the face and he literally fulfilled the gospel precept and turned his other cheek to be slapped also.   But such actions are by no means confined to children who will grow up to be saints, and too much significance must not be attached to them.   When he was fourteen he was sent by his parents to the Jesuit college at Caen.   They wished him to marry and carry on his father's estate ; but John had taken a private vow of celibacy and in 1621 he received minor orders and returned to Caen to study theology, with the idea of enrolling himself among the parochial clergy.   But he decided to offer himself to the Congregation of the Oratory of France, which had been founded in 1611 by M. (afterwards Cardinal) Peter de Bérulle, and after with difficulty obtaining the consent of his parents he was accepted by the superior general at Paris early in 1623.   As he had been an exemplary child and youth, so was he an exemplary cleric, and he made so great an impression upon Bérulle that he permitted him to preach while yet in minor orders.   After a year at Paris John Eudes was sent to Aubervilliers to be under the instruction of Charles de Condren, a priest who, in the words of St Jane Frances de Chantal, was " fit to instruct angels ".   The aim of the Oratory is the perfection of sacerdotal life, and John Eudes was happy in having his first steps along that path directed by two such men as Condren and Bérulle.

Two years later a virulent epidemic of plague broke out in Normandy and St John volunteered to go and work among the sufferers of his own countryside.   He was given permission and Bérulle sent him to the bishop of Séez, with a letter of introduction in which he said, " The order of charity demands that his gifts should be used in the service of the province wherein he received life, grace and holy orders, and that his own diocese should be the first to have the fruits that are to be expected from his ability, goodness, wisdom, energy and life ".   Father Eudes spent two months ministering spiritually and medically to the sick, dying and endangered.   He was then sent to the Oratory of Caen, where he remained quietly till a visitation of plague to that city in 1631 called him out again ; during that time, in order to avoid the danger of infecting his brethren, he lived in a large cask in the middle of a field, receiving his food daily from a nearby convent.   For the following ten years St John was chiefly engaged in giving missions and incidentally gaining much experience for the work which he was afterwards to undertake.   It was a time in which were inaugurated popular missions as we now understand them and, amid many able and some pre-eminent mission-preachers, St John Eudes was the most distinguished ; and from the pulpit he went to the confessional for, as he said, " the preacher beats the bushes but the confessors catch the birds ! "   So competent a judge as Mgr Le Camus, Bishop of Belley, a friend of St Francis de Sales, said of him, " I have heard all the best preachers in Italy and France, but I have never heard anyone who touches the heart so deeply as does this good father ".   He preached in his life-time one hundred and ten missions.

Among the matters that troubled St John during the course of his mission was the difficult position of women and girls who were reclaimed by God's grace from a disorderly life.   For a time he tried to deal with the problem by finding for these penitents temporary homes with religious people, but this arrangement was soon seen to be inadequate.   A certain woman of humble origin, Madeleine Lamy, who had taken charge of several of these girls, strongly realized the unsatisfactoriness of the position and wanted St John to make some more permanent provision. " Where are you off to now ? " she demanded of him one day, " To some church,

I suppose, where you'll gaze at the images and think yourself pious. And all the time what is really wanted of you is a decent home for these poor creatures who are being lost for want of attention and guidance." These words and the laughter of his companions made a deep impression on St John, and in 1641 a house was rented as a refuge for penitent women until honest work could be found for them. But he soon saw that it was necessary for the work to be in the hands of a religious congregation and offered it to the Visitandines of Caen, who accepted it.

In 1643 Father Eudes, after much prayer, consideration and consultation with his superiors and high ecclesiastics, severed his connection with the Oratorians. He had learnt in the course of his missions that the clergy needed reform even more than their flocks, and became convinced that the first necessity was to establish seminaries, and that until this was done the Congregation of the Oratory could not hope to have its full effect. His views were shared by Father de Condren, who had become superior general, but his successor Father Bourgoing would not countenance the plan of a seminary in connection with the Oratory of Caen. Father Eudes then formed the project of a new congregation of secular priests whose object should be the formation of a zealous and virtuous parochial clergy by the conduct of seminaries, and such a congregation was founded at Caen on the feast of the Annunciation, 1643. It was called the Congregation of Jesus and Mary and was modelled on that of the Oratory, consisting of secular priests who were not bound by vows ; the first members were St John Eudes and five others, and they were consecrated to " the Most Holy Trinity as the first principle and last end of priestly dignity and holiness ". The badge by which they were to be distinguished was the hearts of Jesus and Mary regarded as mystically one, symbolizing the eternal love of Jesus. The new venture met with immediate criticism and opposition, particularly from the Jansenists and from the French Oratorians ; and when in 1646 Father Eudes sent Father Maunoury to Rome to try and get papal approval for his foundation the opposition was so strong that he was unsuccessful.

In 1650 the bishop of Coutances invited St John to set up a seminary in that city and in the following year he was invited by M. Olier, who regarded him as " the marvel of his age ", to give a ten weeks' mission at the parish-church of Saint-Sulpice in Paris. During the course of it news was brought that the sisters at the refuge in Caen, having separated from the Visitandines, were recognized by the bishop of Bayeux as a separate congregation, under the name of the Sisters of Our Lady of Charity of the Refuge. St John founded a seminary at Lisieux in 1653 and another at Rouen in 1659, and he then went to Rome, where he made personal representations for the formal approbation of his work ; but even saints do not do everything properly and herein Father Eudes failed, in part through his own disregard for prudence and tact. But a year after his return, in 1666, the Refuge sisters by a bull of Pope Alexander VII were erected as a recognized institute to labour for the reclamation of unchaste women and to care for penitents from among them. This work begun by Father Eudes and the devoted Madeleine Lamy had then been going on for thirty years. St John continued to give long and successful missions and founded two more seminaries, at Evreux in 1666 and at Rennes in 1670.

In the latter year he published a book entitled *The Devotion to the Adorable Heart of Jesus ;* he had already given a feast of the Holy Heart of Mary to his congregation, and in this book was included a proper Mass and Office of the Sacred Heart of Jesus. On August 31, 1670, this feast was first observed in the seminary chapel at Rennes, and other dioceses took it up.   It will be seen therefore that, while St John Eudes can hardly be called the first apostle of devotion to the Sacred Heart as we know it today, nevertheless he was " the institutor of the liturgical *cultus* of the sacred heart of Jesus and the holy heart of Mary ", as Pope Leo XIII called him in 1903 : " He was the first to think—and that not without a divine inspiration—of rendering to them liturgical worship ", says his decree of beatification.   In 1674, the year before St Margaret Mary's " great revelation ", Pope Clement X issued six briefs of indulgences for the confraternities of the Hearts of Jesus and Mary erected in Eudist seminaries.

During the last years of his life St John spent much time on his treatise *The Admirable Heart of the Most Holy Mother of God*, at which he had been working for many years and which he finished less than a month before his death.   His last mission had been at Saint-Lô in 1675, where in wintry weather he had preached in the open *place* nearly every day for nine weeks ; from this ordeal the old man never properly recovered and his days of active work were practically ended.   He died on August 19, 1680, was canonized in 1925, and in 1928 his feast was added to the general calendar of the Western church.   The most famous saying of St John Eudes is that to celebrate the holy sacrifice of the Mass properly three eternities would be required : the first to prepare for it, the second to celebrate it, and the third to give thanks for it ; and in a book which he wrote during the early years of his ministry, *The Life and Reign of Jesus in Christian Souls*, he sums up in a sentence the principle of his own life and of his own works : " Our wish, our object, our chief preoccupation must be to form Jesus in ourselves, to make His spirit, His devotion, His affections, His desires and His disposition live and reign there.   All our religious exercises should be directed to this end.   It is the work which God has given us to do unceasingly."

The later biographers of St John Eudes have done well to draw largely upon his correspondence, much of which still remains unpublished.   The first formal life was written by one of his congregation, Fr Hérambourg, who had not personally known him, but who in joining the institute two years after the founder's death had had abundant opportunities of conversing with those who had lived with him in the most intimate personal relation. No full bibliography can be attempted here.   The most exhaustive study so far published is the life by Fr Boulay in four stout volumes (1905) ; Émile Georges, in his *Saint Jean Eudes, missionaire apostolique* (1925), has sketched on a less ample canvas a very thorough portrait of the saint and of his manifold activities.   Excellent also is the still more handy volume of Henri Joly in the series " Les Saints ".   It must suffice to add a reference to Henri Bremond's chapters on Eudes in his *Histoire littéraire du sentiment religieux en France*, vol. iii, pp. 583–671 ; and to Émile Dermenghem, *La Vie Admirable et les Révélations de Marie des Vallées* (1926).   There is a good article also under the heading " Eudes " in DTC., vol. v, with an adequate bibliography ; and a useful popular work in English by D. Sargent, *Their Hearts be Praised* (1949).

ST ANDREW THE TRIBUNE, Martyr   (*c.* A.D. 300)

So far as the story can be plausibly reconstructed, Andrew was a captain under Antiochus in the army of Galerius sent by Diocletian against the Persians.   During an engagement with the enemy Andrew called on the name of Christ (of whom he had heard as a mighty protector) and told his men to do the same ; when their arms were successful they attributed the victory to these prayers, and Andrew and some others resolved to become Christians.   For this they were denounced to Antiochus, who was not certain what steps he ought to take with regard to this breach of discipline among his troops, and wrote to Galerius to enquire.   The general was unwilling to risk spoiling the *morale* of the army by executing brave soldiers at a moment of victory and so ordered Antiochus to discharge the offenders from the service, but to punish them later on when a more suitable opportunity should arise. Andrew therefore with the other converts made his way to Peter, Bishop of Caesarea in Cappadocia, by whom they were baptized. Seleucus, the military governor of Cilicia, heard of what had happened and sent a detachment to arrest the neophytes, who fled for refuge into the Taurus mountains. Here they were tracked, surrounded and put to death. St Andrew is the object of a great devotion in the East, where he is one having the title of " the Great Martyr ". The number of his companions is not known.

There is no early evidence for the cult of this St Andrew, though the fictitious story of the martyrdom was popular at a later date. The Greek text is given in the *Acta Sanctorum*, August, vol. iii. There is an Andrew in the " Hieronymianum " on July 22, but there is nothing to connect him with this date or with the story told in the alleged " acts ".

SS. TIMOTHY, AGAPIUS AND THECLA, MARTYRS　　(A.D. 304)

WHILST Diocletian signalized his rage and cruelty against the Christians, in the second year of the general persecution, orders were received by Urban, the governor of Palestine, to proceed against Christians in his province. St Timothy for having boldly confessed his faith was inhumanly scourged, his sides were torn with iron combs, and he was at length burnt to death at a slow fire at Gaza. SS. Agapius and Thecla were condemned by the same judge to be exposed to wild beasts. Thecla was despatched by the beasts in the amphitheatre ; but Agapius was kept back for the time being, and detained two years longer in prison. In the amphitheatre at Caesarea he was brought out in company with a common felon, a slave who had murdered his master. This man, not being at once killed by the beasts, was pardoned and set free ; clemency was likewise offered to the innocent Agapius if he would sacrifice to the gods. He refused. He was therefore left to be mauled by a bear, but as the animal did not kill him outright he was taken back to prison, and on the next day drowned in the sea.

Eusebius's *De mart. Palaestinae* is a trustworthy authority for the martyrdom of this group. The *cultus* of Timothy is well attested ; a basilica was built at Gaza in which his remains were venerated.

ST SIXTUS, OR XYSTUS, III, POPE　　(A.D. 440)

SIXTUS was one of the principal clergy of the Roman church before his pontificate, and when he succeeded Pope St Celestine I in 432 St Prosper of Aquitaine wrote that " We trust in the protection of the Lord, and that what He has done for us in Innocent, Zosimus, Boniface and Celestine He will do also in Sixtus ; and as they guarded the flock against declared and openly professed wolves, so he may drive off the hidden ones ", referring to the teachers of Semi-Pelagianism. He was not disappointed ; but St Sixtus was of a peace-loving nature and conciliatory in his policy, so that some of the hot-heads of orthodoxy were dissatisfied and did not scruple to accuse the pope of Pelagian and Nestorian leanings.

Among other buildings in the City, St Sixtus III restored the Liberian basilica, now called St Mary Major, and in it he set up this noble inscription : " O Virgin Mary, I, Sixtus, have dedicated a new temple to thee, an offering worthy of the womb that brought to us salvation. Thou, a maiden knowing not man, didst bear and bring forth our Salvation. Behold ! These martyrs, witnesses to Him who was the fruit of thy womb, bear to thee their crowns of victory, and beneath their feet lie the instruments of their passion—sword, flame, wild beast, water and cruel poison : one crown alike awaits these divers deaths." Over the arch of the apse can still be read the words in mosaic : " Sixtus the bishop for the people of God." This pope consecrated a number of churches, and the dedications of two of them are feasts universal in the Western church, St Peter *ad Vincula* (August 1) and St Mary Major (August 5).

The *Liber Pontificalis,* with Duchesne's notes, vol. i, pp. 232–237, is the most important source. See also Grisar, *Geschichte Roms und der Päpste,* §§ 224–226, and *cf.* § 468. Some further references are given above in the bibliographical notes to St Peter *ad Vincula* and Our Lady of the Snow.

ST MOCHTA, Abbot   (A.D. 535 ?)

Mochta is mentioned in the lives of St Patrick and there is a late Latin life of himself which is " crammed with fables ". He was a Briton by birth and while still a child was brought over to Ireland by his Christian parents. With them travelled a heathen bard, one Hoa, who when a grievous storm sprang up during the voyage wanted to throw young Mochta overboard as a propitiatory sacrifice ; but the tempest was miraculously calmed and later on Mochta converted Hoa. Mochta became a disciple of St Patrick and was sent to Rome where, according to the *vita,* he was made bishop by Pope St Leo I, and he presented to the pope a tablet on which he had learned writing under the tuition of an angel. When he had collected twelve suitable young men as missionaries he returned to Ireland ; one of these got left behind *en route,* so he put to sea on the bough of a tree—and got there first.

St Mochta settled eventually at Louth, where he was soon surrounded by a large community : but the actual figures given are unbelievable—they include 200 bishops. It is recorded that he never uttered a false word nor a foolish one, and that he never ate a morsel of fat—not from finicalness but by way of curbing his appetite for such food. Among the fables told of St Mochta is that he lived for three hundred years : this was in accordance with a sentence pronounced on him by St Patrick because, when reading the Bible, Mochta had questioned the accuracy of the ages attributed to the antediluvian patriarchs. If the evidence which we have may be trusted he probably lived to be ninety, and was the last of St Patrick's personal disciples.

The best text of the Latin life referred to above is that edited by Fr De Smedt from the Codex Salmanticensis, pp. 903–914 ; but it is also printed after Colgan in the *Acta Sanctorum,* August, vol. iii.

ST BERTULF, Abbot   (A.D. 640)

Among the many relatives of St Arnoul of Metz who were venerated as saints Bertulf was one of the chief ; he had been brought up a pagan, but the example and teaching of Arnoul brought him to the Church of Christ, and in 620 (at what age is not known) he became a monk at Luxeuil. Bertulf remained there for several years, learning the principles of the religious life and the discipline of St Columban from his successor, St Eustace. Then he attracted the attention of St Attala, who had succeeded Columban as abbot of Bobbio ; he was given permission to migrate to that monastery, and in 627 became its abbot on the death of Attala. St Bertulf was worthy of his predecessors in holiness, learning and apostolic zeal. Within the monastery he rigorously maintained the austere rule of St Columban ; outside it he vigorously opposed Arianism, which was rife in northern Italy.

The year following St Bertulf's election, Probus, Bishop of Tortona, taking advantage of a new abbot, claimed a wide jurisdiction over the monastery. Bertulf appealed to Ariovald, the Lombard king, who advised that the matter be carried to Rome and paid the expenses of the abbot to go there to state his case ; he took with him the monk Jonas, his secretary, who afterwards wrote the life of St Bertulf. Pope Honorius I, knowing the great reputation of the monastery and the exactness of its observance, declared it to be exempt from episcopal control and immediately subject to the Holy See ; this was the first recorded exemption of its kind and began a new era in the relationship of the " regular " clergy to the bishops. Jonas relates that on the way home Bertulf was stricken down with a fever, from which he seemed likely to die ; but on the vigil of SS. Peter and Paul he fell into a deep sleep, during which he had a vision of St Peter, and upon waking up was completely recovered. Jonas also records a number of miracles of the saint, of which he claims to have been a witness.

There is a short Latin life by Jonas I, abbot of Bobbio, which was printed both by Mabillon and the Bollandists, and finally has been edited by B. Krusch in MGH., *Scriptores Merov.*, vol. iv, pp. 280 *seq.* There is also an encomium in verse by Hodoard. *Cf.* Cipolla and Buzzi, *Codice diplomatico del Monastero di Bobbio* (1918), vol. i.

ST SEBALD (Eighth Century ?)

St Sebald, patron of Nuremberg in Bavaria, lived as a hermit in the Reichswald, preaching the gospel of Jesus Christ among his neighbours, and already in 1072 was recognized as the patron of Nuremberg. His biography is of uncertain date, and full of anachronisms and inconsistencies. According to it he was a solitary near Vicenza for some time and was in Rome both during the pontificate of St Gregory II and when SS. Willibald and Winebald were there ; when St Gregory III sent Willibald into Germany he accompanied him. One of the reliefs on the base of his shrine at Nuremberg, the best-known work of Peter Vischer, on which he was working from 1505 to 1519, represents the miracle of the icicles attributed to St Sebald : one snowy night he took shelter in a peasant's cottage, but found it almost as cold within as without, for the fire was low and small. Sebald suggested that more fuel might be put on, but the man answered that he was too poor to keep up a decent fire, so Sebald turned to the housewife and asked her to bring in a bundle of the long icicles hanging from the eaves ; this she did, Sebald threw them on the fire, and they blazed up merrily. Other miracles of his are recorded on the shrine, namely, giving sight to a blind man, filling a jug with wine from nowhere, and causing a mocker to be swallowed up by the earth.

The very unsatisfactory life mentioned above is printed in the *Acta Sanctorum*, August, vol. iii. See also the *Kirchenlexikon*, vol. xi, cc. 24–26 ; and Stamminger, *Franconia Sancta*, pp. 534 *seq.*

ST LOUIS OF ANJOU, Bishop of Toulouse (A.D. 1297)

This saint was born in 1274, second son to Charles II surnamed the Lame, King of Naples and Sicily, and Mary, daughter of Stephen V, King of Hungary ; he was therefore a grand-nephew of St Louis of France and connected with the family of St Elizabeth of Hungary.

In 1284 Louis's father Charles, then prince of Salerno, was taken prisoner in a sea-fight by the king of Aragon. His father, Charles I, died within a few months, and he was saluted by his friends as king of Sicily, but he remained four years prisoner and was only released on hard conditions : being, moreover, obliged to send into Aragon as hostages three of his sons, of whom Louis was one. He remained seven years at Barcelona in captivity, under which he was always cheerful and encouraged his companions, and as he grew older he took an active part in the sports and manly exercises with which the brothers and other prisoners passed the time. But Louis imposed strict regulations : chess, for instance, was encouraged, but gambling forbidden. He himself gave much time to study and came under the influence of the Friars Minor, so that when he was attacked by a severe illness at the castle of Sciurana he made a vow to join that order if he should recover. He got leave for two Franciscan friars, who were appointed to attend him, to live with him in his own apartments ; he rose to pray with them in the night, and under them he applied himself diligently to the studies of philosophy and theology.*

St Louis was set at liberty in 1295, by a treaty concluded between his father and James II, King of Aragon, and it was proposed that James's sister should be united in marriage with Louis. But the saint's resolution of dedicating himself to God was inflexible, and he resigned his right to the crown of Naples, which his father conferred on his next brother, Robert. Thus it was his ambition to follow Jesus Christ poor and humble, rather than to be raised to honour in the world : " Jesus Christ ", said he, " is my kingdom. If I possess Him alone, I shall have all things : if I have not Him, I lose all." The opposition of his family obliged the superiors of the Friars Minor to refuse for some time to admit him into their body, wherefore he retired to a castle near Naples, where he befriended a poor scholar of Cahors, James d'Euse, who afterwards became Pope John XXII and canonized his benefactor. Pope Boniface VIII gave him a dispensation to receive priestly orders in the twenty-third year of his age, and afterwards for the episcopate, together with his nomination to the bishopric of Toulouse, and a severe injunction in virtue of obedience to accept it. He first went to Rome to fulfil his vow, and made his religious profession among the Friars Minor, in their convent of *Ara Caeli*, on Christmas eve, 1296, and received the episcopal consecration in St Peter's five days later.

Louis travelled to his bishopric as a poor religious, but was received at Toulouse with the veneration due to a saint and the magnificence that became a prince. His modesty and devotion inspired love in all that beheld him. He banished the use of plate and jewelled vessels from his episcopal dwelling, substituting for them pewter and wooden bowls, and wore an old darned habit, as befitting a Franciscan and as an example to his clergy, who gave too much thought to dress. As a bishop he abated nothing of his austerities, celebrated Mass every day, and preached frequently. But within a few months he found the episcopal office too much for him, and asked leave to resign it. He answered to some that opposed his inclination, " Let the world call me mad ; provided I may be discharged from a burden which is too

---

* It is interesting to note that Richard Middleton (de Media Villa), an English Franciscan who was also a famous theologian, became one of St Louis's tutors ; also that St Aloysius Gonzaga's extreme, and as some may well think exaggerated, modesty in avoiding all relations with the opposite sex was apparently imitated from the conduct of his patron, St Louis of Anjou. See *The Month* for August 1924, pp. 158–160.

heavy for my shoulders, I am satisfied.   Is it not better for me to try to throw it
off than to sink under it ? "   God was pleased to grant him what he desired by
calling him to Himself.   Returning from a visit to his sister in Catalonia he fell
sick at Brignoles.   Finding his end draw near, he said to those about him, " After
a dangerous voyage I am arrived within sight of the port which I have long desired.
I shall now enjoy my God whom the world would rob me of ; and I shall be freed
from the heavy charge which I am not able to bear."   St Louis died on August 19,
1297, being only twenty-three years and a half old.   He was buried in the convent of
the Franciscan friars at Marseilles, as he had ordered.   Pope John XXII canonized
him at Avignon in 1317, and addressed a brief thereupon to his mother, who was
still living.

> There is a valuable book by Miss Margaret R. Toynbee on *St Louis of Toulouse and
> the Process of Canonization in the Fourteenth Century* (1929).   We possess in fact a record
> of the depositions of witnesses in the process of canonization, and this important source,
> long ago utilized by the Bollandists (*Acta Sanctorum*, August, vol. iii), is now being critically
> edited by the Franciscans of Quaracchi.   Another principal source, the life written by St
> Louis's confessor, John de Orta, has been printed in the *Analecta Bollandiana*, vol ix (1890),
> pp. 278–353 (*cf.* also vol. xlvi, pp. 344–354).   There is a sketch in French by L. Chancerel
> (1943), and an ample bibliography in U. Chevalier, *Bio-bibliographie*.

BD EMILY OF VERCELLI, Virgin   (A.D. 1314)

EMILY BICCHIERI was born at Vercelli in 1238, and having lost her mother at an
early age put herself under the special protection of the all-holy Mother of God.
She combined a healthy aversion from worldliness with an efficient care for her
widowed father's household, and he, good man, seeing only the one, planned for
her a respectable marriage by which his daughter, himself and the husband-to-be
would all benefit.   But when she was sixteen Emily upset all this by telling him
she wanted to be a nun ; at first Peter Bicchieri would not hear of such a thing,
but he was a Christian and reasonable man and at length gave in to his daughter's
importunities.   He went further, and built and endowed a convent at Vercelli, of
which Sister Emily became prioress at the age of twenty.   These nuns were under
the direction of the Friars Preachers, and according to one of several theories of the
origins of third orders, this was the first convent of Dominican regular tertiaries.
Having been elected prioress against her will, Bd Emily governed with tact and
ability, and was careful to tell no one to do what she would not do herself—except
that she would never interview the fashionable ladies of Vercelli in the parlour if
she could possibly help it.   In directing her sisters she laid particular stress on
" knowing what you were after " and on the purity of that intention : otherwise,
she would say, one is like a person going to market who does not know with whom
to deal or what price to pay ; and God's glory must be the last end of all their
actions and the motive of their religious obedience.

Those were the days, albeit the " ages of faith ", when frequent communion
was not customary, and Bd Emily was remarkable in the practice and privilege of
receiving the Blessed Sacrament three times a week and on all great feast-days.
She was distinguished by a notable spirit of gratitude both to God and man, and
by her love for liturgical prayer.   She is reputed to have had the gift of miracles
and to have stopped by her prayers and the sign of the cross a disastrous fire in the
convent (though that is almost a commonplace of hagiology, and must often be put
down to " common form ") ; to have had frequent visions of our Lord and His

Mother ; and to have participated in the sufferings of the Passion, especially those caused by the crown of thorns. Bd Emily died on her birthday, May 3, at the age of seventy-six. Her *cultus* was approved in 1769.

See the *Acta Sanctorum*, May, vol. vii, in the appendix ; Ganay, *Les bienheureuses dominicaines*, pp. 121 seq. ; Mortier, *Maîtres généraux O.P.*, vol. ii, p. 9 ; and P. B. Berro, *La beata Emilia* (1914). A fuller bibliography will be found in Taurisano, *Catalogus hagiographicus O.P.*, p. 17.

20 : ST BERNARD, ABBOT OF CLAIRVAUX, DOCTOR OF THE CHURCH (A.D. 1153)

ST BERNARD was the third son of Tescelin Sorrel, a Burgundian noble, and Aleth, who was daughter of Bernard, lord of Montbard. He was born in 1090 at Fontaines, a castle near Dijon, a lordship belonging to his father. His parents had seven children, namely, Bd Guy, Bd Gerard, St Bernard, Bd Humbeline, Andrew, Bartholomew and Bd Nivard. They were all well educated, and learned Latin and verse-making before the sons were applied to military exercise and feats of arms ; but Bernard was sent to Châtillon on the Seine, to pursue a complete course of studies in a college of secular canons. He even then loved to be alone, largely at first because of shyness ; his progress in learning was far greater than could be expected from one of his age ; and he was soon alert to listen to what God by His holy inspirations spoke to his heart. One Christmas-eve, while waiting with his mother to set out for Matins, he fell asleep and seemed to see the infant Jesus newly born in the stable at Bethlehem ; from that day he ever had a most tender devotion towards that great mystery of love and mercy, the manhood of Christ. When he was seventeen his mother died. Bernard was greatly attached to Aleth and her loss was a heavy blow ; he was in danger of becoming morbidly despondent, till he was rallied out of his brooding and inertia by his lively sister Humbeline.

Bernard made his appearance in the world with all the advantages and talents which can make it attractive to a young man, or which could make him loved by it. His personal attractiveness and wit, his affability and sweetness of temper, endeared him to everybody ; in these very advantages lay his chief danger, and for a time there was serious risk of his becoming lukewarm and indifferent. But he began to think of forsaking the world and the pursuit of letters, which greatly attracted him, and of going to Cîteaux, where only a few years before SS. Robert, Alberic and Stephen Harding had established the first monastery of that strict interpretation of the Benedictine rule, called after it " Cistercian ". He wavered for some time in his mind, and one day in great anxiety he went into a church by the road and prayed that God would direct him to discover and follow His will. He arose steadily fixed in the resolution of following the severe Cistercian life. His friends endeavoured to dissuade him from it ; but he not only remained firm—he enlisted four of his brothers as well, and an uncle. Hugh of Mâcon (who afterward founded the monastery of Pontigny, and died bishop of Auxerre), an intimate friend, wept bitterly at the thought of separation, but by two interviews was induced to become his companion. Nor were these the only ones who, with apparently no previous thought of the religious life, suddenly decided to leave the world for the austere life of Cîteaux. Bernard induced in all thirty-one men to follow him—he who himself had been uncertain of his call only a few weeks before.   It is a happening unparalleled in Christian history.   Bernard's eloquent appeals were irresistible ; mothers feared for their sons, wives for their husbands, lest they came under the sway of that compelling voice and look.   They assembled at Châtillon, and on the day appointed for their meeting Bernard and his brothers went to Fontaines to take farewell of their father and beg his blessing.   They left Nivard, the youngest brother, to be a comfort to him in his old age.   Going out they saw him at play with other children, and Guy said to him, " Adieu, my little Nivard !   You will have all the estates and lands to yourself."   The boy answered, " What ! you then take Heaven, and leave me only the earth.   The division is too unequal."   They went away ; but soon after Nivard followed them, so that of the whole family there only remained in the world the old father and his daughter, Humbeline.

The company arrived at Cîteaux about Easter in 1112 and the abbot, the English St Stephen, who had not had a novice for several years, received them with open arms.   St Bernard was then twenty-two years old.   He entered this house with the desire to die to the remembrance of men, to live hidden and be forgotten, that he might be occupied only with God.   After three years the abbot, seeing the great progress which Bernard had made and his extraordinary abilities, ordered him to go with twelve monks to found a new house in the diocese of Langres in Champagne. They walked in procession, singing psalms, with their new abbot at their head, and settled in a place called the Valley of Wormwood, surrounded by a forest.   These thirteen monks grubbed up a sufficient area and, with the assistance of the bishop and the people of the country, built themselves a house.   This young colony lived through a period of extreme and grinding hardship.   The land was poor and their bread was of coarse barley ; boiled beech leaves were sometimes served up instead of vegetables.   Bernard at first was so severe in his discipline, coming down upon the smallest distractions and least transgressions of his brethren, whether in confession or in chapter, that although his monks behaved with the utmost humility and obedience they began to be discouraged, which made the abbot sensible of his fault.   He condemned himself for it to a long silence.   At length he resumed his preaching, and provided that meals should be more regular, though the food was still of the coarsest.   The reputation of the house and of the holiness of its abbot soon became so great that the number of monks had risen to a hundred and thirty ; and the name of the valley was changed to Clairvaux, because it was situated right in the eye of the sun.   Bernard's aged father Tescelin and the young Nivard followed him in 1117, and received the habit at his hands.   The first four daughter-houses of Cîteaux became each a mother-house to others, and Clairvaux had the most numerous offspring, including Rievaulx and, in a sense, Fountains in England.

In 1121 Bernard wrought his first miracle, restoring, while he sang Mass, power of speech to a certain lord that he might confess his sins before he died, three days after, having made restitution for numerous acts of injustice.   It is related that other sick persons were cured instantaneously by his making the sign of the cross upon them ; and we are also told that the church of Foigny was infested with flies till, by Bernard saying he " excommunicated " them, they all died.   The male-diction of the flies of Foigny became a proverb in France.   The contemporary William of Saint-Thierry gives a most unpleasant account of the weakness of Bernard's stomach (which was aggravated by insufficient and unsuitable food), and in consideration of his ill-health the general chapter dispensed him from work in the fields and ordered him to undertake extra preaching instead.   This led to his writing a treatise on the Degrees of Humility and Pride, the first of his published works. It includes a study of character which, says the Abbé Vacandard, " the most expert psychologist would not disavow ".

Notwithstanding St Bernard's love of retirement, obedience and the Church's needs frequently drew him from his cell. Like several other great saints who have had in a supreme degree the gift of contemplation and wished only to live alone with God in the retirement of a monastery, he had for years on end to be about his Father's business in active and public, even political, affairs. In 1137 he wrote that his life was " over-run in all quarters with anxieties, suspicions, cares, and there is scarcely an hour that is left free from the crowd of discordant applicants, from the trouble and care of business. I have no power to stop their coming and cannot refuse to see them, and they do not leave me even the time to pray." So great was the reputation of his character and powers that princes desired to have their differences determined by him and bishops regarded his decisions with the greatest respect, referring to him important affairs of their churches. The popes looked upon his advice as the greatest support of the Holy See, and all people had a profound respect and veneration for his person and opinion. It was said of him that he was " the oracle of Christendom ". For Bernard was not only a great monastic founder, theologian and preacher, he was also a reformer and " crusader " : he never refused what presented itself to him as a challenge, whether it came from the abbey of Cluny or from an antipope, from the philosopher Abelard or the call to the Second Crusade. And he was a hard hitter ; to an ecclesiastic in Languedoc he wrote : " You may imagine that what belongs to the Church belongs to you while you officiate there. But you are mistaken : for though it be reasonable that one who serves the altar should live by the altar, yet it must not be to promote either his luxury or his pride. Whatever goes beyond bare nourishment and simple plain clothing is sacrilege and theft."

After the disputed papal election of 1130 the cause of Pope Innocent II took St Bernard up and down France, Germany and Italy. On one of his returns to Clairvaux he took with him a new postulant, a canon of Pisa, Peter Bernard Paganelli, who was to become a beatified pope as Eugenius III ; for the present he was put to stoke the fire in the monastery calefactory. After the general acknowledgement of Innocent II Bernard was present at the tenth general council in Rome, the second of the Lateran, and it was at this period that he first met St Malachy of Armagh ; the ensuing friendship between the two lasted until Malachy's death in Bernard's arms nine years later. All this time Bernard had continued diligently to preach to his monks whenever he was able, notably those famous discourses on the Song of Songs. In 1140 he preached for the first time in a public pulpit, primarily to the students of Paris. They are the two most powerful and trenchant of his discourses preserved to us, in which he says much of " things hellish and horrible " ; they effected some good and a number of conversions among the students, who were at first superior to their fervent " evangelicalism ". But no sooner was the trouble of the papal schism over than he was involved in the controversy with Abelard. If St Bernard was the most eloquent and influential man of his age, the next was the brilliant and unhappy Peter Abelard, who was moreover, of far wider learning. The two were bound to come into collision, for they represented two currents of thought which, not necessarily opposed, were not yet properly fused : on the one hand, the weight of traditional authority and " faith not as an opinion but a certitude " ; on the other, the new rationalism and exaltation of human reason. St Bernard himself has since been grievously criticized for his unrelenting pursuit of Abelard : but it seemed to him he had detected in Abelard vanity and arrogance masquerading as science, and rationalism masquerading as the use of reason, and his ability and learning made him the more dangerous. St Bernard wrote to the pope : " Peter Abelard is trying to make void the merit of Christian faith, when he deems himself able by human reason to comprehend God entirely . . . the man is great in his own eyes."

Probably about the beginning of the year 1142 the first Cistercian foundation was made in Ireland, from Clairvaux, where St Malachy had put some young Irishmen with St Bernard to be trained. The abbey was called Mellifont, in county Louth, and within ten years of its foundation six daughter-houses had been planted out. At the same time Bernard was busied in the affair of the disputed succession to the see of York, set out in the account of St William of York (June 8), in the course of which Pope Innocent II died. His third successor, within eighteen months, was the Cistercian abbot of Tre Fontane, that Peter Bernard of Pisa to whom reference has been made, known to history as Bd Eugenius III. St Bernard wrote a charming letter of encouragement to his former subject, addressed : " To his most dearly loved father and master, Eugenius, by the grace of God Sovereign Pontiff, Bernard, styled Abbot of Clairvaux, presents his humble service." But Bernard was also rather frightened, for Eugenius was shy and retiring, not accustomed to public life ; and so he wrote also to the college of cardinals, a letter beginning : " May God forgive you what you have done. You have put back among the living a man who was dead and buried. You have again surrounded with cares and crowds one who had fled from cares and crowds. You have made the last first, and behold ! the last state of that man is more perilous than the first." Later he wrote for Pope Eugenius's guidance the longest and most important of his treatises, *De consideratione*, impressing upon him the various duties of his office, and strongly recommending him always to reserve time for self-examination and daily contemplation, applying himself to this still more than to business. He proves to him that " consideration " serves to form and to employ in the heart all virtues. He reminds the pope that he is in danger of falling, by the multiplicity of affairs, into a forgetfulness of God and hardness of heart : the thought of which made the saint tremble for him, and tell him that his heart was already hardened and made insensible if he did not continually tremble for himself ; for if the Pope falls, the whole Church of God is involved.

In the meantime the Albigensian heresy and its social and moral implications had been making alarming progress in the south of France. St Bernard had already been called on to deal with a similar sect in Cologne, and in 1145 the papal legate, Cardinal Alberic, asked him to go to Languedoc. Bernard was ill and weak and hardly able to make the journey, but he obeyed, preaching on the way. Geoffrey, the saint's secretary, accompanied him, and relates many miracles to which he was an eye-witness. He tells us that at Sarlat in Périgord, Bernard, blessing with the sign of the cross some loaves of bread which were brought, said, " By this shall you know the truth of our doctrine, and the falsehood of that which is taught by the heretics, if such as are sick among you recover their health by eating of these loaves". The bishop of Chartres, who stood by, being fearful of the result, said, " That is, if they eat with a right faith, they shall be cured ". But the abbot replied, " I say not so ; but assuredly they that taste shall be cured, that you may know by this that we are sent by authority derived from God, and preach His truth ". And a number of sick persons were cured by eating that bread.   Bernard preached against the heresy throughout Languedoc ; its supporters were stubborn and violent, especially at Toulouse and Albi, but in a very short time he had restored the country to orthodoxy and returned to Clairvaux.   But he left too soon, the restoration was more apparent than real, and twenty-five years later Albigensianism had a stronger hold than ever.   Then came St Dominic.

On Christmas-day, 1144, the Seljuk Turks had captured Edessa, centre of one of the four principalities of the Latin kingdom of Jerusalem, and appeals for help were at once sent to Europe, for the whole position was in danger.   Pope Eugenius commissioned St Bernard to preach a crusade.   He began at Vézelay on Palm Sunday 1146, when Queen Eleanor and many nobles were the first to take the cross, and were followed by such large numbers of people, moved by the monk's burning words, that the supply of badges was exhausted ·and he had to tear strips off his habit to make others.   When he had roused France, he wrote letters to the rulers and peoples of western and central Europe, and then went in person into Germany. First he had to deal with a half-crazy monk, called Rudolf, who in his name was inciting the people to massacre the Jews, and then made a triumphant journey through the Rhineland, confirming his appeals by an amazing succession of miracles, vouched for by his companions.   The Emperor Conrad III took the cross from him, and set out with an army in the May of 1147, followed by Louis of France. But this, the second, crusade was a miserable failure ; Conrad's forces were cut to pieces in Asia Minor and Louis did not get beyond laying siege to Damascus.   Its ill success was in no small measure due to the crusaders themselves, of whom a great part were led by no other motive than the prospect of plunder, were lawless, and committed every kind of disorder in their march.   To those who were led by motives of sincere penance and religion, these afflictions were trials for the exercise of their virtue, but the ascetical exercise was dearly bought.   This unfortunate expedition raised a storm against St Bernard, because he had seemed to promise success.   His answer was that he confided in the divine mercy for a blessing on an enterprise undertaken for the honour of the divine name, but that the sins of the army were the cause of its misfortunes ; further, who could judge the extent of its success or failure, and " how is it that the rashness of mortals dares reprove what they cannot understand ? "

Early in the year 1153 St Bernard entered on his last illness.   He had long dwelt in Heaven in desire, though this desire he by humility ascribed to weakness : " The saints ", said he, " were moved to pray for death out of a desire of seeing Christ ; but I am forced hence by scandals and evil.   I confess myself overcome by the violence of the storm for want of courage."   For a time he mended a little in the spring, and was called on for the last time to leave Clairvaux to succour his neighbour.   The inhabitants of Metz having been attacked by the duke of Lorraine, they were vehemently bent on revenge.   To prevent the shedding of more blood the archbishop of Trier went to Clairvaux, and implored Bernard to journey to Metz in order to reconcile the parties that were at variance.   At this call of charity he forgot his infirmity and made his way into Lorraine, where he prevailed on both sides to lay aside their arms and accept a treaty which he drew up.   Back at Clairvaux, his illness returned with more grievous symptoms.   When he received the last sacraments and his spiritual children assembled about him in tears, he comforted and encouraged them, saying that the unprofitable servant ought not to occupy a place uselessly, that the barren tree ought to be rooted up.   His love for them inclined him to remain till they should be gathered with him to God ; but his desire to enjoy Christ made him long for death. " I am straitened between two ", he cried, " and what to choose I know not. I leave it to the Lord ; let Him decide." And God took him to Himself, on August 20, 1153 ; he was sixty-three years old, had been abbot for thirty-eight, and sixty-eight monasteries had been founded from Clairvaux—Bernard may indeed be counted among the founders of the Cistercian Order, who brought it out of obscurity into the centre of western Christendom. He was canonized in 1174, and in 1830 formally declared a doctor of the Church : *Doctor mellifluus*, the Honey-sweet Doctor, as he is now universally called.

St Bernard " carried the twelfth century on his shoulders, and he did not carry it without suffering " ; he was during his life the oracle of the Church, the light of prelates, and the reformer of discipline ; since his death he continues to comfort and instruct by his writings. The great French lay scholar of the seventeenth century, Henry Valois, did not hesitate to say they are the most useful for piety among all the works of the fathers of the Church, though he is the youngest of them in time, and Sixtus of Siena, the converted Jew, said, " His discourse is everywhere sweet and ardent : it so delights and warms that from his tongue honey and milk seem to flow in his words, and a fire of burning love to glow from his breast ". To Erasmus he was " cheerful, pleasant, and vehement in moving the passions ", and in another place, " He is Christianly learned, holily eloquent, and devoutly cheerful and pleasing ". From Pope Innocent II to Cardinal Manning, from Luther to Frederic Harrison, Catholics and Protestants of eminence have recognized the sanctity of St Bernard and the greatness of his writings, in which he is equally gentle and vigorous ; his charity appears in his reproaches, he reproves to correct, never to insult. He had so meditated on the Holy Scriptures that in almost every sentence he borrows something from their language, and diffuses the marrow of the sacred text with which his own heart was filled. He was well read in the writings of the fathers of the Church, especially SS. Ambrose and Augustine, and often takes his thoughts from their writings and by a new turn makes them his own. Though he lived after St Anselm, the first of the scholastics, and though his contemporaries are ranked in that class, yet he treats theological subjects after the manner of the ancients. On this account, and for the great excellence of his writings, he is himself reckoned among the fathers. And though he is the last among them in time, he is one of the greatest to those who desire to study and to improve their hearts in sincere religion.

Almost all the principal materials for the life of St Bernard have been printed in the *Latin Patrology* of Migne, vol. 185. The most important source, known as the *Vita prima* —the best text is that of Waitz in MGH., *Scriptores*, vol. xxvi—is made up of five sections by different authors, his contemporaries, *i.e.* William of Saint-Thierry, Arnold of Bonneval and Geoffrey of Auxerre, supplemented by a collection of the miracles. There are other accounts of his life by Alan of Auxerre, John the Hermit, etc., and a good deal of more or less legendary matter in later compilations, notably the *Exordium magnum* of Conrad of Eberbach, and the *Liber miraculorum* of Herbert. All these sources as well as the saint's correspondence have been very carefully discussed by G. Hüffer in his *Vorstudien* (1886) and in the first chapter of E. Vacandard's *Vie de Saint Bernard* (1910), which last book still remains the most authoritative biography. More popular lives such as those by G. Goyau (1927), F. Höver (1927), and A. Luddy, *Life and Teaching of St Bernard* (1927), are numerous but the accuracy of the rather bulky work last named cannot always be relied upon. Many non-Catholic biographies or histories, notably those of J. Cotter Morison (1877), R. S. Storrs (1893), Watkin Williams (1935), and G. G. Coulton (*Five Centuries of Religion*, vol. i), also pay tribute to St Bernard's greatness.   E. Gilson's *Mystical Theology of St Bernard* appeared in English in 1940.   J. Leclercq's *St Bernard mystique* (1948) includes 200 pp. of passages from his writings.   Dom Leclercq is working on a critical edition of the saint's works.   See also the *recueil* of the Assoc. Bourguignonne des Sociétés Savantes, *St Bernard et son temps* (2 vols., 1928) ; and *cf.* D. Knowles, *The Monastic Order in England* (1949).   An English translation of the saint's letters, by the Rev. B. Scott James, and a valuable volume of biographical material in French, *Bernard de Clairvaux*, ed. by Dom Jean Bouton, were published in 1953, among other relevant works.

ST AMADOUR   (No Date)

St Amadour is honoured in Quercy and the Limousin as founder of the shrine of our Lady now known as Rocamadour, and as the first hermit ot Gaul.   There is in fact nothing whatever known about him, neither of the events ot his life nor the age in which he lived, nor even that he ever existed.   His legend was first written some time after the discovery at Rocamadour in 1166 of an incorrupt body. The hypothesis that St Amadour was an early solitary in the valley of Alzou and gave his name to the spot is not supported by a shadow of evidence.

According to the fiction, Amadour was a servant of the Holy Family and afterwards married St Veronica.   Driven from Palestine by persecution, they landed in Gaul and, under the direction of St Martial (who lived not in the first but in the third century), evangelized the neighbourhood of Bordeaux and Cahors. Amadour was sent to Rome to report Martial's progress to St Peter, where he was present at the martyrdom of the Apostles ; on his return he continued his preaching, founded monasteries, and, after the death of Veronica, retired to his lonely cell in Quercy where he built the chapel of our Lady which became the great sanctuary. In the fifteenth century a fresh turn was given to this legend when St Amadour was gratuitously identified with the Zaccheus of St Luke xix.   The finding of the incorrupt body of " St Amadour " is remembered in the popular saying, " With skin and bones like Amadour ".

The curious and manifestly incredible legend of St Amadour, owing to the popularity of the shrine and pilgrimage of Rocamadour, has attracted much attention in France.   The subject has been critically and soberly dealt with by E. Rupin, first in his monograph *Roc-Amadour ; étude historique et archéologique* (1904) ; and then in his *Légende de Saint Amadour* (1909).   In this last he replied convincingly to the booklet *Notre-Dame de Roc-Amadour* (1908) written by an uncritical assailant, J. T. Layral.   *Cf.* also the article of E. Albe, " La vie et les miracles de S. Amator " in the *Analecta Bollandiana*, vol. xxviii (1909), pp. 57–90. In this the fictitious character of the whole tradition is made apparent by another line of argument.

ST OSWIN, Martyr   (A.D. 651)

When his father Osric, King of Deira, was killed by the British Cadwallon in 633, the young Oswin was taken into Wessex for safety, where he was baptized and educated ; but after the death of the great prince St Oswald in 642 he returned to the north and took possession of his kingdom.   He governed it with virtue, prudence and prosperity.   The Venerable Bede relates how, having rebuked St Aidan for giving away to a beggar a horse the king had given him, Oswin accepted Aidan's correction and apologized.   Whereupon Aidan said to his attendants in the Irish language, which the king and his courtiers did not understand, that he was assured so humble and so good a king would not live long, because the nation was not worthy of such a ruler.

His prediction was soon verified. Oswin incurred the jealousy of his cousin Oswy, King of Bernicia, the two fell out, and Oswy declared a state of open warfare. Oswin, seeing his own weakness and being desirous to spare human blood (or, as St Bede says, from simple prudence, but doubtless for both considerations), dismissed his forces at a place called Wilfaresdon, near Catterick. Attended with one faithful thegn, he retired to Gilling, near Richmond in Yorkshire, which estate he had lately bestowed on one Hunwald. Oswy ordered his reeve, Ethelwin, to find Oswin and kill him. Hunwald treacherously betrayed his guest ; Oswin and his thegn were slain together, and buried at Gilling. Queen Eanfleda, daughter to St Edwin and wife of Oswy, founded a monastery at Gilling, in which prayers might be ever offered up for both kings. It was afterwards destroyed by the Danes, before whose incursions the body of St Oswin, whose shrine was made illustrious by miracles, was translated to Tynemouth. Here it was lost sight of during the Danish troubles, but in 1065 a monk of Tynemouth discovered it in consequence of a vision, and it was accordingly enshrined again in the year 1100.

We know little of St Oswin beyond what is told us in Bede's *Ecclesiastical History*, bk iii, ch. 14. There is, however, a twelfth-century life with two homilies and some liturgical matter. This has been used by Plummer in his notes to Bede. See also Stanton's *Menology*, pp. 401–403.

ST PHILIBERT, Abbot   (c. A.D. 685)

HE was born about 608 in Gascony. His father, Philibaud, having received holy orders, was made bishop of Aire, and the young Philibert was educated under the eyes of his father, who sent him to the court of Dagobert I. Here the example and instructions of the chancellor, St Ouen, made so deep an impression on him that at the age of twenty years he took the habit in the abbey of Rebais, founded by Ouen. He was appointed successor to St Aile in the government of this house, but left it on finding some of the monks refractory, and his own inability through inexperience to deal with them. After having visited many monasteries to study various observances, he retired into Neustria, where Clovis II gave him ground in the forest of Jumièges. Here he founded a monastery in 654, and the community of Jumièges increased in a short time to a large number of monks. He also built a monastery for women, at Pavilly.

St Philibert, having some business at the court, boldly reproached Ebroin, mayor of the palace, for his many acts of injustice. This brought on him the vengeance of that minister, who slandered him to St Ouen ; in consequence Philibert was imprisoned for a time at Rouen and obliged to quit Jumièges. The saint then retired to Poitiers, and afterward to the little island of Herio, on the coast of Poitou, where he founded a monastery later called Noirmoutier. He likewise founded the priory of Quinçay, near Poitiers, the government of which he gave to St Achard, whom he afterwards made abbot of Jumièges. These he peopled with monks from his first foundation. He had a further responsibility put upon him when Ansoald, Bishop of Poitiers, founded a monastery at Luçon, which he put under the supervision of St Philibert, who was remembered for his concern for the spiritual and temporal welfare of the lay neighbours of his various houses.

There is an early life of St Philibert which has been printed both by Mabillon and in the *Acta Sanctorum*, August, vol. iv. But the best text and the most valuable contribution to the subject is that of R. Poupardin, *Monuments de l'histoire des abbayes de Saint-Philibert* (1905), which contains a discussion of the authorship and recensions of the life, as well as the record of the miracles of St Philibert, and much supplementary matter.

BD MARY DE MATTIAS, Virgin, Foundress of the Sisters Adorers of the Precious Blood   (A.D. 1866)

WHEN Mary de Mattias began the work that was to develop into a congregation for adoration of the Precious Blood of Christ and the education of children she met a requirement of her time, which needed, in the words of Pope Pius XI, " a general reform, especially by way of better instruction of minds and a renewed purifying of habits ".

Born in 1805, Mary was the eldest of the four children of a lawyer, John de Mattias, and Octavia de Angelis his wife, who lived at Vallecorsa on the borders of Lazio and Campania.   Shortly after her seventeenth birthday St Caspar del Bufalo gave a mission in the parish church, which was the occasion of her hearing a definite call to some special work for the good of souls.   And within a little time she had come to know the Venerable John Merlini, disciple of St Caspar and his successor at the head of the Missioners of the Precious Blood ; he became her director and adviser, and remained so for the rest of her life.

In 1834 Mary accepted an invitation from her bishop, Mgr Lais, who was also the administrator of Anagni, to take charge of a school at Acuto in that diocese. She went there determined not simply to be a school-mistress but to establish a religious house as well.   In the following year came her first recruit, Anne Farrotti, and they committed themselves to the foundation of a congregation under the inspiration of the example of Canon del Bufalo's missioners.   Mary had already begun to extend her activities from school-children to older girls and to married women.   Six more recruits soon followed.

Mary de Mattias, like St Lucy Filippini, had a great gift of easy and convincing speech, which she used to much advantage in her catechetical and biblical instructions and in the girls' and women's societies that she organized ; and at the end of 1837 she began to conduct " spiritual exercises " for mothers of families, which were a great success.   This evoked the inevitable unfavourable comment and invoking of 1 Corinthians xiv 34 (though they were not in fact held in the church), but after due inquiry Bishop Muccioli approved.   When women began to attend the May devotions in the school the parish-priest objected and put a stop to it : but Mary was vindicated by the rural dean, much to the joy of the mothers.   The canonical process of her beatification makes it plain that Mary's eloquence really was such : she loved quiet and silence, " She was not loquacious ".

In 1840 a second school was taken over, under the auspices of the Missioners of the Precious Blood, in Mary's old home at Vallecorsa, and other foundations followed, the work for adult women and girls increasing at the same time.   Between 1847 and 1851 two houses were founded in Rome itself through the interest of a Russian widow, Princess Zena Volkonska ; and there two English prelates, Mgr George Talbot and Mgr (later cardinal) Edward Howard, became her good friends. It is recorded of an English member of the congregation that Mother de Mattias had gently to rebuke her for her endless boasting about English politeness : " Calvary is the school of good manners ", she said.

The rapid expansion of the Sisters Adorers of the Precious Blood of course did not take place without difficulties and disappointments, so many trials for the faith and spiritual integrity of Mother de Mattias. But at last her robust energy began to tire and her health to weaken, and she died at Rome on August 20, 1866, in her sixty-first year. At the time of her beatification in 1950 her congregation had nearly 400 establishments, many of them in the United States and other countries, including schools of all grades and kinds.

The first biography of Bd Mary de Mattias was by Don Merlini. A full official life was published in Rome in 1950, written by a Benedictine, Dame M. Eugenia Pietromarchi.

21 : ST JANE FRANCES DE CHANTAL, WIDOW, CO-FOUNDRESS OF THE ORDER OF THE VISITATION   (A.D. 1641)

THE father of St Jane de Chantal was Bénigne Frémyot, president of the *parlement* of Burgundy. M. Frémyot was left a widower whilst his children were yet in their infancy ; but he took such care of their education that nothing was wanting for forming them in the practice of every religious duty and preparing them for life. Jane, who at her confirmation was called Frances, profited above the rest and was tenderly beloved by her father, who gave her in marriage when she was twenty years of age to Christopher de Rabutin, Baron de Chantal, then twenty-seven years old, an officer in the French army and an accomplished but penitent duellist ; on his mother's side he was descended from Bd Humbeline, whose feast is kept on this same day. The marriage was solemnized at Dijon, and a few days after Jane Frances went with her husband to his seat at Bourbilly. She found an estate and household which since the death of her husband's mother had not been much accustomed to regularity, and the baroness made it her first care to establish order and good management. After three children had died soon after birth, they were blessed with a boy and three girls who throve. Nothing which the world could afford was wanting to complete their happiness, and they strove to be worthy of God's blessings. When someone commented on the baroness's modest clothes when her husband was away, she replied, " The eyes which I want to please are a hundred leagues from here " ; and the remark of St Francis de Sales was as true in the early days as when he made it, " In Madame de Chantal I have found the valiant woman whom Solomon had difficulty in finding in Jerusalem."

But the happiness of Bourbilly lasted only nine years. One day in the year 1601 M. de Chantal, in company with a friend, went out shooting ; the circumstances are not known, but accidentally M. d'Aulézy shot him in the thigh. He survived nine days, during which he suffered great pain from the efforts of an unskilful surgeon and received the sacraments with edifying resignation. Madame de Chantal's life, thoughts and actions were bound up in her beloved husband, and when she was left a widow at twenty-eight years of age her grief is not to be expressed ; for four months she was sunk in dejection, until she was roused by a letter from her father, who reminded her of her obligations towards her children. To testify her perfect forgiveness of him who had been the cause of her husband's death, she did him every good office in her power, and stood godmother to one of his children. She doubled her alms, and divided her time between the instruction and care of her children, her prayers and her work. It was her earnest and continual prayer that God would show her a truly holy guide, by whom she might be instructed in what manner she might best accomplish His will. One day when she was speaking to our Lord on this matter, she saw suddenly a man of the same stature and features as St Francis de Sales, dressed just as he was the first time she saw him afterwards at Dijon.   Another time, being in a little wood, she seemed to be trying to get into a church that was near, but in vain.   Here it was given her to understand that divine love must consume all the rust of self-love in her, and that she should meet with a great many troubles, both from within and without.

During the year of her mourning her father sent for her to his house at Dijon, where she lived with her children until she had to go with them to Monthelon, near Autun, to live with the old Baron de Chantal, who was then seventy-five years of age.   She gave up her beautiful and deeply-loved Bourbilly for an unprepossessing *château*, occupied by a vain, fierce and extravagant old man and ruled by an insolent housekeeper of bad reputation.   Jane never let fall a word of complaint, and, though she was never allowed to take her rightful place in the house, her compliance in everything was cheerful and agreeable.   It happened in 1604 that St Francis de Sales came to preach the Lent at Dijon, and she went to stay with her father there that she might have the opportunity of hearing so celebrated a preacher.   She at once recognized him as the person she had seen in vision and knew him to be the spiritual director she had long begged of God to send her.   St Francis dined frequently at her father's house, and she gained a great confidence in him.   It was her wish to put her difficulties before him, but she was hindered by a scruple on account of a vow she had made by the advice of an indiscreet religious, her director, not to address herself to any other than to himself for spiritual advice.   She, however, took care to profit by the presence of the bishop, and he in his turn was greatly impressed by and attracted to her.   One day, seeing her dressed better than usual, he said, " Madam, do you wish to marry again ? "   " No, indeed, my lord ! " she replied.   " Very well ", he said with a smile, " but then you should pull down your flag."   She took the hint.

The perplexities about her indiscreet vow being removed, she prevailed on St Francis after some difficulty to undertake her direction.   By his advice she regulated her devotions and other exercises so as to conform herself to what she owed to the world whilst she lived in the houses of her father and father-in-law.   In this she was so successful that the significant remark was made, " Madam prays always, and yet is never troublesome to anybody ".   She followed a strict rule of life, devoting much time to her children, and visited the poor that were sick in the neighbourhood and watched whole nights by those that were dying.   The sweetness and mildness of her temper showed how she had already co-operated with the grace of God ; Madame de Chantal was by nature strong, firm and forceful, but there was a certain hardness and rigidity in her character which was only removed by long years of prayer, suffering and patient guidance.   And this was the work, under God, of St Francis de Sales, whom she visited at Annecy and who corresponded freely with her.   He strictly limited her bodily mortifications, reminding her that St Charles Borromeo, " a man with a true spirit of liberty acting from charity ", did not disdain to drink toasts with his hearty neighbours, and that St Ignatius Loyola ate meat on a Friday on the bare word of his doctor, " when a narrow man would have argued about it for at least three days ".   He never allowed her to forget that she was still a woman in the world, an old man's daughter, and, above all, a mother ; he spoke much to her about her children's upbringing and softened her tendency to over-strictness in their regard, so that they profited almost as much from his friendship as their mother did.

For some time various considerations, including the presence of Carmelite nuns at Dijon, inclined Madame de Chantal to enter a cloister. When she had talked to St Francis about this he took some time to recommend the matter to God, and at length in 1607 he unfolded his project of forming a new establishment, a congregation of the Visitation of the Virgin Mary. St Jane welcomed the proposal with joy ; but the grief of her aged father, the requirements of her children, and the situation of the affairs of her family, raised great obstacles and gave her much suffering. To the objection that the obligation which Madame de Chantal owed her children could not be complied with unless she remained with them in the world, St Francis replied that they were no longer infants and that in a cloister she would be able to watch over them with no less vigilance, and perhaps even with greater advantage to them, than by continuing always with them, especially as the two eldest were about to go " into the world " ; and these and other objections were eventually overcome.

Before she left the world St Jane Frances married her eldest daughter to St Francis's brother, the young Baron de Thorens. Her two younger daughters she determined to take with her : one died in a short time ; the other she afterwards married to M. de Toulonjon. Her son, Celse-Bénigne, was fifteen years old, and him she left under the care of her father and of tutors. At Dijon she had to bid adieu to all her friends, and as she came to leave the room Celse-Bénigne, who had tried in vain to shake her resolution at the last moment, threw himself to the ground across the doorway in a paroxysm of grief. Here was a last inducement to choose the easier way, and stay ; she chose the harder—and stepped over his body. In the porch her aged father was waiting. She fell on her knees with streaming eyes and asked him to bless her. He laid his hands on her head and said, " I cannot blame you for what you do. You go with my consent, and I offer you to God, a daughter dear to me as ever Isaac was to Abraham. Go where God calls you. I shall be happy, knowing you are in His house. Pray for me." St Francis having provided a house, called the Gallery House, on the edge of the lake at Annecy, he inaugurated his convent on Trinity Sunday, 1610. With St Jane Frances were clothed two other sisters, Mary Favre and Charlotte de Bréchard, and a servant, Anne Coste, and they were soon joined by ten others. So far the institute had no name, and indeed the founder had no certain idea of its scope, except that it was to be a haven for those whose health, age or other considerations debarred them from the already established orders, and that he wished the sisters to be unenclosed and so more free to undertake work for souls and bodies.

It encountered much opposition, from the usual failure of the narrow and unimaginative to understand anything new. St Francis changed the plan of the congregation so far as to make it an enclosed religious order, under the Rule of St Augustine, to which he added constitutions admirable in their wisdom and moderation, " not too easy for the strong, nor too hard for the weak ". But he refused to give up the name, " of the Visitation of Our Lady ", which he had chosen for his nuns, and St Jane Frances urged him to make no concessions at all. St Francis would have the two sister virtues of humility and meekness to be the basis of the rule. " In the practice of virtues ", said he to St Jane Frances and her religious sisters, " let humility be the source of all the rest ; let it be without bounds ; make it the reigning principle of all your actions. Let an unalterable meekness and sweetness on all occasions become by habit natural to you." He wrote specifically for St Jane and her more experienced sisters his famous treatise *On the Love of God*.

One saint so far profited by the direction of the other saint that Mother de Chantal, who was fast progressing on the mystical road, was allowed to make a vow always to do what was the more perfect in the sight of God. And she faithfully and prudently governed her community in the spirit of their founder and director.

The affairs of her children and the foundation of new convents obliged her often to leave Annecy. The year after she took the habit, upon the death of her father, she went to Dijon and stayed there some months to settle his affairs and place her son in a college. While at Dijon St Jane Frances was tormented by her relatives to return to the world. " Why do you bury yourself like that under two yards of bombasine ? That ridiculous veil should be torn to bits ! " exclaimed one excitable lady. St Francis de Sales wrote the last word : " If you had married again, some gentleman from the farthest end of Gascony or Brittany, you would have had to leave your family—and no one would have made a single objection. . . ." After convents had been established at Lyons, Moulins, Grenoble and Bourges, St Francis from Paris sent for Mother de Chantal to see about a foundation there, which she was able to bring about in 1619 in the face of open hostility and underhand intriguing ; God strengthened and comforted her under it, and her meekness and patience gained her the admiration of those who had been her bitter adversaries. She governed her convent at Paris for three years, during which St Vincent de Paul directed it at the request of St Francis, and she made the acquaintance of Angélique Arnauld, abbess of Port-Royal, who failed to get permission to resign her office and join the Visitation Order.

In 1622 the death of St Francis was a grievous affliction to her, which her resignation to the divine will made her bear with unshaken constancy ; his body was buried in the church of her convent at Annecy. In 1627 her son was killed fighting against the English and the Huguenots in the isle of Ré, in his thirty-first year, leaving his wife with a daughter not a year old, who became the celebrated Madame de Sévigné. St Jane received this news with heroic fortitude ; she offered her heart to God, saying, " Destroy, cut, burn, whatever opposes thy holy will ". During the following year a terrible plague ravaged France, Savoy and Piedmont, causing great suffering to several Visitation convents. When it reached Annecy St Jane Frances refused to leave the town, put all the resources of her convent at the disposal of the sick, and whipped up the local authorities to greater efforts on behalf of the sufferers. In 1632 came the news of the death of Celse-Bénigne's widow, and then of her much-loved son-in-law, Antony de Toulonjon, and of Michael Favre, the confessor of St Francis and a close and devoted friend of the Visitandines. To these bereavements were added interior anguish, darkness and spiritual dryness which she sometimes experienced to a terrible degree, as appears from several of her letters. Thus does God suffer those souls which are most dear to Him seemingly to lose themselves and wander in mists and darkness, amid disturbance of mind. Yet these are certain and direct paths to happiness, and lead to the source and centre of all light.

During the years 1635–36 St Jane Frances made a visitation of the convents of the order, which now numbered sixty-five and many of which had never seen their spiritual mother ; and in 1641 she went into France on an errand of charity to Madame de Montmorency. It was her last journey. She was invited to Paris by the queen, Anne of Austria, and to her distress was treated there with great distinction and honour. On her return she fell ill on the road, in her convent at Moulins. There it was that she died on December 13, 1641, being sixty-nine years old.   Her body was taken to Annecy and buried near St Francis de Sales ; she was canonized in 1767.   St Vincent de Paul said of her : " She was full of faith, and yet all her life long had been tormented by thoughts against it.   While apparently enjoying that peace and easiness of mind of souls who have reached a high state of virtue, she suffered such interior trials that she often told me her mind was so filled with all sorts of temptations and abominations that she had to strive not to look within herself, for she could not bear it : the sight of her own soul horrified her as if it were an image of Hell.   But for all that suffering her face never lost its serenity, nor did she once relax in the fidelity God asked of her.   And so I regard her as one of the holiest souls I have ever met on this earth."

Apart from her own writings and correspondence and the letters of St Francis de Sales, by far the most important source for any biography of St Jane Frances is the volume of *Mémoires* of Mother de Chaugy.   This book rightly forms the first of the eight volumes which make up the collection *Sainte Chantal, sa vie et ses œuvres* (1874–79).   St Francis's letters have been completely edited in the imposing series of his works (20 vols.) published by the Visitation nuns at Annecy, and these, of course, are of great importance in the light they shed upon the origins of the order.   Moreover, the foundress has been fortunate in finding an almost ideal biographer in modern times : the *Histoire de Sainte Chantal et des origines de la Visitation* by Mgr Bougaud (Eng. trans., 1895), is generally acknowledged to be a *chef-d'œuvre* in hagiographical literature.   Besides this there is an able sketch, *Sainte Chantal*, in the series " Les Saints ", by Henri Bremond ; and the same author has devoted many pages to the saint's spiritual influence and inspiration in his *Histoire littéraire du sentiment religieux en France :* see especially vol. i, pp. 68–127, and vol. ii, pp. 537–584. An interesting episode in St Chantal's story has been treated by A. Gazier, *Jeanne de Chantal et Angélique Arnauld d'après leur correspondance* (1915).   See also a selection of her letters published in English in 1918, a short biography by Emily Bowles in the Quarterly Series, a life by E. K. Sanders (1918), and popular accounts by Janet M. Scott and H. J. Heagney (1950).

SS. LUXORIUS, CISELLUS AND CAMERINUS, MARTYRS
(A.D. 303 ?)

ACCORDING to the unreliable *acta* of these martyrs Luxorius was a Roman soldier who, being able to read, had seen a psalter and was greatly impressed by its contents. When he read in Psalm 85, " There is none among the gods like unto thee, O Lord, and there is none according to thy works.   All the nations thou hast made shall come and adore before thee, O Lord, and they shall glorify thy name ; for thou art great and dost wonderful things : thou art God alone ", he saw that such a god was none other than the Christians' God.   He made the next verse his own, " Conduct me, O Lord, in thy way and I will walk in thy truth ", clumsily he made the sign of the cross upon himself, and made his way to a church, and there heard them singing Psalm 118 : " Give bountifully to thy servant, enliven me, and I shall keep thy words.   Open thou my eyes. . . ."   He borrowed more of the sacred books, and learned the psalms and the words of the prophets by heart, and when at last he was permitted to read the gospels his soul was enlightened by faith, and he believed in Jesus Christ and was baptized.

At that time the persecution of the Emperor Diocletian broke out and Delphius the prefect began to enforce the imperial decrees in Sardinia, where Luxorius was stationed.   The soldier was one of the first to be brought before him, and with him two young boys, Cisellus and Camerinus, still wearing the white garments of baptism.   Delphius ordered Luxorius to deny Christ, and he refused.   So he was tied to a post and scourged, and while this was done he sang psalms, to glorify God, to keep his mind off his own sufferings, and to put heart into his two small companions.   And when he could not move them, Delphius had them all three put to death by the sword.   This martyrdom took place at Forum Trajanum.

It is to be feared that we can be assured of nothing more than the fact of the martyr's existence and early *cultus*.   The story of the two boy companions who suffered with Luxorius seems to be a mere embellishment.   The place of martyrdom, Forum Trajanum, makes one think of Rome, but it is the name of a township in Sardinia now known as Fordingiano. See the *Acta Sanctorum*, August, vol. iv ; and CMH., pp. 454–455.

SS. BONOSUS and MAXIMIAN, Martyrs   (A.D. 363)

THE Emperor Julian the Apostate commanded the cross and monogram of Jesus Christ which Constantine had placed on the standard of the army to be struck off, and had the standards reduced to the form used under the pagan emperors.   There were in the Herculean cohort at Antioch two officers, zealous Christians, named Bonosus and Maximian, who refused to change their standard.   The emperor's uncle, Count Julian, commanded them to give their troops the new ensign, and to worship the same gods which he and the emperor worshipped.   Bonosus answered, " We cannot worship gods which have been made by the hands of men ", and refused to give up the standard to be altered.   The *comes* ordered him to be tied up, and three hundred lashes to be given him.   Under this Bonosus only smiled, and made no answer when asked if he would obey.   The *comes* then turned to Maximian, who said, " Let your gods first hear and speak to you, and then we will worship them ".   Julian then had them both racked, but when he asked again if they would obey, they answered, " We cannot obey the emperor in these matters, because we have before our eyes the invisible God in whom we trust ".   Count Julian threatened the martyrs in a second and a third interrogation, but they answered they were Christians and were determined to continue such.   The *comes* was for having them tortured again ;   but the prefect Secundus, himself a pagan, absolutely refused to hear of it ;   Julian therefore condemned Bonosus and Maximian to be beheaded.

There is tacked on to the narrative of the trial and death of these martyrs an account of the last days of Count Julian, in its details manifestly false.   He is represented as suffering from a disease as revolting as it is impossible ;   his Christian wife tells him in effect that it serves him right, and urges him to bear the hand of the Lord gladly ;   and he dies miserably, but calling on the name of the one God. Alban Butler takes the opportunity for a dissertation on the death of a sinner, which is here omitted together with the occasion of it.

Although the text of this Latin *passio* is printed by Ruinart amongst his *Acta sincera*, we lack any satisfactory guarantee of its authenticity.   There seems to be no oriental *cultus*, though the martyrs suffered at Antioch.   See, however, P. Allard, *Julien l'Apostat*, vol. iii, p. 153.   Dom Leclercq, in his collection *Les Martyrs*, vol. iii, pp. 99–104, has printed a translation of the whole document.

ST SIDONIUS APOLLINARIS, Bishop of Clermont (A.D. 479 ?)

GAIUS SOLLIUS APOLLINARIS SIDONIUS, soldier, poet, statesman, country gentleman, and eventually bishop, was born at Lyons about the year 430, and was of one of the most noble families in Gaul, where his father and grandfather, both named Apollinaris, had been prefects of the praetorium.   He was educated in arts and learning under the best masters, and was one of the most celebrated orators and poets of the age in which he lived.   From his letters it is clear that he was always religious, extremely affectionate, beneficent and compassionate ; on the other hand, he was no rigorous censor, for at a time when Salvian was writing so fiercely of the corruption of southern Gaul, St Sidonius did not raise his voice in vituperation of the iniquities of his times.   He married Papianilla, by whom he had a son and three daughters.   Papianilla was daughter of Avitus, who was raised to the imperial throne at Rome in 455 ; Sidonius wrote a panegyric in honour of his father-in-law, who returned the compliment by putting a statue of him among the poets in the Forum of Trajan.   Avitus, a weak person if no worse, was made to resign the purple after a reign of ten months, and he died on the road to Auvergne.   Majorian, his successor, captured Lyons and threatened severe treatment for the citizens ; but after a time of eclipse and uncertainty Sidonius wrote a panegyric of him too. The new emperor was slain in 461 by Ricimer the Goth, who placed the diadem upon the head of Severus.   Upon this revolution Sidonius left the court, and retired to Auvergne.   Severus was poisoned by Ricimer after a reign of four years, and Anthemius was chosen emperor in 467.   Sidonius went again to Rome, on business of his province ; and hoping for a revival of the empire he wrote another very encouraging panegyric.   The feeble emperors of this age were peculiarly susceptible to compliments, and the poet was made prefect of the city.   But his hopes of Anthemius came to nothing, the position in Rome was difficult, and he returned to Gaul, to his wife and family and the enjoyment of his estates.

Sidonius was soon called from these secular dignities to responsibilities in the Church.   The bishopric of Arvernum, since called Clermont in Auvergne, falling vacant, the people of that diocese and the bishops of the country demanded that he should fill the episcopal office ; they were conscious not only of his high character and abilities, but also of the fact that he was the man best qualified to uphold Gallo-Roman power against the Visigoths.   St Sidonius was very unwilling, deploring his unfitness, but eventually acquiesced ; and from that moment he renounced lighter poetry, which till then had been his delight, to apply himself to those studies which were more required by his ministry.   He was no stranger to them whilst a layman, and he soon became an authority whom other bishops consulted in their difficulties ; he was always reserved and unwilling to decide things and referred them to others, alleging that he was not capable of acting the part of a teacher among the brethren whose direction and knowledge he himself stood in need of.   St Lupus of Troyes, who had always loved and honoured him, on his being made a bishop wrote a letter of congratulation and advice, in which among other things he told him : " It is no longer by show and a stately household that you are to keep up your rank, but by deep humility of heart.   You are placed above others, but must see yourself as below the meanest and last in your flock.   Be ready to kiss the feet of those whom formerly you would not have thought worthy to sit at your own.   You must make yourself the servant of all."

And so St Sidonius did.   He kept a frugal table, fasted every second day and, though of a delicate constitution, seemed to carry his austerities to excess.   He looked upon it as a principal duty to provide for the instruction, comfort and assistance of the poor.   In the time of a great famine he maintained at his own charge, with the charitable help of Ecdicius, his wife's brother, more than four thousand Burgundians and other strangers who had been driven from their own country by misery and necessity ; and when the scarcity was over he helped to send them to their homes.   His reputation was such that, being summoned to Bourges when that see, which was his metropolitan church, was vacant in 472, the assembled prelates referred the election of a bishop to him, and he nominated one Simplicius.   He says that a bishop ought to do by humility what a monk and a penitent are obliged to do by their profession, and he gives an account of Maximus, Bishop of Toulouse, whom he had before known as a very rich man of the world : he found him in his new spiritual dignity wholly changed ; his clothes, mien and conversation savoured of nothing but modesty and piety ; he had short hair and a long beard ; his household stuff was plain ; he had wooden benches, stuff curtains, a bed without feathers, and a table without a covering ; and the food of his household consisted of pulse more than flesh.

Clermont being threatened by Euric, King of the Visigoths, who then controlled the southern provinces of France, the bishop encouraged the people to oppose them. He put his brother-in-law Ecdicius in charge of the defence and instituted rogation processions to implore the mercy of God.   But in 474 Clermont fell ; his previous activities exposed St Sidonius to the reprisals of the conquerors after they were masters of the place, and for a time he was exiled to a fortress near Carcassone. Here he was lodged next door to two bad-tempered old women, who made such a noise that he could neither sleep nor read : " Never ", complained the poor man, " were two such quarrelsome, restless and abusive chatterers ! "   When he was restored to his see he continued to be the protection and support of his people, though grievously troubled by the Goths.   He died in peace in 479, or possibly a decade later.

St Sidonius Apollinaris was one of the principal writers of the beginning of the second age of Christian literature, or he may be regarded as the last of the Gallo-Roman school.   His poetry is inflated and tiresome, but his letters are a valuable witness to the life of Christian gentlemen in southern Gaul during the break-up of the empire ; they were sportsmen, with a taste for literature and the other fine arts, whose Christianity sat rather lightly upon them but was not insincere.   The saint shows us himself in his secular days in Auvergne joining in the recreations, physical and intellectual, of his neighbours ; looking after his estates and the material and moral well-being of his slaves ; and caring for his children : he warns his son against loose talk, forbids *vaudeville* in his house, and declines an invitation to go fishing because his daughter Severiana has a bad feverish cold.   Sidonius Apollinaris may at a first glance seem a surprising character to find in the Roman Martyrology ; as Father M. Van Cutsem has written, he " is one of the many bishops who have reached the honours of the altar because they left no unhappy memory behind and their anniversary was entered in the *Depositio episcoporum* ".

The greater part of our information concerning Sidonius is derived from his letters and other writings.   The best text is that edited in MGH., *Auctores Antiquissimi*, vol. viii. There is an excellent short biography by Paul Allard in the series " Les Saints " (1910) and a longer one in two volumes by the Abbé Chaix (1866).   An English version of the letters of Sidonius was published by O. M. Dalton in 1915, and another by W. B. Anderson in 1936.   An unusually long article has been devoted to him in DCB., vol. iv, pp. 649–661.   See C. E. Stevens, *Sidonius Apollinaris and His Age* (1935).

BD HUMBELINE, MATRON   (A.D. 1135)

BD HUMBELINE was born in 1092, the year after her brother St Bernard, with whom she was always on terms of intimate friendship.   Like him she was of great physical beauty, and had a lovely voice and was skilled in music ; in due course she married a nobleman of the house of Lorraine, Guy de Marcy. Some years after the founding of Clairvaux she went to visit Bernard there and in due course arrived, very stylishly dressed and surrounded by an imposing train of attendants. When St Bernard was told that the Lady Humbeline had come, and with what array, he was not at all pleased and refused to see her : he knew his sister and disapproved of her display, and perhaps thought she was " showing off ", travelling in that style. She at once guessed what had upset him, or, as tradition says, her brother Andrew told her, roughly enough, and she sent in a message that if he would come out she would do just as he told her ; and out of enclosure St Bernard accordingly came. Humbeline's life in the world was more notable for dancing than devotion, and it was Bernard's opinion that the balance needed redressing ; he took the opportunity presented, and gently reasoned with her, particularly reminding her of the virtuous and devoted life of their mother, Aleth. This had its effect (even a sister would hesitate about arguing with a St Bernard), and Humbeline went away, considerably chastened.

A few years later this interview at Clairvaux had a more unexpected result, when Humbeline got her husband's consent to her becoming a nun. She went to the monastery of the nuns at that Jully near Troyes which is called " les-Nonnains " after them ; here her sister-in-law Elizabeth was abbess, and when she left to found a convent near Dijon, Bd Humbeline was appointed in her place. She practised severe physical austerities and when her nuns urged her to moderate them she replied, " That is all very well for you, my sisters, who have been serving God in religion all your lives. But I have lived so long in the world and of the world that no penance can be too much for me." In her last illness three of her brothers, Bernard, Andrew and Nivard, hurried to her bedside, and she died in Bernard's arms in 1135 (or 1136). The *cultus* of Bd Humbeline was approved in 1703.

There is no early life of Bd Humbeline. A short account of her is given in the *Acta Sanctorum*, August, vol. iv, and she stands first in the group of holy women whose history is traced by Henriquez in his *Lilia Cisterciensium* (1633) ; but almost all lives of St Bernard devote more or less space to his relations with his only sister.

ST ABRAHAM OF SMOLENSK, ABBOT   (A.D. 1221)

THIS Abraham has a place apart among the saints of pre-Tartar Russia. He was born at Smolensk during the later part of the twelfth century. While a youth he lost his parents, whereupon he gave away his goods to the needy and became a monk and priest of the Bogoroditskaya monastery at his birthplace. He was like St Theodosius Pechersky in his reverence for St Sabas and the early monks of Palestine, in his insistence on personal poverty, and in his combining the active with the contemplative life, not only doing much manual work within the monastery but preaching and helping the poor and sick outside as well. But Abraham took no part in secular affairs, and further differed from Theodosius in his studiousness. He copied manuscripts, and became a learned and industrious interpreter of the Holy Scriptures and an energetic and vigorous preacher ; he was full of zeal for God's house and the beauty of divine worship, and " strictly forbade talking in church ", especially during the Holy Sacrifice. More remarkable still, for that time and place, he celebrated the eucharistic Liturgy every day.

What distinguished St Abraham from his contemporaries was his sternness and austerity, both in precept and practice : " he slept but little ; kneeling and weeping abundant tears, he beat his breast and called upon God, imploring the Lord to have mercy on His people and to turn away His wrath." His preaching was marked by prophetic solemnity and concern with the " last things " ; he was tireless in his calls to repentance and his warnings of the end of the world and its judgement.* The influence St Abraham exerted was very great, especially among lay people, but his teaching aroused the opposition of some among the clergy and monks ; and, after his abbot had forbidden him to teach and he had suffered " many annoyances ", Abraham migrated to the Holy Cross monastery in Smolensk.

But here things got worse, and the whole city began to turn against him. There is no doubt that the more ignorant of the clergy were jealous of his learning and popularity as a spiritual director, and they stirred up others. Charges were made against St Abraham " on account of women ", of heresy, of claiming to be a prophet, of reading impious books. Eventually he was arrested, dragged through a jeering mob, and on successive days brought before two different tribunals : the first, composed of laymen, acquitted him, and it does not seem certain that the second, of clerics, found him guilty either. But the bishop of Smolensk, Ignatius, sent him back to his first monastery and he was inhibited from celebrating the Holy Mysteries.

There were not wanting those who foretold disaster for Smolensk because of its mistreatment of an innocent and holy man ; and when the city was afflicted with a serious drought Bishop Ignatius decided to re-examine the case of Abraham. The result of his deliberations was to decide that the accusations were all false, and St Abraham was reinstated, with the request that he should pray for the city. " He had not even reached his cell ", writes Ephrem, " before God sent rain." The persecution had lasted for five years, during which he was " insulted and vilified as if he were a felon ". The bishop asked Abraham's forgiveness for the injustice to which he had been a party, and after a time made him abbot of the small monastery of the Mother of God. It was not a very desirable charge, for the monks were few and old and of poor repute ; but St Abraham gladly accepted it, and there spent the rest of his life in peace. He again took up his former work of the ministry of the word and of spiritual wisdom, and died in the year 1221, loved and respected by all. He had been a monk for fifty years, and was stern and uncompromising to the last as he " in great humility and sorrow of heart reminded himself with sighs and groans of the separation of soul from body ".

The contemporary biographer Ephrem says that at St Abraham's trial " God softened the hearts of the prince and the rulers, but the abbots and priests would gladly have eaten him alive ". The less ignorant and malicious among these clergy were probably disturbed by some of St Abraham's biblical exegesis, for that was his great interest, especially as regards the " last things " and their practical significance for human souls. Ephrem repeatedly refers to the divine grace that was given Abraham " not only to read but to interpret, so that nothing in the sacred writings could be hidden from him ". It is not known what the challenged speculations were, nor the nature of the unorthodox books St Abraham was accused of studying, for little of his teaching has come down to us, except one sermon, on the Heavenly Powers, and it is not certain that that is his, though without doubt it reflects his spiritual background accurately, a background wherein mercilessness is regarded as almost the worst of sins and the consummation of the Last Judgement

---

* St Abraham painted two *eikons* : both were concerned with the Last Judgement, the Terrible Judgement as it is called in Russia.

is the transfiguration of the physical earth.   What remains certain is that " Many came to St Abraham from the city, and passed from sin to repentance ".

For bibliographical notes on Russian saints, see under St Sergius on September 25, especially Fedotov's *Russian Religious Mind* there referred to, to which most of the above is indebted.   There are in existence only two detailed *vitae* of pre-Mongol Russian saints, that of this St Abraham being one of them.

BD BERNARD TOLOMEI, ABBOT, FOUNDER OF THE BENEDICTINES OF MONTE OLIVETO   (A.D. 1348)

THIS holy founder was born at Siena in 1272 and was baptized John.   He was educated by his uncle, a Dominican friar, and at the local university ; after receiving his doctorate in law he took up public work in Siena and fulfilled several municipal offices.   He was always a devout man ; but he seems to have undergone some sort of sudden " conversion ", for in 1312 instead of a lecture on philosophy he gave a sermon on contempt of the world, resigned his position and withdrew to a place ten miles from the city and lived there in solitude.   He was joined by two other Sienese, Ambrose Piccolomini and Patrick Patrizi, and the three lived together in the desert land between Siena and the woods of Mont' Amiata, where all was ash-coloured, sterile and desolate.   The reputation of the sanctity of their lives was marred by malicious or mistaken rumours (some thought them mad, others subversive), which caused them to be summoned before Pope John XXII at Avignon to give an account of themselves.   They were able to demonstrate their orthodoxy to the pope's satisfaction, but he instructed them to put themselves under one or other of the approved monastic rules.   They thereupon consulted Guy, Bishop of Arezzo, who gave them the Rule of St Benedict and instructed a Camaldolese monk to clothe them in the monastic habit—but white instead of the usual black.

John Tolomei, who was recognized as their leader, took the name of Bernard, their hermitage at Chiusuri was called Monte Oliveto, and the Benedictine congregation of our Lady of Monte Oliveto came into existence in 1319.   It professed a primitive observance of the rule, to which a number of austerities (including, at first, total abstinence from wine) were added, and its success was instantaneous. Within a few years Bd Bernard had founded a second monastery at Siena, and others followed elsewhere ; their penitential life continued to attract disciples and in 1344 the new congregation was confirmed by Pope Clement VI.   Some time afterwards a bad epidemic of plague broke out around Siena, and the Olivetan monks gave themselves up entirely to the care of the suffering and the burial of the dead ; it seemed as if they were miraculously preserved from contagion, but in August 1348 the first of them was struck down : it was their founder himself.   He died at Monte Oliveto on the 20th, the feast of his patron, St Bernard of Clairvaux. In 1644 the *cultus* of Bd Bernard Tolomei was confirmed, and his name appears in the Roman Martyrology with the title " Blessed " ; but he is venerated by the Olivetans, who still exist as a small independent congregation of Benedictines, as " Saint ", in accordance with the declaration of the Congregation of Sacred Rites that " he was worthy of veneration among the saints ".

The Bollandists in the *Acta Sanctorum*, August, vol. iv, give a long account of Bd Bernard, though there is no formal biography of early date.   The most valuable contribution to the history of the founder of the Olivetani is that of Dom Placid Lugano, *Origine e primordi dell' Ordine di Montoliveto* (1903), who, basing his work upon the relatively early chronicles of Antony de Barga and Alexander da Sesto, has stripped Bernard's life of its legendary accretions, notably of the story which attributes his religious vocation to the miraculous cure of sudden blindness. On the Olivetani as a reformed congregation see Heimbucher, *Orden und Kongregationen der Kath. Kirche*, vol. i, pp. 281–283.

22 : THE IMMACULATE HEART OF MARY

DEVOTION to our Lady's heart is analogous to that to the sacred heart of Jesus, and consists in veneration of her heart of flesh, united to her person, as representing her love, especially her love for her divine Son, her virtues and her inner life. Adumbrations of this devotion can be found in some early commentaries on the Song of Songs, but it was first considerably fostered by St John Eudes in the seventeenth century, and Pope Pius VII gave permission for a feast of the Pure Heart of Mary in 1805. In more recent times words attributed to our Lady at Fatima have had very strong influence in popularizing the devotion, and on October 31, 1942, Pope Pius XII consecrated the whole world to her immaculate heart ; shortly afterwards, on May 4, 1944, he directed that the corresponding feast should be observed throughout the Western church on the octave day of the Assumption.

Mary's office is universal ; " her natural title is that she is the mother of the Word made flesh, and her acquired title is that she gave her all with her Son in the anguish of her sorrows for the redemption of the world. In that work she was admitted as a partner in a very true sense, though we must always remember that she herself differs from her Son as the finite from the infinite, as the created from the uncreated. Moreover, she herself was redeemed and was full of grace at her conception precisely because of the redeeming merit of the Word Incarnate, whose mother she had been chosen to be. It is well to repeat these truths lest we offend the heavenly Mother by untoward exaggeration and careless expression which hinder rather than promote true Catholic piety and devotion " (Archbishop Godfrey).

See *Acta Apostolicae Sedis*, vol. xxxiv (1942), pp. 313–319, 345–346 ; vol. xxxvii (1945), pp. 44–52 ; and an article by Archbishop William Godfrey in the *Clergy Review*, vol. xxiii (1943), no. 5, pp. 193–199 ; Mgr Messner, *The Immaculate Heart* (1950) ; H. Keller, *The Heart of Mary* (1950).

SS. TIMOTHY, HIPPOLYTUS AND SYMPHORIAN, MARTYRS
(SECOND TO FOURTH CENTURIES)

ON this day the Church commemorates three martyrs totally unconnected with one another. ST TIMOTHY was a martyr under Diocletian, who was buried on the Ostian Way at Rome, opposite the basilica of St Paul-outside-the-Walls.

ST HIPPOLYTUS is described both in the lesson at Matins and in the Roman Martyrology as a bishop of Porto, a " man greatly renowned for his learning ", who, either at that place or at Ostia, was for his confession of the faith put to death by drowning ; and was buried in the place of his martyrdom. There is uncertainty as to who this martyr was, but it is possible that he is identical with the St Hippolytus who has been mentioned on the thirteenth of this month.

ST SYMPHORIAN suffered at Autun in the second or third century. The city of Autun was one of the most ancient and famous of Gaul, but at that time particularly addicted to the worship of Berecynthia (Cybele), Apollo and Diana. On a certain day of the year, the statue of Cybele was with great pomp carried through the streets in a chariot. Symphorian, because he had treated the image with disrespect, was seized by the mob and carried before Heraclius, governor of the province. Heraclius asked him why he refused to honour the image of the mother of the gods. He answered, because he was a Christian and worshipped the true God ; and that, moreover, if someone would give him a hammer he was prepared to break up their idol. To the judge this reply savoured of rebellion, as well as being impious, and he inquired of the officers whether he was a citizen of the place. One of them answered, " He is, and of a noble family ". The judge said to Symphorian, " You flatter yourself on account of your birth, or are perhaps unacquainted with the emperor's orders ". He then ordered the imperial edict to be read, and said to him, " What say you to this, Symphorian ? " The martyr continuing to express his abhorrence of the idol, Heraclius commanded him to be beaten, and sent him to prison. Later he was brought out and presented before the tribunal when, Symphorian still being firm, Heraclius condemned him to die by the sword for treason towards gods and men. As he was led out of the town to execution, his mother, standing on the wall of the city to see him pass by, cried out to him, " My son, my son Symphorian ! remember the living God and be of good courage. Fear not ! You go to a death which leads to certain life." His head was struck off and his body buried in a cave, near a fountain, and in the middle of the fifth century St Euphronius, Bishop of Autun, built over it a church in his honour.

The village and church of Veryan in Cornwall have their name from this martyr (Sci Simphoriani in 1278, Severian in 1545), the only church in Great Britain dedicated under his name.

The conjunction of these three wholly unconnected saints in one common prayer, such as that said in the Roman office and Mass on this day, is a curious liturgical feature. Originally the same prayer was said with the name of Timothy alone as may be seen in the Gregorian sacramentary ; the two other names have been subsequently inserted. Whatever may be thought of the story of St Timothy's martyrdom as recounted in the Acts of St Silvester, his name and his burial on the Ostian Way are entered in the *Depositio martyrum* of A.D. 354, not to speak of other early testimonies which Father Delehaye has set out in CMH., pp. 456–457. A mention of Timothy on this day in the famous Carthaginian calendar, and a statement in the chronicle known as " The Barbarus of Scaliger " that " Timothy the bishop gloriously suffered martyrdom at Carthage " has raised a doubt whether there may not be two Timothei ; just as the question of a second Hippolytus (of Porto) has been much discussed. Symphorian again is a martyr whose existence is established by very early allusions and dedications. On his respectable " acts ", printed by Ruinart and elsewhere, see W. Meyer, " Fragmenta Burana ", in the *Festschrift* published for the Göttingen Academy in 1901, pp. 161–163. Further references will be found in Delehaye's commentary just mentioned, pp. 456–458. See also G. H. Doble, *St Symphorian* (1931), in his Cornish Saints series.

ST SIGFRID, ABBOT OF WEARMOUTH   (A.D. 690)

WHILE St Benedict Biscop was away on his fifth visit to Rome his coadjutor abbot at Wearmouth, St Esterwine, died, and the monks, together with St Ceolfrid, coadjutor abbot of Jarrow, elected in his place the deacon Sigfrid. " He was " says St Bede, " a man well skilled in the knowledge of Holy Scripture, of admirable behaviour and perfect continence, but one in whom vigour of mind was somewhat depressed by bodily weakness and whose innocence of heart went along with a distressing and incurable affection of the lungs." Some three years after St

Sigfrid's promotion and St Benedict's return to his monasteries both saints were stricken with sickness and had to take to their beds ; they knew that death was upon them and wished for a last conference about one another's welfare and that of their monks.   Sigfrid therefore was carried on a stretcher to Benedict's cell and laid on his bed, " with their heads on the same pillow ", but they were too weak even to embrace one another unaided.   After consultation with Sigfrid, Benedict sent for Ceolfrid and, with the approval of all, appointed him abbot of both monasteries, that so peace, unity and concord might be preserved.   Two months later St Sigfrid, " having passed through the fire and water of temporal tribulation, was taken to the place of everlasting rest : sending up to the Lord the offerings of praise which his righteous lips had vowed, he entered the mansion of the heavenly Kingdom ".   He was buried in the abbey-church of St Peter beside his master, St Benedict, and his predecessor, St Esterwine.

All our information comes from Bede's *Historia Abbatum* and the anonymous history which covers the same ground.   See the text in C. Plummer and his notes.   It is very questionable how far saintship can be claimed in this and many similar cases.   There is no trace of any liturgical commemoration, not even so much as an entry in church calendars. *Cf.* Stanton's *Menology*, p. 405.

ST ANDREW OF FIESOLE   (NINTH CENTURY ?)

ACCORDING to his worthless *acta* of the fourteenth or fifteenth century this Andrew was a young Irishman who went on a pilgrimage to Rome with his teacher, St Donatus.   On their way back they stopped at Fiesole, where the episcopal see was vacant, and Donatus was miraculously designated to fill it ; he thereupon ordained Andrew deacon and made him his archdeacon.   In this office he served the Church faithfully and holily for some years.   He restored the church of St Martin, which had been destroyed by the Magyars, and founded the monastery there.   St Andrew had a sister called Brigid to whom he was greatly attached and who also is venerated near Fiesole ; she is said to have followed him to Italy and to have lived as a solitary among the mountains of Tuscany, but according to the legend of Andrew she was miraculously transplanted from Ireland to her brother's bedside while he lay dying.

The document which purports to recount the history of St Andrew is printed in the *Acta Sanctorum*, August, vol. iv.   It may be noted that Dom Gougaud in his *Gaelic Pioneers of Christianity* (1923) makes no mention of Andrew ; *cf.* his *Les saints irlandais hors d'Irlande* (1936), p. 77.   No Andrew is mentioned in the life of Donatus.

BB. WILLIAM LACEY AND RICHARD KIRKMAN, MARTYRS (A.D. 1582)

WILLIAM LACEY was born at Horton, near Settle, in the West Riding of Yorkshire ; he was married to the widow of a man of county family named Creswell, and was a lawyer holding an official position.   For long he was reputed to be a Papist at heart and after the visit of Dr (afterwards Cardinal) William Allen to the north of England in 1565 that suspicion became a certainty.   He almost at once lost his office and for fourteen years was subjected to bitter persecution, in which his wife nobly bore her part ; he was repeatedly fined, visited, examined, and once was imprisoned at Kingston-on-Hull, till he eventually fled from his house with his family, and was hunted from place to place.   At last Mrs Lacey broke down under the strain and was taken seriously ill ; this did not deter the archbishop of York, Dr Sandys, from taking steps to have her arrested as a recusant, but the good lady died first.

The next year, 1580, Lacey, already a man of considerable age, entered himself as a student at Rheims, and finally went to Rome, where he was ordained. He arrived in England in 1581, but was destined to work only some twelve months for the Catholics of his native Yorkshire. He, together with Bd William Hart, Mr Thomas Bell, and other priests, was in the habit of visiting the Catholic prisoners in York castle. Now Mr Bell had, before his ordination, been imprisoned and tortured for the faith in that castle, and he conceived the project of now singing a high Mass there, as an act of thanksgiving. In those days prisons were not the efficient institutions that they are today and a little money, carefully distributed to turnkeys, would go a long way. Early on Sunday, July 22, 1582, that Mass was sung in one of the prisoners' cells, with Mr Lacey and Mr Hart assisting as deacon and subdeacon. Just as it was over, an alarm was given and the authorities began to search the building ; Hart and Bell got away, but Lacey was captured. He was examined first by the mayor and then by Dr Sandys, by whom he was committed to solitary confinement in irons, and after three weeks was brought up for trial. His letter of orders was put in against him, and he openly avowed his priesthood (it was not at that time high treason for a priest to come into the country) ; when asked if he acknowledged the queen as head of the Church, he replied, " In this matter, as well as in all other things, I believe as the Catholic Church of God and all good Christians believe ". Whereupon he was convicted and sentenced. On August 22, Bd William Lacey was hanged, drawn and quartered at the Knavesmire, outside the city of York.

There suffered at the same time and place (they confessed to one another on the way to the scaffold) Bd Richard Kirkman, also a secular priest and a Yorkshireman. He was born at Addingham, near Skipton, and was ordained at Rheims in 1579. He appears to have been taken into the household of Robert Dymoke, hereditary Champion of England, at Scrivelsby in Lincolnshire, where he was tutor to Dymoke's three younger sons and pastor to the Catholics of the neighbourhood. After eleven months his patron and his wife were indicted for not going to the Protestant service (Dymoke died in prison for the faith), and Mr Kirkman had to leave Scrivelsby and seek refuge elsewhere. He worked in Yorkshire and Northumberland until he was arrested near Wakefield merely as a suspected person, but his chalice was found on him and he admitted that he was a priest. The very next day he was brought up at the York assizes, and sentenced to death. For four days he shared the cell of Bd William Lacey, but after a private interview with the sheriff and two ministers he was put into a dungeon alone, without light, food or bed. And here he was left till he was brought out to die.

See MMP., pp. 66–70 ; and B. Camm, LEM., vol. ii, pp. 564–588, with the authorities there cited.

BD JOHN KEMBLE, MARTYR   (A.D. 1679)

THIS martyr was the son of John Kemble, gentleman, of a family originally of Wiltshire, and Anne, one of the Morgans of Skenfrith, and was born in 1599, traditionally at Rhydicar farm in the parish of Saint Weonards, Herefordshire, though some say at Pembridge Castle nearby. They were a Catholic family, and there were four other related Kemble priests at this time. In some year unknown

John was smuggled abroad to Douay, where he was ordained in 1625 and in the same year sent on the mission to work in and around his birthplace. Of these labours nothing at all is known except that they extended over a period of fifty-three years, apparently unbroken save that in the archives of the Old Brotherhood of the Secular Clergy there is an entry in or about the year 1649 which suggests that he was then for a time in London ; it is known from the Westminster archives that in 1643 he was recommended as a suitable person to be made archdeacon of South Wales. During these years he gained that reputation for goodness which persisted among the folk of Monmouthshire almost to our own day and, with the help of the Jesuits at the Cwm in Llanrothal, he formed those mission centres, at the Llwyn, the Graig, Hilston, and elsewhere, which lingered on into the nineteenth century and are now represented only by a desolate burying-ground and a ruined chapel at Coed Anghred on a hill above Skenfrith. During most, if not all, of this time he. made his headquarters at Pembridge Castle, the home first of his brother George, and then of his nephew, Captain Richard Kemble. In 1678 the " Oates Plot " terror began and in the autumn it reached Herefordshire : the Cwm was sacked and John Kemble's friend David Lewis, s.j., was taken. He was urged to fly, but he would not : " According to the course of nature I have but a few years to live [he was just on eighty] ; it will be an advantage to suffer for my religion, and therefore I will not abscond."

In November Captain Scudamore of Kentchurch, for all his wife and children were Catholics and ministered to by Mr Kemble, went to Pembridge Castle, arrested the old priest, and dragged him off through the snow to Hereford gaol. There he remained four months, till the March assizes, at which he was condemned to be hanged, drawn and quartered, *pro Sacerd' Seminar.*, " for being a seminary priest ", as it is recorded in the Crown Book of the Oxford Circuit. On April 23 an order was signed for him and Bd David Lewis to be sent to London for examination by the Privy Council ; on the journey he " suffered more than a martyrdom on account of a great indisposition he had, which would not permit him to ride but sideways ; and it was on horseback he was compelled to perform the journey, at least a great part of the way ". " He was strapped like a pack to his horse going there, but allowed to walk most of the way on his journey back ", which he made a few weeks later : as he said at his execution, " Oates and Bedloe not being able to charge me with anything when I was brought up to London (though they were with me) makes it evident that I die only for professing the old Roman Catholic religion, which was the religion that first made this kingdom Christian . . .". That execution was ordered by Scroggs L.C.J., at the summer assizes, and its date fixed for August 22.

When the under-sheriff, one Digges, arrived at the jail Bd John asked for time first to finish his prayers and then to smoke a pipe of tobacco and have a drink. The governor and under-sheriff joined him, Digges in his turn delaying in order to finish *his* pipe.* Towards evening he was dragged on a hurdle to Widemarsh Common, where before a huge crowd he denied all knowledge of any plot and made a final profession of faith. He was allowed to hang till he was dead before the remainder of the sentence was carried out, but the hangman's work was so ill done that, old as he was, he lived for half-an-hour after the cart was withdrawn. With

---

* This curious and pleasing incident originated the Herefordshire custom of calling the last pipe of a sitting " the Kemble pipe ", a custom now fallen into disuse. *Cf.* the footnote on p. 394 of Sir John Hawkins's edition of Izaak Walton's *Compleat Angler* (1808), where Bd John Kemble is made a Protestant martyr under Queen Mary.

the exception of the left hand, now enshrined in the Catholic church at Hereford, Bd John's remains were buried under a flat stone in Welsh Newton churchyard, where they still lie.   The first miracle recorded at the intercession of Bd John was in favour of the daughter of his denouncer, Captain Scudamore, who was cured of an affection of her throat by applying to it the rope with which the martyr was hanged ; and Mgr Matthew Pritchard, Vicar Apostolic for the Western District in 1715, was present when Mrs Catherine Scudamore was cured of long-standing deafness while praying at his graveside.   Protestant witnesses of his execution " acknowledged that they never saw one die so like a gentleman and so like a Christian ", and Bd John Kemble has never been without local veneration ; the annual pilgrimage to his grave is said to have been uninterrupted since his martyrdom.

See MMP., pp. 555–557 ; T. P. Ellis, *Catholic Martyrs of Wales* (1932), pp. 126–129 ; B. Camm, *Forgotten Shrines* (1910), pp. 333–342 ; and an excellent C.T.S. pamphlet by J. H. Canning.   Sarah Siddons, *née* Kemble, was a great-great-grandniece of the martyr.

23 : ST PHILIP BENIZI   (A.D. 1285)

THIS principal ornament and propagator of the religious order of the Servites in Italy was of the noble families of Benizi and Frescobaldi in Florence, and a native of that city.   He was born on August 15, in the year 1233, which is said by some to be the very feast of the Assumption on which the seven Founders of the Servites had their first vision of our Lady.   His parents had been long married but childless, and Philip was a child of prayer.   At the age of thirteen he was sent to Paris to apply himself to the study of medicine, and Galen, though a heathen, was a strong spur to him in raising his heart from the contemplation of nature to the worship and praise of its Author.   From Paris he removed to Padua, where he took the degree of doctor in medicine and philosophy at the age of nineteen.   After his return to Florence he took some time to deliberate with himself what course to steer.   For a year he practised his profession, spending his leisure time in the study of sacred Scripture and the fathers and in prayer for guidance, especially before a certain crucifix in the abbey-church at Fiesole and before a picture of the Annunciation in the Servite chapel at Carfaggio, just outside the walls of Florence.

At this time the Servites, or Order of the Servants of Mary, had been established fourteen years, having been founded by seven gentlemen of Florence as described under their feast on February 12.   At their principal house on Monte Senario, six miles from Florence, they lived in little cells, something like the hermits of Camaldoli, possessing nothing but in common, and professing obedience to St Buonfiglio Monaldi.   The austerities which they practised were great, and they lived mostly on alms.   On the Thursday in Easter Week 1254, Philip was in prayer at Fiesole when the figure on the crucifix seemed to say to him, " Go to the high hill where the servants of my mother are living, and you will be doing the will of my Father ".   Pondering these words deeply Philip went to the chapel at Carfaggio to assist at Mass, and was strongly affected with the words of the Holy Ghost to the deacon Philip, which were read in the epistle of that day, " Go near and join thyself to this chariot ".   His name being Philip he applied to himself these words as an invitation to put himself under the care of the Blessed Virgin in that order, and he seemed to himself, in a dream or vision, to be in a vast wilderness (representing the world) full of precipices, snares and serpents, so that he did not see how it was possible to escape so many dangers. Whilst he was thus in dread he thought he beheld our Lady approaching him in a chariot. Persuaded that God called him to this order as to a place of refuge, Philip went to Monte Senario and was admitted by St Buonfiglio to the habit as a lay-brother : " I wish ", he said, " to be the servant of the Servants of Mary." In consideration of the circumstances in which he had joined the order he retained his baptismal name in religion. He was made gardener and questor for alms, and put to work at every kind of hard country labour ; the saint cheerfully applied himself to it in a spirit of penance and accompanied his work with constant recollection and prayer, living in a little cave behind the church. Philip was sent in 1258 to the Servite house at Siena and on the way there he undesignedly displayed his abilities in a discourse on certain controverted points, in the presence of two Dominicans and others, to the astonishment of those that heard him, and especially of his companion, Brother Victor. The matter was reported to the prior general, who examined St Philip closely and then had him promoted to holy orders, though nothing but an absolute command could extort his consent.

All Philip's hopes of living out his life in quiet and obscurity, serving God and his brethren as a lay-brother, were now at an end. In 1262 he went to the Siena monastery as novice-master and to be one of the four vicars to assist the prior general ; soon after he became himself colleague of the prior general. In 1267 a chapter of the whole order was held at Carfaggio ; at this chapter St Manettus resigned the generalship and, in spite of his protests, St Philip Benizi was unanimously elected in his stead. During his first year of office he made a general visitation of the provinces of northern Italy, which at the time were torn and distracted by the strife of Guelf and Ghibelline. It was on this tour that his first miracle was reported of him, very similar to one attributed to St Dominic and other saints : owing to the troubles the Servites of Arezzo were unable to get food and were on the verge of starvation ; when they assembled for supper there was nothing to eat until, when St Philip had exhorted them to have faith and had prayed before our Lady's image, a knock was heard at the monastery door and two large baskets of good bread were found on the steps. He codified the rules and constitutions of the Servite order and this work was confirmed by the general chapter held at Pistoia in 1268 ; he would on the same occasion have asked leave to give up his office. But he was so warmly dissuaded by his colleague, Brother Lottaringo, that he resigned himself to holding it so long as his brethren should wish, which proved to be for the rest of his life.

Upon the death of Pope Clement IV it was rumoured that Cardinal Ottobuoni, protector of the Servites, had proposed St Philip to succeed him, and that the suggestion was well received. When word of this came to Philip's ears he ran away and hid himself in a cave among the mountains near Radicofani, where he was looked after for three months by Brother Victor until he deemed the danger past. During this retreat St Philip rejoiced in an opportunity of giving himself up to contemplation ; he lived on vegetables and drank at a spring, since esteemed miraculous and called St Philip's Bath. He returned from the desert glowing with zeal to kindle in the hearts of Christians the fire of divine love, and soon set out on a visitation of his order in France and Germany. In 1274 he was summoned by Bd Gregory X to be present at the second general council of Lyons. At it he made a profound impression and the gift of tongues was attributed to him, but his reputation did not serve to obtain for the Servites that formal papal approbation for which St Philip worked continually.

The saint announced the word of God wherever he came and had an extra-ordinary talent in converting sinners and in reconciling those that were at variance. Italy was still horribly divided by discords and hereditary factions. Holy men often sought to apply remedies to these quarrels, which had a happy effect upon some ; but in many these discords, like a wound ill-cured, broke out again with worse symptoms than ever. Papal Guelfs and imperial Ghibellines were the worst offenders, and in 1279 Pope Nicholas III gave special faculties to Cardinal Latino to deal with them. He invoked the help of St Philip Benizi, who wonderfully pacified the factions when they were ready to tear each other to pieces at Pistoia and other places. He succeeded at length also at Forli, where the seditious insulted and beat him ; but his patience at length disarmed their fury. Peregrine Laziosi, who was their ringleader and had himself struck the saint, was so moved by his meekness that he threw himself at his feet and begged his pardon. Being become a model penitent Peregrine was received by Philip into the order of Servites at Siena in 1283, and was canonized by Benedict XIII in 1726. St Philip attracted a number of notably good men to himself. Among them were this St Peregrine and Bd John of Frankfort ; Bd Joachim Piccolomini, who met Philip at Siena ; Bd Andrew Dotti, a soldier, and Bd Jerome, both of Borgo San Sepolcro ; Bd Bonaventure of Pistoia, converted by a sermon of the saint from a life of violence and crime ; Bd Ubald, whose quarrelling had turned Florence upside down ; and Bd Francis Patrizi. In 1284 St Alexis Falconieri put his niece St Juliana under the direction of St Philip, and from his advice to her sprang the third order regular of the Servants of Mary. He was also responsible for sending the first Servite missionaries to the East, where some penetrated to Tartary and there gave their blood for Christ. Throughout his eighteen years of generalship of his order Philip had as his official colleague Lottaringo Stufa, whom he had known and loved from boyhood. They remained the closest friends and the utmost confidence subsisted between them ; their long association was an ideal partnership.

Judging at length by the decay of his health that the end of his life drew near, St Philip set out in 1285 to visit the newly-elected Pope Honorius IV at Perugia, and at Florence convened a general chapter at which he announced his approaching departure and handed over the government to Father Lottaringo. " Love one another ! Love one another ! Love one another ! " he adjured the friars, and so left them. He went to the smallest and poorest house of the order, at Todi, where he was enthusiastically received by the citizens, and when he could escape from them he went straight to the altar of our Lady, and falling prostrate on the ground prayed with great fervour, " This is the place of my rest for ever ". He made a moving sermon on the glory of the blessed on the feast of the Assumption of the Mother of God, but at three o'clock in the afternoon of that day was taken seriously ill. He sent for the community, and again spoke of brotherly love : " Love one another, reverence one another, and bear with one another." Seven days later the end came ; he called for his " book ", by which word he meant his crucifix, and devoutly contemplating it, calmly died at the hour of the evening *Angelus*. St Philip Benizi was canonized in 1671, and his feast was extended to the whole Western church in 1694.

La Vie de St Philippe Benizi (1886 ; new ed., 1913) by Father Soulier (Eng. trans.) must still be regarded as the standard biography of this saint. Though a long list of sources is set out in an appendix, it must be confessed that the early evidence is not quite so full as might be desired.   It is often difficult to decide how large a part legend has played in the story commonly circulated.   Fr Soulier has, however, edited very carefully some of the most important biographical materials : see the *Monumenta Ordinis Servorum Sanctae Mariae*, vols. ii, iii and iv.   The biography by Malaval (1672) has been translated into English in the Oratorian Series.   In the *Acta Sanctorum*, August, vol. iv, a life has been reproduced which is in substance a Latin rendering of the more relevant portions of Giani's (1604).

SS. CLAUDIUS, ASTERIUS, NEON, DOMNINA AND THEO-NILLA, MARTYRS   (A.D. 303 ?)

ACCORDING to Greek tradition the martyrs Claudius, Asterius and Neon were brothers who suffered death by crucifixion in Isauria, but the Latin *acta* locate the martyrdom in Cilicia.   In the judgement of Father Delehaye these *acta* belong to the class which have for their principal source a written document of some value, which has been embellished, *e.g.* by the multiplication of torments patiently borne, or even more seriously modified.   In any case Domnina and Theonilla seem to have been added to the original from some other source.

The *acta* relate that the three brothers were in the time of Diocletian charged as Christians at Aegea, having been denounced by their step-mother.   At the same time two women named Domnina and Theonilla, with a little child, were likewise on account of their faith thrown into prison, and brought to trial before the proconsul of Cilicia, whose name was Lysias.   He, when he came into court, said, " Bring before me the Christians whom the officers have delivered to the city magistrate ".   The gaoler said, " The magistrate of this city having pursuant to your orders made the strictest inquiry after Christians, has apprehended six ; three young men, all brothers, two women, and a small child.   One of them is here before you."   Lysias said to him, " Well, what is your name ? "   He answered, " Claudius ".

LYSIUS : " Do not be such a madman as to throw yourself away in youth ; sacrifice to the gods, and escape the torments prepared for you if you refuse."

CLAUDIUS : " My God requires no such sacrifices ; He delights rather in alms-deeds and holiness of life.   Your gods are unclean spirits, who are pleased with such oblations whilst they are preparing eternal punishments for those who offer them."

LYSIAS : " Let him be bound and beaten ; there is no other way of bringing him to reason."

CLAUDIUS : " Though you inflict upon me the most cruel tortures you will not move or hurt me."

LYSIAS : " The emperors have commanded that Christians sacrifice to the gods, and that they who refuse be punished ; those who obey are to be rewarded."

CLAUDIUS : " Their rewards are temporary and short-lived ; but the confession of Jesus Christ earns everlasting glory."

Then the proconsul commanded him to be tortured.   The martyr said, "Neither your fire nor anything else can hurt those who fear God ; it brings them to eternal life ".   Lysias ordered further torments, but Claudius only said, " I hold it a great benefit to suffer for God, and the greatest happiness to die for Jesus Christ."

LYSIAS : " Take him back to prison, and bring another."   When Asterius was before him he said, " Take my advice and sacrifice to the gods ; you have before your eyes what is prepared for those who refuse."

ASTERIUS : " There is one God, who dwells in Heaven and in the greatness of His power sees the lowest things : Him my parents have taught me to love and worship. I know not those that you worship and call gods."

LYSIAS : " Crush his sides, tear them with hooks, and make him sacrifice to the gods."

ASTERIUS : " I am the brother of him whom you just now questioned. We agree, and we make the same confession. My body is in your power ; but my soul is out of your reach."

LYSIAS : " Bring the pincers and pulleys, bind his feet, squeeze and torture him to teach him I can make him suffer." And when this was done, " Put live coals under his feet, and lash him on the back and belly."

ASTERIUS : " All I ask of you is that you will not spare any part of my body."

LYSIAS : " Take him away, put him with the rest, and bring the third."

When Neon was brought Lysias called him " son ", and treated him with kindness, urging him to sacrifice that he might escape torment. Neon answered that the proconsul's gods had no power if they were not able to defend themselves without having recourse to his authority.

LYSIAS : " Strike him on the neck, and teach him not to blaspheme the gods."

NEON : " You think I blaspheme when I speak the truth."

LYSIAS : " Stretch him on the rack, put burning coals on him, and scourge his back."

NEON : " I will do what is good for my soul, and no man shall ever make me change." When therefore he had been fruitlessly tortured, Lysias dictated this sentence : " Euthalius the gaoler and Archelaus the executioner shall take these three brothers to be crucified outside the town, that the birds of the air may devour their bodies."

Then Euthalius presented Domnina ; whereupon Lysias said to her, " You see, woman, the fire and torments which are prepared for you ; if you would avoid them, draw near and sacrifice." Domnina replied, " I shall not do it, lest I fall into eternal fire and endless torments. I worship God and His Son Jesus Christ, who hath made Heaven and earth and all that is therein." Lysias said, " Strip her and scourge her," While this was done, Archelaus, the executioner, said to Lysias, " Sir, Domnina is dead ", and Lysias replied, " Throw her body into the river and bring the next one." To Theonilla he said, " You have seen the torments with which the others have been punished. Honour the gods and sacrifice."

THEONILLA : " I dread eternal torments, which will destroy both body and soul."

LYSIAS : " Buffet her, lay her flat and bind her ; torture her to the utmost."

THEONILLA : " Are you not ashamed to inflict such punishments on a woman that is free, and a stranger too ? You know it to be shameful, and God sees what you do."

LYSIAS : " Hang her up by the hair and beat her face."

THEONILLA : " Is it not enough that you have stripped me naked ? It is not me only that you injure : your mother and your wife are also put to confusion in my person."

LYSIAS : " Are you married, or a widow ? "

THEONILLA : " I have been a widow these three and twenty years. It is for the love of God that I have continued in this state, in fasting, watching and prayer, ever since I forsook your filthy idols."

LYSIAS : " Let her suffer the last indignity and have her head shaved. Tie brambles round her middle ; stretch out her legs and arms and tie them to ·stakes ; scourge her all over ; put coals on her belly. And let her die."

When Theonilla had soon succumbed to these cruelties, Lysias said, " Sew her body up in a sack, and throw it into the water ", and this was done, that the Christians might not get possession of the martyrs' relics.

These Latin acts will be found printed in Ruinart, and also in the *Acta Sanctorum*, August, vol. iv ; while the Synaxaries (see Delehaye's edition, October 30, p. 178) show that they were known in the Byzantine church. A French translation is in Leclercq, *Les Martyrs*, vol. ii, pp. 182–190. The " Hieronymianum " duly commemorates the saints under this date. And *cf.*, P. Franchi de' Cavalieri, *Note Agiografiche* in *Studi e Testi*, vol. xxvii (1915), pp. 107–118.

ST EUGENE, OR EOGHAN, BISHOP (SIXTH CENTURY)

EOGHAN (the equivalent of which name in English is Owen, not Eugene, as he is generally called) is venerated as the first bishop at Ardstraw in Tyrone, predecessor of the see of Derry. According to his Latin life, on which little reliance can be put, his father was a Leinster man and his mother from county Down, and he was related to St Kevin of Glendalough. While a child he was carried off with two other boys, Tigernach and Coirpre, first to Britain and then to Brittany, where they were sold into slavery and set to grind corn. One day the chieftain found the three reading, the mill meanwhile being worked by angels, and he ordered them to be released. They found their way back to Ireland, where Coirpre became a bishop at Coleraine. St Eoghan was for fifteen years a monk, with St Kevin, at Kilnamanach in county Wicklow, and then set out for the north where, after helping St Tigernach to found the monastery of Clones, he settled with his disciples at Ardstraw in the valley of Mourne in Tyrone and was made a bishop. The feast of St Eoghan is kept throughout Ireland.

The Latin life spoken of above is in the Codex Salmanticensis and has been printed both in the *Acta Sanctorum*, August, vol. iv, and in De Smedt's edition of that codex, pp. 915–924. St Eoghan is also mentioned on this day in the *Félire* of Oengus.

BD JAMES OF BEVAGNA (A.D. 1301)

MEVANIA, now called Bevagna, is a small town in Umbria, and here this James was born in the year 1220, of the family of the Bianconi. His future holiness was foreshadowed in his childhood, and a reconciliation of the Bianconi to the Alberti, with whom they had quarrelled, was attributed to his youthful prayers. When he was sixteen, two Dominicans came to Bevagna to preach during Lent, and the boy was attracted by what he heard of the life of the preachers and by their discourses ; he considered the matter over and over and when, after his communion on Maundy Thursday, he was saying Psalm 118, the appositeness of the thirty-third verse struck him : " Set before me for a law the way of thy justifications, O Lord, and I will always seek after it." He went to one of the friars and opened his mind, and was recommended to watch all that night before the Blessed Sacrament in the Easter sepulchre, asking for light, and to await the will of God. This he did, and as he slept on the eve of Holy Saturday St Dominic appeared to him and said, " Do it ! According to God's will I choose you, and will be ever with you ". And so when the friars returned to their house at Spoleto James went with them.

In due course he was given permission to establish a house of his order at Bevagna, of which he became prior.   The neighbourhood gave ample scope for the labours of the friars, and after the town had been sacked by the Emperor Frederick II in 1248 Bd James more than ever endeared himself to the people by his solicitude for them in their misfortunes.   This was a time of recrudescence of Manichean errors, and a particularly pestilential sect of antinomians was active in Umbria ; James set out to combat it with great energy, and succeeded in inducing one of its leaders to make a public repudiation of his heresy at Orte.   Bd James was very strict in his observance of his vow of poverty, and when his mother gave him some money to buy a new habit, which he badly needed, he got permission from his superior to buy a crucifix for his cell instead.   When his mother saw the worn-out habit again, she remonstrated with him, but he answered with a smile, " I have done as you wished.   St Paul tells us to ' put on the Lord Jesus ', and that is the habit I have bought." But that crucifix was to clothe him in a way he never thought of, for praying before it one day in great dryness and fear of spirit, almost despairing of his salvation, it is said that a spurt of blood miraculously sprang from the image over his face, and he heard a voice saying, " Behold the sign of your salvation ! " Another marvel, reported at his death, is recounted in the notice of Bd Joan of Orvieto, under July 23.   Pope Boniface IX approved the *cultus* of Bd James of Bevagna.

The Bollandists in giving an account of this *beatus* (August, vol. iv) deplore, and not without reason, the lack of any early biography.   The narrative of Father Taigi is certainly full of legendary matter ; neither can one feel any more confidence in the *Vita del B. Giacomo Bianconi* by Father Piergili (1729) or in that compiled by F. Becchetti or in the summary given in Procter, *Lives of Dominican Saints.*   For a fuller bibliography see Taurisano, pp. 23–24.

24 : ST BARTHOLOMEW, Apostle   (First Century)

THE name given to this apostle is probably not his proper name, but his patronymic, meaning the son of Tolmai, and beyond the fact of his existence nothing is certainly known of him.   Many scholars, however, take him to have been the same person as Nathanael, a native of Cana in Galilee, of whom our Lord said, " Behold ! an Israelite indeed, in whom there is no guile ".   Among the reasons advanced for this supposition is that, as St John never mentions Bartholomew among the Apostles, so the other three evangelists take no notice of the name of Nathanael ; and they constantly put together Philip and Bartholomew, just as St John says Philip and Nathanael came together to Christ ; moreover, Nathanael is reckoned with other apostles when Christ appeared to them at the sea of Galilee after His resurrection (John xxi 2).

The popular traditions concerning St Bartholomew are summed up in the Roman Martyrology, which says he " preached the gospel of Christ in India ; thence he went into Greater Armenia, and when he had converted many people there to the faith he was flayed alive by the barbarians, and by command of King Astyages fulfilled his martyrdom by beheading . . .".   The place is said to have been Albanopolis (Derbend, on the west coast of the Caspian Sea), and he is represented to have preached also in Mesopotamia, Persia, Egypt and elsewhere.   The earliest reference to India is given by Eusebius in the early fourth century, when he relates that St Pantaenus, about a hundred years earlier, going into India (St Jerome adds " to preach to the Brahmins "), found there some who still retained the knowledge of Christ and showed him a copy of St Matthew's Gospel in Hebrew characters, which they assured him that St Bartholomew had brought into those parts when he planted the faith among them. But " India " was a name applied indifferently by Greek and Latin writers to Arabia, Ethiopia, Libya, Parthia, Persia and the lands of the Medes, and it is most probable that the India visited by Pantaenus was Ethiopia or Arabia Felix, or perhaps both. Another eastern legend says the apostle met St Philip at Hierapolis in Phrygia, and travelled into Lycaonia, where St John Chrysostom affirms that he instructed the people in the Christian faith. That he preached and died in Armenia is possible, and is a unanimous tradition among the later historians of that country ; but earlier Armenian writers make little or no reference to him as connected with their nation. The journeys attributed to the relics of St Bartholomew are even more bewildering than those of his living body ; alleged relics are venerated at present chiefly at Benevento and in the church of St Bartholomew-in-the-Tiber at Rome.

Although, in comparison with such other apostles as St Andrew, St Thomas and St John, the name of St Bartholomew is not conspicuous in the apocryphal literature of the early centuries, still we have what professes to be an account of his preaching and " passion ", preserved to us in Greek and several Latin copies. Max Bonnet (*Analecta Bollandiana*, vol. xiv, 1895, pp. 353–366) thinks the Latin was the original ; Lipsius less probably argues for the priority of the Greek ; but it may be that both derive from a lost Syriac archetype. The texts are in the *Acta Sanctorum*, August, vol. v ; in Tischendorf, *Acta Apostolorum Apocrypha*, pp. 243–260 ; and also in Bonnet, *Act. Apocryph.*, vol. ii, pt. 1, pp. 128 *seq.* There are also considerable fragments of an apocryphal Gospel of Bartholomew (on which see the *Revue Biblique* for 1913, 1921 and 1922), and traces of Coptic " Acts of Andrew and Bartholomew ". The gospel which bears the name of Bartholomew is one of the apocryphal writings condemned in the decree of Pseudo-Gelasius. The statement that St Bartholomew was flayed alive before being beheaded, though this is not mentioned in the *passio*, is contained in the so-called " Breviarium Apostolorum " prefixed to certain manuscripts of the " Hieronymianum ". It is the flaying which has probably suggested the knife, often associated as an emblem with pictures of the saint ; but on St Bartholomew in art see Künstle, *Ikonographie*, vol. ii, pp. 116–120. The Indian question is examined in some detail by Fr A. C. Perumalil in *The Apostles in India* (Patna, 1953).

THE MARTYRS OF UTICA (A.D. 258 ?)

THE story of these martyrs as known to himself was popularized by the poet Prudentius in one of his hymns, and it is recorded in the Roman Martyrology today in these words : The passion " at Carthage, of three hundred holy martyrs in the time of Valerian and Gallienus. The governor, among other torments, ordered a limekiln to be lighted and charcoal and incense to be at hand near by ; then he said to them, ' Choose one of these two things : either offer incense to Jupiter upon these coals, or be thrown into that lime '. They, armed with faith and confessing Christ the Son of God, on a swift impulse threw themselves into the fire and were reduced to powder in the heat of the lime. Wherefore this white-robed company of the blessed earned for itself the name of the White Mass." That is to say, their ashes made but one common mass cemented with the lime. St Augustine says that this happened at Utica, twenty-five miles from Carthage, and that the martyrs numbered not three hundred but more than one hundred and fifty-three. Prudentius refers to them thus : " Whiteness [*candor*] possesses their bodies ; purity [*candor*] bears their souls to Heaven. Hence they have merited to be for ever called the White Mass [*Massa candida*]."

But, as Father Delehaye points out in his commentary on the " Martyrology of Jerome ", it seems that this poetic description of Prudentius must be set aside. " Massa Candida " is really the name of a place—the White Farm. A number of martyrs were buried there, but there is nothing to show that they suffered under Valerian. There was quite probably something in the nature of a massacre, as an early sermon, formerly without warrant attributed to St Augustine, dwells upon the bloodshed and the readiness of the martyrs to submit their necks to the sword ; but on the other hand there is no evidence that they numbered either 300 or 153, for the latter figure was merely suggested to Augustine by a reference he had just made to the draught of fishes in John xxi 11. There can be little doubt that Prudentius evolved the whole story of the lime out of the name " massa candida ", which he interpreted according to his own exuberant fancy.

See Prudentius, *Peristephanon*, xiii, 76–87 ; P. Franchi de' Cavalieri, in *Studi e Testi*, vol. ix (1902), pp. 37–51 ; G. Morin in *Miscellanea augustiniana*, vol. i (1930), p. 647 ; H. Delehaye, CMH., pp. 449–450, and *Origines du culte des martyrs* (1933), pp. 384–385.

ST AUDOENUS, OR OUEN, BISHOP OF ROUEN   (A.D. 684)

ST OUEN (Dado) was born at Sancy, near Soissons, about 600, of a Frankish family, his father being St Authaire. While he and his brother Ado were still children, living at Ussy-sur-Marne, their father entertained the exiled St Columban in his house. The brothers were educated well and when they were of sufficient age were put at the court of King Clotaire II, where Ouen became one of a group of remarkable young men which included St Eligius, St Wandrille and St Didier of Cahors. Ouen was in great favour with the king and with his son and successor, Dagobert I, who made him his referendary or chancellor ; in this office Ouen steadily opposed the prevalent simony. He obtained of the king a grant of a piece of land situated in the forest of Brie where, in 636, he erected a monastery, called at present Rebais. By the advice of St Faro, Bishop of Meaux, he sent for Aile, a disciple of St Columban from Luxeuil, and had him appointed the first abbot. St Ouen would have retired himself to Rebais, but Dagobert and his nobles could not be induced to give their consent. St Ouen and St Eligius, though yet laymen, were for their zeal, piety and learning considered as equals even of the bishops, and they promoted the cause of religion and virtue through the whole kingdom. Dagobert dying in 639, Clovis II, his son and successor, testified the same esteem for St Ouen, and kept him in the office of referendary. At length Clovis was prevailed upon to give Ouen leave to receive ordination from Dieudonné, Bishop of Mâcon, and he was shortly after elected bishop of Rouen ; at the same time his friend St Eligius was chosen bishop of Noyon. They took a considerable time to prepare themselves for this dignity, by retreat, fasting and prayer, and received the episcopal consecration together at Rheims in 641.

St Ouen in this new office increased his humility, austerities and charities. His zeal was indefatigable, and by his kindness and patience he was truly all things to all men. He encouraged learning by the foundation of monasteries, and sent missionaries to those parts of his diocese that were still pagan ; nor did he slacken his efforts for extirpating simony and other abuses. He was a trusted adviser of King Thierry III and upheld the policy of Ebroin, the mayor of the palace, to such a degree that he was, perhaps inculpably, involved in Ebroin's ill-treatment of St Leger and of St Philibert. Returning from a political mission to Cologne, St Ouen went to Clichy, and there fell ill and died, on August 24, 684.

The earliest of the lives of St Ouen dates from the beginning of the eighth century, and has been critically edited by W. Levison in MGH., *Scriptores Merov.*, vol. v, pp. 536–567. Levison also comments (pp. 548 *seq.*) on the two ninth-century lives, the former of which is printed with the first-named in the *Acta Sanctorum*, August, vol. iv, and the latter in the *Analecta Bollandiana*, vol. v, pp. 76–146.   By far the best modern contribution to the history of St Ouen is that of E. Vacandard, *Vie de Saint Ouen* (1902).   He has in particular rectified in several points the chronology of previous writers.   For miracles attributed to relics of St Ouen at Canterbury, see *Analecta Bollandiana*, vol. li (1933), pp. 285–292, and vol. lxiv (1946), pp. 50–53.

25 : ST LOUIS OF FRANCE   (A.D. 1270)

IN the person of St Louis (Lewis) IX were united the qualities which form a great king, a hero of romance, and a saint.   He was endowed with qualifications for good government, he excelled in the arts of peace and of war, and his courage and greatness of mind received from his virtue the highest setting ; ambition had no share in his enterprises, his only motives in them was the glory of God and the good of his subjects.   Though the two crusades in which he was engaged were failures, he is certainly to be ranked among the most valiant of princes, and a perfect example of the good and great medieval nobleman.   He was son of Louis VIII and was eight years old when the death of his grandfather, Philip II Augustus, put his father in possession of the crown of France.   He was born at Poissy on April 25, 1214.   His mother was Blanche, daughter of Alfonso of Castile and Eleanor of England, and to her care and attention in the education of St Louis we are indebted, under God, for the great example of his virtues.   She used often to say to him when he was a child, " I love you, my dear son, as much as a mother can love her child ; but I would rather see you dead at my feet than that you should ever commit a mortal sin ".   Nor did Louis forget the lesson.   His friend and biographer, the Sieur de Joinville, historian of the crusades, relates that the king once asked him, " What is God ? "   Joinville replied, " That which is so good that there could be nothing better."   "Well said.   Now tell me, would you rather be a leper or commit a mortal sin ? "   " And I, who never told a lie ", says Joinville, " answered, ' I would rather commit thirty mortal sins than be a leper '."   Later Louis led him apart and took him to task for his honest but misguided reply.

King Louis VIII died on November 7, 1226, and Queen Blanche was declared regént for her son, who was then only twelve years old.   The whole time of the king's minority was disturbed by ambitious barons, but Blanche by several alliances and by her courage and diligence overcame them in the field and forced their submission.   Louis rejoiced in his victories chiefly because he procured by them the blessings of peace to his subjects.   He was merciful even to rebels, and by his readiness to receive any proposals of agreement gave the proof that he neither sought revenge nor conquests.   Never had any man a greater love for the Church, or a greater veneration for its ministers.   Yet this was not blind ; he opposed the injustices of bishops, when he saw them betrayed into any, and did not listen to their complaints till he had given a full hearing to the other party, as he showed in the contests of the bishops of Beauvais and Metz with the corporations of those cities.   Louis enjoyed the conversation of priests or other religious men, and he often invited such (*e.g.* St Thomas Aquinas) to his house, but he knew how to observe seasons with a decent liberty.   Once when a friar had started a grave religious topic at table, he turned the discourse to another subject, saying, " All things have their time ".   He celebrated feasts and rejoicings on the creation of knights and other such occasions with magnificence, but banished from his court all diversions dangerous to morals.   And he would tolerate neither vulgar obscenity nor thoughtless profanity ; " I was a good twenty-two years in the holy king's company ", says Joinville, " and never once did I hear him swear, either by God or His mother or His saints.   I did not even hear him name the Devil, except if he met the word when reading aloud, or when discussing what had been read."   And a Dominican testified that he had never heard him speak ill-naturedly of anyone. When he was urged to put to death the son of Hugh de la Marche, who had followed his father in rebellion, Louis refused, saying, " A son cannot refuse to obey his father ".

When he was nineteen St Louis married Margaret, the eldest daughter of Raymund Berenger, Count of Provence, whose second daughter, Eleanor, was married to Henry III, King of England ; his third, Sanchia, to his brother Richard of Cornwall ; and Beatrice, the youngest, to Charles, brother to St Louis.   The marriage was blessed with a happy union of hearts and eleven children, five sons, six daughters, from whose descendants kings were given to France until that January 21, 1793, when the Abbé Edgeworth, it is often stated, said to Louis XVI as the guillotine was about to fall, " Son of St Louis, go up to Heaven ! "*   In 1235, having come of age, St Louis took the government of his kingdom into his own hands.   But he continued to show the greatest deference to his mother, and to profit by her counsel, though Blanche was inclined to be jealous of and unkind to her daughter-in-law.   The first of many religious foundations for which Louis was responsible was the abbey of Royaumont.   In 1239 Baldwin II, the Latin emperor at Constantinople, made St Louis (in gratitude for his largesse to the Christians in Palestine and other parts of the East) a present of the Crown of Thorns, which was then in the hands of the Venetians as a pledge for a loan of money to Baldwin, which Louis had to discharge.   He sent two Dominican friars to bring this treasure to France, and met it himself beyond Sens, attended by his whole court.   To house it he pulled down his chapel of St Nicholas and built the *Sainte Chapelle*, which is now empty of its relic.†   He brought the Carthusians to Paris and endowed them with the palace of Vauvert, and helped his mother in the foundation of the convent of Maubuisson.

Several ordinances of this prince show us how much he applied himself to see justice well administered.   In succeeding reigns, whenever complaints were raised among the people, the cry of those dissatisfied was to demand that abuses should be reformed and justice impartially administered as was done in the reign of St Louis.   In 1230 he forbade all manner of usury, and restrained the Jews in particular from practising it.   He published a law commanding all who should be guilty of blasphemy to be branded, and thus punished a rich and important citizen of Paris ; to some who murmured at this severity he said that he would undergo that punishment himself if thus he might put a stop to the crime.   He protected

* Edgeworth is said to have denied to Lord Holland that he used these words.

† What remains of it is now in Notre-Dame de Paris and is, in fact, only part of the rush foundation, with no thorns thereon.   Several of these were given away by St Louis in golden reliquaries : one such is in the British Museum and appears still to contain the thorn it was made to enshrine.   After the Revolution what remained of the crown, or its rush foundation, was brought to light in 1804 and handed over to the archbishop of Paris.

vassals from oppressive lords, and when a Flemish count had hanged three children for hunting rabbits in his woods, had him imprisoned and tried, not by his peers as he demanded, but by the ordinary judges, who condemned him to death. He afterwards spared his life, but subjected him to a fine which deprived him of the greater part of his estates. This money the king ordered to be expended on religious and charitable works. He forbade feudal lords to make private war upon one another, and his scrupulous fidelity in keeping his word and observing treaties was notable ; this impartial and inflexible integrity made barons, prelates and even foreign kings ask to have him for judge and arbitrator, and put their affairs into his hands.

Hugh of Lusignan, Count of La Marche, made trouble soon after the king's majority ; his estates were a fief of Poitou and he refused to pay homage to the count of Poitiers, the brother of St Louis. Hugh's wife, Isabel, was the widow of King John and mother of Henry III of England, who came over to support his stepfather. St Louis defeated King Henry III (who was never born to be a soldier) at Taillebourg in 1242. Henry fled to Bordeaux and the next year returned to England, having made a truce with the French. Seventeen years later Louis concluded another treaty with Henry III. By it he yielded to England the Limousin and Périgord, King Henry renouncing on his side all pretensions to Normandy, Anjou, Maine, Touraine and Poitou. The French criticized their sovereign's concessions, and Louis replied that he hoped by them to cement a lasting peace between the two nations, and that it was very honourable to his crown to have so great a king as vassal for Guienne. But some historians are of the opinion that had Louis pushed home his advantage the Hundred Years' War would have been averted for his successors.

After an illness in 1244 Louis determined to undertake a crusade in the East, and early the next year he by letter assured the Christians in Palestine that he would make all possible haste to their assistance against the infidels, who a few months before had retaken Jerusalem. But the opposition of his councillors and nobles, the preparation of the expedition, and the settling of his kingdom put off his departure for three and a half years. At the thirteenth general council at Lyons in 1245 all benefices were taxed a twentieth of their income for three years for the relief of the Holy Land (the English representatives strongly protested against this), and this gave encouragement to the crusaders. In 1248 Louis sailed for Cyprus, where he was joined by William Longsword, Earl of Salisbury, and two hundred English knights. The objective was Egypt. Damietta, in the delta of the Nile, was easily taken and St Louis made a solemn entry into the city, not with the pomp of a conqueror but with the humility of a truly Christian prince, walking barefoot with the queen, the princes his brothers and other great lords, preceded by the papal legate. The king ordered that all plundering and other crimes should be strictly inquired into and punished, and that restitution should be made, and he forbade any infidel to be slain whom it was possible to make prisoner. But notwithstanding all his watchfulness many, to his grief, gave themselves up to debauchery and outrageous acts of violence. Owing to the rising of the Nile and the summer heat the crusaders could not follow up their advantage, and it was not till six months had passed that they advanced to attack the Saracens, who were on the other side of the river. Then followed another six months of desultory fighting, in which the crusaders lost many by battle and sickness, until in April 1250 St Louis himself was taken prisoner, and his army routed with frightful slaughter.

During his captivity the king recited the Divine Office every day with two chaplains just as if he had been in perfect health in his own palace, and to the insults that were sometimes offered him he opposed an air of majesty and authority which kept his guards in awe. When he was asked and refused to give up the castles in Syria he was threatened with the most ignominious treatment and with torture ; to which he coolly replied that they were masters of his body, and might do with it what they pleased. The sultan sent to him a proposal by which he demanded a million bezants of gold and the city of Damietta for his ransom and that of the other prisoners. Louis answered that a king of France ought not to redeem himself for money, but that he would give the city for his own release and the million bezants for that of all the other prisoners. The sultan at that time was overthrown by the Mamluk emirs, and these eventually released the king and the other prisoners on these terms, but the sick and wounded crusaders in Damietta they treacherously slew. St Louis then sailed to Palestine with the remainder of his army. There he remained until 1254, visiting all the holy places he could, encouraging the Christians, and strengthening the defences of the Latin kingdom—such as it was. Then, news being brought to him of the death of his mother, who was regent in his absence, he returned to France. He had been away almost six years, but he was oppressed by the memory of the distresses of the Christians in the East and he continued to wear the cross on his clothes to show that he intended to return to their assistance. Their position got rapidly worse : between 1263 and 1268 the Mamluk Baibars took Nazareth, Caesarea, Jaffa and Antioch.

About 1257 Master Robert de Sorbon, a canon and very learned doctor of Paris, laid the foundations of that theological institute in the city which became known after him as the Sorbonne. Master Robert was a personal friend of St Louis and sometimes acted as his confessor, and the king enthusiastically seconded his project and helped to endow it. Louis also founded in Paris, for poor blind men, the hospital of Quinze-Vingts, so called because there were in it at the first foundation three hundred such patients. He likewise made provision of all kinds for the poor ; in addition to thirteen special indigent guests he had daily a large number of poor folk to meals near his own palace, and in Lent and Advent all who presented themselves ; and these he often served in person. He kept lists of needy people, especially *les pauvres honteux*, whom he regularly relieved in every province of his dominions. Though not personally a legislator he had a passion for justice, and he transformed the feudal " king's court " into a highly organized royal court of justice and, as in the case of Henry III and his barons, sovereign princes submitted their difficulties to his ruling ; in all causes he endeavoured to substitute proof by witnesses and decision by judicial process or arbitration for appeal to arms.

Having one day stood godfather to a Jew who was baptized at Saint-Denis, St Louis said to the ambassador of the emir of Tunis that to see his master receive that sacrament he would with joy pass the rest of his life in chains under the Saracens. Accordingly people were not surprised when in 1267 he announced another crusade : nor were they pleased. Among less worthy reasons, they feared to lose so good a king, who if only fifty-two years old was weak with toil, ill-health and austerities. Joinville said bluntly that " those who recommended this voyage to the king sinned grievously ", and excused himself, urging the necessity of his staying at home to protect his vassals from oppression. The king embarked with his army at Aigues-Mortes on July 1, 1270 ; when the fleet was over against

Cagliari in Sardinia it was resolved to proceed to Tunis, where soon after landing the king himself and his eldest son Philip both sickened with typhus. It was soon seen that Louis was dying. He gave his last instructions to his sons and to his daughter, the queen of Navarre, and composed himself for death. On August 24, which was Sunday, he received the last sacraments, and called for the Greek ambassadors, whom he strongly urged to reunion with the Roman Church. He lost his speech the next day from nine till twelve o'clock ; then, recovering it and lifting up his eyes towards Heaven, he repeated aloud the words of the psalmist, " Lord, I will enter into thine house ; I will worship in thy holy temple, and will give glory to thy name ". He spoke again at three in the afternoon, " Into thy hands I commend my soul ", and immediately after breathed his last. His bones and heart were taken back to France and enshrined in the abbey-church of St Denis, whence they were scattered at the Revolution ; he was canonized in 1297.

Authentic materials for the life of St Louis are naturally abundant. We have in the first place the French memoirs of the Sieur de Joinville which have been translated into almost every European language : the English version by Sir Frank Marzials is in the Everyman series, and there is an excellent new one by René Hague (1955). Then, from a more religious point of view, there are somewhat detailed Latin biographies by his confessors and chaplains, Geoffrey de Beaulieu and William de Chartres. The text of these two narratives will be found in the *Acta Sanctorum*, August, vol. v, but they have been printed more than once elsewhere. Most valuable also is the copious French account of the saint compiled by the confessor of the queen ; a Latin version of this life, which contains a good deal of information about the canonization, is printed by the Bollandists. From the king's own hand we have the account of his captivity, and the instructions which he drew up for his son Philip and his daughter Isabel ; these instructions should not be read without reference to the comments of Paul Viollet in the *Bibliothèque de l'École des chartes*, 1869 and 1874. There are excellent modern lives by H. Wallon (1875), and on a smaller scale (in the series " Les Saints ") by Marius Sepet (Eng. trans.). *Cf.* also especially Elie Berger, *Saint Louis et Innocent IV* and the same author's *Histoire de Blanche de Castille ;* and the *Cambridge Mediaeval History*, vol. vi. Among slighter sketches, which are numerous in every language, that of W. F. Knox, *The Court of a Saint*, may be recommended. The French name Louis should properly be rendered in English as Lewis.

ST GENESIUS THE COMEDIAN, Martyr (No Date ?)

FATHER DELEHAYE classes the story of St Genesius in the category of imaginative romances ; it is possible that Genesius never existed at all, but is a western version of St Gelasius of Heliopolis, of whom (and of others) a similar tale is told. The legend of Genesius is narrated by Alban Butler as follows.

The Emperor Diocletian coming to Rome, he was received with great rejoicings. Among other entertainments prepared for him, those of the stage were not neglected. In a comedy which was acted in his presence one of the players took it into his head to burlesque the ceremonies of Christian baptism, which could not fail to amuse the people, who held our religion and its mysteries in contempt and derision. This player therefore, whose name was Genesius and who had learned some things concerning Christian rites from friends who professed that religion, laid himself down on the stage, pretending to be ill, and said, " Ah ! my friends, there is a great weight upon me, and I would gladly be eased ". The others answered, " What shall we do to give you ease ? Would you like us to plane you and reduce the weight that way ? " " Idiots ! " he exclaimed, " I am resolved to die a Christian, that God may receive me on this day of my death as one who seeks His salvation by turning from idolatry and superstition." Then a priest and exorcist were called, that is to say, two players who impersonated these characters. These, sitting down by his bedside, asked, " Well, my child, why did you send for us ? " But here Genesius was suddenly converted by a divine inspiration and replied, not in mockery but seriously, " Because I desire to receive the grace of Jesus Christ and to be born again, that I may be delivered from my sins ".

The other players then went through the whole ceremony of baptism with him ; but he in earnest answered the usual interrogatories, and on being baptized was clothed with a white garment. After this, other players, dressed like soldiers, to carry on the jest, seized him and presented him to the emperor, to be examined as the martyrs were wont to be. Genesius then declared himself openly and seriously, standing upon the stage, " Hear ! O emperor, and all you that are present, officers, philosophers, senators and people, hear what I am going to say. I never yet so much as heard the word Christian but I reviled it, and I detested my very relations because they professed that religion. I learned its rites and mysteries only that I might the better ridicule it, and inspire you with the utmost contempt for it ; but when I was to be washed with the water and examined, I had no sooner answered sincerely that I believed, than I saw a company of angels over my head, who recited out of a book all the sins I had committed from my childhood ; and having plunged the book into the water which had been poured upon me in your presence, they showed me the book whiter than snow. Wherefore I advise you, O great and mighty emperor, and all people here present who have mocked these mysteries, to believe with me that Jesus Christ is the true Lord ; that He is the light and the truth ; and that it is through Him you may obtain the forgiveness of your sins." *

Diocletian, enraged at these words, ordered him to be beaten, and afterward to be put into the hands of Plautian, the prefect of the praetorium, that he might compel him to sacrifice. Plautian put him upon the rack, where he was torn with iron hooks and then burnt with torches ; but the martyr persisted in crying out, " There is no other Lord beside Him whom I have seen. Him I worship and serve, and to Him I will cling, though I should suffer a thousand deaths. No torments shall remove Jesus Christ from my heart and my mouth. Bitterly do I regret that I once detested His holy name, and came so late to His service." At length his head was struck off.

For satisfactory proof that Dom Ruinart blundered in including the story of this probably mythical personage among his *Acta Sincera*, the reader must consult the *Martyrologes historiques* of Dom Quentin, especially pp. 533–541, and also the *Analecta Bollandiana*, vol. xxix (1910), pp. 258–269. The legend of the mock baptism of the comedian Genesius was no doubt in circulation before the sixth century, for " Genesius the actor " is commemorated in the calendar of Carthage. Still the text in Ruinart is certainly not the primitive form of his " acts ". What Ruinart has printed is only a copy of Ado's abridgement of the longer narrative which is known to us through Surius and others. It is not disputed that in early times the Christian rites were often burlesqued upon the stage (though H. Reich in his book, *Der Mimus*, has greatly exaggerated the evidence for this), and early currency was given to the tradition or legend that the practice had resulted in the conversion of an actor, who was thereupon put to death ; but unfortunately what is substantially the same story is connected with four different names, Genesius, Gelasius or Gelasinus, Ardalio and Porphyrius. We have no guarantee in any of these cases that it is not a hagiographical fiction. See further Bertha von der Lage, *Studien zur Genesiuslegende* (1898) ; Mostert

* Assuming the story to be true, the " baptism " administered would not be valid, for lack, on the part of the sacrilegious actor, of any intention even " to do what the Church does " when she baptizes. Genesius received the baptism, not of water, but of desire and of blood.

and Stengel, *L'ystoire et la Vie de Saint Genis* (1895) ; Paul Allard, *La persécution de Dioclétien*, vol. i (1908), pp. 7–9, who argues in favour of the real existence of the martyr ; and CMH., pp. 463–465. *Cf.* also the next notice.

ST GENESIUS OF ARLES, MARTYR   (A.D. 303 ?)

ON this day is commemorated another St Genesius (Genès), the patron of the city of Arles.   He was said to be a catechumen and by profession a notary, one of those *notarii* who took down shorthand notes of judicial proceedings for the public archives to whom reference is several times made in the acts of the martyrs.   His *acta* say that he " studied with great perseverance and exercised with much success that useful art by which he was able at a single stroke to take down words, and by the speed of his hand to equal the rapidity of the discourse of an orator, and to render word for word, with abridged notes, the pleadings of counsel, the deposition of witnesses and the answers of the accused. . . . Now it happened one day that, while he was performing his duties as clerk of the court before the judge at Arles, there was read out an impious and sacrilegious edict which the emperors had published throughout all the provinces [of persecution against the Christians].   The ears of the religious clerk were wounded and his hand refused to trace the words on the wax.   He did more : he got up from his seat, flung his registers at the feet of the judge, and renounced for ever such a wicked occupation."

He then fled secretly, seeking safety from town to town, and, " as he thought that he had need to be fortified in the faith by baptism (for he had not yet been born again by water and the Holy Spirit), he sent his request to the bishop by some faithful persons.   But whether the bishop was meanwhile arrested himself, or that he distrusted the youth of Genesius, would not risk conferring the sacrament, and put it off, he only told him that his blood shed for Jesus Christ would take the place of the baptism he so ardently wished to receive.   And I think myself that it was not without a special dispensation of Providence that the bishop made difficulties : for without doubt Heaven wished alone to consecrate Genesius, and Jesus Christ had prepared for him a double baptism, that of the water and blood which flowed from the side of the divine Saviour."   Genesius was at length overtaken by the persecutors and beheaded on the banks of the river Rhône, during the persecution of Maximian and Diocletian.

The mention of this martyr by Prudentius, by Fortunatus and by others, as well as his inclusion in the " Hieronymianum " on this day, can leave little doubt that the honour paid to him at Arles rested on a sound historical foundation.   The brief " acts " have been printed by Ruinart and again, with a much fuller discussion, in the *Acta Sanctorum*, August, vol. v.   Delehaye in CMH., pp. 463–465, has discussed the case of the two saints called Genesius in some detail.   His conclusion is that the martyr of Arles is alone historical. He became so famous that his cult was adopted in Rome, and thence spread to Africa and other places.   From the fact that a church was built to him in Rome it was rashly announced that his body was buried there and that he was a Roman martyr.   In a short time a story was invented transforming him into an actor who made sport of the Christian religious rites in presence of the emperor himself.

ST PATRICIA, VIRGIN   (DATE UNKNOWN)

ACCORDING to her legend, Patricia was a maiden of noble birth, belonging seemingly to the imperial family of Constantinople.   To avoid marriage with the suitor chosen for her, she fled to Italy, and in Rome took vows consecrating her virginity to God.   She then returned to Constantinople in order to distribute her goods to the poor, but, this done, she again made her way to Italy, and reached Naples, where not long after she died. The miracles which followed led to a *cultus* which was notably revived some centuries later by the discovery and translation of her relics in 1549. Since 1625 she has been honoured as one of the patrons of the city of Naples, and what is believed to be a relic of her blood liquefies there, like that of St Januarius, which is referred to by J. H. Newman when travelling in Italy in 1846.

In the *Acta Sanctorum*, August, vol. v, two short medieval Latin lives are printed, with stories of miracles and other material. The accounts given of her in various pious booklets published in Naples and elsewhere are full of extravagances, describing her absurdly as an empress, or as a daughter of Constantine the Great. *Cf.* Father Thurston's articles on " blood-miracles " in *The Month*, 1927.

ST MENNAS, PATRIARCH OF CONSTANTINOPLE   (A.D. 552)

MENNAS, a native of Alexandria, was a priest in Constantinople until, in the year 536, he was appointed patriarch of that church and consecrated by Pope St Agapitus, who was then in Constantinople. Mennas set himself to repair the harm done by his predecessor Anthimus, who was a monophysite, and to deal with a number of sectaries who, sheltering under the name of Origen, were troubling the East. In 544 the Emperor Justinian who, like most Eastern emperors and with more reason than some, fancied himself as a theologian, sought to conciliate his monophysite subjects by condemning certain writings, called the Three Chapters. All his bishops were ordered to sign the condemnation and St Mennas was the first to obey ; not, however, very happily, for he said that he would withdraw his signature if the pope of Rome did not agree ; but in the event he did not do this.

What followed need not be traced in detail here. Many bishops of the West, although they recognized that the writings were clearly heretical in part, objected to the condemnation because it seemed to compromise the Council of Chalcedon. The pope, Vigilius, was first on one side, then on the other, but eventually in 551 refused to accept Justinian's edict, and sought refuge in St Peter's church in Constantinople (whither he had been peremptorily summoned by the emperor), and then in St Euphemia's at Chalcedon, from whence he excommunicated St Mennas and others who had signed it. Mennas assured Vigilius that he in no way deviated from the acts of the Council of Chalcedon, and the matter of the Three Chapters was referred to an oecumenical council.

This council Mennas did not live to see, for he died on August 24, 552, and the fifth general council did not assemble till the following year. It then condemned the Three Chapters, as the emperor had done, and Pope Vigilius approved and confirmed the condemnation. We thus have the curious and unusual spectacle of a patriarch of Constantinople firmly supporting a policy which was to be eventually confirmed by a general council, as against a feeble pope who allowed his judgement and actions to be swayed from side to side by the conflicting views of Western bishops and Eastern emperor ; it must be borne in mind that the matter at issue was concerned not with any definition of faith, but with the expediency and implications of the proposed condemnation. St Mennas is named in the Roman Martyrology.

A short Greek life with a general discussion of the saint's career is in the *Acta Sanctorum*, August, vol. v, but the story belongs rather to general ecclesiastical history. See Hefele-Leclercq, *Conciles*, vol. iv ; F. Savio, *Il Papa Vigilio* (1904) ; and especially DTC., vol. xi, cc. 1574–1588 ; and Fliche and Martin, *Histoire de l'Église*, t. iv, pp. 453–471.

ST EBBA, Abbess of Coldingham, Virgin　　(A.D. 683)

This St Ebba is sometimes called " the Elder " to distinguish her from the St Ebba, also abbess of Coldingham, said to have been put to death by the Danes about the year 870. She was sister to St Oswald and Oswy of Northumbria, and Oswy wanted her to marry the king of the Scots, but when she refused and took the monastic habit from St Finan of Lindisfarne he gave her a piece of land on the Derwent, where she founded the monastery of Ebbchester. She afterwards moved to Coldingham on the coast of Berwick, and there founded a double monastery, which both in arrangement and situation resembled that of St Hilda at Whitby ; the promontory on which it was built is still called St Abb's Head. Here she was visited by St Cuthbert, and St Etheldreda was a nun under her before becoming abbess of Ely.

Personal sanctity, that is, ability rightly to rule oneself, by no means always involves ability to rule others well and apparently St Ebba was not a very successful abbess. For St Bede relates that St Adamnan (not he of Iona), who was a monk at Coldingham, had a vision in which he learned that the monastery would be destroyed by fire, because its monks and nuns were slack and frivolous : " the cells that were built for prayer or reading are now turned into places for feasting, drinking, talk and other pleasures ; the very maidens, dedicated to God, lay aside the respect due to their profession and employ their leisure in weaving fine clothes, either to adorn themselves like brides, which is dangerous to their state, or to attract the attention of strangers ". Perhaps St Adamnan, being himself a holy man and seeing how things were, cast his prophecy in the form of a vision from God for motives of prudence. For when it came to the ears of St Ebba and she asked for an explanation, he said, " I was afraid to say anything about it before, out of respect for yourself ", and added tactfully, " But this calamity will not happen in your time." The chronicler goes on to say that the religious were frightened and behaved themselves better for a short time, but after the death of St Ebba they became worse than ever, and the house was in fact burned down very shortly after. " That all this fell out thus ", says Bede, " was told me by my very reverend fellow priest, Edgils, who then lived in that monastery. After its destruction he lived for a long time in our monastery and died here."

A life of Ebba by Capgrave, partly based on Reginald of Durham, is printed in the *Acta Sanctorum*, August, vol. v. See also Plummer's Bede ; and DCB., vol. ii, pp. 22–23. Apart from the lessons in the Aberdeen Breviary, there is not much trace of *cultus*.

ST GREGORY OF UTRECHT, Abbot　　(A.D. 775 ?)

This Gregory was born in the territory of Trier about the year 707. One day when he was fifteen years of age he was desired by his grandmother, the abbess of Pfalzel, near Trier, to read to the nuns. St Boniface, who was travelling from Friesland into Hesse and Thuringia, was present. After he had finished reading, Gregory was asked to explain what he had read for the benefit of those who did not understand Latin ; but this he said he was not able to do. Whereupon St Boniface got up and expounded the passages, and added a homily on the need and beauty of an apostolic and virtuous life by way of commentary. Gregory was so moved by his discourse that he resolved upon the spot to follow the holy man wherever he went. St Boniface took him with him, and was himself his master and instructor, made him his constant attendant, and always loved him as his son.   The disciple was a faithful imitator of his spirit and virtues, assisted him in his missions, and accompanied him on his journeys.   St Boniface a little before his death sent Gregory to Utrecht to govern a monastery lately founded there, dedicated in honour of St Martin.   In 754 St Boniface received the crown of martyrdom and at the same time St Eoban, who had administered the see of Utrecht since the death of St Willibrord.   Thereupon St Gregory had to take upon himself the care of that church.   He never received episcopal consecration, though he administered the diocese during twenty years, to his death ; that he never was more than priest appears from his life written by St Ludger, though he is called bishop in the Roman Martyrology and elsewhere.

The abbey of St Martin became a great missionary centre under the rule of St Gregory ;   candidates came to it from all the neighbouring countries, not least from England :   among its *alumni* were St Ludger, just mentioned, St Lebwin and St Marchelm, all three associated with England, the last two as natives and Ludger being a student at York.   By his preaching and care St Gregory made the diocese for which he was responsible a fitting surrounding to the abbey.   St Ludger speaks particularly of his prudence, generous alms-deeds and spirit of forgiveness.   The last trait was exemplified after his two half-brothers had been treacherously killed. When the murderers were sent to him to be put to what death he should think fit, according to the barbarous custom of the country in that age which left the punishment of assassins to the direction of the relations of the deceased person, the saint gave every one of them an alms, and dismissed them with good advice.   For the last three years of his life St Gregory bore with fortitude and patience a creeping paralysis.   He died at Maastricht on August 25, about the year 775, and his feast is kept at Utrecht and Trier as well as by the Canons Regular of the Lateran.

As mentioned above St Ludger wrote a life of Gregory which is our principal source of information.   It has been printed by Mabillon and in the *Acta Sanctorum*, August, vol. v.   Moreover it has been critically re-edited in Pertz, MGH., *Scriptores*, vol. xv.   See further H. Timerding, *Die christliche Frühzeit Deutschlands*, vol. ii, " Die angelsächsische Mission " (1929), and J. A. Coppens, *Kerkgeschiedenis van Noord-Nederland* (1902), pp. 62–70 ; with Hauck, *Kirchengeschichte Deutschlands*, vol. ii.

ST JOAN ANTIDE-THOURET, Virgin, Foundress of the Sisters of Charity under St Vincent's Protection   (A.D. 1826)

Joan Antide-Thouret was born on November 27, 1765, at Sancey-le-Long, near Besançon.   Her father was a tanner, and she was the fifth child of a large family. She lost her mother when she was sixteen, and thereafter took charge of her father's household, which she managed for six years until it was made clear to her that she was called to serve God in the religious life, and she was accepted by the Sisters of Charity of St Vincent de Paul in Paris.   During her period of postulancy and noviceship Sister Joan was twice taken very seriously ill, and when the Revolution began the Sisters of Charity were allowed to carry on their work only on sufferance, so when in 1793 the religious were dispersed she had not yet made her profession. She made her escape from Paris and begged her way on foot to Besançon, and then to her home at Sancey.   Her father was now dead, and to her bitter grief one of her brothers had become a revolutionary.   So she went to live with her godmother and opened a free school, where in the mornings she taught reading, writing and catechism to the village children, and spent the rest of the day, and much of the night, in visiting the sick and needy all over the large parish. She sheltered priests and enabled them to celebrate Mass and administer the sacraments. Joan was denounced to the magistrates for these activities, but her disarming frankness kept her from harm. But in 1796 she took refuge in Switzerland and attached herself to the Sisters of the Christian Retreat, established by the Ven. Antony Receveur at Fribourg ; she accompanied them to Germany, but after a time was advised to return to Switzerland, and again begged her way on foot, this time to Landeron, in the canton of Neufchâtel. Here she met M. de Chaffoy, vicar general of Besançon, who invited her to come back there now conditions were improved and take charge of a school. She at first demurred, pointing out that she had had no proper formation and training in the religious life, but M. de Chaffoy waved aside her scruples : " All that is true, but you can do it, nevertheless. Courage, virtue and trust in God are what are required, and it seems to me that you have these qualities."

In April 1799 the school was opened at Besançon and in the following October, with four other sisters, had to move to a larger house, to which they added a soup-kitchen and a dispensary. In 1800 the community numbered twelve, and a regular novitiate was begun. St Joan was subjected to much adverse criticism for having established this new institute, it being objected that after the Concordat of 1801 she ought to have returned to her own congregation in Paris. She herself had scruples in this matter, but was assured by M. de Chaffoy that she was under no obligation towards the community to which she had formerly belonged : she had taken no vows with them, she had been separated from them by force of the Revolution, and the community was not yet re-established. And she had established the Besançon institute purely and simply in obedience to her ecclesiastical superiors. At the request of the prefect of the city she took charge of the municipal female asylum at Belleveaux, which sheltered orphans, beggars and criminals as well as lunatics, and her acceptance of this charge involved her in a deal of odium and persecution which for a time grievously hampered her work. But this was put on a more secure footing when in 1807 the rule of her sisters was approved by Mgr Le Coz, Archbishop of Besançon. By 1810 they had spread into Switzerland and Savoy, and in that year Joachim Murat, King of Naples, asked St Joan to occupy the convent of Regina Coeli and administer a hospital in his capital city. With seven sisters she accordingly went, and remained there until 1821, laying firm foundations for the educating of girls, the care of the sick, and the spiritual and temporal welfare of her community. One of the first things to be done, and St Joan did it with determination and spirit, was to get rescinded in their favour the local law which put nuns at the mercy of the civil authorities and forbade their dependence on a foreign mother general.

In 1818 Pope Pius VII approved the institute, and confirmed it by a brief in the following year. But this, instead of giving joy and increased stability to the sisters, precipitated a schism that filled with sorrow the remaining years of life of the foundress. In its approbatory brief the Holy See made some small alterations in the rule, and decreed that for the future all the convents of the congregation of the Daughters of Charity under the protection of St Vincent de Paul (as they were to be called) were to be subject to their local bishop and not, as hitherto, to the archbishop of Besançon. The then archbishop, Mgr Cortois de Pressigny, a Gallican-minded prelate, announced that he refused to accept these amendments, and he separated all the convents in his diocese from the rest of the congregation and even forbade them to receive their foundress and mother general within their walls. In 1821 she came to France and passed eighteen months in Paris, trying in vain to smooth out the difficulties. As a last resort she presented herself at the mother-house in Besançon—and was refused admission. Both charity and the facts incline us to the view that this action was prompted not by partizanship but by obedience to their archbishop ; before the schism had hardened many of the sisters of the Besançon diocese openly adhered to their foundress and to the directions of the Holy See. St Joan wrote of these troubles, " As for French affairs, we commit all to divine providence. With the advice of the Holy See we have done all that is possible to achieve unity ; that unity has not yet been effected. We therefore leave it to the mercy of God, in whose hands we long ago placed it. May His will be done and everything be for His glory ! " Then she returned to Naples and, having spent three strenuous years in founding new convents in Italy, she died peacefully on August 24, 1826. St Joan Antide-Thouret was canonized in 1934.

There are biographies in French by P. Bernard and by F. Trochu (the best), and in English by Blanche Anderdon.

ST MARY MICHAELA DESMAISIÈRES, Virgin, Foundress of the Handmaids of the Blessed Sacrament (A.D. 1865)

THIS Spanish lady, who had the title of viscountess and is sometimes referred to by her long family style, is called in the documents of the Congregation of Rites simply Maria Michaela Desmaisières. She was born in Madrid in 1809, lost her mother in childhood, and resisted all attempts to persuade her to marry ; but she lived for some years with her brother while he was Spanish ambassador at Paris and Brussels. Her position necessitated attendance at banquets, state balls and theatrical performances, but she fortified herself against this outwardly worldly life by daily communion and by wearing instruments of penance beneath her dress. All her interest was given to the religious instruction of the ignorant, the rescue of the unprotected and the fallen, and the relief of sickness and poverty.

When she returned to Spain she started more than one organization for work of this kind, but she had to encounter in full measure the contradictions which usually beset such efforts. Her most lasting achievement was the foundation of the congregation of Handmaids of the Blessed Sacrament and of Charity, of which she was elected mother general in 1859. Its work is for women of the streets. This institute was approved by the Holy See for five years in the lifetime of its foundress, and shortly after her death it obtained permanent recognition. It had in the meantime spread widely and was full of promise for the future. In 1865 in connection with this final approbation Mother Michaela had set out on her way to Rome, when an epidemic of cholera broke out in Valencia. Thither she hastened to the succour of her religious daughters, who were attending the plague-stricken. But though she had more than once in previous outbreaks attended cholera patients, she took the infection herself and died, a victim of charity, on August 24. She was canonized in 1934.

The brief of beatification with a biographical summary is printed in the *Acta Apostolicae Sedis*, vol. xvii (1925), pp. 292–296. See also Kempf, *Holiness of the Church in the Nineteenth Century*, pp. 199–201 ; and Angelo Romano di S. Teresa, *La Beata Maria Michelina del Sacramento* (1925).

26 : ST ZEPHYRINUS, Pope and Martyr   (*c.* A.D. 217)

S T ZEPHYRINUS succeeded St Victor I in the pontificate about the year
199. The Church at Rome was disturbed internally during his time of
office by the Montanists, by two sectaries both called Theodotus, and by a
Christological dispute between two parties, one of which was led by the learned
priest Hippolytus (August 13). The last named opposed himself strongly to
Zephyrinus and his deacon and adviser Callistus, the pope refusing to countenance
his teaching on the person of Christ. For this reason the statement that Zephyrinus
was an uneducated man of weak character, a mere tool in the hands of Callistus,
can hardly be accepted on the bare authority of Hippolytus in the *Philoso-
phoumena* : the writer's prejudice is manifest. Eusebius tells us that this pope
exerted his zeal so strenuously against the blasphemies of the two Theodoti that
their followers treated him in the most contumelious manner : but it was his glory
that they called him the principal defender of Christ's divinity.

During the later years of the Emperor Septimius Severus the toleration of
Christians ceased, though it is not known what was the effect in Rome itself of the
edict which laid heavy penalties upon conversion, except that there were many
confessors of the faith. But St Zephyrinus is venerated as a martyr, which title
he might deserve by what he suffered in the persecution, though he probably did
not die by the hand of the executioner.

We know little of St Zephyrinus beyond what may be gathered from a passage or two
in Eusebius and a rather perplexing notice in the *Liber Pontificalis*. Mgr Duchesne has
striven without much success to elucidate the latter (vol. i, pp. 139-140). For the rest
see the *Acta Sanctorum*, August, vol. v ; and DCB., vol. iv, pp. 1215-1220. On the pope's
place of burial see Marucchi in the *Nuovo bullettino di arch. crist.*, 1910, pp. 205-225.

BD HERLUIN, Abbot   (A.D. 1078)

HERLUIN is commonly given the title " Blessed " ; but he received no known *cultus*,
and the Bollandists do not include him in their *Acta Sanctorum*. This great monk
is therefore here passed over with a bare mention.

He was born at Brionne in Normandy in 994. About 1034 he abandoned
knightly service to become a monk, and some five years later founded the abbey of
Bec, which was to become one of the most famous and influential intellectual centres
of the middle ages. Through Lanfranc (also often called Blessed), St Anselm and
others it had an important effect on the ecclesiastical history of England. Herluin,
the rough Norman soldier who desired only to serve God under the Rule of St
Benedict yet fathered so great a foundation, died on August 26, 1078. His abbey
was despoiled at the French Revolution, but it was repeopled by monks in 1948.

Two lives of Herluin have been printed by Mabillon. The earlier is by Gilbert Crispin,
abbot of Westminster, a contemporary who had himself been a monk of Bec. Tooting
Bec in south London was a manor of this abbey, as was Weedon *Beck* in Northamptonshire.

BD TIMOTHY OF MONTECCHIO   (A.D. 1504)

VERY little seems to be recorded concerning the life of this holy Franciscan priest,
although his *cultus* was formally confirmed by Pope Pius IX in 1870. He was, we
are told, of good family and came from the neighbourhood of Aquila in the Abruzzi.

He entered the Franciscan noviceship at an early age and was remarkable from the first for his austerity of life and for his scrupulous observance of the rule. What seems most of all to have impressed his contemporaries was the efficacy of the prayers which he said for those in need of help. He worked many miracles, and it is alleged that he was visited by our Blessed Lady and St Francis and that our Saviour spoke to him audibly from the sacramental species. He died, aged 60, in the friary of St Angelo at Ocra, where his remains are still honoured.

See Mazzara, *Leggendario Francescano* (1680), vol. iii, p. 540 ; and Léon, *Auréole Séraphique* (Eng. trans.), vol. iii, p. 88.

BD THOMAS PERCY, MARTYR   (A.D. 1572)

THE father of this martyr was Sir Thomas Percy, brother and heir-presumptive to the sixth earl of Northumberland, who, if not formally himself a martyr, died for the denial of the ecclesiastical supremacy of King Henry VIII in that he was one of the leaders of the Pilgrimage of Grace, and was hanged at Tyburn in 1537. His elder son, Thomas, was then nine years old and with his brother Henry was removed from the care of his " treasonable " mother. In 1549 the attainder under which they suffered as a result of their father's action was to a certain extent removed, they were " restored in blood"', and eight years later Queen Mary permitted Sir Thomas Percy to succeed to the now vacant earldom of Northumberland. He served the queen well in military and civil affairs on the Scottish border, and in 1558 married Anne Somerset, daughter of the earl of Worcester. During the years following the accession of Elizabeth, while she was consolidating her position and settling the foundations of the Anglican Church, Thomas Percy became a suspect person ; he was " considered very Catholic ", and this in spite of the fact that he used considerable prudence in opposing the queen and, partly on account of his duties in the northern marches, played only a minor part therein ; indeed, the queen gave him the Order of the Garter in 1563, and certain words of the earl during his trial suggest that he was not satisfied with his own behaviour at this time. But he was soon to come to the forefront of affairs.

The north of England was still fairly solidly Catholic : a Protestant observer said of Yorkshire that, " There were scarcely ten gentlemen of note that favour the queen's proceedings in religion " ; and when Queén Mary of the Scots had to take refuge at Carlisle in 1568 she was soon regarded as the Catholic champion. The Earl of Northumberland espoused her cause, hoping by her liberation " to have some reformation in religion, or at the least some sufferance for men to use their conscience as they were disposed ". His support of her attracted attention and he was peremptorily ordered to leave Carlisle, a " gross disrespect " at which he was very indignant. In 1569 the gentlemen of the north began to plan a rising in her favour as next heir to the throne and in order " to restore the Crown, the nobility, and the worship of God to their former estate" ; Northumberland was doubtful about the project, and wished it to be clear that it was not a political one : " we are seeking, I imagine, the glory not of men but of God ". He, therefore, with the earl of Westmorland, Charles Neville, sent a letter to Pope St Pius V, asking for his advice and direction, but they were forced into action before his reply could be received.* The movement was known, and only a few days after they

* The pope's eventual answer was approving and encouraging, and referred to the example of St Thomas Becket. It was dated three days before his bull of deposition of Elizabeth, "*·Regnans in excelsis* ".

had written to the pope the two earls were summoned to appear before Elizabeth ; a hasty meeting of the leaders was called at Brancepeth Castle, they decided (against Northumberland's will and judgement) to ignore the summons, and on November 14 they marched into Durham at the head of their forces. They were welcomed by the townsmen and the cathedral was at once restored to Catholic worship. However inopportune and regrettable the Rising of the North may have been, it at least shows that, after eleven years of forced apostasy, the people of northern England were Catholic at heart, for not only at Durham was the restoration of the religion received with enthusiasm. Mass was celebrated in the parish-churches of Bishop Auckland, Darlington, Ripon, Staindrop, Stokesby and Whitby, and a joyous revival was chronicled at many other places. Meanwhile the earls' forces, under the banner of the Five Wounds and with Bd Thomas Plumtree as chief chaplain, marched into Yorkshire as far as Wetherby, collecting recruits and encouraging the people, but then had to turn back north, where they captured Hartlepool and Barnard Castle. But that was the limit of their success. At the end of a month Elizabeth's troops, under the Earl of Sussex, were in control, the earls disbanded their men at Durham, and with the other leaders fled across the border into Scotland.

The Earl of Sussex took bloody vengeance. People of substance were let off with a good fine, but the common people were hanged in hundreds : every village between the Wear and the Tyne suffered. Westmorland escaped into Flanders ; the Countess of Northumberland, who had been one of the leading spirits of the rebellion, and entirely without her husband's scruples and fears, eventually came under the protection of Lord Home ; and Northumberland himself was captured by the Scottish regent, the Earl of Moray, to whom he was betrayed. He was not willing to hand him over to Elizabeth, but his successor, the Earl of Mar, sold him for £2000—not the first nor the last time in history that a refugee in Scotland was given up for gold. Before this haggling was concluded, the earl had been shut up for two and a half years in Lochleven castle. Dr. Nicholas Sander, a leading Catholic divine of the day, records that he bore this imprisonment and his separation from his wife and four small children with exemplary patience ; he observed all the fasts of the Church, spent much time in prayer and meditation (a book of prayers which he wrote out still exists), and resolutely refused to purchase his pardon (which was offered him) by apostasy. His keeper at Lochleven, William Douglas, was also negotiating for the sale of his prisoner—to the countess his wife, who was scouring Scotland and the Netherlands to raise the ransom. But Elizabeth closed first ; the earl was handed over ; and eventually conveyed to York, where he was lodged in the castle on August 21, 1572.

On the queen's instructions Northumberland had been examined on the way, at Berwick ; a last offer of release on condition of apostasy was made to him ; and when he refused he was told to prepare for death on the very next day. He spent all the night, except for a brief space when sleep overcame him, in prayer, and the next afternoon was marched to The Pavement, where the scaffold was set up. He told the people that he died a Catholic, " as for this new Church of England, I do not acknowledge it " ; and expressed sorrow that he had been the occasion of so many meeting their death in following him for the furtherance of religion, " yet I have no fear but that their souls have obtained the glory of Heaven ". Then his head was struck off, and every drop of his blood was gathered up with handkerchiefs, " for throughout his life he was beyond measure dear to the whole people ". He was forty-four years old. The Countess of Northumberland died in exile at

Namur in 1596 ; two years later their youngest daughter, Mary Percy, whom her father probably never saw, founded at Brussels a monastery of Benedictine nuns, now at Haslemere in Surrey.   Bd Thomas Percy was equivalently beatified in 1896, and his feast is observed in the dioceses of Hexham, Leeds and Middlesbrough.

A full account of this martyr was contributed by G. E. Phillips to the second volume of Camm, LEM., pp. 111–186.   His information is largely drawn, apart from the state papers at the Record Office, from De Fonblanque's *Annals of the House of Percy* (1887), vol. ii, pp. 3–123, and from a Surtees Society publication, *Depositions and Ecclesiastical Proceedings from the Courts of Durham* (1845).   A description of the martyrdom of the earl, written by Nicholas Sander, is in Bridgewater's *Concertatio*.   See also M. M. Merrick, *Thomas Percy, Seventh Earl* (1949).

BD JOHN WALL, MARTYR   (A.D. 1679)

JOHN WALL (*alias* Francis Johnson, Webb, Dormer) belonged to a good Lancashire family and was born in that county (perhaps at Chingle Hall, near Preston) in 1620. He was sent when young to Douay, entered the Roman College in 1641 and was ordained there in 1645.   After a few years on the mission he took the Franciscan habit at St Bonaventure's friary at Douay in 1651, receiving the religious name of Joachim-of-St-Anne, and served there until 1656, when he returned to England. After he had ministered to the Catholics of Worcestershire for over twenty-two years, his headquarters being at Harvington Hall, he was seized in December 1678, at Rushock Court, near Bromsgrove, by a sheriff's officer who had come there to look for a defaulting debtor.   After five months in prison he was tried before Mr Justice Atkins as a priest unlawfully come into the realm ; of the four witnesses brought against him, three had to be subpoenaed, and he defended himself with great prudence.   However, he was sentenced, whereupon he bowed to the judge and said, " Thanks be to God !   God save the king !   And I beseech God to bless your lordship and all this honourable bench."   To which the judge made answer, " You have spoken very well.   I do not intend you shall die, at least not for the present, until I know the king's further pleasure."   " I was not, I thank God for it," wrote Bd John, " troubled with any disturbing thoughts either against the judge for his sentence, or the jury that gave in such a verdict, or against any of the witnesses. . . . And I was, I thank God, so present with myself whilst the judge pronounced the sentence that, without any concern for anything in this world, I did actually at the same time offer myself and the world to God."

In spite of the good will of Mr Justice Atkins, the innocent and beloved Franciscan was not to be reprieved, although after being carefully examined in London for several times by Oates, Bedloe, Dugdale and Prance he was declared by Bedloe in public to be free from any complicity in the Oates " plot ".   He would not renounce his religion, which was what they really wanted, so after a month he was returned to Worcester for execution.   The day before, he was visited in prison by a fellow-Franciscan, Father William Leveson (brother of the venerable martyr, Father Francis Leveson, O.S.F.), who was allowed to spend several hours there and so was able to hear his confession and give him viaticum.   The same friar stood by the scaffold at Redhill the next day and gave him the final absolution when the martyr was hanged and quartered, " thirsting after nothing more than the shedding of his blood for the love of his God ; which he performed with a courage and cheerfulness becoming a valiant soldier of Christ, to the great edification of all Catholics and admiration of all Protestants ".   Bd John Wall was the only one of the English martyrs to be executed at Worcester ; his feast is kept in the arch-diocese of Birmingham.

See Challoner, MMP., pp. 550–555 ; B. Camm, *Forgotten Shrines* (1910), pp. 253–280, and *Bd John Wall* (1932).

BD BERNARD OF OFFIDA (A.D. 1694)

THIS Bernard was born at Appignano in the Marches in the year 1604 of humble parents, and when he was seven years old was set to tend sheep. But he heard the call of God to the religious life, and in 1626 was accepted as a lay-brother by the Capuchins. When he had made his profession he was sent to Fermo and put in charge of the infirmary, and afterwards to other houses of his order, in all of which he laboured with fervour and zeal. Sometimes, some of his brethren thought, with too much zeal, for on one occasion he was reported to the minister provincial for imprudent lavishness in the distribution of alms, whereby his community suffered damage. The provincial called him before a chapter of the house and administered a severe rebuke, which was a matter of great satisfaction to the Franciscan heart of Brother Bernard. When he was sixty years old he was appointed *quaestor*, to beg alms in the streets and from door to door for the friary at Offida, and in this duty he gave more than he received ; people came to him for advice and consolation and help, for his wisdom could not be hid. He had an especial gift for composing quarrels and restoring peace to distracted families, and the most hardened sinners would listen to him and be converted. Bd Bernard's reputation among the people was such that they would come to him and quite simply and confidently ask for a miracle. This sometimes caused difficulties for him. It is said that once a woman came with a very sick baby to be cured, so sick that it died in Bernard's arms. The mother seized his habit and begged and implored him to restore it to life, or she would not let him go. Bernard led her into the church, lay the body on the altar dedicated in honour of St Felix of Can-talice, and exclaiming, " Now, my good St Felix, this is the time to help me ", set himself to prayer. And the child became alive and well. It is also said that our Lady appeared to him one day and told him that all his faults had been forgiven.

Bd Bernard died when he was ninety years old, having spent the last years of his life as door-keeper to his convent, where the poor and unhappy never ceased to crowd to him, on August 22, 1694. He was beatified in 1795.

See Léon, *Auréole Séraphique* (Eng. trans.), vol. iii, pp. 121–123 ; and E. M. de Beaulieu, *Deux émules de St Félix de Cantalice* (1910).

ST ELIZABETH BICHIER DES AGES, VIRGIN, CO-FOUNDRESS
OF THE DAUGHTERS OF THE CROSS OR SISTERS OF ST ANDREW
(A.D. 1838)

THIS holy woman was born at the Château des Ages, at Le Blanc, between Poitiers and Bourges, in the year 1773. Her father was Antony Bichier, lord of the manor of Ages and a public official, and her mother Mary Augier de Moussac, whose father also held public office. The child was christened Jean Elizabeth Mary Lucy, and was commonly called by her second name. Little is known of her childhood, except that she was shy and impressionable, with a heart easily moved by the sight of a beggar or other unfortunate. When she was ten she was sent for schooling to a convent at Poitiers. Her maternal uncle, the Abbé de Moussac, was vicar general at Poitiers, and the superioress of the convent was a relative and Elizabeth seems to have been very happy there.   Her favourite game was building sandcastles, and when in after years she had to be much concerned with building she remembered this and remarked, " It looks as if this was meant to be my trade, seeing I began my apprenticeship to it so young ".

When Elizabeth was nineteen her father died, and a few weeks later, in February 1792, the National Assembly issued a decree against the property of those citizens, the *émigrés*, who had left France in face of the revolution.   Now her eldest brother was among these *émigrés* and, her mother being old and ill, Elizabeth took on herself the job of looking after his interests.   She asked the Abbé de Moussac to instruct her in the law of property and in the keeping of accounts, studies which did not come easy to her but which she was to find again useful later on, and she undertook the defence of her brother and the whole family in a long law case that was eventually decided in their favour.   The village shoemaker was overcome with admiration for Elizabeth's pertinacity, and declared delightedly to her, " Citizeness, all you have to do now is to marry a good republican ! "   But she had no intention of marrying either a " good republican " or a " wicked aristocrat ".   There is still in existence the little picture of our Lady of Help on the back of which she wrote, " I, Joan Elizabeth Mary Lucy Bichier, today dedicate and consecrate myself to Jesus and Mary for ever.   5 May, 1797 ".

In the previous year she and her mother had left the Château des Ages and gone to live at La Guimetière, on the outskirts of Béthines in Poitou.   Here Elizabeth intensified her life of prayer and good works : years later one of the servants said to some Daughters of the Cross, " You've got a great respect for your reverend mother.   But you'd have a twenty times greater respect if you had seen, as I have, what she did for God and His poor when she was young."   The local parish was in a bad way as a result of the revolution, for it had a " constitutional priest " ;* so every night Elizabeth used to collect the farmers and their wives at La Guimetière for prayers and hymns and spiritual reading.   And then she first heard of a priest in a parish twenty-five miles away who was grappling with a similar situation, and had reopened his church in a barn.   It was the Abbé Fournet at Maillé, now known as St Andrew Fournet (May 13).

Elizabeth made her way to Maillé, and the two at once took to one another. She became a frequent visitor to the barn at Petits Marsillys, and Abbé Fournet devised for her a rule of life, at the same time discouraging her suggestion of joining the Trappistines : " Your work is in the world ", he said.   " There are ruins to be rebuilt and ignorance to be remedied."   And so she went on repairing the ravages of religious discord in Béthines, helped by her uncle and her new friend, visiting the sick and needy, and teaching the smaller children.   During the summer months she was helped by two friends, Madeleine Moreau and Catherine Gaschard, and the services of her maid, Mary Anne Guillon, were also enlisted.   Then, in the autumn of 1804, her deeply loved mother died.   The coarse peasant's mourning clothes which Elizabeth then put on, with the approval of Abbé Fournet, raised a curious storm-in-a-teacup.   Her well-dressed and conventional relatives were outraged by it ;   the grave vicar general, M. de Moussac, severely rebuked M. Fournet for allowing it : she must take them off.   Elizabeth refused, obstinately.   The

* The " constitutional clergy " were those who took the oath to maintain the civil constitution drawn up for the Church in France by the National Assembly in 1790.   The constitution and oath were condemned by Pope Pius VI.

cousins went on chattering ; M. de Moussac shrugged, and dropped his opposition, thinking there was probably more in the gesture than met the eye. There was. St Andrew Fournet had had it in his mind for some time that that part of the country needed a small community of nuns to care for the sick and to teach the girls, especially in the rural districts, and that Miss Bichier should be in charge of it. Her reaction to the proposal was that she had never even been a novice, much less a mother superior ; and as this was undeniable St Andrew sent her off to do a year's novitiate with the Carmelite nuns in Poitiers. But, perhaps because he thought she might never come out again, Abbé Fournet soon transferred her to the Society of Providence. Meanwhile he set about forming a community at La Guimetière, consisting of the Madeleine Moreau and Mary Anne Guillon named above and two other young women, and when she had been away hardly six months Elizabeth Bichier was called back to take charge in spite of her protests. As La Guimetière was so far from Maillé, in May 1806 they moved into the Château de Molante, which was quite close. Here they began to teach the children, to give shelter and care to the aged and sick, and to make reparation for the outrages of the revolution against Christ in the Blessed Sacrament.

At first neither St Andrew nor St Elizabeth had in mind anything more than a small local congregation. The foundation members made temporary vows early in 1807, and then looked around for a suitable established congregation to which they could affiliate themselves. But by the end of 1811 it was clear that they would have to stand on their own feet, and they moved into a bigger house, Rochefort, in Maillé itself, for they already numbered twenty-five sisters. Five years later their rule was approved by the diocesan authorities of Poitiers, with the name of Daughters of the Cross,* a name particularly meaningful for the " Good Sister ", Elizabeth Bichier. The fatigues and trials incidental to her position and vocation were considerable ; she did not spare herself in fasting and watching and other austerities ; and St Andrew Fournet, as general superior, did not spare her either.

In 1815 Sister Elizabeth had to go to Paris for an operation, the result of an accident with a vehicle, and the king, Louis XVIII, himself received her at the Tuileries. When the Good Sister returned to Maillé she found her humility and obedience tested to the utmost. The Abbé Fournet received her coldly and informed her she was removed from her office of superioress. It is said that he had been misled by malicious talk ; but it is possible that he acted thus drastically because he feared Elizabeth's success in Paris might go to her head. However, she was restored within a week.

During 1819–1820 thirteen new convents were opened, but at this time a dispute arose about jurisdiction that threatened to disrupt the congregation entirely. However, as things turned out, this unfortunate business did nothing to retard its continued progress. The civil authorities were in favour of small convents dotted about the countryside, their inmates working among the people, and between 1821 and 1825 the Daughters of the Cross opened some fifteen houses in a dozen dioceses. Then the bishop of Bayonne invited them to the Midi, and they spread to Béarn, the Basque country, Gascony and Languedoc. Altogether by 1830 they had over sixty convents, and Sister Elizabeth's record of travelling challenged that of St Teresa herself.

* That is their official designation (there are other congregations with a similar name) but the foundress liked to refer to them as Sisters of St Andrew, after the apostle, patron-saint of Andrew Fournet.

When the Basque house of Igon was opened, the spiritual director appointed was a young curate named Garicoïts : we now know him as St Michael Garicoïts. Elizabeth Bichier greatly encouraged him in the foundation of the Priests of the Sacred Heart of Bétharram, so much so that he declared, " It's all the Good Sister's doing. I had only to do what she told me." When the Good Father, St Andrew Fournet, died in 1834, " the biggest and saddest loss that could happen to us ", wrote Sister Elizabeth, Father Garicoïts became a second Father Fournet to the Daughters of the Cross, at any rate so far as the Basque convents were concerned ; and so he remained till his death. In the autumn of 1836 St Elizabeth's health began seriously to fail. Over and above her state of extreme exhaustion she was afflicted with bad erysipelas of the face, and the hurt that had sent her to Paris over twenty years before broke out afresh. In the spring of 1838 her condition became alarming : she suffered constant and acute pain, and was subject to fits of delirium. Then, after ten days of agony borne with heroic patience, she died peacefully in the evening of August 26.

St Elizabeth Bichier des Ages was canonized in 1947. Numerous anecdotes are told of her goodness and devotion. One of them has special significance for a generation that has known professing Christians wrangle endlessly about whether hungry enemies should be fed, and so on. She once found a miserable-looking man lying ill in a barn, so she had him taken up and brought to the convent, where during the night he died. Next morning she had a visit from the superintendent of police, who told her that she was liable to arrest for sheltering a man who was wanted on a charge of arson. " As you like, sir ", the Good Sister replied. " But allow me to point out that I have only done what you would do yourself in the same circumstances. I found this unfortunate man lying ill ; I took him in ; and I looked after him. Now he is dead. I'm quite ready to tell the magistrate just what happened." This was very characteristic of St Elizabeth's simple straightforwardness of action, the putting into effect of high ideals tenaciously held. Louis Veuillot, whatever objections can be brought against some of his theology and politics, at any rate knew a saint when he saw one, and he said of her, " She is one of the finest-tempered characters ever seen : gentle, resolute, strict, intelligent, industrious, but above all contrite and humble. No difficulty daunts her courage, no lack of strength stops her superhuman labours, no interior distress troubles her outward serenity, no success puffs her up. Whatever happens, she remains undisturbed. Hardships, setbacks, successes, respect, insults—they are all the same to the supreme tranquillity that is rooted in an understanding that sees God in everything, and so must obey."

The first biography of this saint was written by Father L. Rigaud (translated into Italian in 1934) ; he also wrote a life of St Andrew Fournet (1885), who is accounted co-founder of the Daughters of the Cross. The most complete and fully documented biography is that of Father Jules Saubat, but the most handy one is *Ste Jeanne-Elisabeth Bichier des Ages*, by Father Etienne Domec (1947). An essay on the saint by Father Domec appeared in *La Vie Spirituelle*, no. 320 (July 1947).

27 : ST JOSEPH CALASANCTIUS, Founder of the Clerks Regular of the Religious Schools   (A.D. 1648)

JOSEPH CALASANCTIUS was the youngest of five children borne by Maria Gaston to her husband Pedro Calasanz. He was born in his father's castle near Peralta de la Sal in Aragon in the year 1556, and in due course was sent to study the humanities at Estadilla, where his virtue and religious observances were regarded with considerable disrespect by his fellow-students. His father wanted him to be a soldier, but Joseph had other ideas and induced Don Pedro instead to send him to the University of Lerida, where he took his doctorate in law before going on to Valencia. It is said that he left this university in order to escape the attentions of a young kinswoman, who subjected him to a temptation similar to that undergone by his namesake many centuries before at the court of Pharaoh ; certainly he continued his theology at Alcalá, and in 1583 he was ordained priest, being already twenty-eight years old. Soon the fame of Joseph's wisdom, learning and goodness was spread abroad, and after varied experience he was appointed by the bishop of Urgel vicar general of the district of Trempe. He was so successful here that he was sent to deal with the Pyrenean part of the diocese, which comprises the valleys of Andorra of which the bishop of Urgel was joint sovereign prince (he still holds the title) as well as ordinary. This lonely and inaccessible region was in a terrible state of religious and moral disorder, and St Joseph conducted a long and arduous visitation of which the first task was to bring the clergy to a sense of their responsibilities and obligations ; on its completion he returned to Trempe and remained there until he was made vicar general of the whole diocese. But for some time Joseph had been listening to an interior call to undertake a quite different sort of work ; at length he resigned his office and benefices, divided his patrimony between his sisters and the poor, reserving a sufficient income for himself, endowed several charitable institutions, and in 1592 left Spain for Rome.

Here Joseph met an old friend of Alcalá, Ascanio Colonna, already a cardinal, and for five years he was under the direct patronage of the Colonnas. During the plague of 1595 he distinguished himself by his devotion and fearlessness, and entered into a holy rivalry with his friend St Camillus of Lellis as to who should expend himself the more freely in the service of the sick and dying. But during these years St Joseph never lost sight of the work which had drawn him to Rome, namely, the instruction of young children, of whom there were so many, neglected or homeless, in the most urgent need of interest and care. He had become a member of the Confraternity of Christian Doctrine, whose business it was to teach both children and adults on Sundays and feast-days, and in so doing was brought home vividly to St Joseph the state of degradation and ignorance in which so many of the children of the poor lived. He was soon convinced that periodical instruction was utterly inadequate to cope with the situation, and that free day-schools for both religious and secular education were required. He therefore first of all invited the official parish-schoolmasters to admit poor pupils to their schools without payment, but they would not undertake the extra work without a rise in salary, and this the Roman senate refused to grant. He approached the Jesuits and the Dominicans, but neither order could see a way to extending its activities, for their members were already fully engaged. St Joseph then came to the conclusion that it was God's will that he should begin the work himself, single-handed if necessary. Don Antonio Brendani, parish-priest of Santa Dorotea, offered him the use of two rooms and his own services, two more priests joined them, and in November 1597 a public free school was opened.

At the end of a week the school had a hundred pupils and before long many more, and the founder had to engage paid teachers from among the unbeneficed clergy of the city. In 1599 it was moved into new quarters and St Joseph obtained permission from Cardinal Ascanio to leave the Colonna household and take up his residence on the school premises with the other masters ; they lived a quasi-community life and the founder acted as superior. During the following couple of years the pupils increased to seven hundred, and in 1602 another move was made, to a large house adjoining the church of Sant' Andrea della Valle. While hanging a bell in the courtyard St Joseph fell from a ladder and broke his leg, an accident the effects of which were a source of lameness and pain for the rest of his life. Pope Clement VIII having made a grant towards the rent, and people of consequence having begun to send their children to the school, the parish-schoolmasters and others began to criticize it with some vehemence ; complaints of its disorders were made to the pope and he directed Cardinals Antoniani and Baronius to pay it a surprise visit of inspection. This was done and as a result of their report Clement took the institution under his immediate protection. In similar circumstances the same course was taken and the grant doubled in 1606 by Paul V. But these difficulties were the beginning of trials and persecutions which beset St Joseph until the end of his life. Nevertheless during the succeeding five years the work prospered and grew in spite of all opposition, and in 1611 a *palazzo* was purchased to house it near the church of San Pantaleone ; there were about a thousand pupils, including a number of Jews whom the founder himself invited to attend and encouraged by his kindness. Other schools were opened, and in 1621 the teachers were recognized as a religious order, of which St Joseph was named superior general. He did not let the cares of the generalate diminish either his religious observances or his care for the needy, the sick, and any to whom he could be of service. About this time there came to Rome, with his wife and family, an English gentleman, Mr Thomas Cocket, who by abjuring Protestantism had brought himself within reach of the penal laws ; him the saint assisted, and the pope followed his example. assigning a pension to the refugee converts. For ten years the congregation continued to prosper and extend, and spread from Italy into the Empire.

In 1630 was admitted to the institute at Naples one Mario Sozzi, a middle-aged priest, who in due course was professed. For several years his froward and perverse behaviour made him a great nuisance to his brethren but, having by a show of zeal gained the good will and influence of the Holy Office, he contrived to get himself, in 1639, made provincial of the Clerks Regular of the Religious Schools in Tuscany, with extraordinary powers and independence of the superior general. He proceeded to administer the province in the most capricious and damaging way, harmed as much as he could the reputation of St Joseph with the Roman authorities, and at length denounced him to the Holy Office. Cardinal Cesarini, as protector of the new institute and in order to vindicate Joseph, ordered Father Mario's papers and letters to be seized ; these included some documents of the Holy Office and that congregation, spurred on by Sozzi, straightway had St Joseph arrested and carried through the streets like a felon. He was brought before the assessors and only saved from imprisonment by the intervention of Cardinal Cesarini. But Father Mario was unpunished, and continued to plot for control of the whole institute, representing St Joseph to be too old and doddering for the responsibility ; he managed by deceit to get him suspended from the generalate and contrived that a visitor apostolic be appointed who was favourable to himself. This visitor and Father Mario became in effect in supreme command, and St Joseph was subjected by them to the most humiliating, insulting and unjust treatment, while the order was reduced to such confusion and impotence that the loyal members were unable to persuade the superior authorities of the true state of affairs.

Towards the end of 1643 Mario died and was succeeded by Father Cherubini, who pursued the same policy.   St Joseph bore these trials with marvellous patience, urging the order to obey his persecutors for they were *de facto* in authority, and on one occasion sheltering Cherubini from the violent opposition of some of the younger fathers who were indignant at his treachery.   The Holy See had some time previously set up a commission of cardinals to look into the whole matter, and at length in 1645 it ordered the reinstatement of St Joseph as superior general ; this announcement was received with great joy but led at once to renewed efforts on the part of the malcontents, who had the support of an aggrieved female relative of the pope.   They were successful, and in 1646 Pope Innocent X published a brief of which the effect was to make the Clerks Regular of the Religious Schools simply a society of priests subject to their respective bishops.   Thus in his ninetieth year St Joseph saw the apparent overturning of all his work by the authority to which he was so greatly devoted and the indirect disgrace of himself before the world ; when the news was brought to him he simply murmured, " The Lord gave and the Lord hath taken away.   Blessed be the name of the Lord."

The business of drawing up new constitutions and regulations for the shattered institute of Religious Schools was entrusted to Father Cherubini, but within a few months he was convicted by the auditors of the Rota of the maladministration of the Nazarene College, of which he was rector.   He retired from Rome in disgrace, but returned in the following year to die, repentant of the part he had played and re-conciled to St Joseph, who consoled him on his death-bed.   A few months later, on August 25, 1648, St Joseph himself died, and was buried in the church of San Pantaleone ; he was ninety-two years old.   There is an obvious parallel between this history and that of St Alphonsus Liguori and the early days of the Redemptorists, and during the troubles of his young congregation St Alphonsus used to encourage and fortify himself by reading the life of St Joseph Calasanctius ; he was canonized in 1767, six years before the death of Alban Butler, who only gives to him a brief notice, wherein he is referred to as " a perpetual miracle of fortitude and another Job "—a comparison made by Cardinal Lambertini (afterwards Pope Benedict XIV) before the Congregation of Sacred Rites in 1728.   The failure of St Joseph's foundation was only apparent.   Its suppression was strongly objected to in several places, and it was reconstituted with simple vows in 1656 and restored as a religious order in 1669.   Today the Clerks Regular of the Religious Schools (commonly called Piarists or Scolopi) flourish in various parts of the world.

The documents submitted in the process of beatification and canonization have been largely utilized by the biographers of St Joseph Calasanctius, and this is notably the case in the life written in Italian in the eighteenth century, a translation of which was published in the Oratorian Series edited by Father Faber (1850).   The earliest detailed account of Calasanctius seems to have been compiled by one of his religious sons, Father Mussesti, for the information of Pope Alexander VII, less than twenty years after the saint's death. A considerable number of biographies have since appeared in Italian, French, Spanish and German.   Those by Timon-David (1883), Tommaseo (1898), Casanovas y Sanz (1904), Heidenreich (1907), Giovanozzi (1930) and Santoloci (1948) may be specially mentioned. See also Heimbucher, *Orden und Kongregationen der Kat. Kirche*, vol. iii, pp. 287–296 ; and Pastor, *Geschichte der Päpste*, especially vol. xi, pp. 431–433 (Eng. trans.).

SS. MARCELLUS AND HIS COMPANIONS, MARTYRS   (A.D. 287 ?)

THE governor of the Egyptian Thebaïd summoned before him seventeen individuals, the whole Christian congregation of a place, said to be Oxyrynchus, who had been denounced to him as " the only ones in the city who oppose the imperial decree, who are impious towards the worship of the gods, and who despise your tribunal by not obeying your commands ". They were the tribune Marcellus, his wife Mammaea, and their two sons, a bishop and three clerks, a soldier, seven other laymen and a woman. When they had been brought in chains before the governor at Thmuis he tried to move them to obedience, and when he failed condemned them all to the beasts. He made a last attempt to save them the next day, in the amphitheatre itself. " Are you not ashamed ", he cried ," to worship a man who was put to death and buried years ago by order of Pontius Pilate, whose records, I am told, are still in existence ? " The Christians refused to be moved by this appeal, and the writer of their *acta* puts into the mouth of the bishop, Miletius, a confession of faith in the divinity of Jesus Christ in words obviously inspired by the Arian controversy and the definitions of the Council of Nicaea. They were therefore put to death, the *acta* say by beheading, because the bears when let loose would not touch them and a fire could not be kindled to burn them.

The Roman Martyrology refers to these martyrs as Marcellinus and Mannea with their three sons, and puts the place of the passion at Tomi on the Black Sea.

Achelis in his book *Die Martyrologien* (1900), pp. 173–177, adopted a view substantially identical with that expressed above. More recent investigation has questioned his conclusions. Delehaye does not think it probable that Tomi has been substituted for Thmuis, but that the martyrs really belonged to Moesia and were transferred by the hagiographer to Egypt. See the *Analecta Bollandiana*, vol. xxxviii (1920), pp. 384–385, and P. Franchi de' Cavalieri in *Studi e testi*, vol. lxv (1935). The text of the acts is printed in the *Acta Sanctorum*, August, vol. vi, pp. 14–15.

ST POEMEN, Abbot   (Fifth Century)

THE abbot Poemen was one of the most celebrated of the fathers of the desert. He forsook the world and went into the Egyptian desert of Skete, one elder and several younger brothers of his accompanying him. In 408 they were driven away from their first settlement by raids of Berbers, and took refuge in the ruins of a temple at Terenuthis. Anubis, the eldest, and Poemen governed the little community of hermits by turns. Of the twelve hours of the night, four were allotted to work, four to singing office, and four to sleep ; in the day they worked till noon, read till three in the afternoon, and then went to gather firing, food and other necessaries.

St Poemen often passed several days, sometimes a whole week, without eating, but it was his constant advice to others that their fasts should be moderate, and that they should take sufficient nourishment every day : " We fast ", he said, " to control our bodies, not to kill them." But he taught that no monk ought ever to taste wine or to seek any deliberate gratification of the senses : " for sensuality expels the spirit of penance and the holy fear of God from the heart as smoke drives away bees ; it extinguishes grace, and deprives a soul of the comfort and presence of the Holy Ghost ". St Poemen feared the least occasion that could interrupt his solitude, or make the distractions of the world break in upon him ; and on one occasion he even went so far as to refuse to see his mother, foregoing that happiness then that they might enjoy it more hereafter. He is chiefly remembered for his " sayings ". Among them is related that, when one who had committed a fault told him he would do penance for it three years, the saint advised him to confine his penance to three days, but to be very fervent about it. A monk was grievously molested with thoughts of blasphemy ; Poemen comforted him, and bade him confidently say to the Devil, whenever he suggested any abominable thought, " May your blasphemy fall on you ; it is not mine, for my heart detests it ". But to another who spoke of the Devil he said, " Devil ! It's always the Devil that's blamed. I say that it's self-will." And another time, " Never try to have your own way. Those who are self-willed are their own worst tempters, and require no devil to tempt them." St Poemen used strongly to exhort to frequent communion and to a great desire for that divine food, as the stag pants after the water-brooks. " Some aver ", said he, " that stags feel a violent inward heat and thirst because in the desert they eat serpents and their bowels are parched with the poison. Thus souls in the wilderness of this world always suck in something of its poison, and so need perpetually to approach the body and blood of Jesus Christ, which fortifies them against all such venom." To one who complained that his neighbour was a monk of whom derogatory tales were told, and gave the authority of another monk to prove their truth, he said, " There could not be worse evidence than scandalous stories told by a monk ; by telling them he shows himself unworthy of credence ". It was another saying of this abbot that " silence is no virtue when charity requires speech " ; that " people should not waste other people's time by asking advice when no advice is necessary or wanted " ; and that " a living faith consists in thinking little of oneself and having tenderness towards others ".

St Poemen took over complete control of the community on the death of Anubis. " We lived together ", he said, " in complete unity and unbroken peace till death broke up our association. We followed the rule Anubis made for us ; one was appointed steward, and he had care of our meals. We ate such things as were set before us, and no one said : Give me something else ; I cannot eat this." He returned from Terenuthis to Skete but was again driven out by raids. Later he was present at the death of St Arsenius on the rock of Troë, near Memphis : " Happy Arsenius ! " he cried, " who had the gift of tears in this life ! For he who does not weep for his sins on earth will bewail them for ever in eternity." St Poemen himself died very soon afterwards. He is named in the Roman Martyrology and in the Byzantine liturgical books is referred to as " the lamp of the universe and pattern of monks ".

A short Greek life with other miscellaneous references will be found in the *Acta Sanctorum*, August, vol. vi ; but the most convenient source of information concerning Poemen and the other fathers of the desert is the *Vitae Patrum* of Father Rosweyde. His " sayings " are printed in Migne, PG., vol. lxv, cc. 317-368.

ST CAESARIUS, Bishop of Arles　　(A.D. 543)

St Caesarius was born in 470, in the territory of Chalon on the Saône, of a Gallo-Roman family. In his youth he laid a good foundation of learning and determined to become a priest, and at eighteen years of age he asked that he might enter himself in the service of the Church. This was done accordingly ; but two years after Caesarius withdrew to the monastery of Lérins, which had produced many learned and holy men. In this house the abbot appointed him cellarer ; but as human passions creep into places the furthest removed from the incentives of vice, some of the monks were offended at his scrupulously just administration and complained so much that the abbot relieved him of his office. Caesarius was glad to be at liberty to give himself up entirely to contemplation and penance ; but his health gave way and he was sent to Arles to recover. Here his scruples about the use of pagan authors for study by Christian clerics drew the attention of the bishop,

Eonus, to him ; they were kinsmen, and Eonus was sufficiently attracted by the young man to write to the abbot of Lérins asking that he might be released for the episcopal service. Caesarius was then ordained deacon and priest, and put by Eonus in charge of a neighbouring monastery whose discipline was very relaxed. He gave these monks a rule, governed them for three years, and in spite of his youth and inexperience made them a model body of religious. The bishop of Arles on his death-bed recommended him for his successor. The saint fled and hid himself among the tombs ; but he was discovered and obliged to acquiesce in the election of the clergy and the city. He was then thirty-three years old, and he presided over that church forty years.

Caesarius had not the Roman sense of order nor the sumptuous habits by which some bishops of those times supported the temporal importance of their positions, but he had a high and holy religious conscience which made him the leading prelate of Gaul. Among the first things he did was to regulate the singing of the Divine Office, which he ordered to be celebrated publicly, not only on Sundays, Saturdays, and solemn festivals as had been the custom at Arles, but every day as was done in other neighbouring churches ; and he did not scruple to modify the office to encourage the attendance of lay people. He was careful to instruct his flock in prayer, and to teach them to cry to God with earnest desires of the heart : not with their lips only, which can be no prayer but only mockery and an insult to God, for prayer is the raising of the heart and mind to God. " A man ", said he, " worships that on which his mind is intent during prayer. Whoever in his prayers thinks of public affairs, or of the house he is building, worships them rather than God." Caesarius preached on all Sundays and holidays, and often on other days, both morning and evening, and if he was hindered he ordered the priests or deacons to read to the people some homilies of the fathers ; and he had some such homily always read after Matins and Vespers, that the people might never leave church without some instruction. He was opposed to studied discourses, and his own style is plain, natural and pleasing. He used to descend very much to particulars, and spoke chiefly against those vices which prevailed most, especially warning against a delay of repentance, and inculcating fear of Purgatory for venial sins and the necessity of effacing them by daily penance. His ordinary exhortations were on prayer, fasting, alms, the pardon of injuries, chastity and the practice of all manner of good works. He was, in fact, the first " popular " preacher whose words have come down to us ; his discourses are full of homely allusions and illustrations, and they rarely exceeded a quarter of an hour in length. At the same time he urged the value of the corporate worship which he took so much pains to have observed fittingly. " Match your behaviour to the words you sing ", he said. " Let your souls be as pure as the text *Beati immaculati in via*. When you sing the verse *Confundantur superbi*, hate pride and flee from it. And so, while your ears are charmed with melody, you will realize what the Psalmist meant when he said, *Quam dulcia faucibus meis eloquia tua !* "

An early biographer refers to St Caesarius as " another Noah, who built an ark to shelter his daughters against the perils of the times ". This refers to the monastery he established to give a more permanent home to the maidens and widows of southern Gaul who wished to give themselves to God. It was first at Aliscamps, among the Roman tombs, and then removed within the city walls. This monastery was at first called St John's, but afterward took the name of St Caesarius, who committed the government of it to his sister St Caesaria. St

Caesarius drew up a rule for these women, which was one of the principal preoccupations of his life ; in it he put strong emphasis on stability and the completeness and permanence of enclosure. He also drew up a rule for men on the same lines, which he imposed throughout his diocese, whence it spread further. St Caesarius was promoted to the see of Arles when it had just succeeded in maintaining its extensive jurisdiction against the bishop of Vienne, and he found himself metropolitan of many suffragan sees. As such he presided over several synods, of which the most important was that at Orange in 529. This council pronounced against those who blasphemously affirm that God predestines any man to damnation ; on the other side, it declared that according to the Catholic faith God inspires into our souls by His grace the beginning of His faith and love, or the first desire or good disposition of the soul towards it, and that He is the author of our conversion, against the semi-Pelagians.

Side by side with his ecclesiastical labours, St Caesarius had his share in the public upheavals of the age in which he lived. The city of Arles was at that time subject to Alaric II, King of the Visigoths. It was suggested to this prince that the bishop, being born a subject to the king of Burgundy, did all that lay in his power to bring the territory of Arles under his dominion. This was untrue, but Alaric in 505 banished him to Bordeaux. When Alaric discovered his innocence he recalled him from exile and condemned his accuser to be stoned, but pardoned him at the intercession of Caesarius. When the Burgundians besieged Arles and many prisoners were brought into the city, St Caesarius was moved exceedingly at their condition, for they were in want both of clothes and food. He gave them both, and employed in relieving them the treasury of his church. He stripped off silver and melted down censers, chalices and patens, saying, " Our Lord celebrated His last supper on earthen dishes, not on plate, and we need not scruple to part with His vessels for those whom He has redeemed with His own life. I should like to know if those who censure what we do would not be glad to be themselves helped in the same way were the same misfortune to befall them."

After the death of the king of the Visigoths, Theodoric the Ostrogoth, King of Italy, seized those dominions in Languedoc, and St Caesarius came under his suspicion ; so he was apprehended and brought under guard to Ravenna. When the saint came into the king's presence and saluted him, Theodoric, seeing his venerable aspect and intrepid air, rose and returned his courtesy. He then spoke kindly with the bishop on the state of his city and after he had dismissed him said to those about him, " May God punish those who have been responsible for this holy man's undertaking so long a journey without cause. I trembled when he came in ; he has the face of an angel. I can believe no harm of such a person." Theodoric sent to Caesarius a silver basin, with three hundred pieces of gold, and the message, " Receive the offering of the king, your son, and look on it as a token of friendship ". Caesarius sold the basin and ransomed captives with the money. He went on to Rome, where Pope St Symmachus confirmed the metropolitan rights of Arles, recognized him as apostolic delegate in Gaul, and conferred the *pallium*, which St Caesarius is said to have been the first bishop in western Europe to receive.

St Caesarius returned to Arles in 514 and continued to watch over and instruct his people for many years. When the city was taken by the Franks in 536 he retired somewhat from public life and spent much time at the convent of St John. He made a will in favour of those nuns, and in his seventy-third year began to prepare finally for the death which he knew to be near.   He asked how long it was to the festival of St Augustine, saying, " I hope I shall die about that time ; you know how much I always loved his truly Catholic doctrine ".   He caused himself to be carried in a chair to the monastery of his nuns, whom he endeavoured to prepare and comfort for the grief which he knew his death would give them ; they were then above two hundred in number, and their superior was called Caesaria, and had succeeded his sister of the same name.   St Caesarius, " veritable teacher of Frankish Gaul ", died on the eve of the feast of St Augustine in 543.

We possess what may be called two early biographies of St Caesarius.   Both of them, after having been printed by Mabillon and the Bollandists, have been critically edited by B. Krusch in MGH., *Scriptores Merov.*, vol. iii, pp. 457–501.   The authenticity of the saint's last will and testament has been called in question by the same critic, but it has been successfully vindicated by G. Morin in the *Revue Bénédictine*, vol. xvi (1899), pp. 97–112, who also provides a revised text.   Two important monographs dealing with St Caesarius were published in 1894, the first by B. F. Arnold, *Caesarius von Arelate und die gallische Kirche seiner Zeit*, the other by A. Malnory, *St Césaire Évêque d'Arles*, and with these may be coupled a valuable summary by Lejay in DTC., vol. ii, cc. 2168–2185.   But the scholar who had admittedly the most competent knowledge of the life and writings of Caesarius was Dom G. Morin.   A list of his earlier contributions to the subject will be found in his *Études, Textes, Découvertes* (1913), pp. 41–45.   He prepared an edition of the saint's sermons and other works (1937–42), the second volume of which includes the *vita* by Cyprian of Toulon.   Dom Morin proved that Caesarius, if not himself the author, is at least the earliest writer to show familiarity with the so-called Athanasian Creed (*Quicunque vult*) ; and he was at one time inclined to identify him with the important canonical collection *Statuta Ecclesiae antiqua*, but this attribution is much contested.   A useful, but not altogether reliable, modern life of St Caesarius is that of M. Chaillan in the series " Les Saints " ; that by A. Malnory (1934) is fuller and better.

ST SYAGRIUS, Bishop of Autun   (A.D. 600)

SYAGRIUS is supposed to have been by birth a Gallo-Roman, and he was raised to the see of Autun about the year 560.   He exercised great influence both in councils and in the training of persons in the Christian life.   To his prudence was committed the difficult business of re-establishing tranquillity in the convent of the Holy Cross at Poitiers, where two nuns were in rebellion against their abbess ; but the task was too much for him and the other bishops associated with him in it, and the rebels had to be excommunicated by a synod.   Apparently this experience made the good bishop over-careful, for some years later we find him reproved by Pope St Gregory the Great for not preventing the marriage of a nun (named, curiously enough, Syagria) who had been abducted from her cloister.   The pope nevertheless gave distinguishing marks of the esteem he had for the virtue and capacity of Syagrius. When he sent St Augustine with missionaries into England, he recommended them to him, and they were entertained by St Syagrius on their journey.   Moreover, though he was only a bishop he was granted permission to wear the *pallium*, at the instance of Queen Brunhilda.   King Gontran, who also greatly appreciated his abilities, chose St Syagrius for the companion of his journey when going to the baptism of Clotaire II ; this took place at Nanterre in 591.

See the *Acta Sanctorum*, August, vol. vi, and Duchesne, *Fastes Épiscopaux*, vol. ii, p. 173.

LITTLE ST HUGH OF LINCOLN   (A.D. 1255)

THE charge against the Jews of a general practice of ritual murder, a charge which arose from the story of Little St William of Norwich in the twelfth century, has been amply refuted by both Jewish and Christian writers ; nor has any particular sporadic example of it ever been proved. This does not do away with the possibility of accidental or deliberate killing of Christian children by Jews out of hatred for their religion (or even more of hatred for those that professed it), even to the extent of crucifixion and mockery of the passion of Christ ; but this again has never been proved against them in any specific example, nor is there any evidence to show that the famous cases of William of Norwich and Hugh of Lincoln were exceptions to this.

The story is that Hugh was a child of nine years old, the son of a widow. On the occasion of some Jewish gathering at Lincoln one Koppin (or Jopin) enticed him into his house on July 31, 1255, where he was kept until the following August 27, a Friday. On that day Koppin and his fellows tortured and scourged him, crowned him with thorns and finally crucified him in derision. They tried to dispose of the body by burial, but the earth refused to cover it, and it was thrown down a well. Hugh's school-fellows directed suspicion towards the Jew's house and Koppin was arrested, together with ninety-two other Jews of the city. Koppin is alleged to have confessed the crime, to have denounced his accomplices, and to have stated (certainly falsely) that it was Jewish custom to crucify a Christian boy once a year. By an order of King Henry III and his parliament assembled at Reading, Koppin was dragged to death at the heels of a young horse and eighteen others were hanged at Lincoln ; the remainder were imprisoned in London, but set free on payment of large fines. Their release was attributed to the kind offices of the Franciscans, who interceded for them ; but Matthew Paris asserts that they were bribed to do this by the wealth of Jewry. Immediately Hugh's body was recovered from the well a blind woman was restored to sight on touching it and invoking the martyr ; other miracles followed, and the chapter of Lincoln solemnly translated the relics from their parish church to a shrine next to the tomb of Grosseteste. It is impossible to tell now whether the Jews were innocent or guilty of the crime attributed to them ; the widespread antisemitism of the middle ages encouraged the conviction that Hugh suffered *in odium fidei*. The account of Little St Hugh in Chaucer's *Prioresse's Tale* is well known, and both he and St William of Norwich were favourite ballad subjects ; a pathetic song about William, with a sweet simple tune, was sung in country parts within living memory.

The account given above is that of Matthew Paris. The Burton Annalist attributes the intervention in favour of the Jews to the Dominicans, not to the Franciscans, and C. Trice Martin in his preface to the *Registrum Epistolarum J. Peckham* (Rolls Series), vol. ii, pp. lxxxviii and xcvi, seems to agree with him. See also the French account described by T. D. Hardy in his *Catalogue of British History*, vol. iii, p. 144. *Cf.* further what has been said regarding these cases of supposed ritual murder under St Simon of Trent herein on March 24.

BD ANGELO OF FOLIGNO (A.D. 1312)

THIS Angelo must not be confounded with Bd Angela of the same place. He was born at Foligno in 1226, the son of Bernard, Count of Torre and Vignole, and at the age of twenty became an Augustinian friar at Botriolo, near Cesena. In 1248 he was sent to his native town to found a house of the order there ; ten years later, with Bd Ugolino Mevainati, he established another in an abandoned Benedictine house at Gualdo Cattaneo in Umbria ; and in 1275 another at Montefalco, where he remained as prior till 1292.   The last twenty years of his long and arduous life were spent in holy retirement at Foligno, where he died on August 27, 1312. Bd Angelo had as novice-master Bd John Buono, the converted clown, and was bound in friendship to St Nicholas of Tolentino ; he was himself venerated as a saint immediately after his death, and his *cultus* was approved by the Holy See in 1891.

A short biographical notice with indication of authorities will be found in DHG., vol. iii, c. 21.   See also Seeböck, *Herrlichkeit der Katholischen Kirche*, p. 308 ; and Torelli, *Ristretto delle Vite*, etc.

ST MARGARET THE BAREFOOTED, Widow   (A.D. 1395 ?)

She was born of a poor family at San Severino in the March of Ancona in the middle of the fourteenth century, and was married at the age of fifteen to a husband who ill-treated her.   He was particularly annoyed at the nickname which the people gave her because she went about without shoes, making herself like one of those beggars whom she delighted to help.   St Margaret bore this patiently for years until the man died, and she was free to pass the rest of her life unmolested in prayer and alms-deeds.   Her body is entombed in the church of St Dominic at San Severino, and she is named in the Roman Martyrology on this day, having been added thereto by Cardinal Baronius.

A brief, but, in view of the lack of reliable materials, a fairly exhaustive account of this saint is given in the *Acta Sanctorum* in the second volume for August under August 5.   A fragment will there be found of a life by a contemporary, Pompilio Caccialupo, but the editors were unable to obtain a copy of the complete text.

BD GABRIEL MARY   (A.D. 1532)

Gilbert Nicolas was born at Riom, near Clermont, in 1463 and at the age of sixteen sought admission among the Friars Minor at Meung and at Amboise ; he was refused, because he looked a boy of very delicate health, but undeterred by the rebuff he journeyed on across Touraine and Poitou until he came to a friary near La Rochelle, where he again presented himself, without hiding that he had been refused elsewhere.   The father guardian liked his pluck and accepted him.   His novice master " had rather to use a bridle to restrain him from excess than a goad to urge him on ", and Friar Gilbert proved an exemplary Franciscan, " no more kind or charitable man could be found ".   He became a very proficient philosopher and theologian, was made guardian of the friary that had turned him away at Amboise, and filled various other offices among the Friars Minor of France.   In 1517 he attended the general chapter of his order at Rome, where he was elected commissary general for the Observants on this side of the Alps, an office which he held till the end of his life.

Long previously Friar Gilbert had been appointed confessor to St Joan of Valois who, after King Louis XII had obtained in 1498 a declaration that his marriage with her was null, had retired to Bourges and devoted herself to founding the Order of the Annunciation (*Annonciades*).   She was assisted in this by her confessor, who obtained the approbation of the rule by Pope Alexander VI in 1502. He was named visitor general of the order, which he directed for thirty years, and Pope Leo X, struck by his love for the mystery of the Annunciation, gave him the

name of Gabriel Mary by which he has since been called.   He revised the constitutions of the order for the confirmation of Leo X, and he founded six convents
of these nuns in France and the Netherlands.   In 1521 he made a visitation of the
Observant friaries in England.   Throughout his life Gabriel Mary was distinguished by his devotion to our Lady, of whom he frequently preached and was
never tired of speaking ; he died with her *Magnificat* on his lips in the Annonciade
convent of Rodez on August 27, 1532.

This feast does not seem to be kept liturgically by the Franciscans, though the
Annonciades observe it ; but the *cultus* of Gabriel Mary has not been approved.   A
somewhat lengthy account of this servant of God is, however, to be found in Léon, *Auréole
Séraphique* (Eng. trans.), vol. iii, pp. 74–87.   See the article by J. F. Bonnefoy in
Revue d'ascétique et de mystique, t. xvii (1936), pp. 252–273 ; *Vies de la bse Jeanne de
France et du bx Gabriel-Marie* (1937) ; and the bibliographical note to St Joan of France
on February 4.

BD DAVID LEWIS, Martyr   (A.D. 1679)

DAVID LEWIS (*alias* Charles Baker) was a Monmouthshire man, son of Morgan
Lewis, a Protestant member of a recusant family, and Margaret Prichard, a Catholic.
All their nine children were brought up Catholics except, curiously enough, the
future martyr. He was born in 1616 and lived at Abergavenny, where he was
educated at the Royal Grammar School (his grand-uncle, the Venerable Father
Augustine Baker, Bd Philip Powell, and others had preceded him there) ; at the
age of sixteen he was entered at the Middle Temple, but after three years in London
went abroad as tutor to the son of Count Savage, and it is probable that he was
reconciled to the Church while staying in Paris.   He returned home to Abergavenny
for a couple of years, and in 1638 entered the *Venerabile* at Rome.   He was ordained
priest in 1642 and two years later became a Jesuit novice ; in 1646 he was sent to
the mission, but such was the impression he had left behind him that he was almost
at once recalled to Sant'Andrea and made spiritual director of the English College.
In 1648 the Jesuit father general again sent him to Wales and he had his headquarters at the Cwm, an obscure hamlet on the Hereford-Monmouth border ; here
in a large farmhouse was the College of St Francis Xavier, which from 1625 to 1678
was the Jesuit centre in the west of England and the shelter and refuge of hunted
priests for miles around.   For the next thirty-one years he worked in this
border-land, which was full of recusants : " a zealous seeker after the lost sheep,
fearless in dangers, patient in labours and sufferings, and so charitable to his
indigent neighbours as to be commonly called the father of the poor ", in Welsh,
" tad y tlodion ".

In 1678 Titus Oates discovered his " popish plot ".   When the anti-Catholic
panic reached Monmouthshire the Jesuits got ready to leave the Cwm and cover up
their tracks, and they did so only just in time.   The Cwm was sacked by the
sheriff's men, who found pictures of saints, " also crucifixes and bottles of oyle,
reliques, an incense-pot, a mass-bell, surplices and other habits, boxes of white
wafers, stamps with Jesuitical devices ", and a number of books which are still in
the cathedral library at Hereford.   Father Lewis was by then safely in hiding at
Llanfihangel Llantarnam ; but there was a woman, Dorothy James, wife of a
servant of Father Lewis, and now apostates both, who had tried to get some money
from him on false pretences, and she was going about the streets of Caerleon saying
that " she would wash her hands in Mr Lewis's blood, and would have his head to

make porridge of, as a sheep's head ". James found out his refuge, denounced him, and he was taken by six dragoons early on Sunday morning, November 17, just as he was going to celebrate Mass. John Arnold of Llanfihangel Crucorney and two other magistrates conveyed him into Abergavenny, where the recorder was wakened from his Sunday after-dinner nap, and in a room of the Golden Lion inn David Lewis was committed to Monmouth jail. Here he remained till the following January 13 : " I was kept close prisoner, locked up at night and barred up by day, though indeed friends by day had access unto me, with an underkeeper's leave ". Then he was removed to Usk, " and it snowing hard on the way, we alighted at Raglan to warm and refresh ourselves. While I was there a messenger comes to the door and desires to speak to me. His business was that a very good friend of mine, one Mr Ignatius, *alias* Walter Price [S.J.], lay dying about half a mile off thence." Being able to do no more, Father Lewis " sent him his best wishes for his soul's passage out of this turbulent world into an eternity of rest, and so went forward with his keepers to his new prison of Usk ".

He was tried at the March assizes before Sir Robert Atkins, and was condemned for his priesthood, chiefly on the evidence of James and his wife ; though, on the prisoner's strong protest, the judge exonerated him from " a foul aspersion " being circulated in a pamphlet, *viz.* that he had cheated a woman out of £30. The words of the sentence, as used in all such cases, have a grim interest : " David Lewis, thou shalt be led from this place to the place from whence thou camest, and shalt be put upon a hurdle and drawn with thy heels forward to the place of execution, where thou shalt be hanged by the neck and be cut down alive, thy body to be ripped open and thy bowels plucked out ; thou shalt be dismembered and thy members burnt before thy face, thy head to be divided from thy body, thy four quarters to be separated, and to be disposed of at his Majesty's will. So the Lord have mercy on thy soul ! " And so it was done. But not before this old man, together with Bd John Kemble who was much older, had been made to ride up to London to be examined by the Privy Council touching the plot, about which they could tell them nothing because there was nothing to tell ; " and conform I would not, for it was against my conscience ". On August 27, 1679, at some spot on or near the site of the present Catholic church at Usk, the gallows was set up by a bungling amateur (he was a convict, who thus earned his freedom), the official executioner having decamped with his assistants.

From the scaffold Bd David made a ringing speech. " . . . I die for conscience and religion, and dying upon such good scores, as far as human frailty permits I die with alacrity, interior and exterior. . . . Here, methinks, I feel flesh and blood ready to burst into loud cries : ' Tooth for tooth, eye for eye, blood for blood, life for life ! ' ' No ! ' exclaims the holy gospel. ' Forgive and you shall be forgiven ' ; I profess myself a child of the gospel, and the gospel I obey. . . . Friends, fear God, honour your king, be firm in your faith, avoid mortal sin by frequenting the sacraments of Holy Church, patiently bear your persecutions and afflictions, forgive your enemies. Your sufferings are great. I say, be firm in your faith to the end, yea, even to death. . . ." The crowd threatened to stone the proxy hangman, who ran away, and a blacksmith was bribed to take his place—but no one would employ him after at his own trade. The body of Bd David Lewis was buried in the neighbouring churchyard, and within a short time a handkerchief dipped in his blood had been the occasion of the cure of an epileptic child and of other miracles.

In the case of this martyr we are fortunate in possessing his own account of his arrest, imprisonment and trial ; a summary of the proceedings in court, and also a copy of the speech (written out in prison beforehand) which he delivered to the assembled crowd at the time of his execution.   All these have been utilized in the admirable sketch contributed to *St Peter's Magazine* (Cardiff) in 1923 by J. H. Canning under the general title of " The Titus Oates Plot in S. Wales and the Marches ".   See also REPSJ., vol. v, pp. 912 *seq.* ; MMP., pp. 557–561 ; T. P. Ellis, *Catholic Martyrs of Wales* (1932), pp. 129–140 ; and Catholic Record Society *Publications*, vol. xlvii (1953), pp. 299–304.

28 : ST AUGUSTINE, Bishop of Hippo, Doctor of the Church   (A.D. 430)

ST AUGUSTINE, who used commonly to be called Austin in English, was born on November 13 in the year 354 at Tagaste, a small town of Numidia in north Africa, not far from Hippo, but at some distance from the sea, which he had never seen till he was grown up.   His parents were of good position, but not rich ; his father, Patricius, was an idolater, and of a violent disposition ; but through the example and prudent conduct of St Monica, his wife, he was baptized a little before his death.   She bore him several children ; St Augustine speaks of his brother Navigius, who left a family behind him, and of a sister who died a dedicated virgin.   He was entered in his infancy among the catechumens, baptism itself being deferred, according to a common custom of the time ; but in early youth he fell into evil ways and until the age of thirty-two led a life morally defiled by licence and intellectually by Manicheism.   Of this time, up to his conversion and the death of St Monica, Augustine speaks at large in his *Confessions,* a book written for " a people curious to know the lives of others, but careless to amend their own " ; written not indeed to satisfy such curiosity, but to show forth to his fellows the mercy of God and His ways as exemplified in the life of one sinner, and to endeavour that no one should think of him above that which he confessed himself to be.   As a child Monica instructed him in the Christian religion and taught him to pray ; falling dangerously ill, he desired baptism and his mother got everything ready for it : but he suddenly grew better, and it was put off.   This custom of deferring baptism for fear of sinning under the obligations of that sacrament, St Augustine later very properly condemns ; but the want of a sense of its sanctity and the sacrileges of Christians in defiling it, by relapsing into sin, is an abuse which no less calls for our tears.

  " And so I was put to school to learn those things in which, poor boy, I knew no profit, and yet if I was negligent in learning I was whipped : for this method was approved by my elders, and many that had trod that life before us had chalked out unto us these wearisome ways. . . ."   Augustine thanks God that, though the persons who pressed him to learn had no other end in view than " penurious riches " and " ignominious glory ", yet divine Providence made a good use of their error, and forced him to learn for his great profit and manifold advantage.   He accuses himself of often studying only by constraint, disobeying his parents and masters, not writing, reading, or minding his lessons so much as was required of him ; and this he did, not for want of wit or memory, but out of love of play.   But he prayed to God with great earnestness that he might escape punishment at school, for which dread he was laughed at by his masters and parents. Nevertheless, " we were punished for play by them that were doing no better ; but the boys' play of them that are grown up is named *business*. . . . Who is he that, weighing things well, will justify my being beaten when I was a boy for playing at ball, because by that play I was hindered from learning so quickly those arts with which, when grown up, I should play far worse ? " " No one does well what he does against his will ", he says, and takes notice that the master who corrected him for a small fault " if overcome in some petty dispute by a fellow teacher, was more envious and angry than the boy ever was when outdone by a playfellow at ball." He liked Latin very well, having learned that language from his nurses, and others with whom he conversed ; but not the Latin " which the first masters teach ; rather that which is taught by those who are called grammarians ". Whilst he was little he hated Greek, and, for want of understanding it sufficiently, Homer was disagreeable to him ; but the Latin poets became his early delight.

Augustine went to Carthage towards the end of the year 370, in the beginning of his seventeenth year. There he took a foremost place in the school of rhetoric and applied himself to his studies with eagerness and pleasure ; but his motives were vanity and ambition, and to them he joined loose living, though it was acknowledged that he always loved decency and good manners even in his excesses. Soon he entered into relations with a woman, irregular but stable, to whom he remained faithful until he sent her from him at Milan in 385 ; she bore him a son, Adeodatus, in 372. His father, Patricius, died in 371 ; but Augustine still continued at Carthage and, by reading the *Hortensius* of Cicero, his mind was turned from rhetoric to philosophy ; he also read the Christian sacred writings, but he was offended with the simplicity of the style, and could not relish their humility or penetrate their spirit. Then it was that he fell into the error of the Manichees, that infirmity of noble mind troubled by the " problem of evil ", which seeks to solve the problem by teaching a metaphysical and religious dualism, according to which there are two eternal first principles, God, the cause of all good, and matter, the cause of all evil. The darkening of the understanding and clumsiness in the use of the faculties which wait on evil-living helped to betray him into this company, which he kept till his twenty-eighth year ; and pride did the rest. " I sought with pride ", he says, " what only humility could make me find. Fool that I was, I left the nest, imagining myself able to fly ; and I fell to the ground."

For nine years Augustine had his own schools of rhetoric and grammar at Tagaste and Carthage, while his devoted mother, spurred on by the assurance of a holy bishop that " the son of so many tears could not perish ", never ceased by prayer and gentle persuasion to try to bring him to conversion and reform. After meeting the leading Manichean teacher, Faustus, he began to be disillusioned about that sect, and in 383 departed to Rome, secretly, lest his mother should prevent him. He opened a school of rhetoric there, but finding the scholars were accustomed frequently to change their masters in order to cheat them of their fees he applied for and received a post as master of rhetoric in Milan. Here he was well received and the bishop, St Ambrose, gave him marks of respect. Augustine was very desirous of knowing him, not as a teacher of the truth, but as a person of great learning and reputation. He often went to his sermons, not so much with any expectation of profiting by them as to gratify his curiosity and to enjoy the eloquence ; but he found the discourses more learned than those of the heretic Faustus, and they began to make impression on his heart and mind ; at the same time he read

Plato and Plotinus : " Plato gave me knowledge of the true God, Jesus Christ showed me the way." St Monica, having followed him to Milan, wished to see him married, and the mother of Adeodatus returned to Africa, leaving the boy behind ; but neither marriage nor single continence followed. And so the struggle, spiritual, moral, intellectual, went on.

Augustine became convinced of the truth and excellence of that virtue which the divine law prescribes in the Catholic Church, but was haunted with an apprehension of insuperable difficulties in its practice, that kept him from resolutely entering upon it. And so, by listening to St Ambrose and reading the Bible he was convinced of the truth of Christianity, but there was still wanting the will to accept the grace of God. He says of himself : " I sighed and longed to be delivered but was kept fast bound, not with exterior chains but with my own iron will. The Enemy held my will, and of it he had made a chain with which he had fettered me fast ; for from a perverse will was created wicked desire or lust, and the serving this lust produced custom, and custom not resisted produced a kind of necessity, with which, as with links fastened one to another, I was kept close shackled in this cruel slavery. I had no excuse as I pretended formerly when I delayed to serve Thee, because I had not yet certainly discovered thy truth : now I knew it, yet I was still fettered. . . . I had nothing now to reply to thee when thou saidst to me, ' Rise, thou that sleepest, and rise up from the dead, and Christ shall enlighten thee '. . . . I had nothing, I say, at all to reply, being now convinced by thy faith, except lazy and drowsy words, ' Presently, by and by, let me alone a little while longer ' ; but this ' presently ' did not presently come ; these delays had no bounds, and this ' little while ' stretched out to a long time."

He had been greatly impressed by hearing the conversion of the Roman neo-Platonist professor, Victorinus, related by St Simplician ; and soon after Pontitian, an African, came to visit Augustine and his friend Alipius. Finding a book of St Paul's epistles lying on the table, he took occasion to speak of the life of St Antony, and was surprised to find that his name was unknown to them. Pontitian then went on to speak of two men who had been suddenly turned to the service of God by reading a life of St Antony. His words had a powerful influence on the mind of Augustine, and he saw, as it were in a glass, his own filthiness and deformity. In his former half desires of conversion he had been accustomed to beg of God the grace of continence, but was at the same time in some measure afraid of being heard too soon. " In the first dawning of my youth ", says he, " I had begged of thee chastity, but by halves, miserable wretch that I am ; and I said, ' Give me chastity, but not yet awhile ' ; for I was afraid lest thou shouldst hear me too soon, and heal me of the disease which I rather wished to have satisfied than extinguished." He was ashamed his will had been so weak, and directly Pontitian had gone he turned to Alipius : " What are we doing to let the unlearned seize Heaven by force, whilst we with all our knowledge remain behind, cowardly and heartless, wallowing in our sins ? Because they have outstripped us and gone on before, are we ashamed to follow them ? Is it not more shameful not even to follow them ? "

He got up and went into the garden. Alipius, astonished at his manner and emotion, followed, and they sat down as far as they could from the house, Augustine undergoing a violent inward conflict. He was torn between the voice of the Holy Ghost calling him to chastity and the seductive memory of his former sins, and going alone further into the garden he threw himself on the ground under a tree, crying out, " How long, O Lord ? Wilt thou be angry for ever ? Remember not my past iniquities ! " He reproached himself miserably : " How long ? How long ? To-morrow, to-morrow ? Why not now ? Why does not this hour put an end to my filthiness ? " As he spoke these things and wept with bitter contrition of heart, on a sudden he heard as it were the voice of a child singing from a neighbouring house, which frequently repeated these words, *Tolle lege ! Tolle lege !* " Take up and read ! Take up and read ! " And he began to consider whether in any game children were wont to sing any such words ; and he could not call to mind that he had ever heard them. Whereupon he rose up, suppressing his tears, and interpreted the voice to be a divine admonition, remembering that St Antony was converted from the world by hearing a particular passage of the gospel read. He returned to where Alipius was sitting with the book of St Paul's epistles, opened it, and read in silence the words on which he first cast his eyes : " Not in rioting and drunkenness ; not in chambering and impurities ; not in contention and envy ; but put ye on the Lord Jesus Christ, and make not provision for the flesh in its concupiscences." All the darkness of his former hesitation was gone. He shut the book, and with a serene countenance told Alipius what had passed. Alipius asked to see the passage he had read, and found the next words to be : " Him that is weak in faith, take unto you " ; which he applied to himself, and joined his friend in his resolution. They immediately went in and told St Monica, who rejoiced and praised God, " who is able to do all things more abundantly than we desire or understand ". This was in September 386, and Augustine was thirty-two.

He at once gave up his school and retired to a country house at Cassiciacum, near Milan, which his friend Verecundus lent to him ; he was accompanied by his mother Monica, his brother Navigius, his son Adeodatus, St Alipius, and several other friends, and they lived a community life together. Augustine employed himself in prayer and study, and his study was a kind of prayer by the devotion of his mind therein. Here he sought by austere penance, by the strictest watchfulness over his heart and senses, and by humble prayer, to control his passions, and to prepare himself for the grace of leading a new life in Christ and becoming in Him a new creature. " Too late ", he prayed, " have I loved thee, O Beauty so ancient and so new, too late have I loved thee ! Thou wast with me, and I was not with thee ; I was abroad, running after those beauties which thou hast made ; those things which could have no being but in thee kept me far from thee. Thou hast called, thou hast cried out, and hast pierced my deafness. Thou hast enlightened, thou hast shone forth, and my blindness is dispelled. I have tasted thee, and am hungry for thee. Thou hast touched me, and I am afire with the desire of thy embraces." From the conferences and conversations which took place during these seven months St Augustine drew up his three dialogues, *Against the Academicians, Of the Happy Life* and *Of Order.*

St Augustine was baptized by St Ambrose on Easter-eve in 387, together with Alipius and his dearly loved son Adeodatus, who was about fifteen years of age and was to die not long afterwards. In the autumn he resolved to return to Africa. Accordingly he went to Ostia with his mother and several friends, and there St Monica died in November 387. To her life and last days Augustine devotes six moving chapters of his *Confessions.* He returned for a short while to Rome, and went on to Africa in September 388, where he hastened with his friends to his house at Tagaste. There he lived almost three years, disengaged from temporal concerns, serving God in fasting, prayer, good works, meditating upon His law and instructing others by his discourses and books.   All things were in common and were distributed according to everyone's needs ; St Augustine himself reserved nothing which he could call his own.   He had no idea of becoming a priest, but in 391 he was ordained as an assistant to Valerius, Bishop of Hippo.   So Augustine had to move to that city ; and in a house adjoining the church he established a sort of monastery, modelled on his household at Tagaste, living there with St Alipius, St Evodius, St Possidius, and others " according to the rule of the holy Apostles ".   Valerius, who was a Greek, and had, moreover, an impediment in speaking, appointed him to preach to the people in his own presence, as was customary for bishops to do in the East, but till that time was unusual in the West ; more unusual still, he was given permission to preach " on his own " ; he from that time never interrupted the course of his sermons till his death.   We have nearly four hundred extant, though many were not written by him but taken down by others as he delivered them.   During these early days he vigorously opposed the Manicheans and the beginnings of Donatism, as well as effected such domestic reforms as the abolition of feasting in the chapels of the martyrs and of family fights as a public amusement. St Augustine preached always in Latin, though among the peasants of the country in certain parts of his diocese some understood only the Punic tongue, and these he found it difficult to furnish with priests.

In 395 he was consecrated bishop as coadjutor to Valerius, and succeeded him in the see of Hippo on his death soon after.   Augustine established regular and common life in his episcopal residence, and required all the priests, deacons, and subdeacons that lived with him to renounce property and to follow the rule he established there ; nor did he admit any to holy orders who did not bind themselves to a similar manner of life.   His biographer, St Possidius, tells us that the clothes and furniture were modest but decent, and not slovenly.   No silver was used in his house, except spoons ; dishes were of earthenware or wood.   He exercised hospitality, but his table was frugal ; nor was wine wanting, but the quantity was regulated, which no guest was ever allowed to exceed.   At meals he preferred reading to secular conversation.   All his clerks who lived with him ate at the same table and were clothed out of the common stock.   Thus, in the words of Pope Paschal II, " The regular mode of life recognized in the early Church as instituted by the Apostles was earnestly adopted by the blessed Augustine, who provided it with new regulations ".   He also founded a community of religious women to whom, on the death of his sister, the first " abbess ", he addressed a letter on the general ascetic principles of the religious life.   This letter, together with two sermons on the subject, constitutes the so-called Rule of St Augustine, which is the basis of the constitutions of many canons regular, friars and nuns.   St Augustine employed the revenues of his church in relieving the poor, as he had before given his own patrimony, and Possidius says that he sometimes melted down part of the sacred vessels to redeem captives : in which he was authorized by the example of St Ambrose.   In several of his letters and sermons mention is made of the custom he had got his flock to establish, of clothing all the poor of each parish once a year, and he was not afraid sometimes to contract considerable debts to help the distressed. Nor did his zeal and charity for the spiritual welfare of others have bounds.   " I do not wish to be saved without you ", said he to his people, like another Moses or St Paul.   " What shall I desire ?   What shall I say ?   Why am I a bishop ?   Why am I in the world ?   Only to live in Jesus Christ : but to live in Him with you. This is my passion, my honour, my glory, my joy and my riches."

There were few men endowed by nature with a more affectionate and friendly soul than St Augustine. He conversed freely with infidels, and often invited them to his table; but generally refused to eat with Christians whose conduct was publicly scandalous, and was severe in subjecting them to canonical penance and to the censures of the Church. He never lacked courage to oppose iniquity without respect of persons, though he never forgot charity, meekness and good manners. He complains that some sins were by custom become so common that, though he condemned them, he dare not oppose them too strongly for fear of doing much harm and no good. He observed the three rules of St Ambrose: never to make matches for any persons, lest they should prove unhappy; never to persuade any to be soldiers; and never to dine out in his own city, lest invitations should become frequent. The letters of great men are generally interesting both for illustrating their history and throwing light on their minds. Those of St Augustine are particularly so. In his fifty-fourth to Januarius he says that they do well who communicate daily, provided it be done worthily and with the humility of Zaccheus when he received Christ under his roof; but that they are also to be commended who sometimes imitate the humble centurion and set apart Sundays and Saturdays or other days for communicating, in order to do it with greater devotion. He explains the duties of a wife towards her husband in his letter to Ecdicia, telling her that she ought not to wear black clothes, seeing this gave him offence, and she might be humble in mind in rich and gay dress if he should insist upon her wearing such. He tells her she ought, in all things reasonable, to agree with her husband as to the manner of educating their son, and leave to him the chief care of it. In like manner did he impress upon husbands the respect, tender affection and consideration which they owe to their wives. There is a good example of St Augustine's modesty and humility in his discussion with St Jerome over the interpretation of a text of Galatians. Owing to the miscarriage of a letter Jerome, not an easily patient man, deemed himself publicly attacked. Augustine wrote to him: " I entreat you again and again to correct me confidently when you perceive me to stand in need of it; for though the office of a bishop be greater than that of a priest, yet in many things Augustine is inferior to Jerome." He grieved at the violence with which the controversy between St Jerome and Rufinus was carried on. He always feared the deceit of vain-glory in such disputes, in which men love an opinion, as he says, " Not because it is true, but because it is their own, and they dispute, not for the truth, but for the victory ".

Throughout his thirty-five years as bishop of Hippo St Augustine had to defend the Catholic faith against one heresy or another. Serious trouble was given by the Donatists, whose chief errors were that the Catholic Church by holding communion with sinners had ceased to be the Church of Christ, this being confined within the limits of their sect, and that no sacraments can be validly conferred by those that are not in the true Church. These Donatists were exceedingly numerous in Africa, and they carried their fury to the greatest excesses, murdering Catholics and committing all sorts of violence. By the learning and indefatigable zeal of St Augustine, supported by the sanctity of his life, the Catholics began to gain ground; at which the Donatists were so exasperated that some preached publicly that to kill him would be doing service to their religion, and highly meritorious before God. Augustine was obliged in 405 to invoke the civil power to restrain the Donatists about Hippo from the outrages which they perpetrated, and in the same year the Emperor Honorius published severe laws against them. Augustine at first disapproved such measures, though he afterwards changed his opinion, except that he would not countenance a death-penalty. A great conference between the two parties at Carthage in 411 marked the beginning of the decline of these heretics, but almost at once the Pelagian controversy began.

Pelagius is commonly called a Briton, but as St Jerome refers to him as " big and fat, a fellow bloated with Scots porridge ", he has been claimed for Ireland ; he rejected the doctrine of original sin and taught therefore that baptism was simply a title of admission to Heaven, and that grace is not necessary to salvation. In 411 he left Rome for Africa with his friend Caelestius, and during that year their doctrines were for the first time condemned by a synod at Carthage. St Augustine was not at this council, but from that time he began to oppose these errors in his sermons and letters. Before the end of that year he was persuaded by the tribune St Marcellinus to write his first treatises against them. This, however, he did without naming the authors of the heresy, hoping thus more easily to gain them ; he even praised Pelagius by name. " As I hear, he is a holy man, well exercised in Christian virtue : a good man, and worthy of praise." But he was fixed in his errors and throughout the series of disputations, condemnations and subterfuges that followed, St Augustine pressed him relentlessly : to him is the Church indebted as the chief instrument of God in overthrowing this heresy. When Rome was plundered by Alaric the Goth in 410 the pagans renewed their blasphemies against the Christian religion, to which they imputed the calamities of the empire. To answer their slanders, St Augustine began his great work *Of the City of God* in 413, though he only finished it in 426, the work of his which is the most widely read after his *Confessions ;* it goes far beyond simply answering the pagans to a development of his philosophy of God-controlled history.

In the *Confessions* St. Augustine, with the most sincere humility and contrition, lays open the errors of his conduct ; in his seventy-second year he began to do the like for his judgement. In this work, his *Retractations*, he reviewed his writings, which were very numerous, and corrected with candour and severity the mistakes he had made, without seeking the least gloss or excuse to extenuate them. To have more leisure to finish this and his other writings, and to provide against a trouble-some election after his death, he proposed to his clergy and people to choose for his coadjutor Heraclius, the youngest among his deacons, and his election was confirmed with acclamation in 426. But in spite of this precaution Augustine's last years were full of turmoil. Count Boniface, who had been the imperial general in Africa, having unjustly incurred the suspicion of the regent Placidia and being in disgrace, incited Genseric, King of the Vandals, to invade the African provinces. Augustine wrote a wonderful letter to Boniface, recalling him to his duty, and the count sought a reconciliation with Placidia, but could not stay the Vandal invasion. St Possidius, now bishop of Calama, describes the dreadful ravages by which they scattered horror and desolation as they marched. He saw the cities in ruin and the houses in the country razed to the ground, the inhabitants either being slain or fled. The praises of God had ceased in the churches, which had in many places been burnt. Mass was offered up in private houses, or not at all, for in many parts there were none left to demand the sacraments, nor was it easy elsewhere to find any to minister to those who required them. The bishops and the rest of the clergy who had escaped were stripped of everything, and reduced to beggary ; and of the great number of churches in Africa, there were hardly three remaining (namely, Carthage, Hippo and Cirta) whose cities were yet standing.

Count Boniface fled to Hippo, and St Possidius and several neighbouring bishops took refuge in the same place. The Vandals appeared before it about the end of May 430, and the siege continued fourteen months. In the third month St Augustine was seized with a fever, and from the first moment of his illness knew that it was the summons of God to Himself. Ever since he retired, death had been the chief subject of his meditations ; and in his last illness he spoke of it with great cheerfulness, saying, " We have a merciful God ". He often spoke of the joy of St Ambrose in his last moments, and of the saying of Christ to a certain bishop in a vision mentioned by St Cyprian. " You are afraid to suffer here, and unwilling to go hence : what shall I do with you ? " " What love of Christ can that be ", he wrote, " to fear lest He, whom you say you love, shall come ? Brethren, are we not ashamed to say we love, when we add that we are afraid lest He come ? " In this last illness he asked for the penitential psalms to be written out and hung in tablets upon the wall by his bed ; and as he there lay he read them with tears. The strength of his body daily and hourly declined, yet his senses and intellectual faculties continued sound to the last, and he calmly resigned his spirit into the hands of God on August 28, 430, after having lived seventy-six years and spent almost forty of them in the labours of the ministry. St Possidius adds, " We being present, the Sacrifice was offered to God for his recommendation, and so he was buried ", in the same manner as St Augustine says was done for his mother. Whilst the saint lay sick in bed, by the imposition of his hands he restored to health a sick man, and Possidius says, " I know, both when he was priest and when he was bishop, that being asked to pray for certain persons that were possessed, he poured out supplications to our Lord, and the evil spirits departed from them."

It is from St Augustine's own writings, more particularly from his *Confessions*, his *De Civitate Dei*, his correspondence, and his sermons, that we obtain the fullest insight into his life and character. All these are readily accessible both in the original and in translations. The text of the Vienna *Corpus scriptorum ecclesiasticorum latinorum* is generally reliable so far as it is available, but for the *Confessions* that of Pierre de Labriolle, published in 1926 with an excellent French translation, may be preferred. The best English translation of this last work, among many, is probably that of Gibb and Montgomery (1927) ; a more recent one is by F. J. Sheed (1944). A convenient edition of the *De Civitate Dei* with English notes has been published by Dean Welldon (1924) ; W. J. Sparrow Simpson has produced a good translation of the *Letters* (1919), as well as a sympathetic study, *St Augustine's Conversion* (1920). Of all modern contributions to Augustinian literature the most outstanding is the publication, the merit of which mainly rests with Dom Germain Morin, of a revised and much enlarged collection of the sermons. This forms the first volume of the *Miscellanea Agostiniana* (1931) brought out to commemorate the fifteenth centenary of the saint's death. The early life of Augustine by his disciple St Possidius has also been re-edited and translated into German by Adolf Harnack (1930). But the whole literature is too vast for detailed discussion ; to quote only the titles of books produced in the past twenty years would fill several pages. It must suffice here to mention *A Monument to St Augustine* (1930), a volume of essays by English Catholic writers ; H. Pope, *St Augustine of Hippo* (essays ; 1937) ; G. Bardy, *S. Augustin, l'homme et l'œuvre* (1940) ; E. Gilson, *Introduction à l'étude de S. Augustin* (1943) ; and a biography in French by J. D. Burger (1948). For a general account of both life and writings, the article by Fr Portalié in DTC., vol. i, cc. 2208–2472, may be specially recommended ; as also Bardenhewer's *Geschichte der altkirch. Literatur*, vol. iv, pp. 435–511. There are lives of a more popular character in English by Bertrand and by Hatzfeld, and Mary Allies brought out two or three volumes of selections and translations from St Augustine's various works ; more recently translations have begun to appear in U.S.A., edited by competent scholars. There is a translation of the *vita* by Possidius in F. R. Hoare, *The Western Fathers* (1954) ; and see J. J. O'Meara, *The Young Augustine* (1954).

ST HERMES, Martyr   (Second Century ?)

For the martyrdom of St Hermes at Rome and for his early *cultus* there and else-where we have the fullest evidence. He is mentioned in the *Depositio martyrum* of the year 354, and his name occurs in the " Martyrology of Jerome " and in the itineraries of the pilgrims. But upon the Passion of St Hermes, which forms part of the so-called *acta* of Pope Alexander I, no reliance can be placed ; " it is a romance, whose principal heroes are martyrs known to history, but the plot and the parts therein attributed to the different characters are the invention of the hagiographer " (Delehaye).

St Hermes was buried in the cemetery of Basilla on the Old Salarian Way, where the remains of a large basilica have been found over his tomb ; there have also been found fragments of an inscription put up there by Pope St Damasus, containing the martyr's name. What purported to be the relics of this St Hermes were given by Pope St Leo IV to the Emperor Lothair I in 850, and these eventually came to rest in the church of Renaix in Flanders, where they are still an object of pilgrimage. This led to a certain diffusion of *cultus* in western Europe. But by what process St Hermes came to be the titular of three churches in Cornwall—Saint Erme, Saint Ervan, Marazion—is not clear.

See *Acta Sanctorum*, August, vol. vi ; CMH., pp. 472–473 ; and DAC., vol. vi, cc. 2303 *seq.* G. H. Doble in his *·St Hermes* (1935 ; Cornish Saints series) refers to " an excellent little book " on the cult of the saint at Renaix, by Abbé F. d'Hollander (1934).

ST JULIAN OF BRIOUDE, Martyr   (Third Century ?)

This Julian was one of the most famous martyrs of Gaul ; he is sometimes called Julian of Auvergne. His unreliable *passio* tells us that he was a soldier, who knew how to reconcile the profession of arms with the teaching of the gospel. Crispin, governor of the province of Vienne, having declared himself against the Christians, Julian withdrew to Auvergne ; afterwards, learning that he was sought by the persecutors, of his own accord he presented himself before them, saying, " I have been too long in this bad world ; I would be with Jesus ". He had scarce uttered these words, when they fell upon him and cut off his head. This is said to have happened near Brioude. Later a church was built at Brioude (near Clermont-Ferrand) to shelter his relics, and it became a great place of pilgrimage. St Gregory of Tours relates a number of miracles wrought by St Julian's intercession ; he also mentions a church dedicated at Paris under the invocation of the holy martyr : it is that which is now known as St Julien-le-Pauvre, used by the Catholic Melkites of the city.

Apollinaris Sidonius, Gregory of Tours, and the " Hieronymianum " sufficiently attest the early *cultus* of this martyr, but Gregory also lets us know that they were at first in doubt on what day he ought to be venerated. See Delehaye, *Les Origines du Culte des Martyrs*, p. 357. The *passio*, printed in the *Acta Sanctorum*, August, vol. vi, and also by E. Munding (1918), is of little value, but E. C. Babut in the *Revue d'histoire et de littérature religieuses*, vol. v (1914), pp. 96–116, has tried to turn it to historical account.

SS. ALEXANDER, JOHN III and PAUL IV, Patriarchs of Constantinople   (A.D. 340, 577, 784)

Alexander of Byzantium was already seventy-three years old when he was elected to the episcopal throne of Constantinople, and he filled the office for twenty-three years in the troubled days of the heresiarch Arius. Soon after his election the Emperor Constantine ordered a conference between the Christian theologians and a number of pagan philosophers, and the discussion was thrown into confusion by all the philosophers trying to talk at the same time. On St Alexander's suggestion they then chose the most learned among them to voice their views, and while one of them was speaking Alexander suddenly exclaimed, " In the name of Jesus Christ, I command you to be silent ! " Whereupon, it is said, the unfortunate man found his tongue was paralysed and his mouth unable to utter a word until Alexander gave him leave, and by this manifestation of divine power the Christian cause made more impression than by the most solid arguments. In 336 Arius arrived in triumph at Constantinople, with an order from the emperor that St Alexander should receive him into communion. It is said that Alexander shut himself in church and prayed, with St James of Nisibis, that God would remove either himself or Arius. In any case, on the night before the day appointed for his solemn reception, Arius suddenly died. It was natural that many Christians should look on this as a divine intervention at the intercession of St Alexander, and this view is expressed by the Roman Martyrology, which refers to him as, " a glorious old man, on account of whose prayers Arius, condemned by the judgement of God, brake in the middle and his bowels poured out ".

The Byzantine Catholics join in one commemoration with St Alexander two other holy archbishops of Constantinople, John III and Paul IV, called " the Young ". John was born near Antioch, and had been a lawyer before he was ordained. He was sent as patriarchal legate from Antioch to Constantinople, where his learning caused him to be known as " the Scholastic " ; he had already made a collection of canons of ecclesiastical law, which recommended him to the Emperor Justinian I, and in the year 565 he was made patriarch of the imperial city. While he held that office he revised and enlarged his collection of canons, which was the first to be made systematically ; this work grew eventually into the compendium of Eastern church law called the *Nomokanon*. St. John the Scholastic died in 577. St Paul the Young was a native of Salamis who became patriarch of Constantinople in 780, during the last months of the Emperor Leo IV. Directly the Empress Irene became regent he advocated the restoration of holy images and their veneration ; in 784 he withdrew to the monastery of Florus, avowedly as an act of penance for his compromises and lack of boldness during the iconoclast regime. Until his death shortly afterwards he encouraged the assembling of a council for the condemnation of Iconoclasm ; it eventually met in the year 787.

The not entirely concordant stories of St Athanasius and the church historians concerning St Alexander will be found sufficiently illustrated in the *Acta Sanctorum*, August, vol. vi. *Cf.* also DCB., *s. nn.*

ST MOSES THE BLACK   (*c.* A.D. 405)

THIS Moses was an Ethiopian and the most picturesque figure among those remarkable men who are known as the Fathers of the Desert. At first he was a servant, or slave, in the house of an Egyptian official ; the general immorality of his life, but particularly his continual thefts, caused his dismissal—in those days he was lucky to have got off with his life—and he took to brigandage. He was a man of huge stature, with corresponding strength and ferocity, and he soon gathered a gang about him that was a terror to the district. Once some contemplated villainy was spoiled by the barking of a sheep-dog giving the alarm, and Moses swore to kill the shepherd. To get at him he had to swim across the Nile with his sword in his teeth, but the shepherd had hidden himself by burrowing into the sand ; Moses could not find him, so he made up for it by killing four rams, tying them together and towing them back across the river. Then he flayed the rams, cooked and ate the best parts, sold the skins for wine, and walked fifty miles to join his fellows. That was the sort of man Moses was.

Unfortunately the circumstances of his conversion are not known ; it is possible that he hid himself among the solitaries to avoid the law and was touched and conquered by their example, for when next heard of he was at the monastery of Petra in the desert of Skete. Here he was attacked in his cell by four robbers. Moses fought and overpowered them, then tied them together, slung them across his back, and went to the church, where he dumped them on the floor, saying to the astonished monks, " I am not allowed to hurt anybody, so what do you want me to do with these ? " They are said to have reformed their ways and become monks themselves. But Moses did not become well-behaved in a day and, despairing of overcoming his violent passions, he consulted St Isidore. The abbot took him up to the roof of the house at dawn : " See ! " he said, " the light only gradually drives away the darkness. So it is with the soul." Eventually by hard physical labour, especially in waiting on his brethren, hard physical mortification, and persevering prayer he so conquered himself that Theophilus, Archbishop of Alexandria, heard of his virtues and ordained him priest. Afterwards as he stood in the basilica, anointed and vested in white, the archbishop said, " Now, Father Moses, the black man is made white ". St Moses smiled ruefully. " Only outside ! God knows that inwardly I am yet dark ", he replied.

When a raid on the monastery by Berbers was threatened, Moses refused to allow his monks to defend themselves but made them run away before it was too late : " All that take the sword shall perish with the sword." He remained, and seven with him, and all save one were murdered by the infidels. St Moses was then seventy-five years old, and he was buried at the monastery called Dair al-Baramus, which still exists.

A Greek life, said to have been written by Laurence, a monk in Calabria, is printed in the *Acta Sanctorum*, August, vol. vi, with a commentary. But St Moses also figures in Palladius's *Historia Lausiaca* and in some of the early church historians.

THE LONDON MARTYRS OF 1588

WHATEVER the attitude of those on the continent, English Catholics at home did not lag behind in opposition to the Great Armada of Spain or in preparation for defence against it ; nationalist patriotism as we know it today was not then matured, but, even though one of Philip's admitted objects was to re-establish the Church, Catholics no more than anybody else wanted a Spanish invasion of England : the queen persecuted them, but she was still the queen. Nevertheless the defeat of the Armada at the end of July 1588 was followed at once by a more severe persecution, of which the first victims suffered in London on August 28 and 30. Six new gallows were set up in various parts of the city, and each of these received its hallowing of innocent blood. At Mile End Green was hanged BD WILLIAM DEAN, a Yorkshire man born at Linton in Craven. He was a convert minister, who had been ordained at Rheims and already banished once on pain of death if he returned to the country ; but come back he did, and was the first victim after the Armada. At the place of execution he began to speak to the people, " but his mouth was stopped by some that were in the cart, in such a violent manner, that they were like to have prevented the hangman of his wages ". With this remarkably grave and learned man died the Ven. Henry Webley, a layman who had befriended him. A short distance away, at Shoreditch, was hanged BD WILLIAM GUNTER, a Welshman from Raglan in Monmouthshire. He also was a priest from Rheims and had been ordained only the previous year. BD ROBERT MORTON and BD HUGH MORE (see September 1) were both hanged in Lincoln's Inn Fields. Mr Morton was born at Bawtry in Yorkshire, educated and ordained at Rheims and Rome, and sent on the mission in 1587. BD THOMAS HOLFORD (*alias* Acton and Bude) was the son of a minister of Aston in Cheshire. He became tutor in the household of Sir James Scudamore at Holme Lacy in Herefordshire, where he was converted by Mr Davis, a very zealous priest in those parts, who wrote an account of him. From it we learn that he was ordained at Rheims and ministered in Cheshire and London, having many narrow escapes, till he was seen coming out of the house of Bd Swithin Wells after celebrating Mass there, when the pursuivant " dogged him into his tailor's house, and there apprehended him ". He was hanged at Clerkenwell.

BD JAMES CLAXTON (or Clarkson) was sent on the mission from Rheims in 1582 ; he was banished in 1585 but returned, and was hanged at Isleworth, together with BD THOMAS FELTON. Bd Thomas was a Minim friar, the son of Bd John Felton, only twenty years old and not yet a priest, and of him there is an account from the hand of his sister, Mrs Frances Salisbury. She tells us that he came into England to recover his health and was about to return to his monastery when he was arrested and imprisoned for two years. He was twice released and re-arrested, and in Bridewell was confined in the " little ease ", put to labour at the mill, and finally tortured, in order to make him betray the names of priests. When brought up at Newgate after the Armada and asked whether he would have taken the queen's side or that of the pope and the Spaniards, he replied, " I would have taken part with God and my country ". According to Mrs Salisbury he was condemned for denying the Queen's ecclesiastical supremacy : " I have read divers chronicles, but never read that God ordained a woman should be supreme head of the Church " ; but other accounts say it was for being reconciled, and, as Mrs Salisbury certainly fell away from the faith for a time, her brother may have done so too, in spite of their martyred father.

On August 30 six more martyrs were hanged, all at Tyburn. One only was a priest, BD RICHARD LEIGH (*alias* Garth), a Londoner, who had made his studies at Rheims and Rome, been sent to England in 1586, banished in the same year, returned almost at once, and was committed for offering to answer questions put to a Catholic gentleman on his examination by the Protestant bishop of London. Mr Leigh and all the priests mentioned above were condemned for their priesthood. BD EDWARD SHELLEY, BD RICHARD MARTIN, and the Ven. Richard Flower (*vere* Lloyd) all suffered for harbouring or relieving priests. Mr Shelley was a gentleman of Warminghurst in Sussex, son of that Edward Shelley whose name is familiar to men-of-law from " the rule in Shelley's case " ; Mr Martin, born in Shropshire and educated at Broadgates Hall, Oxford, had had the infamy to pay sixpence for a supper for Bd Robert Morton ; Flower was from Anglesey. The other two victims at Tyburn on this day were BD MARGARET WARD and BD JOHN ROCHE (*alias*

Neale). Bd Margaret was a gentlewoman, born at Congleton in Cheshire, in the service of another gentlewoman, Mrs Whitall, in London. She had visited in the Bridewell prison Mr Richard Watson, a secular priest ; to him she smuggled a rope, but in making use of it to escape Watson had fallen and broken an arm and a leg. He was got away by Margaret's young Irish serving-man, John Roche, who, to assist the priest's escape, changed clothes with him and so was himself arrested. When charged, both Bd Margaret and Bd John refused to disclose Mr Watson's whereabouts ; they were offered their liberty if they would ask the queen's pardon and promise to go to church : to which they replied that they had done nothing that could reasonably offend her Majesty, and that it was against their conscience to attend a Protestant church. And so they were condemned. Father Ribadeneira, s.j., wrote that all these martyrs, who suffered with such firm constancy and patience, were forbidden to speak to the people from the scaffold because their persecutors were afraid of the impression they would make ; " but the very death of so many saint-like innocent men (whose lives were unimpeachable), and of several young gentlemen, which they endured with so much joy, strongly pleaded for the cause for which they died."

Three more *beati* achieved their crowns on the following October 5. BD WILLIAM HARTLEY was of yeoman stock, born about 1557 at Wilne, Derbyshire, in the same parish as Bd Edward James. He was educated a Protestant and went up to St John's College, Oxford, where he ultimately became a chaplain. He was ejected by the vice-chancellor in 1579, went to Rheims, was ordained in 1580, and came back to England in the same year. For a time he helped Bd Edmund Campion and Father Persons in their printing and publishing activities, but in eighteen months he was apprehended in the house of the Lady Stonor. For three and a half years he was in prison in London, the last twelve months in irons, having been caught celebrating Mass before other prisoners in his cell. At the beginning of 1585 he was deported, without trial, but he returned secretly to London. In September 1588, Bd William was arrested in Holborn, and a rumour was spread that he had apostatized. This was effectually contradicted by the heroic way in which he met his death, by hanging, " near the Theatre " in Shoreditch, and in the presence of his own mother. " He was a man ", says a contemporary, " of the meekest disposition and naturally virtuous, modest, and grave, with a sober and peaceful look."

BD JOHN HEWETT, who was hanged on the same day at Mile End Green for his priesthood, was son of a York draper and had been a student at Caius College, Cambridge. While yet a deacon he was arrested and banished. After ordination to the priesthood at Rheims in 1586, he came back to London and was seized in Grays Inn Lane in the following year. At that time he went under the name of John Weldon (*alias* Savell) and in that name he was again sent into exile. But he was arrested on a false charge in the Netherlands by the Earl of Leicester, who sent him to London for trial. Here he was tried and sentenced (as John Weldon) for being a seminary priest in England. BD ROBERT SUTTON, a schoolmaster of Paternoster Row, was hanged at Clerkenwell for being reconciled to the Church, he having been brought up a Protestant at his birthplace, Kegwell in Leicestershire. An eye-witness of his martyrdom, William Naylor, wrote : " . . . the sheriff promised to procure his pardon if he would but pronounce absolutely the word *all* : for he would that he should acknowledge the queen to be supreme head in all causes without any restriction ; but he would acknowledge her to be supreme head in all causes temporal ; and for that he would not pronounce the word *all* without any restriction, he was executed. This I heard and saw."

There may also be mentioned with this group of martyrs BD WILLIAM WAY (*alias* Flower). Though Challoner calls him a Cornishman he seems to have been born in Exeter, in 1561. He was trained at Rheims, ordained, and sent on the mission at the end of 1586. Six months later he was in jail in London ; and on September 23, 1588, he was hanged, drawn and quartered for his priesthood at Kingston-on-Thames.

See MMP., pp. 133–146 and 150–151 ; Burton and Pollen, LEM., vol. i, pp. 351–430 and 508–536 ; and *Publications* of the Catholic Record Society, vol. v, pp. 150–159 and *passim*.

BD EDMUND ARROWSMITH, MARTYR (A.D. 1628)

HE was born in 1585 at Haydock, near Saint Helens, the son of Robert Arrowsmith, a yeoman farmer, and his wife Margery, a Gerard of Bryn, both of families which had already suffered for the faith. He was baptized Brian, but took the name of Edmund at confirmation and ever after used it. The recusant Arrowsmiths were subjected to a good deal of persecution : on one occasion their house was searched for priests at night and the father and mother taken off to Lancaster jail, leaving four small children shivering in their shirts. When the father died, his widow confided young Edmund to the care of an old priest who had him educated. The youth was of an unquestionably religious disposition, and he managed to make his way out of the country to Douay in December 1605. His studies there were interrupted by ill-health, and he was not ordained till 1612, and sent to Lancashire in the following year. For ten years he worked there fruitfully and without mishap, in spite of the fact that his enthusiasm for controversy made him in-different ,to its dangers. " Though his presence was very mean, yet he was both zealous, witty and fervent, and so forward in disputing with heretics that I often wished him merrily to carry salt in his pocket to season his actions, lest too much zeal without discretion might bring him too soon into danger, con-sidering the vehement and sudden storms of persecution that often assailed us." " He was a man ", says another contemporary, " of great innocency in his life, of great sincerity in his nature, of great sweetness in his conversation and of great industry in his function. And he was ever of a cheerful countenance— a most probable sign of an upright and unspotted conscience " (Both quoted by Challoner).

About 1622–23 Bd Edmund was taken up and examined before the Protestant bishop of Chester, but King James being at that time interested in a Spanish match for his son, all priests in custody were ordered to be released in order to make a good impression on his Most Catholic Majesty. Dr Bridgeman, the bishop, a kindly old man, was at supper with several ministers when he was brought in, and apologized for eating meat on a Friday because of his age and infirmity. " But who has dispensed these lusty gentlemen ? " inquired Bd Edmund. He decided to offer himself to the Jesuits, and after a retreat of several months in Essex in lieu of a novitiate abroad he was admitted to the order. Five years later he was betrayed to a magistrate by a young man whom he had reproved for his irregular life, and at Lancaster assizes in August 1628 he was indicted before Sir Henry Yelverton on charges of being a priest and a Jesuit and of persuading the king's subjects to join the Church of Rome.   The charges, of course, were true, but he was convicted on grossly insufficient evidence and sentenced to death.   At the express command of the judge he was heavily manacled and put into a cell so small that he could not lie down ; here he was left from two o'clock on Tuesday afternoon till midday on Thursday, apparently without food and with no one allowed to speak to him except a Protestant minister.   When he was passing through the courtyard on his way to execution, there was standing at a window Bd John Southworth, who had been (temporarily) reprieved ; Bd Edmund lifted up his hands to him as a sign of humble contrition, and Bd John gave him absolution before all the people, who had assembled in great numbers.   Up to the last moment before he was thrown off the ladder he was pestered with offers of life and liberty if he would conform, that is, apostatize.   " Tempt me no more," he replied, " I will not do it, in no case, on no condition."   He was allowed to die before the rest of the sentence was carried out ; his last audible words were " Bone Iesu ! "

A relic of this martyr, known as the Holy Hand, is preserved in the church of St Oswald at Ashton-in-Makerfield and is greatly venerated ; it has been and is the occasion of remarkable cures of sickness and disease and of the granting of spiritual requests.

The fullest account of this martyr is probably that preserved in a booklet entitled *A Full and Exact Relation of the Death of Two Catholicks who suffered for their Religion at Lancaster in* 1628 (1737).   It is taken in large part from Henry More, s.j., *Historia Provinciae Anglicanae* (1630).   See also MMP., pp. 362–373 ; Bede Camm, *Forgotten Shrines* (1910), pp. 183–201 ; and G. Burns, *Gibbets and Gallows* (1944).

29 : THE BEHEADING OF ST JOHN THE BAPTIST   (*c.* A.D. 30)

JOHN THE BAPTIST, the preparation of whom for his unique office of forerunner of the Messias has already been referred to on the feast of his birthday (June 24), began to fulfil it in the desert of Judaea, upon the banks of the Jordan, towards Jericho.   Clothed in skins, he announced to all men the obligation of washing away their sins with the tears of sincere penitence, and proclaimed the Messias, who was about to make his appearance among them.   He exhorted all to charity and to a reformation of their lives, and those who came to him in these dispositions he baptized in the river.   The Jews practised religious washings of the body as legal purifications, but no baptism before this of John had so great and mystical a signification.   It chiefly represented the manner in which the souls of men must be cleansed from all sin to be made partakers of Christ's spiritual kingdom, and it was an emblem of the interior effects of sincere repentance ; a type of that sacrament of baptism which was to come with our Lord.   So noteworthy was this rite in St John's ministrations that it earned for him even in his own life the name of " the Baptist ", *i.e.* the baptizer.   When he had already preached and baptized for some time our Redeemer went from Nazareth and presented Himself among the others to be baptized by him.   The Baptist knew Him by a divine revelation and at first excused himself, but at length acquiesced out of obedience.   The Saviour of sinners was pleased to be baptized among sinners, not to be cleansed himself but to sanctify the waters, says St Ambrose, that is, to give them the virtue to cleanse away the sins of men.

The solemn admonitions of the Baptist, added to his sanctity and the marks of his divine commission, gained for him veneration and authority among the Jews, and some began to look upon him as the Messias himself. But he declared that he only baptized sinners with water to confirm them in repentance and a new life : that there was One ready to appear among them who would baptize them with the Holy Ghost, and who so far exceeded him in power and excellence that he was not worthy to untie His shoes. Nevertheless, so strong was the impression which the preaching and behaviour of John made upon the minds of the Jews that they sent priests and levites from Jerusalem to inquire of him if he were not the Christ. And St John " confessed, and did not deny ;, and he confessed, I am not the Christ ", neither Elias, nor a prophet. He was indeed Elias in spirit, being the herald of the Son of God, and excelled in dignity the ancient Elias, who was a type of John. He was likewise a prophet, and more than a prophet, it being his office, not to foretell Christ at a distance, but to point Him out present among men. So, because he was not Elias in person, nor a prophet in the strict sense of the word, he answers " No " to these questions and calls himself " the voice of one crying in the wilderness " ; he will not have men have the least regard for him, but turns their attention to the summons which God has sent them by his mouth. The Baptist proclaimed Jesus to be the Messias at His baptism ; and, the day after the Jews consulted him from Jerusalem, seeing Him come towards him, he called Him, " the Lamb of God ". Like an angel of the Lord " he was neither moved by blessing nor cursing ", having only God and His will in view. He preached not himself, but Christ ; and Christ declared John to be greater than all the saints of the old law, the greatest that had been born of woman.

Herod Antipas, Tetrarch of Galilee, had put away his wife and was living with Herodias, who was both his niece and the wife of his half-brother Philip. St John Baptist boldly reprehended the tetrarch and his accomplice for so scandalous a crime, and told him, " It is not lawful for thee to have thy brother's wife ". Herod feared and reverenced John, knowing him to be a holy man, but he was highly offended at the liberty which the preacher took. Whilst he respected him as a saint he hated him as a censor, and felt a violent struggle between his veneration for the sanctity of the prophet and the reproach of his own conduct. His anger got the better of him and was nourished by the clamour and artifices of Herodias. Herod, to content her, and perhaps somewhat because he feared John's influence over the people, cast the saint into prison, in the fortress of Machaerus, near the Dead Sea ; and our Lord during the time of his imprisonment spoke of him, saying, " What went you out to see ? A prophet ? Yea, I tell you, and more than a prophet. This is he of whom it is written : Behold I send my angel before thy face, who shall prepare thy way before thee. Amen I say to you, amongst those that are born of women there is not a greater than John the Baptist."

Herodias never ceased to endeavour to exasperate Herod against John and to seek an opportunity for his destruction. Her chance at length came when Herod on his birthday gave a feast to the chief men of Galilee. At this entertainment Salome, a daughter of Herodias by her lawful husband, pleased Herod by her dancing so much that he promised her with an oath to grant her whatever she asked though it amounted to half his dominions. Herodias thereupon told her daughter to demand the death of John the Baptist and, for fear the tyrant might relent if he had time to think it over, instructed the girl to add that the head of the prisoner should be forthwith brought to her in a dish. This strange request startled Herod ; as Alban Butler says, " The very mention of such a thing by a lady, in the midst of a feast and solemn rejoicing, was enough to shock even a man of uncommon barbarity ". But because of his oath, a double sin, rashly taken and criminally kept, as St Augustine says, he would not refuse the request. Without so much as the formality of a trial he sent a soldier to behead John in prison, with an order to bring his head in a dish and present it to Salome. This being done, the girl was not afraid to take that present into her hands, and deliver it to her mother. Thus died the great forerunner of our blessed Saviour, the greatest prophet " amongst those that are born of women ". His disciples so soon as they heard of his death came and took his body and laid it in a tomb, and came and told Jesus. " Which when Jesus had heard, He retired . . . into a desert place apart ". Josephus, in his *Jewish Antiquities*, gives remarkable testimony to the sanctity of John, and says, " He was indeed a man endued with all virtue, who exhorted the Jews to the practice of justice towards men and piety towards God ; and also to baptism, preaching that they would become acceptable to God if they renounced their sins and to the cleanness of their bodies added purity of soul ". He adds that the Jews ascribed to the murder of John the misfortunes into which Herod fell.

Although today's feast does not seem to have been adopted in Rome until a comparatively late period, we can trace it at an early date in other parts of the Western church. We find it mentioned not only in the " Martyrology of Jerome " and in the Gelasian sacramentaries of both types, but it occurs in the *Liber comicus* of Toledo belonging to the middle of the seventh century. Moreover, either then or even sooner it had probably established itself firmly at Monte Cassino ; and indeed we may assume that its observance was introduced into England from Naples as early as 668. As we find this special feast, as distinct from that of the Birthday of the Baptist, kept on the same day (August 29) in the synaxaries of Constantinople, it is quite likely that it was of Palestinian origin. In the *Hieronymianum* it is associated with a commemoration of the prophet Eliseus, the link being that both Eliseus and St John Baptist were believed in St Jerome's time to have been buried at Sebaste, a day's journey from Jerusalem. Now the gospel-book of Würzburg, dating from about 700, has an entry " Depositio Helisei et sancti Johannis Baptistae ", and there are other gospel-books which couple the two in the same way.

See the bibliographical note under the Baptist's feast on June 24. For today's feast see also G. Morin in *Revue bénédictine*, 1891, p. 487, 1893, p. 120, and 1908, p. 494 ; F. Cabrol in DAC., vol. v, c. 1431 ; and L. Duchesne, *Christian Worship* (1931), p. 270.

ST SABINA, Martyr   (Date Unknown)

According to her *passio*, which was composed probably in the sixth century and is quite worthless, Sabina was a widow who was converted to the Christian faith by her servant Serapia, a girl from Syria. Serapia was martyred under Hadrian on a July 29, and her mistress received her crown a month later. This Sabina was said to be the titular of the famous church of that name on the Aventine at Rome. But it would seem that we can have no assurance even of the existence of any such martyr. As we hear first of the " titulus Sabinae ", and later always of " titulus Sanctae Sabinae " it remains possible that this was one of the cases in which the founder of a church, whose memory was annually commemorated there, was subsequently mistaken for the patron under whose invocation the church had been built, an appropriate story being invented to do him honour.

In CMH., pp. 475-476, Fr Delehaye discusses the case of St Sabina, quoting the divergent opinions of de Rossi, J. P. Kirsch, Lanzoni and others. The *passio* is in the *Acta Sanctorum*, August, vol. vi.

ST MEDERICUS, OR MERRY, Abbot   (*c*. A.D. 700)

HE was born at Autun, in the seventh century, and from an early age realized that the end of human life is the sanctification and salvation of the soul. That he might wholly give himself to God, when he was still very young he entered a local monastery, probably St Martin's in Autun. In that monastery then lived fifty-four fervent monks, whose penitential and regular lives were an object of edification to the whole country. Merry in this company grew up in habits of virtue, and a scrupulous observance of the rule. Being chosen abbot much against his own inclination, he pointed out to his brethren the narrow path of true virtue by example, walking before them in every duty ; and the reputation of his sanctity drew the eyes of all men upon him. The distractions which continual consultations from all parts gave him, and a fear of falling into vanity, made him resign his office and retire into a forest four miles from Autun, where he lay hid for some time. He earned himself all necessaries of life by the labour of his hands, and found this solitude sweet by the liberty it gave him of employing his time in heavenly contemplation and work. The place of his retreat at length becoming public, and being struck down by sickness, he was obliged to return to the monastery. After having edified his brethren and strengthened them in religious perfection, he again left them in old age in order to make a pilgrimage to the shrine of St Germanus of Paris (also a native of Autun) in that city. There with one companion, St Frou or Frodulf, he chose his abode in a small cell adjoining a chapel dedicated in honour of St Peter, in the north suburb of the city ; and, after two years and nine months during which he bore with patience a painful lingering illness, he died happily about the year 700.

There is a Latin life printed by Mabillon and in the *Acta Sanctorum*, August, vol. vi. It manifests a relative sobriety in the matter of miracles.

BD RICHARD HERST, Martyr   (A.D. 1628)

ON the day following the martyrdom of Bd Edmund Arrowsmith at Lancaster there suffered in the same town Bd Richard Herst, whose story is one of the most remarkable in the histories of the English and Welsh martyrs. He was hanged, ostensibly for wilful murder. Richard Herst (Hurst, Hayhurst) was born in a year unknown, near Preston, probably at Broughton, and was a yeoman farmer, comfortably off. Being a recusant, on a day in 1628 the bishop of Chester sent a pursuivant, Norcross, with two men, Wilkinson and Dewhurst, to arrest him. They found him ploughing, and as Norcross handed him the warrant, Wilkinson struck at him with a stick. A girl at work in another part of the field, seeing this, ran to summon her mistress, who came running out with a farm-servant and another man. The process-servers turned to meet this diversion and Wilkinson knocked the two men down, whereat the girl (unfortunately the name of this spirited young woman is not known) hit Dewhurst over the head. The pursuivant's men then ran away, but Dewhurst,

" partly on occasion of the blow, partly also to apply himself close to Wilkinson, made more haste than good speed, and ran so disorderly over the hard ploughed lands, as that he fell down and broke his leg ". The fracture mortified and thirteen days later Dewhurst died of it, after declaring that his fall had been quite accidental. Nevertheless Herst was indicted for murder before Sir Henry Yelverton and convicted, in defiance of all the evidence, the known facts of the case, and the finding of the coroner's jury ; the criminal jury was unwilling to bring in a verdict of guilty, but the judge told the foreman in private that it must be done " for an example ".

A petition of reprieve was sent to King Charles I, supported by Queen Henrietta Maria, but the contrary influence was too strong ; his life was offered him if he would take the oath which had been condemned by the Holy See, which fact alone shows the humbug of the murder charge. Three short letters are extant from Bd Richard to his confessor. In one he says, " I pray you remember my poor children, and encourage my friends about my debts ; and let it appear that my greatest worldly care is to satisfy them as far as my means will extend " ; in another, " Although my flesh be timorous and fearful, I yet find great comfort in spirit in casting myself upon my sweet Saviour with a most fervent love, when I consider what He hath done and suffered for me, and my greatest desire is to suffer with Him. And I had rather choose to die a thousand deaths than to possess a kingdom and live in mortal sin ; for there is nothing so hateful to me as sin, and that only for the love of my Saviour." On his way to the gallows, he looked up to where Bd Edmund Arrowsmith's head was displayed above the castle ; " I look ", he said, " at the head of that blessed martyr whom you have sent before to prepare the way for us ", and then turned to the minister who was questioning him, and said, " I believe according to the faith of the Holy Catholic Church ". He spent some time in prayer at the foot of the scaffold and then, seeing that the hangman was fumbling over fixing the rope, called up to him, " Tom, I think I must come up and help thee ". He left behind in the world six young children, and one yet unborn.

The printed account of Bd Edmund Arrowsmith mentioned under August 28 supplies in addition full details regarding Richard Herst ; and in MMP. also the two martyrs are noticed together.

30 : ST ROSE OF LIMA, Virgin   (A.D. 1617)

ASIA, Europe and Africa had been watered with the blood of many martyrs and adorned for ages with the shining example of innumerable saints, whilst the vast regions of America lay barren till the faith of Christ began to enlighten them in the sixteenth century, and this maiden appeared in that land like a rose amidst thorns, the first-fruits of its canonized saints. She was of Spanish extraction, born at Lima, the capital of Peru, in 1586, her parents, Caspar de Flores and Maria del Oliva, being decent folk of moderate means. She was christened Isabel but was commonly called Rose, and she was confirmed by St Toribio, Archbishop of Lima, in that name only. When she was grown up, she seems to have taken St Catherine of Siena for her model, in spite of the objections and ridicule of her parents and friends. One day her mother having put on her head a garland of flowers, to show her off before some visitors, she stuck in it a pin so deeply that she could not take off the garland without some difficulty. Hearing others frequently commend her beauty, and fearing lest it should be an occasion of temptation to anyone, she used to rub her face with pepper, in order to disfigure her skin with blotches. A woman happening one day to admire the fineness of the skin of her hands and her shapely fingers, she rubbed them with lime, and was unable to dress herself for a month in consequence. By these and other even more surprising austerities she armed herself against external dangers and against the insurgence of her own senses. But she knew that this would avail her little unless she banished from her heart self-love, which is the source of pride and seeks itself even in fasting and prayer. Rose triumphed over this enemy by humility, obedience and denial of her own will. She did not scruple to oppose her parents when she thought they were mistaken, but she never wilfully disobeyed them or departed from scrupulous obedience and patience under all trouble and contradictions, of which she experienced more than enough from those who did not understand her.

Her parents having been reduced to straitened circumstances by an unsuccessful mining venture, Rose by working all day in the garden and late at night with her needle relieved their necessities. These employments were agreeable to her, and she probably would never have entertained any thoughts of a different life if her parents had not tried to induce her to marry. She had to struggle with them over this for ten years, and to strengthen herself in her resolution she took a vow of virginity. Then, having joined the third order of St Dominic, she chose for her dwelling a little hut in the garden, where she became practically a recluse. She wore upon her head a thin circlet of silver, studded on the inside with little sharp prickles, like a crown of thorns. So ardent was her love of God that as often as she spoke of Him the tone of her voice and the fire which sparkled in her face showed the flame which consumed her soul. This appeared most openly when she was in presence of the Blessed Sacrament and when in receiving It she united her heart to her beloved in that fountain of His love.

God favoured St Rose with many great graces, but she also suffered during fifteen years persecution from her friends and others, and the even more severe trial of interior desolation and anguish in her soul. The Devil also assaulted her with violent temptations, but the only help she got from those she consulted was the recommendation to eat and sleep more ; at length she was examined by a commission of priests and physicians, who decided that her experiences, good and bad, were supernatural. But it is permissible to think that some of them, if correctly reported, were due to natural physical and psychological causes. The last three years of her life were spent under the roof of Don Gonzalo de Massa, a government official, and his wife, who was fond of Rose. In their house she was stricken by her last illness, and under long and painful sickness it was her prayer, " Lord, increase my sufferings, and with them increase thy love in my heart ". She died on August 24, 1617, thirty-one years old. The chapter, senate, and other honourable corporations of the city carried her body by turns to the grave. She was canonized by Pope Clement X in 1671, being the first canonized saint of the New World.

The mode of life and ascetical practices of St Rose of Lima are suitable only for those few whom God calls to them ; the ordinary Christian may not seek to copy them, but must look to the universal spirit of heroic sanctity behind them, for all the saints, whether in the world, in the desert or in the cloister, studied to live every moment to God.   If we have a pure intention of always doing His will we thus consecrate to Him all our time, even our meals, our rest, our conversation and whatever else we do : all our works will thus be full.

The Bollandists in the *Acta Sanctorum*, August, vol. v, after referring to one or two earlier lives of St Rose, in particular that of John de Vargas Machuca in Spanish, and that of D. M. Marchese in Italian, elected to print entire the Latin biography of the saint by Fr Leonard Hansen, o.p.   This has been the backbone of nearly all that has been subsequently written about her.   Moreover, it is supplemented in the *Acta Sanctorum* by the text of Clement X's very ample bull of canonization, which gives full details both of the life of the saint and of her miracles.   In English we have in the Oratorian series a translation of a seventeenth-century French life by J. B. Feuillet, and an attractive sketch by F. M. Capes, *The Flower of the New World* (1899) ; Sara Maynard's attempt to popularize the saint in *Rose of America* (1943) is spoiled by too much " sweetness ".   See also Vicomte de Bussière, *Le Pérou et Ste Rose de Lima* (1863); Mortier, *Maîtres Généraux O.P.*, vol. vii, pp. 76 *seq.*, and the *Monumenta O.P. Historica*, vol. xiii, pp. 22 *seq.*   There are several recent books in Spanish ; and see Sheila Kaye-Smith, *Quartet in Heaven* (1952).

SS. FELIX AND ADAUCTUS, MARTYRS   (A.D. 304 ?)

ST FELIX was a holy priest in Rome, no less happy in his life and virtue than in his name.   Being apprehended in the beginning of Diocletian's persecution, he was put to the torture, which he suffered with constancy, and was condemned to lose his head.   As he was going to execution he was met by a stranger, who, being a Christian, was so moved at the sight of the martyr and the glory to which he was hastening that he cried out aloud, " I confess the same law which this man professes ; I confess the same Jesus Christ ; and I also will lay down my life in His cause ". The magistrates hearing this, caused him forthwith to be seized, and the martyrs were both beheaded together.   The name of this stranger not being known, he was called by the Christians Adauctus, *i.e.* the one added, because he was joined to Felix in martyrdom.

This story, with sundry legendary embellishments, is derived from an inscription of Pope St Damasus, which ran : " O how truly and rightly named Felix, happy, you who, with faith untouched and despising the prince of this world, have confessed Christ and sought the heavenly kingdom.   Know ye also, brethren, the truly precious faith by which Adauctus too hastened, a victor, to Heaven.   The priest Verus, at the command of his ruler Damasus, restored the tomb, adorning the thresholds of the saints."   SS. Felix and Adauctus were buried in the cemetery of Commodilla on the Ostian Way, where a church built over their tomb was uncovered in 1905.

As " Felix and Adauctus, in the cemetery of Commodilla on the Ostian Way " are registered in the *Depositio martyrum* of 354, we have a solid guarantee for their early *cultus*, which is further confirmed by the Leonine sacramentary and many other records.   See the *Analecta Bollandiana*, vol. xvi (1897), pp. 17–43, and the discussions by de Rossi, Wilpert, Marucchi, Bonavenia, etc., to which Delehaye gives references in CMH., pp. 476–478. The *passio* is in the *Acta Sanctorum*, August, vol. vi.

ST PAMMACHIUS   (A.D. 410)

PAMMACHIUS was distinguished alike as a saint, a Roman citizen, a man of learning, and a friend of St Jerome, with whom he had studied in his youth and maintained correspondence all his life.   He belonged to the house of the Furii and was a senator ; in 385 he married Paulina, the second daughter of St Paula, that other great friend of St Jerome. Pammachius was probably one of the religious men who denounced to Pope St Siricius a certain Jovinian, who maintained among other errors that all sins and their punishments are equal ; he certainly sent copies of the heretic's writings to Jerome, who replied to them in a long treatise. This reply did not meet with the entire approval of St Pammachius : he found its language too strong (a failing to which Jerome was very inclined) and that it contained exaggerated praise of virginity and depreciation of marriage ; so he wrote and told him so, and St Jerome replied in two letters, thanking him for his interest and defending what he had written. Jovinian was condemned in a synod at Rome and by St Ambrose at Milan, and nothing more is heard of him ; St Jerome wrote a few years later that he had " belched rather than breathed out his life amidst pheasants and pork ".

In 397 the wife of St Pammachius died, and in a letter of sympathy St Paulinus of Nola wrote to him : " Your wife is now a pledge and an intercessor for you with Jesus Christ. She now obtains for you as many blessings in Heaven as you have offered her treasures from hence : not honouring her memory with fruitless tears only, but making her a partner of your charities. She is honoured by your virtues ; she is fed by the bread you have given to the poor. . . ." St Jerome wrote in the same strain. Pammachius devoted the rest of his life to study and works of charity. Together with St Fabiola he built at Porto a large hospice to shelter pilgrims coming to Rome, especially the poor and the sick ; this was the first institution of its kind, technically called a *xenodochium*, in the west, and received the hearty praise of St Jerome ; Pammachius and Fabiola spent much time thereat, personally looking after their guests. The site of this building has been discovered and its plan laid bare. In his devotion to the suffering Pammachius was following in the footsteps of his dead wife Paulina, and the blind, the incapacitated and the moneyless were declared by St Jerome to be her heirs ; he never went out into the streets but they flocked around him, knowing well that they would not be turned away.

St Pammachius was greatly disturbed by the bitter controversy between Jerome and Rufinus ; he wrote to him urging that he should undertake the translation of Origen's *De principiis*, and gave Jerome very useful help in his controversial writings : but abate the imprudence of expression of much of them he could not. He also wrote to the people living on his estates in Numidia urging them to abandon the Donatist schism and return to the Church, and this action drew a letter of thanks from St Augustine at Hippo in 401. Pammachius had a church in his house on the Coelian hill, consequently called *titulus Pammachii* : its site is now occupied by the Passionist church of SS. Giovanni e Paolo, beneath which remains of the original house have been found. St Pammachius died in 410 at the time Alaric and the Goths captured Rome ; he is often stated to have been a priest but this does not seem to have been so.

A fairly complete account of Pammachius, compiled by Father John Pien, is printed in the *Acta Sanctorum*, August, vol. vi. See also lives of St Jerome.

ST RUMON, OR RUAN (SIXTH CENTURY ?)

BEFORE the dissolution of the monasteries the Benedictine abbey of Tavistock claimed to possess the relics of St Rumon, who in the beginning of the fifteenth century was referred to by a monk of Glastonbury as a brother of St Tudwal, bishop at Tréguier in the sixth century. This Rumon, who gave their names to Romansleigh, Ruan Lanihorne, and other places in Devon and Cornwall, has been believed to be the St Ronan venerated in Brittany. Of his life there is likewise nothing known, though there is a story that he had to defend himself from the charge of being a werewolf and carrying off and eating a child ; this charge was made by a young woman who feared that the missionary (from Ireland, it was said) would make her husband a monk. Ronan's humanness was demonstrated by some wolf-hounds, which refused to touch him.

The arguments against the identification of the British Rumon with the Breton Ronan are very strong, but what does seem certain is that the legend of Ronan was borrowed to do duty for the Rumon across the Channel. Canon Doble adduces reasons for the suggestion that St Rumon and St Kea, who seems to have been the founder of a monastery or hermitage at Street in Somerset, were native monks of the British Glastonbury who went to make settlements in the Dumnonian peninsula.

The best attempt to disentangle the threads of this complicated problem is that of G. H. Doble in his *Four Saints of the Fal* (1930) and his *St Rumon and St Ronan* (1939), wherein he translates the *Vita Rumonis* (which may have emanated from the Glasney college at Penryn) from the Gotha MS. The Breton Ronan's biography is printed in the Bollandist catalogue of Paris hagiographical Latin MSS., vol. i, pp. 438–458. Ernest Renan, as he told the Cambrian Archaeological Association in 1889, claimed him as a patron : " Vous connaissez mon patron Saint Renan sous sa vraie forme Ronan (Locronan, les eaux de St Renan, etc.). C'était un irlandais, un grand original." L. Gougaud in *Les saints irlandais hors d'Irlande* (1936), pp. 159–166, expresses the view that Rumon and Ronan are not the same, and that Rumon was not of Irish origin. For St Ronan, whose feast is on June 1, see A. Thomas, *S. Ronan et la Troménie* (1893). The most recent work on St Rumon is Fr P. Grosjean's long article in *Analecta Bollandiana*, vol. lxxi (1953), pp. 359–414 ; it includes the text of the Gotha *vita*.

ST FANTINUS, ABBOT   (TENTH CENTURY)

THIS Fantinus is said to have been abbot of the Greek monastery of St Mercury in Calabria. After some years he claimed that the voice of God was telling him to leave the monastery and he accordingly did so, wandering about the countryside from place to place, sleeping in the open, and living on fruit and herbs. When he came to a church or monastery he lamented and prophesied woe ; when he met a monk he wept over him as though he were a dead man. When his friends, much upset by this strange behaviour, tried to induce him to return to the monastery, he only replied that there would soon be no monastery to return to and that he would die in a foreign land. In due course the Saracens devastated Calabria, the monastery of St Mercury was destroyed, and St Fantinus with two disciples went overseas and landed in the Peloponnesus. He lived for a time at Corinth and at Larissa in Thessaly, and then moved to Salonika, where his miracles and virtues made him famous. Here he died.

Not much that is reliable is known of this saint, though the Bollandists have devoted a few pages to him in the *Acta Sanctorum*, August, vol. vi. It is apparently this Fantinus who figures in the Constantinople synaxaries on November 14 ; though in an Italo-Greek synaxary he is assigned to August 30. See J. Rendel Harris, *Further Researches into the Ferrar Group* (1900), with Delehaye's comments in the *Analecta Bollandiana*, vol. xxi (1902), pp. 23–28. The story seems to be nothing but legend and confusion, including possibly confusion between two holy men, both named Fantinus.

BD BRONISLAVA, VIRGIN   (A.D. 1259)

IT is related that Bd Bronislava was a cousin of St Hyacinth, and that on the day of his death she saw our Lady in vision receive him into Heaven.   She had joined the Norbertine nuns near Cracow when she was about twenty-five years old, and for some time led the ordinary life of her order.   But her gift of contemplation and consequent love of solitude were so great that she was allowed to withdraw for long periods to a cell in a cave not far from the monastery, and was eventually permitted to live there permanently as a solitary.   After her death on January 18, 1259, her body was buried in the convent church, and when the buildings were destroyed by warfare it was lost ; but in the seventeenth century the relics were discovered again, and carried from church to church throughout Poland for the veneration of the people.   The *cultus* of Bd Bronislava was recognized in 1839, and her feast is observed by the Premonstratensian canons regular.

Most of the accounts of this rather obscure *beata* seem to be written either in Polish or in Flemish (Brabant being at present the stronghold of the Premonstratensian Order) ; but there are short lives published in French by Flambeau (1897) and Van Spielbeeck (1886). Bronislava is also one of the three holy people whose story is told by J. Chrzaszcz in *Drei schlesische Landesheilige* (1897).

31 : ST RAYMUND NONNATUS, CARDINAL OF THE HOLY ROMAN CHURCH   (A.D. 1240)

THE true story of the career of this saint is wrapped in impenetrable mystery for lack of reliable materials, and no confidence can be put in the accuracy of the details furnished by Alban Butler's account, summarized below.

St Raymund was brought into the world at Portello in Catalonia in the year 1204, and was called *non natus*, " not born ", because he was taken out of the body of his mother after her death in labour.   When he grew up he got his father's leave to enter the newly founded Mercedarian Order, and was admitted to profession therein at Barcelona by St Peter Nolasco.

So swift was the progress that he made that within two or three years after his profession he was judged qualified to discharge the office of ransomer, in which he succeeded St Peter.   Being sent into Barbary with a considerable sum of money he purchased at Algiers the liberty of a number of slaves.   When all other resources were exhausted, he voluntarily gave himself up as a hostage for the ransom of others, whose situation was desperate and whose faith was exposed to imminent danger.   The sacrifice which the saint made of his liberty served only to exasperate the Algerians, who treated him with barbarity till, fearing lest if he died in their hands they would lose the ransom stipulated for the slaves for whom he remained a hostage, the magistrate gave orders that he should be treated with more humanity. He was permitted to go about the streets and he made use of this liberty to comfort and encourage the Christians, and he converted and baptized some Mohammedans. When the governor heard of this he condemned him to be impaled.   However, the persons who were interested in the ransom of the captives prevailed that his life should be spared lest they should be losers ; and, by a commutation of his punishment, he was made to run the gauntlet.   This did not daunt his courage. So long as he saw souls in danger, he thought he had yet done nothing ; nor could he let slip any opportunity of ministering to them.

St Raymund had, on one side, no more money to employ in releasing poor captives ; on the other, to speak to a Mohammedan upon the subject of religion was by the Islamic law to court death.   He could, however, still exert his endeavours with hope of some success or of dying a martyr of charity.   He therefore resumed his former method of instructing and exhorting both Christians and infidels.   The governor was enraged, and commanded the servant of Christ to be whipped at the corners of all the streets in the city, his lips to be bored with a red-hot iron, and his mouth shut up with a padlock, the key of which he kept himself and only gave to the gaoler when the prisoner was to eat.   In this condition he was kept in a dungeon, where he lay full eight months, till his ransom was brought by some of his order, who were sent with it by Nolasco.   Raymund was unwilling to leave the country of the infidels, where he wanted to remain to assist the slaves ; but he acquiesced in obedience, begging God to accept his tears, seeing he was not worthy to shed his blood for the souls of his neighbours.

Upon his return to Spain in 1239 he was nominated cardinal by Pope Gregory IX.   But so little was he affected by the unlooked-for honour that he neither changed his dress, nor his poor cell in the convent at Barcelona, nor his manner of living.   The pope called him to Rome.   St Raymund obeyed, but could not be persuaded to travel otherwise than as a poor religious.   He got no farther than Cardona (Cerdagne), which is only six miles from Barcelona ; he was seized with a violent fever and died there, being only about thirty-six years old.   He was buried in the chapel of St Nicholas at Portello, and his name was inscribed in the Roman Martyrology in 1657.   St Raymund Nonnatus is the patron-saint of midwives, from the circumstances of his birth.

It has already been pointed out on January 28, under St Peter Nolasco, how extremely unreliable are the accounts supplied from Mercedarian sources of the beginnings and early developments of the Order of Our Lady of Ransom.   The Bollandists, unable to discover any trustworthy materials for the story of St Raymond Nonnatus, fell back in despair upon the account given by a sixteenth-century writer (Ciacconius) in his series of biographies of the Roman cardinals.   This penury of information has lasted to the present day.   All that can be said is that in the seventeenth and eighteenth centuries a number of books were printed, mostly of small bulk, by Fathers Dathia, Echeverez y Eyto, Juan de la Presentacion, P. E. Menendez, F. T. de Miranda, M. Ulate, and others, purporting to recount the life and miracles of St Raymund Nonnatus, that they repeat with slight variations the story told above, adding, however, numberless miracles, and that they were published with all necessary ecclesiastical sanctions.   See also Gams, *Kirchengeschichte von Spanien*, vol. iii, pt 1.   Pope Benedict XIV's commission proposed to remove this feast from the general calendar.

ST PAULINUS, BISHOP OF TRIER   (A.D. 358)

THIS Paulinus, called by St Athanasius " a truly apostolic man ", and referred to by St Jerome as " happy in his sufferings " for the faith, was educated in the cathedral-school of Poitiers and was a disciple of St Maximinus whom he succeeded in the see of Trier.   During the exile of St Athanasius at Trier Paulinus had become one of his most fervent supporters, and at the arianizing synod of Arles in 353 he stood out boldly for the faith of Nicaea and opposed the papal legates who were prepared to condemn Athanasius.   In the same cause he withstood the intimidation and violence of the Emperor Constantius, and was banished from his see with St Dionysius of Milan, St Eusebius of Vercelli and St Lucifer of Cagliari ; he was sent into Phrygia, to places so remote that Christians had hardly been heard of, and died in exile in the year 358 : as expressed in the Roman Martyrology, " wearied even to death by the changes and chances of exile far beyond Christian lands, he received from the Lord the crown of a blessed passion, dying at length in Phrygia ". His body was brought back to Trier by its bishop St Felix in 396 and enshrined in 402 in the church which bore his name, amid the ruins of which his tomb was found in 1738.

Great interest attaches to St Paulinus from the fact that his skeleton, still wrapped in oriental silk-stuffs with fragments of the wooden coffin in which it had been brought from Phrygia, was in 1883 taken out of the sarcophagus in which it lay and minutely investigated by a committee of archaeologists and other experts. The scientists pronounced the relics to be unquestionably authentic, and satisfied themselves that the saint had not, as some stories alleged, been decapitated.

See the *Acta Sanctorum*, August, vol. vi, where a Latin life is printed dating from the ninth or tenth century. For the relics, see Father Schneider in the *Jahrbüchern des Vereins für Alterthumsfreunden im Rheinlande*, vol. 78 (1884), pp. 167 *seq.* On the life of Paulinus *cf.* P. Diel, *Der hl. Maximinus und der hl. Paulinus* (1875).

ST AIDAN, Bishop of Lindisfarne   (A.D. 651)

When St Oswald had come to the throne of Northumbria in the year 634, and wished to spread the faith among his people, he asked the monks of Iona to send him a bishop to preach to his pagan subjects. The first person who came was of a rough, austere temper, and therefore could do little good ; being soon forced to return home again, he laid the fault on the rude character and indocile disposition of the English. The monks called a synod to deliberate what was best to be done, and Aidan, who was present, told the missionary, on his blaming the obstinacy of the English, that the fault lay rather in him : that he had been too harsh and severe to an ignorant people, who ought first to be fed with the milk of milder doctrine till they should be able to digest more solid food. At this the whole assembly turned their thoughts to the speaker, as one endued with prudence, and he was appointed to the arduous mission.

Aidan was a native of Ireland, and is said to have been a disciple of St Senan on Scattery Island, but nothing else is known with certainty of his early life, before he became a monk of Iona. He was well received by King Oswald, who bestowed on him for his episcopal seat the isle of Lindisfarne. Of his humility and piety St Bede gives a glowing account. He obliged all those who travelled with him to use their spare time either in reading the Bible or in learning the psalms by heart, and he did all his missionary journeys on foot. By his actions he showed that he neither sought nor loved the things of this world ; the presents which were made him by the king, or by other rich men, he distributed among the poor. He rarely would go to the king's table, and never without taking with him one or two of his clergy, and always afterwards made haste away to get on with his work. Bede mentions his apostolic liberty in reproving the proud and the great, and the love of peace, charity, continence and all other virtues which by his spirit and example he communicated to a rough and barbarous nation. " He was a bishop inspired with a passionate love of goodness, but at the same time a man of remarkable gentleness and moderation : zealous in God's cause, though not altogether according to knowledge " (Bede refers to the fact that St Aidan naturally followed the Celtic customs with regard to the date of Easter, etc.). And such a man was wanted for the task in hand, for Penda and Cadwallon had effectually undone much of the work of St Paulinus.

St Aidan supported his preaching with miracles, three of which Bede relates and, in speaking of the state of the country thirty years later, testifies to the effectiveness of his apostolate : " Wherever any cleric or monk came, he was received by all with joy as a servant of God ; and when one was met travelling, they would run up to him and bow, glad to be signed by his hand or blessed by his prayer. They gave diligent attention to the words of exhortation which they heard, and on Sundays flocked to the churches or monasteries to hear the word of God.   If any priest happened to come into a village, the inhabitants gathered together, solicitous to hear from him the words of life, nor did the clergy frequent the villages on any other account but to preach, visit the sick, and take care of souls ; and so free were they from avarice that no one would receive lands or possessions for building monasteries unless compelled to by the secular power."

The centre of St Aidan's activity was the island of Lindisfarne, now generally called Holy Isle, off the coast of Northumberland, between Berwick and Bamburgh.   Here he had his see and established a monastery under the Rule of St Columcille ; it has not improperly been called the English Iona, for from it the paganism of Northumbria was gradually dispelled and barbarian customs undermined.   Dom Gougaud quotes Lightfoot's opinion that " it was not Augustine, but Aidan, who was the true apostle of England " : of northern England this is true.   After the seventeen years of Aidan's rule there was a succession of sixteen bishops of Lindisfarne, of whom St Cuthbert was the greatest, but by no means the only saint connected with the island.   St Aidan took to this monastery twelve English boys to be brought up there, and he was indefatigable in caring for the welfare of children and of slaves, for the manumission of many of whom he paid from alms bestowed on him.   The great king St Oswald assisted his bishop in every possible way, as did St Oswin his successor, and when in 651 Oswin was murdered at Gilling, Aidan survived him only eleven days.   He died at the royal castle at Bamburgh, which he used as a mission centre, leaning against a wall of the church where a tent had been set up to shelter him.   He was first buried in the cemetery of Lindisfarne, but when the new church of St Peter was built there his body was translated into the sanctuary ; no doubt there were further translations when the island was abandoned at the time of the Scandinavian invasions. St Aidan is named in the Roman Martyrology, and his feast is kept in several English dioceses and in Argyll and the Isles.

We know little of St Aidan except what we learn from the third book of Bede's *Ecclesiastical History ;* but the notes of C. Plummer are also valuable.   On points connected with archaeology there is much illustrative matter in Sir Henry Howorth's *The Golden Days of the Early English Church*, vol. i.

BB. LAURENCE NERUCCI AND HIS COMPANIONS, MARTYRS (A.D. 1420)

IN the year 1415 John Hus, the leader of a " nationalist " but heretical party among the Czechs, was tried, condemned and burnt alive at Constance, and the ensuing repressive measures had the effect of increasing and strengthening his followers. In 1419 a former canon regular, John of Selau, stirred up the citizens of Prague to clamour for the release of certain imprisoned Hussites ; carrying the Blessed Sacrament in procession he led them to make their demand of the magistrates, and when it was refused urged the mob on to break into the municipal hall and murder all whom they found therein, blasphemously and sacrilegiously using the presence of the Blessed Sacrament as an incentive to fury and bloody revenge. The victims were thrown out of the windows, to be hacked to pieces by the rioters below (the first " defenestration of Prague ").

For the next twelve months there was civil war, with horrible outrages on both sides, and in March 1420 Pope Martin V called on Christendom to undertake a crusade against the Hussites.   He also sent into Bohemia a number of preachers, among them four Servite friars, all of Tuscan families, namely, Laurence Nerucci, Augustine Cennini, Bartholomew Donati, and John-Baptist Petrucci.   Shortly after they arrived, the monastery in which they were staying at Prague was attacked and set on fire by Hussites, and these four with sixty other friars were burned to death as they were singing the Te Deum in church.

See Giani in his *Annales Ordinis Servorum B.M.V.*, vol. i, pp. 396–400, where some contemporary documents will be found printed.   There was presumably a decree promulgating the *confirmatio cultus* alleged to have taken place in 1918, but it does not seem to have been published in the *Acta Apostolicae Sedis*.

BD JUVENAL ANCINA, BISHOP OF SALUZZO   (A.D. 1604)

ON October 19, 1545, was born at Fossano in Piedmont the first child of Durando Ancina, of a distinguished family of Spain, and his wife Lucy.   The boy was baptized John Juvenal, in honour of St Juvenal of Narni, patron of Fossano.   He was a pious youth, but at first he had no intention of entering upon other than a secular career ; his father proposed that he should be a physician and sent Juvenal at the age of fourteen to begin his studies at the University of Montpellier.   From thence he went to the school of Mondovi in Savoy and, after his father's death, to the University of Padua ; he was a brilliant student, and when only about twenty-four took his doctorate both in philosophy and medicine at Turin.   Here he was appointed to the chair of medicine in 1569 ; and he soon had an extensive private practice, especially among the poor, because he treated them free of charge.   It was noticed that Juvenal never took part in games or recreations ; the only relaxations that he allowed himself were chess and the writing of verse in Latin and Italian : he liked to deal with great affairs of church and state, and publicly declaimed his own ode on the death of Pope St Pius V in 1572.   He continued to write verses and hymns all through his life, and composed two epigrams on St Thomas More.   About this same year he was assisting at a solemn Mass of requiem in a church at Savigliano, when he was suddenly overwhelmed by the tremendous message of the *Dies irae* : he must have heard the hymn often, and as a physician he was very familiar with death, but now he realized as never before that after death comes judgement.   Hitherto his life had been blameless, but now he saw that this was not enough ; God required something more of him, though what it was he did not yet know.   He gave himself more than ever to prayer and meditation, trained himself in detachment from temporal things, and accepted the first opportunity that came along to relinquish his post at Turin.   This was when Count Frederick Madrucci, ambassador of the duke of Savoy to the Holy See, asked him to become his personal private physician.

Juvenal arrived in Rome in 1575, and took a lodging near the church of *Ara Caeli*, in a spot which appealed to him because it was " close to the prisons, the hospital, a multitude of the poor, and the prison for young criminals ".   His official work was not arduous and he set himself to the serious study of theology, having for his master St Robert Bellarmine himself; he became acquainted with Don Caesar Baronius, and by him was introduced to St Philip Neri, and so frequented the most learned and most devout society of Rome. Thus he lived for three years, becoming ever more attracted to the formal religious life, but uncertain what definite step to take. He received minor orders, attended regularly the exercises at the Oratory, and put himself under the direction of St Philip, on whose advice he accepted a benefice at Cherasco in Piedmont; but almost at once legal proceedings were taken to dispossess him and he relinquished it without contesting the suit. The fact was that he was disturbed in mind by the example of a leading lawyer at Turin, who had become a Carthusian monk at Pavia, and thought he saw in that an indication of what he must do. His brother, John Matthew, with whom Juvenal kept up an intimate correspondence from Rome, was of one mind with him, and eventually they together consulted St Philip Neri. He unhesitatingly dissuaded them from the Carthusian life, as being unsuited to their temperament and needs, and recommended to them the newly founded Congregation of the Oratory, over which he himself presided. Juvenal at first dissented, wanting more austerity and solitude, but submitted to his director and on October 1, 1578, was admitted with his brother into the congregation. Baronius said it had that day received a " second St Basil ".

When Bd Juvenal had lived four years at the Oratory he was ordained priest, and in 1586 he was sent to the Oratory at Naples, the first house of his congregation to be founded outside Rome. He was appointed to preach at once, and after a few sermons wrote to his brother, " These Neapolitans require very beautiful things, and they must be substantial as well. Ordinary things are no use here, where even the cobblers can compose sermons, and make a profession of it. One has to keep one's wits about one." But Juvenal succeeded in pleasing even the fastidious Neapolitans, and they remembered the nickname that had been given him by some wit in Rome, " the son of thunder "; " By the grace of God the people are satisfied with me ", he writes. One of his most sensational conversions was that of Giovannella Sanchia, a singer who was known in the city as " the Siren " —and not solely on account of her singing. She was so touched by hearing him speak of the beauty of holiness that she made a vow never again to sing any vain, improper or profane song, but only sacred songs. Bd Juvenal was very fond of music; we are told that " he wished Vespers to be sung with the best music, or if that were not attainable, with Gregorian chant faultlessly executed "—a critical distinction that is not acceptable to everybody. He therefore took a great deal of care with the music at the Naples Oratory, not simply from the point of view of the decencies of Christian worship and the honour due to Almighty God, but also because he had a firm belief in its good effect on the soul; he got hold of all the latest popular airs and wrote devout words to them (whether or not to be sung in the Oratory church does not appear) and published a hymn-book with tunes, called the *Temple of Harmony*. One of the Oratorians, Father Borla, took up his quarters at the Hospital for Incurables, which for long had been grossly neglected. Bd Juvenal supported him and enlisted the interest and assistance of the Neapolitan ladies, whom he formed into a confraternity of " Kind Ladies "; to ensure that the object for which they were banded together should not be lost sight of, it had its headquarters not at a church but in the hospital itself. His own material charity was boundless; its most unusual manifestation (but a very useful one) was to have a deposit account with a barber, to whom he sent any poor man whom he saw with unkempt hair or beard ; and the barber was under orders when he met any such to use his skill on them and " put it down to Father Juvenal ".   How much he was respected and loved by the whole city he betrays himself in a letter written to St Philip, when convalescent from a serious illness.   He obediently accepted the comforts that were provided for him by his brethren and took a reasonable pleasure in them.

About the year 1595, when he had been in Naples nearly ten years, Juvenal was tormented on the one hand by a desire for the cloistered and contemplative life, and on the other by the sight of so much wretchedness and wickedness around him which he could do relatively little to alleviate and reform.   But in 1596 Baronius was made a cardinal and the fathers of the Roman Oratory recalled Bd Juvenal from Naples to fill the vacant place in their community.   Greatly fearing what responsible dignities might be thrust on him in Rome, he obeyed at once, to the great grief of the Neapolitans ;   he carried on quietly for a year and then suddenly three episcopal sees fell vacant.   Bd Juvenal had good reason to think that he would be preferred to one of them ;   he went out from the Oratory one day and did not return, and after hiding for a time in the city fled from Rome.   He spent the next five months wandering from place to place.   At San Severino he received an imperative order to come back to Rome, and found when he got there that the danger of his being made bishop was, for the moment, over.   During the next four years he worked with great energy on behalf of the Piedmontese, and met and entered into intimate friendship with St Francis de Sales.

In 1602 the duke of Savoy asked Clement VIII to fill the two vacant sees in his dominions, and the pope personally charged Bd Juvenal to accept the charge of one of them.   " It is time to obey and not to fly ", said he, and on September 1 was consecrated bishop of Saluzzo by Cardinal Borghese.   His troubles began at once.   When he went to take possession of his see he found that, owing to certain actions of the duke of Savoy, he could do so only either by compromising the rights of the Church or breaking with his prince.   So he withdrew to Fossano, wrote a pastoral letter for his diocese, and devoted himself to good works for the benefit of his native town ;   supernatural gifts and the performance of miracles were, not for the first time, freely attributed to him.   After four months he was able to take possession of his cathedral, and one of his first acts was to observe the " Forty Hours " therein, for the first time in Piedmont.   Towards the end of 1603 Bd Juvenal set out on a visitation of his diocese.   Supernatural happenings again attended his progress, especially by way of healing and prophecy—Juvenal had at all times a disconcerting habit of correctly foretelling people's approaching death. Both before and during this visitation he had foretold his own, and he had only been back in Saluzzo a few weeks when his prophecy came true.

There was in the town a certain friar who was carrying on an intrigue with a nun ;   this came to the ears of Bd Juvenal, who reasoned gently with them both but warned them that if their conduct was continued he would use strong measures to stop it.   On the feast of St Bernard he went to officiate for and to dine with the Conventual Franciscans, it being the name-day of their church, and the criminal friar took the opportunity to poison the bishop's wine.   Before Vespers he was taken ill ;   four days later he had to retire to bed ;   and by the dawn of August 31 Bd Juvenal Ancina was dead.   " He died ", wrote a Carthusian monk, " for virtue, for religion, for Christ, and therefore a martyr's death " ;   like St John the Baptist, he

" received martyrdom as the reward of fearless speech ".   Marvels attended his lying-in-state and burial, Masses of the Holy Ghost were celebrated rather than requiems, and the cause of his beatification was introduced at Rome in 1624 ; this received several set-backs and postponements and was not finally achieved till 1869, when the Vatican Council had just assembled.

A full *Life of Bd John Juvenal Ancina*, with an admirable portrait, was published by Fr Charles Bowden in 1891.   The author in his preface refers to the life by F. Bacci (1671) as his principal authority.   There are other modern lives, in French, by Ingold (1890), Richard (1891), and Duver (1905).   In a review of Fr Duver's book in the *Analecta Bollandiana*, vol. xxviii (1909), p. 243, it is pointed out that some of the most valuable sources for the history of the *beato* have never been utilized, notably a memoir written by Fr B. Scaraggi, who had his work revised by G. M. Ancina, a brother of the holy bishop.

SEPTEMBER

1 : ST GILES, Abbot   (Date Unknown)

THE legend of St Giles (Aegidius), one of the most famous of the middle ages, is derived from a biography written in the tenth century. According to this he was an Athenian by birth, and during his youth cured a sick beggar by giving him his own cloak, after the manner of St Martin. Giles dreaded temporal prosperity and the applause of men which, after the death of his parents, was showered on him because of the liberality of his alms and his miracles. He therefore took ship for the west, landed at Marseilles, and, after passing two years with St Caesarius at Arles, eventually made his hermitage in a wood near the mouth of the Rhône. In this solitude he was for some time nourished with the milk of a hind, which was eventually pursued by a certain king of the Goths, Flavius, who was hunting in the forest. The beast took refuge with St Giles in his cave, and the hounds gave up their chase ; on the following day the hind was found again and the same thing happened ; and again on the third day, when the king had brought with him a bishop to watch the peculiar behaviour of his hounds. This time one of the huntsmen shot an arrow at a venture into the bushes which screened the cave, and when they had forced their way through they found Giles, wounded by the arrow, sitting with the hind between his knees. Flavius and the bishop approached and asked the hermit to give an account of himself, and when they heard his story they begged his pardon and promised to send physicians to attend him. Giles begged them to leave him alone and refused all the gifts they pressed upon him.

King Flavius continued frequently to visit St Giles, who eventually asked him to devote his proffered alms to founding a monastery ; this the king agreed to do provided Giles would become its first abbot. In due course the monastery was built near the cave, a community gathered round, and the reputation of the monks and of their abbot reached the ears of Charles, King of France (whom medieval romancers identified as Charlemagne). Giles was sent for to the court at Orleans, where the king consulted him on spiritual matters but was ashamed to name a grievous sin that was on his conscience. " On the following Sunday, when the holy man was celebrating Mass according to custom and praying to God for the king during the canon, an angel of the Lord appeared to him and laid on the altar a scroll on which was written the sin which the king had committed, and which further said that he would be forgiven at Giles's intercession, provided he did penance and desisted from that sin in the future. . . . When Mass was ended Giles gave the scroll to the king to read, who fell at the saint's feet, begging him to intercede with the Lord for him. And so the man of the Lord commended him to God in prayer and gently admonished him to refrain from that sin in the future." St Giles then returned to his monastery and afterwards went to Rome to commend his monks to the Holy See. The pope granted them many privileges and made a present of two carved doors of cedar-wood ; to emphasize his trust in divine providence St Giles threw these doors into the Tiber, and they safely preceded him to France. After being warned of his approaching end in a dream, he died on a Sunday, September 1, " leaving the world sadder for his bodily absence but giving joy in Heaven by his happy arrival ".

This and other medieval accounts of St Giles, our sole source of information, are utterly untrustworthy ; some of their statements are obviously self-contra-dictory and anachronistic, and the legend is associated with certain papal bulls which are known to be forgeries made in the interests of the monastery of Saint-Gilles in Provence. The most that is known of St Giles is that he may have been a hermit or monk near the mouth of the Rhône in the sixth or eighth century, and that his relics were claimed by the famous monastery that bore his name. The story of the hind is told of several saints, of whom Giles is the best known, and for many centuries he was one of the most popular of saints. He is numbered among the Fourteen Holy Helpers (the only one of them who is not a martyr) and his tomb at his monastery became a place of pilgrimage of the first importance, con-tributing much to the medieval prosperity of the town of Saint-Gilles, which was, however, badly damaged by the crusade against the Albigensians in the thirteenth century. Other crusaders named another town Saint-Gilles (now Sinjil), on the borders of Benjamin and Ephraim, and his cult spread throughout western Europe ; England had so many as 160 parish churches dedicated in his honour, and he was invoked as the patron of cripples, beggars and blacksmiths. John Lydgate, monk of Bury in the fifteenth century, invokes him as

> Gracious Giles, of poor folk chief patron,
> 　　Medicine to sick in their distress,
> To all needy shield and protection,
> 　　Refuge to wretches, their damage to redress,
> 　　Folk that were dead restoring to quickness. . . .

The text of the Latin life of St Giles is printed in the *Acta Sanctorum*, September, vol. i, and another recension in the *Analecta Bollandiana*, vol. viii (1889), pp. 103–120. There is also a metrical version and an adaptation in old French. For these last consult the careful study of Miss E. C. Jones, *Saint Gilles : essai d'histoire littéraire* (1914). For the folklore which has gathered round the name of St Giles see Bächtold-Stäubli, *Handwörterbuch des deutschen Aberglaubens*, vol. i, pp. 212 *seq.*, and, for the treatment in art, Künstle, *Ikonographie*, vol. ii, pp. 32–34 : this saint's distinctive emblem, as might be expected, is a hind with an arrow. For English readers an excellent account of St Giles and his *cultus* is provided in F. Brittain, *Saint Giles* (1928). See also F. Boulard, *Saint Gilles* (1933) ; and A. Fliche, *Aigues-Mortes et Saint-Gilles* (1950). Pope Benedict XIV's commission projected the removal of this feast from the general calendar.

THE TWELVE BROTHERS, Martyrs　　(Date Unknown)

THE twelve martyred brothers mentioned in the Roman Martyrology on this day were, according to their legend, natives of Hadrumetum in proconsular Africa and the children of SS. Boniface and Thecla, whose passion is commemorated on August 30. They were seized at Hadrumetum, brought to Carthage and tortured, and then sent into Italy chained together by the neck as they refused to apostatize. Four of them, Honoratus, Fortunatus, Arontius and Savinian, were put to death by beheading at Potenza on August 27 ; Septiminus, Januarius and Felix at Venosa on the 28th ; Vitalis, Sator and Repositus at Velleiano on the 29th ; and another

Felix and Donatus at Sentiano on September 1. These martyrs of Apulia were not in fact related to one another nor to SS. Boniface and Thecla, and were probably not Africans. But after their relics had been taken up by the Duke Arechis, in the year 760, and enshrined in the church of St Sophia at Benevento, they became associated together in the general mind and the story grew up that they were brothers from across the seas.

What purports to be a brief history of these martyrs will be found in the *Acta Sanctorum*, September, vol. i ; but for an adequate investigation of the composition of this group we must have recourse to CMH., pp. 471–472 and 480–482. *Cf.* also Lanzoni, *Le diocesi d'Italia*, pp. 285–288.

ST VERENA, Virgin   (Date Unknown)

The Roman Martyrology mentions on this day the death of Verena the Virgin at " Aquae Durae " in the neighbourhood of Constance, of whom nothing at all, not even the era of her life, is known. She has been drawn into the legend of the Theban Legion (September 22) and her fictitious " acts " represent her as a native of the Thebaid and a relative of St Victor, who had been her preceptor. She came to Agaunum to venerate the relics of the martyrs there and search for traces of Victor and settled at Solothurn. There is still shown the cave in which she lived and from whence she would go out on errands of mercy among the peasants of the district, for whose personal cleanliness she had a particular care. She is said to have ended her days in a cell built for her at Zurzach in the Aargau, where her tomb shows her holding a comb and a bowl, emblems of her charitable works. St Verena is held in honour throughout Switzerland.

The legendary Life of St Verena is printed in the *Acta Sanctorum*, September, vol. i. A certain respectability attaches to the cult of the saint from the fact that the name appears in the additions to the *Hieronymianum*, *e.g.* in the manuscript of Reichenau and also in the Munich martyrology of the ninth century (MS. Latin 15818). See also Huber, *Das Leben der h. Jungfrau Verena* (1870) ; A. Lütolf, *Glaubensboten der Schweiz* (1871), pp. 182–192, and especially E. A. Stückelberg in his *Schweizerischen Heiligen des Mittelalters*, pp. 127–134, and other publications. *Die heilige Verena von Zurzach*, by A. Reinle, is reviewed in *Analecta Bollandiana*, vol. lxix (1951), pp. 412–415.

ST LUPUS, or LEU, Bishop of Sens   (A.D. 623)

Having succeeded St Artemius in the bishopric of Sens, Lupus distinguished himself by the most zealous discharge of every pastoral duty, and showed that, as no dignity could inspire him with pride, so no application to public employment could divert him from constant attention to God. When the safety of his country demanded his assistance he was active in maintaining public order, and after the death of King Thierry II he supported his son Sigebert to the utmost of his power. Afterwards Clotaire became master of Burgundy and sent the Duke Farulf thither to take care of his affairs. This minister proceeded against St Lupus, who when Sens was besieged had escaped the swords of Clotaire only by ringing the church bell and thereby frightening them off. The bishop neglected the precaution of buying his safety from Farulf, who accused him falsely to the king, and was seconded in his calumnies by Medegislus, abbot of Saint-Remi at Sens, whose aim it was to supplant St Lupus in his see. The wages of the success of this unscrupulous prelate was that the people of Sens broke into his church and there slew him.

Clotaire, being deceived by the slanderers, banished St Lupus to Ausène, a village not far from Lyons. The holy bishop on his arrival found that the people of the country worshipped false gods. By restoring sight to a blind man he converted the governor, and baptized him with several other pagans in the armies of the Franks. In the meantime St Winebald, abbot of Troyes, and the citizens of Sens asked King Clotaire to recall St Lupus. That prince realized the injury he had done the man, and the slanders of his accusers. He therefore sent for St Lupus to ask his forgiveness, and sent him back to his church. The saint never showed the least resentment against his enemies, and by the evenness of temper with which he bore his disgrace gave the highest mark of heroism and virtue. Among the marvels told of this saint is that one day while singing Mass a precious stone dropped miraculously into the chalice. This is referred to in the Roman Martyrology, with the guarded word *refertur*, " it is reported ", which is certainly called for when we consider how easily a jewel might become detached from a vestment. Nevertheless it was kept as a relic in the treasury of the cathedral of Sens, where also was preserved the archbishop's episcopal ring, one of the many in legend that were dropped into water and recovered in the belly of a fish. St Lupus died in the year 623.

The earliest Latin biography of St Lupus of Sens has been critically edited in MGH., *Scriptores Merov.*, vol. iv, pp. 176–178. B. Krusch assigns it no higher date than the ninth century and thinks it historically unreliable. See, however, G. Vielhaber in *Analecta Bollandiana*, vol. xxvi (1907), pp. 43–44 ; and *cf.* H. Bouvier, *Histoire de l'Église de Sens*, vol. i, pp. 101–106, with Duchesne, *Fastes Épiscopaux*, vol. ii, p. 392.

ST FIACRE   (A.D. 670 ?)

St Fiacre (Fiachra) is not mentioned in the earlier Irish calendars, but it is said that he was born in Ireland and that he sailed over into France in quest of closer solitude, in which he might devote himself to God, unknown to the world. He arrived at Meaux, where St Faro, who was the bishop of that city, gave him a solitary dwelling in a forest which was his own patrimony, called Breuil, in the province of Brie. There is a legend that St Faro offered him as much land as he could turn up in a day, and that St Fiacre instead of driving his furrow with a plough turned the top of the soil with the point of his staff. The anchorite cleared the ground of trees and briers, made himself a cell with a garden, built an oratory in honour of the Blessed Virgin, and made a hospice for travellers which developed into the village of Saint-Fiacre in Seine-et-Marne. Many resorted to him for advice, and the poor for relief. His charity moved him to attend cheerfully those that came to consult him ; and in his hospice he entertained all comers, serving them with his own hands, and he sometimes miraculously restored to health those that were sick. He never suffered any woman to enter the enclosure of his hermitage, and St Fiacre extended the prohibition even to his chapel ; several rather ill-natured legends profess to account for it. Others tell us that those who attempted to transgress were punished by visible judgements, and that, for example, in 1620 a lady of Paris, who claimed to be above this rule, going into the oratory, became distracted upon the spot and never recovered her senses ; whereas Anne of Austria, Queen of France, was content to offer up her prayers outside the door, amongst the other pilgrims.

The fame of St Fiacre's miracles of healing continued after his death and crowds visited his shrine for centuries. Mgr Séguier, Bishop of Meaux in 1649, and John de Châtillon, Count of Blois, gave testimony of their own relief. Anne of Austria attributed to the mediation of this saint the recovery of Louis XIII at Lyons, where he had been dangerously ill: in thanksgiving for which she made on foot a pilgrimage to the shrine in 1641. She also sent to his shrine a token in acknowledgement of his intervention in the birth of her son, Louis XIV. Before that king underwent a severe operation, Bossuet, Bishop of Meaux, began a novena of prayers at Saint-Fiacre to ask the divine blessing. His relics at Meaux are still resorted to and he is invoked against all sorts of physical ills, including venereal disease. He is also a patron saint of gardeners and of the cab-drivers of Paris. French cabs are called *fiacres* because the first establishment to let coaches on hire, in the middle of the seventeenth century, was in the rue Saint-Martin, near the hôtel Saint-Fiacre, in Paris. St Fiacre's feast is kept in some dioceses of France, and throughout Ireland on this date.

There is a Latin life of some length printed in the *Acta Sanctorum*, August, vol. vi, but it is difficult to judge of its historical value. See also Gougaud, *Gaelic Pioneers of Christianity*, pp. 135–137 ; L. Pfleger in *Zeitschrift f. die Geschichte des Oberrheins* (1918), pp. 153–173 ; J. F. Kenney, *Sources . . . Ireland*, vol. i, p. 493 ; and Bächtold-Stäubli, *Handwörterbuch des deutschen Aberglaubens*, vol. iii.

ST SEBBE   (*c.* A.D. 694)

THIS prince, in the year 664, which was remarkable for a terrible pestilence, began to reign over the East Saxons, who inhabited the country which now comprises Essex, Middlesex and part of Hertfordshire ; he was co-king of this region with Sighere, who, fearing that the plague was a token of the wrath of the gods whom he had abandoned, apostatized to their worship again, with many of his people. Thereupon a bishop, Jaruman, came from Mercia to show them the error of their ways. On the authority of a priest that was with him, St Bede says he was a very discreet, religious and good man, and was successful in his mission. In it the bishop had the support of Sebbe, who was by his wise government the father of his people, who sanctified his soul by penance, alms-deeds and prayer, so that many said he was more suited by disposition to be a bishop than a king. When he had reigned for thirty years, he resigned his crown, which he had long desired to do in order to be more at liberty to prepare himself for his last hour ; but his queen had resolutely refused to agree to a separation and was only won over at last by the ill-health of her husband, which presaged that his death was not far off. St Sebbe received the monastic habit from Waldhere, successor of St Erconwald in the bishopric of London, whom he charged with the distribution of his personal estate among the poor. " When the aforesaid sickness increased upon him ", says St Bede, " and he perceived the day of his death to be drawing near, being a man of royal disposition he began to apprehend lest, when under pain and the approach of death, he might be guilty of anything unworthy of his person, either in words or any movement of his limbs. Wherefore, calling to him the said bishop of London, in which city he then was, he asked him that none might be present at his death besides the bishop himself and two attendants." Shortly after this truly royal man died, and was buried against the north wall of old St Paul's. He is named in the Roman Martyrology on August 29, having been added thereto by

Cardinal Baronius in the sixteenth century, and his feast is kept in the diocese of Brentwood on September 1.

All that we know of St Sebbe is derived from Bede, *Eccl. Hist.*, bk iii, ch. 30, and bk iv, ch. 11. There would seem to be no trace of liturgical *cultus* until modern times.

ST DRITHELM   (*c.* A.D. 700)

St Bede in the fifth book of his *Ecclesiastical History* relates what he calls " a memorable miracle, like to those of former days ".   It concerns a man called Drithelm, who was a householder in Northumbria and a person of virtuous life, father of a God-fearing family.   Somewhere about the year 693 he was seized with an illness and one evening appeared to be dead, but the next morning he suddenly sat up, to the fear of those mourning around his body, who all fled except his wife. To her he said : " Be not afraid, for I am now truly risen from death and allowed again to live among men.   But hereafter I am not to live as I have been wont but rather in a very different manner."   He then went to pray in the church of the village and afterwards returned to his house where he made a division of his goods, one-third to his wife, one-third to his children, and the remaining third to the poor.   He then made his way to King Aldfrid and told him his story, and at the king's request St Ethelwald, who was then abbot of Melrose, tonsured Drithelm and admitted him among his monks.

Now the things which Drithelm had seen, and which " he would not tell to tepid persons and such as lived negligently, but only to those who, being feared with the dread of Hell or delighted with the hope of heavenly joys, would make use of his words to advance in religion ", were these : After he was dead he had been met by one with a shining countenance and bright garments who led him towards the north-east, where sunrise is at midsummer.   There was a great valley, whereof one side was burning with flames and the other frozen with ice and snow, and everywhere were men's souls which seemed to be tossed from one side to the other as it were by a storm.   Drithelm thought that this might be Hell, but his guide said it was not so and led him on till they came to a great fiery pit, on the edge of which Drithelm was left alone.   The souls of folk were cast about in this pit and Drithelm could discern a priest, a layman, and a woman ; cries and lamentations and a horrible stench rose from the flames, and evil spirits of repulsive aspect were about to push Drithelm in.   But his guide appeared again and led him forward, now towards the south-east, to the quarter where the sun rises in winter, and they came out into an atmosphere of clear light where there was an endless unpierced wall.   He found himself on the top of this wall, and within was a large and delightful field, " so full of fragrant flowers that the smell of their sweetness at once dispelled the stink of the dark furnace, which had pierced me through and through". In this field were innumerable men and women, clothed in white and rejoicing together in groups, so that Drithelm thought that perhaps this was the kingdom of Heaven.   But his guide said : " This is not the kingdom of Heaven as you suppose."   Then they went yet further and came to a place of light and singing and delight, beside which the first field was dull and bleak, and Drithelm was hoping that they would enter into that place, when his guide suddenly stopped, turned round, and led him back by the way they had come to the first field.

Here he turned to Drithelm and said : " The valley of flames and cutting cold is the place where are tried the souls of those who have delayed to repent and confess their sins, but have done so at the point of death.   And they shall be delivered at the day of Judgement, and some before then because of the prayers and alms-deeds and Masses of the living.   The fiery and stinking pit which you saw is the mouth of Hell, into which whosoever is cast shall not be delivered for all eternity.   This flowery place, in which you see these beautiful young people so shining and merry, is that into which are received for a space the souls who depart the body in good works but are not so perfect that they may at once be taken into Heaven.   Whoever leave life perfect in thought, word, and deed are called at once into the kingdom of Heaven, of which you heard the singing, smelled the fragrance, and saw the light.   As for you, who are now to return to your body and live among men again, if you will try nicely to examine your actions and direct your speech and behaviour in righteousness and simplicity, you shall have a place among the blessed souls.   For when I left you for a while it was to learn what was to be your doom."   Then Drithelm, fearing to ask any more questions, found himself living and among men once more.

St Drithelm lived for the rest of his days in a cell on the banks of the Tweed, into the freezing waters of which he would sometimes cast himself by way of penance, and stand reciting his office with ice floating around him.   At which some would say : " It is wonderful, Brother Drithelm, that you can stand such cold."   And he, being a man " of much simplicity and indifferent wit ", would reply simply, " I have seen greater cold."   Or if they said, " It is strange how you can endure such hardship ", he would answer, " I have seen greater hardship ". In such ways he continued to mortify his body till the day of his death and for-warded the salvation of many by his words and example.   One such was a priest and monk called Hemgils, of whom St Bede wrote : " He is still living, and leading a solitary life in Ireland where he supports his declining years with coarse bread and cold water.   He often went to Drithelm and heard of him all the particulars of what he had seen when separated from his body ; by whose relations we also came to the knowledge of the few particulars which we have briefly set down."

There has been no known *cultus* of St Drithelm, but Alcuin refers to him in his poem on the saints of the church of York.   Bishop Challoner mentions him under this date in his *Memorials of Ancient British Piety.*

We know little of Drithelm beyond what is contained in Bede's *Historia Ecclesiastica* (see Plummer's edition and notes) ; but Abbot Aelfric devotes a homily to the vision (ed. B. Thorpe, vol. ii, pp. 348–356).   *Cf.* also St John Seymour, *Irish Visions of the Other World* (1930), especially pp. 154–156.

BB. JOHN OF PERUGIA AND PETER OF SASSOFERRATO,
Martyrs   (A.D. 1231)

Among the Friars Minor whom St Francis of Assisi sent into Spain to preach the gospel to the Moors were Brother John, a priest of Perugia, and Brother Peter, a lay-brother from Sassoferrato in Piceno.   These two friars established themselves at Teruel in Aragon, living in cells near the church of St Bartholomew, and there for some time prepared themselves for their apostolate.   Their poverty and lowliness won the love and attention of the people of the place, and their lives and preaching bore much fruit.   They then went on to Valencia, which was completely under the dominion of the Moors, and took up their quarters quietly at the church of the Holy Sepulchre.   But directly the friars attempted to preach in public the Mohammedans turned against them ; they were arrested and brought before the emir. He asked what had brought them to Valencia, and Bd John replied that they came to convert the Moors from the errors of Islam. They were then offered the usual alternatives of apostasy or death, and when they chose death were condemned to be beheaded. The sentence was carried out then and there in the emir's garden, the martyrs praying aloud for the conversion of their persecutor. This was on August 29, 1231.

Seven years later James I the Conqueror, King of Aragon, drove the Moo. from Valencia with the help of his English and other mercenaries, and in accordance with the martyrs' prayer the emir became a Christian. He gave his house to the Franciscans for a friary, saying to them : " While I was an unbeliever I killed your brethren from Teruel, and I want to make reparation for my crime. Here, then, is my house at your disposal, consecrated already by the blood of martyrs." The bodies of BB. John and Peter had been taken to Teruel, where miracles were reported at their tomb, and so a church was erected at the new friary at Valencia in their honour. They were beatified in 1783.

An account of these martyrs is given in the *Acta Sanctorum*, August, vol. vi, where their story is reproduced as told by St Antoninus of Florence. An older narrative of the martyrdom has been printed in the *Analecta Franciscana*, vol. iii, pp. 186–187. See also Léon, *Auréole Séraphique* (Eng. trans.), vol. iii, pp. 96–97.

BD JOAN SODERINI, Virgin (A.D. 1367)

THE Soderini were a noble family of Florence and Bd Joan was born in that city in the year 1301. From a very early age she showed herself remarkably good and devoted to God, so much so that when she told her governess, Felicia Tonia, that she knew by a revelation that she, Felicia, would shortly die, she is said to have been believed, and the governess began to look around for a successor to take charge of her pupil. As soon as she was adolescent Joan's parents arranged a marriage for her, but the child protested and they, not too well pleased, for she was their only child, reluctantly gave their consent to her becoming a nun. At this time St Juliana Falconieri was organizing the Servite third order regular (" Mantellate ") in Florence, and Joan elected to join this new community. She was soon distinguished by her corporal austerities and perseverance in prayer, but at the same time was active in the work of the house and the care of the sick who came to it for attention and medicine. She voluntarily undertook the most distasteful tasks, and endeared herself to her sisters by her equability and cheerfulness. Joan was visited with hard trials and grievous temptations which she triumphed over, attaining by her faithfulness to a certain gift of prophecy. She was the constant personal attendant of St Juliana during her last long illness, when she was almost continually sick and could digest no food. To Bd Joan is attributed the first discovery of the image of a crucifix, alleged to have been found imprinted on the chest of St Juliana after her death. She survived her beloved prioress for twenty-six years and succeeded her in the government of the community, which she sought to direct according to the example and wishes of St Juliana. Bd Joan died on September 1, 1367, and was buried in the Annunziata at Florence, where her tomb at once became a place of pilgrimage. In 1828 Count Soderini, a relative of Joan, petitioned Pope Leo XII for confirmation of this *cultus*, which was duly granted.

See the *Acta Sanctorum*, October, vol. xii, pp. 398–404 ; and also A. Giani, *Annales Ordinis Servorum*, vol. i, pp. 320–321.

BD HUGH MORE, Martyr   (A.D. 1588)

Bd Hugh More was one of the first group of London Martyrs of 1588 (August 28). He is accorded a separate feast today in the diocese of Nottingham, because he was born within the borders of what is now that diocese, at Grantham in 1563.

He was brought up a Protestant and educated at Broadgates Hall, Oxford, from whence he passed to Gray's Inn. Having been reconciled with the Church by Father Thomas Stephenson, s.j., he went abroad to Rheims, where for a time he studied at the seminary. Upon returning home he was arrested, and arraigned for his reconciliation. He could have saved himself by conforming to the law of attendance at the established church, but this he refused to do ; he was accordingly hanged in Lincoln's Inn Fields on August 28, 1588. This young layman was only twenty-five years old, one of the " several young gentlemen " referred to by Father Ribadeneira in his appendix to Sander's *De Schismate anglicano* whose death " strongly pleaded for the cause for which they died ".

See MMP., p. 136 ; Burton and Pollen, LEM., vol. i.

BD GABRA MICHAEL, Martyr   (A.D. 1855)

After Bd Justin de Jacobis arrived in Ethiopia in 1839 it was not long before he came to know Abba Gabra Michael,* a monk of the dissident Church of Ethiopia, a man some fifty years old who was renowned for his holiness and learning, and who was also suspected of an inclination towards Catholicity, which his fellow monks stigmatized as a taint of Arianism. Gabra Michael was not a priest, but he had studied as deeply in theology as conditions in his church allowed, going from monastery to monastery, teaching and learning. The deputation from Ethiopia to Egypt and Rome, of which Gabra Michael was a member and which Bd Justin accompanied, has been described under July 31 ; and following that experience, and much talk with Father Justin, Gabra Michael eventually in 1844 was received into the visible membership of the Catholic Church.

The learned Abyssinian was a most valuable auxiliary for Father de Jacobis, especially in the training of native aspirants for the priesthood. Together they drew up a catechism of Christian doctrine adapted to local needs and translated a work of moral theology into Amharic, and established a college of which Gabra Michael was put in charge. This was an opportunity for Abuna Salama, head of the dissident Church, to stir up feeling against " the Franks " which led to the ruler banishing their two leaders, who took refuge in the island of Massawa. Here Mgr Massaia consecrated Father de Jacobis bishop ; he returned secretly to the scene of his mission, and his first episcopal act was to ordain Gabra Michael to the priesthood in 1851. There followed a brief period of almost startlingly successful work among the dissidents. But then came the revolt of Kassa and his seizure of the Ethiopian crown as Theodore II, and persecution flared up again.

Gabra Michael and four of his fellow countrymen were thrown into prison and threatened with torture in order to make them apostatize. They refused ; and at intervals over a period of nine months they were dragged from their filthy cell into the presence of Theodore and his metropolitan, Salama, to be browbeaten and cajoled ; and each time when they stood firm they were lashed with a giraffe's tail

* Gabra Mika'el, *i.e.* Servant of Michael ; *cf.* the Scottish " Gilmichael ". The name is sometimes found in a French form, Michel Ghèbrè.

(whose hair is like steel wire) and otherwise tortured. " In matters of faith ", said Gabra Michael to Salama, " I cannot be other then opposed to you. But so far as Christian charity is concerned I think I have never done you anything but good " —and indeed it was due to his intervention that Salama had been exiled instead of executed some years before. In March 1855 Theodore set out on an expedition against the ruler of Shoa, Gabra Michael was taken with him in chains, and on May 31 a last attempt was made to induce him to submit to the king by repudiating the true faith. He refused and was condemned to death.

Among those present was the British consul, Walter Chichele Plowden, who had supported Theodore in his usurpation ; he now came forward with others and begged a reprieve for Gabra Michael, which was granted ; but he was to be a prisoner for life. By the mouth of a friend he sent a message to the other prisoners at Gondar : " Be steadfast to death in your faith. I have no hope of seeing you again on this earth. If they kill me, I shall die testifying to my faith ; if they spare me, I shall go on preaching it." For three more months, decrepit with age and ill-treatment, Gabra Michael was dragged in chains from place to place in the train of the king ; he caught cholera and recovered, giving away his pittance of food to other sufferers and earning the esteem even of his guards ; at last on August 28, 1855, he lay down by the side of the road and died. His guards gently removed his chains and buried his body ; and Bd Gabra Michael was beatified as a martyr in 1926.

There is a French life of this martyr by J. B. Coulbeaux (1902), and one in Italian by E. Cassinari (1926). See also the sketch by G. Goyau in *The Golden Legend Overseas* (1931) ; and the *Book of Eastern Saints* (1938), by D. Attwater, pp. 136–147. *Cf.* bibliography of Bd Justin de Jacobis, July 31.

2 : ST STEPHEN OF HUNGARY   (A.D. 1038)

THE people whom we call Magyars came into the country of Hungary during the last years of the ninth century, settling in the land around the Danube from several districts to the east of it, under the general leadership of a chief called Arpad. They were a fierce and marauding people and met Christianity in the course of their raids into Italy, France and westward generally. St Methodius and others had already planted the faith in Pannonia, but it was not until the second half of the tenth century that the Magyars themselves began to pay any serious consideration to the Church. Geza, the third duke (*voivode*) after Arpad, saw the political necessity of Christianity to his country, and (encouraged by St Adalbert of Prague) he was baptized and a number of his nobles followed his example. But it was largely a conversion of expediency, and had the usual result of such conversions : the Christianity of the converts was largely nominal. An exception to this was Geza's son, Vaik, who had been baptized at the same time as his father and been given the name of Stephen (Istvan) ; he was then only about ten and so had not acquired pagan ways and fixed habits of mind. In the year 995, when he was twenty, he married Gisela, sister of Henry, Duke of Bavaria, better known as the Emperor St Henry II, and two years later he succeeded his father as governor of the Magyars.

Stephen was soon engaged in wars with rival tribal leaders and others ; and when he had consolidated his position he sent St Astrik, whom he designed to be the first archbishop, to Rome to obtain Pope Silvester II's approval for a proper ecclesiastical organization for his country ; and at the same time to ask his Holiness to confer upon him the title of king, which his nobles had long pressed him to assume and which he now asked that he might with more majesty and authority accomplish his designs for promoting the glory of God and the good of his people. Silvester was disposed to grant his request, and prepared a royal crown to send him with his blessing, acting no doubt in concert with political representations from the Emperor Otto III who was then in Rome. At the same time the pope confirmed the religious foundations which the prince had made and the elections of bishops. St Stephen went to meet his ambassador upon his return and listened, standing with great respect, to the pope's bulls whilst they were read ; to express his own sense of religion and to inspire his subjects with awe for whatever belonged to divine worship, he always treated the pastors of the Church with great honour and respect. The same prelate who had brought the crown from Rome crowned him king with great solemnity in the year 1001.*

Firmly to root Christianity in his kingdom and to provide for its steady progress after his own time, King Stephen established episcopal sees only gradually, as Magyar clergy became available ; Vesprem is the first of which there is reliable record, but within some years Esztergom was founded and became the primatial see. At Szekesfehervar he built a church in honour of the Mother of God, in which the kings of Hungary were afterwards both crowned and buried. This city St Stephen made his usual residence, whence it was called Alba Regalis to distinguish it from Alba Julia in Transylvania. He also completed the foundation of the great monastery of St Martin, begun by his father. This monastery, known as Martinsberg or Pannonhalma, still exists, and is the mother house of the Hungarian Benedictine congregation. For the support of the churches and their pastors and the relief of the poor throughout his dominions he commanded tithes to be paid. Every tenth town had to build a church and support a priest ; the king himself furnished the churches. He abolished, not without violence, barbarous and superstitious customs derived from the former religion and by severe punishments repressed blasphemy, murder, theft, adultery and other public crimes. He commanded all persons to marry except religious and churchmen, and forbade all marriages of Christians with idolators. He was of easy access to people of all ranks, and listened to everyone's complaints, but was most willing to hear the poor, knowing them to be more easily oppressed and considering that in them we honour Christ who, being no longer among men on earth in His mortal state, has recommended to us the poor in His place and right.

It is said that one day, while the king was distributing alms in disguise, a troop of beggars crowding round him knocked him down, hustled him, pulled at his beard and hair, and took away his purse, seizing for themselves what he intended for the relief of many others. Stephen took this indignity humbly and with good humour, happy to suffer in the service of his Saviour, and his nobles, when they heard of this, were amused and chaffed him about it ; but they were also disturbed, and insisted that he should no more expose his person ; but he renewed his resolution never to refuse an alms to any poor person that asked him. The example

* The alleged bull of Pope Silvester granting the title of Apostolic King and Apostolic Legate to St Stephen, with the right to have a primatial cross borne before him, is a forgery, probably of the seventeenth century. The upper part of the crown sent by the pope, fitted on to the lower part of a crown given to King Geza I by the Emperor Michael VII, is preserved at Budapest.

of his virtue was a most powerful sermon to those who came under his influence, and in no one was it better exemplified than in his son, Bd Emeric, to whom St Stephen's code of laws was inscribed. These laws he caused to be promulgated throughout his dominions, and they were well suited to a fierce and rough people newly converted to Christianity. But they were not calculated to allay the discontent and alarm of those who were still opposed to the new religion, and some of the wars which St Stephen had to undertake had a religious as well as a political significance. When he had overcome an irruption of the Bulgarians he undertook the political organization of his people. He abolished tribal divisions and divided the land into " counties ", with a system of governors and magistrates. Thus, and by means of a limited application of feudal ideas, making the nobles vassals of the crown, he welded the Magyars into a unity ; and by retaining direct control over the common people he prevented undue accumulation of power into the hands of the lords. St Stephen was indeed the founder and architect of the independent realm of Hungary. But, as Father Paul Grosjean, Bollandist, has remarked, to look at him otherwise than against his historical background gives as false an impression as to think of him as a sort of Edward the Confessor or Louis IX. And that background was a very fierce and uncivilized one.

As the years passed, Stephen wanted to entrust a greater part in the government to his only son, but in 1031 Emeric was killed while hunting. " God loved him, and therefore He has taken him away early ", cried St Stephen in his grief. The death of Emeric left him without an heir and the last years of his life were embittered by family disputes about the succession, with which he had to cope while suffering continually from painful illness. There were four or five claimants, of whom one, Peter, was the son of his sister Gisela, an ambitious and cruel woman, who since the death of her husband had lived at the Hungarian court. She had made up her mind that her son should have the throne, and shamelessly took advantage of Stephen's ill-health to forward her ends. He eventually died, aged sixty-three, on the feast of the Assumption 1038, and was buried beside Bd Emeric at Szekesfehervar. His tomb was the scene of miracles, and forty-five years after his death, by order of Pope St Gregory VII at the request of King St Ladislaus, his relics were enshrined in a chapel within the great church of our Lady at Buda. Innocent XI appointed his festival for September 2 in 1686, the Emperor Leopold having on that day recovered Buda from the hands of the Turks.

There are two early lives of St Stephen, both dating apparently from the eleventh century, and known as the *Vita major* and the *Vita minor*. These texts have been edited in Pertz, MGH., *Scriptores*, vol. xi. A certain Bishop Hartwig early in the twelfth century compiled from these materials a biography which is printed in the *Acta Sanctorum*, September, vol. ii. Other facts concerning the saint may be gleaned from the *Chronica Ungarorum* edited in Endlicher's *Monumenta*, vol. i. Although the supposed bull of Silvester II is certainly spurious, and although very serious doubts have been raised as to the genuineness of the crown alleged to have been sent by the pope, still there does seem to be evidence of special powers conferred by papal authority which were equivalent to those of a legate *a latere*. The belief, however, that St Stephen was invested with the title of " Apostolic King " is altogether without foundation. See *e.g.* the article of L. Kropf in the *English Historical Review*, 1898, pp. 290–295. A very readable, but rather uncritical, life by E. Horn (1899) has appeared in the series " Les Saints ". For more reliable and detailed information we have to go to such Hungarian authorities as J. Paulers, Mgr Fraknoi and Dr Karácsonyi. In a later volume of the *Acta Sanctorum*, November, vol. ii, pp. 477–487, the Bollandists, when dealing with the life of Bd Emeric, have discussed many points which have a bearing on the history of the king, his father. Among the publications marking the ninth centenary of the death of St Stephen were F. Banfi, *Re Stefano il Santo* (1938), and B. Hóman, *Szent István* (1938) ; the last has been translated into German (1941). See also *Archivum Europae centro-orientalis*, vol. iv (1938) ; and C. A. Macartney, *The Medieval Hungarian Historians* (1953).

ST ANTONINUS, MARTYR   (FOURTH CENTURY)

ACCORDING to the eastern legend Antoninus was a Syrian stonemason who, with an especially disinterested zeal, rebuked the idolaters of his native place for worshipping images of stone. He then lived with a hermit for two years, at the end of which time he came back to the town and found the people still worshipping their false gods. So he went into a temple and threw down the idol therein, whereupon he was driven from the place and came to Apamaea. Here the bishop engaged him to build a church, an undertaking which so angered the pagans that they raised a riot and killed Antoninus, who was only twenty years old.

This appears to be the Antoninus the martyr who is stated by the Roman Martyrology to have suffered at Pamiers, where there are local legends about him. Some alleged relics were taken to Palencia in Spain, of which he is the patron, and which has its own version of the Pamiers legend. The name of St Antoninus is associated with those of SS. Almachius and John, who are supposed to have suffered with him, and has by another error become connected also with Capua, where " Antoninus, a boy ", is named with St Aristaeus, bishop and martyr, on September 3.

A great deal of confusion has grown up around the mention of this martyr in the ancient martyrology known as the *Hieronymianum*. Delehaye (CMH., pp. 484–486) points out that there was an unquestionably authentic *cultus* of the Apamaean Antoninus, which is vouched for amongst others by Theodoret. The martyr is honoured, however, in the Greek synaxaries on November 9. See, further, Fr Delehaye, " Saints et reliquaires d'Apamée ", in *Analecta Bollandiana*, vol. liii (1935), pp. 225 *seq.*

ST CASTOR, BISHOP OF APT   (*c.* A.D. 425)

HE was a native of Nîmes and perhaps brother to St Leontius of Fréjus. He began a secular career, having married the daughter of a rich widow from Marseilles. But both were drawn to the life of the cloister, and St Castor founded, near Apt in Provence, the monastery of Mananque, himself becoming the first abbot. Thence he was called to the episcopal chair of Apt, an office he undertook unwillingly but discharged unwaveringly. He bent all his energies to the saving of souls, calling on them to love God with all their hearts, to join with the Church in serving Him who is all-lovely and all-worshipful. St Castor maintained the closest interest in the welfare of his monks, and it was at his request for them that St John Cassian wrote his work on the monastic life, *De institutis coenobiorum*, which was dedicated to St Castor.

See the *Acta Sanctorum*, September, vol. vi ; *Gallia christiana novissima*, vol. i, pp. 192–195 ; and Duchesne, *Fastes Épiscopaux*, vol. i, p. 282.

ST AGRICOLUS, BISHOP OF AVIGNON   (SEVENTH CENTURY)

INFORMATION about this saint is very unreliable, for it is obtained from no document earlier than the sixteenth century, at which time a popular devotion towards him began to grow up. He has been officially recognized as the patron of the city of Avignon only since 1647. These late traditions say that Agricolus was born about the year 630, the son of St Magnus, a Gallo-Roman senator of the *gens Albina*, who after the death of his wife became first a monk at Lérins and then bishop of Avignon. Agricolus himself went to Lérins when he was fourteen and, making great progress in learning and virtue, was advanced to the priesthood. After sixteen years as a monk his father summoned him to the episcopal city. Here he was appointed archdeacon and distinguished himself by his preaching, by his powers of administration, and by his care for the poor, the oppressed and the sick. In 660 St Magnus consecrated his son bishop as his coadjutor. Ten years later Magnus died and St Agricolus succeeded both to his father's see and to the success with which he administered it. He is invoked locally to bring both rain and fair weather.

See the *Acta Sanctorum*, September, vol. i, and more particularly Duprat, *Les origines de l'Église d'Avignon* (1909), pp. 73 *seq.* A full bibliography may be found in DHG., vol. i, c. 1019.

ST WILLIAM, BISHOP OF ROSKILDE   (*c.* A.D. 1070)

THE historians of Denmark relate that St William was an English priest, chaplain to King Canute. In one of the voyages which that prince made from England to Denmark, the zealous servant of God who attended him was so moved with compassion at the sight of the ignorance, idolatry and superstition in which so many of the Danes lived that he decided to stay behind to preach Christ and His gospel. He later was advanced to the episcopal see of Roskilde in the island of Zealand. Most of the things related of St William have reference to his unwearying efforts to reform the behaviour of King Sweyn Estridsen. This prince having once caused some persons to be put to death not only without trial but also within the bounds of a church, the saint met him at the church door the next day and, holding out his pastoral staff, forbade him to enter the house of God till his hands were cleansed from the blood he had unjustly spilt ; and seeing some of the courtiers draw their swords, he presented his neck, saying he was ready to die in defence of the Church of God. Sweyn publicly confessed his crime, and later gave some land to the church of Roskilde as a peace offering.

St William had affection for his troublesome sovereign, and for some years the saint and the penitent concurred to promote the cause of religion. Upon the death of the king his body was temporarily buried in the abbey he had founded at Ringsted, till the cathedral of Roskilde should be ready for its reception. At the same time a tomb was prepared there for St William, and it is said that, while Sweyn's body was being conveyed from Ringsted to Roskilde, St William came out to meet it and himself died at its approach, so that the two friends were borne together to burial. St William is named in Danish calendars but he has never had a liturgical feast in his honour. He has been confused with St William of Eskill (April 6).

There is no separate biography of St William ; his history has to be gleaned from such unsatisfactory chroniclers as Saxo Grammaticus in his *Gesta Danorum*.

BD MARGARET OF LOUVAIN, VIRGIN AND MARTYR   (A.D. 1225 ?)

In the sixth book of his *Dialogue on Miracles*, dealing with Singleness of Heart, the Cistercian monk Caesarius of Heisterbach tells the story of this young girl whose *cultus* in the diocese of Malines was confirmed in 1905. She was born at Louvain about the year 1207 and went into domestic service with a relative named Aubert. He was an innkeeper and a good and charitable man, who would entertain pilgrims and necessitous travellers free of charge. Margaret entered whole-heartedly into these good works, but the recollected way with which she went about them and her indifference to the attentions of men got her the nickname of " the proud Margaret". About the year 1225 Aubert and his wife determined to become religious. Having sold their business and made the necessary preparations, they were spending their last night at home when they were visited by some evil-disposed men under the pretence of saying good-bye. Margaret was sent out to get some wine for the visitors, and while she was gone they set on Aubert and his wife, murdered them, and seized their money which they had by them to take to the monasteries to which they were going. On her return with the wine the robbers carried off Margaret and at a lonely spot near the river Dyle proposed to kill her too, as a witness to their crime. One of them offered to marry her if she would keep silence, but she refused, and thereupon an extra ten marks was added to the share of one of them to make away with her. " He, taking the innocent lamb like a cruel butcher, cut her throat, stabbed her in the side, and threw her into the river." The body was found and, in consequence of the supernatural light and angelic voices that were reported to accompany it, was taken by the clergy to St Peter's collegiate church at Louvain and buried in a special chapel in their churchyard. Miracles were vouchsafed at this tomb and there Bd Margaret has been venerated from that day to this.

Concerning this story the novice in the *Dialogue* asks : " What would you say was the cause of martyrdom in the case of this girl ? " To which his preceptor replies : " Simplicity and an innocent life, as I have already said. There are different kinds of martyrdom, namely, innocence, as in Abel ; uprightness, as in the prophets and St John Baptist ; love of the law, as in the Machabees ; confession of the faith, as in the apostles. For all these different causes Christ the Lamb is said to have been ' slain from the beginning of the world '." All Christian virtues, being protestations of our faith and proofs of our fidelity to God, are a true motive of martyrdom.

The Bollandists, in the *Acta Sanctorum*, September, vol. i, find nothing to add to the account given by Caesarius, but they supply evidence regarding the later *cultus*, and translate from the Flemish a relation of a number of miracles wrought at the shrine. Several booklets of a popular kind have been printed about Bd Margaret in modern times ; the most note-worthy, by M. G. Ollivier, originally appeared as an article in the *Revue Thomiste*, vol. iv (1896), pp. 592–618. The *Dialogue* of Caesarius was published in English in 1929.

ST BROCARD (A.D. 1231 ?)

ON the death of St Berthold about the year 1195 he was succeeded as superior of the Frankish hermits on Mount Carmel by this Brocard or Burchard, who was a Frenchman. As these hermits had no fixed rule of life Brocard asked for instructions from St Albert, a canon regular who was Latin patriarch and papal legate in Palestine. Between 1205 and 1210 Albert gave them a short rule, which St Brocard imposed on his subjects. It bound them to live alone in separate cells, to recite the Divine Office or other prayers, to work with their hands, and to meet together daily for Mass ; to observe poverty, perpetual abstinence and long silences. They were to give obedience to St Brocard as prior during his life, and afterwards to his successors. After the fourth Council of the Lateran had passed a decree against new religious orders these hermits, who had begun to spread in Palestine, were attacked on the ground that they contravened this canon, not having been approved by the Holy See but only by its legate.   According to the tradition of the Carmelite Order Pope Honorius III was going to suppress them, but warned by a vision of our Lady he confirmed their rule instead, about the year 1226.   St Brocard directed his community with virtue and prudence during these difficulties, and died after being prior for some thirty-five years.   One of the few events recorded in his life is that he miraculously restored to health a Mohammedan emir and converted him to the faith.   It is said that St Albert intended to take St Brocard to the Lateran Council, as one well versed in Eastern affairs, understanding Islam, and respected by all.   But Albert was murdered the year before the council assembled.

See the *Acta Sanctorum*, September, vol. i, and more especially the *Monumenta historica Carmelitana* of B. Zimmerman, pp. 276–279.   Some account of St Brocard may also be found in Lezana, *Annales*, vol. iv, p. 244, and in the *Speculum Carmelitanum*, ii, p. 661 ; and *cf.* DHG., vol. xi, c. 1070 *seq.*

BB. JOHN DU LAU, ARCHBISHOP OF ARLES, AND HIS COMPANIONS, THE MARTYRS OF SEPTEMBER   (A.D. 1792)

THERE can be no doubt that at the time of the French Revolution there were conditions in the Church in France which, to phrase it mildly, were regrettable : worldly and domineering bishops and higher clergy who were indifferent to the sufferings of the people, numbers of self-seeking and ignorant rectors and curates who in the hour of trial did not refuse to accept an oath and constitution condemned by the Holy See and their own bishops, and many lay people who were, more or less culpably, indifferent or openly hostile to religion.   The other and better side of the picture may be represented by those *émigré* priests and people who made so good an impression and helped on the cause of Catholic emancipation in our own country, and by those many others who gave their lives rather than co-operate with the forces of irreligion.   Such, for example, were the martyrs who suffered in Paris on September 2 and 3, 1792.   In 1790 the Constituent Assembly had passed the civil constitution of the clergy, which the hierarchy at once condemned as unlawful : all the diocesan bishops except four and most of the urban clergy refused to take the oath imposed by it.   In the following year Pope Pius VI confirmed this condemnation of the constitution as " heretical, contrary to Catholic teaching, sacrilegious, and opposed to the rights of the Church ".   At the end of August 1792 the revolutionaries throughout France were infuriated by the rising of the peasants in La Vendée and the success of the arms of Prussia, Austria and Sweden at Longwy, and, inflamed by fierce rhetoric against the royalists and clergy who upheld their country's foes, over fifteen hundred clergy, laymen and women were massacred. Of these victims 191 individuals were beatified as martyrs in 1926.

Early in the afternoon of September 2 several hundred rioters attacked the Abbaye, the former monastery where priests, loyal soldiers and other disaffected persons were imprisoned.   Led by a ruffian called Maillard, they tendered the constitutional oath to a number of priests, all of whom refused it and were killed on the spot.   A mock tribunal then condemned the rest of the prisoners *en masse*. Among the martyrs here was the ex-Jesuit (the Society was at that time suppressed) BD ALEXANDER LENFANT.   He had been a confessor of the king, and a devoted friend of the royal family in its misfortunes.   This led to his arrest and, in spite of the efforts of an apostate priest to get him released, he suffered martyrdom. Mgr de Salamon tells in his memoirs how he saw Father Lenfant quietly hearing the confession of another priest five minutes before both confessor and penitent were dragged out and slain.

Having been refreshed with wine and encouraged with *pourboires* by the mayor of Paris, a gang then made for the Carmelite church in the Rue de Rennes. Here were imprisoned over one hundred and fifty ecclesiastics, with one layman, BD CHARLES DE LA CALMETTE, Comte de Valfons, an officer in the cavalry who had voluntarily accompanied his parish priest into confinement. This noble company, led by BD JOHN MARY DU LAU, Archbishop of Arles, BD FRANCIS JOSEPH DE LA ROCHEFOUCAULD, Bishop of Beauvais, and his brother BD PETER LOUIS, Bishop of Saintes, led a life of almost monastic regularity and astounded their gaolers by their cheerfulness and good temper. It was a sultry Sunday afternoon and the prisoners were allowed, on this day ordered, to take the air in the garden. While the bishops and some other clergy were saying Vespers in a chapel the murderers broke into the garden and killed the first priest they met. In the resulting panic Mgr du Lau came quietly out of the chapel. " Are you the archbishop ? " he was asked. " Yes, sirs. I am the archbishop." He was cut down by a sword stroke and killed by the thrust of a pike as he lay on the ground. Amid howls of execration shooting began right and left : several were killed and wounded and the Bishop of Beauvais's leg was shattered by a bullet.

But the French sense of good order was outraged. A " judge " was appointed, who sat in a passage between the church and the sacristy, and two by two the confessors were brought in and had the constitutional oath tendered to them. Every one refused it without hesitation, and as each recalcitrant couple passed down the narrow staircase they were hacked to pieces. The Bishop of Beauvais was called for. He replied from where he lay : " I do not refuse to die with the others, but I cannot walk. I beg you to have the kindness to carry me where you wish me to go." There could have been no more telling rebuke than that courteous speech : it did not save him, but silence fell on the murderers as he was brought forward and rejected the proffered oath. BD JAMES GALAIS, who had been in charge of the feeding arrangements of the prisoners, handed to the " judge " 325 francs which he owed the caterer ; BD JAMES FRITEYRE-DURVÉ, ex-Jesuit, was killed by a neighbour whom he knew in his own birthplace ; three other ex-Jesuits and four secular priests were aged men who had only recently been turned out of a house of rest at Issy and made to walk to the Carmelite church ; the Comte de Valfons and his confessor, BD JOHN GUILLEMINET, met death side by side. Thus perished the martyrs who from their place of martyrdom are called " *des Carmes* " : the remaining forty or so were able to make their escape unseen or were allowed to slip away by conscience-stricken soldiers. Among the victims were BD AMBROSE AUGUSTINE CHEVREUX, superior general of the Maurist Benedictines, and two other monks ; BD FRANCIS LOUIS HÉBERT, confessor of Louis XVI ; three Franciscans ; fourteen ex-Jesuits ; six diocesan vicars general ; thirty-eight members or former members of the Saint-Sulpice seminary ; three deacons ; an acolyte ; and a Christian Brother. The bodies were buried some in a pit in the cemetery of Vaugirard and some in a well in the garden of the Carmes.

On September 3 the band of murderers came to the Lazarist seminary of Saint-Firmin, also used as a prison, where their first victim was BD PETER GUÉRIN DU ROCHER, an ex-Jesuit sixty years old. He was asked to choose between the oath and death, and on his replying was thrown out of the nearest window and stabbed in the courtyard below.   His brother BD ROBERT was also a victim, and there were five other ex-Jesuits among the ninety clerics there, of whom only four escaped. The superior of the seminary was BD LOUIS JOSEPH FRANÇOIS, who in his official capacity had advised that the oath was unlawful for the clergy.   He was so well loved in Paris that an official had warned him of the danger and offered to help him to escape.   He refused to desert his fellow prisoners, many of whom he knew had taken refuge at Saint-Firmin out of regard for his own reliability, confidence and example.   Among those who died with him were BD HENRY GRUYER and other Lazarists, BD YVES GUILLON DE KERANRUN, vice-chancellor of the University of Paris, and three laymen.   At the prison of La Force in the Rue Saint-Antoine there was not one survivor to describe the last moments of any of his fellows.

The brief of beatification, in which the names of the martyrs are individually recorded, is printed in the *Acta Apostolicae Sedis*, vol. xviii (1926), pp. 415–425.   Some account of these massacres may be found in most histories of the French Revolution, but the subject of the martyrdoms is dealt with in detail in many separate books, for example, in Lenôtre, *Les massacres de Septembre* (1907) ; P. Caron, *Les massacres de Septembre* (1935) ; H. Leclercq, *Les Martyrs*, vol. xi ; and more concisely in F. Mourret, *Histoire générale de l'Église*, vol. vii (1913).   There are also books devoted to individuals or groups ; for example, G. Barbotin, *Le dernier évêque de Saintes* (1927) ; H. Fouqueray, *Un groupe des Martyrs de Septembre ; vingt-trois anciens Jésuites* (1927) ; anonymous, *Martyrs Franciscains des Carmes* (1926) ; E. Levesque, *Les bx. martyrs du séminaire S.-Sulpice* (1928) ; L. Misermont, *Le bx. L. J. François* (1929) ; C. Clercq, *Le bx. Apollinaire Morel* (1945) ; and others.

3 : ST PIUS X, POPE   (A.D. 1914)

THAT distinguished historian of earlier popes, Baron von Pastor, has written of Pope Pius X :

He was one of those chosen few men whose personality is irresistible. Everyone was moved by his simplicity and his angelic kindness.   Yet it was something more that carried him into all hearts : and that " something " is best defined by saying that all who were ever admitted to his presence had a deep conviction of being face to face with a saint.   And the more one knows about him the stronger this conviction becomes.

He was born in 1835, son of the municipal messenger and postman of the big village of Riese in Venetia, and was then known as Giuseppe Sarto (*i.e.* " Joseph Taylor ") ; he was the second of ten children, and the circumstances of the family were very poor.   Young Joseph went to the local elementary school, from thence, through the encouragement of his parish priest, to the " grammar school " at Castelfranco, walking five miles there and back every day, and then by bursary to the seminary at Padua.   He was ordained priest by dispensation at the age of twenty-three, and for seventeen years gave himself wholeheartedly to the pastoral ministry ; then he became a canon of Treviso, where his hard work and generous charities were very marked, and in 1884 bishop of Mantua, a diocese then in a very low state, with a negligent clergy and two towns in schism.   So brilliantly successful was he in handling this charge that in 1892 Pope Leo XIII appointed Mgr Sarto cardinal-priest of St Bernard-at-the-Baths and promoted him to the metropolitan see of Venice, which carries with it the honorary title of patriarch.   Here he became a veritable apostle of Venetia, his simplicity and forthrightness standing out in a see that rather prided itself on its pomp and magnificence.

On the death of Leo XIII in 1903 it was generally believed that Cardinal Rampolla del Tindaro would succeed him, and the first three ballots of the conclave so far bore this out that Cardinal Puzyna, Archbishop of Cracow, communicated to the electors the formal veto against Rampolla of the Emperor Francis Joseph of Austria. There was a profound sensation, and the cardinals solemnly protested against the interference : but Rampolla withdrew his candidature with great dignity, and after four more ballots Cardinal Sarto was elected.* Thus there came to the chair of Peter a man of obscure birth, of no outstanding intellectual attainments, and with no experience of ecclesiastical diplomacy, but one who, if ever man did, radiated goodness : " a man of God who knew the unhappiness of the world and the hardships of life, and in the greatness of his heart wanted to comfort everybody."

One of the new pope's earliest acts, by the constitution " Commissum nobis ", was to put an end once for all to any supposed right of any civil power to interfere in a papal election, by veto or in any other way ; and later he took a cautious but definite step towards reconciliation between church and state in Italy by relaxing in practice the " Non expedit ".† His way of dealing with the most critical situation that soon arose in France was more direct and assuredly not less effecitve than ordinary diplomatic methods would have been. After a number of incidents the French government in 1905 denounced the concordat of 1801, decreed the separation of church and state, and entered on an aggressive campaign against the Church. For dealing with ecclesiastical property it proposed an organization called *associations cultuelles*, to which many prominent French Catholics wanted to give a trial ; but, after consultation with the French episcopate, Pope Pius in two strong and dignified pronouncements condemned the law of separation and forbade the *associations* as uncanonical. Of those who complained that he had sacrificed all the possessions of the Church in France he said, " They are too concerned about material goods, and not enough about spiritual ". A good aspect of the separation was that the Holy See could now appoint French bishops direct, without nomination by the civil power. " Pius X ", declared the bishop of Nevers, Mgr Gauthey, " at the cost of sacrificing our property emancipated us from slavery. May he be blessed for ever for not shrinking from imposing that sacrifice on us." The pope's strong action caused the French government such difficulties that twenty years later it agreed to another and canonical arrangement for the administration of church property.

The name of Pius X is commonly and rightly associated with the purging of the Church of that " synthesis of all heresies ", somewhat unhappily called Modernism. A decree of the Holy Office in 1907 condemned certain writers and propositions, and it was soon followed by the encyclical letter " Pascendi dominici gregis ", wherein the far-reaching dangerous tendencies were set out and examined, and manifestations of Modernism in every field were pointed out and condemned. Strong disciplinary measures were also taken and, though there was some fierce opposition, Modernism was practically killed in the Church at one blow. It had

* It seems now to be generally agreed that Rampolla would not have been elected anyhow.

† *I.e.* the Holy See's ruling that it was inexpedient for faithful Catholics to associate themselves publicly with the despoilers of the papal states, *e.g.* by voting in parliamentary elections. For what a wise man thought about this policy, *cf.* Bd Contardo Ferrini (October 17).

made considerable headway among Catholics, but there were not wanting those even among the orthodox who thought the pope's condemnation was excessive to the verge of an obscurantist narrowness.* How far he could be from that was seen when in 1910 his encyclical on St Charles Borromeo had been misunderstood and given offence to Protestants in Germany. Pius had his official explanation of the misunderstood passages published in the *Osservatore Romano*, and recommended the German bishops not to give the encyclical any further publication in pulpit or press.

In his first encyclical letter Pius X had announced his aim to be to " renew all things in Christ ", and nothing was better calculated to do that than his decrees concerning the sacrament of the Eucharist. These formally recommended daily communion when possible,† directed that children should be allowed to approach the altar upon attaining the use of reason, and facilitated the communion of the sick. But there is a ministry of the word as well as of the altar, and he also strongly urged daily reading of the Bible—but here the pope's words did not receive so much heed. With the object of increasing the worthiness of divine worship he in 1903 issued on his own initiative (*motu proprio*) an instruction on church music which struck at current abuses and aimed at the restoration of congregational singing of the Roman plainchant. He encouraged the work of the commission for the codifying of canon law, and was responsible for a thorough reorganization of the tribunals, offices and congregations of the Holy See. Pius also set up a commission for the revision and correction of the Vulgate text of the Bible (this work was entrusted to the monks of St Benedict), and in 1909 founded the Biblical Institute for scriptural studies in charge of the Society of Jesus.

Pius X was ever actively concerned for the weak and oppressed. He strongly denounced the foul ill-treatment of the Indians on the rubber-plantations of Peru, and greatly encouraged the Indian missions in that country. He sent a commission of relief after the earthquake at Messina, and sheltered refugees at his own expense in the hospice of Santa Marta by St Peter's, while his general charities, in Rome and throughout the world, were so great that people wondered where all the money came from. The quiet simplicity of his personal habits and the impressive holiness of his character were both exemplified in his custom of preaching publicly on the day's gospel in one of the Vatican courtyards every Sunday. Pius was embarrassed —perhaps a little shocked—by the ceremoniousness and some of the observances of the papal court. At Venice he had refused to let anyone but his sisters cook for him, and now he declined to observe the custom of conferring titles of nobility on his relatives. " The Lord has made them sisters of the pope ", he said, " that should suffice ". " Look how they have dressed me up ", he exclaimed to an old friend, and burst into tears. And to another he said, " It is indeed a penance to be forced to accept all these practices. They lead me about surrounded by soldiers like Jesus when he was seized in Gethsemane."

* Partly because of the excesses of the inevitable groups of those who were " more Catholic than the pope ". These had on their lists of " suspects " Cardinal della Chiesa, who was to become Benedict XV.

† In the middle ages, and later under the influence of Jansenism, communion was a rare occurrence for the ordinary Catholic. Daily or very frequent communion was looked on as extraordinary, and even improper. When the Catholics of the west of England rose against Protestant innovations in 1549 one of their expressed grievances was being expected to communicate more often than at Easter or thereabouts.

Those are not merely entertaining anecdotes. They go right to the heart of Pius's single-minded goodness. To an English convert who wished to be a monk but had made few studies, he said, " To praise God well it is not necessary to be learned ". At Mantua infamous charges were made against him in print. He refused to take any action ; and when the writer went bankrupt, the bishop privately sent him money : " So unfortunate a man needs prayers more than punishment."

Already during his lifetime Almighty God used Pope Pius as an instrument of miracles, and these occurrences are stamped with the same perfection of modest simplicity. A man at a public audience pointed to his paralysed arm, saying, " Cure me, holy Father ". The pope smiled, stroking the arm gently : " Yes, yes, yes ", he said. And the man was healed. A paralysed child, 11-years old, at a private audience, suddenly and unprompted asked the same thing. " May God grant your wish ", said Pius. She got up and walked. A nun, in an advanced stage of tuberculosis, made the same request. " Yes ", was all Pius replied, laying his hands on her head. That evening her doctor verified her recovery.

On June 24, 1914, the Holy See signed a concordat with Serbia ; four days later the Archduke Francis of Austria and his wife were assassinated at Sarajévo ; by the midnight of August 4 Germany, France, Austria, Russia, Great Britain, Serbia, Belgium were at war : it was the eleventh anniversary of the pope's election. Pius X had not merely foreseen this European war—many people had done that— he had foretold it definitely for the summer of 1914, but its outbreak was nevertheless a blow that killed him : " This is the last affliction that the Lord will visit on me. I would gladly give my life to save my poor children from this ghastly scourge." After a few days' illness he developed bronchitis on August 19 : next day he was dead—the first great victim of a war called great. " I was born poor, I have lived poor and I wish to die poor ", he said in his will : and its contents bore out the truth of his words, so that even the anti-clerical press was moved to admiration.

After the funeral in St Peter's Mgr Cascioli wrote, " I have no doubt whatever that this corner of the crypt will before long become a shrine and place of pilgrimage. . . . God will glorify to the world this pope whose triple crown was poverty, humility and gentleness." And so indeed it came about. The pontificate of Pius X had not been a quiet one, and the pope had been resolute in his policies. If he had no enemies—for it takes two to make an enemy—he had many critics, inside the Church as well as outside. But now the voice was unanimous : from all quarters, from high and low, came a call for the recognition of the sanctity of Pius X, once Joseph Sarto, the postman's little boy. In 1923 the cardinals in curia decreed that his cause be introduced, Cardinal Aidan Gasquet representing England among the twenty-eight signatories ; and in 1954 Pope Pius XII solemnly canonized his predecessor before a vast multitude in St Peter's Square at Rome— the first canonized pope since Pius V in 1672.

It is not to be expected that there should be a full and frank biography of a pontiff who died so lately as 1914. A short life by Abbot Pierami, the postulator of the cause, was published in 1928 : it was written in a " devotional " style that the English translation did little to modify, but it is valuable as a reliable factual record. See also Cardinal Merry del Val, *Memories of Pope Pius X* (1939) ; R. M. Huben, *Symposium of the Life and Work of Pius X* (1947) ; V. Marmoiton, *Pie X* (1951) ; and for good popular accounts in English, Katherine Burton, *The Great Mantle* (1951), and E. A. Forbes, *Pope St Pius X* (1954).

See also the 2-volume work in French by Professor Fernessole (1953), and the life by H. Dal-Gal, published in English in 1954. There were of course a number of other new works in various languages during those years.

ST PHOEBE (First Century)

In the last chapter of his letter to the Christians of Rome St Paul sends his greetings to many of his friends there, but first of all refers to one Phoebe, of whom he writes : " And I commend to you Phoebe, our sister, who is in the ministry of the church that is in Cenchrae, that you receive her in the Lord as becometh saints and that you assist her in whatsoever business she shall have need of you. For she also hath assisted many, and myself also." Cenchrae was the port of Corinth from whence the Epistle to the Romans was written about the year 57, and it would appear that St Phoebe was the bearer of the letter. Beyond what St Paul tells us in his testimonial nothing is known of her ; she is named in the Roman Martyrology on this day, and St John Chrysostom eulogized her merits.

The Bollandists devote a few pages to St Phoebe, refuting in particular the allegation that she had been the wife of St Paul, but ministered to him afterwards as a dear sister. The notion that St Paul had been married seems to have been suggested by a phrase in the interpolated letter of St Ignatius to the Philadelphians, and by a remark of Clement of Alexandria. The insertion of Phoebe's name (as well as that of other New Testament characters) in the martyrology is due to Ado in the ninth century. See Dom H. Quentin, *Les martyrologes historiques*, p. 665.

ST MACANISIUS, Bishop (A.D. 514)

The records of St Macanisius (Aengus MacNisse) consist chiefly of miracles, many of them fantastic, and conflicting references. He is said to have been baptized by St Patrick, who in due course consecrated him bishop. It is related that he made a pilgrimage to the Holy Land and on the way back made a stay at Rome. He returned to Ireland, where he established a church and monastery which developed into the diocese of Connor, of which see he is venerated as the first bishop. The original foundation was perhaps not at Connor itself but at Kells, close by, where, according to a Latin life, he changed the course of the river Curi, perhaps by natural means later regarded as miraculous, for the convenience of his monks. While journeying through Munster with St Patrick and St Brigid, Macanisius had a vision of angels at Lynally in Offaly, in consequence of which St Patrick wished to establish a monastery there. But St Macanisius dissuaded him, prophesying that that was to be the work of a bishop who would follow them sixty years after. This prophecy was duly verified in the person of St Colman Elo, who is venerated on the 26th of this month. Among the more incredible legends about St Macanisius is that his reverence for the Holy Scriptures was so great that it would not allow him to carry them in a wallet when on his journey ; instead he proceeded on all fours, balancing the precious book on his back. He is also alleged to have saved the life of the child who was to become St Colman of Kilruaidh. Colman's father was guilty of parricide and was sentenced to lose his own son. Macanisius in vain interceded for his innocent life, so when the child was tossed into the air to be caught on the spear-points of the waiting tribesmen, the saint, standing on an adjacent hillock, prayed with such fervour that Colman's body was blown by the wind safely into his arms, at which miracle the executioners abandoned their purpose. The feast of St Macanisius is kept on this day throughout Ireland.

The Latin legend of St MacNisse has been printed by the Bollandists in the *Acta Sanctorum*, September, vol. i, and again in their edition of the *Codex Salmanticensis*, pp. 925–930. The saint is commemorated in the *Félire* of Oengus. See also O'Hanlon, LIS., vol. ix, pp. 62 *seq.*

ST SIMEON STYLITES THE YOUNGER   (A.D. 592)

SIMEON was born about the year 517 at Antioch, and his mother Martha was revered as a saint. His father, who was from Edessa, was killed in an earthquake when Simeon was five years old. The child, of whom strange things were already recorded, eventually wandered off into the mountains, where he came to a small monastery and put himself in the care of a well known stylite called John. For the rest of his life John looked after the boy, who also had his pillar near by, on which he took up his abode at the age of seven, " before he had lost his first teeth ". The reputation, not simply of his eccentricity, but of his holiness and powers was such that, to avoid if he might the attentions of pilgrims, Simeon retired to live on a rock in a more inaccessible place on another mountain, which became known as the Hill of Wonders. He was then twenty. Ten years later, in consequence of a vision, he established a monastery for his disciples, and had a new column built for himself to which he was solemnly conducted by two bishops.

Simeon lived in this extraordinary but indubitably historically true fashion for another forty-five years ; from time to time he moved to another pillar, and without coming down to the ground he was ordained priest when he was thirty-three, the bishop going up to impose hands on him. Apparently there was a platform on his pillar sufficiently large to enable him to celebrate the Holy Mysteries there, and his disciples climbed up by a ladder to receive communion at his hands. It is recorded that God manifested his sanctity by a number of miracles, which he performed chiefly in curing the sick, foretelling things to come, and knowing the secret thoughts of others. Evagrius, the Syrian historian, was an eye-witness to many and assures us that he had experienced Simeon's knowledge of the thoughts of others in himself, when he visited him for spiritual advice, and that the fame of his holiness was unsurpassed.

Crowds of people of many races flocked to St Simeon for his spiritual advice and hoping to witness or be healed by a miracle. After the death of St John Stylites there was no one who could or would restrain his austerities, and Evagrius says that he supported life entirely on one sort of fruit or vegetable. He wrote to the Emperor Justin II urging him to punish the Samaritans who had attacked their Christian neighbours, and St John Damascene attributes to Simeon a passage praising the veneration of sacred images : there are other writings, homilies and hymns, also attributed to him but without sufficient reason. Simeon had foretold that Justin II would succeed Justinian, and told John the Scholastic that he would be elected to the see of Constantinople : and so he was.

That he became a stylite when a child and displayed spiritual understanding from his tenderest years, that he came to live almost without sleep and nourishment, that the contests with evil spirits, physical mortifications and numerous miracles are of so startling a character, may well make the reader of St Simeon's life ask whether it be not entirely a work of imagination : and Father Delehaye did not fail to remark that it is an unusual document that must be read with corresponding discrimination. But many of its statements can be checked and compared, and it certainly is not entirely wanting in historical value. The saint fell ill in the May of 592, and the Patriarch Gregory of Antioch, being told that he was at the point of death, went in haste to assist at his last moments ; but before he arrived St Simeon was dead.

Dr P. van den Ven has long had in preparation the full Greek text of the contemporary Life of St Simeon ; *cf.* his article in *Analecta Bollandiana*, vol. lxvii (1949), pp. 435–443. Fr Delehaye edited the more historical portions in his *Saints stylites* (1923), pp. 238–271, and he gives a summary account of Simeon's history in the preface (pp. lix–lxxv). There is a Greek life of the saint's mother, St Martha, which, with the biography of Simeon himself by Nicephorus Ouranus, can be found in the *Acta Sanctorum*, May, vol. v. For some particulars of a stylite's pillar see under the elder St Simeon herein, on January 5.

ST REMACLUS, Bishop   (*c.* A.D. 675)

REMACLUS, a native of Aquitaine, became a priest, and after, it is said, having spent some time under St Sulpicius of Bourges, was appointed by St Eligius first abbot of the monastery which he founded at Solignac, near Limoges. The saint was afterwards obliged to take upon him the government of the abbey of Cugnon, in the duchy of Luxemburg ; but was soon after called to the court of King Sigebert III, who followed the advice of St Remaclus in founding the double abbey of Stavelot and Malmedy in Ardenne, to help forward the evangelization of that still pagan district. The direction of these foundations was committed to St Remaclus. It does not appear that he was ever bishop of Tongres-Maestricht, but he may have been a missionary monastic bishop. His association with Stavelot-Malmedy procured him a wide *cultus* in Belgium.

The reputation of his sanctity moved many noblemen and others to embrace a penitential state under his direction. Remaclus walked before them in the narrow paths of Christian perfection, encouraging them both by words and example. He modified nothing of his austerities on account of old age, but rather strove continually to increase his pace as he drew nearer to the end of his course, lest by sloth at the last he should forfeit his crown. He strongly exhorted his religious brethren to perfect self-denial, obedience, poverty, patience in adversity, and constant peace and union, virtues in which he had been to them a shining example, and died about the year 675. He was buried at Stavelot. There are a number of legends and places still connected with the name of St Remaclus in the province of Liège.

No confidence can be placed in any of the medieval biographies which purport to describe the career of St Remaclus. A list of them will be found in BHL., nn. 7113–7141. The more important have been printed by Mabillon and the Bollandists (*Acta Sanctorum*, September, vol. i). G. Kurth seems to have been the first to reveal the untrustworthy character of the principal document. His paper is printed in the *Bulletin de la Commission roy. d'hist. de Belgique*, 4 série, vol. iii. See also Van der Essen, *Étude critique sur les vies des saints méroving.*, pp. 96–105 ; and *Revue bénédictine*, vol. lx (1950), pp. 120–147.

ST AIGULF, Martyr   (*c.* A.D. 676)

AIGULF was born at Blois, and became a monk at Fleury, then in its first fervour of Benedictine observance. About the year 670 a new abbot was required at Lérins, where the passage of time and the ravages of the Moors had impaired discipline, and Aigulf, now a monk of twenty years' experience with a reputation for solid virtue and stability, was sent to fill the office. But as is usual in such circumstances some of the religious were well content with the old ways and willing to go to a good deal of trouble to frustrate the efforts to improve their observance. In this case two of them, Arcadius and Columbus, went too far. They appealed to the local governor against the abbot, and when he sent a company of soldiers to keep order they used them to kidnap St Aigulf and four of his chief supporters and carry them off to sea. They were landed on the island of Capraia, between Corsica and the coast of Tuscany, where their eyes and tongues were torn out and they were put to death. But one of the monks escaped and brought word to Lérins of what had taken place.

It has been suggested, not without reason, that even were the abbot and his companions carried off by the soldiers, it is more likely that they were massacred by some marauding party of Moors. The bodies were brought back to Lérins and their transportation was reported to be the occasion of many miracles. Later, a controversy arose between Lérins and Fleury as to which abbey really possessed the body of St Aigulf.

According to a biography of St Aigulf written by a monk of Fleury about the year 850 the saint was put in charge of the party of monks from Fleury and Le Mans which Mommolus, abbot of the first named, sent to Italy to save the relics of St Benedict from the hands of the Lombards. The rights of this affair and the resting-place or places of the relics of St Benedict do not concern us here. It is sufficient to notice that this St Aigulf almost certainly had nothing to do with it.

A somewhat lyrical account of Aigulf written by Adrevaldus, a monk of Fleury who lived two centuries later, does not inspire confidence. The Bollandists print it in the *Acta Sanctorum*, September, vol. i, together with a shorter narrative which they believe to be of earlier date and more reliable. See also H. Moris, *L'Abbaye de Lérins* (1909), and DHG., vol. i, cc. 1141–1142.

ST HILDELITHA, ABBESS OF BARKING, VIRGIN   (*c.* A.D. 717)

AT a date when there were not many nunneries in England, a young Anglo-Saxon princess called Hildilid or Hildelitha went over to France and took the veil, either at Chelles or at Faremoutier. There she remained until requested by St Erconwald to return to England to train his sister Ethelburga, for whom he had built a convent at Barking, but who was quite inexperienced in the religious life. When the training was completed and St Ethelburga had taken her place as abbess, her instructress became one of the nuns. After the death of St Ethelburga, St Hildelitha was elected her successor, and continued to rule the community for the rest of her life. Her contemporary the Venerable Bede writes of her with great admiration, and St Aldhelm dedicated to her a metrical treatise on virginity. In one of his letters St Boniface speaks of her in the highest terms and mentions a wonderful vision which she had described to him with her own lips. She is known to have lived to extreme old age, but the exact date of her death is uncertain. Her feast is kept in the diocese of Brentwood together with St Cuthburga (below).

See the *Acta Sanctorum*, March, vol. iii, where such casual references to Hildelitha as have been made by Capgrave and other later writers will be found collected. · *Cf.* also Plummer's edition of Bede's *Ecclesiastical History*, and Stanton's *Menology*, p. 131.

ST CUTHBURGA, ABBESS OF WIMBORNE, WIDOW   (*c.* A.D. 725)

THIS saint was sister to the great King Ine of Wessex and was married to Aldfrid, who became king of Northumbria in 685. At her suit he allowed her to retire to the monastery of Barking in Essex, where she was a novice under St Hildelitha. Some time after the year 705 she founded, together with her sister St Quenburga, the abbey of Wimborne in Dorset, of which the rule of enclosure was so strict that not even prelates on their lawful occasions were allowed to enter it.   This abbey St Cuthburga governed, giving herself up totally to fasting and prayer ; humble both to God and man, meek and tender to others, but always austere to herself. Under her successor, St Tetta, Wimborne contributed to the conversion of Germany by sending nuns to assist St Boniface there.   The feast of St Cuthburga is kept in the diocese of Brentwood on September 3 with St Hildelitha (above).

There is an unpublished early life, BHL. 2033 ; see further *Analecta Bollandiana*, vol. lvi (1938), p. 336, and lviii, p. 100.   The summary by Capgrave is printed in the *Acta Sanctorum*, August, vol. vi, with the usual prolegomena.   See also Stanton's *Menology*, pp. 431–432.

BD GUALA, BISHOP OF BRESCIA   (A.D. 1244)

WHEN St Dominic came to Bergamo towards the end of the year 1217 the first there to offer themselves as his disciples and to receive the habit of his new order from his hands were Guala Romanoni, a man already nearly forty years of age, and his brother Roger.   Guala went with St Dominic to Bologna, and afterwards to Brescia for the establishment of the friars there, and of that house he became prior. While he was fulfilling that office St Dominic was struck down by his last sickness, and on August 6, 1221, Bd Guala was praying for his recovery in the church, believing him to be still alive.   Falling asleep, he seemed to see two ladders let down from the heavens, at the top of one of which stood our Lord and of the other His holy Mother.   Angels were going up and down the ladders, and at their foot there sat between them a figure in the Dominican habit, his face covered with his hood as if for burial.   Then the ladders were drawn up and with them the friar, borne up by the angels to the feet of Christ.   This vision would seem to have only one possible meaning, and Guala went in great haste and alarm to Bologna, where he learned that at the very hour of his dream St Dominic had gone to God.   The third antiphon at Lauds in the office of St Dominic refers to this : *Scala caelo prominens fratri revelatur, per quam pater transiens sursum ferebatur :* " A brother is shown a ladder hanging from Heaven, on which our dying father was carried up."   When this office was solemnly sung for the first time, after the canonization of St Dominic in 1234, Bd Guala was present in the choir at Bologna and himself precented this antiphon.

He was, we are told, a man of remarkable prudence and of much experience in the world ; a good religious and eloquent preacher and of impressive personality, qualities sufficiently strong to get him noticed at both the papal and imperial courts. In the midst of the struggle between the Holy See and the Emperor Frederick II, Guala was, about 1230, promoted to the see of Brescia, which he governed successfully for some twelve years, the beloved father of the poor and unfortunate.   But strife continued to distract Lombardy ; Guala was exiled from Brescia and retired to a monastery of the Vallumbrosan Benedictines at Astino.   Here he lived in prayer and study till his death.   The ancient *cultus* of Bd Guala was confirmed in 1868.

See the *Acta Sanctorum*, September, vol. i ; Masetti, *Memorie storico-biografico-critiche del B. Guala Romanoni* (1868) ; and a life in French by J. Kuczynski (1916).   This last writer seems to have been successful in exonerating Bd Guala from the charge of having prompted Pope Gregory IX to enforce throughout Lombardy the death penalty against heretics ; *cf.* the *Analecta Bollandiana*, vol. xxxix (1921), p. 223.   A short account of the career of this holy bishop will be found in Procter, *Dominican Saints*, pp. 247–249.

BD ANDREW OF BORGO SAN SEPOLCRO   (A.D. 1315)

ANDREW DOTTI was born at Borgo San Sepolcro in Tuscany about the year 1250. His family was distinguished (Andrew's brother was a captain in the bodyguard of King Philip the Fair), and the young man was brought up accordingly, with no thought of the religious life.   When he was seventeen he became a secular tertiary of the Servites, and when, a few years afterwards, a general chapter of that order was held at Borgo San Sepolcro, Andrew naturally went to hear the prior general, St Philip Benizi, preach.   His text was, " Every one of you that doth not renounce all that he possesseth cannot be my disciple ", and his eloquence and fire touched Andrew's heart ; he offered himself to St Philip, was accepted, and became a Servite friar.   After he was ordained he was attached to a monastery governed by St Gerard Sostegni, one of the seven founders of the order, and from thence he preached with success throughout the surrounding country and accompanied St Philip Benizi on several of his missionary journeys.   Bd Andrew prepared a number of hermits who were living a rather go-as-you-please life at Vallucola to affiliate themselves to the Servites and submit to their discipline, and over these he was appointed superior, until his services were again required for preaching and as prior of various houses.   In 1310 he was present at the death of St Alexis Falconieri, the principal founder of the Servites, at Monte Senario, and so great was the impression made on him that he asked permission to retire to a hermitage and prepare for his own end, though he was barely sixty.   Bd Andrew lived with great penance and was the recipient of many visions, including a forewarning of his own death ; when the day came he was apparently in good health, and he went out to a certain rock where he was wont to give conferences to his brethren.   When they assembled there they found their beloved father kneeling motionless on the rock apparently in ecstasy ; but he was dead.   He was buried in the church at Borgo San Sepolcro, where the popular veneration for his holiness was confirmed by miracles, and in 1806 Pope Pius VII approved the ancient *cultus*.

A full account is given in A. Giani, *Annales Ordinis Servorum B.V.M.*, vol. i, especially pp. 230–231 ; see also DHG., vol. ii, c. 1663 ; and P. Battini, *Vita del b. Andrea Dotti* (1808).

4 : SS. MARCELLUS AND VALERIAN, MARTYRS   (*c.* A.D. 178 ?)

THE massacre of the martyrs of Lyons with their bishop, St Pothinus, took place during the persecutions of Marcus Aurelius in the year 177.   Marcellus, a priest, we are told in his *passio*, by divine intervention managed to escape to Chalon-sur-Saône, where he was given shelter.   His host was a pagan, and seeing him offer incense before images of Mars, Mercury and Minerva, Marcellus remonstrated with and converted him.   While journeying towards the north the priest fell in with the governor Priscus, who asked him to a celebration at his house. Marcellus accepted the invitation, but when he found that Priscus was preparing to fulfil religious rites he asked to be excused on the ground that he was a Christian. This raised an outcry, and the bystanders tried to kill Marcellus there and then by tying him to the tops of two young trees in tension and then letting them fly apart. The governor ordered him to make an act of worship before an image of Saturn.

He refused peremptorily, whereupon he was buried up to his middle in the earth on the banks of the Saône, and died in three days of exposure and starvation. Alban Butler mentions with St Marcellus the martyr St Valerian, who is named in the Roman Martyrology on September 15. He is said to have escaped from prison at the same time as Marcellus, and was beheaded for the faith at Tournus, near Autun.

It is difficult to say how much confidence can be placed in the two sets of acts (printed in the *Acta Sanctorum*, September, vol. ii) which record the martyrdom of St Marcellus. The eighteenth-century Bollandists seem inclined to defend them from the criticisms of Tillemont. In the second set the name of Valerian is associated with Marcellus, and an inscription in a church near Bagnols (Gard) couples together certain relics of the two saints. The cult of both was certainly early and is indirectly attested by Gregory of Tours. Dom Quentin in his *Martyrologes historiques*, pp. 179–180, provides an interesting illustration of how the long elogium of Marcellus in the Roman Martyrology originated.

ST MARINUS   (FOURTH CENTURY ?)

BETWEEN the Italian provinces of Forli, Pesaro and Urbino lies an area of land of less than forty square miles in extent, having only some 12,000 inhabitants, and yet forming an independent republic, which has retained its sovereignty against all assaults for nigh a thousand years. On the highest of seven hills, Il Titano, is built the capital city of this tiny state, called San Marino ; from this city the whole republic takes its name, and the San Marino referred to is St Marinus the Deacon, named in the Roman Martyrology on this day. His legend, unhappily worthless, is as follows.

Marinus was born on the Dalmatian coast and was by trade a stonemason. Hearing that the walls and town of Rimini were being rebuilt, he went there to find work in company with another mason, St Leo. They were employed at squaring and working stone in the quarries of Monte Titano in what is now San Marino, and met among their fellow workmen a number of Christians of gentle birth who had been sentenced to labour in the quarries because of their adherence to the faith. Marinus and Leo did their best to alleviate the hardships of these unfortunate people, helping them in their work and encouraging them to persevere ; and also made a number of new converts. At the end of three years St Leo was ordained priest by St Gaudentius, Bishop of Rimini, and went to live at Montefeltro (where he is now titular of the cathedral) ; St Marinus was made deacon, and returned to his work that he might continue to look after the confessors and converts. For twelve years he was working on an aqueduct, and was known as a skilled and indefatigable mason and a good man, a model Christian workman. But then a misfortune happened to him. A Dalmatian woman turned up one day at Rimini, saw Marinus, and claimed him as her deserting husband. He lost his head. Escaping out of the city, he made his way to Monte Titano and there hid himself. The woman pursued him and for a week he had to barricade himself into a cave, until she retired for lack of food. Marinus took the opportunity to penetrate further up the mountain, the woman did not find him again, and he chose to pass the rest of his life there as a hermit. On the site of the hermitage first a monastery and then the town of San Marino arose.

The Bollandists print this fabulous story from Mombritius (*Acta Sanctorum*, September, vol. ii ; and *cf.* August, vol. i, the priest Leo being honoured on August 1). See also L. A. Gentili, *Compendio della vita di S. Marino* (1864).

ST BONIFACE I, Pope   (A.D. 422)

It is a piece of hagiographical common form to say of a holy man raised to the episcopate that he accepted the office with the greatest reluctance ; doubtless they (and lesser men) generally did, though frequently there is no evidence either way. But in the case of Boniface I it is certainly true, for he was an old man and he knew that he was faced by a rival, the antipope Eulalius. On the same day, or even the day before, that Boniface was chosen pope by the senior clergy of Rome, a faction, chiefly of deacons, seized the Lateran and elected Eulalius, who had considerable support behind him. The ensuing disorder lasted fifteen weeks, and it required the intervention of the Emperor Honorius before Boniface could take possession of his see.

This pope combined a peaceable disposition with firmness, especially in resisting the encroachments of the Eastern emperor and the Constantinopolitan see, and in other jurisdictional questions. But while reiterating that " the blessed apostle Peter received by our Lord's word and commission the care of the whole Church ", he was careful to vindicate the rights of bishops against the encroachments of papal vicars. St Boniface was a strong supporter of St Augustine in his opposition to Pelagianism, and when letters were sent him by Pelagians slandering their opponent, he forwarded them to Augustine for his information. As a mark of his respect and gratitude St Augustine dedicated to the pope the work he wrote in reply to his critics, and sent it to Rome by the hand of St Alipius.

St Boniface I died in 422, after being pope for not quite four years. He was buried in the cemetery of Maximus on the New Salarian Way, close to the chapel he had built over the grave of St Felicitas, to whose memory he had a warm devotion.

The *Liber Pontificalis* with Duchesne's notes (vol. i, pp. 227–229 and *cf.* p. lxii), and the letters calendared by Jaffé-Kaltenbrunner (vol. i, pp. 52–54) form our most direct source of information. See also the *Acta Sanctorum*, September, vol. ii ; DTC., vol. ii, cc. 988–989, with appended bibliography ; and Grisar, *History of Rome and the Papacy* (Eng. trans.), pp. 219, 226, 466, 471.

ST ULTAN, Bishop   (A.D. 657)

This Ultan is said to have been a maternal uncle to St Brigid, but this cannot have been the case if, as is recorded, he died in the middle of the seventh century. The uncertainty is made worse by confusion with other saints of the name, for instance, the St Ultan who was abbot of Fosses in Belgium. He is supposed to have been bishop in Ardbraccan, whence he evangelized and ministered to the Dal Conchubhair branch of the Desi of Meath. An old quatrain refers to his particular care for children, especially orphans and those sick (he was sometimes responsible for " fifty and thrice fifty " children at a time), and to his fondness for bathing in cold water on a windy day. He also educated and fed numerous poor students, and was a man of letters himself. He is said to have collected the writings of St Brigid, to have written the " third Life " of her, and to have supplied to St Tirechan the materials for his annotations on the life of St Patrick in the Book of Armagh. The hymn in honour of St Brigid, beginning *Christus in nostra insula, Quae vocatur Hibernia*, is often attributed to St Ultan, but was probably written by another. He also, we are told, illuminated his own manuscripts. St Ultan is no longer commemorated liturgically in Ireland, but a holy well at Ardbraccan bears his name.

There is no formal life of St Ultan, either in Latin or Irish, but an unusually copious gloss is appended to his notice in the *Félire* of Oengus. This deals more especially with the proverbial phrase " Ultan's left hand against evil ". The saint was feeding children with his right hand when an appeal reached him to exert his power against the Norse marauders then infesting Ireland. Even with his left hand he put them to flight, and an early Irish poet wrote : " Had it been the right hand that noble Ultan raised against them, no foreigner would ever have come into the land of Erin."

A Latin poem in praise of Ultan has been printed by Dümmler, *Poetae Latini medii aevi*, i, 589. See also the references in *The Irish Liber Hymnorum* (Henry Bradshaw Society) ; and O'Hanlon, LIS., vol. ix, pp. 83 *seq.*

ST IDA OF HERZFELD, WIDOW   (A.D. 825)

THIS noble lady was a great-granddaughter of Charles Martel, and was born in Alsace ; her father was in great favour with Charlemagne, in whose court she had her upbringing. The emperor gave her in marriage to a lord named Egbert, but the death of her husband left Ida a widow whilst she was yet very young. This state she sanctified by redoubling her devotion, self-denial and austerities. The revenues of her estate she chiefly employed in relieving the poor, and she built herself a little chapel within a church which she had founded near her own house at Hofstadt in Westphalia.

When her son Warin, moved by his mother's example, went to be a monk at Corvey, St Ida changed her residence to Herzfeld, where she lived for the remainder of her life, continuing always in good works. It is said that, to remind her both of her earthly end and of her duty to her neighbour, she had a stone coffin made for herself, which was daily filled up with food for distribution to the needy. During her last years she was afflicted with a painful and unremitting illness, which she bore with patience and turned to advantage. St Ida was buried at Herzfeld in the cemetery of the convent she had founded there.

Her life, written a century and a half after her death by Uffing, a monk of Werden, is full of improbable miracles. It is printed in the *Acta Sanctorum*, September, vol. ii. For a modern biography see A. Hüsing, *Die hl. Ida, Gräfin von Herzfeld* (1880) ; and a booklet by J. Herold (1925).

ST ROSALIA, VIRGIN   (A.D. 1160 ?)

THERE were churches dedicated in honour of St Rosalia in Sicily in the thirteenth century, but she was not mentioned in any of the ancient martyrologies and there are no accounts of her life older than the end of the sixteenth century. Her history says Father Stilting, the Bollandist, is put together from the evidence of local tradition, inscriptions and paintings. According to these Rosalia, while yet young, left her home to live as a recluse in a cave on Mount Coschina, near Bivona in Sicily. Later she migrated to a stalagmitic grotto on Monte Pellegrino, three miles from Palermo ; here she died, and in due course a stalactitic deposit completely covered her remains. The inscription to which Father Stilting referred was found carved on the walls of the cave at Coschina, ostensibly by her own hand : *Ego Rosalia Sinibaldi Quisquine et Rosarum domini filia amore Domini mei Iesu Christi in hoc antro habitare decrevi* : " I, Rosalia, daughter of Sinibald, lord of Quisquina and Rosae, decided to live in this cave for the love of my Lord Jesus Christ." St Rosalia has been claimed as a nun both by the Benedictines and, with considerable likelihood, by the Greek religious who formerly flourished in Sicily ; in the Byzantine archabbcy of St Saviour at Messina was a wooden crucifix with the inscription, " I, Sister Rosalia Sinibaldi, place this wood of my Lord, which I have ever followed, in this monastery ". This relic is now at Palermo.

In the year 1624 an epidemic of plague broke out at Palermo. In accordance, it is said, with a vision of St Rosalia that appeared to one of the victims, search was made in the cave on Monte Pellegrino and the bones of the maiden were found. They were put into a reliquary and carried in procession through the city, and the pestilence was stayed. In their gratitude the people of Palmero made St Rosalia their principal patron and built a church over her hermitage. Pope Urban VIII entered her name in the Roman Martyrology, wherein she is mentioned twice, on this date (said to be of her death) and on July 15, the anniversary of the finding of her relics. With the bones were found a crucifix of terra-cotta, a Greek cross of silver, and a string of beads, twelve small and a large one, which was doubtless a rosary in one of its many early forms. The feast of St Rosalia on September 4 is still the principal popular *festa* among the Panormitans, who always look for a cleansing rain on the preceding days.

A multitude of small Italian biographies have been written to do honour to the patroness of Palermo, but they add nothing of value to the account, compiled by the Bollandists and illustrated with several engravings, in the *Acta Sanctorum*, September, vol. ii. See, however, D. M. Sparacio, *S. Rosalia, vergine panormitana* (1924).

ST ROSE OF VITERBO, Virgin   (A.D. 1252 ?)

When the ambitious Frederick II was excommunicated for the second time by Pope Gregory IX the emperor retorted by setting out to conquer the papal states themselves, and in 1240 he occupied Viterbo in the Romagna. A few years previously there had been born in this city, to parents of lowly station, a girl child, who was christened Rose. From babyhood she displayed a far from usual goodness and her childish virtue and devotion made such an impression that in after years some very surprising legends about her grew up, and it is difficult to disentangle truth from error in her story as it has come down to us.

During an illness when she was eight years old Rose is said to have had a vision or dream of our Lady, who told her that she was to be clothed in the habit of St Francis, but that she was to continue to live at home and to set a good example to her neighbours by both word and work. Rose soon recovered her health, received the dress of a lay penitent in due course, and thought more and more about the sufferings of our Lord and the thoughtless ingratitude of sinners. Perhaps inspired by some sermon she heard or the burning words of some indignant Guelf, she began when she was about twelve years old to preach up and down the streets, upbraiding the people for their supineness in submitting to Frederick and urging them to overthrow the Ghibelline garrison. Her simple words did not fail of effect, which was heightened by the rumours of marvels attending her speeches which circulated among the citizens. Crowds would gather outside her house to get a glimpse of her, till her father became frightened, and forbade her to show herself in public ; if she disobeyed she would be beaten. Rose replied gently : " If Jesus could be beaten for me, I can be beaten for Him. I do what He has told me to do, and I must not disobey Him." At the instance of their parish priest her father withdrew his prohibition and for about two years the pope's cause continued to be preached in public by this young girl. Then the partisans of the emperor became alarmed and clamoured that Rose should be put to death as a danger to the state. The *podestà* of the city would not hear of this : he was a just man, and moreover he feared the people ; but instead he passed a sentence of banishment against St Rose and her parents.

They took refuge at Soriano, and here, in the beginning of December 1250, St Rose is said to have announced the approaching death of the Emperor Frederick II. He in fact died in Apulia on the 13th of the month ; the papal party thereupon got the upper hand in Viterbo, and St Rose returned thither. There is a story that before doing so she confuted a zealous female Ghibelline by a successful appeal to the ordeal by fire. She now went to the convent of St Mary of the Roses at Viterbo and asked to be received as a postulant. The abbess refused, for want of a dowry. " Very well ", said St Rose smilingly. " You will not have me now, but perhaps you will be more willing when I am dead." Her parish priest took it upon himself to open a chapel close by the convent, with a house attached wherein St Rose and a few companions might lead a religious life ; but the nuns got an order from Pope Innocent IV for it to be closed, on the ground that they had the privilege of having no other community of women within a given distance of their own. St Rose therefore returned to her parents' house, where she died on March 6 1252, about the age of seventeen. She was buried in the church of Santa Maria in Podio, but her body was on September 4 in 1258 translated to the church of the convent of St Mary of the Roses, as she had foretold. This church was burnt down in 1357 but her body was preserved and is annually carried in procession through the streets of Viterbo. Pope Innocent IV immediately after her death ordered an inquiry into the virtues of St Rose, but her canonization was not achieved until 1457.

If any authentic or early materials for the history of this saint ever existed, they have perished, and legend plays a large part in what is now presented as her life. The Bollandists in the eighteenth century collected what they could, but were ill-satisfied with the result : see the *Acta Sanctorum*, September, vol. ii. They have, however, preserved substantial extracts from the later process of canonization. The best-known biographies in Italian are those of Andreucci (1750) and Mencarini (1828), and in more recent years that of L. de Kerval in French (1896), which has been translated into German and Flemish. A short English life was included in the Oratorian series (1852), and we have also a notice in Léon, *Auréole Séraphique* (Eng. trans.), vol. iii, pp. 98–109. An article in *The Month* (September, 1899) gives an account of the *festa* of the saint at Viterbo and of the famous " Macchina " which is carried in the procession on that occasion. The sources for St. Rose are carefully examined by G. Abate in *S. Rosa da Viterbo* (1952).

BD CATHERINE OF RACCONIGI, Virgin   (A.D. 1547)

RACCONIGI is a small place in Piedmont, and there in 1486 a poor working-man and his wife became the parents of a girl, who was baptized Catherine. She was born in a tumble-down shed, a fact that was symbolic of the whole of the material side of her life throughout which she had to endure indigence, ill-health and misunderstanding ; but spiritually she was enriched with some of the more extra-ordinary favours which God extends to man. It is told of her that already at five years old she believed herself to have been espoused to the child Jesus by His all-holy Mother, and that He gave her as her special patrons and protectors St

Jerome, St Catherine of Siena and St Peter Martyr. When she was nine and one day broke down in tears of tiredness over her work and the wretched state of her home, she was again visited and comforted by the holy Child. On the feast of St Stephen in the year 1500 she was praying to that saint, and reminding him that as a deacon the Apostles had especially entrusted the care of women to him, when he appeared to her and spoke encouraging words, promising that the Holy Spirit would come upon her in a special way. Then it seemed that three rays of light flashed upon her, and a voice exclaimed : " I am come to take up my dwelling in you, and to cleanse, enlighten, kindle and animate your soul." After she had made a vow of virginity the mystical espousals were repeated and the mark of a ring appeared upon her finger, and she suffered the pains of a crown of thorns and of the other *stigmata* of our Lord's passion, without, however, their becoming visible to the eye.

In these and other things reported of Bd Catherine there is a very marked resemblance to what we are told of St Catherine of Siena, and the words of her breviary lessons are often quoted, that " between Racconigi and Siena there is only the difference of canonization ". But this is not meant to be taken too literally. It was not until she was twenty-eight years old that she imitated her patron in becoming a tertiary of the Friars Preachers, continuing to live in the world and work hard for her family, and then she was said to have been girt by angels with a girdle of chastity, after the example of St Thomas Aquinas. Catherine often implored God that the mouth of Hell might be for ever shut, and when she learned that this was impossible she offered herself as a victim for others and by her penances and austerities lightened the burden of many souls in Purgatory. Many miracles are related of her, as that she was carried with great speed from place to place to bring spiritual help ; and she experienced both recognition and persecution. Catherine was profoundly distressed by the evils brought upon her land by warfare, and offered herself to bear them also. A long illness would seem to have been an acceptance of this, and she died at Carmagnola in her sixty-second year, deserted by her friends and without the ministrations of a priest. Five months later her body was translated to Garezzo, amid miracles which gave rise to a *cultus* that has never since ceased. It was confirmed in 1810.

It is regrettable that more satisfactory evidence is not available concerning the life of this interesting mystic. Our primary source of information is the account furnished by John Francis Pico della Mirandola and the Dominican, Peter Martyr Morelli. They knew her intimately, but it is evident that they accepted unquestioningly what she told them about herself, for example, that in some cause of charity she had travelled invisibly to a place 100 miles distant, returning within four hours of the time of starting. The best notice of Bd Catherine is probably that of M. C. de Ganay, *Les Bienheureuses Dominicaines* (1913), pp. 475–502, but *cf. Miscellanea di storia ecclesiastica e di theologia*, vol. ii (1904), pp. 185–191. For a fuller bibliography see Taurisano, *Catalogus hagiographicus O.P.* An English translation of the life by S. Razzi was published in the Oratorian series in 1852 ; and there is a short life in French by J. Christophe (1947).

5 : ST LAURENCE GIUSTINIANI, Patriarch of Venice   (A.D. 1455)

ST LAURENCE was born at Venice in 1381. His father, Bernard Giustiniani, was of illustrious rank among the nobility of the commonwealth and his mother was not less noble. She was early left a widow with a number of young children, and she devoted herself altogether to the upbringing of her children, to works of charity, and the exercise of virtue.   In Laurence she discovered even from the cradle an uncommon docility and generosity of soul ; and, fearing some spark of pride or ambition, she chid him sometimes for aiming at things above his age.   He answered confidently that it was his only desire to become a saint ; and when he was nineteen he was called by God to consecrate himself in a special manner to his service.   He seemed one day to see in a vision the Eternal Wisdom in the guise of a shining maiden, and to hear from her the words : " Why do you seek rest for your mind in exterior things, sometimes in this object and sometimes in that ?   What you desire is to be found only with me : it is in my hands.   Seek it in me who am the wisdom of God.   By taking me for your companion and your lot you shall be possessed of its boundless treasure."   That instant he found his soul so pierced with divine grace that he felt himself warmed with new ardour to give himself entirely to the search of the knowledge and love of God ; and he addressed himself for advice to his uncle, a holy priest called Marino Querini, who was a canon of St George's chapter, established in a little isle called Alga, a mile from Venice.   Don Querini advised him first to make trial of himself at home, and represented to him on one side honours, riches and worldly pleasures, and on the other the hardships of poverty, fasting and self-denial.   " Have you the courage to despise these delights and to undertake a life of penance and mortification ? " After standing some time in consideration, Laurence looked up at a crucifix and said : " Thou, O Lord, art my hope.   In this tree are comfort and strength."   The strength of his resolution to walk in the narrow path of the cross showed itself in the severity with which he treated his body and the continual application of his mind to religion.   His mother, fearing lest his mortifications should damage his health, tried to divert him from that course, and proposed a marriage to him.   He replied by retiring to the chapter of St George in Alga, and was admitted to the community.

His superiors judged it necessary to mitigate the rigours which he used.   He went about the streets begging alms with a sack on his back, and when it was pointed out to him that by appearing thus in public he would expose himself to ridicule, he answered, " Let us go boldly in quest of scorn.   We have done nothing if we have renounced the world only in words.   Let us triumph over it with our sacks and crosses."   Laurence frequently came to beg at the house where he was born, but only stood in the street before the door, crying out, " An alms for God's sake ". His mother always filled his sack, but he never took more than two loaves and, wishing peace to those who had done him charity, departed as if he had been some stranger.   When the storehouse in which were kept the provisions of the community for a year was burnt down, St Laurence, hearing a brother lament the loss, said cheerfully, " Why have we vowed poverty ?   God has granted us this blessing that we may feel it."   When he first renounced the world he often felt a violent inclination to justify or excuse himself upon being unjustly reprehended ; in order to repress it he used to bite his tongue, and so at length obtained mastery over himself.   He so much dreaded the danger of worldly dissipation that from the day on which he first entered the monastery to that of his death he never set foot in his father's house, except to assist his mother and brothers on their deathbeds.   A certain nobleman who had been his intimate friend, returning from the East and hearing of the state he had embraced, determined to try to change his purpose. With this idea he went to St George's, but the issue of the interview proved quite contrary to his expectation.   Upon the first sight of his old friend he was struck by his modesty, gravity and composure, and stood for some time silent. However, at length he spoke and endeavoured to shake the resolution of the young religious. Laurence let him finish, and then he spoke in so persuasive a manner that the nobleman was disarmed and himself resolved to embrace the rule which he came to violate.

St Laurence was promoted to the priesthood in 1406, and the fruit of his spirit of prayer and penitence was a wonderful experimental knowledge of spiritual things and of the paths of interior virtue, and great light and prudence in the direction of souls. The tears which he shed whilst he offered the sacrifice of the Mass strongly affected all the assistants and awakened their faith ; and he often experienced raptures at prayer, especially in celebrating Mass one Christmas night. Soon after his ordination he was made provost of St George's, and the most sincere humility was the first thing in which he grounded his religious disciples. Nor was his teaching confined to his canons. He never ceased to preach to the magistrates and senators in time of war and public calamity that to obtain the remedy of the evils which they suffered they ought in the first place to persuade themselves that they were nothing, for without this disposition of heart they could never deserve the divine assistance.

In 1433 Pope Eugenius IV appointed St Laurence to the bishopric of Castello, a diocese which included part of Venice. He tried hard to avoid this dignity and responsibility, and he took possession of his cathedral-church so privately that his own friends knew nothing of the matter till the ceremony was over. As a religious so as a prelate he was admirable for his sincere piety towards God and the greatness of his charity to the poor. He remitted nothing of the austerities which he had practised in the cloister, and from his prayer drew a light, courage and vigour which directed and animated him in his whole conduct ; he pacified dissensions in the state and governed a diocese in most difficult times with as much ease as if it had been a single well-regulated convent. In the ordering of his household he consulted only piety and humility ; and when others told him that he owed some degree of state to his own birth, to the dignity of his church and to the republic, his answer was that virtue ought to be the only ornament of the episcopal character and that all the poor of the diocese composed the bishop's family. The flock loved and respected so holy and tender a pastor. When any private persons opposed his religious reforms he overcame them by meekness and patience. A certain man who was exasperated at a decree the bishop had published against stage entertainments called him a " scrupulous old monk ", and tried to stir up the rabble against him. Another time he was reproached in the public streets as a hypocrite. The saint heard these complaints without changing countenance or altering his pace. He was no less unmoved amidst commendations and applause ; and indeed all his actions demonstrated a constant peace and serenity of mind. Under his rule the face of his whole diocese was changed. Crowds every day resorted to Laurence's residence for advice, comfort or alms ; his gate and purse were always open to the poor. He gave alms more willingly in bread and clothes than in money, which might be ill spent ; when he gave cash it was always in small sums. He employed married women to find out and relieve the bashful poor or persons of family in decayed circumstances, and in the distribution of his charities he had no regard to flesh and blood. When a poor man came to him, recommended by his brother Leonard, he said to him, " Go to him who sent you, and tell him from me that he is able to relieve you himself ". Laurence had a contempt for finance. He committed the care of his temporals to a steward, and used to say that it is an unworthy thing for a shepherd of souls to spend much of his precious time in casting up farthings.

The popes of his time held St Laurence in great veneration. Eugenius IV, meeting him once at Bologna, saluted him with the words, " Welcome, ornament of bishops ! " His successor, Nicholas V, equally esteemed him and in 1451 recognized his worth in no uncertain fashion. In that year died Dominic Michelli, Patriarch of Grado,* whereupon the pope suppressed the see of Castello and transferred that of Grado to Venice. He named St Laurence as the new patriarch. The senate of the republic, always jealous of its prerogatives and liberty, made difficulties lest his authority should trespass upon their jurisdiction. Whilst this was being debated in the senate-house, St Laurence asked an audience of the assembly, before which he declared his sincere and earnest desire rather to resign a charge for which he was unfit and which he had borne against his will eighteen years, than to feel his burden increased by this additional dignity. His bearing so strongly affected the whole senate that the doge himself asked him not to entertain such a thought or to raise any obstacle to the pope's decree, and he was supported by the whole house. St Laurence therefore accepted the new office and dignity, and for the few years during which he survived to administer it he continually increased the reputation for goodness and charity which he had earned as bishop of Castello. A hermit of Corfu assured a Venetian nobleman, as if by a divine revelation, that Venice had been preserved from the dangers which threatened it by the prayers of the patriarch. His nephew, Bernard Giustiniani, who wrote his uncle's life, narrates certain miracles and prophecies of his which he himself witnessed.

St Laurence left some valuable ascetical writings ; he was seventy-four years old when he wrote his last work, entitled *The Degrees of Perfection*, and he had just finished it when he was seized with a sharp fever. His servants prepared a bed for him, at which the true imitator of Christ was troubled and said, " Are you making up a feather-bed for me ? No ; that shall not be. My Lord was stretched on a hard and painful tree. Do not you remember that St Martin said in his last moments that a Christian ought to die on sackcloth and ashes ? " Nor could he be contented till he was laid on his straw. During the two days that he lived after receiving the last anointing many of the city came in turn according to their different rank to receive his blessing. He insisted on having the beggars admitted, and gave to each class a short instruction. Seeing one Marcello, a young nobleman and his favourite disciple, weep most bitterly, he comforted him and assured him that, " I go before, but you will shortly follow. Next Easter we shall meet again." Marcello in fact fell sick at the beginning of Lent, and was buried in Easter-week. St Laurence died on January 8, 1455, but his feast is kept on this date whereon he received episcopal consecration. He was canonized in 1690.

There is a Latin life by his nephew, Bernard Giustiniani, which is reprinted in the *Acta Sanctorum*, January, vol. i, under January 8. Some other materials may be found

---

* There is only one true patriarch in the Western church, the Pope himself, who is Patriarch of the West. The title of patriarch borne by the former metropolitans of Grado and Aquileia was due to a sixth-century schism of the metropolitans of Illyricum. It was not till 1751 that the patriarchal title of Grado at Venice w as merged in that of Venice, but St Laurence Giustiniani is usually referred to as first patriarch of Venice. This and the other " minor patriarchs " of the West are actually only archbishops with precedence and other honours.

in D. Rosa, *De B. Laurentii Justiniani vita, sanctitate et miraculis, testimoniorum centuria* (1914). There are also several Italian lives, *e.g.* that of Maffei (1819), Regazzi (1856), Cucito (1895), and La Fontaine (1928).   See also DTC., vol. ix, cc. 10–11, and Eubel, *Hierarchia catholica medii aevi*, vol. ii, pp. 130 and 290.

ST BERTINUS, ABBOT   (*c.* A.D. 700)

THIS great abbot was one of three young men—the others were St Mommolinus and St Bertrand—natives of the Coutances country, who were sent from the abbey of Luxeuil to assist St Omer (Audomarus) after he was made bishop of Thérouanne, the centre of the half-heathen Morini in what is now called the Pas-de-Calais.   The Morini had already received the seed of divine faith but only superficially and imperfectly, and had then for almost a whole century been an abandoned field. Great were the fatigues, persecutions and sufferings of these holy men in rooting out vice and idolatry and in civilizing a people who were in a great measure bar-barians, but they were tireless in words and works and they reaped a most abundant harvest.   The three missionaries built their first small monastery on a hill on the banks of the river Aa, where is now the village of Saint-Mommolin ; this was afterwards known as the " Old Monastery ".   The place being very narrow, confined by the river and marshy ground, it soon grew too small for the numbers that came to take the religious habit.   Whereupon a convert named Ardwald gave St Omer some land about four miles away, and this ground, which was a part of the estate of Sithiu, St Omer bestowed on the missionaries, with instructions that they were to colonize it and start another monastery.   St Mommolinus was the first abbot of the Old Monastery and afterwards of Sithiu.   But upon the death of St Giles, Bishop of Noyon, he was chosen to fill that see about the year 661, and St Bertinus, who is said to have been chosen head of the original settlement by St Omer and refused because he was the youngest of the three, was left abbot of Sithiu.

Under his government the reputation of this monastery (first dedicated in honour of St Peter, but after called Saint-Bertin) seemed to equal even that of Luxeuil.   During its early days its claustral activity went'hand in hand with the evangelizing and taming of the Morini and their country, and was a civilizing agency characteristic of the monks of the West (it is likely that during the lifetime of Bertinus they still followed the rule of Columban, though he is numbered among the Benedictine saints).   The country itself was sufficiently bad and discouraging. Even today it is depressing in its low-lying wetness : twelve hundred years ago it was undrained and water-logged.   The monks went from Vieux Moutier to take over Sithiu in a boat, and it is not for nothing that a boat is the emblem of St Bertinus in art.   The amphibious population was wild and dull of understanding. St Bertinus and his companions brought to them the knowledge of the gospel, the light of learning, and the enterprise and energy which drains land and builds solid houses.   If he had setbacks and plenty of discouragement to face among these rough people and places, St Bertinus had the comfort of seeing his monastery flourish with illustrious examples of penance and holiness.

In 663 St Bertinus and St Omer built a church dedicated in honour of our Lady on a hill near Sithiu, which afterwards became the cathedral of the diocese of Saint-Omer ; and when he acquired some land at Wormhout, near Dunkirk, the abbot founded a cell there, putting it in charge of St Winnoc, who with three other Bretons had joined the community at Sithiu.   The exact year of the death of St

Bertinus is not known, but he died at a great age, and was buried in the chapel of St. Martin at Sithiu.

In the fifth volume of MGH., *Scriptores Merov.*, W. Levison has discussed very fully the relative importance and date of the lives of St Bertinus. The oldest (early ninth-century) is unquestionably that which forms one whole with two other lives, the one of St Omer and the other of St Winnoc. The various sources which have a bearing on the holy abbot's history and *cultus* are catalogued in BHL., nn. 763 and 1290–1298. The more important texts were already printed in the *Acta Sanctorum*, September, vol. ii, with a full introduction. See also Van der Essen in *Analectes pour servir à l'hist. ecclés. de Belgique*, vol. xxxii (1905), pp. 6–23. The representation of St Bertinus in art is dealt with by Künstle, *Ikonographie*, vol. ii, pp. 134–135.

BD RAYMUND LULL, Martyr   (A.D. 1316)

AMONG the few really human documents which are attributable to the hagiographers of medieval times, the contemporary life of Ramón Lull may claim exceptional recognition. We do not know the name of the author ; we cannot even be quite sure whether the Latin or the Catalan text is the original ; we learn that the facts were communicated by himself at the solicitation of his followers, though we are not told when or how they were taken down. Still, no one who reads the narrative can fail to be impressed by the absolute candour of the revelation. We see into the soul of the man therein depicted. There is boundless generosity and courage, but also somewhat of extravagance. It is a veritable Don Quixote who stands before us, animated only by the holiest and most unselfish purposes, but paying, to judge from the human standpoint, a pitifully heavy price for all his indiscretions. He is restless, like St Francis Xavier or like Charles de Foucauld, but his energy never flags. The great conceptions which fill his mind are seen so clearly and open out so wonderful a vision that he has not time to reflect. The obstacles which stand in his way are dwarfed, if indeed they are not obliterated altogether.

The limits of this notice do not permit of more than the barest summary of Ramón's strange career. Born in 1232, he was apparently the son of one of the military chiefs who in the first part of the thirteenth century succeeded in reconquering the island of Majorca from its Moslem invaders. He was wealthy, talented, enthusiastic ; he married young, but though at the age of thirty he had a little son and daughter and a charming wife, he was shameless in his pursuit of any new face that attracted him. One night, about 1263, when he was busied in composing an ode to his latest *inamorata*, he suddenly saw beside him the figure of Jesus Christ hanging on the Cross. He was so startled that he could not shake off the impression or go on writing, but had to take refuge in his bed. It was not, however, until this experience had been renewed five separate times that his heart was touched ; but, being the man he was, the conversion was thorough. Reflecting on the words " greater love than this no man hath, that a man lay down his life for his friends ", his mind, from his uninterrupted contact with the Moors, turned to the thought of winning them to the service of Christ Jesus. Here was a cause worthy of the sacrifice of all things, even of life itself. He went on a pilgrimage to Compostela and to Rocamadour to obtain the divine guidance. For such a task systematic preparation was needed. He had first of all to make provision for those dependent on him. He gave the rest of his wealth to the poor, and then, after a period of seclusion and prayer, he set about acquiring the knowledge necessary for an intellectual crusade against Moslem philosophy and religion, against Averroes and the Koran. Nine years were spent in learning Arabic and in making other preliminary studies. From the very beginning he had seen the necessity of establishing Catholic religious centres to train missionaries and disputants for the new campaign. This was, he convinced himself, the only way to cope with an outlandish culture of which the average theologian of western Europe knew next to nothing. But though a foundation of this sort—the first missionary college—was later on (in 1276) begun in Majorca at the charges of his good friend, King James II, and confided to the Friars Minor, it seems to have achieved very little.

Meanwhile Ramón pursued his studies and wrote endless books—one of them, a sort of spiritual romance called *Blanquerna*, has been translated into English. He visited Rome in 1277, in the hope of enlisting the sympathies of the pope, then Paris in 1286, and Genoa in 1290, but always with the purpose of finding at last an opportunity to cross over to Africa himself and begin preaching in Tunis. His fluctuations of mind and resolution are marvellously depicted in the " Contemporary Life ". It was at Genoa that, after receiving somewhat of a rebuff in an application to join the Friars Preachers, he finally offered himself to and was accepted by the Franciscans as a tertiary. He was then very ill, but recovered miraculously when in 1292 he caused himself to be carried on board a galley bound for Africa. He realized his dream of preaching in the streets of Tunis, but after imprisonment and much rough treatment at the hands of the Moslems he was soon forcibly deported out of the country and found himself in Naples. Appeals to Pope Boniface VIII at Rome and subsequently to Clement V at Avignon to obtain papal support for his campaign met with very little response. A journey to Cyprus, under a false impression that the khan of Tartary had made himself master of the Saracens in Syria and Palestine, was equally disappointing. Ramón lectured for a while in Paris and then made a second attempt to gain a hearing among the Moors themselves at Bougie in Barbary, but once more, after much ill-usage and a cruel imprisonment, he was deported, and incidentally suffered shipwreck before he reached Italy. Further appeals to the Holy See and to the Council of Vienne in 1311 brought him no encouragement. He spent some time lecturing at Paris, and finally on a third visit to Africa he was stoned at Bougie and left for dead ; he was rescued by Genoese sailors, but died on shipboard, within sight of Majorca, on June 29, 1316.

Although Ramón's whole life was a record of disappointment, his literary activity was incredible. Three hundred and thirteen different treatises are attributed to him, most of them in Latin or Catalan, but not a few are in Arabic. Some of his writings have been thought to deserve a note of theological censure, but there is also difficulty in determining in certain cases what is authentically his composition. Nearly all of it gives proof of a tender piety, but he speaks fearlessly of the abuses then prevalent in the Church. Lull is celebrated liturgically by the Friars Minor and others, and Pope Pius XI speaks highly of him in bis encyclical letter " *Orientalium rerum* " (1928), but without according him the title Blessed.

The fullest and most satisfactory bibliography of the subject is the contribution of Fr E. Longpré, in DTC., vol. ix (1926), cc. 1072–1141. The more important biographical material may still be found in the *Acta Sanctorum*, July, vol. ii, and it is to be noticed that a critical revision of the Latin text of the " Contemporary Life " has appeared in the *Analecta Bollandiana*, vol. xlviii (1930), pp. 130–178. An admirable translation of the Catalan text has been published in English by E. Allison Peers who has also translated *Blanquerna* and issued a full biography (*Ramón Lull*, 1929). The complete works were published in Spain, ed. by P. M. Bataillon and M. Caldentey, in 1948.

BD GENTILIS, MARTYR   (A.D. 1340)

GENTILIS was born at the end of the thirteenth century at Matelica, near Ancona. He joined the Friars Minor, and after profession and ordination was sent to the convent of Mount Alvernia, where he twice served as guardian. The associations of this place had a strong effect on Gentilis and bred in him a great love of silence and solitude ; but at the same time they fired him with St Francis's own ambition to evangelize the East and Islam. He was eventually sent to Egypt, where he found he could do nothing because not only did he not know Arabic but all his efforts to learn it were without fruit. He was about to return home in despair, but in consequence of a dream or vision persevered and at length overcame his difficulties. He fell in with a Venetian ambassador to the court of Persia, Mark Comaro, who asked the friar to accompany him across Arabia ; while on the journey he tended Comaro in a dangerous illness, and prophesied that he would live to be doge of the republic. Together they visited the shrine of St Catherine of Alexandria in the desert of Sinai, a great resort of Christian pilgrims in spite of its inaccessible situation. One day Bd Gentilis disappeared mysteriously for a week, and on his return it was said that he had been miraculously transported to Italy and back to assist at the death-bed of his father in accordance with a promise he had made him. Arrived in Persia, he preached throughout that country northward as far as Trebizond, and is said to have baptized very many converts. He was put to death for the faith, but the circumstances of his martyrdom are not known. His body was brought back to Europe by some Venetians, and is buried in the church of the *Frati* at Venice. The *cultus* of Bd Gentilis was approved by Pope St Pius V.

Besides Wadding's *Annales* (*sub anno* 1340), consult Mazzara, *Leggendario Francescano*, vol. ii, 1, pp. 409–411, and Marcellino de Civezza, *Missions franciscaines*, vol. iii, p. 650. A short account is also given in Léon, *Auréole·Séraphique* (Eng. trans.), vol. iii, pp. 109–112.

6 : SS. DONATIAN, LAETUS AND OTHERS, BISHOPS AND MARTYRS (*c.* A.D. 484)

IN the year 484 the Arian king of the Vandals, Huneric, ordered that all the Catholic churches of Africa were to be closed and the goods of the clergy to be taken from them and given to the Arian clergy ; the bishops, in particular, who had assembled at the royal command were turned out of the city. Outside of the gates Huneric met a party of them, who appealed against his injustice and cruelty. " Ride them down ! " he said to his mounted followers, and that was all the answer he vouchsafed. St Donatian with four others, all bishops in the province of Byzacene, were cruelly beaten, and then driven into the desert, and died of hunger, thirst and exposure. St Laetus, Bishop of Leptis Minor, whom the Roman Martyrology calls " a zealous and very learned man ", had made himself particularly obnoxious to Huneric by his opposition to Arianism. He therefore was thrown into a filthy dungeon, from which he only emerged to be burnt alive, one of the first martyrs of the persecution. The feast of these martyrs, with St Laetus in chief, is kept by the Canons Regular of the Lateran.

See the *Acta Sanctorum*, September, vol. ii, where we are referred to the *Historia perse-cutionis provinciae Africanae* by Victor of Vita, but it is difficult to identify the particular names set down in the martyrology.

ST ELEUTHERIUS, ABBOT   (SIXTH CENTURY)

" THE holy man, old father Eleutherius ", is spoken of several times in the *Dialogues* of St Gregory, wherein are chronicled certain miracles reported of him by his monks.   He was abbot of the monastery of St Mark, near Spoleto, and once when lodging at a convent of nuns he was asked to take over the care of a boy who was nightly troubled by an evil spirit.   St Eleutherius did so, and for long nothing untoward happened to the boy, so that the abbot said, " The Devil is having a game with those sisters ; but now that he has to deal with the servants of God he daren't come near the child ".   As if in rebuke of a speech that certainly savoured of boasting, the boy was at once afflicted by his former trouble.   Eleutherius was conscious-stricken, and said to the brethren that stood by, " None of us shall eat food to-day until this boy is dispossessed ".   All fell to prayer, and did not cease until the child was cured.

One Holy Saturday St Gregory was ill and could not fast, whereat, he tells us, he was considerably disturbed.   " When I found on this sacred vigil, when not only adults but even children fast, that I could not refrain from eating, I was more grieved thereby than troubled by my illness."   So he asked Eleutherius to pray for him that he might join the people in their penance, and soon by virtue of that prayer Gregory found himself enabled to abstain from food.   St Eleutherius lived for many years in Gregory's monastery at Rome, and died there.

We know practically nothing more about St Eleutherius than St Gregory tells us in his *Dialogues*, notably in bk 3, ch. 33 ; but the story is discussed by the Bollandists in the *Acta Sanctorum*, September, vol. ii.

ST CHAINOALDUS, OR CAGNOALD, BISHOP OF LAON   (*c.* A.D. 633)

THIS saint, commonly called Cagnoald or Cagnou in France, is of interest chiefly on account of his association with St Columban, who stayed at the house of his father near Meaux, and made a deep impression on Chainoaldus and on his brother and sister, Faro and Burgundofara, who followed him in holiness.   He became a monk at Luxeuil, and when St Columban was banished followed his master in all his wanderings and helped him in his preaching and ministry.   The strife going on at the time between Theodebert II of Austrasia and his brother Theoderic gave Columban an occasion to read a lesson in charity to his disciple.   He dreamed one day that he saw the two brothers fighting together, and when he awoke told Chain-oaldus sadly of what he had seen.   " Pray then, father, that Theodebert may beat our enemy Theoderic ", observed Chainoaldus, whose father was at the Austrasian court.   " Not at all ", replied Columban.   " Such prayer would not be pleasing to God, for He tells us to pray for our enemies."   Chainoaldus became bishop of Laon, was present at the Council of Rheims of the year 630, and signed the charter of the abbey of Solignac, which was founded by St Eligius while he was still a layman.

Though there is no proper life of this saint, his activities and *cultus* are discussed at some length in the *Acta Sanctorum*, September, vol. ii.   See also Duchesne, *Fastes Épis-copaux*, vol. iii, p. 139.

ST BEGA, OR BEE, VIRGIN   (SEVENTH CENTURY)

IN the fourth book of his *Ecclesiastical History* St Bede the Venerable refers to St Heiu, who, he says, was regarded as the first woman in Northumbria to become a nun and who founded a monastery at Hartlepool. This was taken over by St Hilda and Heiu went to live at Tadcaster. A little further on he makes mention of St Begu who, after being a religious for over thirty years, had in the nunnery at Hackness a vision of the departing of the soul of its foundress Hilda. St Bega (Begh, Bee) has been identified with either or both of these holy women, as was done by Leland and the Bollandists ; the identification has not been confirmed but rather seems to have been disproved. She is the heroine of a legend which makes her the daughter of an Irish king, sought in marriage by a son of the king of Norway. She had, however, vowed herself a virgin to Christ, and had been given by an angel a bracelet marked with a cross as a token of her heavenly betrothal. The day before she was to be given to the prince, while her suitor and her father were revelling in the hall, she escaped with the help of this bracelet and, seated on a clod of earth, was navigated across the sea and landed safely on the coast of Cumberland. For a time she lived as an anchoress, and the sea-gulls, guillemots and gannets brought food for her sustenance ; but human marauders were less kind, and she was advised by the king of Northumbria, St Oswald, to become a nun. She therefore received the veil from St Aidan (Bede says it was he who consecrated Heiu) and established a monastery at St Bees (Copeland) which afterwards became a cell of the Benedictine abbey of St Mary at York.

Whatever background of truth there may be in the legend of St Bega, there seems no doubt that she existed and was venerated in Northumbria. The promontory on which she lived is named after her St Bee's Head, and she was the patroness of the people of the neighbourhood, ground down between the exactions of their lords and the raids of the border Scots. They claimed even to possess her miraculous bracelet, and treasured equally the stories of how St Bega in her earthly life had been devoted to the poor and oppressed and had cooked, washed and mended for the workmen who built her monastery. St Bega was venerated in Scotland and Norway, and she may be the same as the " Becga, daughter of Gabhran, virgin ", who is named in the Martyrology of Tallaght on February 10. Her feast is observed in the diocese of Lancaster.

It is very difficult to establish the truth where we have no sort of guarantee of the reliability of our sources. The legend of St Bega in its fuller form rests entirely upon one manuscript (Cotton, Faust. B. iv), which Hardy in his *Descriptive Catalogue*, i, p. 223, dates twelfth century. The story is supported by the lessons in the Aberdeen Breviary : see KSS., p. 278, and the *Acta Sanctorum*, September, vol. ii. C. Plummer, a very careful scholar, familiar with Irish as well as Anglo-Saxon sources, says quite positively that the Begu of Bede (bk iv, ch. 23) " is not to be confounded, as is often done, with Heiu, or with the very mythical Irish saint Bega whose name is preserved in St Bees ". In the *Lives of the English Saints*, Faber recounted in graceful terms the legend of St Bega, and cited in an appendix Wordsworth's " Stanza " on the headland of St Bee's. The Latin text of the Cotton manuscript was first printed and translated by G. C. Tomlinson in the *Carlisle Historical Tracts*.

BD BERTRAND OF GARRIGUES   (*c.* A.D. 1230)

AT the end of the twelfth and the beginning of the thirteenth centuries the south of France was ravaged by heresy and civil war. Albigensianism, supported by the nobles and appealing to the people by offering a life of virtuous austerity to the few and of licence to the many, had almost complete control ; the Catholics, rendered impotent by indifference and ill-living, took up arms against the heretics, and the challenge was accepted.   Bd Bertrand was born at Garrigues in the diocese of Nîmes and brought up in the midst of these disturbances ; but he was taught the true faith, and learned the dangers of the heresy that flourished all around.   In the year 1200 the Albigensian Raymund VI of Toulouse marched through Langue- doc, harrying the orthodox monasteries, especially those of the Cistercians, who were the official missionaries against the heretics.   It is said that the convent at Bouchet was saved from destruction by the prompt action of a bee-master, who overturned his rows of hives in the faces of the soldiers.   Bertrand himself became a priest and joined himself as a preacher to the Cistercian mission.   In 1208 the Cistercian legate, Peter of Castelnau, was murdered, the crusade of Simon de Montfort was let loose, and soon after this time probably Bd Bertrand first met St Dominic, who was trying to remedy by prayer and preaching some of the harm that his friend Simon was doing by the sword.

In 1215 Bertrand was one of the group of six preachers gathered round Dominic from which sprang the great order of Friars Preachers ; by the following year they had increased to sixteen, " all in fact and in name excellent preachers ", when they met at Prouille to choose a rule and plan the life of their new society.   After a year of community life at the priory in Toulouse, the founder made his famous bold stroke of dispersing his religious, and Bd Bertrand was sent to Paris with Friar Matthew of France and five others.   There they made a foundation near the university.   But Bertrand did not stay long in Paris.   He was called by St Dominic to Rome and sent thence with Friar John of Navarre to establish the order in Bologna.   Though Bd Reginald of Orleans was the friend who influenced him most, early Dominican writers speak of Bd Bertrand as a beloved companion of St Dominic, the dearest associate in his work, the sharer of his journeys, his prayers and his holiness.   In 1219 he accompanied him on the only visit St Dominic made to Paris ; they went from Toulouse by way of the sanctuary of Rocamadour, and the journey has been surrounded with wonders, such as that they understood German without having learnt it and were not wetted by heavy rain.

At the second general chapter held at Bologna in 1221 the Dominican order was divided into eight provinces, and Bertrand was appointed prior provincial of Pro- vence.   The remaining nine years of his life were spent in energetic preaching throughout the south of France, where he greatly extended the activities of his order and founded the great priory of Marseilles.   There is a story told that on one occasion a Friar Benedict questioned Bd Bertrand because he so rarely celebrated a requiem Mass.   " We are certain of the salvation of the holy souls ", was the reply, " but of the end of ourselves and other sinners we are not certain ".   " Well, but ", persisted Friar Benedict, " suppose there are two beggars, one strong and well, the other disabled.   Which would you be the more sorry for ? "   " The one who can do least for himself."   " Very well then.   Such certainly are the dead. They have neither mouths wherewith to confess nor hands wherewith to work, but living sinners have both and can take care of themselves."   Bertrand was not at all convinced by this argument, and the fact that he afterwards celebrated Mass more frequently for the dead was attributed to his having had enlightenment in the form of a nightmare of a departed soul, which much distressed him.   Bd Bertrand died at the abbey of Bouchet, near Orange, about the year 1230 ; his *cultus* was confirmed in 1881. " By his watchings, his fasts, and his other penances ", wrote Friar Bernard Guidonis, " he succeeded in making himself so like his beloved Father that one might have said of him as he passed by : Of a truth the disciple is like the master ; there goes the very image of the blessed Dominic."

A very full account of Bd Bertrand is given by the Bollandists in the *Acta Sanctorum*, October, vol. xiii, pp. 136–145 and 919–921. Though there was no separate early biography which they could utilize, they at first drew largely from the *Vitae Fratrum* of Gerard de Fracheto and other Dominican chronicles, but in a supplement to their first account they have added many details from documents submitted to the Congregation of Rites in the process for the *confirmatio cultus*. See also a series of papers by J. P. Isnard in the *Bulletin de la Société archéol. de la Drôme*, 1870 to 1872 ; and Procter, *Dominican Saints*, pp. 253–256. A fuller bibliography is provided by Taurisano, *Catalogus hagiographicus O.P.*, p. 9.

BD PEREGRINE OF FALERONE   (A.D. 1240)

PEREGRINE was a young man of good family who was studying with great success at Bologna when St Francis came to preach there in 1220. Both he and a fellow student, Bd Rizzerio, were deeply impressed, and desired to join the friars. St Francis accepted them, but told Peregrine that, in spite of his learning, it was God's will that he should serve as a lay-brother. In this humble condition he persevered to the end. Both before and after death he was famous for miracles.

The Friars Minor join this *beatus* in one feast with Bd Liberatus (below) and BD SANTES of MONTE FABRI who, having killed a man in defending himself, became a lay-brother in the order. After a most holy life he died in 1390 and miracles were wrought at his grave.

The story of Peregrine is told in the documents which Sabatier calls the *Speculum Vitae* and the *Actus b. Francisci et sociorum ejus* (cap. 36). See also Gentili, *Saggio sopra l'ordine serafico*, p. 27 *seq.* ; and Léon, *Auréole Séraphique* (Eng. trans.), vol. i, pp. 527–529. For Bd Santes, see Wadding, *Annales Ord. Minorum*, vol. ix, pp. 94–96, and Léon, vol. iii.

BD LIBERATUS OF LORO   (A.D. 1258 ?)

THE *cultus* of this *beato* was approved by Pope Pius IX in 1868, but his history is involved in a good deal of obscurity. He is said to have belonged to the noble family of Brunforte, to have joined the Order of Friars Minor, but to have led the life of a contemplative and a hermit. He is also supposed to have been associated with Bd Humilis and Bd Pacificus in a project of stricter observance ; but the attempt to identify him with the unnamed friar of Soffiano who had a vision of our Blessed Lady (see the *Fioretti*, chs. 46 and 47) is not free from difficulty.

Bd Liberatus is discussed, with Humilis and Pacificus, in the *Acta Sanctorum*, August, vol. v. See also Salvi, *Cenni storici sul b. Liberato da Loro* (1896), and on this the notice in the *Analecta Bollandiana*, vol. xvii (1898), p. 381. There is also an account in Léon, *Auréole Séraphique* (Eng. trans.), vol. iii, pp. 431–432 ; and an interesting comment by Paul Sabatier, *Actus beati Francisci et sociorum ejus* (1902), p. 195, and p. 215, note.

7 : ST REGINA OR REINE, VIRGIN AND MARTYR   (DATE UNKNOWN)

OF St Regina, mentioned in the Roman Martyrology as having been martyred in the territory of Autun, the true history is not known. French legends represent her as the daughter of Clement, a pagan citizen of Alise, in Burgundy. Her mother died at the child's birth, and Regina was handed over to the care of a Christian woman, who brought her up in the faith.   When Clement discovered this, he refused to receive his daughter, and she went back to live with her nurse, earning her bread as a shepherdess.   She attracted the desire of the prefect Olybrius who, when her good birth was told to him, wanted to marry her. Regina refused him, nor would she listen to the persuasions of her father who, now that his daughter had attracted a distinguished suitor, was willing to own her.   She was therefore locked up in a dungeon, and when her spirit remained unbroken Olybrius vented his rage by having her cruelly tortured.   That night she was consoled in her prison by a vision of the cross and a voice telling her that her release was at hand.   The next day Olybrius ordered her to be tortured again and then that she should be beheaded ; the appearance of a shining dove hovering over her converted many of the onlookers.   This romance invites comparison with the story of St Margaret on July 20.

Though no trust can be placed in what purports to be the *passio* of St Regina (printed in the *Acta Sanctorum*, September, vol. iii), the *cultus* is certainly early, as is vouched for by the fact of the inclusion of her name in the " Hieronymianum ".   The foundations of a basilica dedicated in her honour at Alise have been discovered in comparatively recent times ; see *e.g.* J. Toutain in *Bulletin archéologique du Comité des Travaux historiques*, 1914, pp. 365–387.   The legend has been set out at length, with pictorial illustrations by F. Grignard, *La Vie de Ste Reine d'Alise* (1881) ; and by Quillot, *Ste Reine d'Alise* (1881).

ST SOZON, Martyr   (Date Unknown)

The following is the legend of this young shepherd of Cilicia, who was originally called Tarasius and took the name of Sozon at baptism.   One day while sleeping under a tree our Lord appeared to him, told him to leave his sheep, and to follow Him to death.   Sozon awoke and at once made his way to the nearest town, Pompeiopolis, where he found a pagan festival was being celebrated.   He went straight into the temple of the god and with a mighty blow of his crook knocked down the golden image and broke off its hand.   This hand he took and broke into further small pieces, which he distributed as alms among the poor.   Several innocent persons were arrested for this, whereupon Sozon marched into court and gave himself up as the true culprit.   He was offered pardon and freedom if he would worship the god whose statue he had mutilated, but Sozon mocked at the idea of worshipping a god that could be broken by a sheep-crook.   Nails were then driven, points upward, through the soles of his sandals and he was made thus to walk around the arena.   As Sozon passed before the magistrate he pointed at his blood-stained feet and said, " I have finer red shoes than you ".   " You are a brave fellow ", said the magistrate.   " Play a tune on your pipe and I will let you go."   But Sozon refused, saying that he had often piped to his sheep but would now make music only to God.   So he was sentenced to be burned, and when night had come the Christians of the place collected his charred bones and gave them honourable burial.

Two Greek texts preserve the alleged acts of this martyr.   One has been edited in the *Acta Sanctorum*, September, vol. iii ; the other in vol. cxv of Migne, PG.

ST GRIMONIA, Virgin and Martyr   (Date Unknown)

A French legend relates that St Grimonia was the daughter of a pagan Irish chief, and that when she was twelve years old she was converted to Christianity and made a vow of perpetual virginity. Her father, in defiance of or not understanding such a vow, wished her to marry, and when she refused shut her up. Grimonia escaped and fled to France, where she became a solitary in the forest of Thiérache in Picardy. Here the contemplation of the beauty of created things would often bring her to the state of ecstasy. After a prolonged search the messengers of her father traced her to her retreat, where they put before her the alternatives of return and a forced marriage or death. Grimonia remained firm and so she was beheaded on April 20 in an unknown year. A chapel was built over her grave which became famous for miracles, and around it grew up a town, called from its origin La Chapelle. On September 7, 1231, her relics, together with those of St Proba (Preuve), another Irishwoman, who is supposed to have suffered with Grimonia, were enshrined at Lesquielles. The facts about St Grimonia are hard to come by : she may have been a solitary who lost her life in defending her chastity.

What little is known concerning this saint and her *cultus* may be read in the *Acta Sanctorum*, September, vol. iii.

ST JOHN OF NICOMEDIA, Martyr   (A.D. 303)

WHEN the edict of the Emperor Diocletian against Christians was published in Nicomedia a certain Christian, " a man of secular dignity ", at once tore it down and was punished by death. The name of this man is not known, but his memory is venerated in the Western church under the name of " John ". The Roman Martyrology says that " when he saw the cruel decrees against the Christians displayed in the forum he was fired with zeal for the faith and pulled them down and tore them up with his own hands. When this was told to the emperors, Diocletian and Maximian, who were residing in the city, they ordered that all kinds of sufferings should be inflicted on him. This most noble man endured them with such readiness both of demeanour and spirit that they seemed not at all to disturb him." He was burnt alive, on February 24, 303, according to Lactantius. The unknown man whom we call John has sometimes been erroneously identified with St George, protector of England. The Syrians called him Euhtis (Euetios) and put his feast on February 24.

Eusebius in his *Ecclesiastical History* (bk viii, ch. 5), and also Lactantius, almost certainly make reference to the fate of this martyr, though they do not actually name him. The passages are quoted and commented on in the *Acta Sanctorum*, September, vol. iii. We find the name of John given, and the commemoration assigned to this day, in the so-called " Parvum Romanum ". See Quentin, *Martyrologes historiques*, p. 439.

ST ANASTASIUS THE FULLER, Martyr   (A.D. 304 ?)

THE Roman Martyrology refers today to the passion " of the holy Anastasius the martyr at Aquileia ", though the martyr indicated did not suffer on this date nor at Aquileia. It would appear that vij Idus Septembris has been copied for vij Kalendas Septembris, *i.e.* August 26, the day given in earlier martyrologies and on which his feast is still kept at Split (Spalato). According to his more than doubtful *acta*, Anastasius was born at Aquileia of a good family, but remembering the word of the Apostle to the Thessalonians, " that you do your own business and work with your own hands ", he became a fuller and practised his trade at Salona (Split) in Dalmatia. During the persecution of Diocletian he would not conceal his faith, but boldly painted up a cross on his door, wherefore he was arrested and brought before the governor.   He stood firm, and was therefore thrown into the sea with a stone tied round his neck.   A matron of the city, Asclepia, promised their liberty to any of her slaves who should recover the body, and they eventually came upon it in the hands of some Negroes who had found it in the water.   They threatened the Negroes that if they did not give it up they would be charged with having murdered the man, and so brought the body back in triumph to their mistress.   She buried it honourably in her garden, which later became a Christian cemetery with a basilica.

St Anastasius, martyr at Salona, named in the Roman Martyrology on August 21 is an invention of hagiographers, though attempts have been made to identify him with St Anastasius the Fuller ; he is made to be the converted officer mentioned in the *passio* of St Agapitus (August 18).

That there has been confusion is certain, and it is likely that the acts (in *Acta Sanctorum*, September, vol. iii) are altogether fictitious; but we have good evidence that there was a real martyr Anastasius who was probably a fuller and was honoured at Salona.   His proper day, as the " Hieronymianum " shows, is August 26.   All that we can say is that this one saint has had two different days and two different stories assigned to him.   See CMH., pp. 467–468, 492, and references given.

ST CLODOALD, or CLOUD   (*c.* A.D. 560)

ON the death of Clovis, King of the Franks, in the year 511 his kingdom was divided between his four sons, of whom the second was Clodomir.   Thirteen years later he was killed fighting against his cousin, Gondomar, King of Burgundy (he had first murdered St Sigismund of Burgundy, whom the Roman Martyrology calls a martyr), leaving three sons to share his dominions.   The youngest of these sons of Clodomir was St Clodoald, a name more familiar to English people under its French form of Cloud from the town of Saint-Cloud near Versailles.   The three boys were brought up by their grandmother St Clotilda, widow of Clovis, who lavished much care and affection on them in her home at Paris, while their kingdom was administered by their uncle Childebert.   When Cloud was eight years old, Childebert entered into a plot with his brother, Clotaire of Soissons, to get rid of these boys and partition their kingdom.   A familiar of Childebert was sent to Clotilda asking her to choose whether the three boys should be put to death or forcibly tonsured and shut up in monasteries.   He so twisted the reply of the distracted queen that she was made to appear to choose their death, whereupon Clotaire seized the eldest boy, Theodoald, and stabbed him.   The second, Gunther, fled in terror to his uncle Childebert, whose heart was so softened by fear and sickened at the brutal killing that he tried to protect him.   But Clotaire did not approve of such faintheartedness, dragged Gunther from Childebert's arms and killed him too.   Cloud escaped, and was taken for safety into Provence or elsewhere.

Childebert and Clotaire shared the fruits of their crime, and Cloud made no attempt to recover his kingdom when he came of age.   He had seen quite enough of the politics of the world, and voluntarily hid himself in a hermit's cell.   After some time he put himself under the discipline of St Severinus, a recluse who lived near Paris, and he afterwards went to Nogent on the Seine and had his hermitage where is now Saint-Cloud.   St Cloud was indefatigable in instructing the people of the neighbouring country, and ended his days at Nogent about the year 560 when he was some thirty-six years old.   By a pun on his name St Cloud is venerated in France as the patron of nail-makers.

Understandably distressed by the monstrous brutality of Merovingian politics as exemplified by the fate of the sons of Clodomir, Alban Butler adds the following suitable reflection from the fifteenth-century humanist Pico della Mirandola: " Many think it a man's greatest happiness in this life to enjoy dignity and power and to live amid the riches and splendour of a court.   Of these you know I have had a share ; and I can assure you I could never find in my soul true satisfaction in anything but retreat and contemplation.   I am persuaded that the Caesars, if they could speak from their sepulchres, would declare Pico more happy in his solitude than they were in the government of the world ; and if the dead could return, they would choose the pangs of a second death rather than risk their salvation again in public offices."

There is a life which has been critically edited by B. Krusch in MGH., *Scriptores Merov.*, vol. ii, pp. 350–357, as also at an earlier date by Mabillon and the Bollandists.   But as the life is pronounced to be not older than the close of the ninth century, the data provided by St Gregory of Tours and reproduced in the *Acta Sanctorum* are more trustworthy.   J. Legrand's *St Cloud : prince, moine, prêtre* (1922) is an uncritical booklet.

SS. ALCMUND AND TILBERT, BISHOPS OF HEXHAM   (A.D. 781 AND 789)

No details are known of the lives of these holy bishops, respectively the seventh and eighth occupants of the see of Hexham.   St Alcmund succeeded to St Frithebert in the year 767, and at his death was buried beside St Acca in the cemetery outside the cathedral-church.   During the Danish raids all trace and memory of his grave were lost, but about the year 1032 it is said that the saint appeared in a vision to a man of Hexham, pointed out the place where his body lay, and asked him to tell the sacristan of the church of Durham to have it translated to a more honourable resting-place within the cathedral.   This was accordingly done. Tradition says that during the translation the Durham monk, Alured, secretly abstracted one of Alcmund's bones to take back to his own church ; but the coffin became so weighty that it was found impossible to move it—until Alured restored the stolen relic.   Alban Butler includes St Tilbert with St Alcmund on this day, but the chronicler Simeon of Durham records the date of his death as October 2. In the year 1154 the relics of all the six saints among the twelve early bishops of Hexham, which had then ceased to exist as a bishopric, were collected into one shrine ; they were finally and completely scattered by the Scots when they raided Hexham in 1296.

For historical details consult the volumes of the younger James Raine, *The Priory of Hexham* (1864–65).   Here, as in the *Acta Sanctorum*, September, vol. iii, extracts are given from Simeon of Durham.   There seems to have been no liturgical *cultus*.

BB. MARK, STEPHEN AND MELCHIOR, MARTYRS   (A.D. 1619)

CANON MARK CRISIN (Körösy) belonged to a distinguished Croat family.   Having made his studies at the Germanicum in Rome, he returned to labour in his own country, and under the primate of Hungary, Archbishop Pazmany, he was entrusted with important duties in the archdiocese of Esztergom.   The two other martyrs were Jesuits, Stephen Pongracz, a Hungarian by birth, and Melchior Grodecz, who was a Czech.   In 1619, when these priests were all engaged in apostolic and educational work in the neighbourhood of Kaschau or Kassa (now Kosice in

Slovakia), an army under George Racoczy invaded the district, acting at the instigation of the Calvinist leader, Bethlen Gabor. The troops seized these three influential priests, tortured them for the greater part of the night, and then put them to death under conditions of great barbarity. These martyrs were beatified in 1905.

See Schmidl, *Historia Provinciae Bohemicae S.J.*, vol. iii, pp. 193 *seq.* ; *Études*, vol. civ (1905), pp. 5–27 ; N. Angelini, *I beati Canonico Marco Stefano Crisino* . . . (1904) ; and H. Leclercq, *Les Martyrs*, t. viii, pp. 338–352.

BB. JOHN DUCKETT AND RALPH CORBY, MARTYRS (A.D. 1644)

THE north country family of Duckett had already given one martyr to the Church in the person of Bd James Duckett (April 19). He had a son who became prior of the English Carthusians at Nieuport in Flanders. Whether the James Duckett who fathered Bd John was another son is not certain ; but Bd John was related to Bd James in some way. He was born at Underwinter in the parish of Sedbergh in the west riding of Yorkshire in 1613, went to the English College at Douay, and was made priest there in 1639. He then studied for three years at Paris, where the long periods he passed in prayer were commented on and he was rumoured to have gifts of contemplation of a high order. When he was at length sent to the English mission he passed two months of preparatory retreat with the Carthusians at Nieuport, under the direction of Father Duckett, whom Bishop Challoner refers to as his kinsman but does not specify to have been his uncle. When he had ministered in the county palatine of Durham for about twelve months he was arrested while on his way to baptize two children, on July 2, 1644, the day on which the battle of Marston Moor was fought, together with two laymen. Mr Duckett was examined before a parliamentary committee of sequestrators at Sunderland, and refused to admit that he was a priest, demanding to see their proofs. The holy oils and *Rituale* found on him were pretty clear evidence, but the examiners wanted a personal admission, so they put him in irons and threatened to torture him. When he heard that the two laymen were being questioned and that inquiries were to be made among his friends and associates, he decided he must save them from the possibility of their implicating themselves, and therefore confessed his priesthood. Thereupon he was sent up to London, together with a Jesuit, Father Corby, who had been seized when celebrating Mass at Hamsterley Hall, near Newcastle.

Ralph Corby (or Corbington) came of a Durham family, but was born at Maynooth, in 1598. When Ralph was five his parents returned to England, and after years of persecution every member of the family entered religion. The father, Gerard Corbington, became a temporal coadjutor with the Jesuits and reconciled to the Church his own father when he was a hundred years old. The mother, Isabel Richardson, died a Benedictine at Ghent, and two surviving daughters joined the same order at Brussels, while Ralph's elder and younger brothers also were Jesuits. He himself joined the Society of Jesus at Watten in Flanders, and came on the mission in 1632, ministering for twelve years thereafter with unquenchable zeal among the widely scattered faithful of county Durham. Challoner tells us that " they loved him as their father and reverenced him as an apostle ".

On their arrival in London the two confessors were committed to Newgate to await the September sessions.   There was no doubt what the upshot would be, and the English Jesuits abroad were making feverish efforts in concert with the imperial *chargé d'affaires* in London to get Father Corby exchanged for a Scots colonel who was held prisoner in Germany by the emperor.   When it seemed as if this would be successful, Father Corby offered the reprieve to Mr Duckett.   To which he replied, " This thing is being procured and arranged by your friends.   Be you therefore pleased to accept it."   Corby disclaimed it—Mr Duckett was younger and better qualified for service on the mission than himself.   And thus it was " handed to and fro between them, neither being willing to accept of it, till an expedient was proposed to save them both ; but it succeeded not, for the Parliament, it seems, was resolved they both should suffer ".   At the trial they both pleaded guilty to being priests, but Father Corby claimed that as he was born in Ireland he did not come within the statute.   This plea was overruled (quite properly) and sentence of death was pronounced.

While he was celebrating his last Mass in their Newgate lodging, Father Corby " appeared to be as it were in an agony of sadness and fear ", but the trial passed, and at ten o'clock in the morning of September 7, 1644, they both set out on the journey to Tyburn, " with their crowns shaved, in their cassocks, and with a smiling look ".   Mr Duckett spoke little but to give his blessing to the many who asked it and to say to the Protestant minister that would address him, " Sir, I come not hither to be taught my faith but to die for the profession of it ".   Bd Ralph made a short speech, they lovingly embraced one another, and the cart was drawn away : nor would the sheriff allow them to be cut down and disembowelled before they were both dead.   He took extraordinary precautions to prevent any relics escaping the flames, nevertheless a hand of Bd John and some pieces of their cassocks were saved ; and in the archives of the diocese of Westminster there is treasured a letter written by Bd John on the eve of his passion to Dr Richard Smith, titular Bishop of Chalcedon and vicar apostolic of England, who was then living in Paris.   " I fear not death ", he writes, " nor I contemn not life.   If life were my lot, I would endure it patiently ; but if death, I shall receive it joyfully, for that Christ is my life and death is my gain."

Ralph Corby is included in his brother's *Certamen Triplex* (see biography of Bd Henry Morse on February 1). See also MMP., pp. 457–466 ; REPSJ., vol. iii, pp. 68–96 ; and J. Brodrick, *Procession of Saints* (1949), pp. 111–130.

8 : THE BIRTHDAY OF THE BLESSED VIRGIN MARY

THE birth of the Blessed Virgin Mary announced joy and the near approach of salvation to the lost world, and so this festival is celebrated by the Church with praise and thanksgiving.   It was a mystery of holiness, distinguished by unique privileges.   Mary was brought into the world unlike other children of Adam : not deprived of sanctifying grace and prone to sin, but pure, holy, beautiful and glorious, adorned with all the most precious graces becoming her who was chosen to be the Mother of God.   Man was no sooner fallen in Paradise through the woman led away by Satan, than God promised another woman, whose seed should crush the serpent's head.   At the birth of the Virgin Mary the accomplishment of that promise was begun.

To study the lessons in the life of Mary, to praise God for the graces conferred upon her and the blessings which through her He has bestowed on the world, and to recommend our necessities to so powerful an advocate, we celebrate festivals in her honour.   This of her birthday was kept first in the East.   In the West we know for certain that Pope St Sergius (A.D. 687–701) ordered that four separate feasts of our Lady should be kept in Rome—the Annunciation, the Assumption, the Nativity and the "Hypapante" (*i.e.* the Purification).   But there is much probability that in certain other parts of the West the Nativity was commemorated earlier.   It is clearly entered in the Calendar of St Willibrord (*c.* 704), and the mention in the Auxerre *Hieronymianum* (*c.* 600) is suggestive of a higher antiquity. What strongly supports this view is the fact that a feast of the birthday of St John the Baptist was known in the time of St Augustine, probably as early as 401.   It was inevitable that when people realized that the beheading of the Baptist and his birth were honoured by two separate celebrations, the idea would suggest itself that the birth of the Mother of God ought to be similarly commemorated.   Hence to the feast of her Assumption or Falling Asleep was added that of her Birthday. (*Cf.* the feasts of the conception of St John and of our Lady.)   The birthplace of our Lady is unknown.   An ancient tradition favours Nazareth and this was accepted in the West ; but a parallel tradition named Jerusalem, and specifically the neighbourhood of the pool of Bethesda, where a crypt under the church of St Anne is now venerated as the spot where the Mother of God was herself born.

See G. Morin in the *Revue bénédictine*, vol. v (1888), pp. 257–264 ; vii (1890), pp. 260–270; and xix (1912), pp. 469–470.   See also K. A. Kellner, *Heortology* (1908), pp. 230–231 ; L. Duchesne, *Christian Worship* (1919), pp. 269–272 ; and on the birthplace, *Analecta Bollandiana*, vol. lxii (1944), pp. 272–273.

SS. ADRIAN and NATALIA, Martyrs   (*c.* A.D. 304)

THE *acta* of St Adrian in the romantic and written-up form in which we have them relate that he was a pagan officer at the imperial court at Nicomedia.   He was present at the scourging and ill-treatment of twenty-three Christians, and at the sight of their constancy in suffering Adrian was moved to come forward and say, " Count me in with these men, for I also am a Christian ".   He was at once arrested and imprisoned, and word was brought to his young wife Natalia, who was herself a Christian and to whom he had been married for only thirteen months.   She hurried to the prison and kissed the chains which bound her husband, saying, " You are blessed, Adrian, for you have found the riches which your father and mother did not leave to you, and which the wealthy themselves have need of in the day when neither father nor mother nor children nor friends nor earthly goods are of any avail ".   She recommended him to the care and instruction of his fellows, and then Adrian sent her home, promising to let her know how things went with him.   And when he knew that the time of his passion was at hand, Adrian bribed his gaoler to let him go and take leave of his wife.   When someone told her that he was approaching the house, Natalia jumped to the conclusion that he had saved himself by apostasy and shut the door in his face.   But he explained what had happened and that the other prisoners were hostages for his return, and then they embraced and kissed and Natalia returned with him to the prison.   She stayed there a week, waiting on the confessors and dressing their wounds, till Adrian was brought before the emperor and refused to sacrifice.   Then he was scourged and

carried back to prison.   Meanwhile other women had come to help look after the
sufferers, and when the emperor heard it he forbade that they should be allowed.
Whereupon Natalia cropped her hair, put on male clothes, and bribed her way into
the gaol like any other man ; and she asked Adrian that when he was in the glory
of Heaven he should pray for her that she might live sinless in the world and soon
follow him out of it.   The martyrs were sentenced to have their limbs broken, and
Natalia asked that her husband might suffer first and so be spared the trial of seeing
the agony of the others.   When he was dragged to the block she herself disposed
his legs and arms thereon, and knelt by while the bones were crushed with blows ;
his feet and hands were cut off, and so he died.   Natalia hid one of the severed
hands in her clothes, and when the bodies of the martyrs were heaped up to be
consumed with fire she had to be restrained from jumping in among them.

A sudden storm of rain putting the fire out, the Christians of Nicomedia were
able to gather together many relics of St Adrian and his companions, which were
taken to Argyropolis, on the Bosphorus near Byzantium, and there buried.   Some
months after St Natalia decided to follow them, for she was being persecuted by
an imperial official at Nicomedia who wanted to marry her.   So she went aboard
ship, taking her precious relic, the hand of Adrian ;   and soon after arriving at
Argyropolis she died in peace and was buried with the martyrs, among whom she
is reckoned.   The Roman Martyrology gives March 4 as the day of the death of
St Adrian and December 1 of St Natalia, today being the anniversary of the
alleged translation of their relics to Rome.   St Adrian was one of the great
popular martyrs of the past, a patron of soldiers and butchers and invoked against
plagues.

There is an Adrian, martyr at Nicomedia, mentioned on March 4, and the Roman
Martyrology takes for granted his identity with the saint here spoken of.   Tillemont, it is
true, was of this opinion ;   but the Bollandists, who print the so-called acts both in Latin
and Greek in their third volume for September, strongly urge that the two Nicomedian
Adrians are different ;   *cf.* too, the Roman Martyrology on August 26 and the *Acta Sanctorum*,
August, vol. v, pp. 808–811.   Both martyrs are alleged to have suffered at Nicomedia, and
their remains are said to have been taken to Argyropolis ;   but Adrian, the husband of Natalia,
is stated to have been put to death under Diocletian, the other under Licinius, and the rest
of their stories is entirely different.   S. Salaville has discussed the matter very patiently
in DHG., vol. i, cc. 608–611.   All that we can be sure of is that there was an early and very
considerable *cultus* of an Adrian, martyr of Nicomedia, both in East and West.

SS. EUSEBIUS, NESTABUS, ZENO AND NESTOR, MARTYRS
(*c.* A.D. 362)

IN the reign of Julian the Apostate, Eusebius, Nestabus and Zeno, three Christian
brothers who were said to have been concerned in the destruction of a heathen
temple at Gaza, were carried to prison and scourged.   Afterwards the mob in the
amphitheatre loudly demanded the punishment of the sacrilegious criminals.   It
soon became a tumult, and the people worked themselves into such a ferment that
they ran to the prison, which they forced open and, taking out the three brothers,
began to drag them about, bruising them against the pavement, and striking them
with sticks, stones, or anything that came to hand.   The very women, quitting
their work, ran the points of their spindles into them, and the cooks took the kettles
off the fire, poured scalding water upon them, and pierced them with their spits.
After the martyrs were thus mangled and their skulls so broken that the ground was

smeared with their brains, they were dragged out of the city to the place where dead beasts were thrown.   Here the people lighted a fire, burned the bodies, and mingled the bones that remained with those of the camels and asses, that it might not be easy for the Christians to distinguish them.   But a certain woman came by night and was able to pick out some of their remains, which she conveyed to another Zeno, a relative of the martyrs, who had fled to Majuma.   He kept the relics carefully until, in the reign of Theodosius, he was made bishop ; he then built a church and buried them therein.   With these three brothers there was taken a young man named Nestor, who suffered imprisonment and scourging as they had done.   But as the rioters were dragging him through the street, some took compassion on him on account of his personal beauty and they left him lying outside the gate.   He died of his wounds soon after in the house of Zeno, who afterwards buried his body with the others.

The whole of this story is based upon the church historian, Sozomen (bk v, ch. 9).   The relevant text with a commentary is given in the *Acta Sanctorum*, September, vol. iii.

ST DISIBOD   (*c.* A.D. 674)

HE is said to have been an Irishman and a bishop in his own country.   He was a zealous preacher and apostle, and he laboured hard to reform his flock, but without success ; and about the middle of the seventh century he left Ireland in discouragement to be a missionary in Germany.   With three companions he eventually founded a monastery on a hill in the valley of the Nahe, near Bingen, which became known from its founder as Disibodenberg or Diessenberg (*Mons Disibodi*), and from thence ministered and worked wonders among the surrounding inhabitants.

During the twelfth century this monastery was rebuilt by Benedictine monks from the abbey of Hirschau, and in an adjoining building was a community of nuns presided over by St Hildegard.   After she had removed to the Rupertsberg, the abbot of Mount St Disibod asked her to write a life of the holy founder of his monastery, and this she did in 1170.   The contents of this Life of St Disibod were, like nearly everything St Hildegard wrote, attributed to revelation in her visions ; but most of the so-called biography is taken up with moral and scriptural disquisitions, and the few alleged facts about St Disibod are simply the traditions then current in his monastery and of very little worth.   There is, in fact, practically nothing known certainly about him.

See the *Acta Sanctorum*, September, vol. iii, where St Hildegard's mystical dissertation is reproduced.   Falk has devoted an article to St Disibod in *Der Katholik*, of Mainz, vol. i (1880), pp. 541–547.   Wattenbach declares that down to the eleventh century nothing was known of St Disibod but his name.   He is mentioned neither in the *Félire* of Oengus nor the Martyrology of Tallaght, nor in the Roman Martyrology.

ST SERGIUS I, POPE   (A.D. 701)

DURING the long last illness of Pope Conon his archdeacon, Paschal, offered a big bribe to the imperial exarch John to secure his own succession to the papal chair. When Conon died in 687 the exarch accordingly brought about Paschal's nomination by a faction, to whom a majority opposed the archpriest Theodore; whereupon both were set aside and the priest Sergius canonically elected.   John, who had come to Rome to look after his own interests, gave his approval to Sergius—but not until he had received from him the sum of money which had been offered by

Paschal. Here was no question of simony, but rather of extortion : Sergius had been freely elected and he paid only under strong protest. The man who became pope in such distressing circumstances was a Syrian, son of an Antiochene merchant, who had been brought up in Palermo.

The earlier years of his pontificate were disturbed by troubles arising out of the Council *in Trullo* (*Concilium Quinisextum*), which was convened at Constantinople to supplement the acts of the fifth and sixth oecumenical councils by drawing up some canons of discipline. Over two hundred bishops were present, all orientals except one, and they enacted 102 canons, some of which were inspired by a certain hostility to and defiance of the West. The mischief of this gathering was that it professed to legislate, not for the East alone, but for the whole Church ; and so, when the emperor, Justinian II, in 693 sent its acts for the pope to approve for the Western church, Sergius refused to sign them. So the emperor sent the commandant of his bodyguard, one Zachary, to fetch the recalcitrant pontiff to Constantinople. Sergius appealed to the exarch, and the citizens of Rome, reinforced by troops from Ravenna, gathered in force and made a violent demonstration. Zachary was terrified, fled to Sergius for protection, and hid in the pope's bed. Sergius went out to pacify the people (not, we may suspect, without some quiet feeling of amusement), but they would not disperse until the gallant soldier from Constantinople had been taken from his refuge and escorted from the city. Doubtless this affair would have had serious consequences for Sergius, but Justinian II was deposed soon after. Nor does it appear that any Roman pontiff has done much more about the canons of *Quinisextum* than tacitly to approve them for the Eastern church.

It was during this pontificate that there arrived in Rome the king of the West Saxons, Caedwalla, who had " quitted his crown for the sake of the Lord and His everlasting kingdom ", as has been narrated herein under April 20. St Sergius baptized him on the vigil of Easter in 689. The pope had other contacts with England, and in 695 he consecrated the Northumbrian St Willibrord bishop and gave every encouragement to his mission in Friesland. St Sergius received a deputation of monks from St Ceolfrid, to whom he granted confirmation of the privileges of their abbey of Wearmouth and Jarrow, and in 701 the pope wrote to Ceolfrid asking him to send " that religious servant of God, Bede, a priest of your monastery " to Rome, as he was in need of the advice of learned men. Sergius promised that Bede should be returned as soon as the business was done, but it is certain he did not go, for St Bede himself tells us that he never left his monastery. Sergius was an alumnus of the Roman *schola cantorum*, and he seems to have been actively concerned with the liturgy and its music ; in particular, the *Liber pontificalis* states that he directed that the *Agnus Dei* " should be sung by clergy and people at the breaking of the Lord's body " at Mass, and he ordained that the Roman church should observe the four feasts of our Lady already kept at Constantinople, namely, her birthday, her purification, the Annunciation and her " falling alseep ".

The personal character of St Sergius I can be judged only by his public acts and the tradition of the Church, wherein he appears, in the words of Alcuin, a holy and most worthy successor of St Peter, second to none in piety. He died in the year 701, and was buried in St Peter's.

An entry " Sergii Papae Romae " under September 7 in the first hand of the Calendar of St Willibrord serves as a *terminus a quo* from which to date that document. It also proves that the *cultus* must have begun immediately after the pope's death. The *Liber Pontificalis*, with Duchesne's notes, and the letters calendared in Jaffé are of primary importance as sources ; but Sergius belongs to ecclesiastical history. See, however, the *Acta Sanctorum*, September, vol. iii ; Grisar, *Geschichte Roms und der Päpste ;* and especially Mgr Mann, *Lives of the Popes*, vol. i, part 2, pp. 77–104.

ST CORBINIAN, Bishop (A.D. 725)

THIS early apostle of Bavaria was born at Châtres, near Melun, in France. He was baptized Waldegiso after his father, but his mother afterwards changed his name to Corbinian, after herself. He lived as a recluse for fourteen years in a cell which he built near a chapel in the same place. The fame of his sanctity, which was increased by the occurrence of several miracles and the prudence of the advice which he gave in spiritual matters, made his name famous, and he admitted several persons to form themselves into a religious community under his discipline. The distraction which this gave him made him think of seeking some new place where he might live in obscurity, and he determined to go to Rome. While crossing the Brenner occurred the legendary incident which gave the saint his emblem of a bear. A bear attacked and killed Corbinian's pack-horse, so he ordered his servant to put the leading-rein and pack on the bear. Which was done, and they proceeded, and with the tamed bear arrived at Rome. But not before a certain lord at Trent had stolen the saint's best horse, and another at Pavia stolen his second best. Retribution soon overtook both these thieves, for the one died and the other lost forty-two of his own horses from elephantiasis. Pope St. Gregory II sent Corbinian, who may already have been a bishop, to preach in Bavaria, where he put himself under the protection of Duke Grimoald. After having much increased the number of the Christians, he fixed his headquarters at Freising, in Upper Bavaria, which, however, did not become a regular episcopal see till St Boniface made it such in 739.

St Corbinian discovered that his patron Grimoald, though a Christian, had defied the discipline of the Church by marrying his brother's widow, Biltrudis. Corbinian refused to have anything to do with the duke until they separated. But the lady Biltrudis was not at all satisfied and pursued Corbinian with persecution in the hope that he would allow her to be reinstated ; she abused him as a foreign interloper, specifically, a British bishop —which of course he wasn't. At length she even conspired to have him murdered. The saint took refuge at Meran, and remained in semi-exile until Grimoald (who had rejoined the lady) was killed in battle shortly after and Biltrudis was carried off by the Franks. He was then recalled by Grimoald's successor, and continued his missionary work throughout Bavaria. Corbinian was buried at a monastery he had founded at Obermais, at Meran, but his body was brought to Freising in 765 by Aribo, his second successor and biographer. Aribo says that St Corbinian was a man easily aroused to anger, and a story in illustration is told concerning a woman of Freising who was reported to deal in black magic. Meeting her one day in the street carrying some meat he asked what she was about, and was told that she was going to try and cure a sick man by her art. Corbinian jumped off his horse, gave the woman a sound thrashing with his own hands, and gave the meat away to the poor.

Of Corbinian we have an excellent medieval life by Arbeo or Aribo, who lived in the same century and was one of his successors at Freising. This biography was afterwards interpolated with legendary incidents, the episode of the bear, for example, being one of the additions. After editing the genuine text in the fourth and sixth volumes of MGH., *Scriptores Merov*., Bruno Krusch produced a very handy edition (1920) *in usum scholarum*. See also the *Acta Sanctorum*, September, vol. iii.

9 : ST GORGONIUS, Martyr   (Date Unknown)

THE Western church today keeps the feast of St Gorgonius, who according to the Roman Martyrology and the lesson read at Matins was an official of the Emperor Diocletian at Nicomedia ; with his colleague Dorotheus he was put to death for protesting against the torments inflicted on a certain Christian, one Peter ; and the body of Gorgonius was eventually taken to Rome, and buried on the Via Lavicana (" Latina " by mistake), " between the two laurels ".

There is confusion here between two martyrs, both called Gorgonius. The one buried on the Via Lavicana, the original object of today's commemoration, was not the Gorgonius of Nicomedia, whose body was not translated to Rome. Of the first we know nothing, eecept that his *cultus* is tolerably ancient ; the other, with his companions, is well attested and appears in calendars of both East and West on March 12, under which date he is noticed herein.

The Breviary is unquestionably mistaken here in identifying the Gorgonius of Nicomedia with the Gorgonius who was buried *inter duas lauros* on the Via Lavicana. The two martyrs were distinct, as Delehaye, Quentin and J. P. Kirsch are all agreed ; and Dorotheus was associated not with the Roman Gorgonius, but with the Gorgonius of Nicomedia, of whose sufferings an account has been left by Eusebius. The martyrologist Ado was the author of the confusion, as Quentin, *Martyrologes historiques*, pp. 613–615, has fully demonstrated. See also the paper of Kirsch in *Ehrengabe Deutscher Wissenschaft für J. G. von Sachsen* (1920), pp. 58–84 ; and especially CMH., pp. 497–498. *Cf.* SS. Peter and Gorgonius on March 12.

ST ISAAC, or SAHAK, I, Katholikos of the Armenians   (A.D. 439)

AT the end of the fourth century the state of matrimony was still not a bar to the episcopate in the Armenian church, and St Isaac was the son of the katholikos St Nerses I (though he was probably a widower when ordained). There were indeed families in which the episcopate was hereditary, and Isaac himself was the great-great-great-grandson of St Gregory the Enlightener ; to abolish this abuse and do away with married bishops was to be part of Isaac's work. He studied at Constantinople, where he married. After the death of his wife he became a monk and devoted himself to learning. When Isaac was called to rule the Armenian church both it and the nation were in a very critical state. The two divisions of Armenia were nominally ruled by princes subject to their Byzantine and Persian masters. Some years previously the successor of St Nerses I had repudiated the dependence of his church on Caesarea, of which St Basil was at that time the metropolitan, and the Armenians were in consequence regarded as being more or less in schism. Though St Isaac found a small pro-Caesarean party he disregarded it, and got himself recognized at Constantinople as primate of the Armenian church, which would appear to be an appeal to the imperial power as against the rights of his true patriarch at Antioch. This bold move no doubt was partly due to Persian pressure, but it ushered in a period of some ecclesiastical progress, which was joined with the beginning of the golden age of Armenian letters. His father Nerses had begun the reform of his church by bringing it more into line with Byzantine custom and law, and Isaac completed this work. Byzantine canon law was strictly enforced, which meant the end of married bishops, and Isaac was in fact the last of the house of St Gregory the Enlightener to rule over the church which is sometimes called after him " Gregorian ".   Monasticism began to flourish, schools and hospitals were established, and churches destroyed by the Persians rebuilt.   Isaac had to contend on the one hand with the influence of Persian paganism and on the other with those Christians who resented the enforcement of ecclesiastical discipline.

When Theodosius II came to the throne of Constantinople in the year 408 he adopted the policy of promoting Greek influence throughout Armenia by encouraging the diffusion of Christianity, and he gave invaluable support to the undertakings of St Isaac who, faced with Greek ambitions in the small Byzantine part of his territory and the absolute forbiddance of Greek language and culture in all the rest of it, made this disparity a unity by taking elements from both Byzantine and Syrian sources and giving them an Armenian dress.   For this purpose it was necessary to provide an Armenian alphabet, which was done by St Mesrop.   The first literary work undertaken was a translation of the Bible.   The Armenian version of the Old Testament is valuable for biblical scholars, and several of the translations of other books are of importance because the originals are now lost ; by the time of Isaac's death the Armenians already had the works of Greek and Syrian doctors in their own tongue, and the beginnings of a native literature had been made.   He also contributed to the formation of the national liturgy from that of Caesarea, now represented by the Byzantine " St Basil ".

In the year 428 the Persians drove out the Armenian tributary prince, and Isaac, whose leaning towards Christian Byzantium was notorious, was driven into retirement in the western corner of the country.   There is a story that the Emperor Theodosius told his general Anatolius to build the city of Theodosiopolis (Karin, Erzerum) to shelter the fugitive bishop, but that city has a much older origin and had already been renamed in honour of the emperor thirteen years before.   After some years he was invited to return to his see, but did not at once do so, appointing a vicar in his stead.   Upon his death Isaac resumed the government, but he was now very old and could not for that reason attend the Council of Ephesus, whose acts he accepted in 435.   He seems to have retained the first Armenian ecclesiastical centre at Ashtishat as his see, in which place he died at the age of about ninety-two.   He is named in the great intercession of the Armenian Mass, and is called " the Great ".

The principal sources are Moses of Khoren, Lazarus of Pharp and other chronicles which may be consulted in Langlois, *Collection des historiens de l'Arménie*, vol. ii.   Among modern books Sahak is frequently referred to both in F. Tournebize, *Histoire politique et religieuse de l'Arménie* (1901) and in S. Weber, *Die Katholische Kirche in Armenien* (1903). See also F. C. Conybeare, " The Armenian Canons of St Sahak ", in the *American Journal of Theology*, 1898, pp. 828–848.

ST KIERAN, OR CIARAN, ABBOT OF CLONMACNOIS   (A.D. 556 ?)

KIERAN of Clonmacnois, sometimes called " the Younger " to distinguish him from St Kieran of Saighir, was born in Roscommon or Westmeath.   His father Beoit was a cartwright, but he is also called a carpenter, like the ostensible father of our Lord.   Kieran was said to have died at the age of thirty-three (though he was probably older) and other parallels to the life of Christ can be found in his legends. It has been suggested that these were unconscious inventions on the part of simple people impressed by the holiness of Kieran's character.   His mother was named

Darerca and belonged to the tribe of the Glasraige, granddaughter of a bard called
Glas, and both families may have been of pre-Celtic blood.   Owing to oppression
by his chieftain, Beoit fled from Antrim into Connacht, and there Kieran was born,
one of seven children.

Several fabulous incidents are told of his boyhood, as that he revivified a dead
horse, changed water into honey, and played a practical joke on his mother.   She
was dyeing and turned him out of the house, " for it was thought unbecoming that
males should be in the house when garments were being dyed ".*   Kieran was
annoyed, and " May there be a dun stripe on them ", he exclaimed.   The clothes
came out of the blue dye with a dun stripe accordingly, and they were put in again.
This time they came out white.   But at the third dyeing Kieran had recovered his
temper, and the dye was so blue that not only the clothes but also dogs, cats and
trees that it came into contact with were turned blue.   Kieran had some teaching
from the deacon Uis at Fuerty, and when he was about fifteen he asked his parents
to give him a cow for his support, that he might go to the school of St Finnian at
Clonard.   Darerca refused, so he blessed one of the cows and she followed him
for the rest of his life, the Dun Cow of Kieran.   At Clonard he was one of those
twelve holy ones afterwards known as the Twelve Apostles of Ireland (see St
Finnian, December 12), and at this time was the greatest among them, for whereas
the others had to grind their own corn every day, angels would come and grind it
for Kieran.   St Finnian esteemed him above the rest, so that all the others except
Colmcille were jealous of him, and when the daughter of the king of Cuala was sent
to learn to read, her instruction was confided to St Kieran.   So indifferent was he
to her person that it was said that he saw nothing but her feet.

When the time came for St Kieran to leave Clonard, Finnian wanted to give
up his place to him, but the young disciple refused.   " Leave not your monastery
for any save God only ", he said, " seeing He has favoured you above us all.'   Then
he departed and made his way to the Arans, where St Enda still ruled on Inishmore.
Here he lived for seven years, and became so skilful at threshing and winnowing
that not a grain of corn could be seen in the chaff-heaps.   Then one day Enda and
Kieran saw a vision of a great tree growing beside a river in the middle of Ireland,
whose branches overhung the sea, laden with fruit which the birds pecked.   And
Enda said : " That tree is yourself, for you are great before God and man and
Ireland shall be full of your honour.   It shall be protected under your shadow and
many shall be satisfied with the grace of your fasting and your prayer.   Go,
therefore, at the word of God to the shore of the stream and found a church there."
Then Kieran arose and left Aran and came to Scattery Island, where he visited
St Senan who gave him a new cloak, a kindness which Kieran afterwards repaid
by floating another cloak down the Shannon to Senan.   Afterwards he proceeded
on his journey towards the middle of Ireland and came to a place called Isel where
he stayed in a monastery for a time, but had to leave because the monks complained
that his excessive generosity left them nothing.   He followed a stag, which led him
to Lough Ree, above Athlone, where he went across to Inis Aingin (Hare Island)
and lived in the monastery there.   His holiness and the number of his disciples
excited the envy of a priest, called Daniel and said to be a Briton, who tried to get
him expelled, but Kieran won him over by the gift of a golden cup, as a token of his

* Ingenious explanations and suggestions have been made about this statement.   But
need it be anything more than the gloss of a monastic writer who did not realize that hard-
worked housewives don't want boys messing around when they are busy ?

good will.   At last he set out on his journey again, having eight companions.   He was urged to settle at a beautiful place called Ard Manntain, but he refused, saying, " If we live here we shall have much of the riches of the world, and few souls will go from us to Heaven ".   But when they came to the grassy ridge of Ard Tiprat, on the west bank of the Shannon in Offaly, Kieran said : " We will stay here, for there shall be many souls going to Heaven from this place, and God and man shall visit it for ever."   To Diarmaid MacCerrbeoil was promised the high-kingship of Ireland, and together with St Kieran he planted on his land the first post of the monastery that was to be famous as Clonmacnois.   One account says that as they were about to plant the post a wizard, who feared for his authority, said, " This is not a good hour for beginning, for the sign of the hour is contrary to the beginnings of building ".   To which St Kieran made reply : " Wizard, I fix this post into the ground against your sign.   I care nothing for the art of wizards, but do all my works in the name of my Lord Jesus Christ."

The rest of the records of Kieran are anecdotes concerning his virtues and the miracles to which they gave rise ; one of them, about that " boy of great wit but mischievous and wanton ", Crichidh of Cluain, has already been told in the life of St Kieran of Ossory (March 5).   There is extant a " law " or monastic rule attributed to St Kieran the Younger which consists of moral and ascetical precepts of a very severe kind ; it is probably not of his authorship but accurately represents the spirit that obtained in his and other early Irish monasteries, a spirit of austerity that has characterized Gaelic religion down to our own day.   According to his lives, St Kieran lived to govern his monastery only seven months.   When the time of his death was near he asked to be carried out to the Little Hill.   Then he looked up at the heavens and said, " Awful is this road upward."   " Not for you is it awful ", replied his monks.   " Indeed, I do not know ", said he, " that I have transgressed any of the commandments of God, yet even David the son of Jesse and Paul the Apostle dreaded this way."   They made to take away a stone from under him for his greater comfort, but he stopped them.   " Put it under my shoulders ", he said, " ' He that shall persevere unto the end, he shall be saved.' "—" Then angels filled the space between Heaven and earth to receive his soul."

The account of the death of St Kieran is one of the few almost certainly authentic stories in his *vitae*, but is immediately followed by the statement that he came to life for the space of twenty-four hours to converse with St Kevin of Glendalough.   Clonmacnois remained his living monument for many centuries, the chief school of Ireland and the burial place of princes.   During the evil days of the ninth and tenth centuries its monks must often have called to mind the question put by their predecessors to their dying founder who had prophesied persecution.   " What shall we do in that time ?   Is it by your relics we shall stay, or go elsewhere ? " and his reply : " Arise and leave my bones as the bones of a deer are left in the sun.   For it is better for you to live with me in Heaven than to stay here with my relics."   Under the form *Queranus* the name of St Kieran figures in the Roman Martyrology, and his feast is kept throughout Ireland.

Four short lives of St Kieran have been preserved to us, three in Latin and one in Irish. The first Latin life has been critically edited by C. Plummer in VSH. with occasional illustrations from the others ; the Irish life was made accessible by Whitley Stokes in his *Lives of Saints from the Book of Lismore*.   But translations of all these with much other matter may be found in the admirable little volume of R. A. S. Macalister, *The Latin and Irish*

Lives of Ciaran (1921).   See also the *Acta Sanctorum*, September, vol. iii ; J. Ryan, *Irish Monasticism* ; J. F. Kenney, *The Sources for the Early History of Ireland*, vol. i ; and L. Gougaud, *Christianity in Celtic Lands* (1932).   For the cutting short of Kieran's life, and his elegy on it, see *Analecta Bollandiana*, vol. lxix (1951), pp. 102–106.

ST AUDOMARUS, OR OMER, BISHOP OF THÉROUANNE   (c. A.D. 670)

THE name of St Audomarus is more familiar to English readers in its French form of Omer, on account of the famous penal-times Jesuit college in the then episcopal city of Saint-Omer ; a college which afterwards came into the hands of the secular clergy, over which Alban Butler presided for a time, and at which he died.   The place of Omer's birth was not far from Coutances.   The thoughts of his parents were wholly taken up in him, and his education was their chief care.   He made the most happy progress, and his father upon the death of his wife accompanied his son to the monastery of Luxeuil.   St Eustace, who had succeeded St Columban, the founder, in the government of that house, received them kindly, and they made their religious profession together.   The humility, obedience, devotion and purity of manners which shone forth in Omer distinguished him among his brethren even in that house of saints.   After some twenty years from his becoming a monk, Thérouanne, the capital of the Morini, stood in need of a zealous pastor ; that country, which contained what is now called the Pas-de-Calais, was overrun with vice and error, so that King Dagobert was looking for a person well qualified to establish the faith and practice of the gospel in that district.   St Omer was pointed out as capable for this arduous employment, and proposed to the king by St Achaire, Bishop of Noyon and Tournai, so about 637 Omer, who had been happy and content in his retreat, was suddenly called on to leave his solitude.   Upon receiving the command, he cried out, " How great is the difference between the secure harbour in which I now enjoy calm, and that tempestuous ocean into which I am pushed, against my will and destitute of experience ".

The first undertaking of his pastoral care was to re-establish the faith in its purity among the few Christians he found, whose reformation was a task no less difficult than the conversion of idolaters.   Yet such was the success of his labours that he left his diocese almost equal to those that were most flourishing in France. His sermons were full of a fire which could scarcely be resisted, but his exemplary life preached still more powerfully ; for it encouraged others to spend themselves freely in feeding the poor, comforting the sick, reconciling enemies, and serving everyone without any other view than that of their salvation and the glory of God. This was the character of the holy bishop and his fellow labourers who were employed under his direction.   The chief among these were St Mommolinus, St Bertrand, and St Bertinus, monks whom St Omer invited to his assistance from Luxeuil, and whose association with him has been related in the life of the third-named on the 5th of this month.   St Omer founded with them the monastery of Sithiu, which became one of the greatest seminaries of sacred learning in France. The lives of St Omer recount a number of not very convincing miracles attributed to him.   In his old age he was blind some years before his death, but that infliction made no abatement in his pastoral concern for his flock.   The third and least reliable biography says that when St Aubert, Bishop of Arras, translated the relics of St Vedast to the monastery which he had built in his honour, St Omer was present and recovered his sight for a short time on that occasion.   St Omer died probably soon after 670.

The least unsatisfactory Life of St Omer is that already referred to in the bibliographical note to St Bertinus, on September 5. The edition of that text by W. Levison, there spoken of, is accompanied by a discussion of the relations between the different lives printed in the *Acta Sanctorum*, September, vol. iii.

ST BETTELIN   (EIGHTH CENTURY)

IN the history of Croyland which bears the name of the eleventh-century abbot Ingulf, though compiled after his time, we are told that the great hermit St Guthlac had four disciples, who led penitential lives in separate cells not far from their director in the midst of the fens of Lincolnshire. These were Cissa, Egbert, Tatwin and Bettelin (Beccelin, Berthelm). The last-named, after he had overcome a temptation which once came to him while shaving St Guthlac to cut his throat and succeed to his authority, became of all others the most dear to his master. When St Guthlac was near death he counselled Bettelin with such wisdom that " he never before or after heard the like ", and in his last moments sent him with a loving message to his sister, St Pega. St Bettelin and his companions lived on at Croyland under Kenulf, first abbot of the monastery founded there by King Ethelbald of Mercia, and there died and were buried.

St Bettelin (or another) was honoured as patron of the town of Stafford, which boasted his relics. But the story of his life as told by the chronicler Capgrave is, as Alban Butler says, " of no authority ". It is, in fact, popular fiction, according to which Bettelin was a son of the ruler of Stafford who went on a visit to Ireland. There he fell in love with a princess, who ran away with him to England. While making their way through a forest the princess was overtaken by the pains of child-birth, and Bettelin hurried away to try and find a midwife. While he was gone the girl was found by a pack of hungry wolves, and Bettelin returned only to find them tearing her to pieces. The loss of his bride and baby in so terrible a fashion drove Bettelin to offer himself to God in a solitary life, and he became an anchorite near Stafford. On the death of his father he was induced to leave his cell to help in driving off a usurping invader, which he did by the assistance of an angel sent from Heaven to oppose the demon who led the opposing forces. Then Bettelin returned to his cell and lived there for the rest of his days.

Very little seems to be known of St Bettelin or Berthelm. In the *Acta Sanctorum* an account is printed from a manuscript source which is in substance identical with that preserved by Capgrave in the *Nova Legenda Angliae*. See also Stanton's *Menology*, pp. 389 and 666. Felix, the early writer on St Guthlac, mentions his disciple Bettelin by name ; the Stafford story seems to be concerned with a St Berthelme whose relics were venerated at Fécamp : A. M. Zimmermann, *Kalendarium benedictinum*, vol. ii, p. 564 ; iii, p. 94 ; iv, p. 75.

BD SERAPHINA SFORZA, WIDOW   (*c.* A.D. 1478)

SHE was born at Urbino about the year 1432, the daughter of Guy, Count of Montefeltro, by his second wife, Catherine Colonna. In baptism she received the name of Sueva. Her parents died while she was a child, she was sent to Rome to be brought up in the household of her uncle, Prince Colonna, and at the age of about sixteen she was joined in marriage to Alexander Sforza, Lord of Pesaro. This man was a widower, with two children, and for some years she lived very happily with her husband. Then he was called away to take up arms on behalf of his brother, the duke of Milan, leaving his estate to the care of Sueva, and his absence was prolonged.   On his return, none the better man for so long a period of campaigning and absence from home, Alexander began an intrigue with a woman called Pacifica, the wife of a local physician.   Sueva used all the means at her disposal to win her husband back, but with so little success that he added physical cruelty and insult to unfaithfulness.   He even tried to poison her, and thenceforward the unhappy woman gave up active efforts towards reconciliation, and confined herself to prayer and quietness.   This served only to irritate Alexander, and he at last drove her from the house with violence, telling her to take herself off to some convent.

Sueva was received as a guest by the Poor Clares of the convent of Corpus Christi, where she lived the life of the nuns ; eventually she was clothed and took the name of Seraphina.   This was exactly what Alexander wanted, and, feeling himself free, he went from bad to worse ; Pacifica was flaunted about Pesaro as though she were his lawful wife, and she even had the insolence to visit the convent wearing Sueva's jewels.   Sister Seraphina was an exemplary nun and she did not forget her obligations to her husband.   She never ceased to pray and offer her penances for his conversion, and before his death in 1473 her desire was fulfilled.

That is the substance of Bd Seraphina's story as it is commonly told.   Unhappily further research in contemporary evidence suggests that at the time of her leaving the world she was not so entirely an innocent victim as has been assumed. Even if her husband's charges of unfaithfulness were false, there is some evidence that she was privy to a plot against him.   We find ourselves very much in the Italian *beau monde* of the *quattrocento*.   But Sueva entered the convent in 1457, when she was twenty-five years old, and whatever she may have had to repent of she had more than twenty years in which to grow holy in the living of a most austere religious rule.   This she did, and the local *cultus* of Bd Seraphina was approved by Pope Benedict XIV in 1754.

There is an anonymous life printed with prolegomena in the *Acta Sanctorum*, September, vol. iii.   But in 1903 B. Feliciangeli published his study, *Sulla monacazione di Sueva Montefeltro-Sforza*, *Ricerche*, which made public certain new documents, throwing fresh light on the subject.   This evidence was unknown to such earlier biographers as Mgr Alegiani and Léon, *Auréole séraphique* (Eng. trans.), vol. iii, pp. 114–120.   The problem is discussed by Fr Van Ortroy in *Analecta Bollandiana*, vol. xxiv (1905), pp. 311–313.

BD LOUISA OF SAVOY, WIDOW   (A.D. 1503)

THE very high, mighty and illustrious lady, Madame Louisa of Savoy, who was destined by God to become a humble nun of the Poor Clares, was born in 1461, the daughter of Bd Amadeus IX, Duke of Savoy, grand-daughter through her mother Yolande of King Charles VII of France, niece of King Louis XI, and cousin to St Joan of Valois.   Her father died before she was nine and she was admirably brought up by her mother and showed from a very early age indications of spiritual qualities out of the ordinary ; Catherine de Saulx, one of her maids-of-honour, wrote that " she was so sweet and generous, debonair and gracious, that she gave affection to everyone and was engaging and charming to all ".   At the age of eighteen she married Hugh de Châlons, Lord of Nozeroy, a man as good as he was wealthy and powerful, and together they set themeslves to live a truly Christian life.   Both by example and precept they set a high standard for all living on their estates, and their house seemed a monastery by contrast with many noble establishments of that time ; loose swearing and profanity was particularly discouraged, and Madame Louisa provides the first recorded example of a poor-box into which every person who indulged in bad language had to put a contribution : but men had to kiss the ground because that was a more effective deterrent for them.   Louisa exercised a wide charity towards the sick and needy, widows and orphans, and especially lepers, and she used to say of the dances and shows that took place in her house that they were like mushrooms, " of which the best are not worth much ".

After nine years of wedded happiness her husband died, and, having no children, Louisa began to prepare to retire from the world.   It took two years to set her affairs in order, during which time she wore the Franciscan tertiary habit and learned to recite the Divine Office, getting up at midnight for Matins.   Every Friday she took the discipline, she distributed her fortune, and overcame, or disregarded, the objections of her relatives and friends.   Then with her two maids-of-honour, Catherine de Saulx and Charlotte de Saint-Maurice, she was admitted to the Poor Clare convent of Orbe, which monastery had been founded by the mother of Hugh de Châlons and occupied with a community by St Colette in 1427.   Bd Louisa had been a model for maids, for wives and for widows, and henceforward was to be an exemplary religious.   As with so many of high birth, her humility was sincere and unaffected : if she was to wash dishes, help in the kitchen, sweep the cloisters, well ; if she was to be an abbess, well also.   In this office she was especially solicitous in the service of the friars of her order, and any whose journeyings took them past the convent were always most carefully looked after : the presence of the fathers and brothers was a blessing from God, and nothing would lack that was required for the sons of " our blessed father, Monseigneur St Francis ".   The ancient *cultus* of this servant of God, who was called to Him when only forty-two years old, was approved in 1839.

There is a life by Catherine de Saulx, who had been lady-in-waiting to Louisa and who followed her into the convent at Orbe.   This was edited with annotations, etc., by A. M. Jeanneret (1860).   See also F. Jeunet and J. H. Thorin, *Vie de la bse Louise de Savoie* (1884), and *cf. Revue des questions historiques*, t. xxi, pp. 335–336.   In the English translation of Leon, *Auréole Séraphique*, Bd Louisa occurs in vol. iii, pp. 267–271.   E. Fedelini produced a slight sketch of *Les bienheureux de la maison de Savoie* (1925), in which Bd Louisa finds a place.

ST PETER CLAVER   (A.D. 1654)

In the United States of America, this is the principal feast for this date.

IF to England belongs the honour of having begun the work of abolishing the slave-trade in 1815, it was she also who, in the person of such national heroes as Sir John Hawkins, played a great part in establishing that trade between Africa and the New World in the sixteenth century.   And of the heroes who in the intervening period devoted their lives to the interests of the victims of this nefarious exploitation, the most were from countries which had not received the enlightenment of the Reformers.   Among them none was greater than St Peter Claver, a native of that Spain whose history in his time is represented for most Englishmen solely by the buccaneering of an unscrupulous imperialism and the fantastic cruelty of an ecclesiastical inquisition.   He was born at Verdu, in Catalonia, about 1581, and as he showed fine qualities of mind and spirit was destined for the Church and sent to study at the University of Barcelona.   Here he graduated with distinction and, after receiving minor orders, determined to offer himself to the Society of Jesus. He was received into the novitiate of Tarragona at the age of twenty, and was sent to the college of Montesione at Palma, in Majorca.   Here he met St Alphonsus

Rodriguez, who was porter in the college, though with a reputation far above his humble office, and this meeting was to set the direction of Peter Claver's life.   He studied the science of the saints at the feet of the lay-brother, and Alphonsus conceived a corresponding regard for the capabilities of the young scholastic, and saw in him a man fit for a new, arduous and neglected work.   He fired him with the idea of going to the help of the many who were without spiritual ministrations in the colonies of the New World.

In after years St Peter Claver said that St Alphonsus had actually foretold to him that he would go and the very place wherein he would work.   Moved by the fervour of these exhortations Peter Claver approached his provincial, offering himself for the West Indies, and was told that his vocation would be decided in due course by his superiors.   He was sent to Barcelona for his theology and after two years was, at his further request, chosen to represent the province of Aragon on the mission of Spanish Jesuits being sent to New Granada.   He left Spain for ever in April 1610, and after a wearisome voyage landed with his companions at Cartagena, in what is now the republic of Colombia.   Thence he went to the Jesuit house of Santa Fé to complete his theological studies, and was employed as well as sacristan, porter, infirmarian and cook, and was sent for his tertianship to the new house of the Society at Tunja.   He returned to Cartagena in 1615 and was there ordained priest.

By this time the slave trade had been established in the Americas for nearly a hundred years, and the port of Cartagena was one of its principal centres, being conveniently situated as a clearing-house.   The trade had recently been given a considerable *impetus*, for the local Indians were not physically fitted to work in the gold and silver mines, and there was a big demand for Negroes from Angola and the Congo.   These were bought in West Africa for four crowns a head, or bartered for goods, and sold in America for two hundred crowns.   The conditions under which they were conveyed across the Atlantic were so foul and inhuman as to be beyond belief, and it was reckoned that there would be a loss in each cargo by death during the six or seven weeks' voyage of at least a third ; but in spite of this an average of ten thousand living slaves was landed in Cartagena every year.   In spite of the condemnation of this great crime by Pope Paul III and by many lesser authorities, this " supreme villainy ", as slave-trading was designated by Pius IX, continued to flourish ; all that most of the owners did in response to the voice of the Church was to have their slaves baptized.   They received no religious instruction or ministration, no alleviation of their physical condition, so that the sacrament of baptism became to them a very sign and symbol of their oppression and wretchedness.   The clergy were practically powerless ; all they could do was to protest and to devote themselves to the utmost to individual ministration, corporal and material, among the tens of thousands of suffering human beings.   They had no charitable funds at their disposal, no plaudits from well-disposed audiences ; they were hampered and discouraged by the owners and often rebuffed by the Negroes themselves.

At the time of Father Claver's ordination the leader in this work was Father Alfonso de Sandoval, a great Jesuit missionary who spent forty years in the service of the slaves, and after working under him Peter Claver declared himself " the slave of the Negroes for ever ".   Although by nature shy and without self-confidence, he threw himself into the work, and pursued it not with unreliable enthusiasm but with method and organization.   He enlisted bands of assistants, whether by money, goods or services, and as soon as a slave-ship entered the port he went to wait on its living freight.   The slaves were disembarked and shut up in the yards where crowds came to watch them, " idle gazers ", wrote Father de Sandoval, " drawn thither by curiosity and careful not to come too close ".   Hundreds of men who had been for several weeks shut up without even the care given to cattle in the ship's hold were now, well, ill or dying, herded together in a confined space in a climate that was unwholesome from damp heat.   So horrible was the scene and revolting the conditions that a friend who came with Father Claver once could never face it again, and of Father de Sandoval himself it was written in one of the " relations " of his province that, " when he heard a vessel of Negroes was come into port he was at once covered with a cold sweat and death-like pallor at the recollection of the indescribable fatigue and unspeakable work on the previous like occasions. The experience and practice of years never accustomed him to it."   Into these yards or sheds St Peter Claver plunged, with medicines and food, bread, brandy, lemons, tobacco to distribute among the Negroes, some of whom were too frightened, others too ill, to accept them.   " We must speak to them with our hands, before we try to speak to them with our lips ", Claver would say.   When he came upon any who were dying he baptized them, and then sought out all babies born on the voyage that he might baptize them.   During the time that the Negroes spent in the sheds, penned so closely that they had to sleep almost upon one another and freely handed on their diseases, St Peter Claver cared for the bodies of the sick and the souls of all.

Unlike many, even among the clergy, he did not consider that ignorance of their languages absolved him from the obligation of instructing them in the truths of religion and morals and bringing to their degraded spirits the consolation of the words of Christ.   He had a band of seven interpreters, one of whom spoke four Negro dialects, and with their help he taught the slaves and prepared them for baptism, not only in groups but individually ; for they were too backward and slow and the language difficulty too great for him to make himself understood otherwise.   He made use of pictures, showing our Lord suffering on the cross for them and popes, princes and other great ones of the " white men " standing by and rejoicing at the baptism of a Negro ; above all did he try to instil in them some degree of self-respect, to give them at least some idea that as redeemed human beings they had dignity and worth, even if as slaves they were outcast and despised. Not otherwise could he hope to arouse in them a shame and contrition for their vices more perfect than that evoked by the picture of Hell which he held up as a warning.   He showed them that they were loved even more than they were abused, and that that divine love must not be outraged by evil ways, by cruelty and lust. Each one had to be taken apart and drilled, time and again, even in so simple a matter as making the sign of the cross or in learning the prayer of love and repentance that each had to know : " Jesus Christ, Son of God, thou shalt be my Father and my Mother and all my good.   I love thee much.   I am sorry for having sinned against thee.   Lord, I love thee much, much, much."   How difficult was his task in teaching is shown by the fact that at baptism each batch of ten catechumens was given the same name—to help them to remember it.   It is estimated that in forty years St Peter Claver thus instructed and baptized over 300,000 slaves.   When there was time and opportunity he took the same trouble to teach them how properly to use the sacrament of penance, and in one year is said to have heard the confessions of more than five thousand.   He never tired of persuading them from the occasions of sin or of urging the owners to care for the souls of the slaves ; he became so great a moral force in Cartagena that a story is told of a Negro frightening off a harlot who was pestering him in the street by saying, " Look ! Here comes Father Claver ".

When the slaves were at length allotted and sent off to the mines and plantations, St Peter could only appeal to them for the last time with renewed earnestness, for he would be able to keep in touch with only a very few of them.   He had a steady confidence that God would care for them and, not his least difference from some social-reformers of a later age, he did not regard the most brutal of the slave-owners as despicable barbarians, beyond the mercy or might of God.   They also had souls to be saved, no less than the Negroes, and to the masters St Peter appealed for physical and spiritual justice, for their own sakes no less than for that of their slaves.   To the cynical mind the trust of the saint in the goodness of human nature must seem *naïf*, and no doubt could he have known he would have been far more often disappointed than not.   But the conclusion cannot be avoided that only the worst of the Spanish masters can be compared for iniquity with, say, the English slave-owners of Jamaica in the seventeenth-eighteenth centuries, whose physical cruelty was no less than fiendish and moral indifference diabolical.   The laws of Spain at least provided for the marriage of slaves, forbade their separation from their families, and defended them from unjust seizure after liberation.   St Peter Claver did all he could to provide for the observance of these laws, and every spring after Easter he would make a tour of those plantations nearer Cartagena in order to see how his Negroes were getting on.   He was not always well received. The masters complained that he wasted the slaves' time with his preaching, praying and hymn-singing ; their wives complained that after the Negroes had been to Mass it was impossible to enter the church ; and when they misbehaved Father Claver was blamed.   " What sort of a man must I be, that I cannot do a little good without causing so much confusion ? " he asked himself.   But he was not deterred, not even when the ecclesiastical authorities lent too willing an ear to the complaints of his critics.

Many of the stories both of the heroism and of the miraculous powers of St Peter Claver concern his nursing of sick and diseased Negroes, in circumstances often that no one else, black or white, could face, but he found time to care for other sufferers besides slaves.   There were two hospitals in Cartagena, one for general cases, served by the Brothers of St. John-of-God ; this was St Sebastian's ; and another, of St Lazarus, for lepers and those suffering from the complaint called " St Antony's Fire ".   Both these he visited every week, waiting on the patients in their material needs and bringing hardened sinners to penitence.   He also exercised an apostolate among the Protestant traders, sailors and others whom he found therein, and brought about the conversion of an Anglican dignitary, represented to be an archdeacon of London, whom he met when visiting prisoners-of-war on a ship in the harbour.   Temporal considerations stood in the way of his being then reconciled, but he was taken ill and removed to St Sebastian's, where before he died he was received into the Church by Father Claver.   A number of other Englishmen followed his example.   Claver was less successful in his efforts to make converts among the Mohammedans who came to Cartagena, who, as his biographer remarks, " are well known to be of all people in the world the most obstinate in their errors ", but he brought a number of Moors and Turks to the faith, though one held out for thirty years before succumbing, and even then a vision of our Lady was required to convince him.   Father Claver was also in particular request to minister to condemned criminals, and it is said that not one was executed at Cartagena during his lifetime without his being present to console him ; under his influence the most hardened and defiant would spend their last hours in prayer and sorrow for their sins. But many more, uncondemned by man, would seek him out in the confessional, where he had sometimes to spend fifteen hours at a stretch, reproving, advising, encouraging, absolving.

His country missions in the spring, during which he refused as much as possible the hospitality of the planters and owners and lodged in the quarters of the slaves, were succeeded in the autumn by a mission among the traders and seamen, who landed at Cartagena in great numbers at that season and further increased the vice and disorder of the port. Sometimes St Peter would spend almost the whole day in the great square of the city, where the four principal streets met, preaching to all who would stop to listen. He became the apostle of Cartagena as well as of the Negroes, and in so huge a work was aided by God with those gifts that particularly pertain to apostles, of miracles, of prophecy, and of reading hearts. Few saints carried out their active work in more repulsive circumstances than did he, but these mortifications of the flesh were not enough ; he continuously used penitential instruments of the most severe description, and would pray alone in his cell with a crown of thorns pressed to his head and a heavy cross weighing down his shoulders. He avoided the most innocent gratification of his senses, lest such should divert him from his path of self-imposed martyrdom ; never would he extend to himself the indulgence and kindness he had for others. Once when commended for his apostolic zeal, he replied, " It ought to be so, but there is nothing but self-indulgence in it ; it is the result of my enthusiastic and impetuous temperament. If it were not for this work, I should be a nuisance to myself and to everybody else." And he put down his apparent indifference to handling loathsome diseases to lack of sensibility : " If being a saint consists in having no taste and having a strong stomach, I admit that I may be one."

In the year 1650 St Peter Claver went to preach the jubilee among the Negroes along the coast, but sickness attacked his emaciated and weakened body, and he was recalled to the residence at Cartagena. But here a virulent epidemic had begun to show itself, and one of the first to be attacked among the Jesuits was the debilitated missionary, so that his death seemed at hand. After receiving the last sacraments he recovered, but he was a broken man. For the rest of his life pain hardly left him, and a trembling in his limbs made it impossible for him to celebrate Mass. He perforce became almost entirely inactive, but would sometimes hear confessions, especially of his dear friend Doña Isabella de Urbina, who had always generously supported his work with her money. Occasionally he would be carried to a hospital, a dying prisoner, or other sick person, and once when a cargo arrived of slaves from a tribe which had not been seen in Cartagena for thirty years his old strength returned ; he was taken around till he found an interpreter who spoke their tongue, then baptized all the children, and gave brief instructions to the adults. Otherwise he remained in his cell, not only inactive but even forgotten and neglected; the numbers in the house were much reduced, and those who remained were fully occupied in coping with the confusion and duties imposed by the spreading plague, but even so their indifference to the saint is surprising. Doña Isabella and her sister remained faithful to him, doubtless his old helper, Brother Nicholas Gonzalez, visited him when he could. For the rest, St Peter Claver was left in the hands of a young Negro, who was impatient and rough with the old man, and sometimes left him nearly helpless for days on end without any attention whatever. Once the authorities woke up to his existence, when a complaint was laid that Father

Claver was in the habit of re-baptizing Negroes. This, of course, he had never done, except conditionally in cases of doubt, but he was nevertheless forbidden to baptize in future. " It behoves me " he once wrote, " always to imitate the example of the ass. When he is evilly spoken of, he is dumb. When he is starved, he is dumb. When he is overloaded, he is dumb. When he is despised and neglected, he is still dumb. He never complains in any circumstances, for he is only an ass. So also must God's servant be : ' Ut jumentum factus sum apud te.' "

In the summer of 1654 Father Diego Ramirez Fariña arrived in Cartagena from Spain with a commission from the king to work among the Negroes. St Peter Claver was overjoyed and dragged himself from his bed to greet his successor. He shortly afterwards heard the confession of Doña Isabella, and told her it was for the last time, and on September 6, after assisting at Mass and receiving communion, he said to Nicholas Gonzalez, " I am going to die ". That same evening he was taken very ill and became comatose. The rumour of his approaching end spread round the city, everyone suddenly remembered the saint again, and numbers came to kiss his hands before it was too late ; his cell was stripped of everything that could be carried off as a relic. St Peter Claver never fully recovered consciousness, and died two days later on the birthday of our Lady, September 8 1654. The civil authorities who had looked askance at his solicitude for mere Negro slaves, and the clergy, who had called his zeal indiscreet and his energy wasted, now vied with one another to honour his memory. The city magistrates ordered that he should be buried at the public expense with great pomp, and the vicar general of the diocese officiated at the funeral. The Negroes and Indians arranged for a Mass of their own, to which the Spanish authorities were invited ; the church was ablaze with lights, a special choir sang, and an oration was delivered by the treasurer of the church of Popayan, than whom " no other preacher was more diffuse on the virtues, holiness, heroism and stupendous miracles of Father Claver ". St Peter Claver was never again forgotten and his fame spread through· out the world : he was canonized at the same time as his friend St Alphonsus Rodriguez in 1888, and he was declared by Pope Leo XIII patron of all missionary enterprises among Negroes, in whatever part of the world. His feast is observed throughout the United States.

It would seem that no quite adequate life of St Peter Claver has yet seen the light, though the depositions obtained in the various " processes " conducted in view of his beatification afford a good deal of material. Perhaps the most reliable summary is that set out in chapter 8 of the 5th volume of Astrain, *Historia de la Compañía de Jesús en la Asistencia de España*, pp. 479–495. The best accessible biography is probably that of J. M. Solá, *Vida de San Pedro Claver* (1888), which is based on the early life by J. M. Fernandez. There are a number of other lives, mostly of small compass, amongst which may be mentioned that of J. Charrau, *L'Esclave des Nègres* (1914) ; G. Ledos in " Les Saints " series (1923) ; Höver (in German ; 1905) ; M. D. Petre, *Aethiopum Servus* (in English ; 1896) ; and C. C. Martindale, *Captains of Christ*, pt iii. Claver's story is told in fictional form by M. Farnum in *Street of the Half-Moon*. See Arnold Lunn, *A Saint in the Slave Trade* (1935).

10 : ST NICHOLAS OF TOLENTINO (A.D. 1305)

THIS saint received his surname from the town which was his residence for the most considerable part of his life, and in which he died. He was a native of Sant' Angelo, a town near Fermo in the March of Ancona, and was born in the year 1245. His father lived many years in happiness with his wife.

but when both had reached middle age they were still childless. Nicholas was the fruit of their prayers and a pilgrimage to the shrine of St Nicholas at Bari, in which his mother especially had earnestly begged of God a son who should faithfully serve Him. At his baptism he received the name of his patron. In his childhood he would go to a little cave near the town and pray there in imitation of the hermits who then lived among the Apennines. People now go to pray there in honour of St Nicholas of Tolentino. While still a boy he received minor orders, and was presented to a canonry in the collegiate church of St Saviour at Sant' Angelo ; and there were not wanting those who were willing to use their influence for his promotion within the ranks of the secular clergy. Nicholas, however, aspired to a state which would allow him to consecrate his whole time and thoughts directly to God, and it happened that he one day went into the Augustinian church and heard a friar preaching on the text : " Love not the world nor the things which are in the world. . . . The world passeth away. . . ." This sermon finally determined him absolutely to join the order of that preacher. This he did so soon as his age would allow, and he was accepted by the Augustinian friars at Sant' Angelo. He went through his novitiate under the direction of the preacher himself, Father Reginald, and made his profession before he had completed his eighteenth year.

Friar Nicholas was sent to San Ginesio for his theology, and he was entrusted with the daily distribution of food to the poor at the monastery gate. He made so free with the resources of the house that the procurator complained and reported him to the prior. It was while discharging this labour of love that his first miracle was recorded of St Nicholas, when he put his hand on the head of a diseased child, saying, " The good God will heal you ", and the boy was there and then cured. About 1270 he was ordained priest at Cingoli, and in that place he became famous among the people, particularly on account of his healing of a blind woman, with the same words which he had used to the child above. But he did not stay there long, for during four years he was continually moving from one to another of the friaries and missions of his order. For a short time he was novice-master at Sant' Elpidio, where there was a large community which included two friars who are venerated as *beati* among the Augustinians today, Angelo of Furcio and Angelo of Foligno. While visiting a relative who was prior of a monastery near Fermo, Nicholas was tempted by an invitation to make a long stay in the monastery, which was comfortable and well off compared with the hard poverty of the friaries to which he was accustomed. But while praying in the church he seemed to hear a voice directing him : " To Tolentino, to Tolentino. Persevere there." Shortly after to Tolentino he was sent, and stopped there for the remaining thirty years of his life.

This town had suffered much in the strife of Guelf and Ghibelline, and civil discord had had its usual effects of wild fanaticism, schism and reckless wickedness. A campaign of street-preaching was necessary, and to this new work St Nicholas was put. He was an immediate success. " He spoke of the things of Heaven ", says St Antoninus. " Sweetly he preached the divine word, and the words that came from his lips fell like burning flame. When his superiors ordered him to take up the public ministry of the gospel, he did not try to display his knowledge or show off his ability, but simply to glorify God. Amongst his audience could be seen the tears and heard the sighs of people detesting their sins and repenting of their past lives." His preaching aroused opposition among those who were unmoved by it, and a certain man of notoriously evil life did all he could to shout down the friar and break up his audiences.   Nicholas refused to be intimidated, and his perseverance began to make an impression on his persecutor.   One day when the man had been trying to drown his voice and scatter the people by fencing with his friends in the street, he sheathed his sword and stood by to listen.   Afterwards he came and apologized to St Nicholas, admitted that his heart had been touched, and began to reform his ways.   This conversion made a strong impression, and soon Nicholas had to be spending nearly whole days in hearing confessions. He went about the slums of Tolentino, comforting the dying, waiting on (and sometimes miraculously curing) the sick and bed-ridden, watching over the children, appealing to the criminals, composing quarrels and estrangements : one woman gave evidence in the cause of his canonization that he had entirely won over and reformed her husband who for long had treated her with shameful cruelty. Another witness gave evidence of three miracles due to the saint in his family. " Say nothing of this ", was his usual comment after these happenings (and they were numerous), " give thanks to God, not to me.   I am only an earthen vessel, a poor sinner."

Jordan of Saxony (not the Dominican *beatus*, but an Austin friar) in his Life of St Nicholas, written about 1380, relates a happening which has the distinction of being referred to by the Bollandists as the most extraordinary miracle which they find attributed to the saint.   A man was waylaid by his enemies at a lonely spot on Mont' Ortona, near Padua, and, disregarding his entreaties in the name of God and St Nicholas [of Bari] for mercy, or at least a priest to shrive him, they killed him and threw his body into a lake.   A week later his body was recovered by one wearing the habit of an Austin friar, who led him back alive and well to his family.   He asked for a priest, received the last sacraments, and then, declaring that he had been brought back to make a good end in response to his desperate appeal to St Nicholas, he again died.   His flesh at once shrivelled up and dropped off, leaving only his bare bones for Christian burial.   Many of the marvels attributed to the intercession of St Nicholas are in connexion with the bread blessed on his feast by the friars of his order.   In his later years when he was ill and weak his superiors wished him to take meat and other strengthening food, and St Nicholas was troubled between the obligation of obedience and his desire not to give in to his body.   One night it appeared to him that our Lady was present and that she told him to ask for a small piece of bread, to dip it in water and eat it, and he would recover.   So it fell out, and Nicholas in grateful memory would afterwards bless pieces of bread and give them to the sick, thus originating the Augustinians' custom.*

The final illness of St Nicholas lasted nearly a year, and in the last months he got up from bed only once, to absolve a penitent who he knew intended to conceal a grievous sin from any priest but himself.   The end came quietly on September 10, 1305.   His last words to the community gathered round his bed were : " My dearest brethren, my conscience does not reproach me with anything—but I am not justified by that."   A commission was appointed which at once began to collect evidence for his heroic virtues and miracles, but the

* The spirit in which the Church desires her children to make use of such things is illustrated by the prayer to be said by those who use St Nicholas's bread : " Grant, we beseech thee, Almighty God, that thy Church, which is made illustrious by the glory of the marvels and miracles of blessed Nicholas, thy confessor, may by his merits and intercession enjoy perpetual peace and unity, through Christ our Lord.   Amen."

transfer of the papacy to Avignon intervened and canonization was not achieved till 1446.

There is a life of St Nicholas by a contemporary, Peter of Monte Rubiano. This is accessible in the *Acta Sanctorum*, September, vol. iii. Of the later lives none seem to have treated this work and the other materials there provided in a very critical spirit. The most copious biography is that of Philip Giorgi, *Vita del taumaturgo S. Niccolò da Tolentino* (1856–1859, in 3 vols.). The others are for the most part of a popular character : for example, two in French, by A. Tonna-Barthet (1896), and by " H.P." (1899). At Tolentino itself, in view of the centenary kept in 1905, a sort of periodical was brought out, beginning in 1899, under the title of *Sesto Centenario di San Nicolà da Tolentino*. This includes copies of certain documents preserved in the archives of the city, but it is mainly interesting for the information it provides concerning the later *cultus* of the saint. It must be remembered that the accounts of miracles and wonders belong for the most part to a very uncritical age. Several little booklets, notably one by N. G. Cappi (1725), were published in Italy concerning the alleged bleeding of St Nicholas's severed arms. A short English biography by E. A. Foran was issued in 1920. See also a life in Italian by N. Concetti (1932).

SS. NEMESIAN AND MANY COMPANIONS, MARTYRS   (A.D. 257)

IN the first year of the eighth general persecution, raised by Valerian in the year 257, St Cyprian, Bishop of Carthage, was banished by the proconsul of Africa to Curubis. At the same time the president of Numidia proceeded with severity against the Christians, tortured many, and afterwards put several to barbarous deaths and sent others to work in the mines, or rather quarries. Out of this holy company some were taken at intervals to be tormented afresh or inhumanly butchered, whilst others continued their lingering martyrdom in hunger, nakedness and filth, exhausted with hard labour, persecuted with daily blows, hardships, and insults. St Cyprian wrote from the place of his banishment to comfort and encourage these sufferers for their faith.

Those to whom his noble letter was addressed thanked St Cyprian for it through their leader, Bishop Nemesian. It had, they said, eased the pain of their blows and sufferings, and made them indifferent to the stench and filth of their prison. They tell him that by gloriously confessing his faith in the proconsul's court, and going before them into banishment, he had animated all the soldiers of God for the conflict. They conclude by begging his prayers, and say, " Let us assist one another by our prayers, that God and Christ and the whole choir of angels may send us help when we shall most want it ". This glorious company is commemorated on this day in the Roman Martyrology, nine of them being mentioned by name, all bishops ; but there also suffered, as St Cyprian tells us, lower clergy and lay-people of all ages and states of life. Some were deliberately put to death, a few survived, but the most part died of exposure, hardship, ill-treatment or sickness brought on by their captivity.

The mention of SS. Nemesian, Felix and Companions in the Roman Martyrology on this date seems to be due to a confusion. There was a martyr, Nemesius, who suffered with companions at Alexandria, and he, as the " Hieronymianum " bears witness, belongs to this day, being probably identical with a martyr who in the Syriac *breviarium* appears as " Menmais ", also on September 10. Dom Quentin has shown that Florus, the martyrologist, has identified this group of martyrs of Alexandria with those to whom St Cyprian's letter is addressed (see *Martyrologes historiques*, p. 289). We have no evidence beyond Cyprian's letter that the bishops to whom it was addressed were honoured subsequently as martyrs. The Carthaginian calendar names a Nemesian on December 23, but this may be a boy martyr of whom St Augustine speaks. The text of St Cyprian, with comments, is quoted in the *Acta Sanctorum*, September, vol. iii.

SS. MENODORA, METRODORA AND NYMPHODORA, VIRGINS AND MARTYRS   (*c.* A.D. 304 ?)

THE " acts " of these martyrs are known only in the tenth-century version of Simeon Metaphrastes, wherein they are represented as having been three orphan sisters who lived a life of solitude and good works in Bithynia, " near the Pythian baths ". During the persecution under Diocletian and Maximian they were reported to Fronto, governor of the province, who had them brought before him. The beauty and modest carriage of the three girls touched his heart, and when they made a profession of Christianity he offered to be their protector if they would submit themselves to his gods. They gently refused his offer, asking instead that as they had lived so might they die, all together. When he was unable to make them change their minds, Fronto had Menodora beaten in barbarous fashion before the two others to shake their constancy, but even the sight of her mangled and dead body putrefying in the fierce sun did not move them. " We are three branches of the same good tree ", said Metrodora, " nor will we disgrace the root from which we are sprung by doing as you wish." Then she was tortured with fire after she had been beaten, and was at last beheaded. But Nymphodora, the youngest, died under the blows of the scourges.

The Greek passio, *so called, is printed in Migne, PG., vol. cxv ; a Latin translation in the* Acta Sanctorum, *September, vol. iii.*

ST PULCHERIA, VIRGIN   (A.D. 453)

IT is characteristic of the important part played in religious and ecclesiastical affairs by the Byzantine Roman emperors and of the influence of women at the imperial court (an influence not always, perhaps not even generally, for good) that the fathers of the epoch-making Council of Chalcedon should have hailed the Empress Pulcheria as " Guardian of the faith, peacemaker, religious right-believer, a second St Helen "—for these were not simply the flowery compliments of oriental bishops who knew from experience the importance of keeping the good-will of the imperial sovereign.

Pulcheria was granddaughter to Theodosius the Great and daughter to the Emperor Arcadius, who died in the year 408. She was born in 399, and had three sisters, Flacilla, who was the eldest but died soon, and Arcadia and Marina, who were younger than Pulcheria. Arcadius left a son, Theodosius II, who was mild, humane and devout, incapable in public affairs, and not sufficiently strong for his position ; he was more interested in writing and painting than in the art of government, and was nicknamed " the Calligrapher ". In the year 414 Pulcheria, though only fifteen years of age, was declared, in the name of her young brother, *augusta* and partner with him, and charged with the care of his instruction.

Under Pulcheria's control the court was an improvement on what it had been in the days of her mother, who had incurred the wrath of St John Chrysostom. On becoming *augusta*, Pulcheria made a vow of perpetual virginity and induced her sisters to do the same. Her motive for doing this was probably not even primarily, much less wholly, religious : she was a realistic young woman of affairs, and she did not want her political administration upset and perhaps her brother to lose his throne through the aspirations of ambitious men to marry her or the princesses her sisters. But neither was the vow devoid of religion ; she had called on God to be her witness and she did not take His name in vain : she kept her vow, even after she was in fact married. But to represent the court at this time as a sort of monastery is an exaggeration : the spectacle of the young princesses spending much time spinning and embroidering and in church was nothing out of the ordinary and if Pulcheria forbade men access to her own and her sisters' apartments that was a measure of elementary prudence—tongues will wag and Byzantine court officials were not consistently well behaved. We get the impression of a united and busy family, of which the main domestic concern was the education and training of the young Theodosius. Unfortunately, like so many more than ordinarily capable people, Pulcheria was too self-sufficient, and she (perhaps unconsciously at first) took advantage of her brother's lack of enthusiasm for public affairs : the result was that he grew up virtuous and scholarly but no ruler. As it has been caustically put, " His incapacity for business was so great that he is hardly accused of having augmented the misfortunes of his reign by his own acts "—or the predominant good fortunes either, which can mostly be put down to St Pulcheria. Both her thoroughness and her brother's indifference are illustrated by the story that on one occasion, in order to test him, Pulcheria drew up and presented to him a decree of death against herself. He signed it without reading it.

When the time came for Theodosius to marry, Pulcheria had again in view the avoidance of political complications and, it must be admitted, perhaps the safe-guarding of her own ascendancy, which certainly in the circumstances was for the good of the state. Her choice fell on Athenais, the beautiful and highly accomplished daughter of an Athenian philosopher, who was still a pagan.* She was acceptable to Theodosius and had no objection to becoming a Christian, so in 421 they were married. Two years later Theodosius declared Athenais, or Eudokia as she had been christened, *augusta*. It was inevitable that the Augusta Eudokia should sooner or later attempt to undermine the influence of her sister-in-law, the Augusta Pulcheria, and she worked on her feeble husband till at length Pulcheria was forced into exile at Hebdomon. This lasted for some years. We may well believe that, as Alban Butler says, St Pulcheria " looked upon her retreat as a favour of Heaven and consecrated all her time to God in prayer and good works. She made no complaint of her brother's ingratitude, of the empress who owed everything to her, or of their unjust ministers ". And no doubt she would have been glad " both to forget the world and to be forgotten by it ", but for the fact that she had responsibilities in respect of that great part of the world whose metro-polis was at Constantinople. For a time things went fairly well, but about the year 441 came the fall of Eudokia. She was accused, probably unjustly, of infidelity with a handsome but gouty officer named Paulinus,† and she was exiled to Jerusalem, under the guise of a pilgrimage. She never came back. There was a general shuffling of offices at court, and Pulcheria was recalled ; but not to her old position of control : this was now held by Chrysaphius, an old supporter of Eudokia. Under his administration the Eastern empire went from bad to worse for ten years.

---

* The story of Athenais being sent to Constantinople to seek her fortune throws an interesting sidelight on Greco-Roman society at this period, but to retell it would be out of place here. For a summary, see Finlay's *Greece Under the Romans*, ch. ii, sect. xi.

† For the fantastic story of the Phrygian apple, see Finlay, *loc. cit.*

Under pressure from this man, and with a fine disregard for theological consistency seeing that he had formerly favoured Nestorius, Theodosius gave support to Eutyches and the monophysite heresy.   In 449 Pope St Leo the Great appealed to St Pulcheria and to the emperor to reject Monophysism, and the answer of Theodosius was to approve the acts of the " Robber Synod " of Ephesus, and to drive St Flavian from the see of Constantinople.   Pulcheria was firmly orthodox, but her influence with her brother had been weakened.   The pope wrote again, and the archdeacon of Rome, Hilarus, wrote, and the Western emperor, Valentinian III, with Eudoxia his wife (Theodosius's daughter) and Galla Placidia, his mother —and amid all these appeals Theodosius suddenly died, killed by a fall from his horse while hunting.

St Pulcheria, now fifty-one years old, nominated as emperor a veteran general of humble origin, seven years older than herself.   His name was Marcian ; he was a native of Thrace, and a widower.   Pulcheria, judging it would be of advantage to the state and secure his title to the purple, proposed to marry him, on condition she should be at liberty to keep her vow of virginity.   Marcian agreed, and these two governed together like two friends who had in all things the same views and sentiments, which centred in the advancement of religion and the public weal. They welcomed the legates sent by St Leo to Constantinople, and their zeal for the Catholic faith earned the highest commendations of that pope and of the Council of Chalcedon which, under their protection, condemned the monophysite heresy in 451.   They did their utmost to have the decrees of this synod executed over all the East, but failed lamentably in Egypt and Syria.   St Pulcheria wrote herself two letters, one to certain monks, another to an abbess of nuns in Palestine, to convince them that the Council of Chalcedon did not (as was averred) revive Nestorianism, but condemned that error together with the opposite heresy of Eutyches.   Twice already, in 414 and 443, Pulcheria had been responsible for remissions of arrears of unpaid taxes, covering a period of sixty years, and she and her husband followed a policy of low taxation and as little warfare as possible. The admirable spirit in which they undertook their duties was expressed by Marcian in his *dictum*, " It is our business to provide for the care of the human race ".   But the excellent partnership lasted only three years, for in July 453 St Pulcheria died.

This great empress built many churches, and among them three in honour of the all-holy Mother of God, namely, those of Blakhernae, Khalkopratia and the Hodegetria, that were among the most famous Marian churches of Christendom. In the last she placed a famous picture of the Blessed Virgin, which had been sent from Jerusalem as the reputed work of St Luke the Evangelist.   She and Theodosius were the first rulers of Constantinople who were Greek rather than Latin ; she encouraged the establishment of a university there, with an emphasis on Greek literature and the recognition of Greek as an official language, which her brother carried out ; and she gauged the needs of rulers and people for fixed principles of law which were met by the Code of Theodosius.   If we consider her actions and virtues we shall see that the commendations which St Proclus, in his panegyric on her, Pope St Leo, and the Council of Chalcedon, bestowed on this empress were, so far from being compliments or mere eloquence, thoroughly well deserved.   St Pulcheria is named on this day in the Roman Martyrology, having been inserted by Cardinal Baronius, a happier and more worthy addition than some that we owe to that venerable and learned scholar ; her feast is kept by the Greeks, and at one time she had a certain *cultus* in the West, her feast being observed, *e.g.* throughout Portugal and the kingdom of Naples.

Pulcheria played a prominent part in the ecclesiastical history of her time, but she has no separate biography.   See the *Acta Sanctorum*, September, vol. iii, and also vol. iv, pp. 778–782 ; Hefele-Leclercq, *Conciles*, vol. ii, pp. 375–377, etc., and the usual reference books.   Even Gibbon speaks well of Pulcheria : *cf. Decline and Fall* . . ., ch. xxxii.

ST FINNIAN OF MOVILLE, Bishop   (*c.* A.D. 579)

ULSTER is a name which now has unhappy associations for many Catholics, but its history is no less glorious than that of any other part of Ireland, and one of its greatest sons was this Finnian.   He was said to be of royal race, born in the neighbourhood of Strangford Lough, and he was sent when young to be educated by St Colman at Dromore and St Mochae on Mahee Island.   From thence he went across the sea to Whitern in Strathclyde, and stayed at the monastery founded by St Ninian.   There is a story told that here he attracted the love of a Pictish princess, who for a time was made ill by his indifference.   When she realized that Finnian really meant to be a monk, the young woman quickly recovered and transferred her affections to another youth, and Finnian acted as a go-between between them. Whether by accident, treachery or as a practical joke, he brought about a meeting between the girl and a third young man, and a scandal was raised which made it desirable for Finnian to leave Whitern.   Anyway, he is supposed to have gone to Rome, where he was ordained priest, and then returned to Ulster, bringing with him, perhaps, among other treasures, a copy of the Old Testament.   On his way he is said to have preached in various places, including Anglesey, and to have there founded the church of Llanfinnan.   He established a monastery at Moville (Maghbile) in county Down, and another at Dromin in Louth ; Moville was and continued to be one of the great schools of Ireland, and some of its chief influence was through St Colmcille, who was a disciple of St Finnian.   The incident of the dispute between the saints concerning the copy made by Colmcille of Finnian's psalter is referred to under St Columba on June 9 ; but, as Father John Ryan puts it, " There is something about all this tale that smacks of the inventor's art ".

Finnian found that the observance of his community was considerably hampered by the long distance from the monastery of the mill in which many worked.   He therefore built another mill nearer at hand, and, as there was no stream to work it, prayed beside a stream on a nearby hill which altered its course so as to make a convenient mill-race.   Such a miracle is easily " rationalized ", but is of interest because of its resemblance to the story told in the *Dialogues* of St Gregory of the diverting of the course of the river Serchio by St Frigidian (Frediano) of Lucca. This saint has often been identified with St Finnian of Moville—and still is in Ireland and in the breviary of the Canons Regular of the Lateran—but it is difficult to reconcile what is known of the lives of either of them.   Finnian's death took place about the year 579.   The Breviary of Aberdeen says that he founded a monastery and set up a cross of St Brigid at Holywood in Dumfries, and he is supposed to have changed the course of a river in Scotland as well, namely, the Garnock.   In Ireland the feast of St Finnian of Moville is not observed separately from that of St Frigidian in March.

For any connected life of Finnian we have to turn to such unreliable sources as Capgrave and the Aberdeen Breviary.   But there are several passages which refer to him in such books as Gougaud, *Christianity in Celtic Lands*, and J. Ryan, *Irish Monasticism*. All admit the confusion between the legends which attach to this Finnian and those belonging to other holy men who bear this and similar names. In the *Félire* of Oengus under this day, September 10, we read : " A kingpost of red gold and purity, over the swelling sea he came with law, a sage for whom Ireland is sad, Findbarr of Mag Bile." This seems to endorse the idea of foreign travel and the bringing of some important text from beyond the seas. Most probably it is this Finnian who was credited with the authorship of the *Paenitentiale Vinniani ;* see Esposito, *Latin Learning*, vol. i, pp. 236-240. Under the name " Wynnin " in KSS. there is (p. 465) an interesting note by Dr Reeves who also identifies Finnian of Moville with Frigidian of Lucca.

ST SALVIUS, BISHOP OF ALBI   (A.D. 584)

ST SALVIUS (Salvy) belonged to a family of Albi in France, and was at first a lawyer and magistrate ; but his love for retirement and the desire of being freed from distractions induced him to become a monk, and his brethren afterwards chose him for their abbot. He chiefly confined himself to a cell at a distance from the rest, and here, being seized by a violent fever, he grew so ill that he was dead in the opinion of all about him. Indeed the saint himself was always persuaded that he really died, was vouchsafed an experience of Heaven before due time, and then was restored to life ; be that as it may, he was in the year 574 taken from his retreat and placed in the see of Albi. He lived as austerely as ever ; if anything were forced upon him, he on the spot distributed the whole among the poor. The patrician Mommolus having taken a great number of prisoners at Albi, Salvius followed him and ransomed them all. The king of Soissons, Chilperic, fancied himself as a theologian and was responsible for an unorthodox treatise ; Salvius, together with his friend St Gregory of Tours, succeeded in bringing the monarch back to orthodoxy. In the year 584 an epidemic made great havoc among his flock. It was in vain his friends advised him to be careful of his health ; animated, unwearied, undaunted, he went everywhere he thought his presence necessary. He visited the sick, comforted them, and exhorted them to prepare for eternity by such good works as their condition admitted. When he knew that his own hour was near, he ordered his coffin to be made, changed his clothes, and prepared himself to appear before God, to whom he was called on September 10, 584.

Nearly all we know of St Salvius is contained in the *Historia Francorum* of Gregory of Tours. See also the Bollandists, September, vol. iii.

ST THEODARD, BISHOP OF MAESTRICHT   (A.D. 670 ?)

ST THEODARD was an energetic bishop of Tongres-Maestricht and a man of cheerful and sympathetic disposition, but little of interest is told of his life except his manner of leaving it. Some unscrupulous nobles having taken possession of lands which rightly belonged to his church, he made up his mind to go personally to Childeric II of Austrasia to ask that justice might be done. While passing through the forest of Bienwald near Speyer he was set upon by robbers and killed. His biographer informs us that St Theodard made a long speech to his murderers, to which they replied with a quotation from Horace. As his death was occasioned by a journey undertaken in defence of the rights of the Church he was venerated as a martyr, and his successor, St Lambert, translated his body to the church of Liège. The Roman Martyrology, too, speaks of St Theodard as a martyr " who lay down his life for his sheep and after his death was resplendent with significant miracles ".

There is an anonymous life written in the eighth century, and another, of later date, perhaps by Heriger, Abbot of Lobbes.   The former is printed in the *Acta Sanctorum*, September, vol. iii.   See also G. Kurth, *Étude critique sur St Lambert* (1876), pp. 67 *seq.*, and L. van der Essen, *Étude critique . . .* (1907), pp. 135–143.

ST AUBERT, Bishop of Avranches   (*c.* A.D. 725 ?)

NOTHING definite is known of this saint except that he was the founder of the church of Mont-Saint-Michel early in the eighth century.   Tradition says that an apparition of St Michael the Archangel told St Aubert to build a church on the Rocher de la Tombe on the sea-board of his diocese, which the bishop undertook to do.   The undertaking was beset with great and unexpected difficulties, and it was not until he had received two more visions of the archangel and a divine rebuke for his want of energy that St Aubert was able to carry it through.   The church was dedicated in 709, in honour of St Michael for those in peril on the sea, and it was entrusted to a chapter of canons.   These in later ages were replaced by Benedictines.   On October 16, the traditional anniversary of the dedication of the church, a feast of St Michael *in Monte Tumba* is kept in the diocese of Coutances and at St Michael's Abbey, Farnborough.

Some slight materials for the history of this saint are provided by the Bollandists in the *Acta Sanctorum* on June 18, vol. iii.   See also Motet in *Mém. Soc. archéol. d'Avranches*, 1847, pp. 28 *seq.* ; and C. Claireux, *Les reliques de S. Aubert* (1909).

BB. APOLLINARIS FRANCO, CHARLES SPINOLA AND THEIR COMPANIONS, MARTYRS IN THE GREAT MARTYRDOM IN JAPAN (A.D. 1622)

IN 1867, the same year in which persecution began again in Urakami, though not to blood, Pope Pius IX beatified 205 of the martyrs of Japan, of whom the Franciscan Martyrology today refers to eighteen members of its first order and twenty-two tertiaries.   Owing to various causes—among them it seems we must sadly recognize national jealousies and even religious rivalries between the missionaries of various orders—the *shogun* Ieyasu Tokugawa in 1614 decreed that Christianity should be abolished, and these Franciscan *beati* suffered between the years 1617 and 1632.   The persecution gradually increased in intensity until in 1622 took place the " great martyrdom ", in which BD APOLLINARIS FRANCO was one of the principal victims.   He was a Castilian of Aguilar del Campo, who after taking his doctor's degree at Salamanca became a Friar Minor of the Observance.   In 1600 he went on the Philippine mission and thence to Japan, where after the persecution began he was named commissary general in charge of the mission.   While he was at Nagasaki in 1617 he heard that there was not a single priest left in the province of Omura, where Christians were numerous, and he went thither without disguise to minister to them.   He was thrown into a filthy prison, where he was left for five years.   Father Apollinaris never ceased to comfort his flock by messages and letters, and ministered to those who were able to make their way into the gaol.   A number of other Christians were confined with him, and a fellow-religious, BD RICHARD-OF-ST-ANNE, wrote to the guardian of his friary at Nivelles : " I have been for nearly a year in this wretched prison, where are with me nine religious of our order, eight Dominicans, and six Jesuits.   The others are native Christians who have helped us in our ministry.   Some have been here for five years.   Our food is a little rice and water.   The road to martyrdom has been paved for us by more than three hundred martyrs, all Japanese, on whom all kinds of tortures were inflicted. As for us survivors, we also are all doomed to death. We religious and those who have helped us are to be burnt at a slow fire; the others will be beheaded. . . . If my mother is still alive, I beg you to be so kind as to tell her of God's mercy to me in allowing me to suffer and die for Him. I have no time left to write to her myself."

Early in September 1622, twenty of the prisoners were removed to Nagasaki. On the 12th Bd Apollinaris and the seven remaining with him at Omura were there burnt to death, including BB. FRANCIS-OF-ST-BONAVENTURE and PAUL-OF-ST-CLARE, whom he had clothed with the Franciscan habit while in captivity. Two days previously those who had been removed to Nagasaki had there met the same death. Prominent among the Franciscans were Bd Richard, mentioned above, and BD LUCY DE FREITAS. The last-named was a Japanese of high birth, widow of a Portuguese merchant who had died many years before. She became a Franciscan tertiary and devoted the rest of her life to the cause of the poor and the encouragement and help of persecuted Christians. She was afflicted with this cruel death when she was over eighty years old, because it was in her house that Bd Richard had been captured.

Among the confessors who were taken from prison at Omura to Nagasaki, as mentioned above, were BD CHARLES SPINOLA and BD SEBASTIAN KIMURA of the Society of Jesus. Bd Charles was an Italian by birth who, after a first abortive attempt to reach Japan, landed there in the first years of the seventeenth century and laboured as a missionary for eighteen years. At this time the Jesuits (and after them the Lazarists) in the Far East made a special study and practice of astronomy, which recommended them to the favour of the Chinese and Japanese. Bd Charles was a keen mathematician and astronomer, and in 1612 wrote a technical account of a lunar eclipse as seen from Nagasaki. When he was arrested six years later there was imprisoned with him at Omura Bd Sebastian Kimura, an early Japanese to be ordained priest and a descendant of a Japanese baptized by St Francis Xavier. When on September 10, 1622, these two Jesuits and their companions reached the place of execution, on a hill outside Nagasaki, they had to wait an hour for the arrival of another body of confessors, from Nagasaki itself. It was a moving moment when in the presence of a huge crowd of Christians and pagans these two groups of dedicated ones met and gravely greeted one another. Among the new comers was BD ISABEL FERNANDEZ, a Spanish widow who was condemned for sheltering Bd Charles, whose son he had baptized. " Where is my little Ignatius ? " he asked. " Here he is ", replied the mother, picking up the four-year-old child from amongst the crowd. " I brought him with me to die for Christ before he is old enough to sin against Him." And the boy knelt down for Father Spinola to bless him. He watched his mother's head struck off without flinching, and with his own hands loosed his collar to bare his neck to the sword.

The priests and some of the others were reserved for a more terrible death. They were tied to stakes and large fires lit around them at a distance of some twenty-five feet; when the heat was seen to gain too quickly on its victims, the fires were damped down. Some died within a few hours, suffocated by the atmosphere, and of these were Fathers Charles and Sebastian; others lingered on in the fiercest agony until well into the night or even till the next morning. Two young Japanese wavered and begged for mercy : but they did not ask for life at the price of apostasy, only for an easier and quicker death. It was denied them, and they died with the others.

The scene on this occasion was perhaps the most dramatic and impressive in all the annals of martyrdom. Among the Japanese victims were BD CLEMENT VOM and his son, BD ANTONY ; BD DOMINIC XAMADA and his wife, BD CLARE ; the catechist BD LEO SATZUMA ; five women named MARY, viz., TANAURA,TANACA, TOCUAN, XUM and SANGA, the last four with their husbands ; the children BB. PETER NANGAXI, PETER SANGA and the five-year-old MICHAEL YAMIKI, with his father ; the aged BD THOMAS XIQUIRO ; and a Korean, BD ANTONY, with his wife and young son. These were all beheaded.

Five days later there suffered by fire at Firando BD CAMILLO COSTANZO, an Italian Jesuit from Calabria. He was a missionary in Japan for nine years till he was exiled in 1611. From Macao he wrote several treatises in Japanese defending Christianity from pagan attacks, and in 1621 got back into the country disguised as a soldier. He was captured in the following year. The Society of Jesus keeps his feast on September 25, and joins in it BD AUGUSTINE OTA and BD CASPAR COTENDA, Japanese catechists, BD FRANCIS TAQUEA, aged twelve, and BD PETER KIKIEMON, aged seven, all of whom were slain from hatred of the faith within a few days of one another. Another distinguished Jesuit, BD PAUL NAVARRO, was burned alive at Shimabara on November 1 in the same year. He was an Italian and was in India before coming to Japan, where he mastered the language perfectly and was a zealous missionary at Nagasaki and elsewhere, being rector of the Jesuit house at Amanguchi for twenty years. Some very noble letters written by Father Navarro on the eve of his martyrdom are printed in volume ii of L. Pagès, *Histoire de la religion chrétienne au Japon* (1869).

In such ways was consummated the " great martyrdom " of 1622. An English skipper, Richard Cocks, testified to having seen about this time fifty-five persons martyred together at Miako. " Among them little children five or six years old burned in their mothers' arms, crying out, ' Jesus, receive our souls ! ' Many more are in prison who look hourly when they shall die, for very few turn pagan." And it was in the face of such happenings that certain English and Dutch sailors, having seized a Japanese vessel off Formosa and found missionaries aboard, handed them over to the authorities at Nagasaki to save themselves from a charge of piracy.

There is an interesting association between Bd Charles Spinola and England. While at sea in 1597 his ship was captured by an English vessel, and he was landed at Topsham in Devonshire on November 6. " There he continued for several days ; but was not permitted to extend his excursions beyond one mile from the place. Some, professing themselves Catholics, presented him with money ; others invited him to their houses." (*Cf.* Dr Oliver's *Collections*, p. 3.)

For other martyrs in Japan, see under February 5 and June 1.

See the bibliography for the martyrs of Japan herein on June 1. And also Marcellin de Civezza, *Histoire universelle des Missions franciscaines* (1890), t. ii, pp. 343 *seq.* and 381 *seq.* ; H. Leclercq, *Les Martyrs*, t. ix ; *Analecta Bollandiana*, vol. vi (1887), pp. 53–72, and Léon, *Auréole Séraphique* (Eng. trans.), vol. i, pp. 124–178. For Spinola, see the biographies by E. Séguin, Broeckaert, and the short sketch in English by D. Donnelly, *A Prisoner in Japan* (1928). *Cf.* C. R. Boxer, *The Christian Century in Japan* (1951).

BD AMBROSE BARLOW, MARTYR   (A.D. 1641)

IN the year 1611 Benedictine monks of the reviving English congregation moved into the monastery which the beneficence of Abbot Philip de Caverel had provided for them at Douay, and three years later there offered himself to them as a novice a young cleric who had already been imprisoned in London for his faith. This was Edward Barlow, son of Sir Alexander Barlow of Barlow, near Manchester. He was born, the fourth of fourteen children, in 1585 ; and after ecclesiastical studies abroad and a year's confinement at home he went to St Gregory's, where his brother, Dom Rudesind, was prior, and was clothed with the habit, taking the name of Ambrose. He was ordained priest in 1617, and sent on the mission to work in his native Lancashire.

Father Ambrose's principal headquarters was at Morleys Hall in the parish of Leigh, " where ", wrote Mr Knaresborough at the beginning of the next century, " his memory is held in great esteem to this day by the Catholics of that county, for his great zeal in the conversion of souls and the exemplary piety of his life and conversation." His stipend at this mission-centre was £8 a year, of which three-quarters went in board and lodging, though his duties called him away for three months in the year. A penitent of his wrote of him : " Although God had put into his hands (as I think) enough wherewithal to have played the housekeeper, he chose rather to subject himself, and become a sojourner with a poor man and his wife, to avoid thereby (as I did conceive) distracting solicitude and dangerous dominion, and to expose sensuality to be curbed with the simple provision of poor folks. . . . Notwithstanding his infirmities, I never knew him to tamper with the physicians, surely he was to himself Dr Diet, Dr Quiet and the only Dr Merriman that ever I knew." * He was so " mild, witty, and cheerful in his conversation, that of all men that ever I knew he seemed to me the most likely to represent the spirit of Sir Thomas More. . . . Neither did I ever see him moved at all upon occasions of wrongs, slanders, or threats which were frequently raised against him : but as one insensible of wrong, or free from choler, he entertained them with a jest, and passed over them with a smile and a nod." The writer gives a vivid description of Father Ambrose celebrating Mass of Christmas at Morleys, in a venerable vestment " that came out on great days " at a poor, clean altar, whereon great candles he had himself helped to make. And afterwards they sang carols round a " fair coal fire ". Bishop Challoner from other sources gives a similar account of the work, emphasizing his piety, humility, and temperance at table and in company. " He always abstained from wine, and being asked why he did so, he alleged the saying of the wise man : ' Wine and women make the wise apostatize.' "

In 1628, according to Challoner, Father Ambrose ministered the last sacraments in prison to Bd Edmund Arrowsmith, who after his martyrdom appeared in sleep to Father Ambrose (who knew not he was dead) and said to him, " I have suffered and now you will be to suffer. Say little, for they will endeavour to take hold of your words." And so the monk laboured on for thirteen years in daily expectation of his hour. Four times he was in prison and four times released, till in March 1641 the House of Commons bullied King Charles I into ordering that all priests should leave the realm or incur the penalties of traitors. Six weeks later, the vicar of Leigh, a Mr Gatley, celebrated Easter by leading his congregation, armed with weapons of offence, to Morleys Hall, where they seized Ambrose Barlow while he was preaching to his flock after Mass. They carried him off to a justice of the peace, who committed him to Lancaster Castle. After four months imprisonment he was brought for trial before Sir Robert Heath, and at once acknowledged he

---

* He consulted a doctor once, and was told to " Go into your own country and for your physic drink in the morning a mess of new milk and eat a roasted apple at night ".

was a priest.   When asked why then had he not obeyed the order to leave the kingdom, he replied that the decree specified " Jesuits and seminary priests ", whereas he was neither, but a Benedictine monk ; moreover, he had been too ill to travel far at the time.   To the judge's question as to his opinion of the penal laws he replied that he held them to be unjust and barbarous, and those who condemned the innocent were in danger from the divine judgement.   Sir Robert Heath was surprised at his boldness, but said he would be set free if he undertook " not to seduce the people any more."—" I am no seducer, but a reducer of the people to the true and ancient religion. . . .   I am in the resolution to continue until death to render this good office to these strayed souls."   On September 8 he was condemned in the usual form.   Five days before a general chapter of the English Benedictine Congregation in session at Douay had accepted the resignation by Father Rudesind Barlow of the titular cathedral-priorship of Coventry, and elected his brother, Father Ambrose, in his place.   On that day week, a Friday, Bd Ambrose Barlow, monk of St Benedict and prior of Coventry, was drawn on a hurdle from Lancaster Castle to his place of execution, where, after pacing three times round the gallows saying the psalm *Miserere*, he was hanged, disembowelled and quartered.

The mortuary notice of Bd Ambrose sent round to his brethren contained the request that instead of requiem Masses and prayers for the dead they should offer Masses of the Holy Trinity, *Te Deum*, and other prayers of thanksgiving.   At Wardley Hall, which must have been familiar to the martyr and is now the episcopal residence of the diocese of Salford, is preserved a skull said to be his, and his left hand is at Stanbrook Abbey in Worcestershire.

See MMP., pp. 392–400 ; and, especially, B. Camm, *Nine Martyr Monks* (1931), pp. 258–292.

11 : SS. PROTUS AND HYACINTH, Martyrs   (Date Unknown)

THESE martyrs are mentioned in the *Depositio martyrum* of the middle of the fourth century.   They were buried in the cemetery of Basilla or St Hermes on the Old Salarian Way, and here in the year 1845 Father Joseph archi, s.j., found the burial-place of St Hyacinth undisturbed.   It was a niche closed with a slab bearing the inscription DP III IDUS SEPTEBR/YACINTHUS/MARTYR : Hyacinth the Martyr, buried September 11.   Within it were the remains of the martyr, charred bones and traces of costly material.   He had evidently met his death by fire.   These precious relics were translated to the church of the Urban College in 1849.   Near by was found part of a later inscription, bearing the words SEPULCRUM PROTI M : The tomb of Protus, M[artyr], but no other trace of him. The relics of St Protus are supposed to have been removed into the city by Pope St Leo IV in the middle of the ninth century, and parts thereof have been translated several times since.   In an epitaph by Pope St Damasus, these martyrs are referred to as brothers.

The simple certitude of the passion, burial and finding of St Hyacinth is in marked contrast with the " acts ", which are contained in those of St Eugenia and are entirely fictitious.   The story is that Eugenia, the Christian daughter of the prefect of Egypt, fled from her father's house with Protus and Hyacinth, her two slaves.   Eugenia after various adventures converts her family and many others.   Among them, the Roman lady Basilla is brought to the faith by the efforts of Protus and Hyacinth, and she, Protus and Hyacinth are all beheaded together.

See Delehaye's CMH., pp. 501–502, where there is a succinct but complete statement of the facts, with references ; his *Origines du culte des martyrs* (1933), pp. 72, 272 ; and his *Étude sur le légendier romain* (1936), pp. 174–175, 183–184.   See also J. Marchi, *Monumenti primitivi*, vol. i, pp. 238 *seq.* and 264 *seq.* ; and *cf.* bibliography of St Eugenia on December 25.   On the parish of " St Pratt " (Blisland in Cornwall), see *Analecta Bollandiana*, vol. lxix (1951), p. 443.

ST THEODORA OF ALEXANDRIA   (No Date)

The Roman Martyrology speaks today of the death at Alexandria of St Theodora, " who, having transgressed through carelessness, was repentant therefor and persevered in the religious habit, unknown and with marvellous abstinence and patience, until her death ".   These restrained words are very different in tone from the legends of St Theodora.   They relate that she was the wife of Gregory, prefect of Egypt, and that, having fallen into grave sin, she fled away from her home to expiate it in a monastery of the Thebaid.   Disguised as a man she lived for many years among the monks a life of extraordinary austerity.   Once when she went into Alexandria in charge of some camels she was recognized by her husband, but she insisted on returning to the desert, where she lived for the rest of her life. There was a St Theodora who was known to the fathers of the desert, whose wise sayings they repeated, but the above story, decked out with other fictitious particulars, is nothing but a romance, belonging to that class which Father Delehaye traces to the tale of St Pelagia of Antioch (October 8).   For example, like St Reparata, St Marina, and others who lived as men among monks, St Theodora was accused of being guilty of seduction and was vindicated only after her death.

On September 17 the Roman Martyrology makes mention of another St Theodora, a matron of Rome who zealously ministered to the holy martyrs during the persecution under Diocletian.

The Greek text of the fictitious story of Theodora has been printed by K. Wessely at Vienna, *Die Vita S. Theodorae* (1889).   See also the *Acta Sanctorum*, September, vol. iii ; and Delehaye, *Les légendes hagiographiques* (1927), p. 189 and *passim*.

ST PAPHNUTIUS, Bishop   (*c.* A.D. 350 ?)

The holy confessor Paphnutius was an Egyptian who, after having spent several years in the desert under the direction of the great St Antony, was made bishop in the Upper Thebaid.   He was one of those confessors who under the Emperor Maximinus lost the right eye, were hamstrung in one leg, and were afterwards sent to work in the mines.   Peace being restored to the Church, Paphnutius returned to his flock, bearing all the rest of his life the glorious marks of his sufferings for the name of his crucified Master.   He was one of the most zealous in defending the Catholic faith against the Arian heresy and for his holiness, and as one who had confessed the faith before persecutors and under torments, was an outstanding figure of the first general council of the Church, held at Nicaea in the year 325.

Paphnutius, a man who had observed the strictest continence all his life, is said to have distinguished himself at the council by his opposition to clerical celibacy.

Many of the bishops were for making a general law forbidding all bishops, priests, deacons and subdeacons to live with wives whom they had married before their ordination. Whereupon Paphnutius rose up in the assembly and opposed the motion, saying that it was enough to conform to the ancient tradition of the Church, which forbade the clergy marrying after their ordination. For the married the use of wedlock is chastity, he reminded the fathers, and implored them not to lay the yoke of separation on clerics and their wives. St Paphnutius carried·the council with him, and to this day it is the law of the Eastern churches, whether Catholic or dissident, that married men may receive all holy orders below the episcopate, and continue to live freely with their wives.

St Paphnutius remained always in a close union with St Athanasius and the other orthodox prelates. He and other Egyptian bishops accompanied their holy patriarch to the Council of Tyre in 335, where they found the greater part of the members who composed that assembly to be professed Arians. Paphnutius, seeing Maximus, Bishop of Jerusalem, among them and full of concern to find a prelate who had suffered in the late persecution in such bad company, took him by the hand, led him out, and told him that he could not bear that anyone who bore the same marks as himself in defence of the faith should be led away and imposed upon by persons who were resolved to condemn the most strenuous asserter of its fundamental article. Maximus was overcome by the saint's appeal and let himself be led to a seat among the supporters of St Athanasius, whom he never afterwards deserted.

St Paphnutius is sometimes called " the Great " to distinguish him from other saints of the same name ; the year of his death is not known.

There is no early life of St Paphnutius, but in the *Acta Sanctorum*, September, vol. iii, a number of passages, notably from the historians Socrates and Theodoret, have been brought together. See also DCB., vol. iv, p. 185. The authenticity of the pronouncement attributed to Paphnutius on the celibacy question has been often discussed. Consult on this DTC., vol. ii, c. 2078.

ST PATIENS, Bishop of Lyons   (*c*. A.D. 480)

God was pleased to raise up this holy prelate for the comfort and support of his servants in Gaul under the calamities with which that country was afflicted during a great part of the fifth century. He was about the year 450 promoted to the see of Lyons. An incursion of the Goths into Burgundy brought on a serious famine, during which St Patiens fed thousands at his own expense ; Providence wonderfully multiplied his revenues to furnish him with abundant supplies to build churches, to repair old ones, and to feed the poor wherever they might be in Gaul, as St Sidonius Apollinaris assures us. That illustrious prelate and friend of St Patiens calls him a " holy, active, ascetic and merciful man ", and declares that he knew not which to admire more in him, his zeal for God or his charity for the poor. By his pastoral solicitude and sermons many heretics were converted; a great field was open to St Patiens for the exercise of his zeal in this respect, for theBurgundians, who were at that time masters of Lyons, were infected with the heresy of the Arians, and some of his fellow bishops were not free from it. When the diocese of Chalon-sur-Saône was thrown into confusion and disagreement by the death of its bishop, St Patiens was invited by St Euphronius of Autun to help him in its pacification and the removal of the scandal. At the order of St Patiens, Constantius, a priest among his clergy, wrote the Life of St Germanus of Auxerre, which he dedicated to his bishop.   He seems to have died about the year 480.

There is no ancient life of St Patiens of Lyons, but the Bollandists have collected from Sidonius Apollinaris, Gregory of Tours and others, a sufficient account of his activities. See also S. L. Tatu, *St Patient, évêque de Lyon* (1878), and Duchesne, *Fastes Épiscopaux*, vol. ii, p. 163.

ST DEINIOL, Bishop   (*c.* A.D. 584 ?)

THIS famous bishop, " Daniel of the Bangors ", came of a Strathclyde family.   He went into Arfon and established the monastery of Bangor Fawr on the Menai Straits, which became the nucleus of the medieval diocese of Bangor.   Deiniol was also the founder of the monastery of Bangor Iscoed on the Dee, and is alleged to have been consecrated bishop by St Dyfrig or St Teilo or St David himself, who is said to have sent Deiniol into Gaul to fetch a bishop to help combat a recrudescence of Pelagianism.   The same crisis is put forward to account for a synod at Llanddewi Frefi about the year 545 : Rhygyfarch in his *vita* of St David says that David refused to attend this assembly, whereupon Deiniol and Dyfrig were sent to fetch him and succeeded in persuading him to come ; and David's eloquence swept all before him.   A number of miracles are related of St Deiniol, not always free from that element of haughty pride and revenge which is a characteristic of so many Celtic hagiological stories.   When he died he was buried at Ynys Ynlli, now commonly called Bardsey.   St Deiniol is named on various dates, September 11 being the day on which his feast is now kept in the diocese of Menevia.

Very little can be stated with any certainty about this saint, but Baring-Gould and Fisher, LBS., vol. ii, profess to give an account of him ; and something may be gleaned from A. W. Wade-Evans, *Life of St David* (1923) and *Welsh Christian Origins* (1934).   His name is familiar to generations of grateful students from St Deiniol's Library at Hawarden in Flintshire, founded by W. E. Gladstone in 1896.

ST PETER OF CHAVANON   (A.D. 1080)

THE Canons Regular of the Lateran today keep the memory of this saint, who adorned their order in the eleventh century.   He was born in the year 1003 at Langeac in Haute-Loire, and was given a good education in the course of which he discovered his vocation to the priesthood.   After his ordination he was appointed priest of his birthplace, where he faithfully fulfilled his duties and secretly led a very austere life.   He for long desired to leave pastoral work and submit himself to a rule in community, and eventually found an occasion to do so when he was persecuted by the attentions of a woman who was attracted towards him.   He was given some land at Pébrac in Auvergne.   Here St Peter founded and built a monastery for canons regular under the Rule of St Augustine, and himself governed it as the first provost.   The success of his undertaking caused several bishops to call him in to help them to bring rule and order into the collegiate chapters of their cathedrals.   St Peter of Chavanon died on September 9, 1080, and was buried at Pébrac, of which house the holy M. Olier was made abbot *in commendam* at the age of eighteen, in 1626.

There is a life by Stephen, a canon of Pébrac, who was almost a contemporary.   It is printed in the *Acta Sanctorum*, September, vol. iii, with an ample commentary.

BD LOUIS OF THURINGIA   (A.D. 1227)

IF we were bound to take all the writings of hagiographers at the foot of the letter we should be faced with the conclusion that most women saints who were married were hindered (or helped) on the path of sanctity by the ill-will or general short-comings of their husbands ; the unworthy husband of the holy wife is almost common form, and as such it is to be distrusted.   No one has tried to find such unhappy tension between Elizabeth of Hungary and Louis (Ludwig) of Thuringia, for the good reason that it so obviously did not exist (though even here there is a book by a well-known clerical writer in which the author has been betrayed by careless adhesion to common form into applying it to these two) ; veneration for Louis was as spontaneous among his people as it was for his wife : it is true that the *cultus* has not been officially confirmed (it has not been put forward), but it is nevertheless worthy of respect.

Louis was the eldest son of the Landgrave Herman I and was born in 1200. When he was eleven years old a betrothal was arranged for him with Elizabeth, daughter of King Andrew II of Hungary, who was then four.   Later the child was taken to the Thuringian court, the two grew up together, and in 1221, when Louis succeeded his father, the marriage was ratified.   In its origin this alliance was purely one of political expedience, but it proved to be none the worse for that ; they had a son and two daughters, of whom the younger is known as Bd Gertrude of Altenberg.   Louis in every way encouraged the charity and devotion of his wife.   Once he found a leper, who had come to the castle for relief, laid in their bed ; for a moment he was tempted to anger but then he saw, as it were, not the leper but the crucified Son of God lying there, and he made no complaint but instead paid for the building of a lazar-house on the slope of the Wartburg.   St Elizabeth told him they could serve God better if instead of a castle and a county they had land enough for one plough and a couple of hundred sheep.   Her husband laughed.   " We should hardly be poor ", he said, " with so much land and so many sheep.   And there would be plenty of folk to say we were far too well off."

The landgrave was a good ruler as well as a good man.   In 1225 some Thurin-gian merchants were robbed and beaten over the Polish border.   Louis demanded reparation ; none was forthcoming.   So he rode into Poland and by force extorted satisfaction from the citizens of Lubitz.   The same thing happened at Würtzburg ; he marched into the prince-bishopric to recover the stock of which a trader had been robbed.   In 1226 the Emperor Frederick II sent for the military help of Louis, and he assisted with his counsel at the diet of Cremona.   He was away for a winter, a hard winter, and a spring ; when he returned, Elizabeth " a thousand times and more ", says Berthold, " kissed him with her heart and with her mouth", and when he inquired how his people had fared in the terrible frost, " I gave to God what was His, and God has kept for us what was ours ", she replied.   " Let her do good and give to God whatever she will, so long as she leaves me Wartburg and Neuenburg ", was Louis's answer to a complaining treasurer.   In the following year he volunteered to follow the emperor on the crusade (the story of Elizabeth finding the cross in his purse is well known) ; to rouse men's hearts he had a passion-play presented in the streets of Eisenach, and visited the monasteries of his dominion, asking for prayers.   The Central-German forces concentrated at Schmalkalden, and Louis was in command ; here on the birthday of St John he parted from Elizabeth, and set out towards the Holy Sepulchre.   In August he met the emperor at Troja, and in September the army embarked ; three days later the fleet put into Otranto, and Louis took to his bed.   He had a malarial fever and was dying ; he received the last sacraments, and it seemed to him that the cabin wherein he lay was full of doves.   " I must fly away with these white doves ", he said, and died.   When the news was brought to his wife, " The world is dead to me ", she cried, " and all that was pleasant in it ".   The young landgrave was buried in the Benedictine abbey of Reinhardsbrunn, and there he is popularly called " St Ludwig " to this day.

There is a German fourteenth-century translation of a still earlier Latin life of the Landgrave Louis IV.   This Latin biography, written by Bertoldus, who was Louis's chaplain and a monk of Reinhardsbrunn, seems not to have been separately preserved to us, though some contend that it is practically incorporated in the *Annales Reinhardsbrunnenses* which were edited by Wegele in 1854.   There is an excellent article on Louis by C. Wenck in the *Allgemeine deutsche Biographie*, vol. xix, pp. 589–597, and a biography in German by G. Simon (1854).   See also Michael, *Geschichte des deutschen Volkes seit dem* 13 *Jahrh.*, vol. i, p. 221, and ii, pp. 207 *seq.*   Further, the many lives of St Elizabeth of Hungary all contain some notice of her husband.

BD BONAVENTURE OF BARCELONA   (A.D. 1684)

IN his youth this *beatus* was a shepherd near Barcelona.   He was married when he was seventeen, but within two years his wife was dead and he became a Franciscan lay-brother.   He was a man of the deepest spirituality, and his religious ecstasies became so well known that his superiors sent him far off, to Rome, where he became door-keeper at the friary of St Isidore.   But neither could his light be hidden there ; and it was thanks to the interest taken in him by two cardinals that he was able to establish at Ponticelli the first of several houses of retreat, hermitages, for members of his order, although his superiors were not too favourable to the enterprise.   The best-known of these establishments was at Rome itself, on the Palatine.   Bd Bonaventure died in 1684, and he was beatified in 1906.

See the *Acta Ord. Fratrum Minorum*, vol. xxix (1910) ; and Fr Leonard da Popi, *Il b. Bonaventura* . . . (1906 ; Eng. trans., 1920).

BD JOHN GABRIEL PERBOYRE, MARTYR   (A.D. 1840)

THOUGH John Gabriel Perboyre was the first Christian in China to be beatified (in 1889) he was very far from being the first martyr in that country.   After the re-establishment of the missions there in the beginning of the seventeenth century there were only relatively short periods during which Christians were free from danger.   At the end of the eighteenth century fierce persecution was carried on, and was continued sporadically till after the death of Father Perboyre in 1840, thousands of Christians gladly giving up their lives.   Perboyre was born in 1802, and when he was fifteen he was fired by a sermon with the ambition to be a missionary to the heathen ; he joined the Congregation of the Mission (Lazarists, Vincentians), and was ordained in 1826.   At first his desire to carry the gospel to foreign parts had to give way before the requirements of religious obedience.   His theological course had been a brilliant one, and so after his ordination he was appointed professor in the seminary of Saint-Flour, and two years later rector of the *petit séminaire* in the same place.   His own personal goodness was very apparent in these employments, and in 1832 he was sent to Paris to be assistant-director of the general novitiate of his congregation. At intervals since the taking of his vows twelve years before he had asked to be sent to China, from whence reports of the sufferings and heroic deaths of the local Christians continued to come in, but it was not till 1835 that the permission was given.

In that year he arrived at Macao, and at once was set to learn Chinese, for which he showed such aptitude that at the end of four months he was appointed to the mission of Honan. On the eve of setting out he wrote to his brethren in Paris : " If you could see me now in my Chinese ' get-up ' you would see a very curious sight : my head shaved, a long pig-tail and moustaches, stammering my new language, eating with chop-sticks. They tell me that I don't make a bad Chinaman. That is the only way to begin making oneself all things to all men : may we be able thus to win all to Jesus Christ ! " The Lazarists had elaborated a system of rescuing abandoned children, who are so numerous in China, and bringing them up in the faith. In this work Father Perboyre was especially active, and he devoted much of his time to instructing these children, illustrating his lessons by apt stories to which his very colloquial Chinese gave an added flavour. After two years at Honan he was moved to Hupeh, and here in September 1839 there was a sudden and unexplained renewal of persecution.

The missionaries went into hiding, but a neophyte betrayed Father Perboyre (with a horrid fitness, for thirty *taels*—about £9), and he was dragged in chains from functionary to functionary, each of whom questioned him and sent him on to someone else. Finally he came into the hands of the governor and mandarins of Wuchangfu. These required him to betray the hiding-places of his *confrères* and to trample on the cross. The sufferings endured by Father Perboyre were incredible, in the literal sense of the word. Twenty times he was dragged before his judges to be bullied into compliance, and more than twenty times he was tortured because he refused. The ingenuity of the Chinese in inflicting physical pain is notorious, and Father Perboyre underwent torments beside which those invented by hagiographers for some of the martyrs of the Ten Persecutions are crude and clumsy. He was branded on the face with four characters, which stood for " teacher of a false religion ", and a Chinese priest who bribed his way into his prison described him as a mass of open wounds, his very bones in places exposed. On September 11, 1840, almost a year after his capture, Bd John Gabriel, with bare feet and only a pair of drawers under the red robe of the condemned, was strangled with five common criminals. He was buried beside another Lazarist martyr, Francis Regis Clet, who was also to be beatified. In China the feast of Bd John Gabriel is kept on November 7, the nearest convenient date to that of his beatification in 1889.

The murder of John Gabriel Perboyre was the occasion of the British government insisting on a clause in the Treaty of Nanking in 1842 which provided that any foreign missionary who was arrested should not be dealt with by the Chinese authorities but handed over to the nearest consul of his nation.

See the anonymous volume which appeared in 1853 under the title of *Le disciple de Jésus ;* also the biography by Father Huonder, *Der selige Johann Gabriel Perboyre ;* L. Castagnola, *Missionario martire* (1940) ; and A. Chatelet, *J.-G. Perboyre, martyr* (1943). Accounts will also be found in Leclercq, *Les Martyrs*, vol. x, and in the various works of A. Launay dealing with the Chinese missions. For other martyrs in China see under February 17 and references there.

12 : THE HOLY NAME OF MARY

THE object of this feast is our blessed Lady bearing the name of Mary, and it was instituted that on it the faithful might in a special manner recommend to God, through the intercession of His all-holy Mother, the needs of the Church, and thank Him for His almighty protection and numberless mercies, especially those we receive on account of the graces and mediation of the Blessed Virgin. The feast was allowed at Cuenca in Spain in 1513 ; it spread in that country, and in 1683 Pope Innocent XI extended it to the whole Western church, as an act of thanksgiving for the raising of the siege of Vienna and the defeat of the Turks by John Sobieski, King of Poland ; it was at that time assigned to the Sunday within the octave of our Lady's birthday, but is now kept on the date of Sobieski's triumph. Actually this special commemoration is probably somewhat older than 1513, though definite evidence does not seem to be forthcoming. All we can say is that the great devotion to the holy name of Jesus, which we identify in part with the preaching of St Bernardino of Siena, will naturally have prepared the way for a similar commemoration of the holy name of Mary. One curious point with regard to this name which deserves to be noticed is that while in the case of the other Marys who appear in the New Testament we find in the Greek text simply the form Μαρία, the best manuscripts almost uniformly spell the name of our Blessed Lady as Μαριάμ. This seems to mark at least a sense of her dignity : for her alone the Old Testament form of the name is preferred. There is a similar practice in Ireland, where the form Muire is reserved for our Lady, Maire or Moira being given in baptism.

Our name Mary is derived from Maria and Mariam, later forms of Miryam, which was our Lady's name in Hebrew, but the most learned scholars have been unable certainly to decide what was the derivation and meaning of that name. The prevalent view seems to be that it means " wished-for-child ", or, less likely, " rebellion ". It appears certain that the name of Mary has nothing to do with " bitterness ", " the sea " or " a star ".

The various stages in the adoption of the feast of the Holy Name of Mary are set out in Holweck, *Calendarium liturgicum festorum Dei et Dei matris Mariae* (1925), p. 317, and *cf.* Kellner, *Heortology*, p. 264. *Cf.* E. G. Withycombe, *Oxford Dictionary of Christian Names* (2nd edn.), and Fr E. Vogt in *Verbum Domini*, 1948. Pope Benedict XIV's commission recommended the dropping of this feast from the general calendar.

ST AILBHE, BISHOP   (*c.* A.D. 526 ?)

A COMMEMORATION of St Ailbhe (Ailbe, Albeus) is made throughout Ireland on this date, and in the diocese of Emly his feast is kept as that of its patron and first bishop, but the recorded life of the saint is a confusion of valueless legends and contradictory traditions. One concerns his birth of a serving-girl by a chieftain, who ordered that the baby should be exposed to perish. A she-wolf found him and suckled him along with her own cubs, till a hunter found the child in the wolf's lair and took him away. Years later Ailbhe was present at a run, when an aged she-wolf, hard pressed by hounds, ran to him for protection. The bishop recognized his foster-mother, gave her sanctuary, and every day thereafter fed her at his own table. When Ailbhe was a boy in the north of Ireland, he was one day considering the wonders of the natural world, and said aloud, " I pray that I may know the Creator of all things, and I will believe in Him who made the heavens and the earth. For I perceive that these things did not come into existence without a maker, and no human work could produce them." He was overheard by a Christian priest, who thereupon instructed and baptized him. Another account says he was brought up and baptized by a British colony in Ireland. He is supposed to have gone to Rome and to have been consecrated bishop in the city.

Ailbhe preached up and down Ireland, and with such commanding authority did this apostolic man deliver the eternal wisdom to a barbarous people, such was the force with which both by words and example he set forth the divine law, and so evident were the miracles with which he confirmed the truths which he preached, that the sacred doctrine made its way to the hearts of many of his hearers ; he not only brought over a multitude to the faith of Christ but infused into many the spirit of perfection, for he had a wonderful art of making men not only Christians but saints. In his old age it was his desire to retire to Thule, the remotest country toward the northern pole that was known to the ancients (which seems to have been Shetland or Norway), but the king guarded the ports to prevent his flight. Another legend tells us that from this same king, Aengus of Munster, St Ailbhe begged the Isles of Aran for St Enda. Aengus did not know he had such islands in his dominions until they were shown to him in a dream ; whereupon he handed them over, and at Killeaney on Inishmore was founded a monastery which was so famous for holiness that the island was called " Aran of the saints ". It does not detract from the sanctity of Killeaney to point out that among Celtic peoples " saint " was often used synonymously with " monk " or " recluse " ; on Ynys Ynlli (Bardsey) were buried 20,000 " saints ".

It is often said on the poor authority of Ailbhe's *vita* that he preached in Ireland before St Patrick, but he seems certainly to have died in the sixth century : the date is variously put at 526, 531 and 541.

The life in the *Codex Salmanticensis* was edited in that collection by the Bollandists in 1888, cc. 235–260. A somewhat different version has been printed by C. Plummer in his VSH., vol. i, pp. 46–64 ; and note also what is said in the preface to the same work, pp. xxviii–xxxi. What is of more importance than the extravagant incidents of this mythical life, St Ailbhe is the reputed author of a monastic rule ; it was edited by J. O'Neill in *Ériu*, vol. iii (1907) ; and *cf.* L. Gougaud, *Christianity in Celtic Lands* (1932).

ST EANSWIDA, Virgin   (*c.* A.D. 640)

St ETHELBERT, the first Christian king among the English, was succeeded in the kingdom of Kent by his son Edbald, who, though he was at first impious and idolatrous, became afterwards a Christian. His daughter Eanswida added lustre to her birth by the sanctity of her life. She had to oppose her father's wish that she should marry a pagan prince from Northumbria. " I will marry him ", she said, " when by prayer to his gods he has made this log of wood a foot longer." She obtained her father's consent to found a monastery of nuns upon the sea-coast, hard by Folkestone in Kent. Here she sacrificed herself in penance and prayer, till she was called to rest on the last day of August about the year 640, the date on which she is named in some calendars. Her convent was destroyed by the Danes but was refounded for Benedictine monks in 1095. The sea afterwards swallowed up part of this priory and it was removed into Folkestone, and the saint's relics were deposited in that church which had been built by her father in honour of St Peter ; the successor of this church is now known as SS. Mary and Eanswida's.

September 12 is probably the day of the translation of her relics about the year 1140.　Many legends about the miraculous powers of St Eanswida were current in England in the middle ages, some of which are preserved by the chronicler Capgrave.

St Eanswida (or Eanswitha) seems to have been unknown to Bede, but her connexion with Folkestone is alluded to in an Anglo-Saxon document printed by Cockayne (*Leechdoms*, vol. iii, p. 422).　The mention of her name in certain calendars and martyrologies suggests that there was some *cultus* : see Stanton, *Menology*, p. 432.　The statements made by John of Tynemouth and Capgrave can inspire little confidence.

ST GUY OF ANDERLECHT　　(*c.* A.D. 1012)

ALTHOUGH the accounts of this saint derive from late and not very reliable sources, and have been touched up and filled out with edifying but very doubtfully authentic miracles, it is clear that he belongs to that category of simple, hidden souls who, whether as wanderers or workmen, are familiar to us from St Alexis and St John Calybites through St Isidore of Madrid and St Walstan of Costessey down to St Benedict Joseph Labre and Matt Talbot in our own time.

St Guy (Guidon), called the Poor Man of Anderlecht, was born in the country near Brussels, of poor parents, but both virtuous and consequently content and happy.　They were not able to give their son a school education nor did they let that perturb them, but instead they were diligent in instructing him early in the Christian faith and the practices of our holy religion, often repeating to him the lesson which old Tobias gave his son, " We shall have many good things if we fear God ".　St Augustine says that God ranks among the reprobate, not only those who shall have received their comfort on earth, but also those who shall have grieved to be deprived of it.　This was what Guy dreaded.　In order to preserve himself from it he never ceased to beg of God the grace to love the state of poverty in which divine providence had placed him, and to bear all its hardships with joy. The charity which Guy had for his neighbour was no less active.　He divided his pittance with the poor, and often fed them whilst he fasted himself.

When he grew up St Guy wandered about for a time, until one day he came to the church of our Lady at Laeken, near Brussels, whose priest was struck with the piety and willingness of the man, and retained him in the service of his church as sacristan.　Guy accepted the offer with pleasure ; and the cleanliness and good order that appeared in everything under his direction struck all that came to that church.　But Guy, like other simple folk before and since, was induced by a merchant of Brussels to invest his small savings in a commercial venture, but with the unusual motive of having more at his disposal wherewith to relieve the poor. The merchant offered to put him in a way of thus making more provision for them by admitting him into partnership with himself.　It was not easy for him to throw off the importunities of the merchant : the bait was specious and he was taken by it.　But the ship carrying their goods was lost in going out of harbour, and Guy, whose place in the church of Laeken had upon his leaving been given to another, was left destitute.　He saw his mistake in following his own ideas and in forsaking secure and humble employment to embark, though with a good intention, on the affairs of the world, and he blamed himself for the false step he had taken.

In reparation for his folly Guy made a pilgrimage on foot first to Rome and then on to Jerusalem, and visited all the most celebrated shrines in that part of the

Christian world.   After seven years' absence he again reached Belgium, where he
made his way to Anderlecht, dying from exhaustion and illness brought on by the
fatigue of his journeys and other hardships.   Shortly after he was received into
the hospital of Anderlecht he yielded up his soul to God.   He was buried in the
cemetery of the canons there who, after miracles had taken place at his grave,
translated his body into a shrine.   His popular *cultus* among workers with horses
has persisted through the ages.

St Guy, who is known to the Flemings as St Wye, is honoured in a relatively long
biography, printed in the *Acta Sanctorum*, September, vol. iv.   A good deal of folklore is
associated with his *cultus ;* see E. H. van Heurck, *Les Drapelets de pèlerinage en Belgique ;*
F. Mortier in *Folklore brabançon*, vol. x (1930), pp. 46–55 ; and J. Lavalleye in *Annales de
la Soc. d'archéol. de Bruxelles*, t. xxxvii (1934), pp. 221–248.

BD VICTORIA FORNARI-STRATA, WIDOW, FOUNDRESS OF THE BLUE NUNS OF GENOA   (A.D. 1617)

BD MARY VICTORIA was born at Genoa in the year 1562.   At the age of seventeen
there was some talk of her becoming a nun, but she deferred to the wishes of her
father and married Angelo Strata.   They lived together very happily for nine
years, Angelo joining gladly in his wife's charitable works, and defending her from
the adverse criticism of those who wished to see her take more part in social
pleasures.   They had six children, four boys and two girls.   When Angelo died
in 1587 Victoria was for long inconsolable, both for her own sake and for the sake
of the children, whom she felt she was incapable of properly looking after alone.
A certain nobleman of the city wanted her to marry him and she thought she
perhaps ought to for her children's sake.   But her uncertainty was ended by a
happening of which she wrote down an account by the direction of her confessor.
Our Lady appeared in vision and said to her : " My child Victoria, be brave and
confident, for it is my wish to take both the mother and the children under my
protection ; I will care for your household.   Live quietly and without worrying.
All I ask is that you will trust yourself to me and henceforth devote yourself to
the love of God above all things."   Victoria now saw clearly what she must do and
ceased to be disquieted.   She made a vow of chastity and lived in retirement,
giving her whole time to God, her children and the poor.   She allowed no super-
fluity or luxury in her home, and set herself a standard of severe mortification :
when, for example, the Church directed a fast she would always observe it on bread
and water.

After her children were all provided for, Victoria put before the archbishop of
Genoa a project she had formed for a new order of nuns, who were to be devoted in
a special way to our Lady.   For a time the archbishop withheld his approval, for
there was lack of sufficient funds to support such a foundation.   But when one of
her friends offered to bear the expense of providing a building, the archbishop's
consent also was forthcoming.   In the year 1604 Bd Victoria and ten others were
clothed, and professed in the following year.   Their object was to honour in their
lives and worship our Lady in the mystery of her annunciation and hidden life at
Nazareth ; each nun added Maria Annunziata to her baptismal name and the rule of
enclosure of their convent was particularly strict.   By the enthusiasm and zeal of
Mother Victoria a second house was founded in 1612, and soon after the order
spread to France, but not till an attempt had been made behind the back of the
foundress to affiliate the nuns to another order, on the pretence that they were not

strong enough to exist on their own.   Mother Victoria learned what was happening and appealed for the help of our Lady, who in a vision assured her of her unfailing assistance, and the danger was overcome.   Bd Victoria continued to govern her foundation, encouraging her sisters in their penitential life and setting them an example of complete humility and love, till her death at the age of fifty-five.   This took place on December 15, 1617, but today is her feast in the order that she founded.   These nuns are distinguished from those of the Annunciation (*Annonciades*) founded by St Joan of Valois by the epithet " Sky-Blue ", with reference to the colour of their mantles.

On the occasion of the beatification of Mary Victoria in 1828, an Italian life was printed with the title *Vita della b. Maria Vittoria Fornari-Strata, fondatrice dell' Ordine della Santissima Annunziata detto " Le Turchine "*, in other words, called by Italians " the Blue Nuns ".   This life is anonymous, but official.   See also a French account by Father F. Dumortier, *La bse Marie-Victoire Fornari-Strata* (1902).

13 : ST MAURILIUS, Bishop of Angers   (A.D. 453)

THIS Maurilius was a native of Milan who came into Touraine and became a disciple of St Martin, by whom he was ordained.   He was a vigorous missionary, who knew how to make the most of an opportunity.   When a pagan temple was struck by lightning he showed it to the people as an indication of God's anger, and at once set to work to build a church in its place.   He was made bishop of Angers and governed that see in virtue and prudence for thirty years.

Later writers have embroidered his life with a number of quite false tales, particularly one of a dying boy to whom he did not go to minister till it was too late. Overcome with remorse he deserted his see and made his way to the Breton coast. There, having written on a rock the words, " I, Maurilius of Angers, passed this way ", he took ship for Britain.   In the Channel he accidentally dropped the key of his cathedral into the sea.   The people of Angers were stricken with grief at the loss of their bishop, and eventually traced him to Brittany, where the inscription on the rock was found.   Some of them then passed over into Britain to seek him there, and on the way a fish jumped into the boat ; in its belly was found the key of the cathedral of their city.   St Maurilius was presently found working as a gardener, and they besought him to return.   " I cannot come back to Angers ", he said, " without the key of my church."   But when he was shown that they had the key he gladly went with them, and when they had safely arrived he went to the grave of the boy who by his fault had died unconfirmed and unhouseled, and called him by his name.   The boy rose from the grave and was therefore given the name of Renatus (René), and lived to succeed St Maurilius as bishop of Angers : he is venerated as a saint both there and as bishop of Sorrento in Italy.   The fable of an object recovered from the belly of a fish is found in the legends of St Ambrose of Cahors, St Kentigern, St Maglorius and others, as well as in several non-Christian sources, particularly the story of the ring of Polycrates.   There is a tradition at Angers that St Maurilius introduced the feast of the Birthday of our Lady into that diocese, in consequence of a man having a vision of singing angels on the night of September 8 ; but it deserves no more credence than the other stories told about this holy bishop.

On the 3rd of this month is celebrated the feast of another St MAURILIUS, a bishop of Cahors who died in the year 580.

Deliberate fraud has been associated with what at one time passed current as the Life of St Maurilius.   A certain deacon named Archanaldus in 905 rewrote an earlier account of the saint, and pretended that it had originally been compiled by Venantius Fortunatus and had afterwards been corrected by Gregory of Tours.   The deception was exposed by Launoy in 1649, and the whole matter will be found discussed in the *Acta Sanctorum*, September, vol. iv.   The genuine life by Magnobodus, written *c.* 620, has also in part been edited by B. Krusch when writing of Venantius in·MGH., *Auctores Antiquissimi*, vol. iv, pt 2, pp. 84–101.   See also the *Analecta Bollandiana*, vol. xviii (1899), pp. 417–421, and J. Levron, *Les saints du pays angevin* (1943), pp. 53–64.

ST EULOGIUS, PATRIARCH OF ALEXANDRIA   (*c.* A.D. 607)

St EULOGIUS was a Syrian by birth and while young became a monk, and at length abbot of his monastery of the Mother of God at Antioch.   Amongst the evils with which the Church was then afflicted, the disorder and confusion into which the monophysites had thrown the church of Alexandria called for strong measures, and an able pastor endowed with prudence and vigour to apply them.   Upon the death of the patriarch John, in 579, St Eulogius was raised to that dignity.   Two or three years later Eulogius was obliged to make a journey to Constantinople on the affairs of his church, and there he met St Gregory the Great, who was at that time the papal representative (*apocrisiarius*) at the Byzantine court.   Between the two a friendship soon sprang up, and there are extant a number of letters which in after years Gregory addressed to Eulogius.   In one of these letters St Gregory, now pope, refers to the success of the monk Augustine among the pagan Angli, " living in an angle of the world ", stating that on the preceding Christmas-eve ten thousand of them had been baptized ; he goes on to use this as an encouragement for Eulogius in his efforts against the monophysites.   One passage almost seems to imply that St Eulogius had something to do with originating St Augustine's mission to England.   St Gregory, who had already had to rebuke the patriarch of Constantinople, John IV the Faster, for assuming the pompous title of " Oecumenical Patriarch " and had thenceforward in protest signed himself " Servant of the Servants of God ", likewise reproved St Eulogius for addressing him as " Oecumenical Pope ".   " I do not wish to be exalted in words but in virtue ", he wrote.   " Away with these words which puff up pride and offend charity."   Of the numerous writings of St Eulogius, chiefly against heresies, only a sermon and a few fragments remain ; one treatise was submitted to St Gregory before publication, and he approved it with the words, " I find nothing in your writings but what is admirable ".   St Eulogius did not long survive his friend, dying at Alexandria about the year 607.

Besides the *Acta Sanctorum*, September, vol. iv, an account of Eulogius will be found in Bardenhewer's *Patrology* (Eng. trans.), pp. 575–576, and in DCB., vol. ii, p. 283.   His works are printed in Migne, PG., vol. lxxxvi.   See also the *Theologische Quartalschrift*, vol. lxxviii, pp. 353–401.   Pope Gregory I's letter about the English mission is in lib. viii, ind. i, no. 30 of his *Epistolae*.

ST AMATUS, or AME, ABBOT   (*c.* A.D. 630)

THE first in time of the two saints of this name commemorated today was born of a Gallo-Roman family at Grenoble.   While still a child he was taken to the abbey of Agaunum where he passed over thirty years of his life, first as a schoolboy, then as a religious in the community, and finally as a hermit in a cell on the cliff behind the monastery. There he lived alone, supporting himself by the cultivation of a small patch of land, helped therein, it was said in after ages, by divine intervention. Persevering and improving in every grace and virtue, he in the year 614 attracted the attention of St Eustace, when he visited Agaunum on his way back from a visit to Italy. He induced Amatus to return with him to Luxeuil and become a monk in that monastery.

The most important external achievement of St Amatus was the conversion of Romaric, a Merovingian nobleman who had a castle at Habendum, on the Moselle. This conversion was begun when one day St Amatus was dining at the table of Romaric, who asked the question of another certain ruler : " What shall I do to possess everlasting life ? " Amatus pointed out a silver dish as representing the possessions to which his questioner was enslaved, and added the words of our Lord : " Sell all whatever thou hast and give to the poor, and thou shalt have treasure in Heaven. And come, follow me." Romaric took these words to heart and was given the grace to interpret them literally : he manumitted his serfs, gave most of his goods, except Habendum, to the poor and the Church, and became a monk at Luxeuil. Then, about the year 620, the converted nobleman himself founded a double monastery under the Columbanian rule, St Amatus being appointed its first abbot. This monastery was on his estate at Habendum, and was afterwards called after the founder Remiremont (*Romarici Mons*). Its early days are said to have been darkened by a sad quarrel between Amatus and Romaric on the one hand and Eustace on the other, in which a monk of Luxeuil, named Agrestius, was deeply implicated. But that unhappy man came to a bad end : he was murdered (it is said by a wronged husband) and after his death peace was gradually restored. St Amatus died about the year 630, in love and charity with St Eustace and the monks of Luxeuil. During his last years he reverted to the solitary life of his earlier ones, living in a cell apart, cultivating his garden and looking after their bees for the nuns, and coming to choir only on Sundays and great feasts. His friend and convert Romaric took over the direction of the two communities, and in due course he too was venerated as a saint.

The Latin life, which was formerly accepted (*e.g.* in the *Acta Sanctorum*, September, vol. iv) as written by a monk of Remiremont who was practically a contemporary of the saint, has been re-edited by B. Krusch in MGH., *Scriptores Merov.*, vol. iv, pp. 215–221 ; Krusch arrives at the conclusion that the document is quite untrustworthy and fabricated in the ninth century. The matter is not altogether clear, though the life must in any case have been written as much as fifty years after the death of St Amatus. As against Krusch, see Besson in the *Zeitschrift für Schweitzerische Kirchengeschichte*, vol. i (1907), pp. 20–51, and *cf.* the *Analecta Bollandiana*, vol. xxvi, pp. 342–343.

ST AMATUS, OR AMÉ, BISHOP OF SION IN VALAIS (*c.* A.D. 690)

THIS other Amatus became bishop of Sion (Sitten), in what is now Switzerland, about the year 660. We hear little of him till some sixteen years later when, for reasons unknown, King Thierry III of Austrasia banished him to the monastery at Péronne, where St Ultan, brother of its founder St Fursey, was then abbot. After the death of St Ultan, St Amatus was in 686 given into the care of St Maurontus at his newly founded abbey at Breuil in Flanders. On his way thither the bishop, while vesting himself in the church at Cambrai, emulated St Goar and other saints by hanging his cloak not on a beam but on a sun-beam.   But it was the holiness of St Amatus and the injustice of his position, rather than this imaginary incident, that caused St Maurontus to kneel at his feet and apologize for being his guardian.   At Breuil St Amatus both by words and example excited the monks to fervour and humility.   He himself lived in a cell near the church, and occupied his soul in heavenly contemplation.   Thus he lived some years with these monks, and only left them to become an intercessor with Christ in His glory for them about the year 690.

The Roman Martyrology implies that St Amatus was bishop of Sens, as indeed he is generally called ; there has been confusion between *Senonensis* and *Sedunensis*, and his name was interpolated in the episcopal lists of that see during the tenth century.   Nevertheless his attribution to Sion in Valais is not without its difficulties.

There are two Latin lives of the saint, the one printed in the *Acta Sanctorum*, September, vol. iv, the other in the Catalogue of the Hagiographical MSS. of Brussels, ii, pp. 44–55.   The Bollandists formerly described him as bishop of Sens, not Sion, and this view has been supported in modern times by H. Bouvier, *Histoire de l'Église de Sens*, vol. i (1906), pp. 457–460.   On the other side see Besson, *Monasterium Agaunense* (1913), p. 171.   *Cf.* also Duchesne, *Fastes Épiscopaux*, vol. i, p. 246, and ii, p. 239.

14 : THE EXALTATION OF THE HOLY CROSS, COMMONLY CALLED HOLY CROSS DAY   (A.D. 629)

ON this day the Western church celebrates, as we learn from the Roman Martyrology and the lessons at Matins, the veneration of the great relics of Christ's cross at Jerusalem after the Emperor Heraclius had recovered them from the hands of the Persians, who had carried them off in 614, fifteen years before.   According to the story, the emperor determined to carry the precious burden upon his own shoulders into the city, with the utmost pomp ; but stopped suddenly at the entrance to the Holy Places and found he was not able to go forward. The patriarch Zachary, who walked by his side, suggested to him that his imperial splendour was hardly in agreement with the humble appearance of Christ when He bore His cross through the streets of that city.   Thereupon the emperor laid aside his purple and his crown, put on simple clothes, went along barefoot with the procession, and devoutly replaced the cross where it was before.   It was still in the silver case in which it had been carried away, and the patriarch and clergy, finding the seals whole, opened the case with the key and venerated its contents.   The original writers always speak of this portion of the cross in the plural number, calling it the pieces of the wood of the true cross.   This solemnity was carried out with the most devout thanksgiving, the relics were lifted up for the veneration of the people, and many sick were miraculously cured.

In the Eastern church the feast of the World-wide Exaltation of the Holy and Life-giving Cross is one of the greatest of the year, and principally commemorates the finding of the cross and (now on the previous day) the dedication of Constantine's churches at the Holy Sepulchre and Calvary.   The pilgrim Etheria in the fourth century tells us that these dedications were fixed for the same day as that on which the cross was found ; and in early times in the East the feasts of the cross were connected more with the finding, the dedications, and a vision accorded to St Cyril of Jerusalem in 351, rather than with the recovery by Heraclius.   It would appear certain that September 14 was the original date of the commemoration of the finding even at Rome, but that the Exaltation under Heraclius took its place and the Finding was fixed for May 3, according to a Gallican usage.   Mgr Duchesne states that this Holy Cross day in September was a festival of Palestinian origin, " on the anniversary of the dedication of the basilicas erected by Constantine on the sites of Calvary and the Holy Sepulchre ", and he adds : " This dedication festival was celebrated in 335 by the bishops attending the Council of Tyre, who had pronounced upon Athanasius the sentence of deposition.   There was associated with it also the commemoration of the discovery of the true cross ", which was " exalted " before the assembled people.

See L. Duchesne, *Christian Worship* (1919), pp. 274–275, 522–523 and 570–571 ; and Bludau, *Die Pilgerreise der Etheria* (1927), pp. 185–190.   The earliest mention in the West of the feast of the Exaltation of the Cross, under this name, appears to be in the notice of Pope St Sergius I (d. 701) in the *Liber pontificalis*, ed. Duchesne, vol. i, pp. 374–378.   See also K. A. Kellner, *Heortology* (1908), pp. 333–341 ; DAC., vol. iii, cc. 3131–3139 ; and a most useful summary in Baudot and Chaussin, *Vies des saints . . .*, t. v (1947), pp. 63–78. *Cf.* also what is said herein under May 3.

ST MATERNUS, Bishop of Cologne   (Fourth Century)

Maternus was the first bishop of Cologne of whom there is any certain knowledge : he is heard of in connexion with the Donatist controversy.   The schismatic bishops in Africa presented to the Emperor Constantine a petition against the Catholic bishop, Caecilian, asking that the case might be judged by bishops from Gaul, who had no practical interest in the matters at issue.   Constantine sent for three Gallic bishops to assist at the trial in Rome : these were Reticius of Autun, Marinus of Arles and St Maternus of Cologne.   In the year 313 Caecilian was unanimously vindicated.   The Donatists demanded a fresh trial and the emperor directed that a council be held to deal with the matter.   This took place in the follow-ing year, at Arles, and St Maternus was again one of the bishops present. It is possible that at one time he was bishop at Trier, where he seems to have died.

But the legends of Cologne and Trier, accepted in their liturgical books and referred to by the Roman Martyrology, make of St Maternus a very different figure.   Many ancient sees have naturally sought to find for themselves an apostolic or sub-apostolic origin, and among those that have associated themselves with St Peter are Cologne and Trier—the first named claims two bishops called Maternus, in the first and the fourth centuries.   He was, asserts the apocryphal story, the resurrected son of the widow of Naim, who was sent by St Peter himself with St Eucharius and St Valerius to evangelize the Gauls.   When they got so far as Ehl, in Alsace, Maternus died, and his companions returned to Rome, where St Peter gave them his staff, with instructions to lay it upon the dead man.   This was done, and St Maternus underwent another resurrection, and lived to bring the gospel to " the peoples of Tongres, Cologne and Trier and other neighbouring parts ". Almost exactly the same tale is related of other apostolic missionaries to Gaul, and it is of course quite worthless.   There is no reason for supposing that this St Maternus is other than the bishop who attended the Synod of Arles in 314.

The extravagant legend summarized above seems to have been fabricated towards the close of the ninth century by one Eberhard, a monk at Trier.   It is discussed at some length in the *Acta Sanctorum* for September, vol. iv. The text is printed in January, vol. ii (January 29). See also DCB., vol. iii, p. 862 ; Hauck, *Kirchengeschichte Deutschlands*, vol. i, pp. 46–47 ; W. Neuss, *Die Anfänge des Christentums im Rheinlande* (1923), pp. 13–20, and Duchesne, *Fastes Épiscopaux*, vol. iii, pp. 34 and 178.

ST NOTBURGA, Virgin   (*c.* A.D. 1313)

Some fourteen years before the death of St Zita at Lucca there was born at Rattenberg in Tirol a girl who was to become as well known as a patron of domestic servants in her own neighbourhood as is St Zita in a more extended area. This girl, Notburga by name, was the daughter of a peasant, and at the age of eighteen entered the service of Count Henry of Rattenberg and was employed in the kitchen. There was a good deal of food left over from the tables of this feudal establishment, and Notburga used to take it to one of the side doors of the castle and give it away to the poor people who daily waited there. Not content with this, she would even stint her own meals to increase the portion of the poor. When Count Henry's mother died, his wife, the Countess Ottilia, looked less favourably on the charity of the kitchen-maid, and gave orders that the broken food was to go into the pigbuckets as heretofore, and be fed to the swine. For a time Notburga did as she was told, and gave to the poor only what she could save from her own food and drink, but she soon began secretly to continue her old practice, till one day her mistress caught her at it and she was dismissed. The Countess Ottilia died shortly after, and the victims of her parsimony, with that whimsical realism with which the poor watch the antics of the rich, said that her ghost haunted the pigsties of Rattenberg castle, and that the count had had to have the place exorcized.

Notburga now hired herself to a farmer at Eben, and a legendary incident during her time with him is familiar to all good Tirolese children. One Saturday afternoon in the harvest-time Notburga was reaping, when the church bell rang for Vespers, indicating that Sunday was begun. Notburga stopped work and was preparing to go to church, when her employer came along and told her to go on working. She refused : Sunday begins with Saturday Vespers, and good Christians do not reap on Sundays in fine weather. The farmer argued ; the weather might change. " Very well ", replied St Notburga, " let this decide it." Picking up the sickle, she threw it into the air—and there it remained suspended, looking like the first quarter of the harvest moon against the evening sky.

Count Henry in the meantime had been suffering considerably in the strife between the count of Tirol and the duke of Bavaria, and St Notburga's biographer, who wrote in the seventeenth century and had a lively and credulous imagination, says that Henry attributed all his misfortunes to the meanness of his late wife and the consequent dismissal of Notburga. So, when he married a second time and somebody was required to manage the household, she was installed as housekeeper and lived a happy and holy life at Rattenberg for the rest of her days. Before she died she particularly recommended her beloved poor to her master, and asked him to lay her body on a farm-wagon and bury it wherever the oxen should finally rest. This was done, and after a journey of which the usual miraculous accompaniments are recorded, the oxen brought the burden to a halt before the door of the church of St Rupert at Eben. Here accordingly St Notburga was buried. In 1862

Pope Pius IX confirmed her local *cultus* as patroness of poor peasants and hired servants.

Although we are dependent almost entirely upon the life originally published in German in 1646 by H. Guarinoni, still there seem, as we learn from Rader's *Bavaria Sancta* and other sources, to have been materials of earlier date. In the *Acta Sanctorum*, September, vol. iv, Guarinoni's narrative is translated into Latin, and accompanied with full prolegomena and a number of curious engravings of the *cultus* of St Notburga.

15 : THE SEVEN SORROWS OF THE BLESSED VIRGIN MARY

TWICE during the year the Western church commemorates the sorrows of the Blessed Virgin Mary, on the Friday in Passion week and again on this September 15. The first is the older feast, instituted at Cologne and elsewhere during the fifteenth century. It was then called the Commemoration of the Distress and Sorrow of the Blessed Virgin Mary, and had in view specifically our Lady's suffering during the passion of her divine Son. When the feast was extended to the whole Western church in 1727 under the title of the Seven Sorrows, the original reference of the Mass and Office to the Crucifixion was retained, and the commemoration is still called the Compassion of our Lady in some calendars *e.g.* those of the Benedictines and Dominicans, as it was in many places before the eighteenth century.

In the middle ages there was a popular devotion to the five joys of Mary, and this was soon complemented by another in honour of five of her sorrows at the Passion. Later, these were fixed at seven, and extended back from Calvary to embrace her whole life. The Servite friars, who from their beginning had a particular devotion to the sufferings of Mary, were in 1668 granted a feast for the third Sunday in September on which these Seven Sorrows should be commemorated, and this feast also was extended to the Western church in 1814. For long there were several different ways of enumerating these mysteries, but since the composition of the liturgical office they have been fixed by the responsories at Matins as : (i) The prophecy of holy Simeon. " There was a man named Simeon, and this man was just and devout ; and he said unto Mary : Thine own soul also a sword shall pierce." (ii) The flight into Egypt. " Arise, and take the Child and His mother and fly into Egypt ; and be there until I shall tell thee." (iii) The three days' disappearance of the boy Jesus. " Son, why hast thou done so to us ? Behold thy father and I have sought thee, sorrowing." (iv) The painful progress to Calvary. " And bearing His own cross He went forth. And there followed Him a great multitude of people, and of women who bewailed and lamented Him." (v) The crucifixion. " And when they were come to the place which is called Calvary, they crucified Him there. Now there stood by the cross of Jesus His mother." (vi) The taking down from the cross. " Joseph of Arimathaea begged the body of Jesus. And taking it down from the cross His mother received it into her arms." (vii) The entombment. " What a sadness of heart was thine, Mother of sorrows, when Joseph wrapped Him in fine linen and laid Him in a sepulchre."

Much has been written about the gradual evolution of this consecrated number of our Lady's sorrows or " dolours ", but the subject ha by no means been exhausted. One of the most valuable contributions to the history is an article in the *Analecta Bollandiana* (vol. xii, 1893, pp. 333–352), under the title " La Vierge aux Sept Glaives ", written in reply to a foolish attempt of the folklorist H. Gaidoz to connect the devotion with a Chaldean cylinder at the British Museum. It bears a representation of the Assyrian goddess Istar ; around this is a sort of trophy of arms, which can be resolved into seven separate weapons. The coincidence is by no means striking in itself, and there is not a shadow of evidence to suggest any link between Assyria and this very late western devotion. We know for certain that in the middle ages a recognition of five joys and then of seven preceded any specified numbering of our Lady's sorrows. Moreover, before a settled convention was arrived at we hear occasionally of nine joys, fifteen sorrows, or twenty-seven sorrows, etc. On all this consult S. Beissel, *Geschichte der Verehrung Marias in Deutschland*, vol. i (1909), pp. 404–413, and, on the liturgical commemoration, vol. ii of the same work (1910), pp. 364–367. Further information as to the local observance of the feast in the past is afforded by Holweck, *Calendarium liturgicum festorum* . . . (1925). Although its general observance was then quite new, Benedict XIV's commission advocated the removal of this feast from the general calendar.

ST NICOMEDES, .Martyr   (Date Unknown)

Nicomedes was a martyr of the Roman church who was buried in a catacomb on the Via Nomentana, just outside the Porta Pia. There was a church dedicated in his honour, and there is good evidence of his early *cultus*. The Roman Martyrology says that, " on saying to those who tried to make him sacrifice, ' I do not sacrifice except to the almighty God who reigns in Heaven ', he was for a long time beaten with leaded whips and under this torture passed to the Lord ". But this is derived from an account of him in the worthless *acta* of SS. Nereus and Achilleus,wherein he is represented as a priest who buried the body of St Felicula, was arrested and put to death, and his body thrown into the Tiber whence it was recovered by the deacon Justus. Another recension of his passion makes him suffer in the third-fourth century, under the Emperor Maximian. His catacomb was discovered in 1864.

It is curious that the name of Nicomedes does not occur in the Roman list, *Depositio martyrum*, of 354 ; but the Itineraries, as well as the Sacramentaries, authenticate his early *cultus* in Rome. The evidence has been set out in Delehaye's CMH., p. 510.

ST NICETAS THE GOTH, Martyr   (A.D. 375)

Saints Sabas and Nicetas are the two most renowned martyrs among the Goths. The former is honoured on April 12, the latter, whom the Greeks place in the class of the " great martyrs ", is commemorated on this day. He was a Goth, born near the banks of the Danube, and converted to the faith in his youth by Ulfilas, a great missionary among those people, and translator of the Bible into the Gothic tongue. By him Nicetas was ordained priest. In the year 372 Athanaric, king of the Eastern Goths who bordered upon the Roman empire toward Thrace, raised a persecution against the Christians, occasioned by the ill-treatment by the Roman authorities of a number of Goths who had taken refuge in Moldavia from the Huns. By his order an idol was carried in a chariot through all the towns and villages where it was suspected that any Christians lived, and all who refused to worship it were put to death. The usual method of the persecutors was to burn the Christians with their children in their houses or in the churches where they were assembled together. In the army of martyrs which glorified God on this occasion, St Nicetas sealed his faith and obedience with his blood, and triumphing over sin passed to eternal glory by the death of fire. His relics were taken to Mopsuestia in Cilicia and there enshrined, whence it came about that this Visigothic martyr is venerated throughout the Byzantine and Syrian churches.

On September 12 the feast is observed at Venice of another St Nicetas, a martyr under Diocletian.

The Greek text of the *passio* of St Nicetas, as presented by the Metaphrast, was printed with a commentary in the *Acta Sanctorum*, September, vol. v.   But in the *Analecta Bollandiana*, vol. xxxi (1912), pp. 209–215, the earlier original of this account has been critically edited, with a commentary which occupies pp. 281–287 of the same volume.

ST AICHARDUS, or ACHARD, Abbot   (*c.* A.D. 687)

It is related that Aichardus at the age of ten was taken to be educated at a monastery at Poitiers.   Here he remained till his father thought it was time for him to come home and be introduced to the life of court and camp ; but his mother was concerned that he should become a saint, and that this end alone should be considered in it.   This led to considerable disagreement between the parents, and to end it Aichardus himself was called in to give his opinion.   This he expressed to his father with so much earnestness and in so dutiful a manner that he gained his consent upon the spot : Aichardus went without delay to the abbey of St Jouin at Ansion in Poitou.

St Aichardus had been at Ansion for thirty-nine years when the priory of St Benedict at Quinçay was founded by St Philibert, who peopled it with fifteen monks from Jumièges and made Aichardus their superior.   Under his rule the new house prospered and soon augmented its numbers.   When St Philibert finally retired from Jumièges he resigned that abbacy to St Aichardus, whose nomination was accepted by the community in consequence of a vision granted to one of their number.   This was not the only occasion in the career of Aichardus that, according to tradition, a vision was vouchsafed at a particularly useful moment.   There were then at Jumièges nine hundred monks, among whom he promoted monastic perfection by his example, and this manner of exhorting proved most effectual for some of them.   But others were not so easily led, until their abbot had a dream of the approaching death and judgement of 442 of them : this had a great effect in heightening their observance.

St Aichardus was forewarned of the death of St Philibert very shortly before his own, and when his time came he was laid on ashes and covered with sackcloth, and said to the monks : " My dear children, never forget the last advice and testament of your most loving father.   I implore you in the name of our divine Saviour always to love one another, and never to suffer the least coldness toward any brother to be for a moment in your breasts, or anything by which perfect charity may suffer any harm in your souls.   You have borne the yoke of penance and are grown old in the exercise of religious duties in vain, if you do not sincerely love one another.   Without this, martyrdom itself cannot make you acceptable to God.   Fraternal charity is the soul of a religious house."   Having spoken these words, he happily surrendered his soul into the hands of his Creator.

The Cistercian menology on this same day commemorates a Bd Aichardus who was evidently a man whose virtues and abilities were equally above the average for he was master of novices at Clairvaux and was used by St Bernard in the work of his foundations.   He died about 1170.

A full account of St Aichardus is given in the *Acta Sanctorum*, September, vol. v, but little trust can be placed in the published lives of the saint.

ST MIRIN   (SEVENTH CENTURY ?)

ST MIRIN (Meadhran) was an Irish missionary in Scotland, who was buried at Paisley, where his shrine became a place of pilgrimage.   He was co-titular of the medieval abbey there, and other churches in Scotland bore his name.   According to the Aberdeen Breviary, Mirin was a disciple of St Comgall and was for a time abbot of Bangor.   Characteristic of the vindictive strain in some Celtic hagiology, it is related that Mirin laid the pains of childbirth on an Irish king who had opposed him.

His feast, as a bishop, is observed in the diocese of Paisley, where the cathedral church is dedicated in his honour.

See the *Acta Sanctorum*, September, vol. v ; KSS., pp. 397, 406.   *Cf.* M. Barrett, *A Calendar of Scottish Saints* (1904), p. 123, and *Footprints of the Ancient Scottish Church* (1914), p. 184 ; and LIS., vol. ix, p. 377.   Mirin is not to be confused with the eponymous saint of Saint Merryn in Cornwall, apparently a woman, and not certainly identified.

ST CATHERINE OF GENOA, WIDOW   (A.D. 1510)

THE Fieschi were a great Guelf family of Liguria, with a long and distinguished history.   In 1234 it gave to the Church the vigorous Pope Innocent IV, and in 1276 his nephew, who ruled for a few weeks as Adrian V.   By the middle of the fifteenth century it had reached the height of its power and splendour in Liguria, Piedmont and Lombardy ; one member was a cardinal, and another, James, descended from the brother of Innocent IV, was viceroy of Naples for King René of Anjou.   This James Fieschi was married to a Genoese lady, Francesca di Negro, and to them was born at Genoa in the year 1447 the fifth and last of their children, Caterinetta, now always called Catherine.   Her biographers give particulars of her promising childhood which may perhaps be dismissed as common-form panegyric, but from the age of thirteen she was undoubtedly strongly attracted to the religious life. Her sister was already a canoness regular and the chaplain of her convent was Catherine's confessor, so she asked him if she also could take the habit.   In consultation with the nuns he put her off on account of her youth, and about the same time Catherine's father died.   Then, at the age of sixteen, she was married. It is alleged of many saints, both male and female, that, though wishing to enter a monastery, they married in obedience to the will of those in authority over them, and of some of them these circumstances are only doubtfully true.   But about St Catherine of Genoa there is no question.   The star of the Ghibelline family of the Adorni was in decline, and by an alliance with the powerful Fieschi they hoped to restore the fortunes of their house.   The Fieschi were willing enough, and Catherine was their victim.   Her bridegroom was Julian Adorno, a young man with too poor a character to bring any good out of his marriage as a marriage. Catherine was beautiful in person (as may be seen from her portraits), of great intelligence and sensibility, and deeply religious ; of an intense temperament, without humour or wit.   Julian was of very different fibre, incapable of appreciating his wife, and to that extent to be commiserated ; but if he failed to win more than her dutiful submission and obedience it was either because he did not try, or because he set about it in the wrong way.   He was, on his own admission, unfaithful to her; for the rest, he was pleasure-loving to an inordinate degree, undisciplined, hot-tempered and spendthrift.   He was hardly ever at home, and for the first five years of her married life Catherine lived in solitude and moped amid vain regrets. Then for another five she tried what consolations could be found in the gaieties and recreations of her world, and was little less sad and desperate than before.

She had, however, never lost trust in God, or at least so much of it as was implied in the continued practice of her religion, and on the eve of the feast of St Benedict in 1473 she was praying in a church dedicated in his honour near the sea-shore outside Genoa. And she asked that saint, " St Benedict, pray to God that He make me stay three months sick in bed ". Two days later she was kneeling for a blessing before the chaplain at her sister's convent when she was suddenly overcome by a great love of God and realization of her own unworthiness. She repeated over and over interiorly, " No more world ! No more sins ! " and she felt that " had she had in her possession a thousand worlds, she would have cast them all away ". She was able to do nothing but mumble an excuse and retire, and within the next day or two she had a vision of our Lord carrying His cross which caused her to cry out, " O Love, if it be necessary I am ready to confess my sins in public ! " Then she made a general confession of her whole life with such sorrow " as to pierce her soul ". On the feast of the Annunciation she received holy communion, the first time with fervour for ten years, and shortly after became a daily communicant, so remaining for the rest of her life—a most rare thing in those days, so that she used to say she envied priests, who could receive our Lord's body and blood daily without exciting comment.

At about this time his luxury and extravagance had brought Julian to the verge of ruin, and his wife's prayers, added to his misfortunes, brought about a reformation in his life. They moved from their *palazzo* into a small house, much more humble and in a poorer quarter than was necessary ; agreed to live together in continence ; and devoted themselves to the care of the sick in the hospital of Pammatone. Associated with them was a cousin of Catherine, Tommasina Fieschi, who after her widowhood became first a canoness and then a Dominican nun. This went on for six years without change, except in the development of St Catherine's spiritual life, till in 1479 the couple went to live in the hospital itself, of which eleven years later she was appointed matron. She proved as capable an administrator as she was a devoted nurse, especially during the plague of 1493, when four-fifths of those who remained in the city died. Catherine caught the distemper off a dying woman whom she had impulsively kissed, and herself nearly died. During the visitation she first met the lawyer and philanthropist Hector Vernazza, who was soon to become her ardent disciple (and also the father of the Venerable Battista Vernazza) and to whom is due the preservation of many precious details of her life and conversation. In 1496 Catherine's health broke down and she had to resign the control of the hospital, though still living within the building, and in the following year her husband died after a painful illness. " Messer Giuliano is gone ", she said to a friend, " and as you know well he was of a rather wayward nature, so that I suffered much interiorly. But my tender Love assured me of his salvation before he had yet passed from this life." Julian provided in his will for his illegitimate daughter Thobia, and her unnamed mother, and St Catherine made herself responsible for seeing that Thobia should never be in want or uncared for.

For over twenty years St Catherine had lived without any spiritual direction whatever, and going only rarely to confession. Indeed, it is possible that, having no serious matter on her conscience, she did not always make even an annual confession, and she had, without fussiness, found no priest who understood her spiritual state with a view to direction. But about 1499 a secular priest, Don Cattaneo Marabotto, was made rector of the hospital, and " they understood each other, even by just looking each other in the face without speaking ". To him she said, " Father, I do not know where I am, either in soul or body. I should like to confess, but I am not conscious of any sin." And Don Marabotto lays bare her state in a sentence : " And as for the sins which she did mention, she was not allowed to see them as so many sins thought or said or done by herself. She was like a small boy who has committed some slight offence in ignorance, and who, if someone tells him, ' You have done wrong ', starts and blushes, yet not because he has now an experimental knowledge of evil." We are also told in her life " that Catherine did not take care to gain plenary indulgences. Not that she did not hold them in great reverence and devotion and consider them of very great value, but she wished that the selfish part of her should be rather chastised and punished as it deserved. . . ." In pursuance of the same heroic idea she but rarely asked others, whether on earth or in Heaven, to pray for her ; the invocation of St Benedict mentioned above is a very notable exception and the only one recorded as regards the saints. It is also noteworthy that throughout her widowhood St Catherine remained a lay-woman. Her husband on his conversion joined the third order of St Francis (and to become a tertiary of any order was in those days a far more serious matter than it is now), but she did not do even that. These peculiarities are mentioned neither for commendation nor reprobation ; those to whom they appear surprising may be reminded that those who examined the cause of her beatification were perfectly well aware of them : the Universal Church does not demand of her children a uniformity of practice compatible neither with human variousness nor the freedom of the Holy Spirit to act on souls as He wills.

From the year 1473 on St Catherine without intermission led a most intense spiritual life combined with unwearying activity on behalf of the sick and sad, not only in the hospital but throughout Genoa. She is one more example of the Christian universality which those who do not understand call contradictions : complete " other-worldliness " and efficient " practicality " ; concern for the soul and care for the body ; physical austerity which is modified or dropped at the word of authority, whether ecclesiastical, medical or social ; a living in the closest union with God and an " all-thereness " as regards this world and warm affection for individuals in it. The life of St Catherine has been taken as the text of a most searching work on the mystical element in religion—and she kept the hospital accounts without ever being a farthing out and was so concerned for the right disposition of property that she made four wills with several codicils.

Catherine suffered from ill health for some years and had to give up not only her extraordinary fasts, but even to a certain extent those of the Church, and at length in 1507 her health gave way completely. She rapidly got worse, and for the last months of her life suffered great agony ; among the physicians who attended her was John-Baptist Boerio, who had been the principal doctor of King Henry VII of England, and he with the others was unable to diagnose her complaint. They eventually decided " it must be a supernatural and divine thing ", for she lacked all pathological symptoms which they could recognize. On September 13, 1510, she was in a high fever and delirium, and at dawn of the 15th " this blessed soul gently breathed her last in great peace and tranquillity, and flew to her tender and much-desired Love ". She was beatified in 1737, and Benedict XIV added her name to the Roman Martyrology, with the title of saint. St Catherine left two written works, a treatise on Purgatory and a Dialogue of the soul and the body, which the Holy Office declared were alone enough to prove her sanctity. They are among the more important documents of mysticism, but Alban Butler says of them very truly that " these treatises are not writ for the common ".

Apart from a short notice by Giustiniano, Bishop of Nibio, in his *Annali di Genova* (1537), the earliest biographical account of St Catherine seems to be preserved in manuscripts varying considerably in their Italian text and belonging to the years 1547–1548. From these in the main was compiled the first book concerning her which was printed in any detail. It is commonly known as the *Vita e Dottrina*, and was issued in 1551. This work, which has been often reprinted, is our principal source of information concerning the saint, and it contains also a collection of her sayings and meditations. The many problems connected with its text have been discussed in great detail by Baron Friedrich von Hügel in his important work, *The Mystical Element of Religion* (2 vols., 1908) ; see especially vol. i, pp. 371–466. His conclusions are beyond doubt justified in the main, but there is room for some difference of opinion as to details, as noted, *e.g.* in *The Month*, June, 1923, pp. 538–543. See also the *Acta Sanctorum*, September, vol. v. The numerous modern lives of St Catherine are based on the *Vita e Dottrina ;* among the more recent are Lili Sertorius, *Katharina von Genua* (1939), and L. de Lapérouse, *La vie de ste Catherine de Gênes* (1948). A new translation of the Purgatory treatise and the Dialogue was published in 1946, made by Helen Douglas Irvine and Charlotte Balfour.

16 : ST CORNELIUS, POPE AND MARTYR (A.D. 253)

OWING to the violence of the Decian persecution the Roman see was vacant for over twelve months after the martyrdom of Pope St Fabian, when at length the priest Cornelius was elected, " by the judgement of God and of Christ, by the testimony of most of the clergy, by the vote of the people, with the consent of aged priests and of good men, to the vacant place of Peter ", says St Cyprian. " He bravely accepted the episcopate, courageously seating himself in the sacerdotal chair, strong of mind, firm of faith, at a time when the tyrant [Decius] was, in his hatred of bishops, uttering unspeakable threats against them and was more concerned about a new bishop of God in Rome than about a rival prince in the empire." But the immediate troubles of the new pope were due not so much to the secular power as to internal dissension, though that dissension was brought about by persecution, or rather, by its temporary cessation.

During the papal vacancy a dispute had arisen in Africa concerning the way in which repentant apostates should be treated, and an indulgent party had arisen which threatened both canonical discipline and episcopal authority. The bishop of Carthage, St Cyprian, had written to Rome for support of his contention that such penitents could be readmitted to communion only by a free decision of the bishop ; and a certain priest called Novatian, a leader among the Roman clergy, had replied approvingly, but with a hint of a more severe attitude. A few weeks after the election of Cornelius, this Novatian set himself up as bishop of Rome in opposition ; and he denied that the Church had any power at all to pardon *lapsi*, however repentant they might be and whatever penance they had undergone. Murder, adultery, fornication and a second marriage were by him added to apostasy as " unforgivable sins ". Like Hippolytus before him, Novatian was superior in natural ability to the pope whom he opposed ; but he was undone by pride and ambition, and thus became the first formal antipope and the leader of an heretical sect that persisted for several centuries, at any rate in Africa. In his stand that the Church has the power to forgive repentant apostates, and that she should readmit them to communion after due penance, Pope Cornelius had the support of St Cyprian and the other African bishops, and of most of those of the East ; and at a synod of Western bishops in Rome the teaching of Novatian was condemned, and he and his followers excommunicated.

Persecution of Christians was intensified again at the beginning of 253, and the pope was banished to Centumcellae (Civita Vecchia). Cyprian, who had a great admiration for St Cornelius, wrote him a congratulatory letter upon his happiness in suffering for Christ, and even more upon the glory of his church, for not a single Roman Christian had apostatized : " With one heart and one voice the whole Roman church confessed. Then was seen, most dear brother, that faith which the blessed Apostle praised in you [*Cf.* Romans i 8], for even then he foresaw in spirit your glorious fortitude and firm strength." He clearly foretells the approaching conflicts of them both, and adds : " Whoever of us shall be first taken hence, let our charity persevere in never-ceasing prayer to the Father for our brethren and sisters." St Cornelius was the first to be called, in June of the same year, 253. St Cyprian often refers to him as a martyr, but, though later accounts say he was beheaded, he was probably not put directly to death but died of hardships at Centumcellae. His body was taken to Rome and buried, not in the papal cemetery proper but in the near-by crypt of Lucina, which was perhaps the burying-place of the *gens Cornelia*, to which this pope is said to have belonged.

The great supporter of Pope St Cornelius, both as supreme pontiff and as defender of the Church against Novatian's rigorism, was Cyprian of Carthage, and their close association has ever since been recognized. St Cyprian's memory was kept at the tomb of Cornelius in the fourth century and his image painted on the wall of the crypt in the eighth ; they are named together in the canon of the Mass and in the Roman Martyrology on September 14, the date of Cyprian's martyrdom ; and two days later their joint feast is kept by the whole Western church.

The story of St Cornelius forms an important episode in ecclesiastical history, and from Eusebius downwards it has engaged the attention of all writers who deal with the Christian Church in the early centuries. Besides the *Acta Sanctorum*, September, vol. iv, and the works of Grisar, Duchesne, J. P. Kirsch, etc., see especially A. d'Alès, *Novatien* (1925) and J. Chapman, *Studies on the Early Papacy* (1928), pp. 28 *seq.* As for the " martyrdom ", the place of interment, and the inscription and fresco of St Cornelius in the catacombs, see Wilpert, *La cripta dei Papi e la cappella di santa Cecilia* (1910) ; Franchi de' Cavalieri, *Note agiografiche*, vol. vi, pp. 181–210 ; and Delehaye in the *Analecta Bollandiana*, vol. xxix (1910), pp. 185–186. Leclercq in DAC. (vol. iii, cc. 2968–2985) reproduces several illustrations from de Rossi and Wilpert. The so-called *passio* of St Cornelius (the various redactions of which are catalogued in BHL., nn. 1958–1966) is an historically worthless document.

ST CYPRIAN, Bishop of Carthage, Martyr   (A.D. 258)

ST CYPRIAN played an important part in the history of the Western church and the development of Christian thought in the third century, particularly in Africa where his influence was preponderant. By his personal prestige, even more than by that of his see, he became recognized as in fact the primate of the African church, and he is daily named in the canon of the Roman Mass. He was called officially Caecilius Cyprianus, popularly known as Thascius, and was born about the year 200, probably at Carthage ; certainly he was, according to St Jerome, a native of

Proconsular Africa. Very little is known of his pre-Christian life ; he was a public orator, teacher of rhetoric, and pleader in the courts, and engaged to the full in the life of Carthage, both public and social. God's instrument of his conversion, somewhere about middle age, was an old priest, Caecilian, and Cyprian ever after reverenced him as his father and guardian angel. Caecilian, in turn, had the greatest confidence in his virtue and on his death-bed recommended his wife and children to Cyprian's care and protection. A complete change came over Cyprian's life. Before his baptism he made a vow of perfect chastity, which greatly astonished the Carthaginians and drew even from his biographer St Pontius the exclamation, " Who ever saw such a miracle ! "

With the study of the Holy Scriptures St Cyprian joined that of their best expositors, and in a short time became acquainted with the works of the greatest religious writers. He particularly delighted in the writings of his countryman Tertullian, scarce passed a day without his reading something in them, and when he wanted them he used to say, " Reach hither my master ". Not the least of his sacrifices was the renouncement of all profane literature, and in his own extensive writings there is not a single quotation from any pagan author ; in the earlier centuries of Christianity such a policy had a value which it no longer has today. Cyprian was soon made priest, and in 248 he was designated for the bishopric of Carthage. At first he refused and sought to fly, but finding it in vain he yielded and was consecrated. A few priests with some of the people opposed his election, which, however, was validly carried out, " after the divine judgement, the choice of the people, and the consent of the episcopate ". Cyprian administered his office with charity, goodness, and courage mixed with vigour and steadiness. His aspect was reverent and gracious beyond what can be expressed, says Pontius, and no one could look him in the face without awe ; his countenance had a mixture in it of cheerfulness and gravity, so that a person who beheld him might doubt whether he should love or respect him most : but this was certain, that he deserved the highest degree both of respect and love.

The Church continued to enjoy peace for about a year after St Cyprian's pro- motion to the see of Carthage, till the Emperor Decius began his reign by raising a persecution. Years of quietness and prosperity had had a weakening effect among the Christians, and when the edict reached Carthage there was a stampede to the capitol to register apostasies with the magistrates, amid cries of " Cyprian to the lions ! " from the pagan mob. The bishop was proscribed, and his goods ordered to be forfeited, but Cyprian had already retired to a hiding-place, a proceeding which brought upon him much adverse criticism both from Rome and in Africa. He felt put on his defence, and set out justifying reasons for his action in several letters to the clergy. And there is no doubt that he did right to hide in the cir- cumstances. He supplied the want of his personal presence with his flock by frequent letters. He exhorted them to continual prayer, saying, " What has moved me more particularly to write to you in this manner was an admonition which I received in a vision from Heaven saying to me : ' Ask and you shall receive.' " " Let each of us ", he wrote, " pray to God not for himself only but for all the brethren, according to the pattern which our Lord gave us wherein we are taught to pray as a common brotherhood, for all, and not as individuals, for ourselves alone. When the Lord shall see us humble, peaceable, in unity among ourselves, and made better by our present sufferings, he will deliver us from the hands of our perse- cutors." He assured them that this storm had been revealed by God, before it happened, to a devout person at Carthage in a vision of the enemy under the figure of a *retiarius** watching to destroy the faithful, because they did not stand upon their guard.   In the same letter he mentions another revelation of God, which he himself had concerning the end of the persecution and the restoration of peace to the Church.   By such letters he warned and encouraged his flock, heartened the confessors in prison, and took care that priests in turns should visit them and give them holy communion in their dungeons.

During the absence of St Cyprian one of the priests who had opposed his episcopal election, named Novatus, went into open schism. Some among the lapsed, and confessors who were displeased at St Cyprian's discipline towards the former, adhered to him, for Novatus received, without any canonical penance, all apostates who desired to return to the communion of the Church.   St Cyprian denounced Novatus, and at a council convened at Carthage when the persecution slackened he read a treatise on the unity of the Church.   " There is ", said he, " one God and one Christ and but one episcopal chair, originally founded on Peter, by the Lord's authority.   There cannot therefore be set up another altar or another priesthood.   Whatever any man in his rage or rashness shall appoint, in defiance of the divine institution, must be a spurious, profane and sacrilegious ordinance " ; as Peter is the earthly foundation of the whole Church, so is its lawful bishop of each diocese.   The leaders of the schismatics were excommunicated, and Novatus departed to Rome to help stir up trouble there, where Novatian had set himself up as antipope.   Cyprian recognized Cornelius as the true pope and was active in his support both in Italy and Africa during the ensuing schism ; with St Dionysius, Bishop of Alexandria, he rallied the bishops of the East to Cornelius, making it clear to them that to adhere to a false bishop of Rome was to be out of communion with the Church.   In connexion with these disturbances he added to his treatise on Unity one on the question of the Lapsed.

St Cyprian complains in many parts of his works that the peace which the Church had enjoyed had enervated in some Christians the watchfulness and spirit of their profession, and had opened a door to many converts who had not the true spirit of faith, so that there was much relaxation and, their virtue being put to the test in the persecution raised by Decius, many lacked courage to stand the trial. These, whether apostates who had sacrificed to idols or *libellaticii* who, without sacrificing, had purchased for money certificates that they *had* offered sacrifice, were the lapsed (*lapsi*), concerning the treatment of whom so great a controversy raged during and after the Decian persecution : on the side of excessive lenience Novatus went into schism, while Novatian's severity crystallized into the heresy that the Church cannot absolve an apostate at all.   At this time those guilty of less heinous sins than apostasy were not admitted to assist at the holy Mysteries before they had gone through a rigorous course of public penance, consisting of four degrees and of several years' continuance.   Relaxations of these penances were granted on certain extraordinary occasions, and it was also customary to grant " indulgences " to penitents who received a recommendation from some martyr going to execution, or from some confessor in prison for the faith, containing a request on their behalf, which the bishop and his clergy examined and often ratified.†   In St Cyprian's time this custom degenerated in Africa into an abuse, by

---

* A gladiator who was armed with a net (*rete*) wherein he tried to entangle his opponent.
† The terms of time (300 days, 7 years, etc.) in which indulgences are granted today is a survival from the days when the discipline of public penance was still in force in the Church.

the number of such *libelli martyrum*, and their often being given in too vague or peremptory terms, and without examination or discernment.

Cyprian condemned these abuses severely, but though it would appear that he himself tended to severity he in fact pursued a middle way, and in practice was considerate and lenient.   After he had consulted the Roman clergy he insisted that his episcopal rulings must be followed without question until the whole matter could be brought up for discussion by all the African bishops and priests.   This was eventually done in 251, at the council at Carthage mentioned above, and it was decided that, whereas *libellaticii* might be restored after terms of penance varying in length according to the case, *sacrificati* could receive communion only at death. But in the following year the persecution of Gallus and Volusian began, and another African council decreed that " all the penitents who professed themselves ready to enter the lists afresh, there to abide the utmost heat of battle and manfully to fight for the name of the Lord and for their own salvation, should receive the peace of the Church ".   This, said the bishop, was necessary and desirable in order " to make a general rendezvous of Christ's soldiers within His camp for those who are desirous to have arms put into their hands and seem eager for the engagement.   So long as we had peaceable times there was reason for a longer continuance of peni- tents under a state of mortification, to be relaxed only in the case of sickness and danger.   Now the living have as much need of communion as the dying then had, otherwise we should leave naked and defenceless those whom we are exhorting and encouraging to fight the Lord's battle : whereas we should rather support and strengthen them with the Body and Blood of Christ.   The object of the Eucharist being to be a defence and security for those who partake of it, we should fortify those for whose safety we are concerned with the armour of the Lord's banquet. How shall they be able to die for Christ if we deny them the Blood of Christ ? How shall we fit them for drinking the cup of martyrdom, if we do not first admit them to the chalice of the Lord ? "

Between the years 252 and 254 Carthage was visited by a terrible plague, of the ravages of which St Pontius has left a vivid description.   In this time of terror and desolation St Cyprian organized the Christians of the city and spoke to them strongly on the duty of mercy and charity, teaching them that they ought to extend their care not only to their own people, but also to their enemies and persecutors.   The faithful readily offered themselves to follow his directions.   Their services were severally distributed : the rich contributed alms in money ; the poor gave their personal labour and attendance.   How much the poor and necessitous were, not only during this pestilence, but at all times the objects of Cyprian's care appears from the concern he expressed for them and the orders he frequently gave about them in his letters during his absence.   It was one of his sayings : " Do not let that sleep in your coffers which may be profitable to the poor.   That which a man must of necessity part with some time or other it is well for him to distribute volun- tarily that God may recompense him in eternity."   To comfort and fortify his flock during the plague, Cyprian wrote his treatise *De mortalitate*.

Whereas St Cyprian so strongly supported Pope St Cornelius, in the closing years of his life he was moved to oppose Pope St Stephen I in the matter of baptism conferred by heretics and schismatics—he and the other African bishops refused to recognize its validity.   This disagreement is referred to under St Stephen I, on August 2 above.   Though during its course Cyprian published a treatise on the goodness of patience, he displayed considerable warmth during this controversy, an excess for which, as St Augustine says, he atoned by his glorious martyrdom. For in August 257 was promulgated the first edict of Valerian's persecution, which forbade all assemblies of Christians and required bishops, priests and deacons to take part in official worship under pain of exile, and on the 30th the bishop of Carthage was brought before the proconsul. The source for what followed comprises three distinct documents, namely, a report from official sources of his trial in 257, which resulted in banishment; the same of the second trial, in 258, at which he was condemned ; and a short account of his passion : the compiler adds a few words to connect the three parts into one narrative. It runs as follows :

" When the Emperor Valerian was consul for the fourth time and Gallienus for the third, on August 30 [A.D. 257], Paternus the proconsul said to Cyprian the bishop, in the audience-chamber : ' The most sacred emperors Valerian and Gallienus have deigned to give me letters in which they command those who do not follow the Roman religion to observe that ceremonial henceforth. For this reason I have enquired about you. What do you answer me ? '

CYPRIAN : I am a Christian and a bishop. I know no other gods but the one and true God who made Heaven and earth, the sea, and all that is in them. This God we Christians serve ; to Him we pray day and night, for ourselves and for all men and for the safety of the emperors themselves.

PATERNUS : Do you persist in this intention ?

CYPRIAN : A good intention which acknowledges God cannot change.

PATERNUS : You will, then, according to the edict of Valerian and Gallienus, go into exile at Curubis.

CYPRIAN : I will go.

PATERNUS : The emperors have deigned to write to me not only about the bishops but also about the priests. I wish therefore to know from you who are the priests who live in this town.

CYPRIAN : By your laws you have wisely forbidden any to be informers, so I am not able to reveal their names. But they can be found in their towns.

PATERNUS : I will to-day seek them out here.

CYPRIAN : Our discipline forbids that any should voluntarily give himself up, and this is contrary to your principles ; but you will find them if you look for them.

PATERNUS : I will find them. The emperors have also forbidden any assemblies to be held in any place, and also access to the cemeteries. If any one then has not observed this salutary decree, he incurs the penalty of death.

CYPRIAN : Do what is ordered you.

" Then Paternus the proconsul ordered the blessed Cyprian to be exiled, and when he had already been some time in his place of exile, the proconsul Galerius Maximus succeeded to Aspasius Paternus. The first-named ordered the holy bishop Cyprian to be recalled from exile and brought before him [August 258]. When Cyprian, the holy martyr chosen by God, had returned from the city of Curubis* (where he had been in exile according to the decree of the then proconsul Aspasius Paternus), he remained in his own gardens according to the imperial decree, hoping daily that they would come for him as had been revealed to him in a

---

* Curubis was a small town fifty miles from Carthage, on a peninsula of the coast of the Libyan sea, not far from Pentapolis. The place was pleasant and healthy, with good air and, though in desert country, green fields and plenty of fresh water. Cyprian was accompanied by his deacon, St Pontius, and others, and his banishment was attended with that consideration which characterized the official attitude towards him throughout.

dream.* And while he was staying there, suddenly on September 13, in the consulship of Tuscus and Bassus, two officers came to him : one was the chief gaoler of the proconsul Galerius Maximus, and the other was marshal of the guard of the same office. They put him between them in a carriage, and took him to Villa Sexti, whither Galerius Maximus the proconsul had retired to recover his health. This same proconsul ordered the trial to be deferred to the next day, and the blessed Cyprian was taken to the house of the chief gaoler and remained as a guest with him in the quarter called Saturn, between the temple of Venus and the temple of Public Welfare. Thither all the brethren came together. And when the holy Cyprian learnt this he ordered that the young girls should be protected, since all remained together in that quarter before the gate of the officer's house. The next day, September 14, in the morning, a great crowd came together to Villa Sexti according to the command of Galerius Maximus, who ordered Cyprian on that same day to be brought before him in the court called Sauciolum. When he was brought in, Galerius Maximus the proconsul said to Cyprian the bishop : ' You are Thascius Cyprianus ? '

CYPRIAN : I am.

MAXIMUS : You are the father (*papa*) of these sacrilegious men ?

CYPRIAN : Yes.

MAXIMUS : The most sacred emperors order you to sacrifice.

CYPRIAN : I will not sacrifice.

MAXIMUS : Think about it.

CYPRIAN : Do what is required of you ; there is no room for reflexion in so clear a matter.

" Galerius Maximus consulted his assessors, and then gave sentence, most reluctantly, as follows : ' You have lived long in sacrilege ; you have gathered round you many accomplices in unlawful association ; you have made yourself an enemy of the Roman gods and their religion : and our most pious and sacred princes, Valerian and Gallienus the *Augusti* and Gallienus the most noble *Caesar*, have not been able to recall you to the practice of their rites. Therefore, since you are found to be the author and ringleader of shameful crimes, you yourself shall be made an example to those whom you have joined with you in your wickedness : your blood shall be the confirmation of the laws.' At these words he read the decree from a tablet : ' Thascius Cyprianus shall be put to death by the sword.' Cyprian answered, ' Thanks be to God.'

" When this sentence was passed the assembled brethren said : ' Let us be beheaded with him.' A great crowd followed him tumultuously to the place of execution, which was surrounded by trees into which some climbed to get a better view. So was Cyprian led out into the plain of Sextus, and there he took off his cloak and knelt down and bowed himself in prayer to God. And when he had taken off his dalmatic† and given it to his deacons, he stood up in his linen under-garment and waited for the executioner. When he had come, Cyprian ordered his friends to give him twenty-five pieces of gold. Linen cloths and napkins were laid down before Cyprian by the brethren, and then he bandaged his eyes with his

---

* He had been brought back in accordance with a further edict which ordered that bishops, priests and deacons should be at once put to death (Pope St Sixtus II was one of the first to suffer) and the persecution in other ways aggravated.

† A pattern of tunic originating in Dalmatia. At this time it had not yet become a distinctively ecclesiastical garment.

own hand.   When he could not himself fasten the ends of the handkerchief Julian
the priest and Julian the subdeacon fastened them for him.   So suffered blessed
Cyprian ; and his body was laid in a place near by to satisfy the curiosity of the
pagans.   It was carried away thence by night with candles and torches, with
prayers and with great triumph, to the graveyard of Macrobius Candidianus the
procurator, which is on the road to Mappalia near the reservoirs.   A few days later
Galerius Maximus the proconsul died."

The letters of St Cyprian, a brief notice in the *De viris illustribus* of St Jerome, the *passio*
of the saint, and a biographical sketch ascribed to his deacon Pontius, form the main sources
of our information.   The *passio* and the Pontius life have been much discussed.   Harnack
in the thirty-ninth volume of *Texte und Untersuchungen* has devoted a paper to " Das Leben
Cyprians von Pontius ", and describes it as the earliest Christian biography in existence.
Reizenstein, on the other hand, in the Heidelberg *Sitzungsberichte*, Phil.-Hist. Klasse, 1913,
takes a less favourable view.   For him it is unimportant as a historical source.   See upon
the whole matter H. Delehaye, *Les passions des martyrs et les genres littéraires* (1921), pp.
82–104.   If Delehaye is right, we cannot describe the so-called " Proconsular Acts " of
St Cyprian as " an unique record of the trials and death of a martyr in its authenticity and
purity ".   Trustworthy as the document may be, it is not an exact copy of the official record.
The same writer, in the *Analecta Bollandiana*, vol. xxxix (1921), pp. 314–322, has also drawn
attention to the curious confusion which has arisen between the story of St Cyprian of
Carthage and the fictitious legend of Cyprian of Antioch.   See also the *Acta Sanctorum*,
September, vol. iv ; P. Monceaux, *St Cyprien*, in the series " Les Saints " ; and J. H.
Fichter, *St Cecil Cyprian* (1942).   The literature which has grown up around the writings
of St Cyprian is extensive and highly controversial.   In connexion with the well-known
work, *St Cyprian*, of Archbishop Benson, consult Abbot J. Chapman's articles on the *De
unitate ecclesiae* in the *Revue Bénédictine* for 1902 and 1903.   A fuller bibliography is provided
in Bardenhewer, in DTC., and in the *Lexikon für Theologie und Kirche*, vol. iii, pp. 99–102.

ST EUPHEMIA, Virgin and Martyr   (*c.* A.D. 303 ?)

THE city of Chalcedon was the scene of St Euphemia's martyrdom ; when she
refused to attend a pagan festival in honour of the god Ares, she was apprehended
by the persecutors and cruelly tortured by the command of an inhuman judge named
Priscus.   The torments she underwent were represented in a series of frescoes in
her church at Chalcedon, described by St Asterius of Amasea in his panegyric of
the saint.   Whilst one soldier pulled her head back, another with a mallet beat out
her teeth and bruised her mouth, so that her face, her hair and her clothes were
covered with blood.   After having suffered many other torments, she was killed
by a bear, while the other beasts fawned harmlessly around her feet.   The *acta*
of St Euphemia are worthless, consisting principally of a catalogue of the tortures
which she miraculously overcame ; the Roman Martyrology summarizes them,
" imprisonments, stripes, the wheel, fire, heavy stones, beasts, scourging, sharp
nails and burning pans ".   But there undoubtedly was a martyr at Chalcedon of
this name, whose *cultus* was formerly exceedingly popular throughout the Church.

Evagrius, the historian, testifies that emperors, patriarchs and all ranks of people
resorted to Chalcedon to be partakers of the blessings which God conferred on men
through her patronage, and that manifest miracles were wrought.   A great church
was erected there in her honour and in it was held in the year 451 the fourth general
council, which condemned Monophysism.   A legend says that at this council the
Catholic fathers agreed with their opponents that each side should write down its
views in a book, lay them down, and ask Almighty God to show by a sign which
expressed the truth.   This was done and the two books were sealed up in the

shrine of St Euphemia.   After three days of prayer the shrine was opened : the monophysite book lay at the feet of the martyr but the Catholic book was held in her right hand.   It is hardly necessary to say that this great council reached its conclusions by no such methods ; but it seems that the fact that this epoch-making synod was held in the church of St Euphemia accounts for some of the remarkable prestige that she formerly enjoyed, and Pope Pius XII invoked her name in his encyclical letter " Sempiternus Christus rex " on the fifteen hundredth anniversary of the council in 1951.   The martyr is often referred to in the East as Euphemia the Far-renowned, and she is among the saints named in the canon of the Milanese Mass and in the preparation according to Russian usage of the Byzantine rite.

Famous as St Euphemia was, her *acta*, from which some particulars are given above, are correctly described as worthless.   Beyond the fact of her martyrdom we know nothing whatever about her, except that her *cultus* from an early date was widespread.   Pope St Sergius (687–701) restored in Rome the church dedicated to her, which even in his time had fallen into ruin.   See the *Acta Sanctorum*, September, vol. v, and CMH., pp. 187, 515.

SS. ABUNDIUS, ABUNDANTIUS AND THEIR COMPANIONS, MARTYRS   (*c.* A.D. 304 ?)

IN the Lateran museum is part of an epitaph found at Rignano, twenty-six miles from Rome, which the archaeologist de Rossi believed to appertain to the martyr Abundius referred to in the Roman Martyrology on this day.   " At Rome, on the Flaminian Way, the holy martyrs Abundius the priest and Abundantius the deacon, whom, together with the distinguished man Marcian and his son John, who had been raised from the dead by Abundius, the Emperor Diocletian ordered to be slain by the sword at the tenth milestone from the City."   The unhistorical " acts " of these martyrs relate that St Abundius and his deacon were ordered to worship Hercules and refused ; they were then thrown into the Mamertine prison, and a month later were brought out, tortured and condemned.   While on their way to the place of execution they met the senator Marcian, who was mourning the death of his son, John.   St Abundius asked for the boy's body to be brought, and when this was done he prayed over it and life returned.   Marcian and John thereupon both confessed Christ, and were beheaded on the same day and in the same place as Abundius and Abundantius.   They were buried in the cemetery of the matron Theodora, near Rignano on the Via Flaminia.   Their relics with those of St Theodora (whom the Roman Martyrology names on September 17) were afterwards translated to Rome, and SS. Abundius and Abundantius eventually found a resting-place in the church of the Holy Name of Jesus in 1583.   It was at their shrine here that St Aloysius Gonzaga assisted at Mass before entering the Society of Jesus two years later.

A summary, with a discussion of the relics, will be found in the *Acta Sanctorum*, September, vol. v.   Of greater interest is the inscription now preserved in the Christian Museum at the Lateran ; its authenticity is accepted by de Rossi, but rejected by Mgr Wilpert.   See Delehaye, *Origines du culte des martyrs*, p. 322.

ST NINIAN, BISHOP   (A.D. 432 ?)

THE Church in Scotland, and the English dioceses of Hexham and Lancaster, today keep the feast of St Ninian (Ninias, Ninnidh, Ringan, etc.), " the first authentic personage that meets us in the succession of Scottish missionaries ", of whom the most reliable source of information is a short passage in St Bede's *Ecclesiastical History :* " The southern Picts who dwell on this side of those mountains had, it is reported, long before forsaken the errors of paganism and embraced the truth by the preaching of Ninias, a most reverend bishop and holy man of the British nation, who had been regularly instructed at Rome in the faith and mysteries of the truth. His episcopal see, named after St Martin the Bishop and famous for a church dedicated in his honour (wherein Ninias himself and many other saints rest in the body), is now in the possession of the English nation. The place belongs to the province of the Bernicians and is commonly called the White House, because he there built a church of stone, which was not usual amongst the Britons." St Bede states definitely that St Ninian was a Briton, and there is no good reason for believing that he was ever in Ireland, but some Irish writers have identified him with Moinenn of Cluain Conaire in county Kildare.

More details of the life of St Ninian are given by St Aelred in the twelfth century, who claims to have had the help of " a book of his life and miracles, barbarously written ", but Aelred's *vita* is clearly untrustworthy. He states that St Ninian was the son of a converted chieftain of the Cumbrian Britons, and that he spent some years studying in Rome. Before returning home to preach the gospel to his countrymen he was consecrated bishop by the pope. St Ninian came back by way of Tours, where he made the acquaintance of St Martin, who greatly befriended him. Ninian had already determined to build a church of stone, in the likeness of those he had seen at Rome, and while at Tours borrowed some masons from St Martin for the purpose. When he got back he established his see and built his church at the place now called Whithorn or Whitern, in Wigtownshire, " which place, situated on the shore, while it runs far into the sea on the east, west and south, is closed in thereby. From the north only can it be approached by land. There he built the first stone church in Britain. . . ."

This famous church may have been the first built of stone in Strathclyde, but it was certainly not the first in Britain. It became known as the White House (Whitern) ; it was the centre of the most ancient ecclesiastical foundation in Scotland, and *Candida Casa* is still the official name of the Catholic diocese of Galloway. The monastery attached was distinguished as the Great Monastery, and from it St Ninian and his monks set out not only to preach to the Britons of the neighbourhood but also to the Picts of the former Roman province of Valentia ; they may even have penetrated to the northern Picts beyond the Grampians. The mission received an impetus from Ninian's cure of the blindness and subsequent conversion of a local chieftain. The Britons and Picts received baptism in large numbers and Ninian consecrated bishops to minister to them ; St Aelred recounts many miracles by which the saint was reported to confirm his message. Through the foundation of Whitern, St Ninian's effect on Celtic Christianity was considerable, but his success among the Picts seems to have been rather short-lived : St Patrick in his letter to Coroticus refers to them as apostates. But he had paved the way for St Columba and St Kentigern, and it has been suggested that he had indirect influence on Wales, by the conversion of the family of Cunedda, which probably came from the district of Kyle, in Ayrshire.

The notes in C. Plummer's edition of Bede's *Ecclesiastical History* (vol. ii, pp. 128–130) tell us all that is to be known about St Ninian. See, however, A. P. Forbes, *Lives of St*

Ninian and St Kentigern (1874) ; L. Gougaud, *Christianity in Celtic Lands* (1932) pp. 26–27 and *passim* ; J. Ryan, *Irish Monasticism* (1931), pp. 105–107 ; and W. D. Simpson, *St Ninian and the Origins of the Christian Church in Scotland* (1940). *Cf.* N. K. Chadwick, preliminary study of the sources in the *Transactions* of the Dumfriesshire and Galloway Nat. Hist. and Ant. Socy., vol. xxvii (1950) ; O. Chadwick's reference in *Studies in Early British History* (ed. N. K. Chadwick, 1954), pp. 177 *seq.* ; and S. G. A. Luff in *Irish Eccl. Record*, July–December 1953. See also W. Levison's edition of an eighth-century poem on Ninian, and his conclusions therefrom, in *Antiquity*, 1940, pp. 280–291. Aelred's statement that Ninian dedicated his church at Whithorn in honour of St Martin, a confessor, can hardly be true at so early a date.

ST LUDMILA, MARTYR   (A.D. 921)

LUDMILA was born about the year 860, the daughter of a Slav prince in the country between the confluence of the Elbe and the Moldau.   She married Borivoy, Duke of Bohemia, and when her husband was baptized by St Methodius she followed him into the Church.   They built the first Christian church in Bohemia, at Levy Hradec to the north of Prague.   The princely neophytes had a very difficult time, for most of the leading families were utterly opposed to the new religion.   In accordance with the all-too-common practice of those days Borivoy tried to force Christianity on his people, which led to much discontent and increased his diffi-culties.   After his death he was succeeded by his sons Spytihinev and Ratislav. The latter had married a Slav " princess ", Drahomira, who was only nominally Christian, and when a son, Wenceslaus, was born to them, Ludmila was entrusted with his upbringing.   She was now about fifty years of age, a woman of virtue and learning, and it was to her unfailing care and interest that Wenceslaus in a large measure owed his own sanctity.

The premature death of Ratislav and the consequent regency of Drahomira removed Wenceslaus from Ludmila's immediate charge.   The regent was in the hands of the anti-Christian party in Bohemia, and was, moreover, not unnaturally, jealous of the responsibility which had been confided to Ludmila and of the influence she exercised over her grandson.   St Ludmila's gentleness and charity had made her greatly beloved among the people, and probably she hoped that, if young Wenceslaus could be persuaded to seize the government before his time, they would rally to him, and Christianity in Bohemia, now threatened, be saved.   The opposing party saw this possibility clearly, and every effort was made to keep Wenceslaus and Ludmila apart.   The more desperate characters decided to take no risks ; on September 16, 921, two of them came to the castle of Tetin, near Podybrad, and there strangled Ludmila.   That this crime was instigated by Drahomira is often asserted, but it is not certain, nor is she surely known to have been privy to it.   St Ludmila was acclaimed as a martyr, and her body was trans-lated, perhaps by St Wenceslaus himself, to St George's church at Prague.   She is still venerated in Czechoslovakia.

What purports to be the *passio* of St Ludmila exists in more than one form and has been printed in the *Acta Sanctorum*, September, vol. v, and in Pertz, MGH., *Scriptores*, vol. xv, pp. 573–574.   An account in much greater detail (which is attributed to one Christian de Scala, alleged to have been a great-grand-nephew of the saint, but which many scholars believe to date only from the thirteenth century) has been edited by the Bollandists in the same 5th volume for September.   For a sober and reasoned defence of the authenticity of these materials see J. Pekar, *Die Wenzels und Ludmila Legenden und die Echtheit Christians* (1906).   The question has given rise to much controversy, but see the *Analecta Bollandiana*, vol. xxv (1906), pp. 512–513, and vol. xlviii (1930), pp. 218–221.   A little book on St Wenceslaus by F. Dvornik (1929) also touches on the Ludmila legend.

ST EDITH OF WILTON, Virgin   (A.D. 984)

St Edith was the daughter of King Edgar and Wulfrida (also sometimes called Saint) in circumstances that are obscure and, according to some reports, exceedingly scandalous.*   Soon after she was born, in the year 962 at, according to tradition, Kemsing in Kent, she was taken by her mother to Wilton Abbey which she never left, so that the words of the Roman Martyrology are literally true : " She was dedicated to God from her earliest years in a monastery and rather knew not this world than forsook it."

When she was less than fifteen years old, her royal father visited Wilton on the occasion of her profession.   He had a carpet laid down before the altar on which were put gold and silver ornaments and jewels, while Wulfrida stood by with a nun's veil, a psalter, a chalice and paten.   " All prayed that God, who knows all things, would show to one still at so wayward an age what life she should choose." Perhaps Edgar was trying to avoid the foregone conclusion.   Certainly he shortly after offered Edith the abbacy of three different houses (Winchester, Barking and another) which she obviously was not old enough to govern other than nominally. But she declined all superiority and chose to remain in her own community, subject to her mother, who was now abbess there.   But the nuns insisted on giving her the honorary title of abbess, though she remained as before " serving her sisters in the most menial offices like a very Martha ".   Soon after, King Edgar died, and was succeeded by his son, Edward the Martyr.   Upon the death of the latter, the nobility who adhered to the murdered king wanted Edith, his half-sister, to quit her monastery and ascend the throne : but she preferred a state of humility and obedience to the prospect of a crown.   Edith built the church of St Denis at Wilton, to the dedication of which she invited the archbishop of Canterbury, St Dunstan. He was observed to weep exceedingly during Mass, the reason of which he after-wards said was because he learned that Edith would shortly be taken out of this world, whilst we, said he, shall still continue sitting here below in darkness and in the shadow of death.   According to this prediction, forty-three days after this solemnity, she happily reposed in the Lord, on September 16, 984, being but twenty-two years old.   A pleasing story is told of St Edith appearing after her death at the baptism of a child for whom she had promised to stand godmother, holding the baby in her arms at the font.   She also appeared, but rather indig-nantly, to King Canute, who had had the temerity to doubt some of the marvels attributed to her.   St Edith is commemorated today in the diocese of Clifton.

Our main authorities are William of Malmesbury, Simeon of Durham and Capgrave. But see *Analecta Bollandiana*, vol. lvi (1938), pp. 5–101 and 265–309, where Dom A. Wilmart prints and discusses the legend, in prose and verse, by Goscelin (dedicated to Lanfranc of Canterbury), from the Rawlinson MS. in the Bodleian, which is quite different from the short version in the *Acta Sanctorum*, September, vol. v, p. 369.

BD VICTOR III, Pope   (A.D. 1087)

The young man who was to become pope as Victor III was known in secular life as Daufar, and he belonged to the Lombard family of the dukes of Benevento.

* King Edgar too was venerated at Glastonbury.   He was a notable sovereign ; but his elevation to sainthood seems to have been no more than part of what the usually temperate Dr Plummer calls " that huge system of monastic lying in which Glastonbury had a bad pre-eminence " (Plummer's " Bede ", vol. ii, p. 167).

As he was an only son his father was particularly anxious for him to marry, but Daufar, whose "nobility of soul was greater even than that of his birth", was confident that he was called to serve God as a monk. His father was killed in battle in 1047 and Daufar, who was about twenty years old, took the opportunity to slip away from his family and take up his residence with a hermit. His relatives found him, tore his religious habit off his back, and forced him to return to his home at Benevento. A sharp watch was kept on him, but after twelve months he managed to escape and entered the monastery of La Cava. His family then accepted the fact of his vocation, only stipulating that he should leave La Cava and come to the abbey of St Sophia at Benevento. To this he agreed, and his new abbot gave him the name of Desiderius. But for some years the young monk seemed unable to find stability : he was at a monastery on an island in the Adriatic, he studied medicine at Salerno, he was a hermit in the Abruzzi. He had attracted the favourable notice of Pope St Leo IX, and about 1054 he was at the court of Victor II. Here he met monks from Monte Cassino, went on a pilgrimage to that cradle of Benedictine monasticism, and joined the community. In the year 1057 Pope Stephen X summoned Desiderius to Rome, intending to send him as his legate to Constantinople. Stephen had been abbot of Monte Cassino and had retained the office on his elevation to the papacy, but now, believing himself to be dying, he ordered the election of a successor. The choice fell on Desiderius, and he had got to Bari on his way to the East when he learned of the pope's death and was told to return. There was a disputed succession to Stephen X, in which Desiderius supported Pope Nicholas II, who made him a cardinal before he was permitted to go and take up his duties at his monastery.

Desiderius was one of the greatest of the abbots of Monte Cassino, and under his rule the archcoenobium reached the height of its glory. He rebuilt first the church and then the whole range of buildings on a larger and more convenient scale than those of St Petronax and Abbot Aligernus, who had restored them after the Lombard and Saracenic spoliations. The basilica in particular Desiderius made of the greatest beauty ; "by influence and money" he procured fine materials from Rome and sent for workmen from Lombardy, from Amalfi, from Constantinople itself. Under the combined Lombard and Byzantine influences new forms emerged which had far-reaching effect on building, mosaic, painting and illuminating, the activity of the monks of Monte Cassino themselves doing much to spread it. All this magnificence was no empty show or to house "vile bigots, hypocrites externally devoted". The number of monks at Monte Cassino rose to two hundred, and Desiderius insisted on the most strict observance of the rule. Among those whom he attracted thither was Constantine Africanus, the best known physician of the early Salerno school and a personal friend of Desiderius. On the side of manual work the buildings gave continual employment, and the Cassinese *scriptorium* was famous both for its illuminating and for the books copied therein. As well as abbot and cardinal, Desiderius was papal vicar for Campania, Apulia, Calabria and Capua, and so well was he regarded by the Holy See that he was authorized to appoint prelates for vacant bishoprics and abbeys.

Desiderius was much used by Pope St Gregory VII as his intermediary with the Normans in Italy. He was a very different type of man from Gregory, gentle by nature and afterwards much weakened by ill-health, but he had shown himself a determined upholder of the papacy against the emperor, and perhaps was one of the people named by Gregory on his death-bed as a suitable successor. During the vacancy Desiderius fled from Rome to Monte Cassino in order to avoid election, but in May 1086 he was chosen by acclamation and the papal red cope forced upon his shoulders in the church of Santa Lucia. He was given the name of Victor. Four days later a rising gave him the excuse again to flee to his monastery, where he laid aside the papal insignia and could not be induced finally to take up the office until Easter of the following year. Rome was by then occupied by the imperial antipope, Guibert of Ravenna (" Clement III "). Norman troops drove him out of St Peter's long enough for Victor to be consecrated there, after which he went back again to Monte Cassino. He was again in Rome, for the last time, a few weeks later when the Countess Matilda of Tuscany made a strong effort to dislodge Guibert. The peace-loving pope, so ill that he rarely celebrated Mass, could not bear to see the apostolic city turned into a battlefield, and left it finally towards the end of the summer. After a synod over which he presided at Benevento, Victor was carried back dying to his monastery. Stretched on a couch in the chapter-house he gave final directions to be observed by his monks, and recommended Eudes, Cardinal-Bishop of Ostia, to fill the apostolic see ; and two days later died, September 16, 1087. ·He had been pope for four months. The *cultus* of Bd Victor III was approved by Pope Leo XIII, who added his name to the Roman Martyrology.

A detailed account of Bd Victor occupies considerable space in the *Chronica Monasterii Casinensis*, bk iii. The text has been published in MGH., *Scriptores*, vol. vii, pp. 698–754 ; and also in the *Acta Sanctorum*, September, vol. v. See further Mgr H. K. Mann, *Lives of the Popes*, vol. vii, pp. 218–244.

BD VITALIS OF SAVIGNY, Abbot   (A.D. 1122)

A RATHER florid account of the life of Bd Vitalis is extant from which we learn that he lived for some time as a hermit, then gathered disciples around him, and eventually founded the abbey of Savigny on the confines of Normandy and Brittany. As abbot he seems to have travelled about a great deal and to have become famous as a preacher. In early life, before the years he spent in solitude as a hermit, he acted as chaplain to Robert, Count of Mortain, the half-brother of William the Conqueror. Vitalis visited England more than once, and the story was told of him that on one of these occasions, when preaching in church to a crowded assembly, he was understood by all his hearers, though he spoke in French and they, for the most part, knew nothing but English. The Savigny " reform " was very popular for a time (it was followed at Buckfast), but its houses joined Cîteaux in 1147. Its founder died, his biographer tells us, on September 16, 1122, while he was presiding in choir at the recitation of the office of the Blessed Virgin.

The chief authority for Bd Vitalis is a biography compiled by Stephen de Fougères, who was first one of King Henry II's chaplains and afterwards bishop of Rennes ; he died in 1178, and may consequently be regarded almost as a contemporary. This life is printed in the *Analecta Bollandiana*, vol. i (1882), pp. 355–390. We have also a good deal of information in the Mortuary Roll of Abbot Vitalis, printed by L. Delisle, *Rouleaux des Morts*, p. 282 *seq*. See also *Acta Sanctorum*, January 7 ; and D. Knowles, *The Monastic Order in England* (1949), pp. 202, 227.

BD LOUIS ALLEMAND, Archbishop of Arles and Cardinal (A.D. 1450)

THE history of this holy prelate is a striking example of how the Church, looking so far as possible at the souls rather than the exterior actions of men, raises to the honours of her altars those whom she judges to have been interiorly holy, whatever and however serious the errors of action or of judgement apparent in their lives : always provided that she finds those errors to have been due to *bona-fide* mistake, inculpable ignorance, or otherwise made in good faith. This particular example, Louis Allemand (or Aleman) was born near the end of the fourteenth century in the diocese of Beiley. He read law at the University of Avignon and, having taken his degrees, he received through the influence of his uncle, a chamberlain at the papal court, a number of ecclesiastical benefices. Young Louis in 1409 accompanied his uncle to the Synod of Pisa, an assembly which vainly tried to cure the scandalous and terrible rivalry between claimants to the papal throne (the " Great Schism of the West ") by deposing both Gregory XII and Benedict " XIII " and electing a third " pope " ; and in 1414 he was present at the gathering, summoned by King Sigismund and John " XXIII ", which was to become the oecumenical Council of Constance, and two years later was vice-chamberlain in charge of the conclave that elected Pope Martin V and put an end to the " great schism ".

Louis was attached to the court of the new pope, who named him bishop of Maguelonne and entrusted him with very responsible missions. In 1423 he was promoted to the archbishopric of Arles, appointed governor of Romagna, Bologna and Ravenna, and soon after his services were recognized by making him cardinal-priest of St Cecilia-in-Trastevere. But a rising of the Canetoli faction drove him from Bologna, he was unable to retake the city, and retired to Rome in political disgrace. An envoy of the Order of Teutonic Knights writes at this time of five cardinals who were well disposed towards his order, but " they dare not speak before the pope, save what he likes to hear, for he has so crushed the cardinals that they say nothing before him except as he wishes, and they turn red and white when they speak in his hearing ". Louis Allemand was one of these five cardinals. When Martin V died in 1431 he was succeeded by Eugenius IV, who had been Louis's predecessor at Bologna and with whom he was at variance both personally and in policy. Louis had come more and more to identify himself with the party, now waxing very strong, that maintained the supremacy of a general council over the pope and practically reduced him to the position of a servant of the council. During the last year of his pontificate Martin V had convened a general council at Basle, and one of the first acts of Eugenius was to issue a bull dissolving it. The few fathers assembled refused to separate and announced their intention of carrying on the council.

Louis was then in Rome, and, on account of his known sympathies, was forbidden to leave. But he made an adventurous escape, boarded a Genoese ship in the Tiber, and went to his episcopal city of Arles. Perhaps his object was to avoid having to declare himself openly against the Holy See, in the hope that the troubles would blow over. But in 1434 he was at Basle, daily becoming more clearly the leader of the extreme majority who opposed Cardinal Cesarini, the pope's representative—for Eugenius had withdrawn his decree of dissolution. The anti-papal activities of the council became so strong that in 1437 the pope himself was summoned to appear before it to answer charges. He refused, and ordered the council to reassemble at Ferrara ; Cardinal Cesarini and his other adherents obeyed, leaving an illegal assembly at Basle under the skilful direction of Cardinal Allemand. In 1439 it went to the extreme length of declaring Eugenius deposed in consequence of his opposition to the council, and electing Amadeus of Savoy in his stead as Felix " V ", the last of the antipopes. This was the work principally of Cardinal

Allemand and only eleven bishops, and Louis himself consecrated Amadeus bishop and crowned him.   In the following year Eugenius IV pronounced Louis Allemand to be excommunicated and deprived of his cardinalate.

It cannot be questioned that many of the " conciliar party " at the Council of Basle were sincerely animated by zeal for the improvement of the condition of the Church, for the conversion of those in error, and for the restoration of peace and unity.   Nor must it be supposed that Bd Louis was the only good man to be grossly mistaken as to the right methods to be employed to attain these ends.   For a long time he had the support of the holy and learned Cardinal Nicholas of Cusa, and also of Aeneas Sylvius Piccolomini, who, though at that time a layman and certainly not a holy one, afterwards himself became pope, as Pius II.   The council, after it had become a rebellious assembly, discussed the doctrine of the Immaculate Conception of our Lady, and with the vigorous encouragement of Bd Louis declared it to be consonant with Catholic faith and worship, right reason and Holy Scripture. Basle for a time was visited by the plague, and Cardinal Allemand was foremost in organizing relief for the victims, encouraging the other bishops to join with him in ministering to the sick and dying.   During all this time he disregarded the suspension that had been pronounced against him by Pope Eugenius, and was zealous in the service of the antipope Felix.   But in 1447 Eugenius died, and Felix declared his willingness to resign in favour of the duly elected Nicholas V.   Thereupon Nicholas with a magnificent gesture of peace revoked all suspensions, excommunications and other penalties incurred by the antipope, the recalcitrant council and their adherents, and Bd Louis was restored to his cardinalatial dignity. He was profoundly repentant for the part he had taken in involving the Church in schism, and retired to his see of Arles where he spent the remaining year of his life in those exercises of prayer and penance that had always characterized his private life.   He was buried in the church of St Trophimus, where his tomb was the scene of many miracles, and the *cultus* that then began was approved by Pope Clement VII in 1527.   The feast of Bd Louis Allemand is observed in several dioceses of southern France.

Some considerable biographical materials will be found, with prolegomena, in the *Acta Sanctorum*, September, vol. v.   But see more particularly G. Pérouse, *Le Cardinal Louis Aleman* (1904) ; N. Valois, *Le Pape et le Concile* (1909) ; and the various writings of Professor H. Finke on the period of the schism.

17 : THE IMPRESSION OF THE STIGMATA UPON ST FRANCIS   (A.D. 1224)

IN the month of August 1224 St Francis of Assisi withdrew himself from the world for a while to commune with God on the summit of La Verna, a lonely mountain in the Apennines.   He was accompanied by Brother Leo and five or six others, but he chose a hut apart, under a beech tree, and gave instructions that no one was to come near him except Leo when he brought him food or other ministrations.   About the feast of the Exaltation of the Holy Cross, Francis, being in prayer on the side of the mountain, raised himself towards God with seraphic ardour and was transported by a tender and affective compassion of charity into Him who out of love was crucified for us.   In this state he saw as it were a seraph, with six shining wings, bearing down from the highest part of the heavens towards him with a most rapid flight, and placing himself in the air near the saint. There appeared between his wings the figure of a man crucified, with his hands and feet stretched out, and fastened to the cross. The wings of the seraph were so placed that two he stretched above his head, two others he extended to fly, and with the other two he covered his body. At this sight a sudden joy, mingled with sorrow, filled Francis's heart. The close presence of his Lord under the figure of a seraph, who fixed on him His eyes in the most gracious and loving manner, gave him great joy, but the sorrowful sight of His crucifixion pierced his soul with compassion. At the same time he understood by an interior light that, though the state of crucifixion in no way agreed with that of the immortality of the seraph, this wonderful vision was manifested to him that he might understand he was to be transformed into a resemblance with Jesus Christ crucified, not by the martyrdom of the flesh, but in his heart and by the fire of love. Suddenly, in a moment of great pain, the seraph smote him as it were in body and soul, and Francis had great fear, till the seraph spoke and made plain many things which had hitherto been hidden from him. Then, after a moment which seemed an age, the vision vanished.

But the saint's soul remained interiorly burning with ardour, and his body appeared exteriorly to have received the image of the crucifix, as if his flesh had received the marks of a seal impressed upon it. For the scars of nails began to appear in his feet and hands, resembling those he had seen in the vision of the man crucified. His hands and feet seemed bored through in the middle with four wounds, and these holes appeared to be pierced with nails or hard flesh ; the heads were round and black, and were seen in the palms of his hands and in his feet in the upper part of the instep. The points were long, and appeared beyond the skin on the other side, and were turned back as if they had been clinched with a hammer. There was also in his right side a red wound, as if made by the piercing of a lance, and this often shed blood, which stained the clothes of the saint. This wonderful miracle was performed whilst Francis's understanding was filled with the most vivid ideas of Christ crucified, and his love employed in the utmost strength of its will in directing its affections on that object and assimilating them to his Beloved in that suffering state ; so that in the imaginative faculty of his soul he seemed to form a second crucifix, with which impression it acted upon and strongly affected the body. To produce the exterior marks of the wounds in the flesh, which the interior love of his heart was not able to do, the fiery seraph, or rather Christ Himself in that vision, by darting piercing rays from His wounds represented in the vision, really formed exteriorly in St Francis those signs which love had interiorly imprinted in his soul.

Whether or no St Francis was the first person to be thus marked with the *stigmata* (Gk. marks) of our crucified Lord, his is unquestionably the most famous example, and the best authenticated until we come to recent and contemporary times ; moreover, it is the only occurrence of the sort to be celebrated by a liturgical feast throughout the Western church. The happening and general nature of the phenomenon are beyond doubt. It is referred to by Brother Leo in the note which he wrote with his own hand on the " seraphic blessing " of St Francis, a document preserved by the Conventual friars at Assisi, and in announcing the death of their patriarch to the friars of France Brother Elias wrote in 1226 : " From the beginning of ages there has not been heard so great a wonder, save only in the Son of God who is Christ our God. For a long while before his death, our father and brother appeared crucified, bearing in his body the five wounds which are verily the Stigmata of the Christ ; for his hands and feet had as it were piercings made by nails fixed in from above and below, which laid open the scars and had the black appearance of nails ; while his side appeared to have been lanced, and blood often trickled therefrom." In the earliest life of the saint, written between two and four years after his death, the stigmata are described thus : " His hands and feet seemed pierced in the midst by nails, the heads of the nails appearing in the inner part of the hands and in the upper part of the feet and their points over against them. Now these marks were round on the inner side of the hands and elongated on the outer side, and certain small pieces of flesh were seen like the ends of nails bent and driven back, projecting from the rest of the flesh. So also the marks of nails were imprinted in his feet, and raised above the rest of the flesh. Moreover his right side, as if it had been pierced by a lance, was overlaid with a scar, and often shed forth blood. . . ." *The Book of Miracles*, probably written by the same eyewitness about twenty years later (Thomas of Celano), adds that the crowds who flocked to Assisi " saw in the hands and feet not the fissures of the nails but the nails themselves marvellously wrought by the power of God, indeed implanted in the flesh itself, in such wise that if they were pressed in on either side they straightway, as if they were one piece of sinew, projected on the other ". The statement, repeated above by Alban Butler from the *Fioretti*, that the points of the nails were " bent back and clinched on such wise that under the clinching and the bend, which all stood out above the flesh, it would have been easy to put a finger of the hand, as in a ring ", can be traced back to before 1274, but the most careful critics are inclined to reject its truth as a literal statement ; nothing of the like kind is reported of any other well-attested cases of stigmata. There is not, of course, any suggestion that the " nails " referred to were other than fleshy or sinewy substances, and that they were even this (rather than part of the appearance and shape of the wounds or raised scars) is hardly warranted by the evidence, and not at all by comparison with the stigmata of others.

The fact of stigmatization has been confirmed by modern examples ; the stigmata often bleed periodically, especially on Fridays, and in no recorded case do the wounds suppurate. It would appear then that God singles out certain noble souls to be united more closely with the sufferings of His Son, souls who are willing and in some degree worthy to expiate the sins of others by bearing before the world the form of Jesus crucified, " not portrayed upon tables of stone or wood by the hand of an earthly artist but drawn in their flesh by the finger of the living God ". In the large number of reported stigmatizations in the past seven hundred years only some fifty or sixty are at all well attested, and some of these are explainable by fraud or other natural means, so the valid phenomenon remains a rare and remarkable indication by God of some of those who are heroically His servants. With some few exceptions the best-known *stigmatisés* were either friars, nuns or tertiaries of one or other of the mendicant orders, and nearly all of them women.

Nearly all the many published Lives of St Francis give prominence to the stigmata. The contemporary evidence, notably that of Brother Elias, of the document called the " Blessing " of Brother Leo, and of the *Vita prima* by Thomas of Celano, is quite conclusive as to the existence of these wound marks. Paul Sabatier, Dr J. Merkt (*Die Wundmale des Franziskus von Assisi*, 1910), and others have propounded a naturalistic explanation, on which see Bihl in *Archivum Franciscanum Historicum,* July, 1910, and Königer in the *Historisches Jahrbuch,* 1910, pp. 787 *seq.* In the collection *Studi Francescani* (1924) a volume was devoted to the seventh centenary of the stigmatization. This contains an important article (pp. 140–174) by A. Gemelli on " Le Affirmazione della Scienza intorno alle Stimmate di S. Francesco ". *Cf.* also V. Facchinetti, *Le Stimmate di S. Francesco* (1924) ; and Faloci Pulignani, *Miscellanea Francescana,* vol. xv, pp. 129–137. For stigmatization in general see H. Thurston, *The Physical Phenomena of Mysticism* (1952) ; and *Douleur et stigmatisation* (1936) in the series " Études carmélitaines ". This contains an excellent article by Fr P. Debongnie on stigmatization in the middle ages ; he sharply criticizes the work of Dr Imbert-Gourbeyre (*La stigmatisation . . .,* 2 vols., 1894), following, among others, Fr Gemelli and Fr Thurston. See also F. L. Schleyer, *Die Stigmatisation mit den Blutmalen* (1948), who examines the very frequent coincidence of stigmatization and serious nervous disorders.

SS. SOCRATES AND STEPHEN, MARTYRS   (DATE UNKNOWN)

NOTHING whatever is known of these martyrs and they are only of interest because the Roman Martyrology, following the " Martyrology of Jerome ", says that their passion took place in Britain. Dom Serenus Cressy refers to them in his *Church History* as " two noble British Christians ", disciples of " St Amphibalus ". They are supposed to have suffered in the persecution of Diocletian, and Monmouth is put forward as the place because, it is said, there were churches dedicated in their honour in that neighbourhood, but these churches have not been identified. The *Britannia* of the martyrologists may have been a mistake for *Abretannia,* in Asia Minor, or it may have been Bithynia.

Fr Delehaye has discussed this entry in a paper printed in the *Proceedings of the British Academy,* vol. xvii (1932). He abandons the suggestion made by D. Serruys that " Britannia" has been written by mistake for Abretannia, and suggests that the original reading was probably Bithynia.

ST SATYRUS   (*c.* A.D. 379)

SATYRUS was the elder brother of St Ambrose, born sometime before the year 340, probably at Trier. The sister, St Marcellina, was the eldest. When their father, who was prefect of the *praetorium* of the Gauls, died about 354 the family moved to Rome, where the two boys were well educated under the watchful eyes of their mother and sister. Satyrus undertook a public career, practised as a lawyer, and became prefect of an unnamed province. When St Ambrose was elected bishop of Milan in 374, Satyrus resigned his post to undertake the administration of the temporal concerns of the see for his brother. He made several voyages to Africa, on the last of which he nearly lost his life through shipwreck, and in consequence took the first opportunity to receive baptism, having hitherto been only a catechumen. Before jumping overboard from the wrecked vessel he was given a particle of the Blessed Sacrament by one of his fellow voyagers, which he wrapped in a scarf and fastened about his neck. He died suddenly at Milan, in the arms of his sister and brother, who distributed his estate among the poor in accordance with his wish that they should deal with it as they thought best. The mighty merits of St Satyrus, his integrity and his kindness, were eulogized by St Ambrose in his funeral sermon, in the course of which he asks God mercifully to accept the priestly sacrifices which he offers for his dead brother.

The passages in the writings of St Ambrose, upon which all our knowledge of St Satyrus is based, are printed in the *Acta Sanctorum,* September, vol. v.

ST LAMBERT, BISHOP OF MAESTRICHT, MARTYR   (*c.* A.D. 705)

ST LANDEBERT, called in later ages Lambert, was a native of Maestricht, and born of a noble and wealthy family between the years 633 and 638.   His father sent him to St Theodard to perfect his education.   This holy bishop had such an esteem for his pupil that he spared no trouble in instructing and training him in learning and Christian virtue, and he was a credit to his master : his biographer, who was born soon after Lambert's death, describes him as, " a prudent young man of pleasing looks, courteous and well behaved in his speech and manners ; well built, strong, a good fighter, clear-headed, affectionate, pure and humble, and fond of reading ".   When St Theodard, who was bishop of Tongres-Maestricht, was murdered, Lambert was chosen to succeed him ; but the tyrannical Ebroin was reinstated as mayor of the palace when the Austrasian king, Childeric II, was slain in 674, and he at once began to revenge himself on those who had supported Childeric.   This revolution affected St Lambert, who was expelled from his see. He retired to the monastery of Stavelot, and during the seven years that he con- tinued there he obeyed the rule as strictly as the youngest novice could have done. One instance will suffice to show how he devoted his heart to serve God according to the perfection of his temporary state.   One night in winter he let fall his shoe, so that it made a noise.   This the abbot heard, and he ordered him who was responsible for that noise to go and pray before the great cross, which stood outside the church door.   Lambert, without making any answer, went out as he was, barefoot and covered only with his shirt ; and in this condition he prayed, kneeling before the cross, three or four hours.   Whilst the monks were warming themselves after Matins, the abbot inquired if all were there.   Answer was made that he had sent someone to the cross who had not yet come in.   The abbot ordered that he should be called, and was surprised to find that the person was the Bishop of Maestricht, who made his appearance almost frozen.

In 681 Ebroin was assassinated, and Pepin of Herstal, being made mayor of the palace, expelled the usurping bishops and, among other exiled prelates, restored St Lambert to Maestricht.   The holy pastor returned to his flock animated with redoubled fervour, preaching and discharging his other duties with wonderful zeal and fruit.   Finding there still remained many pagans in Kempenland and Brabant he applied himself to convert them to the faith, softened their barbarous temper by his patience, regenerated them in the water of baptism, and destroyed many superstitious observances.   In the neighbourhood of his own see he founded with St Landrada the monastery of Munsterbilzen for nuns.

Pepin of Herstal, after living many years in wedlock with St Plectrudis, entered into adulterous relations with her sister Alpais (of whom was born Charles Martel), and St Lambert expostulated with the guilty couple.   Alpais complained to her brother Dodo, who with a party of his followers set upon St Lambert and murdered him as he knelt before the altar in the church of SS. Cosmas and Damian at Liège. That is the later story of the circumstances of St Lambert's death, but his earliest biographers, writing in the eighth and tenth centuries, tell a quite different tale. According to them, two relatives of Lambert, Peter and Andolet, killed two men who were making themselves obnoxious to the bishop.   When Dodo, a kinsman of the men thus slain, came with his followers to take revenge, Lambert told Peter and Andolet that they must expiate their crime.   They were killed on the spot ; and when the bishop's room was found to be barred, one of Dodo's men climbed to the window and cast a spear which killed Lambert too, as he knelt in prayer. This took place at a house where is now the city of Liège.

Lambert's death, suffered with patience and meekness, joined with the eminent sanctity of his life, caused him to be venerated as a martyr. His body was conveyed to Maestricht. Several miracles which ensued excited the people to build a church where the house stood in which he was slain, and his successor, St Hubert, translated thither his relics. At the same time he removed to the same place the episcopal see of Tongres-Maestricht, and around the cathedral which enshrined the relics of St Lambert the city of Liège grew up. He is to this day the principal patron of that place.

There are several medieval lives of St Lambert, and most of them may be found printed in the *Acta Sanctorum*, September, vol. v. The earliest in date, and much the most important, has been critically edited by Bruno Krusch in MGH., *Scriptores Merov.*, vol. vi, the text being supplemented by notable extracts from the later biographies written by Stephen, Sigebert of Gembloux and Nicholas. The long-standing controversy regarding the precise cause which brought about the assassination of St Lambert has been very well stated in the *Analecta Bollandiana*, vol. xxxiii (1914), pp. 247–249 ; but see also pp. 219–347 in the second volume of Kurth's *Études franques* (1919). This last scholar many years before, in the *Annales de l'Académie archéol. de Belgique*, vol. xxxiii (1876), had set the whole controversy in a new light. *Cf.* further Hauck, *Kirchengeschichte Deutschlands*, vol. i, pp. 400–401, and J. Demarteau, *Vie la plus ancienne de S. Lambert* (1890).

ST COLUMBA, Virgin and Martyr   (A.D. 853)

This Columba was one of the victims of the persecution of Christians in Spain begun by the Moors in the year 850. According to St Eulogius, who wrote an account of those who suffered, called *The Memorial of the Saints*, and then himself gave his life for the faith, Columba was a native of Cordova. Her brother Martin was an abbot and her sister Elizabeth had, with her husband Jeremy, founded a double monastery at Tabanos, whither they both retired with their children. Inspired by these examples Columba determined to give herself to God in the cloister, but was hindered by her widowed mother, who wished her to marry. The mother tried to prevent her visiting her sister, where she knew Columba got her encouragement to persevere, but her efforts were fruitless and the girl became a nun at Tabanos. In the year 852 the persecution drove the religious away from this place, and the nuns took refuge in a house at Cordova, near the church of St Cyprian. In spite of the fact that in the same year a council at Cordova had forbidden Christians to provoke persecution, Columba secretly left this house, presented herself before the Moorish magistrate, and openly and deliberately denied Mohammed and his law. She was beheaded for her temerity, and her body thrown into the river Guadalquivir, whence it was recovered and buried.

The notice of St Columba in the *Acta Sanctorum*, September, vol. v, reproduces all that St Eulogius has recorded concerning her history.

ST HILDEGARD, Virgin   (A.D. 1179)

St Hildegard, Abbess of Rupertsberg, called in her own day the " Sibyl of the Rhine ", was one of the great figures of the twelfth century and one of the most remarkable of women. She was the first of the great German mystics, a poet and a prophet, a physician and a political moralist, who rebuked popes and princes, bishops and lay-folk, with complete fearlessness and unerring justice. She was born in the year 1098 at Böckelheim, on the Nahe, and when she was eight years old her parents confided her to the care of Bd Jutta, sister to Count Meginhard of Spanheim, who was living as a recluse in a cottage adjoining the church of the abbey founded by St Disibod on the Diessenberg close by her home. The child was sickly, but she continued her education, learning to read and sing Latin and other things appertaining to a nun, as well as those domestic accomplishments which adorned all medieval women, from queens to peasants. By the time Hildegard was old enough to receive the veil of a nun the hermitage of Bd Jutta had received several recruits so that it had become a community, following the Rule of St Benedict. She was clothed when she was fifteen, and continued for another seventeen years to lead an uneventful life ; exteriorly uneventful only, for she grew in the grace of God, unusual experiences which she had known from very early years continued, and " it became habitual with me to foretell the future in the course of conversations. And when I was completely absorbed in what I saw I used to say many things that seemed strange to those who heard me. This made me blush and cry, and often enough I would have killed myself had that been possible. I was too frightened to tell anyone what I saw, except the noble woman to whom I was entrusted, and she told a little to a monk whom she knew." In 1136 Bd Jutta died, and Hildegard became prioress in her place.

Her revelations and visions pressed more and more upon her. There was a continual interior urging that she should write them down, but she feared what people would say, their mockery, and her own inadequate Latin. But the voice of God seemed to say to her : " I am the living and inaccessible Light, and I enlighten whomever I will. According to my pleasure I show forth through any man marvels greater than those of my servants in times past." At last she opened her heart fully to her confessor, the monk Godfrey, and authorized him to refer the matter to his abbot, Conon, who after careful consideration ordered Hildegard to write down some of the things she said God had made known to her. They dealt with such matters as the charity of Christ and the continuance of the kingdom of God, the holy angels, the Devil and Hell. These writings Conon submitted to the archbishop of Mainz, who examined them with his theologians and gave a favourable verdict : " These visions come from God." The abbot then appointed a monk named Volmar to act as secretary to Hildegard, and she at once began the dictation of her principal work, which she called *Scivias*, for *Nosce vias* [*Domini*]. In the year 1141, she tells us, " a shaft of light of dazzling brilliancy came from the opened heavens and pierced my mind and my heart like a flame that warms without burning, as the sun heats by its rays. And suddenly I knew and understood the explanation of the psalms, the gospels, and the other Catholic books of the Old and New Testaments, but not the interpretation of the text of the words or the division of the syllables or the cases and tenses." This book took ten years to complete, and consists of twenty-six visions dealing with the relations between God and man by the Creation, the Redemption and the Church, mixed with apocalyptic prophecies, warnings, and praises expressed in symbolical fashion. She reiterated time and again that she saw these things in vision, and they were the inspiration of all her active work. In 1147 the pope, Bd Eugenius III, came to Trier and the archbishop of Mainz referred St Hildegard's writings to him. Eugenius appointed a commission to examine both them and her, and on receiving a favourable report he read and discussed the writings himself with his advisers, including St Bernard of Clairvaux, who wished him to approve the visions as genuine.   The pope then wrote to Hildegard expressing wonder and happiness at the favours granted her by Heaven, and warning her against pride ; authorizing her to publish, with prudence, whatever the Holy Ghost told her to publish ; and exhorting her to live with her sisters in the place she had seen in vision in faithful observance of the Rule of St Benedict.   St Hildegard wrote a long letter in reply, full of parabolic allusions to the troubles of the times and warning Eugenius against the ambitions of his own household.

The place to which Bd Eugenius referred was the new home which Hildegard had chosen for her community, which had outgrown its accommodation at the Diessenberg.   The migration was stoutly opposed by the monks of St Disibod's, whose abbbey owed much of its importance to the neighbouring convent, with its relics of Bd Jutta and the growing reputation of Hildegard.   The abbot accused her of acting from pride, but she claimed that God had revealed to her that she should move her nuns and the place to which they should go.   This was the Rupertsberg, an exposed and unfertile hill above the Rhine, near Bingen.   During the dispute with the monks of St Disibod's Hildegard was reduced to a very bad state of weakness and ill-health.   Abbot Conon, perhaps doubting the reality of her illness, visited her and, when he saw she was not " putting it on ", he told her to get up and prepare to visit the Rupertsberg.   Immediately she was cured and got ready to obey.   This was enough for Conon, who withdrew his objections ; but the strong feeling of his monks in the matter was by no means allayed, though the leader of the opposition, one Arnold, was won to Hildegard's side by being cured of a painful malady in her church.   The move was made some time between 1147 and 1150, the nuns exchanging their convenient house on the vine-clad Diessenberg for a dilapidated church and unfinished buildings in a deserted spot.

The energy of St Hildegard was responsible for the building of a large and convenient monastery, " with water piped to all the offices ", we are told, which housed a community of fifty nuns.   For the recreation of these the versatility of Hildegard provided a large number of new hymns, canticles and anthems, of which she wrote both the words and the music, and a sort of morality play, or sacred cantata, called *Ordo Virtutum*, and for reading in the chapter-house and refectory she composed fifty allegorical homilies.   Her Lives of St Disibod and St Rupert were claimed to be revelations (in common with a good deal else that was probably a purely natural production), gratuitously, for they bear the marks of local tradi-tions.   Among the diversions of her leisure hours—though it is hard to believe that St Hildegard ever had any leisure—is the so-called " unknown language ", a sort of Esperanto, of which nine hundred words and a made-up alphabet have come down to us.   These words seem to be simply assonant versions of Latin and German words with a liberal addition of final zeds.   From the Rupertsberg St Hildegard conducted a voluminous correspondence, and nearly three hundred of her letters have been printed, though doubt has been thrown on the authenticity of some of them and of the letters she received.   Except when writing to one or other of the numerous abbesses that consulted her, the letters are rather in the nature of homilies, prophecies and allegorical treatises.   They were addressed to popes and emperors, to kings (including Henry II of England, before he had slain Becket), to bishops and abbots.   She wrote once to St Bernard and received a reply, to St Eberhard of Salzburg, and frequently to the Cistercian mystic, St Elizabeth of Schönau.   In two letters to the clergy of Cologne and Trier she rates the carelessness and avarice of so many priests, and foretells, in what are for her unusually clear terms, the scourges that will follow.

Her letters are very full of these prophecies and warnings, and they soon made her notorious. On the one hand people of all kinds came from all parts to consult her ; on the other she was denounced as a fraud, a sorceress, a demoniac. Though her meaning was often wrapped up in difficult symbolism, she always made it quite clear when she was reproving, which she most frequently found occasion to do. Henry, Archbishop of Mainz, wrote rather brusquely requiring St Hildegard to allow one of her nuns, Richardis, to become abbess of another monastery. She replied : " All the reasons given for the promotion of this young woman are worthless before God. The spirit of this jealous God says : Weep and cry out, ye pastors, for you know not what you do, distributing sacred offices in your own interest and wasting them on perverse and godless men. . . . As for yourself, arise !— for your days are numbered." He was in fact deposed and died soon after. To the bishop of Speyer she wrote that his deeds were so evil that his soul was scarcely alive, and told the Emperor Conrad III to reform his life lest he have to blush for it. But she did not pretend to make these judgements on her own. " I am a poor earthen vessel and say these things not of myself but from the serene Light ", she writes to St Elizabeth of Schönau. Nevertheless such a disclaimer could not save her from criticism, and she had trouble even with some of her own nuns, high-born German girls in whom personal pride and vanity were still strong. " Some of them persist in regarding me with an unfavourable eye, pulling me to pieces with malicious tongues behind my back, saying that they cannot stand this talk about discipline that I keep on dinning into them, and that they won't let themselves be ruled by me."

In spite of all her work and continual sickness the activities of St Hildegard were not confined to her convent, and between 1152 and 1162 she made numerous journeys in the Rhineland. She founded a daughter-house at Eibingen, near Rudesheim, and did not hesitate roundly to rebuke the monks and nuns of those monasteries whose discipline she saw to be relaxed ; indeed, her expeditions were rather in the nature of the progress of an " abbess visitor ". At Cologne, Trier, and elsewhere, she addressed herself to selected representatives of the clergy, imparting to them the divine warnings she had received, and exhorted bishops and lay folk with equal ease and straightforwardness. Probably the first of these journeys was the one she made to Ingelheim to meet Frederick Barbarossa, but what took place at that interview is not known. She also visited Metz, Würzburg, Ulm, Werden, Bamberg and other places, and with all this travelling, penetrating in spite of her weakness and the bad conditions into inaccessible spots to visit remote monasteries, she continued to write. Among other works she wrote two books of medicine and natural history. One of these treats of plants, elements, trees, minerals, fishes, birds, quadrupeds, reptiles and metals, and is distinguished by careful scientific observation ; the other treats of the human body, and the causes, symptoms and treatment of its ailments. Some modern methods of diagnosis are at least adumbrated, and she came near to certain later discoveries, such as the circulation of the blood. She deals with normal and morbid psychology, refers to frenzy, insanity, dreads, obsessions and idiocy, and says that " when headache, vapours and giddiness attack a patient simultaneously they make him foolish and upset his reason. This makes many people think that he is possessed by an evil spirit, but that is not true."

During the last year of her life St Hildegard was in great trouble on account of a young man who, having been at one time excommunicated, died and was buried in the cemetery at St Rupert's.   The vicar general of Mainz ordered that the body be removed.   St Hildegard refused, on the grounds that the man had received the last sacraments and that she had been favoured with a vision justifying her action. Thereupon the church was put under an interdict ; and Hildegard wrote to the chapter of Mainz a long letter about sacred music—" A half-forgotten memory of a primitive state which we have lost since Eden "—" symbol of the harmony which Satan has broken, which helps man to build a bridge of holiness between this world and the World of all Beauty and Music.   Those therefore who, without a good reason, impose silence on churches in which singing in God's honour is wont to be heard, will not deserve to hear the glorious choir of angels that praises the Lord in Heaven."   Apparently she was doubtful of the effect of her touching eloquence on the canons of Mainz, for at the same time she wrote very energetically to the archbishop himself who was in Italy.   He thereupon removed the interdict, but, in spite of a promise, he did not fulfil Hildegard's other request, to leave fighting and intriguing and come and govern his diocese.   St Hildegard was now broken by infirmity and mortifications, she could not stand upright and had to be carried from place to place.   But the broken instrument, in the phrase of her friend and chaplain, Martin Guibert, still gave out melody ; to the last she was at the disposition of everybody, giving advice to those that sought it, answering perplexing questions, writing, instructing her nuns, encouraging the sinners who came to her, never at rest.   She survived her trouble with the chapter of Mainz a very little time, and died peacefully on September 17, 1179.   Miracles, of which a number are recorded of her during her life, were multiplied at her tomb, and the process of her canonization was twice undertaken.   It was never achieved, but she is named as a saint in the Roman Martyrology and her feast is kept on this day in several German dioceses.

The visions and revelations claimed by or for St Hildegard are among the best known in this class of phenomena, and her actualization of ideas in symbols and images has provoked comparison both with Dante and William Blake.   She thus describes the fall of the angels : " I saw a great star, most splendid and beautiful, and with it a great multitude of falling sparks which followed it southward.   And they looked on Him upon His throne as it were something hostile, and turning from Him they sought rather the north.   And suddenly they were all annihilated and turned into black coals . . . and cast into the abyss, so that I could see them no more."   In the drawings which illustrate some of the manuscripts these fallen angels are shown as black stars with points of white in the centre and a gold disc surrounded by white points in one of them, while above the horizon other stars still shine in golden light.   In many of them " a prominent feature is a point or a group of points of light, which shimmer and move, usually in a wave-like manner, and are most often interpreted as stars or flaming eyes. . . .   Often the lights give that impression of working, boiling, or fermenting, described by so many visionaries from Ezekiel onwards."   " These visions which I saw ", wrote St Hildegard, " I beheld neither in sleep nor dreaming nor in madness nor with my bodily eyes or ears, nor in hidden places ; but I saw them in full view and according to God's will, when I was wakeful and alert, with the eyes of the spirit and the inward ears. And how this was brought about is indeed hard for human flesh to search out." The visions recorded in the *Scivias* received the guarded approbation of Pope

Eugenius III, but this and similar approvals of private revelations impose no obligation of belief.   The Church receives them only as probable, and even those most worthy of faith may be prudently rejected by individuals.

A great part of our information concerning the life of St Hildegard is derived from her own correspondence and writings, but there are also two or three formal biographies, as biography was understood in the middle ages.   The most noteworthy is that by two monks, Godefrid and Theodoric, printed in the *Acta Sanctorum*, September, vol. v.   Another, by Guibert of Gembloux, was edited by Cardinal Pitra in his *Analecta Sacra*, vol. viii.   Also there are remnants of an inquisition made in 1233 with a view to her canonization, most of which has been published by the Bollandists.   Moreover, in recent times, a considerable literature has grown up dealing with this remarkable mystic.   See in particular J. May, *Die hl. Hildegard von Bingen* (1911) ; and for a fuller bibliography DTC., vol. vi, cc. 2468–2480.   But now almost every aspect of St Hildegard's activities is being independeutly studied.   Her work as a pioneer in science has attracted attention in England, as may be noted in C. Singer, *Studies in the History and Method of Science* (1917).   A number of monographs have appeared in Germany and France, dealing not only with her medical speculations, but also with her musical and artistic compositions.   The illustrations, for example, which adorn the *codex minor* of the *Scivias* have been reproduced by L. Baillet in *Monuments et Mémoires publiés par l'Académie des Inscriptions et Belles-lettres*, vol. xix (1911).   A short popular account of St Hildegard is provided in F. M. Steel's *Life and Visions of St Hildegarde* (1914).   See also J. P. Schmelzeis, *Das Leben und Wirken der hl. Hildegardis* (1879) ; and J. Christophe, *Ste Hildegarde* (1942).

ST PETER ARBUES, MARTYR   (A.D. 1485)

ONE of the chief problems of church and state in medieval Spain was how to deal with the Jews and the Mohammedans who were so numerous in the country : a problem complicated by the active hatred against them displayed by the common people, who shared neither the Christian sentiments of the more tolerant ecclesiastics nor the material interest involved for the civil authorities.   During the fourteenth century Jews in particular had acquired great influence, not only the underground influence of finance but also the open power of high secular and even ecclesiastical offices.   This had been attained, could be attained, only by profession of Christianity, a profession to a considerable extent false, and when genuine often superficial and unreliable.   Two classes who gave particular trouble and were regarded as especially dangerous were the Maranos and the Moriscos, Jews and Moors respectively who, having for one reason or another, good or bad, been converted to Christianity and received baptism, subsequently relapsed, either openly or secretly.   In the year 1478 Pope Sixtus IV, at the urgent request of King Ferdinand of Aragon and Queen Isabella of Castile, issued a bull empowering them to appoint a tribunal to deal with Jewish and other apostates and sham converts.   Thus was established the institution known in history as the Spanish Inquisition.   It may be noted in passing that, though primarily an ecclesiastical tribunal, it acted independently and often in defiance of the Holy See ; and that though it was undoubtedly often brutal, harsh and cruel in its methods, yet its theoretical basis was **not indefensible**.   It was not concerned with *bona-fide* Jews and Mohammedans, and those who voluntarily confessed apostasy and promised amendment were reconciled, with a light penance.

A few years before the establishment of this Inquisition there was professed with the canons regular at Saragossa a certain Peter Arbues.   He had been born at Epila in Aragon about the year 1440, and had graduated brilliantly in theology and canon law in the Spanish College at Bologna.   His virtue and enthusiasm had turned him to the religious life, but the reputation of his learning and zeal caused him to be called from his cloister some years after his profession.　The organization of the nascent Inquisition was in the hands of the Dominican friar Thomas Torquemada, and he, looking about for a provincial inquisitor for the kingdom of Aragon, selected Peter Arbues, who took up his appointment in 1484.　During the few months that he discharged this office Peter preached and worked unwearyingly against the sham Christians and apostates, and their characteristic vices of perjury, usury and sexual immorality.　His zeal made him many enemies, who traduced his character and started the legend of his cruelty, a legend familiar to many, who have not otherwise heard of Peter Arbues, from the picture painted by Wilhelm von Kaulbach, in which the forty-four-year-old canon is represented as an aged and sadistic tyrant.　Apart from the fact that in St Peter's day the Spanish Inquisition was still more or less in the control of the more humane spirit of Rome, no sentence of death or torture has been proved against him.　But the Maranos were determined to get rid of him.　St Peter was aware of what was going on, but refused to take any extraordinary precautions, even after an unsuccessful attempt had been made on his life.　But on the night of September 14–15, 1485, three men entered the cathedral of St Saviour at Saragossa and stabbed the canon as he knelt in prayer.　He died two days later, and was at once acclaimed throughout the land as a martyr ; as such he was canonized in 1867.

　　A sufficient account of St Peter is given in the *Acta Sanctorum*, September, vol. v.　We have no formal biography of early date, but a good deal of information is provided by the chronicles of the time.　See also G. Cozza, *Della vita, miracoli e culto del martire S. Pietro de Arbues* (1867).

ST FRANCIS OF CAMPOROSSO　(A.D. 1866)　　*(Transferred to September 25)*

CAMPOROSSO is a small town on the coast of Liguria, and there was living there at the beginning of the last century a family called Croese, who were farmers and olive-cultivators in a small way.　To the master and mistress was born in 1804 a son, whom they had baptized John.　He was one of four children and had a simple and religious upbringing, and as a matter of course began to work on his father's farm. When he was about eighteen, however, John met a lay-brother of the Conventual Friars Minor, who gave him the idea of the same vocation.　John presented himself at the friary at Sestri Ponente and was accepted as a tertiary and given the name of Antony.　He spent two years in the service of that house, and then, desiring a life of greater austerity, he offered himself to the Capuchin Friars Minor.　He was sent to their novitiate at Genoa and in 1825 was clothed as a lay-brother, with the names Francis Mary.　In the following year he was professed and set to work in the infirmary, from whence he was taken to be questor, whose office it is to beg food from door to door for the community.　This was a new experience for Brother Francis, and he disliked it so much that he thought of asking to be relieved of it. But instead, when the guardian asked him if he would undertake to beg in the city of Genoa itself, he accepted with alacrity.　The Genoese were not invariably well disposed towards the religious, and Brother Francis sometimes received stones instead of bread, but he persevered for ten years and became the best-known and most welcome questor in the place.　He was a particularly familiar figure in the dockyard, where people would come to ask of him news of their friends and relatives overseas, for he was reputed to be able to give correct information about people in distant lands, whom he had never seen.　Miracles of healing too were attributed to him and, though there were some still who insulted and jeered at him, to the majority he was known as " Padre santo ".   It was in vain that he protested that he was a lay-brother and not a priest—" good father " he remained, and he was indeed a father to the poor and afflicted who flocked to him.

During two years Brother Francis suffered from varicose veins, of which he told nobody till his limp betrayed him, and he was found to be in a most shocking state.   By the time he was sixty he was nearly worn out, and his leg had to be operated on, without much effect.   In August 1866 Genoa was devastated by cholera.   The Capuchins and other religious of the city were out among the sufferers at once, and Bd Francis was so moved by all he saw around him that he solemnly offered his own life to God that the epidemic might cease ; and he accurately predicted the circumstances of his approaching death.   On September 15 he was himself smitten by the disease, and two days later he was called to God. From that time the cholera began to abate.   The tomb of St Francis became famous for miracles. He was beatified in 1929 and canonized in 1962.

The decree of beatification, printed in the *Acta Apostolicae Sedis*, vol. xxi (1929), pp. 485–488, includes a biographical sketch of his life.   Several biographies were issued or republished at the same time.   The most considerable is one in Italian by Fr Luigi da Porto Maurizio ; another, also of some length, is in French, by Fr Constant de Pélissanne (1929).

18 : ST JOSEPH OF CUPERTINO   (A.D. 1663)

JOSEPH DESA was born June 17, 1603, at Cupertino, a small village between Brindisi and Otranto.   His parents were poor and unfortunate.   Joseph himself was born in a shed at the back of the house, because his father, a carpenter, was unable to pay his debts and the home was being sold up.   His childhood was unhappy.   His widowed mother looked on him as a nuisance and a burden, and treated him with great severity, and he developed an extreme absent-mindedness and inertia.   He would forget his meals, and when reminded of them say simply, " I forgot ", and wander open-mouthed in an aimless way about the village so that he earned the nick-name of " Boccaperta ", the gaper.   He had a hot temper, which made him more unpopular, but was exemplary and even pre-cocious in his religious duties.   When the time came for him to try and earn his own living, Joseph was bound apprentice to a shoemaker, which trade he applied himself to for some time, but without any success.   When he was seventeen he presented himself to be received amongst the Conventual Franciscans, but they refused to have him.   Then he went to the Capuchins, and they took him as a lay-brother ; but after eight months he was dismissed as unequal to the duties of the order : his clumsiness and preoccupation made him an apparently impossible subject, for he dropped piles of plates and dishes on the refectory floor, forgot to do things he was told, and could not be trusted even to make up the kitchen fire. Joseph then turned for help to a wealthy uncle, who curtly refused to aid an obvious good-for-nothing, and the young man returned home in despair and misery.   His mother was not at all pleased to see him on her hands again and used her influence with her brother, a Conventual Franciscan, to have him accepted by the friars of his order at Grottella as a servant.   He was given a tertiary habit and put to work in the stables.   Now a change seems to have come over Joseph ; at any rate he was more successful in his duties, and his humility, his sweetness, his love of mortification and penance gained him so much regard that in 1625 it was resolved he should be admitted amongst the religious of the choir, that he might qualify himself for holy orders.

Joseph therefore began his novitiate, and his virtues rendered him an object of admiration ; but his lack of progress in studies was also remarked.   Try as he would, the extent of his human accomplishments was to read badly and to write worse.   He had no gift of eloquence or for exposition, the one text on which he had something to say being, " Blessed is the womb that bore thee ".   When he came up for examination for the diaconate the bishop opened the gospels at random and his eye fell on that text : he asked Brother Joseph to expound it, which he did well.   When it was a question of the priesthood, the first candidates were so satisfactory that the remainder, Joseph among them, were passed without examination.   After having received the priesthood in 1628 he passed five years without tasting bread or wine, and the herbs he ate on Fridays were so distasteful that only himself could use them.   His fast in Lent was so rigorous that he took no nourishment except on Thursdays and Sundays, and he spent the hours devoted to manual work in those simple household and routine duties which he knew were, humanly speaking, all he was fitted to undertake.

From the time of his ordination St Joseph's life was one long succession of ecstasies, miracles of healing and supernatural happenings on a scale not paralleled in the reasonably authenticated life of any other saint.   Anything that in any way could be particularly referred to God or the mysteries of religion was liable to ravish him from his senses and make him oblivious to what was going on around him ; the absent-mindedness and abstraction of his childhood now had an end and a purpose clearly seen.   The sight of a lamb in the garden of the Capuchins at Fossombrone caused him to be lost in contemplation of the spotless Lamb of God and, it is said, be caught up into the air with the animal in his arms.   At all times he had a command over beasts surpassing that of St Francis himself ; sheep were said to gather round him and listen to his prayers, a sparrow at a convent came and went at his word.   Especially during Mass or the Divine Office he would be lifted off his feet in rapture.   During the seventeen years he remained at Grottella over seventy occasions are recorded of his levitation, the most marvellous being when the friars were building a calvary.   The middle cross of the group was thirty-six feet high and correspondingly heavy, defying the efforts of ten men to lift it.   St Joseph is said to have " flown " seventy yards from the door of the house to the cross, picked it up in his arms " as if it were a straw ", and deposited it in its place.   This staggering feat is not attested by an eye-witness, and, in common with most of his earlier marvels, was recorded only after his death, when plenty of time had elapsed in which events could be exaggerated and legends arise.   But, whatever their exact nature and extent, the daily life of St Joseph was surrounded by such disturbing phenomena that for thirty-five years he was not allowed to celebrate Mass in public, to keep choir, to take his meals with his brethren, or to attend processions and other public functions.   Sometimes when he was bereft of his senses they would try to bring him to by hitting him, burning his flesh or pricking it with needles, but nothing had any effect except, it is said, the voice of his superior.   When he did come back to himself he would laughingly apologize for what he called his " fits of giddiness ".

Levitation, the name given to the raising of the human body from the ground by no apparent physical force, is recorded in some form or other of over two hundred saints and holy persons (as well as of many others), and in their case is interpreted as a special mark of God's favour whereby it is made evident even to the physical senses that prayer is a raising of the heart and mind to God.   St Joseph of Cupertino, in both the extent and number of these experiences, provides the classical examples of levitation, for, if many of the earlier incidents are doubtful some of those recorded in his later years are very well attested.   For example, one of his biographers states that : " When in 1645 the Spanish ambassador to the papal court, the High Admiral of Castile, passed through [Assisi] he visited Joseph of Cupertino in his cell.   After conversing with him he returned to the church and told his wife : ' I have seen and spoken with another St Francis.'   As his wife then expressed a great desire to enjoy the same privilege, the father guardian gave Joseph an order to go down to the church and speak with her Excellency.   To this he made answer : ' I will obey, but I do not know whether I shall be able to speak with her.'   In point of fact no sooner had he entered the church than his eyes rested on a statue of Mary Immaculate which stood over the altar, and he at once flew about a dozen paces over the heads of those present to the foot of the statue. Then after paying homage there for some short space and uttering his customary shrill cry he flew back again and straightway returned to his cell, leaving the admiral, his wife, and the large retinue which attended them, speechless with astonishment."   This story is supported in two biographies by copious references to depositions, in the process of canonization, of witnesses who are expressly stated to have been present.

" Still more trustworthy ", says Father Thurston in the *Month* for May 1919, " is the evidence given of the saint's levitations at Osimo, where he spent the last six years of his life.   There his fellow religious saw him fly up seven or eight feet into the air to kiss the statue of the infant Jesus which stood over the altar, and they told how he carried off this wax image in his arms and floated about with it in his cell in every conceivable attitude.   On one occasion during these last years of his life he caught up another friar in his flight and carried him some distance round the room, and this indeed he is stated to have done on several previous occasions.   In the very last Mass which he celebrated, on the festival of the Assumption 1663, a month before his death, he was lifted up in a longer rapture than usual.   For these facts we have the evidence of several eye-witnesses who made their depositions, as usual under oath, only four or five years later.   It seems very difficult to believe that they could possibly be deceived as to the broad fact that the saint did float in the air, as they were convinced they had seen him do, under every possible variety of conditions and surroundings."   Prosper Lambertini, afterwards Pope Benedict XIV, the supreme authority on evidence and procedure in canonization causes, personally studied all the details of the case of St Joseph of Cupertino.   The writer goes on : " When the cause came up for discussion before the Congregation of Rites [Lambertini] was ' promotor Fidei ' (popularly known as the Devil's Advocate), and his ' animadversions ' upon the evidence submitted are said to have been of a most searching character.   None the less we must believe that these criticisms were answered to his own complete satisfaction, for not only was it he himself who, when pope, published in 1753 the decree of beatification, but in his great work, *De Servorum Dei Beatificatione*, etc., he speaks as follows : ' Whilst I discharged the office of promoter of the Faith the cause of the venerable servant of God, Joseph of Cupertino, came up for discussion in the Congregation of Sacred Rites, which after my retirement was brought to a favourable conclusion, and in this *eyewitnesses of unchallengeable integrity* gave evidence of the famous upliftings from the ground and prolonged flights of the aforesaid servant of God when rapt in ecstasy.' There can be no doubt that Benedict XIV, a critically-minded man, who knew the value of evidence and who had studied the original depositions as probably no one else had studied them, believed that the witnesses of St Joseph's levitations had really seen what they professed to have seen."

There were not wanting persons to whom these manifestations were a stone of offence, and when St Joseph attracted crowds about him as he travelled in the province of Bari, he was denounced as " one who runs about these provinces and as a new Messias draws crowds after him by the prodigies wrought on some few of the ignorant people, who are ready to believe anything ". The vicar general carried the complaint to the inquisitors of Naples, and Joseph was ordered to appear. The heads of his accusation being examined, the inquisitors could find nothing worthy of censure, but did not discharge him ; instead they sent him to Rome to his minister general, who received him at first with harshness, but he became impressed by St Joseph's innocent and humble bearing and he took him to see the pope, Urban VIII. The saint went into ecstasy at the sight of the vicar of Christ, and Urban declared that if Joseph should die before himself he would give evidence of the miracle to which he had been a witness. It was decided to send Joseph to Assisi, where again he was treated by his superiors with considerable severity, they at least pretending to regard him as a hypocrite. He arrived at Assisi in 1639, and remained there thirteen years. At first he suffered many trials, both interior and exterior. God seemed to have abandoned him ; his religious exercises were accompanied with a spiritual dryness that afflicted him exceedingly and terrible temptations cast him into so deep a melancholy that he scarce dare lift up his eyes. The minister general, being informed, called him to Rome, and having kept him there three weeks he sent him back to Assisi. The saint on his way to Rome experienced a return of those heavenly consolations which had been withdrawn from him. Reports of Joseph's holiness and miracles spread over the borders of Italy, and distinguished people, such as the Admiral of Castile mentioned above, would call at Assisi to visit him. Among them was John Frederick, Duke of Brunswick and Hanover. This prince, who was a Lutheran, was so struck with what he had seen that he embraced the Catholic faith. Joseph used to say to some scrupulous persons who came to consult him : " I like neither scruples nor melancholy ; let your intention be right and fear not ", and he was always urging people to prayer. " Pray ", he would say, " pray. If you are troubled by dryness or distractions, just say an Our Father. Then you make both vocal and mental prayer." When Cardinal Lauria asked him what souls in ecstasy saw during their raptures he replied : " They feel as though they were taken into a wonderful gallery, shining with never-ending beauty, where in a glass, with a single look, they apprehend the marvellous vision which God is pleased to show them." In the ordinary comings and goings of daily life he was so preoccupied with heavenly things that he would genuinely suppose a passing woman to be our Lady or St Catherine or St Clare, a strange man to be one of the Apostles, a fellow friar to be St Francis or St Antony.

In 1653, for reasons which are not known, the Inquisition of Perugia was instructed to remove St Joseph from the care of his own order and put him in charge of Capuchins at a lonely friary among the hills of Pietrarossa, where he was to live in the strictest seclusion. " Have I got to go to prison then ? " he asked, and departed at once—leaving his hat, his cloak, his breviary and his spectacles behind him. To prison, in effect, he had gone. He was not allowed to leave the convent enclosure, to speak to anyone but the friars, to write or to receive letters ; he was completely cut off from the world. Apart from wondering why he should be sundered from his fellow Conventuals and treated like a criminal, this life must have been particularly satisfactory to St Joseph. But soon his whereabouts was discovered and pilgrims flocked to the place ; whereupon he was spirited away to lead the same sort of life with the Capuchins of Fossombrone. The rest of his life was spent like this. When in 1655 the chapter general of the Conventual Franciscans asked for the return of their saint to Assisi, Pope Alexander VII replied that one St Francis at Assisi was enough, but in 1657 he was allowed to go to the Conventual house at Osimo. Here the seclusion was, however, even more strict, and only selected religious were allowed to visit him in his cell. But all this time, and till the end, supernatural manifestations were his daily portion : he was in effect deserted by man but God was ever more clearly with him. He fell sick on August 10, 1663, and knew that his end was at hand ; five weeks later he died, at the age of sixty. He was canonized in 1767.

There is a printed *summarium* prepared for the Congregation of Rites in 1688, containing an abstract of the depositions of witnesses in the process of beatification. It is stated, however, that only two copies are now known to exist, and it does not seem to have been accessible to the Bollandists. In the *Acta Sanctorum*, therefore (September, vol. v), they contented themselves with translating from previously published biographies such as those of Pastrovicchi (1753) and Bernino (1722). The two lives last named have been translated into French and other languages. A convenient version or adaptation of Pastrovicchi in English was brought out by Father F. S. Laing (1918). The bull of canonization, a lengthy document, containing many biographical data, is printed in the later Italian lives, and in the French translation of Bernino (1856). In this the story of St Joseph's aerial flights, as recounted above, is told in detail and emphasized. *Cf.* H. Thurston, *The Physical Phenomena of Mysticism* (1952).

ST FERREOLUS, MARTYR   (THIRD CENTURY ?)

ACCORDING to his *passio*, St Ferreolus was a tribune who lived at Vienne in Gaul, and was secretly a Christian. St Julian of Brioude, a native of that city, lodged in his house and made public profession of the faith. When persecution began and St Julian had been put to death, Crispin, governor of that part of Gaul, had St Ferreolus apprehended for failing to arrest Christians. Crispin told him that, as he was paid by the state as a military officer, it became him to set to others an example of obedience. The martyr answered : " I do not so much overrate money. If I may be allowed to live and serve God, I am well satisfied. If even this seem too much, I am willing to resign life itself rather than abandon my religion." The judge commanded that he should be scourged, and then confined him in that inner pit of the prison into which the rest of the place drained. On the third day his chains fell off his hands and legs by the power of God, and he made his escape and went out of the city by the gate which led to Lyons. He swam over the river Rhône and got as far as the river Gère which falls into the Rhône just above Vienne, when he fell again into the hands of the persecutors, who bound him and led him away to death. He was beheaded on the banks of the Rhône and the Christians of Vienne interred his body with great veneration near the same river. A church was built over his burying-place, from whence his relics were removed by St Mamertus about the year 473 to a church built to shelter them within the city of Vienne.

On this same day is commemorated another St Ferreolus, a bishop of Limoges who died in 591 or thereabouts.

The " acts " of St Ferreolus (printed in the *Acta Sanctorum*, September, vol. v) are, as Delehaye states, " of little worth ". But his martyrdom is authentic, and his *cultus*, to which both St Gregory of Tours and Venantius Fortunatus bear witness, very ancient. See CMH., pp. 517–518.

ST METHODIUS OF OLYMPUS, Bishop and Martyr   (*c.* A.D. 311)

St Jerome states that this Methodius was bishop first of Olympus in Lycia and then of Tyre, and that he was crowned with martyrdom at Khalkis in Greece at the very end of the last persecution. These statements are reproduced in the Roman. Martyrology, but it is practically certain that he was never bishop of Tyre ; Greek writers refer to him as bishop of Patara in Lycia. We have no particulars of his life or martyrdom and his fame rests on his writings. Against Origen's teaching that man's risen body is not the same as his earthly body he wrote a dialogue *On the Resurrection*. He wrote on free will against the Valentinians, and other works which caused St Jerome to refer to him as " the most eloquent Methodius ", and the Roman Martyrology to call him " most renowned for the brilliance of his preaching and his learning ". Methodius himself, however, gave support to the error of Millenarianism *i.e.* Christ's temporal reign of a thousand years before the general resurrection, in his *Symposium*. The best-known of his works is this *Symposium* or Banquet of the Ten Virgins, written in imitation of the *Banquet* of Plato. As an imitation it is hardly a success (Alban Butler calls his style " diffusive, swelling, and full of epithets "), but as an ascetical treatise on virginity it was formerly famous. In it a matron is introduced to tell her friend Eubulus (the surname of St Methodius himself) the conversation of ten maidens at a festive meal in the garden of Arete (Virtue). A discourse is put into the mouth of each of these in commendation of virginity. The symposium ends with a hymn to our Lord as the Bridegroom of the Church, in which the maiden Thecla sings a series of alphabetical strophes and is answered by the others with a refrain. This forms one of the earliest of Christian hymns.

The slender data available concerning the life of St Methodius of Olympus have been collected in the *Acta Sanctorum*, September, vol. v. With regard to his literary work, research in modern times has brought to light a Slavonic text of several of his writings which has been turned to profit by N. Bonwetsch in his *Methodius von Olympus* (1891). See also Bardenhewer, *Altkirchliche Literatur* (1913), vol. ii, pp. 334 *seq.*, and DTC., vol. x, cc. 1606–1614.

ST RICHARDIS, Widow   (*c.* A.D. 895)

When she was twenty-two years old Richardis, daughter of the Count of Alsace, was married to Charles the Fat, son of King Louis the German. Nineteen years later, in 881, she accompanied him to Rome, to be crowned emperor and empress of the Holy Roman Empire by Pope John VIII. Hitherto they had lived together in amity but a few years later Charles, either because his suspicions were genuinely aroused or else in order to serve some unworthy purpose of his own, charged his wife with unfaithfulness.   He named as her accomplice his chancellor, Liutward, who was bishop of Vercelli and a man greatly esteemed both for his abilities and his virtue.   Richardis and Liutward appeared before the imperial assembly and solemnly denied the allegation ; the bishop purged himself by an oath and the empress appealed to the judgement of God by claiming an ordeal, either by fire or (by proxy) of battle.   It is said that the ordeal by fire was accepted and that St Richardis, with bare feet and wearing an inflammable smock, walked unharmed across burning embers.   Liutward was nevertheless deprived of his chancellorship and, it not being decent after so public an exhibition that they should continue to live together, Richardis was allowed to separate from Charles.   She went for a time to a nunnery at Hohenburg and then to the abbey of Andlau, which she had herself founded.   Here she lived in peace until her death about the year 895, joining in the life of the nuns, interesting herself on their behalf with the Holy See, caring for the poor, and writing verses.   When Pope St Leo IX visited Andlau in 1049, on his way from a council at Mainz, he ordered her relics to be disinterred, enshrined, and exposed for the veneration of the faithful.   This *cultus* has continued and the feast of St Richardis is observed in the diocese of Strasburg.

There is no formal life of St Richardis, but a few breviary lessons, panegyrics, etc., have been brought together in the *Acta Sanctorum*, September, vol. v.   See also the *Allgemeine Deutsche Biographie*, vol. xxviii, pp. 420 *seq.* ; and M. Corbet, *Ste Richarde* . . . (1948).

BD JOHN MASSIAS   (A.D. 1645)

THE lessons of his office state that the parents of Bd John Massias (or Masias) were representatives of noble and ancient families, who " had been deprived of rank and wealth by the various misfortunes of an unreliable world ".   He was born at Ribera in Estramadura in 1585 and was left an orphan whilst still young, being looked after by an uncle, who made the boy earn his living as a shepherd.   During the long hours when there was nothing particular to do except keep his eyes open John would say his rosary and meditate on the Christian mysteries, and it sometimes appeared that the holy ones were there, visible and talking to him, especially our Lady and St John the Evangelist.   He attributed to an instruction of the last named his sudden decision to go to the Americas, as so many others of his countrymen were then doing.   He landed in Peru and got work on a cattle-ranch, where he stopped for over two years and saved a little money with which he made his way to Lima.   Here he decided to become a religious and, having given away what was left of his savings, he was accepted as a lay-brother by the Dominicans of St Mary Magdalen's.   Brother John's austerities exceeded the bounds of prudence, and his prior had to insist on moderation : for he would content himself with one hour of sleep, and that on his knees with his head on the bed, and brought on himself a disease which required a painful and dangerous operation.   He was made porter and his lodge soon became the meeting-place for the poor, the sick and the wretched of the city ; following the example of his friend Bd Martin de Porres, he begged alms with which to feed and physic them, and accompanied his ministrations with good advice and exhortations to good life and the love of God.   Those who were too shy to beg he sought out in their homes, and to save time in begging from door to door he trained the priory donkey to go round by itself and receive in its panniers food and clothing for his beloved poor.   Many and remarkable were the miracles attributed to Bd John Massias, and his death at the age of sixty was mourned by the whole city. He was beatified in 1837.

On the occasion of the beatification an Italian life, *Vita del Beato Giovanni Massias* was published by the Dominicans in Rome. See also Procter, *Lives of Dominican Saints*, pp. 263–274. There is a fuller bibliography in Taurisano, *Catalogus Historicus O.P.*

19 : SS. JANUARIUS, BISHOP OF BENEVENTO, AND HIS COMPANIONS, MARTYRS   (*c.* A.D. 305 ?)

ST JANUARIUS (Gennaro), a native some say of Naples, others of Benevento, was bishop of this latter city when the persecution of Diocletian broke out. Sossus, deacon of Miseno, Proculus, deacon of Pozzuoli, and Euticius and Acutius, laymen, were imprisoned at Pozzuoli by an order of the governor of Campania, before whom they had confessed their faith. Sossus by his wisdom and sanctity had earned the friendship of St Januarius, and upon the news that this servant of God and several others were fallen into the hands of the persecutors, the bishop determined to make them a visit to comfort and encourage them. He did not escape the notice of the keepers, who gave information that someone from Benevento had visited the Christian prisoners. The governor gave orders that Januarius, whom he found to be the person, should be arrested and brought before him at Nola, which was accordingly done. Festus, the bishop's deacon, and Desiderius, a lector of his church, were also taken, and had a share in the interrogatories and torments which the good bishop underwent at Nola. Some time after the governor went to Pozzuoli, and these three confessors, loaded with irons, were made to walk before his chariot to that town, where they were thrown into the same prison where the four martyrs already mentioned were detained. They had been condemned to be torn in pieces by wild beasts, and were then lying in expectation of the execution of their sentence. The day after the arrival of St Januarius and his two companions all these champions of Christ were exposed to the beasts in the amphitheatre, but none of the animals could be provoked to touch them. The people were amazed and imputed their preservation to magic, and the martyrs were condemned to be beheaded. This sentence was executed near Pozzuoli, and the martyrs were buried near that town.

The city of Naples eventually got possession of the relics of St Januarius, which in the fifth century were brought from the little church of San Gennaro near the Solfatara. During the wars of the Normans they were removed, first to Benevento, and some time after to the abbey of Monte Vergine ; but in 1497 they were brought back to Naples, where he has long been honoured as principal patron.

No reliance can be placed upon the above particulars of the martyrdom of St Januarius ; all the recensions of his " acts " are late and untrustworthy ; nothing certain is known of him or of those who suffered with him. All the fame of Januarius rests upon that " standing miracle " (as Baronius called it), the liquefaction of the alleged relic of his blood which is preserved in the chapel of the treasury of the cathedral-church of Naples, a happening of which there are records for the past four hundred years. The relic consists of a dark, solid, opaque mass which half fills the small glass phial in which it is contained, the phial itself being fixed in a metal reliquary. Eighteen times a year, in connexion with the feast of the translation of the relics to Naples (Saturday before the first Sunday in May), the feast of the saint (September 19), and the anniversary of the averting of a threatened eruption of Vesuvius in 1631 (December 16), this relic is brought out and held by a priest in the presence of what is believed to be the martyr's head, exposed in a silver reliquary on the altar. Prayers are said by the people, especially as represented by a number of poor women who have a privileged position in the church and are known as the " aunts of St Januarius " (*zie di San Gennaro*). After a varying interval, from two minutes to an hour as a rule, the priest from time to time turning the reliquary upside down, the dark mass, hitherto solid and immovable, detaches itself from the sides of the glass, becomes liquid and reddish in colour, and sometimes froths, bubbles up, and increases in volume. This takes place not only in full view of the people but in close proximity to any accredited persons who may have been admitted to the sanctuary. The priest then announces, " The miracle has happened ", *Te Deum* is sung, and the relic venerated by the congregation and clergy. Few, if any, alleged miracles have been examined more carefully, more often, or by people of more divergent views than this of the blood of St Januarius, and it may be safely affirmed that no expert inquirer, however rationalist in temper he may be, now denies that what is said to take place *does* take place. There is no trick, and there is as yet no completely satisfactory explanation (though many have been advanced, both by Catholics and others), except the explanation of miracle. But before a miracle may be certainly recognized all natural explanations must have been examined and found wanting, and all objections answered. Among the undoubted facts concerning this relic are the following :

1. The dark substance alleged to be the blood of St Januarius (which for more than 300 years has remained sealed up in a glass phial immovably set in a metal reliquary) does not always occupy the same volume. Sometimes the black and hard mass is seen almost completely to fill the phial, at other times there is a vacant space above it of more than a third of its bulk.

2. Concurrently with this variation in volume there is a variation in weight, which of late years has been tested in an accurate chemical balance. Taking the extremes which have been recorded, this variation has amounted to as much as 27 grammes.

3. The rapidity of the liquefaction seems to bear no ratio to the temperature of the atmosphere. Sometimes when the temperature has stood as high as 86° Fahrenheit, more than two hours have passed before any signs of liquefaction were observed. On the other hand, when the temperature has been 15° or even 20° lower than this, complete liquefaction has occurred in from 10 to 15 minutes.

4. The liquefaction does not always take place in the same way. Instances are recorded in which the liquefied contents seem almost to boil and are of a vivid crimson colour, while in other cases the colour is dull and the movement sluggish.

On the other hand, among the difficulties in the way of accepting the phenomenon as a miracle the following have been pointed out. The fact that a very large majority of all other blood-relics of which similar behaviour seems to be true are found in the neighbourhood of Naples ; and some of the relics, *e.g.* those of St John Baptist, St Stephen, St Ursula, are almost certainly spurious. The relic has seven times been known to liquefy while a jeweller was repairing the reliquary, but often during the December exposition it has failed to liquefy at all. The authenticity of the relic itself is extremely problematical ; we have no record of the *cultus* of St Januarius before the fifth century.   Moreover there is the consideration, of yet greater weight if the relic be not authentic, of the seeming purposelessness of the marvel.   Such a criticism may be levelled at many other alleged miracles ; we cannot search the ways of God ; and it is true that for centuries the liquefaction has been a standing manifestation of His omnipotence for thousands of Neapolitans. But it must also be remembered that marvels of this kind, so far from being a help, are a definite hindrance to the faith of other people, of different temperament but of no less good will : and these also have souls to be saved.

Miracles recorded in Holy Scripture are revealed facts and an object of faith. Other miracles are not considered in the same light, neither does our faith in part rest upon them as upon the former, though they illustrate and confirm it ; nor do they demand or admit any higher assent than that which prudence requires and which is due to the evidence of human authority, upon which they depend.   When such miracles are propounded, they are not to be rashly admi tted : the evidence of the fact and circumstances ought to be examined to the bottom, and duly weighed ; where that fails it is the part of prudence to suspend or refuse our assent.   If human evidence set the certainty of a miracle above the reach of doubt, it must more powerfully excite us to raise our minds to God in humble worship, love and praise, and to honour Him in His saints, when by such wonderful means He gives us tangible proofs of the glory to which He exalts them.

The unsatisfactory " acts " of St Januarius and companions are preserved to us in varying forms.   The texts printed in the *Acta Sanctorum*, September, vol. vi (but out of place, at the end of the volume), sufficiently illustrate this diversity.   On the other hand there can be no serious doubt that a bishop named Januarius was really martyred somewhere near Naples, and that he was venerated at an early date.   Not only does the priest Uranius, shortly after the year 431, allude to him in terms which imply that he was a saint in Heaven, on a footing with the famous St Martin of Tours, but a fifth-century representation of him in the so-called " catacomb of St Januarius " at Naples depicts him with a nimbus.   His name also is entered on this day in the early calendars both of East and West.   See the *Acta Sanctorum*, November, vol. ii, part 2, p. 517 ; and Pio Franchi de' Cavalieri, in *Studi e Testi*, vol. xxiv (1912), pp. 79–114.   The question of the liquefaction of the blood has of course been discussed again and again.   For a vindication of the supernatural character of the prodigy, consult especially Taglialatela, *Memorie storico-critiche del culto e del sangue di S. Gennaro* (1893) ; Cavène, *Le célèbre miracle de S. Janvier à Naples et à Pouzzoles* (1909) ; Alfano e Amitrano, *Il miracolo di S. Gennaro* (1924)—this last includes a bibliography of 1346 entries—and for English readers, Bishop E. P. Graham, *The Mystery of Naples* (1909) ; and Ian Grant, *The Testimony of Blood* (1929).   The view of those who question the miraculous nature of the liquefaction is set out in Isenkrahe, *Neapolitanische Blutwunder* (1912), and in *The Month*, January, February and March 1927 and February 1930, by Fr Thurston, who also contributes the article in the *Catholic Encyclopaedia*, vol. viii, pp. 295–297. The *Kirchliches Handlexikon* states (vol. ii, col. 25), " a conclusive judgement in this matter can hardly be arrived at, but so far no natural explanation has been found ".

SS. PELEUS AND HIS COMPANIONS, MARTYRS   (A.D. 310)

THE confessors who were condemned to the minés (*i.e.* quarries) in Palestine during the course of the last general persecution built little oratories where they met for divine service, which · was their chief comfort under their sufferings. Firmilian, governor of Palestine, informed the Emperor Galerius of the liberty they had taken, and the tyrant sent an order that they should be sent, some to the mines in Cyprus, others to those in the Lebanon, and others to other places.   The officer upon whom the command devolved removed the servants of God to the new places of banishment ; but first he caused four of their number to be burnt alive.   These were Peleus and Nilus, two Egyptian bishops, Elias, a priest, and an Egyptian layman.   These probably suffered at Phunon, near Petra, at the same time as St Tyrannio of Gaza and his companions.

Eusebius, *De Martyribus Palaestinae* (xiii, 3), is the main authority.   See also B. Violet, *Die palästinischen Märtyrer des Eusebius von Cäsarea*, pp. 105–107.

ST SEQUANUS, or SEINE, Abbot   (*c.* A.D. 580)

THIS holy monk was born in the little town of Mesmont in Burgundy.   He was for a time a solitary at Verrey-sous-Drée, where he lived in a hut that he built himself from forest timber, and was said to break his fast every day only after having recited the whole psalter.   The bishop of Langres promoted him to the priesthood at a very early age.   The saint having suffered some persecution in consequence from the local clergy, he put himself under the direction of the holy abbot John, who governed the monastery of Réomé.   Here he perfected himself in the study of the Holy Scriptures, and in the practice of all religious virtues. After some time he built a monastery in the forest of Segestre, near the source of the river Seine, and the monks did much to civilize the people of the neighbourhood, who were said to be cannibals.   A village which grew up around the abbey became known as Saint-Seine, after the founder, and the regular discipline which he established there rendered it famous and drew to it a number of disciples.   God was pleased to honour him with the gift of miracles.   He is mentioned in early martyrologies under the name of St Sigon.

Under the form " depositio sancti Sigonis, presbyteri et confessoris ", St Sequanus was commemorated in the *Hieronymianum ;* but he is called " Sequanus " by St Gregory of Tours, who mentions him at a still earlier date.   There is an anonymous life printed in the *Acta Sanctorum*, September, vol. vi, but its value as an historical source is very questionable.

ST GOERICUS, or ABBO, Bishop of Metz   (A.D. 647)

DURING the seventh century there were two great saintly families in Aquitaine, Salvia and Ansbertina, and in the second of these was born St Goericus.   He became an officer in the palace of Dagobert I and was a soldier of distinction, when he was suddenly smitten with blindness.   After bearing his affliction with patience for a time he decided to make a pilgrimage to the church of St Stephen at Metz, of which city his relative St Arnulf was bishop, in consequence of a vision which he believed he had had.   He therefore set out with his two daughters, Precia and Victorina, and, while praying in the church, his sight was restored.   In thanksgiving Goericus became a priest, and when St Arnulf resigned his see in the year 629 he succeeded to it.   St Goericus as a bishop followed the golden example of his predecessor, whom he would often visit in his retreat at Remiremont ; and when Arnulf died he translated his body to his cathedral city, an occasion said to have been marked with miracles.   St Goericus founded a nunnery at Epinal, of which his daughter Precia was first abbess.

A medieval life of the usual unsatisfactory type is printed in the *Acta Sanctorum*, September, vol. vi.   Goericus was in correspondence with St Desiderius of Cahors (Migne, PL., vol. lxxxvii, cc. 218 *seq.*).   See also Duchesne, *Fastes Épiscopaux*, vol. iii, p. 56.

ST THEODORE, ARCHBISHOP OF CANTERBURY   (A.D. 690)

THEODORE was a Greek, born at Tarsus in Cilicia (the birthplace of St Paul) and a student at Athens : the last early bishop of foreign birth to occupy the metropolitan throne of Canterbury and one of the greatest of its archbishops.   After the death of St Deusdedit, sixth archbishop, in 664, Oswy, King of Northumbria, and Egbert, King of Kent, sent a priest named Wighard to Rome that he might be consecrated and duly confirmed to the see by the pope himself.   Wighard died in Italy, and St Vitalian, who then sat in St Peter's chair, chose Adrian, abbot of a monastery near Naples, to be raised to that dignity.   This abbot was by birth an African, understood Greek and Latin perfectly, was thoroughly versed in theology and in the monastic and ecclesiastical discipline.   But so great were his fears of the office that the pope was compelled to yield to his excuses.   He insisted, however, that Adrian should find a person equal to the charge, and Adrian first named a monk called Andrew ; but he was judged incapable on account of his bodily infirmities ; Adrian then suggested another monk, Theodore of Tarsus.   He was accepted, but on condition that Adrian should accompany him to Britain, because he had already travelled twice through France and also to watch over Theodore lest he introduce into his church anything contrary to the faith (" as the Greeks have a habit of doing ", comments St Bede).

Theodore was at that time sixty-six years old, well instructed in secular and sacred learning, and of exemplary life, and was not in holy orders.   Being ordained subdeacon, he waited four months for his hair to grow, that it might be shaved in the form of a crown according to the Roman custom : from which it may be gathered that he had hitherto been a monk of the Eastern obedience and that his promotion involved what we should now call a " change of rite "*   At length Pope Vitalian consecrated him bishop, and recommended him to St Benedict Biscop, who was then in Rome and whom the pope obliged to return to England with SS. Theodore and Adrian in order to be their guide and interpreter.   They set out on May 27, 668, went by sea to Marseilles, and from thence by land to Arles, where they were entertained by the archbishop, John.   St Theodore passed the winter at Paris with St Agilbert, who had formerly been bishop of Wessex. From his conversation the new archbishop informed himself of the circumstances and necessities of the church of which he was going to take charge, and he also began to learn the English language.   Egbert, King of Kent, hearing his new archbishop had arrived at Paris, sent his reeve to meet him, who took him to the port of Quentavic, now called Saint-Josse-sur-Mer ; Theodore, falling sick, was obliged to stay there some time.   As soon as he was able to travel he proceeded on his voyage with St Benedict Biscop, and took possession of his see of Canterbury on May 27, 669, a year to a day after leaving Rome.   St Adrian meanwhile was detained in France some time.

St Theodore made a general visitation of all the churches of the English nation, taking Abbot Adrian with him.   He was everywhere well received and heard with attention ; and wherever he came he taught sound morality, confirmed the discipline of the Church in the celebration of Easter, and introduced the Roman chant in the divine offices, till then known in few of the English churches except those of Kent.   He regulated other things belonging to the divine service, reformed abuses,

* The first Catholic church of Byzantine rite in England, in Saffron Hill, London, was appropriately given St Theodore as its titular saint in 1949.

and ordained bishops in places where they were wanting. When he came into Northumbria he had to deal with the difficulties that had arisen between St Wilfrid and St Chad, both of whom laid claim to the see of York. St Theodore judged that Chad had been improperly consecrated, to which he replied that he had been ordained against his inclination, and retired to his monastery of Lastingham. But St Theodore made him bishop of the Mercians when that see became vacant. St Wilfrid was confirmed as the true bishop of York, to ensure the support of whose pro-Roman policy against the Celtic elements in Northumbria was probably the principal reason for St Adrian's being sent to England with Theodore. Theodore penetrated to the stronghold of Celtic influence at Lindisfarne and there consecrated the church in honour of St Peter. During these journeys he is said to have ordered that every head of a household should each day say with his family the Lord's Prayer and the Creed in the vulgar tongue.

St Theodore was the first bishop whom the whole English church obeyed, the first metropolitan of all England, and his fame penetrated into the remotest corners of the land. Many students gathered round these two foreign prelates who knew Greek as well as Latin, for Theodore and Adrian themselves expounded the Scriptures and taught the sciences, particularly astronomy and arithmetic (for calculating Easter), and to compose Latin verse. Many under them became as proficient in Latin and Greek as they were in their own tongue. Britain had never been in so happy a condition as at this time since the English first set foot in the island. The kings were so brave, says Bede, that the barbarous nations dreaded their power ; and men such good Christians that they aspired only after the joys of the kingdom of Heaven which had been but lately preached to them. All who desired to learn could find instructors.

Theodore gave the long vacant see of Rochester a bishop in the person of Putta, and authorized the inclusion of all Wessex in the see of Winchester. Then, in 673, he held the first national council of the English Church, at Hertford. There were present at this council Bisi, Bishop of the East Angles, Putta of Rochester, Eleutherius of Wessex, Winfrid of the Mercians, and the proxies of St Wilfrid. St Theodore addressed them, saying : " I beseech you, most dear brethren, in the love and fear of our Redeemer, that we may all treat in common of our faith to the end that whatsoever has been decreed and defined by the holy and venerable fathers may be inviolably observed by all." He then produced a book of ecclesiastical canons of which ten were marked as being of special importance to England. The first one was that Easter should everywhere be kept on the Sunday after the full moon which occurs on or next after March 21, in accordance with the Council of Nicaea and against the Celtic recalcitrants. Other canons had the effect of consolidating in England the common diocesan system of the Church ; and their adoption by the bishops can be looked on as the first legislative act, ecclesiastical or civil, for the whole English people. With these canons was approved one that provided for an annual synod of the bishops, to meet every August 1 at Clovesho.* Another provincial council held by St Theodore, seven years later at Hatfield, was convened in order that he might safeguard the purity of the faith of his clergy from any taint of monophysite error. After discussing the theology of the mystery of the

---

* The identity of this place has never yet been discovered, but a number of these synods were held there. The first of which we have any authentic evidence was, however, sixty-nine years after the Council of Hertford, in 742 ; between that date and 825 six more are known, and they are of considerable importance in the history of the early English church.

Incarnation the members of the council expressed their adherence to the five oecumenical councils and their abhorrence of the heresies condemned thereat.

Two years previously, 678, " the year of the comet ", trouble had arisen between Egfrid, King of the Northumbrians, and St Wilfrid, who had supported the king's wife, St Etheldreda, in her desire to retire to a convent. St Wilfrid's adminis- tration of his huge diocese had not been altogether well received, even by those who sympathized with his aims, and St Theodore took this to be a good opportunity to assert his metropolitan authority in the north. He therefore ordered that three sees should be carved out of the diocese of York, and in concert with King Egfrid proceeded to appoint bishops thereto. St Wilfrid objected and appealed to Rome, going off to conduct his case in person, while Theodore consecrated new bishops in the cathedral of York. Pope St Agatho decided that Wilfrid was to be restored to his see but that he should choose suffragan bishops to assist in its government. However, King Egfrid refused to accept the pope's decision on the charge that it had been bought, and St Wilfrid went into exile, eventually to evangelize the South Saxons. St Theodore, so far as is known, did not attempt to stop Egfrid's high- handed action, and a few years later consecrated St Cuthbert as bishop of Lindis- farne in the cathedral of York. Any injustice that he may have been guilty of herein was atoned for in the closing years of his life, when with St Erconwald he met St Wilfrid in London, and it was agreed that he should again govern York but in its smaller extent ; St Theodore wrote to King Ethelred of Mercia and to King Aldfrid of Northumbria recommending St Wilfrid to them, and to St Elfleda, abbess of Whitby, and others who had opposed Wilfrid or were interested parties.

St Theodore's great achievements were all in the sphere of active organization and administration, and the only literary work that bears his name is a collection of disciplinary decisions and canons called the *Penitential of Theodore*, and this was his work only in part, if that. It is sometimes said that St Theodore of Canterbury organized the parochial system in England, but this is far from being true. The parish system in this country was one of very slow growth, over a long period of time and under several influences, and was not the work of any one man. What he did do was to find the Church in this country a missionary body, distressed by faction and with no particular cohesion, and to leave it, after twenty-one years' episcopate, a properly organized province of the Catholic Church, divided into dioceses which looked to Canterbury as their metropolitan see. The work he did remained for eight hundred and fifty years his monument, and is still the basis of the hierarchical organization of the Established Church of England. He died on September 19, 690, and was buried in the abbey-church of SS. Peter and Paul at Canterbury, the Greek monk nigh to his first predecessor the Roman monk, Augustine. " To say all in a few words ", says St Bede, " the English churches prospered more during the pontificate [of Theodore] than ever they had done before " ; and Stubbs writes that " It is difficult, if not impossible, to overstate the debt which England, Europe and Christian civilization owe to the work of Theodore ". This has not been forgotten, and his feast is today observed in six of our English dioceses and by the English Benedictines.

The main authority, of course, is Bede's *Ecclesiastical History*, which has been in many points elucidated by C. Plummer's valuable commentary ; and second to this Eddius's *Vita Wilfridi*. Much has been published in England bearing upon the period of St Theo- dore's activities, but, apart from some fresh archaeological illustrations, such books as G. F. Browne's *Theodore and Wilfrith*, Sir Henry Howorth's *Golden Days of English Church History* and Canon Bright's *Chapters on Early English Church History* are apt to exhibit a pronounced anti-Roman bias. As for Theodore's share in the " Penitential " attributed to him, the researches of Paul Fournier, culminating in his *Histoire des Collections canoniques en Occident* (1931–32), tend to render the archbishop's personal connexion with even that part of the code assigned him by Wasserschleben and Stubbs extremely doubtful. See W. Stubbs in DCB., vol. iv, pp. 926–932 ; F. M. Stenton, *Anglo-Saxon England* (1943), pp. 131–141 and *passim*. A biography by Dr W. Reany was published in 1944.

ST MARY OF CEREVELLON, Virgin (A.D. 1290)

This Mary is venerated as the first nun of the Order of our Lady of Ransom (Mercedarians). She was the daughter of a Spanish nobleman of Barcelona, and is said to have been born to her childless parents at the prayer of St Peter Nolasco, who is credited with founding that order. A sermon by the Mercedarian Bernard Corbaria on the hardships and outrages suffered by Christian slaves at the hands of the Moors and Saracens inspired her to devote her life to their cause. In 1265 she joined a community of women who lived under the direction of Bernard and reinforced the work of the Mercedarians by their prayers. These were formed into a third order regular of our Lady of Ransom, and Mary of Cerevellon was their first prioress. The assiduity of her prayers and her generosity in temporal good works caused her to be called *Maria de Socós*, Mary of Help, the name by which she is still commonly known in Spain, where she is venerated also as a patroness of seamen, especially those in danger of shipwreck. St Mary died at Barcelona in 1290. Many miracles were claimed at her tomb and her *cultus* was confirmed in 1692. The Roman Martyrology says that she is called Mary of Help " because of her present aid to them that call upon her ".

A short Latin life by Juan de Laes and Guillermo Vives was printed in the *Acta Sanctorum*, September, vol. vii, but its apocryphal character is now hardly disputed by serious investigators. The fact is that the story of Maria de Socós has got mixed up with the notorious forgeries which marked the attempts to create an imposing record for the early developments of the Mercedarian Order : see January 28, under Peter Nolasco. It was in the folio *Vida de Maria de Corveilon*, by Estevan de Corbera (1639), that many of the impugned documents, together with that known as " de los sellos ", first saw the light. The author of the life, and other biographers who followed, may have been imposed upon, but it is only too plain that the *hechos maravillosos* attributed to Maria de Socós must be for the most part suspect.

SS. THEODORE, DAVID and CONSTANTINE (A.D. 1299, 1321)

St Theodore, called " the Black ", duke of Yaroslavl and Smolensk, was a great-grandson of that Kievan prince, Vladimir Monomakh, whose " Charge to my Children " is one of the most precious documents of early Russian Christianity. As a ruler Theodore was sincerely concerned for the poor and the uncared-for ; he defended his people against the Tartars ; and did all he could for the promotion of religion, building a church in honour of St Michael and several others. A few days before his death, which happened on September 19, 1299, he was clothed with the monastic habit, and was buried in the monastery of the Transfiguration at Yaroslavl. On the death of his first wife, mother of his son Michael, Theodore married again, and of this second wife his sons David and Constantine were born. They died in 1321 and were buried with their father, and were equally with him venerated as saints, the relics of all three being solemnly enshrined in 1464. Throughout their lives Theodore and his sons walked worthily of their calling, both as Christians and as noblemen ; they were forgiving of injuries, and more mindful of their own obligations than of the delinquencies of others.   Accordingly a *troparion* (hymn) of their office says of them : " From your youth up you loved Christ with all your heart, most carefully did you observe His law and ordinances : therefore have you received the gift of miracles, and do pour out healing benefits upon us, O ye holy ones, Theodore, David and Constantine."

See Martynov's *Annus ecclesiasticus Graeco-Slavicus*, in *Acta Sanctorum*, October, vol. xi ; and *cf.* note to St Sergius on September 25.   Vladimir Monomakh, referred to above, married Gytha, daughter of Harold II Godwinson, king of the English, who was slain at Hastings in 1066.

BD ALPHONSUS DE OROZCO   (A.D. 1591)

IN the task of maintaining a high standard of austerity and devotion among a sixteenth-century aristocracy no Spanish churchman was more enthusiastic or more effective than this Augustinian friar, Alphonsus (Alonso) de Orozco.   He was born at Oropesa in the diocese of Avila in the year 1500, and so early as six years of age made up his mind that he wanted to be a priest.   He studied at Talavera and Toledo, and then went on to the University of Salamanca, where he attended the sermons of St Thomas of Villanova.   By him he was attracted to the religious life and to the Hermits of St Augustine in particular, and when he was twenty-two he was clothed with the habit of that order.

For thirty years after his profession Friar Alphonsus was engaged in teaching, preaching, and the other activities of his state, and his success and shining goodness made him in great request as a confessor.   He was four times prior of different houses, and then in 1554, the year in which Philip II married Queen Mary of England, he was sent to take charge of the Augustinian priory in the royal city of Valladolid.   Two years later he was appointed court preacher.   He at once began exercising his beneficent influence over the nobility, attracting them to his sermons by the quality both of his preaching and of his music, of which he was very fond. In 1561 King Philip established his court at Madrid, and Bd Alphonsus went along with the court.   He had a cell in the friary of San Felipe el Real, where he lived a life of great austerity and simplicity, in sharp contrast with the official functions of the court in which of necessity he had to take part.   While he was prior at Seville in his earlier days Bd Alphonsus had had a vision of our Lady, in which she had told him that he was to use his pen for the glory of God and the salvation of souls. This he did thenceforth with great application.   Every year he produced a work on the Mother of God herself, and was the author of numerous mystical and other treatises which fill seven large volumes, and range him among the great Spanish mystics of the sixteenth century.   At the order of his superiors he also wrote an account of his own religious experiences which, lest he should seem to lack in humility, he called his " Confessions ".   For thirty-five years he continued his good work in maintaining Christian life among the nobility and gentry and also among the lesser folk of the Spanish court ; they flocked to his sermons and his confessional, and read his writings, and when he died at the age of ninety-one followed his coffin to its burial with unfeigned lamenting.   Bd Alphonsus was beatified in 1881.

The literary quality of the Augustinian friar's writings as well as their devotional appeal have helped to make him well remembered.   T. Cámara in 1882 brought out a volume dealing with his *Vida y Escritos*, which has been translated into German.   See also J. A. Fariña, *Doctrina de Oración del B. Alfonso* (1927), and further a sketch in the *Katholik* of Mainz, 1882, vol. ii, pp. 375–411.

ST EMILY DE RODAT, VIRGIN, FOUNDRESS OF THE CONGREGATION OF THE HOLY FAMILY OF VILLEFRANCHE   (A.D. 1852)

FACING the plateau on which stands the ancient city of Rodez in the south of France is a handsome manor-house called Druelle, and it was here that Marie Guillemette (Wilhelmina) Emilie de Rodat was born in 1787.   When she was only eighteen months old Emily was taken to live with her maternal grandmother in the château of Ginals, on a hill outside Villefranche-de-Rouergue, and she was here at the time of the revolution, which passed lightly over the household in that somewhat remote spot.   Though by no means free from youthful tantrums Emily was certainly what would be called a pious child, and a cousin who tried to kiss her received an impressively heavy smack.   But when she was sixteen she began to see something of life in society, and her devotion cooled a little : she found her confessor over-strict, and sought another, she made her prayers as short as possible and so on.   The vigilant grandmother did not fail to notice this and, as she rejected the company of " nuns and pious females " in Villefranche, Emily had to go back to the austere and monotonous life at Ginals, where her parents were now living. But here she gradually realized where her happiness and duty really lay, and from about Corpus Christi 1804, when she underwent a sudden and definitive spiritual experience, she never looked back : " I was so wrapped-up in God that I could have gone on praying for ever, especially in church. . . .   I was bored only once in all my life, and that was when I had turned away from God."

In the following year, when she was eighteen, Emily returned to Villefranche to help the nuns at the establishment, Maison Saint-Cyr, where she had herself been to school.   No doubt she hoped to find her own vocation there, but the community was not an entirely satisfactory one, being composed of nuns of some age dispersed from various convents at the revolution and now gathered fortuitously under one roof.   Their lack of internal unity was reflected in their treatment of Emily : some approved of her, others found her enthusiasms exaggerated.   She had charge of the children's recreation, prepared them for first communion, and taught them geography ; and the second of these duties spilled over into the third, for the names of saints in places were made the occasion of drawing edification from the life of the saint concerned—a proceeding for which the place-names of France give ample scope.   But the important thing that happened was her meeting with the Abbé Marty, the spiritual director of the establishment.   Three times during her eleven years at the Maison Saint-Cyr Emily left, with his permission, to try elsewhere : at Figeac with the Ladies of Nevers, at Cahors with the Picpus Sisters, at Moissac with the Sisters of Mercy ; and each time she was disappointed and restless, and came back to Villefranche reproaching herself for instability.

Then one day in the spring of 1815 Emily de Rodat, calling on a sick woman, found a number of the neighbours there ; they were discussing (with more vigour than discretion and charity) the near impossibility of getting schooling for their children because they had no money for it.   In a flash it came to her : " I will teach these poor children ", she said to herself, and straightway opened her mind to the Abbé Marty.   This was the very thing he had been hoping for, and within a few weeks Emily had started teaching in her own room at the Maison Saint-Cyr.

It was only a small room, but somehow she got forty children into it, as well as three young women to help her with the teaching. This was the beginning of what was to become the Congregation of the Holy Family,* and there was the usual opposition. The parents of one of the assistants, Eleanor Dutriac, threatened legal proceedings to get her away since she was only sixteen ; some of the other inmates of the house behaved very unkindly ; public opinion was critical, and some of the clergy did not recognize a good thing when they saw it. But, with the quiet encouragement of the Abbé Marty, Emily went ahead, rented premises on her own, and in May 1816 her free school was started. Meanwhile the community at the Maison Saint-Cyr was breaking up, and less than eighteen months after leaving it Sister Emily (who had now taken public vows) returned to take possession of that house, with eight other sisters and a hundred pupils. People no longer laughed at them in the street or let their children follow them with cat-calls and jeering.

Two years later Sister Emily was enabled to buy better buildings, a disused monastery with its chapel and garden, but there soon followed a disaster that threatened to put an end to the growing community. Starting with Sister Eleanor Dutriac there was a series of deaths that physicians were unable properly to account for and that the famous priest Mgr Alexander von Hohenlohe attributed to diabolic influence. Sister Emily was inclined to take this as a sign that she was not called to make a foundation, and she seriously thought of uniting her community with the Daughters of Mary, newly established by Adèle de Batz de Trenquelléon. This probably would have happened but that the Villefranche sisters refused any mother superior but Emily de Rodat, and so the installation in the new house was carried through ; in the autumn of 1820 perpetual vows were taken, and the habit adopted of which the distinguishing feature is the transparent edge of the veil covering the upper part of the face.

During the next seven years Mother Emily suffered cruelly in body, firstly from cancerous growths in the nose and then from a complaint which left her with permanent and incurable noises in the ears (from the description it sounds rather like the obscure Menier's Disease). It was this ill-health that led to the establishment of the first daughter house, at Aubin, whither Mother Emily had gone to consult a doctor. The Abbé Marty was not altogether in favour of this foundation, because of legal difficulties, but Mother Emily, although she had not hitherto envisaged more than a single community and school, followed her own judgement. Afterwards she blamed herself for insufficient docility, declaring that " The word ' Aubin ' sounds in my ears like the crowing of a cock ". A few months afterwards M. Marty's direct supervision was withdrawn from the congregation, he having been appointed vicar general to the bishop of Rodez.†

There was now added to Mother Emily's physical ill-health a prolonged and severe " dark night of the soul ", but she continued to expand her congregation and to make further foundations (there were thirty-eight of them before her death).

---

* There are other congregations of this name, *e.g.* the one founded by the Abbé Noailles and his sister in 1820, and the Negro sisters at New Orleans in 1842.

† Near Aubin was a coal-mining centre where there was a number of English workers with their families. These were among the beneficiaries of the convent, and indirectly they contributed to the formation in the new congregation of unenclosed as well as enclosed choir-sisters, to meet their needs at a distance from the convent. England repaid her debt when she welcomed the Sisters expelled from France in 1904.

To teaching were added sick-nursing and other good works, and the strain on the sisters' resources was often considerable ; but Mother Emily always had complete faith that the needs of their poor would be met, and so they were, sometimes by a multiplication of resources both of money and goods that had every mark of the miraculous. She insisted on the most rigorous simplicity and plainness in her establishments, every possible penny must be available for the needs of the poor, and this applied to the chapel no less than to the refectory : Mother Emily realized that costly marbles and expensive statues do not necessarily do honour to God, as the Cistercians and Franciscans had emphasized in the middle ages. The Abbé Marty was of another mind ; but this was but a slight difficulty compared with those that attended the beginnings of some of the convents—difficulties compendiously attributed by one of her biographers, the Abbé Raylet, to " la rage du démon ". However, aspirants continued to come in, for all that Mother Emily but rarely directly encouraged girls to " leave the world ". She had a great respect for personal freedom and individual responsibility, and would often remind people that " Religious vocations are brought about by the grace of God, not by any words of ours ".

In 1843 the sisters at Villefranche began to visit the prison, with encouraging results, and two years later there was an important development when their first " rescue-home " for women was opened. And then there was what Mgr Gély called " l'Hôtel des Invalides ", a place of retirement for aged religious, to which was added a novitiate house and another for orphans. But with all these and other developments the enclosed sisters of the congregation were not neglected. Mother Emily never lost an opportunity to open a cloistered convent, seeing in the two branches a personification of Martha and Mary : Martha's active work in the world was upheld and blessed by Mary's work in the cloister, recollected and interceding at the feet of the Saviour of all.

Mother Emily had a gift for pithy apophthegms. " There are some people who are not good for a convent, but a convent is good for them ; they would be lost in the world and they don't do much good in a convent—but at least they keep out of mischief." If a novice looked round when anyone entered the class-room she was sent at once to kiss the foot of the crucifix : " And that is not meant as a reward." " If I meet an angel with a priest, I bow to the priest first." " The evangelists report four occasions when our Lady spoke, but they don't tell us a single word of St Joseph's utterance. Rightly understood, there's a valuable lesson in that." " Confession is an accusation, not a conversation." There is something almost dour about these remarks, picked out at random, and St Emily was not by nature inclined to merriment ; but the joy of the saints is a well-known phenomenon and she had it as an inner characteristic, one, moreover, that she was conscious of and valued. " Keep your enthusiasm ", she wrote to a postulant. " Be brave. Put all your trust in God. And always maintain a holy cheerfulness." And to the sisters at Aubin, " Be gay, be gay. We must keep away all gloom." In the younger days of Emily de Rodat her besetting sin had been personal pride, and later she put before herself that " I must try to be humble in the same degree that I feel pride." She succeeded in this, and far over-passed it, to the extent of a carelessness of appearances in her manner and clothes that, writes the Abbé Raylet with unwonted candour, was sometimes ridiculous. It is interesting to find in nineteenth-century France this echo—if such it was—of the " fools for Christ's sake " of the East.

" It is good to be an object of contempt ", St Emily declared, and certainly the slanders and misunderstandings that gathered round her from time to time showed contempt in those who circulated them. People used to write her abusive letters, and when her secretary protested at her respectful and gentle replies, Mother Emily answered, " Don't you know that we are the scum of the earth, and that anyone is entitled to tread on us ? " Such abnegation can be sustained by no ordinary means, and it is not surprising to learn that it was often impossible to interrupt St Emily at prayer until her state of ecstasy had passed.

The Sisters of the Holy Family lost the care and love of the Abbé Marty, so far as this world is concerned, when he died in 1835. He had not always seen eye-to-eye with Mother Emily, nor had she always dissembled her disagreement (" A saint, but a headstrong saint ", as somebody said of her to his successor). But affection, respect and common purpose had bound them together, and not the least thing that Mother Emily owed to the Abbé Marty was a deep appreciation of the abiding presence of the Holy Spirit and His significance for Christians. Mother Emily outlived her old friend by seventeen years.

It was in April 1852 that a cancerous growth appeared in her left eye, and she knew that her course was nearly run. She resigned the government of the congregation into the hands of Mother Foy, leaving herself, as she said, nothing else to do but to suffer. And it was so, for her physical sufferings and weakness increased terribly day by day. For nearly three weeks from September 3 Mother Emily lay patiently awaiting the day that should be her last. Among the things she thought of was the Confraternity of the Holy Childhood and its work for abandoned babies in China : " Keep up interest in that among the children, and teach them to love it ", she said to her daughters. " The wall is crumbling ", she told them in the evening of September 18 ; and on the following day it fell, to be rebuilt in the streets of the heavenly Jerusalem where play those children to whom she had devoted her earthly life. Emily de Rodat was canonized in 1950.

There are lives in French by L. Aubineau (1891), by L. Raylet (1897), by Mgr Ricard in the series " Les Saints " (1912), by the Abbé Barthe, *L'Esprit de . . . Emilie de Rodat* (2 vols., 1897), and by M. Arnal (1951). Her letters were published separately in 1888. But for ordinary purposes the most useful and readable book is *Marie-Emilie de Rodat*, by Marguerite Savigny-Vesco (1940). In addition to all the printed sources the authoress had access to certain manuscript material, and it may be questioned if she makes the best possible use of her opportunities ; but the work has been crowned by the French Academy. In English, Doris Burton's *St Emilie de Rodat* (1951) is useful for the facts.

20 : SS. EUSTACE AND HIS COMPANIONS, MARTYRS (DATE UNKNOWN)

ST EUSTACE (Eustachius, Eustathius) is among the most famous martyrs of the Church, venerated for many centuries in both East and West. He is one of the Fourteen Holy Helpers, a patron of hunting men, and at least since the eighth century has given his name to the titular church of a cardinal-deacon at Rome. But there is nothing that can be said of him with any sort of certainty. His worthless legend relates that he was a Roman general under Trajan, by name Placidas, and while out hunting one day he saw coming towards him a stag, between whose antlers appeared a figure of Christ on the cross (which story appears also in the legend of St Hubert and other saints), and a voice issuing therefrom calling him by name.   This is said to have occurred at Guadagnolo, between Tivoli and Palestrina.   Placidas was at once converted by the vision and received baptism with his whole family.   His own name he changed to Eustachius, that of his wife to Theopistis, and his sons' to Agapitus and Theopistus.   Eustace soon after lost all his wealth, and in a series of misadventures was separated from the members of his family.   Then he was recalled to command the army at a critical moment, and was romantically reunited with his wife and sons.   But Eustace refused to sacrifice to the gods after his victory for the imperial arms, and he and his family were martyred by being confined in a brazen bull wherein they were roasted to death.

Popular as was the legend of St Eustace—the number of different recensions both in prose and verse prove this—even the historical existence of the martyr must remain a matter of doubt.   The cult is not early, nor can its origins be clearly located.   It probably came from the East ; but it had been adopted in Rome before the first half of the eighth century. The legend has been very thoroughly analysed by Delehaye in the *Bulletin de l'Académie royale de Belgique*, Classe des Lettres, 1919, pp. 175–210.   The attempt of A. H. Krappe, *La leggenda di S. Eustachio* (1929), to link it up with the Dioscuri is altogether futile.   For St Eustace in folklore see Bächtold-Stäubli, *Handwörterbuch d. deutsch. Aberglaubens*.

ST VINCENT MADELGARIUS, ABBOT   (*c.* A.D. 687)

THE feast of this saint, under the name of Madelgaire (or Mauger), is kept in Artois and Hainault on the date of his death, July 14, but in Flanders, as Vincent of Soignies, he is venerated on September 20.   He was born about the year 615, and became the husband of St Waldetrudis (Waudru).   They had four children, all venerated as saints, namely Landericus or Landry, Madelberta, Aldetrudis and Dentelinus.   About 653 his wife became a nun, and Madelgarius took the Benedictine habit and the name of Vincent in the monastery of Hautmont, which he founded.   He later established another abbey on his estate at Soignies, where he died.

His biography was written in the abbey of Hautmont in the tenth or eleventh century, and in his *Légendes Hagiographiques* Father Delehaye refers to it at some length *à propos* of deliberate plagiarisms in the lives of saints, as distinct from accidental coincidences.   He says (Mrs Crawford's translation) :

The naïve hagiographers of the middle ages, compelled to supplement the paucity of primitive sources by more or less legitimate means, do not introduce us to any very embarrassing dilemmas.   As a rule their methods are simple, and their secrets are easily surprised.   The following, for example, shows the process by which the biographer of St Vincent Madelgarius honoured his patron with a literary composition of adequate dimensions.

In the preface he begins by transcribing the prologue from the Life of St Erminus, to which he adds a phrase from Sulpicius Severus ; there follows a second introduction which reproduces, word for word, St Gregory of Tours's preface to the Life of St Patroclus.   In order to describe the birth and early years of the saint, he accumulates reminiscences from the Life of St Erminus, without speaking of others from members of St Vincent's own family, St Waldetrudis and St Aldegondis, while the history of his marriage is extracted literally from the *Vita Leobardi* by Gregory of Tours.   Vincent's son Landry embraces the ecclesiastical state : this is taken from the Life of St Gall by

Gregory of Tours.   The same author furnishes him with the greater part of a vision, which fills one of the chapters in the Life of St Leobardus.   St Vincent enters on the religious life and trains his followers : taken from the lives of SS. Martius and Quintianus by Gregory of Tours.   He gives himself up to prayer and penance and practises all the religious virtues : taken from the Life of St Bavo.   Knowing himself to be on the point of death he confides his spiritual children to his son Landry : taken from the Life of St Ursmar. He is buried within his monastery where he exercises his power on behalf of the faithful who invoke him : taken from the Life of St Bavo.   A blind cleric recovers his sight on his tomb : this miracle is appropriated in its entirety from Gregory of Tours, who relates it of St Martin.   We must add, moreover, to our plagiarist's account six chapters from the Life of St Waldetrudis, which, it is true, served him as an historic source, but which he transcribes word for word, besides numerous other reminiscences which it would take too long to enumerate.

The lives of saints filled with extracts from other lives of saints are exceedingly numerous, and some are nothing more than a mere hagiographic anthology. . . .

One biography of the saint was printed by the Bollandists in their third volume for July ; but a somewhat older version, possibly of the tenth century, has been edited by them in *Analecta Bollandiana*, vol. xii (1893), pp. 422–440.   In this on p. 425 the dependence of the life on other texts has been pointed out in detail.

BD FRANCIS DE POSADAS   (A.D. 1713)

HE was born at Cordova in 1644 and brought up by his parents, who were greengrocers, to the idea that he should become a religious, in particular a Friar Preacher, a prospect that was more than attractive to him.   But on the death of his father his mother married again, and his stepfather decided that the studies on which he was engaged were a waste of time.   He therefore made Francis give them up and apprenticed him to a trade.   His master at first treated him very roughly, but Francis won him over by patience and good temper and by sticking to his work, and eventually the master even helped him to get on with his studies in his spare time.   When his stepfather also died, Francis had to devote himself to the care of his mother for a time, but in 1663 was able to enter the Dominican noviciate at the convent of Scala Caeli in Cordova.   For a time his experience here was not happy.   He was misunderstood by his fellows and made the butt of ridicule and petty persecution ; he persevered, was professed, and admitted to the priesthood. Francis at once made his mark as a preacher and he was hailed as a second Vincent Ferrer.   He gave missions all over the south-west of Spain, adding to the fatigues of preaching, hearing confessions, and travelling on foot voluntary mortifications of a most rigorous kind.   His combination of example and precept won him a great influence over all with whom he came in contact, and in his native city he brought about a much-needed reform and improvement in public and private morals ; disorderly places of amusement shut up for lack of business.   He was always at the service of the poor and learned from them an humility that made him avoid not only the offices of his order but also bishoprics that were offered to him.   Bd Francis wrote several books—*The Triumph of Chastity*, lives of St Dominic and other holy ones of his order, moral exhortations—and died at Scala Caeli after

forty years of uninterrupted work for souls on September 20, 1713.   He was
beatified in 1818.

Following close upon the beatification Father V. Sopena published in Rome a *Vita del
B. Francesco de Posadas.*   It contains amongst other things an interesting account of his
levitations when he was celebrating Mass (pp. 42–45), and of his sensations in endeavouring
to resist this lifting of his body into the air.   See also Martinez-Vigil, *La Orden de Predicadores*
(1884), pp. 352 *seq. ;* and a short notice in Procter, *Dominican Saints*, pp. 263–265.   For
a fuller bibliography consult Taurisano, *Catalogus Hagiographicus O.P.*

21 : ST MATTHEW, Apostle and Evangelist   (First Century)

ST MATTHEW is called by two evangelists Levi, and by St Mark " the son
of Alpheus " ; it is probable that Levi was his original name and that he took,
or was given, that of Matthew (" the gift of Yahveh ") when he became a
follower of our Lord.   But Alpheus his father was not he of the same name who
was father of St James the Less.   He seems to have been a Galilaean by birth, and
was by profession a publican, or gatherer of taxes for the Romans, a profession
which was infamous to the Jews, especially those of the Pharisees' party ; they were
in general so grasping and extortionate that they were no more popular among the
Gentiles.   The Jews abhorred them to the extent of refusing to marry into a family
which had a publican among its members, banished them from communion in
religious worship, and shunned them in all affairs of civil society and commerce.
But it is certain that St Matthew was a Jew, as well as a publican.

The story of Matthew's call is told in his own gospel.   Jesus had just confounded
some of the Scribes by curing a man who was sick of the palsy, and passing on saw
the despised publican in his custom-house.   " And He saith to him, ' Follow me '.
And he arose up and followed him."   Matthew left all his interests and relations
to become our Lord's disciple and to embrace a spiritual commerce.   We cannot
suppose that he was before wholly unacquainted with our Saviour's person or
doctrine, especially as his office was at Capharnaum, where Christ had resided for
some time and had preached and wrought many miracles, by which no doubt
Matthew was in some measure prepared to receive the impression which the call
made upon him.   St Jerome says that a certain shiningness and air of majesty
which appeared in the countenance of our divine Redeemer pierced his soul and
strongly attracted him.   But the great cause of his conversion was, as St Bede
remarks, that " He who called him outwardly by His word at the same time moved
him inwardly by the invisible instinct of His grace ".

The calling of St Matthew happened in the second year of the public ministry
of Christ, who adopted him into that holy family of the apostles, the spiritual
leaders of His Church.   It may be noted that whereas the other evangelists in
describing the apostles by pairs rank Matthew before St Thomas, he places that
apostle before himself and in this list adds to his own name the epithet of " the
publican ".   He followed our Lord throughout His earthly life, and wrote his
gospel or short history of our blessed Redeemer, doubtless at the entreaty of the
Jewish converts, in the Aramaic language which they spoke.   We are not told that
Christ gave any charge about committing to writing His history or doctrine, but it
was nevertheless by special inspiration of the Holy Ghost that this work was
undertaken by each of the four evangelists, and the gospels are the most excellent

part of the sacred writings. For in them Christ teaches us, not by His prophets but by His own mouth, the great lessons of faith and of eternal life ; and in the history of His life the perfect pattern of holiness is set before our eyes for us to strive after.

It is said that St Matthew, after having made a harvest of souls in Judea, went to preach Christ to the nations of the East, but of this nothing is known for certain. He is venerated by the Church as a martyr, though the time, place and circumstances of his end are unknown. The fathers find a figure of the four evangelists in the four living animals mentioned by Ezechiel and in the Apocalypse of St John. The eagle is generally said to represent St John himself, who in the first lines of his gospel soars up to the contemplation of the eternal generation of the Word. The ox agrees to St Luke, who begins his gospel with the mention of the sacrificing priesthood. Some made the lion the symbol of St Matthew, who explains the royal dignity of Christ ; but St Jerome and St Augustine give it to St Mark, and the man to St Matthew, who begins his gospel with Christ's human genealogy.

The account of St Matthew furnished in the *Acta Sanctorum*, September, vol. vi, is largely taken up with the discussion of his alleged relics and their translations to Salerno and other places. How little trust can be placed in such traditions may be judged from the fact that four different churches in France have claimed to be in possession of the head of the apostle. A long apocryphal narrative of his preaching and martyrdom has been edited by M. Bonnet, *Acta Apostolorum apocrypha* (1898), vol. ii, pt 1, pp. 217–262, and there is another, much shorter, in the Bollandists. The Roman Martyrology describes his martyrdom as having taken place " in Ethiopia ", but in the *Hieronymianum* he is said to have suffered " in Persia in the town of Tarrium ". This, according to von Gutschmid, is a misreading for Tarsuana, which Ptolemy places in Caramania, the region east of the Persian Gulf. In contrast to the varying dates assigned to the other apostles, St Matthew's feast seems uniformly to have been kept in the West on this day (September 21). Already in the time of Bede, we find a homily of his assigned for this particular feast : see Morin in the *Revue Bénédictine*, vol. ix (1892), p. 325. On the symbols of the evangelist see DAC., vol. v, cc. 845–852.

ST MAURA OF TROYES, VIRGIN   (*c.* A.D. 850)

SHE was born at Troyes in Champagne in the year 827, and in her youth obtained of God by her prayers the conversion of her father, who had till then led a worldly life. After his death, Maura continued to live in dutiful obedience to her mother, Sedulia, and by the fervour of her example was the sanctification of her brother Eutropius, who became bishop of Troyes, and of the whole family. The maiden's whole time was consecrated to prayer, to offices of obedience or charity in attending on her mother and serving the poor, or to her work, which was devoted to the service of the needy and of the Church. As order in what we do leads a soul to God, according to the remark of St Augustine, Maura was regular in the distribution of her time and in all her actions. She spent almost the whole morning in the church worshipping God, praying to her divine Redeemer, and meditating on His passion. Every Wednesday and Friday she fasted, allowing herself no other food than bread and water, and she sometimes walked barefoot to the monastery of Mantenay, two leagues from the town, to open the secrets of her soul to the holy abbot of that place. The profound respect with which she was penetrated for the word of God is not easily to be expressed, and so wonderful was her gift of tears that she seemed never to fall upon her knees to pray but they streamed from her eyes. God performed miracles in her favour, but it was her care to conceal His gifts, because she dreaded human applause. In her last moments she said the Lord's Prayer, and died as she pronounced the words, " Thy kingdom come ", being twenty-three years old.

The *Acta Sanctorum*, September, vol. vi, prints a short life by St Prudentius of Troyes, who died in 861. See also E. Socard, *Ste Maure de Troyes* (1867).

ST MICHAEL OF CHERNIGOV AND ST THEODORE, MARTYRS (A.D. 1246)

THE Church in Russia had no martyrs, properly speaking, before the Tartar invasions of the thirteenth century. The number who then gave their lives for Christ was very large, and the first to receive both popular and liturgical veneration were those among them who were also nobles and military leaders against the barbarian invaders. Thus was reinforced the regard already felt for these men, not as aggressive " crusaders against the infidels ", but as selfless warriors who were ready to give their lives in defence of their people : the palm of martyrdom for Christ was added to the halo of self-sacrifice for others. Outstanding in popularity among these was Michael, Duke of Chernigov.

The first we hear of him is unpromising. He showed cowardice in face of the enemy and fled from Kiev, abandoning the city to the Tartars. But then, hoping to attract their violence to himself and distract it from the people, he returned of his own will and made his way into the camp of the Horde. Their leader, **Bati,** tried to persuade Michael to treachery, making great promises if he would only make an act of **idolatrous** worship. St Michael refused : he was not willing to be a Christian only in name. His friends then formed a plan for his escape from the camp, but this also he refused, lest they should suffer **Bati's** reprisals. So the Tartars tortured and then beheaded him, on September 20, 1246, and there suffered with him one of his nobles, St Theodore.

The Russians looked on such **martyrs** as their special representatives before the throne of God at a time when all the people were crushed by the most hideous sufferings. St Michael and St Theodore of Chernigov and others responded by anticipation to the challenge of another martyred prince, St Michael of Tver, seventy-five years later : " It is not a matter of giving one's life for one friend or for two, but for a whole enslaved people. Many of them are murdered, their wives and daughters are outraged by the foul heathen—and nobody offers his life for them."

For bibliographical notes on Russian saints, see under St Sergius on September 25 ; and *cf.* C. Dawson, *The Mongol Mission*, (1955), p. 10.

BB. LAURENCE IMBERT AND HIS COMPANIONS, THE MARTYRS OF KOREA   (A.D. 1839)

KOREA is one of the few countries in the world to which Christianity was first introduced otherwise than by Christian missionaries. During the eighteenth century some Chinese Christian books were brought into the country, and a man who had read them joined the embassy from Seoul to Peking in 1784, sought out Mgr de Gouvea there, and from him received baptism. He returned to his own country and when, ten years later, a Chinese priest came to Korea he found four thousand Christians awaiting him. He was their only pastor for seven years, and after he was killed in 1801 they were without a priest for thirty years. A letter is extant written by the Koreans to Pope Pius VII, imploring him to send them priests at once ; their little flock had already given martyrs to the Church. In 1831 the vicariate apostolic of Korea was created, but the first vicar never reached there. His successor, Mgr Laurence Joseph Mary Imbert, Titular Bishop of Capsa and a member of the Paris Foreign Missions, who had been in China for twelve years, entered the country in disguise at the end of 1837, having been preceded by BD PETER PHILIBERT MAUBANT and BD JAMES HONORÉ CHASTAN, priests of the same missionary society.

Christianity was now definitely proscribed in Korea, and for two years the missionaries went about their work with complete secrecy. Of its circumstances and difficulties Mgr Imbert wrote : " I am overwhelmed with fatigue and in great danger. I get up at half-past two every morning. At three I call the people of the house to prayers, and at half-past I begin the duties of my ministry by baptizing, if there are any converts, or by giving confirmation. Then come Mass, communion, and thanksgiving. The fifteen to twenty people who have received the sacraments can thus get away before daybreak. During the day about as many come in, one by one, for confession, and do not go until the next morning after communion. I stay two days in each house, where I get the Christians together, and before it is light I go on to another. I suffer a great deal from hunger : for it is no easy matter in this cold and wet climate to get up at half-past two and then wait until noon for a meal which is poor, insufficient, and lacking in nourishment. After dinner I rest a little until I have to take my senior scholars in theology, and finally I hear confessions again until nightfall. At nine o'clock I go to bed—on a mat on the floor with a Tartary-wool blanket ; there are no bedsteads or mattresses in Korea. In spite of my weak body and poor health I have always led a hard and very busy life : but here I think I have reached the positive limit of work. You will well understand that, leading a life like this, we scarcely fear the sword-stroke that may at any time end it."

By these heroic means the Christians in Korea were increased by a half, roughly from 6000 to 9000, in less than two years. What was going on soon became known, and a decree for their extermination was published. An example of the horrors that took place is provided by BD AGATHA KIM, one of the seventy-six Koreans beatified with the three priests. She was asked if it were true that she practised the Christian religion. " I know Jesus and Mary ", she replied, " but I know nothing else."—" If you are tortured you will give up this Jesus and Mary."— " If I have to die I will not." She was long and cruelly tormented and at last sentenced to death. A tall cross of wood was fixed to a cart and to this cross Agatha was hung by her arms and hair. The cart was driven off and at the top of a steep and very rough slope the oxen were pricked up and the cart sent lurching and jolting down, the woman swinging at every movement with all her weight on her hair and wrists. At the place of execution she was stripped naked, her head forced down on to a block, and there cut off. BD JOHN RI wrote from prison : " Two or three months passed before the judge sent for me, and I became sad and anxious. The sins of my whole life, when I had so often offended God from sheer wickedness, seemed to weigh me down like a mountain, and I wondered to myself, ' What will be the end of all this ? ' But I never lost hope. On the tenth day of the twelfth moon I was brought before the judge and he ordered me to be bastinadoed. How could I have borne it by my own strength alone ? But the strength of God and the prayers of Mary and the saints and all our martyrs upheld me, so that I believe I scarcely suffered at all. I cannot repay such a mercy, and to offer my life is only just."

To avert a general massacre and its attendant danger of apostasy, Mgr Imbert allowed himself to be taken and recommended M. Maubant and M. Chastan to do the same. This they did, after writing letters to Rome explaining their action and giving an account of their charge. They were all three bastinadoed, then carried on chairs to the banks of the river which flows around Seoul, tied back to back to a post, and there beheaded. This was on September 21, 1839, but their feast is kept by the Paris Foreign Missions on the 26th. In the year 1904 the relics of eighty-one martyrs of Korea were translated to the episcopal church of the vicar apostolic at Seoul, and in 1925 Bd Laurence and his companions were beatified. The first Korean priest martyr was BD ANDREW KIM in 1846.

In C. Dallet, *L'Histoire de l'Eglise de Corée* (1874), especially vol. ii, pp. 118–185, the life and sufferings of these martyrs are recounted in detail. See also A. Launay, *Les Missionnaires français en Corée* (1895), and *Martyrs français et coréens* (1925) ; and E. Baumann in *The Golden Legend Overseas* (1931).

22 : ST THOMAS OF VILLANOVA, ARCHBISHOP OF VALENCIA   (A.D. 1555)

S T THOMAS, a glory of the Church of Spain, was born at Fuentellana in Castile in 1488, but received his surname from Villanueva de los Infantes, a town where he was brought up. His parents were also originally of Villanueva ; the father was a miller ; their state was not affluent, but solid, and their charitable disposition was the most valuable part of their son's inheritance. At the age of sixteen he was sent to the University of Alcalá, and he pursued his studies there with success ; he became master of arts and licentiate in theology and, after ten years at Alcalá, was made professor of philosophy in that city, being then twenty-six years old ; among those who attended his lectures was the famous Dominic Soto.

In 1516 Thomas joined the Augustinian friars at Salamanca, and his behaviour in the novitiate showed he had been long inured to austerities, to renouncing his own will, and to the exercise of contemplation. In 1518 he was promoted to priestly orders and employed in preaching, and he taught a course of divinity in his convent. His text-books were Peter Lombard and Aquinas, and students from the university soon sought permission to attend his lectures. He was exceptionally clear-headed, with a firm and solid judgement, but had always to cope with absent-mindedness and a poor memory. He was afterwards prior in several places, and was particularly solicitous for those friars who were sick ; he would often tell his religious that the infirmary was like the bush of Moses, where he who devotes himself to the sick will assuredly find God among the thorns with which he is surrounded. In 1533, while provincial of Castile, he sent the first band of Augustinians to the Americas, where they established their order as missionaries in Mexico. Thomas fell into frequent raptures at prayer, especially at Mass ; and though he endeavoured to hide such graces he was not able to do it : his face after the holy Sacrifice shone, and as it were dazzled the eyes of those that beheld him.

Preaching once in the cathedral-church at Burgos, reproving the vices and ingratitude of sinners, he held in his hand a crucifix and cried out, " Christians, look here ! "—and he was not able to go on, being ravished in an ecstasy.   Once while addressing a community at the clothing of a novice he was rapt and speechless for a quarter of an hour.   When he recovered himself he said : " Brethren, I beg your pardon.   I have a weak heart and I feel ashamed of being so often overcome on these occasions.   I will try to repair my fault."

Whilst St Thomas was performing a visitation of his convents, he was nominated by the Emperor Charles V to the archbishopric of Granada, and commanded to go to Toledo.   He obeyed ; but undertook the journey with no other object than that of declining the dignity, in which he succeeded.   When, some years later, Don George of Austria resigned the archbishopric of Valencia, the emperor thought of not offering St Thomas this see because he knew how grievous a trial it would be to him.   He therefore, it is said, ordered his secretary to draw up a letter of nomination in favour of a certain religious of the Order of St Jerome.   Afterwards, finding that the secretary had put down the name of Brother Thomas of Villanova, he asked the reason.   The secretary answered that he thought he had heard his name, but would rectify the mistake.   " By no means ", said Charles.   " This has happened by a particular providence of God.   Let us therefore follow His will."   So he signed the appointment for St Thomas and it was forthwith sent to Valladolid, where he was prior.   The saint used all means possible to excuse himself, but had to accept the appointment and was consecrated at Valladolid.   Thomas set out very early next morning for Valencia.   His mother, who had converted her house into a hospital for the use of the poor and sick, had asked him to take Villanueva on the way ; but Thomas applied literally the words of the gospel, " a man shall leave his father and mother and shall cleave to his wife ", and hastened direct to the see with which he was now wedded, convinced that his office obliged him to postpone all other considerations to that of going to the flock committed to his care (later on he spent a month's holiday with his mother at Liria).   He travelled on foot in his monastic habit (which was very old) with the hat he had worn ever since his profession, accompanied by one religious and two servants.   Upon his arrival at Valencia he retired to an Augustinian friary where he spent several days in penance and prayer to beg the grace of God by which he might be enabled worthily to acquit himself of his charge.   He took possession of his cathedral on the first day of the year 1545 amidst the rejoicings of the people.   The chapter, in consideration of his poverty, made him a present of four thousand crowns towards furnishing his house, which he accepted in a humble manner and thanked them for their kindness, but he immediately sent the money to the great hospital with an order to lay it out in repairing the house and for the use of the patients.   He explained to the canons that " our Lord will be better served and glorified by your money being spent on the poor in the hospital, who need it so much, than if it had been used by me. What does a poor friar like myself want with furniture ? "

It is often said that " Honours change manners ", but St Thomas kept not only the same humility of heart but as much as possible the same exterior marks of contempt of himself.   He even kept for some years the very habit which he brought from his monastery, which he sometimes mended himself as he had been wont to do.   One of his canons, surprising him one day at this, said he wondered he could so employ his time which a tailor would save him for a trifle.   The archbishop replied that he was still a friar and that that trifle would feed some poor man.

Ordinarily he wore such clothes that his canons and domestics were ashamed of him.   When he was pressed by them to put himself into a dress suitable to his dignity his answer was, " Gentlemen, I am much obliged to you for the care you take of my person, but really I do not see how my dress as a religious interferes with my dignity as archbishop.   You know well enough that my position and duties are quite independent of my clothes, and consist in taking care of the souls committed to me."   The canons eventually induced him to cast away his cloth hat and wear one of silk.   He used afterwards sometimes to show this hat and say merrily, " Behold my episcopal dignity.   My masters the canons judged it necessary that I should wear this silk hat that I might be numbered among the archbishops." St Thomas discharged all the duties of a good pastor and visited the churches of his diocese, preaching everywhere in the towns and villages with zeal and affection. His sermons were followed by·a wonderful change in the lives of men, so that one might say he was a new apostle or prophet raised by God to reform the people. He assembled a provincial council (the first for many years) wherein with the help of his fellow bishops he made ordinances to abolish the abuses he had taken notice of in his visitation of his clergy.   To effect that of his own chapter cost him much difficulty and time.   At all times he had recourse to the tabernacle to learn the will of God ; he often spent long hours in his oratory and, perceiving that his servants were unwilling to disturb him at his devotions when persons came to consult him, he gave them strict instructions that as soon as anyone asked for him they should immediately call him, without making the visitor wait.

There came to St Thomas's door every day several hundred poor people, and each of them received an alms, which was ordinarily a meal with a cup of wine and a piece of money.   He took destitute orphans under his particular care, and for the eleven years that he was archbishop not one poor maiden was married who was not helped by his charity.   To his porters, to make them more keen in finding children that were exposed by their parents, he gave a crown for every foundling they brought him.   When in 1550 pirates had plundered a coast town in his diocese the archbishop immediately sent four thousand ducats and cloth worth as much more to furnish the inhabitants with necessaries and to ransom the captives.   Like many good men before and since, St Thomas was remonstrated with because a number of those whom he relieved were idle fellows who abused his kindness. " If ", he replied, " there are vagabonds and work-shy people here it is for the governor and the prefect of police to deal with them : that is their duty.   Mine is to assist and relieve those who come to my door."   Nor was he only the support of the poor himself, but he encouraged the great lords and all that were rich to make their importance seen not in their luxury and display but by becoming the protectors of their vassals and by their liberality to the necessitous.   He exhorted them to be richer in mercy and charity than they were in earthly possessions. " Answer me, sinner," he would say, " what can you purchase with your money better or more necessary than the redemption of your sins ? "   At other times : " If you desire that God should hear your prayers, hear the voice of the poor.   If you desire that God should forestall your wants, prevent those of the indigent without waiting for them to ask you.   Especially anticipate the necessities of those who are ashamed to beg ; to make these ask an alms is to make them buy it."

St Thomas was always averse from using the coercive weapons of the Church in bringing sinners to reason before methods of appeal and persuasion had been tried to the utmost. Of a theologian and canonist who objected to the archbishop's delay in taking threatened strong measures to put down concubinage, he said : " He is without doubt a good man, but one of those fervent ones mentioned by St Paul as having zeal without knowledge. Is the good man aware of the care and pains I have taken to correct those against whom he fulminates ? . . . Let him inquire whether St Augustine and St John Chrysostom used anathemas and ex-communication to stop the drunkenness and blasphemy which were so common among the people under their care. No ; for they were too wise and prudent. They did not think it right to exchange a little good for a great evil by inconsider-ately using their authority and so exciting the aversion of those whose good will they wanted to gain in order to influence them for good." He invited a canon, in whom he had long tried in vain to procure an amendment of life, to come and stay in his own house under pretext of preparing to go on an errand to Rome for the archbishop. Part of the preparation was to consist of a good confession. At the end of one, of two, of three months, the business for Rome was still not ready and all the time the canon was having unobtrusively put before him the fruits and bene-fits of penance. At the end of six months he left the saint's house a changed man, his friends all supposing he had just returned from Rome. Another priest of irregular life upon being rebuked abused St Thomas to his face and left his presence in a rage. " Do not stop him," said the archbishop to his chaplains, " it is my fault. My remonstrances were a little too rough."

St Thomas wished to extend the same sort of methods to the *nuevos Cristianos* or *Moriscos*, Moors who were converted to Christianity but whose conversion was often unreal or who lapsed into apostasy and so were brought under the brutal juris-diction of the Spanish Inquisition. He was never able to achieve much for them in his large diocese, but he induced the emperor to provide a fund to support special priests for work among them and himself founded a college for the children of the newly converted. He also founded a college for poor scholars at his old university at Alcalá, and then, having scruples at having expended money outside his own diocese, he endowed another at Valencia. His material charity was equalled by his charity of judgement. Detraction he abhorred and he would always defend the cause of the absent. " Sir ", he would say, " you do not look at this from a right point of view. You are wrong, because he may have had a good intention. For myself, I believe that he had." Many examples are recorded of St Thomas's supernatural gifts, such as his power of healing the sick and of multiplying food, and numerous miracles were attributed to his intercession both before and after his death.

It is not known for certain why St Thomas did not attend the Council of Trent ; he was represented thereat by the bishop of Huesca, and most of the Castilian bishops consulted with him before they left. He impressed on them that it was at least as necessary for the council to legislate for an internal reformation in the Church as against the Lutheran heresy, and made two interesting suggestions neither of which was in fact acted upon. One was that all benefices having the cure of souls should be filled by incumbents native of the place, so far as possible and providing they were well qualified, especially in rural districts ; the other was that the ancient canon which forbade the translation of a bishop from one see to another should be re-enforced. The idea of the union of a bishop with his see as with a bride was always present to the saint, and he lived in perpetual concern for the proper discharge of his own episcopal duties. " I was never so much afraid ", he would

say, " of being excluded from the number of the elect as since I have been a bishop ".
Several times he petitioned for leave to resign, and God was pleased at length to
hear his prayer by calling him to Himself.   He was seized by *angina pectoris* in
August 1555.   Having commanded all the money then in his possession to be
distributed among the poor, he ordered all goods to be given to the rector of his
college, except the bed on which he lay ; he gave this bed to the gaoler for the use
of prisoners, but borrowed it of him till such time as he should no longer require
it.   On September 8 the end was at hand.   He ordered Mass to be offered in his
presence, and after the consecration recited the psalm *In te, Domine, speravi :* after
the priest's communion he said that verse, " Into thy hands, O Lord, I commend
my spirit ", at which words he rendered his soul into the hands of God, in the
sixty-seventh year of his age.   He was buried, according to his desire, in the church
of the Austin friars at Valencia ; and he was canonized in 1658.   St Thomas of
Villanova was called in his lifetime " the pattern of bishops ", " the almsgiver ",
" the father of the poor ", and nothing can be more vehement or more tender than
his exhortation to divine love.   " Wonderful beneficence ! " he cries, " God
promises us Heaven for the recompense of His love.   Is not His love itself the
greatest reward, the most desirable, the most lovely, and the most sweet blessing ?
Yet a further recompense, and so immense a recompense, waits upon it.   Wonderful goodness !   Thou givest thy love, and for this thy love thou bestowest on us
Paradise."

In setting out the history of St Thomas of Villanova (*Acta Sanctorum*, September,
vol. v) the Bollandists translated the Spanish life by Miguel Salon, a contemporary who,
after a first biography published in 1588, utilized the materials furnished by the canonization
processes to produce a more complete work in 1620.   They also printed the memoir by
his friend and fellow Augustinian, Bishop Juan de Muñatones.   This had been prefixed
to an edition of St Thomas of Villanova's sermons, etc., which Muñatones edited in 1581.
Some other sources, including a summary of the depositions in the Valencia and Castile
processes, were also available, and these are used in the Bollandist prolegomena and annotations.   The whole is supplemented by a notice of the saint's relics and miracles.   Not much
fresh biographical material seems to have added to our knowledge since the Bollandists
published their account in 1755.   There is a brief sketch by Quevedo y Villegas, which was
translated into English through a French channel for the Oratorian series in 1847.   There
is also a German life by Poesl (1860), and one in French by Dabert (1878).   The writings
of St Thomas of Villanova, however, have been collected and more carefully edited, and
some of them have been translated into other languages.

ST PHOCAS THE GARDENER, Martyr   (Date Unknown)

St Phocas dwelt near the gate of Sinope, a city of Paphlagonia on the Black Sea, and
lived by cultivating a garden.   In his humble profession he imitated the virtue of
the most holy anchorites, and seemed in part restored to the happy condition of
our first parents in Eden.   To prune the garden without labour and toil was their
sweet employment and pleasure.   Since their sin, the earth yields not its fruit but
by the sweat of our brow.   But still, no labour is more useful or necessary or more
natural to man, and better adapted to maintain in him vigour of mind and health
of body, than that of tillage ; nor does any other part of the universe rival the
charms which a garden presents to our senses, by the fragrance of its flowers and
the sweetness and variety of its fruits ; by the melody of its musicians, by the worlds
of wonders which every stem, leaf, and fibre exhibit to the attention of the inquisi-
tive philosopher, and by that beauty and variegated lustre of colours which clothe

the numberless tribes of its smallest inhabitants and adorn its shining landscapes, vying with the brightest splendour of the heavens and in a single lily surpassing the lustre with which Solomon was surrounded on his throne in the midst of all his glory.   And what a field for contemplation does a garden offer to our view, raising our souls to God in love and praise, stimulating us to fervour by the fruitfulness with which it repays our labour and multiplies the seed it receives, and exciting us to tears of compunction for our insensibility to God by the barrenness with which it is changed into a desert unless subdued by ceaseless toil.   St Phocas, joining prayer with his labour, found in his garden an instructive book and an inexhaustible fund of meditation.   His house was open to strangers and travellers who had no lodging in the place ; and after having for many years liberally bestowed the fruit of his labour on the poor, he was found worthy also to give his life for Christ.

When a cruel persecution was suddenly raised against the Church, Phocas was impeached as a Christian, the formality of a trial was dispensed with, and soldiers were despatched with an order to kill him wherever they should find him.   Arriving near Sinope, they could not enter the town, but stopping at his house without knowing it, at his invitation they took up their lodging with him.   They at supper disclosed to him the errand upon which they were sent, and desired him to inform them where this Phocas could be found.   He told them he was well acquainted with the man, and would give them news of him next morning.   After they had retired to bed he dug a grave, prepared everything for his burial, and spent the night in disposing his soul for his last hour.   When it was day he went to his guests, and told them Phocas was found and in their power whenever they pleased to apprehend him.   They inquired where he was.   " He is here ", said the martyr. " I myself am the man."   Struck by his undaunted resolution and composure they did not at first know what to do with this man who had so generously entertained them ; he, seeing their trouble, told them that he looked upon such a death as the greatest of favours and his highest advantage.   At length, recovering from their surprise and scruples, they struck off his head.   The Christians of that city afterwards built a stately church which bore his name.   St Asterius, Bishop of Amasea, about the year 400 pronounced the panegyric of this martyr on his festival in a church which possessed a small part of his relics, and said that " Phocas from the time of his death has become a pillar and support of the churches on earth.   He draws all men to his house ; the highways are filled with persons resorting from every country to this place of prayer.   The magnificent church which is possessed of his body is the comfort and ease of the afflicted, the health of the sick, the storehouse plentifully supplying the wants of the poor.   If in any other place, as in this, some small portion of his relics be found, it also becomes admirable and most desired by Christians."   He adds that the sailors in the Euxine, Aegean and Adriatic seas, and in the ocean, sing hymns in his honour, and that the martyr has often succoured and preserved them.

Alban Butler's account of St Phocas has been set out above, with some verbal alterations and omissions, because it will touch the heart of all gardeners.   But it must be added that all that can be safely said of Phocas of Sinope is that he lived, was martyred, and was widely venerated.   Much false and allusive matter has accrued to his story, and the name Phocas figures in calendars on various dates. In the Roman Martyrology St Phocas, martyr at Antioch on March 5, and St Phocas, Bishop of Sinope and martyr under Trajan, on July 14, are probably both derivatives of Phocas the Gardener.   His relics, or parts of them, were claimed by Antioch, Vienne in France and other places.

The panegyric of St Asterius is printed in the *Acta Sanctorum*, September, vol. vi, and in Migne, PG., vol. xl, cc. 300–313.   St Phocas has been much discussed by students of folklore anxious to elucidate his popularity with sea-faring people ; the explanation is perhaps to be found in the resemblance of his name to the word φώκη, meaning a seal. See Radermacher in *Archiv f. Religionswissenschaft*, vol. vii (1904), pp. 445–452.   On the other hand E. Maas, O. Kern, and Jaisle suggest quite untenable solutions.   St Phocas has a full notice in the *Synaxarium Constantinopolitanum* (ed. Delehaye), cc. 67–68, under September 22 ; and see CMH., pp. 128, 374–375.

SS. MAURICE AND HIS COMPANIONS, MARTYRS OF THE THEBAN LEGION   (*c.* A.D. 287 ?)

A NUMBER of the Gauls, called Bagaudae, having risen in revolt, the *Augustus* Maximian Herculius marched against them with an army, of which one unit was the Theban Legion.   This had been recruited in Upper Egypt and was composed entirely of Christians.   When he arrived at Octodurum (Martigny), on the Rhône above the lake of Geneva, Maximian issued an order that the whole army should join in offering sacrifice to the gods for the success of their expedition.   The Theban Legion hereupon withdrew itself, encamped near Agaunum (now called St Maurice-en-Valais), and refused to take any part in these rites.   Maximian repeatedly commanded them to obey orders, and upon their constant and unanimous refusal sentenced them to be decimated.   Thus every tenth man was put to death, according as the lot fell.   After the first decimation, a second was commanded, unless the soldiers obeyed the orders given ; but they cried out that they would rather suffer all penalties than do anything contrary to their religion.   They were principally encouraged by three of their officers, Maurice, Exuperius and Candidus, referred to respectively as the *primicerius*, the *campiductor* and the *senator militum*. Maximian warned the remainder that it was of no use for them to trust to their numbers, for if they persisted in their disobedience not a man among them should escape death.   The legion answered him by a respectful remonstrance : " We are your soldiers, but are also servants of the true God.   We owe you military service and obedience ; but we cannot renounce Him who is our Creator and Master, and also yours even though you reject Him.   In all things which are not against His law we most willingly obey you, as we have done hitherto.   We readily oppose all your enemies, whoever they are ; but we cannot dip our hands into the blood of innocent persons.   We have taken an oath to God before we took one to you : you can place no confidence in our second oath if we violate the first.   You command us to punish the Christians ; behold, we are such.   We confess God the Father, author of all things, and His Son, Jesus Christ.   We have seen our companions slain without lamenting them, and we rejoice at their honour.   Neither this nor any other provocation has tempted us to revolt.   We have arms in our hands, but we do not resist because we would rather die innocent than live by any sin."

This legion consisted of about six thousand six hundred men, and Maximian, having no hopes of overcoming their constancy, commanded the rest of his army to surround them and cut them to pieces.   They made no resistance but suffered themselves to be butchered like sheep, so that the ground was covered with their dead bodies, and streams of blood flowed on every side.   Maximian gave the spoils of the slain to his soldiers for their booty, and they were sharing it out when a veteran named Victor refused to join in.   At this the soldiers inquired if he was also a Christian.   He answered that he was, upon which they fell upon him and slew him.   Ursus and another Victor, two straggling soldiers of this legion, were found at Solothurn and there killed, and according to local legends many others elsewhere, such as St Alexander at Bergamo, SS. Octavius, Adventor and Solutor at Turin, and St Gereon at Cologne.   The Roman Martyrology mentions Vitalis and Innocent, as well as the above three and Victor, today, SS. Ursus and Victor on September 30, and St Antoninus at Piacenza, wrongly associated with the Theban Legion, on the same date.   St Eucherius, speaking of their relics preserved at Agaunum in his time, says, " Many come from divers provinces devoutly to honour these saints, and offer presents of gold, silver and other things.   I humbly present this monument of my pen, begging intercession for the pardon of my sins, and the perpetual protection of my patrons."   He mentions many miracles to have been performed at their shrine and says of a certain woman who had been cured of a palsy by them : " Now she carries her own miracle about with her."

This St Eucherius is the principal witness for the story which has just been related.   He was bishop of Lyons during the first half of the fifth century, and wrote down for a Bishop Salvius an account of these martyrs of Agaunum, in whose honour a basilica had been built there towards the end of the previous century, in consequence of a vision of their place of burial vouchsafed to the then bishop of Octodurum, Theodore.   Eucherius says he had the story from informants of Isaac, Bishop of Geneva, who, Eucherius thought, was told it by Theodore.   It will be noticed that, as related above, the legionaries in their manifesto speak of refusing to spill the blood of innocent Christians.   This protest was doubtless composed by St Eucherius himself, who states that they were killed for refusing to undertake the massacre of Christians and does not mention the revolting Bagaudae ; other accounts of the martyrs say they suffered for not sacrificing.   St Maurice and his companions have been the subject of much discussion.   That a whole legion was put to death is highly improbable ; Roman imperial generals were not incapable of such a wholesale slaughter, but the circumstances of the time and the lack of early evidence of an entirely satisfactory sort are all against it.   Alban Butler notes with pain that " the truth of this history is attacked by some Protestant historians ", but it has been questioned by Catholic scholars as well, and some have even gone so far as to reject the whole of it as a fabrication.   But it seems clear that the martyrdom at Agaunum of St Maurice and his companions is an historical fact : what was the number of men involved is another matter ; in the course of time a squad could easily be exaggerated into a legion.

The church built at Agaunum by St Theodore of Octodurum later became the centre of an abbey, which was the first in the West to maintain the Divine Office continually by day and by night by means of a cycle of choirs.   This monastery came into the hands of the canons regular, and is now an abbey-*nullius*.   Relics of the martyrs are preserved here in a sixth-century reliquary, but veneration of the Theban Legion has spread with other relics far beyond the borders of Switzerland.   They are commemorated in the liturgy of the whole Western church, and St Maurice is patron of Savoy and Sardinia and of several towns, as well as of infantry soldiers, sword-smiths, and weavers and dyers.

The text of St Eucherius which has suffered many interpolations will be found in Ruinart, and in the *Acta Sanctorum*, September, vol. vi ; but the critical edition by B. Krusch in

MGH., *Scriptores Merov.*, vol. iii, pp. 32–41, is of first importance.   On the whole question of the martyrdom the volume of M. Besson, *Monasterium Acaunense* (1913), is perhaps the most sober and reliable.   He dissents from the extreme views of Krusch, though he is in some matters himself open to criticism (*cf.* the *Analecta Bollandiana*, vol. xxxiii, pp. 243–245). The subject is also treated at great length by H. Leclercq in DAC., vol. x (1932), cc. 2699–2729.   The bibliography which he supplies extends to four closely-printed columns, and shows impressively the interest which the controversy has excited.   See also O. Lauterburg and R. Marti-Wehren, *Martyrium von sankt Mauritius . . . Die Legende* (1945).

ST FELIX III (IV), POPE   (A.D. 530)

UPON his return from his visit to Constantinople in the year 526, Pope St John I was imprisoned by the Gothic king Theodoric at Ravenna, and died very shortly afterwards.   When therefore Theodoric caused the priest Felix to be nominated as his successor, the clergy and people at Rome were relieved that the royal choice had fallen upon so blameless and otherwise suitable a person and that they could without hesitation proceed to elect him.   The new pope used his favour with the court to promote the interests of the Church, and obtained a decree imposing a fine on those who should disregard the ancient custom that a layman should cite a cleric only before the pope or his delegates.   Fines levied for this offence were to be at the disposal of the Holy See for distribution among the poor.   St Felix approved the writings of St Caesarius of Arles on grace and free will against St Faustus of Riez, and sent to the second Synod of Orange in 529 a number of propositions about grace drawn from the works of St Augustine, and so led up to the condemnation of Semi-Pelagianism by the council.   Having been given two ancient buildings in the Roman Forum, Felix built on their site the basilica of SS. Cosmas and Damian ; the mosaics to be seen today in the apse and on the triumphal arch of that church are those made at his direction.

After he had occupied the apostolic chair for four years St Felix died in 530. He was revered in his day as a man of great simplicity, humility and kindness to the poor.

Though described in the Roman Martyrology as Felix IV, it is now decided that he is properly Felix III, a previous antipope having no right to figure in the numbering : see Felix " II " herein on July 29.   A short account of his pontificate is given by the Bollandists under January 30.   See also the *Liber Pontificalis* (Duchesne), vol. i, pp. 270 *seq.* ; Grisar, *Geschichte Roms und der Päpste*, vol. i, pp. 183 *seq.*, and 495 *seq.*

ST SALABERGA, MATRON, AND ST BODO, BISHOP   (c. A.D. 665 AND c. 670)

ST EUSTACE of Luxeuil, travelling from Bavaria back to his monastery, was entertained in a household where one of the children, a small girl called Salaberga, was blind.   He took oil, blessed it, and anointed her sightless eyes.   Then he prayed over her, and her sight was restored.   When she grew up Salaberga was married to a young man, who, however, died two months after the wedding.   She took this to be a sign that she was called to serve God in a monastery, but her parents thought otherwise and she married again, a nobleman called Blandinus.   By him she had five children, of whom two, Bauduin and Anstrudis, are venerated as saints. Salaberga had endowed a convent at Poulangey, and when they had lived in happy wedlock for a number of years she and her husband agreed both to withdraw from the world.   Blandinus became a hermit and is venerated as a saint in the diocese of Meaux.   Salaberga went to Poulangey first, and then, by the advice of St Walbert, abbot of Luxeuil, founded a new monastery at Laon about the year 650. This abbey was a very extensive establishment and had provision for both monks and nuns.   St Salaberga had a married brother named Bodo, and him she persuaded to become a monk, his wife joining the community at Laon.   He was made bishop of Toul, and founded three monasteries, of one of which his own daughter was the first abbess.   St Bodo's feast is observed on the 11th of this month.   During the last two years of her life St Salaberga suffered continually from very great pain which she bore with corresponding courage and patience ; after her death her daughter St Anstrudis took up the government of the community.   St Salaberga was buried at the abbey, and St Bodo's body was later exhumed at Toul and brought to be laid beside that of his sister.

A life, previously printed in the *Acta Sanctorum*, September, vol. vi, has been critically edited by B. Krusch in MGH., *Scriptores Merov.*, vol. v, pp. 40–66.   He shows that the correct form of the name is Sadalberga ; but, what is more important, that the life, which professes to have been written by a contemporary, is really a compilation of the beginning of the ninth century.   Certain references made to Sadalberga by Jonas, Abbot of Bobbio, in his Life of St Columban, are, however, more trustworthy.   For Bodo (Leudin) see the *Acta Sanctorum*, September, vol. iii.

ST EMMERAMUS, Bishop   (Seventh Century)

This holy missionary preached the gospel with indefatigable zeal around Poitiers, of which city he is often stated to have been bishop ; but his name does not appear in the episcopal lists of that or any other see.   After having laboured thus several years, St Emmeramus was so touched with compassion for the unhappy state of so many thousands of idolaters in Germany and beyond the Danube that he went to preach the gospel in Bavaria.   Duke Theodo detained him at Regensburg, as he was later to try to detain St Corbinian, to minister to his subjects.   Emmeramus, after having preached there three years and gained to God a number of infidels and sinners, undertook a pilgrimage to Rome.   He set out on his journey south but when he had reached Kleinhelfendorf, between Munich and Tirol, he was overtaken by, apparently, some representatives of Duke Theodo, who brutally mishandled him.   The saint managed to reach Feldkirchen, but there died of the injuries he had received.   His body was shortly afterwards translated to Regensburg.   It is not known that he was ever bishop of that city or founder of the monastery there that bore his name.

The motive and circumstances of the murder of St Emmeramus are a mystery (the Roman Martyrology says oracularly that he " patiently suffered a most cruel death for Christ's sake that he might set others free ").   Less than a century after, his life was written by Aribo, Bishop of Freising, who gives an account of it that is a characteristic example of hagiographical invention, exaggeration, embroidery, or all three, for the sake of popular edification.   We are told that before St Emmeramus left for Italy the daughter of Duke Theodo, Oda, confided to him that she was with child by a nobleman of her father's court, and she feared the duke's anger both for herself and her lover.   Emmeramus authorized her to state that he himself was the partner of her guilt.   The pious Aribo expects the reader to admire the magnanimity and self-sacrifice of Emmeramus, but, quite apart from the fact that he was recommending a lie, and a lie that would cause great scandal, it is difficult to see what would be gained by it except protection for the guilty man.   However,

the lady Oda acted accordingly when her secret was discovered, and her brother
Lantbert and his men set off in pursuit of Emmeramus. When they came up with
him at Kleinhelfendorf they tied him to a ladder, tore out his eyes and tongue, cut
off his members, and left him to die amid an outbreak of supernatural marvels.
St Emmeramus was at once acclaimed a martyr by the people.

Much has been written about St Emmeram (perhaps more correctly spelt " Haimhram-
mus "). There are lives by Bishop Arbeo or Aribo (in two recensions), another by Meginfrid
of Magdeburg, and a third by Arnold, who belonged to the monastery called by the name
of the saint himself. In the critical edition of Arbeo prepared for MGH., *Scriptores Merov.*,
vol. iv, pp. 452–520, B. Krusch has shown that the text printed by the Bollandists (in *Acta
Sanctorum*, September, vol. vi) represents substantially Arbeo's genuine work and that it
was written about the year 772. But even in its authentic form the data provided by Arbeo's
life are not trustworthy. See also A. Bigelmair, " Die Anfänge des Christentums in Bayern,"
in *Festgabe A. Knöpfler* (1907), and J. A. Endres in the *Römische Quartalschrift* for 1895
and 1903. The genuine tomb of the saint is believed to have been discovered in 1894 ;
on this see especially J. A. Endres, *Beiträge zur Geschichte des M. A. Regensburgs* (1924).

23 : ST LINUS, POPE AND MARTYR   (c. A.D. 79 ?)

IT is now not disputed that St Linus was the first successor of St Peter in the
see of Rome, but practically nothing is known about him. St Irenaeus,
writing about the year 189, identifies him with the Linus mentioned by St
Paul in his second letter to Timothy (iv 21), and implies that he was appointed
bishop before the death of Peter. St Linus is named among the martyrs in the
canon of the Mass and his feast as a martyr is kept throughout the Western church
today, but his martyrdom is very doubtful as no persecution is recorded in his
time ; moreover, Irenaeus names only St Telesphorus as a martyr among the
earliest popes after Peter.

See the *Liber Pontificalis* (ed. Duchesne), vol. i, p. 121 ; Grisar, *Geschichte Roms und
der Päpste*, p. 220 ; Lightfoot, *St Clement of Rome*, vol. i, p. 201.

ST THECLA OF ICONIUM, VIRGIN AND MARTYR   (FIRST CENTURY ?)

THECLA, referred to liturgically in the East as " protomartyr among women and
equal with the Apostles ", was one of the most revered heroines of the earlier ages
of the Church. St Methodius of Olympus in his *Banquet of the Ten Virgins* tells
us that she was well versed in profane philosophy and literature, and he commends
the ease, strength, sweetness and modesty of her speech, having received her
instruction in divine and evangelical knowledge from St Paul. St Augustine, St
Epiphanius, St Ambrose and other fathers mention that St Paul by his preaching
converted her to the faith, and that his discourses kindled in her a love of virginity.
St Gregory of Nyssa says that she undertook the sacrifice of herself by a life dead
to the senses, so that nothing seemed to remain living in her but reason and spirit.
    It is, however, by no means certain that this St Thecla ever existed ; there may
have been a convert of St Paul of that name who devoted herself to the service of
the Church, but if there was we know nothing about her. Her widespread and
popular legend depends entirely on a romance composed at the end of the second
century and known as the *Acts of Paul and Thecla*. St Jerome recognized this

work as apocryphal, and Tertullian tells us that it was written by a presbyter of Asia who, on being convicted of having falsely used St Paul's name, was deposed from his office.   In spite of this the book continued to be popular in the Church, and its incidents were referred to by a long succession of fathers, of whom some are mentioned above.   It relates how St Paul (who is described as " a little man, bald-headed, bow-legged, stoutly built, with eyebrows meeting, rather long-nosed, graceful "), preaching in the house of Onesiphorus at Iconium, attracts the attention of the maiden Thecla, who determines to put into practice his teaching on virginity. She therefore broke off her engagement to marry a certain Thamyris.   Her parents were indignant, Thamyris sought to move her with flatteries and caresses, her servants entreated her with tears, her friends and neighbours argued with her, and the authority and threats of the magistrate were employed to bring her to change her mind.   Thecla, strengthened by the arm of the Almighty, was proof against all this.   Thamyris thereupon laid an information against St Paul, who was sentenced to be scourged and cast out of the city for persuading maidens from marriage and wives from their husbands.   Thecla was ordered to be burnt, but a storm from Heaven put out the fire and she escaped to Paul and accompanied him to Antioch.   Here the Syriarch Alexander tried to abduct her in the street.   In defending herself, Thecla tore off his cloak and rolled his crown in the dust, and he, furious at being made a public laughing-stock, haled her before the governor, and she was condemned to the beasts.   For a time she was sheltered in the house of a certain Queen Tryphaena (an historical personage), whose dead daughter had told her in a dream to adopt Thecla, for the reason that " she may pray concerning me and that I may be transferred to the place of the just ".

When the time came for her execution she was exposed in the amphitheatre. But the lions walked gently up to the maiden and, laying themselves down at her feet, licked them as if it had been respectfully to kiss them, and the other beasts fought among themselves, so that the keepers had to turn others into the arena. Then Thecla saw a ditch full of water and was reminded thereby that she was not yet baptized.   And she threw herself in, saying : " In the name of Jesus Christ I am baptized on my last day."   The seals that were in the water floated about dead, and when Thecla came out there was a cloud of fire around her, so that the animals could not reach her nor the people see her naked.   Then Alexander suggested to the governor that goaded bulls should be tried, " and the governor, looking gloomy, said : ' Do as you like.' "   But the fire consumed the ropes which bound Thecla to the bulls, and at this moment Queen Tryphaena fainted.   Then the governor put a stop to the games, for Tryphaena was a kinswoman of Caesar*, and amid the applause of the multitude Thecla was released.   Dressed as a boy she rejoined St Paul at Myra in Lycia and was by him commissioned to teach the word of God, which she did to her mother in Iconium, and then retired to live in a cave at Seleucia for seventy-two years.   Then it was rumoured among the Greek physicians of the city that " this Thecla is a virgin, and serves Artemis, and from this she has power of healing," for many miracles were done by her ; and they were jealous and sent a band of young men to slay (or to ravish) her.   And Thecla praying to the Lord, the rock opened to receive her, and so she was taken to Him.   But another account says that within the rock she found a passage and thence made her way to Rome, where she found that St Paul was dead.   " And after staying there

* She was second cousin to the Emperor Caligula.

a brief space she rested in a glorious sleep ; and she is buried about two or three stadia from the tomb of her master, Paul."

That this story is a romance in at least its details is apparent on the face of it. It was written to a considerable extent in praise of virginity and to impress on its hearers the Christian teaching about chastity.   But even herein the text of the *Acts of Paul and Thecla* is somewhat extravagant, making St Paul teach that salvation is hardly possible without virginity, so that some commentators suppose it to have been written under the influence of the Encratites, an heretical sect which reprobated the use of wine, flesh-meat and marriage.   St Thecla did not actually give her blood for Christ ; her martyrdom consists in the reproaches she received from her lover and her mother, her trial at the stake, and her trial among the lions. These are the three torments referred to in the *Rituale Romanum* where, in the recommendation of a departing soul, occurs the prayer : " And as thou didst deliver the blessed virgin and martyr Thecla from three most cruel torments, so deign to deliver the soul of this thy servant and bring him to rejoice with thee in heavenly happiness."   From the great church built over her alleged cave at Meriamlik, near Seleucia, veneration for St Thecla spread over all Christendom ; she has a commemoration in the Roman liturgy, and she is named in the canon of the Ambrosian Mass.

The Greek text of the *Acts of Paul and Thecla* was edited by Tischendorf in 1851 ; and again by Lipsius-Bonnet in their *Acta Apostolorum Apocrypha*, 1891, vol. i.   The Syriac version was rendered accessible by W. Wright in 1871 and the Armenian by F. C. Conybeare in *The Apology and Acts of Apollonius and other Monuments of Early Christianity* (1894). See also Pirot, *Supplément au Dictionnaire de la Bible* (1926), vol. i, cc. 494–495.   Sir W. M. Ramsay in his book *The Church in the Roman Empire* committed himself to the view that there was a real person of the name of Thecla who embraced the teaching of the apostle St Paul.   There is a very long discussion in DCB., vol. iv, pp. 882–896, and an English translation of the " Acts " in J. Orr, *New Testament Apocryphal Writings* (1903).

ST ADAMNAN, OR EUNAN, ABBOT OF IONA   (A.D. 704)

ADAMNAN, whom St Bede calls " a good and wise man, remarkably learned in the Holy Scriptures ", was born about the year 624 at Drumhome in the county of Donegal.   He entered a monastery which had been founded there.   Afterwards, following the steps of his holy kinsman Columba, he retired to the monastery of Iona, of which he became ninth abbot in the year 679.   On the death of Oswy, King of Northumbria, his son Aldfrid had had to fly from the usurper Egfrid, and had taken shelter at Iona, where he met Adamnan.   When in 686, Aldfrid being then on his throne, someone was required to go on behalf of the Irish to the Northumbrians to negotiate for the release of some captives, it was therefore natural that St Adamnan should be chosen for the mission.   He succeeded, and while he was in England again in 688 he visited the monasteries of Wearmouth and Jarrow, and was seen by the young Bede, who was then a boy of thirteen.   The important result of this visit was that, by the persuasion of St Ceolfrid, he laid aside the custom of his predecessors and conformed to the true time of celebrating Easter.   Upon his return home he used his utmost endeavours to guide his monks at Iona into the same practice, but without success.

After his failure to convert his monks from Celtic to Roman customs, St Adamnan spent a good deal of time in Ireland.   At the Council of Birr he was instrumental in persuading the assembly that women should not take part in warfare and that they and their children should be neither killed nor taken as prisoners ; this decision was called after him, Adamnan's Law.   All the time he was zealously propagating the observance of the true Easter, which was accepted nearly wherever he went, except where the influence of Columban monasteries was strong, and notably in his own Iona.   He made a final fruitless attempt to overcome the opposition of his community ;   " and it so happened that he departed this life before the next year came round, the divine Goodness so ordaining that, as he was a great lover of peace and unity, he should be received into everlasting life before he should be obliged, by the return of the time of Easter, to dispute yet more seriously with those who would not follow him ".   This was on September 23, 704.

St Adamnan, " a man of tears and penitence, devoted in prayer, diligent, mortified, and learned in God's holy scriptures ", was after St Columba Iona's brightest light and most accomplished scholar.   He himself refers to the writing-tablets, the pens and *stili* and ink-horns, in the monastic scriptorium, and of these he made full use himself.   His own name is remembered for, more than anything, his Life of St Columba, one of the most important hagiographical documents in existence and the most complete biography of the early middle ages.   He wrote it in Latin at the request of his brethren.   In the latter part of the seventh century a Frankish bishop called Arculf went on pilgrimage to Jerusalem, and on the way back his ship was so driven by contrary winds that he was eventually cast up on the western coast of Britain (which, unless they were trying to make a port on the west coast of France, seems a very remarkable occurrence).   Arculf " after many adventures " found himself at Iona, where he was warmly received by Adamnan and gave a long account to the monks of all he had seen in the East.   St Adamnan wrote this narrative down, and so composed his other well-known work, *De locis sanctis*, " beneficial to many and particularly to those who, being far from those places where the patriarchs and apostles lived, know no more of them than they can learn by reading ".   This book was presented by Adamnan to King Aldfrid, " and through his bounty it came to be read by lesser persons ", even to the present day.

Among the popular tales told of this saint is that, to provide wood for his monastery, he felled with his own hands enough oak trees on a neighbouring island to load twelve boats.   He is also said one day to have been missing from choir, and when his brethren sought him they found him in ecstasy before a vision of the Holy Child.   St Adamnan was very greatly venerated among the people of Scotland, and the common Scots baptismal name of Adam is a corruption of his own. His feast is still observed in the diocese of Argyll and the Isles.   Throughout Ireland he is commemorated on this day as St Eunan, and celebrated at Raphoe as its first bishop ; but it is not certainly established that this Eunan and Adamnan are one and the same.   That he was ever bishop in Raphoe is unlikely.

Our most reliable information about Adamnan comes from Bede, *Ecclesiastical History ;* see Plummer's edition and notes.   But, though of a more legendary character, Irish materials are also available, at least in the form of casual anecdotes : Plummer's *Miscellanea Hagiographica Hibernica* supplies references to many of these.   There is even a short Irish Life of St Adamnan, of which a translation has been printed in the *Celtic Review*, vol. v (1908), pp. 97–107.   The best text of Adamnan's *De locis sanctis* is that of Geyer in the Vienna *Corpus Scriptorum*, vol. xxxix, while the *Life of St Columba* has been well edited by J. T. Fowler (1920).   See also L. Gougaud, *Christianity in Celtic Lands* (1932) ; and J. F. Kenney, *The Sources of the Early History of Ireland*, vol. i, 1929.

BD MARK OF MODENA   (A.D. 1498)

THIS Mark was born at Modena and entered the Dominican order, in which he became a renowned preacher throughout northern Italy. He was for many years prior of the friary at Pesaro and whilst there was credited with the working of many miracles. Bd Mark died at Pesaro on September 23, 1498. His body, buried in the church of his order, was afterwards solemnly transferred to the Lady chapel, where it was venerated every year on Whit Monday. His *cultus* was approved in 1857.

See the *Acta Sanctorum*, September, vol. vi ; L. Alberti, *De viris illustribus O.P.*, fol. 248 ; *Année Dominicaine*, vol. vii, p. 49 ; L. Vedriani, *Vita . . .* (1663) ; Taurisano, *Catalogus hagiographicus O.P.*, p. 49.

BD HELEN OF BOLOGNA, WIDOW   (A.D. 1520)

BD HELEN DUGLIOLI has been selected by popular acclamation from among the unknown numbers of those who have served God heroically " in the world " to be exalted at the altars of the Church. She was born at Bologna, and when she was about seventeen years old married Benedict dall' Oglio. Husband and wife lived together for thirty years in amity and happiness, supporting and encouraging one another in the life of Christians, and when Benedict died, Helen shortly after followed him to the grave. The common people, who have an almost unerring instinct for detecting true holiness, knew she was a saint, and the continual *cultus* they had given her was confirmed in 1828.

The most important part of the notice devoted to her by the Bollandists consists of an extract from the *De Servorum Dei beatificatione* of Prosper Lambertini (afterwards Pope Benedict XIV), written when he was archbishop of Bologna. In this he quotes the tributes paid to Bd Helen at Bologna as an almost typical case of a spontaneous and immemorial *cultus*, and refers to sundry local publications which bore witness to the devotion of the citizens. Among other evidence cited by the Bollandists it is curious to find a passage from the *Ragionamenti* of Pietro Aretino, of all people, a contemporary of the *beata*, who refers satirically to the crowds of candles, pictures and *ex votos* deposited " alla sapoltura di santa Beata Lena dall' Olio a Bologna ".

See the *Acta Sanctorum*, September, vol. vi.

24 : OUR LADY OF RANSOM

THE first entry in the Roman Martyrology today is, " The feast of blessed Mary the Virgin, called of Ransom, institutress of the Order for the Redemption of Captives under that title. Her Appearing is mentioned on August 10 ", and accordingly under that date we find, " The Appearing in Spain of blessed Mary . . .", etc. In the account of St Peter Nolasco on January 28 we have referred to the difficulties surrounding the history of the foundation of this order (*vulgo* Mercedarians), particularly the unsatisfactory nature of the evidence for the apparitions of our Lady to St Peter and others. The date of the order's first foundation in Spain was August 10 (in 1218 or 1223 or 1228), but the feast commemorating this event, under the name of the Solemnity of the Coming-down of Our Lady of Ransom, was kept by the Mercedarians on the Sunday nearest to August 1. The feast was granted to Spain at large in 1680, and extended to the whole Western church, for its present date, in 1696.

The invocation of our Lady under this title for the conversion of England has nothing to do with the historical and liturgical aspects of the feast. Our Lady of Pity was an old name for her in this country, expressing a cognate idea to " ransom ", and she may be regarded as interceding for our country's release from the bonds of religious error, just as in the prayer of the Mass today we ask for the deliverance of the faithful people from the bonds of sin.

See F. G. Holweck, *Calendarium festorum Dei et Dei Matris* (1925), p. 327, who seems to accept the Mercedarian traditions a little too trustfully ; he also appeals to D. Perez Sanjulian, *Historia de la SS. Virgen Maria* (1912), vol. ii, p. 645. It was a project of Pope Benedict XIV's commission for the reform of the Roman Breviary to suppress this feast of our Lady of Ransom, a project to which effect has been given in the calendar approved for the Benedictines in 1915.

ST GEREMARUS, OR GERMER, ABBOT   (*c.* A.D. 658)

THIS saint was one of the numerous Frankish noblemen of whom we are told that, after marrying and following a secular career, they left the world and became distinguished in the monastic or other ecclesiastical life of their time. He belonged to the territory of Beauvais, and was attached in his youth to the court of Dagobert I, where he met his wife Domana, who was herself venerated as a saint in the diocese of Evreux. Their two girl children predeceased them, and their boy being grown up they, under the influence of St Audoenus, Bishop of Rouen, determined to embrace the religious life. Geremarus had already built a monastery near his birthplace, but he himself chose to receive the monastic habit at Pentale on the Risle, near Brionne. He was a model religious and became abbot of the house. But strictness and regularity which are admired in a subject are not always so popular in a superior, and some of the monks at Pentale were very discontented under their new father. They were themselves such bad religious and even bad men that it is said they attempted to take the life of St Geremarus by fastening a sharp knife point upwards in the boards of his bed under the blanket—though unless he were a heavy man or in the habit of throwing himself into his bed, such a device was not likely to inflict a mortal wound. Whether for this reason or because of his unpopularity and lack of success in improving discipline, the abbot resigned his office and went to live as a hermit in a cave on the banks of the river. Here he passed five contented years, communing with God, working with his hands, and ministering to his neighbours, until one day news was brought to him of the death of his only son, Amalbert. " O my God ", he cried, " I thank thee that thou hast shown thy mercy towards me by calling my son to thy glory ". With the young man's estate which now reverted to him he founded a monastery at Flay, on the river Epte between Beauvais and Rouen, which was afterwards called Saint-Germer. St Geremarus abandoned the solitary life to direct the new monastery till his death.

The Life of St Geremarus printed in the *Acta Sanctorum* (September, vol. vi) is not the earliest. That which B. Krusch has edited for MGH., *Scriptores Merov.* (vol. iv, pp. 626–633), is of older date, but Krusch shows that even this can only have been written a little before 851, and that as a source of history it is quite untrustworthy. That printed by the Bollandists was compiled in the eleventh century. There are other accounts such, for example, as that written by Guibert of Nogent, but all are legendary.

ST GERARD, BISHOP OF CSANAD, MARTYR (A.D. 1046)

ST GERARD, sometimes surnamed Sagredo, the apostle of a large district in Hungary, was a Venetian, born about the beginning of the eleventh century. At an early age he consecrated himself to the service of God in the Benedictine monastery of San Giorgio Maggiore at Venice, but after some time left it to undertake a pilgrimage to Jerusalem. While passing through Hungary he became known to the king, St Stephen, who made him tutor to his son, Bd Emeric, and Gerard began as well to preach with success. When St Stephen established the episcopal see of Csanad he appointed Gerard to be its first bishop. The greater part of the people were heathen, and those that bore the name of Christian were ignorant, brutish and savage, but St Gerard laboured among them with much fruit. He always so far as possible joined to the perfection of the episcopal state that of the contemplative life, which gave him fresh vigour in the discharge of his pastoral duties. But Gerard was also a scholar, and wrote an unfinished dissertation on the Hymn of the Three Young Men (Daniel iii), as well as other works which are lost.

King Stephen seconded the zeal of the good bishop so long as he lived, but on his death in 1038 the realm was plunged into anarchy by competing claimants to the crown, and a revolt against Christianity began. Things went from bad to worse, and eventually, when celebrating Mass at a little place on the Danube called Giod, Gerard had prevision that he would on that day receive the crown of martyrdom. His party arrived at Buda and were going to cross the river, when they were set upon by some soldiers under the command of an obstinate upholder of idolatry and enemy of the memory of King St Stephen. They attacked St Gerard with a shower of stones, overturned his conveyance, and dragged him to the ground. Whilst in their hands the saint raised himself on his knees and prayed with St Stephen, " Lord, lay not this sin to their charge. They know not what they do." He had scarcely spoken these words when he was run through the body with a lance ; the insurgents then hauled him to the edge of the cliff called the Blocksberg, on which they were, and dashed his body headlong into the Danube below. It was September 24, 1046. The heroic death of St Gerard had a profound effect, he was revered as a martyr, and his relics were enshrined in 1083 at the same time as those of St Stephen and his pupil Bd Emeric. In 1333 the republic of Venice obtained the greater part of his relics from the king of Hungary, and with great solemnity translated them to the church of our Lady of Murano, wherein St Gerard is venerated as the protomartyr of Venice, the place of his birth.

The most reliable source for the history of St Gerard is, it appears, the short biography printed in the *Acta Sanctorum*, September, vol. vi (pp. 722–724). Contrary to the opinion previously entertained, it is not an epitome of the longer life which is found in Endlicher, *Monumenta Arpadiana* (pp. 205–234), but dates from the twelfth, or even the end of the eleventh, century. This, at least, is the conclusion of R. F. Kaindl in the *Archiv f. Oesterreichische Geschichte*, vol. xci (1902), pp. 1–58. The other biographies are later expansions of the first named, and not so trustworthy. St Gerard's story and episcopate have also been discussed by C. Juhász in *Studien und Mittheilungen O.S.B.*, 1929, pp. 139–145, and 1930, pp. 1–35 ; and see C. A. Macartney, in *Archivum Europae centro-orientalis*, vol. iv (1938), pp. 456–490, on the Lives of St Gerard, and his *Medieval Hungarian Historians* (1953).

BD ROBERT OF KNARESBOROUGH   (A.D. 1218 ?)

LIKE his fellow hermit and fellow Yorkshireman Richard Rolle, Robert Flower, the " Holy Hermit of Knaresborough ", enjoyed a considerable *cultus* in medieval England which was never confirmed or made public by canonization. His name has not been found in calendars, but the Trinitarian church at Knaresborough was called St Robert's, and Matthew Paris mentions him with St Edmund of Abingdon and St Elizabeth of Hungary as one of the holiest persons of his time. He was born about the year 1160 at York, of which city his father was a citizen and at one time aspired to be a priest. But he never proceeded beyond the subdiaconate, " for what cause God best knoweth ", as Leland says. His brother was a Cistercian in Newminster Abbey at Morpeth and Robert followed him there, but four and a half months of novitiate was enough to demonstrate that his vocation was not to the cenobitical life. He was convinced that God was calling him to a dedicated life of some sort, and so, forgoing his patrimony as eldest son, he went to live in a cave adjoining a poor chapel called St Giles's below a cliff by the river Nidd, near Knaresborough. This cave was already occupied by a knight who, it is stated, was hiding from the wrath of his king rather than seeking the love of God, for immediately on the death of Richard I he deserted his cave and his companion and went home to his wife. Robert remained there till the offer of a cell and chapel of St Hilda at Rudfarlington enticed him further into the forest; his life here was rudely interrupted by the burglary and destruction of his hermitage by robbers. So he moved a few miles away to Spofforth, under the protection of the Percys, but he was beginning to become known as a holy man, and to avoid the people who insisted on coming to see him he fled in desperation to the priory of Hedley, near Tadcaster. But Robert was no more successful as a Black than as a White monk, and when he took the liberty openly to criticize their interpretation of the Rule of St Benedict the monks dismissed him. He now went back to Rudfarlington, where his patroness gave him a barn and other buildings, some land, and four hinds to help him work it, and all went well for a year till he attracted the attention of William de Stuteville, constable of Knaresborough. He suspected the hermit of giving shelter to thieves and outlaws and had his buildings pulled down about his ears. Robert fled back to St Giles's chapel where he had started, but was pursued by the wrath of the constable who found him there and intended to have him ejected. However, he changed his mind, because he had a dream in which three demons of most terrifying aspect threatened his life on account of his wrongs to the man of God.

De Stuteville gave to Robert all the land between his cave and Grimbald's Crag, and also two horses, two oxen and two cows, which he was to farm for his own sustenance and the relief of the poor. Robert was now well provided for and left in peace, except that people of all degrees came to visit him " for to be edified ". Another brother, Walter, a prosperous burgess and mayor of York, urged him to go into a monastery—perhaps he thought a hermit brother, however holy, did not consort with his own dignity—but Robert replied in the words of the psalmist, " Hic habitabo, quoniam elegi eam ". So Walter agreed to send workmen to build a chapel of the Holy Cross, traces of which still remain beside the cave which the hermit enlarged by his own labour. Unhappily the place is now more associated with the crime of Eugene Aram in 1745 than with Robert Flower, for in it the body of the murdered Daniel Clark was hidden. Several miracles of the hermit passed into the memory of the countryside and he was popularly esteemed to have waged long warfare with visible manifestations of the Devil ; he is also said to have had a vision of his mother, asking him to pray for her in Purgatory and afterwards assuring him that his prayers were efficacious. Robert had a disciple called Yve who, after an early attempt to run away was spoiled by his breaking his leg, persevered in this solitary life and succeeded to Robert's hermitage after his death. From his master he learnt that a hermit's first duty, after his own sanctification, is to care for the poor and oppressed ; Robert sheltered all unfortunates, whether " deserving " or not, who came to him, and collected alms and worked hard on his land for the relief of the needy. He refused to pay tithes of corn and hay to the parson of Knaresborough, pointing out in rather forcible language that his land was already the patrimony of the poor.

When King John was staying at Knaresborough Castle he visited the hermit, and is said to have found him at prayer. When Sir Brian de l'Isle called him to the king's presence, Robert presented him with an ear of corn, saying, " My lord king, can you with all your power make such a thing as this out of nothing ? " John accepted the lesson in silence, but sycophantic (or kindly tactful) bystanders were quick to point out that Robert was mad. The king asked if there was anything he could give him, and the hermit replied there was nothing. But directly John was gone Yve rebuked his master for missing an opportunity of benefiting the poor ; Robert ran after the king, and a plow-land of the adjoining wood was granted. While Robert lay dying, monks came from Fountains Abbey, offering him the Cistercian habit, which he refused, warning Yve what would happen after his death. And directly he was dead the monks again came, and wished to have his body for burial in their great minster. But Robert had said that he was to be buried in his own chapel of Holy Cross, and soldiers were sent from the castle to guard the body until it was buried in the appointed place in the presence of crowds of weeping people, mourning the " devout, debonair and discreet man, than whom a milder could not be met ". After the death of Yve, Robert's hermitage came into the hands of the Trinitarian order, whose canons seem eventually to have removed his body into their own church at Knaresborough.

In *Analecta Bollandiana*, vol. lvii (1939), pp. 364–400, Fr P. Grosjean printed the prose life from the B.M. manuscript Egerton 3143, and an earlier but fragmentary life from Harleian MS. 3775. These texts (with other matter) are given in a slightly shortened form in the appendices to the *Metrical Life of St Robert of Knaresborough* (E.E.T.S. 1953), ed. by Joyce Bazire ; this Middle English metrical life is also from Egerton 3143, which has been dated as late fifteenth century. See also A. F. Pollard in DNB., vol. xlviii ; R. M. Clay, *Hermits and Anchorites of England* (1914) ; and Abbot J. I. Cummins in *Yorkshire Archaeological Journal*, vol. xxviii (1926), pp. 80–88, and his *Legends, Saints and Shrines of Knaresborough* (1928). Robert Flower (who is often called Saint) has sometimes been confused with St Robert, Abbot of Newminster (d. 1159).

ST PACIFICO OF SAN SEVERINO   (A.D. 1721)

IN the year 1653 there was born to Antony Divini and Mary Bruni, at San Severino in the March of Ancona, a son, who was baptized under the names of Charles Antony. When he was about five both his parents died, leaving him to the care of his maternal uncle, a harsh and disagreeable man. He used the boy simply as a servant about the house and treated him with something less than the consideration due to a servant, all of which Charles bore with patience and humility until, in his seventeenth year, he offered himself to the Friars Minor of the Observance. In 1670 he was clothed in their monastery at Forano and received the name of Pacifico. After the usual course of studies he was ordained at the age of twenty-five. For the two following years he taught philosophy to the junior friars and then, representing to his superiors that preaching was a more suitable employment for him, he was sent out on mission work in the neighbouring villages and hamlets. His sweet and simple discourses were everywhere well received, and were strengthened in their effect by his ability to read the consciences of his penitents. He reminded one James Sconocchia at Cingoli that he had forgotten to confess two sins of profanity, and another penitent said that the friar had brought back to his memory occasions on which he had been unkind to his mother and had entertained unchaste thoughts. But the public apostolate of Brother Pacifico was destined to last only for six or seven years, for when he was thirty-five he was overtaken by both deafness and blindness and by a chronic ulceration of his legs which almost crippled him. He continued to live at Forano, passing his time in prayer, penance and almsdeeds, but having for a short time filled the offices of vicar and guardian of the friary of San Severino, he was in 1705 transferred to that house where, amid the friends and scenes of his childhood, he passed the rest of his life.

On several occasions St Pacifico displayed the gift of prophecy, as, for example, in 1717 when he foretold the victory of Prince Eugene of Savoy over the Turks at Belgrade. As though his natural bodily afflictions were not enough, he still further mortified himself with hair-shirt and discipline, and his superiors had to interfere to limit his fasts. At Mass he was often rapt in ecstasy, sometimes for several hours. During the month of July 1721 he received a visit from the bishop of San Severino, and as he was leaving St Pacifico suddenly cried out : " My lord—Heaven, Heaven ! And I shall soon follow you." Within fifteen days the bishop was dead, and on the following September 24 St Pacifico died also. Miracles took place at his tomb, as they had done in his lifetime, and in 1752 his cause was begun ; Cardinal Henry of York was *ponente* and Mgr (afterwards Cardinal) Erskine promoter of the faith. He was canonized in 1839.

Several biographies have been published since the saint was canonized, notably those of Melchiorri (1839), Bernardino da Gajoli (1898), and Diotallevi (1910). See also Léon, *Auréole Séraphique* (Eng. trans.), vol. iii, pp. 224–229.

25 : ST FIRMINUS, Bishop and Martyr (Fourth Century ?)

ACCORDING to his worthless " acts ", he was a native of Pampeluna, in Navarre, initiated in the Christian faith by St Honestus, a disciple of St Saturninus of Toulouse, and consecrated bishop of Toulouse by St Honoratus to preach the gospel in the remoter parts of Gaul. Being arrived at Amiens, Firminus there chose his residence and founded a church of faithful disciples. He received the crown of martyrdom in that city, where the bishop St Firminus II (who is honoured on September 1) built a church over his tomb, dedicated under the invocation of the Blessed Virgin, but now known as St Acheul's. It is possible that Firminus I and Firminus II were only one man ; they are both unheard of before the ninth century, the first known bishop of Amiens being Eulogius in the middle of the fourth century. Firminus was probably simply a missionary bishop in Gaul.

Two texts are known which claim to represent the " acts " of St Firminus. The Bollandists (September, vol. vii) print one entire with extracts from the other. See also C. Salmon, *Histoire de S. Firmin* (1861), and Duchesne, *Fastes Épiscopaux*, vol. iii, pp. 122–127. For Firminus II, see Duchesne, *loc. cit. ;* the *Acta Sanctorum*, September, vol. i. For both a popular account is provided by J. Corblet, *Hagiographie du diocèse d'Amiens* (1870), vol. ii, pp. 31–216.

ST CADOC, ABBOT   (*c.* A.D. 575)

ST CADOC (Cadog, Catwg) was one of the most celebrated of the Welsh saints, but the earliest accounts of him were not written till some 600 years after the events they claim to record. According to these he was the son of St Gundleus and St Gwladys, and was baptized by the Irish St Tatheus, to whom Gundleus entrusted the boy's education, " in preference to all the other teachers of Britain ", in his school at Caerwent. At Llancarfan (formerly Nantcarfan), between Cardiff and Llantwit Major, Cadoc founded a monastery, and then passed over to Ireland, where he spent three years in study. On his return he went into Brecknock, for further study under a rhetor named Bachan ; here he miraculously relieved a famine by the discovery of an unknown store of wheat, and at the scene of this find founded the church of Llanspyddid, which still bears his name.

Cadoc then went back to Llancarfan, which was the resort of many because of its fame for holiness and learning. We are particularly told that he gave his disciples (St Gildas is said to have been one of them) the example of living by the work of his own hands and not those of others, for " he who does not work shall not eat ". His biographer Caradoc gives some details of the teaching methods at the monastery, which clearly represent his own practice in the eleventh century at Llancarfan, not Cadoc's. The monastery fed five hundred dependants and poor every day, and its abbot had authority over all the surrounding country. During Lent Cadoc would retire from all this activity to the solitude of the islands of Barry and Flatholm, but always came back to his monastery in time for Easter. Another place of retreat, bearing his name, is now called Cadoxton, by Neath.

There is evidence that St Cadoc visited Brittany, Cornwall, and Scotland, founding a monastery at Cambuslang ; and he is said to have been present at the synod of Llandewi Frefi, and to have made the common-form pilgrimage to Rome and Jerusalem. Very surprising are the circumstances of his death, as reported by his biographer Lifris. Warned by an angel in a dream on the eve of Palm Sunday, he was transported " in a white cloud " to Benevento in Italy, where he was made bishop and met his death by martyrdom. Caradoc, too, takes him to Benevento, not miraculously but by road, and says nothing about martyrdom : he died peacefully, and all the city accompanied him to burial, " with hymns and songs and lights ". It is not unlikely that the actual place of St Cadoc's death was at Llansannor, a few miles from Llancarfan. His feast is observed today throughout Wales.

St Cadoc's biographers were both clerics of Llancarfan : Lifris wrote his *vita* (text and translation in A. W. Wade-Evans, *Vitae sanctorum Britanniae*, 1944) between 1073 and 1086, and Caradoc his about 1100. This long-lost life by Caradoc, found in the Gotha MS. I. 81, is printed in *Analecta Bollandiana*, vol. lx (1942), pp. 35–67, with an introduction by Father

P. Grosjean. There are two interesting notices of " King " Arthur in Lifris. See A. W.
Wade-Evans, *Welsh Christian Origins* (1934), pp. 126–132 ; LBS., vol. ii, pp. 14–42 ; G. H.
Doble, *St Cadoc in Cornwall and Brittany* (1937) ; KSS., pp. 292–293 ; J. Barrett Davies
in *Blackfriars*, vol. xxix (1948), pp. 121 *seq.* ; J. S. P. Tatlock, " Caradoc of Llancarfan "
in *Speculum*, vol. xiii (1938), pp. 138–152. For the influence of Cadoc in Ireland, see J.
Ryan's *Irish Monasticism* (1931).

ST AUNACHARIUS, OR AUNAIRE, BISHOP OF AUXERRE (A.D. 605)

HE was born of a family of the Orléanais distinguished alike for its nobility and
virtue ; his sister St Austregildis was the mother of St Lupus of Sens.   Aunacharius
passed his youth at a royal court, but renounced the world and put himself under
the direction of St Syagrius, Bishop of Autun.   By him he was ordained priest,
and in 561 was elected to the see of Auxerre.   St Aunacharius was one of the most
influential and respected bishops of his time in France in both civil and religious
affairs, but it was in ecclesiastical discipline that he was particularly active.   He
attended the synod of Paris under St Germanus in the year 573, and those at Mâcon
in 583 and 585, which among other things forbade clerics to summon one another
before the civil courts, established the right of bishops to interfere on behalf of
widows, orphans and freed slaves, and enforced Sunday observance and the payment
of tithes.

Aunacharius, zealous for discipline in his own diocese, tireless in his vigilance
over public morals, and anxious to instruct his people in everything that affected
their lives as Christians, himself held two synods at Auxerre in which the above
legislation was applied to his own church.   In the first of these forty-five canons
were enacted, some of which throw interesting light on the manners and customs
of the place and time, when superstitious survivals of paganism and abuse of
Christian practices had not yet attained the harmless respectability of " folk-
survivals ".   People were forbidden, for example, to use churches for dancing and
to sing ribald songs or give entertainments therein ; they were not to dress themselves up as stags or calves on New Year's day or to exchange " evil gifts ", or to
make vows or oaths before " holy " bushes, trees and wells, or to practise sympathetic magic, or to meet together in private houses to celebrate the vigils of feasts
(*cf.* the abuse of " wakes " in England and Ireland).   For the edification and
encouragement of the faithful St Aunacharius caused biographies of his two distinguished predecessors St Amatus and St Germanus to be written, and he increased
the revenues of his church in order that divine worship might be conducted with
more order and decency.   Secular clergy as well as monks were bound to assist
at the Divine Office daily, and solemn litanies of intercession were to be carried
out by each church and monastery in turn, by the larger ones once every month.
St Aunacharius died on September 25 in the year 605.

There are two short lives printed in the *Acta Sanctorum*, September, vol. vii, with the
usual prolegomena.   See also Cochard, *Les Saints d'Orléans*, pp. 272–277, and Duchesne,
Fastes Épiscopaux, vol. ii, pp. 435–437.   Cf. R. Louis, *Antessiodorum Christianum* (1952),
and in *St Germain d'Auxerre et son temps* (1948), pp. 39 *seq.*

ST FINBAR, BISHOP   (*c.* A.D. 633)

FINBAR, or Bairre, founder of the city and see of Cork, is said to have been the
natural son of a royal lady and of a master smith.   He was baptized Lochan, but

the monks who educated him at Kilmacahill in Kilkenny changed his name to *Fionnbharr*, Whitehead, because of his fair hair. Legends say that he went to Rome on pilgrimage with one of his preceptors, and on his way back passed through Wales and visited St David in Pembrokeshire. As he had no means of getting to Ireland, David lent him a horse for the crossing, and in the channel he sighted and signalled St Brendan the Navigator, voyaging eastward. St Finbar is fabled to have gone again to Rome, in company with St David and others, when Pope St Gregory would have made him a bishop but was deterred by a vision in which he learned that Heaven had reserved this prerogative for itself. Accordingly when Finbar returned to Ireland our Lord brought a miraculous flow of oil from the ground, caught him up into Heaven, and there consecrated him bishop, anointing him with the oil which flowed round the feet of the onlookers. After preaching in various parts of southern Ireland, and living as a hermit on a small island at Lough Eiroe, he established a monastery on low marshy ground on the south side of the mouth of the river Lee, the *corcagh mor* from which the city of Cork takes its name. The monastery soon attracted disciples and its school exerted an influence all over the south of Ireland ; " to this house, as an abode of wisdom and sacred storehouse of all Christian virtues, so many came through zeal of leading a holy life that it changed a desert into a great city, from the number of its cells and of the holy men inhabiting them ".

Accounts of St Finbar are full of conflicting statements and decorated with surprising wonders. There is a charming story that when he was visited by St Laserian the two monks sat together under a hazel bush, talking of the things of God. Presently Laserian asked Finbar for a sign that God was with him. Finbar prayed, and the spring catkins on the bush above them fell off, nuts formed, grew and ripened, and he gathered them in handfuls and poured them into Laserian's lap. The death of St Finbar was the occasion of a very unusual marvel, for when he was taken to God the sun did not set for a fortnight. It would appear that the saint visited and preached in Scotland. There was formerly considerable devotion to him there, and the island of Barra in the Western Isles, as well as other places, has its name from him. Kintyre was apparently the scene of his labours. He is said to have died at Cloyne, and his body was taken for burial back to his church in Cork. The feast of St Finbar is kept on this day throughout Ireland.

There are both Irish and Latin lives of St Finbar. The primary Irish text has been edited by C. Plummer in his *Bethada Náem nÉrenn*, with a translation in vol. ii, pp. 11–21. The best Latin life has also been edited by Plummer, VSH., vol. i, pp. 65–74. See further Caulfield, *Life of St Fin Barre* (1864). Some other Latin materials, more or less dependent upon these, will be found in the *Acta Sanctorum*, September, vol. vii. See also Forbes, KSS., pp. 275–276 ; O'Hanlon, LIS., vol. ix, pp. 547 *seq. ;* and J. F. Kenney, *Sources for the Early History of Ireland*, vol. i. Cf. W. D. Simpson, *The Origins of Christianity in Aberdeenshire* (1925) ; and for the lives of the saint, P. Grosjean in *Analecta Bollandiana*, vol. lxix (1951), pp. 324–347.

ST CEOLFRID, ABBOT OF WEARMOUTH   (A.D. 716)

CEOLFRID was born in the year 642, probably in Northumbria. When he was eighteen he became a monk in his kinsman Tunbert's monastery at Gilling, but soon migrated to St Wilfrid's monastery at Ripon, where the Rule of St Benedict had been introduced, and was ordained there. Soon afterwards he went to Canterbury to visit the communities of Christ Church and SS. Peter and Paul's, and then spent some time with St Botulf at his newly founded monastery at Icanhoe in East Anglia. He returned to Ripon " so well instructed that no one could be found more learned than he in either ecclesiastical or monastic traditions ". He was made novice-master, and the fame of his virtues and learning presently reached the ears of St Benedict Biscop at Wearmouth. At St Benedict's request St Wilfrid released Ceolfrid from his obedience at Ripon, and he went to Wearmouth, where he was soon appointed prior. When the abbot left on a journey to Rome, Ceolfrid was put in sole charge, a responsibility that accorded ill with his personal preferences. Some of the monks complained of the strictness with which he administered the house, and in consequence of the dissension so caused St Ceolfrid went back for a time to Ripon. St Benedict induced him to return, and about the year 678 took him with him to Rome.

In 685 Benedict founded another monastery, dedicated in honour of St Paul, at Jarrow, on the Tyne six miles from Wearmouth. The two houses in effect were one abbey, under the rule of St Benedict Biscop, but it was necessary to have a local superior at the new foundation. Ceolfrid was therefore appointed deputy abbot of St Paul's, and given seventeen monks from St Peter's at Wearmouth as the nucleus of a community. While St Benedict was absent in Rome for the fifth time an epidemic ravaged Tyneside. In it perished St Esterwine, deputy-abbot at St Peter's and a great part of his community, and at Jarrow every single monk died except St Ceolfrid and a young *alumnus* who was being educated at the monastery. It is recorded that Ceolfrid could not bear to give up celebrating the Divine Office in choir, so he and the boy continued to sing it alone together until a new community was formed. In the year 690 St Benedict Biscop died, after having, with the agreement of the monks, nominated Ceolfrid as his successor. St Ceolfrid was diligent and active in everything he took in hand, of a sharp wit, mature in judgement and fervent in zeal. St Bede, who had the happiness to live under this great man, has left authentic testimonies of his learning, abilities and sanctity. He was a great lover of sacred literature, and enriched the libraries of his two monasteries with a large number of books. To how high a pitch he carried the sacred sciences in his monasteries St Bede himself is the foremost example. He says of St Ceolfrid that : " Whatever good works his predecessor had begun he with no less energy took pains to finish."

In the year 716 Ceolfrid, finding himself old and infirm and no longer able to teach his subjects by word and example, decided to resign his office and told his unwilling and protesting monks that they must elect somebody in his place. He himself was determined to end his days in Rome and, fearful that he would die before arriving there, as in fact happened, he set out only three days after his decision was made known. Early in the morning of Wednesday, May 4, after the six hundred monks had assisted at Mass and received communion, they all assembled in St Peter's church at Wearmouth. St Ceolfrid, when he had lighted the incense and sung a prayer, gave his blessing to them all, standing at the altar-steps with the thurible in his hand. Then in the chapel of St Larence he addressed them for the last time, urging them to keep charity with one another and lovingly to correct those who were in fault ; he forgave whatever wrongs might have been done him, and asked them all to pray for him and to pardon him if he had ever reprimanded them too harshly. They then went down to the shore where, amid tears and lamentation, he gave them the kiss of peace and prayed aloud for them, and went aboard a boat, preceded by ministers with lighted candles and a golden crucifix. Having crossed the river, he kissed the cross, mounted his horse, and departed.

Among the treasures which St Benedict Biscop had brought from Rome, or received from his friend St Adrian of Canterbury, was a copy of St Jerome's Vulgate, and of this precious manuscript St Ceolfrid had had three copies made. One was given to the library at Wearmouth, one to that at Jarrow, and the third he now took with him as a present to the pope. But he was not destined to deliver it. During his journey in spite of his weakness and the rigours of travel he relaxed none of his old discipline. Every day he said the Divine Office, and even when he had to be carried in a horse-litter he celebrated Mass, " except one day which was passed at sea and the three days immediately before his death ". After travelling for just on fifteen weeks he reached Langres in Champagne, where he died on the day of his arrival, September 25, 716. He was buried the next day, amid the sorrow not only of his companions but also of the people of the place, " for it was almost impossible not to weep at the sight of part of his company continuing their journey without their holy father, whilst part returned home to relate his death and burial, and others again lingered in grief at his grave among strangers speaking an unknown tongue ".

The immediate fate of the Bible which St Ceolfrid was taking to St Gregory II is not known ; in all probability it never reached the pope. But there is in the Bibliotheca Laurentiana at Florence a manuscript, called Codex Amiatinus, which has been known since the sixteenth century as one of the finest books in the world and as probably the purest text of the Vulgate extant. It was given by a Lombard abbot called Peter to the monastery of St Saviour on Monte Amiata, near Siena, in the ninth century and remained there till 1786 when, on the dissolution of the abbey, it was taken to Florence. For a time it was accepted that this codex was written in southern Italy during the sixth century, it having been found that the donor's inscription was partly written over, partly composed of, an older one. But the archaeologist J. B. de Rossi was not satisfied with the received reconstruction of the original dedication ; about 1885 he came to connect it with Ceolfrid. His conjectures were confirmed by the researches of the Cambridge exegete, Dr. F. J. E. Hort, and it is now established beyond doubt that Codex Amiatinus was written (not necessarily by an Englishman) in the abbey of Wearmouth or Jarrow at the beginning of the eighth century and is the very book which St Ceolfrid carried with him to give to Pope St Gregory II.

St Ceolfrid was buried at Langres ; thence his relics were later translated to Wearmouth, and finally, during the Danish invasions, to Glastonbury. His feast-day is still kept, by a commemoration on this day, in the diocese of Langres, where he is known as St Ceufroy ; it is the only place where his memory is observed liturgically.

Besides the account which Bede gives of Ceolfrid in his *Historia Abbatum*, we have the anonymous original from which he largely drew his information. Both texts are printed at the conclusion of C. Plummer's edition of the *Ecclesiastical History*, vol. i, pp. 364–404. Little can be added to these sources and to the material collected in Plummer's notes. A certain amount of further illustration, chiefly archaeological, may be obtained from Sir Henry Howorth's *The Golden Days of Early English History*, vol. ii. Of the Codex Amiatinus an exact description is given in the new critical edition of the Vulgate, vol. i (1926), pp. xx–xxvi. *Cf.* the DAC., vol. ii, cc. 3260–3267.

BD HERMAN THE CRIPPLE (A.D. 1054)

A BRIEF notice must be given to this well-known Herman for he is commonly called Blessed and his feast is observed in certain Benedictine monasteries, this being allowed by the Holy See.

He was born in Swabia of the house of Altshausen in 1013, and from his birth was not simply a cripple but was practically helpless, so deformed (*Contractus*) was he. As a child charge was taken of him by the abbey of Reichenau on an island of Lake Constance, where he spent all his forty years, being professed a monk at the age of twenty. As not infrequently happens with the physically disabled, Herman's mind was as good an instrument as his body was a useless one, and his will bent it to the service of learning and of God. Among his works was one of the earliest medieval world-chronicles, a long unfinished poem on the deadly sins, and a mathematico-astronomical treatise which begins, " Herman, the rubbish of Christ's little ones, lagging behind the apprentices of philosophy more slowly than a donkey or a slug . . .". But the unforgotten and unforgettable things that we owe to this bedridden monk are the two anthems of our Lady, " Alma Redemptoris mater " and, probably, " Salve regina ". It is only fitting that he also made, as well as astronomical, musical instruments.

This holy monk, whom his own age admired as " the wonder of the times ", died in 1054.

See *Die Kultur der Abtei Reichenau* (2 vols., 1925). The best text of the chronicle is in MGH., *Scriptores*, vol. v, and it has been translated into German. F. A. Yeldham contributed an article on Herman's fraction-tables to *Speculum*, vol. iii (1928), pp. 240 *seq.* There is a short essay on Herman in Fr C. C. Martindale's *What are Saints ?* (1939). For the authorship of " Salve regina ", see H. Thurston, *Familiar Prayers* (1953), pp. 119-125.

ST ALBERT, PATRIARCH OF JERUSALEM (A.D. 1214)

WHEN the Latin kingdom of Jerusalem was set up in 1099 by the crusaders under Godfrey de Bouillon, the Greek hierarchs were driven from their principal sees and churches and replaced by bishops from the West, whose only subjects were in the ranks of the crusaders themselves. Thus there came to be a Latin patriarch in Jerusalem, and it must be regretfully recorded that most of the prelates who held this office in crusading times were as equivocal in character as they were in position. When therefore the Patriarch Michael died in the year 1203 the canons regular of the Holy Sepulchre, supported by King Amaury II de Lusignan, petitioned Pope Innocent III to send to succeed him a prelate whose holiness and abilities were well known even in Palestine. This was Albert, Bishop of Vercelli. He belonged to a distinguished family of Parma, and after brilliant theological and legal studies had become a canon regular in the abbey of the Holy Cross at Mortara in Lombardy. When he was about thirty-five years old, namely in 1184, he was made bishop of Bobbio and almost at once translated to Vercelli. His diplomatic ability and trustworthiness caused him to be chosen as a mediator between Pope Clement III and Frederick Barbarossa. By Innocent III he was made legate in the north of Italy, and in that capacity he brought about peace between Parma and Piacenza in 1199. Innocent did not want to spare him for Jerusalem, but approved the choice of the canons ; he invested him with the *pallium* and created him his legate in Palestine, and in 1205 St Albert set out.

Already in 1187 the Saracens had retaken Jerusalem, and the see of the Latin patriarch had been moved to Akka (Ptolemais), where the Frankish king had set up his court.   At Akka accordingly St Albert established himself, and set out to gain the respect and trust not only of Christians but of the Mohammedans as well, which his predecessors had conspicuously failed to do.   As patriarch and legate he took a foremost part in the ecclesiastical and civil politics of the Levant, and over a period of nine years had to deal with a variety of matters which exercised his patience and prudence to the utmost ; in the first place and continually he was faced with the almost impossible task of keeping the peace between the Frankish leaders and their followers, within the factions themselves, and between the invaders and the natives of the country.   But Albert is best remembered now for a quite different work.   Between 1205 and 1210 St Brocard, prior of the hermits living on Mount Carmel, asked him to embody the life they were leading in a rule for the observance of himself and his subjects.   This St Albert did in a document of sixteen very short and definite " chapters ".   He provided for complete obedience to an elected superior ; a separate dwelling for each hermit, with a common oratory ; manual work for all ; long fasts and perpetual abstinence from flesh-meat ; and daily silence from Vespers till after Terce.   " Let each hermit remain in or near his cell, meditating day and night on the law of the Lord and persevering in prayer, unless engaged in some legitimate occupation."   This rule was confirmed by Pope Honorius III in 1226, and modified by Innocent IV twenty years later.   Whoever may have been the founder of the Carmelite Order, there is no doubt that St Albert of Jerusalem, an Augustinian canon, was its first legislator.

Innocent III summoned St Albert to the forthcoming council of the Lateran ; but he did not live to be present at that great assembly, which opened in November 1215.   For twelve months he faithfully supported the pope's hopeless efforts to get back Jerusalem, and then his life was suddenly and violently cut short. He had found it necessary to depose from his office the master of the Hospital of the Holy Ghost at Akka, and the man was nursing his resentment.   On the feast of the Exaltation of the Cross in 1214 St Albert officiated at a procession in the church of the Holy Cross at Akka, and in the course of it he was attacked and stabbed to death by the deposed hospitaller.   His feast was first introduced among the Carmelites in 1411.   The anomaly to which the Bollandists draw attention by which he was not honoured liturgically in his own order no longer exists, for the Canons Regular of the Lateran now keep his feast on April 8.

A short early Life of St Albert is printed with ample prolegomena in the *Acta Sanctorum*, April, vol. i.   See also the *Analecta Ordinis Carmelitarum Discalceatorum*, vol. iii (1926), pp. 212 *seq. ;* and DTC., vol. i, cc. 662–663.   Some other data are supplied by B. Zimmerman, *Monumenta historica Carmelitarum* (1907), pp. 277–281.   The rule compiled by St Albert is also edited in this last-named work, pp. 20–114 ; and see Fr François de Ste-Marie, *La Règle du Carmel et son esprit* (1949).

ST SERGIUS OF RADONEZH, ABBOT   (A.D. 1392)

WHEN in 1940 the Holy See authorized a liturgical calendar for the use of the few Russian Catholics it included, among other Slav modifications of the Byzantine calendar, the feasts of some thirty Russian saints, twenty-one of whom had not previously figured in any calendar in use today among Catholics.   These last all lived after the trouble between Rome and Constantinople in 1054. Their admission to Catholic recognition is a further example of the Holy See's practical judgement that the separation of the Eastern Orthodox Church was not fully consummated till long after the excommunication of the patriarch Cerularius of Constantinople in that year, and in any case the consummation became complete in different places at different times. The choice of these saints, as Father Cyril Korolevsky has remarked (in *Eastern Churches Quarterly*, July 1946, p. 394), " based upon impartial judgement, does not exclude the possibility of still other Russian saints being admitted when more progress has been made in the study of Slav hagiography ".

According to Father Korolevsky this has no connexion, whether direct or indirect, with canonization. " When a dissident Eastern church [or part thereof] comes into the Catholic Church she brings into it all her rites and all her liturgy ; so also her menology or liturgical calendar. Only what is directly or indirectly against faith is excluded—but this does not prevent the need for there being well-chosen critical standards for the moral, historical and hagiographical aspects, so that the inclusion or exclusion of certain saints in a Catholic calendar can be decided upon, and so that the position of others can be submitted to fresh examination in accordance with developments in hagiographical studies." This of course is true. Nevertheless, from the point of view of the Church's present practice, it would canonically seem to be a case either of equivalent (" equipollent ") canonization or of confirmation of *cultus*.

Of these twenty-one Russians, the best known and most important is certainly St Sergius of Radonezh, a monk. In its earlier days the great centres of Russian monasticism were in or near the towns ; but the Tartar invasion of the thirteenth century destroyed the urban culture of the southern part of the country, and the state of the monasteries suffered accordingly. Many of them continued to exist, but their life was weak and degenerate, and those men looking for a more perfect life began to move out into the country, particularly to the vast solitudes of the northern forests. These sylvan hermits were called *pustiniky*, that is to say, men of the wilderness. St Sergius of Radonezh is often looked on as the beginner of this movement. Actually he was only one in a general movement that broke out in several places simultaneously and gave rise to a number of new centres of monastic life. But if only one among many, he was the outstanding figure, and many regard him as the most resplendent of all Russian saints. And he was not only a great monk. The imposition of Tartar sovereignty and the continuance of waves of invasion, massacre and plunder (they went on from 1237 for a century) had reduced the Russian people to the depths of misery and demoralization ; and St Sergius probably more than any other single man was able by his example and influence to unify them in the face of their oppressors and to restore their self-respect and trust in God. The historian Kluchevsky declared that the Russians owe their liberation to the moral education and spiritual influence of Sergius of Radonezh.

He was born into a noble family round about 1315 near Rostov, and was christened Bartholomew ; and of three boys he seems to have been the least bright and quick. This preyed on his mind, so that when a monk whom he had met in the fields asked him what gift he desired, he replied that he wanted to be able to learn to read and write, especially in order to study the Bible. Whereupon the monk gave him a piece of sweet-tasting bread to eat, and from that hour he could read and write, as the biographer tells us.

This was the time of the beginning of the growth of the principality of Moscow, one step in which was the destruction of the power and influence of Rostov, and among the victims of this policy were Bartholomew's parents, Cyril and Mary. When he was still little more than a boy the whole family had to flee, and eventually found a refuge in the little village of Radonezh, fifty miles north-east of Moscow. Henceforward they had to live the life, not of nobles, but of peasant farmers working in the fields. Then, in 1335, his parents being dead, Bartholomew carried out his long-cherished plan of pursuing a solitary life. He was accompanied by his widowed brother, Stephen.

The place they chose for their hermitage was a piece of rising ground called Makovka, in the forest and several miles from the nearest neighbour. They built a hut and a chapel of timber, and at their request the metropolitan of Kiev sent a priest to dedicate it to the Most Holy Trinity, a very unusual dedication in Russia at that time. Shortly afterwards Stephen went away to live in a monastery at Moscow, and for years the now completely solitary Bartholomew almost disappears from sight.

His biographer tells us of onslaughts by demonic powers successfully beaten off, of threatening wild beasts reduced to docility, of hunger and hard tillage, of nights of prayer and growth in holiness. It is all very reminiscent of the early desert fathers. But there is one important point of difference. We in the West, associating the eremitical life chiefly with St Antony and other saints of Egypt and Syria, think of one of its hardships in terms of sandy and rocky wastes, of fierce heat and lack of water. For Bartholomew, or Sergius as we may now call him, for he had received the monastic tonsure from a visiting abbot, it was very different: his physical foes were ice and snow, fierce winds and lashing rain and dripping trees. The attitude of these hermits to wild nature has been likened to that of St Francis of Assisi. Paul of Obnorsk made friends with the birds, St Sergius with bears, and he called fire and light his friends (as well he might). But physically they were of a different type from Francis (at any rate as shown in his later representations), a big strong northern peasant type, bearded, sparing of speech and gesture. St Sergius " smells of fresh fir wood ".

As in so many other similar instances, it was only a matter of time before the young hermit's reputation spread and disciples gathered round him. Each built his own hut, and the monastery of the Holy Trinity had begun. When they numbered twelve, at their request and by direction of the nearest bishop, Sergius agreed to be their abbot ; he was ordained priest at Pereyaslav Zalesky, and there he offered the Bloodless Sacrifice for the first time. " Brethren ", he said, epitomizing a whole chapter of the Rule of St Benedict, " pray for me. I am completely ignorant, and I have received a talent from on high for which I shall have to give an account and of the flock committed to me."

The monastery flourished in all but worldly goods and increased in numbers, among its recruits being the archimandrite of a monastery at Smolensk. The forest was cleared, a village grew up and, most unwelcome, a road was beaten out along which visitors began to arrive. And in all this development the abbot remembered that he was only first among equals, and set a shining example of assiduity whether at work or in the church.

Then the question arose which of the two forms of monastic life prevalent in the East should be followed at the Holy Trinity. Hitherto the monks had followed the individual pattern, " hermits in community ", each having a separate free-

standing cell and plot of ground. Sergius, however, was in favour of properly
cenobitical, communal, life, and in 1354 this reform was carried out, partly as a
result of a personal letter of recommendation of this course from the oecumenical
patriarch at Constantinople, Philotheus. Unhappily this led to trouble. Some
of the monks were discontented at the change, and found a leader in Sergius's
brother Stephen, who had come back to the monastery. The upshot was that,
one Saturday after Vespers, whereat there had been an " incident ", St Sergius,
rather than quarrel with his brother, quietly left the monastery and did not return.
He settled down by the river Kerzhach, near the monastery of Makrish.

But some of the brethren of the Holy Trinity soon followed him there, and the
parent monastery began to degenerate, so that the Metropolitan Alexis at Moscow
sent two archimandrites with a message asking St Sergius to return. This he did,
after appointing an abbot for the new settlement at the Kerzhach, and after four
years' absence he arrived back at the Holy Trinity where the brethren came out
to meet him, " so filled with joy that some of them kissed the father's hands, others
his feet, while others caught hold of his clothing and kissed that ".

Like St Bernard of Clairvaux two centuries earlier, and like other holy monks
in East and West before and since, St Sergius came to be consulted by the great
ones of church and state ; he was appealed to as a peace-maker and arbitrator, and
more than one vain attempt was made to get him to accept the primatial see of the
Russian church. Then, between 1367 and 1380, came the great " show-down "
between Dmitry Donskoy, Prince of Moscow, and Khan Mamai, leader of the
Tartar overlords. Dmitry was faced with making a decision of final defiance which,
should it fail, would bring greater miseries on Russia than it had ever known
before. He went to ask the advice of St Sergius, and St Sergius blessed him and
said, " It is your duty, sir, to care for the flock which God has entrusted to you.
Go forth against the heathen, and conquer in the might of God's arm. And may
you return in safety, giving God the glory."

So Prince Dmitry set out, accompanied by two of Sergius's monks who had
formerly been fighting men. At the last moment, seeing the enemy's strength, he
again hesitated. But at that moment arrived a messenger from St Sergius, saying,
" Do not fear, sir. Go forward with faith against the foe's ferocity. God will
be with you." And so on September 8, 1380, was fought the battle of Kulikovo
Polye, which has an equal significance for Russia with Tours and Poitiers for western
Europe (and in reverse, Kossovo for the Balkans nine years later) : for the Tartars
were beaten and scattered. " At that same time the blessed Sergius with his
brethren was praying to God for victory. And within an hour of the overthrow
of the heathen he had announced to the community what had happened—for he
was a seer."

Thus did Sergius of Radonezh have a decisive part in beginning the break-down
of Tartar power in Russia. But he was not then allowed to remain in his monastery
in peace, for his services were required for both political and ecclesiastical missions :
the one particularly to help on peace and concord amid the rivalries of the Russian
princes, the other particularly in connection with other monastic foundations to
which his own community gave rise in one way or another. And it is recorded
of all these journeyings that he made them on foot.

His biographer speaks in general terms of Sergius's " many incomprehensible
miracles " but particularizes only a few marvels in the course of his narrative,
emphasizing that the saint commanded reticence about these things. But he gives

a clear and convincing account of a vision of the all-holy Mother of God (one of the earliest recorded in Russian hagiography), when with the apostles Peter and John she appeared to Sergius and another monk and assured him of the flourishing future that was before his monastery. The objectiveness of this vision is characteristic of Russian hagiology : we hear rarely of rapts and ecstasies but rather of the Holy Spirit enabling people to see realities, whether earthly or heavenly, hidden from the eyes of those less holy.

Six months before his death St Sergius saw his approaching end. He resigned his office, appointed a successor, and was then taken ill for the first time in his life. " As his soul was about to leave his body, he received the sacred Body and Blood, supported in the arms of his disciples ; and, raising his hands to Heaven with a prayer on his lips, he gave up his pure and holy spirit to the Lord, in the year 1392, September 25, probably at the age of seventy-eight."

In the words of Dr Zernov, " It is difficult to define exactly what made people crowd round St Sergius. He was neither an eloquent preacher nor a man of great learning, and although there were several cases when people were cured by his prayers yet he could not be described as a popular healer. It was primarily the quality of his personality which attracted everybody to him. It was the warmth of his loving attention which made him so indispensable to others. He possessed those gifts which they lacked, he had the confidence in God and trust in men which the world around him was seeking in vain, and without which it could not find rest." Like so many monks in Christian history from the earliest to the latest times, St Sergius looked on direct active service for others as part of his monastic vocation. And so he, like them, was sought out by high and low as a healer of soul and body, a friend of those who suffer, as one who fed the hungry, defended the unprotected, and counselled the wavering. The emphasis of these northern monks was laid particularly on poverty, both personal and corporate, and solitude, so far as a communal life and the requirements of brotherly charity would allow. Sergius urged them " to keep before their eyes the example of those great light-bearers the monks of Christian antiquity, who while still in this world lived like the angels : such men as Antony, Euthymius, Sabas. Plain men and monarchs came to them ; they healed disease and helped the suffering ; they fed the needy and were the widows' and orphans' treasure-house."

The body of St Sergius was enshrined in the principal church of his monastery, where it remained until the revolution of 1917. The monastery was then forcibly closed by the bolshevists, and the saint's relics deposited in the local " antireligious museum ". In 1945 permission was given to the authorities of the Russian Orthodox Church to reopen the monastery, and the relics were restored. The Russians mention St Sergius of Radonezh in the preparation of the holy things at the Eucharistic Liturgy.

There is a large manuscript literature of Russian saints' lives, of which the medieval ones belong to three distinct areas. Those of *Kiev and the Ukraine* are the earliest, and are concerned particularly with the " holy princes " and the " holy monks ". The monastery of the Caves at Kiev led in this work, and there was produced the first *paterik*, that is, a collection of short lives of saints concerned with one particular district or monastery. But there are extant only two detailed lives of pre-Mongol saints, *viz.* of St Theodosius and of St Abraham of Smolensk. After the Tartar conquest a new hagiographical " school " developed in the *North*, with its centres at Novgorod and further north. Its accounts are distinguished by their shortness and austerity of manner, often containing no more than is said in the proper office " hymn ". The third, *Central*, school grew up around Moscow with that city's rise to power, and it eventually popularized the " dressing-up " of a few facts with devotional rhetoric and edifying commonplaces, in the manner so familiar in the medieval West.   It was in this form that the lives were in the sixteenth century collected into the *Cety Miney* (" Menology for Reading ").   Though these accounts were often written by contemporaries and friends of their subjects, they are nevertheless generally conventional and uninformative, lacking in personal and historical information—Russian hagiography has indeed been aptly likened to Russian eikonography.   Most of these ancient documents were carefully studied, edited and printed during the nineteenth century ; but this work being in Russian it is still virtually unknown outside Slavonic-speaking lands, and the Western contribution to Russian hagiology is negligible.   It is regrettable that the Bollandist fathers have not extended their work in Byzantine hagiography further north-east. The notices of Russian saints in their *Acta Sanctorum*, volume xi of October, *Annus ecclesiasticus graeco-slavicus*, were the work of a Russian, Father Ivan Martynov (d. 1894), and have been subjected to unfavourable criticism ; but this he in a measure met by anticipation in his explanation of his method of work.   A far better work is said to be that by an Old-Catholic priest, L. Götz, *Das kiewer Höhlenkloster als Kulturzentrum des vormongolischen Russlands* (1904).   So far as St Sergius of Radonezh is concerned, his biography was written at length, and soberly if rather conventionally, by one of his own monks, Epiphanius the Wise.   This work was shortened and rewritten in the fifteenth century by a Serbian monk, Pakhomius, whose version is still current.   We are fortunate to have in English a book by an Orthodox writer, Dr Nicholas Zernov, on *St Sergius, Builder of Russia* (1939) ; the third part of this book is an English translation of the Pakhomian life, made by Miss Adeline Delafeld from Professor Fedotov's modern Russian version of the original.   There is a still more abbreviated version, by Helen Iswolsky, in G. P. Fedotov's *Treasury of Russian Spirituality* (1950).   For Russian saints in general, there is an excellent series of articles by Mrs E. Behr-Sigel in *Irenikon*, vol. xii, nos. 3 and 6, vol. xiii, nos. 1 and 3, vol. xiv, no. 4, and vol. xv, no. 6 (1935–38), to which the present writer is indebted for the substance of this note.   These articles, with additions, were published in book form by Editions du Cerf, in 1950, *Prière et Sainteté dans l'Église russe*.   See also articles by Arseniev in *Der christliche Osten* (1939) and by Danzas in *Russie et Chrétienté*, no. 3 of 1937, and *Menologium der Orthodox-Katholischen Kirche des Morgenlandes* (1900), by Alexis Maltsev.   The pertinent parts of vol. iii of Leroy-Beaulieu's *La Russie et l'empire des Tsars* (Eng. trans., 1896) are superficial and misleading in the light of later knowledge.   See, too, Sipiaguin, *Aux sources de la piété russe*, Irenikon Collection, vol. i, no. 2 (1927), for the Kievan saints.   The so-called *Chronicle of Nestor*, often referred to in early Russian ecclesiastical history, is now generally called the " Russian Primary Chronicle " (ed. S. H. Cross, 1930 ; contains the Kiev *paterik*). In 1946 there was published G. P. Fedotov's *The Russian Religious Mind : Kievan Christianity*.   This is valuable for SS. Abraham of Smolensk, Antony and Theodosius Pechersky, Boris and Gleb, Cyril of Turov and Vladimir and for the pre-Mongol saints in general. In reading and writing of such men as St Sergius and St Theodosius one is very conscious of how suited to Alban Butler's style they would have been, and of how he would have delighted in men so obviously absorbed in " the one thing necessary " : but no doubt he had not even heard the names of most of them.   The only Russians to whom he accorded a notice were SS. Romanus and David (*i.e.* Boris and Gleb) on July 24.   In the course of it he mentions St Olga, St Vladimir, St Antony Pechersky, St Sergius and the revered prince Alexander Nevsky ; but it is only to be expected that Butler's information about " the Russians (now called Muscovites) " is far from satisfactory.   Two valuable books were published in 1953 : *Essai sur la sainteté en Russie*, by Fr Ivan Kologrivof, and *Russische Heiligenlegenden*, translations and notes by E. Benz and others.

ST VINCENT STRAMBI, Bishop of Macerata and Tolentino (A.D. 1824)

VINCENT STRAMBI, the son of a druggist in Civita Vecchia, was born on January 1, 1745.   He seems to have been a very lively child who loved to play boyish pranks, but amongst these pranks we are told that he would take off his own overcoat or his shoes to give to some little ragamuffin whom he saw going barefoot.   His parents, seconding the religious bent of mind which soon became manifest in

Vincent, decided that he should study for the diocesan priesthood.   However, when making a retreat before his ordination, he came under the influence of St Paul-of-the-Cross, the founder of the Passionists, and on September 20, 1768, after a painful struggle with parental opposition, he entered the noviceship of that congregation.   Important charges were confided to him almost from the outset. After many public missions attended with immense gain of souls, he was made professor of theology and sacred eloquence, but from the age of thirty-five onwards he filled one post of authority after another in the congregation.   He was made provincial in 1781, and after twenty years of labour, during which he had to contend with endless difficulties caused by the distracted state of Italy, he was in 1801, sorely against his will, appointed bishop of Macerata and Tolentino.

The indefatigable zeal for God's glory and for regular discipline which St Vincent displayed as a bishop led to a wonderful renewal of fervour both among clergy and laity in that part of Italy.   Refusing to take the oath of allegiance to Napoleon in 1808, he was expelled from his diocese and had to carry on the administration as best he could by letter.   After the fall of Napoleon in 1813, his return to Macerata was marked by popular demonstrations of joy : but his troubles were not at an end.   After Napoleon's escape from Elba, Murat, with an army of 30,000 men, made Macerata his headquarters.   His troops were defeated by the Austrians, and would have sacked the town in their disorderly retreat had not Bishop Strambi gone out, like another St Leo, and pleaded with their commander. The intrepidity of this devoted pastor was successful both with Murat and with the Austrians, who followed in pursuit ; to him alone Macerata owed its safety. Later there was an outbreak of typhus and a dearth of provisions which bordered on famine, but in all these emergencies the bishop set an heroic example.   In the fierce resentment excited by some of his reforms his life is said to have been more than once attempted.   On the death of Pope Pius VII he resigned his see, and at the instance of Leo XII, who was Strambi's devoted friend, he took up his quarters at the Quirinal, where he acted as the pope's confidential adviser.   During all these vicissitudes he had never relaxed anything of the austerity of his private life ; but his strength was now exhausted, and, as Bd Anna Maria Taigi, his penitent, had prophesied, he received holy communion for the last time on December 31, and passed away on his seventy-ninth birthday, on January 1, 1824.   St Vincent Strambi was canonized in 1950.

See biographies in Italian by Father Stanislaus (1925) and Mgr F. Cento (1950), and in French by the same (1950) and by Father Joachim (1925).

26 : ST FRANCIS OF CAMPOROSSO   (*See pp. 586-7*)

THE MARTYRS OF NORTH AMERICA   (A.D. 1642–1649)

THE good intentions of the explorer James Cartier, to whom redounds the credit of having tried in 1534 to bring Christianity to Canada, as well as the later efforts of Samuel Champlain who founded Quebec in 1608, remained without permanent result.   Nevertheless by the wish of the French King Henry IV, in this same year 1608, two Jesuits, Peter Biard and Ennemond Massé, had sailed from Europe, and on their arrival in Acadia (Nova Scotia) began work among the Souriquois Indians at Port Royal (now Annapolis).   Their first task was to learn the language.   Massé went into the woods to live with these nomad tribes and to pick up what he could of their speech, while Biard stayed at the settlement and bribed with food and sweets the few Indians who remained, in order to induce them to teach him the words he required. After a year they were able to draw up a catechism and to begin to teach. They found one of the two tribes they had to do with—the Etchemins—averse to Christianity, and the Souriquois, though more favourably disposed, lacking in the religious sense. All were given to drunkenness and sorcery, and all practised polygamy. Nevertheless by the time the missionaries were joined by fresh colonists and by two more Jesuit priests, as well as by a lay-brother, the work of evangelization seemed well inaugurated. But in 1613 a raid was made from the sea by the piratical English captain of a merchant vessel, who descended with his crew on the unfortunate inhabitants, pillaged the settlement, and set adrift fifteen of the colony, including Massé. He then sailed back to Virginia with Biard and Quentin on board. Eventually the missionaries found their way back to France, but their work of preaching the gospel was brought to a standstill.

In the meantime Champlain, now governor of New France, was continually imploring that good religious should be sent out, and in 1615 several Franciscans arrived at Tadroussac. They laboured heroically, but finding that they could not obtain enough men or enough money to convert the Indians, they invited the Jesuits to come to their assistance. In 1625 three priests of the Society of Jesus landed in Quebec in time to meet the Indian traders who had just murdered the friar Vial and his catechist and had thrown them into that part of the rapids which is still known as Sault-au-Récollet. Of the three new-comers one was Massé, returning to his former labours, but the two others, Brébeuf and Charles Lalemant, were new to the work. When John de Brébeuf entered the Jesuit seminary in Rouen, at the age of twenty-four, his constitution was so feeble that he could not pursue the usual courses of study, nor could he teach for any length of time. It seems almost incredible that this tuberculous invalid should have developed within a very few years into the giant apostle of the Hurons, whose powers of endurance and courage were so outstanding that the Indians who killed him drank his blood to infuse themselves with his valour.

As Brébeuf was unable to trust himself at once to the Hurons he wintered with the Algonquins, learning their speech and their customs under conditions of appalling discomfort, dirt and occasionally of hunger. The following year he went with a Franciscan and a fellow Jesuit to the Huron country. On the journey of 600 miles they were obliged, owing to the rapids, to carry their canoes thirty-five times and to drag them repeatedly, and all their baggage had to be carried by hand at these numerous portages. The Jesuits settled at Tod's Point, but Brébeuf's companions were soon recalled and Brébeuf was left alone with the Hurons, whose habit of living, less migratory than that of other tribes, gave the missionaries a better prospect of evangelizing them. He soon discovered that he was a source of constant suspicion to his hosts, who blamed him for every mishap that befell them and had a superstitious terror of the cross on the top of his cabin. During that period he failed to make a single convert among them. His stay was, however, cut short. The colony was in distress : the English closed the St Lawrence to all relief from France and obliged Champlain to surrender. Colonists and missionaries were forced to return to their own country, and Canada became, for the first time and for a short period, a British colony. Before long the indefatigable Champlain brought the matter to the law courts in London, and was able to prove so conclusively that the seizure of the colony was unjust that in 1632 Canada reverted to France.

Immediately the Franciscans were invited to return, but they had not enough men, and the Jesuits took up the work of evangelization once more. Father Le Jeune, who was placed in charge of the mission, came to New France in 1632, Antony Daniel soon followed, and in 1633 Brébeuf and Massé arrived with Champlain, the governor. Le Jeune, who had been a Huguenot in early life, was a man of extraordinary ability and of wide vision. He considered the mission not merely a matter for a few priests and their supporters, but as an enterprise in which every French Catholic ought to be interested. He conceived the plan of keeping the entire nation informed of the actual conditions in Canada by a series of graphic descriptions, beginning with his own personal experiences on the voyage and his first impressions of the Indians. The earliest reports were written and despatched to France within two months and were published at the end of the year. These missives, known as " The Jesuit Relations ", continued to pass from New to Old France almost without interruption, and often embodied the letters of other Jesuits, such as Brébeuf and Perrault. They awakened interest not only in France but in all Europe. Immediately on their appearance a stream of emigration began to flow from the old country, and religious—both men and women—soon came to labour among the Indians, as well as to render spiritual help to the colonists. Father Antony Daniel, who was to be Brébeuf's companion for some time, was, like him, a Norman by birth. He was studying law when he decided to become a Jesuit, and previous to his departure for the New World had been in contact with those who had much to tell about the Canadian mission.

When the Hurons came to Quebec for their annual market they were delighted to meet Brébeuf and to be addressed by him in their own language. They wished him to go back with them, and he was eager to do so, but they were frightened at the last moment by an Ottawa chieftain, and for the time refused. The following year, however, when they came again, they agreed to take Brébeuf, Daniel and another priest named Darost, and after a most uncomfortable journey in which they were robbed and abandoned by their guides, the three Jesuits reached their destination, where the Hurons built a hut for them. Brébeuf gave his companions lessons in Huron, and Daniel, who proved himself an apt pupil, could soon lead the children in chanting the Lord's Prayer when Brébeuf held assemblies in his cabin. Religion, as the Indians understood it, was solely based on fear, and the missionaries found it desirable to start with what they could apprehend. As Brébeuf writes : " We began our catechizing with the memorable truth that their souls, which are immortal, all go after death either to paradise or hell. It is thus we approach them in public or in private. I explained that it rested with them during life to decide what their future lot was to be." A great drought parched the land and threatened famine : the sorcerers could do nothing and the Indians were in despair. Brébeuf, to whom they appealed, told them to pray, and began a novena, at the close of which rain fell in abundance and the crops were saved. The Hurons were impressed, but the older members held fast to their old traditions and the middle-aged were indifferent and fickle. The Jesuits decided never to confer baptism on adults without long preparation and proof of constancy, but they baptized the sick near to death—of whom there were always a number, owing to the prevalence of epidemics. The children, on the other hand, were teachable and well disposed, though vice was so general that it was well-nigh impossible to preserve them from the contamination of their elders. It was therefore resolved to establish a seminary at Quebec for Indians, and Daniel started back with two or three children to found the new institution which became the centre of the mission-aries' hopes. Daniel himself was not only the children's father, but their teacher, nurse and playmate. For a short time Brébeuf was again alone among the Hurons and he then wrote for those who were to come to the Huron mission an instruction which afterwards became famous.

In 1636 arrived five more Jesuits, two of whom were destined to be numbered among the martyrs—Jogues, who was to become the apostle of a new Indian nation, and Garnier. Isaac Jogues had been born at Orléans, and after entering the Jesuit novitiate at Rouen at the age of seventeen had studied at the royal college of La Flèche, which Descartes considered one of the first schools of Europe. After his ordination he was appointed to Canada and sailed with the governor of New France, Huault de Montmagny. Charles Garnier was a Parisian, educated at the Clermont college. At nineteen he became a Jesuit, and after his ordination in 1635 he volun-teered for the Canadian mission. He sailed with Jogues in 1636. Garnier was then thirty years of age, Jogues was twenty-nine.

While Brébeuf was alone with the Hurons he had gone through the excitement of a threatened invasion by their bitter enemies the Iroquois, and had to witness the horrible sight of an Iroquois tortured to death. He could do nothing to avert this ; but, as he had baptized the captive shortly before, he was determined to stand by to encourage him. He saw an aspect of Indian character which was a revelation to him. " Their mockery of their victim was fiendish. The more they burned his flesh and crushed his bones, the more they flattered and even caressed him. It was an all-night tragedy." Brébeuf was witnessing what he himself would afterwards suffer. Five of the new-comers went almost at once to join Father de Brébeuf, and Jogues, who had not been intended at first for the Huron mission, followed a few months later. An epidemic which was raging in the village prostrated most of the missionaries for a time, and although even the convalescents ministered to the Indian sick, the village sorcerer spread the suspicion—which they were only temporarily able to allay—that the foreigners were the cause of the visitation.

Nevertheless in May 1637 Brébeuf felt free to write to the father general of his order : " We are gladly heard, we have baptized more than 200 this year, and there is hardly a village that has not invited us to go to it. Besides, the result of this pestilence and of these reports has been to make us better known to this people ; and at last it is understood from our whole conduct that we have not come hither to buy skins or to carry on any traffic, but solely to teach them, and to procure for them their souls' health and in the end happiness which will last for ever." Again, however, the hopes of the missionaries received a check in consequence of a new outbreak of suspicion, culminating in a tribal council of twenty-eight villages which was practically a trial of the priests. Brébeuf defended himself and his companions with spirit, but they were informed that they must die. They drew up a last statement for their superiors, and Brébeuf invited the Indians to his farewell feast. There he harangued them about life after death, and so wrought upon them that he was adopted by them, and his companions were left in peace.

A second mission was established at Teanaustaye, and Lalemant was appointed in charge of both stations, whilst Brébeuf at his own wish undertook the care of a new location, called Sainte-Marie, at some distance from the Indian villages. This settlement acted as a central bureau for missions and as a headquarters for priests and their attendants, as well as for the Frenchmen who served as labourers or soldiers. A hospital and a fort were erected and a cemetery established, and for five years the pioneers worked perseveringly, often undertaking long and perilous expeditions to other tribes—to the Petun or Tobacco Indians, the Ojibways, and to the Neuters north of Lake Erie—by whom they were more often than not very badly received. The first adult to be baptized (in 1637) was followed by over eighty, two years later, and by sixty in 1641. It did not seem much, but it proved that genuine conversion was possible. Lalemant, in his relation for 1639, wrote, " We have sometimes wondered whether we could hope for the conversion of this country without the shedding of blood ", and at least two of the missionaries, Brébeuf and Jogues, were praying constantly to be allowed a share in the glory of suffering—if not of martyrdom. In 1642 the Huron country was in great distress : harvests were poor, sickness abounded, and clothing was scarce. Quebec was the only source of supplies, and Jogues was chosen to lead an expedition. It reached its objective safely and started back well supplied with goods for the mission, but the Iroquois, the bitter enemies of the Hurons, and the fiercest of all Indian tribes, were on the war-path and ambushed the returning expedition. The story of the ill-treatment and torture of the captives cannot here be told. Suffice it to say that Jogues and his assistant René Goupil, besides being beaten to the ground and assailed several times with knotted sticks and fists, had their hair, beards and nails torn off and their forefingers bitten through. What grieved them far more was the cruelty practised on their Christian converts. The first of all the martyrs to suffer death was Goupil, who was tomahawked on September 29, 1642, for having made the sign of the cross on the brow of some children. This René Goupil was a remarkable man. He had tried hard to be a Jesuit and had even entered the novitiate, but his health forced him to give up the attempt. He then studied surgery and found his way to Canada, where he offered his services to the missionaries, whose fortitude he emulated.

Jogues remained a slave among the Mohawks, one of the Iroquois tribes, who, however, had decided to kill him. He owed his escape to the Dutch, who, ever since they had heard of the sufferings he and his friends were enduring, had been trying to obtain his release. Through the efforts of the governor of Fort Orange and of the governor of New Netherlands he was taken on board a vessel and, by way of England, got back to France, where his arrival roused the keenest interest. With mutilated fingers he was debarred from celebrating Mass, but Pope Urban VIII granted him special permission to do so, saying, " It would be unjust that a martyr for Christ should not drink the blood of Christ ". Early in 1644 Jogues was again at sea on his way back to New France. Arriving at Montreal, then recently founded, he began to work among the Indians of that neighbourhood, pending the time when he could return to the Hurons, a journey which was becoming yearly more perilous because Iroquois Indians were everywhere along the route. Unexpectedly the Iroquois sent an embassy to Three Rivers to sue for peace : Jogues, who was present at the conference, noticed that no representative came from the chief village, Ossernenon. Moreover, it was clear to him that the Iroquois only desired peace with the French—not with the Hurons. However, it was considered desirable to send a deputation from New France to meet the Iroquois chiefs at Ossernenon, and Jogues was selected as ambassador, together with John Bourdon, who represented the government of the colony.

They went by the route of Lake Champlain and Lake George, and after spending a week in confirming the pact they returned to Quebec, Jogues leaving behind a box of religious articles because he was resolved later to return to the Mohawks as a missionary, and was glad to be relieved of one of his packages. This box proved the immediate cause of his martyrdom. The Mohawks had had a bad crop, and soon after Jogues's departure an epidemic broke out which they attributed to a devil concealed in the box. So when they heard that Jogues was paying a third visit to their villages, they waylaid, stripped and ill-treated him and his companion Lalande. His captors were members of the Bear clan, and although the other clans tried to protect the prisoners, the Bear family refused to allow their fate to be decided in council. Some of them treacherously invited Jogues to a meal on the evening of October 18 and tomahawked him as he was entering the cabin. His head they cut off and placed on a pole facing the route by which he had come.* The following day his companion Lalande and the Huron guide were likewise tomahawked and beheaded, their bodies being afterwards thrown into the river. John Lalande was, like René Goupil, a *donné* or oblate of the mission. The martyrdom of Jogues sealed the fate of the Hurons, whose only hope of peace had lain in his success as a missionary among their ferocious enemies, the Iroquois. They had begun to receive the faith in considerable numbers, and there were twenty-four missionaries working amongst them, including Father Daniel. The Hurons, in fact, were gradually becoming Christian, and with a period of peace the whole tribe would have been converted, but the Iroquois were unremitting in their hostilities. They began to attack and pillage the Huron villages, sparing no one, and on July 4, 1648, they appeared at Teanaustaye, just as Daniel had finished celebrating Mass. A great panic ensued, but the father threw himself amongst them and baptized all he could. There were so many who cried to him that he was constrained to dip his handkerchief in water and baptize them by aspersion. When he saw that the Iroquois were becoming masters of the place, instead of escaping, as his converts urged him to do, he remembered some old and sick people he had long ago prepared for baptism, and went through the cabins to encourage them to be steadfast. Then, betaking himself to the church, which he found filled with Christians, he warned them to fly while there was yet time, and went forth alone to meet the enemy. They surrounded him on all sides, covering him with arrows till he fell dead, pierced through the breast. They stripped him and threw his body into the church, which they set on fire. As the narrator of this martyrdom writes, " He could not have been more gloriously consumed than in the conflagration of such a *chapelle ardente* ".

Within a year, on March 16, 1649, the Iroquois attacked the village at which Brébeuf and Lalemant were stationed. Gabriel Lalemant was the last of the martyrs to reach New France. Two of his uncles had been Canadian missionaries, and he, after taking his vows in Paris as a Jesuit, had added a fourth vow—to sacrifice his life to the Indians—a vow which had to wait fourteen years for its fulfilment. The torture of these two missionaries was as atrocious as anything recorded in history. Even after they had been stripped naked and beaten with sticks on every part of their bodies, Brébeuf continued to exhort and encourage the Christians who were around him. One of the fathers had his hands cut off, and

* Ossernenon, the scene of these martyrdoms, was ten years later the birthplace of Kateri Tekakwitha, the Mohawk girl whose beatification is looked forward to.

to both were applied under the armpits and beside the loins hatchets heated in the fire, as well as necklaces of red-hot lance blades round their necks.   Their tormentors then proceeded to girdle them with belts of bark steeped in pitch and resin, to which they set fire.   At the height of these torments Father Lalemant raised his eyes to Heaven and with sighs invoked God's aid, whilst Father de Brébeuf set his face like a rock as though insensible to the pain.   Then, like one recovering consciousness, he preached to his persecutors and to the Christian captives until the savages gagged his mouth, cut off his nose, tore off his lips, and then, in derision of baptism, deluged him and his companion martyrs with boiling water.   Finally, large pieces of flesh were cut out of the bodies of both the priests and roasted by the Indians, who tore out their hearts before their death by means of an opening above the breast, feasting on them and on their blood, which they drank while it was still warm.

The murder of the missionaries and the havoc wrought amongst the Hurons, far from satisfying the ferocious Iroquois, only whetted their thirst for blood. Before the end of the year 1649 they had penetrated as far as the Tobacco nation, where Father Garnier had founded a mission in 1641 and where the Jesuits now had two stations.   The inhabitants of the village of Saint-Jean, hearing that the enemy was approaching, sent out their men to meet the attackers, who, however, having elicited from fugitives information of the defenceless condition of the settlement, took a roundabout way and arrived at the gates unexpectedly.   An orgy of incredible cruelty followed, in the midst of which Garnier, the only priest in the mission, hastened from place to place, giving absolution to the Christians and baptizing the children and catechumens, totally unmindful of his own fate. While thus employed he was shot down by the musket of an Iroquois.   He strove to reach a dying man whom he thought he could help, but after three attempts he collapsed, and subsequently received his death-blow from a hatchet which penetrated to the brain.   Some of his Indian converts buried him on the spot where the church had stood.

Father Noel Chabanel, the missionary companion of Garnier, was immediately recalled.   He had started on his way back with some Christian Hurons when they heard the cries of the Iroquois returning from Saint-Jean.   The father urged his followers to escape, but was too much exhausted to keep up with them.   His fate was long uncertain, but a Huron apostate eventually admitted having killed the holy man out of hatred of the Christian faith.   Chabanel was not the least heroic of the martyrs.   He possessed none of the adaptability of the rest, nor could he ever learn the language of the savages, the sight of whom, their food—everything about them—was revolting to him.   Moreover, he was tried by spiritual dryness during the whole of his stay in Canada.   Yet in order to bind himself more inviolably to the work which his nature abhorred, he made a solemn vow, in the presence of the Blessed Sacrament, to remain till death in this mission to the Indians.   Little did these noble martyrs who saw such scanty results accruing from their labours foresee that within a short time after their death the truths they proclaimed would be embraced by their very executioners, and that their own successors would visit and christianize almost every tribe with which the martyrs had been in contact.

These martyrs of North America, viz. SS. John de Brébeuf, Isaac Jogues, Antony Daniel, Gabrial Lalemant, Charles Garnier, Noel Chabanel, René Goupil and John Lalande, were canonized in 1930.   Their feast is observed

throughout the United States and Canada on this day and on March 16 by the
Society of Jesus.

The primary source of information concerning these martyrs must of course be the
letters of the missionaries themselves.   These are accessible to all and equipped with an
English translation in the great series of R. G. Thwaites, *Jesuit Relations* (73 vols., 1897–
1901).   Of the many books which provide a more compendious account may be mentioned
J. Wynne, *The Jesuit Martyrs of North America* (1925) ; E. J. Devine, *The Jesuit Martyrs
of Canada* (1925) ; and T. J. Campbell, *Pioneer Priests of North America*.   In French we
have Rigault and Goyau, *Martyrs de la Nouvelle France ;* and more especially H. Fouqueray,
Martyrs du Canada (1930), which last may be recommended for its excellent bibliography.
There are also some biographies of the individual martyrs, particularly those of Jogues,
Brébeuf, and Garnier by F. Martin.   Needless to say that many non-Catholic historians
have also paid a generous tribute of respect to these heroic missionaries, notably Francis
Parkman in *The Jesuits in North America* (1868).   More recent American works are J. A.
O'Brien, *The American Martyrs ;* F. X. Talbot, *A Saint Among the Savages* and *A Saint
Among the Hurons ;* and W. and E. M. Jury, *Sainte-Marie among the Hurons* (1953).   See
also L. Pouliot, *Étude sur les Relations des Jésuites de la Nouvelle-France* (1940) ; and R.
Latourelle, *Étude sur les écrits de S. Jean de Brébeuf* (2 vols. 1953).

SS. CYPRIAN AND JUSTINA, MARTYRS   (NO DATE)

THE legend of this St Cyprian, distinguished as " of Antioch ", is a moral tale,
utterly fabulous (if there ever were a martyred Cyprian and Justina on whom the
story was built all trace of them has been lost), composed in order to impress on
the listener or reader the powerlessness of the Devil and his angels in the face of
Christian chastity defending itself with the might of the Cross.   The tale has been
worked up from various sources, and was known at least as early as the fourth
century, for St Gregory Nazianzen identifies this Cyprian with the great St Cyprian
of Carthage ; the poet Prudentius makes the same mistake.   The story as told by
Alban Butler is as follows :

Cyprian, surnamed " the Magician ", was a native of Antioch who was brought
up in all the impious mysteries of idolatry, astrology and black magic.   In hopes
of making great discoveries in these infernal arts, he left his native country when he
was grown up and travelled to Athens, Mount Olympus in Macedonia, Argos,
Phrygia, Memphis in Egypt, Chaldaea, and the Indies, places at that time famous
for superstition and magical practices.   When Cyprian had filled his head with all
the extravagances of these schools of wickedness and delusion he stuck at no crimes,
blasphemed Christ, and committed secret murders in order to offer the blood and
inspect the bowels of children as decisive of future events ; nor did he scruple to
use his arts to overcome the chastity of women.   At that time there lived at Antioch
a lady called Justina, whose beauty drew all eyes upon her.   She was born of
heathen parents but was brought over to the Christian faith by overhearing a deacon
preaching, and her conversion was followed by that of her father and mother.   A
young pagan, Aglaïdes, fell deeply in love with her, and finding himself unable to
win her to his will he applied to Cyprian for the assistance of his art.   Cyprian was
no less enamoured of the lady than his friend, and tried every secret with which he
was acquainted to conquer her resolution.   Justina, finding herself vigorously
attacked, armed herself by prayer, watchfulness and mortification against all his
artifices and the power of his spells, suppliantly beseeching the Virgin Mary that
she would succour a virgin in danger.   Three times she overcame the assaults of
demons sent by Cyprian by blowing in their faces and making the sign of the cross.

Cyprian, finding himself worsted by a superior power, threatened his last

emissary, who was the Devil himself, that he would abandon his service. The
Devil, enraged to lose one by whom he had made so many conquests, assailed
Cyprian with the utmost fury, and he was only repulsed by Cyprian himself making
the sign of the cross. The soul of the penitent sinner was seized with a gloomy
melancholy, which brought him almost to the brink of despair, at the sight of his
past crimes. God inspired him in this perplexity to address himself to a priest
named Eusebius, who had formerly been his school-fellow, and by the advice of
this priest he was comforted and encouraged in his conversion. Cyprian, who in
the trouble of his heart had been three days without eating, by the counsel of this
director took some food, and on the following Sunday was conducted by him to
the assembly of the Christians. So much was Cyprian struck by the reverence and
devotion with which their divine worship was performed that he said of it, " I saw
the choir of heavenly men—or of angels—singing to God, adding at the end of
every verse in the psalms the Hebrew word Alleluia, so that they seemed not to be
men ".* Everyone present was astonished to see Cyprian introduced among them
by a priest, and the bishop was scarce able to believe that his conversion was sincere.
But Cyprian gave him a proof the next day by burning before his eyes all his magical
books, giving his goods to the poor, and entering himself among the catechumens.

After due instruction and preparation, he received the sacrament of baptism
from the hands of the bishop. Aglaïdes was likewise converted and baptized.
Justina herself was so moved at these wonderful examples of the divine mercy that
she cut off her hair as a sign that she dedicated her virginity to God, and disposed
of her jewels and all her possessions to the poor. Cyprian was made door-keeper
and then promoted to the priesthood, and, after the death of Anthimus the bishop,
was placed in the episcopal chair of Antioch. [No known bishop of Antioch in
Syria or Antioch in Pisidia was called either Cyprian or Anthimus.] When the
persecution of Diocletian began, Cyprian was apprehended and carried before the
governor of Phoenicia, who resided at Tyre. Justina had retired to Damascus,
her native country, which city at that time was subject to the same authority and,
falling into the hands of the persecutors, was presented to the same judge. She
was inhumanly scourged, and Cyprian was torn with iron hooks. After this they
were both sent in chains to Diocletian at Nicomedia who, upon reading the letter
of the governor of Phoenicia, without more ado commanded their heads to be struck
off. This sentence was executed upon the banks of the river Gallus, after a vain
effort had been made to slay the martyrs by boiling them in a cauldron of pitch.

This legend was widely popular, as the many texts in Latin and Greek, not to speak of
other languages, abundantly attest. Some part of the story was certainly known before the
time of St Gregory Nazianzen, for the orator, preaching about the year 379, attributes to
St Cyprian of Carthage a number of incidents which are taken from the legend of Cyprian
of Antioch. None the less no shred of evidence can be produced to justify the belief that any
such persons as Cyprian of Antioch, the quondam magician, and Justina the virgin martyr,
ever existed. See on this especially Delehaye, " Cyprien d'Antioche et Cyprien de Carthage"
in the *Analecta Bollandiana*, vol. xxxix (1921), pp. 314–332. Apart from the text of the
legend, which may be read in the *Acta Sanctorum* (September, vol. vii), and elsewhere in
other forms, the story has given rise to a considerable literature. See, for example,

* In the course of a footnote Butler here tells a story which admirably illustrates an
eighteenth-century deist's knowledge of and attitude towards Catholic worship. Lord
Bolingbroke, being one day present at Mass in the chapel at Versailles and seeing the bishop
elevate the host, was much impressed and whispered to his companion, the Marquess de ——,
" If I were king of France, I would always perform that ceremony myself " !

T. Zahn, *Cyprian von Antiochien und die deutsche Faustsage* (1882) ; R. Reitzenstein, *Cyprian der Magier* in the Göttingen *Nachrichten*, 1917, pp. 38–79 ; and Rademacher, " Griechische Quellen zur Faustsage " in the Vienna *Sitzungsberichte*, vol. 206 (1927). This legend was taken by Calderon as the theme for one of the most famous of his dramas, *El Magico Prodigioso*, and passages from this were selected by Shelley in his " Scenes from Calderon ".

ST COLMAN OF LANN ELO, Abbot (A.D. 611)

THERE are dozens of saints of the name of Colman who have been or are still venerated in Ireland ; twelve are mentioned in calendars in this month of September alone, and of them the most important one is St Colman of Lann Elo.   He belonged to a family of Meath, but was born in Glenelly in Tyrone, about the year 555.   He came under the influence of St Colmcille, who was his maternal uncle. Colman visited him at Iona, and is said to have been delivered from the perils of the voyage by his uncle's prayers.   About the year 590 land was given to him in Offaly, where he founded a monastery and so fulfilled the prophecy made by St Macanisius sixty years earlier.   (He is sometimes referred to as " Coarb of Mac-Nisse ", perhaps because he exercised some authority at Connor in Antrim, where he stayed for a time and Macanisius was buried.)   Colman's famous monastery was called Lann Elo, now Lynally.   Near the end of his life he made a pilgrimage to Clonard, where he had a vision of St Finnian, and on his return announced his approaching death to his monks.   A number of miracles of a familiar type are attributed to St Colman Elo, and to him is attributed the authorship of the tract called *Aibgitir in Chrabaid*, the Alphabet of Devotion.   He is also said to have been deprived for a while of his memory in punishment of his pride of intellect, and then to have recovered it again by a miracle.

There is both an Irish and a Latin life of St Colman Elo.   The former has been edited by C. Plummer in his *Bethada Náem nÉrenn* (Eng. trans. in vol. ii, pp. 162–176) ; and the latter by the same scholar in VSH., vol. i, pp. 258–273.   See also Canon E. Maguire, *St Barron* (1923) ; and J. Ryan, *Irish Monasticism* (1931).

ST NILUS OF ROSSANO, Abbot (A.D. 1004)

NILUS, sometimes called " the Younger ", was born of a Greek family of Magna Graecia at Rossano in Calabria about the year 910, and was baptized Nicholas.   So far from being in his youth " fervent in religious duties and in the practice of all virtues ", as Alban Butler avers, he was at least lukewarm and careless in his early life ; it has even been questioned whether the lady with whom he lived, and who bore him a daughter, was married to him.   But when he was thirty she and the child died, and this double bereavement, aided by a serious sickness, recalled him to a sense of his responsibilities and brought about a complete turning to God.   At that time there were a number of monasteries of monks of the Byzantine rite in southern Italy, and Nicholas received the habit at one of them, taking the name of Nilus.   At different times he lived in several of these monasteries, after being for a period a hermit, and became abbot of St Adrian's, near San Demetrio Corone. The reputation of his sanctity and learning was soon spread over the country and many came to him for spiritual advice.   On one occasion the archbishop, Theophylact of Reggio, with the *domesticus* Leo, many priests, and others went to him, rather desiring to try his erudition and skill than to hear any lessons for their edification.   The abbot knew their intention, but having saluted them courteously and made a short prayer with them, he put into the hands of Leo a book in which were contained certain theories concerning the small number of the elect, which seemed to the company too severe.   But the saint undertook to prove them to be clearly founded on the principles laid down not only by St Basil, St John Chrysostom, St Ephrem, St Theodore the Studite, and other fathers, but by St Paul and the gospel itself, adding at the close of his discourse, " These statements seem dreadful, but they only condemn the irregularity of your lives.   Unless you be altogether holy you will not escape everlasting torments."   One of them then asked the abbot whether Solomon were damned or saved ?   To which he replied, " What does it concern us to know whether he be saved or no ?   But it is needful for you to reflect that Christ pronounces damnation against all persons who commit impurity."   This he said knowing that the person who put the question was addicted to that vice.   And he added, " I would know whether *you* will be damned or saved.   As for Solomon, the Bible makes no mention of his repentance, as it does of that of Manasses."   Euphraxus, a vain and haughty nobleman, was sent as governor of Calabria from the imperial court of Constantinople.   St Nilus made him no presents upon his arrival, as other prelates did, and so the governor sought every occasion of mortifying the servant of God.   But shortly after, falling sick, he sent for Nilus and begged his pardon and prayers, and asked to receive the monastic habit from his hands.   St Nilus refused a long time to give it him, saying, " Your baptismal vows are sufficient for you.   Penance requires no new vows but a sincere change of heart and life."   Euphraxus was not satisfied and continued so urgent that the saint at length gave him the habit.   The governor made all his slaves free, distributed his estate among the poor, and died three days later with holy resignation.

About the year 981 the Saracen incursions into south Italy compelled St Nilus to flee, and with many of his monks this representative of Eastern monachism threw himself upon the hospitality of the headquarters of Western monachism at Monte Cassino.   They were received " as if St Antony had come from Alexandria, or their own great St Benedict from the dead ", and after living in the house for a time and celebrating their Greek offices in the church, the Benedictine abbot, Aligern, bestowed upon the fugitives the monastery of Vallelucio.   There they lived for fifteen years, and then moved to Serperi, near Gaeta.   When in the year 998 the Emperor Otto III came to Rome to expel Philagathos, Bishop of Piacenza, whom the senator Crescentius had set up as antipope against Gregory V, St Nilus went to intercede with the pope and emperor that the antipope might be treated with mildness.   Philagathos (" John XVI ") was a Calabrian like himself, and Nilus had tried in vain to dissuade him from his schism and treason.   The abbot was listened to with respect, but he was not able to do much to modify the atrocious cruelty with which the aged antipope was treated.   When a prelate was sent to make an explanation to Nilus, who had protested vigorously against the injuries done to the helpless Philagathos, he pretended to fall asleep in order to avoid an argument about it.   Some time after Otto paid a visit to the *laura* of St Nilus ; he was surprised to see his monastery consisting of poor scattered huts, and said, " These men who live in tents as strangers on earth are truly citizens of Heaven." Nilus conducted the emperor first to the church, and after praying there entertained him in his cell.   Otto pressed the saint to accept some spot of ground in his dominions, promising to endow it.   Nilus thanked him and answered, " If my brethren are truly monks our divine Master will not forsake them when I am gone ". In taking leave the emperor vainly asked him to accept some gift : St Nilus, laying his hand upon Otto's breast, said, " The only thing I ask of you is that you would save your soul. Though emperor, you must die and give an account to God, like other men."

In 1004 (or 1005) Nilus set out to visit a monastery south of Tusculum and on the journey was taken ill among the Alban hills. Here he had a vision of our Lady, in which he learned that this was to be the abiding home of his monks. From Gregory, Count of Tusculum, he got a grant of land on the lower slopes of Monte Cavo and sent for his community to establish themselves there. But before the work could be begun he was dead. It was carried on by his successors, especially by St Bartholomew, who died about 1050; the monastery of Grottaferrata (of which St Nilus is generally accounted the first abbot as well as founder) has existed from that day to this, peopled by Italo-Greek monks, who thus have maintained the Byzantine life and liturgy within a few miles of the heart, not merely of the Latin, but of the Catholic world.

A life of serious value as a historical source, which was written in Greek by one of his disciples, is printed with a Latin translation in the *Acta Sanctorum*, September, vol. vii. This biography has more than once been translated into Italian, *e.g.* by G. Minasi, *San Nilo di Calabria* (1893), and by A. Rocchi, *Vita di San Nilo abate* (1904). St Nilus was also a writer of liturgical poetry, and his compositions have been edited by Sofronio Gassisi, *Poesie di S. Nilo juniore* (1906). On the question of Nilus's alleged marriage see U. Benigni in *Miscellanea di storia e coltura ecclesiastica* (1905), pp. 494–496. His view is adverse to the existence of any legitimate union. See also J. Gay, *L'Italie méridionale et l'Empire byzantin* (1904), pp. 268–286.

ST JOHN OF MEDA (A.D. 1159 ?)

THERE is considerable discussion about the origins of the penitential association of lay-people who were in the middle ages called *Humiliati*, and the quite unreliable legend of St John of Meda does little but add to the confusion. In the earlier part of the twelfth century numbers of persons of good position in northern Italy, while still living " in the world ", gave themselves up entirely to works of penance and charity; and we are told that in the year 1134 some of the men, on the advice of St Bernard, gave up secular life altogether and began community life at Milan. At this time, it is said, there was a certain secular priest from Como, John of Meda, who had been a hermit at Rodenario and then joined the *Humiliati*. He belonged to the Oldrati of Milan, and was a welcome recruit for the new community. On his recommendation they chose to live under the Rule of St Benedict, which St John adapted to their needs, but they nevertheless called themselves " canons ". Among the peculiar observances which St John is supposed to have introduced was the daily recitation of the Little Office of our Lady and the use of a special Divine Office, called simply the " Office of the Canons ". Whatever the early history of the *Humiliati*, the order eventually went into a bad decline and was suppressed by the Holy See in 1571.

In the *Acta Sanctorum*, September, vol. vii, the Bollandists have published a short medieval life, introducing it with lengthy prolegomena. It is much to be feared that this pretended biography and indeed the whole traditional early history of the Humiliati is no better than a romance. A review of the controversy is impossible here, but it has been excellently summarized, with abundant bibliographical references, by F. Vernet in DTC., vol. vi, cc. 307–321. It must suffice to mention the important work of L. Zanoni, *Gli Umiliati nei loro rapporti con l'Eresia* (1911); the earlier investigation of Tiraboschi, *Vetera Humiliatorum Monumenta* (1766–1768); and the perhaps hypercritical article of A. de

Stefano, " Le Origini dell' ordine degli Umiliati " in the *Rivista storico-critica delle scienze teologice*, vol. ii (1906), pp. 851–871.

BD LUCY OF CALTAGIRONE, Virgin   (Thirteenth Century?)

CALTAGIRONE, a town in Sicily well-known in later times as the home of Don Luigi Sturzo, was the birthplace of this *beata*, but she seems to have spent her life in a convent of Franciscan regular tertiaries at Salerno. Very little is known about her. She became mistress of novices, and instilled into her charges her own special devotion to the Five Wounds ; and miracles were attributed to her both before and after her death, the date of which is not known. Bd Lucy's *cultus* seems to have been approved by Popes Callistus III and Leo X.

See the *Acta Sanctorum*, September, vol. vii.

BD DALMATIUS MONER   (A.D. 1341)

THE life of this confessor of the order of Friars Preachers was passed in the obscurity of his cell and the quiet discharge of his ordinary duties ; he was concerned in no public affairs whether of an ecclesiastical or secular nature. He belonged by birth to the village of Santa Columba in Catalonia and was eventually sent to the University of Montpellier. Here he had to struggle hard lest he be drawn into the disorderly life led by so many of the students ; with the aid of grace he triumphed and, after finishing his studies, was accepted by the Dominicans at Gerona. Bd Dalmatius was then twenty-five and after profession was employed for many years in teaching, and became master of the novices. To those prescribed by his rule he added voluntary mortifications, such as abstaining from drink for three weeks on end and sleeping in an old chair, and he loved to pray out of doors in places where the beauty of nature spoke to him of the glory of God. It is said that one day, when Brother Dalmatius was missing and another friar was sent to find him, he was found to be literally caught up in esctasy, and three people saw him gently floating down to the ground. The lessons of his office say that he was familiarly known as " the brother who talks with the angels " ; but with women he would not talk at all, except over his shoulder. We are told that his personal appearance was somewhat unattractive

It was a great desire of Bd Dalmatius to end his days at La Sainte Baume, where the legend of Provence says thirty years were spent by St Mary Magdalen, patroness of the Dominican Order, to whom he had an intense devotion. This was not to be, but he was allowed to hollow out for himself a cave in the friary grounds at Gerona and he lived in that uncomfortable place for four years, leaving it only to go to choir, chapter and refectory. Bd Dalmatius died on September 24, 1341, and his *cultus* was confirmed in 1721.

The Bollandists, writing of Bd Dalmatius in the *Acta Sanctorum*, September, vol. vi, were unable to procure the original Latin life of this holy ascetic which they knew had been compiled by his contemporary and fellow religious, the famous inquisitor, Nicholas Eymeric. They therefore reproduced in Latin the Spanish translation, or rather adaptation, of the original, which had been made by Francis Diego for his history of the Aragon province of the Friars Preachers. In the early years, however, of the present century a copy of Eymeric's work was identified and it was edited by Fr van Ortroy in the *Analecta Bollandiana*, vol. xxxi (1912), pp. 49–81. This memoir is extremely interesting because we have evidence that, unlike most hagiographical documents, it was written within ten years of the death of its subject.

BD TERESA COUDERC, Virgin, Co-Foundress of the Congregation of Our Lady of the Retreat in the Cenacle * (A.D. 1885)

In the year 1824 the Reverend J. P. E. Terme and other priests were sent by their bishop to La Louvesc, in the Vivarais in south-eastern France, to do missionary work among the peasants and to look after the pilgrim shrine of St John Francis Regis. It was soon found urgently necessary to open a hostel for women pilgrims ; and to look after this hostel Father Terme turned to a community of sisters whom he had established to teach school in his former parish of Aps. Three young women were accordingly sent to La Louvesc in 1827, among them Sister Teresa Couderc. Sister Teresa, born in 1805 and christened Mary Victoria, came of good farming stock at Sablières, and had been one of the first members of the community at Aps.

Father Terme said that Sister Teresa had " a sound head, sound judgement, and a power of spiritual discrimination rare in a woman " ; and in the very next year, when she was only twenty-three, he made her superioress at La Louvesc, where under considerable difficulties (especially from the climate which, at 4000 feet up, is fierce in winter) the community was already showing signs of growth. The year after that came its turning-point. Father Terme went to a retreat at a Jesuit house near Le Puy : and on his return he announced that the Daughters of St Regis (as they were then called) should add to their work the giving of retreats for women—not, of course, with spiritual direction or anything like that, but to begin with spiritual reading and simple instruction on the fundamentals of Christianity. This was at that time a most remarkable innovation ; it was an immediate success, especially among the countrywomen, and in years to come it was to spread across the world. But meanwhile, on December 12, 1834, Father Terme died.

The shrine and parish of La Louvesc had recently been taken over by the Jesuit fathers ; and with their advice it was decided to separate the work of school-teaching from that of retreats. Twelve carefully-chosen sisters were therefore withdrawn from the Daughters of St Regis and, with Mother Teresa Couderc at their head, installed at La Louvesc, under the direction of Father Rigaud, s.j. The giving of retreats according to the method of St Ignatius went ahead, and a new house and church for the convent soon became necessary. But the source on which reliance had been put to meet these and other expenses suddenly failed, and the community was left with very large debts and nothing to pay them with. Mother Teresa blamed herself—quite unnecessarily—for what had happened, and in 1838 she resigned her office as superioress. Thereupon the bishop of Viviers named in her place a wealthy widow who had been in the community less than a month.

Thus began a long, complex and not always edifying story, which is a matter of the history and development of the Society of the Cenacle (as it was soon to be known), rather than of its holy foundress. Mother Teresa was sent to make a new foundation at Lyons, in most difficult conditions ; but she more and more dropped

---

* This name has reference to the period between our Lord's Ascension and the day of Pentecost, when the Apostles " were persevering with one mind in prayer, with the women and Mary the mother of Jesus, and with His brethren ", in the upper room at Jerusalem. *Cénacle* is the French form of Latin *cenaculum*, literally a " dining-room ". " Upper room " is the traditional rendering in English.

into obscurity, living the words she uttered on her death-bed : " I ask of God that we shall never do anything out of ostentation ; but that we should on the contrary do our good in the background, and that we should always look on ourselves as the least of the Church's little ones."

It was nearly twenty years before Mgr Guibert, bishop of Viviers, declared once and for all that the founder of the Cenacle was Father John Terme and the foundress Mother Teresa Couderc, and nobody else ; and at that time she was sent to the Paris convent as temporary superioress at a moment of crisis.   Then she sank into the background again, so that Cardinal Lavigerie on a visit to the nuns, at once detecting holiness in her face, had to ask who was the one that had been *left out*.

Bd Teresa Couderc was a foundress, yet for well over half of her eighty years her life was a hidden one, forwarding the work of her foundation in hiding as it were, with her prayers, her penances, her humiliations.   In herself she saw " only feebleness and incapacity, uselessness and a complete lack of virtue ".   No criticism was heard from her of so much that seems to deserve criticism.   She was content. " God has always given me peace of soul, the grace to leave myself in His hands and to want nothing but to love Him and be ever closer to Him."   The word *bonté* recurs on the lips of those who knew her ; and in English the simple word " good- ness " expresses the depth and nature of her quality better than all the superlatives of hagiographers.

Towards the end of her life Mother Teresa's health began to fail badly, and for the last nine months she suffered terribly in body.   At Fourvière on September 26, 1885, Mary Victoria Couderc, Mother Teresa, died ; and in 1951 she was beatified.

See, in French, E. M. I., *La Mère Thérèse Couderc* (1911) ;   H. Perroy, *Une grande humble* (1928) ;   S. Dehin, *L'esprit de la vén. Mère Thérèse Couderc* (1947) ;   P. Vernion, *La Cénacle et son message* (1948) :   in English : C. C. Martindale, *Marie Thérèse Couderc* (1921) ;   R. Surles, *Surrender to the Spirit* (1951), an American adaptation of Fr Perroy's book.   See also G. Longhaye, *La Société de N.-D. du Cénacle* (1898), and M. de Sailly, *J. P. E. Terme* (1913).

27 : SS. COSMAS AND DAMIAN, Martyrs   (Date Unknown)

COSMAS and Damian are the principal and best known of those saints venerated in the East as ἀνάργυροι, " moneyless ones ", because they practised medicine without taking reward from their patients.   Though some writers have professed to be able to extract from their very extravagant and historically worthless *acta* fragments of lost and authentic originals, it is the opinion of Father Delehaye that their " origin and true history will probably always evade research ".   Alban Butler summarizes the core of their story thus :

Saints Cosmas and Damian were twin brothers, born in Arabia, who studied the sciences in Syria and became eminent for their skill in medicine.   Being Christians, and full of that holy temper of charity in which the spirit of our divine religion consists, they practised their profession with great application and success, but never took any fee for their services.   They lived at Aegeae on the bay of Alexandretta in Cilicia, and were remarkable both for the love and respect which the people bore them on account of the good offices which they received from their charity, and for their zeal for the Christian faith, which they took every opportunity their profession gave them to propagate.   When persecution began to rage, it was impossible for persons of so distinguished a character to lie concealed. They were therefore apprehended by the order of Lysias, governor of Cilicia, and after various torments were beheaded for the faith. Their bodies were carried into Syria, and buried at Cyrrhus, which was the chief centre of their *cultus* and where the earliest references locate their martyrdom.

The legends pad out this simple story with numerous marvels. For example, before they were eventually beheaded they defied death by water, fire and crucifixion. While they were hanging on the crosses the mob stoned them, but the missiles recoiled on the heads of the throwers ; in the same way the arrows of archers who were brought up to shoot at them turned in the air and scattered the bowmen (the same thing is recorded of St Christopher and others). The three brothers of Cosmas and Damian, Anthimus, Leontius and Euprepius, are said to have suffered with them, and their names are mentioned in the Roman Martyrology. Many miracles of healing were ascribed to them after their death, the saints sometimes appearing to the sufferers in sleep and prescribing for them or curing them there and then, as was supposed to happen to pagan devotees in the temples of Aesculapius and Serapis. Among the distinguished people who attributed recovery from serious sickness to SS. Cosmas and Damian was the Emperor Justinian I, who out of regard for their relics honoured the city of Cyrrhus ; and two churches at Constantinople are said to have been built in honour of the martyrs in the early fifth century. Their basilica at Rome with its lovely mosaics was dedicated *c.* 530. SS. Cosmas and Damian are named in the canon of the Mass, and they are, with St Luke, the patrons of physicians and surgeons. By an error the Byzantine Christians honour three pairs of saints of this name. " It should be known ", says the Synaxary of Constantinople, " that there are three groups of martyrs of the names of Cosmas and Damian : those of Arabia who were beheaded under Diocletian [October 17], those of Rome who were stoned under Carinus [July 1], and the sons of Theodota, who died peacefully [November 1] ", but these are all actually the same martyrs.

As has been said, physicians honour Cosmas and Damian as their patrons, with St Pantaleon and after St Luke. Happy are they in that profession who are glad to take the opportunities of charity which their art continually offers, of giving comfort and corporal, if not often also spiritual, succour to the suffering and distressed, especially among the poor. St Ambrose, St Basil and St Bernard warn us against too anxious a care of health as a mark of untrustingness and self-love, nor is anything generally more hurtful to health. But as man is not master of his own life or health, he is bound to take a reasonable care not to throw them away ; and to neglect the more simple and ordinary aids of medicine when they are required is to transgress that charity which every one owes to himself. The saints who condemned difficult or expensive measures as contrary to their state were, with St Charles Borromeo, scrupulously attentive to prescriptions of physicians in simple and ordinary remedies. But let the Christian in sickness seek in the first place the health of his soul by penitence and the exercise of patience.

The many recensions of the *passio* of these saints are catalogued in BHG. and BHL. The texts printed in the *Acta Sanctorum*, September, vol. vii, serve abundantly to illustrate their fabulous nature, though others have come to light in recent years. See with regard to the early *cultus* the references given in CMH., pp. 528–529 ; and also Delehaye, *The Legends of the Saints, Les origines du culte des martyrs*, and other works. The data supplied in L. Deubner, *Kosmas und Damianus* (1907) deserve special notice. *Cf.* also Fr Thurston in the *Catholic Medical Guardian*, October 1923, pp. 92–95.   SS. Cosmas and Damian are named in the preparation of the Byzantine Mass.

ST ELZEAR AND BD DELPHINA   (A.D. 1323 AND 1360)

ST Elzear of Sabran was born in 1285 at Ansouis in Provence, a castle belonging to his father.   The lessons in virtue he received from his mother were perfected by his uncle, William of Sabran, Abbot of St Victor's at Marseilles, under whom he had his education in that monastery.   The abbot had to reprove him for the austerities which he practised, yet secretly admiring so great fervour in a young noble.   While he was still a child he was affianced to Delphina of Glandèves, daughter and heiress to the lord of Puy-Michel.   She had been left an orphan in her infancy and was brought up by her aunt, an abbess, under the guardianship of her uncles.   When they were both about sixteen years old the marriage took place. It is said that the girl, encouraged by a Franciscan friar, asked her husband to agree to a virginal union, but it was some time before he would do so.   In the lives of this holy couple the world saw religious devotion in the midst of secular dignities, contemplation amid the noise of public life, and in conjugal friendship a holy rivalry in goodness and charity.   St Elzear recited the Divine Office every day and communicated frequently.   " I do not think ", he said one day to Delphina, " that any man on earth can enjoy a happiness equal to that which I have in holy communion."

Elzear was twenty-three years old when he inherited his father's honours and estates, and he found it necessary to go into Italy to take possession of the lordship of Ariano.   He found his Neapolitan vassals badly disposed towards him, and it required all his tact and gentleness to satisfy them.   His cousin one day told him that his mild methods hurt the common cause, and said, " Let me deal with these people for you.   I will hang up half a thousand, and make the rest as pliant as a glove.   It is fit to be a lamb among the good, but with the wicked you must play the lion.   Such insolence must be curbed.   Say your prayers for me, and I will give so many blows for you that this rabble will give you no more trouble."   Elzear smilingly replied, " Would you have me begin my government with massacres and blood ?   I will overcome these men by good.   It is no great matter for a lion to tear lambs ; but for a lamb to pull a lion in pieces is another thing.   Now, by God's assistance, you will shortly see this miracle."   The effect verified the prediction. To mention one other instance of his Christian forbearance.   Among the papers which his father left, Elzear found the letters of a certain gentleman under his command, filled with calumnies against him and persuading his father to disinherit him as one fitter to be a monk than to bear arms.   Delphina was indignant at reading such impudence, and said she hoped her husband would deal with the man as he deserved.   But Elzear reminded her that Christ commands us not to revenge but to forgive injuries, and to overcome hatred by charity : therefore he would destroy and never make mention of these letters.   He did so, and when their writer came to wait upon him he affectionately greeted him and won his good-will.

It is a dangerous mistake to imagine that one can be devout merely by spending much time in prayer, and that pious persons should fall into careless neglect of their temporal concerns.   On the contrary, solid virtue is also able to do business and to despatch it well.   St Elzear was rendered by his piety faithful, prudent and dexterous in the management of temporal affairs, both domestic and public : valiant in war, active in peace, faithful in every trust, and diligent in the care of his household for which he drew up careful regulations.   He himself set the example in everything which he prescribed to others, and Bd Delphina concurred with her husband in all his views and was perfectly obedient to him.   No coldness interrupted the harmony or damped the affections of this holy pair.   The countess never forgot that the devotions of a married woman ought to be ordered in a different manner from those of a nun, that contemplation is the sister of action and that Martha and Mary must mutually help one another.

About 1317 Elzear returned to Naples, taking with him Delphina, who waited upon Queen Sanchia, wife of King Robert, and the tutorship of their son Charles was entrusted to Elzear.   This young prince was sprightly, understood too well his high position, was intractable, and had all the airs of the court.   The count saw his pupil's dangerous inclinations but took no notice of them till he had won his affection and gained credit with him.   Then did St Elzear lead young Charles into more sober and fruitful ways, and when his father had need of a new justiciar in the southern Abruzzi, Elzear was named to the office.   Some years later King Robert sent St Elzear to Paris to ask for the hand of Mary of Valois for his son. Bd Delphina was a little nervous for her husband amid the dangers of the French court, but he replied drily that since by the grace of God he had kept his virtue in Naples he was not likely to come to any harm at Paris.   In fact, the danger that awaited him was quite other.   After he had carried through his commission he fell sick and it was the sickness of death.   He at once made a general confession and he continued to confess almost every day of his illness, though he is said never to have offended God by any mortal sin.   The history of Christ's passion was every day read to him, and in it he found great comfort amidst his pains.   Receiving viaticum, he said with joy, " This is my hope ; in this I desire to die ", and on September 27, 1323, he died in the arms of a Franciscan friar who had been his confessor.   About the year 1309 St Elzear had assisted as godfather at the baptism of William of Grimoard, his nephew, a sickly child whose health was restored at the prayers of his sponsor.   Fifty-three years later this William became pope as Urban V, and in 1369 he signed the decree of canonization of his godfather Elzear, who is named in the Roman Martyrology on this day.

Bd Delphina survived her husband thirty-seven years.   At the death of King Robert, Queen Sanchia put on the habit of a Poor Clare in a nunnery at Naples. In this state she lived with great fervour, learning from Delphina the exercises of a spiritual life.   After her death Delphina returned into Provence and led the life of a recluse, first at Cabrières and then at Apt.   She gave away all she could to the poor, and during her last years was afflicted with a painful illness which she bore with heroic patience.   She died in 1360 and was buried with her husband at Apt. An old tradition says that both St Elzear and Bd Delphina were members of the third order of St Francis, and they are therefore particularly venerated by the Franciscans ; in their supplement to the martyrology Bd Delphina is named on December 9, though she appears to have died on November 26.

The manuscript materials collected and printed by the Bollandists in their vol. vii for September are of considerable interest.   From these sources P. Girard compiled a popular biography, *Saint Elzéar de Sabran et la B. Delphine de Signe* (1912).   A liturgical office formerly in use for their feast day will be found in the *Archivum Franciscanum Historicum*, vol. x (1917), pp. 231–238.   There is another good popular account in French by G. Duhamelet (1944).

28 : ST WENCESLAUS OF BOHEMIA, Martyr   (A.D. 929)

THE baptism of the ruler of Bohemia, Borivoy, and his wife St Ludmila was not by any means followed by the conversion of all their subjects, and many of the powerful Czech families were strongly opposed to the new religion. From the year 915 Duke Borivoy's son Ratislav governed the whole country. He married a nominally Christian woman, Drahomira, daughter of the chief of the Veletians, a Slav tribe from the north, and they had two sons, Wenceslaus (Vaclav), born in 907 near Prague, and Boleslaus. St Ludmila, who was still living, arranged that the upbringing of the elder might be entrusted to her, and she undertook with the utmost care to form his heart to the love of God. Ludmila joined with herself in this task a priest, her chaplain Paul, who had been a personal disciple of St Methodius and had baptized Wenceslaus ; under his tuition the boy, by the time he was ready to go to the " college " at Budech, " understood Latin as if he were a bishop and read Slavonic with ease ", while the example of both the priest and his good grandmother had grounded him equally well in virtue. He was still young when his father was killed fighting against the Magyars, and his mother Drahomira assumed the government, pursuing an anti-Christian or " secularist " policy. In so doing she was probably acting chiefly at the instigation of the semi-pagan elements in the nobility, and these encouraged her jealousy of St Ludmila's influence over her son, and represented him as being more suitable for a cloister than for a throne. St Ludmila, afflicted at the public disorders and full of concern for the interest of religion, which she and her consort had established with so much difficulty, showed Wenceslaus the necessity of taking the reins of government into his own hands. Fearing what might happen, two nobles went to Ludmila's castle at Tetin and there strangled her, so that, deprived of her support, Wenceslaus should not undertake the government of his people. But it turned out otherwise : other interests drove Drahomira out, and proclaimed Wenceslaus. He straightway announced that he would support God's law and His Church, punish murder severely, and endeavour to rule with justice and mercy. His mother had been banished to Budech, so he recalled her to the court, and there is no evidence that for the future she ever opposed Wenceslaus.

At a meeting of rulers presided over by the German king, Henry I the Fowler, St Wenceslaus arrived late and kept everybody waiting. Some of the princes took offence and the king, saying he was probably at his prayers, suggested that no one should greet him when he did arrive. Nevertheless, Henry himself, who really respected his devotion, received him with honour, and at the end bade him ask whatever he pleased, and it should be granted him. The saint asked an arm of the body of St Vitus, and to shelter it he began the building of a church at Prague, where now stands the cathedral. The political policy of St Wenceslaus was to cultivate friendly relations with Germany, and he preserved the unity of his country by acknowledging King Henry I as his over-lord, about the year 926, seeing in him the legitimate successor of Charlemagne. This policy, and the severity with which he checked oppression and other disorders in the nobility, raised a party against him, especially among those who resented the influence of the clergy in the counsels of Wenceslaus. Then, when the young duke married and had a son, his jealous brother Boleslaus lost his chance of the succession, and he threw in his lot with the malcontents.

In September 929 Wenceslaus was invited by Boleslaus to go to Stara Boleslav to celebrate the feast of its patron saints Cosmas and Damian. On the evening of the festival, after the celebrations were over, Wenceslaus was warned he was in danger. He refused to take any notice. He proposed to the assembly in the hall a toast in honour of " St Michael, whom we pray to guide us to peace and eternal joy ", said his prayers, and went to bed. Early the next morning, as Wenceslaus made his way to Mass, he met Boleslaus and stopped to thank him for his hospitality. " Yesterday ", was the reply, " I did my best to serve you fittingly, but this must be my service to-day ", and he struck him. The brothers closed and struggled ; whereupon friends of Boleslaus ran up and killed Wenceslaus, who murmured as he fell at the chapel door, " Brother, may God forgive you ".

At once the young prince was acclaimed by the people as a martyr (though it seems that his murder was only very indirectly on account of religion), and at least by the year 984 his feast was being observed. Boleslaus, frightened at the reputation of many miracles wrought at his brother's tomb, caused the body to be translated to the church of St Vitus at Prague three years after his death. The shrine became a place of pilgrimage, and at the beginning of the eleventh century St Wenceslaus, *Svaty Vaclav*, was already regarded as the patron saint of the Bohemian people ; and as the patron of modern Czechoslovakia devotion to him has sometimes been very highly charged with nationalist feeling. It must not be inferred from the existence of a vernacular Christmas carol that there was formerly a widespread popular devotion to this saint in England : the words of " Good King Wenceslaus " were written by the nineteenth-century hymn-writer J. M. Neale to fit a thirteenth-century air (" *Tempus adest floridum* ").

In a contribution to the *Analecta Bollandiana*, vol. xlviii (1930), pp. 218–221, Fr Paul Peeters reviews the more outstanding features of the literature produced in Czechoslovakia, and mostly written in the Czech language, to do honour to the millenary of St Wenceslaus, celebrated in 1929. It is unfortunate, as he points out, that a good deal of this literature was coloured by racial and political prepossessions. The slight, but judicious, life of St Wenceslaus, by F. Dvornik (1929), appeared both in French and in English as well as in Czech. The German biography by A. Naegle, *Der hl. Wenzel, der Landespatron Böhmens* (1928), is representative of a point of view which is somewhat adverse to that of Dvornik, with whose estimate of the authenticity of the Life of Wenceslaus by the monk Christian not all scholars are in agreement. Wenceslaus has a specially long notice in the Bollandist commentary on the *Mart. Rom.* (1940), pp. 421–422. See also *Acta Sanctorum*, September, vol. vii ; J. Pekar, *Die Wenzels und Ludmila Legenden und die Echtheit Christians* (1906) ; DHG., t. ix, cc. 426–427 ; and F. Dvornik, *The Making of Central and Eastern Europe* (1949), pp. 25–30 and *passim*. Benedict XIV's commission recommended the removal of this feast from the general calendar. *Cf.* St Ludmila above, September 16.

ST EXSUPERIUS, Bishop of Toulouse   (*c*. A.D. 412)

HE was probably born at Arreau in the High Pyrenees, where a chapel dedicated in his honour is a place of pilgrimage, and succeeded to the see of Toulouse on the death of St Silvius about the year 405. He completed the great church of St Saturninus (Sernin), begun by his predecessor. Generosity seems to have been the outstanding characteristic of this bishop. He sent gifts so far away as to the monks of Egypt and Palestine, thereby earning the thanks and commendation of St Jerome, who dedicated to him his commentary on Zacharias and wrote of him : " To relieve the hunger of the poor he suffers it himself. The paleness of his face shows the rigour of his fasts, but he is grieved by the hunger of others. He gives his all to the poor of Christ : but rich is he who carries the Body of the Lord in an osier-basket and His Blood in a glass vessel.   His charity knew no bounds.   It sought for objects in the most distant parts, and the solitaries of Egypt felt its beneficial effects."   At home as well as abroad there was ample scope for his benefactions, for in his time Gaul was overrun by the Vandals.

St Exsuperius wrote to Pope St Innocent I for instruction on several matters of discipline and enquiring about the canon of Holy Scripture.   In reply the pope sent him a list of the authentic books of the Bible as they were then received at Rome, and that list was the same as today, including the deuterocanonical books. The place and year of the death of Exsuperius are not known, but he seems to have suffered exile before the end.   St Paulinus of Nola referred to him as one of the most illustrious bishops of the Church in Gaul, and by the middle of the sixth century he was held in equal honour with St Saturninus in the church of Toulouse.

It seems curious that St Exsuperius, whose fame had reached Rome and Palestine, finds no place in the *Hieronymianum*.   What has been recorded concerning him is gathered up in the *Acta Sanctorum*, September, vol. vii ; and there is a very full notice in DTC., vol. v, cc. 2022–2037.   See also Duchesne, *Fastes Épiscopaux*, vol. i, p. 307.

ST EUSTOCHIUM, Virgin   (*c.* A.D. 419)

EUSTOCHIUM JULIA, whose memory is rendered illustrious by the pen of St Jerome, was daughter of St Paula, whose life is related on January 26 ; its exterior events and circumstances conditioned those of Eustochium, who was the third of four daughters and the only one to share her mother's life till its end.   St Paula, upon the death of her husband Toxotius, devoted herself wholly to God in a life of simplicity, poverty, mortification and prayer.   Eustochium, who was about twelve years old when her father died, shared all the views of her mother and rejoiced to consecrate the hours which so many spend in vain amusements to works of charity and religion.   When St Jerome came to Rome from the East in the year 382 she, with St Paula, put herself under his spiritual direction, and its trend soon alarmed some of her friends and relatives.   An uncle, Hymettius, and his wife Praetextata tried to dissuade the young girl from a life of austerity and attempted to entice her into participation in the pleasures of ordinary life.   Their efforts were wasted, for before very long Eustochium had taken the veil of perpetual virginity, the first noble Roman maiden so to do.   To commend her resolution and to instruct her in the obligations of that state St Jerome addressed to her on this occasion his famous letter called Concerning the Keeping of Virginity, which he wrote about the year 384.   The venerable author, however, does not confine his letter to ascetic teaching but writes passages of satire which suggest it was intended for a wider public than one young girl ; he is merciless in his criticism of the behaviour of certain virgins, widows and priests.

Much of the formation of Eustochium had been at the hands of St Marcella, that " glory of the Roman ladies ", but when St Paula decided to follow St Jerome to Palestine she elected to go with her mother.   With other maidens who aspired to the religious life, they met St Jerome at Antioch, visited the Holy Places, Egypt, and the monks of the Nitrian desert, and finally settled down at Bethlehem.   Three communities of women were established, in the direction of which Eustochium assisted St Paula, and St Jerome has left us an account of the simple devoted lives that were passed therein.   When his sight began to fail, these two women, who had learnt Greek and Hebrew, helped in the work of the translation of the Bible, the Vulgate ; at their request he wrote commentaries on the epistles to Philemon, the Galatians, the Ephesians and Titus, and dedicated some of his works to them, for, as he said, " these women were more capable of forming a judgement on them than most men ". Other duties of St Eustochium were to sweep out the house, trim and fill the lamps, and cook.

In 403 St Paula was taken ill, and Eustochium spent long hours between waiting on her and praying for her in the cave of the Nativity. At her death on January 26, 404, Eustochium, " like a baby weaned from her nurse, could scarcely be drawn away from her mother. She kissed her eyes and clung to her face and caressed her whole body and would even have been buried with her." Paula was succeeded as directress by her daughter, who found the communities not only destitute but much in debt. With the encouragement of St Jerome and her own quiet intrepidity she faced the situation and retrieved it, with the assistance of funds brought by her niece, another Paula, who had joined the Bethlehem maidens. In 417 a band of roughs burnt down her monastery and committed many outrages : of which St Jerome, St Eustochium, and the younger Paula informed Pope St Innocent I by letter, who wrote in strong terms to John, Bishop of Jerusalem. St Eustochium did not long survive this terrible shock. We have no account from St Jerome of her death as we have of that of her mother, but he wrote to St Augustine and St Alipius that " such a sorrow caused him to disdain the outrageous writings of the Pelagian Anianus ". She died peacefully about 419, and was buried in the same tomb as St Paula in a grotto adjoining the spot in which our Lord was born. There their tomb may still be seen, but it has long been empty and the fate of their relics is not known.

St Jerome's letters and other writings furnish almost all that we know concerning St Eustochium. The material has been gathered up in the *Acta Sanctorum*, September, vol. vii. All the lives of St Jerome tell us a good deal about Eustochium (see, *e.g.* F. Cavallera, *St Jérôme*, 1922), and she also figures prominently in F. Lagrange's delightful *Histoire de Ste Paule* (1868).

ST FAUSTUS, BISHOP OF RIEZ　　(*c.* A.D. 493)

REFERENCES are often made to Faustus of Riez as a chief exponent and defender of what is now called Semi-Pelagianism but it is more often forgotten he was a holy man whose name appears in several martyrologies and that his feast is observed in several churches of southern France. He was born in the early years of the fifth century, his contemporaries St Avitus and St Sidonius Apollinaris say in Britain, but more likely in Brittany. He is said to have begun life as a barrister, but can hardly have gone far in that profession because he became a monk of Lérins before the founder of that house, St Honoratus, had left it in 426. He was ordained to the priesthood, and after seven or eight uneventful years in the monastery he was elected abbot after St Maximus, who was promoted to the see of Riez. He was greatly respected by St Honoratus and St Sidonius, who says that his monastic observance and regularity were worthy of the fathers of the desert, and he had a great gift of extempore preaching ; Sidonius relates in a letter how he shouted himself hoarse at the sermons of Faustus. Applause—and dissent—in church was not uncommon in those, and other, days.

As he had followed St Maximus as abbot, so Faustus followed him as bishop, going to Riez after he had governed Lérins for about twenty-five years. In his panegyric on his predecessor, Faustus exclaimed : " Lérins has sent two successive bishops to Riez.   Of the first she is proud ; for the second she blushes."   She had no need to blush.   Faustus was as good a bishop as he had been an abbot, and encouraged the opening of new monasteries throughout his diocese.   He continued his former mortified life, adding thereto the manifold duties of the episcopate and an apostolic concern for the purity of the faith, opposing himself vigorously to Arianism and the errors of him whom he called " that pestiferous teacher Pelagius ".

A certain priest called Lucidus having been preaching the heretical doctrine which denies that God has a true will to save all men, asserting that salvation or damnation depends on His will alone, irrespective of the action of man's free will and his consequent merits or demerits, two synods met at Arles and Lyons in 475 to deal with him.   St Faustus induced Lucidus to retract his errors, and the bishops asked him to write a treatise against this predestinarian teaching, as " erroneous, blasphemous, heathen, fatalistic and conducive to immorality ".   Faustus complied with two treatises on free will and grace in which he refuted as well Pelagianism as Predestinarianism.   In these he had occasion to deal with certain views of St Augustine, and in so doing himself propounded the semi-Pelagian error that, though grace is necessary for the accomplishment of good works, it is not necessary for their initiation.   St Faustus erred in good faith and in the holy company of St John Cassian, but, though he was vehemently attacked directly his books appeared, their errors were not finally condemned until the Council of Orange in 529.   But his theological activity raised up for him an enemy of a cruder sort, in another quarter. Euric, King of the Arian Visigoths, who seems to have received a certain political support from Faustus, was in occupation of a large part of southern Gaul and was offended by the attacks of Faustus on Arianism.   He was therefore driven from his see about 478 and had perforce to live in exile until the death of Euric some years later.   He then returned and continued to direct his flock until his death at about the age of ninety.   His memory was greatly revered by his people, who built a basilica in his honour.   St Faustus was among the principal of the writers for whom the abbey of Lérins was famous, and some of his letters, discourses and other works are yet extant.

The life and activities of Faustus of Riez occupy sixty pages of the *Acta Sanctorum*, September, vol. vii.   There is also a monograph by A. Koch, *Der hl. Faustus von Riez* (1895).   The edition of the works of Faustus prepared for the Vienna *Corpus Scriptorum* by A. Engelbrecht has met with somewhat damaging criticism from Dom G. Morin in the *Revue Bénédictine*, vol. ix (1892), pp. 49–61, and vol. x (1893), pp. 62–78.   See further F. Wörter, *Zur Dogmengeschichte des Semipelagianismus* (1899), pp. 47 *seq.* ; and DTC., vol. v, cc. 2101–2105.

ST ANNEMUND, Bishop of Lyons   (A.D. 658)

ANNEMUND gives the name Saint-Chamond to a town near Vienne and is principally remembered as the friend and patron of St Wilfrid of York when he was a young man.   He belonged to a Gallo-Roman family, his father being prefect at Lyons. Annemund was trained in the court of Dagobert I and was an adviser of Clovis II. A few years after he was appointed to the see of Lyons there came to his episcopal city St Benedict Biscop, on his way to Rome for the first time, accompanied by St Wilfrid of York, who was then about twenty years old.   Benedict hastened on towards Rome but Wilfrid lingered at Lyons, whose prelate, says St Bede, " was pleased with the youth's wise conversation, the grace of his appearance, his eager

manner, and the maturity of his thoughts.   He therefore supplied Wilfrid and his
friends with all they required so long as they stayed with him."   Annemund even
offered to adopt the young Englishman, to give him his niece to wife, and a post of
honour for his maintenance.   Wilfrid thanked him for his great kindness to a
stranger, and explained that he was determined to serve God in the clerical state
and was for that very reason travelling to Rome.   Whereupon St Annemund made
provision for the rest of his journey, and pressed him to come back through Lyons
when he returned to England.   This Wilfrid did and stayed three years with the
archbishop, by whom he was tonsured.   He might have stayed on indefinitely and
with very important results, for Annemund is said to have had thoughts
of Wilfrid as his successor, but for the untimely and tragic death of the
archbishop.   On September 28, 658, in the disturbances that followed the death
of Clovis II, he was slain by soldiers at Mâcon.   Wilfrid was present and offered
to die with him, but when the executioners heard that he was a foreigner and an
Englishman they let him go.   Eddius, the biographer of St Wilfrid, lays the
assassination of St Annemund (and of nine other French bishops) at the door of
the queen-regent, St Bathildis, and his statement has been copied by St Bede.
But it is improbable that she was guilty of this crime (*cf.* her notice under January
30).   St Wilfrid helped to bury the body of St Annemund at Lyons, where he was
at once venerated as a martyr, and departed to his own country.   Eddius calls
St Annemund *Dalfinus*, which was perhaps a surname, or a confusion with his
brother, and St Bede refers to him by this name.

A brief *passio* of St Annemund is printed in the *Acta Sanctorum*, September, vol. vii,
with the usual prolegomena ; but the principal authorities are Eddius and Bede.   See
Plummer's edition of the latter and his notes ; and MGH., *Scriptores Merov.*, vol. vi, pp.
197 *seq.*

ST LIOBA, Virgin   (A.D. 780)

THE active participation of nuns and religious sisters in the work of the foreign
missions has so greatly developed and extended in our own time that we have come
to regard it as a modern innovation altogether.   It is, of course, nothing of the sort
and, allowing for a certain difference of method consequent on the development of
" unenclosed active congregations ", we find just the same sort of thing happening
during the evangelization of barbarians in Europe during the dark ages.   An
outstanding example is the request of St Boniface that took SS. Lioba, Thecla,
Walburga and others from their quiet abbey at Wimborne to the wilds of heathen
Germany.   Lioba was of a good Wessex family, and Ebba, her mother, was related
to St Boniface.   Lioba was placed while young in the monastery of Wimborne in
Dorsetshire, under the care of the abbess St Tetta.   The girl had been baptized
Truthgeba but came to be called Liobgetha (Leofgyth), abbreviated to Lioba, " the
dear one ", a name which was fitting to one so precious in the eyes of God and man
and which has been used of her ever since.   When she came to the requisite age
Lioba elected to remain in the monastery, wherein she was duly professed and
made progress in virtue and knowledge.   Her innocence and single-mindedness
were an example even to her seniors, and reading and books were her delight.

In the year 722 St Boniface was consecrated bishop by Pope St Gregory II and
sent to preach the gospel in Saxony, Thuringia and Hesse.   He was a native of
Crediton, not very far from Wimborne, and when accounts of his labours and

successes reached the nuns there his young relative Lioba made bold to write to him, in the following terms :

> To the most reverend Boniface, bearer of the highest dignity and well-beloved in Christ, Liobgetha, to whom he is related by blood, the least of Christ's handmaids, sends greetings for eternal salvation.
>
> I beg you of your kindness to remember your early friendship in the west country with my father, Dynne, who died eight years ago and from whose soul, therefore, I ask you not to withhold your prayers.   I also commend to your memory my mother Ebba, who still lives, but painfully ; she is, as you know, related to you.   I am the only child of my parents and, unworthy though I be, I should like to look on you as my brother, for I can trust you more than anyone else of my kinsfolk.   I send you this little gift [the letter itself ?] not because it is worth your consideration but simply so that you may have something to remind you of my humble self, and so not forget me when you are so far away ; may it draw tighter the bond of true love between us for ever. I beseech you, dear brother, help me with your prayers against the attacks of the hidden enemy.   I would ask you, too, if you would be so good as to correct this unlearned letter and not to refuse to send me a few kind words, which I eagerly look forward to as a token of your good will.   I have tried to compose the subscribed lines according to the rules of verse, as an exercise for my poor skill in poetry, wherein also I have need of your guidance.   I have learned this art from my mistress Edburga, who is ever in mind of God's holy law.
>
> Farewell !   May you live long and happily, and pray for me always.

> Arbiter omnipotens, solus qui cuncta creavit
> in regno Patris semper qui lumine fulget
> qua iugiter flagrans, sic regnat gloria Christi,
> illaesum servet semper te iure perenni.

> (May the almighty Maker of the world,
> Shining for ever in the heavenly realm
> Where Christ in glory reigns for endless days,
> Keep you in safety with sustainéd care.)

St Boniface was not unmoved by so touching an appeal, and entered into a correspondence of which the upshot was that in 748 he asked St Tetta that St Lioba might be sent to him with certain companions, in order to settle some monasteries as centres of religion for women in the infant church of Germany. Tetta accordingly sent out some thirty nuns, including SS. Lioba, Thecla and Walburga, who joined St Boniface at Mainz.   He settled St Lioba and her little colony in a monastery which he gave her, and which was called Bischofsheim, that is, Bishop's House, which suggests that he may have given up his own residence to the nuns.   Under Lioba's care this nunnery became in a short time very numerous, and out of it she peopled other houses which she founded in Germany.

Rudolf, a monk of Fulda, who within sixty years of St Lioba's death wrote an account of her from the testimonies of four of her nuns, says that nearly all the convents of that part of Germany asked for a nun trained at Bischofsheim to guide them.   The saint herself was so wrapped up in her work that she seemed to have forgotten Wessex and her own folk.   Her beauty was remarkable ; she had a face " like an angel ", always pleasant and smiling, but rarely laughing outright.   No one ever saw her in a bad temper or heard her speak an uncharitable word, and her patience and intelligence were as large as her kindness. We are told that her cup was a " little one ", and its small size witnessed to her own abstemiousness in a community which kept to St Benedict's provision of two meals a day. All the nuns engaged in manual work, whether in bakehouse, brewhouse, household duties or otherwise, and at the same time had what today would be called " higher education " ; all had to know Latin, and their scriptorium was kept busy. St Lioba would allow no imprudent austerities, such as deprivation of sleep, and insisted on the observance of the midday rest prescribed by the rule. She herself spent this hour lying down, while one of the novices read to her from the Bible, and if it appeared that Mother Abbess had gone to sleep and the reader became careless, she would soon find herself corrected for a mispronunciation or a false quantity. Afterwards Lioba would devote two hours to private talk with any of the sisters who wished to see her. All this activity subserved the main business of public prayer and worship of Almighty God, and the spiritual support of the missionary monks who worked in the land around them. A letter is extant from St Boniface to the " reverend and most dear sisters Lioba, Thecla, Cynehild, and those who dwell with them ", asking for the continuance of their prayers. St Lioba's fame was widespread ; her neighbours came to her in peril of fire and tempest and sickness, and men of affairs in church and state asked her counsel.

St Boniface, before his mission into Friesland in 754, took a moving farewell of Lioba and recommended her to St Lull, a monk of Malmesbury and his episcopal successor, and to his monks at Fulda, entreating them to care for her with respect and honour, and declaring it his desire that after her death she should be buried with him, that their bodies might wait the resurrection and be raised together in glory to meet the Lord and be for ever united in the kingdom of His love. After St Boniface's martyrdom she made frequent visits to his tomb at the abbey of Fulda, and she was allowed by a special privilege to enter the abbey and assist at divine service and conferences, after which she went back to her own nunnery. When she was grown very old, and had been abbess at Bischofsheim for twenty-eight years she settled all the nunneries under her care and, resigning their government, came to reside at the convent of Schönersheim, four miles from Mainz. Her friend Bd Hildegard, Charlemagne's queen, invited her so earnestly to the court at Aachen that she could not refuse to go, but had to insist on being allowed to return to her solitude. Taking leave of the queen, embracing and kissing her, she said, " Farewell, precious part of my soul ! May Christ our Creator and Redeemer grant that we may see each other without confusion of face in the day of judgement, for in this life we shall never more see each other." And so it was. For St Lioba died a very short while after and was buried in the abbey-church of Fulda, not in the tomb of St Boniface, for the monks feared to disturb his relics, but on the north side of the high altar. She is named in the Roman Martyrology, and her feast is kept at several places in Germany, but, rather surprisingly, nowhere in England.

There is a biography, said to have been compiled by Rudolf, a monk of Fulda, before 838, which has been printed by Mabillon and the Bollandists (September, vol. vii) ; and, as pointed out above, a good deal of reliable information comes to us through the correspondence of St Boniface and of St Lull. This has been edited in modern times by Jaffé, and still more recently in MGH., first by Dümmler and again by Tangl. See also H. Timerding, *Die christliche Frühzeit Deutschlands*, vol. ii, *Die angelsächsische Mission* (1929);

L. Eckenstein, *Woman under Monasticism*, ch. iv; and W. Levison, *England and the Continent in the Eighth Century* (1946). Rudolf's Life of Lioba is translated in C. H. Talbot's *Anglo-Saxon Missionaries in Germany* (1954).

BD LAURENCE OF RIPAFRATTA   (A.D. 1457)

THE so-called Great Schism of the West, during which the papacy underwent a " Babylonian captivity " at Avignon, was inevitably a time of great trial and difficulty for all Catholic institutions, and among them the Order of Preachers went through a period of relaxation of its earlier fervour.   In Italy and other places this was aggravated by outbreaks of plague which depopulated the houses of the order, but there also God raised up Bd Raymund of Capua to lead a movement of reform. Among those who supported him was Bd John Dominici, Archbishop of Ragusa, who discovered the abilities and virtues of Friar Laurence of Ripafratta.   He had entered the order at Pisa when he was already a deacon, and after studying and preaching for some years he was appointed master of novices in the priory of Cortona.   It was an office for which Bd Laurence was peculiarly well qualified. He was a champion of rigorous observance but understood how properly to make use of the adaptability of the constitutions of his order ; and he knew that if once the hearts of his novices were fired with the love of God respect for and obedience to the least provisions of their rule would follow.   Among those who made their novitiate under his direction were St Antoninus, Fra Angelico, and his supposed brother, Benedict of Mugello.   Laurnece encouraged these last two to paint, seeing that preaching may be done as well by pictures as by word of mouth, and in one respect more advantageously : " The most persuasive tongue becomes silent in death, but your heavenly pictures will go on speaking of religion and virtue throughout the ages."

For his biblical knowledge Bd Laurence was, like St Antony of Padua, called the " Ark of the Testament ", and he used his learning in preaching up and down Etruria with much effect.   When he was made vicar general of the priories that had taken up the reform he went to live at Pistoia, where almost at once there was a sharp outbreak of plague.   Laurence immediately turned from his administrative duties to give himself to the service of the sufferers, and, as always, many who were deaf to the appeals of the preacher were moved to penitence by the example of priests moving fearlessly among the infected to minister to their souls and bodies.   After the death of Bd Laurence at an advanced age St Antoninus wrote to the Dominicans of Pistoia, condoling them on their loss and eulogizing the memory of their leader. " How many souls have been snatched from Hell by his words and example and led from depravity to a high perfection ; how many enemies he reconciled and what disagreements he adjusted ; to how many scandals did he put an end.   I weep also for my own loss, for never again shall I receive those tender letters wherewith he used to stir up my fervour in the duties of this pastoral office."   His tomb was the scene of many miracles, and in 1851 Pope Pius IX confirmed his *cultus*.

See V. Marchese, *Cenni storici del b. Lorenzo di Ripafratta* (1851) ; a short life by M. de Waresquiel (1907) ; and Procter, *Dominican Saints*, pp. 38–41.

BD JOHN OF DUKLA   (A.D. 1484)

AMONG the many Poles in the Franciscan Order who adopted the stricter constitutions of the Observant friars in consequence of the preaching of St John of

Capistrano was this John, who was born at Dukla in the year 1414. For long he lived the life almost of a recluse, but after being appointed guardian of the friary at Lwów he gave himself to apostolic activity, and by his preaching and example brought back many to the Church from among the Ruthenians and from the Hussite and other sects ; neither old age nor blindness could curb his zeal. He died on September 29, 1484, and the devotion of his people was answered with miracles ; in 1739 Pope Clement XII approved his *cultus* as a principal patron of Poland and Lithuania.

A tolerably full account of Bd John is given by Dr Kamil Kantak in the *Archivum Franciscanum Historicum*, vol. xxii (1929), pp. 434–437. Writing with a thorough knowledge of Polish sources, he complains of the scantiness of historical material. The facts he cites are drawn from the chronicle of John Komorowski, which was edited by Liske and Lorkiewicz in vol. v of their *Monumenta Poloniae Historica* (1888), see especially pp. 246–249. See also Léon, *Auréole Séraphique* (Eng. trans.), vol. ii, pp. 507–509.

BD BERNARDINO OF FELTRE (A.D. 1494)

THE fifteenth century in Italy was a period of incessant warfare and internal disorder; not the defence of a united nation against aggression, but the outcome of commercial rivalry and political disputes between neighbouring states, the quarrels of princes carried on to a great extent by hired mercenaries, who cared nothing for the goodness or badness of their cause and who would always rather plunder than fight, and fight than work honestly. The people of the peninsula were at the mercy of tyrants and demagogues, demoralized by fighting and political uncertainty, weakened by the refinement of the Renaissance, divided by factions and parties whose differences penetrated into the Church and enfeebled her influence ; faith tended to degenerate into superstition, and morality became more and more corrupt. Of the saints whom this state of things did not fail to bring forth to cope with it, many were members of the Franciscan order in one or other of its branches, and foremost among them Bd Bernardino Tomitani, called " of Feltre ", preacher and practical economist. His coming had been foretold by another Benrardino, of Siena, who, preaching at Perugia, had said : " After me will come another Bernardino, dressed in this same habit, who will do great things. Many, I know, will not listen to him, but do you believe his words and conform to his teaching."

He was born in 1439, at Feltre in Venezia of the noble family of Tomitani (though some have claimed for him a more humble origin at Tome), the eldest of ten children, and received at baptism the name of Martin. Martin was the studious one of the family. When he was twelve he could write Latin verse, and his mother had to force him to play games for the good of his health ; and he cut off his luxuriant hair, saying he would rather use a pen than a comb. In 1454 his father got him admitted into the local college of notaries, and after two years sent him to the University of Padua where he plunged ardently into the study of philosophy and law, and began that acquaintance with the fashionable thought of his time which was afterwards valuable to him as a preacher. The sudden death of two of his professors at Padua had a profound effect on the young student, and soon after he came under the influence of the Franciscan St James of the March, who preached the Lent at Padua in 1456. In May of the same year Martin was clothed as a novice among the Friars Minor of the Observance, and took the name of Bernardino, after him of Siena who had just been canonized. " We have to-day ", said St

James, " enrolled in the militia of Jesus Christ a soldier who will shed a lustre over our order and contribute mightily to the glory of God and the confusion of Satan." Among the delights and interests which he cut himself off from was music. " Above all ", he wrote, " music is not suitable for those consecrated to God. Those chants which please the hearers by the harmony of the voices are not pleasing to the Lord. I should not wish to listen to a *Kyrie* in [figured] music, but I gladly hear it sung in plain chant. In all our monasteries of the Observance [figured] music is forbidden ; we regard it as scandalous to do anything like a concerted piece." Friar Bernardino was ordained priest in 1463, and for six more years continued quietly in study and prayer.

Hitherto Friar Bernardino had done no public preaching, and when in 1469 a chapter at Venice appointed him a preacher he was much troubled. He was nervous, lacked confidence in himself, and seemed physically ill-equipped, for he was very short in stature. This was sufficiently noticeable to earn him the nick-name of *Parvulus* from Pope Innocent VIII, and he used to sign himself " piccolino e poverello ". He therefore consulted his director, Sixtus of Milan, pointing out his lack of experience, his ignorance, his disabilities. Sixtus bade him kneel down, and signing him on the lips with the cross said, " God will take away all hindrance from your tongue to show you that the gift of preaching is from Him alone. Do not fear, my son ! You will learn more from your crucifix than from books." Bernardino felt no more doubt or hesitation ; God had spoken through the holy friar Sixtus. Nevertheless when he first went into the pulpit before a large con-gregation at Mantua on the feast of his patron, he was seized with panic ; he forgot everything, what he wanted to say, how he wanted to say it, all his carefully prepared points and periods. But he remembered his love and admiration for the virtues of St Bernardino of Siena, and he spoke of those, spontaneously, easily and compel-lingly. He never again tried to preach a sermon prepared in detail, but trusted to his heart made virtuous by prayer. " Prayer ", he said, " is a better preparation than study : it is both more efficacious and quicker." Bd Bernardino preached up and down Italy for twenty-five years. Crowds acclaimed him ; the wise and holy, popes, bishops, other great preachers praised him ; the wicked raged against him ; all proclaimed his power. Churches were too small to hold the crowds who wanted to hear him. At Florence and Pavia his congregations covered the main square, and all could hear ; at Padua and Feltre people from afar booked up all the lodgings throughout his stay ; three thousand people followed him through the night from Crema that they might hear him again the next day at Lodi. It has been estimated that Bd Bernardino preached over three thousand six hundred times, but only some 120 of his sermons are extant.* From these it can be judged that he spoke simply, with liveliness, and without any oratorical flourishes. He even eschewed quotations in Latin, because, as he said, " Ostentation never does any good. A sermon of which the thread is often broken by quotations does not ' get across ', it moves nobody."

Bernardino was sent to minister to a society that was in great part selfish, proud and depraved ; he opposed to its vices charity, humility and austerity. He never forgot he was a Friar Minor : he washed the feet of visitors when he was at home, refused the hospitality of the rich, and lodged in lowly places when abroad. But a good example alone is not always enough ; he had to inveigh plainly and often

---

* Bd Bernardino has often been credited with the authorship of *Anima Christi*, but this prayer was written at least ninety years before he was born.

against the evils he saw around him. " When he attacks vice ", wrote Jerome of Ravenna, " he does not speak—he thunders and lightens." Twice this slightly-built little man broke a blood-vessel in the fury of his denunciation of public scandals. " He has a heavy hand and he does not know how to flatter ", said Cardinal d'Agria. Naturally he made enemies for himself, and several attempts were made on his life, but he pursued his way unperturbed. He got the disorders of carnival time controlled and public gambling establishments suppressed in several cities ; the races at Brescia on the feast of the Assumption were abolished because of their abuses; in many places vicious images and books were destroyed by the public authorities ; and, of course, he had continually to attack the extravagances of female dress. Like St Bernardino of Siena before him and Savonarola contemporaneously he finished each mission by having a public bonfire of cards, dice, obscene books and pictures, useless finery, false hair, superstitious philtres, badges of factions, and other vanities. This he called the " burning of the Devil's stronghold ", and it was designed not so much to be a practical removal of occasions of sin as to be a gesture forcibly to strike the imagination of the public. At his appeal civil authorities enacted or repealed laws. Men and women were separated in the public gaols ; the Married Women's Property Act was anticipated and husbands were prevented from wasting the goods of their wives ; the senates of Venice and Vicenza ceased to grant immunity to transgressors who should bring the heads of outlawed relatives.

Bd Bernardino was no respecter of persons when it was a question of the moral law. He reproved the prince of Mantua, a liberal patron of the Friars Minor, for not restraining the rapacity and oppression of his courtiers ; he preached at Milan in defiance of the duke, Galeazzo Visconti ; he denounced the Oddi and the Baglioni, heads of the factions in Perugia ; and when Ferdinand I of Naples ordered him to come from Aquila to answer before the courts, Bernardino refused to give an account of his words unless commanded by his own superiors. The wiser princes trusted and admired him, and when it served their purpose made use of his services as a peacemaker. At Brescia, at Narni, at Faenza and other places he healed public strife and brought tranquillity for a time, and Pope Innocent VIII sent him on a mission of pacification into Umbria. But the feuds of one town defied all his efforts. Three times, in 1484, in 1488, and again in 1493, the year before he died, he went to Perugia to try and compose its dissensions ; and each time he failed. As a contribution towards making peace lasting he encouraged the formation of associations of tertiaries, who were under obligation not to take up arms. Unlike many lesser preachers and moralists in his time Bd Bernardino did not allow his personal successes and consciousness of ecclesiastical abuses to lead him into an independent attitude towards the church authorities. When the Holy See offered him faculties to absolve from sins reserved to the bishops, he replied : " The bishops are the ordinary shepherds of the clergy and the people, and I would rather depend on them in all those circumstances where the law of the Church requires it."

From time to time we hear much of the hardships which the Jews suffered at the hands of Christians in the middle ages, and it cannot be denied that monstrous injustices were perpetrated against them. On the other hand the problem of how to deal with the " anti-social " activities of some Jews was a real one, and most inadequately met by the device of so far as possible isolating them from the life of their Christian surroundings. Bd Bernardino of Feltre was, throughout his career, in conflict with Jews, not as Jews but as the cause and occasion of some of the worst of the abuses which it was his business to combat. He spoke of them at Crema thus : " Jews must not be harmed either in their persons or their property or in any way whatever. Justice and charity must be extended to them, for they are of the same nature as ourselves. I say this everywhere and I repeat it here at Crema in order that it may be acted upon, because good order, the sovereign pontiffs, and Christian charity alike require it. But it is not less true that canon law expressly forbids too frequent dealings, too great familiarity with them. . . . To-day no one has any scruples in this matter, and I cannot be silent about it. Jewish usurers exceed all bounds ; they ruin the poor and get fat at their expense. I, who live on alms and myself eat the bread of poverty, cannot be a dumb dog before such outrageous injustice. The poor feed me and I cannot hold my tongue when I see them robbed. Dogs bark to protect their masters, and I must bark in the cause of Christ." The lending of money at usury, with huge rates of interest, to which Bernardino refers above, was the chief (but not the only) complaint against Jews, who had thus succeeded in making themselves hated by the poor and necessary to the rich.*

A century earlier a bishop of London, Michael of Northborough, had left a thousand silver marks to be lent to the needy without interest, on the security of deposited articles, and among several experiments of the sort this was the first true *mons pietatis*.† In 1462 the Franciscan Barnabas of Terni founded at Perugia a " pawnshop " which should make small loans to the poor upon pledged objects at a low rate of interest. It was immediately successful, and in the following year another was established, at Orvieto, and the institution soon spread to the Marches, the Papal States, Tuscany and elsewhere. The scheme was taken up, organized, and perfected by Bd Bernardino. In 1484 he opened a *mons pietatis* at Mantua (it soon succumbed to the hostility of usurers), and was responsible for twenty more during the following eight years. The details of the organization varied, but they were generally administered by mixed committees of friars and laymen representative of different trades, and some were municipally controlled. The initial capital fund was obtained in part from voluntary subscriptions and in part by loans from the Jews themselves ; all profits were added to capital and applied to the reduction of rates of interest. It was natural that Bernardino should be fiercely attacked by the Jews and Lombards, who succeeded in getting some of his *montes pietatis* closed ; but a more serious and no less inevitable opposition came from some canonists and moral theologians who insisted that the interest charged was usurious within the meaning of canon law and therefore sinful. They wished the loans to be free. This would have meant that the *montes* could not be self-supporting, and Bd Bernardino stood firmly for the charging of small interest. The controversy was fierce and was never settled in his time. But the fifth General Council of the Lateran decreed in 1515 that *montes pietatis* were lawful and worthy of all encouragement, and thereafter they became common throughout western

---

* Jews were not the only offenders. There were, for example, also the Lombard bankers and the *Caorcini* (from Cahors in France?). Bd Bernardino was a child of his age and believed the charges brought against the Jews of Trent in 1475 in respect of Little St Simon. See an account of him herein under March 24.

† *Monte di pietà, mont-de-piété.* Literally a " heap of money of piety ", *mons* signifying an accumulation of wealth, capital, and *pietatis* that it was not a commercial concern ; but the meaning " pity, compassion " is also involved.

Europe, except in the British Isles. His struggle for these institutions is the work for which Bd Bernardino of Feltre is best remembered, and he is often represented in art with a little green hill of three mounds, each surmounted by a cross, with the legend *Curam illius habe :* a more pleasing and good-omened device than the three bezants borrowed by English pawnbrokers from the arms of Lombardy—though this was the badge of Savonarola's *mons pietatis* at Florence.

Bd Bernardino worked up to the last. Early in 1494 he told the Florentines he would never see them again, and when he arrived in Siena he heard a report of his own death. " I'm always dying, if one can believe all one hears ", he observed. " But the day will come, and come soon, when it will be true." He welcomed Cardinal Francis Piccolomini (afterwards Pope Pius III), who wished to be his penitent : " We are both of us little men *(piccolomini)* ", was his remark to his Eminence. At the end of August he dragged himself to Pavia to preach, and warned the city that he could " hear the French shoeing their horses for the invasion of Italy "—which within a few months King Charles VIII did. But Bernardino did not live to see it, for he died at Pavia on September 28 following. His *cultus* was approved in 1728.

Materials for the life of this holy Franciscan are fairly abundant, as Father Suyskens pointed out nearly two centuries ago in the long notice of one hundred folio pages accorded to him in the *Acta Sanctorum*, September, vol. vii. The most complete modern biography seems to be that of L. Besse, *Le bx Bernardin de Feltre et son œuvre*, in 2 volumes (1902). But even here an important manuscript source seems to have been but little used, to wit, the journal of Father Francis of Feltre, who for twelve years acted as the great preacher's secretary (see the *Analecta Bollandiana*, vol. xxii, 1903, pp. 118–119). Other documents have since been brought to light, for example, a number of letters concerning Fra Bernardino's preaching in Reggio (Emilia), which are now printed in the *Archivum Franciscanum Historicum*, vol. xix (1926), pp. 226–246. A conveniently brief account of Bd Bernardino is that of E. Flornoy in the series " Les Saints " (1897). See also Léon, *Auréole Séraphique* (Eng. trans.), vol. iii, pp. 243–266 ; and Italian lives by A. Pellin (1938) and F. Casolini (1939).

BD FRANCIS OF CALDEROLA (A.D. 1507)

THE feast of this *beato* is kept by the Friars Minor and the Capuchins. He was born at Calderola in the Italian diocese of Camerino and became a Friar Minor of the Observance of the province of the Marches. Bd Francis was a great missioner, with an unwearying zeal for the reform of sinners and he was known for the long hours he spent hearing confessions. He had an especial gift, both natural and supernatural, for the reconciling of enemies and the settlement of disputes. He was active with Bd Bernardino of Feltre in the establishment of charitable pawn-shops. Francis died at the friary of Colfano on September 12, 1507, and the *cultus* that at once manifested itself was confirmed by Pope Gregory XVI.

There is a short account of Bd Francis of Calderola in the *Acta Sanctorum*, October, vol. xi, though no contemporary life was available. Such chroniclers as Mark of Lisbon, *Chroniche*, lib. viii, cap. 26, and Mazzara, *Leggendario Francescano*, pt 2, vol. i (1679) p. 440, devote a paragraph or two to this *beato*. See also Léon, *Auréole Séraphique* (Eng. trans.), vol. iii, pp. 421–422 ; H. Holzapfel, *Die Anfänge der Montes Pietatis* (1903) ; and a popular account in Italian by G. Stacchiotti (1937).

BD SIMON DE ROJAS (A.D. 1624)

FROM being an exemplary friar of the Trinitarian order, Bd Simon was called to the court of Philip III, King of Spain. Here he was chosen to be confessor to the king's wife, Isabella of Bourbon.   When an epidemic of plague broke out at Madrid, Bd Simon prepared to go to the help of the sufferers, but the king forbade him, fearing that infection might be brought to the court.   " Sick-beds are more fitting places for me than royal palaces ", replied the friar, " and if I must give up one I will give up the court."   Like Bd Alphonsus de Orozco, another chaplain, Simon de Rojas exercised a strong influence in the royal entourage and contributed much to the high standard of religion and morality maintained therein.   He was a great missionary, founded a confraternity of the *Ave Maria*, and wrote an office for the feast of the Holy Name of Mary, to which his order had a special devotion. Bd Simon died ten days after the then date of this feast in 1624, and was beatified in 1766.

Several references to the beatification process of this friar occur in the great work of Benedict XIV, *De . . . beatificatione*, bk ii.   When Bd Simon was beatified there was published in Rome a *Compendio della Vita del B. Simone de Roxas* (1767).   See also P. Deslandres, *L'Ordre des Trinitaires* (1903), vol. i, p. 618, etc.

29 : THE DEDICATION OF THE BASILICA OF ST MICHAEL THE ARCHANGEL, COMMONLY CALLED MICHAELMAS DAY

IT cannot be disputed that in the apocryphal literature, which, both before and after the coming of Christ, was so prevalent in Palestine and among the Jewish communities of the Diaspora, the archangel Michael (Michael= who is like to God ?) played a great part.   A starting-point may be found in the authentic scriptures, for the tenth and twelfth chapters of the Book of Daniel speak of Michael as " one of the chief princes ", the special protector of Israel, and describe how at that time shall Michael rise up, " the great prince who standeth for the children of thy people " (Dan. xii 1).   In the *Book of Henoch*, which is regarded as the most important and influential of all the Old Testament apocrypha, Michael comes before us repeatedly as " the great captain ", " the chief captain ", he " is set over the best part of mankind ", *i.e.* over the chosen race who are the inheritors of the promises.   He is merciful, and it is he who will explain the mystery which underlies the dread judgements of the Almighty.   Michael is depicted as ushering Henoch himself into the divine presence, but he is also associated with the other great archangels, Gabriel, Raphael and Phanuel, in binding the wicked potentates of earth and casting them into a furnace of fire.   The merciful conception of the leader's office is, however, especially emphasized in the *Testaments of the Twelve Patriarchs* and in the *Ascension of Isaias (c.* A.D. 90 ?) in which last we read of " the great angel Michael always interceding for the human race ", but in this same work he is further presented as the scribe who records the deeds of all men in the heavenly books.

In New Testament times it is written in the Apocalypse of St John (xii 7–9) that " there was a great battle in Heaven.   Michael and his angels fought with the dragon, and the dragon fought and his angels ; and they prevailed not, neither was their place found any more in Heaven.   And that great dragon was cast out, that old serpent who is called the Devil and Satan, who seduceth the whole world : and he was cast unto the earth, and his angels were thrown down with him."   Still more significant of the close association of a cult of St Michael with Jewish traditions or folk-lore is the mention of his name in the Epistle of St Jude (v 9) : " When Michael the archangel, disputing with the Devil, contended about the body of Moses, he durst not bring against him the judgement of railing speech, but said : ' The Lord rebuke thee.' " Whether this is a direct quotation from the apocryphal writing known as *The Assumption of Moses* may be disputed, because we do not possess the text of the latter part of that work ; but Origen expressly states that it is a quotation and names this book.   The story there recounted seems to have been that when Moses died, " Samael " (*i.e.* Satan) claimed the body on the ground that Moses, having killed the Egyptian, was a murderer.   This blasphemy kindled the wrath of Michael, but he restrained himself, saying only : " The Lord rebuke thee, thou slanderer (*diabole*)."   What seems certain is that *The Assumption of Moses* did give prominence to the part played by St Michael in the burial of Moses, and also that this same book was cited by certain fathers at the Council of Nicaea in A.D. 325.   It was probably of pre-Christian origin, but we find in the *Shepherd of Hermas*, dating from the early part of the second century A.D., an illustration of the veneration in which St Michael was held by those who were undoubtedly Christians.   In the eighth " similitude " we have the allegory of the twigs cut from the great willow tree, some of which sprout into vigorous life when planted and watered, while others droop or wither away.   An angel of majestic aspect presides over the awards when these twigs are brought back for inspection and judgement is passed upon them.   This, we are told, is " the great and glorious angel Michael who has authority over this people and governs them ; for this is he who gave them the law and implanted it in the hearts of believers ; he accordingly superintends them to whom he gave it to see if they have kept the same ".

The *Shepherd of Hermas* was treated by some of the early fathers as if it formed part of the canon of scripture, but it hardly seems to have been so widely popular as a very extravagant apocryphal writing of Jewish origin known as the *Testament of Abraham*, which is probably not very much later in date.   In this the archangel Michael throughout plays almost the leading part.   His difficult task is to reconcile Abraham to the necessity of death.   Michael is presented to the reader as God's commander-in-chief, the organizer of all the divine relations with earth, one whose intervention is so powerful with God that at his word souls can be rescued even from Hell itself.   We have, for example, passages like the following :

> And Abraham said to the chief-captain [*i.e.* St Michael], " I beseech thee, archangel, hearken to my prayer, and let us call upon the Lord and supplicate His compassion and entreat His mercy for the souls of the sinners whom I formerly in my anger cursed and destroyed, whom the earth swallowed up and the wild beasts tore in pieces and the fire consumed through my words. Now I know that I have sinned before the Lord our God.   Come then, Michael, chief captain of the hosts above, come let us call upon God with tears, that He may forgive my sins and grant them to me."   And the chief captain heard him and they made entreaty before the Lord, and when they had called upon Him for a long space there came a voice from Heaven, saying : " Abraham, Abraham, I have hearkened to thy voice and to thy prayer, and I forgive thee thy sin, and those whom thou thinkest that I destroyed I have called up and brought them into life by my exceeding kindness, because for a season I have requited them in judgement and those whom I destroy living upon earth I will not requite in death."

Whether this and similar *apocrypha* were based on Jewish traditions or not there can be no doubt that they were read by Christians. In most of them there is nothing so glaringly unorthodox as to stamp them as attacks upon the Christian faith. What is more, the thinly disguised fictional element, which is predominant in most of the hagiographical literature even of the early centuries, must infallibly have dulled the critical sense of the great majority of readers, however piously inclined. To this we may safely attribute the fact that these apocryphal writings were very widely circulated and that we find echoes of them even in a canonical epistle like that of St Jude and still more in several of the early Greek fathers. The liturgy itself was imperceptibly coloured by them. A most conspicuous example is the still existing offertory chant in Masses for the dead :

> Lord Jesus Christ, king of glory, deliver the souls of all the faithful departed from the pains of Hell and from the deep pit ; deliver them from the mouth of the lion that Hell may not swallow them up and that they may not fall into darkness, but may the standard-bearer Michael conduct them into the holy light, which thou didst promise of old to Abraham and his seed. We offer to thee, Lord, sacrifices and prayers ; do thou receive them in behalf of those souls whom we commemorate this day. Grant them, Lord, to pass from death to that life which thou didst promise of old to Abraham and to his seed.

There are many reminiscences here of the type of apocryphal literature which has just been spoken of. The association of St Michael with Abraham is full of significance for anyone who is acquainted with the so-called *Testament of Abraham*. To enter into details would here be out of place, but it must suffice to point out that from the prominence thus given to St Michael, further developments followed very naturally, as has been pointed out herein under the Appearing of St Michael, on May 8.

Today's festival has been kept with great solemnity at the end of September ever since the sixth century at least. The Roman Martyrology implies that the dedication of the famous church of St Michael on Mount Gargano gave occasion to the institution of this feast in the West, but it would appear that it really celebrates the dedication of a basilica in honour of St Michael on the Salarian Way six miles north of Rome. In the East, where he was regarded as having care of the sick (rather than, as today, captain of the heavenly host and protector of soldiers), veneration of this archangel began yet earlier and certain healing waters were named after him, as at Khairotopa and Colossae. Sozomen tells us that Constantine the Great built a church in his honour, called the Michaelion, at Sosthenion, some way from Constantinople, and that in it the sick were often cured and other wonders wrought. Many churches in honour of St Michael stood in the city of Constantinople itself, including a famous one at the Baths of Arcadius, whose dedication gave the Byzantines their feast of November 8.

Though only St Michael be mentioned in the title of this festival, it appears from the prayers of the Mass that all the good angels are its object, together with this glorious tutelary angel of the Church. On it we are called upon in a particular manner to give thanks to God for the glory which the angels enjoy and to rejoice in their happiness ; to thank Him for His mercy in constituting such beings to minister to our salvation by aiding us ; to join them in worshipping and praising God, praying that we may do His will as it is done by these blessed spirits in

Heaven ; and lastly, we are invited to honour them and implore their intercession and succour.

Apart from the veneration of St Michael, the earliest liturgical recognition of the other great archangels seems to be found in the primitive Greek form of the Litany of the Saints. Edmund Bishop was of opinion (*Liturgica Historica*, pp. 142–151) that this may be traced back to the time of Pope Sergius (687–701). In it St Michael, St Gabriel and St Raphael are invoked in succession just as they are today, the only difference being that they there take precedence, not only of St John the Baptist, but also of the Blessed Virgin herself. See *Dictionnaire de la Bible*, vol. iv, cc. 1067–1075 ; DAC., vol. xi, cc. 903–907 ; DTC., vol. i, cc. 1189–1271 ; *Acta Sanctorum*, September, vol. vii ; K. A. Kellner, *Heortology* (1908), pp. 328–333 ; and on the archangels in art it is sufficient to give a reference to Künstle, *Ikonographie*, vol. i, pp. 239–264, though the subject has also been fully treated by A. Didron, van Drival, and others. For the angels in the church fathers, see J. Daniélou, *Les anges et leur mission* (1952).

SS. RHIPSIME, GAIANA, and their Companions, Virgins and Martyrs   (*c.* A.D. 312 ?)

ALTHOUGH these maidens, apparently the protomartyrs of the Armenian church, are mentioned in the Roman Martyrology on this date as suffering under King Tiridates, nothing at all is known of their history or the circumstances of their passion. They are referred to in the legend of St Gregory the Enlightener, and may have been put to death during the persecution which preceded the baptism of Tiridates and his family by Gregory, but more likely later : their *acta* is a romance of the most barefaced kind.

These legends tell us that Rhipsime (Hrip'sime) was a maiden of noble birth, one of a community of consecrated virgins at Rome presided over by Gaiana. The Emperor Diocletian, having made up his mind to marry, sent a painter around Rome to paint the portraits of all those ladies who seemed to him eligible, and he did his work with such thoroughness that he penetrated into the house of Gaiana and made likenesses of some of her Christian maidens. When Diocletian examined the portraits his choice fell on Rhipsime, and she was informed of the honour that had befallen her. It was not at all to her liking, and Gaiana was so afraid of what the emperor might do that she summoned her charges at once from Rome, went aboard ship, and proceeded to Alexandria. From thence they made their way through the Holy Land to Armenia, where they settled down at the royal capital, Varlarshapat, and earned their living by weaving. The great beauty of Rhipsime soon attracted attention, but the noise of it apparently reached back to Rome before it came to the ears of King Tiridates, for Diocletian wrote asking him to kill Gaiana and send Rhipsime back—unless he would like to keep her for himself. Tiridates thereupon sent a deputation to fetch her to his palace with great magnificence, but when it arrived at the convent Rhipsime prayed for deliverance, and so fierce a thunderstorm at once broke out that the horses of the courtiers and their riders were scattered in confusion. When Tiridates heard this and that the girl refused to come he ordered her to be brought by force, and when she was led into his presence he was so attracted by her beauty that he at once tried to embrace her. Rhipsime not only resisted but threw the king ignominiously to the floor, so that in a rage he ordered her to prison. But she escaped and returned to her companions during the night.

At morning when they found her gone the king sent soldiers after her with orders that she was to die, and all the other maidens with her. St Rhipsime was roasted alive and torn limb from limb, and St Gaiana and the others to the number of thirty-five likewise were brutally slain.   St Mariamne was dragged to death from a bed of sickness, but one, St Nino, escaped and became the apostle of Georgia in the Caucasus.   This massacre took place on October 5, on which date the martyrs are named in the Armenian menology.   A week later retribution overtook the brutal Tiridates who, as he was setting out to hunt, was turned into a wild boar. He was brought back to nature by St Gregory the Enlightener, who had been confined in a pit for fifteen years.   These martyrs figured in the fabulous vision of St Gregory at Etshmiadzin, and around the great church there are three smaller churches on the alleged site of the martyrdom of St Rhipsime, of St Gaiana and of the others.

Extravagant as the legend is, there can be no question that the *cultus* of these martyrs meets us at an early date in Armenia, and that it was very widely diffused.   We find Rhipsime mentioned in Egypt under the Coptic form " Arepsima " (see *Analecta Bollandiana*, vol. xlv (1927), pp. 157 and 395), as well as in Arabic texts and in the Syriac martyrology of Rabban Sliba.   From the testimony of the Armenian historians Faustus and Lazarus, it seems safe to state that the martyrs were venerated before the middle of the fifth century. See Tournebize, *Histoire politique et religieuse d'Arménie*, pp. 452 *seq.* and *passim*.   One Greek version of their " acts ", attributed to Agathangelus, is printed in the *Acta Sanctorum*, September, vol. viii, associated with those of St Gregory on September 30 : all students of his legend agree that the Rhipsime part of it is pure fable.   *Cf.* also S. Weber, *Die katholische Kirche in Armenien* (1903), p. 117, etc., and the *Analecta Bollandiana*, vol. lx (1942), pp. 102–114.   In the opinion of Fr Paul Peeters " It would perhaps be going too far to deny the existence of these martyrs. . . .".

ST THEODOTA, Martyr   (*c.* A.D. 318 ?)

THIS Theodota is supposed to have suffered at Philippopolis in Thrace during the persecution raised by the *Augustus* Licinius when he professed paganism and went to war with Constantine the Great.   Her quite unreliable " acts " are full of exaggeration and embroidery.   According to them, Agrippa the prefect at a festival of Apollo commanded that the whole city should offer sacrifice with him. Theodota was accused of refusing to conform and, being called upon by the president, answered him that she had indeed been a grievous sinner, but could not add sin to sin or defile herself with a sacrilegious sacrifice.   Her constancy encouraged seven hundred and fifty people to step forward and, professing themselves Christians, to refuse to join in the sacrifice.   Theodota was cast into prison where she lay twenty days.   Being brought to the bar again she burst into tears and prayed aloud that Christ would pardon the crimes of her past life, and arm her with strength that she might be enabled to bear with constancy the torments she was going to suffer.   In her answers to the judge she confessed that she had been a harlot but that she had become a Christian, though unworthy to bear that sacred name.   Agrippa commanded her to be scourged.   Those that stood near exhorted her to free herself from torments by obeying the president : for one moment would suffice.   But Theodota remained constant.

The president then ordered her to be put on the rack and her body to be torn with an iron comb.   Under these tortures she prayed and said, " I worship you, O Christ, and thank you, because you have made me worthy to suffer this for your name ".   The judge, enraged at her resolution and patience, ordered the executioner to pour vinegar and salt into her wounds.   But she only said, " I fear your torments so little that I ask you to increase them, that I may find mercy and attain to the greater crown." Agrippa next commanded the executioners to pull out her teeth, which they did violently, one by one. The judge at length condemned her to be stoned to death. She was led out of the city and during her martyrdom prayed, " O Christ, who showed favour to Rahab the harlot and received the good thief, turn not your mercy from me ". In this manner she died and her soul ascended triumphant to Heaven.

This extravagant legend has not been included by the Bollandists in the *Acta Sanctorum*. The Syriac text was first published by Assemani in his *Acta Sanctorum Orientalium et Occidentalium*, vol. ii, pp. 210–226, and since then by other scholars. Mrs A. Smith Lewis, in *Studia Sinaitica*, vol. x, has printed some better readings of the text.

BD RICHARD OF HAMPOLE (A.D. 1349)

THE authority for the attribution of the title Blessed to Richard Rolle is no more than that given by a considerable popular *cultus* in the past, which has never yet been confirmed by the competent authority. After his death the honour in which he was held and the miracles reported at his tomb caused preparations for his canonization to be made, but the cause was never prosecuted. The Breviary of the Church of York had an office prepared for his feast, to which this warning was attached : " The Office of Saint Richard, hermit, after he shall be canonized by the Church, because in the meantime it is not allowed to sing the canonical hours *de eo* in public, nor to solemnize his feast. Nevertheless, having evidence of the extreme sanctity of his life, we may venerate him and in our private devotions seek his intercession, and commend ourselves to his prayers." The Matins lessons of this office are the principal source for the life of Richard, in whom more interest has been taken in recent years than in any other English uncanonized saint on account of the unique position which he holds among English mystical writers.

Richard was born about the year 1300 at Thornton in Yorkshire, traditionally identified as Thornton-le-Dale in the North Riding. With the help of Master Thomas Neville, afterwards archdeacon of Durham, his parents sent him to Oxford, which he left in his nineteenth year. The *officium* tells us that he went home, begged two of his sister's gowns, and made out of them so well as he was able a habit which roughly resembled that of a hermit. His sister thought he was mad and told him so, and he fled away lest his friends should prevent him, for he was acting without his father's knowledge and against his wish. On the vigil of our Lady's Assumption he turned up in the church of a neighbouring parish (Topcliffe ?) at Vespers, and knelt down at the bench reserved to the squire, John of Dalton. He was recognized by the squire's sons, who had been with him at Oxford. Next day he was in church again and, vested in a surplice, assisted at the singing of Matins and Mass. After the gospel he came and asked the celebrant's blessing, and went into the pulpit and " gave the people a sermon of wonderful edification, in so much that the crowd that heard it was moved to tears, and they all said that they had never before heard a sermon of such virtue and power ". After Mass John of Dalton asked Richard to dinner, and when he had convinced himself of the youth's good faith and honesty of purpose he offered him a suitable place to live in and gave him proper clothes, food and all else that he required. " Then he began with all diligence by day and night to seek how to perfect his life and to take every opportunity to advance in contemplation and to be fervent in divine love."

On the face of it there are certain features in this narrative appropriate to a more primitive age of Christianity than England in the fourteenth century, and there is reason to think that the author of the *officium* has somewhat " telescoped " events, with the usual object of making his story more edifying to the faithful. In his own works Richard Rolle refers to his youth as having been unclean and sinful, which, even after allowing for the self-depreciation of holiness, does not accord with the tone of the *officium*.

Therefore when his sudden appearance in a Yorkshire parish church and subsequent events took place he was not a youth fresh from Oxford but an experienced man of twenty-seven or twenty-eight ; not, as is usually supposed, a relatively unlearned layman, but perhaps a priest, even a doctor of theology. " He was first a Doctor, and then leaving the world became an Eremite ", wrote the priest John Wilson, who published an English martyrology in 1608. For some years Richard continued his eremitical life on the Daltons' estate. Writers on mysticism have described from his own writings his progress in contemplation, and brought it into accord with the now classical scheme of the purgative, illuminative and unitive ways, though the terms which he uses, *dulcor, canor* and *calor* or *fervor* do not correspond with these stages. The last is undoubtedly the state of passive contemplation or mystical union where, as he says, the soul " ascends not into another degree, but as it were confirmed in grace, so far as mortal can be, she rests ". " I did not think anything like it or anything so holy could be received in this life." But Richard claims no direct revelations or visions such as are apparently granted to so many of the mystics, and his spiritual experiences were, so far as we know, unaccompanied by any unusual physical phenomena. His seeing the Devil in a certain woman who tempted him seems to be a figure of speech, as perhaps were the demons who left the death-bed of Dame Dalton only to infest his own cell.

Richard himself tells us something of his early difficulties and discouragements. " Rotten rags hardly covered me, and in my nakedness I was annoyed with the bites of the flies which no comfortable covering prevented from walking over me, and my skin became rough with ingrained dirt ; and yet in warm weather I was tormented by the heat, among men who were enjoying all the shade that they desired ; and my teeth chattered with the cold while they were indulging in rich adornments and rejoicing in superfluities—although nevertheless they loved not the Giver of these things." " Indeed, I have so weakened my body and suffer so from headaches in consequence that I cannot stand, so bad are they, unless I am strengthened by wholesome food." Later in life he wrote from experience, " It behoves him truly to be strong that will manfully use the love of God. The flesh being enfeebled with great disease oft-times a man cannot pray, and then much more he cannot lift himself to high things with hot desire. I would rather therefore that man failed for the greatness of love than for too much fasting. . . ." For many years he was troubled by mischief-making tongues, and learned that this too was a mortification to be turned to good account. " This have I known, that the more men have raved against me with words of backbiting, so much the more I have grown in spiritual profit. Forsooth, the worst backbiters I have had are those which I trusted before as faithful friends. Yet I ceased not for their words from those things that were profitable to my soul. . . ." At first Richard lived in the Daltons' house, but afterwards removed to a hermitage at some distance on their estate. But its proximity drew down ill-natured criticism ; " my detractors say that I am led astray by the pleasures in which the rich delight, and am unworthy of God ". He provoked the resentment of some of the clergy including, it would seem, his own bishop, for he did not hesitate to attack those who lived evilly or were worldly, and particularly those who discharged their duties mechanically and did not encourage those who were sincerely concerned for the good of souls.

After the death of Dame Dalton, Richard " for most urgent and practical reasons " went to live in the district of Richmondshire, where one Maundy Thursday he was summoned to Dame Margaret Kirkby, a recluse and dear friend, who had been seriously ill for a fortnight and quite speechless. " And as she sat by the window of her dwelling and they were eating together, it befell at the end of the meal that the recluse desired to sleep and, so oppressed by sleep, she drooped her head at the window where Richard leaned. And after she had slept thus for a short time, leaning slightly upon Richard, suddenly a violent convulsion seized her. . . . She awoke from sleep, the power of speech was restored to her, and she burst forth, ' Gloria tibi Domine '. And Richard finished the verse which she had begun, saying, ' Qui natus es de Virgine ', with the rest of the Compline hymn. Then said he to her, ' Now your speech is come back to you, use it as a woman whose speech is for good.' " From time to time Richard visited various places in Yorkshire, " so that dwelling in many places he might benefit many unto salvation . . . for it is not ill for hermits to leave cells for a reasonable cause, and afterwards, if it accord, to turn again to the same ", and eventually settled at Hampole, on the Wakefield road four miles from Doncaster, where he had a cell near the priory of Cistercian nuns. Whether he was their accredited chaplain or simply an unofficial adviser and friend is not known.

Some think that Richard Rolle's best-known work, *Incendium amoris*, was written here, the book in which " I here stir all manner of folk to love, and am busy to show the hottest and supernatural desire of love ". But it is more likely that he was now writing only, or mostly, in English. He had already translated and commented on the psalms for Margaret Kirkby (a chained copy was kept at Hampole Priory) and written a little book in English for a Benedictine nun at Yedingham, and he now wrote for one of the Hampole nuns the *Commandment of Love to God*, a fruit of the experience of middle age and one of the most moving of all his works. Any further details of his life we do not know, but it is abundantly clear from his own writings that he had reached those heights of contemplation and joyful resignation to God's will that are hardly attainable without an exercise of virtue not less than heroic. " As death slays all living things in this world, so perfect love slays in a man's soul all earthly desires and covetousness. And as Hell spares nought to dead men but torments all that come thereto, so a man that is in this degree of love not only forsakes the wretched solace of this life but also he desires to suffer pains for God's love."

Richard Rolle died at Hampole on September 29, 1349 ; the circumstances are not known but it is extremely likely that he was a victim of the Black Death which raged in Yorkshire in that year. The sort of man Richard was, as seen in his written works, is no less attractive than the works themselves : he was the opposite of all those qualities which ignorance and prejudice attribute to those who choose to be hermits and seek God alone rather than in company. " The holy lover of God shows himself neither too merry nor full heavy in this habitation of exile, but he has cheerfulness with maturity. Some, indeed, reprove laughter and some praise it. Laughter therefore which is from lightness and vanity of mind is to be reproved, but that truly which is of gladness of conscience and spiritual mirth is to be praised ; the which is only in the righteous, and it is called mirth in the love of God. Wherefore if we be glad and merry the wicked call us wanton ; and if we be heavy, hypocrites."

Miss Hope Emily Allen has of all other investigators rendered the greatest service to students in her books, *Writings ascribed to Richard Rolle and Materials for his Biography* (1927) and his English Writings (1931). See also F. Comper, *Life and Lyrics of Richard Rolle* (1928) ; R. M. Woolley, *Richard Rolle of Hampole* (1919) ; C. Horstman, *English Works of Richard Rolle*, 2 vols. (1896)—an uncritical compilation ; M. Deanesly, the *Incendium amoris* (1926) ; G. C. Heseltine, *Selected Works of Richard Rolle* (1930) ; and a French translation of sundry works by Dom Noetinger, in his *Mystiques anglais* (1928). See too an article by this last writer in the *Month*, January 1926, pp. 22 *seq.*

BD CHARLES OF BLOIS (A.D. 1364)

THIS royal saint has a particular interest for English people as he had the misfortune to spend nine years in our country—as a prisoner in the Tower of London. He was born in 1320, son of Guy de Châtillon, Count of Blois, and Margaret, the sister of the king of France, Philip VI, and as a young man showed himself both virtuous and brave and unusually worthy of his high rank. In 1337 he married Joan of Brittany, and by this marriage himself claimed the dukedom of Brittany. His claim was disputed by John de Montfort, and he was immediately involved in warfare that continued to the end of his life. Charles did all in his power to allay the stress of war for his subjects, and is said to have offered to settle the succession by single combat in his own person. The first thing he did after the capture of Nantes was to provide for the poor and suffering, and he showed the same solicitude at Rennes, Guingamp and elsewhere. To pray for his cause and the souls of those who were slain he founded religious houses, and in general behaved so that the less devout of his followers complained that he was more fit to be a monk than a soldier. He went on pilgrimage barefooted to the shrine of St Ivo at Tréguier, and when he held up the siege of Hennebont that his troops might assist at Mass one of his officers was moved to protest. " My lord ", retorted Charles, " we can always have towns and castles. If they are taken away from us, God will help us to get them back again. But we cannot afford to miss Mass." Charles was, in fact, as good a soldier as he was a Christian, but the weight of arms against him was too heavy. He had the support of the French king, but his rival John was helped by Edward III of England, who for his own reasons had announced his intention of winning back his " lawful inheritance of France ". For four years Charles was able to keep his enemies at bay, but 1346 was a year of piled-up misfortune. France was beaten by England at Crecy, Poitiers was sacked, and Poitou overrun ; then Charles in a great battle at La Roche-Derrien, not far from Tréguier, was defeated, captured and shipped across to England.

He was housed in the Tower and a huge sum of money was asked for his ransom, so that it was nine years before Charles regained his liberty. Like many prisoners in the Tower before and since his time, he sanctified his confinement by patience and prayer and earned the ungrudging admiration of his gaolers. He pursued his struggle for the defence of his duchy another nine years, with varying fortunes but with ever growing respect and admiration from his people. At one time it was even thought that the pilgrimage of *Bonne Nouvelle* at Rennes commemorated one of the battles, but this has been shown not to be so. The last engagement took place at Auray on September 29, 1364, a battle in which the English forces were commanded by Sir John Chandos, and Bertrand du Guesclin was taken prisoner. Charles, the man who would always rather have been a Franciscan friar than a prince, was killed on the field.   Numerous and remarkable miracles were reported at his tomb at Guingamp, and there was a strong movement for his canonization in spite of the opposition of John IV de Montfort, whose cause in Brittany might suffer were his late rival to be canonized.   Pope Gregory XI seems in fact to have decreed it, but in the turmoil of his departure from Avignon in 1376 the bull was never drawn up.   The people nevertheless continued to venerate Bd Charles, his feast was celebrated in some places, and finally in 1904 this ancient *cultus* was confirmed by St Pius X.

The Bollandists mention Charles of Blois among the *praetermissi* of September 29 in the *Acta Sanctorum*, and refer to Pope Benedict XIV's *De . . . beatificatione*, bk ii, ch. 8. See A. de Sérent, *Monuments du procès de canonisation du bx Charles de Blois* (1921), which includes Dom Plaine's account of Charles of 1872 ; G. Lobineau, *Histoire de Bretagne* (1744), vol. ii, pp. 540–570 ; and N. Maurice-Denis-Boulet, " La canonisation de Charles de Blois " in the *Revue d'histoire de l'Église de France*, t. xxviii (1942), pp. 216–224.

30 : ST JEROME, Doctor of the Church   (A.D. 420)

JEROME (EUSEBIUS HIERONYMUS SOPHRONIUS), the father of the Church most learned in the Sacred Scriptures, was born about the year 342 at Stridon, a small town upon the confines of Pannonia, Dalmatia and Italy, near Aquileia.   His father took great care to have his son instructed in religion and in the first principles of letters at home and afterwards sent him to Rome.   Jerome had there for tutor the famous pagan grammarian Donatus.   He became master of the Latin and Greek tongues (his native language was the Illyrian), read the best writers in both languages with great application, and made progress in oratory ; but being left without a guide under the discipline of a heathen master he forgot some of the true piety which had been instilled into him in his childhood.   Jerome went out of this school free indeed from gross vices, but unhappily a stranger to a Christian spirit and enslaved to vanity and other weaknesses, as he afterward confessed and bitterly lamented.   On the other hand he was baptized at Rome (he was a catechumen till he was at least eighteen) and he himself tells us that " it was my custom on Sundays to visit, with friends of my own age and tastes, the tombs of the martyrs and apostles, going down into those subterranean galleries whose walls on either side preserve the relics of the dead ". After some three years in Rome he determined to travel in order to improve his studies and, with his friend Bonosus, he went to Trier.   Here it was that the religious spirit with which he was so deeply imbued was awakened, and his heart was entirely converted to God.

In 370 Jerome settled down for a time at Aquileia, where the bishop, St Valerian, had attracted so many good men that its clergy were famous all over the Western church.   With many of these St Jerome became friendly, and their names appear in his writings.   Among them were St Chromatius, then a priest, who succeeded Valerian ; his two brothers, the deacons Jovinian and Eusebius ; St Heliodorus and his nephew Nepotian ; and, above all, Rufinus, first the bosom friend and then the bitter opponent of Jerome.   Already he was beginning to make enemies and provoke strong opposition, and after two or three years an unspecified conflict broke up the group, and Jerome decided to withdraw into some distant country. Bonosus, who had been the companion of his studies and his travels from childhood, went to live on a desert island in the Adriatic.   Jerome himself happened to meet a well-known priest of Antioch, Evagrius, at Aquileia, which turned his mind towards the East.   With his friends Innocent, Heliodorus and Hylas (a freed slave of St Melania) he determined to go thither.

St Jerome arrived in Antioch in 374 and made some stay there.   Innocent and Hylas were struck down by illness and died, and Jerome too sickened.   In a letter to St Eustochium he relates that in the heat of fever he fell into a delirium in which he seemed to himself to be arraigned before the judgement-seat of Christ.   Being asked who he was, he answered that he was a Christian.   " Thou liest ", was the reply, " Thou art a Ciceronian : for where thy treasure is, there is thy heart also." This experience had a deep effect on him which was deepened by his meeting with St Malchus, whose strange story is related herein under October 21.   As a result, St Jerome withdrew into the wilderness of Chalcis, a barren land to the south-east of Antioch, where he spent four years alone.   He suffered much from ill health, and even more from strong temptations of the flesh.

" In the remotest part of a wild and stony desert ", he wrote years afterwards to St Eustochium, " burnt up with the heat of the scorching sun so that it frightens even the monks that inhabit it, I seemed to myself to be in the midst of the delights and crowds of Rome. . . .   In this exile and prison to which for the fear of Hell I had voluntarily condemned myself, with no other company but scorpions and wild beasts, I many times imagined myself witnessing the dancing of the Roman maidens as if I had been in the midst of them.   My face was pallid with fasting, yet my will felt the assaults of desire : in my cold body and in my parched-up flesh, which seemed dead before its death, passion was able to live.   Alone with this enemy, I threw myself in spirit at the feet of Jesus, watering them with my tears, and I tamed my flesh by fasting whole weeks.   I am not ashamed to disclose my temptations, but I grieve that I am not now what I then was.   I often joined night to day crying and beating my breast till calm returned."   Thus does God allow His servants to be from time to time severely tried ; but the ordinary life of St Jerome was doubtless quiet, regular and undisturbed.   To forestall and ward off the insurgence of the flesh he added to his corporal austerities a new study, which he hoped would fix his rambling imagination and give him the victory over himself. This was to learn Hebrew.   " When my soul was on fire with bad thoughts," says he writing to the monk Rusticus in 411, " as a last resource I became a scholar to a monk who had been a Jew, to learn of him the Hebrew alphabet ; and, from the judicious rules of Quintilian, the copious flowing eloquence of Cicero, the grave style of Fronto, and the smoothness of Pliny, I turned to this language of hissing and broken-winded words.   What labour it cost me, what difficulties I went through, how often I despaired and left off, and how I began again to learn, both I myself who felt the burden can witness, and they also who lived with me.   And I thank our Lord, that I now gather such sweet fruit from the bitter sowing of those studies."   However, he still continued to read the pagan classics from time to time.

The church of Antioch was at this time disturbed by doctrinal and disciplinary disputes.   The monks of the desert of Chalcis vehemently took sides in these disputes and wanted St Jerome to do the same and to pronounce on the matters at issue.   He preferred to stand aloof and be left to himself, but he wrote two letters to consult St Damasus, who had been raised to the papal chair in 366, what course he ought to steer.   In the first he says : " I am joined in communion with your holiness, that is, with the chair of Peter ; upon that rock I know the Church is built.   Whoever eats the Lamb outside of that house is a profane person.   Whoever is not in the ark shall perish in the flood.   I do not know Vitalis ; I disown Meletius ; Paulinus * is a stranger to me.   Whoever gathers not with you, scatters ; he who is not Christ's belongs to Antichrist. . . .   Order me, if you please, what I should do."   Not receiving a speedy answer he soon after sent another letter on the same subject.   The answer of Damasus is not extant : but it is certain that he and the West acknowledged Paulinus as bishop of Antioch, and St Jerome received from his hands the order of priesthood when he finally left the desert of Chalcis. Jerome had no wish to be ordained (he never celebrated the holy Sacrifice), and he only consented on the condition that he should not be obliged to serve that or any other church by his ministry : his vocation was to be a monk or recluse.   Soon after he went to Constantinople, there to study the Holy Scriptures under St Gregory Nazianzen.   In several parts of his works Jerome mentions with satisfaction and gratitude the honour and happiness of having had so great a master in expounding the divine writings.   Upon St Gregory's leaving Constantinople in 382, St Jerome went to Rome with Paulinus of Antioch and St Epiphanius to attend a council which St Damasus held about the schism at Antioch.   When the council was over, Pope Damasus detained him and employed him as his secretary ; Jerome, indeed, claimed that he spoke through the mouth of Damasus.   At the pope's request he made a revision, in accordance with the Greek text, of the Latin version of the gospels, which had been disfigured by " false transcription, by clumsy correction, and by careless interpolations ", and a first revision of the Latin psalter.

Side by side with this official activity he was engaged in fostering and directing the marvellous flowering of asceticism which was taking place among some of the noble ladies of Rome.   Among them are several of the most famous names of Christian antiquity : such were St Marcella, who is referred to herein under January 31, with her sister St Asella and their mother, St Albina ; St Lea ; St Melania the Elder, the first one of them to go to the Holy Land ; St Fabiola (December 27) ; and St Paula (January 26) with her daughters St Blesilla and St Eustochium (September 28).   But when St Damasus died in 384, and his protection was consequently withdrawn from his secretary, St Jerome found himself in a very difficult position.   In the preceding two years, while impressing all Rome by his personal holiness, learning and honesty, he had also contrived to get himself widely disliked ; on the one hand by pagans and men of evil life whom he had fiercely condemned and on the other by people of good will who were offended by the saint's harsh outspokenness and sarcastic wit.   When he wrote in defence of the fashionable young widow, Blesilla, who had suddenly renounced the world, he was witheringly satirical of pagan society and worldly life, and opposed to her lowliness the conduct of those who " paint their cheeks with rouge and their eyelids with antimony ; whose plastered faces, too white for those of human beings, look like idols, and if in a moment of forgetfulness they shed a tear it makes a furrow where it rolls down the painted cheek ; they to whom years do not bring the gravity of age, who load their heads with other people's hair, enamel a lost youth upon the wrinkles of age, and affect a maidenly timidity in the midst of a troop of grandchildren."   In the letter on virginity which he wrote to St Eustochium he

* Rival claimants to the see of Antioch.

was no less scathing at the expense of Christian society, and made a particular attack on certain of the clergy. "All their anxiety is about their clothes. . . . You would take them for bridegrooms rather than for clerics ; all they think about is to know the names and houses and doings of rich ladies " ; and he proceeds to describe a particular individual, who hates fasting, looks forward to the smell of his meals, and has a barbarous and froward tongue.   Jerome wrote to St Marcella of a certain man who wrongly supposed that he was an object of attack : " I amuse myself by laughing at the grubs, the owls and the crocodiles, and he takes all that I say to himself. . . . Let me give him some advice.   If he will only conceal his nose and keep his tongue still he may be taken to be both handsome and learned."

It cannot be matter of surprise that, however justified his indignation was, his manner of expressing it aroused resentment.   His own reputation was attacked with similar vigour ; even his simplicity, his walk and smile, the expression of his countenance were found fault with.   Neither did the severe virtue of the ladies that were under his direction nor the reservedness of his own behaviour protect him from calumny : scandalous gossip was circulated about his relations with St Paula.   He was properly indignant and decided to return to the East, there to seek a quiet retreat.   He embarked at Porto in August 385.   Before he left he wrote a fine *apologia*, in the form of a letter to St Asella.   " Salute Paula and Eustochium ", it concluded, " mine in Christ whether the world wills it or no . . . say to them, we shall all stand before the judgement seat of Christ, and there it shall be seen in what spirit each has lived."   At Antioch nine months later he was joined by Paula, Eustochium and the other Roman religious women who had resolved to exile themselves with him in the Holy Land.   Soon after arriving at Jerusalem they went to Egypt, to consult with the monks of Nitria, as well as with Didymus, a famous blind teacher in the school of Alexandria.

With the help of Paula's generosity a monastery for men was built near the basilica of the Nativity at Bethlehem, together with buildings for three communities of women.   St Jerome himself lived and worked in a large rock-hewn cell near to our Saviour's birthplace, and opened a free school, as well as a hospice, " so that ", as St Paula said, " should Mary and Joseph again visit Bethlehem there would be a place for them to lodge in ".   Here at last were some years of peace. " The illustrious Gauls congregate here, and no sooner has the Briton, so remote from our world, made some progress in religion than he leaves his early-setting sun to seek a land which he knows only by reputation and from the Scriptures. And what of the Armenians, the Persians, the peoples of India and Ethiopia, of Egypt, of Pontus, Cappadocia, Syria and Mesopotamia ? . . .   They throng here and set us the example of every virtue.   The languages differ but the religion is the same ; there are as many different choirs singing the psalms as there are nations. . . .   Here bread, and vegetables grown with our own hands, and milk, country fare, afford us plain and healthy food.   In summer the trees give us shade. In autumn the air is cool and the fallen leaves restful.   In spring our psalmody is sweeter for the singing of the birds.   We do not lack wood when winter snow and cold are upon us.   Let Rome keep its crowds, let its arenas run with blood, its circuses go mad, its theatres wallow in sensuality and, not to forget our friends, let the senate of ladies receive their daily visits."

But Jerome could not stand aside and be mute when Christian truth was threatened.   He had at Rome composed his book against Helvidius on the perpetual virginity of the Blessed Virgin Mary, Helvidius having maintained that Mary had

other children, by St Joseph, after the birth of Christ.   This and certain associated errors were again put forward by one Jovinian.   St Paula's son-in-law, St
Pammachius, and other laymen were scandalized at his new doctrines, and sent
his writings to St Jerome who in 393 wrote two books against Jovinian.   In the
first he shows the excellence of virginity embraced for the sake of virtue, which had
been denied by Jovinian, and in the second confutes his other errors.   This
treatise was written in Jerome's characteristically strong style and certain expressions in it seemed to some persons in Rome harsh and derogatory from the honour
due to matrimony ;   St Pammachius informed St Jerome of the offence which he
and many others took at them.   Thereupon Jerome wrote his Apology to Pammachius, sometimes called his third book against Jovinian, in a tone that can hardly
have given his critics satisfaction.   A few years later he had to turn his attention
to Vigilantius—Dormantius, sleepy, he calls him—a Gallo-Roman priest who both
decried celibacy and condemned the veneration of relics, calling those who paid it
idolaters and worshippers of ashes.   St Jerome in his answer said : " We do not
worship the relics of the martyrs ;   but we honour them that we may worship
Him whose martyrs they are.   We honour the servants that the respect which is
paid to them may be reflected back on the Lord."   He vindicates the honour paid
to martyrs from idolatry because no Christian ever worshipped them as gods, and
in order to show that the saints pray for us he says :   " If the apostles and martyrs
while still living upon earth can pray for other men, how much more may they do
it after their victories ?   Have they less power now they are with Jesus Christ ? "
He defends the monastic state, and says that a monk seeks security by flying occasions
and dangers because he mistrusts his own weakness and knows that there is no
safety if a man sleeps near a serpent.   St Jerome often speaks of the saints in
Heaven praying for us.   Thus he entreated Heliodorus to pray for him when he
should be in glory, and told St Paula, upon the death of her daughter Blesilla, " She
now prays to the Lord for you, and obtains for me the pardon of my sins ".   But
the general tone of his reply to Vigilantius is even more vehement than that to
Jovinian.

     From 395 to 400 St Jerome was engaged in a war against Origenism, which
unhappily involved a breach of his twenty-five years friendship with Rufinus.
Years before he had written to him the doubtful statement that " friendship which
can perish has never been a true one ", as Shakespeare would write twelve hundred
years later :

           . . . Love is not love
           Which alters when it alteration finds
           Or bends with the remover to remove ;

and now his affection for Rufinus was to succumb to his zeal for truth.   Few
writers made more use of Origen's works and no one seemed a greater admirer of
his erudition than St Jerome ;   but finding in the East that some had been seduced
into grievous errors by the authority of his name and some of his writings he joined
St Epiphanius in warmly opposing the spreading evil.   Rufinus, who then lived
in a monastery at Jerusalem, had translated many of Origen's works into Latin
and was an enthusiastic upholder of his authority :   though it does not appear that
he had any intention of upholding those heresies which are undoubtedly contained,
at least materially, in Origen's writings. St Augustine was not the least of the good
men who were distressed by the resulting quarrel, which, however, he the more

easily understood because he himself became involved in a long controversy with St Jerome arising out of the exegesis of the second chapter of St Paul's epistle to the Galatians. By his first letters he had unintentionally provoked Jerome, and had to use considerable charitable tact to soothe his easily wounded susceptibilities. St Jerome wrote in 416 : " I never spared heretics and have always done my utmost that the enemies of the Church should be also my enemies " ; but it seems that sometimes he unwarrantably assumed that those who differed from himself were necessarily the Church's enemies. He was no admirer of moderation whether in virtue or against evil. He was swift to anger, but also swift to remorse, even more severe on his own shortcomings than on those of others. There is a story told that Pope Sixtus V, looking at a picture of the saint which represented him in the act of striking his breast with a stone, said : " You do well to carry that stone, for without it the Church would never have canonized you."

But his denunciations and controversies, necessary as most of them were, are the less important part of his activities : nothing has rendered the name of St Jerome so famous as his critical labours on the Holy Scriptures. For this the Church acknowledges him to have been raised by God through a special providence, and she styles him the greatest of all her doctors in expounding the divine word. Pope Clement VIII did not scruple to call him a man divinely assisted in translating the Bible. He was furnished with the greatest helps for such an undertaking, living many years upon the spot where the remains of ancient places, names, customs which were still recent, and other circumstances set before his eyes a clearer representation of many things recorded in holy writ than it is possible to have at a greater distance of place and time. Greek and Aramaic were then living languages, and Hebrew, though it had ceased to be such from the time of the captivity, was not less understood and spoken among the doctors of the law. It was thought that he could not be further instructed in the knowledge of Hebrew, but this was not his own judgement of the matter and he applied again to a famous Jewish master, called Bar Ananias, who came to teach him in the night-time, lest the Jews should know it. Above other conditions it is necessary that an interpreter of the Bible be a man of prayer and sincere piety. This alone can obtain light and help from Heaven, give to the mind a turn and temper which are necessary for being admitted into the sanctuary of the divine wisdom, and furnish the key. Jerome was prepared by a great purity of heart and a life spent in penance and contemplation before he was called by God to this undertaking. We have seen that while in Rome under Pope St Damasus he had revised the gospels and the psalms in the Old Latin version, followed by the rest of the New Testament. His new translation from the Hebrew of most of the books of the Old Testament was the work of his years of retreat at Bethlehem, which he undertook at the earnest entreaties of many devout and illustrious friends, and in view of the preference of the original to any version however venerable. He did not translate the books in order, but began by the books of Kings, and took the rest in hand at different times. The only parts of the Latin Bible called the Vulgate which were not either translated or worked over by St Jerome are the books of Wisdom, Ecclesiasticus, Baruch and the two books of Machabees. The psalms he revised again, with the aid of Origen's *Hexapla* and the Hebrew text, and this is the version included in the Vulgate and used in the Divine Office.* The first revision, called the Roman Psalter, is still

* Since 1945 there is an alternative Latin version for this purpose, made principally from the Hebrew Masoretic text.

used for the invitatory psalm at Matins and throughout the Missal, and for the Divine Office in St Peter's at Rome, St Mark's at Venice, and in the Milanese rite. St Jerome's Vulgate was declared by the Council of Trent to be the authentic or authoritative Latin biblical text of the Catholic Church, without thereby implying any preference of this version above the original text or above versions in other languages. In 1907 Pope Pius X entrusted to the monks of St Benedict the duty of restoring so far as possible St Jerome's text of the Vulgate, which during fifteen centuries of use has become considerably modified and corrupted. The version of the Bible ordinarily used by English-speaking Catholics is the translation of the Vulgate made at Rheims and Douay towards the end of the sixteenth century, as revised by Bishop Challoner in the eighteenth ; and the English version officially made by Monsignor Ronald Knox was also from the Vulgate.

In the year 404 a great blow fell on St Jerome in the death of St Paula and a few years later in the sacking of Rome by Alaric ; many refugees fled into the East, and he wrote of them : " Who would have believed that the daughters of that mighty city would one day be wandering as servants and slaves on the shores of Egypt and Africa ? That Bethlehem would daily receive noble Romans, distinguished ladies brought up in wealth and now reduced to beggary ? I cannot help them all, but I grieve and weep with them, and, completely given up to the duties which charity imposes on me, I have put aside my commentary on Ezekiel and almost all study. For to-day we must translate the words of the Scriptures into deeds, and instead of speaking saintly words we must act them." Again towards the end of his life he was obliged to interrupt his studies by an incursion of barbarians, and some time after by the violence and persecution of the Pelagians who sent a troop of ruffians to Bethlehem to assault the monks and nuns who lived there under the direction of St Jerome, who had opposed them. Some were beaten, and a deacon was killed, and they set fire to the monasteries. In the following year St Eustochium died and Jerome himself soon followed her : worn out with penance and work, his sight and voice failing, his body like a shadow, he died peacefully on September 30, 420. He was buried under the church of the Nativity close to Paula and Eustochium, but his body was removed long after and now lies somewhere in St Mary Major's at Rome. He is often represented in art habited as a cardinal, because of the services he discharged for Pope St Damasus, and also with a lion from whose paw he was said to have drawn a thorn. This story has been transferred to him from the legend of St Gerasimus, but a lion is a far from inapt emblem of this fearless and fierce defender of the faith.

During recent years much advance has been made in the study of the life of St Jerome. Of special value is the volume *Miscellanea Geronimiana* which was published at Rome in 1920 to do honour to the fifteenth centenary of his death. In this a number of eminent scholars, including Duchesne, Batiffol, Lanzoni, Zeiller and Bulic, contribute studies on moot points of particular interest in connection with the saint. Then in 1922 appeared the best modern life, that of F. Cavallera, *Saint Jérôme, sa vie et son œuvre* (1922, 2 vols.), though the criticisms of Father Peeters in *Analecta Bollandiana*, vol. xlii, pp. 180–184, claim careful attention. At an earlier date we have the discovery by G. Morin of Jerome's *Commentarioli* and *Tractatus* on the psalms, with other finds (see his *Études, textes, découvertes*, pp. 17–25). Further, a very full article on St Jerome by H. Leclercq figures in DAC., vol. vii, cc. 2235– 2304 ; and another by J. Forget in DTC., vol. viii (1924), cc. 894–983. In the eighteenth century we have the painstaking labours of Vallarsi, and of the Bollandists (September, vol. viii). The early accounts of St Jerome, with the exception perhaps of the chronicle of Marcellinus (edited by Mommsen in MGH., *Auctores antiquissimi*, vol. ii, pp. 47 *seq.*), do not offer much of value. Jerome's correspondence and works must always remain the principal source for a study of his life.   See also P. Monceaux, *St Jerome : the Early Years* (1935) ;   J. Duff, *Letters of St Jerome* (1942) ;   A. Penna, *S. Girolamo* (1949) ;   P. Antin, *Essai sur S. Jérôme* (1951) ;   and *A Monument to St Jerome* (1952), essays ed. by F. X. Murphy.

ST GREGORY THE ENLIGHTENER, Bishop of Ashtishat
(*c.* A.D. 330)

THE Christian faith was first preached in Armenia during the second or third century, probably by missionaries from Syria and Persia, but the local beliefs concerning this first evangelization are different and contradictory.   These worthless legends give the credit for it to the apostles SS. Bartholomew and Thaddeus, and together with Thaddeus have appropriated the story of King Abgar the Black and the likeness of our Lord, which really belongs to Edessa and St Addai.   Nevertheless, the Armenians also venerate St Gregory of Ashtishat as the apostle who brought the light of the gospel to their country, whence he is named " the Illuminator " or " Enlightener " and regarded as their principal national saint and patron.   He was born in the third century, at a time when the Persians had invaded Armenia.   His origin and even nationality are uncertain.   According to unreliable Armenian tradition he was a son of that Parthian Anak who murdered King Khosrov I of Armenia.   When the dying Khosrov ordered the extermination of Anak's family, the baby Gregory was smuggled away by a merchant of Valarshapat to Caesarea in Cappadocia.   Here certainly he was baptized, and in due course married and had two sons, St Aristakes and St Vardanes.   Tiridates, a son of King Khosrov, who had been in exile among the Romans, returned with an army and regained his father's throne.   Gregory was given a place at the court of Tiridates (an unlikely thing if he were really a son of his father's murderer), but soon incurred the displeasure of the king by the encouragement he gave to the Armenian Christians and by his zeal in making converts.   Active persecution began, and Gregory himself suffered greatly.   But eventually he triumphed.   Tiridates himself was converted (he is venerated as a saint), and while Christians in the Empire were suffering under the persecution of Diocletian, Christianity was proclaimed the official religion of Armenia, which thus became—superficially—the first Christian state in the world's history.

St Gregory went to Caesarea and there was consecrated bishop by the metropolitan Leontius.   He established his see at Ashtishat and then set himself with the aid of Greek and Syrian missionaries to organize his church, instruct the new converts, and win over waverers.   To recruit a clergy he took a number of youths, instructed them in the Holy Scriptures and Christian morality, and taught them Greek and Syriac ; but the episcopate became hereditary, and the chief bishop of Armenia was a direct descendant of St Gregory for a century after.   " Invincibly did our Illuminator carry the life-giving name of Jesus from end to end of the land, in all seasons and weathers, untiring and earnest in the duties of an evangelist, repelling adversaries, preaching before chieftains and nobles, and enlightening every soul which by the new birth of baptism was made a child of God.   To show forth the glory of Christ he rescued prisoners and captives and those oppressed by tyrants ; he destroyed unjust contracts and liabilities ; he comforted by his words many who were afflicted or living in fear, putting before them the hope of the glory of God and planting our Lord Jesus Christ in their souls so that they became truly glad."   Gregory sent his son St Aristakes to represent him at the first oecumenical council at Nicaea, and when Gregory read the *acta* of that assembly he is said to have exclaimed : " As for us, we praise Him who was before time, worshipping the Holy Trinity and the one Godhead of the Father, the Son and the Holy Ghost, now and throughout all ages." Whether or no St Gregory actually made use of these words, they are still repeated by the celebrant in the Armenian eucharistic liturgy when the deacon has recited the conciliar anathema after the creed. Shortly after Gregory consecrated Aristakes to succeed him, and himself retired to a hermitage on Mount Manyea in the province of Taron. In the following year he was found dead by a shepherd and was buried at Thortan.

The above particulars of this saint are all quite uncertain, but if authentic information is scarce legends are not wanting, which are set out at length in a history written by one who called himself Agathangelus and averred that he was secretary to King Tiridates. Actually it was not composed earlier than the second half of the fifth century. According to this work, Gregory first got into trouble with Tiridates for refusing to lay a garland of flowers on the image of the goddess Anahit in her temple at Ashtishat. When he could by no means persuade him to this act of worship, Tiridates had him tortured in twelve different ways, ways of a cruel ingenuity differing considerably from those usually recorded of martyrs under the Romans. Gregory was then thrown into a noisome pit, stinking with corpses, filth and vermin, where he was left and forgotten for fifteen years. But he was kept alive by the ministrations of a kindly widow. After the martyrdom of St Rhipsime (September 29), King Tiridates was turned into a wild boar, roaming about the woods with others of his kind, and it was revealed in a vision to his sister that he would be restored to his natural shape only by the prayers of Gregory. Whereupon the pit was searched, he was found and released from confinement, and at once healed the king who in repentance and gratitude was baptized with his wife and sister. Gregory then fasted without food, prayed, and preached for seventy days, and had a vision at Valarshapat near Mount Ararat in which our Lord came down from Heaven and showed him that He wanted the chief cathedral-church of Armenia to be built there where he was. Which was done and the place called Etshmiadzin, which means " the Only-begotten has descended " ; but the story of the vision was probably really invented to bolster up the claim of the Armenian church to be independent of Caesarea. Each of these marvels, namely, the Twelve Torments, the Casting into the Pit, the Release from the Pit, and the Vision, is commemorated by a separate feast among the Armenians, who keep other feasts of St Gregory as well. He is sometimes erroneously venerated as a martyr, *e.g.* among the Greeks. Devotion to St Gregory is found in southern Italy, where it was introduced by Armenian " colonists ". A church in Naples indeed claims some of his relics, but it is most doubtful that they ever left Armenia. The saint is commemorated in the canon of the Armenian Mass.

Those who are not specialists in oriental languages have to be content, in the case of Armenian and Georgian saints, to consult second-hand sources. Even the Bollandists in the eighteenth century (*Acta Sanctorum*, September, vol. viii) had to do the best they could with the aid of a Greek version or abridgement by the Metaphrast of the unreliable and often fabulous Armenian narrative attributed to Agathangelus. The genuine Armenian Agathangelus, if he ever existed, cannot be traced, but we possess an Arabic version of an earlier stage in the development of the pseudo-Agathangelus. This is in a letter, *c.* 714, of the Arabian bishop George to the priest Joshua. See von Ryssel, *Ein Brief Georgs an den Presb. Joshua* (1883) ; A. von Gutschmid, *Kleine Schriften*, vol. iii (1892), pp. 339–420 ; Gelzer in the *Berichte* of the Sächsischen Gesellschaft, 1895, pp. 109–174 ; P. Peeters in the *Analecta Bollandiana*, vol. xxvi (1907), pp. 117–120 and vol. l (1932), pp. 3–58 ; G.

Garitte in *Documents pour l'étude du livre d'Agathange*, " Studi e testi ", no. cxxvii (1946) includes an unpublished Greek text of Agathangelus from which the Arabic is derived. See also a long article by Fr Paul Peeters in *Analecta Bollandiana*, vol. lx (1942), *à propos* the marble calendar of Naples ; the notice in the Bollandist commentary on the *Mart. Rom.* (1940), pp. 426–427 ; S. Weber, *Die Katholische Kirche in Armenien* (1903), pp. 115 *seq.* ; F. Tournebize, *Histoire . . . de l'Arménie* (1901), pp. 423 *seq.* ; and L. Duchesne, *Histoire ancienne de l'Église*, vol. iii (1911), pp. 528–536.

ST HONORIUS, Archbishop of Canterbury   (a.d. 653)

This apostolic man was a Roman by birth, and a monk by profession. St Gregory the Great, from the experience which he had of his virtue and skill in sacred learning, made choice of him for one of the missionaries which he sent to convert the English, though whether he was of St Augustine's original company or came over with the second band in 601 is not known.   Upon the death of St Justus in 627 St Honorius was chosen archbishop of Canterbury.   He was consecrated at Lincoln by St Paulinus, Bishop of York, and received the *pallium* sent by Pope Honorius I together with a letter, in which his Holiness ordained that whenever either the see of Canterbury or York should become vacant, the other bishop should ordain the person that should be duly elected, " because of the long distance of sea and land that lies between us and you ".   And to confirm this delegation of the patriarchal power of consecrating all bishops under him, a *pallium* was sent also to the bishop of York.

The new archbishop saw with joy the faith of Christ extending daily in many different parts of this island and the spirit of the gospel taking root in the hearts of many servants of God.   His own zeal and example contributed to so great an increase throughout an episcopate of some twenty-five years.   One of the first and most important of his acts was to consecrate the Burgundian St Felix as bishop of Dunwich and send him on his mission to convert the East Angles.   After King Edwin was slain in battle and Cadwallon of Wales, " more cruel than any pagan" says St Bede, " and resolved to cut off every Englishman in Britain ", ravaged Northumbria, St Paulinus fled with Queen Ethelburga and was given shelter by St Honorius, who appointed him to the vacant see of Rochester.   When Paulinus died there in 644 Honorius consecrated in his place St Ithamar, a man of Kent, the first English bishop.   St Honorius died on September 30, 653, and was buried in the abbey-church of SS. Peter and Paul at Canterbury.   He is named in the Roman Martyrology and commemorated in the dioceses of Southwark and Nottingham.

For all this see Bede, *Eccles. Hist.*, bks ii and iii, with Plummer's notes.

ST SIMON OF CRÉPY   (a.d. 1082)

Simon, Count of Crépy in Valois, was a relative of Matilda, wife of William the Conqueror, in whose court he was brought up.   He was favoured by William and fought against Philip I of France to keep the Vexin for Normandy, but he desired to be a monk, moved thereto, it is said, by the sight of the decomposing body of his father which he was taking from Montdidier to be buried at Crépy.   There is a story told of his persuading his *fiancée*, a daughter of Hildebert, Count of Auvergne, to be a nun, and of a romantic flight from their respective homes just before the wedding.   But Simon's intention was frustrated for a time by King William, who wished him to marry his daughter Adela.   He was afraid directly to refuse his powerful benefactor, and went off to Rome on the pretext of finding out if the projected marriage were lawful, as the lady was his kinswoman.   On the way he went to the abbey of Saint-Claude at Condat in the Jura, and there received the habit.   Like other royal monks he was called on by his superiors and relatives to use his influence to bring about reconciliations and restorations of rights.   St Hugh of Cluny sent him to the king of France to recover lands that had been taken from his monastery, and he intervened in the troubles between William the Conqueror and his sons.   When Pope St Gregory VII, in view of his conflict with the emperor, determined to come to terms with Robert Guiscard and his Normans in Italy, he sent for St Simon to help him in the negotiations.   These were brought to a successful conclusion at Aquino in 1080, and the pope kept Simon by his side. He died in Rome shortly afterwards, receiving the last sacraments from the hands of St Gregory himself.

Many of Simon's contemporaries have sung his praises.   Bd Urban II compiled a eulogistic epitaph for his tomb, and Guibert de Nogent, who denounced so uncompromisingly the corruption of the age, wrote enthusiastically of the good example set by Simon.   These and many other testimonies have been collected in the *Acta Sanctorum*, September, vol. viii, together with a separate biography, anonymous but written not long after his death.   See also G. Corblet, *Hagiographie d'Amiens*, vol. iii, pp. 491–519.

THE virtue of the most fervent novices in the service of God is very imperfect so long as entire self-denial and a great assiduity in prayer have not yet prepared their souls for, and called down upon them, a plentiful inpouring of the Holy Ghost, who fills their understanding with a clear and heavenly light, and by the fire of His charity consumes the rust of worldly affections, and fills them with His grace. In this state the moral virtues acquire an heroic and infused degree of perfection. Humility gives the soul a more clear knowledge of her own infirmities and imperfections, with stronger contempt of herself ; and the like is to be said of divine and fraternal charity, and all other virtues ; so that the soul seems to herself translated into a region of new light, in which by continual exercise of these virtues, and especially of prayer and contemplation, she makes wonderful progress.

THE END OF VOLUME III

INDEX

Individual members of groups, e.g. of martyrs, are not entered in this index if they have only a bare mention in the text.